Peter Norton's Complete Guide to DOS 6.22

Peter Norton

SAMS
PUBLISHING

201 West 103rd Street,
Indianapolis, Indiana 46290

Copyright © 1994 by Peter Norton

FIRST EDITION

International Standard Book Number: 0-672-30614-X

Library of Congress Catalog Card Number: 94-67510

98 97 96 95   4 3 2

Interpretation of the printing code: the rightmost double-digit number is the year of the book's printing; the rightmost single-digit, the number of the book's printing. For example, a printing code of 95-1 shows that the first printing of the book occurred in 1995.

Composed in Goudy and MCPdigital by Macmillan Computer Publishing

Printed in the United States of America

Trademarks

What's New in this Edition

- Two books in one: now covers all advanced DOS topics

- Highlights new DOS 6.22 features and incompatibilities with earlier DOS versions

- Shows you how to upgrade from DoubleSpace to DriveSpace

- Separate chapters on Windows use, Multimedia and the Internet

- Step-by-step hands-on tutorial approach in practically every chapter

- Peter's Principles for the most intelligent use of DOS commands

- On Your Own exercises to consolidate your grasp of each chapter

- Tear-out Survival Guide that you'll want to stick to your monitor

- Easy-to find general procedures for most common tasks

- Problem-Solvers for immediate lookup when you're in trouble

- Tips and Cautions for Windows (and network) users throughout the book

- Even more Tips that put DOS commands at **your** command

- Comprehensive and detailed Command Reference now enhanced with chapter cross-references

- Retains thorough coverage of DOS 6.0, 6.2, DoubleSpace and the DOSSHELL

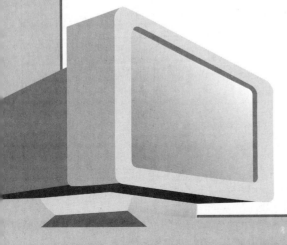

Publisher
Richard K. Swadley

Acquisitions Manager
Stacy Hiquet

Managing Editor
Cindy Morrow

Acquisitions Editor
Sunthar Visuvalingam

Development Editor
Sunthar Visuvalingam

Production Editor
James Grass

Editor
Ryan Rader

Editorial Coordinator
Bill Whitmer

Editorial Assistants
Carol Ackerman
Sharon Cox
Lynette Quinn

Technical Reviewers
Gordon Arbuthnot
Ruth Ashley

Marketing Manager
Gregg Bushyeager

Assistant Marketing Manager
Michelle Milner

Cover Designer
Tim Amrhein

Book Designer
Alyssa Yesh

Director of Production and Manufacturing
Jeff Valler

Imprint Manager
Juli Cook

Manufacturing Coordinator
Paul Gilchrist

Production Analysts
Dennis Clay Hager
Mary Beth Wakefield

Graphics Image Specialists
Teresa Forrester
Clint Lahnen
Tim Montgomery
Dennis Sheehan
Greg Simsic
Susan VandeWalle
Jeff Yesh

Page Layout
Rob Falco
Aleata Howard
Ayana Lacey
Shawn MacDonald
Casey Price
Clair Schweinler
Susan Shepard
Dennis Wesner

Proofreading
Michael Brummit
Cheryl Cameron
Kimberly K. Hannel
Donna Harbin
Brian-Kent Proffitt
S.A. Springer

Indexer
Chris Cleveland

Overview

Quick Reference   ix

Acknowledgments   xvi

Introduction   xvii

Part 1   Getting Acquainted   **1**

  1   Getting Acquainted with Your System   3

  2   Getting Acquainted with DOS   19

  3   How DOS Organizes Data   31

  4   Setting Up Your System   45

Part 2   DOS Shell   **59**

  5   Getting Acquainted with DOS Shell   61

  6   Managing Directories   77

  7   Selecting Files in the Shell   93

  8   Copying and Moving Files in DOS Shell   103

  9   Additional File Management in the Shell   119

 10   Running Programs from DOS Shell   135

 11   Customizing the Shell   151

Part 3   DOS Commands   **169**

 12   Working at the Command Prompt   171

 13   DOSKEY   197

 14   Managing Directories   211

 15   Copying and Moving Files   229

 16   Additional File Management   245

 17   Formatting and Unformatting Disks   265

 18   Additional Disk Management   283

 19   The DOS Editor   297

20	Basic Batch Programs	317
21	Configuring Your System	333

Part 4   Managing Your System   345

22	Avoiding Disaster: An Overview	347
23	MSBACKUP and MWBACKUP	353
24	Restore and Compare	391
25	DOS's Antivirus Programs	415
26	Using UNDELETE	437
27	CHKDSK and SCANDISK	461
28	Optimizing Your System	473
29	Managing Memory	477
30	Additional Memory Facilities for 386, 486, and Pentium Computers	479
31	Caching the Drives	499
32	RAM Drives	515
33	Defragmenter	521
34	DriveSpace and DoubleSpace	535
35	Putting It All Together before Advancing	549

Part 5   Advanced DOS   557

36	DOS at Your Command	559
37	Programming Logic in Batch Programs	583
38	Starting Up DOS	609
39	Directory Management	621
40	Advanced Copying Techniques	631
41	INTERLNK	649
42	Windows on DOS	663
43	DOS and the Environment	687
44	Squeezing Even More Out of Memory	705
45	A Second Look at DrvSpace and DblSpace	717
46	Additional Techniques for Handling Data	735

47	Advanced Rescue Techniques	745
48	Console Control	761
49	Another Country Heard From	785
50	Printing Through DOS	805
51	Configuring Disks and Networks	823
52	The Multimedia PC	835
53	Upgrading to QBASIC	843
54	FDISK	867
55	Riding the Internet with DOS	875
Part 6	**Command Reference**	**885**
	Command Reference	887
A	Device Drivers	1065
B	Exit Codes	1089
C	IBM Extended Characters	1093
	Glossary	1097
	Index	1115

Quick Reference

Procedure Quick Reference

Procedure	Page
How to Move the Focus in DOS Shell	67
How to Scroll with the Keyboard	69
How to Scroll with the Mouse	70
How to use Menus	72
How to Change Drives in DOS Shell	78
How to Create a New Directory in DOS Shell	83
How to Expand and Collapse DOS Shell's Directory Tree	86
How to Rename a Directory in DOS Shell	88
How to Delete a Directory in DOS Shell	90
How to Select Files in DOS Shell	95
How to Move or Copy a Single File in DOS Shell	106
How to Move or Copy Multiple Files in DOS Shell	110
How to Move or Copy Files by Dragging in DOS Shell	112
How to View a File's Attributes in DOS Shell	121
How to Change File Attributes in DOS Shell	122
How to Rename Files in DOS Shell	125
How to Initialize the PRINT Program	128
How to Launch a Program from DOS Shell's File List	137
How to Associate a File Extension with a Program	141
How to Terminate a Malfunctioning Program while Task Swapping in DOS Shell	148

Procedure	Page
How to Create and Manage a DOS Shell Program Group	153
How to Create and Manage a DOS Shell Program Item	156
How to Run One Command at a Secondary Command Prompt from within DOS Shell	175
How to Copy a Block of Text to Another Location in DOS's Text Editor	305
How to Move a Block of Text to Another Location in DOS's Text Editor	305
How to Rerun the Compatibility Test	362
How to Reconfigure a Floppy Drive	363
How to Create a New Backup Setup	365
How to Select Files for a Backup Setup	366
How to Run a Backup	380
How to Copy a Huge File to Another Computer via Floppy Disks	389
How to Open a Backup Catalog	395
How to Select Files to be Compared or Restored	396
How to Fall Back to an Older Version of a File	400
How to Restore the Latest Versions of Individual Files	406
How to Restore a File after Its Catalog Has Been Deleted from the Hard Drive	406
How to Restore an Entire Drive	408
How to Restore Files to Different Drives and Directories	409
How to Rebuild a Catalog	410
How to Compare Backed Up Files to Their Originals	412
How to Scan Your Hard Drive for Viruses	420
How to Load MWAVTSR.EXE from WIN.INI	429

Procedure	Page
How to Unload VSAFE	433
How to Recover a File Using Delete Sentry	441
How to Purge the SENTRY Directory	445
How to Recover a Deleted Directory and Its Files	446
How to Recover a File Using Deletion-Tracking	448
How to Recover a File from the DOS Directory	452
How to Configure Undelete	457
How to Recover Cross-Linked Files with CHKDSK	469
How to Optimize Your Hard Drive	523
How to Sort Directory Entries	532
How to Compress Your First Hard Drive	539
How to Compress Additional Drives	541
How to Break Command Output into Pages	562
How to Bypass the Startup Files during Booting	610
How to Empty a Directory without Deleting the Directory	623
How to Switch Drives A and B	628
How to Copy a Large Set of Files to Floppy Disks using XCOPY	634
How to Prune and Graft a Directory	636
How to Link Two Computers before Booting the Client Computer	653
How to Link Two Computers after Booting the Client Computer	659
How to Compress an Additional Hard Drive	720
How to Convert a DoubleSpace Floppy to DriveSpace	724
How to Completely Defragment a Compressed Drive	729
How to Uncompress a Drive with DOS 6.0	733
How to Install a New Device Driver	838

Tips Quick Reference

Tip	Page
Preparing for a CMOS battery failure by noting your hard drive code number	7
Adding DOSSHELL to the end of the AUTOEXEC.BAT	65
Changing current drive with Ctrl key irrespective of context	80
Expanding/collapsing directory tree without activating it	86
Using DELTREE instead of DEL to remove directories quickly	90
Heeding the Confirm Mouse Operation box while copying/moving files	114
Press Ctrl or Alt to change the drag procedure in mid-drag	115
Initializing the PRINT command in the AUTOEXEC.BAT	129
Keeping Confirm on Delete on, before deleting files	132
Not associating extensions with Windows program files	141
Using the period (.) to indicate blank extensions for file associations	141
Saving your files before switching away from a task	146
Cycling backward through a long task list with Shift+Alt+Tab, Tab, ...Tab	146
Type a caret (^) followed by M in Help Text box to start a new paragraph	155
Include complete path in the Commands box	158
Saving display mode and screen color choices in DOSSHELL.INI	160
Unseen files resulting in message No files match file specifier in the file list	165

Tip	Page
Opening Help window with the Syntax topic for the requested command	190
Moving from one command to another in HELP by searching for the command name	191
Optimizing the PATH command	194
Using DELTREE for one-step deletion of directories and branches	227
Using Norton Utilities' Unerase utility to retrieve an overwritten file	234
Avoiding "file or directory?" question with XCOPY	238
Using the default destination for COPY or XCOPY	243
Bypassing the "Make directory" question in the MOVE command	243
When to use Ctrl+Break to cancel a program in midstream	254
Clearing the print queue and adding new files to it in one command	258
Configuring the PRINT TSR to control print jobs	258
When to include the /U switch in the FORMAT command	272
Avoiding the "volume label" question during the formatting process	274
Using both /Q and /U for the fastest possible format	278
Write-protecting the source disk during DISKCOPY	287
Including the new filespec in the EDIT command to create a new file	300
Deleting all occurrences of a string in the DOS Editor	306
Avoiding spaces in your find string so that the DOS Editor can find it	307
Search Find as a handy way to move the cursor long distances in the Editor	308

Tip	Page
Ensuring quick and easy access to batch files	319
Adding REM, ECHO, CLS, and PAUSE commands to your AUTOEXEC.BAT file	331
Speeding up the backup process with two identical floppy drives	360
Undoing file selections in Backup with a single safe step	372
Using IF ERRORLEVEL 86 with MSAV to determine if any viruses were detected	427
Deleting files without letting UNDELETE preserve them	447
Optimizing memory after installing compression software	541
Assigning the extension .TXT to files created by redirection	561
Making custom commands more handy with DOSKEY macros	573
Adding explanatory comments to label lines to document your program logic	594
Checking for existence of subdirectories with IF EXIST	596
Using the % symbol in a batch file without having it deleted	603
Eliminating the pause after the Starting MS-DOS... message	613
Making it difficult for novice users to bypass the startup	613
Avoiding confirmation when deleting a directory with DELTREE in a batch file	623
Telling Windows which drive to use for its swap files	665
Using WINPMT variable to customize DOS running under Windows	668
Clearing the Clipboard to make room in memory for loading another application	669

Tip	Page
Controlling the size of the text displayed in the DOS window	672
Using an environment variable instead of a filename in a PIF	674
Using an environment variable instead of a title in a PIF	675
Using an environment variable instead of parameters and switches in a PIF	675
Using an environment variable instead of a directory path name in a PIF	676
Changing an application's execution settings while the application is running	679
Troubleshooting a DOS application that refuses to load under Windows	679
Permitting a DOS application under Windows to print screens on the printer	682
Deleting a shortcut key for a DOS application under Windows	682
Checking the setting of a particular variable without viewing the entire list	689
Using CONFIG to personalize messages to the user in a multi-user environment	695
Precaution for using FORMAT'S /AUTOTEST switch to format a disk	738
Repeatedly inserting extended characters without reusing Alt+key combination	767
Determining which line settings are valid for your screen	779
Finding the optimal location in upper memory for the PRINT command	813

Problem Solver Quick Reference

Problem	Page
DOSSHELL command results in `Bad program or file name`	63
I can't read the screen in DOS Shell	64
DOS Shell shows drive B, but I have only one floppy drive	79
Switching to floppy drive results in an error message	79
The File, Create Directory command is dimmed in DOS Shell	83
Creating a directory results in `Access denied`	84
Renaming a directory results in `Access denied`	89
Deleting a directory results in `You cannot delete a non-empty directory`	91
DOS Shell's File, Copy and File, Move commands are dimmed	107
Nothing happens when I choose DOS Shell's File, Copy and File, Move commands	107
Copying or moving a file results in `Access Denied`	109
Copying a file results in `File can't be copied onto itself`	109
Copying or moving files results in `You have more than one file selected`	111
Renaming a file results in Access Denied	126
Computer hangs when I try to switch tasks in DOS Shell	147
I can't find DOS Shell's File, New command	153
My customized DOS Shell program list reverted to the default list	161
Exiting DOS Shell results in `Unable to update DOSSHELL.INI`	161

Problem	Page
My command prompt doesn't show the current drive and directory	173
Changes to a disk don't show up in DOS Shell's Directory Tree or File List	174
A command results in `Bad command or file name`	178
My printer does not print or prints all but the last page	181
Renaming a directory with MOVE results in `permission denied`	225
Deleting a directory results in `Invalid path, not directory, or directory not empty`	226
Attempting to access a file results in `File not found`	231
Copying a group of files results in `Disk full`	233
Attempting to access a file results in `Access denied`	234
Trying to create a new directory with XCOPY results in `Unable to create directory`	239
`MOVE` command results in `Too many parameters`	242
Moving a file results in `Unable to create destination`	242
Moving files results in `Cannot move multiple files to a single file`	243
Moving files results in `Unable to open source`	244
Renaming a file results in `Duplicate file name or file not found`	247
Changing or deleting a file results in `Write-protect error writing drive`	251
TYPE dumps strange characters onto the screen, accompanied by beeping	256
FC dumps strange characters onto the screen, accompanied by beeping	260

Problem	Page
Acessing a file results in `Sector not found`	267
Accessing a file results in `Read error` or `Write error`	268
Formatting a disk results in `Invalid media or Track 0 bad - disk unusable, Format failure`	273
Formatting a disk results in `Insert DOS disk in drive and strike any key when ready`	275
Formatting a disk results in `Drive d error. Insufficient space for the MIRROR image file`	278
Duplicating a disk with DISKCOPY results in `Unrecoverable read error on drive d; Side x`	285
Duplicating a disk with DISKCOPY results in `Unrecoverable write error on drive d; Side x`	286
Duplicating a disk results in `Error creating image file; Diskcopy will revert to multiple-pass copy`	288
Duplicating a disk results in `TARGET diskette bad or incompatible; Copy process ended`	290
Duplicating or comparing disks results in `Specified drive does not exist or is non-removable`	292
MWBACKUP can pass the compatibility test in Standard Mode but not in Enhanced Mode	363
Backup takes a long time reading a disk drive that isn't included in the setup	380
Backup freezes up in the middle of a backup	382
Restore or Compare does not show all of my hard drives in the drive list	395

Problem	Page
Restore can't read compressed files backed up by DOS 6.0 or 6.2	404
Starting Windows results in a hard disk error or a write-protected message	431
UNDELETE doesn't list files deleted by DOS Shell	449
I can't boot after adding a command to CONFIG.SYS to load HIMEM	486
Running a program results in `Packed file corrupt`	487
My system froze in the middle of running MEMMAKER	494
Concatenating files results in `Content of destination lost before copy`	639
My mouse won't work with my DOS applications when I run them under Windows	672
When I try to boot, DOS says `Bad or missing command interpreter`	696
After compressing my hard drive, one of my applications issues a copy-protection message	725
When I tried to use FC, I got the message `FC: Out of memory`	740
My screen froze up when I pressed PrintScreen	808
I entered `PRINT` as a command and nothing printed	816
I installed a new (or used) floppy drive and DOS doesn't recognize it	831

Peter's Principle Quick Reference

Peter's Principle of...	Page
Naming Files: Give files meaningful names	34
Directory Names: Directory name should be short and meaningful	83
Copying/Moving Files: Use DOS Shell—it's safer	104
Loading TSRs: Always load TSRs from the command prompt	128
Rebooting: Reboot from the primary command prompt only	175
Renaming Files: Keep group renames simple	248
Deleting Files: Always use the /P switch on the DEL command	253
Saving Files: Save early and save often	310
Batch Filespecs: Always use absolute path names in batch programs	319
Selecting Files for Backup: Use the Include/Exclude list	372
Backup Types: Don't mix differential and incremental types	374
Keeping Backups: Don't delete a backup until you know the next one is good	385
Deletion Protection: Use it, but don't count on it	438
Concatenation: Use the original application to concatenate files	640
Updating Time/Date Stamps: Always use the /B switch	644
Replacing Files: Always use the /P switch	646

Contents

Part 1 Getting Acquainted — 1

1 Getting Acquainted with Your System — 3

Your Hardware 4
    The System Unit 4
    The Keyboard 8
    The Mouse 12
Software 13
    System Software 13
    Applications 14
Disks 14
Your Data 15
    How Data Is Stored 15
    Kilobytes, Megabytes, Gigabytes, and Beyond 16
The User 16
On Your Own 17

2 Getting Acquainted with DOS — 19

What is DOS? 20
What Does DOS Do? 20
    The Command Prompt 20
    DOS Shell 22
DOS Features 24
    Command Prompt Features 24
    Batch Program Features 25
    Disk and Data Management Features 25
    Protecting and Recovering Your Data 25
    Memory Facilities 26
    Optimizing Your System's Performance 27
    Hardware Features 27
    Miscellaneous Services 28
What's New in DOS 6? 28
On Your Own 30

3 How DOS Organizes Data — 31

How DOS Controls Data 32
Files 33
    Filespecs 33
    Global Filespecs 34
    Attributes 35
Directories 37
    The Root Directory 37
    The Directory Tree 37

The Current Directory 39
Path Names 40
Paths in Filespecs 41
Allocation Units and the File Allocation Table 41
How DOS Deletes a File 42
On Your Own 43

4   **Setting Up Your System**   **45**
Basic Assumptions 46
Getting Ready for Installation 46
Making a Decision about Backups 48
Running SETUP 49
Dealing with Problems During SETUP 50
Understanding What SETUP Does 51
Looking at Additional Documentation 52
Scanning for Viruses 52
Starting Delete Sentry 53
Making an Emergency Startup Disk 56
Uninstalling DOS 6 56
DELOLDOS 57
Using Expand 57

Part 2   **DOS Shell**   **59**

5   **Getting Acquainted with DOS Shell**   **61**
Deciding When to Use the Shell 62
Starting the Shell 62
Exploring the Shell Screen 65
Using DOS Shell's On-Screen Help 68
Dialog Boxes 68
Command Buttons 68
Scrolling 69
Using the Help Menu 72
Exiting DOS Shell 76
On Your Own 76

6   **Managing Directories**   **77**
Managing Directories 78
Selecting a Drive 78
Selecting an Empty Drive 80
Refreshing Drives 81
Repainting the Screen 82
Creating Directories 82
Selecting Directories 85
Collapsing and Expanding the Directory Tree 86
Renaming Directories 88
Deleting Directories 90
On Your Own 92

7   **Selecting Files in the Shell**   93

Selecting Files in the Shell 94
Selecting a Single File 94
Selecting Multiple Files..95
    Selecting Multiple Files with the Mouse 96
    Combining Selection and Deselection 97
    Selecting Multiple Files with the Keyboard....................................98
    Selecting and Deselecting All Files 99
When No Files Are Selected 99
Selecting from Multiple Directories...100
On Your Own 101

8   **Copying and Moving Files in DOS Shell**   103

Copying and Moving Files in DOS Shell 104
Using Replacement Confirmation 104
Copying a Single File 105
Moving a Single File 110
Copying and Moving Multiple Files 110
Dragging Files 112
    Alternate Views 115
Understanding Copy 116
Moving and Copying Files from One Floppy to Another 117
Moving and Copying a Large Group of Files to Several Floppies 118
Miscellaneous Problems 118
On Your Own 118

9   **Additional File Management in the Shell**   119

File Management in the Shell...120
Creating Practice Files 120
Managing Attributes 120
    Viewing Attributes 121
    Changing Attributes 122
    Changing Multiple Attributes 123
Renaming Files 125
Viewing Files 126
Printing Files 128
    Printing Through the Shell...129
    Working with the Print Queue 130
    Choosing a Print Program 131
Deleting a Single File 131
Deleting Multiple Files 132
On Your Own 134

10   **Running Programs from DOS Shell**   135

Executing Programs from the Shell 136
Opening Objects 136
Launching a Program from the File List 137
Dropping a Data File on a Program File 138
Opening an Associated File 140

Launching Programs from the Program List 142
Working at the Command Prompt 143
Task Swapping 143
    Starting Tasks 144
    Switching Tasks 145
    Ending a Task 148
    Ending the Task Swapper 149
On Your Own 149

11   Customizing the Shell   151

Overview 152
Managing the Program List 152
    Working with Groups 153
    Defining a Group 153
    Defining a Program Item 156
    Copying Program Items 159
Choosing Display Options 162
Customizing the Screen Colors 162
Customizing the File List 163
    Filtering the File List 164
    Displaying All the Files on the Drive 164
    Locating Misplaced Files 165
    Displaying Hidden and System Files 165
    Locating Files on a Set of Floppies 166
    Sorting the File List 166
On Your Own 167

Part 3   DOS Commands   169

12   Working at the Command Prompt   171

Understanding Commands 172
Getting to the Command Prompt 172
    Interpreting the Command Prompt 173
    Secondary Command Prompts 174
    The File, Run Command 174
    Advantages and Disadvantages of
        Primary and Secondary Command Prompts 175
Understanding Command Syntax 176
    The Name of the Program 177
    Parameters and Switches 177
    Using Paths in Commands 178
Redirecting Command Output 180
Introduction to the Command Reference 183
Getting On-Screen Help with Commands 185
    Getting On-Screen Help with Command Syntax 185
    Getting On-Screen Help with Complete Command Information ... 186
The PATH Program 193
The PROMPT Command 195
On Your Own 196

13 DOSKEY   **197**

Understanding What DOSKEY Does 198
Loading the DOSKEY TSR 198
Using the Command History 200
Editing Commands 201
    The Insert and Overtype Editing Modes 202
Combining Commands 203
Using Macro Power 204
    Using Replaceable Parameters 207
    Controlling the DOSKEY Buffer Size 208
    Loading DOSKEY in AUTOEXEC.BAT 208
Reviewing Commands and Macros 209
    Revising and Deleting Macros 210
On Your Own 210

14 Managing Directories   **211**

Overview 212
Changing the Default Drive and Directory 212
    Displaying the Name of the Default Directory on Another Drive 214
    Changing a Default Directory on Another Drive 214
Displaying the Directory Tree 214
Listing a Directory 216
    Selecting Files According to Attributes 218
    Sorting the Listing 220
    Filtering Names 221
    Listing Branches 221
    Finding a Lost File 222
Creating a Directory 223
Renaming Directories 224
Deleting a Directory 225
Deleting a Branch 226
On Your Own 228

15 Copying and Moving Files   **229**

Overview 230
Using the COPY Command 230
    Copying More Than One File 232
    Replacing Existing Copies 233
    Printing Text Files Quickly with COPY 235
Using the XCOPY Command 236
    Specifying a Directory or a File 237
    Using XCOPY with Multiple Files 239
    Copying Entire Branches 240
Moving Files 241
    Moving Multiple Files 243
    Using MOVE to Rename Files 244
Cleaning Up Your Directories 244
On Your Own 244

16   Additional File Management   245

Overview 246
Creating Some Practice Files 246
Using REN To Rename Files 247
Managing Attributes with the *ATTRIB* Command 248
    Changing the Attributes of Hidden and System Files 250
    Setting Attributes Throughout a Branch 251
    Working with Directory Attributes 251
Deleting Files 252
    Deleting Multiple Files...253
    Deleting Protected Files 254
    Deleting All the Files in a Directory..254
Displaying Files with the *TYPE* Command 255
Printing Files with PRINT 256
Comparing Files with FC 258
    Binary Comparisons 259
    ASCII Comparisons 260
    Resynchronization 262
    Comparison Options 263
On Your Own 263

17   Formatting and Unformatting Disks   265

Overview 266
Understanding How Formatting Works 266
    Formatting New Floppy Disks 266
    Formatting New Hard Disks 268
    Reformatting Floppy Disks 269
    Using FORMAT to Prepare a New Disk 271
    Using FORMAT to Reformat a Disk 275
FORMAT in DOS Shell 279
Using UNFORMAT to Restore a Reformatted Disk 280
On Your Own 282

18   Additional Disk Management   283

Overview 284
Copying Disks with DISKCOPY 284
    Copying Disks with a Single Drive in DOS 6.0 or Earlier............287
    Copying Disks with a Single Drive in DOS 6.2 or Later 288
    Copying Disks with Two Drives 289
    Verifying the Copy 290
Copying Disks in the Shell 291
Comparing Disks with DISKCOMP 291
Managing Internal Labels with VOL and LABEL 293
On Your Own 296

19   The DOS Editor   297

Working with DOS Editor 298
Starting DOS Editor 299
Lines Versus Paragraphs 300

Editing Text 301
    Cursor Movement 301
    Inserting Text 302
    Selecting Text 303
    Deleting Text 303
    Cutting and Pasting 304
Finding and Replacing 306
Using Find without Replace 307
Managing Files 308
    Saving a New File 309
    Saving a File That Already Has a Name 310
    Opening Files 311
Printing Files 311
Getting Help 312
Customizing the Editor Screen 314
EDIT Command Switches 314
On Your Own 314

20   **Basic Batch Programs**   **317**

Creating Your Own Programs 318
Creating a Batch File 318
Running a Batch Program 319
Locating the Batch File 320
Understanding How the Batch File Executes 321
Stopping the Batch File 321
Using Special Batch Commands 321
    Clearing the Screen 322
    Annotating the Program 322
    Controlling Messages 323
    Pausing the Program 325
    Calling Other Batch Programs 327
Using Replaceable Parameters 329
Understanding Your AUTOEXEC.BAT File 331
Using Batch Files in DOS Shell 332
On Your Own 332

21   **Configuring Your System**   **333**

Booting DOS 334
Taking Care of Your Startup Files 334
Bypassing the Startup Files 336
Understanding What Is in CONFIG.SYS 338
Loading Device Drivers 338
Understanding the *DEVICE* Command 339
    Using SETVER 339
    Using HIMEM.SYS 340
    Using ANSI.SYS 340
    Other Device Drivers 340
Loading DOS High 340
Using Buffers 341

Allocating File Handles 342
Defining a Command Processor 342
Allocating Stacks 342
On Your Own 343

Part 4   Managing Your System   345

22   Avoiding Disaster: An Overview   347

Overview 348
Coping with Viruses 348
Dealing with Misbehaving Software 349
Coping with Hardware Failure 350
Coping with Deletions 350
Dealing with Reformatting 351
Dealing with Damaged Disks 351
On Your Own 351

23   MSBACKUP and MWBACKUP   353

Backing Up Your Files 354
Getting Ready for the Practice Exercises 355
Choosing MSBACKUP or MWBACKUP 355
Starting Backup 356
Configuring Backup 357
    Beginning the Tests 357
    Determining the Video and Mouse Configuration 358
    The Floppy Drive Change Line Test 359
    The Floppy Disk Compatibility Test 359
    Coping with Configuration Problems 362
    Retesting Your System 363
Choosing the Backup Function 364
Working with Setup Files 365
    Selecting Files for the Setup 366
    Other Selection Functions 373
    Choosing a Backup Type 373
    Identifying the Backup Drive 375
    Selecting Backup Options 376
    Managing Setup Files 379
Running a Backup 380
Working with Backup Catalogs 382
Taking Care of Your Backup Disks 384
Managing Backup's Files 385
    Where Setup and Catalogs Files Are Stored 386
    Printing Setup Files 387
    Deleting Setups 388
    Deleting Catalogs 388
Copying Huge Files via Floppies 389
On Your Own 390

24   Restore and Compare   **391**

Restoring and Comparing 392
Restoring from Backups Made with Previous Versions of DOS 392
Restoring Files 393
    Opening a Catalog 394
    Selecting Files 395
    The Restore Options 400
    Running Restore 403
    Using Restore for Common Tasks 405
Compare 411
Restoring from Backups Made before DOS 6 412
On Your Own 412

25   DOS's Antivirus Programs   **415**

Why Virus Protection? 416
Microsoft Antivirus Features 416
    The Virus Scanning Programs 417
    Monitoring for Viruses 418
When to Use the Antivirus Programs 418
Using MSAV 419
    Selecting a Drive 421
    Selecting Options 421
    Running the Scan 424
How to Handle a Virus 425
Other MSAV Commands 425
Using MSAV in Batch Mode 426
Using MWAV 428
Using VSAFE 428
    The VSAFE Options 429
    Unloading VSAFE 432
    Options for Loading VSAFE 434
Updating Your Virus List 434
On Your Own 435

26   Using UNDELETE   **437**

Deleting and Undeleting Files 438
    Using Delete Sentry 439
    Checking the Drive List 441
    Listing Files Available for Recovery 441
    Undeleting with Delete Sentry 444
    Purging the SENTRY Directory 445
    What's in SENTRY? 446
UNDELETE's Destination Directory 446
When UNDELETE Can't Recover a File 447
Using Deletion-Tracking 448
    Listing Files Protected by Deletion-Tracking 449
    Recovering Partial Files 450
    Recovering Files Deleted under DOS 5 451

Using the DOS Directory Method 452
    Deleted Directories 454
    Problems with the Directory Method 454
Undeleting Files without Prompts 454
Undeleting Files from DOS Shell 455
Working with Windows Undelete 455
    Windows Undelete Features 456
    Undeleting Directories 457
Working with UNDELETE.INI 457
On Your Own 459

27   **CHKDSK and SCANDISK**   **461**
What CHKDSK and SCANDISK Do 462
When To Use CHKDSK or SCANDISK 462
Checking a Drive for Problems 463
    Handling Disk Problems 465
    Dealing with Lost Clusters with CHKDSK 466
    Dealing with Lost Clusters with SCANDISK 467
    Cross-Linked Files 468
Archaic CHKDSK Functions 469
SCANDISK's Surface Scan 470
On Your Own 470

28   **Optimizing YourSystem**   **473**
What Can DOS Do? 474
    Better Memory Management 474
    Defragmenting 475
    Data Compression 476

29   **Managing Memory**   **477**
DOS's Memory Crunch 478
What Is Memory? 479
    The Types of Memory 479
    Expanded Memory 480
    Extended Memory 481
    The High Memory Area 482
Viewing Your Memory Layout 482
    Loading HIMEM 484
    Loading DOS into the HMA 485
On Your Own 487

30   **Additional Memory Facilities for
      386, 486, and Pentium Computers**   **489**
DOS and 386, 486, and Pentium Machines 490
Providing Expanded Memory 490
    Using Upper Memory Blocks 491
Using MEMMAKER 493
MEMMAKER's Changes 495
    Loading HIMEM and EMM386 496
    The *DOS* Command 496
    The *DEVICEHIGH* Commands 496

The AUTOEXEC.BAT File 496
    Undoing MEMMAKER 497
On Your Own 498

31   Caching the Drives   499

About Caching 500
What Does SmartDrive Do? 500
Caches and Buffers 502
Starting SmartDrive 502
    SmartDrive's Double-Buffering Feature 503
    Choosing the Caching for Drives 504
    Changing Drive Caching after SmartDrive is Installed 505
    SmartDrive Results 505
    Forcing SmartDrive to Write Cached Data 506
    Windows and SmartDrive 506
Controlling the Cache Size 507
    Tailoring SMARTDRV 507
Measuring SmartDrive's Performance with SMARTMON 509
    Logging 510
    SmartMon Options 510
Disk Buffers 511
On Your Own 513

32   RAM Drives   515

About RAM Drives 516
Deciding Where to Place the RAM Drive 516
Setting Up a RAM Drive 517
Using the RAM Drive 518
Directing Temporary Files to a RAM Drive 519
Overriding the Default Parameters 519
On Your Own 520

33   Defragmenter   521

About File Fragmentation 522
Preparing to Run DEFRAG 523
Starting DEFRAG 527
Interpreting the Drive Map 529
Optimization Progress 529
The Optimize Menu 530
Sorting Directory Entries 531
Other DEFRAG Command Options 533
Running DEFRAG in Batch Mode 534
On Your Own 534

34   DriveSpace and DoubleSpace   535

DOS 6 and Data Compression 536
How Data Compression Works 537
The Compressed Drive 537
Compressing an Existing Drive 538
Setting Up DriveSpace or DoubleSpace 538

Getting Started 539
    During Compression 541
    Compressing Additional Drives 541
    Selecting a Drive 543
Interacting with Other DOS Utilities 544
Converting from DoubleSpace to DriveSpace 544
Working with Compressed Drives 545
DIR and Compressed Drives 546
Additional DriveSpace and DoubleSpace Features 546
On Your Own 547

35   Putting It All Together before Advancing   549

A Look at CONFIG.SYS and AUTOEXEC.BAT 550
Setting Up a 286 System 550
Setting Up a 386 or Higher System 552
Daily Shutdown 554
Weekly Shutdown 554
Introduction to the Advanced Chapters 554
On Your Own 555

Part 5   Advanced DOS   557

36   DOS at Your Command   559

Getting the Most out of the Command Prompt and DOS Shell 560
Redirecting Input and Output 560
    Paging with MORE 561
    The Temporary Pipe Files 563
    Adding Comments to a Text File 563
    What Happens When You Redirect Input and Output? 564
    Standard Error Output 565
    Redirecting Output to PostScript Printers 566
    Using ECHO to Automate Commands 566
The DOS Filters 566
    What's a Line? 567
    Sorting Lines with SORT 567
    Locating Lines with FIND 571
Working with DOS Shell 574
    Defining Program Items 575
    A Trip Through DOSSHELL.INI 578
On Your Own 582

37   Programming Logic in Batch Programs   583

Introduction to Programming Logic 584
Linking Batch Files 584
    Chaining Versus Calling 585
    Chaining 585
    Calling 586
    Passing Replaceable Parameters 587
    Multiple Links 587

Recursion 588
Killing a Batch Job with Links 588
Branching 588
Types of Branches 589
The *IF* Command 590
Exit Codes 591
The ERRORLEVEL Condition 591
Testing for Files 596
Comparing Text Strings 596
Testing for Null Values 597
Nested IFs 598
Loops 598
Sample Loop 599
Loops Involving SHIFT 600
Using FOR to Create Loops 601
The *CHOICE* Command 603
CHOICE Variations 605
Using DOSKEY Macros to Override DOS Commands 605
Floppy Batches 606
Clobbering the Batch File 606
On Your Own 607

38   Starting Up DOS   609
Controlling the Booting Process 610
Bypassing the Startup Files 610
Prompting for *CONFIG.SYS* Commands 613
Using Configuration Blocks 613
The Configuration Blocks 615
Defining a Menu 615
Submenus 616
Adding Color to the Menu 618
On Your Own 619

39   Directory Management   621
Advanced Techniques for Managing Directories 622
Recommendations for Directory Structure 622
Using DELTREE to Delete Files Instead of Branches 623
Emptying a Directory Without Deleting the Directory 623
Deleting the Files but Retaining the Directories 624
Restructuring a Directory Tree 625
Why APPEND Is Dangerous 625
Making a Directory Look Like a Drive 626
Creating a Virtual Drive with SUBST 627
Choosing a Drive Name for SUBST 627
TRUENAME 629
On Your Own 630

40   Advanced Copying Techniques   631

Handling Those "Other" Copying Tasks 632
The XCOPY Command 632
  XCOPY Versus DISKCOPY 633
  Avoiding Disk Full Termination 634
  Pruning and Grafting 636
Concatenating Files 637
  Appending Files 638
  The Effect of Concatenation on Certain File Types 640
  Updating Date/Time Stamps 640
  Matched Concatenations 642
  The ABCs of /A and /B 642
The REPLACE Command 644
  Replacing Missing Files 645
  Replacing Existing Files 646
On Your Own 647

41   INTERLNK   649

Linking Two Computers via INTERLNK 650
Overview of the INTERLNK Procedure 651
Cabling the Two Computers 651
Setting Up the Server 652
Setting Up the Client 655
  Identifying the Connected Port 656
  Redirected Drives 658
Completing the Connection with INTERLNK 658
Breaking the Link 660
Copying the INTERLNK Software 661
On Your Own 661

42   Windows on DOS   663

DOS and Windows Working Hand-in-Hand 664
Optimizing Windows 664
  Freeing Up Memory 664
  Freeing Up Disk Space 665
  Using SmartDrive 666
Running DOS Applications under Windows 667
  Starting a DOS Application 668
  Running a DOS Task in a Window 670
  Program Information Files 672
  The PIF Editor 673
  Real and Standard Mode PIF Options 683
On Your Own 686

43   DOS and the Environment   687

DOS's Environment 688
Environment Variables 688
  Displaying Environment Variables 688
  DOS's Environment Variables 689
  Creating an Environment Variable 691

Modifying and Deleting Environment Variables 692
Accessing Environment Variables 692
Controlling the Command Interpreter and the Environment 695
Environment Size 697
Command Interpreter in Another Location 697
Using a Third-Party Command Interpreter 698
Loading a Secondary Command Interpreter 698
Specifying COMSPEC 700
Omitting COMSPEC 700
Dynamic Environment Allocation 701
Starting COMMAND.COM when
   Another Command Interpreter Is Primary 701
Loading a New Primary Command Interpreter 702
Executing a Command with COMMAND.COM 702
Testing a Batch Program with COMMAND.COM 703
On Your Own 704

44   Squeezing Even More Out of Memory   705

Customizing Upper Memory 706
Problems in Using HIMEM.SYS 706
Loading the Correct Driver for the HMA 708
Controlling the Clock Speed 708
Making Memory beyond 16MB Available in EISA Computers 708
Controlling Older Programs that Address Extended Memory Directly 709
Making Sure that DOS Loads into the HMA 709
Shadowing ROM-BIOS 709
Finding Extra Space in Upper Memory 710
Aggressive Scan 711
Use Monochrome Region 711
Excluding Upper Memory Regions 712
Turning Expanded Memory On and Off 713
Problems with UMBs 715
Handling TSRs 715

45   A Second Look at DrvSpace and DblSpace   717

Beyond the Basics with DrvSpace and DblSpace 718
The DriveSpace or DoubleSpace Core Program 718
The *DRVSPACE* or *DBLSPACE* Command 719
Compressing Additional Hard Drives 719
Compressing a Floppy 721
Files on the Host Drive 724
Maintaining Compressed Drives and Their Hosts 725
Caching a Compressed Drive 725
Viewing Compressed Drive Information 726
Resizing the Drive 727
Defragmenting a Compressed Drive 728
Changing the Estimated Compression Ratio 729
Formatting a Compressed Drive 731
Scanning the Drive for Errors 731
Freeing Up Memory 732

Deleting a Compressed Drive 732
Uncompressing a Drive 733
On Your Own 733

46   Additional Techniques for Handling Data   735

Beyond the Basics 736
Formatting at Nondefault Capacities 736
Formatting for Older Versions of DOS 738
Expanding FC's Resynchronization Buffer 739
Comparing Two Files for Sense 742
Understanding DOS's Verification 743
    CRCs 743
    DOS's Verification 744
On Your Own 744

47   Advanced Rescue Techniques   745

DOS's Recovery Tools 746
Handling Structural Problems with SCANDISK and CHKDSK 746
    Invalid Allocation Units 746
    How SCANDISK and CHKDSK Fix Invalid Allocation Units 748
    Allocation Errors 749
    Invalid Subdirectory Entry 750
    Bad Sectors in the Disk's Administrative Areas 752
Rebuilding Disks without Mirror Image Information 753
    How UNFORMAT Rebuilds a Disk 755
    Starting the Rebuilding Process 755
Using MSD 757
On Your Own 759

48   Console Control   761

Dressing Up DOS 762
DOS and Your Video Monitor 762
    The CON Driver 762
    The Video Buffer 763
    What ANSI.SYS Offers 763
The ANSI.SYS Device Driver 764
Sending Commands to ANSI.SYS 765
    Typing the Escape Character 765
    Using PROMPT 766
    Using a Text File 767
    Using a Batch File 768
The ANSI.SYS Codes for Screen Colors 768
Screen and Cursor Control 770
    Creating a Banner 771
    Displaying a Message Box 772
    Character Wrap 774
    Screen Mode (Graphics) 774
ANSI Keyboard Control 775
    Remapping Individual Keys 777
    Assigning Strings to Keys 778

Controlling the CON (Console) Mode 779
    Specifying Lines and Columns 779
    Controlling Keyboard Response 779
Switching the Standard Console Devices 781
Preserving Your Laptop Batteries 782
    The POWER Command 782
On Your Own 783

49   Another Country Heard From   785

Communicating in Other Languages 786
Overview 786
International Formats 787
Typing International Characters 789
Using International Keyboard Layouts 791
    The KEYB Command 792
Using Code Pages 794
    How to Load a Code Page 795
    Monitor Code Pages 795
    Preparing Code Pages 797
    Switching Code Pages 798
    Complete Code Page Example 799
    National Language Support 800
    Another Complete Code Page Example Using NLSFUNC and CHCP 801
    Manipulating Code Pages 802
    Displaying Code Page Information 802
On Your Own 803

50   Printing Through DOS   805

DOS's Very Basic Printing Services 806
Printer Types 806
    Echo Printing 806
    Text Screen Printing 807
Configuring a Printer 808
Using Serial Printers 809
    Configuring the Serial Port 809
    Redirecting a Serial Printer 812
    Viewing Redirection Status 812
The PRINT Command 813
    Configuring PRINT 813
    Controlling the Print Queue 815
Printing GRAPHICS Screens 816
    How GRAPHICS Works 817
    The GRAPHICS Command 817
    GRAPHICS Switches 818
    Aspect Ratio 820
On Your Own 820

51   Configuring Disks and Networks   823

Defining Drives for DOS 824
Configuring Physical Disks 824

Change-Line Support 827
Configuring Logical Floppy Disks 827
    Creating an Alternate Drive Name 828
    Setting Up Two Alternate Drive Names 829
    Adding an External Floppy Disk Drive 830
    Choosing between DRIVER.SYS and DRIVPARM 830
Running DOS on a Network 831
    Upgrading a Networked System to DOS 6.22 832
    DOS Command Limitations 832
    Sharing and Locking Files 833
On Your Own 834

52   The Multimedia PC   835

New Concepts in Multimedia 836
Multimedia Hardware 836
The Software 838
    The MSCDEX Program 839
    Choosing an IRQ 841
    Optimizing CONFIG.SYS and AUTOEXEC.BAT 842

53   Upgrading to QBASIC   843

QBASIC Features and Facilities 844
QBASIC's Interface 845
    The QBASIC Editor 845
    Smart Editor Effects 847
Converting a GW-BASIC or BASICA Program 849
    Running Programs 849
    Line Numbers 850
New Constant and Variable Types 850
    Constants 851
    Numeric Variables 851
    String Variables 851
    Additional String Functions 852
    Array Variables 852
    Record Data Type 852
New Flow of Control Facilities 854
    Expanded *IF* Statement 854
    Using a Case Structure 855
    Loop Structures 856
    Contents of Loop 857
Modular Programming 857
    Examining a Modular Program 858
    Creating a Procedure 858
    Global Variables 859
    Subprograms 860
    Passing Values 861
    Functions 862
    Creating a Function 863
Debugging Innovations 863
    The Immediate Window 863

Tracing a Program 863
Breakpoints 864
Running QBASIC Programs Directly from the DOS Prompt 865
On Your Own 865

54 FDISK   **867**
Partitioning Your Hard Drive with FDISK 868
Starting FDISK 868
Creating a DOS Partition 869
Creating the Primary Partition 870
Creating the Extended Partition 870
Setting the Active Partition 871
Deleting a Partition 871
Viewing Partition Information 872
Exiting FDISK 873
On Your Own 874

55 Riding the Internet with DOS   **875**
What Is Internet? 876
Internet Resources 876
Databases 877
Newsgroups 877
E-mail 877
Mailing Lists 878
Chatting 878
Other Services 879
Accessing Internet 879
A Word about Modems 880
Telecommunications Software 881
The Gateway to Internet 882
Some Internet Warnings 882
How Do I Access Internet through DOS? 883

Part 6 Command Reference   **885**

Command Reference   **887**
Conventions 888

A Device Drivers   **1065**
ANSI.SYS 1066
CHKSTATE.SYS 1067
DBLSPACE.SYS 1067
DISPLAY.SYS 1068
DRIVER.SYS 1069
DRVSPACE.SYS 1071
EGA.SYS 1072
EMM386.EXE 1073
HIMEM.SYS 1078
INTERLNK.EXE 1081
POWER.EXE 1083

RAMDRIVE.SYS 1084
SETVER.EXE 1086
SIZER.SYS 1086
SMARTDRV.EXE 1087

B   Exit Codes   1089

C   IBM Extended Character Set   1093

Glossary   1097

Index   1115

Acknowledgments

Special thanks to Judi Fernandez for her masterful work on this completely new edition.

Thanks also to my literary agent, Bill Gladstone at Waterside Productions and to Donna Tabler, Scott Clark, and Keven Goldstein for their invaluable assistance.

Their contributions are greatly appreciated.

Introduction

Many new personal computer users try to ignore DOS. They concentrate on learning just the one or two applications they work with every day. A word processor or database manager, however, can't locate and correct errors in the disk directory structure; these programs can't rescue a file that you deleted by mistake, and they can't detect and remove a virus that has infected your disk. The more you know about DOS, the safer your data will be. You also can significantly improve the overall performance of your system with DOS. For example, you can make your applications run faster, and you can squeeze almost twice as much data onto your hard disk.

What You Will Learn

In this book, you learn how to do the following:

- Upgrade your system to DOS 6.22
- Use DOS's on-screen Help system
- Protect your system from viruses
- Protect your data from accidental deletions
- Manage your disks, directories, and files by using DOS Shell or the DOS command prompt
- Set up DOS Shell to make your everyday tasks easier (if you don't have Windows or a third-party shell)
- Use several programs at the same time under DOS Shell
- Use DOS's full-screen editor to create and modify text files
- Write your own simple miniprograms using DOS's batch programming commands
- Understand and take full advantage of the CONFIG.SYS file
- Use DOS's new backup system to protect and restore files
- Optimize the way your system uses memory
- Optimize your hard disk; you can minimize the time it takes to read and write data as well as double the amount of usable space
- Use DOS with Windows
- Use DOS on the Internet
- Use DOS with a multimedia PC
- Upgrade to QBASIC, if you have been programming with an earlier form of BASIC
- Connect two computers together via DOS's INTERLNK facility
- Manage the DOS environment

- Take full advantage of your hardware, including your printer, monitor, keyboard, and disk drives
- Set up your system for the conventions and character set of another country

At the back of the book, you will find a complete command reference for all the DOS commands and device drivers. With DOS 6, Microsoft decided to cut down on the amount of printed documentation. Most of the commands and device drivers are described only in the on-screen Help system, and that information is often incomplete. When you are ready to move beyond the basics, and dig into the nuts and bolts of DOS commands and drivers, you will find the Command Reference and Appendix A, "Device Drivers," two of your best resources.

This book explains the DOS basics and advanced techniques, as well as the major new utilities released with DOS 6, such as MEMMAKER (DOS 6.0) and SCANDISK (DOS 6.2). Whether you are a new DOS user or have just upgraded from an earlier DOS version, you will find all the information you need to gain mastery of your new operating system.

What's New in This Edition?

I have added DOS 6.22 into this edition of the DOS Guide, and I have also made some other, rather sweeping changes. I have combined two books into one, incorporating the former *Peter Norton's Advanced DOS* into this book, so that you will find both basic and advanced information in one complete guide. Parts 1 through 4 of this new edition cover DOS basics, and Part 5 presents a wealth of advanced techniques for those readers who are ready to progress beyond the basics.

In addition, I have added several new features to the book:

- Look throughout the book for numbered lists of steps included directly in the text. These are hands-on practical exercises that guide you in trying out most of the DOS facilities. If you follow the steps carefully, you'll see for yourself exactly how DOS works—and, on occasion, doesn't work, which is just as important.

  The exercises within each chapter are cumulative. By that I mean that the earlier exercises often set up your system for later ones. You might, for example, create a file early in a chapter, rename it a few pages later, move it to another directory a little later, and delete it toward the end of the chapter. So, when you read a chapter, either do all the exercises, or don't do any. If you skip some exercises, you might find that you don't have the files or directories you need to successfully complete the remaining ones.

  But, you don't have to work through all the chapters in the book in sequence. Each chapter's exercises are independent of any other chapter's, so that you can pick and choose the order in which you read the chapters in this book. Also, by the end of any chapter, you will have removed any changes you have made to your system, except those that you choose to keep. (There is one exception to this rule: The exercises in Chapter 23, "MSBACKUP and MWBACKUP," continue into Chapter 24, "Restore and Compare," so that you can practice backing up and restoring files.)

To create the exercises, I had to make some basic assumptions about your PC. The exercises assume that you have upgraded to DOS 6.2 or 6.22, that drive C is your boot drive, that you have installed DOS in a directory named DOS on that drive, that you have not deleted any of the files that came with DOS (especially the .TXT files), and that you have at least 1MB of free space on the same drive. They also assume that drive A is a floppy disk drive. If these basic assumptions are not met, you will need to adapt the exercises for your system. If you have installed DOS on drive D, for example, you would adapt all drive references to D.

- I have included itemized Procedures for the most frequently performed DOS tasks such as deleting a file, copying a file, and creating a new directory. The Procedures summarize the discussion in the accompanying text, so they help to provide an overview of a new task that you're learning. But, more importantly, they serve as a quick review and expert guide when you actually need to perform a task several months after reading the chapter. The Procedures are set off in special boxes (an example follows) so that you can find them easily.

How to Create a New Directory in DOS Shell

1. Activate the directory tree.

2. Select the desired parent directory.

3. Choose File, Create Directory.

4. Make sure that the Parent Name field is correct. (If not, choose Cancel and try again.)

5. Enter the desired name in the New Directory Name text box.

6. Choose OK.

- I have also added Problem Solvers for the most common DOS problems such as not being able to boot, or getting an error message when you try to use a DOS utility. Each Problem Solver explains why the problem occurs and guides you in solving it. Problem Solvers are also set off on the page; the following is an example of a Problem Solver from Chapter 6, "Managing Directories":

Problem: When I try to switch to my floppy drive, I get an error message, even though there's a disk in the drive.

Either your floppy disk has never been formatted for DOS (it might be formatted for some other operating system), or it is so badly damaged that DOS can't read it.

If you're trying to read a disk provided by someone else, ask that person to make another one, being sure to format it for DOS.

If you're trying to use a new, blank disk, you must format it first. Chapter 18, "Additional Disk Management," explains how to format disks.

- I have added several new types of notes. Peter's Principles suggest good DOS practices, such as making file names meaningful. Network notes advise you on how to apply the current topic to a networked PC. Looking Ahead notes let you know that there's more information on a topic (usually advanced techniques) in later chapters.

- I have added chapters on Internet, using DOS with Windows, and the multimedia PC.

Conventions Used in This Book

The following conventions are used in this book:

italics	Expressions in italics indicate variables to be replaced by specific values. In the example "SCANDISK creates generic file names in the form FILE*nnnn*.CHK," the *nnnn* indicates four characters that change from file name to file name. The actual file names generated by SCANDISK are FILE0000.CHK, FILE0001.CHK, FILE0002.CHK, and so on. (Italics also are used when introducing new terms, and occasionally for emphasis.)
ALL CAPS	In regular text, commands, file names, directory names, drive names, and program names are shown in all caps to make them stand out from the context. The expression "the copy program," for example, refers to any program that makes a copy, but "the COPY program" refers specifically to the DOS program named COPY.
	Commands are shown in ALL CAPS, even though DOS usually ignores case. You can enter commands in any mixture of cases, and many users prefer to work with all lowercase characters. The few places in which DOS is case-sensitive are pointed out in the appropriate chapters.

Keys linked with the plus sign (+)	Two or more key names joined by a + indicates that you hold down the first key while you press the second key. "Ctrl+Break," for example, indicates that you hold down the Ctrl key while pressing the Break key.
`Special typeface`	Screen displays and on-screen messages appear in a special typeface.
Filespecs	The expression *filespec* is used to indicate the conglomeration of elements that identifies a file or set of files. It can include a drive name, a path name, a file name, and/or an extension. In many cases, a drive name alone is sufficient; all files in the current directory of that drive are selected. In other cases, you may find it necessary to specify a directory, a file name, and perhaps an extension to identify the files you want.

Icons

These icons are used in the book to identify various types of notes.

This icon identifies a *Note*, which presents an interesting side fact about the topic being discussed.

This icon identifies a *Tip*, a technique that saves you time or hassle.

Watch especially for this icon, which identifies a *Warning*. Warnings alert you to the possibility of losing data, damaging your system, or wasting money.

This icon identifies a *Network Note*, which advises you how to apply DOS techniques on a network.

This icon identifies a *Peter's Principle*, which suggests intelligent PC management.

This icon identifies a *Looking Ahead* note, which alerts you that more information on a topic appears later in the book.

This icon identifies a *Problem Solver*, which helps you over a DOS pitfall.

This icon identifies information pertaining to Windows.

This icon identifies information that is unique to DOS 6.2

This icon identifies information that is unique to DOS 6.22

1

Getting
Acquainted

1

Getting Acquainted with Your System

Introduction

Your personal computer system isn't just hardware; it's also the software that makes the system work for you, the data it processes, the media on which it stores information, and, most important of all, you.

Your Hardware

Hardware refers to the physical pieces of your system: at the very least, the system unit, monitor, and keyboard. You probably also have a mouse and printer, and maybe a few bells and whistles.

The System Unit

The *system unit* houses the heart of your computer. This unit is where the microprocessor chip, disk drives, and the power supply are located. Personal computers are made to be opened by their owners, so feel free to take the case off; but, be careful not to touch or remove anything unless you know what you're doing.

Warning: Be sure to unplug your system unit before you open it.

To open your system unit, remove the screws around the outside edges of the back panel and slide the case off. Figure 1.1 shows the inside of a typical system unit.

Figure 1.1.
The inside of the system unit.

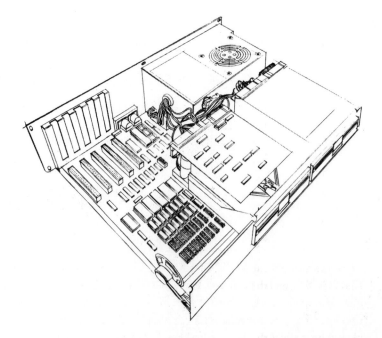

Tip: While the case is open, vacuum or blow out the dust.

Inside, you see the system board (or *mother board*), the power supply, some expansion boards, the disk drives, and lots of ribbon cables. The system board is the large circuit card that everything else plugs into. It holds the microprocessor module, memory, possibly some other chips, and all the circuitry to connect them.

The Microprocessor

The *microprocessor* provides the brains of your computer, an amazing conglomeration of electronic circuits microminiaturized into a single silicon chip. The microprocessor executes the program commands that make up a word processor, a CAD/CAM system, a solitaire game, and the many other programs that run on your computer. You should be able to see the chip on your system board, which is probably near the center. Figure 1.2 shows what the newer ones look like.

Figure 1.2.
A *microprocessor module*.

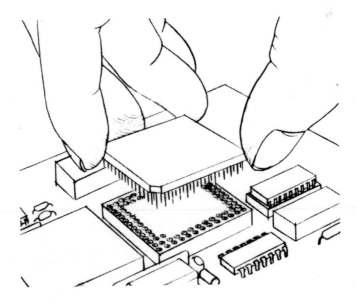

The terms *286*, *386*, and so on refer to the type of microprocessor your system contains. The original IBM PCs, XTs, and their clones featured Intel Corporation's 8088 microprocessor. ATs use the 80286 chip, known familiarly as the 286. Newer machines contain 386 or 486 chips, or the Pentium chip, which is the newest member of the Intel family of chips designed for PCs. Each new microprocessor more than doubles the capacity and speed of its predecessor, with the exception of the Pentium — some 486 chips can meet or beat the Pentium's speed. Suffixes such as the SX in 386SX indicate variations of the chip's basic architecture.

Coprocessor

Your system also might have a math *coprocessor*. The coprocessor handles math better than the main processor does, significantly speeding up programs that must do a lot of heavy calculating. Surprisingly, spreadsheets and scientific calculators aren't the only beneficiaries. A great deal of math is required to control margins, to manage fonts, to position the cursor in a drawing or document, to zoom in and out of a drawing, and so on. Programs like word desktop publishers and graphic developers may speed up noticeably when you install a coprocessor—if they're designed to use that coprocessor. Some versions of the newer chips, like the 486, include a math coprocessor with the processor (but the 486SX has its math coprocessor turned off).

Memory

Your *memory* components store the programs and data currently in use. These components provide short-term, high-speed storage closely linked to the microprocessor for fast retrieval. However, most memory requires a constant supply of electricity to hold data. When the computer's power goes out, intentionally or accidentally, the memory component drops its data.

Many people find memory the most confusing component in their computer system—both to understand and to control. Chapter 30, "Additional Memory Facilities for 386, 486, and Pentium Computers," and Chapter 31, "Caching the Drives," explain terms like *RAM, ROM, extended memory*, and *expanded memory* in detail. These chapters also show you how to get the most out of your system's memory with DOS.

Buses

In computer terms, a *bus* is a circuit that carries data from one component to another. A bus transfers data between memory and the microprocessor, for example. Even the simplest operations such as adding two numbers involve several data transfers, so the size and speed of a computer's buses have enormous impact on the overall speed of the computer.

For example, a 386 has 32-bit architecture, meaning that its basic data storage unit—called a *word* —can hold 32 digits. A full 386 machine (the 386DX) includes 32-bit buses, so data can be transferred a whole word at a time. A 386SX saves money by using 16-bit buses internally, so it takes two trips to transfer a complete word. Therefore, a 386SX is cheaper but slower than a 386DX.

CMOS and Its Battery

The CMOS or *complementary metal-oxide semiconductor* module (pronounced sea-moss) first appeared in 286s to retain information about the computer's hardware configuration. This information becomes crucial during the startup process. If the system doesn't know what type of hardware it has, it can't read the disk drives and it can't load DOS.

Because the CMOS must retain its information when the computer's power is off, a small battery provides it with constant power. Most new computers have a lithium battery with a life expectancy of several years. When the battery dies, you see CMOS error messages when you try to boot. You can still boot by running your hardware's SETUP program and manually setting the drive types, the date, and the time. Your hardware manuals should tell you how to use the SETUP program; if not, call your dealer or the manufacturer. When you get the battery replaced, your technician may substitute a regular battery pack for the lithium battery. Regular batteries don't last as long, but you can replace them yourself. The CMOS battery also supplies your clock/calendar chip so that the time and date remain current when the machine is turned off or the power goes out.

Tip: Now is a good time to prepare for a CMOS battery failure. Your hard drive is identified by a code number. If you don't know that code number, you can't complete the SETUP program and boot your computer when your battery dies. Write down your code number now and attach it to your system unit. If your hardware manual doesn't tell you the number, DOS 6 includes a diagnostic program called MSD that can tell you what it is. Start MSD and look in the disk drive section for the message `CMOS type nnn`. (MSD is explained in Chapter 47, "Advanced Rescue Techniques.")

Jumpers and Dip Switches

Jumpers and dip switches weren't developed just to torture innocent PC owners. (See Figure 1.3.) They are designed to make your hardware more flexible by reconfiguring it when you change its basic setup. For example, if you add more memory, you may have to reset a dip switch to tell the system how much memory is present. If you change from a lithium battery to a battery pack, you probably have to move a jumper to redirect the circuit to the new power source. You shouldn't change jumpers or dip switches without knowing what you're doing. Your hardware manual probably has instructions on what needs to be done. If you can't figure it out, see your dealer or repair technician.

Note: Systems featuring Plug and Play don't need jumpers and dip switches. As soon as you install a new device, you can begin using it.

Figure 1.3.
A jumper (inset) and a dip switch.

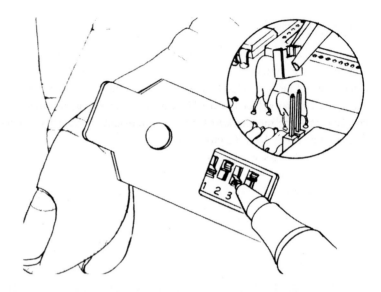

Tip: Printers often have dip switches, which are used to select options such as the default font, vertical spacing, and the emulation of a standard printer.

The Keyboard

Your keyboard works much like a typewriter, with some important differences. In addition to the regular typing area, it has function keys, a keypad, and some special-purpose keys.

Function Keys

The function keys are labeled F1, F2, and so on, and are located to the left of the typing area or across the top. You may have 10 or 12 of them (or more). Each program uses the function keys for whatever it wants. Throughout this book, you will learn what they do in DOS; but they have different functions in Windows, WordPerfect, Lotus 1-2-3, and every other program you use.

Tip: With many programs, F1 brings help information to the screen.

The Keypad

The keypad has two functions. When NumLock is on, it works like a 10-key adding machine. The numbers appear in the uppercase positions on the key caps. When NumLock is off, the keypad becomes a cursor-movement pad. (The *cursor* is the indicator on your monitor screen showing where the next character will be typed.) The cursor movements appear in the lowercase positions on the key caps; only the number keys have cursor-movement functions, but the 5 key has none. What these keys do depends on the program currently in control; but, generally, you can count on the up-arrow key moving the cursor toward the top of the screen, the left-arrow key moving the cursor to the left, and so on. The gray keys on the keypad have only one function, which works whether NumLock is on or off.

Try using your keypad with NumLock on and off:

1. There is a NumLock light on your keyboard, somewhere near the keypad. If the light is off, press the NumLock key to turn it on.

    The light is on when NumLock is on.

2. Press 1, 2, 4, /, and *.

3. The characters you typed should appear on your monitor.

4. Press NumLock once to turn the light off.

    NumLock is off when the light is off.

5. Press the 4 key. Notice that it no longer types a 4. Instead, it moves the cursor to the left, and repositions it under that character.

    When NumLock is off, the number keys have their cursor movement functions.

6. Press the * key. Notice that it still types an asterisk.

    The gray keys have the same function whether NumLock is on or off.

Extra Cursor Keys

Most modern computers have a keyboard with either 101 or 102 keys (the original keyboards had only 84 keys). The newer type of keyboard, known as an enhanced keyboard, has an extra set of cursor-movement keys so that you can leave the keypad locked in the numeric position. Again, the meaning of these keys and whether they duplicate the functions of the keypad keys depends on the program.

The Locking Keys

Your keyboard has three locking keys: NumLock, ScrollLock, and CapsLock. As you have seen, *NumLock* locks the keypad into uppercase (numerics) or lowercase (cursor movement) functions. *ScrollLock* has no function with most software; many spreadsheet programs use it, however. *CapsLock* locks the letter keys into uppercase (capitals). Unlike Shift Lock on a regular typewriter, CapsLock has no effect on number or symbol keys (or any keys other than letters).

Try CapsLock on your keyboard:

1. Find the CapsLock light on your keyboard. If it's off, press the CapsLock key to turn it on.

   CapsLock is on when the light is on.

2. Type **A**, **B**, and **c**.

   Notice that these keys produce capital letters.

3. Type **1**, **2**, and **3**. Also type a comma, a period, and a slash (/).

   Notice that these keys produce their lowercase characters even though CapsLock is on.

4. Hold down shift and type **!**, **@**, and **#**. Also type **<**, **>**, and **?**.

   As you can see, you need to use the Shift key to type the uppercase symbols on these keys.

5. Press CapsLock once to turn off the light.

   CapsLock is off when the light is off.

6. Type **a**, **b**, **c**, **1**, **2**, **3**, and a comma, period, and slash.

   With CapsLock off, letters appear in lowercase. Numbers and symbols are not affected by the CapsLock key.

A locking key is a *toggle* key; press the key once to turn it on. It stays on until you press it again to turn it off.

The Shifting Keys

Your keyboard has three shifting keys — Shift, Ctrl, and Alt — that produce no characters of their own, but alter the function of other keys. For example, in a word processing program, the unshifted G key probably types the lowercase letter g. If you press Shift with G, which is written as Shift+G, an uppercase G probably results. Ctrl+G may have some other function, as may Alt+G, Shift+Ctrl+G, Shift+Alt+G, Ctrl+Alt+G, and Shift+Ctrl+Alt+G. The Ctrl key is used a lot with DOS, as in Ctrl+G or Ctrl+Alt+G. Using various combinations of the shifting keys, a program can assign eight different functions to one key.

The Shift key generally reverses the effect of a locking key. If CapsLock is on for a word processor, the unshifted G key probably types an uppercase G, and Shift+G types a lowercase g. The same is true for the keypad; if it's set for numeric functions, Shift produces the cursor functions and vice versa.

Try the Shift key in combination with CapsLock and NumLock:

1. Press CapsLock to turn it on.

2. Type G.

   The capital letter G results.

3. Now type Shift+G.

   The lowercase letter g results.

4. Press NumLock to turn it on.

5. Type 4 on the numeric keypad.

   The number 4 results.

6. Now type Shift+4 on the numeric keypad.

   The cursor moves one character to the left.

Tip: In many programs, Shift+Tab is the opposite of Tab. That is, it tabs backwards.

Special-Purpose Keys

Several of your keyboard keys have special purposes for your system. The *Pause* key generally interrupts the current program until you press any other key, at which time the program continues where it left off. The same key, when pressed with Ctrl, generates a Break signal that kills the current program (although you can't do this in some programs). The PrintScreen key (which may be Shift+PrintScreen on your keyboard) generally prints whatever is on your screen, although it may have trouble if your screen is currently in graphics mode. (Chapter 50, "Printing Through DOS," shows how you may be able to print graphics screens too.) The *Esc* key generally cancels whatever is happening without actually killing the current program.

Note: Ctrl+S functions the same as Pause, and Ctrl+C functions the same as Ctrl+Break. If you are an experienced typist, you might prefer these keys because you don't have to move your hands from the home keys to use them.

Try out the Pause and Esc keys on your PC:

1. You have typed several characters on your screen. Press Esc to tell DOS to ignore them.

   DOS displays a backslash (\ ) and the cursor moves to a new line.

2. Locate the Pause key and be ready to press it when you do the next step.

3. You will display some data on your computer and pause it. Type the following command to display the contents of a file. As soon as the data starts appearing on your screen, press the Pause key.

```
TYPE C:\DOS\README.TXT
```

When you press Pause, the data should stop scrolling onto the screen.

4. Press any other key to release the pause, then press Pause to interrupt the data again.

5. Find the Ctrl key and hold it down while you press the Break key (which is also the Pause key) *twice*.

The first time you press Ctrl+Break, you merely release the pause. The second time, you kill the program. DOS displays its command prompt again.

The Typematic Feature

The character and cursor-movement keys repeat themselves if you hold them down. For example, you can type a row of asterisks by holding down the * key. Some programs, such as Windows and DOS, enable you to adjust how long you must hold a key down before it starts repeating, and how fast it repeats. Chapter 48, "Console Control," shows you how to adjust the typematic rate for DOS.

Try out the typematic feature on your keyboard:

1. Press and hold down the T key to type a string of Ts.

2. Press and hold down the Backspace key to delete the string of Ts.

The Mouse

Your keyboard interactswith all programs, but graphical programs such as Windows also work with a mouse. A mouse accomplishes functions visually instead of verbally. You point to the thing you want to do and click a button. You sometimes grab an object and drag it around on-screen. It's often faster and easier to accomplish tasks using a mouse.

Many older DOS programs don't use the mouse. You can't use it on your DOS command prompt screen, for example. But, most newer applications include mouse manipulation. All Windows programs use the mouse.

Your mouse comes with a vocabulary of its own:

- **Pointer.** The graphic symbol on your screen that indicates where the mouse is; the pointer moves as you move the mouse. There is no standard pointer symbol. Each program decides for itself how to display the mouse pointer. Often the shape of the pointer changes as you move it around the screen, to indicate the various functions that are available to you.

- **Point.** To point at an object, move the pointer close to or on top of the object.

- **Click.** To click, you press and release a mouse button without moving the mouse. To click an object, point at it and click. Generally, you click the left button, but some functions need the right button or both buttons together. The mouse is designed so that you click the mouse button with the index finger of your right hand. If you prefer to use your left hand, you may be able to swap the functions of the left and right mouse buttons. Your mouse manual can tell you how.

- **Double-click.** To double-click, you click twice in rapid succession without moving the mouse.

- **Drag.** To drag an object, you point at the object and press and hold down the mouse button while you move the mouse, so that the object also moves. When the object reaches the desired new location, you release the mouse button to drop it there. (This technique is also called *drag-and-drop*.)

Your mouse doesn't work on the DOS command prompt screen, which was not designed for mouse interactions. However, it should work with DOS Shell, DOS utilities such as MSBACKUP and DEFRAG, and with many of your DOS-based applications such as Microsoft Word for DOS. In order to make your mouse work with DOS, you must load a mouse driver—a program that tells DOS how to control a hardware device. If your mouse isn't working when it should, you probably have not loaded the driver. See the manual that came with your mouse for information on loading the driver. (If you don't have a manual, your dealer may be able to help you get your mouse driver loaded.)

Note: If you use your mouse only with Windows, you do not need to load a mouse driver. Windows loads its own mouse driver when it starts up.

Software

The term *software* refers to programs, without which your computer would be a large lump gathering dust in the corner. Two primary categories of software exist: system and application. The difference between them lies in whether they solve a problem within the computer system, or in the external, workaday world of the user.

System Software

System software controls your computer system and its resources: memory, the disk drives, and the microprocessor. System software includes operating systems such as DOS, shells such as Windows, device drivers, and *utilities* —separate programs that help you manage your system. The DOS package includes dozens of utilities to do such things as format disks, manage disk directories, copy files, and print files.

Applications

Applications turn your computer into a work tool. Applications include programs such as word processors, spreadsheets, and database managers. An application program helps you *apply* your computer system to problems outside the computer.

Disks

Disks are used for permanent storage of your programs and data. You keep the programs and data you use most often on your hard disk because it is faster and holds much more data than a floppy disk. Floppy disks generally are used for transferring data between two computers—for example, for shipping programs and data to customers—and for long-term, off-line storage.

DOS assigns single-letter names to your disk drives. Your first floppy drive is called A. If you have a second floppy drive, it's called B; otherwise, drive A can also be referred to as drive B. Your first hard drive is C. Additional hard drives are named D, E, and so on. Other types of drives such as CD-ROM drives, RAM drives, and network drives receive higher letters. In commands, you often have to put a colon after a drive name to distinguish it from some other type of name. For example, to format the floppy disk in drive A, you must enter the following command (do NOT do this now):

FORMAT A:

Whether it's a hard disk, a floppy, or something in between, a computer disk consists of a round platter that spins, much like an audio disk. It uses magnetic technology to record data in concentric circles called *tracks*.

Note: CDs and "Flopticals" use optical technology rather than magnetism to read and write data.

Each recording surface on the disk has its own read-write head. The arm that holds the head moves back and forth over the surface of the disk to locate a desired track. Then, the disk drive waits for the desired area to spin under the head, and reads or writes the data as appropriate. Because the disk spins so fast, the drive can't read or write just one character or one number, so it divides the tracks into *sectors* and reads or writes one sector at a time. The disks in common use today have 512-byte sectors. (A byte is the storage space for one character.)

Not all of the disk stores data; some of it holds system information. Every sector has an *address*, which is a number that identifies it. Each sector address appears in an area preceding the sector; the drive hardware reads the sector addresses to locate the sector it wants.

Also stored with the sector address is a special value called a CRC (which stands for *cyclic redundancy check*) that helps to validate the data in the sector. When it writes data in a sector, the drive controller performs a special calculation on the data to arrive at the CRC value, which it stores with the sector address. When the drive controller reads a sector, it recalculates the CRC value and compares it to the stored one. If they don't match, the drive controller knows that something is wrong with the data and refuses to use it; you see an error message on your monitor when this happens. Chapter 27, "CHKDSK and SCANDISK," shows you how to deal with disk problems such as this.

Disk data goes bad for a variety of reasons. A disk could have manufacturing defects that were too slight to be detected; such defects sometimes crop up after DOS has stored data on the disk. In addition, the magnetic spots that represent the data sometimes begin to drift after a while; if they drift far enough, the data can no longer be read. But, the most common cause of data loss on disks is mishandling by users. You can protect your disks by following these sensible guidelines:

- Never expose them to magnetism. You must avoid not only those obvious magnets stuck to your refrigerator, but also audio speakers, telephone receivers, most screwdrivers, magnetic paper clip holders, and even electrical wires.
- Keep your computer and its disks in a clean environment. Dust, smoke, and other ambient particles can prevent a drive from reading a disk.
- Keep disks cool and dry.
- Never touch the recording surface.
- For a 5 1/4-inch floppy, don't write on the stick-on label after attaching it to the disk. Also, don't bend the disk.

Your Data

Whether it's a doctoral dissertation, a client database, a five-year plan, or the great American novel, your data is one of the most crucial parts of your system. The hardware, software, and disks can be replaced. But, it could be very difficult, if not impossible, to replace your data unless you keep a good set of backup copies, as explained in Chapter 23, "MSBACKUP and MWBACKUP."

How Data Is Stored

You probably have heard the terms *bits* and *bytes*. *Bit* stands for *binary digit*, which is the way computers represent data internally. A binary digit can have only two values, 0 and 1; so, it can be represented in a computer by a magnetized or demagnetized spot on a disk, an electric pulse or no pulse in a circuit, and so on.

To create meaningful data out of 1s and 0s, eight bits are grouped into a *byte*. When a byte is used to store numeric data, it can handle any value between 0 (binary 00000000) and 255 (binary 11111111); bytes are combined to represent larger numbers. When a byte is used to store character data, it can hold one character. The meaning of each byte depends on which character set is being used. Many different character sets are common, although most of them are based on a code called the *American Standard Code for Information Interchange* (ASCII, which is pronounced ASK-key).

ASCII code is based on 7 bits, not 8. The high-order bit (on the left) is always 0, so only 128 characters are possible in ASCII code. All the lowercase and uppercase letters in the American English alphabet, the 10 digits, and a collection of symbols (such as the period and the comma) are included in the 128 characters. Today's word processors and other text-based software need more characters, and they assign values to the remaining 128 byte values from 10000000 to 11111111. The problem is, those *extended* characters aren't standardized by ASCII, so one program may treat 10001010 as an ë, and another may treat it as a ç. In fact, the same program may interpret it differently depending on which font is in use.

Kilobytes, Megabytes, Gigabytes, and Beyond

The capacity of a computer's disks or memory is expressed in kilobytes, megabytes, and gigabytes. In the outside world, *kilo* means 1,000; but in computers, where everything must be based on powers of 2, it means 1,024 (that's 2^{10}). So a 360KB disk holds 368,640 bytes. A megabyte is 1,024 kilobytes or 1,048,576 bytes, so an 80MB hard disk holds 83,886,080 bytes. A gigabyte is 1,024 megabytes or 1,073,741,824 bytes, so 4 gigabytes of memory holds 4,294,967,296 bytes. For convenience's sake, you can think of a kilobyte as a thousand bytes, a megabyte as a million bytes, and a gigabyte as a billion bytes. In the near future, you may be measuring memory in terabytes, which is more than a trillion bytes.

The User

In general terms, the person who operates a personal computer is referred to as the *user*—that's you. The rest of your system depends on you to tell it what to do and when to do it. The real purpose of this book is to help you make intelligent decisions about managing your hardware, software, data, and storage media. The key to doing that lies in understanding how your system works, what can go wrong, how you can use the tools that DOS provides to prevent problems as well as recover from them, and, occasionally, when to turn to outside sources for help.

On Your Own

- For a detailed description of your hardware components and peripherals—the underlying technology, standards, and specifications—you may want to consult the *Winn L. Rosch Hardware Bible*, Third Edition, SAMS Publishing (1994).

- For a better understanding of how the different components within your computer work together, and what goes on underneath the high-level DOS commands you will be using in this book, you may also want to consult *Peter Norton's Inside the PC*, 5th Edition, Brady Publishing.

2

Getting Acquainted with DOS

Introduction

The better you understand DOS, the more control you will have over your computer.

What is DOS?

An operating system is a set of system programs that makes it possible for you to use your computer. It provides the links among you, the hardware, and other software. The Disk Operating System (DOS) was developed by IBM and Microsoft for the original IBM PCs. As personal computers have evolved into today's 486 and Pentium machines, DOS has grown along with them. The latest version of DOS, called DOS 6.22, is much more sophisticated and powerful than the original DOS. It's also a lot easier to use.

> **Note:** In this book, the term *DOS* (without a version number) refers to any and all versions of DOS. The term *DOS 6* refers to the newest version of DOS, which was originally released as DOS 6.0, was upgraded to 6.2 about a year later, and has now been upgraded to DOS 6.22. The terms *DOS 6.2* and *DOS 6.22* are used when discussing those features that appear only in the 6.2 and 6.22 upgrades.

DOS has three main functions: it manages your system's resources (such as memory and disks); it gives you access to your programs and data; and it helps you manage your system.

This chapter introduces you to your operating system. You'll learn a bit more about each of the three main functions mentioned previously and see an overview of some of the specific features that you'll learn to manage throughout this book. In this chapter, you will learn:

- How you interact with DOS via the command prompt or DOS Shell.
- Major features of DOS, such as its disk and data management facilities and its data protection facilities.
- What's new in DOS 6.0, DOS 6.2, and DOS 6.22.

What Does DOS Do?

As soon as you boot, DOS seizes control of every part of your system except one. You, the user, are in control of DOS. How do you interact with and control DOS? You can choose between two methods: the traditional DOS command prompt and DOS Shell.

The Command Prompt

The command prompt has been around since DOS 1 and has more than its share of faults, both major and minor. But many people like working with the command prompt in spite of its shortcomings. Figure 2.1 shows an example of a command prompt interaction. When DOS displays the command prompt, it is saying, in effect, "I'm ready for your next command." In the figure, the user entered a command requesting a listing of the files on drive A; DOS's DIR program displayed the listing. Then DOS displayed the next command prompt.

Figure 2.1.
Sample command prompt interaction.

```
C:\>DIR A:

 Volume in drive A has no label
 Volume Serial Number is 252B-0FEA
 Directory of A:\

SACK-EGA SEC      37178 12-24-91    8:54p
SACK-TDY SEC      50784 12-24-91    8:54p
DEMO         <DIR>        02-23-93  10:37p
        3 file(s)         87962 bytes
                         908800 bytes free

C:\>
```

For many people, the major problem with the command prompt is having to remember DOS commands. Intelligence in software is often measured by its capability to comprehend free-form language, and by that standard DOS is pretty dumb. You must speak to it in much the same way that you would a well-trained dog: with a limited vocabulary and a strict syntax. For example, the command in Figure 2.1 would have failed if the user had typed **LIST**, **SHOW**, or even **DIRECTORY** instead of **DIR**. It also would have produced a different result if the user had omitted the colon after the **A**.

It's easy to get commands wrong, and even experienced people have to look up commands that they don't use very often. DOS includes an on-screen help facility so that you can look up commands without leaving your computer. You'll learn how to use it in Chapter 12, "Working at the Command Prompt."

Note: If you can't find the information you want from DOS's help facility, a complete command reference is located at the back of this book.

Another major problem with the command prompt is that DOS doesn't always provide as much feedback as you would like. The following is another sample command interaction in which a user asks DOS to delete all files ending in .BAK. The entire interaction is shown.

```
C:\>DEL *.BAK
C:\>
```

DOS erased the files but displayed no message about how many files were erased, what their names were, whether any .BAK file couldn't be erased, and so on. Even a simple message such as Done would be better than absolutely nothing. You get much better feedback from the other user interface, DOS Shell.

DOS Shell

The last few years have witnessed the growth in popularity of graphical user interfaces (GUI, pronounced *goo-ey*), which are oriented toward the mouse rather than the keyboard. Instead of typing a command, you choose it from a menu. You can examine a directory and click the files you want to use. When you delete them, you see the files disappear from the list. When you move or copy files, you see the results on your screen. Many actions can be done without even using a menu. You drag objects around on your screen to accomplish your work. These types of actions are more natural for most people than entering commands with a strict vocabulary and syntax.

DOS first introduced its graphical user interface—called DOS Shell—with DOS 4. The Shell was significantly improved with DOS 5. DOS 6.0 made no major changes to it. With DOS 6.2, it was eliminated from the primary DOS package because of the increasing popularity of Windows, which is a much better GUI. But, if you can't use Windows, DOS Shell is still available, and it's better than no GUI at all. If you don't have the Shell program left over from an earlier version of DOS, you can order a copy from Microsoft; see your DOS *User's Guide* for details.

Figure 2.2 shows an example of the DOS Shell screen. The menus are at the top—named File, Options, and so on. Underneath the menus, you can see a list of all the drives belonging to this system. Each drive is represented by a small picture, called an *icon*, that identifies the type of drive: the figure shows floppy, hard, and RAM drives.

Underneath the drive list is a directory tree and file list, which display the contents of the selected drive. At the bottom, the areas labeled Main and Active Task List are lists of commands that start up programs when you select them.

At the command prompt, you can execute only one command at a time. The next command prompt doesn't appear until the preceding one is completed (except for memory-resident programs, which

Figure 2.2.
A DOS Shell screen.

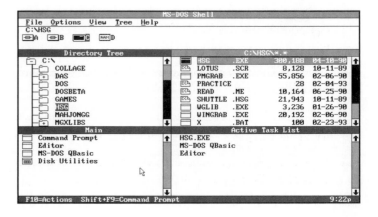

are in a class of their own and are discussed in Chapter 30, "Additional Memory Facilities for 386, 486, and Pentium Computers"). In DOS Shell, you can launch several programs concurrently and switch back and forth among them; this technique is called *task swapping*. Notice the Active Task List in the lower right corner of Figure 2.2. It shows that three programs are currently loaded: HSG.EXE, MS-DOS QBasic, and Editor.

An example should help to explain why you would want to swap tasks. Suppose that you are working on a document with your word processor when you realize you need some information from a spreadsheet. If you are working at the command prompt, where task swapping is not available, you must do the following:

1. Exit your word processor (being sure to save the document).
2. Open the spreadsheet program.
3. Open the desired worksheet.
4. Find the needed data and copy it by hand.
5. Close the spreadsheet.
6. Open the word processor.
7. Open the document.
8. Find your former place in the document.
9. Type the data from the spreadsheet.

Now suppose that you're working in DOS Shell with task swapping. The task is much simpler and faster:

1. Switch from the word processor to the DOS Shell screen. (Leave the word processor running and the document open.)
2. Start up the spreadsheet program.
3. Open the desired worksheet.
4. Find the needed data and copy it by hand.
5. Switch back to the word processor; you'll return to the same place in the same document you left.
6. Enter the spreadsheet data.

Now that the spreadsheet is open, the next time you want to consult it, it's even easier:

1. Switch directly from the word processor to the open worksheet. (You don't have to go through the Shell screen.)
2. Find the desired data and copy it by hand.

3. Switch back to the word processor document.

4. Type the data from the spreadsheet.

I said earlier that Windows was a better GUI than DOS, and this process serves as a perfect case in point. With Windows, you just open the spreadsheet in a second window and copy the desired data electronically (using the Windows clipboard) to the word processor. Unfortunately, DOS Shell doesn't have a direct copy facility; you have to do it by hand.

Many people who have been using DOS since its early days prefer the command prompt because they are used to it. However, new users will find the Shell much easier to learn and use, at least at first. Many experienced users also prefer the Shell for tasks such as moving and copying files. This book emphasizes using the Shell for new users that don't have Windows (or another more sophisticated interface provided by a third-party vendor, such as Norton Desktop for DOS).

As you become more familiar with DOS, however, you'll find yourself learning more and more commands, because you have a lot more control over DOS when you can use its commands. You'll learn how to work at the command prompt in later chapters.

DOS Features

DOS provides facilities to help you with the tasks you must do every day, such as managing files. It also provides help for the less common tasks that you may have to do when trouble develops in your system.

Command Prompt Features

When you're working at the command prompt, DOS helps you out in many ways:

- You can recall and modify a former command rather than having to type a new one from scratch.

- You can create macros to simplify often-used commands.

- You can display documentation on your monitor to help you with command usage and syntax.

- You can design your own command prompt.

- If a command produces so much output that it won't fit on one screen, you can break it into pages.

- You can redirect command messages from the screen to a file, a printer, or someplace else. You can even feed them to another command as input.

- You can cause a command to be repeated automatically for a set of files.

Batch Program Features

DOS enables you to create your own mini-programs, called *batch programs*, by combining DOS commands. You don't have to be a programmer to write batch programs; many people who know absolutely nothing about applications or systems programming write batch programs.

- You can test a condition (such as whether the AUTOEXEC.BAT file exists) and decide what command to execute based on the next statement.
- You can display messages to the user.
- You can read a character from the keyboard and decide what to do next, based on what the user typed.

Disk and Data Management Features

One of DOS's major functions is to manage your disks so that all programs use the same storage techniques on all disks and a well-coordinated system results. Any software that runs under DOS doesn't read or write on your disks directly; the software asks DOS to do it. Most of the time, you aren't even aware that DOS is doing this for you—it works behind the scenes.

In general, you access your disk files through your favorite applications, such as your word processor and database manager. However, DOS gives you a number of facilities that you won't find in most applications:

- It provides several commands to manage disks. For example, you can prepare a new disk for use with the FORMAT program and make a backup copy of a complete floppy disk with the DISKCOPY program.
- DOS uses a system of directories to track where files are stored on the disks. You can create and manage directories with such commands as MD (make a directory), DIR (display a directory), and RD (remove a directory).
- Perhaps the largest category of DOS commands helps you manage your files. You can move and copy them, view them, print them, delete them, and sort them. There's even an editor, named EDIT, so that you can create and modify simple files.
- In case you lose track of a file—which happens more than you might think, especially with a large hard disk—you can search for it by name or by its contents.

Protecting and Recovering Your Data

Literally millions of people have used personal computers in the past 10 years or so, and they have discovered literally hundreds of ways to lose data. Some methods are quite easy, such as deleting the wrong files. Others take real dedication: one friend's son decided to drop a few coins in that interesting looking slot in Daddy's new computer; another friend tried to remove the label from a 5 1/4-inch floppy with a razor blade; and another friend put a valuable floppy exactly where she would find it in the morning—attached to the refrigerator with a magnet.

Such mishaps are not the only way to lose data. Hardware and media malfunctions probably account for most problems, and viruses are gaining in (un)popularity.

Every new version of DOS adds a few new utilities to help you protect your data against loss and to recover it when necessary. DOS 6 now includes the following features:

- You can preserve information about deleted files for a few days so that you can undelete them (get them back) if you change your mind.

- Microsoft Anti-Virus detects and removes computer viruses, hopefully before they have time to do any damage.

- Every disk must be formatted before you use it, but sometimes you accidentally format a disk that already contains data. You can unformat disks to recover the former data on them.

- You can write-protect individual files to prevent them from being changed or deleted.

- You can hide files so that others can't see them in your directory lists.

- If bad data gets into a disk's directories and tables, DOS can't find some files even though the files are perfectly fine. The CHKDSK program can identify and fix such problems.

- DOS 6.2 adds SCANDISK, which not only can detect and repair problems with the directories and tables, but also can scan the disk's physical surface for flaws and rescue data from damaged sectors.

- Perhaps most important of all (because you can't possibly prevent all data loss), DOS 6 makes it easy for you to make backup copies of your important files. If you do this regularly, you can recover from any loss, including having your entire computer stolen or melted in a fire.

Note: DOS gives you the tools to protect your data, but it's up to you to use them. This book shows you how.

Memory Facilities

The other day, I got a frantic call from a friend who had just upgraded to a spanking new Pentium with 16MB of memory. When he tried to run his old software, which ran fine on his ancient 286, he got a message saying there wasn't enough memory. How could he be out of memory with 16MB, he wailed! His problem was that he didn't understand how DOS uses memory and how he could rearrange things to free up more than enough space for his applications. Within a few minutes, we had his old applications up and running.

Memory is another area where DOS is always at work behind the scenes, controlling access to the portion of memory, called *conventional memory*, where most programs run. DOS also can control other areas of memory in 286 and higher machines. DOS 6 includes commands and facilities to do the following:

- Manage the memory area outside of conventional memory.
- Load software into parts of memory that were once reserved for system use only; this faculty gives you a lot more room in conventional memory to run your application programs.
- Display reports telling you exactly what's located where in memory.
- Configure your system to get the most out of the memory space you have.

Optimizing Your System's Performance

Even if you have the very latest in hardware, you can improve your system's performance with a little attention to DOS's optimizing facilities. DOS includes several features that make your system run faster and give you more disk space:

- DOS's DEFRAG program reorganizes your disk data for the fastest possible access. You should run DEFRAG regularly to keep your hard disk in tip-top shape.
- You can create RAM drives that work much faster than real drives. A RAM drive uses a memory area to simulate a disk drive without any moving parts.
- DOS's SmartDrive program duplicates disk data in memory so that DOS can read and write in memory instead of on the disk. This duplication makes all your programs run faster because they aren't impeded by the relative slowness of the disk drive.
- In addition, DOS 6.0 introduced a new facility called DoubleSpace that compresses the data on your hard disk so that you can store approximately twice as much data as before— effectively doubling the size of your hard disk. DOS 6.2 improved the DoubleSpace facility and DOS 6.22 replaced it with DriveSpace.

Hardware Features

DOS also is responsible for most interactions with your hardware. Many applications do not access your keyboard, monitor, or printer directly, but ask DOS to do it for them. (This is not a hard and fast rule, however.)

DOS interacts with hardware through *device drivers*, programs that actually control the devices. For example, when a program wants to print a line on the printer, the printer driver supplies the codes that position the print head, select the font, print the data, and so on.

Drivers make DOS more flexible in the types of hardware it can access. If hardware management was built into DOS, the operating system would be able to handle only those printers, monitors, and keyboards already built into the operating system. By using drivers instead, DOS can access any piece of hardware for which you have a driver.

DOS enables you to do the following:

- Specify what device drivers you want to load during booting
- Control the communications settings (baud rate, and so forth) on your serial port
- Set up your hardware to display and print non-English characters, such as Ñ
- Use a device other than the keyboard-monitor combination to communicate between the user and DOS
- Fine-tune a variety of hardware settings for the best system performance

Miscellaneous Services

DOS includes a variety of other facilities:

- It includes features that make installing DOS 6 easy; you can even uninstall the operating system if it doesn't work out for you.
- It includes a program to test your system and provide diagnostic information.
- You may have some software designed for an earlier version of DOS that doesn't recognize DOS 6. You can set up DOS 6 to lie about its version number to such programs.
- You can set the system date and time through DOS.
- The POWER program helps preserve your notebook's battery.

What's New in DOS 6?

If you're already familiar with DOS 5, you may be curious about what's new in DOS 6. The basics of DOS have stayed the same. DOS 6 adds a handful of new utilities to make your job easier:

- **Data compression.** Compresses data so that you can squeeze nearly twice as much onto a disk
- **INTERLNK.** Enables you to hook up two computers with a cable and copy files directly from one to the other.

- **Anti-Virus.** Detects and removes viruses from your system. (A DOS and a Windows version are included in the DOS 6 package.)

- **MEMMAKER.** Makes loading drivers and TSRs into upper memory blocks easier. Essentially, it does all the decision-making for you.

- **DEFRAG.** Reorganizes a disk to eliminate file fragmentation.

- **POWER.** Saves battery power in your laptop.

In addition to the new utilities, DOS has improved a number of older ones:

- **BACKUP.** The old DOS BACKUP program has been completely replaced with a new GUI facility that has many more features and is a lot easier to work with. A DOS version and a Windows version of the backup program are included in DOS 6. (The old RESTORE is still available, so that you can restore from backups you made in an earlier version of DOS.)

- **UNDELETE.** DOS 6's UNDELETE includes Delete Sentry, which preserves deleted files for a few days. This safety feature makes it much easier to recover files accurately. DOS and Windows versions of UNDELETE are included in DOS 6.

- **DEVICEHIGH** and **LOADHIGH.** These two commands now include switches that enable you to control exactly where a TSR is loaded in upper memory. The new MEMMAKER program determines the best location for each TSR and creates the `DEVICEHIGH` and `LOADHIGH` commands for you.

- **On-screen command help.** A completely new command help utility that provides complete on-line documentation for DOS commands (not just the format summaries that DOS 5 provided).

The major purpose of the DOS 6.2 step release was to improve the reliability of DoubleSpace, which experienced problems on some systems. DOS 6.22 step release replaces DoubleSpace with DriveSpace, not for technical reasons but for legal ones.

DOS 6.2 and 6.22 also include a number of other enhancements to DOS:

- **SCANDISK.** SCANDISK examines drives looking for problems on the physical surface and in the directory structure; it can fix most of the errors it finds.

- **Overwrite Protection.** COPY, XCOPY, and MOVE now warn you before overwriting a file.

- **SmartDrive.** SmartDrive now caches CD-ROM drives and has been enhanced in several other ways.

- **Interactive Startup.** When you press F8 during booting, DOS now executes AUTOEXEC.BAT line-by-line, as well as CONFIG.SYS.

- **Interactive Batch Programs.** You can now execute any batch file on a line-by-line basis.

- **DISKCOPY.** You no longer have to keep swapping diskettes to copy a floppy disk in a single drive.

- **Enhanced Readability.** DOS now inserts commas in numbers greater than 999 in messages from programs like DIR and FORMAT.

- **DEFRAG.** You can now defragment a larger number of files.

On Your Own

I said in the introduction to this book that it doesn't make sense to learn only your applications and ignore DOS. This chapter has pointed out some of the ways that being able to use DOS pays off for you. See if you can find at least two DOS features in each of these areas:

- Protecting your data from accidental or intentional damage
- Recovering data if an accident does occur
- Avoiding out of memory messages
- Managing disks and their data files
- Making your system run faster and smarter
- Squeezing as much data as possible onto your disks

3

How DOS Organizes Data

Introduction

If you know how DOS organizes data on disks, you have a better chance of working with DOS instead of fighting it.

How DOS Controls Data

One of DOS's main responsibilities is controlling all the data stored on your disks. If an application wants to read, write, or delete a file, it asks DOS to do the actual disk access. This way, DOS can guarantee that no application will overwrite or damage another application's files.

DOS stores data in a very structured way. If you know how DOS organizes your disks, you have a better chance of working with DOS instead of fighting it. In this chapter, you will learn:

- How to name a file
- How to write a filespec to access a group of related files at the same time
- How DOS protects (and doesn't protect) your files with attributes
- How DOS keeps track of files on a disk
- How to access a file that isn't in the current directory
- How DOS deletes (and doesn't delete) a file

You will also learn to recognize the following terms:

.

..

archive

attribute

branch

chain

child directory

cluster

current directory

default directory

default drive

directory tree

end-of-file (EOF)

File Allocation Table (FAT)

filename

filespec

global filespec

parent directory

path name

root directory

slack

subdirectory

wildcard character

Files

When you want to store something on a disk, you have to place it in a *file*. A file is similar to a piece of paper in a file folder. It might contain a letter, database, spreadsheet, graphic, chapter, program, font, or other item.

Filespecs

In DOS, every file must have a file name of up to eight characters in length. You can use letters, digits, and the following symbols:

_ ^ $ ~ ! # % & - { } ( ) @ ' '

DOS doesn't see any difference between uppercase and lowercase letters. The names TechData, TECHDATA, and techdata are all the same; DOS stores the name as TECHDATA no matter how you type it.

> **Note:** The following special file names are reserved for DOS's use: CLOCK$, CON, AUX, COM1 through COM4, LPT1 through LPT3, NUL, and PRN.

The eight-character file name is just part of a *filespec* (an abbreviation for file specifier). The filespec also can have an *extension* of up to three letters, which is connected to the file name by a period, as in TECHDATA.JUN or DESIGN.1. It's common practice, but not a requirement, to use extensions to identify file types. Microsoft Word, for example, adds the extension .DOC to every document file it creates. DOS uses .TXT for text files, and HotShot Graphics uses .HSG for its graphics files.

Your life will be less complicated if you avoid using your applications' extensions for other files. If you use Microsoft Word, you shouldn't use the .DOC extension for files you create with DOS's EDIT program, because Microsoft Word will not be able to open or work with them correctly.

DOS attaches special meaning to the following extensions; never use these extensions for other types of files:

.COM	One type of executable program file
.EXE	Another type of executable program file
.BIN	Another type of program file
.SYS	One type of device driver or configuration file
.BAT	A batch program file
.HLP	A file containing help information

Peter's Principle: Give files meaningful names.

If you name a file C23F4-XT.D#2, you might remember that name while you're actively working with the file; but, a year from now when you're trying to find it among thousands of files on your hard disk, you could end up wasting a lot of time searching for it because you can't remember the name. If you name the file BUDGET94.DAT, you'll have a much better chance of finding it later.

Names such as C23F4-XT.D#2 have the added disadvantage of being difficult to type, which increases the probability of a typo that would cause a DOS command to fail. A name such as BUDGET94.DAT is much less error prone.

Global Filespecs

When you want to access a specific file, you reference it by its filespec. The filespec TECHDATA.JUN, for example, refers to just one file. Sometimes, though, it's convenient to process a whole group of related files, and you often can do this by using a *global filespec*. A global filespec contains *wildcard characters* that stand for any other characters. The DOS wildcard characters are ? and *.

The ? Wildcard

The ? character matches any single character except a blank. The global filespec TR?CK, for example, matches TRACK, TRICK, and TRUCK, but not TRCK or TRUELUCK. Notice that it also doesn't match TRACK.100, TRICK.DAT, or any other filespec with an extension, because TR?CK specifies no extension.

When the question mark comes at the end of the file name or extension, it also matches a blank. The global filespec GRAD?, for example, matches GRAD, as well as GRADE and GRADY.

You can use more than one question mark in a global filespec. The name ?ART??.?? matches any filespec containing ART in the second, third, and fourth character positions; up to two more characters in the file name itself; and up to two characters in the extension.

> **Warning:** A global filespec like ?ART??.?? might access more files than you intended. It's always a good idea to enter DIR ?ART??.?? first so that DOS will list all the filenames that match the filespec. Chapter 14, "Managing Directories," explains the DIR command.

The * Wildcard

The * wildcard matches any number of characters, including blanks. The global filespec TR* matches TR, TRY, TREK, TRIAD, TRADER, TRUDEAU, and TRIPTALK; but not TRUST.ME, because no extension is specified.

You can use up to two asterisks in a global filespec, one in the file name itself and one in the extension. DOS ignores any characters following an asterisk in either part of the filespec. Therefore, RE*.T* is a legitimate global filespec, but *RE*.TMP is not. In fact (and unfortunately), there's no direct way in DOS to specify a global filespec containing the letters RE (for example) anywhere in the name.

> **Tip:** When creating a group of related files, plan the names so they can be accessed by a global filespec, and so they will appear together in an alphabetical listing of filespecs. For example, the names DAY1.DAT through DAY7.DAT are better than SUN.DAT through SAT.DAT.
>
> If you're using more than nine sequential numbers in a set of filespecs, use 01 through 09 to keep the first nine files in alphabetical order. For example, the names TRIAL1 through TRIAL12 would be listed in this order: TRIAL1, TRIAL10, TRIAL11, TRIAL12, TRIAL2, TRIAL3, and so on. But TRIAL01 through TRIAL12 would be listed in the correct numerical order.

Attributes

Every file has five attributes: read-only, hidden, system, archive, and directory. These attributes control how DOS and other programs access the files. Each attribute can be on or off. When an attribute is on, programs are supposed to pay attention to it (but see the following warning). When an attribute is off, programs ignore it.

> **Warning:** Do not trust attributes alone to protect your files from accidental or malicious damage. Many programs ignore or override the attributes. Furthermore, anyone who knows DOS basics knows how to change a file's attributes.

Read-Only

When the *read-only* attribute is turned on, the file should not be modified or deleted. Most of the DOS utilities display an `Access denied` message if you try to modify or delete a file with a positive read-only attribute. (You'll see some exceptions later in this book.) Most programs also respect the read-only attribute, but be warned that some programs don't.

Although the read-only attribute can't do much when someone wants to damage a file on purpose, it is good protection against accidental erasure. The `DOS DEL` command, for example, refuses to erase a read-only file, and the `DOS COPY` command refuses to overwrite it with another file.

Hidden

A positive *hidden* attribute means that a program should ignore the file when looking for files to process. The `DIR` command, for example, normally won't list a hidden file (but you can override that). The `DEL` command won't delete a hidden file because it can't see it; you get a `File not found` message instead. Only the most uninformed DOS users, however, will be unable to find a file simply because it is hidden. Once again, the attribute is mostly a protection against accidents rather than maliciousness. Hide a file if you want to avoid accidentally moving, copying, deleting, or otherwise processing it.

System

The *system* attribute combines features of the read-only and hidden attributes; a system file normally can't be modified or erased, and it usually can't be seen by programs when searching for files.

Very few people use the system attribute. In fact, until DOS 5, you couldn't control the attribute yourself, because Microsoft saw no need for nonprogrammers to do that. DOS's core program files, IO.SYS, MSDOS.SYS, and DBLSPACE.BIN or DRVSPACE.BIN, have the system attribute. Other system programs might have a few system files as well. Very few applications need to protect their files this way.

Archive

The *archive* attribute indicates that a file has been modified since the last time you made back-up copies. This attribute signifies that the file needs to be backed up (archived). DOS's back-up programs, and most other back-up programs, can select files to be backed up on the basis of their archive attributes. They turn the archive attribute off after making a back-up copy, because at that point the file doesn't need to be archived.

DOS automatically turns on a file's archive attribute when it creates the file or modifies it in any way. Both of these actions mean that the file needs to be archived. Later in this book, you'll learn how to turn a file's archive attribute on and off manually to control whether the next back-up cycle picks up the file.

Directories

DOS uses directories to keep track of files. A *directory* is somewhat like a telephone book, but instead of name, address, and phone number, each entry contains these items:

File name

Extension

File size

Date last modified

Time last modified

Starting location of the file on the disk

Attributes

DOS uses this information to locate each file. You also can view a directory to see what files it contains. A typical listing looks like this:

```
BUDNEWA   BAK     124,788 04-29-93  12:23a
SCRIPT    STY         512 07-24-90   9:23p
BUDNEWA   DOC     120,653 08-23-93  10:42a
FLOOD1    BAK      41,210 08-23-93  10:10a
FLOOD1    DOC      42,008 08-23-93  10:29a
```

Each line describes one file. You can see its file name, extension, size (in bytes), and the date and time it was last modified. In a listing of this type, DOS doesn't show you the attributes or the starting location on the disk.

The Root Directory

Every disk must have at least one directory, called the *root directory*, which must be located in the first track. DOS installs the root directory when it prepares the disk. The root directory can have a limited number of entries, determined by the size of the disk. On a hard disk, you probably need more directory space than the root directory permits. The next section explains how you can get that space.

The Directory Tree

You can create your own directories that are subdirectories of the root directory. A *subdirectory* acts something like a file folder; you group related files together in the subdirectory to keep them separated from other files and to make them relatively easy to find. You may, for example, want to create separate subdirectories on your hard disk for all your major programs: DOS, Windows, your word processing application, your spreadsheet, and so on. You can create as many subdirectories as you want.

A subdirectory also can have subdirectories, which in turn can have subdirectories. Your word processing subdirectory may have subdirectories for correspondence, artwork, style sheets, the chapters in a report you're working on, and so forth.

A disk's entire directory structure looks something like an upside-down tree: the root directory is at the top and branches into a first level of subdirectories, which in turn branch into a second level of subdirectories, and so on. Figure 3.1 shows an example of a disk directory structure. You can see the root directory at the top; its name is always \ (backslash). DOS assigns this name, and you can't change it. The subdirectories have names just like files do, including an extension if you want. (Most people don't include extensions in subdirectory names.)

Figure 3.1.
A sample directory tree.

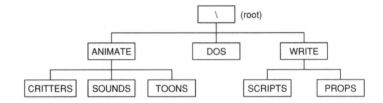

Note: Subdirectories have attributes just as files do, but most people don't use them.

When a directory has subdirectories, the directory is called a *parent*, and the subdirectories are its *children*. In Figure 3.1, ANIMATE is the parent of CRITTERS, SOUNDS, and TOONS. They are the children of ANIMATE.

A structure with a parent plus all its children and all their children is called a *branch*. In Figure 3.1, the ANIMATE branch includes ANIMATE plus its three children. The highest level branch on every drive is headed by the root directory and includes all the directories on the drive.

Tip: In general, try to keep your files in subdirectories, not the root directory. Not only is space in the root directory limited, but in some cases the UNFORMAT program can't recover files in the root directory, should that become necessary.

When you list a directory, its subdirectories appear with <DIR> in the size column. The date and time show when the directory was created, not when it was last modified. Here's a sample directory listing:

```
.                <DIR>         10-05-93    10:32p
..               <DIR>         10-05-93    10:32p
FLOOD3   DOC         42,496    10-06-93     7:52p
JULY             <DIR>         10-07-93    10:38p
FLOOD3   STY            640    10-06-93     7:52p
TREAT    DOC        116,608    10-06-93     7:56p
```

```
FLOOD1    DOC      140,416    10-06-93     8:01p
BUDDY1    DOC       94,080    10-06-93     8:15p
JUNE              <DIR>       10-15-93    10:38p
```

This directory contains five files and four directory entries. JULY and JUNE are its children. The two directory entries at the top appear in every subdirectory to help DOS keep track of the directory tree. The first entry, identified by a single period, always refers to this directory itself. The second entry, identified by two periods, always refers to this directory's parent. You can't see the parent directory's real name, but you can see that it was created on October 5, 1993, at 10:32 p.m. What you can't see, but DOS can, are the starting locations for these two directories, which help DOS link the directories together.

> **Tip:** You can use the names . and .. to refer to the current directory and its parent, respectively. Sometimes that's easier than typing out the directory's real name.

The Current Directory

Every one of your drives has a *default directory*. This is the directory that DOS accesses if you reference that drive but don't specify which directory to use. If you copy a file to drive A without specifying a directory, for example, DOS copies the file to the default directory on drive A. When you boot, the root directory on each drive becomes the default directory for that drive. You'll learn later in this book how to make another directory the default directory.

In addition, one drive is always the *current drive*. DOS accesses this drive when you don't specify another one. If you copy a file to the directory named BACKUPS without specifying the drive, DOS assumes that BACKUPS is on the current drive. The default directory on the current drive is called the *current directory*.

When you boot, the boot drive becomes the current drive. You'll learn later in this book how to switch to another drive.

When you specify neither a drive nor a directory in a DOS command, DOS assumes the current directory. For example, if you enter a command to delete PCLIST.TXT without specifying a drive or directory, DOS looks for it in the current directory.

The DOS command prompt usually shows the name of the current drive and directory, so you always know which drive and directory you're about to access. For example, the following command prompt indicates that the DOS directory on drive C is the current directory:

```
C:\DOS>
```

In the DOS Shell, you know the current directory because it's the one that's displayed on-screen.

Path Names

When you want to access a nondefault directory, you must use its *path name*. The path name shows DOS how to get to the desired directory. The path name may include a drive name (if you don't want the current drive) and a series of directory names separated by backslashes. For example, the following expression is the correct path name for the TOONS directory in Figure 3.1:

```
C:\ANIMATE\TOONS
```

This name tells DOS to go to drive C, start at the root directory (the first backslash), find its child named ANIMATE, and find ANIMATE's child named TOONS. You can omit the `C:` at the beginning of this path name if C is the current drive.

You also can start a path at the current or default directory, instead of the root directory. Suppose that the current directory is C:\, and you want to use the TOONS directory. This path name will do it:

```
ANIMATE\TOONS
```

Because the path name doesn't start with a backslash for the root directory, DOS knows to start with the current directory. If the current drive is A and you want to access TOONS on drive C, all you have to do is add the drive name to the path:

```
C:ANIMATE\TOONS
```

Once again, because the root directory is not specified as the starting point, DOS starts with the default directory on the specified drive.

Now suppose that TOONS is the current directory, and you want to get to CRITTERS. You can start at the root directory, as follows:

```
\ANIMATE\CRITTERS
```

But DOS offers you a shortcut. You're allowed to use the `..` name to tell DOS to start with the current directory's parent, as in:

```
..\CRITTERS
```

A subdirectory's complete path name, starting with the backslash representing the root directory, must not exceed 63 characters. As you design your directory structure, however, you'll probably want to keep your path names a lot shorter than that. A 63-character path name would be a bear to work with in a command. As a rule of thumb, don't create more than four levels in your directory structure.

Paths in Filespecs

A filespec can include a path name along with the file name and extension to completely identify the location of the desired file. If the current directory is C:\ANIMATE and you want to access the file named NEWBUMPS.WAV in A:\SOUNDS, use this filespec:

```
A:\SOUNDS\NEWBUMPS.WAV
```

Allocation Units and the File Allocation Table

You have seen that your disk drive divides tracks into sectors and reads and writes one sector at a time. But if DOS had to keep track of every sector in every file on a disk, its system tables would take up more room than the files themselves. To keep its system tables down to a reasonable size, DOS groups sectors together into *allocation units* (also called *clusters*) and keeps track of the allocation units instead.

The size of an allocation unit depends on the overall size of the disk; DOS decides on the best size when it prepares the disk for use. Floppy disks have one or two sectors per allocation unit. A high-capacity hard drive may have four or more sectors per allocation unit.

Because DOS tracks allocation units instead of sectors, it can't assign part of an allocation unit to a file. It always allocates file space in whole allocation units; that's why they call them *allocation* units. Even if a file contains only one byte, DOS gives it a complete allocation unit; the rest of the space, which is often referred to as *slack*, is wasted. When the file expands, however, there's plenty of room for it. If the file expands beyond the first allocation unit, DOS assigns it a second complete allocation unit.

Obviously, the allocation unit method wastes space, but DOS must compromise between wasting space in slack and taking up too much time tracking files.

The DOS allocation unit system yields some apparent disparities that confuse many DOS users. For example, when you copy a small file (say, 200 bytes) from a disk with 1KB allocation units to a hard disk with 4KB allocation units, the file's size is still 200 bytes but it uses up 4KB of space on the hard disk. If you try to copy a group of 20 small files whose file sizes add up to less than 1KB, you may not have enough space for them on a hard drive with 40KB available.

This section looks at how DOS keeps track of a file's allocation units. Figure 3.2 shows an example of a *file allocation table* (FAT); this is DOS's system table. It contains one entry for every allocation unit on the disk.

Figure 3.2.
A sample file allocation table
(first 38 entries).

		EOF	0	0	6	10	EOF
EOF	0	11	EOF	13	14	15	EOF
0	0	BAD	20	21	EOF	23	24
37	0	0	0	0	0	31	32
33	34	35	36	54	38	39	EOF

Each allocation unit on the drive has a numeric address, starting with 2 and continuing through the end of the disk. The file's directory entry shows the address of the first allocation unit in the file. In the FAT, the entry for that allocation unit shows the address of the next allocation unit. That entry shows the address of the next allocation unit. This pattern continues until you reach the last allocation unit in the file, which contains a special code that means end-of-file. Because the FAT entries link to each other in chain-like fashion, the set of entries for one file is called a *file chain*.

Suppose that the directory entry for GROWTH92.DB shows that it starts in allocation unit 5. Find allocation unit 5 in the FAT in Figure 3.2 (remember that allocation unit numbers start with 2, not 1). You see that it contains a 6, so 6 is the next allocation unit. Allocation unit 6 chains to 10, and 10 chains to 11. Allocation unit 11 shows the end-of-file mark. This file, then, occupies four allocation units. That should be confirmed by the file's actual size, which is stored in the directory entry.

The GROWTH92.DB example also demonstrates a *fragmented* file. Instead of being located in adjacent allocation units, its allocation units form two chunks, or fragments. DOS frequently fragments files to use up available space on the disk. Fragmentation is especially likely to occur when you expand a file. If, for example, you expand GROWTH92.DB so that it needs another allocation unit, it can't expand into allocation unit 12 because that currently belongs to another file. It has to use the next available allocation unit, indicated by a 0 in the FAT, which is allocation unit 16 in this case. Thus, another fragment is born.

Many files need only one allocation unit. Suppose that the file named ALLISON.MEM starts in allocation unit 2. In the sample FAT, allocation unit 2 contains an EOF mark; this is the only allocation unit in the file.

Because the FAT is so important to controlling both the files and the empty space on a disk, DOS maintains two identical FATs—one as a backup of the other. Every time you create a new file, or expand or contract an existing one, DOS needs to update both FATs. If you interrupt it before it can complete the update, you throw the FATs out of whack, and you may not be able to access your files correctly. To avoid this problem, don't reboot or turn the power off when a drive light is on (unless you need to interrupt a virus at work). The drive lights indicate that DOS is currently accessing the drive.

How DOS Deletes a File

When you ask DOS to delete a file, it doesn't erase the file's data from the disk immediately. It simply puts a special delete code in the first character of the file's directory entry and changes the file's FAT entries to 0. This makes the directory entry and allocation units available to other files. When you expand another file, it may take up one or more of the released allocation units, destroying that much of the deleted file's data. When you create a new file, it may use the deleted file's directory entry and some of its former allocation units. Eventually all trace of the former file disappears, but it may take a while. In the meantime, the possibility exists that you can undelete all or part of the file's data. Chapter 26, "Using UNDELETE," discusses the DOS UNDELETE facility.

On Your Own

The rest of the chapters in this book assume that you understand data storage concepts such as filespecs, path names, and the File Allocation Table. You can use the following questions to make sure you're ready to move on:

Which is the better set of filespecs? JAN.BAT...DEC.BAT, MONTH01.BAT...MONTH12.BAT, or MONTH1.BAT...MONTH12.BAT?

Suppose you copy a file to drive A without specifying a directory name. Which directory on A will receive the file?

Write a path name for the SCRIPTS directory in Figure 3.1, shown previously. Assume that the DOS directory is the current directory.

What is the name of the table on each drive where DOS keeps track of the allocation units for that drive?

Utilities like UNDELETE are able to restore files after they have been deleted. What is it about the way that DOS deletes a file that makes this possible?

4 Setting Up Your System

Introduction

This chapter guides you through the installation process if you are upgrading from an earlier version of DOS.

Basic Assumptions

This chapter assumes that you are upgrading to DOS 6.22 from an earlier version. If you are changing to DOS 6.22 from OS/2 or another operating system, the procedures you should follow are explained in your *User's Guide*. This chapter also assumes that your boot drive is drive C, and that your current version of DOS is installed in the directory named C:\DOS; if not, you need to adapt the various commands shown in the instructions to use your boot drive name and DOS directory name.

Note: If you have never used DOS before, you probably won't know how to do most of the following tasks. If you can, you should ask an experienced DOS user to assist you. If you try to run SETUP without doing the recommended preparation, you increase the risk of something going wrong and losing the data on your hard drive.

Getting Ready for Installation

The steps in this section help you prepare your PC for SETUP. You will do such things as back up all your data and prepare an emergency boot disk (in the rare event that SETUP fails and you have to restore your hard disk), prepare for some of the decisions that you must make during installation, and prepare the floppy disk that you need.

1. Make sure that you have enough empty space on your boot drive. You need 5MB to 7MB to upgrade to DOS 6.22, depending on which options you choose. If you do not have that much space, delete unnecessary files to make the room. If you can't delete enough files, move some files to floppy disks while you install DOS and then restore the files to the hard drive. (If your boot drive is compressed, the space must be available on the compressed drive, not the host drive.)

2. Back up your hard drives using your current backup program. If you can, back up all files, including program files. If SETUP fails and you need to restore a hard drive, it will be easier if you have all the files you need in one place. If you can't back up the entire drive for some reason, leave out any program files that you can reinstall from their original disks.

3. Make an emergency startup disk for your current DOS version by formatting a floppy disk in drive A using the following command. Use a brand new disk or one that contains no essential data.

   FORMAT A: /S

Warning: This procedure will destroy any data currently on the floppy disk.

4. Copy the FDISK, FORMAT, and SYS programs to the disk using the following commands. You need these programs if you have to restore your hard drive from scratch because SETUP fails.

```
COPY C:\DOS\FDISK.EXE A:
COPY C:\DOS\FORMAT.COM A:
COPY C:\DOS\SYS.COM A:
```

5. If you used DOS's BACKUP program (from DOS 5 or earlier) to make the backups in step 2, you need to copy the RESTORE program to the emergency startup disk so you can restore the backed up files in case SETUP fails. Type the following command at the command prompt and press Enter:

```
COPY C:\DOS\RESTORE.EXE A:
```

6. If you're stepping up from DOS 6.0 or 6.2 and you used MSBACKUP or MWBACKUP to make the backups in step 2, you will need all the MSBACKUP programs on the emergency startup disk. Enter the following command:

```
COPY C:\DOS\MSB*.* A:
```

Note: The MSBACKUP program files won't all fit on a 360KB disk. Be sure to use a larger capacity disk if your drive A can handle it. If drive A is a 360KB drive, you'll have to put some of the files on a second floppy.

7. Put the emergency startup disk in a safe place; hopefully, you will never have to use it. When your new version of DOS is safely installed and running properly, your floppy will no longer be valid because it is set up for your earlier version of DOS. Don't discard it, however, until after you have done your first full backup with DOS 6.22. Until then, there's always a chance you may need to use the backup programs you put on it.

8. Disable any program that might try to display a message on-screen while SETUP is running. For example, if you use a pop-up alarm to remind you of appointments, you should turn it off. If you have a communication program that runs in the background to receive faxes or mail, turn that off also.

9. Disable all disk caching, deletion protection, and antivirus programs. Programs of this type can prevent SETUP from working properly. (You don't need to disable DOS's SmartDrive.) If your CONFIG.SYS and AUTOEXEC.BAT files load such programs, follow these steps to unload them:

   a. Use an ASCII text editor such as DOS's EDIT to open C:\CONFIG.SYS for editing. (If you use a word processor, be sure to work on the file in ASCII text mode; don't treat it as a document file.)

   b. Insert the word REM in front of every command that loads a disk-caching, deletion-protection, or antivirus program.

    c. Save the file.

    d. Do the same thing in C:\AUTOEXEC.BAT.

    e. Exit the editor.

    f. Press Ctrl+Alt+Delete to reboot.

       Rebooting should remove the indicated programs from memory.

> **Note:** After successfully upgrading, remove all the REMs you inserted and reboot to reload your disk caching, deletion protection, and antivirus programs.

10. Exit DOS Shell or Windows. You must run SETUP from the DOS command prompt.

11. If your hard disk is not compressed by a third-party compression program such as Stacker, SETUP asks for one or two floppy disks so that it can create Uninstall disks. The Uninstall disks help you restore your former DOS version in case the new version does not work with your system. Make sure that you have a blank floppy disk that fits in your drive A. If your drive A is a 360KB drive (double-density 5 1/4-inches), you need two blank floppies.

12. If you use Windows, decide whether you want to install the DOS or Windows versions of UNDELETE, BACKUP, and Anti-Virus. You can choose either version, both versions, or none.

    You really need only the Windows or DOS version of BACKUP and Anti-Virus, but it makes some sense to install both versions of UNDELETE for the following two reasons:

    • You can do an immediate UNDELETE no matter where you're working; if you're not using Delete Sentry, it's very important not to start up Windows when you need to delete a file.

    • The Windows version has some features that the DOS version doesn't have.

> **Note:** If you later change your mind about which versions of these programs you want, you can rerun SETUP with /E to add the DOS or WINDOWS versions of BACKUP, UNDELETE, and/or Anti-Virus. (See the Command Reference for SETUP in the back of this book for an explanation of /E.)

Making a Decision about Backups

During the upgrade process, you must decide whether you want to upgrade your backup program to DOS 6.22. I recommend that you do; but, in certain cases, you should also keep a copy of the old backup program. Under certain conditions, DOS 6.22 can't restore from the backups that you have already made and you must restore using your former backup program.

DOS changed its compression method with DOS 6.22, and the new MSBACKUP and MWBACKUP can't read compressed backups made by DOS 6.0 or 6.2 unless one of the following conditions is true:

- One of your hard drives is currently compressed by DoubleSpace. (If you upgrade to DOS 6.22's DriveSpace, you'll lose the ability to read your old backups.)

- You have DBLSPACE.BIN in your DOS directory along with a file called DRVSPACE.MR1. These two files give DOS 6.22 the ability to read compressed backups made by DOS 6.0 or 6.2. If you're upgrading from 6.0 or 6.2, you already have DBLSPACE.BIN in your DOS directory (as long as you haven't already deleted it) and SETUP won't harm it. SETUP will install the .MR1 file in your DOS directory only if you are using the Stepup version of DOS 6.22, not the Upgrade version, or if you are upgrading using a non-English version of the upgrade program. The English language Upgrade package does not include the .MR1 file. (If you want this file, you can order it from Microsoft.)

If you think that DOS 6.22 won't be able to read your former backups, or if you're not sure, I recommend that you make your own copy of your current backup programs right now using the following two commands:

```
MD \OLDBACKS
```

```
XCOPY \DOS\MSB*.* \OLDBACKS
```

Now you can safely upgrade to DOS 6.22's backup program. If you ever need to restore from your old compressed backups, switch to the OLDBACKS directory and run MSBACKUP from there. (If you need to restore from backups made by DOS 6.22, don't switch to OLDBACKS; run MSBACKUP or MWBACKUP from your DOS directory.) When you no longer need your backups made with DOS 6.0 or 6.2, you can delete the OLDBACKS directory.

Running SETUP

Note: You can use the installation disks in drive A or B. If you need double-density disks (360KB or 720KB) instead of high-density, you must send for them using the order form at the back of the *User's Guide.*

Put the disk labeled Disk 1–Setup into drive A or B. Then, enter one of these commands:

```
A:SETUP
```

or

```
B:SETUP
```

SETUP displays information and instructions on your video screen. After choosing which versions of UNDELETE, BACKUP, and Anti-Virus you want to install, you probably do not have to make any more decisions. However, you do have to insert disks upon request. If your boot drive is not compressed with a third-party compression program, SETUP will tell you when to insert a blank disk to be used as the Uninstall disk.

Dealing with Problems During SETUP

If SETUP encounters problems after making an Uninstall disk, it probably will ask for the Uninstall disk so that it can restore your former DOS version. The chapter titled "Diagnosing and Solving Problems" in your *User's Guide* includes procedures for dealing with common SETUP problems. If you can't make SETUP work, contact Microsoft's Product Support Services for help; the *User's Guide* tells you how to contact them.

If SETUP leaves your boot drive in an unusable state, you may need to restore the drive. If you followed the recommended preparation steps in this chapter, you have the necessary data to do that. Your best bet is to call Microsoft's Product Support Team for assistance. In general, you will probably need to repartition and reformat the drive, then reinstall DOS and restore all your files from their backups.

Note: The emergency disk you made earlier contains the necessary information to:

- Boot using your old system.

- Repartition the hard drive using FDISK.EXE, which is explained in Chapter 54, "FDISK." Repartitioning may not be necessary. If FDISK shows that the partition(s) already exist, you don't need to change them.

- Reformat the hard drive using FORMAT with the /s (for system) switch, which is explained in Chapter 17, "Formatting and Unformatting Disks." This installs your former version of DOS on the hard drive. (You may want to run SETUP right away to upgrade to DOS 6.22 before starting to restore files.)

- Restore all your other files to the drive using your old backup/restore program, as explained in Chapter 24, "Restore and Compare." (If your drive was compressed before, you may not be able to fit all your old files on it until you install your compression software and compress the drive.)

Understanding What SETUP Does

The SETUP program replaces the old files in your C:\DOS directory with the newer versions. If possible, it moves the old files to a directory called OLD_DOS.n; preserving these files enables you to uninstall if you find that necessary. Any files in the C:\DOS directory that are not upgraded are not touched, so that any files you happened to store in C:\DOS are unharmed.

In addition, some of the older DOS programs that have been dropped by DOS 6, such as RECOVER and ASSIGN, live on in your DOS directory because the upgrade doesn't replace them. DOS 6 has dropped these programs for a good reason. Most of the discontinued programs were extinct, replaced by better ones. After you have used your new version of DOS for a while and are sure that you want to keep it, you might want to delete the following files from your C:\DOS directory; you will not need them with your new version of DOS.

4201.CPI

4208.CPI

5202.CPI

ASSIGN.COM

COMP.EXE

DOSSHELL.* (if you use Windows or another graphical interface program)

EDLIN.EXE

EXE2BIN.EXE

GRAFTABL.COM

JOIN.EXE

LCD.CPI

MIRROR.COM

MSHERC.COM

PRINTER.SYS

RECOVER.EXE

SMARTDRV.EXE

DBLSPACE.* (If you don't use DoubleSpace)

Looking at Additional Documentation

You will find some .TXT files in your DOS directory that supplement the *User's Guide*. You should take a look at each .TXT file to see whether it contains anything about your system.

To view .TXT files:

1. Enter the following command at the DOS command prompt:

   DIR C:\DOS*.TXT /OD

   This command lists all the .TXT files in the DOS directory in chronological order. If any files have a date before May 1994, they predate DOS 6.22 and are no longer pertinent. You can delete or ignore them.

2. Follow these steps for each file that you want to read:

   a. Enter the following command, where **filename** is the name of the file you want to read, as in README.TXT or NETWORKS.TXT:

   EDIT C:\DOS*filename*.TXT

   This command opens the file in DOS's editor.

   b. Press PgDn and PgUp to move around in the file.

   c. To print the file, press Alt+F followed by a P. (See Chapter 19, "The DOS Editor," to print just part of the file.)

   d. Press Alt+F, then press X to exit the editor.

Scanning for Viruses

As soon as you upgrade to DOS 6.22, why not take advantage of one of its most powerful new features, Microsoft Anti-Virus? If you have never scanned your system for viruses, you should do so immediately, even if your system is new. (If you have been using an antivirus program fairly regularly, you can safely skip this section.) You learn more about using Microsoft Anti-Virus in Chapter 25, "DOS's Antivirus Programs."

To scan for viruses using the command prompt version of Microsoft Anti-Virus:

1. At the DOS command prompt, type the following command and press Enter:

   MSAV /L /C /P /F

   This command causes all your local drives, except for floppy drives, to be scanned for viruses. If any viruses are found, they are removed. A report is displayed at the end.

2. If the report shows that any viruses were detected, shut down your system and read Chapter 25 immediately.

To scan for viruses using the Windows version of Anti-Virus:

1. Start Windows.

2. Open the Microsoft Tools group. The Anti-Virus (Microsoft Windows Anti-Virus) icon should be there.

> **Note:** If you cannot find the Microsoft Tools group or the Anti-Virus icon, you didn't install the Windows version of Microsoft Anti-Virus.

3. Open the Anti-Virus program. (The Anti-Virus window should open.)

4. Select all your local nonfloppy drives.

5. Press the Detect and Clean button.

6. If any viruses are reported, press the Stop button, exit Anti-Virus, close any other programs that are running, exit Windows, and shut down your system. Read Chapter 25 immediately.

Starting Delete Sentry

DOS 6.22 includes another feature that you should install right away, if you're not already using it. Delete Sentry protects your deleted files for a few days so that you can undelete them easily. Delete Sentry is explained in Chapter 26, "Using UNDELETE," but you should set it up now (if you haven't already done so).

To set up Delete Sentry from the DOS command prompt:

1. Type the following command and press Enter:

   `EDIT C:\AUTOEXEC.BAT`

   This command opens the AUTOEXEC.BAT file for editing by DOS's editor.

2. Press the down-arrow key to move the cursor to the first blank line in the file.

3. Type the following command on the blank line:

   `UNDELETE /SC`

   This command starts Delete Sentry to protect drive C. If you have more than one hard drive, add an /S*drive* switch for each one. For example, if you have drives C, D, and E, the command would appear as follows:

   `UNDELETE /SC /SD /SE`

4. Press Alt+F, press X, and then press Y. This keystroke sequence exits the editor and saves the changes in AUTOEXEC.BAT.

5. Remove any disk in drive A and press Ctrl+Alt+Del to reboot your system. Delete Sentry will be installed during booting.

To set up Delete Sentry from Windows:

1. Start Windows.

2. Open the Microsoft Tools group window. (See Figure 4.1.) The Undelete icon should be there.

Figure 4.1.
The Microsoft Tools group window.

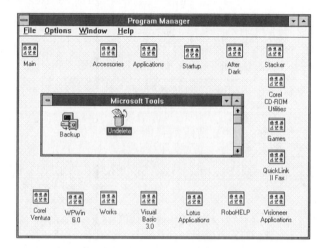

Note: If you cannot find the Microsoft Tools group or the Undelete icon, you didn't install the Windows version of UNDELETE.

3. Open Undelete. The Microsoft Undelete window should open. (See Figure 4.2.)

Figure 4.2.
The Undelete window.

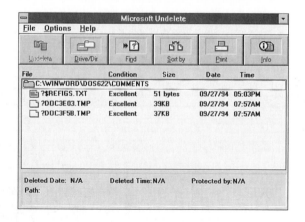

4. Pull down the Options menu and choose the Configure Delete Protection item. The Configure Delete Protection dialog box opens. (See Figure 4.3.)

Figure 4.3.
The Configure Delete
Protection dialog box.

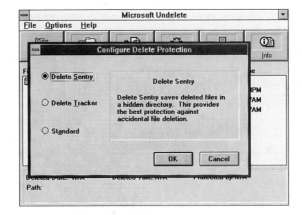

5. Click the Delete Sentry radio button. Then, click OK. This procedure opens the Configure Delete Sentry dialog box. (See Figure 4.4.)

Figure 4.4.
The Configure
Delete Sentry
dialog box.

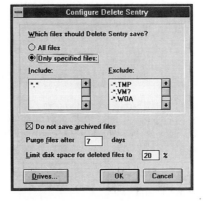

6. Press the Drives button to open the Choose Drives for Delete Sentry dialog box. (See Figure 4.5.)

Figure 4.5.
The Choose Drives for
Delete Sentry dialog box.

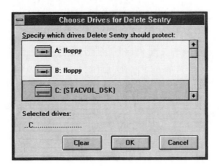

7. Select all your hard drives and press OK several times to return to the main Microsoft Undelete window.

8. Exit Undelete. Close any other programs and exit Windows.

9. Remove any disk from drive A and press Ctrl+Alt+Del to reboot DOS. Delete Sentry will be installed during booting.

With Delete Sentry installed, you should find it easy to undelete files if that becomes necessary. Chapter 26 explains how.

Making an Emergency Startup Disk

Now that your new version of DOS is up and running, you need to make an emergency boot disk for it. Follow steps 3 and 4, under "Getting Ready for Installation" earlier in this chapter, to make the disk. You could reuse the same disk you used before, because you don't need that one anymore.

Uninstalling DOS 6

Unless your hard drive is compressed by a third-party compression program, SETUP recorded uninstall information so that you could return to your former DOS version. If you have an application that will not run under the new version, and SETVER as explained in Chapter 21, "Configuring Your System," does not solve the problem, you may find it necessary to return to your earlier version while you resolve the problem. (You might have to upgrade the application to a version compatible with DOS 6.22.)

Note: You can't uninstall DOS if you have repartitioned or reformatted your boot drive since installing the new version of DOS. Nor can you uninstall DOS if you have deleted or moved DOS's two core program files (MSDOS.SYS and IO.SYS), deleted the OLD_DOS.*n* directory, run DELOLDOS, installed DriveSpace or DoubleSpace, or installed a third-party compression program.

To uninstall DOS 6.22:

1. Insert the Uninstall disk into drive A.

2. Reboot.

3. Follow the instructions on your screen.

DELOLDOS

When you are sure that you want to keep your new version of DOS, the program named DELOLDOS removes any former versions from your hard drive, which will free up several megabytes of space. Enter the following command:

```
DELOLDOS
```

Warning: After you run DELOLDOS, you can't uninstall DOS 6.22.

DELOLDOS simply removes any and all OLD_DOS.n directories from your hard drive. (You can do it without DELOLDOS. Just use DELTREE OLD_DOS.1; then, if necessary, DELTREE OLD_DOS.2, and so on.)

Using Expand

If you did not install all of DOS 6.22, or if you deleted some files after installation, you might find yourself needing to copy some files from the installation disks to your hard drive. Most of the files are compressed on the disks, and you have to expand them before you can use them. (These files are not compressed using DoubleSpace or DriveSpace; they use a different compression technique.) Compressed files have an underscore as the last character of their extension. DOS 6.22 includes an EXPAND program to decompress them. (See Figure 4.6.) For example, to expand MSAV.EX_ from drive A to MSAV.EXE in C:\DOS, you could enter the following command:

```
EXPAND A:\MSAV.EX_ C:\DOS\MSAV.EXE
```

You can specify more than one compressed filespec, but not a global filespec. If you specify multiple filespecs, the destination must not include a filename. EXPAND will use the compressed filenames, including the underscores, and you will have to rename each one on the hard drive.

EXPAND

Expands compressed file(s).

Syntax:

```
EXPAND [filespec ... [destination]]
```

Parameters:

none   Prompts for *filespec* and *destination*.

filespec	Identifies a compressed file that you want to expand.
destination	Specifies the location and/or name of the expanded file(s).

Figure 4.6.   *EXPAND command summary.*

2

DOS Shell

5

Getting Acquainted with DOS Shell

Introduction

DOS Shell is a pale substitute for Windows, but if you don't have Windows, you'll find the Shell more intuitive and easier to use than the DOS command prompt.

Deciding When to Use the Shell

DOS Shell is DOS's graphic user interface (GUI). It enables you to see the drive and directory you're working with and makes it easy to manage disks, directories, and files, as well as to start programs such as the DOS Editor or your favorite game. You interact with the Shell by using your mouse or keyboard, selecting items from lists, choosing commands from menus, and choosing options in dialog boxes. You can even drag files around to move or copy them from one place to another.

Perhaps the most important Shell feature is task swapping, which enables you to start several programs simultaneously and switch around among them. This can save you mounds of time and frustration if you need to consult a spreadsheet while working on a document, or you want to make some room on the hard drive before saving the graphic that you have just spent two hours developing.

Still, you don't really need DOS Shell if you have a more sophisticated third-party shell such as Norton Desktop for DOS, or a true multitasking program such as Windows. If you have one of these programs, skip to Part III of this book now.

If you don't have a more sophisticated program, then you should start by using the Shell for most of your DOS tasks. Later on in this book, you'll learn how to use the command prompt for tasks you can't accomplish in the Shell.

In this chapter, you will learn how to:

- Start and exit the Shell
- Work with the various parts of the Shell screen
- Get on-screen help while working with the Shell
- Scroll around in a list
- Work with menus and dialog boxes

Starting the Shell

Before you can start the Shell, you should be at the DOS command prompt. If you haven't booted yet, go ahead and boot now. If your system is already booted, exit any programs you have started, such as a word processor or spreadsheet.

After booting or exiting all programs, you should see a command prompt similar to the one that follows (it might show a different letter):

```
c:\>
```

If not, someone has modified your system and you will need to find out how to get to your command prompt. Talk to the person who worked on your system to find out what you should do.

To start the shell:

1. Type the following word at the command prompt:

   DOSSHELL

2. Press the Enter key.

A screen similar to the one shown in Figure 5.1 should appear. (The content might be different, but the general appearance should be the same.) You might also see a message telling you that DOS Shell is reading your directories. The message disappears when DOS Shell is ready to go.

Figure 5.1.
An example of the DOS
Shell screen.

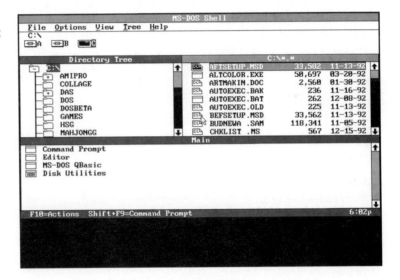

Note: The DOSSHELL command includes several parameters that most people will never need. The complete syntax for the DOSSHELL command is included in the Command Reference at the back of this book.

Problem: When I enter the DOSSHELL command, I get the message Bad program or file name.

Because Windows has become so popular, the Shell is not as necessary as it once was and DOS discontinued it starting with version 6.2. If you installed DOS 6.2 or 6.22 from scratch instead of upgrading, you don't have the Shell software. Your DOS *User's Guide* includes instructions for ordering or downloading the Shell program files.

If you upgraded from any version of DOS from 4.0 through 6.0, you should have the Shell. Try entering the **DOSSHELL** command again to make sure you spelled it correctly. (Notice that it has two Ss.)

If you're sure you're spelling it correctly and DOS still can't find the Shell, try typing the command **MEM** and pressing Enter. Don't worry about the messages that are displayed; you'll learn about MEM in Chapter 29, "Managing Memory." Right now, you're just trying to see if it works at all.

If MEM also produces the message Bad command or file name, DOS can't find your DOS directory. You'll learn how to deal with that in Chapter 12, "Working at the Command Prompt." In the meantime, use the following command to start DOS Shell. (If you did not install DOS in a directory named DOS on drive C, you should substitute the correct name for your DOS directory in place of c:\DOS.)

```
C:\DOS\DOSSHELL
```

If MEM works but DOSSHELL doesn't, or if the above command also fails, someone may have removed the Shell from your system and you need to order the free copy from Microsoft.

Problem: When DOS Shell starts, I can't read the screen.

Your monitor might not be able to display the default Shell screen, which requires a color graphics monitor. Press F3 to exit the Shell and get back to the command prompt.

To start the Shell in black and white instead of color, use this command:

```
DOSSHELL /B
```

To start it in text mode (which is more plain) instead of the normal graphics mode, use this command:

```
DOSSHELL /T
```

You can use both /B and /T if necessary:

```
DOSSHELL /B /T
```

If you have to use text mode, your screen will look somewhat different from the ones shown in this book. For example, it won't have any icons (small drawings that symbolize drives, directories, and files). But, it is close enough to graphics mode that you won't have any trouble learning to use it by following the examples in this book.

Chapter 11, "Customizing the Shell," shows you how to adapt DOS Shell, so you don't have to use /B and /T anymore.

Tip: If you plan to use DOS Shell all the time, you can start it up automatically every time you boot by inserting the DOSSHELL command as the last command (that's important) in your AUTOEXEC.BAT file. Chapter 20, "Basic Batch Programs," explains more about AUTOEXEC.BAT and how to insert commands in it.

Exploring the Shell Screen

The Shell screen is your main work area when you use DOS Shell. The title bar at the top (see Figure 5.2) reminds you that you're using DOS Shell. Underneath is the menu bar, which you'll learn to use a little later in this chapter. The status bar at the bottom displays messages to help you with your current task. You'll learn more about these messages as you learn to use the Shell functions in the upcoming chapters.

Figure 5.2.
The three bars on the Shell screen.

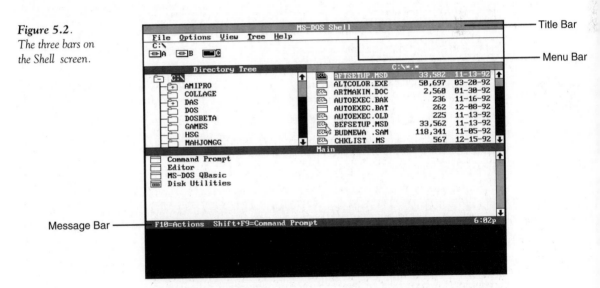

Figure 5.3.
DOS Shell's lists.

Drive List ——

Directory Tree ——

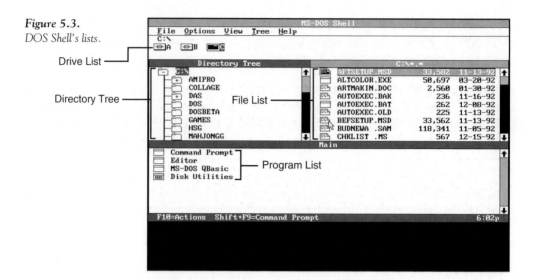

The body of the screen contains four major lists (see Figure 5.3):

- The *drive list* shows all the disk drives available to you, including RAM drives and logged-on network drives. If you're using a data compression system such as DriveSpace, it shows you both the compressed drive and the host drive. The highlight marks the currently selected drive (C in Figure 5.3). In graphics mode, each icon indicates the drive type. In text mode, drive names appear in square brackets without indicating the drive type.

- The *directory tree* displays the directory structure for the selected drive. In the example, you can see that the root directory is C:\, and its children are AMIPRO, COLLAGE, DAS, DOS, and so on. The highlight indicates the current directory, which is C:\ in the example.

Note: In its default status, the directory tree displays only the first level of subdirectories. Directories marked with plus signs (+) have children you can't see. Chapter 6, "Managing Directories," explains how to display them.

The text mode directory tree looks much like the graphics mode tree except that square brackets appear in place of the file folder icons.

- The *file list* shows the files in the currently selected directory. You see an icon in graphics mode that indicates the type of file (program or data), the file name, its size, and the date it was last modified. The highlight marks currently selected files. In the example in Figure 5.3, if you choose the File Delete command right now, you will delete the AFTSETUP.MSD file. Text mode displays no icons and indicates selected files with arrowheads.

- The *program* list shows programs that you can execute merely by choosing them from this list. You can start the DOS full-screen editor, for example, by choosing Editor from the list in Figure 5.3. This is often the easiest way to execute a program in DOS Shell.

One of these sections must always be active, meaning it must contain the cursor or *focus*. We use the word focus because the active list is the focus of any commands you execute. Suppose, for example, that you press the Delete key. If the focus is in the file list, you delete a file; but if the focus is in the directory tree, you delete an entire directory. You move the focus by using either your keyboard or mouse.

How to Move the Focus in DOS Shell

To move the focus using the keyboard: Press Tab or Backtab (Shift+Tab) until you reach the desired list.

To move the focus using the mouse: Click the desired list.

You use the Tab key to move the focus from your keyboard:

1. Press the Tab key several times while you watch the screen.

   You should see the focus move from list to list. The title bar of each list is highlighted when it contains the focus, except for the drive list, which has no title bar.

2. Press Shift+Tab (also called Backtab) several times.

   You should see the focus move again, but in the reverse direction.

You don't think so much about moving the focus when you work with a mouse. When you want to select an item, you click it and the focus moves automatically to that list.

Try moving the focus with your mouse:

1. Click drive C in the drive list.

   You should see the focus move to the drive list and drive C become highlighted. If drive C wasn't current before, the directory tree and file list change to reflect the new drive.

2. Click DOS in the directory tree.

   You should see the focus move to the directory tree and DOS become the selected directory. If it wasn't the current directory before, the file list changes to reflect the new directory.

3. Click ANSI.SYS in the file list.

   You should see the focus move to the file list and ANSI.SYS become the selected file.

4. Click Editor in the program list.

You should see the focus move to the program list and Editor become the selected program. (This does not start up the program, however. You'll learn how to do that in Chapter 10, "Running Programs from DOS Shell.")

Feel free to try out a few more changes, but don't change drives until you read the next chapter.

Using DOS Shell's On-Screen Help

Suppose you're working on a DOS Shell task and you can't remember what to do next. You could look it up in this book, but there's a faster way.

1. Press F1.

DOS Shell opens a *dialog box* to display help information for whichever list currently contains the focus.

2. Choose Esc to close the Help dialog box.

The F1 key requests *context-sensitive* help, meaning that DOS Shell considers the location, or context, of the focus in selecting a help topic. It can respond to any of the main lists, a command on a menu, or a dialog box.

Dialog Boxes

DOS Shell uses dialog boxes to display information that's not part of its lists. When a dialog box opens, you must respond to it. You can't pull down any menus, select items from the main Shell screen, or perform any other actions until you either complete or cancel the dialog box. You use the command buttons, explained in the next section, to do that.

Command Buttons

Every dialog box has at least one *command button*, which causes some kind of action to take place. You'll learn about all five of the Help command buttons as you learn how to use Help. (See Figure 5.4.)

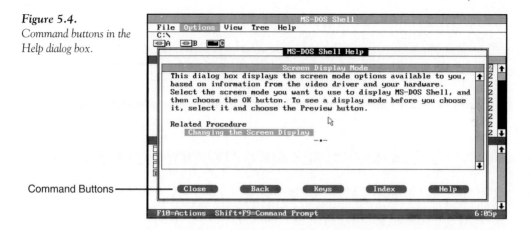

Figure 5.4.
*Command buttons in the
Help dialog box.*

Command Buttons

To choose a command button with the keyboard, press Tab or Shift+Tab until the cursor (which looks like an underline) appears in the button; then press Enter.

Tip: You never need to tab to the Close command button in the Help dialog box because the Esc key does the same thing with only one keypress.

To choose a command button with the mouse, simply click it.

Scrolling

Many Help topics are longer than the dialog box can show. You have to *scroll* the topic to see it all. Scrolling moves the text in the box. Scrolling up takes you toward the beginning of the topic, and scrolling down takes you toward the end.

How to Scroll with the Keyboard	
Key	*Function*
up-arrow	Moves the cursor up one line
down-arrow	Moves the cursor down one line
Home	Moves the cursor to the first line
End	Moves the cursor to the last line
PgUp	Moves the cursor up one page

PgDn	Moves the cursor down one page
character	Moves the cursor to the next item starting with that character

Scrolling with the mouse requires the scroll bar (see the drawing in the following procedure. The scroll box always indicates the position of the current page within the entire list (even when you're scrolling from the keyboard). Clicking the arrows at the ends of the scroll bar scrolls up or down one line at a time. Clicking the bar itself scrolls one page toward the place where you clicked. (A page constitutes the number of lines you can see in the visible area.) If you want to scroll longer distances, drag the scroll box to the position that represents the page you want to see. Holding down the mouse button on the arrow icons or the bar itself scrolls repeatedly and rapidly in the indicated direction, much as holding down a cursor key does.

Note: A horizontal scroll bar works just like a vertical one except the movements are sideways instead of up and down.

There's a major difference between scrolling with the keyboard and scrolling with the mouse. When you scroll with the keyboard, the cursor moves up or down in the list, changing the item that's selected. But when you use the mouse, the cursor stays with the item it was on; as the item moves, the cursor might scroll right out of the visible area. Scrolling with the mouse never changes the selected item; you must click another item to change the selection. Sometimes you want to change the selection as you scroll; sometimes you don't. After you get used to the difference, you will choose the keyboard or mouse, depending on which is more convenient for you.

How to Scroll with the Mouse

A scroll bar appears when there is too much information to fit in the available list. You must use the scroll bar to scroll with the mouse. (See Figure 5.5.)

Figure 5.5.
The anatomy
of the scroll bar.

Click here to scroll
up one line

Click here to scroll
up one page

Scroll box: drag up or
down to move long
distances

Click here to scroll
down one page

Click here to scroll
down one line

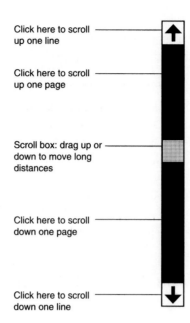

Let's take a look at the entire topic entitled File List Overview:

1. Activate the file list.

2. Press F1 to open the Help dialog box.

   The topic called File List Overview appears in the dialog box.

3. Press down-arrow a few times to scroll down a few lines.

4. Press Page Down a few times to scroll down a page at a time.

5. Press End to scroll to the end of the topic.

6. Now try up-arrow, Page Up, and Home.

Notice that the scroll box moves up and down in the scroll bar to show which part of the topic you're looking at.

If you have a mouse, try scrolling through the topic with it:

1. Click the down arrow at the bottom of the scroll bar to scroll down one line.

2. Click the dark part of the bar below the scroll box to scroll down one page.

3. Drag the scroll box down to the bottom of the bar.

4. Now try the various methods of scrolling up.

5. Press Esc to close Help.

Tip: If you hold down a scrolling key, or if you hold down the mouse button while clicking the scroll bar, the action is repeated rapidly, causing the text to run through the window. When you see the area you want to read, release the key or the button.

Using the Help Menu

Sometimes you want to select your own help topic instead of letting DOS Shell do it for you. The Help menu gives you access to the entire help library. (See Figure 5.6.)

Figure 5.6.
The Help menu.

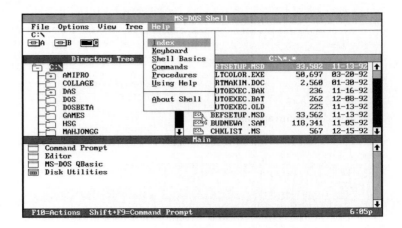

How to Use Menus

From the keyboard:

- Pull down a menu by pressing Alt+*letter*, where *letter* is the first letter of the menu name.

- When a menu is down, pull down the neighboring menu by pressing right-arrow or left-arrow.

- Choose a command by pressing the underlined letter of the command name.

- Close the menu without choosing a command by pressing Esc.

- If a command has a shortcut key listed next to it, you can choose the command without pulling down the menu by pressing the shortcut key.

From the mouse:

- Pull down a menu by clicking its name in the menu bar.

- Choose a command by clicking its name.

- Close a menu without choosing a command by clicking its name in the menu bar again.

Some commands on the menu may appear dimmed (printed in gray). Dimmed commands are not available because some required condition for using them has not been met.

You must pull down the Help menu to use it. To pull down a menu with your keyboard, press Alt+*letter*, where *letter* is the first letter of the menu name. You pull down a menu using your mouse by clicking the menu name.

Try pulling down the Help menu with your keyboard:

1. Press Alt+H.

   The Help menu appears.

2. Press Esc.

   The Help menu disappears.

You can also pull down a menu with your mouse:

1. Click the word Help on the menu bar.

   The Help menu appears.

2. Click the word Help on the menu bar again.

   The Help menu disappears.

Tip: You can close a menu by clicking anywhere outside the menu; but, because you might accidentally select something with your click, develop the safe habit of closing a menu by clicking its name a second time.

The Help Index

You should start exploring the Help system with the Help index (see Figure 5.7), which provides a general index to all the topics. It groups the topics into several categories, such as Keyboard Help, Commands Help, and Procedures Help. There's even a category on how to use the help system itself. Many topics in this index lead to more detailed indexes.

Figure 5.7.
The Help Index.

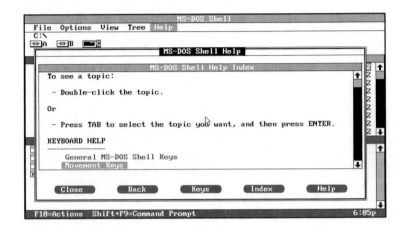

Try opening the Help Index with your keyboard:

1. Press Alt+H to pull down the Help menu.

2. Press I to choose the Index.

    You choose an item in a menu by typing the letter that is underlined in the item's name, which is I in the case of the Index command.

Scroll through the index to see all the categories and topics it contains. Topics are shown in a different color. To select a topic, double-click it or tab to it and press Enter.

1. Scroll the index until you see the topic General MS-DOS Shell Keys.

2. Press Tab until General MS-DOS Shell Keys is highlighted.

    Notice that the cursor goes from the help topics to the command buttons and back again.

3. Press Enter to see the selected topic.

This topic documents the various keys you can use with DOS Shell. Scroll through it to see what it contains. When you're done, you can return to the Help Index by choosing the Index command button. This command button is available in every Help dialog box so that you can always get back to the index.

1. Press Tab until the cursor is in the Index command button.

2. Press Enter to return to the Help Index.

Now try the preceding two exercises using your mouse:

1. Double-click General MS-DOS Shell Keys to open that topic.

2. Click the Index button to return to the Help Index.

The help system keeps track of the windows that you view and you can revisit former ones by choosing the Back button, which appears in every window.

1. Choose Back to return to the previous topic. (Use your mouse or keyboard, whichever you prefer.)

2. Choose Back again.

3. Press Esc or choose Close to close the Help dialog box.

Note: Unfortunately, you can't keep the help window on-screen while you work on the Shell screen.

Other Help Options

The other commands in the top portion of the Help menu access portions of the Help Index. If you know that you want the Keys Index, for example, you can go right to it without having to go through the Help Index. These detailed indexes are the following:

Keyboard Lists topics on how to use your keyboard with DOS Shell, such as Movement Keys and File List Keys. This Keys Index also can be accessed by pressing the Keys command button in the Help dialog box.

Shell Basics Lists general topics on using the Shell, such as Dialog Boxes and the program list.

Commands Lists topics on the Shell menus and their commands, such as the File Menu and the Tree Menu.

Procedures Provides access to step-by-step procedures for how to do things in the Shell. For example, you can see how to use the file list and how to run programs.

Using Help Lists topics on the help system itself, such as Using Help Buttons and Using Help Menu Commands. You can access this same index by pressing the Help button on the Help dialog box.

About Shell

The About Shell command appears below the dividing line in the Help menu because it's quite different from the other Help options. Choosing this command opens a box that shows your DOS version number. If you call Microsoft for technical support on DOS, you may be asked for this number.

1. Choose Help About Shell to see your DOS version number.

2. Press Esc to close the Help dialog box.

Exiting DOS Shell

You can exit DOS Shell temporarily or permanently. A temporary exit takes you to the DOS command prompt so that you can enter some commands without closing down the Shell; when you return to the Shell, the screen appears just as you left it. A permanent exit also goes to the DOS command prompt, but it closes down the Shell. If you restart the Shell, it will be in its initial state again.

You press Shift+F9 key to make a temporary exit to the command prompt (notice the reminder on the status bar). You have to use the EXIT command to return to the Shell again.

1. Press Shift+F9.

   The command prompt screen appears.

2. Type the word **EXIT** and press Enter.

   The Shell screen returns.

> **Note:** You may need to refresh the drive after returning from the DOS prompt if you made any changes to your drives while you were working at the command prompt.

The F3 key or the File Exit command exits the Shell permanently. Press F3 now to exit the Shell on your system.

On Your Own

You'll get plenty of practice in starting and exiting the Shell in upcoming chapters and in your everyday work. But you might not have the opportunity to practice using the Help system until you need it on the job. On your own, continue exploring the Help system so that you know where to find topics when you need them. Some suggested practice tasks:

- Find and read about the Exit command on the File menu.
- Find and read about how to work with a mouse in DOS Shell.

6 Managing Directories

Introduction

The Shell's directory tree makes it easy to create, delete, and otherwise manage directories.

Managing Directories

The Shell makes it easy to manage your drives and directories by displaying them on the Shell screen. You can easily select the item you want to work with, then select commands from the Shell's menus to manage it. Even better, some functions (such as deleting a directory) can be done with shortcut keys so that you don't have to bother with a menu.

In this chapter, you will learn how to:

- Select a drive to make it the current drive
- Force DOS Shell to reread the current drive
- Create a new directory
- Select a directory to make it the current directory
- Rename a directory
- Manipulate the directory tree
- Delete a directory

Selecting a Drive

The drive list shows all your drives, including network drives and pseudodrives such as a RAM drive. (Each icon depicts the drive's type.) You switch to a drive simply by selecting it in the drive list.

How to Change Drives in DOS Shell

To select a drive with the keyboard:

1. Activate the Drive List.

2. Press left-arrow or right-arrow as needed to highlight the drive.

3. Press Enter to select and refresh the drive, or press the spacebar to select it without refreshing it.

To select a drive (without refreshing it) from any area on the screen:

- Press Ctrl+*letter*, as in Ctrl+A to select drive A.

To select a drive with the mouse:

- Click the drive in the Drive List to select it without refreshing it.

- Or, you can Double-click the drive in the Drive List to select and refresh it.

To refresh the current drive (without selecting a new one):

- Press F5 from anywhere on the Shell screen.

To repaint the screen without selecting a new drive:

- Press Shift+5.

Problem: I have only one floppy drive, but DOS Shell shows a drive B in my drive list.

When you have just one floppy drive, DOS lets you use the drive name B as an alternate name for that drive. (Drive B is called the *phantom drive*.) This makes it possible to copy files from one disk to another in the same drive. Chapter 8, "Copying and Moving Files in DOS Shell," shows you how to use the phantom drive for copying files.

Note: If one of your drives doesn't show up in the list, DOS doesn't recognize it. See "Defining Drives for DOS" in Chapter 51, "Configuring Disks and Networks," for suggestions on how to make the drive available.

Try selecting drives with your keyboard:

1. Put a disk in drive A (so it's not empty). Use any disk that has been formatted.
2. Activate the drive list.
3. Press left-arrow until the letter A is highlighted.
4. Press the spacebar to select drive A.

   The directory tree and file list change to show the contents of the new current drive.
5. Press right-arrow until drive C is highlighted.
6. Press the spacebar to select drive C.

Problem: When I try to switch to my floppy drive, I get an error message, even though there's a disk in the drive.

Either your floppy disk has never been formatted for DOS (it might be formatted for some other operating system), or it is so badly damaged that DOS can't read it.

If you're trying to read a disk provided by someone else, ask that person to make another one, being sure to format it for DOS.

If you're trying to use a new, blank disk, you must format it first. Chapter 17, "Formatting and Unformatting Disks," explains how to format disks.

There's an even easier way to select a drive from your keyboard. All you have to do is press the Ctrl key plus the letter of the drive you want, as in Ctrl+A. Try selecting drives using this shortcut:

1. Press Ctrl+A to select drive A.
2. Press Ctrl+C to select drive C.

Tip: The drive list doesn't have to be active to use the Ctrl+*letter* shortcut. You can do it from any part of the Shell screen, so you can change drives while staying in the file list or the directory tree. This is the fastest way to change drives while working in the Shell.

Don't forget that you can also select drives with your mouse:

1. Click drive A to select it.

   Notice that the focus moves to the drive list when you do this.

2. Click drive C to select it.

Selecting an Empty Drive

If you should happen to select an empty drive, you'll see an error message like the one in Figure 6.1. You can place a disk in the drive and choose option 1, Try to read this disk again. Or, choose option 2, Do not try to read disk again, then select a different drive.

Figure 6.1.
Drive Not Ready *warning*
message.

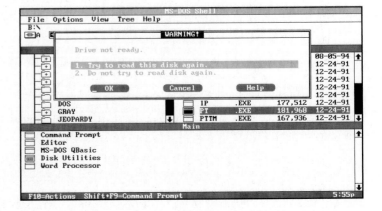

Try out each of the empty drive options:

1. Remove the disk from drive A.

2. Select drive A. (Use whatever technique you like.)

   The `Drive Not Ready` warning message appears.

3. Double-click option 2 or press down-arrow to highlight option 2 and press Enter.

   The warning message disappears and drive A becomes the current drive even though it is empty.

4. Select drive A again.

   The warning message appears again.

5. Place a disk in drive A.

6. Option 1 is already highlighted. Just press Enter to select it. Or, if you prefer to use the mouse, double-click it.

   Drive A becomes the current drive.

Note: When the `Drive Not Ready` warning message appears, you can press the Esc key (or choose Cancel in the dialog box) to cancel the drive change and stay with the current drive.

Refreshing Drives

The first time you select a drive after booting, DOS Shell reads the drive's directory structure. You might see a message while this happens. (On a fast system and a small disk, the message flashes past so quickly that you can't see it.) From then on, DOS Shell remembers the directory structure. If you switch away from that drive and return to it later, the directory tree and file list reappear instantaneously because DOS doesn't have to reread them.

But suppose you change the disk in a floppy drive. You need to see the new disk's directory structure, but DOS Shell continues to display the old one. Then you need to force the Shell to reread the drive. This is called *refreshing* the drive.

The techniques that you have used to select drives so far do not refresh the drives. You must press the Enter key or double-click the drive name to refresh a drive as you select it.

1. Insert a different disk in drive A. You can use any formatted disk.

2. Select drive A using the spacebar (not Enter).

   Notice that the directory tree and file list show the old disk's directory structure.

3. Now select drive A using the Enter key.

DOS Shell reads and displays the new disk's directory structure.

Now try refreshing drives with your mouse:

1. Change the disk in drive A again.

2. Double-click drive A in the Drive List.

   DOS Shell reads and displays the new disk's directory structure.

If you want to refresh the current drive, you don't have to reselect it. Just press F5 from any area of the screen. Try refreshing the current drive:

1. Change the disk in drive A again.

2. Press F5.

   DOS Shell reads and displays the new disk's directory structure.

Repainting the Screen

Sometimes the Shell screen becomes obstructed with part of a leftover dialog box that didn't completely close. Press Shift+F5 or choose View Repaint Screen to clean up the screen without refreshing the current drive. Try pressing Shift+F5 now; you should see the screen flash off and on as it is repainted.

Creating Directories

You create new directories right in the directory tree by using the File, Create Directory command. Whenever a command name is followed by an ellipsis (...) in a DOS Shell menu, as Create Directory is, a dialog box opens when you select the command. Figure 6.2 shows the dialog box that opens when you select File, Create Directory.

Figure 6.2.
The Create Directory dialog box.

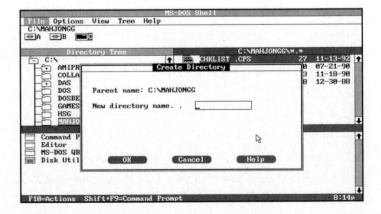

Note: You can't create a new directory on a read-only drive such as a read-only CD-ROM drive.

How to Create a New Directory in DOS Shell

1. Activate the directory tree.

2. Select the desired parent directory.

3. Choose File, Create Directory.

4. Make sure that the Parent Name field is correct. (If not, choose Cancel and try again.)

5. Enter the desired name in the New Directory Name text box.

6. Choose OK.

Problem: I want to create a new directory, but the File, Create Directory command is dimmed.

This command is available only when the directory tree contains the focus. Activate the directory tree and try again.

In the Create Directory dialog box, the field labeled `Parent Name` shows you the name of the currently selected directory, which will be the new directory's parent. If it's the wrong directory, choose Cancel, select the correct parent, and try again.

The smaller box in the middle of the dialog box, labeled `New Directory Name`, is a *text box*. You can type in this box. When the dialog box first appears, the cursor is positioned at the beginning of the text box. All you have to do is type the name of the new directory in the box.

It doesn't matter what case you use to type the directory name. DOS automatically converts it to uppercase letters in the directory tree. You can use Backspace, Home, End, left-arrow, right-arrow, and Delete as needed to correct any typographical errors.

Peter's Principle: Directory names should be short but meaningful.

When you're working at the command prompt, you often have to specify a chain of directory names in front of a file name, as in `C:\WORK\JUNE\BACKUP\OLDORDER.DAT`, where `C:\`, `WORK`, `JUNE`, and `BACKUP` are directory names and `OLDORDER.DAT` is the file name. If you use long directory names complete with extensions, or obscure directory names such as CZ15T25%, you make your job much harder. And, you stand the chance of creating an expression that's too long for DOS to handle.

The three command buttons are the most common ones in DOS Shell dialog boxes. You choose the OK button after you have filled in the text box and are ready to create the new directory. Or, you choose the Cancel button if you change your mind and want to close the dialog box without creating the directory. The Help button takes you directly to the Help topic for this dialog box; it's the same as pressing F1.

You will create an entire branch of directories for the practice sessions in this chapter. The branch looks like this:

PRACTICE

       OTHER
       PLAY
       WORK

              LATER
              NOW

Create the PRACTICE directory now:

1. Select drive C.
2. Activate the directory tree.
3. Press the Home key to select the root directory.
4. Choose the File, Create Directory command.

    The Create Directory dialog box appears.
5. Make sure that Parent Name says c:\. If not, choose Cancel and go back to step 3.
6. Type **PRACTICE** in the text box.
7. Choose OK to create the new directory.

    You should see the PRACTICE directory appear in the directory tree. It will be in alphabetical order, so if you have a lot of directories under the root directory, you might have to scroll to see it.

Problem: I tried to create a new directory and got an Access Denied message.

Each directory name must be unique within its parent directory. It can't duplicate another directory name or a file name in the same parent. If you try to assign a non-unique name, the `Access Denied` message appears in the Create Directory dialog box.

The first option, `Skip this file or directory and continue,` has the same effect as Cancel. It cancels the `Create Directory` command and returns to the Shell screen. You may want to choose this option to take another look at the directory tree and the file list before trying again.

The second option, `Try this file or directory again,` returns to the Create Directory dialog box so that you can try another name right away.

To choose an option, double-click the option or highlight the option and press OK.

Selecting Directories

When you select a directory, you make it the current directory and its files appear in the file list. To select a directory with the keyboard, just move the cursor to it.

Try selecting some directories with the keyboard:

1. Make sure that drive C is selected.
2. Press Home to select the root directory.
3. Press D to select the DOS directory. If D selects another directory starting with D, press it as many times as necessary to reach the DOS directory.

   Watch the file list change as you move from directory to directory.

If you're using a mouse, all you have to do is click a directory to select it. You might have to scroll to find the directory before you can click it.

1. Click C:\ to select the root directory.
2. Click DOS to select the DOS directory.

Now create the rest of the PRACTICE branch that you need for this chapter:

1. Select the PRACTICE directory.
2. Choose File, Create Directory.

   The Create Directory dialog box appears.
3. Type **WORK** and press Enter.

   The WORK directory appears as a child of PRACTICE. (You might have to scroll down to see it.)
4. Repeat steps 2 and 3 to create the PLAY and OTHER directories.
5. Select the WORK directory and create LATER and NOW underneath it.

Did you notice the minus signs appear in the file folder icons next to the PRACTICE and WORK directories? They are explained in the next section.

Collapsing and Expanding the Directory Tree

After you have created a few dozen directories in four or five levels, you might have trouble finding things in the tree. Most of the time, it is much easier to find the branches you want to work with if the lower levels of subdirectories don't appear in the tree. The Tree menu gives you control over the branches that appear. (See Figure 6.3.)

Figure 6.3.
The Tree menu.

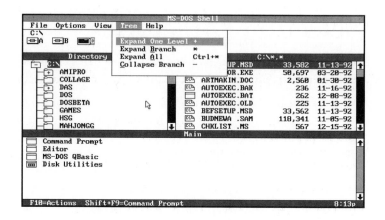

In the directory tree, each directory is represented by an icon shaped like a file folder. A plus sign in the file folder indicates a directory with unseen children; you can expand this directory to display its children. A minus sign in the file folder indicates a directory with at least one child displayed; you can collapse it to hide its children. A blank folder means the directory has no children.

How to Expand and Collapse DOS Shell's Directory Tree

The Tree menu and the shortcut keys used in this procedure work on the current directory when the focus is in the drive list, directory tree, or file list.

Expanding the tree:

To expand the first level of children for the current directory: Press the + key or click the + in the file folder icon.

To expand all levels for the current directory: Press the * key.

> To expand the entire directory tree: Press Ctrl+*.
>
> Collapsing the tree:
>
> To collapse the current directory: Press the - key or click the - in the file folder icon.

Suppose you want to collapse the PRACTICE directory so that none of its children are showing. From the keyboard, you would have to do it this way:

1. Select the PRACTICE directory.
2. Press the – (minus or hyphen) key. You can use the – key on the regular keyboard or the numeric keypad.

   PRACTICE's children disappear and a plus sign appears in its file folder icon.

Now suppose you want to see its first level of children.

1. Make sure PRACTICE is still selected.
2. Press the + (plus) key. You can use the + key on the regular keyboard or the numeric keypad.

   The OTHER, PLAY, and WORK directories appear under PRACTICE. You might have to scroll to see them.

If you want to see the entire PRACTICE branch, use the * key instead of +.

1. Make sure that PRACTICE is still selected.
2. Press * on the regular keyboard or the numeric keypad.

   The LATER and NOW directories appear under WORK. You might have to scroll down to see them.

Tip: You may not have to activate the directory tree to expand or contract it. The Tree menu and its shortcut keys work on the current directory when the directory tree, drive list, or file list is active. But when the program list is active, the Tree menu disappears from the menu bar and none of its commands (or shortcut keys) are available.

To expand the entire tree so that you can see all the directories on the drive, press Ctrl+* or choose Tree Expand All.

1. Press Ctrl+* on the regular keyboard or the numeric keypad. (On the regular keyboard, you must press Ctrl+Shift+*, because * is an uppercase key.)

   The entire directory tree expands.
2. Scroll through the entire directory tree to see all the levels of all the branches.

When you're using a mouse instead of the keyboard, you expand and collapse branches by clicking + and − in the file folder icons.

1. Click − in the file folder next to the root directory.

    The entire directory tree collapses so that only the root directory is showing. A + appears in the icon.

2. Click the + sign.

    The first level of directories appears under the root directory. You have now restored the directory tree to its default condition.

Renaming Directories

You may find it necessary to rename a directory on occasion. You use the File, Rename command to do so. Figure 6.4 shows the dialog box that opens when you choose File, Rename while the cursor is in the directory tree. The current directory's name appears in the Current Name field.

Figure 6.4.
*The Rename Directory
dialog box.*

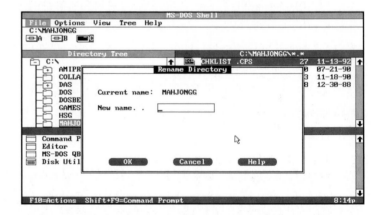

Note: You can't rename or delete directories on a read-only drive such as a CD-ROM drive. If you try, you get the Access Denied message.

How to Rename a Directory in DOS Shell

1. Activate the directory tree.

2. Select the directory to be renamed.

3. Choose File, Rename.

The Rename Directory dialog box opens.

4. Make sure that Current Name shows the correct directory name. (If not, press Cancel and try again.)

5. Type the new name in the New Name text box.

6. Press OK.

Practice by renaming the WORK directory as DETAIL:

1. Select the WORK directory.

2. Choose File, Rename.

   The Rename Directory dialog box opens.

3. Make sure that the Current Name field says WORK. If not, choose Cancel and try again.

4. Type DETAIL in the New Name text box.

5. Choose OK.

   DOS Shell renames WORK to DETAIL and moves it to the correct alphabetical order under PRACTICE.

When a renamed directory moves to its new alphabetical position, you might have to scroll to see it.

Note: File, Rename is not available when the root directory is selected because you're not allowed to rename the root directory.

Problem: I tried to rename a directory in DOS Shell and got an Access Denied message.

Each directory name must be unique within its parent directory. It can't duplicate another directory name or a file name in the same parent. If you try to assign a nonunique name, the Access Denied message appears in the Rename Directory dialog box. You also could get an Access Denied message if the directory is read-only.

The first option, Skip this file or directory and continue, has the same effect as Cancel. It cancels the Rename command and returns to the Shell screen. You may want to choose this option to take another look at the directory tree and the file list before trying again.

The second option, Try this file or directory again, returns to the Rename Directory dialog box so that you can try another name right away.

To choose an option, double-click the option or highlight the option and press OK.

Deleting Directories

A directory must be completely empty before you can delete it by using DOS Shell, which means that the directory must contain neither files nor subdirectories. If you want to delete an entire branch, you have to start at the lowest level and work your way up.

> **Tip:** The DELTREE command is a much faster way to delete a directory. It's explained in Chapter 14, "Managing Directories."

You delete an empty directory by pressing the Delete key while the directory is selected. If DOS Shell's Delete Confirmation feature is enabled, a dialog box opens so that you can confirm the deletion or cancel it. If the Delete Confirmation feature is disabled, the directory is deleted without giving you a chance to change your mind. You'll learn how to enable and disable Delete Confirmation in Chapter 9, "Additional File Management in the Shell." It is enabled by default, so unless someone has modified your system you will see the Delete Directory Confirmation dialog box when you press the Delete key. (See Figure 6.5.)

Figure 6.5.
The Delete Directory
Confirmation dialog box.

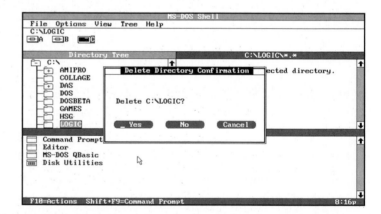

How to Delete a Directory in DOS Shell

Note: The directory must be empty before it can be deleted using this technique. It must contain neither files nor subdirectories.

1. Activate the directory tree.
2. Select the directory to be deleted.
3. Press the Delete key.

4. If the Delete Directory Confirmation dialog box opens, make sure that it displays the correct directory name. If so, choose Yes. (If not, choose No or Cancel.)

You should see the selected directory disappear from the directory tree; the next higher directory becomes selected.

Delete the directories that you created earlier in this chapter:

1. Select the LATER directory.

2. Press the Delete key.

The Delete Directory Confirmation dialog box appears.

3. Make sure the directory name is LATER. If not, choose Cancel and try again.

4. Choose Yes.

5. Delete NOW, DETAIL, PLAY, OTHER, and finally PRACTICE.

Warning: Be sure to select the desired directory before pressing the Delete key. If DOS Shell's delete confirmation feature is disabled, the selected item will be deleted before you get a chance to change your mind.

Problem: I tried to delete an empty directory in DOS Shell, but a message says `You cannot delete a non-empty directory`.

This message is often a surprise because it can happen when you thought the directory was empty. In fact, the directory may contain files and subdirectories that you can't see in the current directory tree or file list.

If the directory you want to delete has a plus sign next to it, it has subdirectories that you can't see. Press the * key to display the entire branch. Delete the branch from the bottom up.

A directory also may have files that you can't see. By default, DOS Shell does not display hidden and system files. If the message in the file list reads `No files match the file specifier` instead of `No files in selected directory`, the directory still contains files. You must display and delete the files before you can delete the directory; Chapter 9 shows you how. Chapter 11, "Customizing the Shell," deals with seeing and deleting hidden files.

On Your Own

This chapter has guided you through the process of changing drives and directories; and creating, renaming, and deleting directories. Try these tasks on your own. Some suggested practice activities:

- Create a complete branch on a floppy disk
- Rename each directory in the branch
- Delete the branch

Selecting Files in the Shell

Introduction

In the Shell, you select files in the file list to be processed by File menu commands such as Print, Copy, and Delete.

Selecting Files in the Shell

You select files in much the same way as directories, with one important difference—you can select more than one file at a time, even across multiple directories. So if you need to delete all the .BAK files on your hard drive, for example, you can select and delete them all with a single command.

In this chapter, you will learn to:

- Select a single file
- Select several adjacent files
- Select several nonadjacent files
- Deselect individual files when multiple files are selected
- Select files in more than one directory

Selecting a Single File

You will often want to process just one file at a time. For example, you may want to view or print a single file. Selecting one file is as easy as selecting a directory—simply click the file or move the cursor to it. The file that's highlighted is the one that's selected; this file becomes the target of any File menu command you invoke while the file list is active. For example, if you press Delete, the selected file is deleted.

Try selecting a single file using the keyboard:

1. Select the DOS directory.

   The files in the DOS directory are displayed in the file list. Notice that they are in alphabetical order (unless someone has modified your DOS Shell).

2. Activate the file list.

   The first file in the list is selected.

3. Press M to jump the cursor to MEM.EXE. If another file starting with M is selected instead, keep pressing M until you reach MEM.EXE.

   Whichever file is highlighted is the currently selected file. Notice that, as you move the cursor, the previous file is deselected.

Deselecting means removing the selection status of a file so that it is no longer selected. Whenever you select one file, you deselect the previous one. If multiple files were selected previously, they are all deselected. It's important to remember that every time you move the cursor or click an entry in the file list, you select a new file and deselect all previous files. Changing to another directory also deselects whichever files were selected in the previous directory. (The first file in the new directory is selected by default.)

Note: Scrolling with the mouse does not affect file selection, but scrolling with the keyboard does, because it moves the cursor.

Selecting Multiple Files

Sometimes it's handy to select a group of files for processing. There's quite a difference in how you select multiple files with the mouse and with the keyboard.

How to Select Files in DOS Shell

To select adjacent files with a mouse:

1. Click the first file.

2. Hold down the Shift key and click the last file.

To select nonadjacent files with a mouse:

1. Click the first file.

2. Hold down Ctrl and click each subsequent file.

To select a mixture of adjacent and nonadjacent files with the mouse:

1. Click the first file in a range of adjacent files.

2. Shift+Click the last file in the range. (The range is now selected.)

3. Ctrl+Click each additional file to be selected.

To select a range of adjacent files with the keyboard:

1. Move the cursor to the first file in the range.

2. Hold down Shift and move the cursor to the last file in the range.

To select nonadjacent files when using the keyboard:

1. Select the first file.

2. Press Shift+F8 to enter Add mode. (The word ADD appears on the status line.)

3. Move the cursor to the next file to be selected.

4. Press the spacebar to select it.

5. Repeat steps 3 and 4 to select all desired files.

6. Press Shift+F8 to exit Add mode.

To deselect an individual file in Add mode:

1. Move the cursor to the selected file name.

2. Press the spacebar.

To select all files, press Ctrl+/.

To deselect all files, press Ctrl+\ .

Selecting Multiple Files with the Mouse

The technique you use to select multiple files with the mouse depends on whether the files you want are adjacent to each other in the file list.

Use the Shift key to select multiple files. Try selecting all the files in the DOS directory from APPEND.EXE through CHKDSK.EXE:

1. Scroll the file list if necessary and click APPEND.EXE.

2. Scroll the file list again if necessary, hold down Shift, and click CHKDSK.EXE.

   All the files between APPEND.EXE and CHKDSK.EXE should be highlighted.

You can create the range of selected files from the top down or the bottom up; that is, you can start by selecting either the first file or the last file in the range, and then Shift+Click the other end of the range.

Shift+Click does not move the cursor, which remains on the first file in the range. You can adjust the other end of the range by using Shift+Click again.

You have to use Ctrl instead of Shift to select nonadjacent files. Try selecting APPEND.EXE, CHKDSK.EXE, and MEM.EXE:

1. Click APPEND.EXE.

   Notice that you deselected the previous range of files when you did this.

2. Scroll if necessary, hold down Ctrl, and click CHKDSK.EXE. (It's very important to scroll with the mouse in this situation. If you try to scroll using the keyboard, you will deselect APPEND.EXE.)

   CHKDSK.EXE is highlighted while APPEND.EXE remains highlighted.

3. Scroll again, if necessary. Hold down Ctrl and click MEM.EXE.

MEM.EXE is highlighted while the other two files remain highlighted (even if you can't see them because they are off the screen).

Each time you Ctrl+click a file, it is highlighted without deselecting any of the previous files.

If you want to select a mixed group of files, some adjacent and some not, you can combine the two methods, but you can use Shift+click only to select the first range. After that, you can use Ctrl+Click to select individual files and Ctrl+Shift+Click to select additional ranges.

Try selecting APPEND.EXE through CHKDSK.EXE plus MEM.EXE through MODE.COM:

1. Scroll the file list, if necessary, and click APPEND.EXE.
2. Scroll the file list again, if necessary. Hold down Shift and click CHKDSK.EXE. (Be sure to scroll using the mouse.)

    All the files between APPEND.EXE and CHKDSK.EXE should be highlighted.

3. Scroll the file list, if necessary. Hold down Ctrl and click MEM.EXE.
4. Scroll the file list again, if necessary. Hold down Ctrl+Shift and click MODE.COM. (Be sure to scroll using the mouse.)

    All the files between MEM.EXE and MODE.COM should highlight. You now have two selected ranges.

Combining Selection and Deselection

If you want to deselect an individual file without deselecting them all, Ctrl+Click the file. Ctrl+Click toggles individual file selection on and off without affecting any other selected files.

Suppose that you want to select every file in the DOS directory except APPEND.EXE:

1. Scroll the file list as necessary and click the first file in the directory.
2. Scroll the file list to the end, hold down Shift, and click the last file in the directory. (The fastest way to scroll to the end is to drag the scroll box all the way to the bottom of the scroll bar.)

    All the files in the directory are highlighted.

3. Scroll up until you see APPEND.EXE, hold down Ctrl, and click APPEND.EXE.

    APPEND.EXE is deselected and its highlight is removed. The rest of the files remain highlighted.

Selecting Multiple Files with the Keyboard

As with the mouse, when you select files with the keyboard, there's a difference between how you select a range of adjacent files and how you select nonadjacent files.

You select a range of files by holding down the Shift key while you scroll from one end of the range to the other. Try selecting from APPEND.EXE to CHKDSK.EXE with your keyboard:

1. Press the letter A to select APPEND.EXE. Keep pressing A until APPEND.EXE is the selected file.

2. Hold down Shift and press C until you see the highlight extend through CHKDSK.EXE.

   All the files from APPEND.EXE through CHKDSK.EXE are highlighted.

You can use any method to move the cursor while you hold down the Shift key: the up- and down-arrow keys, PgUp or PgDn, Home or End, or the first letter of the file name. You also can adjust the end of the range by holding down Shift while you move the cursor again. Suppose that you want to select all the files in the list except the first and the last. You can select the second file, press Shift+End to select the rest of the list, and then press Shift+up arrow to deselect the last file.

Remember that selecting any individual file deselects all others, so be sure not to move the cursor without Shift until you're ready to deselect the range.

To select nonadjacent files when using the keyboard, you must use a special file selection mode called *Add mode*. Add mode enables you to move the cursor in the file list without selecting or deselecting files. The Shift+F8 key combination toggles Add mode on and off; when it's on, the word ADD appears in the status bar.

1. Press Shift+F8.

   The word ADD appears in the status bar and Add mode is enabled.

2. Press up-arrow several times.

   Notice that the previously selected files are not deselected, nor are any files selected as you move the cursor.

3. Press M to scroll to MEM.EXE, then press the spacebar to select it.

   MEM.EXE is highlighted without deselecting any of the previous files.

When you're in Add mode, you also can select a range of files by holding down Shift while you move the cursor. Alternatively, you can select one end of the range by pressing the spacebar, then move the cursor to the other end of the range, and press Shift+spacebar. It's possible to select multiple ranges in Add mode because moving the cursor does not deselect files.

You don't have to exit Add mode before processing the selected files. For example, you can press the Delete key to delete all the selected files, and then select some more files and choose File, Print.

The spacebar acts as a selection toggle in Add mode, just as Ctrl+Click does when you're using a mouse. You can deselect a file by moving the cursor to it and pressing the spacebar. Only that file is deselected; all others remain selected.

1. Press A until the cursor is on APPEND.EXE.

2. Press the spacebar.

   APPEND.EXE is deselected and its highlight is removed. Because the cursor is still on the file, the only way you can tell that the highlight has been removed is to look at the icon at the beginning of the line, which is no longer highlighted.

Selecting and Deselecting All Files

The File menu enables you to select or deselect all files with the `Select All` and `Deselect All` commands. Their hot keys, however, are much faster: Ctrl+/ selects all files; Ctrl+\ deselects all files.

1. Press Shift+F8 to exit ADD mode.

   The word `ADD` disappears from the status bar.

2. Press Ctrl+/ to select all files.

3. Press Ctrl+\ to deselect all files.

   Notice that one file stays selected—the file that the cursor is on.

When No Files Are Selected

It's possible in the Shell to deselect all files. If you accidentally (or intentionally) deselect the last remaining selection by using Ctrl+Click or the spacebar, most of the commands on the File menu go dim. (See Figure 7.1.) To make the commands available again, select any file.

Figure 7.1.
The File menu when no files are selected.

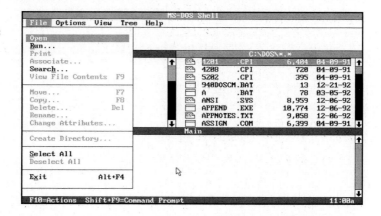

Selecting from Multiple Directories

So far, you have learned how to select files in one directory only. But if you have a large task involving files in several directories, you can handle them all at once using the Shell. (You wouldn't be able to do that at the command prompt.)

There are two ways to select from multiple directories in the Shell. One way, called Select Across Directories, is so awkward that many people have accidentally lost files by using it; therefore, this book does not show you how to use it. The other method, called View All Files, is much safer, although it also involves some risk.

View All Files displays all the files on a drive in one file list. (See Figure 7.2.) In this view, the directory tree and program list are eliminated. The file list includes the names of all the files on the drive, in alphabetical order. You can select any combination of files without regard to directory. To try out View All Files, follow these steps:

1. Choose View All Files.

   The screen changes to show all the files in one file list.

2. Scroll through the file list to see the extent of the files on your hard disk.

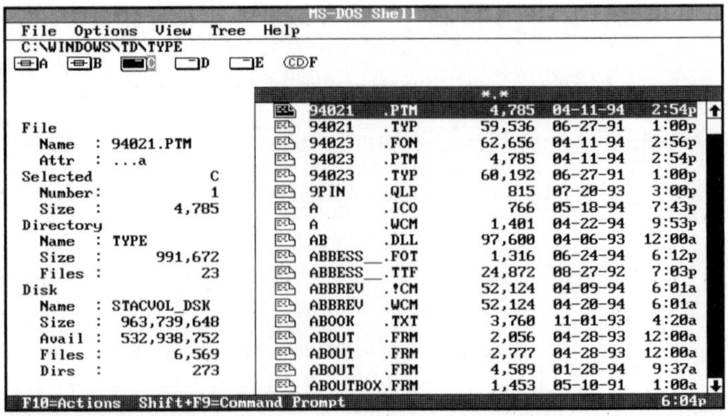

Figure 7.2.
The View All Files list.

A slight danger with View All Files arises when you have two or more files in different directories with the same name. For example, if PROFILE.DOC appears in three different directories, they might be three completely different files, three identical copies of the same file, three different versions of a file, or some combination of these possibilities. In the View All Files list, you would just see the three names, one after the other, along with the details from their directory entries. If you wanted to select just one of these files, it would be very easy to select the wrong one.

The box at the left in the View All Files display can help you decide which file you want to select. It shows information about the drive and the selected files. The Directory Name field shows what directory the most recently selected file is in. If the list shows several files of the same name and you're not sure which one you want, select each one and look at the Directory Name field to find out which directory it's in. This should help you figure out which file is the one you want.

You select files from the View All Files display just as you do from the normal file list. You can select a single file, adjacent files, nonadjacent files, or a combination of adjacent and nonadjacent files.

To return to the usual DOS Shell screen, choose View Program/File Lists.

1. Choose View Program/File Lists.

    The screen returns to normal.

On Your Own

You'll get plenty of chances to use these techniques in upcoming chapters as you learn to move, copy, delete, and otherwise manage files. To make sure that you can comfortably select files, try each of the items below:

1. Select a single file.
2. Select several nonadjacent files.
3. Select a range of adjacent files.
4. Select two or more ranges of adjacent files.
5. Deselect some individual files in your selected ranges.
6. Deselect one of your ranges without deselecting the others.
7. Select two ranges and some individual files.
8. Select all the files in a directory.
9. Deselect all the selected files except for the one that the cursor is on.
10. Select several files in the DOS directory and in the root directory.
11. Deselect all but one file (and restore the normal view) before continuing to the next chapter.

8

Copying and Moving Files in DOS Shell

Introduction

It's amazing how often you must copy or move files. DOS Shell makes it easy and (almost) safe.

Copying and Moving Files in DOS Shell

One of the most common DOS tasks is copying or moving a file, and DOS Shell makes it much easier than using the command prompt. But even in the Shell, problems will crop up and you'll want to be ready to deal with them. In this chapter, you will learn how to:

- Turn replacement confirmation on and off
- Copy a single file to another directory or even to the same directory
- Move a single file to another directory
- Copy and move multiple files to another directory
- Drag files to another directory or drive
- Use alternate views of the Shell screen to make copying and moving files easier

Using Replacement Confirmation

It seems like the most innocent task possible, but copying or moving a file can actually be dangerous—you stand the chance of losing data without any warning. When the destination directory (the directory to receive the file) already contains a file of the same name, DOS might replace that file with the new one. It can't evaluate whether the two files are identical or are two versions of the same file; if the name's the same, DOS replaces it. This is often referred to as *clobbering* the file.

Warning: DOS's UNDELETE program can't recover a file that was clobbered by a COPY, XCOPY, or MOVE command. (But, the Norton Utilities' Unerase program can.)

Peter's Principle: Use DOS Shell to copy and move files—it's safer (for versions of DOS before 6.2).

Prior to DOS 6.2, the COPY, XCOPY, and MOVE commands would clobber files without warning, but DOS Shell wouldn't. DOS 6.2 finally improved these commands. If you haven't yet upgraded from an earlier version and don't have Windows or a third-party shell, use DOS Shell to move and copy files whenever possible.

Figure 8.1 shows the dialog box that opens when you choose the Options Confirmation command. This dialog box contains check boxes. A check box acts like a toggle switch: if you select it when it's on, you turn it off; select it again to turn it on. An X in the box indicates that it's on.

Figure 8.1.
The Confirmation dialog
box.

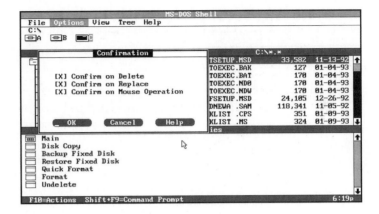

The second option, Confirm on Replace, controls whether the Shell warns you before replacing a file. Check to make sure your Confirm on Replace option is enabled:

1. Choose Options Confirmation.

   The Confirmation dialog box opens.

2. If Confirm on Replace has an X, the option is enabled. Choose OK to close the dialog box.

3. If Confirm on Replace does not have an X, click it once to turn it on. From the keyboard, press the up-arrow twice to move the cursor to it; then, press the spacebar to turn it on.

   When you see the X appear in the box, the option is enabled.

4. Choose OK to close the dialog box.

It's a good idea to keep replacement confirmation on at all times. Turn it off only for an isolated task when you actually intend to replace several files and don't want to be bothered confirming each one. Always turn this feature on again as soon as possible.

Copying a Single File

When you copy a file to a different directory, you can give it a new name or keep its original name. But, when you copy a file to the same directory, you must give it a new name, because a directory can't have two files with the same name.

Note: You can copy files from, but not to, read-only drives such as CD-ROM drives.

How to Move or Copy a Single File in DOS Shell

To copy a file to the same directory:

1. Select the file.

2. Choose File, Copy or press F8 (the file list must be active).

3. Check the file name in the From box. (If it's wrong, press Cancel and try again.)

4. Press End to move the cursor to the end of the text in the To box.

5. If the path name in the To box does not end with a backslash, type a backslash.

6. Add a file name to the path name.

7. Press OK.

To copy a file to a different directory:

1. Select the file.

2. Choose File, Copy or press F8 (the file list must be active).

3. Check the file name in the From box. (If it's wrong, press Cancel and try again.)

4. Edit or replace the path name in the To box.

5. Add a file name and extension (optional) if you want to give the copy a new name.

6. Press OK.

To move a file:

1. Select the file.

2. Choose File, Move or press F7 (the file list must be active).

3. Check the file name in the From box. (If it's wrong, press Cancel and try again.)

4. Edit or replace the default path name in the To box.

5. Add a file name and extension (optional) if you want to give the file a new name.

6. Select OK.

To copy a file, you select it and choose the File, Copy command (or press its shortcut key, F8). Figure 8.2 shows the dialog box that opens when you choose this command. The path name of the current directory appears in the To box. If you want to make a copy in the same directory, you must add a filespec to the path name. Or, you can change the path name to copy the file to a different directory, with or without a new file name. If you omit the file name, the copy receives the same name as the original.

Problem: The Copy and Move commands are dimmed on my File menu and I can't copy or move any files. Or, I pressed F7 or F8 to move or copy some files, but the computer just beeped at me.

Either you didn't select a file first or you didn't activate the file list. Activate the file list and select at least one file, and both commands will be available.

Problem: I chose the Copy command on the File menu, but nothing happened.

You're probably in the program list instead of the file list. Press Esc, then activate the file list, select at least one file and try again.

Figure 8.2.
The Copy File dialog box.

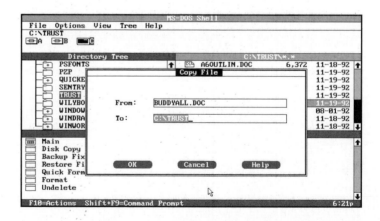

For this chapter, you'll make two practice directories to receive files, so that you don't add any unwanted files to your working directories. Create the directories now, then copy C:\DOS\HELP.COM to the first one. (This is a small file that fits into one allocation unit. It won't take much time to copy, and it won't take up much space on your hard disk.)

1. Create directories called PRAC1 and PRAC2 as children of the root directory.

2. Select the DOS directory.

3. Choose HELP.COM.

4. Press F8 to open the Copy File dialog box.

   The Copy File dialog box uses a text box to collect information from you. When the dialog box first appears, DOS highlights all the text in the To box, indicating that it is selected. If you want to replace the entire value, just start typing. The first character you type replaces everything in the box.

5. Type **PRAC1**.

   The path name C:\DOS is replaced by \PRAC1.

6. Press Enter to complete the copy. (Enter chooses the OK button.)

   DOS copies the HELP.COM file to the \PRAC1 directory.

7. Select the PRAC1 directory to see the new file.

Note: The From box looks like a text box, and you can place the cursor in it, but DOS beeps if you try to type in it.

Suppose that, instead of copying to PRAC1, you want to copy to C:\DOS\OLDPROGS. The To box already contains C:\DOS, so you don't have to type out the entire new value. You can edit the existing value instead of replacing it. If you press a horizontal cursor key first (left-arrow, right-arrow, Home, or End), the highlight disappears. The End and right-arrow keys leave the cursor where it is (at the end); the Home and left-arrow keys move the cursor to the beginning. Either way, you're ready to start editing.

Continue pressing the left- or right-arrow keys to position the cursor where you want it. (After the highlight disappears, pressing the left-arrow and right-arrow keys moves one character at a time.) DOS inserts whatever you type at the cursor. So, to change C:\DOS to C:\DOS\OLDPROGS, you could press End and type \OLDPROGS.

Tip: Another way to start editing is to click the position where you want to place the cursor, and you're ready to go.

If the name of the copy duplicates an existing file name and you're using Confirm on Replace, the Replace File Confirmation dialog box appears. (See Figure 8.3.) It shows you the names, dates, and sizes of both files to help you decide what to do. Choose Yes to make the replacement; choose No or Cancel to cancel it.

Figure 8.3.
The Replace File Confirma-
tion box.

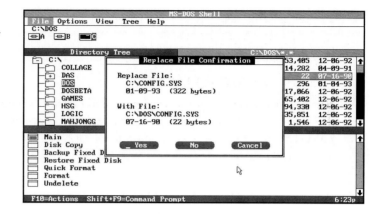

Try copying HELP.COM to \PRAC1 again. This time, you should get the Replace File Confirmation box because \PRAC1 already contains a file named HELP.COM.

1. Select the DOS directory and select the HELP.COM file again.

2. Press F8 to select the COPY command again.

   The Copy File dialog box appears.

3. Type \PRAC1 and press Enter.

   The Replace File Confirmation box appears because the PRACTICE directory already
   contains a file named HELP.COM.

4. Choose Yes.

   DOS copies HELP.COM to \PRAC1, replacing the existing file in that directory.

Problem: I tried to move or copy a file to a floppy disk and got an Access Denied message.

The floppy is write-protected. You can solve this problem by changing disks or removing
the write-protection. Then choose option 2, Try this file again.

Problem: I tried to copy a file and got the message File can't be copied onto itself.

You forgot to change the name in the To box. If you want to copy to the same directory,
you must supply a new file name. If you want to move or copy to a different directory, you
must supply the path name. You cannot move a file to the same directory that it is already
in.

The only thing you can do now is cancel the operation and start over, being more careful
to type the correct filespec or path name.

Moving a Single File

Moving a file is similar to copying it, except DOS removes it from the source directory after completing the copy. You must move the file to a different directory; moving it to the same directory makes no sense. Follow these steps to move a file:

1. Select the PRAC1 directory.

2. Select HELP.COM.

3. Press F7 to choose the Move command.

   The Move File dialog box appears. (If DOS Shell just beeps, the file list is not active. Activate the file list and try again.)

4. This time, you will move the file to PRAC2 and change its name to MYFILE.XXX. Edit C:\PRAC1 to say C:\PRAC2\MYFILE.XXX and press Enter.

   DOS moves the file from PRAC1 to PRAC2. You should see it disappear from the PRACTICE directory.

5. Select the PRAC2 directory.

   You should see MYFILE.XXX in this directory.

Note: You cannot move a file from or to a read-only drive such as a CD-ROM drive.

Copying and Moving Multiple Files

When you select multiple files to move or copy, you can't rename them. They must keep their original names, which means that you must copy them to another directory.

How to Move or Copy Multiple Files in DOS Shell

1. Select the files (make sure that no other files are selected).

2. Choose File, Copy (F8) or File, Move (F7).

3. Scroll through the list in the From box. (If it's not correct, press Cancel and try again.)

4. Edit or replace the path name in the To box to identify the destination directory.

5. Select OK.

Figure 8.4 shows what the Copy File dialog box looks like when you select multiple files. You can see the last few file names in the From box, but you must scroll to see the rest. To be safe, you should examine all the names before continuing. It's easy in the Shell to select more files than you intended.

Figure 8.4.
Copying multiple files.

You use the cursor keys to scroll through the From box. Try copying a set of files to the PRAC1 directory:

1. In the DOS directory, select HELP.COM, LOADFIX.COM, and MSD.COM.

2. Press F8.

   The Copy File dialog box opens.

3. Press Home and right-arrow to scroll through the list in the From box. (If it's not correct, press Cancel and try again.)

4. Press down-arrow to move the cursor to the To box.

5. Type **\PRAC1** and press Enter.

If the Replace File Confirmation dialog box appears when you're moving or copying multiple files (see Figure 8.3, shown previously), No and Cancel have different effects. As always, Cancel ends the entire command; no more files are copied. But No cancels only the current file; DOS continues with the next file in the list, if there is one.

Problem: I tried to move or copy several files and got the message You have more than one file selected.

If you specify a path name for a target directory that doesn't exist, DOS assumes that the name is a file name rather than a path name, and that you want to rename the copied or moved file. But when you're moving or copying more than one file, you're not allowed to specify a new file name. So DOS Shell displays the message You have more than one file selected in the dialog box. What this message really means is, "The name you entered doesn't exist, so I'm assuming that it's a file name." If you really meant it to be a path name, correct the name and try again.

Dragging Files

Now that you know the hard way to move and copy files, you should learn the easy way. If you have a mouse, you can select the files you want and drag them to a new location. You must drag them to a different directory, and you get no opportunity to rename them.

How to Move or Copy Files by Dragging in DOS Shell

To move files to another directory on the same drive:

1. Scroll the directory tree and expand subdirectories as needed to reveal the desired destination directory in the directory tree, but don't actually select the destination directory. (The source directory should be selected for the following steps.)

2. Select the files.

3. Drag any selected file to the desired destination directory (in the directory tree).

4. Drop the files by releasing the mouse button.

5. Confirm the move, if necessary.

To move files to a different drive:

1. Select the destination drive (in the drive list).

2. Select the destination directory (in the directory tree) to make it the default directory for the drive.

3. Select the source drive (in the drive list).

4. Select the files to be moved.

5. Press Alt and drag any selected file to the desired drive (in the drive list).

6. Drop the files by releasing the mouse button.

7. Release the Alt key.

8. Confirm the move, if necessary.

To copy files to another directory on the same drive:

1. Scroll the directory tree and expand subdirectories as needed to reveal the desired destination directory in the directory tree, but don't actually select the destination directory. (The source directory should be selected for the following steps.)

2. Select the files.

3. Press Ctrl and drag any selected file to the desired target directory (in the directory tree).

4. Drop the files by releasing the mouse button.

5. Release the Ctrl key.

6. Confirm the copy, if necessary.

To copy files to a different drive:

1. Select the destination drive (in the drive list).

2. Select the destination directory (in the directory tree) to make it the default directory for the drive.

3. Select the source drive (in the drive list).

4. Select the files to be copied.

5. Drag any selected file to the desired drive (in the drive list).

6. Drop the files by releasing the mouse button.

7. Confirm the copy, if necessary.

To drag files, select them first. Then, point to any selected file, hold the mouse button down, and move the pointer to the desired directory (in the directory tree) or drive (in the drive list). If the destination directory is on a different drive, DOS automatically copies the files to that drive. But, if the directory is on the same drive, DOS moves them instead of copying them. You can override the default action by pressing Ctrl or Alt. Ctrl forces DOS Shell to copy files, while Alt forces it to move them.

Try moving MSD.COM from PRAC1 to PRAC2:

1. Select the PRAC1 directory.

2. Move your mouse pointer over MSD.COM. Press and hold down the mouse button.

3. Keep holding the mouse button down as you move the pointer to the PRAC2 directory in the directory tree.

   Notice that the mouse pointer changes shape as you move it around the screen. You'll learn about the shapes in the next section.

4. When the pointer (which now looks like a file icon) is over the PRAC2 directory, release the mouse button.

   The Confirm Mouse Operation dialog box asks if you're sure you want to move the selected files to C:\PRAC2. If the wrong operation or the wrong target directory are specified, choose No and try again.

Tip: Always read the Confirm Mouse Operation box carefully to make sure it specifies the desired action (move or copy) and the desired directory.

5. If the right action and the right directory are specified in the confirmation box, choose Yes.

   DOS moves the file to the PRAC2 directory. You should see it disappear from the PRAC1 directory.

6. Select the PRAC2 directory to see the moved file.

The Shell gives you many visual clues to confirm what you're doing. The mouse pointer becomes a single file icon or a set of file icons depending on how many files you're dragging. As you move the pointer across areas where you can't drop files (like the program list), the pointer turns into a No symbol—a circle with a line through it. When it becomes a file icon again, you have reached a legitimate destination. In addition, the status bar displays `Cancel` when you can't drop the files and `Move files to directory` or `Copy files to directory` when you can.

Note: You can scroll the directory tree while you're dragging files. Just move the mouse pointer to the arrows on the scroll bar and you'll see the list scroll.

If Confirm on Mouse Operation is enabled (see Figure 8.1, shown previously), a dialog box asks whether you're sure that you want to move or copy the files. This confirmation feature is not nearly so important as Confirm on Replace. Keep it on if you like a chance to change your mind. If you frequently mix moves with copies or drop files in the wrong place, you may appreciate a confirmation step. But if the extra step irritates you, go ahead and turn it off.

Tip: Keep your eye on the message line. If it displays Move when you want to copy, or vice versa, you can press Ctrl or Alt to change the procedure in mid-drag. You don't have to start over.

Note: You'll notice as you drag files around that you can drop them on program files in the file list. Chapter 10, "Running Programs from DOS Shell," explains what happens when you do this.

Alternate Views

You can set the Shell screen up to be more helpful when you're dragging files. Figure 8.5 shows what it looks like without the program list. The larger directory tree could make it easier to reach a destination directory.

Figure 8.5.
Eliminating the Program List.

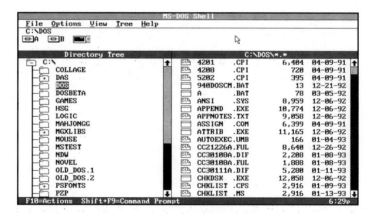

- Choose View Single File List to see what the file list looks like on your screen.

Figure 8.6 shows another view of the Shell screen, in which you can see two directories. You can set up the source directory in the top half of the screen and the target directory in the bottom half. This view is particularly handy when two drives are involved, as shown in the example; it can even be helpful with two directories on the same drive. This view has the added bonus of letting you see the files that already exist in the destination directory.

Figure 8.6.
Dual file lists.

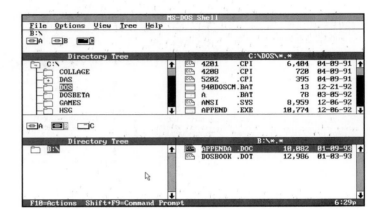

Try viewing two directories at once:

1. Choose View, Dual File Lists. (A second drive list, directory tree, and file list appear on the bottom half of the Shell screen.)

2. Select the PRAC1 directory in the top half of your screen and the PRAC2 directory in the bottom half.

3. Drag LOADFIX.COM from PRAC1 to PRAC2. You can drag it to the file list in the bottom half of the screen.

    You should see the file disappear from the PRAC1 directory and appear in the PRAC2 directory.

4. Choose View Program/File Lists to return to the normal view.

    DOS Shell eliminates the bottom set of lists.

Understanding Copy

When DOS copies a file, it also copies the source file's date and time stamp rather than assigning the current date and time to the new copy. The reason is that the date and time stamp identifies the file's version—for example, the version created on March 13th at 3:10 p.m. As long as you don't revise either copy, they both have the same date and time stamp and you know they're identical. When you revise one or the other, the date and time stamps no longer match, and you can see not only that they're different, but also which one is newer.

DOS Shell can be a little too forgiving when copying and moving files with hidden, system, and read-only attributes. The Shell ignores a source file's attributes, even if that means removing a hidden or read-only file from its original directory. Perhaps even worse, the Shell replaces a hidden or system file in the destination directory without warning you about the attribute.

Figure 8.7.
A Read Only warning.

When the Shell is about to replace a read-only file, a confirmation box mentions (in parentheses) the read-only attribute. (See Figure 8.7.) This box appears regardless of whether or not Confirm on Replace is on, but it doesn't prevent you from clobbering the file.

Moving and Copying Files from One Floppy to Another

When you have only one floppy drive, it can be called drive A or drive B; drive B is called the *phantom drive*. When you boot, DOS assumes that it is drive A. If you select drive B in the drive list (or reference drive B in a command), DOS beeps and asks you to insert a floppy that represents drive B. You can change the floppy in the drive at this time if you wish. If you want to continue using the same floppy that you were using in drive A, you can press Enter without changing the disk. From then on, the drive is considered to be drive B until you reference drive A. Then, DOS beeps once again and asks for the drive A floppy. In DOS shell, the message that requests the floppy appears on the status bar.

If you have only one floppy drive, you can move and copy files from one floppy to another by using the phantom drive. When you move or copy files between A and B, DOS Shell beeps and displays a message on the status bar to tell you when to insert the "Drive A" floppy and when to insert the "Drive B" floppy. You have to remember which disk is which.

When you're done with the operation, if you leave the drive in its "Drive B" status, DOS Shell remembers that it is currently acting as drive B. If you later select drive A, DOS Shell beeps and asks for the drive A disk.

Moving and Copying a Large Group of Files to Several Floppies

If the destination disk doesn't have enough room for the new files, DOS displays the message `The disk is full`. If the destination is a hard drive, you must cancel the operation while you figure out what to do. But if you're copying or moving to a floppy disk, you can change the disk and select option 1, `Skip this file and continue`, to continue with the copy operation. (It won't skip any files.)

Suppose you want to move or copy a large group of files to floppy disks. Select all the files at once and start the move or copy operation. When each floppy disk is full and the `disk full` message appears, insert an empty disk, select option 1, and continue.

Miscellaneous Problems

You can encounter several problems when you are moving and copying files. You might, for example, type a drive or directory name that doesn't exist, or drag files to an empty floppy disk drive. A floppy disk might be damaged—so might a hard drive, for that matter. In every case, the Shell displays some kind of message and gives you the chance to fix the problem. If you end up copying files to the wrong destination, don't worry; the next chapter shows you how to delete them.

On Your Own

Try copying more files to your PRAC1 directory, then moving them to PRAC2. Also try moving and copying files from PRAC1 and PRAC2 to a floppy disk. (Be careful not to move files from any of your real directories.)

When you're ready to go on, delete all the files in PRAC1 and PRAC2, and delete those directories. Also delete any files that you copied to floppy disks.

9

Additional File Management in the Shell

Introduction

One reason for learning DOS is that it enables you to do things that you can't do through your applications, such as assign attributes to files and rename files.

File Management in the Shell

The Shell provides several file-management functions in addition to moving and copying. Some of them are duplicate functions that you have in many of your applications, such as the capability to view and print files. But when you're working on the Shell screen, sometimes it's more convenient to just use a Shell function rather than start up an application. Other functions probably can't be found in your applications, such as the capability to view and change a file's attributes. This chapter shows you how to use the remaining Shell file management functions. You will learn how to:

- View and change attributes
- Rename files
- View text files
- Print text files
- Delete files

Creating Practice Files

You'll learn many different file-management tasks in this chapter, and you'll need some files to practice on. Take the time now to set up a practice directory with some practice files:

1. Create a directory named PRACTICE as a child of the root directory.
2. Copy HELP.COM, LOADFIX.COM, and MSD.COM to the PRACTICE directory.

Managing Attributes

You have seen how a file's attributes are supposed to control the way programs handle it (although even DOS doesn't always comply). Table 9.1 summarizes the four attributes. DOS Shell enables you to view and change a file's attributes.

Table 9.1. File Attributes.

Attribute	Function
Archive	Indicates that the file needs to be backed up.
Read-Only	Prevents the file from being modified or erased.
Hidden	Prevents the file from showing up in the directory.
System	Combines hidden and read-only characteristics.

Viewing Attributes

You might occasionally need to take a look at a file's attributes to find out, for example, if it needs to be backed up, or if it will be deleted in a group delete command. Figure 9.1 shows the Show Information dialog box that opens when you choose Show Information from the Options menu. This dialog box gives you some statistics about the current file, the entire set of selected files, the current directory, and the current drive. Also included in the statistics are the currently selected file's attributes.

Figure 9.1.
The Show Information dialog box.

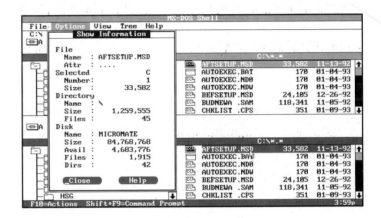

How to View a File's Attributes in DOS Shell

1. Select the file.

2. Choose Options, Show Information. You can see which attributes, if any, are on by looking at the Attr field.

3. Choose Close to return to the Shell screen.

Warning: Be sure you know which file you're seeing. The file displayed in the first section is the file you most recently selected or deselected. For example, if you selected FILEA and FILEB, and then deselected FILEA, the File section would give you information about FILEA (because it's the last file you deselected). The Selected section, however, would tell you about FILEB (because it's the selected file).

The Attr field shows the status of the four attributes. When the letters r (read-only), h (hidden), s (system), or a (archive) are displayed, it indicates that their respective attributes are on. A dot means that an attribute is off. In Figure 9.1, all attributes are off.

Try viewing file information for C:\PRACTICE\MSD.COM:

1. Select the PRACTICE directory.

2. Select MSD.COM.

3. Choose Options, Show Information.

    The Show Information dialog box opens on your screen. You should be able to see the attributes for MSD.COM.

4. Choose Close to close the dialog box.

Changing Attributes

Sometimes, you might find it necessary to change a file's attributes. You might, for example, want to turn off a file's hidden attribute so that you can copy it, or turn on its archive attribute so that it will be backed up. You use the File, Change Attributes command to do this.

How to Change File Attributes in DOS Shell

To change a single file's attributes:

1. Select the file in the file list.

2. Choose File, Change Attributes. (The file list must be active.)

3. Click an attribute to toggle it on or off. Or, you can use the Tab key to move to an attribute, use the arrow to select one, and press the spacebar to toggle it on or off.

4. When all the attributes are set as you want them, select OK.

To set the same attributes for a group of files:

1. Select all the files (and deselect all others).

2. Choose File, Change Attributes. (The file list must be active.)

3. Choose option 2, `Change all selected files at the same time`.

4. Select the desired attributes and toggle it.

5. Choose OK.

Figure 9.2 shows the Change Attributes dialog box. When only one file is selected, this dialog box shows the current attributes of that file (Read only, in the figure). You toggle attributes on and off by selecting them. With the mouse, you click an attribute to toggle it on or off. With the keyboard, you use the Tab key to move to the attribute, the arrow to highlight, and the spacebar to toggle it on or off.

Figure 9.2.
The Change Attributes
dialog box.

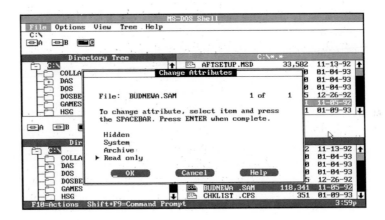

Try changing the attributes for C:\PRACTICE\MSD.COM:

1. Select MSD.COM in the PRACTICE directory.

2. Choose File, Change Attributes. (The file list must be active.)

    The Change Attributes dialog box opens.

3. Click Read only. From the keyboard, you can also tab to Read only and press the spacebar.

    An arrowhead appears next to Read only, indicating that it is turned on.

4. Choose OK to close the dialog box.

5. With MSD.COM still selected, choose Options, Show Information to see the new attribute.

    You should see an r indicating that the Read only attribute is turned on.

6. Choose Close to close the dialog box.

Note: You cannot change the attributes of a file on a read-only drive such as a CD-ROM drive.

Changing Multiple Attributes

When you choose File, Change Attributes with multiple files selected, the Change Attributes dialog box is displayed. (See Figure 9.3.)

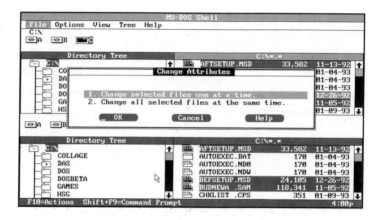

Figure 9.3.
Changing the attributes of
multiple files.

You must choose between two options. If you decide to change the selected files one at a time, the dialog box shown previously, in Figure 9.2, appears for each selected file. You can see in the upper-right corner of this dialog box how many files are selected and which one you're currently working on (1 of 1, or 4 of 7, for example).

If instead you decide to change all the selected files at once, DOS immediately clears all their attributes. Then, it displays the dialog box shown in Figure 9.2, (without the first line) so that you can set the attributes for the entire group.

Suppose you want all the files in the PRACTICE directory to be Read only and to have no other attributes:

1. Select all the files in the PRACTICE directory. (Remember the Ctrl+/ shortcut to select all the files in a directory.)

2. Choose File, Change Attributes.

    The Change Attributes dialog box appears.

3. Choose option 2, Change all selected files at the same time.

    The dialog box changes to show the list of attributes, all of which are turned off.

4. Select Read only.

    An arrowhead appears next to Read only.

5. Choose OK.

    DOS sets the Read only attributes for all the selected files and clears all other attributes.

Note: If you want to set a specific attribute for a group of files without changing their other attributes, you must process the files one at a time. If you choose to do them all at once, DOS automatically clears all their current attributes.

Renaming Files

It's pretty simple to rename a file using the File, Rename command. When you choose the command, a dialog box appears in which you enter a new name for the file. When multiple files are selected, the same dialog box appears repeatedly until all the files are renamed. You can't rename them all at once in the Shell.

How to Rename Files in DOS Shell

To rename one or more files:

1. Select the file(s).

2. Choose the File, Rename command (the file list must be active).

3. In the dialog box, make sure that the file's current name is correct. (If not, press Cancel and try again.)

4. Type the new name and select OK.

5. Repeat steps 3 and 4 until all the files have been renamed.

Try renaming the files in the PRACTICE directory:

1. Select all the files in the PRACTICE directory.

2. Choose the File, Rename command (the file list must be active).

   The Rename File dialog box opens for the first selected file.

3. In the dialog box, make sure that the file's current name is correct. (If not, press Cancel and try again.)

4. Type the name **MYFILE1.XXX** and press Enter.

   The next selected file appears in the dialog box.

5. Repeat steps 3 and 4 until all the files have been renamed. Name the other two files MYFILE2.XXX and MYFILE3.XXX.

   When the last file has been renamed, the dialog box closes and the new filenames appear in the file list.

The new filenames move to their correct alphabetical position in a longer file list. You might have to scroll to see them.

Note: You can't renames files on a read-only drive such as a CD-ROM drive.

Problem: When I tried to rename a file in DOS Shell, I got an `Access Denied` message.

The name you requested already exists in the directory, either as a filename or as the name of a subdirectory. It may be the name of a file that is currently not showing in the file list.

If you have selected several files to rename and want to finish the other files before resolving this one, choose option 1, `Skip this file or directory and continue`. When you choose this option, the current file is not renamed, but DOS shows you the next selected file (if any).

If you want to assign another name to the current file before going on, choose option 2, `Try this file or directory again`.

If you want to cancel the job until you can figure out what the problem is, choose Cancel.

Looking Ahead: You can't do a group rename in the Shell, but you can at the command prompt. You can, for example, rename all *.SAV files to *.OLD. Chapter 16, "Additional File Management," shows you how to do this.

Viewing Files

Sometimes, it is convenient to see the contents of a file while working with the Shell. You can always view a data file by starting up the application that created it. But it's often faster and easier to view it through the Shell. Of course, when you view a file through the Shell, you can't edit it as you can when you start up the file's application.

To view a file, select it and choose File, View File Contents or press F9. The Shell's file viewer takes over the entire screen. (See Figure 9.4.) You can scroll in the file with the cursor keys. (Enter acts like PgDn, as you can see by the note on the status bar.) There aren't any scroll bars, but you can scroll with the mouse by clicking PgUp, PgDn,↑, and ↓ in the message at the top of the screen.

Figure 9.4.
Viewing a file in the Shell.

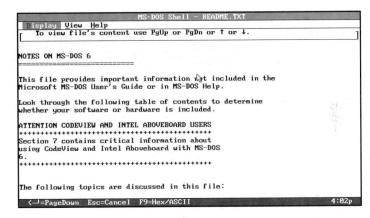

Try viewing the README.TXT file from your DOS directory:

1. Select the DOS directory.

2. Select README.TXT.

3. Press F9.

   DOS Shell's file viewer takes over the screen and displays the README.TXT file.

4. Press Page Down several times.

   Each time you press Page Down, you scroll down one page in the file.

5. Press down-arrow a few times.

   Each time you press down-arrow, you scroll down one line in the file.

6. If you have a mouse, click PgUp at the top of the screen.

   You scroll up one page.

7. If you have a mouse, click ↑ at the top of the screen.

   You scroll up one line.

   The file viewer offers two short menus in addition to the usual Help menu. The Display menu contains two commands, ASCII and Hex, which control how the Shell displays data. ASCII displays the file as text, as shown in the example. Hex displays the bytes stored in the file in hexadecimal, which means something to programmers but almost no one else. You don't really need the Display menu to switch back and forth from ASCII to Hex mode; the F9 key toggles between them, as you can see on the status bar.

Note: The Shell automatically displays text files in ASCII mode and all other types of files in Hex mode.

The View menu contains two commands: Repaint Screen and Restore View. Repaint Screen (Shift+F5) does the same thing it does on the Shell menu; it cleans up a messy screen. The Restore, View command (Esc) exits the viewer and returns to the Shell screen. (Notice the reminder Esc=Cancel on the message line.)

8. Press Esc now to close the viewer and return to the Shell screen.

Printing Files

You saw in the last section how DOS Shell can display a text file. You also can print text files through DOS Shell, but you must load a small TSR into memory first. You should do this from the DOS command prompt before you start DOS Shell.

How to Initialize the PRINT Program

How to Initialize the PRINT Program

1. Exit the Shell, if necessary.

2. Type **PRINT** at the command prompt and press Enter.

3. To use the standard printer attached to LPT1, press Enter. Otherwise, type the name of the print device and press Enter.

Peter's Principle: Always load TSRs from the command prompt.

A TSR (terminate-and-stay-resident) is a program that stays in memory once you load it, ready to provide you with a service if you need it. A program such as DOS's DOSKEY, which keeps track of all the commands you enter at the command prompt, is a TSR. A pop-up alarm program is another example of a TSR.

If you load a TSR after starting up a program such as DOS Shell or Windows, it doesn't make efficient use of memory and could cause you to run out of memory later on. So, always load all your TSRs before starting DOS Shell or Windows.

Load the PRINT TSR now, so you can practice printing files from the Shell.

1. Press F3 to exit the Shell. (Be sure to use F3 for a permanent exit; don't do a temporary exit.)

   The command prompt returns.

2. Type **PRINT** and press Enter.

   If you get the message `PRINT queue is empty`, the PRINT TSR is already loaded. If you get the message `Name of list device [PRN]`, the TSR is not loaded. Go on to step 3.

3. PRINT needs to know where your printer is. If it is attached to your first (or only) parallel port, just press Enter. If it is attached to a different port, type **LPTn** (for parallel ports) or **COMn** (for serial ports), where *n* is the number of the port; then press Enter. If you're not sure, just press Enter.

   You see this message, which confirms that the TSR was loaded and that you are not currently printing anything:

   ```
   Resident part of PRINT installed

   PRINT queue is empty
   ```

Tip: If you will be using PRINT on a regular basis, you can place the command to initialize it in AUTOEXEC.BAT so that it's initialized every time you boot. Chapter 20, "Basic Batch Programs," shows you how to modify AUTOEXEC.BAT.

Printing Through the Shell

After you have initialized the PRINT program, you can print files through the Shell's File, Print command. PRINT does its work in the background, allowing you to continue to work on other tasks, stealing just a little time here and there to send a character to the printer. (Printers are so slow compared to the rest of the computer that PRINT can keep a printer fully occupied while you get most of the processing time for whatever else you're working on.)

Note: Before you can use it, your printer must be cabled to the computer, plugged in, turned on, and online (or selected). Your printer must also have paper, a ribbon, toner or an ink cartridge, and possibly a font cartridge or print wheel.

The best kinds of files to print via the PRINT command are ASCII text files. An ASCII text file is a file that contains only the characters you can type on a standard American keyboard without using the Ctrl or Alt keys. The file doesn't contain any special codes for such things as boldface and italic type, tabs, and graphic characters. Nor does it contain extraneous administrative information that most applications insert in a file. An ASCII text file isn't very fancy, but it is compatible with every editor, word processor, and desktop publisher. Files that DOS must be able to read, such as CONFIG.SYS, AUTOEXEC.BAT, and all batch program files, must be ASCII text files. DOS's EDIT program creates and edits ASCII text files.

You can print any kind of files, but non-ASCII files tend to have bizarre effects. Many non-ASCII bytes print as graphic or foreign-language characters; others trigger printer functions such as beeping its alarm, ejecting incomplete pages, or changing fonts. This is true in nontext files, such as graphic and program files, as well as document files prepared by a word processor. A word processor's formatting codes for functions such as word wrapping and bold-faced type are usually non-ASCII codes.

Most files with the extension .TXT are ASCII text files and print nicely with the PRINT program. Try printing README.TXT from the DOS directory:

1. Prepare the printer, if necessary.
2. Select README.TXT in the DOS directory.
3. Choose File, Print.

A confirmation message appears on-screen, but you might not see anything more than a flash on a fast system. Your file should start printing shortly. If not, the printer probably isn't ready. Check that the cable is tightly connected at both ends and that your printer is turned on.

Working with the Print Queue

PRINT maintains a print queue, which is a list of files waiting to be printed. You can line up 10 files in the queue. Every time you choose File, Print, PRINT adds the selected files to the end of the queue.

Figure 9.5 shows the Print File dialog box, which opens when the print queue has no more room. PRINT continues to print while you make up your mind what to do. You can leave the message on-screen while some files finish printing, and then choose option 1 to add more files to the print queue; however, this ties up the computer and defeats the entire purpose of using PRINT to print in the background. Or, you can choose option 3 (or press Cancel), let PRINT finish the current queue while you do other work, and then select the unprinted files and try again. (Option 2 doesn't make much sense when the print queue is full; it won't have room for the next file either.)

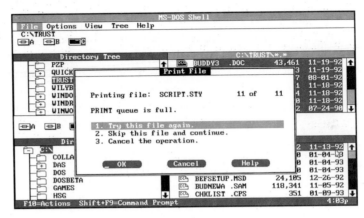

Figure 9.5.
The *Print queue is full* message.

Choosing a Print Program

As print functions go, PRINT is kind of primitive. It can't do many of the things that text editor and word processor print functions do, such as numbering pages or enabling you to print multiple copies. It does break the text into pages, but that's about it. PRINT's main advantage is that, after initialization, you don't have to wait while a program loads before you can use it. And, it prints in the background so that you can continue with other work.

When you want to print several all-ASCII text files and don't care about page numbers, headers, footers, and so on, loading and using PRINT makes sense. For other types of print jobs, you're better off using the print facility of applications such as DOS's editor, your word processor, or one of your other applications.

Looking Ahead: If you find that you make heavy use of PRINT, you might want to learn more about it. There's quite a bit more to the PRINT command than you have seen here. You can, for example, enlarge the print queue or allot more time to printing (giving less to your other work). When you're working at the command prompt, you can view the print queue, remove files from it, and add other files to it. Chapter 16 explains more about the PRINT command.

Deleting a Single File

Deleting a file is as simple as selecting the file and pressing the Delete key (or choosing File, Delete). If Confirm on Delete is enabled, a dialog box asks whether you want to delete the file. Without Confirm on Delete, DOS deletes files the instant you press the Delete key.

Tip: Because it's easy to select the wrong file or bump the Delete key without meaning to, you would be wise to keep Confirm on Delete on. If you want to turn it off to delete a group of files without having to bother with confirmation, be sure to turn it back on again immediately.

Follow these steps to make sure Confirm on Delete is on:

1. Choose Options Confirmation.

   The Confirmation dialog box opens.

2. If Confirm on Delete does not have an X, click it to turn on the X. If you don't have a mouse, tab to it and press the spacebar to turn it on.

3. Choose OK to close the dialog box.

Now delete MYFILE1.XXX from the PRACTICE directory:

1. Choose MYFILE1.XXX.

2. Press the Delete key.

   The Delete File Confirmation dialog box opens. Notice the warning that the file is Read Only. You marked all these files as Read Only earlier in this chapter. DOS Shell enables you to delete the file anyway.

   Make sure that the dialog box refers to C:\PRACTICE\MYFILE1.XXX. If not, choose Cancel and try again.

3. Choose Yes to delete the file.

   The dialog box closes and the file disappears from the PRACTICE directory.

Looking Ahead: Almost every DOS user since caveman days (pre-1980) occasionally needs to recover files after deleting them. DOS 6 includes an UNDELETE facility that might do the trick. Chapter 26, "Using UNDELETE," shows you how to use it.

Deleting Multiple Files

To delete multiple files, select them all. Make sure that no others are selected—watch out particularly when you're selecting across directories. When you press Delete, the dialog box shown in Figure 9.6 is displayed. You should scroll through the list to make sure that it's correct.

Figure 9.6.
The Delete File dialog box.

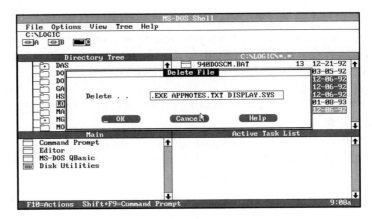

When you select OK, a confirmation dialog box appears for each selected file if Confirm on Delete is on. You must choose Yes or No for each file. Choosing No bypasses that file and goes on to the next file in the list. Select Cancel to stop the entire process.

Try deleting the rest of the files in the PRACTICE directory:

1. Select MYFILE2.XXX and MYFILE3.XXX.

2. Press Delete.

   The Delete File dialog box opens.

   Make sure that the files shown in the Delete box are correct. If not, choose Cancel and try again.

3. Choose OK.

   The Delete File Confirmation dialog box appears for MYFILE2.XXX.

4. Choose Yes.

   The Delete File Confirmation dialog box appears for MYFILE3.XXX.

5. Choose Yes.

   The dialog box closes and the two files are deleted from the directory.

Warning: The delete confirmation feature gives you a second chance to notice that you have selected a file you did not intend to delete. Many people become impatient and start rapidly choosing Yes without reading the file name in each confirmation box. If you get into that habit, you're more likely to delete a file accidentally. Develop the habit of checking the names in each confirmation box.

If you're trying to delete files from a write-protected disk or a read-only drive such as a CD-ROM drive, you see the Write Protection Warning dialog box. (See Figure 9.7.) You can't delete the files as long as the disk is write-protected. There's nothing you can do about a read-only drive, but you can remove the write-protection from a regular floppy disk and try again.

Figure 9.7.
The Write-Protected message.

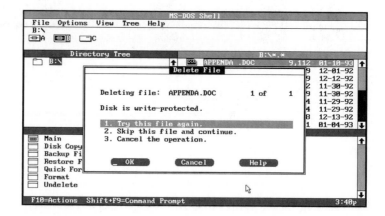

On Your Own

This chapter has shown you a variety of file-management techniques. If you would like to practice them one more time, try your hand at the following items:

1. Copy all the .TXT files from C:\DOS to C:\PRACTICE. (The easiest way to find all the .TXT files in C:\DOS is to limit the file list to .TXT files only.)

All the following steps should be performed on the .TXT files in C:\PRACTICE.

2. Make them all hidden.

3. Remove the hidden attributes. (You'll need to include hidden and system files in the file list before you can select them.)

    Briefly examine the .TXT files. Do any of them contain information pertinent to your system?

4. If you find any files that pertain to your system, print them.

5. Delete the files from your PRACTICE directory. (DO NOT delete them from your DOS directory.)

6. Delete the PRACTICE directory.

10 Running Programs from DOS Shell

Introduction

You don't have to exit DOS Shell to run a program. In fact, it's often better to run programs from within the Shell.

Executing Programs from the Shell

When you use the Shell as your primary interface with DOS, you start up your applications from the Shell screen. When you exit an application, you return to the Shell screen for your next task. If you need to run a DOS utility such as FORMAT (to format a floppy disk) or MS Anti-Virus (which scans for viruses), you can run it directly from the Shell screen also.

> **Warning:** Utilities that work outside DOS's directory structure, such as SCANDISK (which analyzes and repairs the directory structure) and DEFRAG (which reorganizes the allocation units on a drive) should never be run from within the Shell or Windows. Always exit all programs before running such a utility.

There are a variety of ways to start up a program from the Shell screen. Each way has some advantages and disadvantages, as you will learn in this chapter. You will learn to:

- Launch a program from the file list
- Launch a program by dropping a data file on it
- Associate files with programs
- Launch a program from an associated file
- Launch a program from the program list
- Enable and disable task swapping
- Start up and terminate tasks
- Switch among tasks

Opening Objects

This chapter frequently asks you to *open* an object instead of just selecting it. You open an object by double-clicking it or by selecting it and pressing Enter.

You have already seen the difference between selecting an object and opening it in the drive list. If you select a drive, you switch to it without refreshing it; but, if you open it, you also refresh it.

In this chapter, you'll learn how to launch a program by opening its program file, by opening a data file that belongs to it, or by opening an item in the program list.

Launching a Program from the File List

One way to start a program is to open its executable file from the file list. You can't do this unless you know the name of its program file, but that's usually not too hard to figure out. It's usually the program name with an .EXE extension, as in WORD.EXE (for Microsoft Word) or 123.EXE (for Lotus 123). Some programs use .COM or .BAT instead of .EXE.

When you start a program by opening its executable file, the Shell screen is replaced by the program's screen (or the DOS command prompt screen if the program doesn't have a screen of its own). When the program ends, a message asks you to press any key to return to MS-DOS Shell.

How to Launch a Program from DOS Shell's File List

To launch a program by opening its program file:

1. Open the directory containing the program.

2. Double-click the program's .EXE, .COM, or .BAT file. Or, you can select the program's .EXE, .COM, or .BAT file and press Enter.

3. When you're finished with the program, press a key to return to the Shell screen.

To launch a program by dropping a data file on it:

1. Select the data file.

2. Drag it to the program file's entry, scrolling as necessary.

3. Drop the data file on the program file.

4. Choose Yes in the confirmation dialog box.

5. When the program terminates, press a key to return to the Shell screen.

To launch a program from an associated file use one of these methods:

- Double-click the associated file.

- Select the associated file and press Enter (or choose File, Open).

You'll practice launching a program from the file list by running the DOS Editor, which you use to create and edit text files. In this case, you'll just start up the editor and exit it again without working on any files.

1. Select the DOS directory.

2. Scroll the file list to EDIT.COM.

3. Double-click EDIT.COM. Or, you can select EDIT.COM and press Enter.

   Edit's screen replaces the Shell screen. Don't worry about what this screen means now. You'll learn how to use the editor in Chapter 19, "The DOS Editor."

4. To exit the editor, press Esc, followed by Alt+F, followed by X.

   The editor screen closes and a message asks you to press any key to return to MS-DOS Shell.

5. Press a key to return to the Shell screen.

You can't run every program this way. Windows applications, for example, can't start without Windows. You receive an error message if you try. Many DOS commands, such as DIR and COPY, are built into DOS's command processor and don't have their own program files. Also, any program that requires a startup parameter, such as a filespec, cannot be launched from the file list because there is no chance to enter the startup parameter. The FORMAT program, for example, requires a drive name. If you try to run it from the file list, you receive the error message Required parameter missing.

Dropping a Data File on a Program File

Another way to launch a program from the file list is to use your mouse to drop a data file on the program file. This procedure starts the program using the dropped file as the initial data file.

If, for example, you drag the file name APPNOTES.TXT and drop it on PRINT.EXE, the Confirm Mouse Operation dialog box appears. (See Figure 10.1.) When you choose Yes, the PRINT program adds the APPNOTES.TXT file to its print queue. As another example, you could drop the file named MEMO.DOC on WORD.EXE to start Microsoft Word with the MEMO.DOC file open.

Figure 10.1.
The Confirm Mouse Operation dialog box.

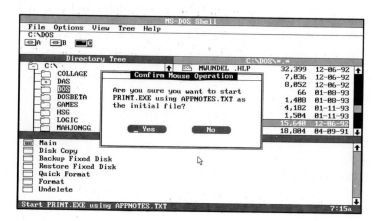

Microsoft included some last-minute documentation for your DOS version in a text file named README.TXT. Try starting up DOS's editor with the README.TXT file:

1. Make sure the DOS directory is selected.

2. Scroll the file list until you can see README.TXT.

3. Start dragging README.TXT upward. (Because the files are in alphabetical order, EDIT.COM is above README.TXT in the list.)

   Your mouse pointer turns into a file icon when you're over any executable file and a "no" icon when it's over any other type of file.

4. Because you can't see the EDIT.COM file, you must scroll the file list while dragging. Move the mouse pointer over the upward-pointing arrow on the scroll bar. (Don't let go of the README.TXT file.)

   The file list starts scrolling upward.

5. Move away from the arrow when you see the EDIT.COM file. (If you go too far, use the downward-pointing arrow to adjust your position, but don't let go of the mouse button.)

   The file list stops scrolling when you move the pointer off the scroll bar.

6. Move the pointer over the EDIT.COM file and release the mouse button.

   A Confirm Mouse Operation dialog box asks if you're sure you want to start EDIT.COM using README.TXT as the initial file.

7. Choose Yes.

   The DOS Shell screen disappears and the Edit screen appears displaying the text of README.TXT.

Ordinarily you would read the file at this point. You might even print all or part of it. But for now, just close it and return to the Shell screen.

1. To exit the program, press Alt+F followed by X.

   The Edit screen disappears and the message `Press any key to return to MS-DOS Shell` appears.

2. Press any key.

   The Shell screen returns.

As you drag a data file around in the file list, the mouse pointer changes from the "no" symbol to a file icon when you cross over an executable program file. Don't mistake this as a signal that the program is appropriate for the data file. DOS permits you to drop a data file on any program file, regardless of appropriateness.

Because it edits files, Edit is designed to accept an initial data file. This procedure will not work with programs that don't work on data files. DOS's FORMAT program, for example, prepares a disk for use by DOS; it has nothing to do with data files. If you drop a data file on the FORMAT.COM program file, you'll get an error message.

Suppose the data file and the program file are in two different directories, perhaps even on different drives. You can't change drives or directories while dragging the data file, so how can you drop the data file on the program file? There is a way. Use View, Dual File Lists to open a second set of lists in the bottom half of the screen. Set up the top half of the screen for the data file's directory and the bottom half for the program file's directory. Then drag the data file to the bottom half and drop it on the program file.

Opening an Associated File

Did you find it awkward to drag README.TXT to EDIT.COM? There's an easier way to start up a program with an initial file, but it only works with certain programs. Some file extensions are *associated* with the applications that use them. This means that you can launch the program with an initial data file simply by opening the data file in the file list. By default, DOS Shell associates all .TXT files with the EDIT program and all .BAS files with QBASIC. If, for example, you open README.TXT, DOS starts EDIT with README.TXT as the initial file.

Try starting the EDIT program by opening the README.TXT file:

1. Double-click README.TXT or select it and press Enter.

   The DOS Shell screen disappears and the EDIT screen appears displaying the text of README.TXT.

2. To exit the program, press Alt+F followed by X.

   The Edit screen disappears and the message `Press any key to return to MS-DOS Shell` appears.

3. Press any key.

   The Shell screen returns.

This is one of the easiest ways to run a program from the Shell. You might want to establish more file associations than the two that DOS provides. You might, for example, want to associate your document files with your word processor, your worksheet files with your spreadsheet, your databases with your database manager, and so on.

You use the `File Associate` command to create an association. Figure 10.2 shows the Associate File dialog box that opens when you select this command.

Figure 10.2.
The Associate File dialog box.

How to Associate a File Extension with a Program

1. Select the program file.

2. Choose File, Associate.

3. Add the extension to the dialog box. (You can add more than one if you want to associate more than one type of file with the program.)

4. Choose OK.

You can associate as many extensions with a program as you want, but not vice versa. An extension can be associated with only one program; otherwise, DOS Shell wouldn't know what program to start when you opened the associated file.

Tip: If you use Windows, don't take the time to associate Windows applications with their files. You can't start Windows applications under the Shell.

Tip: To associate the blank extension with a program, type just a period (.) in the Associate File dialog box. For example, if you associate the blank extension with EDIT.COM, opening files with names such as OCTOBER, MYDAY, and FORM10 (all of which have no extension), would start up the DOS editor.

Launching Programs from the Program List

Another way to start programs is to open items in the program list. Opening the Editor item, for example, starts the DOS editor.

An item in the program list might be defined to display a dialog box so that you can enter startup parameters, such as a filespec or drive name. Figure 10.3 shows the File to Edit dialog box, which appears when you open the Editor item. In this dialog box, you can enter the name of an initial file for the EDIT program.

Figure 10.3.
Starting EDIT from the program list.

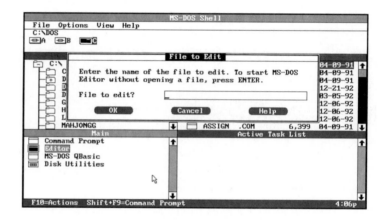

Try starting the Editor from the program list:

1. Double-click the word Editor, or select it and press Enter.

   A dialog box asks for the name of a file.

2. Type \DOS\README.TXT in the dialog box and press Enter. (Remember that DOS ignores case, so you can type in lowercase if you prefer.)

   The Editor opens and displays README.TXT.

3. Press Alt+F followed by X to close the editor.

   You return immediately to the Shell screen; you don't have to press a key to return.

You also can request help for many program items. Just select the item (but don't open it) and press F1. The help information should explain something about the program and its parameters.

1. Select Editor in the program list. (Don't open it.)

2. Press F1.

3. The Help dialog box displays information about the Editor program item.

4. Press Esc to close the dialog box.

When the program terminates, you may or may not have to press a key to return to DOS Shell. Some programs return directly to the Shell. But, the ones that leave a final message on your screen usually let you decide when to return.

> **Note:** Chapter 11, "Customizing the Shell," explains how to add your own items to the program list.

Working at the Command Prompt

Another way to execute a program from the Shell is to go to the command prompt, enter a command, let it execute, and return to the Shell when it's done. You'll learn this technique in Chapter 12, "Working at the Command Prompt," after you've learned more about using the DOS command prompt.

Task Swapping

You can start more than one program at a time with DOS Shell. You might, for example, start a word processor, a spreadsheet, a database, and a graphics program. Then, you can switch among them as needed for the work you're doing.

With task swapping, only one task at a time can be active. The other tasks lie dormant while you work on the active one. You don't lose your place in the dormant tasks, but they can't do any processing when they're not active. This is a distinct difference from a multitasking system, such as Windows, in which several programs can be active at once, sharing processing time so that one program can be printing or calculating (for example) while you are entering data in another.

Another difference between the Shell's task swapper and Windows is that you can't copy data from one task to the other electronically with the task swapper. If you want to copy a name and address from a database into the letter that you're writing, you either must memorize, print, or copy the address down on paper; then, switch to the word processor and type in the data. By comparison, Windows copies the name and address for you.

There's another major difference between Windows and the task swapper. You can see several programs on-screen at the same time with Windows. With the task swapper, you see only the active task.

But even though task swapping does not provide a true multitasking environment, it offers some real advantages over systems that do no multitasking at all.

To start task swapping, choose the `Enable Task Swapper` command from the Options menu. Your DOS Shell screen changes to show the task list, which is empty at first. (See Figure 10.4.) Each program you start from here on will be added to the task list. In Figure 10.4, three programs have been started.

Figure 10.4.
The Shell screen with task swapping enabled.

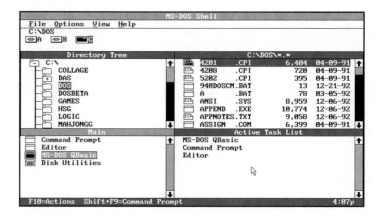

Enable task swapping on your system now by choosing Options, Enable Task Swapper. You should see the task list added to your screen.

Starting Tasks

To start a task, simply start a program. The program automatically becomes a task and is added to the task list. Of course, at first you can't see the task list because you're looking at the program's screen. You learn later in this chapter how to switch back to the Shell screen from a program.

You also can start a task without leaving the Shell screen by holding down Shift while you start the program.

Without leaving the Shell screen, try starting two programs, Editor and HELP.COM (which displays information about DOS's commands):

1. Hold down Shift while you double-click the word Editor. Or, select Editor and press Shift+Enter.

   A dialog box asks for the name of a file. (You can let go of the Shift key now.)

2. Type \DOS\README.TXT and press Enter.

   The dialog box closes. The Editor task appears on the task list.

3. In the DOS directory, hold down Shift while you open the HELP.COM file in the file list.

   HELP.COM appears at the top of the task list.

You can start the same program several times, and each copy becomes a separate task. You could, for example, have one Editor task working on AUTOEXEC.BAT, another Editor task working on CONFIG.SYS, and a third Editor task working on REPORT.TXT. The first task would be displayed as Editor in the task list, the second as Editor. (with a dot), and the third as Editor.. (with two dots).

Switching Tasks

To switch to a particular task from the Shell screen, open the task in the task list. Or, if the task has a shortcut key listed next to it, press the shortcut key. When you're working in a task, you can switch back to the Shell screen by pressing Ctrl+Esc.

Try switching to DOS's editor and back again:

1. Double-click the word Editor in the task list, or select it and press Enter.

   The Editor screen appears with the README.TXT file open.

2. Press Ctrl+Esc.

   The Shell screen returns.

Note: Some programs (such as DOS 6's INTERSVR) inhibit task switching. But, these always are programs for which it is pointless or dangerous to switch away without terminating the program.

You don't have to go through the Shell screen to switch from task to task. Table 10.1 shows the complete set of keys you can use to switch from one task directly to another. (Unfortunately, there are no mouse equivalents for these functions.)

Table 10.1. Task switching hot keys.

Key Combo	Effect
Ctrl+Esc	Switch to DOS Shell
Alt+Tab	Switch to previously opened task
Alt+Tab, Tab, ...	Cycle forward through task list
Shift+Alt+Tab, Tab, ...	Cycle backward through task list
Alt+Esc	Switch to next task in list
Shift+Alt+Esc	Switch to preceding task in list

Tip: Develop the habit of saving your files before switching away from a task, just in case something goes wrong and you can't get back again.

Suppose that you have started five tasks. You are now working in your word processor and want to switch to your graphics program for a moment. Your word processor is task 1, and your graphics program is task 4. Save your current file. Then hold down Alt and press Tab several times, until you see the name of the graphics program on your screen. When you see the name of the desired task, release Alt, and that task is opened and moves to the top of the task list.

When you're finished with the graphics program, the fastest way to get back to your word processor is by pressing Alt+Tab. This always returns you to the previously opened task and moves that task to the top of the list. You can now switch back and forth between the word processor and the graphics program simply by pressing Alt+Tab.

Note: DOS Shell counts as a task even though it doesn't appear in the task list. It's always at the bottom of the list.

Try switching between the Editor task and the HELP.COM task:

1. Press Alt+Tab to return to the Editor task.

    The Editor appears on your screen.

2. Hold down Alt and press Tab once. Don't release the Alt key.

    The message MS-DOS Shell appears on your screen.

3. Keep holding Alt and press Tab again.

    The message HELP.COM appears on your screen.

4. Release the Tab key to switch to the HELP.COM task.

    The HELP screen takes over the monitor. (Don't worry about the contents of this screen now. It is explained in Chapter 12.)

5. Press Alt+Tab to switch to the Editor task.

6. Press Alt+Tab again to switch back to the HELP task.

7. Press Ctrl+Esc to switch to the Shell screen.

Tip: When your task list is long, you might be able to get where you're going faster by cycling backward through the list with Shift+Alt+Tab, Tab, ...Tab.

Problem: I tried to switch tasks but my computer hung up and now I can't do anything.

You'll have to reboot to free up your computer.

You may need to install the correct *grabber* file for your video card. Get out your DOS program disks and look through them for files named MONO.IN_, EGA.IN_, VGA.IN_, and so on. They may not be on your step upgrade disks; you might have to go back to the disks you used to install or upgrade to DOS 6.0.

Before you try installing a grabber file, rename your current DOSSHELL.GRB file as BACK.GRB. If installing a new grabber file doesn't work, rename this file to DOSSHELL.GRB to return your system to its current condition.

When you find the grabber files, try to figure out from their names which is the correct one for your video card. (If you're not sure, there's no harm in trying out several of them.) To install a file, enter the following command, where filespec is the name of the file that you want to install, such as EGA.IN_:

```
EXPAND A:\filespec C:\DOS\DOSSHELL.GRB
```

Then try task swapping again.

If you still can't switch tasks, you'll need to get help from Microsoft. See your DOS *User's Guide* for instructions on how to get technical support.

In Table 10.1, you can see that Alt+Esc and Shift+Alt+Esc also cycle through the task list. But, they have two important differences from Alt+Tab and Shift+Alt+Tab:

- When you use the Esc key, each task is opened as you cycle to it so that you can see it on-screen. This takes more time, but it's nice if you can't remember the name of the task you want.

- The order of tasks is not changed by the Esc key, although the entire list is cycled so that the currently open task appears at the top.

If any of your active tasks has a shortcut key, you can switch directly to that task from any other task by pressing the shortcut key. If two or more active tasks have the same shortcut key, pressing the shortcut key cycles through only those tasks. In some cases, the shortcut key might not work because the program that's currently on the screen uses that key combination for one of its own functions.

Looking Ahead: You'll learn how to define shortcut keys in Chapter 11.

Ending a Task

When you end a program, DOS Shell closes its task and removes it from the task list. Exit each program just as you would if you weren't using task swapping.

Terminate your Editor task now by following these steps:

1. Switch to the Editor task.

    The Editor screen appears.

2. Press Alt+F followed by X.

    The Editor closes and the Shell screen returns. Notice that the Editor has been removed from the task list.

Note: You must end all tasks before you can exit DOS Shell. But, you don't have to turn off task swapping. If you use task swapping regularly, just leave it enabled all the time.

Every once in a while, a program hangs up. That is, it stops functioning properly; in most cases, it stops functioning altogether and you can't even terminate it normally. The most common solution to this problem is to reboot, which kills the malfunctioning program. That's fine if it's the only program that you're running. But, if task swapping is enabled and other tasks have been started, don't get rid of a malfunctioning program by rebooting unless you have no other choice. Rebooting terminates all the current tasks before they have a chance to save and close their files properly, so you could lose some of your data.

How to Terminate a Malfunctioning Program while Task Swapping in DOS Shell

1. Return to the Shell screen, if possible.

2. Select the misbehaving task.

3. Press Delete to abort the task. (A warning box appears.)

4. Choose OK in the warning box.

5. Close all other tasks normally, if possible.

6. Exit DOS Shell.

7. Reboot.

If you really need to kill a task, you can terminate it from the Shell screen. Afterward, all other programs are suspect. You should terminate them, exit the Shell, and reboot as quickly as possible.

Ending the Task Swapper

Task swapping stays on until you turn it off, even if you exit the Shell and reboot. Because the Task Swapper takes up memory space, you might want to disable it when you don't need it. To disable task swapping in your system, first terminate all tasks. Follow these steps to disable task swapping in your system:

1. Open the HELP.COM task.

   The HELP screen appears.

2. Press Alt+F followed by X to exit the program.

   The message `Press any key to return to MS-DOS Shell` appears on your screen.

3. Press any key.

   The Shell screen appears.

4. Choose Enable Task Swapper from the Options menu.

   Notice the bullet next to Enable Task Swapper, which indicates that this option is currently enabled. When you select it again, the menu disappears and the active task list disappears from your screen.

On Your Own

If you would like some more practice at running programs from DOS Shell, try the following activities:

1. Enable task swapping.

2. Launch your word processor (or another one of your applications) by dropping a data file on it.

3. Switch to the Shell screen (without exiting your word processor), and launch another copy of the same program with a different data file.

4. Practice switching between the two word processing tasks.

5. Close all your tasks and disable task swapping.

11 Customizing the Shell

Introduction

You can add your own customization to the Shell screen to tailor it to your own work style.

Overview

So far, you have been working with the standard Shell screen. But you can tailor the screen to make your life even easier. You can define your own program items, for example, and alter the display mode and colors.

In this chapter, you will learn how to:

- Define and use your own program groups
- Define and use your own program items
- Copy items from one group to another
- Delete program items and program groups
- Change the video display mode
- Select a different color scheme for the Shell screen
- Filter the names in the file list
- Change the sort order of the file list
- Locate a specific file or group of files anywhere on your hard drive
- Locate files on a set of floppies
- Display hidden and system files in the file list

Managing the Program List

The program list is the easiest and most flexible way to start programs. When you first install the Shell, the program list contains a number of items in two groups: the Main group (which you have seen on your screen) and a group called Disk Utilities. If the Shell is your main interface with DOS, you probably will want to add your own groups and items to the list. You may even want to redefine the items provided by Microsoft.

Suppose that you manage three databases: CUSTOMER.DB, ORDERS.DB, and SUPPLIER.DB. You also work on several other databases on occasion. You might want to set up a separate Database group with several items, as follows:

- Customers database (opens CUSTOMER.DB)
- Orders database (opens ORDERS.DB)
- Suppliers database (opens SUPPLIER.DB)
- Other databases (lets you enter the name of the desired database file in a dialog box)

You may create similar groups for your major word processing projects, spreadsheets, and other applications you work with frequently.

Working with Groups

The program list shows one group at a time. You've seen the Main group; now, let's take a look at the Disk Utilities group. Notice the Disk Utilities item has a different icon than Command Prompt, Editor, and so on. This icon tells you that it is a group instead of a program item. Try opening the Disk Utilities group:

1. Open the program group called Disk Utilities.

    The program list changes to the Disk Utilities group. The title Disk Utilities appears in the program list's title bar. The program items include such things as Disk Copy and MS-Anti-Virus. You'll learn how to use these programs in later chapters.

2. Leave the group open while you read the following section.

Notice that the first item on the list is Main, which has the group logo. Open Main now to return to the Main group.

Groups are organized similarly to directories on a disk. The Main group is the highest level group; it cannot be deleted or renamed. It can have children (such as the Disk Utilities group), which in turn can have children. The first item in each child's list is always the parent group so that you can return to the parent.

Defining a Group

When the focus is in the program list, the menu selections File, New are used to create a new group or program item. The new item is added to the current group.

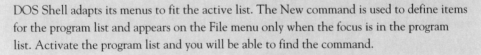

Problem: I can't find DOS Shell's File, New selections; they're not on my File menu.

DOS Shell adapts its menus to fit the active list. The New command is used to define items for the program list and appears on the File menu only when the focus is in the program list. Activate the program list and you will be able to find the command.

How to Create and Manage a DOS Shell Program Group

To create a new group:

1. Open the group that will be the parent of the new group.

2. Choose File, New. (The program list must be active.)

3. In the first dialog box, choose Program Group.

---

continues

4. In the next dialog box, type a title up to 23 characters long.

   You can enter some help text (up to 255 characters long) if you want. You also can define a password (up to 20 characters long).

5. Choose OK.

To modify a group definition:

1. Select the program group (in its parent list).

2. Choose File, Properties. You might need to enter a password. (The Program Group Properties dialog box shows your definition of the group. It looks exactly the same as the Add Group dialog box.)

3. Change the definition as desired.

4. Choose OK to close the dialog box.

To delete a program group:

1. Open the group.

2. Delete all program items and subgroups. (Don't try to delete the parent group name.)

3. Return to the parent group.

4. Select the subgroup without opening it.

5. Press the Delete key.

6. Choose Delete This Item in the confirmation box and choose OK.

Try creating a new group now. You will create a group called Practice as a child of the Main group. To create a new group, follow these steps:

1. Make sure that the focus is in the program list and that the Main group is open.

2. Choose File, New.

   The New Program Object dialog box opens with two options: Program Group or Program Item.

Note: The items in the New Program Object dialog box are called *option buttons* because one, and only one, item must be selected. The black dot in the circle indicates the selected item. To select an item with your mouse, click it. To select an item with your keyboard, tab to the box labeled New and use up-arrow or down-arrow to move the black dot.

3. Select Program Group and press Enter.

   The Add Group dialog box appears. (See Figure 11.1.)

Figure 11.1.
The Add Group dialog box.

```
┌══════════════ Add Group ══════════════┐
│ Required                               │
│                                        │
│   Title . . . .    [                 ] │
│ Optional                               │
│                                        │
│   Help Text . .    [                 ] │
│                                        │
│   Password  . .    [          ]        │
│                                        │
│                                        │
│      ( OK )      ( Cancel )   ( Help ) │
└════════════════════════════════════════┘
```

You must provide a name for the group. All other items are optional. The name can be up to 23 characters long, including spaces. Whatever you enter here appears in the program list. To provide a name for the group, follow these steps:

1. Type **Practice** in the Name box.

2. Press Enter.

   The dialog box closes and Practice group appears in the program list.

You may want to provide a help topic if other people will be using the new group. The help text can be up to 255 characters long, including spaces. DOS Shell displays the help topic when someone selects the group name and presses F1.

Tip: Don't press Enter in the Help Text box to start a new paragraph; Enter closes the dialog box. To start a new paragraph in the help text, type a caret (^) followed by an M. Two ^M codes in a row insert a blank line between paragraphs, which makes a paragraph break more obvious.

If you accidentally close the dialog box before you're done with it, select the new item in the program list and choose File Properties to reopen it.

You also can assign a password (up to 20 characters) to the new group. When a group is password protected, DOS Shell displays the Password dialog box whenever anyone tries to open or modify the group. (See Figure 11.2.) You must enter the correct password to continue.

Warning: DOS Shell's password protection is not very powerful. A savvy user can find out the password by examining the DOSSHELL.INI file. (You can, too, if you forget a password.)

Figure 11.2.
The Password dialog box.

The password is case-sensitive. For example, if you type Jane's Coffee Shop as your password, variations such as Jane's coffee shop or JANE'S COFFEE SHOP won't work. This is one of the few times
that DOS pays attention to case.

You probably won't find much cause to modify a group definition, but if you need to, open the group's
parent, select the group (but don't open it), and choose File, Properties. The Program Group Properties dialog box, which looks just like the Add Group dialog box, displays your current definition
so that you can modify it.

Defining a Program Item

Now that you have a new group, you might want to add some items to it. Figure 11.3 shows the Add
Program dialog box, in which you define a program item. You must define a Program Title and
Commands; the other fields are optional.

Figure 11.3.
*The Add Program dialog
box.*

```
┌──────────────────────── Add Program ────────────────────────┐
│                                                              │
│   Program Title . . . . [                              ]      │
│                                                              │
│   Commands  . . . . . . [                              ]      │
│                                                              │
│   Startup Directory . . [                              ]      │
│                                                              │
│   Application Shortcut Key      [                      ]      │
│                                                              │
│   [X] Pause after exit      Password . .  [            ]      │
│      ( OK )     ( Cancel )    ( Help )    ( Advanced... )     │
└──────────────────────────────────────────────────────────────┘
```

How to Create and Manage a DOS Shell Program Item

To define a new program item:

1. Open the group that is to contain the item.

2. Choose File, New. (The program list must be active.)

3. In the first dialog box, select Program Item and choose OK.

4. In the next dialog box, enter a program title (up to 23 characters long) and startup
   command (up to 25 characters long).

5. Enter a startup directory, define a shortcut key, uncheck Pause After Exit, or enter a
   password if desired.

6. If you want to enter help text, choose Advanced, enter the help text in the Advanced dialog box, and choose OK to return to the Add Program dialog box.

7. Choose OK to close the Add Program dialog box.

To modify the definition of a program item:

1. Select the item.

2. Choose File, Properties. You might have to enter a password. (The Program Item Properties dialog box opens and displays your definition of the item.)

3. Change the definition as needed.

4. Choose OK.

To delete an item:

1. Select the item without opening it.

2. Press the Delete key.

3. Select Delete This Item in the confirmation box and choose OK.

To copy an item:

1. Select the item.

2. Choose File, Copy. (The program list must be active.)

   A note on the status bar tells you to press F2 to complete the copy.

3. Open the destination group.

4. Press F2.

The program title can have up to 23 characters, including spaces. Whatever you type here appears in the program list. The Commands box defines the command to be submitted to DOS when someone opens the item. To start Microsoft Word, for example, you would type WORD in the Commands box. You can enter up to 25 characters in the box, including spaces.

To add an item to your Practice group that displays your system's memory usage, follow these steps:

1. Open the Practice group.

   The program list contains only one item, Main, which takes you back to the Main group.

2. Choose File, New.

   The New Program Object dialog box opens. The Program Item option is selected by default.

3. Press Enter.

   The Add Program dialog box opens.

4. Type **Display Memory** in the Program Title box.

5. Click the Commands box or tab to it.

6. Type **MEM** in the Commands box.

   This is the command to run DOS's MEM program.

7. Choose OK.

   The dialog box closes and Display Memory appears on your program list.

> **Tip:** Always include a complete path, including the drive name, with any filespecs in the Commands box. You don't know what drive or directory will be active when the program item is opened, but if you include a complete path you're assured that DOS can find the file.
>
> You can ignore this rule, however, if you also specify a startup directory for the program item. If the desired file is in the startup directory, then you don't need to provide a path name for it. (Startup directories are discussed in the next section.)

Now try out your new program item:

1. Open the Display Memory item.

   The Shell screen disappears. MEM displays your system's memory layout on the screen. A note at the bottom says Press any key to return to MS-DOS Shell.

2. Press any key.

   The Shell screen returns.

If you specify a startup directory while still in the File, New dialog, DOS Shell switches to that directory before starting the program. If you're starting up a program that maintains files such as EDIT, a word processor, or a database, it's a good idea to identify the directory where you keep the data files for that application. That makes it easier to open and save files while you're using the application. This option changes the current directory in the Shell, and some people find that annoying.

The Application Shortcut Key field is used for task swapping, as you learned in Chapter 10, "Running Programs from DOS Shell." To assign a shortcut key to the item, place the cursor in the text box and press the key combination you want to use. The shortcut key must use Ctrl, Shift, and/or Alt plus a character, function, or cursor key (but not an arrow key). The Shell spells out the key combination you press. For example, if you press Ctrl+E, the expression CTRL+E appears in the text box. If nothing appears, your key combination is not a legitimate shortcut key; try another one.

The Pause After Exit box is checked by default. This causes DOS Shell to display the message `Press any key to return to MS-DOS Shell` when the program terminates. If you uncheck this box, the Shell screen returns automatically as soon as the program terminates. Unchecking the box eliminates an extra step, but be sure that the program doesn't issue any kind of final message that you might want to read. If you discover that you can't read all the messages you need, check this box again.

You can password protect the program item (somewhat weakly) by entering a password of up to 20 characters in the Password box.

You also can provide help text. Selecting the Advanced button opens another dialog box that contains advanced options along with the Help text box. You can enter up to 255 characters, including spaces, in the Help text box. (Use ^M to start a new paragraph.)

> **Looking Ahead:** Chapter 36, "DOS at Your Command," shows you how to use the other items in the Advanced dialog box, as well as how to create a dialog box such as the one you saw for the Editor program item.

If you find later on that you need to modify the item's definition, open the item's parent group, select the item (but don't open it), and choose File, Properties. The Program Item Properties dialog box, which looks just like the Add Program dialog box, displays your current definition so that you can modify it.

Copying Program Items

Suppose you have created an item called Word Processor in Shelly's group, and now you want to create the same item in Donna's and Charles's groups. You can save time and hassle by copying the item instead of defining it two more times. Even if the items are to be defined somewhat differently in the three groups (different passwords and startup directories, for example), it can be faster to copy and modify an item rather than defining it from scratch.

> **Note:** The F8 shortcut for the File, Copy menu items is not available in the program list.

To copy the Display Memory item to the Disk Utilities group follow these steps:

1. Open the Practice group and select (but don't open) the Display Memory item.

2. Choose File, Copy.

   A note on the status bar says `Display the group to copy to, then press F2. Press ESC to cancel.`

3. Return to the Main group and open the Disk Utilities group.

   The note remains on the status bar.

4. Press F2.

   The Display Memory item appears in the Disk Utilities program list. The note disappears from the status bar.

There is no File, Move command for the program list. If you want to move an item instead of copying it, simply return to its original group and delete it.

Now that you can create and manage program groups and program items, delete the objects you have created before going on to the next topic. To delete the objects you've created, follow these steps:

1. In the Disk Utilities group, select the Display Memory item and press the Delete key.

   The Delete Item dialog box opens.

2. Choose option 1, Delete this item.

   The Display Memory item is removed from the list.

3. Return to the Main group.

A group must be empty before you can delete it, so you must delete the items in the Practice group next.

1. Open the Practice group.

2. Delete the Display Memory item.

The Practice group still contains Main, but you can't delete the parent group. It will be deleted automatically when you delete the group.

1. Return to the Main group.

2. Delete the Practice group.

Tip: DOS Shell saves your display mode and screen color choices in a file called DOSSHELL.INI. DOSSHELL.INI is used to initialize your screen each time you start up the Shell. When you've found the display mode and colors you like, the Shell will always start up with those options.

If you have been using the /T switch (for text mode) or the /B switch (for black-and-white color scheme) on your DOSSHELL startup command, choose the appropriate options in the Screen Display Mode dialog box and the Color Scheme dialog box. DOS Shell will remember your choices and you won't have to use the switches anymore.

Problem: I customized my DOS Shell program list and now it has gone back to the default list. How can I get my customized list back?

Any customizations you make to the DOS Shell screen, such as new program groups and items, are saved in a file named DOSSHELL.INI. If DOS Shell can't find that file when it starts up, it reverts to its default setup.

If you (or someone else) moved DOSSHELL.INI, move it back to the DOS directory. If you deleted DOSSHELL.INI, either undelete it or restore it from its most recent backup. If you didn't delete or change DOSSHELL.INI, it might have become corrupted somehow; again, you should restore it from its most recent backup.

If you can't undelete or restore DOSSHELL.INI from a recent backup, you won't be able to recover your customized items.

Problem: I get the message `Unable to update DOSSHELL.INI` when I exit DOS Shell.

DOS Shell saves its current settings in DOSSHELL.INI each time you exit. If it can't find DOSSHELL.INI, if the file has been marked hidden, system, or read-only, or if the disk is full, the Shell displays this message. In this case, any changes you make to the program list, the screen display mode, and the color scheme are forgotten when you exit.

Make sure that DOSSHELL.INI is in your DOS directory and that its read-only, hidden, and system attributes are turned off. Also, make sure there is some free space on the drive. This should fix the problem.

If DOSSHELL.INI is in the right place and is not write-protected, but you're still getting the error message, it may be that your DOS directory is not in your program search path. Check the PATH command in your AUTOEXEC.BAT file. It should include a path name for your DOS directory, among others. If not, add a semicolon and the correct path name at the end of the command, as in:

```
PATH=other-path-names;C:\DOS
```

If your DOS directory appears in the PATH command, it may be that your PATH command is too long. It should not exceed 127 characters. If it does, you must figure out some directories to remove from the command. Chapter 12, "Working at the Command Prompt," explains the PATH command.

Choosing Display Options

Today's monitors are capable of displaying a lot more than the old standard 25 lines per screen, but many people don't take advantage of the increased capability. The more information you can squeeze on your screen at once, the less you must scroll to find the items you want. A longer list can also make it easier to drag a data file to a program file in the same directory; if both files appear on the screen at once, you don't have to scroll to find the program file.

Figure 11.4 shows the Screen Display Mode dialog box that opens when you choose Options, Display. This dialog box shows you the display options for your monitor. You can experiment with the options and select the one that works best for you.

Figure 11.4.

The Screen Display Mode dialog box.

Try out some of the options for your monitor:

1. Choose Options, Display.

   The Screen Display Mode dialog box opens.

2. Select an option you want to try.

3. Choose Preview.

   The screen changes to show the selected display mode, but the dialog box remains open.

4. Repeat steps 2 and 3 until you decide which option you want to use.

5. Choose OK.

   The dialog box closes and the screen changes to the new display mode.

Customizing the Screen Colors

Figure 11.5 shows the Color Scheme dialog box, which opens when you choose Options, Colors. The Shell offers several color schemes, including black and white. Some combinations might work better on your monitor than others. You can try them using the Preview button and select the one you like best.

Figure 11.5.
The Color Scheme dialog box.

Try out some of the options for your monitor:

1. Choose Options, Colors.

    The Color Scheme dialog box opens.

2. Select an option you want to try.

3. Choose Preview.

    The screen changes to show the selected color scheme, but the dialog box remains open.

4. Repeat steps 2 and 3 until you decide which option you want to use.

5. Choose OK.

    The dialog box closes and the screen changes to the new scheme.

Note: Changing DOS Shell's display mode and color scheme does not affect any programs that you start up from the Shell. Nor does it affect the command prompt screen when you exit the Shell.

Customizing the File List

So far, you have worked with the default file list: all files except hidden and system files are displayed, and they are sorted in alphabetical order. However, you can tailor the file list to show a different subset of files, and they can be sorted in a different order. Figure 11.6 shows the File Display Options dialog box that opens when you select Options, File Display Options.

Figure 11.6.
The File Display Options dialog box.

Filtering the File List

You don't have to display all the files in a directory. You can enter a file name in the Name box to filter out any files that don't match that name. To display only the .TXT files in the current directory, follow these steps:

1. Choose Options, File Display Options.

    The File Display Options dialog box opens.

2. Type ***.TXT** and press Enter.

    The dialog box closes. The title bar for the file list now says C:*.TXT. (It always said C:*.* before.) Depending on which directory is current, the file list might show some .TXT files, or it might say `No files match file specifier`.

Displaying All the Files on the Drive

You can combine a file filter with the View All Files display to locate all the files of a particular type on a drive. Suppose, for example, that you want to delete all .BAK files on the drive. You could enter *.BAK in the Name box and then choose View, All Files to display all .BAK files on the drive. Pressing Ctrl+/ selects them all without selecting any other files on the drive, because you can select listed files only. Then, all you have to do is press Delete to erase them all.

Tip: You may want to turn the Confirm on Delete option off for this operation. But, if you do, be sure you turn it on again afterward.

To display a list of all the .TXT files on drive C, follow these steps:

1. Make sure that you are displaying .TXT files only.

2. Choose View, All Files.

    The screen changes to the All Files display. You probably have a list of several .TXT files from all over your hard drive. There might be several with the name README.TXT, because many software manufacturers included a file of that name with their applications.

Note: Changing drives and views doesn't affect the filter, but the default *.* filter is restored when you terminate DOS Shell.

Locating Misplaced Files

Combining View All Files with a file filter is also useful for finding a misplaced file. Suppose you know you had a .TXT file somewhere, but you can't remember its exact name or location. You could probably pick it out from the list on your screen.

If you're trying to find a file that starts with JUNE but can't remember the rest of the name, you could enter JUNE*.* as the file filter to display all files that start with JUNE.

You can even use a specific filename as a filter. Try displaying a list of all the README.TXT files on your hard drive:

1. Choose Options, File Display Options.

   The File Display Options dialog box opens.

2. Type **README.TXT** and press Enter.

   The file list shows all the README.TXT files on your hard drive. You can select individual files and examine the information pane on the left to see which directories they belong to.

It's easy to forget that a file filter is in effect. If you can't find a file that you know exists in the current directory, or if a message says that a directory isn't empty when no files are listed in it, check the title bar to see whether you're filtering the list. If it says anything other than *.*, the directory probably has files that you can't see.

> **Tip:** A sure clue that a directory has unseen files is the message `No files match file specifier` in the file list. This message tells you that the directory contains files but they're being filtered out. When a directory is truly empty, the message says `No files in selected directory`.

Displaying Hidden and System Files

Files with hidden and system attributes should not normally be accessible for operations such as deleting, moving, and copying. For that reason, DOS Shell does not display them by default in the file list. But, you may want to display them, especially if you're trying to empty a directory so that you can delete it.

In the File Display Options dialog box, you can select Display Hidden/System Files to include the files in your file list. Uncheck the box again to hide them. Remember that if a file is not displayed, you can't select it. But, be aware that some programs might access and process those files even if you can't see them in the file list.

There are several hidden and system files in your root directory. To take a look at them, follow these steps:

1. Choose View, Program/File Lists.

   The screen returns to the normal display mode.

2. Select the root directory.

3. Choose Options, File Display Options.

   The File Display Options dialog box opens.

4. Enter ***.SYS** in the Name box.

5. Select Display Hidden/System Files.

   An X should appear in the check box.

6. Press Enter.

   Your file list should show IO.SYS and MSDOS.SYS. These are your core DOS program files.

Warning: Never move, erase, rename, or otherwise tamper with any of the hidden and system files in your root directory. You could disable DOS or make it difficult to reach the files on your hard disk.

As mentioned previously, the message `No files match file specifier` appears when files you can't see exist in the directory. If you get this message when the file filter is `*.*`, the unseen files have either the hidden or the system attribute, or both.

Locating Files on a Set of Floppies

Suppose you stored a file named MISSING.TXT on one of your floppies and now you can't remember which floppy it's on. How can you find the file? Set the file filter to MISSING.TXT. Then place the first floppy in drive A and select the drive. Refresh the drive if necessary to force DOS to read the directory.

Keep inserting floppies in the drive and pressing F5 to refresh the drive until MISSING.TXT shows up in the file list.

Sorting the File List

By default, DOS Shell displays the file list sorted by name in ascending alphabetical order. There are several other ways to arrange the file list. In the File Display Options dialog box, you can choose to sort in alphabetical order by extension (instead of file name), in chronological order by date and time, or in numeric order by file size. Even the DiskOrder option occasionally is useful. This option displays the file list in the order that the files actually appear in the directory as it is stored on the disk.

Try sorting your current display in date order. To do this, while at the same time restoring your normal file filter and removing hidden and system files from the display, follow these steps:

1. Choose Options, File Display Options.

   The File Display Options dialog box opens.

2. Enter *.* in the Name box.

3. Select Display Hidden/System Files to remove the X from the check box.

4. Select the Date option button and press Enter.

   The dialog box closes and the file list is displayed in ascending order by date.

The Descending Order option reverses the order of the list. For example, if you select Size and check Descending Order, the file list is displayed from the largest to the smallest file. If you reverse Date order, files are displayed from the newest to the oldest.

If you display two file lists with View Dual File Lists, both lists are affected by the display options. When you exit DOS Shell, the default file filter is restored, but the other display options are remembered and will be in effect the next time you start DOS Shell.

Before finishing this chapter, return to the normal view of the file list. To return to the normal view, follow these steps:

1. Choose Options, File Display Options.

   The File Display Options dialog box opens.

2. Select the Name option button and press Enter.

   The dialog box closes. The file list displays all files (except hidden and system files) in ascending alphabetical order by name.

On Your Own

The following items will help you practice tailoring your DOS Shell screen on your own:

1. Create a program group called MYGROUP.

2. Copy a couple of items into MYGROUP from other groups.

3. Create an item that starts up your own word processor.

4. Delete MYGROUP.

5. Locate .CPI files on your drive.

6. Restore your screen to its normal view.

3

DOS
Commands

12

Working at the Command Prompt

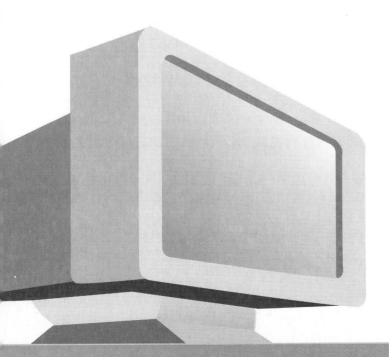

Introduction

Working at the command prompt is quite different from using the Shell screen. This chapter shows you some of the basics.

Understanding Commands

You can do many things from the command prompt that you can't do in the Shell. DOS 6, for example, includes a DELTREE command that deletes an entire directory branch without making you empty all the directories first. DOS utilities such as FORMAT, UNFORMAT, UNDELETE, DEFRAG, and SCANDISK are started by commands. In fact, the last two utilities should be started only from the command prompt, never from Windows or the Shell because they can damage open files.

When you know how to use commands, you can create your own program items for the Shell's program list, as well as batch programs that can be started from the Shell's file list, run at the command prompt, and passed around to other users.

In addition, you can understand batch programs that you receive from other people. You'll understand your own AUTOEXEC.BAT program, which is executed every time you boot and helps to set up your system—an important benefit because this program is crucial to your system. Whenever you're working with your PC, the more you understand what's happening in your system, the better.

In this chapter, you will learn how to:

- Access the command prompt
- Read a command syntax statement
- Redirect command output
- Get on-screen help with commands
- Define a program search path
- Design your own command prompt

In later chapters, you'll learn how to use specific commands such as DELTREE, and how to create and use batch program files such as AUTOEXEC.BAT.

Getting to the Command Prompt

You can get to the command prompt in several ways, each with different effects. The primary way, of course, is to boot or reboot. If your AUTOEXEC.BAT file doesn't start Windows or DOS Shell (or some other program), the command prompt appears.

If your AUTOEXEC.BAT file starts another program, you must terminate that program to get to the command prompt. If a program is running on your computer right now, exit the program to get to your command prompt. To exit the program, follow these steps:

1. If you are in DOS Shell, close any programs that are running and press F3 to exit to the command prompt.

2. If you are in Windows, close any programs that are running and choose File, Exit from Program Manager's menu bar.

3. If you are using some other program, close any files that are open, and exit the program normally.

The command prompt that you get to this way is called the *primary command prompt*. You're at the top of DOS, so to speak. You can do things at this command prompt that you shouldn't do in other command prompt situations, as you'll soon learn.

Interpreting the Command Prompt

The command prompt usually consists of the path name of the current directory followed by a greater-than sign. The following command prompt, for example, tells you that the root directory of drive C is the current directory:

```
C:\>
```

For this chapter, you should be in the root directory of drive C. If your command prompt shows that another directory is current, change to `C:\` by following these steps:

1. Type **c:** and press Enter. (The colon after the C is important; be sure to type it.)

   DOS switches to drive C and displays a new command prompt for you. You should see the drive letter C in the new command prompt.

Note: Remember that this book assumes that drive C is your DOS boot drive. If not, be sure to adapt all these examples for your DOS boot drive.

2. To switch to the root directory, type **CD** \ and press Enter. (Be sure to type a space and then a backslash, not a forward slash, after the letters CD.)

   DOS switches to the root directory and displays a new command prompt. The command prompt should now show `C:\>`.

Problem: My command prompt doesn't show the current drive and directory; it shows different information or no information at all.

Someone has adapted your command prompt. You can learn to live with the adapted command prompt, or change it back to the default one by typing **PROMPT PG** at the prompt and pressing Enter. (Look up the **PROMPT** command in the Command Reference for an explanation of what this command does.)

Secondary Command Prompts

Many programs let you access a command prompt temporarily so that you can run a command or two and then return to the program without losing your place. Windows, for example, offers an MS-DOS Prompt program item in the Applications group. In DOS Shell, you can open the Command Prompt item in the Main program group or press the Shift+F9 shortcut key. When you go to a command prompt this way—under the wings of another program that is still open—the prompt is a *secondary command prompt.*

No matter what program you came from, you always return from the command prompt the same way. You enter the EXIT command with no parameters and the command prompt disappears, leaving you back in your former program.

In general, you can enter commands at a secondary command prompt just as at the primary one, but there are some important exceptions:

- Don't load any TSRs (terminate-and-stay-resident programs) from a secondary command prompt. Doing so could cause you to run out of memory later on or could cause a program to hang up. That's why Chapter 9, "Additional File Management in the Shell," tells you to exit DOS Shell to initialize the PRINT program, and then to restart the Shell.

- Don't run any program that deals directly with the FAT and directory structure of a disk and counts on all files being closed. The program that's paused, such as DOS Shell, may have several files open. Several DOS utilities should not be run from a secondary command prompt for this reason. The CHKDSK and SCANDISK programs (discussed in Chapter 27, "CHKDSK and SCANDISK"), for example, analyze the FAT and directory structure for errors and inconsistencies and correct them; these programs could damage open files. As another example, the DEFRAG program (discussed in Chapter 33, "Defragmenter") reorganizes the data in the clusters to make more efficient use of the hard disk; this program definitely will damage open files.

Problem: I made some changes to a disk and they're not showing up in my DOS Shell Directory Tree or File List.

You probably made your changes from a secondary command prompt or an application program, where DOS Shell is not aware of them. Press F5 to force DOS to reread the current drive and your changes will show up on the Shell screen.

The File, Run Command

Many applications offer a way of accessing a secondary command prompt just long enough to run one command. Figure 12.1 shows DOS Shell's Run dialog box, which opens when you choose File,

Run. You'll find a similar feature in many of your applications. When you enter a command in the box (up to 127 characters), DOS Shell opens a secondary command prompt, executes the command, and then displays the message `Press any key to return to MS-DOS Shell`.

How to Run One Command at a Secondary Command Prompt from within DOS Shell

1. Choose File, Run.
2. Type the command in the Run dialog box.
3. Press OK.
4. When the program terminates, press a key to return to the Shell screen.

Figure 12.1.
The Run dialog box.

```
                          Run
   Command Line . .   MEM /C_

              OK              Cancel
```

Advantages and Disadvantages of Primary and Secondary Command Prompts

Each method of accessing a command prompt has its advantages and disadvantages. Use the primary command prompt when you want to load a TSR such as PRINT, or run a program that manipulates the disk structure, such as SCANDISK. The disadvantage is that you have to completely exit the Shell and restart it when you're done.

You use File, Run from DOS Shell when you want to run just a single command. The advantage is that you don't have to type EXIT to return to the Shell. The disadvantage is that you can run only one command.

Exit to a secondary command prompt when you want to run several commands. The advantage is that you can enter as many commands as you want before returning to the Shell. The disadvantage is that you have to type EXIT to return to the Shell, and you should not run certain types of programs.

Peter's Principle: Reboot (or shut off your computer) from the primary command prompt only.

When you're working with a program such as Word, Windows, or DOS Shell, it may have files open (even if you're not working on any data files). The program needs to close those files properly before you reboot or shut down. Exit the program normally to give it a chance to close its files. Wait until the drive light stops flashing. Then it's safe to reboot or shut down.

When you're working at a secondary command prompt, there's a paused program that's waiting to be resumed. It probably has open files that need to be closed. Be sure to exit from the secondary command prompt to the paused program and end it normally before rebooting or shutting down. The general rule is to reboot or shut down only from the primary command prompt.

There is an important exception to this rule. If a program has hung up—that is, it has stopped functioning and has completely tied up your computer so that you can't do anything else—your only recourse is to reboot. In some cases, even rebooting won't work and you will have to press your reset button or turn the power off and on again. Be prepared to lose whatever data the program was working on (or any other program) when you have to reboot or restart.

Understanding Command Syntax

A DOS command has the following general syntax:

```
command-name [parameters] [switches]
```

Note: In a syntax statement, italics indicate where you must substitute a word or some other data when you actually type the command. Square brackets enclose optional items. Anything not in square brackets is required.

DOS ignores case in commands. This book shows commands in uppercase merely to make them stand out in the text. You'll probably find it slightly more convenient to type them in lowercase. So when an instruction says, for example, "Type VER and press Enter," you can type VER, Ver, ver, or any other combination of uppercase and lowercase. It's all the same to DOS.

A command is limited to 127 characters. (That's about one and a half lines on a typical 80-column monitor.) Most commands never come near that limit, although you'll see some later in this book that do.

You use spaces to separate the various words and expressions in a command. For example, in the command CD DOS (which changes to the DOS directory), it's important that at least one space follow the word CD. DOS cannot interpret CDDOS (without a space).

> **Note:** On some systems, you don't need a space after the command name if the next expression is a path name starting with \. For example, DOS may be able to interpret CD\DOS correctly as CD \DOS on your PC.

The Name of the Program

The *command-name* is the name of the program that you want to execute. For example, if the program file is named FORMAT.COM, the command name would be FORMAT. If the program file is named RUNOUT.BAT, the command name would be RUNOUT.

Try entering the VER command to find out what DOS version you're using:

1. Type **VER** at the command prompt.
2. Press Enter.

   VER displays your DOS version and terminates itself. Then DOS displays another command prompt, ready for your next command.

Programs that have their own files, such as DOSSHELL.EXE and EDIT.COM, are called *external programs*. Your DOS package includes a number of external programs; in addition, your application software provides external programs.

DOS also includes a number of functions within its COMMAND.COM program, such as the VER program that you just tried. Because these functions are internal to COMMAND.COM and don't have their own program files, they are called *internal commands* or *internal programs*. You run both external and internal programs by entering commands at the command prompt.

Parameters and Switches

Many programs include parameters and switches in their commands. A *parameter* is some kind of variable information that tells the program what you want to do. When starting DOS's text editor program, for example, you can include a filespec to open a document for editing.

Try starting up DOS's text editor (called EDIT) with the README.TXT file as the initial file:

1. Type the following command at the command prompt and press Enter:

```
EDIT README.TXT
```

The Editor screen appears on your monitor with the README.TXT file open. (If the current directory does not contain a README.TXT file, EDIT creates a new, empty one.)

If instead you get the message `Bad command or file name`, don't worry about it now. This message is explained in the next section. Just skip the rest of this exercise and go on.

2. Press Alt+F followed by X to exit EDIT.

    EDIT terminates and DOS displays another command prompt for you.

A switch is a particular kind of parameter, usually in the form of a word or letter prefixed by a slash that selects a particular option for the program. The DIR program, for example, lists the files in a directory with only one entry per line. If you add a /W switch to the command, `DIR` displays the filenames in several columns across the screen.

Try displaying the files in the current directory with and without the /W switch:

1. Type **DIR** and press Enter.

    `DIR` displays the file list and terminates. (If it's a long list, the top scrolls off the screen before you have time to read it. You'll learn how to deal with that in Chapter 14, "Managing Directories," when you learn more about `DIR`.) Then DOS displays a new command prompt for you.

2. Now type **DIR** /W and press Enter.

    You should immediately see the effect of the /W switch. The filenames are listed across the screen instead of down. Information such as file size and date is not displayed.

Using Paths in Commands

When you enter a command, DOS makes a valiant effort to find the program that the command requests. It looks first in its own COMMAND.COM file to see if the program is internal. Then it looks in the current directory for an executable file (with the extension .EXE, .COM, or .BAT) with the correct file name.

What happens if DOS doesn't find the executable file in the current directory? DOS maintains a list of directories, called the *program search path*, to search for programs. DOS looks in each search path directory in turn until it finds the necessary executable file. You'll learn how to create your own program search path a little later in this chapter.

Problem: I entered a command and got the message `Bad command or file name`. What's wrong and how can I run my program?

DOS can't find the program file for the command you entered. Make sure first of all that you spelled the command name correctly. If not, try again with the correct spelling.

If you're sure the command name is correct, see if you can find the program file yourself. Enter the following command to see a list of all files on drive C that start with the command name:

```
DIR \command-name /S /B
```

For example, if the command name is WORD, you would enter DIR \WORD /S /B. (See DIR for an explanation of this command.)

In the resulting list, look for a file with the extension .COM, .EXE, or .BAT. If you can't find one, the program is not installed on your hard disk. Install the program and try again.

If you can find a .COM, .EXE, or .BAT file, notice the path name of the directory it is in. Use the CD command to switch to that directory. Then, try your command again and it should work. For example, suppose the directory listing says:

```
C:\MS-WORD\WORD.EXE
```

You would enter CD C:\MS-WORD to switch to the correct directory. Then the WORD command should work. (See "CD" in Chapter 14 for an explanation of this command.)

If you use this command often, you should add its directory to your program search path so that you don't have to switch to its directory every time you want to start the program. See "The PATH Program" in this chapter for an explanation of how to add a program to your program search path.

You can override DOS's usual routine and tell it exactly where to look for a program by attaching a path to the command name. You can reach files in any directory this way. Even if a directory is in the program search path, including the path with the command name saves DOS from having to search for the program in other directories first.

Try adding the C:\DOS path name to the EDIT command:

1. Enter the following command:

   ```
   C:\DOS\EDIT README.TXT
   ```

   DOS locates EDIT a little more quickly this time, although you probably won't notice the difference.

2. Press Alt+F followed by X to exit the editor.

Attaching a path to the command name affects only where DOS searches for the program file. It does not affect filespecs included as parameters in the command. If you want to open a file that's not in the current directory, you can add the path name to the filespec too.

Try opening the README.TXT file in the DOS directory:

1. Enter the following command:

   `C:\DOS\EDIT C:\DOS\README.TXT`

   This time, EDIT opens the README.TXT file that was provided with DOS.

2. Press Alt+F followed by X to exit the editor.

As you can see, locating files this way can get quite awkward, and people often make mistakes. There are other, better ways to help DOS find a program file:

* Add the desired program's directory to the program search path. This makes it easier to locate the program, but doesn't affect the location of data files.

* Switch to the desired directory so that it's the current directory before entering the command (you'll learn the CD command for changing directories in Chapter 14). This affects the location of both the program file and the data file.

Try switching to the DOS directory and opening the editor again:

1. Enter the following command to switch to the DOS directory:

   `CD DOS`

   You should see the new current directory name in your command prompt.

2. Enter the following command to start up the DOS editor with the README.TXT file:

   `EDIT README.TXT`

   The editor starts up with the README.TXT file from the DOS directory.

3. Press Alt+F followed by X to exit the editor.

Redirecting Command Output

Many DOS commands display messages. The DIR (directory) command, for example, lists the contents of a directory. The PATH command, with no parameters, displays the current search path. Under ordinary circumstances, such messages are displayed on your monitor. But you can redirect them to a file or an external device, such as a printer. The greater-than symbol (>) is used to redirect command messages. The following command saves the current directory listing in a file named DIRC.TXT:

```
DIR > DIRC.TXT
```

> **Warning:** This command would replace an existing DIRC.TXT file.

If you have a parallel printer attached to your first (or only) parallel port, try printing a directory listing on it:

1. Make sure your printer is ready. (See the note in "Printing Through the Shell" in Chapter 9 for a list of details.)

2. Enter the following command:

```
DIR > LPT1
```

The DOS directory should print on your printer. You should get at least two pages of data. If not, see the Problem Solver that follows.

Problem: I redirected a command to my printer, but it didn't print, or it printed all but the last page.

If nothing printed and your computer is now hung up, DOS is spending all its time trying to find your printer. This probably means that the printer is not turned on, not cabled to the computer properly, or not online. If you can find and fix the problem, you will free up your computer. If not, you'll have to reboot to get your computer back.

If your computer isn't hung up, DOS shipped the data, but your printer didn't print it. Check the printer's control panel to make sure that it is not out of ink or paper.

If the printer is ready but still doesn't print the page, it is probably waiting for a page eject signal. Most laser and ink jet printers store up a full page of data before printing, unless they receive a page eject signal. DOS does not send a page eject signal when redirecting data, so if the last page of the output is short of a full page, the printer simply holds it and waits for more. If your printer has a page eject button, try pressing that button. If not, enter the following command at the DOS prompt, where ^L indicates that you should press Ctrl+L (don't type ^L):

```
ECHO ^L > PRN
```

Table 12.1 shows names of devices to which you can redirect output.

Table 12.1. Output device names.

Name	Device
LPT*n*	Parallel printer port *n*; LPT1 is the first parallel printer port.
PRN	Same as LPT1.
COM*n*	Serial (communications) port *n*; COM1 is the first serial port.
AUX	Auxiliary port.
NUL	Nowhere; the output is suppressed.
CON	Monitor screen.

DOS commands produce ASCII text messages. When you redirect the messages to a file, a standard ASCII text file is created. When you redirect them to an output device, that device must be set up to handle ASCII text. Most devices can handle it. But you could not, for example, redirect command messages to a PostScript printer unless you can set the printer to handle ASCII text.

Not all command messages are redirected by >; just the standard messages. Error messages are still sent to the monitor. This can create an interesting situation with a program like DIR. When DIR can't find a file to list, it normally displays a set of messages something like this:

```
Volume in drive C is MICROMATE

Volume Serial Number is 199A-59E3

Directory of C:\NEWBOOK

File not found
```

The first three lines are standard messages; the last line is an error message. If you redirect the output to a file, the first three lines are stored in the file, but the last line is displayed on your screen.

Many programs produce output that is not a standard message and is not redirected by >. The COPY program, for example, creates a file on the target directory or device. If you redirect the output of COPY, only its standard messages (such as 1 Files Copied) are redirected; the new file is not redirected.

Note: You can redirect the output of any program that produces standard messages on the monitor. It doesn't have to be one of the DOS utilities.

Looking Ahead: The > symbol is only one of four redirection symbols for DOS commands. Chapter 36, "DOS at Your Command," shows you the other three, which are used much less often.

Introduction to the Command Reference

The back part of this book is a complete DOS Command Reference, arranged in alphabetical order by command name. For each command, the Command Reference documents the command syntax, the parameters and switches, and any notes pertaining to the command. A complete set of examples also is provided.

The Command Reference includes all DOS commands and options, even the intermediate and advanced ones that aren't discussed in the tutorial part of this book. The Command Reference doesn't attempt to explain commands and options in a tutorial fashion; it just documents them.

The Command Reference uses several typographical conventions to portray command syntax. Words and phrases in capital letters must be entered just as shown in the command. The VER command's syntax, for example, looks like this:

```
VER
```

This command displays the current DOS version number. To use it, type the word VER and press Enter. (It doesn't have to be in all uppercase letters. Remember that DOS ignores case most of the time.)

Words and phrases in lowercase italics must be replaced with specific information when you enter the command. The DEL command, for example, is used to delete files. Its syntax looks like this:

```
DEL filespec
```

You must type the word **DEL** followed by a filespec, as follows:

```
DEL C:\CONFIG.OLD
```

Words and phrases enclosed in square brackets are optional. They make a difference in the effect of the command. The DATE and TIME commands, for example, let you examine and change the system date and time. Their syntaxes look like this:

```
DATE [date]
```

```
TIME [time]
```

If you enter DATE without a date, DOS displays the current system date and asks whether you want to change it. If you add a date to the command, DOS changes the system date without asking. Similarly, TIME without a time displays the current time and asks whether you want to change it; but if you specify TIME 3:00, DOS changes the system time to 3:00 without asking.

Sometimes options have options, causing a nest of square brackets. The DIR command includes a /A switch with this syntax:

```
DIR [/A[attributes]]
```

When you include the optional /A switch in a DIR command, DIR lists files with certain attributes. You can specify the attributes or simply use /A by itself. If you use /A by itself, files with all attributes are listed. But, if you add specific attributes, only files with those attributes are listed. The following command, for example, lists only files with the read-only attribute:

```
DIR /AR
```

In some cases, a parameter can be used only with another parameter. This also causes a nest of square brackets. For example, the DEVICEHIGH command (which loads device drivers into upper memory) looks like this:

```
DEVICEHIGH=filespec [/L:region[,min] [/S]]
```

The /L:region parameter is optional. If you use it, you also can add a comma and a min parameter, and you can follow it with the /S switch. Notice that the /S is enclosed within the brackets that contain /L:region. You can't use /S without /L:region.

An ellipsis (...) is used to indicate parameters that can be repeated. The PATH command, for example, looks like this:

```
PATH [pathname[;pathname]...]
```

If you specify one path parameter, you can add a second one separated by a semicolon. The three dots indicate that you can repeat the ;pathname parameter as many times as you want (up to the 127 character limit for DOS commands) to add more directories to the command.

Sometimes you can choose between two or more mutually exclusive parameters, indicated by a vertical bar (¦). The VERIFY command, for example, looks like this:

```
VERIFY [ON ¦ OFF]
```

This command controls whether DOS verifies everything it writes on disk. VERIFY ON turns verification on; VERIFY OFF turns it off. VERIFY without a parameter displays the current verification status.

When you combine several of these elements, command syntax can get pretty complex. In the command reference, the notes and examples should help you understand how you can use the commands in practice.

Getting On-Screen Help with Commands

Suppose you want to delete your current search path, but you can't remember the necessary syntax of the PATH command. If you don't want to reach for the Command Reference at the back of this book, you can look up the command without lifting your hands from the keyboard. DOS includes two on-screen help facilities: FASTHELP and HELP. FASTHELP displays a brief command syntax for a command, while HELP accesses a library of much more complete command documentation.

Getting On-Screen Help with Command Syntax

When you enter any DOS command name followed by /?, DOS displays a brief syntax statement for the command. Suppose you want to know how to eliminate your program search path. To display a brief syntax for the PATH command, type PATH /? and press Enter. DOS displays the command syntax for the PATH command. (See Figure 12.2.)

Figure 12.2.
PATH on-screen help summary.

```
C:\>path /?
Displays or sets a search path for executable files.

PATH [[drive:]path[;...]]
PATH ;

Type PATH ; to clear all search-path settings and direct MS-DOS to search
only in the current directory.
Type PATH without parameters to display the current path.

C:\>
```

You don't find out very much about the command this way, but it's a good reminder when you've simply forgotten the name of a switch or some such detail. In this case, it's enough to tell you that entering PATH followed by a semicolon (;) eliminates the search path.

DOS's syntax statements use a format similar to the one in this book. Phrases in all caps (such as PATH) must be typed as is, although they can be typed in either uppercase or lowercase. Where this book uses lowercase combined with italics to represent replaceable items, DOS uses just lowercase (as in drive:). Items in square brackets are optional, and an ellipsis (...) indicates a repeatable item.

The syntax statements in this book often look slightly different than the ones you get at the command prompt. In many cases, both versions mean the same thing, but this book tries to present the syntax in a simpler, clearer way. In a few cases, the DOS version is slightly inaccurate and this book presents a correct version. For the most part, the DOS version is good enough to remind you of the name of a switch or a parameter.

Note: If you're upgrading from DOS 5, you may be used to entering HELP followed by a command name to display the brief syntax message. The HELP program has been improved with DOS 6, as you'll see in the next section. This more brief facility has been renamed as FASTHELP. So if you don't want to use the /? switch, enter **FASTHELP** *command* to see the brief syntax.

FASTHELP with no parameters displays a complete list of DOS commands with a brief explanation of each. The list is automatically paged on a video screen, but it is printed without paging when redirected to a printer as follows:

```
FASTHELP > PRN
```

Tip: If you are responsible for helping a group of inexperienced people to use DOS, you might want to adapt the Help list to include your own notes, comments, and warnings; to document batch commands and macros that you have created; and most particularly, to modify the explanations of commands you have replaced with DOSKEY macros. You can modify the command list by editing the file named DOSHELP.HLP. The beginning of the file explains the proper way to edit the list.

Getting On-Screen Help with Complete Command Information

For more complete on-screen documentation, type **HELP** with or without a command name. The HELP program starts up and displays a window from which you can access information about any internal command, external command, batch command, or device driver supplied with DOS. (FASTHELP does not include the device drivers and batch commands, but HELP does.)

Note: For on-screen help on how to use the Help system itself, press F1 while the Help window is open.

The Contents List

When you enter just the word HELP with no command name, the Help window opens and displays a list of contents. (See Figure 12.3.) Each item in angle brackets, such as <What's New in MS-DOS 6.22>, is called a *jump*. You can jump to the indicated topic by clicking anywhere within the brackets. Or you can move the cursor to a jump and press Enter to view the topic.

Figure 12.3.
Help contents.

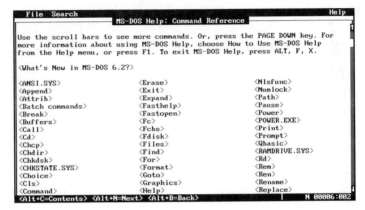

To open the contents list on your screen:

1. Enter **HELP** with no parameters.

   The Help Contents list opens on your screen.

2. Leave the list on your screen while you read the next section.

Moving around the Help Window

Table 12.2 shows the keys you can use to move the cursor among jumps. Unfortunately, the topics are listed alphabetically down columns, but the Tab key moves across rows. So if you want to get from <Call> to <Chdir>, for example, you have to press the Tab key nine times. It's faster to press the letter C or the down-arrow key three times. Of course, it's even faster to just click the item you want with your mouse.

Table 12.2. Moving the cursor in the Help window.

Key	Action
Tab	Moves to the next jump going across rows
Shift+Tab	Moves to the preceding jump going across rows
↓	Moves down one row
↑	Moves up one row

continues

Table 12.2. continued

Key	Action
Letter	Moves to the next jump starting with *letter*
Shift+*letter*	Moves to the preceding jump starting with *letter*
Page Down	Moves down one window
Page Up	Moves up one window

The cursor movement keys such as down-arrow and Page Down do not necessarily move from jump to jump; they simply move the cursor around in the window. If the cursor happens to land in a jump, fine. Otherwise, you may have to move the cursor to the jump yourself. (The other cursor movement keys such as the left arrow key and Home also work in the screen, but they're practically useless for moving from jump to jump.)

1. Use the cursor keys to move to <Exit>.
2. Now move to <Choice>.

   Leave the contents list on your screen while you read the next section.

Scrolling the Help Window

As you can see in the Figure 12.3, the entire Contents list doesn't fit in the window. You have to scroll to see it all. When you move the cursor by using any of the techniques in Table 12.2, the list automatically scrolls as necessary to show you the new position of the cursor.

Try scrolling around in the list with your keyboard:

1. Press Page Down until you reach the bottom of the list.

   A small diamond indicates the bottom of the list.
2. Use Shift+Tab to move to the preceding jump.
3. Press C to move to the first command starting with C.
4. Press Shift+C to move to the last command starting with C.
5. Press Shift+C several more times to back up through the commands starting with C.

You can also scroll without moving the cursor by using the scroll bar and a mouse. Refer to the procedure called "How to Scroll with the Mouse" in Chapter 5, "Getting Acquainted with DOS Shell," for instruction on using the scroll bar.

If you have a mouse, try scrolling the contents list with it:

1. Click the up-arrow at the top of the scroll bar several times and watch the list scroll up line by line.

2. With the pointer positioned over the up-arrow, hold down the mouse button and watch the list scroll up rapidly.

3. Click the bar under the scroll box twice and watch the list scroll down a window at a time.

4. Drag the scroll box to the bottom of the scroll bar to see the end of the list.

The Topic Screens

When you select a command such as <PATH> from the Help window, you see that it has three topics: Syntax, Notes, and Examples. When you first select a command, the Syntax topic appears. (See Figure 12.4.) The other two topics are referenced in jumps at the beginning of the topic. Select one just as you select a jump in the contents list. If you scroll down in the topic, the jumps scroll off the top of the screen. You can get back to them again by scrolling up; by pressing Tab or Shift+Tab until the cursor reaches the desired jump; or by pressing N (for Notes), E (for Examples), or S (for Syntax) to move the cursor to the desired jump.

Figure 12.4.
The PATH—Syntax topic.

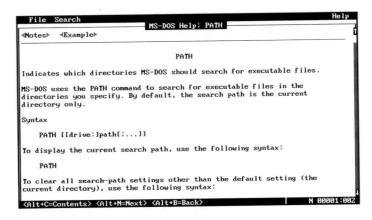

Take a look at the PATH command:

1. Click <Path> or press P to move to it and press Enter.

    The Path--Syntax topic opens.

2. Scroll to the bottom of the topic.

    Don't worry about reading the topic now; you'll learn about PATH later in this chapter.

Now try looking at the Path--Notes topic:

1. Press N to move to the <Notes> jump.

    The list scrolls back to the top automatically.

2. Click <Notes> or press Enter to open the Path--Notes topic.

3. Scroll down to the bottom of this topic.

    Notice that it is a collection of notes related to the PATH command.

Now try the Path--Example topic:

1. Click `<Example>` or press E followed by Enter.

    The Path--Example topic appears. Notice that it is an example of a `PATH` command.

Other Help Jumps

To get back to the Contents list, click `<Alt+C=Contents>` in the status bar at the bottom or press Alt+C. Press Alt+N or click `<Alt+N=Next>` to see the next topic in the library. Press Alt+B or click `<Alt+B=Back>` to back up through the topics you have looked at.

Try these jumps:

1. Click `<Alt+N=Next>` or press Alt+N.

    The Pause--Syntax topic appears. This is the next topic after Path--Example in the help library.

2. Click `<Alt+B=Back>` or press Alt+B.

    The Path--Example topic reappears. This was the previous topic you viewed. You can keep choosing Back to back up through your entire help session.

3. Click `<Alt+C=Contents>` or press Alt+C.

    The Contents list appears.

Tip: You don't have to start with the Contents list to see a specific command. Entering `HELP command` at the command prompt opens the Help window with the Syntax topic for the requested command. To see the syntax for the `PATH` command, for example, you would enter `HELP PATH`.

If you want to go straight to the Notes or Example for a command, add two hyphens followed by `NOTES` or `EXAMPLE`, as in `HELP PATH--NOTES` or `HELP PATH--EXAMPLE`.

The Help Menus

Help's three menus provide the following facilities:

Print (File menu)	Prints the current help topic; you can choose to print it on your printer or save it in a file.
Exit (File menu)	Exits the Help program.

Find (Search menu)	Searches through all the Help topics for whatever phrase you specify. If you're not sure what command deletes files, for example, you could search for the word `delete`.
Repeat Last Find (Search menu)	Repeats the last search command; you may need to repeat the search for `delete` several times, for example, until you find the command you want.
How to Use MS-DOS Help (Help menu)	Displays a list of topics on how to use the Help program.
About (Help menu)	Displays copyright and version information for the Help program.

Tip: A quick way to move from one command to another without returning to the Contents list is to search for the command name. If you search for PATH, for example, HELP does not show you the next instance of the word path in the Help library. Instead, it jumps to the Path--Syntax topic. Repeat Last Find does not work after you do this, since there is only one Path--Syntax topic.

The Search Facility

If you're not sure which command you want to look up, you can search for a word or phrase throughout the entire help library. Suppose, for example, that you want to find out which commands pertain to CD-ROM drives. Try finding any reference to CD-ROM in the help library:

1. Click the word Search on the menu bar or press Alt+S.

   The Search menu pulls down.

2. On the Search menu, click the Find command or press F.

   The Find dialog box opens. (See Figure 12.5.)

Figure 12.5.
Help's Find dialog box.

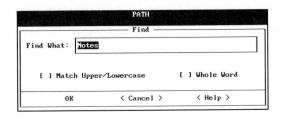

3. Type CD-ROM and press Enter.

DOS searches through the Help library for the next instance of the word CD-ROM. It may take a few moments, so be patient. The message Searching—press Esc to Cancel on the bar at the bottom of the screen tells you that DOS is still searching for CD-ROM.

Eventually, a new topic appears on the screen. The cursor is poised under the C of CD-ROM.

Note: You can type search text in any combination of uppercase and lowercase letters. We show uppercase in this book for clarity. DOS ignores case unless Match Upper/Lowercase is selected in the Find dialog box.

When the text has been found, the topic name at the top of the screen tells you what command deals with this topic. You can scroll to read the rest of the topic and jump to related topics to find the information you need.

If the selected topic is not the one you want, it's simple to continue your search through the library. You can select the Repeat Last Find command from the Search menu, or you can simply press F3. Try finding the next instance of CD-ROM:

1. Press F3.

DOS finds the next instance of CD-ROM and places the cursor under the C. (If the topic doesn't change, look for the new position of the cursor on the same page.)

2. Keep pressing F3 to see more instances of CD-ROM.

Sometimes the topic will scroll, sometimes a new topic appears, and sometimes the cursor simply moves down to the next instance of CD-ROM on the same screen.

Now try printing a topic:

1. Click File or press Alt+F to pull down the File menu.

2. Click Print or press P to choose the Print command.

The Print dialog box opens. (See Figure 12.6.) The default option is to print to the printer on LPT1.

3. Click < OK > or press Enter.

The Help topic should start printing. If not, see the Problem Solver under "Redirecting Command Output" in this chapter.

Now that you've had a chance to explore the Help system, close the Help window and return to the command prompt so that you can begin learning some DOS commands:

1. Click File or press Alt+F to pull down the File menu.

2. Click Exit or press X to choose the Exit command.

The Help window closes and the command prompt returns.

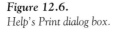

Figure 12.6.
Help's Print dialog box.

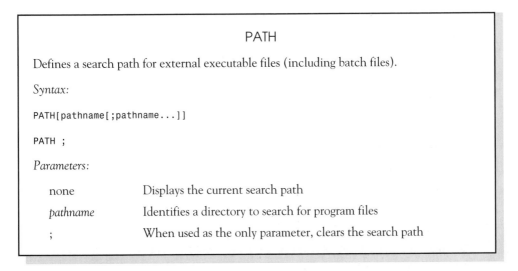

The PATH Program

The PATH program sets the program search path. Figure 12.7 shows the syntax of this command. If you enter just the word PATH with no parameters, PATH displays the current search path, which may look something like this:

```
PATH C:\DOS;C:\;C:\WP;C:\MAILING
```

PATH

Defines a search path for external executable files (including batch files).

Syntax:

```
PATH[pathname[;pathname...]]
```

```
PATH ;
```

Parameters:

none	Displays the current search path
pathname	Identifies a directory to search for program files
;	When used as the only parameter, clears the search path

Figure 12.7. *The PATH command summary.*

Note: The command syntax shown in these chapters is often more brief than the full syntax. See the Command Reference section for complete command information, including advanced parameters, examples, and considerations.

To replace the current path with a new one, follow the word PATH with a list of path names separated by semicolons. Don't include any spaces in the parameter; as ugly as it looks, the whole string of path names must all be one parameter. The order in which you list the directories determines the order in which DOS searches them when it's looking for a program. To search the DOS directory, the WP directory, and the root directory (in that order), you would enter this command:

```
PATH C:\DOS;C:\WP;C:\
```

Tip: Try to arrange the path names in your PATH command from the most used to the least used so that DOS finds programs as quickly as possible.

When you boot, there is no search path. Most users set up the path they want to use all the time in AUTOEXEC.BAT. Your AUTOEXEC.BAT file probably already contains a PATH command inserted by DOS's Setup program. When you install a new program, its INSTALL or SETUP program may add its directory to your PATH command in AUTOEXEC.BAT.

Review your AUTOEXEC.BAT file every once in a while, and edit the PATH command to remove directories for programs that you no longer work with and to change the order of the directories to reflect the way you use your system.

DOS commands are limited to 127 characters, so you can't let your PATH command get too long, or the directories at the end will be ignored.

When you enter the PATH command, DOS doesn't check to make sure that the directories are legitimate. It simply ignores invalid directories when searching for a program file.

Note: Remember that you can override the search path by including a path name with the program name, as in D:\DAS\FLICK.

Try viewing your current search path:

1. Enter **PATH** with no parameters.

   DOS displays your search path.

2. Examine your search path and decide if you want to change it. Is there a better order for the paths' names? Does it include any directories you don't use anymore? Does it omit directories that you use regularly—especially the DOS directory?

3. If you decide that you want to change it, enter the PATH command to define the search path that you want to use. Be sure to spell out each path name completely and correctly, including the drive name. Be sure to separate the path names with semicolons. And, be sure there are no spaces in the parameter.

   If you enter a new PATH command, the old search path is completely replaced by the new one.

> **Note:** If you want to use a different program search path on a permanent basis, you should replace the PATH command in your AUTOEXEC.BAT file. Chapter 20, "Basic Batch Programs," explains how to edit AUTOEXEC.BAT.

The *PROMPT* Command

The command prompt usually takes the form of the current drive and directory followed by a greater-than sign (>). However, you can set up any prompt you want. Just enter a command in this format:

```
PROMPT [text]
```

If you don't specify any text, the current prompt is removed and a stripped down prompt is established. You've probably never seen the stripped down prompt, which is just the drive name followed by a greater-than sign. Try this for yourself:

1. Enter **PROMPT** with no parameters.

   The next command prompt that DOS displays shows just your drive name and a greater-than sign.

Because most people want to know not only the current drive but also the current directory, DOS by default displays the command prompt that you're used to.

You can change the prompt to any text you want. Try creating a prompt that says, What's next?:

1. Enter the following command at the command prompt:

   ```
   PROMPT What's next?
   ```

   DOS displays the new command prompt.

> **Note:** This is another place where DOS pays attention to case. It uses whatever case you specify in the PROMPT text.

Table 12.3 shows some special codes you can use in your PROMPT commands. Some of these codes insert DOS information into the prompt, such as the date or the current directory. Others make certain characters available in the prompt text that otherwise would be interpreted as part of the PROMPT command. You already have learned that > is the redirection symbol, so you can't use it in prompt text. But you can use $G (the G stands for greater-than) to ask for a > symbol. The default prompt is expressed as PG, where $P requests the current drive and directory, and $G displays the greater-than sign.

Table 12.3. Special Prompt command codes.

Code	Meaning
$G	Greater-than (>)
$$	Dollar sign ($)
$P	Current drive and directory
$D	Current date
$T	Current time

Take the time now to restore your default prompt:

1. Enter the following command:

   PROMPT PG

   The standard prompt returns.

On Your Own

This chapter has shown you how to work at the command prompt. If you would like some more practice in the techniques that you have learned in this chapter, try your hand at the following exercises:

1. Make sure you understand the difference between a primary and secondary command prompt. Make sure you know how to get to the primary command prompt. Also make sure you know how to get to a secondary command prompt from DOS Shell or Windows (whichever one you use).

2. Print your DOS version number by redirecting the output of the VER command to the printer.

3. Look up VER in FASTHELP and in HELP.

4. Display your current program search path.

5. Change your command prompt to show the current date and time, as well as the current directory.

6. Restore the normal command prompt.

13

DOSKEY

Introduction

Working at the command prompt used to be awkward and confusing until DOS introduced DOSKEY. Now it's simple.

Understanding What DOSKEY Does

Often, it is handy to be able to recall and edit a former command rather than typing a new one from scratch. Earlier versions of DOS let you do this to a limited extent, but you had to work blind (you couldn't see the former command). Now you can load a terminate-and-stay-resident program (TSR) named DOSKEY that makes command editing easy. Note that when you start a new DOS command session from Windows or OS/2, the DOSKEY list starts over.

DOSKEY does more than mere command editing. It also can do the following:

- Recall a previous command and rerun it as is
- Combine two or more commands in one
- Create command macros, which are complex commands that can be executed by entering a simple name

If you plan to work at the command prompt on a regular basis, you should use DOSKEY. It will save you a lot of time and aggravation.

In this chapter, you will learn how to:

- Load the DOSKEY TSR
- Recall and edit commands
- Combine two or more commands
- Define and use DOSKEY macros
- Manage the macro list
- Manage the command list
- Override DOS commands with macros

Loading the DOSKEY TSR

Figure 13.1 shows the syntax of the command that starts DOSKEY. If your system is set up for it, you can load DOSKEY into upper memory, as explained in Chapter 30, "Additional Memory Facilities for 386, 486, and Pentium Computers."

DOSKEY

Saves and provides access to commands and macros entered at the DOS command prompt.

Format:

```
DOSKEY [/BUFSIZE=size] [/INSERT ¦ /OVERSTRIKE] [/REINSTALL]
```

Parameters and Switches:

none	Loads the DOSKEY TSR with default values for BUFSIZE and INSERT I OVERSTRIKE; immediately begins recording commands in the DOSKEY buffer.
/BUFSIZE=*size*	Specifies the size of the DOSKEY buffer. This parameter is effective only when loading or reinstalling the DOSKEY TSR. The default size is 512 bytes.
/INSERT	Sets default typing mode to insert.
/OVERSTRIKE	Sets default typing mode to overstrike. This is the usual default.
/REINSTALL	Installs a new copy of DOSKEY.

Figure 13.1.   *The DOSKEY command summary (to load DOSKEY).*

Try loading DOSKEY using all the default options:

1. Enter **DOSKEY** without any parameters.

   Unfortunately, you don't get any kind of message when DOSKEY loads without problems. All you see is a new command prompt. (This is one of those cases where no news is good news.)

2. So that you'll have some commands to work with on DOSKEY, enter the **VER** command (no parameters).

   DOS displays the current DOS version number.

3. Enter the **PATH** command (no parameters).

   DOS displays the current program search path.

4. Enter the **PROMPT** command (no parameters).

   DOS changes to the basic prompt with drive letter and > only.

Did you notice that you can't see DOSKEY at work? But it is working, as you will see in the next section.

Note: With the default setup that you are using, DOSKEY takes up 4KB of memory. If you increase or decrease the size of the buffer, which is explained under "Controlling the DOSKEY Buffer Size" later in this chapter, the memory required changes as well. DOSKEY can be loaded into upper memory, as explained in Chapter 30.

Using the Command History

DOSKEY has already recorded three commands in your command history. Table 13.1 shows the keys you use to recall commands from the history. Most often you will simply press the up-arrow key to get back to the command you want. Each time you press up-arrow, DOSKEY moves back one more command in the buffer and displays it at the command prompt. If you go back too far, you can move forward again by pressing the down-arrow key. When you see the command you want, edit it as necessary and press Enter.

Table 13.1. Recalling commands from the DOSKEY history.

Key	Action
↑	Recalls the preceding command in the buffer.
↓	Recalls the next command in the buffer.
PgUp	Recalls the oldest command in the buffer.
PgDn	Recalls the newest command in the buffer.
F8	Recalls the preceding command in the buffer that starts with the letters on the command line.
F7	Displays a numbered list of all saved commands.
F9	Prompts for a command number, then recalls that command.
Alt+F7	Deletes all the commands in the buffer.

Try recalling the commands that you entered before:

1. Press up-arrow.

   DOSKEY displays the PROMPT command. Notice that the command is not executed at this time. It is merely displayed on the command line. You can edit it, enter it, or recall another command.

2. Press up-arrow again.

   DOSKEY displays the PATH command.

3. Press up-arrow again.

   DOSKEY displays the VER command.

4. Press Enter to execute the VER command.

   DOS displays the current version number.

If you want to go back more than a few commands, it's often convenient to type the first few letters of the desired command and press F8. Try recalling the PATH command:

1. Type **PA** and press F8.

   DOSKEY displays the PATH command.

2. Type **V** and press F8 to recall the VER command.

Another way to get back to an earlier command is to press F7, which displays all the commands in the buffer, assigning a number to each one. After you decide which command you want from the list, you press F9. DOSKEY asks for a command number, then it displays the command associated with that number. Try recalling the PROMPT command by using F7 and F9:

1. Press F7.

   DOSKEY displays a numbered list of all the commands in its buffer.

2. Find the number of the PROMPT command.

3. Press F9.

   DOSKEY asks for a command number.

4. Type the number of the PROMPT command and press Enter.

   DOSKEY displays the PROMPT command.

Obviously, it's easier to just press up-arrow a few times. But, if you need to go back 25 or 30 commands, then the F7–F9 combination can be much faster. (If you already know the command number, you just use F9; F7 is not required.)

Editing Commands

Now that you have some text on the command line, how do you edit it? Simply move the cursor back and forth with the cursor keys and insert, delete, and overtype characters. When the command is ready, you press Enter to process it. DOSKEY saves it again as the most recent command in your history.

Adapt your earlier PROMPT command to restore the usual command prompt:

1. If the PROMPT command is not shown on your command line, use DOSKEY to recall it.

2. Position the cursor at the end of the command (press End) and edit it to read:

```
PROMPT $P$G
```

3. Press Enter to execute the command.

   The familiar command prompt is restored.

The Insert and Overtype Editing Modes

If you have ever done word processing or even text editing with an editor like DOS's EDIT, you know the difference between insert and overstrike mode. DOSKEY also offers both modes when you are editing commands. You toggle between them with the editing key.

Right now, overtype mode is your default mode because you didn't specify the /INSERT switch when you loaded DOSKEY. Try overtype mode:

1. Press up-arrow to recall the last PROMPT command.

2. Press left-arrow to move the cursor to the first $ in the command.

3. Overtype the $P with $D.

   Because you are in overtype mode, not insert mode, the $D replaces the $P. (If it gets inserted instead, then your default mode is insert mode. This might be true if someone placed a DOSKEY /INSERT command in your AUTOEXEC.BAT file to load DOSKEY in insert mode each time you boot. Delete this command, enter the command DOSKEY /OVERTYPE, and do this exercise over again.)

4. Press Enter to execute the command.

   The next command prompt displays the date followed by a greater-than sign.

Now try insert mode:

1. Press Insert once to turn on insert mode.

   Notice that the cursor turns into a rectangle instead of the normal underline. This tells you that you're in the nondefault editing mode.

2. Press up-arrow to recall the previous PROMPT command.

3. Press left-arrow to position the cursor on the first $.

4. Type $P followed by a space.

   The $P is inserted in front of the $D.

5. Press Enter to execute the command.

   The new prompt shows the current drive and directory, followed by today's date, followed by a greater-than sign. The cursor has become an underline again, indicating that the default editing mode has been restored.

If you would prefer insert to be your default editing mode, enter a DOSKEY command with the /INSERT switch. You can include /INSERT on the DOSKEY command when you load DOSKEY, or you can enter another DOSKEY command at any time to change it.

1. Make insert your default editing mode by entering the following command:

   DOSKEY /INSERT

2. Press up-arrow twice to recall the previous PROMPT command.

3. Use left-arrow to position the cursor under the first $ in the command.

4. Type **$T** followed by a space.

   Notice that the $T is inserted into the command, because insert mode is now the default mode.

5. Press the Insert key.

   The cursor becomes a flashing rectangle indicating that the nondefault typing mode is in effect.

6. Type **$$** (two dollar signs in a row) followed by a space.

   Notice that these characters *overtype* the former text ($D) in the command. Because insert is now the default editing mode, overtype is the nondefault mode.

7. Press Enter to execute the command.

   The next prompt displays the current time, a dollar sign, and the current date, followed by a greater than sign. The cursor becomes a flashing underline again as the default editing mode (which is now insert mode) returns.

Now straighten out your command prompt:

1. Press up-arrow to recall the previous command.

2. Edit the command to read PROMPT PG.

3. Press Enter to restore your normal command prompt.

4. Enter **DOSKEY /OVERTYPE** to restore overtype as the default editing mode.

Combining Commands

Suppose that you want to see your system date and time. One way to do it would be to change the command prompt to show the date and time, then immediately change the command prompt back to the normal prompt again. You could enter two separate commands to do this, but with DOSKEY you can combine them on one command line by separating them with ¶.

> **Tip:** Press Ctrl+T to type the ¶ symbol.

Try entering both commands in one:

1. Enter the following command:

   PROMPT Date: $D Time: T_$_ ¶ PROMPT PG

   The first PROMPT command causes DOS to display this line:

   Date: Fri 08-19-94 Time: 10:27:15.88

   It is followed by two blank lines (because of the $_$_). Then the second PROMPT command is displayed and executed, returning the normal command prompt.

There are two advantages to combining commands. First, it is slightly faster than entering two separate commands. Second, the commands are recorded as one command in the DOSKEY command buffer; when you recall them, you get two commands for the price of one.

You can now see the system date and time whenever you want by recalling the previous command. Try it now:

1. Press up-arrow to recall the previous command.

   DOSKEY displays the double PROMPT command on your command line.

2. Press Enter to execute it.

   DOS displays the date and time, then restores the normal command prompt.

You're not limited to two commands on a command line. You can combine as many commands as you can squeeze into 127 characters. (The ¶ doesn't count as a character.)

Using Macro Power

Suppose that you execute the preceding command many times a day. DOSKEY lets you assign a name, such as DT (for date and time), to the command and execute it simply by entering DT at the DOS prompt. This is called a *macro*. A macro saves time, energy, and mistakes in typing frequently used commands. You also can use the macro for a longer period of time than you can a command in the command history, which is eventually replaced by newer commands.

Figure 13.2 shows the DOSKEY command syntax for creating macros.

DOSKEY

Defines a macro.

Syntax:

```
DOSKEY macroname=text
```

Parameters:

macroname	Names the macro.
text	Defines a command to be associated with *macroname*.

Notes:

Macro definitions can contain these special characters:

$G	Redirects output; equivalent to the redirection symbol for output (>).
$T	Separates commands; equivalent to the DOSKEY command separator (Ctrl+T).
$$	Specifies the dollar sign character.
$n	Represents a parameter to be specified when the macro is run; n may be 1 through 9. These are similar to the batch parameters %1 through %9.
$*	Represents all parameters. $* is replaced by everything on a command line following a macro name.

Figure 13.2. The `DOSKEY` command summary (for creating macros).

Let's begin with a simple macro to replace the VER command with the letter V:

1. Enter the following command to define the V macro:

   DOSKEY V=VER

   DOSKEY does not confirm the macro definition, so all you get in response is another command prompt.

2. To run the new macro, enter **V**.

   DOS displays the version number.

You can't include any symbols such as ¶ or > in a macro definition, because DOSKEY would interpret them as soon as you enter the command and would not store them in the macro. Instead, you must use the special symbols shown in Figure 13.2.

Suppose you want to revise the V macro to print the version number instead of displaying it. It should also print your DOS search path. At the command prompt, the command would look like this:

```
VER > PRN ¶ PATH > PRN
```

To turn this command into a macro definition, you must replace the > with $G and the ¶ with $T.

1. Enter the following command to define the macro:

   VER $g PRN $T PATH $G PRN

2. Make sure your printer is ready.

3. Enter **V** to execute the macro.

   DOS should print your version number and search path. (If nothing happens, see the Problem Solver in "Redirecting Command Output" in Chapter 12, "Working at the Command Prompt.")

Now let's try a more useful macro. Earlier, you used a combined command to display the date and time:

```
PROMPT Date: $D  Time: $T$L$L ¶ PROMPT $P$G
```

This is a command that you might want to use several times a day. Let's turn it into a macro called DT. In the definition, each dollar sign must be doubled so that DOSKEY stores it in the macro instead of trying to interpret it immediately. This means that $D must be changed to $$D, $T to $$T, and so on. In addition, the ¶ must be replaced by $T. Notice that the command will include $$T as part of the PROMPT command (to display the time) as well as $T to act as a command separator between the two PROMPT commands.

Follow these steps to define the macro:

1. Enter the following command to define the DT macro. (Reminder: Recall your preceding PROMPT command and edit it. You'll save a lot of time and hassle.)

   ```
   DOSKEY DT=PROMPT Date: $$D  Time: $$T$$_$$_$TPROMPT $$P$$G
   ```

2. Try out the new command by entering the command **DT** (which you have just created).

   DOS should display the date and time, then restore the normal command prompt. If it doesn't work properly, go back to step 1 and try again.

Using Replaceable Parameters

Sometimes you want to leave variable parameters out of a macro and supply them when you execute the macro. This makes the macro more flexible, and therefore more useful. Suppose you want to create a macro named PS (for Print Syntax) that prints the command syntax (from FASTHELP) for any DOS command. It redirects the output from *command* /? to the printer.

You use the symbols $1 through $9 in a macro definition to indicate where to plug in variable information. To supply the command name when you execute PS, for example, you could use $1 for the command name:

1. Enter the following command to define PS:

   ```
   DOSKEY PS=$1 /? $G PRN
   ```

2. Enter **PS PATH** to print the command syntax for the PATH command.

   DOSKEY substitutes PATH for $1 in the macro and sends the following command to DOS:

   ```
   PATH /? > PRN
   ```

   As a result, DOS prints the PATH command syntax. (If nothing prints, see the Problem Solver in "Redirecting Command Output" in Chapter 12.)

If you use more than one replaceable variable in a macro, DOSKEY replaces $1 with the first parameter on the command line, $2 with the second parameter, and so on. Be sure to place your parameters in the correct order when you execute the command, or they'll be inserted into the wrong places in the macro. Also, you can't omit any parameters except at the end. If a macro calls for two parameters, for example, there's no way to omit the first one but include the second one, because DOSKEY reads the parameters from left to right on the command line. But you could omit the second parameter if that was appropriate, and you could omit both parameters.

What happens when you omit a parameter? DOSKEY replaces it with a null value (that is, nothing). If you just enter the word PS without a command name, for example, DOSKEY creates this command:

```
/? > PRN
```

The result is a `Bad command or file name` message.

> **Tip:** If you see that a long macro is going wrong because you forgot to include a variable parameter when you executed it, you can stop it by pressing Ctrl+C. If the macro contains multiple commands, you must press Ctrl+C once for each remaining command.

Controlling the DOSKEY Buffer Size

When you load DOSKEY it sets aside a certain amount of memory space for a *buffer* (which is just a storage area in memory). The size of the buffer determines how many commands and macros DOSKEY can store. The default configuration of DOSKEY can store about 50 commands, if you don't define any macros. Every macro, however, takes away space from commands. DOSKEY won't let you fill more than half the buffer with macros; the other half is reserved for commands. So, if you plan to define macros, the default configuration has room for about 25 commands, which should be more than enough for most people.

If, after using DOSKEY for a while, you find that you need more commands, you can request more buffer space the next time you load DOSKEY by including the /BUFSIZE switch. For example, the command DOSKEY /BUFSIZE=1024 would double the size of the buffer. But, increase the size of the buffer only if you have to; it steals valuable memory from your other programs. If instead you find that you need only about 10 commands and a few macros, you should free up the unneeded memory space: Reduce the buffer to its minimum size of 256 bytes by loading DOSKEY with the command DOSKEY /BUFSIZE=256.

> **Note:** Unfortunately, there's no way to unload DOSKEY except to reboot or shut down, so the only good way to change the buffer size is by rebooting. You can reinstall DOSKEY without rebooting by using /REINSTALL, but this technique abandons your first copy of DOSKEY and its buffer in memory, which wastes a lot of valuable memory space. It's much better to reboot if you want to change the buffer size.

Every time you save a new macro, it overwrites some of the commands in the buffer—not necessarily the oldest commands, either. Therefore, you lose some of your command history. But the reverse is not true—new commands do not overwrite macros. If you save a macro, it stays there until you reboot.

Loading DOSKEY in AUTOEXEC.BAT

Each time you boot, DOS looks in the root directory of the boot drive for a file named AUTOEXEC.BAT and executes all the commands it finds in that file. You store any commands you want executed at boot time in AUTOEXEC.BAT. You should include your command to load DOSKEY in AUTOEXEC.BAT, so that DOSKEY is always available to you and you don't have to think about it. Be sure to include /BUFSIZE in the command if you want to use a nondefault buffer size, and the /INSERT switch if you want to make insert the default editing mode. Chapter 20, "Basic Batch Programs," explains more about AUTOEXEC.BAT and how to add commands to it.

Macros are stored in memory, not on disk, and that has both good and bad aspects to it. On the plus side, a macro runs very quickly because it doesn't have to be loaded from disk. On the minus side, all your macros are lost when you reboot or power down. But why not add your favorite macro definitions to AUTOEXEC.BAT so that they will be defined every time you boot?

If you decide to define macros in AUTOEXEC.BAT, keep in mind that the first DOSKEY command that DOS encounters loads the TSR. It can also define a macro, if you wish. But, if you want to specify the buffer size, you must include the /BUFSIZE parameter on that first command.

> **Looking Ahead:** If you give a macro the same name as another program, the macro overrides the program. For example, if you name a macro FORMAT, when you type **FORMAT**, you will access the macro instead of the DOS FORMAT program. Chapter 37, "Programming Logic in Batch Programs," shows you how to use this feature to replace or supplement certain DOS commands.

Reviewing Commands and Macros

Figure 13.3 shows two more DOSKEY switches used to review your commands and macros. The nice thing about these two features is that you can redirect them to print. Try reviewing and printing your history list:

DOSKEY

Displays the command history and macro list.

Format:

DOSKEY [/HISTORY] [/MACROS]

Parameters and Switches:

/HISTORY	Lists all commands in the Doskey buffer; abbreviate as /H.
/MACROS	Lists all current macros; abbreviate as /M.

Figure 13.3.   *DOSKEY command summary (reviewing commands and macros).*

1. To see the history list, enter the command **DOSKEY /H**.

2. To print the macro list, enter the command **DOSKEY /M > PRN**.

Looking Ahead: Chapter 20 shows you how to redirect your command list or your macro list to a file, and turn it into a batch program.

Revising and Deleting Macros

Suppose that you decide you don't like a macro. You can replace it by entering another macro definition for the same macro name, which you have done several times in this chapter. Or, you can remove it altogether by entering a macro definition with no command. Try deleting the macros you have created in this chapter:

1. Enter **DOSKEY DT=** to delete the DT macro.

2. Enter **DOSKEY PS=** to delete the PS macro.

On Your Own

You have learned quite a bit about using DOSKEY in this chapter. The following exercises will help you review what you have learned:

1. Exit any programs you are using and reboot to unload DOSKEY.

2. Load DOSKEY with the minimum buffer size and insert default editing mode.

3. Enter one command line that displays the DOS version number and your program search path.

4. Define and test a macro to print your program search path.

5. Display your command history and your macro list.

6. Delete your macro.

7. Define your macro again by recalling the definition command from the command history.

8. Change the default editing mode to overtype if you prefer.

You'll get a lot more practice in recalling and editing commands in upcoming chapters. I'll remind you every so often that this is the best way to create a new command. I'll also remind you later on to update your AUTOEXEC.BAT file to load DOSKEY and your favorite macros.

14

Managing Directories

Introduction

At the DOS prompt, you can do any directory management you can perform in the Shell—and even more.

Overview

You can't keep all your files in your root directory. Even if its space weren't limited, a directory containing thousands of files would be completely unmanageable. The larger your hard drive, the more important it is to organize your files into a well-designed hierarchy of subdirectories.

You must be able to create directories, manage your directory tree, move around in it at will, and locate the files that you want to work with. This chapter shows you how. You will learn how to:

- Change the default drive and directory
- Display a directory tree
- List the contents of a directory
- List specific files in a directory
- Find a file that you have lost on the hard disk
- Create a new directory
- Rename a directory
- Delete a directory

Network Note: You can create and manage the directory structure on your local drives with no restrictions. But, you may or may not be able to create, list, search, rename, or delete directories on a network drive, depending on your access rights.

Changing the Default Drive and Directory

Every time you boot, the root directory of the current drive becomes your current directory, unless your AUTOEXEC.BAT file changes to another directory. You'll probably want to change to other drives and directories to work with your applications and their data files.

To change drives, enter the desired drive name followed by a colon, as in A: or D:.

Note: Drive names are usually followed by colons in DOS commands so that DOS recognizes them as drive names, not file names.

Try changing to drive A and back:

1. Insert a disk in drive A. (Any disk will do, as long as it's formatted.)

2. Enter **A:**.

   DOS makes drive A the default drive and the default directory on drive A (probably the root directory) the current directory. You see the new current drive and directory in your command prompt.

3. Enter **C:**.

   DOS makes drive C the default drive and the default directory on drive C the current directory. You see the new current drive and directory in your command prompt.

You use the CD command to change the default directory. (See Figure 14.1.) You may see CHDIR used as an alternative for CD. It's the same command.

CD

Changes a default directory or displays the name of a default directory.

Syntax:

`CD [drive] [pathname]`

Parameters:

none	Displays the name of a default directory on the current drive.
drive	Displays the name of the default directory on the specified drive.
pathname	Specifies the name of a new default directory. *Pathname* must represent an existing directory.

Figure 14.1. *CD command summary.*

Try using CD to change directories on your hard drive:

1. Enter **CD ** to switch to your root directory.

2. Enter **CD DOS** to switch to your DOS directory.

Note: Don't forget that a path name must show how to get to the desired location *from the current directory*. The path name DOS works only when the root directory is current. From other directories, you would have to use \DOS.

Displaying the Name of the Default Directory on Another Drive

Normally, the command prompt shows you the name of the current directory (that is, the default directory on the current drive). But what if you want to know the name of the default directory on another drive? The following interaction, complete with command prompts, shows how you would display the name of the default directory on drive D:

```
C:\DOS>CD D:
D:\ORDERS\BACKLOGS

C:\DOS>
```

In this case, the default directory on D is \ORDERS\BACKLOGS. Notice that the command prompt continues to show the current directory. The default directory on the other drive is displayed in a message only. If you have another drive, try CD *d*: to find out what directory is current on that drive.

Changing a Default Directory on Another Drive

The CD command doesn't have to be used on the current directory. Sometimes it's convenient to change the default directory on another drive. Try changing the directory on another drive:

1. Make sure there is a disk in drive A.
2. Switch to drive A.

   The command prompt should show that A is the default drive.
3. Enter **CD C:\DOS** to make the DOS directory the current directory on drive C.

   You won't see any evidence of the change. The command prompt does not change.
4. Switch to drive C.

   Now you see in the command prompt that the DOS directory is the current directory.

Displaying the Directory Tree

When your directory structure starts to get complicated, it's easy to forget how it all fits together. You can use the TREE command to get a picture of a directory structure. (See Figure 14.2.) TREE diagrams the relationships between the directories in the structure, much as they're depicted in the Shell's directory tree.

TREE

Graphically displays a directory structure.

Syntax:

```
TREE [drive¦pathname]
```

Parameters and Switches:

none	Displays the directory structure starting with the current directory.
drive	Displays the directory structure for the specified drive.
pathname	Displays the directory structure for the specified directory.

Figure 14.2. *TREE command summary.*

To display the entire tree for your hard drive, enter **TREE** \.

> Your directory tree displays on your monitor. (See Figure 14.3 for an example.) If it's a long tree, the top scrolls right off the top of the screen.

Figure 14.3.
A *TREE listing.*

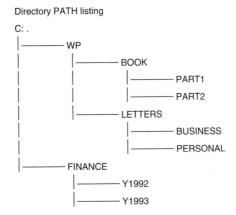

Directory PATH listing
C: .

Tip: If your directory tree scrolls off the top of the screen before you get a chance to read it, there are several things you can do:

- Poise a finger over the Pause key before you enter the command. As the information scrolls onto your screen, press Pause to pause it and any other key to release it again. The success of this venture depends on your system's speed and your speed. You might find the other two techniques more to your liking.

- Redirect the output to your printer, as in TREE \ > PRN.

- Pipe the output to MORE, as in TREE \ | MORE . Piping and MORE are explained in Chapter 36, "DOS at Your Command."

If you request a tree for a directory that has no sub-directories, such as your DOS directory, you see the message No sub-directories exist.

Looking Ahead: TREE has two parameters that are rarely used. /A asks for text characters instead of graphics characters for the connecting lines; the result might be better on printers that can't handle graphics characters. /F lists the files contained in each directory. See the Command Reference for complete details of these parameters.

Listing a Directory

You can see the contents of a directory by using the DIR command. (See Figure 14.4.)

Try listing the contents of some of your directories:

1. Enter **DIR** \ to list the root directory.

    DOS displays the contents of the root directory on your monitor.

2. Enter **DIR** \DOS to list the DOS directory. (Reminder: Try recalling the previous command from DOSKEY and editing it to create this command.)

    DOS has so many files that the beginning of the list scrolls off your screen before you have a chance to see it.

3. To page through the DOS directory list, enter **DIR** \DOS /P. (Reminder: Recall and edit the previous command.)

    DOS displays the first page of the directory list. On the last line is the message Press any key to continue.

4. Press any key.

    DOS displays the next page of the directory list.

5. Keep pressing a key until the list is completed and the command prompt returns.

DIR

Displays the contents of one or more directories.

Syntax:

`DIR [filespec] [/P] [/W] [/A] [/O] [/S] [/B]`

Parameters and Switches:

none	Lists the current directory.
filespec	Identifies the directory and/or file(s) to be listed.
/P	Displays one page at a time.
/W	Displays the listing in wide format, with as many as five names per line.
/A	Lists all files regardless of attributes; without /A, hidden and system files are not listed.
/O	Sorts the listing.
/S	Lists the contents of subdirectories.
/B	Suppresses heading and summary information and lists full filespecs (including path) for all listed entries.

Figure 14.4. DIR *command summary.*

A directory listing looks something like this:

```
Volume in drive C is MY HARDDISK
Volume serial number is 152C-B387
Directory of C:\WP\LETTERS\PERSONAL
.            <DIR>       01-17-90     6:21a
..           <DIR>       01-17-90     6:21a
JANJOHNS LET      1,152 02-22-94    12:08p
FOLK-FEB LET      3,840 02-28-94    10:49a
DOR-BDAY FAX      1,792 03-15-94    12:07p
CONGRESS    <DIR>       01-19-94     7:30p
FOLK-MAR LET      1,787 03-06-94     9:30a
CONNIE   FAX      1,659 03-04-94     9:31a
FOLK-APR LET      1,280 04-10-94    11:48a
MOM-BDAY LET      1,244 09-12-94     9:30a
      10 file(s)    1,2754   bytes
              52,318,464   bytes free
```

Note: The preceding example shows a newer DIR listing. Before DOS 6.2, the byte values were not separated by commas and were much harder to read. Many DOS users have smudged their screens by separating numbers like 10057238 into groups of three with their fingers to find out if they have 1MB or 10MB left on a drive.

The heading shows the volume label, the serial number, and the name of the directory being listed. The main body shows the contents of the directory. Every subdirectory contains the first two entries: . for the directory itself and .. for its parent. The <DIR> shows that these are directories, not files. Notice that this directory also has a child named CONGRESS, shown further down in the list.

For directory entries, the date and time stamp shows the date and time that the directory was created. For files, it shows the date and time that the file was created or last modified. The size gives the actual number of bytes contained in the file, not the amount of space that it occupies on the disk. The actual drive space is affected by such things as the size of the drive's allocation unit and whether the drive is compressed. That figure would not be relevant if you were to copy or move the file to another drive.

The summary lines at the end of the listing show the number of entries that are listed (including both files and directories), and the number of bytes in those files (the files in sub-directories aren't counted in this total). Also shown is the number of free bytes on the drive. Don't expect the total bytes and the free space to add up to the size of your disk. There may be many more files on the disk than are listed.

If you want to see a long directory all on one screen, you could request the wide listing format with the /W switch. This format doesn't show sizes and times, but it manages to squeeze a lot more files onto the screen by listing them in five columns. Try it with the DOS directory:

1. Enter the command **DIR \DOS /W**.

   A wide list of the files in the DOS directory appears on your screen. It's still too long to fit on the screen, and the top scrolls off before you can see it.

2. Enter the command **DIR \DOS /W /P** to page the wide listing on your screen.

   Now you can see the entire list in two pages.

Selecting Files According to Attributes

The DIR command, by default, doesn't list system or hidden files. If you want to see every file regardless of attributes, use the /A switch. You can't see the attributes in the directory listing, but they are still used to control the contents of the listing. Chapter 16, "Additional File Management," explains how to use the ATTRIB command to display and manage attributes at the command prompt.

Try out the /A switch on your root directory:

1. Switch to the root directory on your boot drive.

2. Enter **DIR** /P to list all the files that are not hidden or system files.

3. Enter **DIR** /P /A to list all the files in the directory, including hidden and system files.

   You should see the DOS core program files, such as MSDOS.SYS and IO.SYS, in this second listing. These are hidden and system files, so they don't show up unless you use the /A switch.

Directories can have any of the attributes that files can have. A few applications (notably the De-lete Sentry deletion protection utility) place hidden directories on your drive. You don't see these directories in a DIR listing unless you use the /A switch. (Hidden directories don't show up in a TREE listing either—there's no way around that.)

You can add attribute codes to the /A switch to request files having particular attributes. (See Table 14.1.) For example, /AH causes DIR to list hidden files. When you include one or more attribute codes, only the requested files are listed. Try out the attribute codes for yourself:

1. Make sure you are in the root directory.

2. Enter **DIR** /AH to see only the hidden files in the directory.

   Notice how this listing differs from those in the previous exercise. Only the hidden files are included in the listing.

3. Enter **DIR** /AD to list all the subdirectories of the current directory.

4. You can use multiple codes to limit the listing to files (or subdirectories) that have a combination of attributes. Enter **DIR** /AHD to see entries that have both the hidden and the system directory—in other words, hidden directories.

   You'll see the message File not found, unless your root directory has some hidden subdirectories.

5. You can use a minus sign to list files that *don't* have the specified attribute. Enter **DIR** /A-D /P to see all files except subdirectories.

6. Enter **DIR** /AH-D to see hidden files but not hidden subdirectories.

Table 14.1. Attribute codes for the DIR command.

Code	Meaning
A	Archive attribute
D	Directory attribute
H	Hidden attribute
R	Read-only attribute
S	System attribute

Sorting the Listing

By default, DOS does not sort the directory listing. The files and subdirectories are presented in the order that they actually appear in the directory. Because of the way that DOS manages its directories, this order often appears to be completely arbitrary. Most of the time, you'll find it more useful to sort the listing in some kind of order. The /0 switch causes DOS to sort the listing in alphabetical order by filename, with all subdirectories listed at the beginning. Try out the /0 switch on your system by entering **DIR /0 /P.**

Notice the difference in the order of the entries from the previous exercises.

You can add order codes to the /0 switch to specify the order of the listing. (See Table 14.2.) Try out a few of the order codes on your system:

1. Enter **DIR /ON** to sort the entries by name.

2. Enter **DIR /OS** to sort the entries by size.

3. You add a minus sign to a code to reverse the order of the entries. Enter **DIR /O-S** to sort the entries in descending order by size.

4. If you specify multiple order codes, DOS sorts the entries by the first code. When two or more entries have the same sort data, DOS sorts them by the second code. Enter **DIR /O-DNE** to sort the entries in descending order by date; for files with the same date, in ascending order by name; for files with the same date and name, in ascending order by extension.

5. The G order code places all the subdirectory listings at the beginning of the listing. Enter **DIR /OGNE** to sort the listings by name and extension, with subdirectories first. (This is the default order that results if you enter /0 with no order codes.)

Table 14.2. Order codes for the DIR command.

Code	Meaning
C	Numeric order by compression ratio
D	Numeric order by date
E	Alphanumeric order by extension
N	Alphanumeric order by name
S	Numeric order by size
G	Group directories at the beginning of the listing

Filtering Names

Sometimes you want to see a directory listing of only one file or a set of files. Perhaps you want to find out whether a file exists in the directory, or find its size or date and time stamp. When you add a filespec to a DIR command, DIR lists only the files that match that filespec; it filters out any other files.

The HELP.HLP file contains information for the HELP program that you learned about in Chapter 12, "Working at the Command Prompt." Try listing its directory entry:

1. Enter the command **DIR \DOS\HELP.HLP** to see a listing for the file named HELP.HLP in the DOS directory.

   You see the header lines, a listing for the HELP.HLP file, and the summary lines.

2. If you're going to enter several DIR commands for one directory, it's often easier to switch to that directory so that you don't have to enter path names with every filespec. Enter **CD \DOS** to switch to the DOS directory.

   The command prompt shows that DOS is the current directory.

3. Enter **DIR HELP.HLP** to see the HELP.HLP file again. (Reminder: Recall the previous DIR command from your command history and edit it to create this command, if DOSKEY is loaded.)

You can enter a global filespec to see a list of all the files that match the filespec.

1. Enter **DIR *.HLP** to see a listing of all the .HLP files in the DOS directory.

   There should be quite a few of them. These files contain help information for several of your DOS utilities.

2. There are probably no .XXX files in your DOS directory. Try entering the command **DIR *.XXX** to see what happens.

   You should get a `File not found` message. In this case, DIR displays the heading information but not the summary, so you don't find out how much space is available on the drive.

Listing Branches

You may want to list entries throughout a branch. A quick way is to start at the top of the branch and use the /S switch. Using the /B switch with /S makes the listing much easier to handle because it suppresses the headings and summaries. You see just entries, including full paths, so that you know where each file can be found.

Try listing all the .HLP files on your hard drive:

1. Enter **DIR *.HLP /S** to start at the root directory and display a full listing for each directory on the drive.

   Most of the information scrolls off the screen before you get a chance to read it. However, the last lines of the listing show the total number of .HLP files listed, the number of bytes they include, and the space left on the drive. If all you want to know is how many .HLP files are on the drive and how many bytes they represent, this is a good way to find out.

2. You can use the /P switch with the preceding command to page through the display. Enter **DIR *.HLP /S /P**.

   DOS displays the listing of .HLP files one page at a time.

3. Now try adding the /B switch to the command: **DIR *.HLP /S /P /B**.

> **Note:** Switches can be entered in any order.

A completely different display appears. There are no heading or summary lines, and each line shows the complete path name in the filespec. File size, date, and time are not displayed with /B or /W.

Finding a Lost File

If you misplace a file on a drive, which is easier to do than you might think, the /S and /B switches can help you find it. The command **DIR *filespec* /S /B** starts at the root directory (because the filespec starts with a backslash) and searches through all the directories on the drive, listing every file with the requested filespec. The /B switch causes DOS to include the full path name with each entry, so it's easy to find the file you want.

Try to find the COMMAND.COM file on your hard drive by entering **DIR \\COMMAND.COM /S /B**.

> You see a listing of two or three copies of COMMAND.COM in different directories. From this listing, it would be easy to identify the file that you're looking for.

> **Looking Ahead:** The DIR command has some advanced features that you'll learn about later in this book. For example, you'll learn how to include compression information in the directory listing when you learn about DriveSpace in Chapter 34, "DriveSpace and DoubleSpace." You'll also learn how to set your own default options for DIR in Chapter 43, "DOS and the Environment."

Creating a Directory

How do directories come about in the first place? Some of them, of course, are created when you install programs, but you will create many directories yourself. Figure 14.5 shows the command summary for the MD (Make Directory) command, which creates a directory. (MKDIR is a synonym for MD.)

MD

Creates a new directory.

Syntax:

MD *pathname*

Parameters:

pathname   Identifies the name and location of the new directory.

Notes:

The new directory's full path name including backslashes, from the root directory up to and including the directory, cannot be more than 63 characters.

Pathname must be unique to the parent. You can't duplicate a directory or file name belonging to the parent.

Figure 14.5. *MD command summary.*

As you can see, it's a pretty simple matter to create a new directory. As with any other directory command, though, you need to make sure that your path name tells DOS exactly how to get to the desired location. You can start from the current directory, but if in doubt, specify the full path name for the directory, starting at the root directory.

Note: You can list the directories of a read-only drive, such as a CD-ROM drive, with DIR and TREE. You can switch to a read-only drive, but you can't change the directory structure in any way. You can't use MD, MOVE, or RD on these drives.

Try creating a directory named PRACTICE as a child of the DOS directory:

1. Enter the command MD \DOS\PRACTICE.

   No news is good news; if you didn't get an error message, the directory was successfully created.

2. Try switching to the new directory. Enter **CD \DOS\PRACTICE**.

The command prompt should show that you are in the new directory.

Renaming Directories

A command new with DOS 6 enables you to change the name of a directory. Before DOS 6, you had to use the Shell or some other program to rename a directory. Now you can do it at the command prompt with the MOVE command. (See Figure 14.6.) Chapter 15, "Copying and Moving Files," explains how this command is used to move files from one directory to another. But, when you use it with a directory name instead of a filespec, it simply renames the directory.

MOVE

Renames a directory.

Syntax:

MOVE *pathname newname*

Parameters:

pathname   Identifies the directory you want to rename.

newname   Specifies the new name.

Notes:

If *pathname* includes a parent directory, *newname* should include the same parent directory. If *pathname* is C:\DOS\PRACTICE, for example, *newname* must be C:\DOS*name*.

Figure 14.6. *MOVE command summary (for renaming directories).*

Try changing the name of your PRACTICE directory.

1. You can't rename the current directory, so if PRACTICE is the current directory, switch to its parent with the CD .. command.

Your command prompt should show that C:\DOS is the current directory. If not, enter **CD \DOS** to get to the DOS directory.

2. Enter the command **MOVE PRACTICE EXERCISE**.

You should get the message c:\dos\practice => c:\dos\exercise [ok].

Problem: I tried to rename a directory with MOVE and got the message permission denied. What's wrong?

First, make sure that you're not trying to rename the current directory. If you are, switch to another directory and try again.

Second, make sure that you did not try to change the location of the directory. Both the current name and the new name must specify the same parent directory on the same drive. If you're not sure how to identify the location, switch to the parent directory and specify the directory name without showing its path, as in MOVE PRACTICE EXERCISE.

Third, make sure that you did not specify a global path name. MOVE can change only one directory name per command.

Deleting a Directory

If you have an empty directory you want to delete, you can use the RD (Remove Directory) command. (See Figure 14.7.) RMDIR is a synonym for this command. If you want to delete a directory that contains files or subdirectories, you're better off using the DELTREE command, which is discussed next.

RD

Deletes a directory.

Syntax:

RD *pathname*

Parameter:

pathname   Identifies the directory you want to delete. It must not be the default directory on its drive.

Figure 14.7. *RD command summary.*

Try deleting the EXERCISE directory that you created earlier:

1. A directory must be empty before you can delete it. List the contents of EXERCISE to make sure it's empty.

   You should get the heading lines followed by the File not found message.

2. Switch to the DOS directory, which is the parent of EXERCISE. (Reminder: If EXERCISE is the current directory, you can switch to its parent by entering **CD ..** instead of spelling out the directory name.)

   The command prompt should show that C:\DOS is the current directory.

3. Now delete the EXERCISE directory by entering **RD EXERCISE**.

   If you don't get an error message, the directory was successfully deleted.

4. Enter **DIR EXERCISE** to make sure there is no more EXERCISE directory.

   You should get the message `File not found`.

Problem: I tried to delete a directory and got the message `Invalid path, not directory, or directory not empty`.

First, make sure you typed the path name correctly. If not, try again.

Next, make sure you are not trying to delete the current directory. If you are, enter **CD ..** to switch to the parent directory, then try your **RD** command again.

Finally, the directory may not be truly empty. If `DIR` shows that the directory is empty but you still cannot delete it, try using the `DIR /A` command to see whether some hidden files, system files, or subdirectories are in the directory.

If you still want to delete the directory after seeing what it contains, use the `DELTREE` command to delete the entire branch, files and all.

Deleting a Branch

Before DOS 6, you could delete only one directory at a time, and it had to be empty. But DOS 6 has a new command, `DELTREE`, that deletes the whole branch, including hidden, system, and read-only entries, at one fell swoop. (See Figure 14.8.) You can see that this is a powerful, but dangerous, facility; if you use it, please exercise caution.

In this exercise, you will create a branch, then delete it:

1. Create a directory called EXERCISE as a child of the root directory.

2. Create a directory called PRAC1 as a child of EXERCISE.

3. Create a directory called PRAC2 as a child of EXERCISE.

4. To see the difference between `RD` and `DELTREE`, try `RD` first. Try to delete EXERCISE using the `RD` command.

   You get the message `Invalid path, not directory, or directory not empty`, because `RD` cannot delete a directory that has subdirectories.

5. Enter **DELTREE EXERCISE** to delete the entire branch.

   ```
   Delete directory "exercise" and all its subdirectories? [y/n]
   ```

6. Press **Y**.

   You see this message:

   ```
   Deleting exercise...
   ```

DELTREE

Deletes a directory and all its files and subdirectories.

Syntax:

```
DELTREE [/Y] pathname ...
```

Parameters and Switches:

pathname	Identifies the directory at the top of the branch that you want to delete.
/Y	Bypasses the confirmation step.

Figure 14.8. *DELTREE command summary.*

It can take a while to delete a large branch with all its files. The command prompt returns when DELTREE is done.

You can include more than one path name in the DELTREE command to delete more than one branch. No matter how many path names you include, you can use the /Y switch to bypass the confirmation step.

1. Create three directories: PRAC1, PRAC2, and PRAC3. Each directory should be a child of the root directory, so that they are all on the same level.

2. Enter **DELTREE /Y PRAC1 PRAC2 PRAC3** to delete all three directories without having to confirm them.

   You see these messages:

   ```
   Deleting prac1...

   Deleting prac2...

   Deleting prac3...
   ```

Tip: DELTREE comes in handy even when a directory has no subdirectories. It deletes the directory without making you empty it first.

Looking Ahead: DELTREE can also be used to delete specific files from a branch without deleting the branch. DELTREE also lets you delete a hidden or read-only file without any special effort. Chapter 39, "Directory Management," shows you how to do that.

On Your Own

This chapter has shown you a number of directory management techniques. The following items will help you practice them one more time:

1. Create directories named ONMYOWN and NOHELP as children of the root directory.

2. Create directories named MYDIR, YOURDIR, and OURDIR as children of ONMYOWN.

3. Display the directory tree for the ONMYOWN branch.

4. Display the contents of the DOS directory, one page at a time.

5. Locate the file named CONFIG.SYS on your hard drive.

6. Rename NOHELP as NEWNAME.

7. Delete the ONMYOWN branch and the NOHELP directory in one command.

15

Copying and Moving Files

Introduction

Copying and moving files at the comand prompt has traditionally involved a number of pitfalls. DOS 6.2 includes some enhancements that make it considerably safer.

Overview

DOS gives you a variety of ways to copy and move files. This chapter shows you the three most general commands: COPY and XCOPY to copy files, and MOVE to move them. You will learn to:

- Copy a single file to the same directory, giving the file a new name
- Copy files to another directory, with or without new names
- Copy files to your printer or other devices
- Copy files from one branch to another
- Move files to another directory

Network Note: The procedures and commands in this chapter work on local drives. They may or may not work on a network drive, depending on your access rights. For example, you may be able to copy a file from a network drive to your local drive but not move it to your local drive because you do not have permission to delete a file from the network drive.

Using the COPY Command

DOS's original copying command was COPY (see Figure 15.1), which can be used to copy one or more files from a source to a destination.

COPY

Syntax:

`COPY source [destination] [/[-]Y]`

Parameters and switches:

source	Identifies file(s) to copy.
destination	Identifies location and/or name of copy.
/Y	Replaces destination files without confirmation.
/-Y	Requires confirmation to replace destination files.

Figure 15.1. COPY *command summary.*

Probably the simplest use of COPY is to make a copy of one file, keeping the copy in the same directory but giving it a new name. Try making a copy of HELP.COM:

1. Enter CD \DOS to switch to the DOS directory. (You could make the copy without being in the source directory, but it's a lot more difficult because you have to include path names on both the source and destination filespec.)

2. Enter COPY HELP.COM PRACTICE.XXX.

   You should get the message 1 file(s) copied.

It's almost as easy to copy a file to another directory:

1. Make a new directory called TRIAL as a child of the DOS directory by entering the command MD TRIAL.

2. Enter COPY PRACTICE.XXX TRIAL to copy PRACTICE.XXX to the new directory.

Because the command doesn't specify a destination file name, the new copy also is named PRACTICE.XXX. If you want the new copy to have a different name, include the new name in the destination:

1. Enter COPY PRACTICE.XXX TRIAL\FILE1.XXX to copy the file to the TRIAL directory and name it FILE1.XXX.

   You should get the message 1 file(s) copied.

2. Enter DIR TRIAL to list the files in your TRIAL directory.

   You should see PRACTICE.XXX and FILE1.XXX.

In these examples, the original file is unchanged. The copy has the same date and time stamp as the original file. The archive attribute of the copy is turned on and the hidden, system, and read-only attributes are turned off.

Problem: I tried to access a file and got the message File not found. Why can't DOS find my file?

Check first to make sure that you have typed the file name correctly. If you made a typing error, correct the command and try again.

Next, check to make sure that you are referencing the right directory. If the file is not in the current directory, you must prefix the file name with the path name to tell DOS where to find the file. For example, if the current drive is C:\DOS and you want the file named RUNYMEDE in the root directory of drive A, you must reference the file as A:\RUNYMEDE.

Finally, check to see if the file is a hidden or system file. Many DOS commands, including COPY, XCOPY, MOVE, REN, and DEL, do not recognize a hidden or system file. To check the file's attributes, enter **ATTRIB** *filespec*. If the file has a positive hidden or system attribute and you decide that you still want to process it, enter **ATTRIB** *filespec* **-H** (if it's hidden), or **-S** (if it's a system file) to turn off the attribute. Use both –H and –S in the same command if it's both hidden and system. (See ATTRIB to learn more about these commands.) After you have turned off the attribute, you can process the file as a normal file.

When you don't specify a destination directory, COPY places the new file into the current directory. Try copying FILE1.XXX from TRIAL to the current directory:

1. Enter the command **COPY \TRIAL\FILE1.XXX**.

   You should get the message 1 file(s) copied.

2. Enter **DIR FILE1.XXX** to see the FILE1.XXX file in the current directory.

Problem: I tried to copy a file and got the message File cannot be copied onto itself. What's wrong?

You can't copy a file within its own directory without changing its name. Be sure to specify a new file name, a different directory name, or both, in the destination parameter of the COPY or XCOPY command.

Note: You can copy files from, but not to, a read-only drive such as a CD-ROM drive. And, you can't move files either from or to a read-only drive.

Copying More Than One File

You can copy several files at once by using a global filespec. Try copying a few of the .HLP files from the DOS directory to the TRIAL directory. To keep the task fairly short, just copy files whose names start with D:

1. Make sure you are in the DOS directory.

2. Enter **COPY D*.HLP TRIAL** to copy some .HLP files to the TRIAL directory.

   You should see a list of files as DOS copies them.

Note: Each copy is given the same name as the original, the date and time stamp of the original, a positive archive attribute, and negative read-only, hidden, and system attributes.

Problem: I was in the middle of copying a group of files when I got a `Disk full` message and the copy job stopped. How can I finish copying the files?

First, you need to free up some space on the disk. Delete any unnecessary files or compress the disk. (You don't necessarily have to delete files from the copy task's destination directory. Deleting files from any directory on the drive will free up the space you need.) If you can't find some space, you won't be able to complete the job with this disk.

One special note: If you usually use DOS's Delete Sentry but you have disabled it momentarily, your drive may appear full when it isn't. Enable Delete Sentry to free up the space so that you can complete your copy task.

There is no good way to resume this job in the middle. You will have to start again from the beginning, recopying the same files that you have already copied. Consider using the /Y switch on the `COPY` or `XCOPY` command so that you don't have to confirm each file as it is copied again. However, if there's a chance that the destination directory contains some other files that should not be replaced, omit the /Y switch so that you can review each replacement.

You can change file names when you make multiple copies by including a global filespec for the destination. Try copying all .HLP files that start with M to TRIAL, but change their extensions to XXX:

1. Enter the command **COPY M*.HLP TRIAL*.XXX**.

    You should see a list of files as they are copied. You'll see the source file names, not the new ones.

2. Enter **DIR TRIAL** to see all the files in your practice directory.

    You should see the D*.HLP files and the M*.XXX files.

Replacing Existing Copies

Sometimes when you try to copy a file to a different directory, that directory already has a file of the same name. DOS doesn't let you have two files with the same name in a directory, so something has to give. There's a big difference between how DOS 6.0 and DOS 6.2 handle this situation.

In DOS 6.0 (and earlier versions), `COPY` automatically replaces the existing file without warning unless it has the read-only attribute. UNDELETE doesn't perceive the replacement as a deletion, so it doesn't preserve any information about the former copy. Basically, once `COPY` clobbers it, you can't recover the data through any DOS facility.

Tip: If you accidentally overwrite an important file in a move or copy operation, The Norton Utilities' Unerase utility can sometimes recover all or part of the clobbered file's data. But *don't do anything else* with your computer until you have rescued the data. In fact, I wouldn't even turn it off. Just leave it running until you have the chance to recover the needed data. (If you have to wait more than a few minutes and don't have a screen saver, you should turn off your monitor until you're ready to run Unerase.)

With DOS 6.2 and 6.22, COPY has been changed to protect existing files. When you're working at the command prompt, it asks if you want to overwrite the existing file. If you type **Y**, the file is replaced. If you type **N**, the copy is canceled and you can try again with another name. You can also answer A, for *All*, which cancels the protection feature for the rest of the job. That is, any subsequent files accessed by the current command are overwritten without warning. If you know that you're going to overwrite one or more files and want to inhibit the protection feature right from the start, include the /Y switch in the command.

Problem: I tried to access a file and got the message Access denied. Why won't DOS process my file?

The file's read-only attribute is positive. Many DOS commands, including MOVE, REN, and DEL, will not process a read-only file. COPY and XCOPY won't overwrite one.

If you're sure that you want to process the file, you must remove its read-only attribute first. Enter the command **ATTRIB *filespec* -R** to remove the attribute. Then, you can process the file as a normal file. (Look up ATTRIB to see more about this command.)

Try copying the D*.HLP files from DOS to TRIAL again:

1. Make sure you're in the DOS directory.

2. Enter **COPY D*.HLP TRIAL** to start the copy process.

   If you're using DOS 6.0 or earlier, the copies are made without further ado; skip the rest of this exercise. If you're using DOS 6.2 or later, the message Overwrite TRIAL*filename* (Yes/No/All) appears.

3. Enter **Y** to overwrite the first file.

   The message Overwrite TRIAL*filename* (Yes/No/All) appears for the next file.

4. Enter **N** to skip the next file.

   The message Overwrite TRIAL*filename* (Yes/No/All) appears for the next file. (It appears faster this time because DOS didn't have to take time to copy the file.)

5. Enter **A** to overwrite all the remaining files.

The remaining files are listed, followed by the number of files copied.

Now try the same task again, but this time use the /Y switch to disable the confirmation feature:

1. Make sure you're in the DOS directory.

2. Enter `COPY D*.HLP TRIAL /Y` to start the copy process.

   The copies are made without further ado.

Note: DOS's overwrite protection works differently with commands in a batch file, where it is automatically turned off and you must use the /-Y switch to enable it. Chapter 20, "Basic Batch Programs," discusses batch programs.

Looking Ahead: If you don't like the default overwrite protection of the newer DOS versions, you can change it. Chapter 43, "DOS and the Environment," shows you how.

Printing Text Files Quickly with COPY

The source or destination for `COPY` can be a device, such as COM1 (the first serial port), or PRN (the default printer). Refer back to Table 13.1 in Chapter 13, "DOSKEY," for the complete set of device names.

Network Note: If the device in question is a shared resource, your network software will direct the output to the correct printer, placing it in the queue to await its turn to print.

The most common way to use a device with `COPY` is to make a quick-and-dirty printout of an ASCII text file. Try printing README.TXT:

1. Make sure your printer is ready. (See the note in "Printing through DOS Shell" in Chapter 9, "Additional File Management in the Shell," for a list of items to check.)

2. Enter `COPY README.TXT PRN` to print README.TXT.

   If it doesn't print, see the Problem Solver in the section titled "Redirecting Command Output" in Chapter 12, "Working at the Command Prompt."

A printout produced this way is completely unformatted. `COPY` doesn't even break it into pages like the `PRINT` function does; it prints over the perforated edges of continuous-form paper. The only advantage to printing files this way is that you don't have to load and initialize `PRINT`.

Note: Sometimes a software package will include a README text file that has headings, page numbers, and spacing inserted so that it will copy nicely to your printer, as long as you're using standard size paper and it is lined up fairly accurately.

Looking Ahead: COPY has several features that can be helpful. For example, it can concatenate (combine) two or more files into one. Chapter 40, "Advanced Copying Techniques," covers COPY's advanced features.

Using the *XCOPY* Command

DOS includes a newer, faster, and more powerful command for copying files called XCOPY (for extended copy). One factor that makes XCOPY so much faster than COPY is how it handles multiple files. COPY copies each one individually. XCOPY copies as much data into memory in one move as it can, then writes that amount to the destination directory. Sometimes it can do the entire job in two steps. Figure 15.2 shows the XCOPY command summary.

XCOPY

Copies files and subdirectories.

Syntax:

```
XCOPY source [destination] [/S] [/E][/[-]Y]
```

Parameters and Switches:

source	Identifies the file(s) you want to copy.
destination	Specifies the location where the copy should be written; the default is the current directory.
/S	Extends copying to the entire branch headed by the source directory.
/E	Copies empty subdirectories when copying to the entire branch. You must select /S if you use /E.
/Y	Replaces destination files without confirmation.
/-Y	Requires confirmation to replace destination files.

Figure 15.2. *XCOPY command summary.*

In addition to outright speed, one of XCOPY's major advantages over COPY is that it copies subdirectories. XCOPY can duplicate an entire branch on the target drive.

> **Warning:** Like COPY, XCOPY before DOS 6.2 overwrites a file in a destination directory without warning if it has the same name as the intended copy. You can't undelete a file overwritten this way with DOS 6's UNDELETE facility. Starting with DOS 6.2, XCOPY protects files in the same way that COPY does.

Try copying HELP.COM from DOS to TRIAL using XCOPY:

1. Make sure that DOS is the current directory. (You don't have to copy from the current directory all the time. But, the command in step 2 assumes that DOS is the current directory.)

2. Enter **XCOPY HELP.COM TRIAL**.

   This command produces these messages:

   ```
   Reading source file(s)...

   HELP.COM

           1 File(s) copied
   ```

The first line appears while XCOPY locates and reads MYFILE.DAT; the second line appears while it writes MYFILE.DAT; and the last line appears when the job is finished. When multiple files are involved, XCOPY reads as many files as it can into memory while you see the `Reading source file(s)` message. Then, it writes those files, displaying the name of each file in turn. It repeats this process as many times as necessary to complete the job. The summary line appears only once, at the end of the job.

> **Tip:** The more memory available to XCOPY, the faster it works.

Specifying a Directory or a File

Suppose you specify a destination that doesn't exist. XCOPY doesn't know whether you want to create a new file of that name or a new directory of that name. (COPY doesn't have the same problem, because COPY can't create directories.) XCOPY displays the following message (where TEMPY is the requested destination):

```
Does TEMPY specify a file name
or directory name on the target
(F = file, D = directory)?
```

Note: XCOPY asks this question even if the destination identifies an existing file; it suppresses the question only if the destination identifies an existing directory.

If you press **F**, XCOPY creates a new TEMPY file or overwrites the existing TEMPY file in the current directory. If you press **D**, XCOPY creates a new TEMPY subdirectory as a child of the current directory and copies the file (with the original name) to it.

Try copying HELP.COM to a new directory named TRIAL2:

1. Make sure that DOS is the current directory.

2. Enter **XCOPY HELP.COM TRIAL2**.

   XCOPY asks if TRIAL2 is a file or directory.

3. Press **D** for directory. (You don't have to press Enter.)

   XCOPY creates the new directory and copies HELP.COM to it.

4. Enter **DIR TRIAL2** to list the contents of the new directory.

   You should see that HELP.COM is the only file in the directory.

Tip: You can bypass the "file or directory" question by including a backslash as the last character of the destination parameter, as in **TRIAL2**. Then XCOPY knows that you want a new directory. It creates the directory and copies the requested files to it.

If you want the copy to have a new name, such as NEWFILE.DAT, you could enter the following command:

```
XCOPY HELP.COM TRIAL2\NEWFILE.DAT
```

Again, XCOPY asks you whether NEWFILE.DAT is a file or a directory (even if \TRIAL2\NEWFILE.DAT already exists as a file) and proceeds according to your answer. Try copying HELP.COM to TRIAL2 again, but this time name it NEWFILE.DAT:

1. Enter **XCOPY HELP.COM TRIAL2\NEWFILE.DAT**.

   XCOPY asks if NEWFILE.DAT is a file or directory.

2. Press **F** for file.

   XCOPY copies the file to TRIAL2 and names it NEWFILE.DAT.

3. Enter **DIR TRIAL2** to see the directory listing.

   You should see HELP.COM and NEWFILE.DAT.

Note: As with COPY, when XCOPY copies a file, the original file is unchanged; the copy receives the same date and time stamp as the original; the archive attribute of the copy is turned on; and the hidden, system, and read-only attributes are turned off. XCOPY can't copy hidden or system files.

Problem: I tried to create a new directory with XCOPY and got the message Unable to create directory. What's wrong?

The new directory name you requested already exists in the parent directory, either as a file or as a directory. In DOS, a directory cannot contain a file and a subdirectory with the same name. You can resolve the problem by deleting or renaming the file, or by using a different subdirectory name.

Using XCOPY with Multiple Files

You should always use XCOPY instead of COPY for multiple files because XCOPY is so much faster. The command syntaxes are similar. Suppose you want to copy all the D*.HLP files from DOS to a new directory named TRIAL3, which you want XCOPY to create:

1. Make sure that DOS is the current directory.
2. Enter **XCOPY D*.HLP TRIAL3**\. (The trailing backslash avoids the "file or directory" question.)

   XCOPY creates the new directory and copies the requested files to it.
3. Enter **DIR TRIAL3** to list the contents of the new directory.

   It should contain several D*.HLP files.

An XCOPY command, with wildcards in both the source and destination, has the same effect as the COPY command. In the following example, XCOPY knows that the destination is a file name, so it doesn't ask the "file or directory" question:

```
XCOPY *.BAT *.SAV
```

If you try to copy multiple files to a single destination, you might think XCOPY would realize the destination is a directory, but it doesn't. Suppose that you enter this command:

```
XCOPY *.BAT \NEW
```

XCOPY asks the familiar "file or directory" question. What's more, if you indicate that \NEW is a file, XCOPY copies each .BAT file to \NEW in turn. The final content of \NEW is a copy of the last source file copied. This is probably not what you had in mind.

Copying Entire Branches

One major advantage of XCOPY over COPY is that it works with entire branches. When you include the /S switch in the XCOPY command, XCOPY searches an entire branch for files that match the source filespec. It copies them to the target branch, creating subdirectories as needed to receive the copies.

Suppose, for example, that you copy C:*.SAV to the floppy in drive A using the /S switch. And, suppose that drive C contains .SAV files in the following directories:

```
\ (the root directory)
\BUDGET
\BUDGET\BACKUP
\BANDS\LETTERS
```

XCOPY copies the .SAV files from the root directory of C to the root directory of A. It creates A:\BUDGET (unless it already exists) and copies the .SAV files from C:\BUDGET to A:\BUDGET. Similarly, it creates A:\BUDGET\BACKUP and copies the necessary files to it from C:\BUDGET\BACKUP. XCOPY must create A:\BANDS in order to create A:\BANDS\LETTERS, unless those directories already exist on A. Then, it copies the .SAV files from C:\BANDS\LETTERS to A:\BANDS\LETTERS.

Note: If the command includes the /E switch instead of /S, XCOPY duplicates the entire directory structure of the source branch, even if some of the directories receive no copied files. In the preceding example in which the root directory heads the source branch, the entire directory structure of drive C would be recreated on A, but only the .SAV files would be copied. In versions of DOS before 6.2, you can't use /E unless you specify /S too.

Network Note: Depending on your access rights, you may not be permitted to create a new directory on a network drive. If not, you won't be able to use XCOPY to duplicate a branch on the drive, even though you can use XCOPY to copy files to it if it already exists.

Suppose that you're ready to put all your 1992 financial records onto a floppy disk for permanent storage and remove them from your hard disk. You can do it with only the following two commands, provided that the whole 1992 branch fits on one disk, and that no hidden or system files or subdirectories are involved:

```
XCOPY C:\FINANCE\Y1992\*.* A:\ /S
DELTREE C:\FINANCE\Y1992
```

Try copying all the .XXX files from the practice branch headed by your DOS directory to a disk in drive A:

1. Insert a formatted but unused floppy disk into drive A. (If you don't have a floppy that has been formatted but not used, skip this exercise.)

2. Make sure that C:\DOS is the current directory.

3. Enter **XCOPY *.XXX A:\ /E**.

   XCOPY lists the files with their path names as it creates the directories and copies the files.

4. To see the result on A, enter **TREE A:\ /F**.

   TREE displays the directory structure of drive A, including the files in each directory (because of the /F switch). You should see that the root directory and the TRIAL directory contain some .XXX files, but the TRIAL2 and TRIAL3 directories are empty.

Looking Ahead: XCOPY offers some advanced features that you may occasionally find useful. For example, you can select files to be copied based on their archive attributes, date stamp, or time stamp.

If you need to copy a huge file to a floppy, and COPY or XCOPY can't fit it on the disk, MSBACKUP can span it over two or more disks. Chapter 23, "MSBACKUP and MWBACKUP," explains MSBACKUP.

The REPLACE command, described in Chapter 40, can select files for copying by comparing the source and target directories.

Moving Files

Until DOS 6, you moved files from the command prompt by copying them, making sure that the copy was completed successfully, and then deleting the originals. This process was not as simple as it sounds; it's not easy to determine whether all requested files are successfully copied to the destination before deleting them from the source.

DOS 6.0 introduced a new command, MOVE, that moves files in one step. (It's the same MOVE command that you used to rename directories in Chapter 14, "Managing Directories.") DOS 6.2 enhanced the MOVE command with the same overwrite protection that COPY and XCOPY have. Figure 15.3 shows the command summary for the file move function of MOVE.

MOVE

Moves one or more files and renames a file.

Syntax:

```
MOVE [/[-]Y] filespec [...] destination
```

Parameters and switches:

filespec	Identifies the file(s) you want to move or rename.
destination	Identifies the file or directory to which you want to move the file(s), or the new name of the file.
/Y	Replaces destination files without confirmation.
/-Y	Requires confirmation to replace destination files.

Figure 15.3. *MOVE command summary (to move files).*

Try moving some files one at a time:

1. If you are not in the DOS directory, switch to it now.

2. Enter **MOVE PRACTICE.XXX TRIAL2**.

   DOS moves the PRACTICE.XXX file to the TRIAL2 directory.

3. Enter **MOVE FILE1.XXX TRIAL**.

   Since TRIAL already has a file named FILE1.XXX, DOS asks if you want to overwrite it.

4. Enter **Y** to replace the file.

Problem: I entered a MOVE command and got the message Too many parameters.

You included /Y as the last parameter on the command line. MOVE treats the last parameter on the line as the destination, so you must put /Y earlier in the command.

Problem: I tried to move a file and got the message Unable to create destination. How can I move my file?

There's a read-only file in the destination directory with the same name as the file you're trying to move. Either turn off the read-only attribute of the destination file so that it can be overwritten, change the name of the destination file, or change the name of the source file.

Moving Multiple Files

You can use wildcards in the source file name to move more than one file. The destination must be a directory, however; you can't specify a destination file name, even with wildcards.

Try moving a group of files:

1. Switch to the TRIAL directory.
2. Enter **MOVE *.XXX TRIAL2** to move all the .XXX files to the TRIAL2 directory.

Problem: I tried to move a set of files to another directory and got the message `Cannot move multiple files to a single file`. What's wrong, and how can I move my files?

DOS doesn't recognize the destination directory name that you specified. If the directory already exists, you either misspelled the name or misstated the path. Fix the command and try again.

If the directory doesn't exist and you're trying to create it with this command, when MOVE asks `Make directory "name"? [yn]`, be sure to enter **Y** to create the new directory.

You also can use a list of source file names followed by a destination. The following example moves all MY*.* files from the current directory, along with YOURFIL.TXT and \OURFIL.DAT, to the \NEW directory:

```
MOVE MY*.* YOURFIL.TXT \OURFIL.DAT \NEW
```

Tip: If you omit the destination for COPY or XCOPY, the current directory is assumed as the destination. MOVE requires a destination parameter, but you can use a single dot (.) to specify the current directory as the destination.

MOVE always assumes that the last parameter on the command line is the destination; every filespec before that is a source file. As always, when more than one file is being moved, the destination must be a directory. If the directory does not exist, MOVE asks `Make directory "name"? [yn]`. If you answer **Y**, MOVE creates the directory and moves the files to it.

Tip: You can bypass the "Make directory" question by including the /Y switch in the MOVE command.

Try moving some files to a new directory created by MOVE:

1. Switch to the TRIAL2 directory.

2. Enter **MOVE *.* \DOS\TRIAL4**.

   MOVE asks `Make directory "\c:\dos\trial4"? [yn]`.

3. Enter **Y**.

   MOVE makes the directory and moves the requested files. You see the list of files as they are moved.

Problem: I tried to move all the files from a directory and got the message `Unable to open source`.

MOVE displays this message when it encounters a subdirectory in the source directory. The message simply tells you that the subdirectory was not moved. You can safely ignore the message.

Using MOVE to Rename Files

If you move a file to its own directory, the effect is to rename it. Unfortunately, before DOS 6.2, MOVE replaced an existing file of the desired name without warning, and the file couldn't be undeleted by DOS 6's UNDELETE facility (even with Delete Sentry). This makes the pre-6.2 MOVE dangerous compared to the REN command, which refuses to rename a file when the new name already is in use in the directory. The REN command is explained in Chapter 16, "Additional File Management."

Cleaning Up Your Directories

You have created a number of directories in this chapter. Enter the following command to remove them, as well as the files they contain:

DELTREE \DOS\TRIAL*

On Your Own

You have learned how to use COPY, XCOPY, and MOVE to copy and move files. The following items will help you practice these techniques on your own:

1. Copy all the COMMAND.COM files on your hard drive to comparable directories on drive A.

2. List a directory of drive A to see the new structure and files.

3. Move all the files from A:\ to A:\dos.

4. Delete the structure on A.

16

Additional File Management

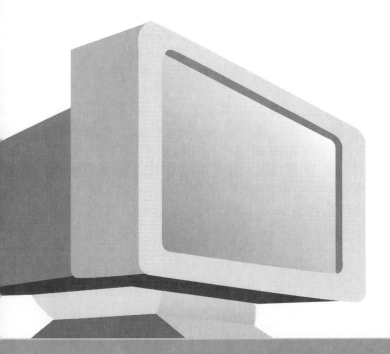

Introduction

DOS includes a number of commands and utilities for managing files from the command prompt and from within batch programs.

Overview

Most applications give you a limited ability to manage files, but you usually can't do such things as set attributes, compare two versions of a file, or even delete a file. DOS provides commands for all these tasks. And, because it can be a pain to wait for an application to load just to take a quick look at a file, DOS will also display and print a text file.

In this chapter, you will learn how to:

- Rename files
- View and change file and directory attributes
- Delete files
- Display text files on your monitor
- Print text files
- Compare two files and display the differences

Network Note: You won't have any trouble working on files on your local drives, but you may or may not be able to change or delete files on a network drive, depending on your access rights.

Note: Because you can't write on a read-only drive, you can't change attributes, or rename or delete files on a CD-ROM drive. But you can view attributes, display and print text files (such as README files), and compare files.

Creating Some Practice Files

Before you start learning how to manage files, you'll need some files to practice on. Create them now:

1. Switch to the root directory.
2. Create a new directory named \PRACTICE and copy all the \DOS*.HLP files to it. (Reminder: You can do this in one command with XCOPY.)

Using REN To Rename Files

When you want to rename one or more files at the command prompt, you use the REN command. (See Figure 16.1.)

REN

REN filespec newname

Parameters:

filespec   Identifies the file(s) to be renamed.

newname   Specifies the new name(s) for the file(s).

Figure 16.1. REN *command summary.*

REN has a small advantage over the Shell's rename feature. You can't perform a group rename in the Shell, but you can with the REN command. Try renaming all the .HLP files in your PRACTICE directory as .XXX files:

1. Enter **CD \PRACTICE** to switch to your practice directory.

   It's very important to be in the PRACTICE directory for this exercise. You don't want to rename any .HLP files in a real directory.

2. Enter **DIR** to make sure that you are in the PRACTICE directory and that the only files present are .HLP files.

   If you find that you are in another directory, go back to step 1.

3. Enter **REN *.HLP *.XXX** to rename all the .HLP files.

   If you don't get an error message, the files were renamed.

4. Enter **DIR** again to see the renamed files.

   You should see that all your files now have the .XXX extension.

Problem: I tried to rename a file and got the message `Duplicate filename or file not found`. What does this mean?

Unfortunately, REN combines two problems into one message, leaving you to figure out for yourself which problem you're facing. Either the filespec that you entered does not identify an existing file, or the new name that you requested already exists in the directory.

Check the original filespec first. Did you misspell it or forget to include a path name? Try `DIR filespec` to make sure the file exists. If you find that the name is wrong, correct the command and try again.

If you're sure that the original filespec is correct, there must already be a file or subdirectory with the name that you're trying to assign. (You can use the `/A` switch on the `DIR` command to list all the files and subdirectories in a directory, including hidden and system ones.) Re-enter the command using a different new name.

If you're sure that the original filespec is correct and the new name doesn't duplicate an existing name, the file must be a hidden or system file. Use `ATTRIB filespec` to find out the file's attributes. Then, use `ATTRIB filespec` with the `-H` switch and/or the `-S` switch to turn off the hidden and system attributes. After you have renamed the file, use `ATTRIB filespec` with the `+H` switch and/or the `+S` switch to restore the hidden and system attributes.

Peter's Principle: Keep group renames simple.

Because `REN` doesn't have a confirmation option, you can end up with unexpected results if you try to get too fancy or do too much with one command. For example, suppose you want to rename CH01.DOC through CH15.DOC as OLD01.DOC through OLD15.DOC. If you enter the command **REN CH*.DOC OLD*.DOC**, CH01.DOC through CH10.DOC will be renamed as OLD1.DOC through OLD0.DOC, and CH11.DOC through CH15.DOC produce error messages because the names OLD1.DOC through OLD5.DOC already exist.

Managing Attributes with the ATTRIB Command

File attributes affect most of the other commands that you'll learn in this chapter. For example, you can't delete or rename a file with a positive hidden or system attribute. You examine and change attributes with the `ATTRIB` command. (See Figure 16.2.) `ATTRIB` can be used for both files and directories.

When you enter a specific or global filespec without any switches, ATTRIB displays the attributes of those files. Try displaying the attributes of the files in the PRACTICE directory:

1. If you're not in the \PRACTICE directory, change to it now so that you don't have to include path names with your filespecs.

2. Enter **ATTRIB HELP.XXX** to see the attributes of that specific file.

ATTRIB displays a message something like this:

```
A       C:\PRACTICE\HELP.XXX
```

The attributes are shown on the left. An A means that the file has a positive archive attribute. S, H, and R mean positive system, hidden, and read-only attributes, respectively. If a letter is missing, as in the preceding example, that attribute is negative.

3. Enter **ATTRIB M*.*** to see the attributes of those files starting with M in the current directory. (Reminder: You can recall the previous ATTRIB command and edit it.)

   ATTRIB displays the requested attributes.

4. Enter **ATTRIB** with no parameters to see the attributes of all the files in the directory.

   ATTRIB displays the requested attributes.

ATTRIB

Displays or changes file and directory attributes.

Syntax:

```
ATTRIB [+R ¦ –R] [+A ¦ –A] [+H ¦ –H] [+S ¦ –S] [filespec [/S]
```

Parameters and Switches:

none	Shows the attributes of all files in the current directory.
+R ¦ –R	Turns on or off the read-only attribute.
+A ¦ –A	Turns on or off the archive attribute.
+H ¦ –H	Turns on or off the system hidden attribute.
filespec	Identifies the file(s) to process.
/S	Processes all files in the branch headed by the current or specified directory.

Figure 16.2. *ATTRIB command summary.*

To change attributes, you include attribute switches in the command. A switch preceded by + turns on an attribute; a switch preceded by – turns it off. Suppose that you want to turn off the archive attribute and turn on the hidden attribute for HELP.XXX:

1. Enter **ATTRIB HELP.XXX -A +H**.

   Unfortunately, ATTRIB does not confirm the changed attributes.

2. Enter **DIR HELP.XXX** to see if the file is truly hidden.

   You should get the File not found message.

3. Enter **ATTRIB HELP.XXX** to see the attributes for the file. (Last reminder for this chapter: If you have installed DOSKEY, you can recall the previous ATTRIB command and edit it.)

    ATTRIB will display a file's attributes even though the file is hidden. The message should look something like this:

    ```
    H    C:\PRACTICE\HELP.XXX
    ```

4. Enter **ATTRIB MW*.XXX +S** to make some of the files in your directory system files.

5. Enter **ATTRIB DOS*.XXX +R** to make some of the files in your directory read-only files.

6. Enter **ATTRIB** (with no parameters) to list the attributes of all the files in the directory.

Changing the Attributes of Hidden and System Files

It takes a little extra work to change the attributes of a hidden or system file. ATTRIB won't change any other attributes unless you deal with the hidden/system attribute also. The long way around this complication is to turn off the hidden/system attribute, change the attributes you want, and then turn on the hidden/system attribute again. But there's an easier way. You can confirm the hidden or system attribute while changing whatever other attributes you want in the same command.

Try making HELP.XXX a read-only file:

1. Enter **ATTRIB HELP.XXX +R**.

    Because HELP.XXX is a hidden file, you should get an error message:

    ```
    Not resetting hidden file C:\PRACTICE\HELP.XXX
    ```

2. Add the +H switch to the command, as in ATTRIB HELP.XXX +R +H.

    This time, you get no error message.

3. Enter **ATTRIB HELP.XXX** to see the attributes of the file.

    You should see that it is both hidden and read-only.

If you want to turn off the hidden/system attribute while setting another attribute, you can use -H or -S instead of +H or +S. As long as you deal with the hidden/system attribute in the command—by either confirming it or turning it off—you can set other attributes too.

When a file's hidden and system attributes are both positive, ATTRIB reports the hidden attribute but not the system one. So, if you get the message Not resetting hidden file *filespec*, the file might also be a system file. (Many hidden files are also system files.) If both attributes are positive, you must deal with them both in the command.

Suppose all four attributes are turned on for SECRET.TXT. To turn off the read-only attribute while leaving the others on, you would have to enter **ATTRIB SECRET.TXT +H +S -R**. The archive attribute does not need to be confirmed. To turn off the system attribute but not the hidden attribute, you would enter **ATTRIB SECRET.TXT +H -S**. (Neither the archive attribute nor the read-only attribute need to be confirmed.)

> **Problem:** I tried to change or delete a file and got the message Write-protect error writing drive A, Abort, Retry, Fail? How can I process this file?
>
> You can't change or delete a file on a write-protected disk because you're physically blocked from writing on the disk. You can't even change its name or attributes.
>
> If you decide that you really want to change or delete the file, take the disk out of the drive, remove its write-protection, and reinsert it in the drive. Then press R for Retry.
>
> If you decide that you don't want to change the file after all, or if you want to take the time to find out why the disk is write-protected before deciding, press A for Abort to cancel the command and get back to the command prompt.

Setting Attributes Throughout a Branch

When you use a global filespec, you can view or change several files' attributes with one command. The /S switch extends the range of the command throughout the entire branch headed by the specified directory. Fortunately, you'll see a Not resetting... message for each hidden/system file that you try to change. You need to treat those files separately.

Working with Directory Attributes

Directories can have attributes just as files can. You can, for example, hide a directory and it will not show up in DIR or TREE listings. ATTRIB works with a directory only if you supply its specific name; global filespecs never access directories with ATTRIB.

Try hiding the PRACTICE directory:

1. Switch to the parent directory. (You can't change the attributes of the directory you're in.)
2. Enter **TREE** to display the complete branch.

   You should see PRACTICE in the directory tree.
3. Enter **ATTRIB PRACTICE +H** to hide the directory.
4. Enter **TREE** again.

   This time, PRACTICE should not show up.

DIR won't list a hidden directory when you display the parent's contents. But, if you reference the directory by name, you can list it, switch to it, and so on. Thus, if you know its name, you can access it; if you don't, you can't. Try it yourself:

1. Enter **DIR**.

   PRACTICE should not show up in the directory listing.

2. Now enter **DIR PRACTICE**.

   DOS lists the contents of the DIR directory, even though it's hidden.

3. Enter **CD PRACTICE** to switch to the PRACTICE directory.

   You won't have any trouble entering the directory, even though it's hidden.

> **Warning:** Don't count on hiding a directory as a security measure. Most programs (including DOS Shell) ignore directory attributes. And, anyone with a little knowledge of DOS knows how to use the /A switch to find out what hidden and system subdirectories and files a directory contains.

Deleting Files

The command prompt is not the best place to delete files. Programs such as Windows and DOS Shell protect your files by making you confirm deletions. And, for multiple files, you can select the specific files to delete rather than using a global filespec that might delete more files than you intended. If you really want to delete files at the command prompt, the DEL command includes a safety switch, called /P, that you should make it a habit to use. (See Figure 16.3.) With /P, DEL asks for confirmation before deleting a file.

DEL
Syntax:
DEL *filespec* [/P]
Parameters and Switches:
filespec   Identifies the file(s) to delete.
/P   Prompts for confirmation before each deletion.

Figure 16.3.   *DEL command summary.*

Whenever you use DEL, keep its limitations in mind:

- If you don't use the /P switch, DEL deletes files without warning or confirmation; it doesn't even display the names of the files that it deletes.

- A global filespec could easily delete more files than you intended. On the other hand, it could delete fewer files than you intended, as the following two items explain.

- DEL will not delete hidden or system files. When you use a specific filename, you see a `File not found` message for a hidden or system file. But with a global filename, even if you use /P, DEL doesn't display any message about the files that it skips.

- DEL also will not delete a read-only file. With a specific filespec, you see an `Access denied` message. The same is true if you use a global filespec with /P. But, if you use a global filespec without /P, you receive no warning that read-only files were skipped.

Bearing all these limitations in mind, suppose that you want to delete EDIT.XXX from the PRACTICE directory:

1. Enter **DEL EDIT.XXX /P**.

   DOS displays this message:

   ```
   C:\PRACTICE\EDIT.XXX,    Delete (Y/N)?
   ```

2. Make sure the path name and filename are both correct. If not, enter N and try again.

3. When the path name and filename are both correct, enter Y to delete the file.

   If you don't get any error message, the file was deleted.

> **Peter's Principle:** Always use the /P switch on the DEL command.
>
> Even when you're deleting a single file, /P protects you from misspelling the filespec and accidentally deleting the wrong file. When you're deleting a group of files with a global filespec, it's doubly important to use /P so that you can confirm each file that will be deleted.
>
> But /P doesn't do you any good if you fall into the habit of pressing Y without inspecting each filespec that is displayed. Try to convince yourself to read each filespec carefully before pressing Y.

Deleting Multiple Files

You can delete a group of files with a global filespec:

1. Enter **DEL MS*.XXX /P** to delete all .XXX files starting with MS in the PRACTICE directory.

   DOS asks you to confirm the first file that matches the filespec.

2. Check the filespec carefully. If it's wrong, press Ctrl+Break to cancel the entire command and start over.

Tip: Ctrl+Break cancels many programs in midstream. It generally works with the older style of program that just displays messages on the command prompt screen and doesn't open up any kind of GUI. For example, it works with DEL, REN, and TYPE, but not with DOSSHELL or MSBACKUP.

If you see that a program such as DEL or TYPE is accessing the wrong directory or files, press Ctrl+Break to kill it and get back to the command prompt.

3. If the path name and the filename are correct, press Y to delete the file.

   DOS asks you to confirm the next file that matches the filespec.

4. Repeat step 3 until all the files are deleted.

Deleting Protected Files

If you see the message `Access denied`, the file is read-only and can't be deleted until you change that attribute. You might also get the message `File not found`; this message means either that it's a hidden or system file, or that the file doesn't exist in the current (or specified) directory.

Try deleting some files that are protected by attributes:

1. Try to delete DOSHELP.XXX.

   DOSHELP.XXX should be a read-only file, so you should get the `Access denied` message.

2. Try to delete HELP.XXX.

   HELP.XXX should be a hidden file, so you should get the `File not found` message.

Note: DOS 6 includes an `UNDELETE` command to recover files if you change your mind after deleting them. Chapter 26, "Using UNDELETE," shows you how to use `UNDELETE`.

Deleting All the Files in a Directory

To delete all the files in a directory, you don't have to include a filespec. If you enter just the path name, DELETE assumes that you mean all the files in the directory. So, to delete all the files in the root directory of drive A, you would enter **DEL A:**. To delete all the files in the current directory, you can enter just **DEL .** or **DEL *.***; both commands have the same result.

When you try to empty a directory, DOS gives you a chance to change your mind by displaying this message:

```
All the files in the directory will be deleted!
Are you sure (Y/N)?
```

You must enter Y to continue.

Try deleting all the files in the current directory:

1. Make sure that the \PRACTICE directory is the current directory.

2. Enter **DEL .** to delete all the files.

   DOS asks if you're sure.

3. Enter N to cancel the command.

Looking Ahead: DEL can handle only one directory at a time, but the DELTREE command can delete files throughout a branch, regardless of attributes. Chapter 39, "Directory Management," shows you how to do this.

Displaying Files with the *TYPE* Command

The TYPE command displays a file on the command prompt screen. (See Figure 16.4.) TYPE can be handy to take a quick peek at a short ASCII text file such as CONFIG.SYS. In other situations, you might not be very happy with the results, because TYPE simply dumps the text onto the screen with no formatting, and you can't scroll around in the file.

TYPE

Displays the contents of a file.

Syntax:

TYPE *filespec*

Parameter:

filespec   Identifies the file that you want to view.

Figure 16.4.   *TYPE command summary.*

If a file is too long to fit on your screen, the beginning disappears off the top of the screen before you have a chance to read it. You might be able to control the text with the Pause key, but the faster your system, the harder that is. Because TYPE can't go backward, once text has disappeared off the top of the screen, you can't get it back without re-entering the command. You're better off examining longer ASCII text files in the Shell (see the Shell's File, View File Contents command) or with EDIT (explained in Chapter 20, "Basic Batch Programs"); both of these programs give you scrolling capabilities.

> **Problem:** I tried to display a file on my command prompt screen, but TYPE started dumping silly characters onto the screen, accompanied by a lot of beeping. What should I do?
>
> If you haven't already done so, press Ctrl+Break to stop TYPE and get back to the command prompt.
>
> This file is not an ASCII text file—it contains binary data. Your computer interpreted the binary data as extended characters such as smiley faces, and control signals such as beeps.
>
> You can't display this file using TYPE. You'll have to open the application that created the file and view it that way.

Files that contain non-ASCII codes don't display well with TYPE. The non-ASCII codes may appear as graphics characters, beep the computer's alarm, or terminate the command before the entire file has been displayed. The best way to view a non-ASCII file is with the application that created it in the first place.

Printing Files with PRINT

There are several ways to print an ASCII text file with DOS. You could redirect the output of TYPE to the printer port, as follows:

```
TYPE AUTOEXEC.BAT > PRN
```

This is fine for a short file; but, because TYPE doesn't do any formatting, a long file runs off the end of the page. COPYing a file to the printer port has the same problems. For longer ASCII text files, the PRINT command is the best choice, as it breaks the text into pages.

> **Network Note:** If your printer is shared with others on a network, you may or may not be able to use the PRINT command. Your network administrator can tell you what command, if any, you can use to print files from the DOS prompt. If you cannot use the PRINT command, skip this section, or print with EDIT.

PRINT must be initialized before you can use it the first time. The procedure called "How to Initialize the Print Program" in Chapter 9, "Additional File Management in the Shell," shows you how to do that. Figure 16.5 shows how to print one or more files with PRINT after it has been initialized.

PRINT

Syntax:

```
PRINT [/T] [filespec]
```

Parameters and Switches:

none	Displays the contents of the print queue or loads the TSR.
/T	Removes all files from the print queue.
filespec	Identifies a text file to place in the print queue.

Figure 16.5. *PRINT command summary.*

You can't print any of the .XXX files in your PRACTICE directory, because they're not ASCII text files. But, you can print README.TXT from your DOS directory:

1. Make sure your printer is ready. (See the note under "Printing through the Shell" in Chapter 9 for an explanation of all the things you should check.)

2. Enter **PRINT \DOS\README.TXT**.

   If you get the message `C:\DOS\README.TXT is currently being printed`, skip to step 4.

   If the following message is displayed, go on to step 3:

   `Name of list device [PRN]:`

3. You must tell PRINT where your printer is located. If your printer is attached to your first parallel port, press Enter. If it's attached to some other port, enter the name of the port, as in LPT2 or COM1. If you're not sure, press Enter.

   You should get these messages:

   `Resident part of PRINT installed`

   `C:\DOS\README.TXT is currently being printed`

4. If you are not on a network, the file should start printing. If it doesn't, see the Problem Solver under "Redirecting Command Output" in Chapter 12, "Working at the Command Prompt."

If your printer is local to your computer—that is, if it's not a shared resource on a network—PRINT maintains a queue of up to ten files waiting to be printed. You can add files to the queue and you can remove all the files in it.

Network Note: If the printer in question is a shared resource on a network, your network software maintains the queue and it probably holds many more than ten files. You won't be able to empty the queue yourself. Your network administrator can tell you how to remove files from the queue or move a high-priority job up in the queue.

1. Enter **PRINT *.TXT** to add several files to the queue.

   You should see a list of files added to the queue.

2. Enter **PRINT** (with no parameters) to see the status of the queue.

   The status report tells you which file is printing and which files are waiting.

3. If your printer is not a shared network resource, enter **PRINT /T** to remove all files from the queue.

   You should get the message Print queue is empty.

Note: The printer might continue printing from its own memory after you clear the print queue. Turn the printer off to clear its memory.

Tip: You can clear the print queue and add new files to it in one command; but, be sure to put the /T before the new filespecs, because the parameters are processed from left to right. The following command clears the queue and adds new files to it:

```
PRINT /T TRY*.TXT SAVE*.TXT
```

Tip: PRINT enables you to configure the PRINT TSR to control such factors as the size of the print queue and the amount of time devoted to print jobs. You also can remove individual files from the queue without clearing the entire queue.

Comparing Files with FC

Suppose you find two files in two different directories that have the same name and the same size, but different date/time stamps. Are they different? Do you want to keep them both? If not, which one do you want to delete? The FC (file comparison) command can help you decide by comparing the two files and displaying their differences.

FC can do two basic types of comparisons: binary and ASCII. In binary mode, FC compares the two files byte by byte, displaying any mismatched bytes. In ASCII mode, FC compares the two files line by line and displays mismatched lines. Binary comparisons are much simpler than ASCII comparisons, but they are also less useful when you are trying to find how two text files differ.

Binary Comparisons

Figure 16.6 shows the syntax of the FC command for binary comparisons. FC automatically uses binary mode for files that it knows to be program files; that is, for .COM, .EXE, .BIN, .SYS, .OBJ, and .LIB files. Any other files are compared in ASCII mode by default; you must use the /B switch if you want the comparison done in binary mode.

FC

Compares two files and displays lines or bytes that don't match.

Syntax:

`FC [/B] filespec1 filespec2`

Parameters and Switches:

filespec1	Identifies first file to compare.
filespec2	Identifies second file to compare.
/B	Compares files in binary mode, byte by byte, without attempting to resynchronize after a mismatch. This is the default mode with files having the extensions .EXE, .COM, .SYS, .OBJ, .LIB, or .BIN.

Figure 16.6. *FC command summary (for binary comparisons).*

Try comparing HELP.XXX in your PRACTICE directory with some other files:

1. Switch to the PRACTICE directory.
2. Remove the hidden attribute from HELP.XXX so that FC can find it.
3. Enter **FC HELP.XXX \DOS\HELP.HLP /B** to compare two files that match.

   You'll see these messages:

   ```
   Comparing files HELP.XXX \DOS\HELP.HLP

   FC: no differences encountered
   ```

4. Enter `FC HELP.XXX MEMMAKER.XXX /B` to compare two files that don't match.

   A whole stream of data begins scrolling on your screen.

5. Press Ctrl+Break to interrupt the comparison.

Because the two files are completely different, FC found and reported a difference in every byte; that's why FC sent so many message to your screen. The FC messages look something like this:

```
00000002: 15 14
00000003: 60 00
```

This means that byte 2 contains 15 in the first file, but 14 in the second file. Byte 3 of the first file contains 60, but byte 3 of the second file contains 00. The addresses and byte values are all reported in hexadecimal numbers, which have different meanings from the decimal numbers that we're used to. The listing goes on like this for several thousand lines.

Obviously, this is information that only a programmer could love. What it tells a normal person is that the two files are different. In this case, very different.

Suppose that you have just copied a set of files and want to make sure that the copies are exact. A binary FC comparison is the perfect choice for this task. You'll quickly find out whether the files are the same or different.

Problem: I tried to compare two files, but FC started dumping strange characters onto my screen, accompanied by a lot of beeping. Have I damaged my computer somehow?

Your computer is working perfectly! At least one of your files contains binary data, and you did an ASCII comparison. When FC tried to display binary data as ASCII text, your computer interpreted it as extended characters such as smiley faces, and control signals such as beeps. Try adding /B to the command to request a binary comparison and the problem will go away.

ASCII Comparisons

An ASCII comparison tells you which lines in two files are different. Figure 16.7 shows the syntax of the FC command for ASCII comparisons. FC automatically does an ASCII comparison for any file that doesn't have one of the program extensions .EXE, .COM, .SYS, .OBJ, .LIB, or .BIN.

ASCII comparisons can be useful to identify changes made to a text file. Suppose that you have an AUTOEXEC.BAT and an AUTOEXEC.BAK file, and you want to see what the differences are. An ASCII comparison displays the exact differences.

FC

Compares two files and displays lines that don't match.

Syntax:

```
FC [/L] [/C] [/N] filespec1 filespec2
```

Parameters and Switches:

filespec1	Identifies the first file to compare.
filespec2	Identifies the second file to compare.
/L	Compares files in ASCII mode, comparing line by line and attempting to resynchronize after a mismatch.
/C	Ignores case.
/N	Displays line numbers when showing mismatched lines during an ASCII comparison.

Figure 16.7. *FC command summary (for ASCII comparisons).*

If you want to do an ASCII comparison for a file with a program extension, you must use the /L switch. Most program files are binary files and do not have lines; an ASCII comparison would make no sense on such files. But, CONFIG.SYS is an ASCII text file with a program's extension, so it makes sense to use the /L switch with this file.

When FC finds a mismatch in an ASCII comparison, it displays a set of lines for each file. Each set starts with the last matching line. Next, it shows all the unmatched lines. Then, it shows the first line that matches again (unless the end of the file was reached first). Here's an example using two AUTOEXEC files:

```
***** AUTOEXEC.BAT
PATH C:\DOS;C:\WINWORD;C:\NDW;C:\WINDOWS
mouse\mouse bon

***** AUTOEXEC.NDW
PATH C:\DOS;C:\WINWORD;C:\NDW;C:\WINDOWS
cls
mouse\mouse bon
*****
```

The first set of lines, identified by the header ***** AUTOEXEC.BAT, shows what's in AUTOEXEC.BAT. The lines following ***** AUTOEXEC.NDW show what's in the other file. The line starting with PATH is the last matching line. You can see it in both files. The line beginning with mouse in each set shows the first line that matches after the mismatched lines. AUTOEXEC.BAT has no lines between these two, but AUTOEXEC.NDW has a CLS command. That command is the difference between the two files. In other words, AUTOEXEC.NDW contains a line that is missing from the other file.

If two files have more than one mismatch, you will see several mismatch reports like this. Each report starts with ***** followed by the name of the first file.

Resynchronization

When FC finds a mismatch during an ASCII comparison, it tries to find a place where the two files match up again so it can continue the comparison. This is called *resynchronizing* the files. By default, FC doesn't consider a single matching line enough evidence of resynchronization. It requires two matching lines in a row to continue the comparison. Look at these "files," for example:

GARDEN	*PRODUCE*
Apples	Apples
Bananas	Pears
Peaches	Plums
Tomatoes	Artichokes
Plums	Peppers
Cherries	Figs
Figs	Onions
Onions	Carrots
Carrots	

The first line matches; then a mismatch starts. Scanning down the GARDEN file, you can see that *Plums* on line 5 matches line 3 in PRODUCE. But, the next lines don't match, so FC would not restart the comparison at that point. Further down in GARDEN, *Figs* on line 7 matches line 6 of PRODUCE. The next lines (*Onions*) also match. Because two lines in a row match, FC would continue the comparison at that point. The message from FC would look like this:

```
***** GARDEN
Apples
Bananas
Peaches
Tomatoes
Plums
Cherries
Figs

***** PRODUCE
Apples
Pears
Plums
Artichokes
Peppers
Figs
*****
```

As usual, the message shows the last line that matches (*Apples*), the mismatched lines, and the first line that matches again (*Figs*).

The information produced by FC tells you exactly where the two files are different so that you can decide what to do about the differences. In most cases, it tells you which file to keep and which to delete. But, sometimes, it identifies data to copy from one file to the other. How you use the FC report depends on the situation, obviously.

In many cases, you might need a printed copy of the report to work from. You can redirect the messages from FC to your printer using the command syntax FC *parameters* > PRN.

Comparison Options

FC is sensitive to case; ordinarily, *Figs* does not match *figs* or *FIGS*. But, you often don't care about case when comparing two files, especially if they're programs. If the only difference between AUTOEXEC.BAT and AUTOEXEC.SAV, for example, is that CLS is capitalized in one and lowercase in the other; the two files would produce exactly the same results. You can tell FC to ignore case with the /C switch when you don't care about case differences.

In long files, seeing the mismatched lines themselves might not be enough. You can add line numbers to the display with the /N switch. This could help you identify which lines you want to edit in the files.

Looking Ahead: FC includes several parameters to control how an ASCII comparison is done and how two files are resynchronized. You can, for example, control how far FC searches for resynchronization and how many lines must match for the comparison to continue. Chapter 46, "Additional Techniques for Handling Data," explains the advanced features of the FC command.

On Your Own

You have learned how to accomplish a variety of file management tasks in this chapter. Use the following items to practice on your own:

1. In your PRACTICE directory, rename all .XXX files to .OMO. (Hint: You'll have to change the attributes of some of the files in order to rename them.)

2. Delete all the files in your PRACTICE directory and remove the directory.

3. Take a quick look at each .TXT file in your DOS directory and print the ones that pertain to your system.

4. If you have an OLD_DOS.1 directory, read the filenamed README.NOW.

5. If you have an OLD_DOS.1 directory, compare some of the files with identical names in your current DOS directory. They will probably be very different files.

6. Do you have any files that appear in both your DOS directory and your root directory? COMMAND.COM, for example, might appear in both places. Compare the files that appear in both directories to make sure they are identical.

7. Do you have several CONFIG.*xxx* files and AUTOEXEC.*xxx* files in your root directory? Do an ASCII comparison of them to find out the differences. Ignore white space and capitalization.

17 Formatting and Unformatting Disks

Introduction

You must format every disk before you can use it (unless you buy pre-formatted disks). And, because everyone makes mistakes, DOS also can unformat a disk if necessary.

Overview

Before DOS can store data on a disk, the disk must be prepared with sectors, a root directory, the FAT, and other administrative information. You must *format* a disk to prepare it. You can also *reformat* a disk to eliminate all its old data, so that you can reuse it. And, in case you accidentally reformat a disk that contains valuable data, you may be able to *unformat* the disk to recover its former data.

In this chapter, you will learn:

- The steps involved in formatting a floppy disk and a hard disk
- How to format a floppy disk
- How to reformat a floppy disk
- How to unformat a floppy disk

Because formatting eliminates the data on a disk, you will not learn how to format your hard disk. If you have been using DOS, your hard disk is already formatted and you probably will never have to reformat it for any reason.

> **Note:** You cannot format a disc in a read-only drive such as a CD-ROM drive or a disk that is write protected.

Understanding How Formatting Works

It's important for you to understand how formatting works before you try your hand at it because you have to make a number of decisions as you go along. This section explains the process of formatting a floppy disk for the first time, as well as reformatting a floppy disk. It also describes hard disk formatting, although you will not practice formatting your hard drive for obvious reasons.

Formatting New Floppy Disks

A new floppy disk needs two levels of formatting. First, it must be *physically* formatted (also called *low-level* formatting), which establishes the disk's sectors. Then, it must be *logically* formatted (also called *high-level* formatting), which installs DOS's system information on the disk: the boot record, an empty root directory, and the initial FAT. (Actually, a logical format installs two duplicate FATs for safety's sake.) It also assigns a serial number that helps DOS identify the disk internally. You can request two optional features:

- Formatting can store an internal label to help you identify the disk. Most people would rather deal with a label such as FEB ORDERS than a DOS serial number such as 57A4-8C14.

- Formatting can install the DOS core program files (IO.SYS, MSDOS.SYS, and COMMAND.COM) so that you can boot from the floppy disk.

Not all disks are perfect, and weaknesses in the magnetic recording surface can cause problems in storing data reliably. The physical formatter tests the disk surface and makes note of any bad spots. Then, the logical formatter marks those spots as bad in the FAT so that DOS will never attempt to store data there.

DOS's FORMAT program handles both low-level and high-level formatting for common disk types. DOS 6 can handle anything from a 360KB 5 1/4-inch diskette to a 2.88MB 3 1/2-inch disk. It can even prepare a disk for a system that's using an earlier version of DOS; for example, DOS 6 can format a 360KB disk as a 320KB disk to work with a DOS 1.0 system. And, to a certain extent, it can prepare a lower capacity disk (such as a 720KB disk) in a higher capacity drive (such as a 1.44MB drive).

Problem: When I try to access a certain file, I get a `Sector not found` error and I can't read the file. How can I access my data?

A `Sector not found` error means that the drive controller can no longer read the sector information that was installed by the physical formatter. This usually happens because the physical formatting on the disk has begun to deteriorate—a natural process if you keep the disk long enough. Even if only one sector is bad, DOS refuses to read the entire file when it encounters a `Sector not found` error.

DOS does not offer a good solution to this problem. Your best bet is a third-party package such as The Norton Utilities, which includes programs to refresh the physical formatting on hard disks and floppies while preserving the existing data. You can almost always re-establish the ability to read your files by refreshing the physical formatting.

After you have recovered the data on a floppy disk, my recommendation is that you copy it to a new disk and throw the old one away. Floppies are cheap when compared to the cost of losing a file because of physical problems with the disk.

Problem: When I try to access a certain file, I get a `Read error` or `Write error` message, and DOS won't read or write the file. How can I access my data?

A `Read error` or `Write error` indicates that DOS has found discrepancies in the sector. This could be a fault of damaged physical formatting or of a bad spot in the sector. In any case, DOS refuses to access the entire file, even though only a small part may actually be damaged.

If you have DOS 6.2 or later, run SCANDISK on the disk to look for a bad spot and rescue as much data as possible from around it. Be sure to select the surface scan option so that SCANDISK will test the surface of the disk.

If you have DOS 6.0 or earlier, your best bet is to upgrade your DOS to get SCANDISK or run a third-party surface scanning utility such as The Norton Utilities' Disk Doctor, which also rescues data from a bad sector.

If the surface scan doesn't solve the problem, you may need to refresh the physical formatting on the disk. DOS does not include a utility to do this without destroying the data on the disk. You need a third-party package such as The Norton Utilities, which includes utilities to refresh the physical formatting on a hard disk and on a floppy.

If the disk is a floppy, don't keep using it. After recovering the data, copy all the files to a new disk and throw the old one away. You don't want to take the chance of losing another file and not being able to recover it.

Formatting New Hard Disks

Hard drive formatting is a little different than formatting a floppy disk. It starts with physical formatting, just as floppy disk formatting does, but DOS's FORMAT program can't handle this job—too many different types of hard disks exist. Low-level formatting usually is done at the factory; if you must redo it for any reason, you might have to buy a special program. (Some systems include a physical formatting program, so check your system documentation to see whether you already have one.)

For hard disks, the second formatting step is *partitioning*, performed by DOS's FDISK program. Partitioning divides the disk into partitions, which you can think of as separate disks even though they're located on the same physical device. You must partition a hard disk; but, if you want, you can set up only one partition that contains all the sectors on the hard disk (most DOS users do this). The maximum partition size with DOS 6 is 2 gigabytes. FDISK stores a *partition table* in the first sector of the disk. The partition table, which is used by DOS during booting, shows which sectors belong to which partitions.

> **Looking Ahead:** Chapter 54, "FDISK," shows you how to partition a hard drive using FDISK.

Each DOS partition can contain one or more logical drives. A logical drive behaves just like a physical drive such as a disk unit. Each logical drive has its own boot record, root directory, and FAT; and, each logical drive is referred to by a drive name, such as C or D.

Many dealers routinely partition a hard disk before delivering it to a customer. This has two benefits: it lets the dealer install software on the hard disk as part of the package, and it avoids making a new computer user perform a rather high-level procedure right off the bat. Unfortunately, if you don't like the way your dealer partitioned your hard disk, you will have a difficult time changing the partitioning once the disk contains data. Repartitioning a disk can cause you to lose access to all its data.

> **Looking Ahead:** Chapter 54 shows you how to repartition a hard disk if you really need to do so.

After you have established one or more logical drives on the hard disk, you must use the FORMAT program to logically format them before you can store data on them. The formatting process is the same as logically formatting a floppy, except that it takes considerably longer. After the logical formatting is complete, the hard disk is ready to go.

Reformatting Floppy Disks

When you don't need the data on a floppy anymore, you can reformat the disk and use it for something else. Reformatting restores a disk to its original, unused condition.

> **Note:** After a hard disk has been formatted and contains data, you probably won't want to reformat it, because doing so would destroy all the data on it. If a hard disk crashes and requires invasive repairs, then you must reformat it from the beginning, just as if it was new.

You can redo both the physical and the logical formatting on a floppy. When you redo the logical formatting, you get a new root directory and FAT, as well as a new internal label, a new serial number, and a new boot record. When you redo the physical formatting, the sectors are reworked and retested. Redoing the logical format doesn't actually erase any data from the clusters; all it does is mark the clusters as available for new data. But, when you redo the physical format, the surface test actually erases the existing data from the clusters; the data can't be recovered.

In certain cases, DOS's FORMAT program tries to protect you from accidentally wiping out valuable data by storing unformatting information on the disk. The unformatting file, called a *mirror image file*, provides DOS's UNFORMAT program the information it needs to recover the former data on the disk.

When reformatting a disk, you can choose from three levels of formatting: quick, safe, and unconditional. Each has its own characteristics, and each is appropriate under certain circumstances.

Quick Format

A quick format simply stores the mirror file and replaces the root directory and FATs without checking the sectors for reliability. This takes almost no time at all, although it's not a good idea when you have had any kind of errors on the disk. However, if all you want to do is reuse the disk for new data, a quick format is often the best choice.

A quick format makes the disk appear blank because its root directory contains no entries; but, in reality, all the former data still exists in the clusters and can be recovered by UNFORMAT before you put anything new on it.

Safe Format

A safe format does the same thing as a quick format but, in addition, checks the sectors for validity. Although this is not the same as a physical formatter's surface test, it can locate and block out clusters that have been causing read-and-write errors. The validity check does not actually write in the sectors, so the former data still exists on the disk and can be unformatted if necessary.

Unconditional Format

An unconditional format performs a physical format followed by a logical format on a floppy disk. The physical format destroys all the data on a disk so that the disk can't be unformatted. DOS's FORMAT program doesn't perform an unconditional format on a hard disk, of course, because DOS can't physically format a hard disk. But, you can do unconditional formats on floppy disks.

> **Warning:** Don't count on an unconditional format to protect confidential data. An expert using the right equipment can still read old data from a physically reformatted disk. To eliminate classified data, you need a program that removes the data according to government standards. The Norton Utilities include a program to do just that.

You must use an unconditional format in two cases:

- When the disk has never been formatted before, you must do an unconditional format to install sectors on it.

- When you want to change the capacity of the disk, it needs new sectors. For example, if a disk is formatted for 720KB and you now want to format it for 1.44MB, you must do an unconditional format.

In other cases, you might want to do an unconditional format to refresh the physical formatting on a disk before using it again. As long as you're sure that you won't want to unformat the disk later on, refreshing the physical formatting on an older disk is always a good idea. (Throwing older disks away is an even better idea. Disks are cheap; data isn't.)

Using FORMAT to Prepare a New Disk

Figure 17.1 shows the FORMAT command summary to format a new, unformatted disk.

FORMAT

Prepares a disk for use.

Syntax:

```
FORMAT drive [/V:label] [/S] [/U]
```

Parameters and Switches:

drive	Identifies the drive to format.
/V:label	Specifies the volume label for the formatted disk. The label can be up to 11 characters long. If you omit /V, DOS prompts you for the volume label during the format process.
/S	Makes the disk bootable.
/U	Specifies an unconditional format.

Notes:

FORMAT also includes several advanced switches that are not shown here. They are all described in the Command Reference at the back of the book. Chapter 46, "Additional Techniques for Handling Data," shows you how to use some of these advanced switches.

Figure 17.1. *FORMAT command summary (for formatting a new disk).*

Tip: If you don't include the /U switch in the FORMAT command, FORMAT tries to perform a safe format, discovers that the disk is unformatted, and switches to an unconditional format. As long as you're sure the disk is new and unused, you can save that extra time by including /U in the command.

Try formatting a new disk:

1. Get a new, completely unused floppy disk. If you don't have an unused one, use a disk that contains data you don't need anymore.

Warning: An unconditional format destroys any existing data on a disk.

2. Enter FORMAT A: /U or FORMAT B: /U, depending on which drive you want to use.

   You see the following message:

   ```
   Insert new disk for drive d:

   and press ENTER when ready.
   ```

3. Insert the floppy disk that you want to format and press the Enter key.

   You see the following message:

   ```
   Formatting 1.44M

           0 percent completed.
   ```

   The first line tells you what capacity FORMAT is preparing the disk for; it might be a different capacity on your drive. When the disk has never been formatted before, FORMAT automatically prepares the disk for the maximum capacity of the drive (even if that's not appropriate for the disk), unless the command explicitly specifies the correct capacity.

   The percent completed counts up as FORMAT lays out the sectors on the disk. When it is finished, you see these messages:

   ```
   Format complete.

   Volume label (11 characters, ENTER for none)?
   ```

4. You could enter a volume label for the disk at this time. (Volume labels are explained in the next section.) But, for now, just press Enter to bypass the volume label and go on.

   You see messages similar to the following (your numbers are probably different):

   ```
       1,457,664 bytes total disk space

           1,024 bytes in bad sectors

       1,456,630 bytes available on disk

             512 bytes in each allocation unit.

           2,845 allocation units available on disk.
   ```

These lines tell you the storage capacity of the disk in terms of bytes and allocation units. This particular disk has some bad sectors, and the number of bytes they occupy is also shown. The total `bytes available on disk` shows how much usable space there is on the disk after the bad sectors were subtracted out.

Next, FORMAT displays the Volume Serial Number that is assigned to the disk:

`Volume Serial Number is 2A46-17F8`

Finally, FORMAT asks if you would like to format another disk:

`Format another (Y/N)?`

5. You do not want to format another disk at this time, so enter `N` to end the FORMAT program.

   The command prompt returns.

If you answer Y in step 4, FORMAT returns to step 3 automatically. You do not get the chance to change any of the formatting parameters such as the drive name or the `/U` switch.

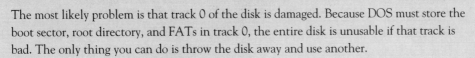

Problem: I tried to format a disk and got the message `Invalid media or Track 0 bad - disk unusable, Format failure`. How can I format this disk?

The most likely problem is that track 0 of the disk is damaged. Because DOS must store the boot sector, root directory, and FATs in track 0, the entire disk is unusable if that track is bad. The only thing you can do is throw the disk away and use another.

Volume Labels

A *volume label* is an electronic label for the disk. It is stored in the root directory, and displayed in DIR listings and in messages from many of your application programs. The volume label helps you identify the disk. When you have a lot of floppy disks, I recommend that you use volume labels in addition to external stick-on labels to avoid mixing up your disks.

Because the formatting command in the preceding example did not specify a volume label, FORMAT asked for one. You can bypass this step by specifying `/V:label` in the original command. Place the label in quotation marks if it contains spaces, as in `/V:"MY DISK"`. Without the quotation marks, a space causes an error message. Spaces count in the 11 character limit, but the quotation marks don't. DOS translates labels to uppercase characters. If you specify `/V:"My Disk"`, DOS stores the label as `MY DISK`.

> **Tip:** If you don't want a volume label, you can enter /V:"" (in other words, a null label in quotation marks). By including a null label in the command, you avoid having to answer the "volume label" question during the formatting process.

You can view a label with the VOL command and change it with the LABEL command, both of which are discussed in Chapter 18, "Additional Disk Management."

System Disks

You most likely boot every day from your hard drive. But, if there's a disk in drive A, your system tries to boot from that disk instead of the hard drive. Normally, you make sure that drive A does not contain a disk before you boot or reboot.

However, you should have at least one floppy disk around that you can boot from in case of a problem with the hard drive. Chapter 4, "Setting Up Your System," includes complete instructions for making an emergency startup disk. If you have not already done so, you should do it now.

To make an emergency startup disk, you must place the disk in drive A and use the /S switch on the FORMAT command. This switch makes the new disk bootable. FORMAT copies the DOS core program files and COMMAND.COM to the disk after formatting it.

Try formatting a system disk in drive A. (If you have been working with drive A on earlier exercises, you can continue using the same disk.) Label the volume BOOT FLOPPY.

1. Enter **FORMAT A: /S /U /V:"BOOT FLOPPY"**.

   You see the following message:

   ```
   Insert new disk for drive A:
   and press ENTER when ready...
   ```

2. The disk is already in the drive this time, so just press Enter.

   You see the following messages:

   ```
   Formatting 1.44M
             0 percent completed.
   Format complete.
   System transferred.
   ```

   The System transferred message tells you that the system files have been copied to the disk from your boot drive.

The next messages tell you the disk capacities:

```
1,457,664 bytes total disk space
   18,432 bytes used by system
    1,024 bytes in bad sectors
1,438,208 bytes available on disk


      512 bytes in each allocation unit.
    2,845 allocation units available on disk.
```

Notice that the space occupied by the system files has been subtracted from the bytes available on the disk.

Next, FORMAT displays the Volume Serial Number and asks if you would like to format another:

```
Volume Serial Number is 2A46-17F8

Format another (Y/N)?
```

If you answer Y here, FORMAT formats another disk with the system files and the same volume label. You do not get a chance to change any parameters.

3. Enter N to conclude the FORMAT program.

The command prompt returns.

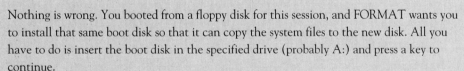

Problem: I tried to format a system disk and got the message Insert DOS disk in drive and strike any key when ready. Is there something wrong?

Nothing is wrong. You booted from a floppy disk for this session, and FORMAT wants you to install that same boot disk so that it can copy the system files to the new disk. All you have to do is insert the boot disk in the specified drive (probably A:) and press a key to continue.

Using FORMAT to Reformat a Disk

Figure 17.2 shows FORMAT command parameters for reformatting a disk.

```
                              FORMAT
Prepares a disk for reuse.

Syntax:

FORMAT drive [/V:label] [/S] [/Q] [/U]

Parameters and Switches:

drive       Identifies the drive to format.

/V:label    Specifies the volume label for the formatted disk.

/S          Makes the disk bootable.

/Q          Does a quick format.

/U          Does an unconditional format.
```

Figure 17.2. *FORMAT command summary (for reformatting a disk).*

As you can see, most of the command is exactly the same as the previous FORMAT command summary, but you can add a /Q switch to request a quick format. If you don't use either /Q or /U, FORMAT does a safe format.

Try reformatting the floppy disk that you formatted in the preceding exercises. This time, do not use a volume label.

1. Enter **FORMAT A:** **/V:""** or **FORMAT B:** **/V:""**, depending on which drive the disk is in.

   You see the following message:

   ```
   Insert new disk for drive d:

   and press ENTER when ready...
   ```

2. Press Enter.

   You see the following message:

   ```
   Checking existing disk format.

   Saving UNFORMAT information.

   Verifying 1.44M

              0 percent completed.
   ```

Because the command did not specify /Q, /S, or /U, FORMAT checked the existing disk to see if it was already formatted. When it found that the disk was formatted, it saved the UNFORMAT information and then did a safe format.

The next line tells you what capacity FORMAT is preparing the disk for; it might be a different capacity on your disk. When the disk has been formatted before, FORMAT automatically prepares the disk for the same capacity that it already has.

For a safe format, FORMAT verifies the reliability of the sectors but doesn't actually physically format the disk. It takes much less time to verify the sectors, and the existing data is not destroyed. The percent completed counts up as FORMAT verifies the sectors. When it is finished, you see these messages:

```
Format complete.


        1,457,664 bytes total disk space
        1,457,664 bytes available on disk


            512 bytes in each allocation unit.
        2,845 allocation units available on disk.


Volume Serial Number is 2A46-17F8


Format another (Y/N)?
```

3. Enter N to end the FORMAT program.

    The command prompt returns.

If you don't want to use the default formatting level, you can specify another level. Try doing a quick reformat on the same disk:

1. Enter **FORMAT A:** /**Q** /**V:""** or **FORMAT B:** /**Q** /**V:""**, depending on which drive you're using.

    You see the following message:
    ```
    Insert new disk for drive d:
    and press ENTER when ready...
    ```

2. Press the Enter key.

    You see the following messages:
    ```
    Checking existing disk format.
    Saving UNFORMAT information.
    QuickFormatting 1.44M
    Format complete.
            1,457,664 bytes total disk space
              1,024 bytes in bad sectors
    ```

```
                  1,456,630 bytes available on disk


                     512 bytes in each allocation unit.
                  2,845 allocation units available on disk.


        Volume Serial Number is 2A46-17F8


        Format another (Y/N)?
```

FORMAT checks the disk to make sure that it has been formatted before; if not, QuickFormatting is not possible. Then, it saves the UNFORMAT information. Next, it displays the disk capacity that it is using, which is the same as the current capacity. There is no percentage count this time, because the sectors are not verified in a quick format.

3. Enter N to end the FORMAT program.

Tip: If you're positive that you will not want to unformat the disk and that its sectors are in good condition, use both /Q and /U. This is the fastest possible format. The /Q causes FORMAT to do a quick format, and the /U keeps FORMAT from storing the unformatting file. Other than that, the /Q invalidates the /U—FORMAT does not reinstall the sectors.

Problem: I tried to do a safe or quick format and got these messages:

```
Drive d error. Insufficient space for the MIRROR image file.
There was an error creating the format recovery file.
This disk can't be unformatted.
Proceed with Format (Y/N)?
```

In a safe or quick format, FORMAT tries to store unformatting information—called a mirror image file—on the disk, so you can unformat it later if necessary. You get this message when there is not enough room left on the disk to store the mirror image file.

If you're sure you won't want to unformat the disk later, enter Y to go ahead with the formatting without storing the unformatting information. You won't be able to unformat the disk later, however.

If you're not sure, enter N to end the FORMAT program. Then, delete some files on the disk to make room for the UNFORMAT information. (The amount of space you need depends on the disk, but it's probably more than 10KB for a 1.44 floppy.)

Looking Ahead: Chapter 46 explains the advanced features of the FORMAT command, such as formatting a disk with only eight sectors per track for very early DOS systems and specifying a nondefault capacity.

FORMAT in DOS Shell

DOS Shell contains two formatting program items in the Disk Utilities group. The first, called Quick Format, is defined as FORMAT %1 /Q. When you open it, a dialog box opens to collect the drive name, showing A: as the default. (See Figure 17.3.) If you want to format drive B: instead, replace the A: with B:. Any other information that you type in the dialog box is also included in the FORMAT command that is submitted to DOS when you choose OK. You could, for example, add the /V switch to define the volume label, the /S switch to make the disk bootable, or the /U switch to suppress the mirror image file.

Figure 17.3.
Quick Format dialog box in DOS Shell

```
╔═══════════════════ Quick Format ═══════════════════╗
║                                                      ║
║   Enter the drive to quick format.                   ║
║                                                      ║
║   Parameters . . .   a:_____     ║
║                                                      ║
║   (    OK    )      ( Cancel )      (  Help  )        ║
╚══════════════════════════════════════════════════════╝
```

If you have only one floppy drive, you might want to adapt the definition to read FORMAT A: /Q so that you don't have to deal with the dialog box. But, if you do, you won't have the opportunity to add switches to the command in the dialog box. That's probably a minor price to pay for the added convenience of eliminating the dialog box. Chapter 11, "Customizing the Shell," shows you how to define and modify program items.

The second item, called simply Format, is defined with the command FORMAT %1. When you open it, a dialog box asks for the drive name, with A: as the default. Here again, you have the opportunity to add switches to the command by typing them in the dialog box. If you have only one drive, you could redefine the item as FORMAT A: to do away with the dialog box.

In both cases, if you redefine the item, you can use other FORMAT switches by choosing File, Run to open a dialog box where you can enter any command you want. Chapter 12, "Working at the Command Prompt," shows you how to use the File, Run command.

Using UNFORMAT to Restore a Reformatted Disk

Suppose that you have formatted a disk. You take it out of the drive and see the label—uh oh! It's the wrong disk. The UNFORMAT command may be able to recover the data. (See Figure 17.4.)

UNFORMAT

Restores a disk reformatted by the FORMAT command.

Syntax:

UNFORMAT *drive*

Parameters:

drive Identifies the drive to be unformatted.

Figure 17.4. *UNFORMAT command summary.*

UNFORMAT recovers the data on a disk by restoring the former root directory and FAT, which are stored in the mirror image file. As long as nothing was added to the disk after the reformatting, this should completely restore its former contents. But, if anything was added, you might find that some files have been ruined. Even so, that might be better than losing all the former data on the disk.

Unformatting can encounter two major problems. The first comes when UNFORMAT can't find the mirror file. UNFORMAT can try to rebuild the disk's directory structure from scratch by searching the clusters for directory entries, but this process does not produce the best results. It's a desperation measure, at best. You'll learn how to attempt it in Chapter 47, "Advanced Rescue Techniques."

The other unformatting problem comes when you have added data to the disk after formatting it. Even making a disk bootable adds DOS's core program files to the disk after formatting it. That new data would have overwritten some of the former data that you're trying to rescue. You can't recover the overwritten data, of course. UNFORMAT doesn't identify this problem. It's up to you to be aware that, if you added data to the disk after formatting it, you might have lost some of the original data. And, by the way, you'll lose the new data when you unformat the disk.

Let's add some data to the floppy disk you have been practicing on, then format it, and finally unformat it.

1. Copy a few files from your hard disk to the floppy. Any files will do.

2. List the directory of the floppy to see the files you copied.

3. Format the disk using the /Q switch for a quick format.

4. List the directory of the floppy again.

   You should see that it contains no files.

5. Now enter **UNFORMAT A:** or **UNFORMAT B:**, depending on which drive contains the floppy.

   The first message you see is:

   ```
   Insert disk to rebuild in drive d:

   and press ENTER when ready.
   ```

6. The disk is already in the drive, so just press Enter.

   Next, you see a whole screenful of messages:

   ```
   Restores the system area of your disk by using the image file created by the MIRROR
   command.

   WARNING !!        WARNING !!

   This command should be used only to recover from the inadvertent use of the FORMAT
   command or the RECOVER command.  Any other use of the UNFORMAT command may cause
   you to lose data!  Files modified since the MIRROR image file was created may be
   lost.

   Searching disk for MIRROR image.

   The last time the MIRROR or FORMAT command was used was at 22:14 on 10-16-94.

   The MIRROR image file has been validated.

   Are you sure you want to update the system area of your drive (Y/N)?
   ```

   These messages refer to MIRROR and RECOVER programs that used to be in DOS but were dropped. Only the FORMAT program stores a mirror image file now.

7. Enter Y to proceed with the format.

   You will see the following messages next:

   ```
   The system area of drive d has been rebuilt.

   You may need to restart the system.
   ```

8. It's always a good idea to reboot after UNFORMAT to flush any leftover directory data out of the system's caches and buffers. Remove the disk in drive A. Then, press Ctrl+Alt+Delete.

   DOS reboots.

Looking Ahead: If you're really, really desperate, you can unformat a disk without the mirror image file. But, many of your files will not be completely recovered. Chapter 47 explains how to unformat when the mirror image file is missing.

On Your Own

You have learned how to format, reformat, and unformat a floppy disk in this chapter. You have also learned what steps are involved in formatting a hard drive, although you haven't actually practiced them. If you want to practice on a few more floppies on your own, you can use the following steps as a guide:

1. Do an unconditional format of the floppy disk in drive A or B. Name it ON MY OWN 1.

2. Do a safe reformat of the same disk, naming it ON MY OWN 2.

3. Add some files to the floppy, then do a quick reformat on it. Name it ON MY OWN 3.

4. Unformat the floppy to recover the files that were eliminated in step 3.

5. Make sure you understand the steps involved in preparing a hard disk for use. What program does the physical formatting? The partitioning? The logical formatting?

18 Additional Disk Management

Introduction

Occasionally, you will need to duplicate disks, and sometimes you may want to change a label that you assigned during formatting. This chapter discusses methods for accomplishing these tasks.

Overview

DOS includes several commands that enable you to manage your disks. Most of them apply to floppy disks only. You can, for example, duplicate a floppy disk, then compare the duplicate to the original to make sure that it's a perfect copy. DOS also includes two commands to view and change a disk's label. These commands can be used on either floppy or hard drives.

In this chapter, you will learn how to:

- Make a duplicate copy of a floppy at the command prompt
- Make a duplicate copy of a floppy in DOS Shell
- Define your own disk copying program items for DOS Shell
- Compare two floppies
- View and change a disk's volume label

Copying Disks with DISKCOPY

Whenever you buy a new software program, you should protect your investment by making backup copies of all the disks. Put the originals away and use the copies to install the software. I recommend that you keep the two sets in different places so that a fire or flood doesn't destroy both sets.

Note: You can't duplicate disks in a read-only drive such as a CD-ROM drive.

Figure 18.1 shows the DISKCOPY command, which you use to copy disks. DISKCOPY makes an identical copy of each track of the disk. Because DISKCOPY copies the source disk's physical and logical formatting by virtue of copying whole tracks, the destination disk doesn't have to be formatted first. In fact, the copying process replaces any formatting that has already been done on the disk.

Duplicating a disk has quite a different effect from copying all the files from one disk to another. A file-by-file copy doesn't duplicate the source disk's system area; it doesn't delete existing data from the destination disk, except to overwrite destination files of the same name; and, it stores the copies wherever it can find available clusters, which might fragment or defragment them differently than they are on the source disk. A track-by-track copy, on the other hand, overwrites the entire destination disk, including the system area at the beginning and any empty tracks at the end. The clusters end up in the same order on the destination disk as the source disk, reproducing any file fragmentation from the source to the destination disk.

DISKCOPY

Copies one floppy disk to another.

Syntax:

```
DISKCOPY [source] [destination] [/V]
```

Parameters and Switches:

source	Identifies the drive holding the source disk.
destination	Identifies the drive holding the destination disk.
/V	Verifies that the copied data is correct.

Figure 18.1. `DISKCOPY` *command summary.*

When you're copying software disks, it could be important that you make a track-by-track copy so that the application's Install or Setup program works correctly. Some installation programs, for example, check the volume labels of the disks that you insert. If the volume label is not what they are expecting, they continue asking for the correct disk.

Note: DISKCOPY can't be used to copy hard disks, only floppy disks. Both disks must be identical in size and capacity.

Copying a disk's formatting can create some problems. If the source disk has some bad sectors blocked out, those same sectors will be blocked out in the destination disk, even though they are not bad on the destination disk. This isn't a big problem; it just wastes a little space. But, suppose that the reverse is true—the destination disk has bad spots that aren't on the source disk. If DISKCOPY identifies this problem because it finds an area that it can't write in, it displays an error message. If it doesn't notice the bad spots, you could end up losing some data later.

Problem: While duplicating a disk, DISKCOPY displayed the message `Unrecoverable read error on drive d; Side x, track xx; Target disk may be unusable`. What's wrong?

Because DISKCOPY copies disks track by track, it does not read the source disk's FAT. If the source disk has bad spots blocked out in the FAT, DISKCOPY is unaware of them and attempts to copy them anyway. When it encounters a read error, it displays this message. In all likelihood, the bad spots do not contain any valid data and there is no problem on the destination disk. However, there is a small chance that a read error on the source disk is a new trouble spot and one or more files have been damaged. To make sure, try copying all the files from the source disk to another disk with XCOPY. If they copy all right, there is no problem with the disk.

Problem: While duplicating a disk, DISKCOPY displayed the message `Unrecoverable write error on drive d; Side x, track xx; Target disk may be unusable.` What's wrong?

DISKCOPY found a faulty area on the destination disk during a copying operation. Because of the error, it was unable to duplicate one or more tracks correctly. The destination disk is surely unusable in this case. Recopy the source disk using another destination disk.

The disk with the bad spot is not completely unusable. Do an unconditional format on it to locate and block out the problem area. It can then be used normally for data, but not as a duplicate disk.

You need two disks to practice making a duplicate copy, one that contains data and one that is blank (or reusable). Both disks must be the same size and capacity, as in two 3 1/2-inch 1.44M disks.

Warning: DISKCOPY destroys all the data on the destination disk, and this data cannot be recovered by any means. So, be sure that the destination disk does not contain any valuable data.

Because both disks must be the same size and capacity, the command that you enter to start DISKCOPY depends on the number and type of floppy drives that you have:

- If you have only one drive, see "Copying Disks with a Single Drive in DOS 6.0 or Earlier" or "Copying Disks with a Single Drive in DOS 6.2 or Later," depending on which version of DOS you have.

- If you have two identical drives, you can use both drives to make the copy. See "Copying Disks with Two Drives."

- If you have a high-density drive and a low-density drive of the same size (either 3 1/2-inch or 5 1/4-inch), you can use two drives to copy a low-density disk, but you must use only the high-density drive to copy a high-density disk. See the appropriate section according to which type of disk you want to copy and your version of DOS.

- If you have two drives of different sizes, such as a 3 1/2-inch drive and a 5 1/4-inch drive, you can't use both drives to make a copy. See "Copying Disks with a Single Drive in DOS 6.0 or Earlier" or "Copying Disks with a Single Drive in DOS 6.2 or Later," depending on which version of DOS you have.

Tip: It's easy to get the two disks mixed up. Always write-protect the source disk to avoid accidentally copying tracks from the destination to the source.

Copying Disks with a Single Drive in DOS 6.0 or Earlier

When you copy disks with a single drive, you must swap the source disk and destination disk in the same drive. For a one-drive copy using DOS 6.0 (or earlier), you must swap the source and destination disks several times. DISKCOPY tells you when to insert each disk.

Try making a copy using only drive A:

1. Write-protect the source disk.

2. Enter **DISKCOPY A: A:**.

   DISKCOPY asks you to `Insert SOURCE disk in drive A:, Press any key to continue.`

3. Insert the source disk in drive A and press any key.

   DISKCOPY displays the disk's parameters, as in:

   `Copying 80 tracks, 18 sectors per track, 2 side(s)`

   `Reading from source diskette...`

   DISKCOPY copies as much data as possible from the source disk into memory and displays this message next:

   `Insert TARGET diskette into drive A:`

   `Press any key to continue...`

4. Insert the destination disk in drive A and press a key.

   DISKCOPY writes the copied data on the destination disk. Then, it asks for the SOURCE disk again.

5. Repeat steps 3 and 4 until the disk copy is complete.

   DISKCOPY assigns a new volume serial number to the destination disk and displays the number. Then, it asks `Copy another diskette?`.

6. You don't want to copy another disk now, so enter N to end the DISKCOPY program.

7. Remove the write-protection from the source disk unless you decide that you want to keep it write-protected.

8. Label the destination disk. If it is a 5 1/4-inch floppy, be sure to write the label before you attach it to the disk, so that you don't press on the disk with a pen.

Copying Disks with a Single Drive in DOS 6.2 or Later

When you copy disks with a single drive, you must swap the source disk and destination disk in the same drive. With DOS 6.2 and 6.22, you only have to swap disks once. DISKCOPY copies all the source data to a temporary file, then copies it to the destination disk. (Chapter 43, "DOS and the Environment," explains where DOS places its temporary files.)

Problem: I tried to make a disk copy and got the message `Error creating image file; Diskcopy will revert to multiple-pass copy`.

In a single-drive copy with DOS 6.2 and later, DISKCOPY copies the data from the source disk to a temporary file. But, DISKCOPY was unable to create the temporary file for some reason. In all likelihood, the disk where your system stores temporary files is full.

Because it can't create the temporary file, DISKCOPY reverts to the older style of copy procedure, which requires you to swap the disks several times to complete the copy. You'll have no trouble making the copy, but it will be somewhat less convenient than usual.

After you complete the copy, you should try to find out why the system could not create a temporary file. Other DOS procedures also need to make temporary files and cannot work around them as DISKCOPY can. See Chapter 43 for a complete explanation of temporary files in DOS.

Try making a copy using only drive A:

1. Write-protect the source disk.

2. Enter **DISKCOPY A: A:**.

   DISKCOPY asks you to `Insert SOURCE disk in drive A:, Press any key to continue`.

3. Insert the source disk in drive A and press any key.

   DISKCOPY displays the disk's parameters, as in:

   `Copying 80 tracks, 18 sectors per track, 2 side(s)`

```
Reading from source diskette...
```

DISKCOPY copies all the data from the source disk into a temporary file and displays this message next:

```
Insert TARGET diskette into drive A:
```

```
Press any key to continue...
```

4. Insert the destination disk in drive A and press a key.

   DISKCOPY writes the copied data on the destination disk. Because it has the data in a temporary file, DISKCOPY can make another copy of the same disk quickly and easily. It displays this message next:

   ```
   Do you wish to write another duplicate of this disk?
   ```

5. If you wanted to make a second duplicate, you would enter Y here. But, for this practice exercise, enter N.

   DISKCOPY assigns a new volume serial number to the destination disk and displays the number. Then, it asks `Copy another diskette?`.

6. You don't want to copy another disk now, so enter N to end the DISKCOPY program.

7. Remove the write-protection from the source disk unless you decide that you want to keep it write-protected.

8. Label the destination disk. If it is a 5 1/4-inch floppy, be sure to write the label before you attach it to the disk, so that you don't press on the disk with a pen.

Copying Disks with Two Drives

When you copy disks with two drives, you place the source disk in one drive and the destination disk in the other. If the two drives have different capacities, such as a 720KB drive and a 1.44MB drive, you should only copy a double-density disk from the high-density drive to the low-density drive. A high-density drive can write a low-density disk, but the results can be unreliable.

Try making a copy using both drives:

1. Write-protect the source disk.

2. If both disks are the same capacity, enter **DISKCOPY A: B:**. If drive A is high-density and drive B is double-density, enter **DISKCOPY A: B:**, so that you're writing on drive B (the double-density drive). If drive A is double-density and drive B is high-density, enter **DISKCOPY B: A:** so that you're writing on drive A (the double-density drive).

   DISKCOPY displays these messages:

   ```
   Insert SOURCE disk in drive x,
   ```

```
Insert TARGET disk in drive y

Press any key to continue.
```

3. Insert the source and destination disks in the designated drives and press any key.

DISKCOPY displays the disk's parameters, as in:

```
Copying 80 tracks, 18 sectors per track, 2 side(s)
```

Then, it displays messages as it copies the data:

```
Reading from source diskette...
```

```
Writing to target diskette...
```

DISKCOPY writes the copied data on the destination disk.

DISKCOPY assigns a new volume serial number to the destination disk and displays the number. Then, it asks Copy another diskette?.

5. You don't want to copy another disk now, so enter N to end the DISKCOPY program.

6. Remove the write-protection from the source disk, unless you decide that you want to keep it write-protected.

7. Label the destination disk. If it is a 5 1/4-inch floppy, be sure to write the label before you attach it to the disk, so that you don't press on the disk with a pen.

Problem: While duplicating a disk with DISKCOPY, I got the message TARGET diskette bad or incompatible; Copy process ended.

Either the destination disk is the wrong size or capacity, or it contains surface faults in vital areas. You will have to use another destination disk for the duplicating process.

Verifying the Copy

The verification switch (/V) can add an extra measure of protection to the copy. Your drive controller automatically verifies all the data it stores. But, some errors may creep in before the data reaches the drive controller. (Such errors are unusual; they are mostly a matter of power fluctuations or malfunctioning hardware.) DOS's verification feature compares the written copy to the copy in memory and corrects any errors it finds. Frankly, this type of error is so rare that you might not think it's worthwhile to slow down DISKCOPY to look for it.

Note: If you keep DOS's general verification feature on (see the VERIFY command), you don't need the /V switch. They both have the same function.

DOS verification does not catch errors that occur before the data leaves memory. The DISKCOMP command, discussed later in this chapter, is one way to do that.

Copying Disks in the Shell

If you use DOS Shell, you can duplicate disks from the Disk Utilities group. The program item named Disk Copy generates the command DISKCOPY %1. When you select it, a dialog box opens so that you can enter the drive names. (See Figure 18.2.) The dialog box suggests A: and B: as the default drive names, as you can see in the figure. You can edit the drive names as needed for your system before you choose the OK button.

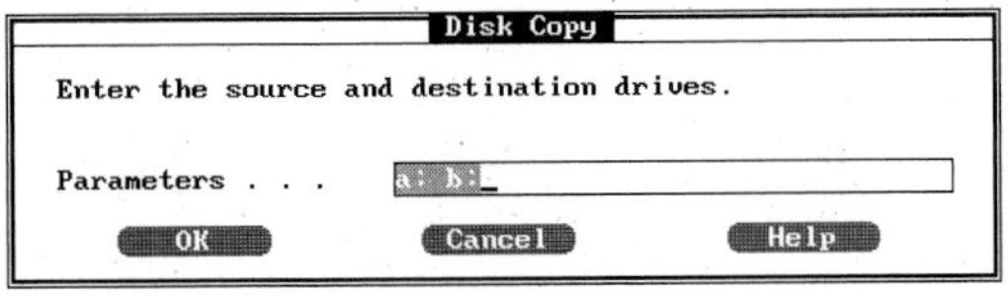

Figure 18.2.
Disk Copy dialog box in
DOS Shell

```
                              Disk Copy
    Enter the source and destination drives.

    Parameters . . .    a: b:

         OK             Cancel              Help
```

In my opinion, you should edit or replace this program item with one that's tailored for your system. You shouldn't have to go through a dialog box to specify the disk drives, because your drive setup isn't variable. Chapter 11, "Customizing the Shell," shows you how to define and edit program items for the Shell's program list.

If you have just one drive, change the definition from DISKCOPY %1 to DISKCOPY A: A:. Similarly, if you have two drives that are the same size and capacity, change the definition to DISKCOPY A: B: to eliminate the dialog box.

If you have two drives that are the same size but different capacities, delete this item and create two others. The first item, which you might call Disk Copy Double Density, should copy from the high density disk to the double density disk. The second item, which you might call Disk Copy High Density, should copy on the high density drive only.

If you have two drives of different sizes, delete this definition and create an item called Disk Copy A: (defined as DISKCOPY A: A:) and another item called Disk Copy B: (defined as DISKCOPY B: B:).

Comparing Disks with DISKCOMP

As you have seen, DOS's verification feature doesn't really guarantee that a copy matches the original; it only verifies the written version against what's in memory. For complete verification of a copied disk with its original, you must compare them with DISKCOMP.

The DISKCOMP command has nearly the same syntax as DISKCOPY, but instead of copying disks, it compares them. Figure 18.3 shows the syntax of the command. Unlike DISKCOPY, DISKCOMP was not improved with DOS 6.2; so, for a single-drive comparison, you still must swap disks several times.

DISKCOMP

Compares two floppy disks.

Syntax:

`DISKCOMP [drive1] [drive2]`

Parameters and Switches:

    drive1   Identifies one drive that holds a disk for comparison.

    drive2   Identifies a second drive that holds a disk for comparison.

Figure 18.3. `DISKCOMP` *command summary.*

Try comparing the two disks that you just copied:

1. If you did a single-drive copy, enter **DISKCOMP** *d:* *d:*, where *d* is the drive name. If you did a two-drive copy, enter **DISKCOMP A:** **B:**. (For DISKCOMP, it doesn't matter which drive is the high-density and which is the double-density.)

   DISKCOMP will tell you when to insert each disk.

2. Follow the directions on the screen.

   Eventually, DISKCOMP displays the message `Compare OK`. Then, it asks if you want to compare another.

3. Enter **N** to terminate DISKCOMP and return to the command prompt.

If DISKCOMP discovers an error, it displays a message like the following for each mismatched track:

```
Compare error on side x, track xx
```

If DISKCOMP finds mismatches in a copy that you have just made with DISKCOPY, the file may be copy protected. Check the vendor's documentation to find out. If it's not copy protected, the problem may be due to a hardware malfunction such as a failing memory chip; or, it could have been caused by a power fluctuation during the copy process. Try making the copy again. If you can't get a perfect disk copy with your system, it probably needs repairs.

DISKCOMP compares disks track by track, not file by file. When you use COPY or XCOPY to copy all files from one disk to another, the result is not a track-by-track copy, and DISKCOMP will find many mismatches.

> **Note:** You cannot compare two CDs with DISKCOMP, even though DISKCOMP doesn't try to write on the disks. If you address a CD-ROM drive with DISKCOMP, you get the message `Cannot DISKCOMP to or from a network drive`. (DISKCOMP is obviously a little confused about what the problem is. Nevertheless, the message is clear—you can't use DISKCOMP on this drive.)

Managing Internal Labels with VOL and LABEL

You can create a volume label for a disk when you format it. The label is stored internally (in the root directory), and appears in such places as directory and tree listings. DOS does not use the label; it identifies disks by their serial numbers. The label is mostly for your use. Other programs, however, might pay attention to disk labels. Some Install or Setup programs, for example, check disk labels to make sure that the correct disks have been inserted.

Some applications display the label in drive lists. For example, Figure 18.4 shows WordPerfect for Windows 6.0's File Open dialog box. You can see the list of drives under the word Drives. The labels of the hard drives are shown in the list.

You can view the label of a disk with the VOL command. (See Figure 18.5.) Try viewing the label of your disk:

Figure 18.4.
A typical drive list showing volume labels as well as drive names.

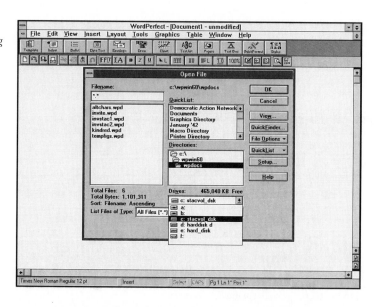

VOL

Displays a disk's volume label and serial number, if they exist.

Syntax:

VOL [*drive*]

Parameters and Switches:

none Displays the volume label and serial number, if any, of the current drive.

drive Specifies a drive whose volume label and serial number you want to see.

Figure 18.5. *VOL command summary.*

1. Enter **VOL** to see the label of the current disk.

   DOS displays a message something like this (your label and serial number will be different):

   ```
   Volume in drive C is MY HARD DRIVE

   Volume Serial Number is 1CFB-7D56
   ```

2. Enter **VOL A:** to see the label of the disk in drive A.

To change a label, you use the LABEL command. (See Figure 18.6.) You can include the new label in the command or let LABEL prompt you for it. Try changing the label of the disk in drive A to PRACTICE:

LABEL

Displays and changes the volume label of a disk.

Syntax:

`LABEL [drive] [label]`

Parameters:

none Displays the volume label of the current drive and lets you change or delete it.

drive Identifies the location of the disk whose label you want to display and/or change; the default is the current drive.

label Specifies a new volume label for the disk; the label may contain up to 11 characters.

Figure 18.6. *LABEL command summary.*

1. Enter **LABEL A: PRACTICE**.

   You can hear the drive working and see the light come on, but you won't get any confirmation message from DOS.

2. Enter **VOL A:** to see the new label.

You don't use quotation marks in the LABEL command as you do with FORMAT, even if the new label contains a space. This means that you can't eliminate a label by including a null label on the command line; without quotation marks, there's no way to specify the null label. Instead, you enter the LABEL command with no label text and wait for LABEL to ask you for a label.

Network Note: You can most likely view the volume labels of your network drives, but you probably can't change them.

Note: You can view the label of a disk in a read-only drive, but you can't change it. If you try to change the label of a CD, for example, you get the message `Cannot label a network drive`.

Try removing the label from the disk in drive A:

1. Enter **LABEL** *drive* with no label parameter.

   DOS displays the current label and asks for a new one.

2. Press Enter.

3. When LABEL asks whether you want to delete the current label, enter Y.

On Your Own

In this chapter, you learned how to make duplicate copies of disks, compare the copies to the originals, and view and change a disk's volume label. If you would like to practice these techniques on your own, you can use the following steps as a guide:

1. Make a duplicate copy of a floppy in drive A.

2. If you have a drive B that is a different size or capacity than drive A, make a duplicate copy of a floppy in drive B.

3. Compare the duplicates from steps 1 and 2 to their originals.

4. Change the labels on the duplicates to read ON MY OWN 1 and ON MY OWN 2.

19

The DOS Editor

Introduction

DOS's Editor makes it easy to manage those pesky little text files that are so surprisingly hard to handle with most word processors.

Working with DOS Editor

DOS has always included a text editor so that people can edit simple ASCII text files, such as AUTOEXEC.BAT and CONFIG.SYS, without bothering with a word processor. But, DOS's original editor was so unfriendly that only a dedicated programmer could love it. DOS 5 finally introduced an easy-to-use, full-screen, graphic-interface editor called DOS Editor (or just EDIT).

DOS Editor makes it easy not only to create and modify text files, but also to view them. With DOS Editor, you can open a document such as README.TXT, scroll back and forth in it, print all or a portion of it, add your own notes, and so on.

If you use a word processor on a regular basis and you're used to its way of doing things, you might prefer it, even for editing text files. But, there are good reasons to use DOS Editor. DOS Editor was designed specifically for text files; most of the leading word processors format their document files so that they contain non-ASCII characters. You have to go out of your way to avoid this formatting and store a file in ASCII format. If you forget and let your word processor format the file, DOS can't read it; if it's a .BAT file or CONFIG.SYS, it won't work.

Even though DOS Editor is not as full-featured as the average word processor, it has more facilities than many text editors:

- DOS Editor's graphic user interface enables you to use your mouse or keyboard to edit text and access menus and dialog boxes
- DOS Editor has a complete online help system to guide you through unfamiliar procedures
- DOS Editor includes a Clipboard so that you can cut, copy, and paste text in a document, or from document to document
- You can search for text and replace it with other text

In this chapter, you will learn how to:

- Start up EDIT
- Insert, delete, and overtype text
- Cut and paste text
- Find and replace text
- Save a file
- Open a file for editing
- Print files
- Get on-screen help while using the editor

Warning: DOS's Editor is a function of the QBASIC programming system. You can't use EDIT if you delete QBASIC.EXE.

Starting DOS Editor

You can start DOS Editor in several ways. You can use these techniques from the Shell:

- Choose Editor (in the Main group)
- Open EDIT.COM in the DOS directory
- Drop an ASCII text file on top of EDIT.COM
- Open a .TXT file. (All .TXT files are associated with EDIT.COM.)
- Use File, Run to enter an EDIT command at the DOS prompt

From the DOS command prompt, you start the editor using the EDIT command. (See Figure 19.1.) If you don't include a filespec, DOS Editor starts with an empty, untitled document.

EDIT

Starts DOS's full-screen editor, which creates, modifies, and displays ASCII text files.

Syntax:

EDIT [*filespec*]

Parameter:

none	Starts the editor with default screen characteristics and no startup file.
filespec	Opens an ASCII text file. If the file does not exist, creates it; if it does exist, displays its contents.

Figure 19.1. *EDIT command summary.*

Try starting up the editor now:

1. If you are not at the primary DOS command prompt, exit your current program and get to the command prompt.
2. Enter **EDIT** to start up the editor.

An initial dialog box tells you to press Enter for help, or Esc for the editing screen. If you press Enter, some initial help information is displayed. When you press Esc, you see a blank editing screen and you can start creating a new document.

3. Press Esc to clear the dialog box.

Tip: When you want to create a new file, you can include the new filespec in the EDIT command to start up the editor. EDIT creates the new file right away, even though it contains no text.

Figure 19.2 shows what DOS Editor's screen looks like when a document is open for editing. At the top is the menu bar. The main portion, in the middle, is the document editing area. The bottom line is a status bar. Two scroll bars provide mouse control.

Figure 19.2.
The DOS Editor screen.

```
   File  Edit  Search  Options                                    Help
                           README.TXT
 README.TXT
 NOTES ON MS-DOS 6.22
 =====================
 This file provides important information not included in the
 MICROSOFT MS-DOS USER'S GUIDE or in MS-DOS Help.

 This file is divided into the following major sections:

 1. Setup
 2. MemMaker, EMM386, and Memory Management
 3. Windows
 4. Hardware Compatibility with MS-DOS 6.22
 5. Microsoft Backup, Defrag and Anti-Virus
 6. Third-Party Programs
 7. DriveSpace

 If the subject you need information about doesn't appear in
 this file, you might find it in one of the following text
 files included with MS-DOS:

                                                       C  00001:001
```

Lines Versus Paragraphs

If you're used to a word processor, you're used to working with paragraphs. But, a text editor works with lines, not paragraphs. A line is a string of up to 255 characters terminated by a carriage return. DOS Editor does not wrap lines; if a line is longer than the viewing area, it continues off into the void. You must scroll sideways to see the entire line. Use the horizontal scroll bar (at the bottom of the editing area) to scroll sideways, or simply move the cursor in the desired direction.

Try typing a long line to see the screen scroll; type the first sentence of Lincoln's Gettysburg Address, as follows. (Don't worry about typos. This is just an exercise, not a civics lesson.)

```
Four score and seven years ago, our fathers brought forth on this continent a new
nation, conceived in liberty and dedicated to the proposition that all men are
created equal.
```

You should see the screen start to scroll by the time you get to new nation.

Editing Text

You edit an existing document by inserting, deleting, overtyping, copying, and moving text. This means that you need to be able to move the cursor, select text, switch between Insert and Overstrike mode, cut and paste, and search and replace. You can do much of this with your mouse. If you prefer the keyboard, DOS Editor recognizes not only the standard keyboard cursor keys such as the up-arrow and down-arrow keys, but also the WordStar control keys such as Ctrl+E and Ctrl+X.

Tip: Many of the keys on your keyboard execute functions, such as cursor movement functions, when combined with the Ctrl key. But if you press Ctrl+P first, and then Ctrl+*letter*, a special character often results. For example, Ctrl+P followed by Ctrl+Y inserts a downward pointing arrow (↓) in your document.

When you type Ctrl+P, the symbol ^P appears in the status bar to remind you that the next thing you type will insert a special character into your document. When you type the next character, the ^P is removed from the status bar.

Another way to type special characters is to hold down the Alt key while you type a numeric code. You can type any character in your system's code page this way. Chapter 49, "Another Country Heard From," explains code pages and how to use them.

Cursor Movement

To move the cursor with your mouse, scroll as necessary and click the position you want. If you prefer the keyboard, Table 19.1 shows the cursor-movement keys. Notice that the WordStar keys give you some functions that the standard keys don't. But, don't worry about memorizing unfamiliar key combinations. You can always get where you're going with the standard keys, even if it takes a little longer.

Table 19.1. Cursor-movement keys.

Standard Key	WordStar Key	Function
↑	Ctrl+E	Up one line
↓	Ctrl+X	Down one line
←	Ctrl+S	Left one character
→	Ctrl+D	Right one character
Ctrl+←	Ctrl+A	Left one word
Ctrl+→	Ctrl+F	Right one word
Home	Ctrl+Q,S	Beginning of line
End	Ctrl+Q,D	End of line
Ctrl+Enter	Ctrl+J	Beginning of next line
(none)	Ctrl+Q,E	Top of window
(none)	Ctrl+Q,X	Bottom of window
Ctrl+Home	Ctrl+Q,R	Beginning of file
Ctrl+End	Ctrl+Q,C	End of file

Practice moving around in the file that you have created so far:

1. Press Home to jump to the beginning of the line.
2. Press right-arrow to move the cursor to the right.
3. Press Ctrl+right-arrow to move to the right word by word.
4. Press left-arrow to move to the left.
5. Press Ctrl+left-arrow to move to the left word by word.

If you have a mouse, practice scrolling to the left and right, and clicking on a position to place the cursor there.

Inserting Text

By default, you are in Insert mode. Press the Ins key or Ctrl+V to switch back and forth between Insert and Overstrike modes. The cursor changes to a flashing rectangle when you're in Overstrike mode.

To insert text, position the cursor where you want it, make sure that you're in Insert mode, and start typing. The new characters shove the rest of the line to the right. DOS Editor beeps and refuses to accept any more characters when the line reaches the 255 character limit.

Try inserting some carriage returns in the text that you have already typed to shorten the lines:

1. Move the cursor to the end of the word `continent`.

2. Press Enter.

    EDIT inserts a carriage return after the word `continent`. The rest of the sentence moves down to the next line.

3. Insert a carriage return after the word `proposition`.

    Now the sentence takes 2 1/2 lines and you can read it all on your screen.

Selecting Text

There are many occasions when you need to select text. You might, for example, select a block of text to be moved, copied, or printed. You can select part of a line; or, if you want to select text from more than one line, you must select whole lines.

You drag the pointer with your mouse to select text. Drag the pointer left or right to select part of a line. If you drag the pointer up or down, you select whole lines. To select text with the keyboard, hold down the Shift key while you move the cursor. To deselect text, click somewhere, move the cursor without holding down Shift, or press Esc.

Try your hand at selecting some text in the file that you are creating:

1. Press Ctrl+Home to move the cursor to the beginning of the file.

2. Hold down the Shift key and press right-arrow until you have selected `Four score and seven`.

    You see a selection highlight grow as you move the cursor.

3. Press Esc to release the selection.

    The cursor remains at the end of the word `seven`.

4. Hold down Shift and press down-arrow once to select the first two lines.

    Both lines are selected in their entirety.

5. Press Esc to release the selection.

If you have a mouse, repeat the previous exercise using your mouse.

Deleting Text

You can delete text in several ways. Table 19.2 shows various keys you can use. Keep in mind that, if you hold down a key, it repeats and you can delete a string of text.

Table 19.2. Deleting keys.

Standard Key	WordStar Key	Function
Backspace	Ctrl+H	Delete one character to the left
Delete	Ctrl+G	Delete one character (or delete the selected block)
(none)	Ctrl+T	Delete the remainder of the current word
Shift+Tab	(none)	Delete the leading spaces from the selected lines

Try deleting some text:

1. Select score and seven from the first line.

2. Press Delete to delete the selected text.

   The first line now reads Four years ago....

3. Position the cursor at the beginning of the word conceived.

4. Hold down the Delete key until you have deleted conceived in liberty and. (If you go too far, don't worry about it now.)

   The second line now reads, a new nation, dedicated to the proposition....

Cutting and Pasting

When you cut a block, you delete it from where it is but save it in a special memory area called a Clipboard. You also can copy a block to the Clipboard, which saves it in the Clipboard without removing it from its present location. You can't see the Clipboard, but it always contains the last thing that you cut or copied. You can paste the contents of the Clipboard anywhere you want. Table 19.3 shows the keys that cut and copy blocks to the Clipboard and paste things from the Clipboard. Many of these functions are also available from the Edit menu if you prefer to use your mouse.

Table 19.3. Clipboard keys.

Key	Function
Shift+Del	Cut block to Clipboard
Ctrl+Y	Cut current line to Clipboard
Ctrl+Ins	Copy block to Clipboard
Ctrl+Q,Y	Cut to Clipboard from cursor to end of line
Shift+Ins	Paste block from Clipboard

How to Copy a Block of Text to Another Location in DOS's Text Editor

1. Select the block.

2. Choose Edit Copy or press Ctrl+Ins.

3. Move the cursor to the desired destination.

4. Choose Edit Paste or press Shift+Ins.

5. Repeat steps 3 and 4 as often as desired.

How to Move a Block of Text to Another Location in DOS's Text Editor

1. Select the block.

2. Choose Edit, Cut or press Shift+Del.

3. Move the cursor to the desired destination.

4. Choose Edit, Paste or press Shift+Ins.

Try moving some text in the file that you are creating:

1. Select a new nation. Include the space before the word a so that it will be moved too.

2. Press Shift+Del or choose Edit, Cut to cut the text to the Clipboard.

   The block disappears from the file.

3. Position the cursor on the space before on this continent.

4. Press Shift+Ins or choose Edit, Paste to insert the block from the Clipboard into the file.

   The first line now reads, ...our fathers brought forth a new nation on this continent....

5. Move the cursor down to the beginning of the first blank line.

6. Paste the text two more times.

   The fourth line now reads, a new nation a new nation.

When you move and copy text, you should consider the spacing that surrounds it. You would normally include either the space that precedes it or the one that follows it, depending on the punctuation in both the old and the new locations. In the preceding example, you selected the preceding space because the phrase was followed by a comma. Then, you positioned the cursor to insert the block so that there would be a space following it also. Sometimes you just can't work out the spacing correctly and you have to adjust it after you paste the block. (In this example, you would have to fix the comma that now starts the second line if you weren't just practicing.)

Finding and Replacing

Suppose that you use DOS Editor to create a 19-page README.TXT document, and then discover that you used the term *block* when you should have said *handle*. You may need to make dozens of changes to correct the error. DOS Editor's find-and-replace feature can make the changes for you. All you have to do is fill in the Change dialog box. (See Figure 19.3.)

Figure 19.3.
The Change dialog box.

```
┌─────────────────────── Change ───────────────────────┐
│                                                       │
│ Find What: ┌─────────────────────────────────────┐   │
│            └─────────────────────────────────────┘   │
│                                                       │
│ Change To: ┌─────────────────────────────────────┐   │
│            └─────────────────────────────────────┘   │
│                                                       │
│                                                       │
│     [ ] Match Upper/Lowercase        [ ] Whole Word   │
│                                                       │
├───────────────────────────────────────────────────────┤
│   Find and Verify    < Change All >  < Cancel > < Help >│
└───────────────────────────────────────────────────────┘
```

You enter the string of text to be replaced in the Find What box, and enter the replacement string in the Change To box.

> **Tip:** To delete a string instead of replacing it, leave the Change To box blank.

Try changing `nation` to `country`:

1. Press Alt+S or click Search to pull down the Search menu.

2. Press C or click Change to select the `Change` command.

   The Change dialog box opens.

3. Type **nation** in the Find What box

4. Press Tab to move to the Change To box. Or click the Change To box.

5. Type **country** in the Change To box.

6. Press Alt+C or click Change All to choose the Change All button.

   EDIT changes every occurrence of `nation` to `country`. A message box tells you that the change is complete.

7. Press Enter or click OK to close the message box.

If you don't check Match Upper/Lowercase, DOS Editor ignores case when searching for the string; that is, BLOCK, Block, and block will all be found. But, DOS Editor replaces all occurrences with the exact string, including case, that you specify in the Change To box. So, if you want to change BLOCK to HANDLE, Block to Handle, and block to handle, you must use three separate Change commands.

When you check Match Upper/Lowercase, DOS Editor finds only those strings that match the case shown in the Find What box. Suppose that you want to change all instances of DOSKEY to DosKey, but you want to leave DOSkey alone. You must check the Match Upper/Lowercase box to avoid changing DOSkey too. Figure 19.4 shows how to set up the dialog box for this replacement task.

Figure 19.4.
Changing DOSKEY *to*
DosKey.

```
┌───────────────────────── Change ─────────────────────────┐
│                                                           │
│ Find What:  │DOSKEY                                      │ │
│                                                           │
│ Change To:  │DosKey                                      │ │
│                                                           │
│                                                           │
│     [X] Match Upper/Lowercase        [ ] Whole Word       │
├───────────────────────────────────────────────────────────┤
│   Find and Verify   < Change All >  < Cancel >  < Help >  │
└───────────────────────────────────────────────────────────┘
```

The Whole Word option also might be necessary. When you're changing new to country, for example, you probably don't want to change newly to countryly or knew to kcountry. If Whole Word is checked, DOS Editor finds only instances of new that are surrounded by spaces and punctuation marks.

When you have filled in the boxes, you must choose a command button to start the replacement. Find and Verify shows you each found string and lets you decide whether to replace it. You could call this the tortoise method; it's slow but sure. Change All makes all the replacements without asking for confirmation. This is the hare method; it's fast, but it can make some strange substitutions, especially if you don't check Whole Word.

> **Tip:** Avoid using spaces in your find string. A phrase containing spaces might be split over the end of a line in the document, and DOS Editor wouldn't find it.

Using Find without Replace

Suppose that, instead of replacing instances of new, you simply want to look at them. You could use the Search Find command, which opens the dialog box shown in Figure 19.5. The Find What box and the two check boxes are the same as in the Change dialog box. When you select OK, DOS Editor locates the next matching string, marks it as a block, and terminates the search. When you're finished working with that string, press F3 (or choose Edit, Repeat Find) to find the next occurrence.

Figure 19.5.
The Find dialog box.

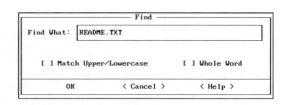

Try finding the word country in your file:

1. Choose the Search, Find command.

   The Find dialog box opens. A default value appears in the Find What box.

2. Delete the default value in the Find What box and type **country**.

3. Press Enter or click OK.

   EDIT highlights the next occurrence of the word country and places the cursor under the letter c.

4. Press F3.

   EDIT highlights the next occurrence of the word country.

5. Press F3 several more times.

   Each time, EDIT highlights the next occurrence of the word.

Tip: Search Find can be a handy way to move the cursor long distances in a document, as long as you can come up with a unique text string, contained in one line, to search for.

DOS Editor remembers the last Find What and Change To text you entered. The next time you open either dialog box, the most recent Find What text appears as the default. You can use the text as is, edit it, or replace it. When you open the Change box, the most recent Change To text appears as the default replacement text.

Managing Files

As you have seen, you can open a file when you start DOS Editor, or you can use the empty editing space to create a new file. The File menu provides the commands that open and save files, print files, and exit DOS Editor. (See Figure 19.6.)

Figure 19.6.
The File menu.

```
  File Edit  Search  Options                                    Help
 ┌────────────────────┐     README.TXT
 │ New                │
 │ Open...            │
 │ Save               │
 │ Save As...         │
 ├────────────────────┤ mportant information not included in the
 │ Print...           │ SER'S GUIDE or in MS-DOS Help.
 ├────────────────────┤
 │ Exit               │  into the following major sections:
 └────────────────────┘
 1. Setup
 2. MemMaker, EMM386, and Memory Management
 3. Windows
 4. Hardware Compatibility with MS-DOS 6.2
 5. Microsoft Programs
 6. Third-Party Programs
 7. DoubleSpace

 If the subject you need information about doesn't appear in
 this file, you might find it in one of the following text
 files included with MS-DOS:
                                                       N 00001:001
```

Saving a New File

When you're ready to save an untitled document—one that's never been saved before—choose File, Save or File, Save As.... Figure 19.7 shows the Save As dialog box that opens in either case. You select the drive and directory in which you want to save the file and then enter a name in the File Name box; or, you can type the complete filespec in the File Name box.

Figure 19.7.
The Save As dialog box.

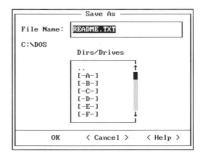

In the example in Figure 19.7, the current directory is C:\DOS. (Look at the line just below File Name.) To change drives, double-click the desired drive name, [-A-], [-B-], and so on. The directories related to the current directory appear in the same dialog box. In the example, the only directory name in the list is the parent directory (..). If the current directory had children, they would also be listed. To change directories, double-click the name of the desired directory. Because only direct relatives of the current directory are listed, you sometimes must change directories several times to reach the one you want.

Save the file that you have been creating:

1. Choose File, Save.

   The Save As dialog box opens.

2. Type **C:\PRAC1.TXT** in the File Name box.

3. Press Enter or click OK.

   DOS creates the new file in the designated directory.

Note: You can't save a file to a write-only drive such as a CD-ROM drive.

Network Note: You won't have any trouble saving files on your local drives; but you may or may not be able to save a file on a network drive, depending on your access rights for that drive.

You can replace an existing file with the new file. Just enter its name in the File Name box; be sure to include the path name if it's not in the current directory. When DOS Editor asks whether you want to replace it, choose Yes.

File, Save As doesn't apply to new files only. For example, you could open README.TXT, add your own comments to it, and save it as MYREADME.TXT. README.TXT would continue to exist in its unedited form. MYREADME.TXT would be a new file (unless it replaced an existing one).

Saving a File That Already Has a Name

The File, Save command saves your current work in the open file. For example, if you open AUTOEXEC.BAT, make some changes, and choose File, Save, the changes are saved in AUTOEXEC.BAT. No dialog box is displayed.

Peter's Principle: Save early and save often.

If your system freezes up or if the power blacks out, you lose whatever data is in memory only, but you don't lose what's on disk. Don't wait to complete a whole file before saving it. Save it for the first time as soon as you start creating it, and save it every few minutes as you work. I save a file at the end of every paragraph and every time I stop to think.

If you're working in DOS Shell or Windows, always save your file before switching away from the editor to another application. There's always a chance that your system will hang up and you won't be able to get back to the file to save it properly.

Opening Files

You can open and work on as many documents as needed, but only one at a time. Choose File, Open to open an existing document. In the dialog box displayed, you can choose the drive, directory, and file; or, you can just type the filespec in the File Name box.

If you want to create a brand new document instead, choose File, New. The document is an untitled document until you save it the first time. Whenever you open a new or existing document, if the current document has been changed since the last time you saved it, DOS Editor asks whether you want to save it before opening the new one.

Try opening a new file:

1. Choose File, New.

2. The PRAC1.TXT file closes and a new, untitled document opens.

3. Type **Now we are engaged in a great civil war**.

Try returning to the PRAC1.TXT file. (Don't save the current file first.)

1. Choose File, Open.

   The Open dialog box appears.

2. Type **C:\PRAC1.TXT** in the File Name box.

   A dialog box warns you that the loaded file is not saved and asks if you want to save it now.

3. Press Enter or click Yes.

   The Save As dialog box opens.

4. Type **C:\PRAC2.TXT** in the File Name box.

5. Press Enter or click OK.

   PRAC2.TXT closes and PRAC1.TXT opens.

Note: DOS Editor also asks whether you want to save the current file if there are unsaved changes when you choose File, Exit.

Printing Files

You use the File, Print command to print the current document. Try it with PRAC1.TXT:

1. If your printer is a local printer (as opposed to a shared printer on a network), make sure it's ready. (See the note in "Printing through the Shell" in Chapter 9, "Additional File Management in the Shell.")

2. Choose File, Print.

   A dialog box asks if you want to print selected text only or the complete document. A dot indicates the default option. In this case, the complete document is the default option because no text is selected.

3. Press up-arrow and down-arrow a few times to move the dot that indicates the selected option. Leave the dot on Complete Document.

4. Press Enter or click OK to print the text.

   If the file doesn't print, see the Problem Solver in "Redirecting Command Output" in Chapter 12, "Working at the Command Prompt."

Getting Help

DOS Editor's Help system provides on-screen guidance as you work with the DOS Editor functions. Figure 19.8 shows what the DOS Editor screen looks like with Help activated. A Help menu or topic appears in the top window, and the open document appears in the bottom. You can keep the Help topic on-screen to guide you as you work in the document.

Figure 19.8.
The DOS Editor screen with an open Help window.

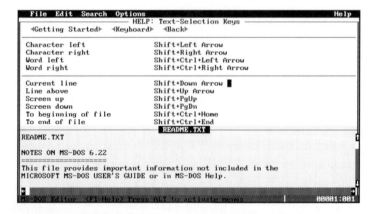

Note: The EDIT.HLP file contains the help information. By default, DOS looks for EDIT.HLP first in the current directory, then in the program search path. If your EDIT.HLP file is located elsewhere, use the Options, Help Path command to tell DOS where to find EDIT.HLP.

DOS Editor's Help system has three main sections: Keyboard, Getting Started, and Survival Guide. The Keyboard section documents the keys that you can use with DOS Editor; it offers such topics as Text Scrolling Keys and Delete Keys. (In the example, you can see the Text-Selection Keys topic.)

The Getting Started section shows you how to get started in DOS Editor and includes general editing topics, such as Using a Dialog Box and MS-DOS Editor Options. The Survival Guide is just one topic that documents a few of the most important actions, such as how to pull down a menu and how to exit Help. Each section provides a means to link to the other two sections.

There are several ways to get Help in DOS Editor:

- Press Enter (instead of Esc) when DOS Editor first starts without opening a document. The Survival Guide opens.

- Choose one of the commands in the Help menu.

- Press F1 to display the appropriate Help topic for the command or dialog box you're working on. (If no Help topic exists for that command or dialog box, the Getting Started topic opens.)

- Press Shift+F1 or click F1=Help on the status bar to open the Survival Guide.

Try opening Keyboard Help:

1. Press Alt+H or click Help to pull down the Help menu.
2. Press K or click Keyboard to choose the Keyboard command.

    The first topic in the Keyboard Help library opens.

If you press F1 from a dialog box, you don't really enter the Help system; you just see an explanation of that dialog box and you press OK to close it. But, all the other methods take you into the Help system and, once there, you easily can get to any topic.

The labels enclosed in highlighted arrowheads, such as <Getting Started> in the figure, are jumps to other topics. To use one, double-click it, click the right mouse button on it, or use the Tab key to move to it and press F1.

Try jumping to the Shortcut Keys topic. To do this tab to Shortcut Keys and press Enter, or click the right mouse button on Shortcut Keys. The Shortcut Keys topic opens.

The status bar shows other commands that you can use in the Help system. Press F6 or click F6=Window to toggle the cursor between the editing window and the Help window. You also can click the position where you want the cursor to be. Press Shift+F1 to display the next Help topic in sequence (Help decides what the sequence is). Press Alt+F1 to display the previous topic in the list of topics that you have viewed. You can back up 20 topics this way. The Back jump also does this. You can print a Help topic just like a document. The Esc key closes the Help window and returns the document to the full screen. Close the Help window now:

1. Press Esc to close the Help window.
2. Press Alt+F, X to exit the Editor.

Customizing the Editor Screen

By default, the editor screen is displayed on a color monitor with white text on a blue background. If that color scheme doesn't work for you, you can choose any other combination of foreground and background. Choose Options, Display while in the Editor to open a dialog box where you can select the colors you want to use.

The Options, Display feature also lets you suppress scroll bars, if you wish, and set tab stops. By default, there are tab stops in every eighth column. You can change that to some other number. For example, if you set tab stops to 10, there will be tab stops in columns 10, 20, 30, and so on.

EDIT Command Switches

The EDIT command includes these optional switches in case the default settings don't work on your system:

/B	Displays the editor in monochrome if you have a color monitor.
/G	Speeds up the editor with a CGA monitor. (If your monitor experiences snow with this option, restart the editor without using /G.)
/H	Displays the highest number of lines per screen that your monitor can handle.
/NOHI	Tells the editor that your monitor does not have a high intensity feature. (Don't use this switch with a Compaq laptop.)

On Your Own

You have learned how to use the DOS text editor in this chapter. The following items will help you practice using the editor on your own:

1. Start the editor and start a new file.
2. Type the introduction to this chapter as text for your new file.
3. Save the file as C:\PRAC3.TXT.
4. Open PRAC1.TXT and edit it back to its original content—the first sentence of the Gettysburg Address. (See "Lines Versus Paragraphs" near the beginning of this chapter.)
5. Save PRAC1.TXT.

6. Look up the Delete Keys in the Help system.

7. Print the Delete Keys topic.

8. Print PRAC1.TXT.

9. Exit the editor.

10. Delete the files you have created in this chapter: C:\PRAC1.TXT through C:\PRAC3.TXT.

20 Basic Batch Programs

Introduction

You can create your own programs out of the everyday commands that you enter at the command prompt, plus a few special commands. Batch programs can save you time, energy, and typing errors.

Creating Your Own Programs

Do you use a certain series of commands over and over? You're probably tired of typing them repeatedly (and of making typing errors). You already have learned how to create a DOSKEY macro out of a short series of commands. Another way to store and recall commands is in a batch program file, which is an ASCII text file with the extension .BAT.

Batch programs offer several advantages over macros:

- You can use as many lines as you need in a batch file (a DOSKEY macro must fit on one command line)
- You can include some commands and parameters that are not available in macros
- You save batch files permanently on disk; they aren't lost when you shut down or reboot your system
- You can distribute the batch files to other people

The major disadvantage of a batch file compared to a DOSKEY macro is in the way you access it. Because the batch file is stored on disk, DOS must search for it and load it into memory just like any other program. Therefore, it takes longer to load, and DOS could fail to find it.

In this chapter, you will learn how to:

- Create a batch program file
- Run a batch program
- Clear the command prompt screen
- Annotate a batch file
- Control messages displayed by a batch program
- Pause a program until the user presses any key
- Call one batch program from another batch program
- Use replaceable parameters in a batch program
- Understand your AUTOEXEC.BAT file
- Use Batch Files in DOS Shell

Creating a Batch File

A batch program file must be an ASCII text file with the extension .BAT. Most people use DOS's text editor to create their batch files. You type one command per line in the file.

Try your hand at creating a batch file:

1. Start up the editor for a new document named C:\FINDBIN.BAT.

2. Type the following command:

    ```
    DIR C:\*.BIN /S /B
    ```

    This command lists all the .BIN files on your hard drive.

3. Save the file and exit the editor.

Peter's Principle: Always use absolute path names in batch programs.

You don't know which drive and directory will be current when a batch file is executed, so make sure that DOS can find the necessary files by including absolute path names in every filespec. Rather than using \DOS\README.TXT, for example, specify C:\DOS\README.TXT.

Tip: You can create a batch file from your DOSKEY macro set using the command `DOSKEY /M > filename`. The contents of the file will look like like this:

macroname1=macrodefinition1

macroname2=macrodefinition2

and so on. To execute the macros as a program, edit the file and remove *macroname=* from each line. To use the file as a batch program to define these macros, edit the file and insert DOSKEY in front of each line.

Similarly, you can create a batch file from your DOSKEY history using the command `DOSKEY /H > filename`. You probably will need to edit the file to insert `ECHO` commands, to delete unwanted commands, and perhaps to make other changes as well. Then you can edit the file like any other batch program.

Running a Batch Program

You run a batch file like any other program, by typing its name with or without the extension at the command prompt. Try executing FINDBIN.BAT:

1. Type **FINDBIN**.

    DOS lists the command, followed by .BIN files on your hard disk.

Locating the Batch File

When you enter a command such as FINDBIN at the command prompt, DOS follows a standard order of processing:

1. If any TSRs that process keyboard input are loaded, they get first access to the newly entered command (in the order they were loaded). For example, if DOSKEY is loaded and currently has a macro named FINDBIN, DOSKEY processes the command.

2. If no TSR claims the command, DOS's command processor must handle it. First, DOS looks for an internal command named FINDBIN.

> **Note:** Internal commands are built into the command processor (COMMAND.COM), and reside in memory with DOS. Your most common DOS commands, such as DIR and CD, are internal commands.

3. Because FINDBIN isn't an internal command, DOS looks next in the current directory for a file named FINDBIN.COM, FINDBIN.EXE, or FINDBIN.BAT, in that order. Notice that .BAT files come at the end of the pecking order.

4. If DOS can't find a FINDBIN program in the current directory, it looks in the first directory in the program search path. If the program file isn't there, DOS looks in the second directory in the path, and so on. In each directory, it looks first for FINDBIN.COM, then for FINDBIN.EXE, and finally for FINDBIN.BAT.

5. If DOS doesn't find a FINDBIN program, you see the message Bad command or file name and you return to the command prompt.

As you can see, it's important to choose your batch file names carefully. For best results, don't duplicate the name of a DOSKEY macro, internal command, or .COM or .EXE program that exists in any directory in the search path. If you're going to use the program often, you might want to keep its name short, as in FB.BAT. Otherwise, make it easy to remember—for example, FINDBIN.BAT.

> **Tip:** For maximum convenience, keep all batch files in a single directory and include that directory near the beginning of your program search path.

Understanding How the Batch File Executes

When DOS executes a batch file, it carries out the commands in the order they appear in the file. For each command, DOS displays a blank line, displays the command prompt, fills in the command, and then executes it. Displaying the blank line, the command prompt, and the command is called *echoing the command*. At the end of the program, DOS might display one or two command prompts as it reads empty lines from the end of the file. Then, DOS terminates the batch file and displays a command prompt for you to use.

All those echoed commands and empty command prompts can be confusing to an inexperienced user. You'll learn how to suppress them later in this chapter.

Stopping the Batch File

Suppose that one of the commands in a batch file displays an error message, and you realize that you need to cancel the rest of the program. You can stop a batch file by pressing one of the break key combinations, Ctrl+C or Ctrl+Break. When interrupted, the batch file displays the message `Terminate batch job (Y/N)?`, and waits for an answer. If you press N, the program terminates the current command but continues with the next one; if you press Y, the entire batch file ends and you return to the command prompt. Some commands can't be interrupted at all; others respond immediately to the break keys. Sometimes a break key stops the current command only; you need to repeat it to cancel each subsequent command until you see the `Terminate batch job (Y/N)?` message.

Note: You can interrupt programs faster when DOS's Break feature is on. See the `BREAK` command.

Using Special Batch Commands

Any command that you can enter at the command prompt you also can put into a batch file, except for DOSKEY macros. DOS offers several commands that are particularly useful in batch files. The `CLS`, `REM`, `ECHO`, `PAUSE`, and `CALL` commands are almost always used in batch files rather than at the command prompt.

Clearing the Screen

CLS (CLear Screen) clears the screen and puts the cursor in the top left corner. This command has no parameters. You also can enter CLS at the command prompt to clean up your screen or hide your work.

Try clearing your screen:

1. Type **CLS**.

   The screen clears.

People often use CLS near the beginning of a batch program to remove any previous information from the screen before displaying new messages. You also might want to clear the output from one command in the program before starting the next command.

Annotating the Program

The REM command creates notes or comments in your batch program files. These notes help document what a program does, why certain commands use the options they do, and so on. Try adding CLS and a comment to your program and running it again:

1. Open FINDBIN.BAT for editing.

2. Insert the following lines at the beginning of the file:

   ```
   REM This program lists all the .BIN files on your hard drive

   CLS
   ```

3. Save the file and exit the editor.

4. Enter **FINDBIN** to execute the program.

   This time, DOS displays the comment, then quickly clears the screen before displaying the file list. If you have a reasonably fast computer, it probably happens too fast for you to see. You'll learn how to control the display shortly.

Note: FINDBIN.BAT should now look like this:

```
REM This program lists all the .BIN files on your hard drive.
CLS
DIR C:\*.BIN /S /B
```

Suppose that you have a batch file called FRESHA.BAT that redoes the physical format on the disk in drive A without destroying its files. FRESHA.BAT might contain these commands:

```
XCOPY A:\*.* C:\TEMPTEXT\ /E
FORMAT A: /U /V:""
XCOPY C:\TEMPTEXT\*.* A:\ /E
DELTREE /Y C:\TEMPTEXT
```

This program would be much easier to interpret if it included a few remarks, as follows:

```
REM This program refreshes the disk on drive A
REM Prepared by D. Tabler, ext. 423

REM Copy the tree from A to temporary branch in C:
XCOPY A:\*.* C:\TEMPTEXT\ /E

REM Refresh the sectors:
FORMAT A: /U /V:""

REM Restore the tree:
XCOPY C:\TEMPTEXT\*.* A:\ /E

REM Remove the temporary branch from C:
DELTREE /Y C:\TEMPTEXT
```

REM is often used to disable commands temporarily in a batch file. Inserting REM in front of a command turns it into a comment that DOS ignores when executing the program. If your program doesn't work properly, you can convert one line at a time to a remark until you find out where the problem is. It's easy to restore a command by removing the REM.

Controlling Messages

Use the ECHO command to turn command echoing on or off. DOS doesn't echo commands that follow ECHO OFF in a batch file. Suppressing echoing results in a much neater screen display and is much less confusing to inexperienced users.

Note: When a batch file ends, echoing reverts to the same status it had when the program started.

The ECHO OFF command itself is echoed, because DOS echoes it before turning echoing off. If you don't want to echo the ECHO OFF command, place an @ in front of it. This symbol suppresses echoing for a single command line.

Note: If you enter ECHO OFF at the command prompt, the command prompt itself disappears. Just enter ECHO ON to get it back.

You may want to display your own messages as the program runs. You can do this by using a command with this syntax:

```
ECHO message
```

Try adding some ECHO commands to your FINDBIN.BAT program:

1. Open FINDBIN.BAT for editing.
2. Insert the following command at the beginning of the file:

   ```
   @ECHO OFF
   ```

3. Insert the following commands after the CLS command:

   ```
   ECHO    **************************************
   ECHO     A List of the .BIN Files on Drive C
   ECHO    **************************************
   ```

4. Save the file and exit the editor.
5. Execute the file.

   This time, the commands don't echo, but you see the ECHO messages at the beginning of the list of files.

> **Note:** FINDBIN.BAT should now look like this:
>
> ```
> @ECHO OFF
> REM This program lists all the .BIN files on your hard drive.
> CLS
>
> ECHO    **************************************
> ECHO     A List of the .BIN Files on Drive C
> ECHO    **************************************
> DIR C:\*.BIN /S /B
> ```

Notice the difference in the way this program uses ECHO and REM messages. The ECHO messages both document the program and display messages to a user. With echoing off, the REM comments don't display, so they provide documentation only when you read the program file.

You might like to set off some of the messages with blank lines. You can type **ECHO.** to display a blank line. Be sure that the period immediately follows ECHO, with no space between. You may also want to use spaces to center a message, display asterisks to highlight a message, or even draw a box around a message to make it stand out on-screen. Combining some of these techniques, you could create a batch file like this:

1. Type **ECHO.** after each of the three ECHO commands that display a message.

2. Run the program.

   There should be a blank line after each message line.

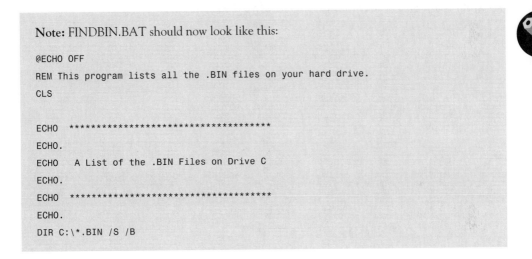

Note: FINDBIN.BAT should now look like this:

```
@ECHO OFF
REM This program lists all the .BIN files on your hard drive.
CLS


ECHO ***********************************
ECHO.
ECHO  A List of the .BIN Files on Drive C
ECHO.
ECHO ***********************************
ECHO.
DIR C:\*.BIN /S /B
```

Pausing the Program

The PAUSE command, which has no parameters, stops the progress of the batch program until you press a key. Some programs have built-in pauses. The FORMAT command, for example, always gives you a chance to change disks before starting to format. XCOPY has a special /W (wait) switch you can use to generate a pause before copying begins; in a batch program that works on floppies, this switch is useful to give someone a chance to change floppy disks. Most commands, though, begin working immediately. If you need a chance to change disks, load special paper in the printer, read messages before they scroll off the top of the screen, or even to decide whether to continue the program, a PAUSE command gives you the opportunity to do so.

Let's change FINDBIN.BAT into FBINSYS.BAT, which finds both .BIN and .SYS files on your drive:

1. Make a copy of FINDBIN.BAT named FBINSYS.BAT.

2. Open FBINSYS.BAT for editing.

3. Add the following lines at the end. (Hint: Copy the earlier lines and edit them so they say SYS instead of BIN.)

   ```
   ECHO.
   ECHO Are you ready to see the .SYS files?
   ```

```
        PAUSE


        ECHO   ************************************
        ECHO.
        ECHO   A List of the .SYS Files on Drive C
        ECHO.
        ECHO   ************************************
        ECHO.
        DIR C\*.SYS /B /S /P
```

4. Save the file and exit the editor.

5. Run FBINSYS.

   This time, DOS displays the .BIN files, then asks if you're ready to see the .SYS files, and waits for your answer.

6. Press any key.

   DOS lists your .SYS files, one at a time.

Note: FBINSYS.BAT should now look like this:

```
@ECHO OFF
REM This program lists all the .BIN files on your hard drive.
CLS


ECHO   ************************************
ECHO.
ECHO   A List of the .BIN Files on Drive C
ECHO.ECHO   ************************************
ECHO.
DIR C:\*.BIN /S /B


ECHO.
ECHO Are you ready to see the .SYS files?
PAUSE


ECHO   ************************************
ECHO.
```

```
ECHO    A List of the .SYS Files on Drive C
ECHO.
ECHO    ***********************************
ECHO.
DIR C\*.SYS /B /S /P
```

Note: You can use command redirection in a batch file. For example, you could redirect the output of the DIR commands in the preceding file to the printer. But, you can't redirect the output of the batch file itself. If you enter the command **FBINSYS > PRN**, DOS ignores the redirection.

Calling Other Batch Programs

You can start a batchprogram from another batch program. For example, rather than including the commands from FINDBIN.BAT in FBINSYS.BAT, you could call FBINSYS.BAT. Try this:

1. Open FBINSYS.BAT for editing.

2. Delete lines 3 (CLS) through 9 (DIR).

3. Insert the following command on the third line (after REM):

   FINDBIN

4. Save the file and exit the editor.

5. Run FBINSYS.

   DOS displays the *.BIN files and terminates. It does not ask if you're ready to see the *.SYS files.

Note: FBINSYS.BAT should now look like this:

```
@ECHO OFF
REM This program lists all the .BIN files on your hard drive.
FINDBIN

ECHO.
ECHO Are you ready to see the .SYS files?
PAUSE
```

```
ECHO    **************************************
ECHO.
ECHO    A List of the .SYS Files on Drive C
ECHO.
ECHO    **************************************
ECHO.
DIR C\*.SYS /B /S /P
```

Why didn't DOS complete the FBINSYS program? When you run one batch file from another, DOS transfers to the second program and never returns to the first one. In this case, when DOS processes the FINDBIN command, it starts that program and returns to the command prompt; the remaining commands in FBINSYS.BAT are never executed.

You can use the CALL command to execute another batch file without completely transferring to it. When you call a batch file, DOS returns to the original program after finishing the called program. Try using CALL to execute FINDBIN from FBINSYS.BAT:

1. Open FBINSYS.BAT for editing.

2. Insert CALL in front of the FINDBIN command.

3. Save the file and exit the editor.

4. Run FBINSYS.

    This time, the entire program runs.

Note: FBINSYS.BAT should now look like this:

```
@ECHO OFF
REM This program lists all the .BIN files on your hard drive.
CALL FINDBIN

ECHO.
ECHO Are you ready to see the .SYS files?
PAUSE

ECHO    **************************************
ECHO.
ECHO    A List of the .SYS Files on Drive C
```

```
ECHO.
ECHO  *************************************
ECHO.
DIR C\*.SYS /B /S /P
```

Using Replaceable Parameters

In Chapter 13, "DOSKEY," you learned how to make macros more flexible by using replaceable parameters. Batch files also use replaceable parameters, but they're written with a percent sign instead of a dollar sign.

A batch program can have up to 10 replaceable parameters, from `%0` to `%9`. `%0` stands for the first word in the command, which is always the name of the batch file. (If you use `%0` at all, it's usually as part of an ECHO message.)

Let's turn FINDBIN into FINDFILE, which lets you enter the desired filespec when you execute the program:

1. Make a copy of FINDBIN.BAT called FINDFILE.BAT. (Be sure to copy FINDBIN.BAT, not FBINSYS.BAT.)

2. Open FINDFILE.BAT for editing.

3. In the `DIR` command, change `*.BIN` to `%1`. Also add a `/P` to the end of the command so that a long list of files will be paged.

   The `DIR` command should now look like this:

   ```
   DIR C:\%1 /S /B /P
   ```

4. Edit the `REM` command to say:

   ```
   REM This program lists all the %1 files on your hard drive
   ```

5. Edit the third `ECHO` command to say:

   ```
   ECHO A List of the %1 Files on Drive C
   ```

6. Save the file and exit the editor.

7. Try out your new program. Type **FINDFILE COMMAND.COM**.

   DOS lists all the files on your hard drive named COMMAND.COM.

8. Try it a few more times with these filespecs:

   ```
   F*.COM
   ```

   ```
   *.HLP
   ```

   ```
   DOSSHELL.*
   ```

9. What would happen if you entered **FINDFILE** without a filespec? Try it and see.

   DOS lists all the files on the hard drive, a page at a time. Don't forget that you can press Ctrl+Break to kill the program without paging all the way through the list.

> **Note:** FINDFILE.BAT should look like this:
>
> ```
> ECHO OFF
> REM This program lists all the %1 files on your hard drive.
>
> ECHO  ************************************
> ECHO.
> ECHO   A List of the %1 Files on Drive C
> ECHO.
> ECHO  ************************************
> ECHO.
> DIR C\%1 /B /S /P
> ```

When you enter a command such as FINDFILE COMMAND.COM, DOS substitutes the parameter, COMMAND.COM, for %1 everywhere in the program. So, the commands as executed look like this:

```
@ECHO OFF
REM This program lists all the COMMAND.COM files on your hard drive.

ECHO  ************************************
ECHO.
ECHO   A List of the COMMAND.COM Files on Drive C
ECHO.
ECHO  ************************************
ECHO.
DIR C:\COMMAND.COM /B /S /P
```

As you can see, this results in listing all the COMMAND.COM files on drive C.

By making FINDFILE.BAT more flexible, you have made it much more useful than FINDBIN.BAT or FBINSYS.BAT. Take the time now to delete FINDBIN.BAT and FBINSYS.BAT. You might want to keep FINDFILE.BAT, as it can actually help you find a file on your hard disk.

Understanding Your AUTOEXEC.BAT File

Almost every system has an AUTOEXEC.BAT file. When DOS boots or reboots, it looks for this file in the root directory of the boot drive. If AUTOEXEC.BAT is there, it runs immediately after CONFIG.SYS, before you get a chance to do anything from the command prompt.

Note: Without AUTOEXEC.BAT, DOS asks for the date and time when you boot. But, AUTOEXEC suppresses the date and time functions. If your system doesn't keep track of the date and time, you probably want to include DATE and TIME commands in AUTOEXEC.BAT so that you can set the correct date and time during booting.

During installation, DOS 6 puts several commands in your AUTOEXEC.BAT file. Most people who use DOSKEY start it with a command in AUTOEXEC.BAT. A very basic AUTOEXEC.BAT file might look like this:

```
@ECHO OFF
PATH C:\; C:\DOS;
DOSKEY
```

Most AUTOEXEC.BAT files are much more complex than this. You may want to include commands to start antivirus and undelete programs from AUTOEXEC. You learn more about these commands in Chapter 25, "DOS's Antivirus Programs," and Chapter 26, "Using UNDELETE."

Tip: You can add REM, ECHO, CLS, and PAUSE commands to your AUTOEXEC.BAT file to make it easier to live with.

Take a look at your own AUTOEXEC.BAT:

1. Open C:\AUTOEXEC.BAT for editing.

   You should now understand any REM, CLS, PAUSE, and ECHO commands contained in the file. There may be commands that you don't recognize yet. Be careful not to change any commands that you don't understand. They might be essential to the running of your system.

2. Review your PATH command. Does it contain the directories you want to include in your search path, in the order of most used to least used? If not, edit or replace the command. But, don't remove any directories from the search path unless you're sure you don't need them anymore. (PATH is explained in Chapter 12, "Working at the Command Prompt.")

3. If you want a different command prompt than the one you use now, insert or replace the PROMPT command. (PROMPT is also explained in Chapter 12.)

4. If you want to start up DOS Shell or Windows automatically when you boot, insert your DOSSHELL or WIN command as the last line in the file. (Note that it's important to make this the last command in the program.) Include whatever parameters and switches you use when starting up the program at the command prompt.

5. Save the file and exit the editor. Then, reboot so that DOS will execute the new AUTOEXEC.BAT.

Looking Ahead: Now that you have mastered the basics of batch files, other commands can make your batch files more flexible. You can make decisions in a batch program, repeat a set of commands several times, and display menus to a user. Chapter 37, "Programming Logic in Batch Programs," explains the advanced functions of batch files.

Using Batch Files in DOS Shell

You can start up your batch programs from DOS Shell. If you open a .BAT entry in the file list, the program is executed, but you don't get a chance to include any parameters for the replaceable variables. For example, if you double-click FINDFILE.BAT in the file list, you'll get a list of all the files on your hard drive. Of course, in the Shell, choosing the View, All Files menu items is a better choice, as it lets you select and process files from the list.

If you use the File, Run menu items to execute a batch program, you can include parameters in the command line. And, if you create some batch files that you use regularly in DOS Shell, consider defining your own program items for them.

On Your Own

You have learned the basics of writing batch programs in this chapter. The following exercises will help you practice on your own:

1. Write a batch program called PRINTF that prints a list of all the %1 files on drive %2. (Hint: Redirect the output of a DIR command to your printer. Use ECHO to print a title for the printout and to display informational messages on the monitor.)

2. Write a batch program called VAULT that copies all the %1 files to a floppy disk in your highest capacity floppy drive. (Hint: Use XCOPY to copy files throughout the branch, creating directories on the target drive as needed. Use ECHO to display informational messages on the screen while the program is working.)

21

Configuring Your System

Introduction

The CONFIG.SYS file is essential to your system, yet many DOS users have no idea what its commands do. This chapter explains some of the mysteries.

Booting DOS

When you boot or reboot DOS, it loads its core program files into memory. Then, it looks in the root directory of the boot drive for a file called CONFIG.SYS. Commands in CONFIG.SYS help DOS set up, or configure, the system. Most of the commands are concerned with defining and managing your hardware, especially memory. Some of the commonly used commands tell DOS:

- How much memory to reserve for certain functions
- Which command processor to use
- Which device drivers to load

After carrying out all the commands in CONFIG.SYS, DOS looks for and runs AUTOEXEC.BAT. Then, DOS turns control over to you, either from the command prompt or from a program such as DOS Shell or Windows.

In this chapter, you will learn to:

- Protect your startup files (CONFIG.SYS and AUTOEXEC.BAT)
- Bypass the startup files in case of problems during booting
- Understand the structure and contents of your CONFIG.SYS file
- Understand the function of common DOS device drivers: SETVER.EXE, ANSI.SYS, HIMEM.SYS, and EGA.SYS
- Interpret the following CONFIG.SYS commands:

  ```
  DEVICE

  DOS=HIGH

  BUFFERS

  FCBS

  FILES

  SHELL

  STACKS
  ```

Taking Care of Your Startup Files

You might have an occasion to edit one or both of your startup files (CONFIG.SYS and AUTOEXEC.BAT). These files are so important to your system that you must take extra care to protect them. I recommend that you make backup copies before making any changes to them.

The location of your startup files depends on whether you use a disk compression program and, if so, whether it loads as part of the DOS core system. Your startup files are in the root directory of your boot drive (probably drive C) in either of the following cases:

- You don't use data compression on your boot drive
- You use DblSpace or DrvSpace to compress your drive

If your boot drive is compressed by Stacker 3.0 or earlier, or by any other third-party compression program, DOS boots from the root directory of the *host drive*, not the compressed drive. You might have copies of CONFIG.SYS and AUTOEXEC.BAT on the compressed drive also, so be sure to edit the ones that are in the root directory of your host drive.

If your boot drive is compressed by Stacker 3.1 or later, and you have DOS 6 or later, the location of the startup files depends on whether Stacker is loaded with the DOS core system or loaded from CONFIG.SYS. You can find out by entering the command:

STACKER

which returns a message that looks something like this:

```
Stacker drive map:
   Drive A was drive A at boot time
   Drive B was drive B at boot time
   Drive C was drive C at boot time  [ E:\STACVOL.DSK = 327.6MB  ]
   Drive D was drive D at boot time
   Drive E was drive E at boot time
```

Assuming that drive C is the compressed drive, as in the example, and that you boot from drive C, if the drive map says `Drive C was drive C at boot time`, your startup files are in the root directory of drive C. If it says `Drive C was drive x at boot time`, your system actually boots from drive *x* and that's where your startup files are located. You should preserve and edit *x*:\CONFIG.SYS and *x*:\AUTOEXEC.BAT.

Make backup copies of both files right now:

1. Make sure you know which drive your system actually boots from.
2. Switch to the root directory of that drive.
3. Enter **XCOPY CONFIG.SYS CONFIG.SAV** to back up your CONFIG.SYS file.
4. Enter **XCOPY AUTOEXEC.BAT AUTOEXEC.SAV** to back up your AUTOEXEC.BAT file.

Note: Always include both startup files when you back up your hard drive. DOS's backup utility is discussed in Chapter 23, "MSBACKUP and MWBACKUP."

After editing either startup file, reboot to try out the changes. Rebooting forces DOS to read and execute the two startup files. Changes to AUTOEXEC.BAT and CONFIG.SYS do not go into effect until you reboot.

Even if everything goes all right with your new configuration, keep the backup files around for a few days until you're sure that you like your new setup. If you decide that you want to return to the former startup file, use COPY or XCOPY to replace the current file with the former one. To restore AUTOEXEC.BAT, for example, you could enter this command:

```
COPY AUTOEXEC.SAV AUTOEXEC.BAT
```

Bypassing the Startup Files

It's not always easy making changes to your startup configuration. Sometimes a small, seemingly innocent change throws some other part of the configuration out of whack, and DOS ends up not being able to boot. The problem is, when you can't boot, you can't open up your editor; so, you can't fix the problem. But, you don't have to reach for your emergency boot floppy just yet. DOS gives you a way out of the dilemma.

If you can't boot after changing one of your startup files, reboot and press the F8 key when you see the Starting MS-DOS... message. This key asks DOS to execute your startup files line by line, giving you a chance to bypass any command in the files. With DOS 6.0, CONFIG.SYS is executed line by line, but AUTOEXEC.BAT is executed normally. With DOS 6.2 and later, both startup files are executed line by line.

> **Note:** DOS displays the Starting MS-DOS... message for several seconds, giving you plenty of time to notice the message and find the F8 key.

What good does it do to execute the startup files line by line? If you know which lines you changed and what the likely problem is, you can bypass those lines. You might end up with only part of your system, but it could be enough to give you access to your editor so that you can change CONFIG.SYS and AUTOEXEC.BAT. If you can't access the editor, you can at least use the COPY command to copy CONFIG.SAV to CONFIG.SYS and AUTOEXEC.SAV to AUTOEXEC.BAT, which will restore your previous versions of those files. The COPY command, which is an internal command, is always available as long as DOS is available. After restoring your previous startup files, you can reboot to get back to your former system.

Try executing your startup files line by line:

1. Exit any programs that are running and get back to the primary command prompt.

2. Press Ctrl+Alt+Delete to reboot.

3. When you see the message `Starting MS-DOS...`, press F8.

   You see the message `MS-DOS will prompt you to confirm each CONFIG.SYS command`. On the next line, you see the first command followed by `[Y,N]?`.

4. Press Y for each command.

   Some commands produce messages on your screen as their programs are started up. If you're having trouble starting up your system, you should scan each message for any indications of problems. After each message, DOS displays the next command in CONFIG.SYS and asks `[Y,N]?`.

   When it finishes CONFIG.SYS, DOS asks `Process AUTOEXEC.BAT [Y,N]?`. If you press N, DOS bypasses AUTOEXEC.BAT entirely. If you press Y, DOS 6.0 executes AUTOEXEC.BAT normally, but 6.2 and later process AUTOEXEC.BAT line by line.

5. If you are using DOS 6.2 or later, press Y for each command in AUTOEXEC.BAT.

   Eventually, you'll reach the end of the file and get to your normal command prompt.

If you can't get your system started using F8, DOS gives you a desperation measure. Press F5 instead of F8 when you see the `Starting MS-DOS...` message. This action bypasses the startup files entirely, giving you a very primitive system. Many of your device drivers will not be available, so you may not be able to use your mouse or your printer. But, you will be able to use the `COPY` command to restore your former startup files. Then, you can reboot and try again.

Try booting without your startup files:

1. Exit any programs that are running and get back to the primary command prompt.

2. Press Ctrl+Alt+Delete to reboot.

3. When you see the message `Starting MS-DOS...`, press F5.

   You see the message `MS-DOS is bypassing your CONFIG.SYS and AUTOEXEC.BAT files.` Then, you see the version number and the command prompt.

4. Reboot to restore your normal configuration.

> **Note:** When you bypass the startup files, DOS establishes a default command prompt of `$P$G` and a default search path of `C:\DOS` so that you can access your DOS utilities (such as the editor) easily.

Understanding What Is in CONFIG.SYS

CONFIG.SYS is an ASCII text file, somewhat like a batch file, that contains special configuration commands. Most of these commands are unique to CONFIG.SYS; you can't use them anywhere else. Nor can you use ordinary commands, such as DIR or FORMAT, in CONFIG.SYS.

Like a batch file, you can create or modify CONFIG.SYS using an ASCII editor. Unlike a batch file, you can't run CONFIG.SYS from the command prompt. CONFIG.SYS is used only during booting.

> **Note:** CONFIG.SYS runs before you have a chance to establish a search path or change the current directory. You need to include in CONFIG.SYS the full path name for any files or programs that aren't in the root directory of the boot drive.

The following is a sample CONFIG.SYS file:

```
DEVICE=C:\DOS\SETVER.EXE
DEVICE=C:\DOS\HIMEM.SYS
DEVICE=C:\DOS\ANSI.SYS
DOS=HIGH
BUFFERS=50
FILES=30
SHELL=C:\DOS\COMMAND.COM C:\DOS /P
STACKS=9,256
```

This example includes six different types of commands: DEVICE, DOS, BUFFERS, FILES, SHELL, and STACKS. These are all commands that you can use only in CONFIG.SYS. Notice their general syntax. In each case, an equal sign (=) follows the command name. To the right of the equal sign are filespecs, parameters, and/or switches.

Loading Device Drivers

DOS includes built-in software to control the basic hardware components of your system: keyboards, disk drives, memory below the 1MB limit, dot-matrix printers, and so on. But, if you have any devices beyond the basics, such as a mouse or an expanded memory board, you probably need to load device drivers to control them. You also might load a device driver to provide extra features for an ordinary device; for example, the ANSI.SYS driver lets you add color to the DOS command prompt.

Some device drivers simulate devices where there are none. The RAMDRIVE.SYS driver, for example, uses part of memory to simulate a hard disk; the DRIVER.SYS driver makes one floppy disk drive look like two.

DOS 6 includes several optional device drivers; you will find full descriptions of them in Appendix A, "Device Drivers," and many of them are described in the chapters. In addition, you might have device drivers that came with your hardware. You also can buy device drivers that have more features than the basic drivers provided by DOS. Many memory managers on the market, for example, have features you don't find in DOS.

You load a device driver with a DEVICE command in CONFIG.SYS. After it's loaded, the driver remains in memory until you remove the command from CONFIG.SYS and reboot the system.

Understanding the *DEVICE* Command

The DEVICE command has this general syntax:

```
DEVICE=filespec [parameters] [switches]
```

The DEVICE command must include the device driver's filespec followed by any necessary parameters or switches. Remember that the filespec must include the drive and path names if the file isn't in the root directory of the boot drive.

The CONFIG.SYS example earlier in the chapter loads three device drivers: SETVER.EXE, HIMEM.SYS, and ANSI.SYS. Each of these drivers is explained in the following sections.

Using SETVER

Some programs expect to run under a particular version of DOS. Many programs use techniques that were not available in early DOS versions. A program written for DOS 3, for example, might be programmed to refuse to run under any other DOS version. It might display an error message such as Incorrect DOS Version and quit. DOS 6, however, still includes most DOS 3 facilities. Programs that require earlier versions often have no problem running under DOS 6.

The SETVER driver (called SETVER.EXE) includes a version table that lists the required version numbers for many such programs. When one of these programs checks for the current version number, SETVER lies and reports the version the program expects. Your CONFIG.SYS probably includes a DEVICE command to load SETVER.EXE, placed there by DOS 6's SETUP program. To add a program to the SETVER table, enter a command using this syntax:

```
SETVER filename.ext version
```

For example, the command SETVER PLACER.EXE 5.0 reports the DOS version number 5.0 to the program named PLACER.EXE. The command causes a new entry to be added to the SETVER table. You must reboot to put the updated table into effect.

Using HIMEM.SYS

If your system includes extended memory, you need to load a device driver to manage it. HIMEM.SYS is the extended memory manager provided with DOS 6 (as well as Windows). DOS 6's SETUP may put a DEVICE command into your CONFIG.SYS file to load HIMEM.SYS. You'll learn how to use and control HIMEM.SYS when you learn how to use extended memory in Chapter 29, "Managing Memory." If you have a HIMEM.SYS in both DOS and Windows directories, use the latest one.

Using ANSI.SYS

The ANSI.SYS device driver provides a set of enhanced functions for your monitor and keyboard. ANSI.SYS lets programs display color and graphics on the command prompt screen, for example, and redefines the meanings of your keyboard keys. Many applications use these functions and will not work right without ANSI.SYS. Even some DOS utilities require ANSI.SYS. You'll learn how to take advantage of ANSI.SYS features in Chapter 48, "Console Control."

Other Device Drivers

Your system might load several other device drivers, depending on your hardware. You might need drivers for your sound board, CD-ROM drive, scanner, fax/modem, and network card, for example. These drivers are not provided by DOS; they're proprietary software that comes with your hardware. You might have to insert the necessary DEVICE commands into CONFIG.SYS yourself, following the instructions in the hardware user manual. Or your hardware might come with a setup program that inserts the appropriate command in CONFIG.SYS for you (making a backup copy of CONFIG.SYS just in case).

If you're using data compression, you might need to load one or more drivers to support the data compression software. You'll use drivers provided with your compression system. DOS provides special drivers for DblSpace and DrvSpace, and third-party compression systems such as Stacker provide drivers for their systems. The appropriate DEVICE commands are inserted in CONFIG.SYS when you install the compression software.

Loading DOS High

Ordinarily, DOS loads itself in the first 640KB of memory. (This area is called *conventional memory*.) Most non-Windows applications must also use this part of memory, and you can run out of space there. If your system has extended memory, you can save some conventional memory by loading DOS into extended memory using a CONFIG.SYS command like this:

```
DOS=HIGH
```

You must load the HIMEM.SYS device driver (or an equivalent memory manager) on a line preceding the DOS=HIGH command in CONFIG.SYS.

You might also see the command DOS=UMB or DOS=HIGH,UMB. The UMB parameter tells DOS to make upper memory (the memory area beyond conventional memory) available for running programs. It is explained in Chapter 30, "Additional Memory Facilities for 386, 486, and Pentium Computers."

Using Buffers

When DOS reads data from a disk, it stores the data in buffers. A *buffer* is a section of memory that DOS has reserved for this purpose. Each buffer is the size of a disk sector, usually 512 bytes. DOS fills as many buffers as necessary to provide the data the program asks for. Then, it passes the data to the program.

Whenever an application requests data, DOS looks in the buffers to see whether the data is already there. If it finds the data, it doesn't have to access the disk, which can save a considerable amount of time.

In the same way, DOS stores output disk data in buffers before writing it to disk. Then, if it needs to reread that data (which happens more often than you might think), it can read the data from the buffers instead of the disk.

Because memory access is so much faster than disk access, buffering can save much time. The BUFFERS command tells DOS how many buffers it should use. A reasonable number, from 10 to 50, improves performance. If you use too many, searching all the buffers may take longer than accessing the disk. Too many buffers might also use more memory than you can spare.

If DOS is loaded into extended memory, the buffers are located there too, if they fit. Otherwise, they're placed in conventional memory.

The BUFFERS command can reserve additional buffers so that DOS can actually read ahead in a file. This feature could make your system run even faster. (See BUFFERS in the Command Reference for details.)

If you don't include a BUFFERS command in CONFIG.SYS, DOS uses default values based on the amount of conventional memory your system has. A system with 512KB to 640KB (the maximum possible) has a default of 15 buffers. You probably can benefit from more buffers than that unless you're using a hard disk-caching system such as SMARTDRV.SYS, which is explained in Chapter 31, "Caching the Drives."

Some applications recommend a certain number of buffers for efficient operation. When these applications are installed, they may place a BUFFERS command into CONFIG.SYS, change the existing BUFFERS command, or their documentation may ask you to do one of these.

Allocating File Handles

DOS reserves an area of memory for a table of file handles. Each file handle contains information about an open file. The FILES command tells DOS the maximum number of files you expect to have open at one time. Some applications require a minimum number of open files. During installation, an application may place a FILES command into CONFIG.SYS, change the existing FILES command, or its documentation may ask you to insert the FILES command.

Some older applications use *File Control Blocks (FCBS)* instead of file handles. Look up the FCBS command in the Command Reference if an application asks you to install some FCBs on your system.

Defining a Command Processor

A command processor interprets commands entered from the command prompt or a batch program. The command processor provided with DOS is COMMAND.COM. DOS expects to find COMMAND.COM in the root directory of the boot drive. If you've moved COMMAND.COM, or if you want to use a different processor, you need a SHELL command in CONFIG.SYS. The following command loads the COMMAND.COM processor from the DOS directory instead of the root directory:

```
SHELL=C:\DOS\COMMAND.COM  C:\DOS /P
```

The first word following SHELL= identifies the filespec of the command processor. The other parameters are unique to the command processor being loaded. The parameters in the example pertain to COMMAND.COM. The C:\DOS parameter tells DOS where to find COMMAND.COM if it needs to reload it. The /P switch tells DOS to make COMMAND.COM the permanent command processor.

You'll learn how to create your own SHELL command in Chapter 43, "DOS and the Environment," when you learn how you can manipulate the DOS environment.

Allocating Stacks

DOS must set aside a certain amount of memory to handle hardware functions. The reserved memory is called a *stack*. You can control how much stack space DOS allocates with a STACKS command in CONFIG.SYS. DOS usually creates enough stack space by default, but some programs might insert a STACKS command in CONFIG.SYS or modify the existing one. Unless you understand how DOS uses stacks and what your hardware and software needs are, you should leave any existing STACKS commands alone.

> **Tip:** If you have certain programs that seem to freeze up often, or if you get occasional Stack error or Stack fault messages, talk to the Microsoft product support team. The problem might be solved with a STACKS command.

On Your Own

This chapter has provided an overview of your CONFIG.SYS file. You might want to take a look at CONFIG.SYS and see how many of its commands you can interpret. Use DOS's editor to browse through the file.

1. Can you find commands that load your extended memory manager, and load DOS into extended memory?
2. Can you identify the commands that load device drivers for hardware devices such as your CD-ROM drive or fax/modem?
3. Does your CONFIG.SYS include commands to load DOS's read-write buffers, and space for file handles and stacks?
4. Is there a command to identify your command processor?
5. Does your system load SETVER.EXE to control version numbers and ANSI.SYS to provide enhanced keyboard and monitor functions?

Don't worry about any commands in CONFIG.SYS that you don't understand yet. As long as your system is functioning, your CONFIG.SYS is fine as it is for now. You'll be learning some ways to improve your system configuration, especially in memory usage, in later chapters.

If you have opened CONFIG.SYS in your editor, be sure to close it without making any changes to it.

4

Managing Your System

22 Avoiding Disaster: An Overview

Introduction

Using just the tools, included with DOS, you can do much to protect your data from all the things that can go wrong in your system.

Overview

As you learn in this chapter, DOS includes several facilities to help you prevent and recover from specific problems such as FAT errors or accidental deletions. But, the most important tool DOS offers—the tool that provides the best protection against data loss of any kind—is MSBACKUP (or its Windows counterpart, MWBACKUP). This program helps you keep up-to-date backups of all your important files so that you can recover from any kind of loss. No matter what type of mishap you run into—if your hard drive crashes, if Delete Sentry purges a file before you realize you want to recover it, even if your computer is stolen—you can recover your data by restoring it from your backup copies, which you have prudently saved in a separate location.

DOS 6 makes it easy to establish and maintain a regular backup cycle at the command prompt, in the Shell, or under Windows, whichever environment you prefer. Chapter 23, "MSBACKUP and MWBACKUP," shows you how to set up and maintain your backup system, and Chapter 24, "Restore and Compare," shows you how to recover files when that becomes necessary.

This chapter reads somewhat like a catalog of disaster, but keep in mind as you read that, if you have a good set of backups, you can recover from anything that happens to your system. In this chapter, you'll see what facilities, if any, DOS provides to cope with:

- Viruses
- Software failure
- Hardware failure
- Deleted files
- Reformatted disks
- Physically damaged disks

Coping with Viruses

A *virus* is a program that sneaks itself into your system, hides somewhere, is triggered by an event, and does something unexpected. Some of the less harmful viruses display a silly message or play a little tune. But, a truly malicious virus might trash your partition table or physically reformat your hard disk; either action wipes out all the data on your hard disk. DOS 6 includes several programs to help you protect your system against viruses.

The MSAV (Microsoft Anti-Virus) program, which runs from the command prompt or the Shell, scans memory and your drives for viruses. It can safely remove many viruses from your system; for other viruses, it deletes the infected file (the file the virus is hiding in), if you decide that's what you want to do. MWAV (Microsoft Windows Anti-Virus) is the Windows version of this program.

The VSAFE program operates as a terminate-and-stay-resident program (TSR) to monitor your system constantly for virus-like activity, such as physically reformatting the hard disk. VSAFE blocks any suspicious activity, warns you what's happening, and lets you decide what to do next. VSAFE can operate under DOS, DOS Shell, and Windows.

Chapter 25, "DOS's Antivirus Programs," explains DOS's antivirus programs. If you use them regularly, your system will be nearly invulnerable to virus attack. But there's always the possibility of a new type of virus managing to sneak past all the safeguards. And, of course, if you choose not to maintain a constant watch for viruses (the antivirus programs take up both space and time), your chances of being attacked by a virus increase dramatically. Your backups provide the ultimate line of defense against viruses; if a virus does manage to damage some of your data, you can restore the data from your backups (after making sure that they aren't also infected).

Dealing with Misbehaving Software

Any program can cause problems in your system. Back in the old days (that is, the late 1970s), when personal computers typically came with 16KB of memory and could be expanded to a whopping 64KB, software was fairly simple—it had to be, or it wouldn't fit in the available memory space. But, nowadays, programs can be wonderfully complex. Software such as an animation studio, a music sequencer, or even everyday word processor or database manager applications, take huge staffs and perhaps several years of effort to develop. Unfortunately, mistakes happen. Even when the testing and debugging process is quite rigorous, a small error in some esoteric corner of a program can be overlooked. This is complicated by the fact that, in the world of IBM PC-compatibles, so many combinations of hardware and software exist that there is no way to test a new program in every environment in which it will be used.

Problems also can occur with programs that were developed to run under an earlier version of DOS. Microsoft's technicians test each new DOS version on thousands of systems, with every variation of hardware and software that they can get their hands on, in an effort to make it error-free. But, 100-percent reliability cannot be guaranteed.

Smaller products may also have their problems. Many products developed by one or two people may not have been as rigorously tested as a program like DOS. The program may have been tested on two or three systems, perhaps even a dozen or more, but probably not 10,000. On the other hand, because such programs are smaller, they're less complex and therefore less likely to conceal problems, especially if they have a national reputation and are sold in reliable stores. Still, there's no guarantee that such a product will not trip over something in your system. The more widespread a program is, however, the less likely it is to cause problems.

Then there's the wide world of cheap software: freeware, publicware, and shareware. Part of the reason it's cheap is because the developers haven't spent money on packaging, marketing, or distribution. But, a few developers occasionally cut corners during the development and testing process. The result could be a program that works fine on one system but causes problems on another. Widely used shareware, such as PKZIP and its sister programs from PKWARE, has received extensive testing in the field, which makes it just as safe as more expensively packaged programs.

If a program malfunctions in your system, it could cause you to lose data. It might freeze your system and force you to reboot at an inconvenient time. Or, worse, the program could actually damage the system area or the data on your hard disk.

There's very little you can do to avoid all program glitches. Certainly you should stay away from those programs most likely to bring problems with them. For the rest, your up-to-date backups are your best defense.

Coping with Hardware Failure

Any kind of hardware failure, from a momentary power fluctuation to a head crash, could damage your system areas and make your hard disk data inaccessible; or, it could damage specific files.

Several hardware solutions are available to protect your system from hardware malfunctions. A surge protector, for example, prevents power surges from reaching your hardware. You can even buy a battery-powered board that swings into action when the power goes out, giving you a minute or so to save all your files and shut down your system properly. If power fluctuations and outages are a problem in your area, talk to your hardware dealer about what's available to protect your data.

But nothing can protect your system from a hard disk failure; and hard disks always fail in the end. When yours does, you'll be glad you have a full set of backups to restore your files after you get the disk repaired or replaced. (A good disk technician can rescue most or all of your files from a dead disk.)

Coping with Deletions

You probably know how easy it is to delete the wrong file or to change your mind after deleting a file. DOS's UNDELETE facility both protects files from deletion and helps you to recover them, if that becomes necessary. Chapter 26, "Using UNDELETE," details how to set up and use UNDELETE.

However, even DOS's top level of deletion protection, Delete Sentry, cannot guarantee recovery of every file. Again, a good set of backups can help you recover a file that cannot be recovered by any other means. Use deletion protection only to protect those files that have not yet been backed up.

Dealing with Reformatting

You've learned how easy it is to reformat the wrong disk, and you've learned about DOS's UNFORMAT facility. But, UNFORMAT counts on two factors. First, the mirror image file must be present. Second, no new data can be added to the disk after formatting. UNFORMAT works without these two conditions, but not as well; you're better off restoring the missing files from their backups.

Dealing with Damaged Disks

The directory tree and the *File Allocation Table* (FAT) are essential to accessing the data on a disk. If either one becomes damaged, you could lose contact with some—and perhaps—all of your files. This vital system information can become damaged in many ways. Malfunctioning hardware, power fluctuations, viruses, and not waiting for the drive light to go out before rebooting are just some of the possibilities.

DOS includes a program called SCANDISK that analyzes the FAT and directory structure, reports problems, and repairs most of the problems it finds. In addition, it tests the surface of the disk for physical flaws and rescues any data from flawed areas. SCANDISK, which is discussed in Chapter 27, "CHKDSK and SCANDISK," is one of the maintenance facilities that you should run on a regular basis to keep your hard disk in good running order.

Versions of DOS before 6.2 do not include SCANDISK. An earlier DOS program, called CHKDSK (check disk), checks and fixes the directory structure but cannot scan the disk surface. If you have not yet upgraded to 6.2 or 6.22, you will use CHKDSK instead of SCANDISK to keep your disks in shape.

CHKDSK and SCANDISK cannot handle every problem they find; there are times when you must restore damaged files from their backups.

On Your Own

A wise person uses, on a regular basis, the preventive programs overviewed in this chapter (and described in detail in the next few chapters). VSAFE and Delete Sentry should be loaded as TSRs every time you boot. MSAV or MWAV should be run daily, perhaps every time you boot. CHKDSK and SCANDISK don't need to be run daily; weekly is probably good enough. Finally, you need to use MSBACKUP at least daily to keep your backups up-to-date.

23 MSBACKUP and MWBACKUP

Introduction

A good backup system is
the most important way to
protect your data. DOS 6
gives you a useful tool,
but it's up to you to use it.

Backing Up Your Files

DOS 6 replaced the backup utility from earlier DOS versions with a much more modern, GUI facility that makes backups almost simple. There are even two versions of the program—one that runs at the command prompt (MSBACKUP), and one that runs under Windows (MWBACKUP). The new backup facility includes a host of features to make your life easier:

- It can compress the backup data to save space on the storage disks
- It can store error correction information with the backup data, so that your data can be recovered even if the backup files are damaged
- It can warn you if a floppy already contains data
- It maintains a set of catalogs to keep track of your backed up files
- It can compare your backed up files to the files on your hard disk and warn you of any disparities
- It can back up to floppy, or to a DOS drive\directory name (such as a tape drive or a network drive)
- You can run your daily backups with just a couple of mouse clicks or keystrokes
- You can select any one or more files to restore from the backup; you could recover a deleted file, fall back to an earlier version of a file, or restore your entire hard disk after a crash

This chapter shows you how to make backups. You will learn how to:

- Decide between MSBACKUP (for DOS) and MWBACKUP (for Windows)
- Start MSBACKUP or MWBACKUP
- Run the backup configuration tests so that backup knows how to access your hardware
- Create and manage setup files so that you only have to define a backup once
- Use a backup setup file to back up your files
- Interpret a backup catalog name
- Manage backup catalogs

Warning: MSBACKUP and MWBACKUP are new with DOS 6 and can't restore files backed up by earlier DOS versions. DOS 6 includes the old RESTORE as a separate program, in case you need to restore files from an earlier backup. You should back up your files with the new Backup as soon as possible and eliminate your old backups. Then, you can delete C:\DOS\RESTORE.EXE.

DOS 6.22's compression techniques are different from those in DOS 6.0 and 6.2. If you made backups using DOS 6.0 or 6.2 and then upgraded to DOS 6.22, you may or may not have trouble restoring from the backups that you made earlier. Chapter 24, "Restore and Compare," explains the conditions under which you can restore easily, as well as how to restore from those files in other cases. In the meantime, however, you should replace your old backups as soon as possible by making new complete or full backups using DOS 6.22.

Getting Ready for the Practice Exercises

You'll need some practice directories and files for the exercises in this chapter. As always, it's better to create a PRACTICE branch, rather than work with your real files:

1. Create a directory named PRACTICE that's a subdirectory of the root directory. Copy all the .HLP files from DOS to PRACTICE, renaming them as .XXX files. (Reminder: You can do this all with one XCOPY command.)

2. Create a directory named \PRACTICE\EXER1 and copy all the \DOS*.COM files to it, renaming them as *.YYY.

3. Create a directory named \PRACTICE\EXER2 and copy all the \DOS*.INI files to it, renaming them as *.ZZZ.

Choosing MSBACKUP or MWBACKUP

DOS 6 includes two versions of its backup program: MSBACKUP (Microsoft Backup) runs at the command prompt or under a shell, and MWBACKUP (Microsoft Backup for Windows) runs under Windows. So, no matter which environment you prefer, you have a backup tool available. Both versions feature a graphical user interface to make it easy to set up and run backups. The Windows version is fancier looking than the DOS version—as you might expect—and a little bit easier to use, but the functions are the same. Figure 23.1 shows MWBACKUP's window; the figures throughout the rest of this chapter are from MSBACKUP.

When you install DOS 6 on a system with Windows, SETUP gives you the choice of installing MSBACKUP, MWBACKUP, or both. You probably don't need both, so you can save some disk space by installing only the one you'll use. If you change your mind later, rerun SETUP to install the other version.

Figure 23.1.
The MWBACKUP
window.

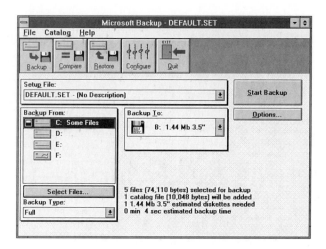

Figure 23.1.
The MWBACKUP
window.

Note: To avoid the awkwardness of saying "MSBACKUP or MWBACKUP" over and over, this chapter uses "Backup" to mean either program.

Starting Backup

There are several ways to start the backup software, depending on which environment you're using. Try starting your version now:

1. If you plan to make your backups from the DOS prompt, enter **MSBACKUP**.

   If you get the message `Backup requires configuration for this computer`, your backup program has never been used before. Read the section titled "Configuring Backup." If you don't get this message, go on to "Choosing the Backup Function."

2. If you plan to make your backups from DOS Shell, start up the Shell. Then, open the Disk Utilities program group and open the MS Backup program item. Or, you can choose File, Run and enter **MSBACKUP** in the Run dialog box.

   If you get the message `Backup requires configuration for this computer`, your backup program has never been used before. Read the section titled "Configuring Backup." If you don't get this message, go on to "Choosing the Backup Function."

Note: The MS Backup program item is defined so that you can't switch away from the task when task switching. Once you have started MS Backup, let it complete its work before switching to another task.

3. If you plan to make your backups under Windows, start up Windows. Then, open the Backup program item (in the Microsoft Tools group).

   If you get the message `Microsoft Backup has not been configured. Do you want to automatically configure it now?`, your backup program has never been used before. Read the section titled "Configuring Backup." If you don't get this message, go on to "Choosing the Backup Function."

Configuring Backup

The first time you start either version of the backup program, you see a message telling you that you have not yet configured the software. You must do this first. During configuration, Backup tests your system to make sure that it can produce reliable backups. Several tests are involved:

- It tries to sense what type of hardware (video, mouse, and disk drives) you have. If it identifies them incorrectly, you have the chance to correct them.

- It checks to see whether it can sense when you have changed a floppy disk. If so, you don't have to choose an OK button every time you insert a new disk.

- It tests memory and your hard disk to make sure that it can read data reliably at high speeds.

- It makes a practice backup with a little more than one floppy disk's worth of data, so that you must change disks once. This small backup should reveal incompatibilities with any part of your system: the drives, memory, any TSRs that conflict with Backup's process, and so on. Backup can avoid some incompatibilities by slowing itself down. Other problems (such as incompatible TSRs) you must fix yourself before you can use Backup.

- It compares all the files in the practice backup to their originals on the hard disk. Again, this should reveal any problems in making reliable backups on your system.

Beginning the Tests

Let's run the configuration tests right now. The following exercise describes the MSBACKUP version. The MWBACKUP version is very similar.

1. If you haven't already done so, start MSBACKUP or MWBACKUP, as described earlier.

   A message warns you that you need to do the configuration tests.

2. Choose Start Configuration to begin the tests.

   You see some dialog boxes flash past as Backup makes choices for you. Then, Backup shows you its assessment of your video and mouse configuration. (See Figure 23.2.)

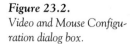

Figure 23.2.
Video and Mouse Configu-
ration dialog box.

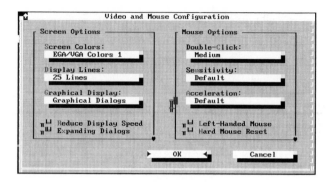

Determining the Video and Mouse Configuration

The Video and Mouse Configuration dialog box gives you a chance to change any configuration items that are incorrect. If you want to change one of the items at the top of the box, such as Screen Colors, you select it so that another dialog box displays the options for that item.

The four items at the bottom of the dialog box, such as Expanding Dialogs, are check boxes; they can be enabled or disabled. Select an item once to enable it; a check mark or X appears in the box to indicate that it's enabled. Select the item again to disable it; the check mark or X disappears.

Note: To select an item in the Video and Mouse Configuration dialog box, or one of its subsidiary dialog boxes, click the item or type **Alt** plus its highlighted letter. For example, to change Screen Colors, you click the box underneath the label Screen Colors, or you simply press Alt+S.

Note: When any dialog box is open in Backup, press F1 to get on-screen help with the options it contains.

You probably won't need to change most of the items in this dialog box. But, if "snow" appears on your screen when you're using MSBACKUP, there are a couple of options that might eliminate it. If the snow appears to be related to mouse movements, change Graphical Display to use fewer graphics. If that doesn't work, enable Reduce Display Speed at the bottom of the dialog box. If you're having any other kind of trouble using your mouse—if it moves erratically, for example—try enabling Hard Mouse Reset.

If you are having trouble double-clicking with your mouse, you might try a different double-click speed. When the slow speed is selected, you don't have to click as quickly to send a double-click.

This speed is the right speed for people who find it difficult to double-click rapidly. It's the wrong speed for many people, it causes clicks that they intend as two separate clicks in a row to be interpreted as a double-click. If you move quickly and want DOS to keep up with you, try selecting the fast double-click speed.

By default, a dialog box doesn't just appear on your screen. It starts as a small box and "grows" into its full size. Disable Expanding Dialog Boxes if your system is slow and if you don't like waiting for a dialog box to "grow" on your screen. When this option is disabled, dialog boxes just pop onto the screen.

If you would like to make any changes to the Video and Mouse Configuration, do so now. Then, choose OK to continue.

The Floppy Drive Change Line Test

After the video and mouse configuration, more dialog boxes flash past. Then, Backup is ready to do the floppy drive change line test. This test determines whether Backup can sense when you have changed the disk in a floppy drive:

1. Remove the disks from every floppy drive.

2. Choose Start Test when you're ready to continue.

   The Backup Devices dialog box displays Backup's analysis of your floppy drives. (See Figure 23.3.) Each drive button is labeled with the current device setting for that drive.

Figure 23.3.
The Backup Devices
dialog box.

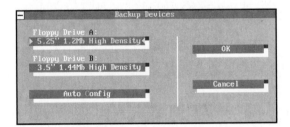

3. If the Backup Devices are correct, choose OK to continue with the next test. If not, take the time to correct them now. To select a device, choose the drive button and select the correct description from the list that is displayed.

The Floppy Disk Compatibility Test

Next, you see Backup conduct some more tests. All you can do is sit and watch until it's ready for the floppy disk compatibility test. (See Figure 23.4.) This test does a practice backup and compare.

You have the option of skipping this test, but you shouldn't skip it the first time you configure. (If you're rerunning the configuration tests for some reason, you might not need to redo the compatibility test.)

Figure 23.4.

The Floppy Disk Compatibility Test dialog box.

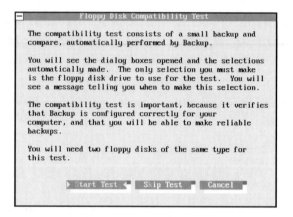

1. Choose Start Test to start the floppy disk compatibility test.

   A series of dialog boxes flashes past as Backup sets up the test. (You'll learn how to use all of these dialog boxes in this chapter, but you don't have any choices now.) Finally, Backup asks you to select the floppy drive and capacity you want to test.

2. Select the drive that you want to test. Be sure to test the drive that you will use for your real backups. However, even if you plan to back up to a network drive or some other device, you must select a floppy drive for the compatibility test. Remember that you must provide two disks for the drive and capacity you select.

Tip: If you have two identical floppy drives, you can opt to use them both. This speeds up the entire backup process, because you can change the disk in one drive while Backup writes to the other. Backup doesn't have to wait for you to change disks.

   After you select the drive, more dialog boxes flash past. Then, Backup asks you to insert the first disk.

3. Insert the first floppy in the indicated drive and choose Continue. (The disk may be formatted but does not have to be.)

   Backup examines the disk and displays an alert box if the disk contains data. You can replace the disk and choose Retry, or simply choose Overwrite to continue with the current disk.

Warning: Backup replaces all the existing data on a disk. Even if you back up only one file, all existing data will be destroyed.

Next, you see a progress screen as the backup takes place. The progress screen is explained in the section "Running a Backup," later in this chapter. Eventually, you are asked to insert the second disk.

If Backup is configured to sense disk changes, the message to insert the next disk appears directly on the progress screen, not in a dialog box. The drive light remains lit as Backup waits for the new disk. This is the only time while using DOS that you should change disks while a drive light is on.

If you don't change disks within a few seconds, Backup stops testing for the changed disk and displays a dialog box. Backup also displays the dialog box if it can't sense changed floppies in your drive.

4. Insert the second disk. If a dialog box is on your screen, choose Continue.

    When the backup is complete, Backup displays a summary dialog box. Backup examines the disk and displays an alert box if the disk contains data. You can replace the disk and choose Retry, or simply choose Overwrite to continue with the current disk.

5. Choose OK to continue.

    Then, the Compare function starts. A series of dialog boxes flash past, as before. Finally, Compare asks you to insert the first backup disk.

6. Insert the first backup disk (from step 3), and choose Continue.

    Compare reads the backed up files and compares them to the originals on the hard drive. Eventually, it asks for the second backup disk.

7. Insert the second backup disk (from step 4). If a dialog box is on your screen, choose Continue.

    At the end, Compare displays a Compare Summary dialog box.

8. Choose OK.

    A message tells you that the compatibility test was successful. (See the next section if Backup or Compare encountered any problems during your test.)

9. Choose OK.

    The Configure dialog box appears on your screen.

10. Choose Save.

    Backup saves the results of the configuration and compatibility tests.

Note: It's very important to save the test results. If you don't, you must rerun the tests the next time you start your backup program. But, you don't need to save the backup floppies that you just created. You can reuse them immediately.

11. Choose OK to exit the Configure dialog box. (If you're using MWBACKUP, skip this step.)

MSBACKUP's main menu appears.

Coping with Configuration Problems

Of course, the configuration tests don't always go smoothly. If Backup encounters trouble, it reports the problem and suggests a solution, if possible. It might, for example, ask you to remove a TSR and try again.

If you don't understand an error message, copy it down verbatim, make a note of where you were in the configuration process (such as "just about to start the practice backup"), and call Microsoft's Product Support team. They should be able to help you identify the problem and finish configuring your system.

If the compatibility test fails, you can go on to make backups, but you shouldn't—they will not be reliable. After you have identified and fixed the problem, you should rerun the compatibility test.

How to Rerun the Compatibility Test

1. Choose Configure to open the Configure dialog box.

2. Choose the Compatibility Test button.

3. Follow the directions on your screen.

If any other part of the configuration tests fails, you must locate and fix the problem before you can use the backup program. In most cases, the problem will be in your hardware or an incompatible TSR. The messages that you receive during the configuration test should help you identify the problem and may even suggest how to fix it.

The configuration alert box appears every time you start the backup program, until you have successfully passed every test except the compatibility test. A different alert box warns you when your system has passed all the other configuration tests but failed the compatibility test.

Problem: When Windows is running in Enhanced Mode, MWBACKUP can't pass the compatibility test, but it can pass the test in Standard Mode.

Some other Windows application is installing a device driver that conflicts with MWBACKUP. It might be easier for you to use MSBACKUP. But, if you really want to use the Windows version, restart Windows without loading any other applications, and try again.

To disable applications that are loaded automatically during Windows startup, create a new group called Tempsave and move all the program icons from the Startup group to Tempsave. Then, restart Windows and try the compatibility test again.

If it still doesn't work, copy the file named WIN.INI as WIN.SAV, then edit WIN.INI to remove every line that starts with LOAD= or RUN=. Then, restart Windows and try again.

If Windows can't start after you edit WIN.INI, copy C:\WINDOWS\WIN.SAV to C:\WINDOWS\WIN.INI (to restore your old WIN.INI), then restart Windows. Then, edit WIN.INI to remove only one item, restart Windows, and try the compatibility test. Eventually, you should discover the item that is conflicting with the compatibility test.

When you make the compatibility test work, make a note of which items you had to remove from your normal Windows configuration. You must remove the same items each time you run Backup.

Retesting Your System

You can use the same procedure to rerun the compatibility test if you change your system configuration in any way. You should rerun the test, for example, if you install a new TSR or change the configuration of a TSR.

Note: Many people don't remember to rerun the configuration and compatibility tests when they install a new TSR. Both backup programs check to see if the configuration has changed and, if so, warn you that a new test is needed.

How to Reconfigure a Floppy Drive

1. Choose Configure to open the Configure dialog box.

2. For MSBACKUP, select Backup Devices, and then press Auto Config.

> For MWBACKUP, press Auto Floppy Configure.
>
> 3. Follow the directions on your screen.
>
> 4. If Backup misidentifies any drives, correct them.

Choosing the Backup Function

After completing the configuration tests, you're ready to try your first backup. From now on, when you start MSBACKUP, you'll see a dialog box in which you can choose one of MSBACKUP's four functions (Backup, Restore, Compare, and Configure) or Quit. (See Figure 23.5.)

Figure 23.5.
MSBACKUP's main menu.

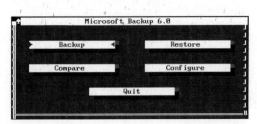

Note: For MWBACKUP, the functions appear as buttons near the top of the window. You can see them in Figure 23.1, shown previously.

The Backup function archives selected files from the hard disk to a backup medium such as a floppy disk or second hard drive. Backup is capable of compressing the backed up data to save space, and you can configure it for maximum speed, maximum reliability, or somewhere between these two extremes.

The Compare function compares backed up files to their hard disk originals. Compare is useful to verify the accuracy of the backups, or to identify files that have changed since they were backed up.

The Restore function returns backed up files to the hard disk. If your hard disk fails, you can use Restore to place all your files on your new or repaired drive. But, you also can use Restore to recover a file that you deleted accidentally, or to return to an earlier version of a file that you trashed, somehow.

Compare and Restore are explained in Chapter 24. This chapter shows you how to use the Configure and Backup functions. You start the Backup function by selecting Backup from the main menu. The Backup dialog box then appears. (See Figure 23.6.)

Figure 23.6.
MSBACKUP's *Backup dialog box.*

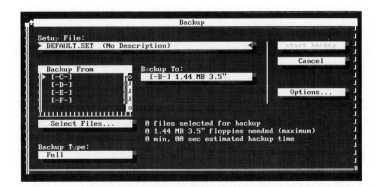

Working with Setup Files

When you define a backup that you want to perform—you select files to be backed up, select a drive to receive the backed up files, select various backup options, and so on—you save your work in a *setup file.* The next time you want to run the same backup, all you have to do is open the setup file and press the Start Backup button. Because you probably repeat the same backup every day, the setup file lets you accomplish your task in just a few keystrokes or mouse clicks after the first day.

Backup setups have other advantages. They can be handed out to other users, or stored on a network drive to make sure that everyone in a work group is conforming to the same backup standards. You can have more than one setup on your PC, if that's appropriate. For example, if several people share one computer, each can have his or her own setup. You might have one setup for each of your major applications. However, many people use just one setup to back up everything.

How to Create a New Backup Setup

1. Open a setup that is similar to the one you want to create.

2. Choose File, Save Setup As.

   The Save Setup As dialog box opens.

3. Specify a name and a description for the new setup and choose OK.

   The dialog box closes, and Backup opens the new setup.

4. Select files for the new setup.

5. Select options for the new setup.

6. Select a backup type for the new setup.

7. Select the drive(s) to back up to.

8. Choose File, Save Setup to save the new setup.

Each new setup must be based on an existing one. Backup provides one setup called DEFAULT.SET, which you use to create your first setup. By default, DOS stores your new setup file in the same directory as the current setup. If you're basing the new setup on DEFAULT.SET, C:\DOS is the default directory. For now, you'll create a practice setup and store it in C:\DOS.

Create a new setup named PRACTICE, based on DEFAULT.SET:

1. Start the Backup function. DEFAULT.SET is opened automatically.

2. Choose File, Save Setup As. A dialog box asks for the name of the new setup, showing DEFAULT.SET as the default. The default directory is C:\DOS.

3. Enter **PRACTICE.SET**.

4. Click the Description box, or press Alt+C to jump to it.

5. Enter **Practice with DOS program files** in the Description box.

6. Choose Save.

    The dialog box closes and PRACTICE.SET becomes the current setup.

At this point, PRACTICE.SET has the same definition as DEFAULT.SET. You will modify it to create the setup you want.

Selecting Files for the Setup

A backup setup must identify the files to be backed up. For example, you could back up all of drive C, all nonprogram files, or all files in certain directories. DEFAULT.SET does not select any files; so, when you create a new setup based on DEFAULT.SET, the new setup doesn't select any files either, at first.

How to Select Files for a Backup Setup

1. Open the setup file.

2. To select all the files on a drive, select the drive in the Backup From box. (Note: Double-click the drive name, or highlight the drive and press the space bar.)

    The Backup dialog box shows the number of selected files (plus one for the catalog). An arrowhead and the words All files appear next to the drive name.

3. To include or exclude files by filename, choose Select Files.

    The Select Backup Files dialog box opens.

4. Choose the Include or Exclude button.

    The Include or Exclude dialog box opens.

---

5. Enter the path name and the filespec in the appropriate boxes.

6. Enable or disable All Subdirectories, according to whether you want to include or exclude files throughout the branch.

7. Choose OK to close the Include or Exclude dialog box.

   The number of selected files appears at the bottom of the Select Backup Files dialog box, and selected files have a check mark next to them in the file list. If the backup type is Incremental or Differential, only files with a positive archive attribute have a check mark. Other selected files have a dot, because they are selected but won't be backed up unless you change the backup type to Full.

8. Repeat steps 3 through 7 until you have included and excluded all necessary files.

9. To select or deselect individual directories and files, choose Select Files again.

   The Select Backup Files dialog box opens.

10. To select or deselect an entire directory, scroll the directory tree until you find it; then, double-click the directory, or highlight it and press the space bar.

    The directory name turns red to show that it has been selected or deselected. If selected, a solid arrowhead appears next to it, and all the files in the file list have check marks to indicate that they are selected.

11. To select or deselect individual files, highlight the directory name; then, double-click the individual names in the file list, or highlight them and press the space bar.

    The directory name turns red to show that at least some of its files have been individually selected or deselected. A chevron appears next to the directory name to show that only some of its files are selected. The individual filename receives a check mark if you selected it, or loses its check mark if you deselected it.

12. To exclude files by date, attributes, or filespec (for copy protected files), choose the Special button.

    The Special Inclusions dialog box opens.

13. Fill out the dialog box as appropriate.

14. Choose OK to close the dialog box.

    Excluded files have a dot next to them in the file list.

Some people back up every file on their hard disk; this makes it simple to restore the entire disk, if that becomes necessary. Other people prefer to back up only those files that are created or modified after an application is installed (such as document files), but not the original program files, which usually don't change and can be reinstalled from their original disks if necessary. Skipping program files significantly reduces backup time and media space, but makes it harder to completely restore the hard disk. The Backup function can be set up easily for either method. Either way, you can eliminate nonessential files such as scratch pads, personal memos, to-do lists, and so on. Throughout this chapter, the phrase *selected files* refers to the set of files that you have selected to be backed up, whether or not that includes all the files on your hard drive.

Selecting an Entire Drive

In the Backup dialog box, the Backup From box lists your hard drives. If you want to back up all the files on a drive, select the drive in this box. You can select as many drives as you want; potentially, you could back up every file in your system in one setup.

Note: You select a drive by double-clicking the drive name or pressing Alt+K to select the Backup From box, typing the letter of the drive to highlight that drive, and pressing the space bar. When the entire drive is selected, the words All files appear next to the drive name.

Note: Your CD-ROM drives appear in the drive list, and you can select them for backup, but there's very little reason to do so. If the files on a CD are damaged, you would not be able to restore them from the backup, because you cannot write on the CD.

For this exercise, you don't want to select all the files on a drive. Don't select a drive name in the Backup From box.

Including and Excluding Files

Most people don't want to back up entire drives. As mentioned earlier, many files don't need to be backed up, and there's no sense in wasting time and space on them. Another way to select files in a setup is to include or exclude them by their filespecs. You might, for example, want to include all DOC files, but exclude MEMO*.DOC and TEMPY.DOC.

Figure 23.7 shows the dialog boxes that you use to include and exclude files in a setup. As you can see, you specify a path and a global or specific filespec for each type of file you want to include or exclude. If you enable Include or Exclude All Subdirectories, files matching the indicated filespec are selected throughout the specified branch. You use these dialog boxes over and over again to create the complete list of inclusions and exclusions.

Figure 23.7.
The Include and Exclude
dialog boxes.

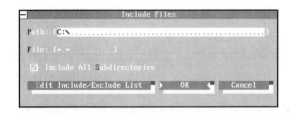

For this practice setup, you will include all the files in the PRACTICE branch except D*.* and M*.* files.

Note: The order of inclusions and exclusions is important. Each new specification overrides all preceding specifications. So, in this exercise, you must include *.* before you exclude D*.* and M*.*.

1. Click Select Files or press Alt+L.

   The Select Backup Files dialog box opens. (See Figure 23.8.)

Figure 23.8.
Select Backup Files
dialog box.

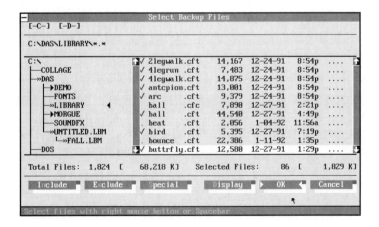

2. Choose Include.

   The Include Files dialog box opens. The default path is the current directory, and the default filespec is *.*.

3. Edit the default path to read C:\PRACTICE. Also enable Include All Subdirectories.

4. Choose OK to return to the Select Backup Files dialog box.

   The Include Files dialog box closes. Notice that the numbers in the Selected Files field have changed in the Select Backup Files dialog box. Notice also the arrowhead next to PRACTICE, EXER1, and EXER2 in the directory tree, indicating that these directories are currently selected.

5. To see the selected files in the PRACTICE directory, move the highlight to PRACTICE in the directory tree. Either press down-arrow to move the highlight, or click PRACTICE in the directory tree.

   In the file list, a check mark indicates a selected file. Right now, all the files are selected, so they all have check marks.

6. Now choose Exclude, so that you can exclude D*.* and M*.* files.

   The Exclude Files dialog box opens.

7. Make sure the path is C:\PRACTICE.

8. Enter D*.* in the File box. Also enable Exclude All Subdirectories.

9. Choose OK.

   The dialog box closes. The number of Selected Files changes. The solid arrowheads next to the PRACTICE, EXER2, and EXER2 directories change to chevrons, indicating that only some of the files in these directories are selected. You can also see in the file list that the D*.* files are not checked.

10. Repeat steps 6 through 9 for M*.*.

Note: You can examine and edit the entire Include and Exclude list by choosing Edit Include/Exclude List in the Include or Exclude dialog box. Editing possibilities include modifying an entry in the list, copying an entry so that you can use it as the basis for a new entry, and deleting entries from the list.

11. Choose OK to close the Select Backup Files dialog box.

    The Backup dialog box returns. In the lower right portion, Backup displays the number of files that are selected, an estimate of the number of floppies needed, and an estimate of the time the backup will take.

    Notice also the arrowhead next to drive C in the drive list, accompanied by the note Some files, indicating that some files on drive C are selected.

Note: The number of files in the Backup dialog box is always one more than the number of selected files. That extra file is the backup catalog, which also must be written to the backup media. Catalogs are explained in the section "Working with Backup Catalogs," later in this chapter.

Overriding the Include/Exclude List

The Include and Exclude dialog boxes create an Include/Exclude list that establishes the basic file selections for the setup. You can then override them by selecting or deselecting individual directories or files in the Select Backup Files dialog box. To toggle a directory or file selection status, double-click it, or highlight it and press the space bar.

Try deselecting some files in your PRACTICE directory:

1. Choose Select Files.

   The Select Backup Files dialog box opens.

2. Highlight the PRACTICE directory.

   The file list shows the contents of the PRACTICE directory.

3. You can rearrange the file list so that all the selected files are displayed at the beginning of the list. This makes it easier to review your selected files. Choose the Display button.

   The Display Options dialog box opens.

4. Enable Group Selected Files.

   A check appears in the check box.

5. Choose OK.

   The dialog box closes. The file list now shows all the selected files first.

6. To deselect the first file in the list, double-click it, or move the highlight to it and press the space bar.

   The check mark disappears from a file name when you deselect the file. You should also see the number of Selected Files decrease.

7. Choose OK to close the dialog box.

When you override the selection of a file or directory, you remove it from the control of the Include/Exclude list. You can subsequently toggle its status between selected and deselected by selecting it again. If any file in a directory has been overridden, the directory name turns red in the directory tree. Unfortunately, in MSBACKUP the file name doesn't turn red, so it's sometimes hard to determine which files have been manipulated this way. (Affected file names do turn red with MWBACKUP.)

When a directory name appears in red, you can return the entire directory to the control of the Include/Exclude list, undoing all manual selections and deselections in the directory, by clicking both mouse buttons simultaneously (this is called *chording*) on the directory name or by highlighting the directory name and pressing Alt+Spacebar. In MWBACKUP, where individual files do appear in red in the file list, you can return an individual file to the control of the Include/Exclude list by the same techniques.

Tip: If you really goof up your file selections, you can undo them all by deleting the file named *setup*.SLT. This deletes individual file and directory selections, but it doesn't touch the Include/Exclude list.

Peter's Principle: Use the Include/Exclude list as much as possible when selecting or deselecting files for Backup.

Selecting individual directories and files is relatively easy, and you might be tempted to do all your file selections this way, but it's not as good a technique as building an Include/Exclude list. The Include/Exclude list affects directories and files added to the drive in the future, whereas selecting files directly affects those files only. Selecting or deselecting a directory affects all current and future files in that directory only.

Making Special Exclusions

There's one more way to exclude files that overrides every other method. Figure 23.9 shows the Special Selections dialog box that opens when you press the Special button in the Select Backup Files dialog box. This feature enables you to exclude files by date, attribute, or file name.

Figure 23.9.
The Special Selections dialog box.

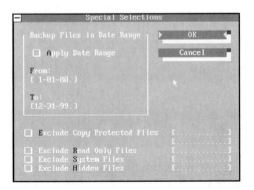

Excluding Files by Date

When you enter a date range in the Backup Files In Date Range area, you exclude all files outside that range. If you want to exclude files created or last modified before 9/10/92, you would enter 9/10/92 in the From box, and any date far in the future in the To box (the maximum is 12/31/99, which is also the default). You also need to check the Apply Date Range box. The exclusions are applied when you choose OK to close the dialog box, but the number of selected files isn't updated until you close the Select Backup Files dialog box.

Entering a date range in this dialog box does not automatically include all the files in that date range (despite the name of the dialog box). Instead, it excludes any files outside that range. You must still select files for inclusion by other methods.

Excluding Files by Attribute

You can exclude hidden, system, or read-only files by checking the appropriate boxes.

Excluding Copy-Protected Files

In an effort to avoid piracy, some applications protect their files from being copied. If you try to copy them or back them up, you could invalidate the entire application. Usually, the application's documentation warns you about copy protection. If you have such an application, you can prevent its files from being backed up by checking the Exclude Copy Protected Files box, and entering up to five filespecs in the boxes to the right.

Other Selection Functions

The Display button opens a dialog box in which you can choose the sort order for the file list, or enter a filename filter for the file list.

Choosing a Backup Type

Most people like to do their backups in cycles, starting by backing up all selected files, whether or not they have changed since the last time they were backed up. This starting point, which is called a *full backup*, gives you a complete set of your selected files to restore from, if necessary.

Between full backups—perhaps on a daily basis—you back up only those selected files that have been created or modified since the last backup, using archive attributes as your guide. These partial backups take much less time and media space than full backups; by combining the last full backup with subsequent partial backups, you have complete coverage of all your selected files. With the Backup function, you can switch between full and partial backups simply by selecting the type of backup you want.

Backup offers three backup types: full, incremental, and differential. A *full backup* backs up all selected files, regardless of their archive attribute. It also turns off the archive attribute of every file it backs up. This begins a new backup cycle. Depending on how active your system is, you might want to do this once a week, once every two weeks, or simply when the incremental or differential backups are getting too long.

Between full backups, you do incremental or differential backups. These partial backups archive only those files that have been modified since the last full backup. A *differential backup* archives those selected files with positive archive attributes, without turning off their archive attributes. Each differential backup, therefore, archives all the selected files that have been created or modified since the last full backup. Thus, the last full backup, together with the most recent differential backup, represents the complete set of files that you need in order to restore the selected files to the hard disk.

An *incremental backup* archives all selected files with positive archive attributes and turns off their attributes. In other words, each incremental backup archives only those selected files that were created or modified since the last full or incremental backup. If you run an incremental backup every day, each day's run backs up only the files created and modified that day. In order to have a complete set of files, you must keep the last full backup, plus each subsequent incremental backup.

Peter's Principle: Don't mix differential and incremental backup types in one setup.

Each kind of partial backup has its advantages and disadvantages. A differential backup enables you to reuse the same disks every day, but backups take longer and longer as the cycle progresses. An incremental backup requires that you use a fresh disk every day, but each day's backup is relatively short. If you revise a file several times during a cycle, incremental backups save every version of the file; differential backups save only the most recent version. Unless you want to be able to fall back to earlier versions, differential backups have the advantage when you work on the same few files every day. But, if you handle different files every day—especially if you work on many of them—incremental backups are the better choice. At any rate, when the differential backup becomes too long, or you have piled up too many incremental backup disks, it's time to restart the cycle with a new full backup.

If you mix incremental and differential backups in one setup, you will end up with an incomplete set of backed up files. If you find that you'd rather do incremental backups after starting to make differential backups, or vice versa, do a full backup before switching to the other type of partial backup.

Once you have created a backup setup for a group of files, use the same setup for both full and partial backups. Simply switch the Backup Type between Full and Incremental or Differential as needed. That way, you know that you're selecting the same files every day.

In this practice backup, you will do a full backup:

1. Choose the Backup Type button.

   The Backup Type dialog box opens, showing the three backup types.

2. Select Full and choose OK.

   The dialog box closes. The Backup Type button now says Full.

When the Backup Type is Incremental or Differential, only selected files with a positive archive attribute are actually backed up. Examine the file list in the Backup File Selection dialog box; a dot appears next to those selected files that will not be backed up, either because they have been excluded by the Special Inclusions dialog box, or because their archive attributes are off.

Note: You might see the number of files to be written change dramatically as you switch between full and partial backups.

Identifying the Backup Drive

In the Backup dialog box, the Backup To box enables you to select where you want the backups written. If you're backing up to floppy disk, be sure to select the disk drives you tested in the compatibility test.

For this practice backup, you will use the same floppy drive that you used during the compatibility test:

1. Choose the Backup To button to open the Backup To dialog box.

   All your floppy drives are listed in the box, plus `MS-DOS Drive` and `Path`.

2. Choose the same floppy drive that you tested during the compatibility test.

3. Choose OK.

Tip: If you have two identical disk drives, Backup includes the option of using them both for the backup. You should choose this option for a speedier backup.

To back up to another type of device, it must be accessible by a DOS drive and path name. Suppose, for example, that you want to back up to a directory on a network drive. You would choose MS-DOS Drive and Path, then type the path name in the text box that appears.

Selecting Backup Options

Backup includes several options to tailor it for speed, reliability, and minimum media usage. You can, for example, choose to compress the backed up data, which not only takes up less media space, but also saves backup time. You can choose to verify all written data against the original files as you go; this type of verification takes much more backup time but guarantees a restorable product. Other options let you password protect your backup files, unconditionally format all backup disks, and so on.

Before reading about the individual options, open the dialog box to see the complete list by choosing the Options button. The Disk Backup Options dialog box opens. (See Figure 23.10.)

Figure 23.10.
The Disk Backup Options dialog box.

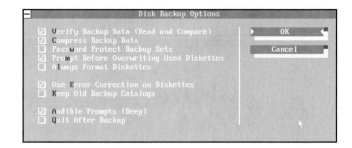

Verify Backup Data

Verify Backup Data slows your backup down quite a bit but helps to ensure a perfect result. Each file is reread and compared to the original as soon as it is written. Errors are corrected immediately. If Backup can't write a perfect copy after several attempts because of bad spots on the target media, it asks you to change the media so that it can try again.

> **Note:** This is a much more thorough verification than DOS's general verification feature. Do not count on the DOS verification to adequately verify your backup files.

Another way to verify your backed up files is to compare them to the originals with the Compare function, which is explained in Chapter 24. This function also repairs errors, if possible. But, if you wait until the backup is completed to check for errors, you must rerun the backup completely if an error can't be repaired. When you verify the backup as you go, you don't have to repeat the entire backup when an uncorrectable error is encountered. I recommend that you always use this Verify option.

Compress Backup Data

This option saves space on the target media and backup time. Backup compresses the data being backed up as much as possible, without actually taking extra processor time to do so. Because it doesn't take extra time to do compression, and because it ends up writing much less data, the overall result is that the backup takes less time.

As you have seen, Backup indicates in the Backup dialog box how many disks are needed for the backup. But, this estimate does not account for compression. If you're using compression, you probably need about half of the predicted number of disks. (The actual number depends on the type of files being backed up. Some types compress more readily than others.)

> **Warning:** Don't forget that DOS 6.22's compression method is incompatible with earlier versions. If you have been using the compression option with DOS 6.0 or 6.2, see the Problem Solver in "Running Restore" in Chapter 24 for more information on how to restore files. If you are backing up files to be restored on another computer that uses an earlier release of DOS 6, do not use the compression option.

Password Protect Backup Sets

If you're backing up confidential data, you might want to password protect it, so that an unauthorized person can't get at your files by gaining access to your backup disks. When you check this option, Backup asks you for a password of up to seven characters. You can't see the password as you type it, so you must type it twice, the second time to confirm the first. The password is case-sensitive; Dagwood is not the same as DAGWOOD.

When you assign a password to a backup, you must supply the password whenever you want to access the backed up files, either to compare them or to restore them. You can, however, delete or overwrite them without the password. So, the password doesn't protect your data from someone who wants to sabotage it.

Prompt Before Overwriting

It's just as easy to insert the wrong disk when making backups as it is at other times. When you check the Prompt Before Overwriting option, Backup warns you when a disk already contains data. You can see what data is on the disk, and choose to overwrite it or change disks.

This step is time-consuming; it takes Backup some time to analyze each new disk; then it must wait for you to respond. If you're planning to reuse former backup disks, and you're sure that you never make a mistake, you might want to disable this option to take less time and less user involvement. I recommend that you always use this option, however. It's too easy to mix up your disks and overwrite something important.

Always Format Diskettes

A disk with new physical formatting is always more reliable than one on which you have simply overwritten previous data. When you check the Always Format Diskettes option, Backup unconditionally formats every disk you use. Otherwise, it formats only unformatted disks. But, as you know, an unconditional format takes a long time. Imagine waiting while Backup formats 30 or more disks. You might not think the slight increase in reliability is worth that much extra time.

> **Note:** When you choose to back up to an MS-DOS drive and path, the options pertinent only for floppies, such as Always Format Diskettes, are dimmed and cannot be selected.

Use Error Correction

When you check the Use Error Correction option, Backup writes special error correction code on the backup media. This code helps the Compare and Restore functions recover data, even when the media is damaged. It doesn't take much additional time or space, so most people think it's worthwhile. I recommend that you leave it on; but, if you're trying to trim your backup time and media usage to a minimum, you might want to take the chance of turning this option off.

Keep Old Backup Catalogs

Backup records a catalog whenever it does a backup; the catalog documents the contents of the backup for use by the Compare and Restore functions. By default, these catalogs stay on your hard disk until you delete them. But, if you disable this option, Backup automatically deletes old catalogs from your hard disk when it creates newer catalogs. (Backup catalogs are discussed further in "Working with Backup Catalogs," later in this chapter.)

> **Note:** Backup stores a copy of the catalog on the backup media, too, so you can always retrieve a catalog from the media after you have eliminated it from the hard disk.

Audible Prompts

If you're going to sit and watch your screen while the backup progresses, you don't need Backup to beep when it wants you to do something (such as change disks). But, if you want to wander away, check the Audible Prompts option so that Backup can call your attention to a message.

Quit After Backup

If you will be exiting Backup as soon as it completes making a backup, you can have Backup do it for you by enabling the Quit After Backup option. This option is particularly useful if you run Backup as part of a batch program, such as AUTOEXEC.BAT or a shutdown routine. If you disable it, you return to the main Backup menu when the backup finishes.

Now that you understand the options, it's time to select the ones you'll use in your practice backup:

1. Enable the following options:

    Verify Backup Data

    Compress Backup Data

    Prompt Before Overwriting Used Diskettes

    Use Error Correction on Diskettes

    Audible Prompts

    A check mark appears next to each enabled option.

2. Disable all other options.

    Disabled options have no check mark.

3. Choose OK to close the dialog box.

Congratulations! You have finished defining your first backup setup. It takes a while, as you have seen, but you only have to do it once per setup. From then on, you just open the setup and choose Start Backup. You'll see how to do this next.

Managing Setup Files

Once you have tailored the setup as you want, you should save it for future use. If you already have used File, Save Setup As to create the setup file, all you need to do is choose File, Save Setup to save any changes to the setup file. Anytime you change the current setup, choose File, Save Setup to make the change permanent. If you make a temporary change—changing the backup type from Differential to Full for this backup only, for example—the change will be forgotten when you exit Backup without saving the setup.

Save your practice backup setup now by choosing File, Save Setup.

When you start Backup, DEFAULT.SET is opened by default. There are three ways to open a different setup. You can choose File, Open Setup, and select the setup you want to open. Or, you can press the Setup File button to display a list of setup files, select the setup you want, and choose Open to open it. It's even more convenient, however, to include the setup name in the startup command, as follows:

```
MSBACKUP DAILY.SET
```

Note: Backup assumes .SET when you omit the extension in the setup filename, so you can omit the extension, if you wish.

Problem: When I open a setup, Backup takes a long time reading a disk drive that isn't included in the setup. Why does it do this, and how can I make it stop?

At some time, you included files from that drive in the setup. Once you have done that, Backup always reads the drive when you open the setup. This can be especially annoying when the drive is a CD-ROM drive, because Backup forces you to place a CD in the drive (or suffer through repeated error messages) just to open the setup.

If DEFAULT.SET is involved, you have to wait for the excess drive to be read every time you start Backup, unless you specify another setup in the command that starts Backup. That can also be irritating.

To make it stop reading the drive, specifically exclude the drive from the setup. In the Backup From drive list (in the Backup dialog box), select the drive once to select all the files in the drive, then select it again to deselect them all. When you've done it right, an arrowhead should appear next to the drive name, but the entry should not say `Some files` or `All files`.

If you create DOS Shell or Windows program items for your backups, you can build the setup file into each program item definition. If you create a program item named Daily Backups, for example, you might define the item as MSBACKUP DAILY.SET or MWBACKUP DAILY.SET.

Running a Backup

When you're ready to back up files, start Backup, open the setup file, check to make sure that the backup type is what you want, and then press Start Backup. If the Start Backup button is dimmed, there are no files to be backed up according to the current setup—probably because either Incremental or Differential type is selected, and there are no modified files to be backed up.

How to Run a Backup

1. Start Backup.

2. Choose the Backup function.

3. Open the desired backup setup.

4. Choose Select Files, and adjust file selections as necessary.

5. Confirm or change the Backup Type.

6. Choose Start Backup, and follow the directions on the screen.

   Be sure to write down the name of the backup catalog while the backup is being performed.

7. Exit Backup when the job is done.

8. Label the backup media and store carefully.

Try running your practice backup now:

1. You will need some floppy disks. You can reuse the ones you used for the compatibility test, if you wish.

Warning: Backup replaces all the existing data on a disk. Even if you back up only one file, all existing data will be destroyed.

2. Choose the Start Backup button.

   A progress screen appears. (See Figure 23.11.) Then, a dialog box asks you to insert diskette #1.

Figure 23.11.
The Backup progress screen.

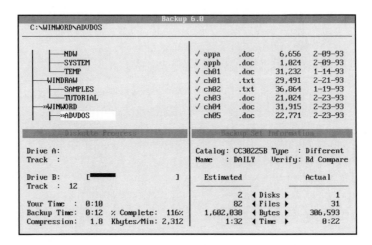

3. Write down on a slip of paper the catalog name from the progress screen. (In Figure 23.11, it is CC30225B.) You will need this catalog name later.

4. Insert a disk in the backup drive and choose Continue.

   Backup examines the disk and displays an alert box if the disk contains data. You can replace the disk and choose Retry, or simply choose Overwrite to continue with the current disk.

5. Insert additional disks as requested.

   When all the data has been backed up, Backup displays a summary dialog box.

6. Choose OK to close the summary box.

   Backup's main menu returns.

Figure 23.11 shows the screen that appears while the backup is in progress. As you can see, this screen keeps you advised of how the backup is progressing. The differences between the estimated and actual time and space requirements (in the lower right panel) result from backup options such as compression, the need to format disks, the amount of time that Backup has to wait for you to change disks, errors that Backup had to correct, and so on.

Problem: Backup freezes up in the middle of a backup.

One of your device drivers or TSRs is conflicting with Backup. Try booting without any TSRs or device drivers that aren't essential to your system. You could, for example, leave out your mouse driver, your virus monitor, your fax-modem driver, your CD-ROM driver, and so on. But, if your hard drive is compressed, be sure to load your compression software.

There are a couple of ways you can bypass items from your startup files:

- Reboot and press F8 to execute CONFIG.SYS, and perhaps AUTOEXEC.BAT, on a line by line basis. Chapter 21, "Configuring Your System," explains how to do this.

- Edit CONFIG.SYS and AUTOEXEC.BAT to insert REM in front of all nonessential commands. Chapter 20, "Basic Batch Programs," explains how to do this.

Be sure to restore your original configuration after you have successfully run Backup. You will have to disable the same programs each time you want to run Backup. (Chapter 38, "Starting Up DOS," shows you how to set up your CONFIG.SYS file so that you can select from alternate configurations when you boot.)

Working with Backup Catalogs

Each time you run a backup, Backup creates a catalog documenting the date, time, setup, and files included in the backup. Both the Compare and the Restore functions use the catalog, as you'll learn in Chapter 24. Backup stores the catalog on the hard disk, as well as on the backup media.

Figure 23.12 shows how to interpret the name Backup assigns to each catalog. You can identify the date, the drives, and the type of backup from the catalog name; but, you can't tell which setup was used. Backup maintains another catalog on the hard disk, called the *master catalog*, which identifies the catalogs belonging to each setup. The master catalog, named *setup*.CAT, simply lists the names of all the current catalogs belonging to the setup.

Figure 23.12.
Anatomy of a catalog name.

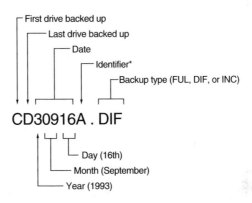

A typical master catalog looks like this:

```
All word processing files on C
CC50724B.FUL    7-24-95  4:59a
CC50805A.DIF    8-05-95  7:53a
```

The first line always shows the description of the setup, so you can check that you're looking at the right catalog. Then, the individual catalogs are listed. In this case, there are two of them, one from a full backup on July 24, 1995, and one from a differential backup on August 5, 1995.

Take a look at the master catalog you have created so far:

1. Exit Backup, saving all changes to your setup.
2. Enter **TYPE C:\DOS\PRACTICE.CAT** to display the catalog on your monitor.

   If you get the message `File not found`, your catalogs are not stored in your DOS directory, probably because you're on a network. Don't worry about looking at PRACTICE.CAT now. You'll learn how to locate your catalogs shortly.

Each time Backup creates a new catalog for a setup, it adds that catalog's name to the setup's master catalog. If you're maintaining the catalogs yourself, when you delete old catalogs, you should delete their names from the master catalog, too. (If you disable Keep Old Backup Catalogs, Backup deletes them from the master catalog automatically.)

Taking Care of Your Backup Disks

Once you have made your backups, you should label the backup disks and put them in a safe place. Include the setup name and the catalog name on the label. (If you find the catalog names hard to interpret, you might also write the date and type of backup on the label.) Label your practice backup disks now:

1. Label each disk with the following information:

    Backup Setup Name: PRACTICE.SET

    Catalog Name: *xxxxxxxx*.FUL

    (optional) Date: *xx/xx/xx*

    (optional) Backup Type: FULL

> **Note:** If you forget to write down the catalog name while you're making the backup, you can find out the name from the backup media. See "Managing Backup's Files," later in this chapter.

Where do you store your backup disks? I recommend that you make duplicate copies. Keep one set near your computer for easy retrieval when you need to restore some files. Store the other set in a fireproof vault, or take it to another location, so that you don't lose all your backups at once in a fire, flood, or other calamity.

Sometimes you change your mind after modifying a file. You might, for example, enter the wrong figures into a spreadsheet or post the wrong updates to a database. If you do your backups regularly, it's easy to fall back to the former version of the file by restoring it from its backup. If you made the faulty modifications several days ago, you might have to go back to an earlier backup to restore the file. If you don't keep old backups, you might not be able to get back to the unmodified file.

You also might encounter a situation in which you deleted a file quite some time ago, and now find that you want to restore it. You would have to restore it from backups that you made before the deletion. You might need to go back several months to find the file. Again, if you don't save your old backups, you won't be able to restore the necessary file.

If you want to be able to restore earlier versions of files, or recover deleted files from, say, six months ago, then you should keep your old backup media. I have one friend who keeps all his old backup disks forever. He has several years' worth stacked up on a closet shelf, so that he never takes the chance of losing a file. I'm not recommending that you be quite that rigorous about saving your backups, but you might consider keeping them for awhile. You must decide what method is best for your data.

If you decide to keep old backups for a long time, you don't need to keep their catalogs on the hard disk. Backup can retrieve catalogs from the backup media.

> **Peter's Principle:** Don't delete a backup until you know the next one is good.
>
> Even if you never need to go back to earlier files, don't reuse your old backup disks until you have a newer backup that you know is good. For example, if you do a full backup each Monday morning, don't reuse the first Monday's disks until at least the third Monday. That way, if the second Monday's backup turns out to be bad, you can fall back to the first Monday's. Similarly, if you make a differential backup every day, don't reuse Tuesday's differential backup until Thursday so that you can fall back to it if Wednesday's turns out to be bad.

Managing Backup's Files

Backup creates .SET, .SLT, .CAT, .FUL, .INC, and .DIF files on the hard drive. On the backup media, it packs as many of the backed up files as possible into a single file called *catalog.nnn*, where *catalog* is the catalog name, and *nnn* is a sequential number. The first or only file in a set might be named CC50107A.001, for example.

If you back up to a DOS directory, only one backup file is created, named *catalog*.001. All the backed up files are combined in this one file. (With Restore and Compare you can extract them.) If the specified backup directory is named JNFBACK, the setup is named DAILY, and the catalog is named CC50105A.FUL, Backup creates a branch like this:

```
JNFBACK  (the specified directory)
¦
¦ ──DAILY  (subdirectory)
        ¦ ──CC50105A.FUL  (subdirectory)
                ¦ ──CC50105A.001  (the backup file)
```

This branch structure makes it easy for you to find your backup files when you want to delete old ones. After a few days of backing up to the same path name from two different setups, your directory tree looks something like this (the backup files are not shown, just the subdirectories):

```
JNFBACK
¦
¦ ──DAILY
¦       ¦ ──CC50105A.FUL
¦       ¦ ──CC50106A.DIF
¦       ¦ ──CC50107A.DIF
¦
¦ ──SPECIAL
        ¦ ──CC50105B.FUL
        ¦ ──CC50106B.INC
        ¦ ──CC50107B.INC
```

As you can see, it would be very easy to find and delete the differential backup you made for the DAILY setup on January 6th, 1995.

If you back up to floppy disks, Backup creates one file per disk, naming them *catalog*.001; *catalog*.002; and so on, and packing as many backed up files as possible into each one. It fills each disk to the last byte, continuing the last file over to the next disk, if necessary. Only the final disk in the set might not be completely full of data. Backup assigns the label *setup type* to each disk, as in PRACTICEFUL.

Where Setup and Catalogs Files Are Stored

By default, Backup stores catalog and setup files in the same directory where the backup program is located, which is C:\DOS in a typical, non-network system. If you're not on a network, and you are the only person using your computer, you'll find it most convenient to let Backup use this default directory.

If you share your computer with others, you might want to keep your catalog and setup files in separate directories, so that each person sees only their own files when using Backup, Compare, or Restore. You can do this by setting an environment variable named MSDOSDATA, which identifies the default directory for all of Backup's files (as well as Microsoft Anti-Virus files, as you'll learn in Chapter 25, "DOS's Antivirus Programs"). For example, to set MSDOSDATA for a directory named C:\JNFBACK, you would enter this command:

```
SET MSDOSDATA=C:\JNFBACK
```

When MSDOSDATA has been set, Backup automatically looks in the indicated directory for any setup or catalog files that you want to open, and it automatically stores any new setups or catalogs there.

 Note: You'll learn how to use variables such as MSDOSDATA in Chapter 43, "DOS and the Environment." In Chapter 38, you'll learn how you can set MSDOSDATA during booting, according to which person is doing the booting.

If you're on a network, you may need to use MSDOSDATA to access a different drive or directory for your setup and catalog files. Your backup software might be located on a read-and-execute-only drive, for example. Your network administrator or work group leader should be able to tell you how to set MSDOSDATA. In fact, your AUTOEXEC.BAT probably has already been set up to define the environment variable properly each time you boot.

You can easily find out what directory your backup program is using by default:

1. Start your backup program and choose the Backup function.
2. Choose File, Open Setup.

    The Open Setup dialog box opens, listing the setups available to you by default. The default directory is shown at the top of the dialog box, next to the label Dir:.

Printing Setup Files

The .SET file contains all your setup information, except the individual directories and files that you have selected or deselected, which are stored in the .SLT file. The File, Print Setup command prints your .SET file, but not your .SLT file, which is not an ASCII text file.

Note: If you print your setup using MWBACKUP instead of MSBACKUP, you can choose between graphics and text mode for the printout.

Try printing your PRACTICE.SET file now:

1. Make sure your printer is ready.
2. Start Backup and open the PRACTICE setup.
3. Choose File, Print Setup.

    The setup should start to print.

You'll be able to recognize many of the items in the setup file, because they are the result of your choices in defining the setup. For example, you might see this line, indicating that the error correction option is enabled:

```
Error correction:      Yes
```

There are also variables in the setup file that you can't control from the Backup window. For example, you'll find the following lines that affect the appearance of the file list:

```
Show File Size:      Yes
Show File Date:      Yes
```

You can edit the .SET file, using an ASCII text editor such as EDIT to change the settings of these variables, which can't be changed any other way.

Note: The MWBACKUP version of the setup file contains somewhat different variables than MSBACKUP's version.

Note: If you decide to edit the .SET file, keep a backup copy, so that you can fall back to your old version if you don't like the results of your changes.

Deleting Setups

Backup's File menu includes a command to delete a backup setup. Both the .SET and .SLT files are deleted in one operation. You can't delete the current setup, so you must make sure that some other setup is open before you try to delete a setup. Try deleting the PRACTICE setup that you created in this chapter:

1. Make sure that PRACTICE is not the current setup. If it is, open the DEFAULT setup.

2. Choose File, Delete Setup.

   The Delete Setup dialog box opens, listing all your setups in the default directory.

3. Select the setup that you want to delete.

Warning: This function deletes the setup with the check mark. Be sure to double-click the setup name, or highlight it and press the space bar to select it. It should have a check mark next to it before you go on.

4. Choose the Delete button.

   A dialog box asks you to confirm your choice. Make sure the dialog box shows the PRAC-TICE setup. If not, choose Cancel and go back to step 2.

5. Choose Delete to delete the setup.

Deleting Catalogs

The Keep Old Backup Catalogs option controls whether Backup automatically deletes old catalogs as you make new ones. If you disable the option, Backup deletes catalogs according to these rules:

• When you make a new full backup, all old catalogs for that setup are deleted from the default directory, and their entries are deleted from the master catalog. Only the new full catalog remains.

• When you make a new differential backup, all previous differential catalogs for that setup are deleted from the default directory, and their entries are deleted from the setup's master catalog. Only the full catalog and the new differential catalog remain. (If there are incremental catalogs for the setup, they are not deleted.)

• When you make a new incremental backup, no catalogs are deleted.

If you enable the Keep Old Backup Catalogs option, Backup does not delete any catalogs automatically. You must decide when to delete catalogs, manually.

You should delete catalogs when you eliminate the backups themselves. But, if you keep your backups for many months, you might not want to keep your catalogs that long. Don't worry about losing the ability to restore files by deleting a catalog. If you need to restore a file from a backup set after its catalog has been deleted from your hard drive, you can retrieve the catalog from the backup set itself. You'll have to decide for yourself how long you want to keep your catalogs. When you delete a catalog, don't forget to delete its entry from the master catalog, which you can edit with EDIT.

Copying Huge Files via Floppies

Suppose that you need to transfer to another computer a copy of a really huge file, one that won't fit on a single floppy even if you use data compression. Suppose further, that you can't link the two computers together, network them, or transfer the file via modem, and that both computers have only the usual floppy drives—no removable cartridges or other high capacity devices. You'll have to figure out a way to transfer the file via floppy disks.

Neither COPY nor XCOPY can span a file over two or more diskettes, but Backup can. All you have to do is back the file up to a floppy drive, then restore the file to the other computer.

If you plan to use the compression option, be sure that both computers use compatible versions of Backup. That is, if computer A uses DOS 6.0 or 6.2, computer B must also have DOS 6.0 or 6.2, but not DOS 6.22 (except under the circumstances described in the Problem Solver in "Running Restore" in Chapter 24). If computer A uses DOS 6.22, computer B must have DOS 6.22 also. If the DOS versions are not compatible, don't use the compression option.

How to Copy a Huge File to Another Computer via Floppy Disks

1. Start Backup.

2. Choose the Backup function.

3. Create a new setup. (Don't use Default setup, or Backup will read the entire drive every time you start backup from now on. See the Problem Solver "Managing Setup Files" earlier in this chapter.)

4. For the new setup, select only the file you want to copy. Also, choose the floppy drive you want to copy it to, and the full backup type.

Note: Don't use the compression option unless the computers are using compatible versions of the Backup.

5. Start the backup and follow the directions on the screen.

6. On the other computer, start Backup.

7. Choose the Restore function.

8. Retrieve the catalog from the disk.

9. Because the catalog includes only one file, you can simply select the entire drive in the Restore Files box.

    The dialog box should show that one file is selected for restoration.

10. Select options to restore the file to the same drive and directory, or to a different drive and directory, as appropriate.

11. Choose Start Restore and follow the directions on the screen.

On Your Own

The next chapter shows you how to compare and restore files from your backups. You will need some backups to practice on, in addition to the one that you made in this chapter. The following items help you create the necessary backups:

1. Copy all the files from EXER1 to PRACTICE, renaming them as .XXX files. (Replace existing files where the names are the same.)

2. Redefine the PRACTICE setup to back up all files in the PRACTICE branch with dates between 1/1/94 and 1/1/95. Exclude files in the EXER1 directory whose names begin with C.

3. Run the PRACTICE backup again, but change the backup type to incremental.

4. Copy all the files from EXER2 to PRACTICE, renaming them as .XXX files. (Replace existing files where the names are the same.)

5. Run another incremental PRACTICE backup.

6. Keep the full backup disk and the two incremental disks for the next chapter.

24 Restore and Compare

Introduction

You can use your backups to restore deleted files, recover from a virus attack or a hard drive crash, and much more.

Restoring and Comparing

With a good set of backups, you are prepared for almost any kind of hard drive emergency. Suppose that you mistakenly delete a branch and can't undelete it; you can restore the entire branch—directories and files—from your backups. Suppose that you modify a spreadsheet and then decide that you want to remove the modifications; you can restore the unmodified version from its backup. Suppose that your hard disk dies and you have to buy a new one; you can restore all the backed up directories and files to the new drive after it has been formatted.

The Compare function notifies you when it detects a difference between the backup version and the hard drive version of a file. It's a good way to verify files if you didn't use the verification option while doing the backup or restore. In general, the verification option is a better choice, because it identifies and corrects errors as it goes. Compare can only identify a problem; you have to take other steps—such as redoing the backup or restore—to fix it.

Compare also comes in handy for identifying files that have been moved or deleted since the backups were made. It tells you when a backed up file no longer exists in its original hard drive directory.

You also can use Compare to determine if a file has been modified or corrupted since its last backup. Compare can tell you if files on different computers are identical; back up the files on computer A, then compare them to the files on computer B. (If you can connect the two computers in some way, it would be easier to compare the files with FC. Use Backup and Compare when there's no possibility of linking or networking the two computers.)

You follow the same general steps to compare or restore one file, a set of files, or all files in a backup: open a backup set catalog, select the files you want to restore or compare, and respond to prompts.

In this chapter, you will learn how to:

* Open a backup set catalog
* Select files to be restored or compared
* Select from among several versions of a file
* Select Restore or Compare options
* Run the Restore or Compare job

Restoring from Backups Made with Previous Versions of DOS

If you need to restore files from a backup that you made before upgrading your DOS system, you might encounter some problems. If you made the backups with DOS 5 or earlier, then upgraded to one of the DOS 6 releases, you can't use MSBACKUP or MWBACKUP to restore from the old backups. See "Restoring from Backups Made before DOS 6," near the end of this chapter, for instructions on how to restore from these backups.

If you made backups using DOS 6 or 6.2, and then upgraded to DOS 6.22, you won't have any trouble restoring from your earlier backups if any one of the following conditions is true:

- You did not use the compression option when you made the backups. (The compression option is the default in the earlier versions of Backup, so the files are compressed unless you specifically turned off the compression option.)

- You chose not to upgrade your Backup program when you upgraded the rest of DOS.

- You installed DblSpace under DOS 6 or 6.2 and have not upgraded your compressed drives to DrvSpace.

- Your old Backup program is still available somewhere on your hard drive, and you can run that version instead of DOS 6.22's. (It might be in OLD_DOS.1, for example.)

- You still have DBLSPACE.BIN in your DOS directory, along with a new file called DRVSPACE.MR1. (DRVSPACE.MR1 is included only in non-English language versions of DOS 6.22.)

If none of these conditions are true, you will need to take some extra steps to restore from your former backups. See the Problem Solver in "Running Restore" later in this chapter for detailed instructions on how to proceed.

Restoring Files

You start Restore by choosing the Restore button in MSBACKUP's main menu, or in the main MWBACKUP dialog box. This chapter assumes that you are using MSBACKUP. If you prefer MWBACKUP, you won't have much trouble adapting to the slight differences. Try starting Restore now:

1. Start up your backup program, if it isn't already started.

2. Choose the Restore button.

    The Restore dialog box opens. (See Figure 24.1.)

Figure 24.1.
The Restore dialog box.

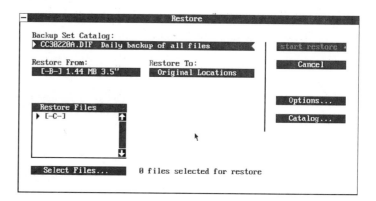

Opening a Catalog

The Backup Set Catalog button shows the name and description of the current backup catalog. The default catalog is the most recent one you have made. If you don't want to work with that catalog, you can choose another from a list of all your catalogs.

Try opening the catalog for the PRACTICE backup that you made in Chapter 23, "MSBACKUP and MWBACKUP." (If the PRACTICE catalog is already open, do this exercise anyway so that you know how to open another catalog.)

1. Choose the Backup Set Catalog button (it's the box containing the name of the current backup catalog).

    The Backup Set Catalog dialog box opens. (See Figure 24.2.) The descriptions next to each catalog name help you identify the catalog's setup. You can see both master catalogs (such as DAILY.CAT) and individual catalogs (such as CC30108A.FUL) in the list.

Figure 24.2.
The Backup Set Catalog dialog box.

Notice the check mark next to the catalog that is currently open.

2. Find the individual catalog for the last backup you did using the PRACTICE setup. Its name should be CC*xxxxxx*.INC. (Don't use the master catalog yet. We'll get to that later.)

3. To open the catalog, you must either double-click it, or highlight it and press the space bar.

   The check mark moves to the catalog that you select, indicating that it is now the open catalog. (If the check mark doesn't move, try again.)

4. Choose Load to complete the dialog.

   The dialog box closes and the Restore dialog box returns. The information in the dialog box, such as the drive list and the Restore From box, reflect the contents of the open catalog. So far, no files are selected and the Start Restore button is dimmed.

How to Open a Catalog

1. In the Restore dialog box, press the Backup Set Catalog button.

   Restore lists all the available catalogs.

2. Select a catalog by double-clicking it, or by highlighting it and pressing the space bar.

   Restore puts a check mark next to the selected catalog.

3. Choose the Load button.

Selecting Files

You don't have to deal with include/exclude lists when you are selecting files to restore. You can select whole drives on the Restore screen, or you can press the Select Files button to work with a drive list, directory tree, and file list.

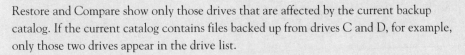

Problem: Restore or Compare does not show all of my hard drives in the drive list. Why can't it find all of my hard drives?

Restore and Compare show only those drives that are affected by the current backup catalog. If the current catalog contains files backed up from drives C and D, for example, only those two drives appear in the drive list.

Selecting Whole Drives

When you select a whole drive, all the directories and files in the backup catalog for that drive are selected. If more than one drive appears in the Restore Files box, you can select any or all of them. When you select a drive, you do not select all the files that are currently on that drive. Instead, you select all the files that were backed up from that drive and appear in the backup catalog.

How to Select Files to be Compared or Restored

To select a complete drive:

1. Double-click the drive name in the Restore Files dialog box, or highlight the drive name and press the space bar.

To select or deselect a directory:

1. Choose Select Files in the Restore dialog box.

   The Select Restore Files dialog box opens.

2. In the directory tree, double-click the directory name, or highlight it and press the space bar.

To select or deselect individual files:

1. Choose Select Files in the Restore dialog box.

   The Select Restore Files dialog box opens.

2. In the directory tree, highlight the directory.

   The directory's contents are listed in the file list.

3. Double-click each file name, or highlight it and press the space bar.

To exclude files by date range:

1. Choose Select Files in the Restore dialog box.

   The Select Restore Files dialog box opens.

2. Choose Special.

   The Special Inclusions dialog box opens.

3. Enable Apply Date Range.

4. Enter the date range in the From and To boxes.

To exclude copy protected files:

1. Choose Select Files in the Restore dialog box.

   The Select Restore Files dialog box opens.

2. Choose Special.

   The Special Inclusions dialog box opens.

3. Enable Exclude Copy Protected Files.

4. Enter up to five file names (which can be generic or specific) in the text boxes to the right of Exclude Copy Protected Files.

To exclude files by attributes:

1. Choose Select Files in the Restore dialog box.

   The Select Restore Files dialog box opens.

2. Choose Special.

   The Special Inclusions dialog box opens.

3. Enable Exclude Read-Only Files, Exclude System Files, and/or Exclude Hidden Files as appropriate.

Try selecting all the backed up files from drive C:

1. If you have a mouse, double-click drive C in the drive list. If you're using the keyboard, press Alt+I to select the Restore Files box. Because only one drive appears in the box, it is highlighted automatically. Press the space bar to select it.

   A solid arrowhead and the words All files indicate that all the files on the drive have been selected. You should see the number of selected files change and the Start Restore button become available.

2. Repeat step 1 to *de*select the drive.

   The arrowhead disappears, the number of selected files reverts to 0, and the Start Restore button becomes dimmed.

Selecting or Deselecting Individual Files

When you choose the Select Files button, you can individually select directories or files to be restored. If you select a whole drive first, you can use Select Files to deselect specific directories or files.

Try selecting some files to be restored:

1. Choose the Select Files button.

   The Select Restore Files dialog box opens. (See Figure 24.3.) The directory tree shows the entire directory structure of the hard drive at the time of the backup, even though files were backed up only from the PRACTICE branch.

Figure 24.3.
The Select Restore Files
dialog box.

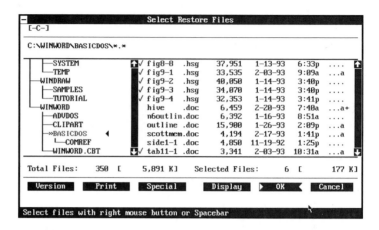

```
┌─┐                    Select Restore Files
│ │ [-C-]
└─┘
 C:\WINWORD\BASICDOS\*.*

     ├──SYSTEM          ▲√ fig8-8  .hsg   37,951   1-13-93    6:33p  ....  ▲
     ├──TEMP             √ fig9-1  .hsg   33,535   2-03-93    9:09a  ...a
   ──WINDRAW             √ fig9-2  .hsg   40,050   1-14-93    3:40p  ....
     ├──SAMPLES          √ fig9-3  .hsg   34,070   1-14-93    3:40p  ....
     └──TUTORIAL         √ fig9-4  .hsg   32,353   1-14-93    3:41p  ....
   ──WINWORD              hive     .doc    6,459   2-20-93    7:40a  ...a+
     ├──ADVDOS            n6outlin.doc     6,392   1-16-93    8:51a  ....
     ├──CLIPART           outline .doc   15,900   1-26-93    2:09p  ...a
     ├─»»BASICDOS    ◄    scottmem.doc    4,194   2-17-93    1:41p  ...a
     │    └──COMREF       side1-1 .doc    4,050  11-19-92    1:25p  ...a
     └──WINWORD.CBT     ▼√ tab11-1 .doc    3,341   2-03-93   10:31a  ...a  ▼

 Total Files:    350 [    5,891 K]   Selected Files:    6 [     177 K]

 ┌─────────┐ ┌───────┐ ┌─────────┐ ┌─────────┐ ┌────────┐ ┌────────┐
 │ Version │ │ Print │ │ Special │ │ Display │▶│   OK   │◄│ Cancel │
 └─────────┘ └───────┘ └─────────┘ └─────────┘ └────────┘ └────────┘

 Select files with right mouse button or Spacebar
```

> **Note:** The drive list, directory tree, and file list are taken from the backup catalog. They reflect the directory structure and files that were backed up, not the current structure of your hard drives.

2. Move the highlight around in the directory tree by pressing up-arrow and down-arrow, or by clicking various directories.

   Notice that there are no files in most of the directories. That's because you didn't back up any files from those directories.

3. Now move the highlight to the PRACTICE directory.

   The file list shows all the files that were backed up from this directory.

4. Double-click the PRACTICE directory, or press the space bar to select the entire directory.

   A solid arrowhead appears next to the directory name in the directory tree, check marks appear next to all the file names in the file list, and the Selected Files field in the bottom right corner shows the number of files you have selected.

5. Move the highlight to the EXER1 directory.

6. Double-click two files. If you're using the keyboard, press tab to move the highlight into the file list, press down-arrow to highlight a file, and press space bar to select it.

   Check marks appear next to the selected files, a chevron appears next to the directory name in the directory tree, and the Selected Files field in the bottom right corner shows the total number of files you have selected.

> **Tip:** You can choose the Print button to print the contents of the catalog.

7. Choose OK to return to the Restore dialog box.

Notice that the words Some files appear next to drive C. You can also see the number of selected files.

Note: Unlike the Backup function, Restore does not save your file selections. Each time you start Restore, you must select the files you want to restore.

Restoring Older Versions

When you open a master catalog, a file might have several versions available. For example, suppose that you modified HIVE.DOC every day for a week, making an incremental backup each day. There would be seven versions of HIVE.DOC in the master catalog.

By default, the file list shows only the latest version of each file in the catalog, but a plus sign next to the file entry indicates that multiple versions are available. The Version button, which is available only for a master catalog, opens a version list for whatever file is currently highlighted in the file list, enabling you to select the version you want.

If you followed all the practice exercises in Chapter 23, you have at least two versions of some files in the PRACTICE master catalog. Take a look at those versions now:

1. Open the PRACTICE master catalog.

2. Choose Select Files.

3. Choose the PRACTICE directory.

Notice the + sign next to some files.

4. Highlight a file with a + sign.

The Version button becomes available.

5. Choose the Version button.

A dialog box shows you a list of all the versions in the catalog. You can tell the difference between the versions by their date and time stamps.

6. Select the earliest version by double-clicking it, or by highlighting it and pressing the space bar.

A check mark appears next to the selected version.

7. Choose OK to close the Version dialog box.

The selected version appears in the file list and is selected to be restored.

How to Fall Back to an Older Version of a File

1. Start your backup program and choose Restore.

2. Open the master catalog for the backup set.

3. Choose Select Files.

   The Select Restore Files dialog box opens.

4. Highlight the directory containing the file.

5. Highlight the file.

   If the file has a + sign next to it, several versions are available in the catalog and the Version button becomes available.

6. Choose Version.

   The Version List dialog box opens.

7. Double-click the version you want, or highlight it and press the space bar.

   A check mark appears next to the selected version.

8. Choose OK.

   The selected version appears in the file list.

9. Choose OK to return to the Restore dialog box.

10. Choose Start Restore.

   Restore will tell you which disks to insert.

The Restore Options

Restore offers a number of options to ensure a successful restoration. But, before you consider the options, you should take a look at which backup setup is currently open, because any changes to the options are stored in the current setup.

Changing the Backup Setup from the Restore Window

When you start MSBACKUP, DEFAULT.SET is opened by default unless you include another setup filespec on the startup command. If you go immediately into the Restore function, where you can't see the name of the backup setup, you might think that the current backup setup is related to the current backup catalog. That's not necessarily true.

Opening a catalog does not cause its setup to be opened. For example, you might have DEFAULT.SET open as the setup file, but DAILY.CAT (from the DAILY setup) open as the catalog file. In that case, any changes you make to the options are stored in DEFAULT.SET, not DAILY.SET.

If you will use the same restore options most of the time, no matter what catalog is involved, store them in DEFAULT.SET. That way, you won't have to open a different setup just for the restore options. But, to relate the restore options to a particular setup, you must open that setup before setting the options, and open it again when you want to use them.

Opening a setup from the Restore dialog box is somewhat different than opening a setup from the Backup dialog box. Because there is no Setup button in the dialog box, you have to use the File menu.

Try opening your PRACTICE setup:

1. Choose File, Open Setup.

    The Open Setup dialog box opens.

2. Double-click the PRACTICE setup file, or highlight it and press the space bar.

    A check mark appears next to the selected setup file.

3. Choose Open to open the setup.

    If you changed any Restore options while the other setup was open, Restore asks if you want to save your changes to that setup. You can answer Yes to save them, or No to drop them. Then, the new setup opens and establishes its own settings for the Restore options.

Now you're ready to select options for the setup you have opened:

1. Choose the Options button to open the Restore Options dialog box. (See Figure 24.4.) Leave it open while you read about the options.

Figure 24.4.
The Disk Restore Options dialog box.

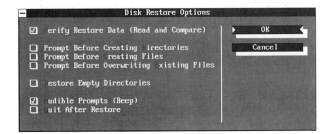

Verify Restore Data

When you enable Verify Restore Data, Restore takes the time to compare each restored file to the backed up version and correct any errors it encounters.

Note: You also can verify the restored files after the restoration is complete by using the Compare function, which is explained under "Compare," later in this chapter.

Prompt before Creating Directories

When you restore one or more files to a directory that no longer exists, Restore re-creates the directory for the restored files. When Prompt before Creating Directories is disabled, Restore creates directories without warning. But, when you enable this option, Restore asks you to confirm each directory it must create. If you choose No, Restore skips any files belonging to that directory.

Prompt before Creating Files

Suppose that you want to restore a file that was deleted from a directory. By default, Restore returns the file to the directory with no warning. But, if you enable Prompt before Creating Files, Restore asks your permission when it must create a file in a directory. If you choose No, Restore skips that file.

Prompt before Overwriting Existing Files

If a destination directory already contains a file of the same name as a file to be restored, Restore overwrites the existing file with the restored file. Disabling Prompt before Overwriting Existing Files lets Restore overwrite existing files without warning. When this option is enabled, Restore asks for permission to overwrite a file. If you choose No, the backup version is not restored.

Restore Empty Directories

Backup always records the entire directory structure of a drive, even if some of the directories contain no files to be backed up. You can re-create a drive's former directory structure, including empty directories, by enabling Restore Empty Directories. If you disable this item, Restore creates directories only for the files it is restoring.

Audible Prompts

Just like Backup, Restore prompts you for backup media. It may display other prompts, depending on which options you have selected. Enable Audible Prompts if you want Restore to beep when it displays a prompt.

Quit after Restore

If you enable Quit after Restore, the backup program terminates itself when the restoration is finished; you return to whatever program you were using when you started backup. If you don't enable this option, you return to the Restore dialog box when the restoration is finished.

Selecting Restore Options

You should have the Disk Restore Options dialog box open on your screen. Try choosing the options for the PRACTICE setup:

1. Enable the following options:

   Verify Restore Data

   Prompt before Creating Directories

   Prompt before Overwriting Existing Files

   Audible Prompts

   Check marks appear next to the enabled options.

2. Disable all other options.

   Disabled options have no check marks.

3. Choose OK to close the dialog box.

You could save these options in the setup right now by choosing File Save Setup; or, you could wait until you exit Restore, or switch to another setup. If you try to exit or change setups without saving option changes, Restore asks if you want to save them to the current setup. (The message tells you the name of the setup.) All you have to do is choose Yes to save them or No to drop them. For this practice exercise, you'll wait until you exit to save the options.

Running Restore

After you have opened the catalog, selected the files, and chosen your Restore options, you're ready to run the Restore job.

1. Press Start Restore to begin restoring files.

   Restore asks for the backup media by catalog name; if floppy disks are involved, it also asks for specific disk numbers. For example, it might ask for disk #2 of backup set CC50510A.FUL.

2. Insert the requested disk in the specified drive and choose Continue.

   Figure 24.5 shows the progress box that appears during the restoration. The top half shows the directory and files that Restore is currently working on. The bottom half shows Restore's progress and results.

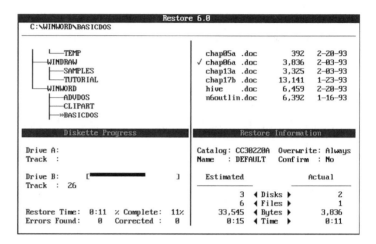

Figure 24.5.
The Restore progress box.

Note: If Backup stored error correction code on the backup disks, Restore can detect and correct errors due to bad sectors, read/write errors, and other physical problems.

At the end, a summary box shows you how many files were restored, how many files were skipped (because you chose not to overwrite an existing file, for example), how many errors in the backup files were detected and repaired, and so on.

3. Choose OK to close the dialog box.

4. Exit the backup program.

   Restore asks whether you want to save changes to the current setup.

5. Choose Yes to save the current Restore options in the PRACTICE setup.

Problem: I tried to restore some files that I backed up with DOS 6.0 or 6.2, and Restore says that it can't read the compressed files.

DOS 6.22 uses a different compression technique than DOS 6.0 and 6.2. It won't be able to read files that you backed up under the earlier DOS version unless you're still using DblSpace on your hard drive. You can use one of the following methods to restore your older backups:

- If you still have the OLD_DOS.1 directory on your hard drive, switch to that directory and try running MSBACKUP. If you can run your former version of MSBACKUP, it should be able to read your older backup files.

- If you still have your installation disks from your former version of DOS, you can copy the former program files to your hard drive and run the former backup program that way. Some of the necessary files are compressed on the installation disks, and you will have to use the EXPAND program to copy them to your hard drive. Follow the steps below:

1. Create a directory called OLDBACK (or whatever name you would like to use).

2. (For MS-DOS 6.2 on 1.2MB disks, go on to step 3.) For MS-DOS 6.0, or for MS-DOS 6.2 on 1.44MB disks, insert Setup Disk 1 from your old DOS version in the appropriate drive and enter the following commands, where *d* is the name of the drive containing the Setup disk:

```
XCOPY d:*.OVL C:\OLDBACK
EXPAND d:MSBACKUP.EXE C:\OLDBACK
EXPAND d:MSACKUP.HLP C:\OLDBACK
EXPAND d:MSBCONFG.HLP C:\OLDBACK
```

3. For MS-DOS 6.2 on 1.2MB disks, insert Setup Disk 2 in the appropriate drive and enter the following commands, where *d* is the name of the drive containing the Setup disk:

```
XCOPY d:*.OVL C:\OLDBACK
EXPAND d:MSBACKUP.EXE C:\DOS
```

Then, insert Setup disk 3 in the drive and enter the following commands:

```
XCOPY d:*.OVL C:\OLDBACK
EXPAND d:MSACKUP.HLP C:\OLDBACK
EXPAND d:MSBCONFG.HLP C:\OLDBACK
```

4. Switch to C:\OLDBACK and start up MSBACKUP.

   From now on, whenever you want to restore files backed up by your previous version of DOS, switch to C:\OLDBACK and start MSBACKUP from there. When you want to restore files backed up by DOS 6.22, make sure you are not in C:\OLDBACK; start MSBACKUP or MWBACKUP from any other directory.

5. If you do not have your former DOS installation disks, you can still restore from your old compressed backups, if you have the DBLSPACE.BIN and DRVSPACE.MR1 files on your hard drive. To obtain DRVSPACE.MR1 if it didn't come with your version of DOS 6.22, send in the coupon at the back of your DOS *User's Guide*.

Using Restore for Common Tasks

You probably will use Restore most often to restore the latest versions of individual files. For example, suppose that you delete all your *.DOC files in a directory, and you can't undelete them reliably. You should be able to restore them. All you have to do is start Restore, open the correct catalog, choose the desired files, select the desired options, and choose Start Restore. Then, you just insert disks as requested.

How to Restore the Latest Versions of Individual Files

1. Start your backup program.

2. Choose the Restore button.

3. Open the master catalog for the setup that includes the files you want.

4. Choose the Select Files button.

5. Select the files to be restored, and choose OK to return to the Restore dialog box.

6. If desired, choose Options to review, and set the options for the restoration.

7. Choose Start Restore.

8. Insert backup media as requested.

9. When the restoration is complete, choose OK to clear the summary report.

Restoring Files from an Older Backup

If you need to restore a file that you deleted a long time ago, you might have to go back to an earlier catalog. If the catalog has already been deleted from the hard drive, you can retrieve it from the backup media. You might have some trouble deciding which backup set contains the last version of the file before it was deleted. You might have to retrieve several catalogs until you find the right one. Once you have found the correct catalog, select the file and choose Start Restore.

How to Restore a File after Its Catalog Has Been Deleted from the Hard Drive

1. Choose Catalog to open the Select Catalog dialog box.

2. Choose Retrieve to retrieve the catalog from the backup media.

   The Retrieve Catalog dialog box opens.

3. If you're retrieving from floppy disks, choose the floppy drive for the backup media. When Restore asks you to, insert the last disk in the backup set in the drive and choose Continue.

If you're retrieving from a DOS directory, enter the drive and path name in the text box. Be sure to include all the subdirectories in the path to the directory that actually contains the catalog file, so that Restore knows exactly which catalog you want. A complete path name looks something like this:

L:\JNFBACK\DAILY\CC50429A.FUL.

Restore displays the message `Path name is entered incorrectly`, if the path name doesn't end with a subdirectory name in the form CATALOG.TYPE.

Restore retrieves the catalog into your default directory for Backup catalogs and selects it, but doesn't open it.

4. Choose Load to load the catalog.

   The Restore dialog box returns. The retrieved catalog is open, but no files are selected as yet.

5. Select the file to be restored.

6. Check the selected options and change them, if desired.

   Suggested option: Verify Restore Data.

7. Choose Start Restore and follow the directions on your screen.

   Restore restores the selected file from the backup set to the hard drive.

Restoring an Entire Drive

If your hard drive fails and you need to replace the entire drive, you must first format the hard drive and reinstall DOS on it (so that MSBACKUP is available). You should also reinstall any other software that you have not included in your backups. Then, you are ready to start restoring backups.

Your catalogs are no longer available on your hard drive, so you must retrieve them from the backup media. Unfortunately, this means that you won't have any master catalogs, and you can't readily identify the latest version of each file.

The easiest way to make sure that you restore the latest versions of all files is to restore the last full backup, followed by your partial backups in chronological order. If you have been doing differential backups, all you have to do is restore the last full backup, followed by the last differential backup, and the job is complete. If you have been doing incremental backups, restore the last full backup, followed by the first incremental backup after it, the next incremental backup after that, the next one, and so on, until you have restored all the incremental backups in chronological order. This guarantees that, if several versions of a file were backed up, the later ones overwrite the earlier ones.

How to Restore an Entire Drive

1. Format the drive and reinstall DOS on it. Also, reinstall any software that you have not backed up.

   Reinstalling DOS makes MSBACKUP available, so that you can restore from your backups.

2. Start MSBACKUP or MWBACKUP, and choose the Restore function.

3. Choose Catalog to open the Select Catalog dialog box.

4. Choose Retrieve to retrieve the catalog from the backup media.

   The Retrieve Catalog dialog box opens.

5. If you're restoring from floppy disks, choose the floppy drive for the backup media. When asked to do so, insert the last disk of that set in the drive and choose Continue.

   If you're restoring from a DOS directory, choose MS-DOS Drive and Path, and enter the drive and path name of your *last full backup* in the text box. Be sure to include all the subdirectories in the path to the directory that actually contains the catalog file, so that Restore knows exactly which catalog you want. A complete path name looks something like this:

   L:\JNFBACK\DAILY\CC50429A.FUL.

   Restore displays the message `Path name is entered incorrectly`, if the path name doesn't end with a subdirectory name in the form CATALOG.TYPE.

   Restore retrieves the catalog into the default directory for your backup catalogs.

6. Choose Load to load the catalog.

   The Restore dialog box returns. The retrieved catalog is open, but no files are selected as yet.

7. Select all the files on the drive.

8. Suggested options: Verify Restore Data, Restore Empty Directories, and Audible Prompts.

9. Choose Start Restore and follow the directions on your screen.

   Restore restores all the files from the backup set to the hard drive.

10. If you made differential backups after the last full backup, repeat steps 3 through 9 for the last differential backup only. If you made incremental backups after the last

full backup, repeat steps 3 through 9 for each incremental backup in chronological order.

11. If you have made backups based on more than one setup, repeat steps 3 through 10 for each setup.

If you have been doing backups based on more than one setup, you'll need to restore the backups from all the setups to complete the job of restoring your hard drive. When you have finished all the setups, your hard disk is completely restored to the condition of your last backup, with one minor exception. You might have restored some directories and files that you had erased. All you have to do is erase them again.

Restoring Files to a Different Drive and Directory

If you're using backup to copy or move files to a different computer—from office to home, for example—the destination computer might have a different directory structure. You can restore files to different drives and directories by selecting Other Drives or Other Directories in the Restore To field.

When you choose Other Drives, Restore asks for a drive name and a path name for each directory represented by the restored files. When you choose Other Directory, Restore asks only for a path name for each directory.

You don't have to use Other Drives and Other Directories just because you're restoring the files to a different computer. The Other Drives and Other Directories options are required only if you want to supply different drive names or directory names for the restored files. If the files came from drive C, for example, and are being restored to drive C on a different computer, you don't need to use Other Drives. If the files are being restored to the same path names on a different computer, you don't need to use Other Directories.

How to Restore Files to Different Drives and Directories

1. Start MSBACKUP or MWBACKUP, and choose the Restore function.

2. Choose Catalog to open the Select Catalog dialog box.

3. Choose Retrieve to retrieve the catalog from the backup media.

   The Retrieve Catalog dialog box opens.

4. Choose the floppy drive for the backup media. When asked to do so, insert the last disk of that set in the drive and choose Continue.

   Restore retrieves the catalog into the default directory for your backup catalogs.

5. Choose Load to load the catalog.

   The Restore dialog box returns. The retrieved catalog is open, but no files are selected as yet.

6. Select the files to be restored.

7. Suggested options: Verify Restore Data, Prompt before Creating Directories, Prompt before Overwriting Existing Files, and Audible Prompts.

8. Choose the Restore To button.

   The Restore To dialog box opens.

9. Select Other Drives or Other Directories and choose OK.

10. Choose Start Restore and follow the directions on your screen.

    Restore asks for drive and/or directory names to substitute for the drive and directory names in the backup set.

Rebuilding a Missing Catalog

Let's take a worst case scenario: You need to restore some files from an older backup, the catalog has been removed from the hard drive, and the last floppy disk in the backup set has been lost or damaged. You have no catalog for this backup. All is not lost. You can ask Restore to examine the backup set and build a new catalog based its contents. Just choose the Catalog button, choose Rebuild, select the drive for the backup set, and insert disks as instructed. Restore reads through the entire backup set to rebuild the catalog.

Warning: If some disks in the backup set are missing or damaged, the files you want to restore may not be available.

How to Rebuild a Catalog

1. Start MSBACKUP or MWBACKUP, and choose the Restore function.

2. Choose Catalog to open the Select Catalog dialog box.

3. Choose Rebuild.

   Restore asks for the drive name for the backup set.

4. Choose the floppy drive for the backup media.

   Restore asks for the first disk in the backup set (unless you have chosen an MS-DOS directory for the backup set).

5. Insert disks as requested.

   Restore rebuilds the catalog in the default directory for your backup catalogs.

6. Choose Load to load the catalog.

   The Restore dialog box returns. The retrieved catalog is open, but no files are selected as yet.

7. Once the catalog is open, choose files and options as with other restoration tasks.

Compare

Figure 24.6 shows the dialog box that opens when you select the Compare function. In terms of your actions, a comparison is nearly identical to a restoration. You open a catalog, select the files to be compared, choose options, and respond to prompts. Compare offers only two options: Audible Prompts and Quit after Compare.

Figure 24.6.
The Compare dialog box.

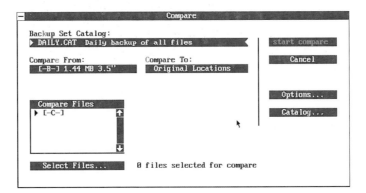

Compare corrects errors when it encounters physical problems on the backup media and has error correction code available. It does not correct disparities between the backup version and the hard drive version of a file, however; it merely displays alert boxes so that you know a problem exists. Make your own notes about any mismatches that Compare reports. The summary report at the end does not list the names of files that were found to be different, although it does show you how many there were.

How to Compare Backed Up Files to Their Originals

1. Start Backup.

2. Choose the Compare button.

3. Open the desired catalog.

4. Select the files to be compared.

5. Set up the compare options as desired.

6. Choose Start Compare.

7. Insert backup media as requested.

Restoring from Backups Made before DOS 6

If you need to restore files made by an earlier DOS backup, use the RESTORE command shown in Figure 24.7. For example, suppose you want to restore all the CHAP*.TXT files from an old backup set to drive C. You would enter the following command:

```
RESTORE A: C:\CHAP*.TXT /S
```

On Your Own

This chapter has shown you how to compare and restore files from backups made by MSBACKUP or MWBACKUP. If you would like to practice these techniques, you can use the following items as a guide:

1. Delete the entire PRACTICE branch from your hard drive and restore it.

2. Compare the restored branch to the backup versions to make sure they are the same.

3. Restore an older version of a file in the PRACTICE branch.

Before going on to the next chapter, you might want to remove from your hard disk all the files that you have created in Chapter 23 and this chapter:

1. Delete the PRACTICE branch from your hard drive.

2. Delete the PRACTICE setup.

3. Delete the catalogs for the PRACTICE setup. (Hint: Print the PRACTICE.CAT master catalog as a guide to the names of the catalogs to be deleted.)

RESTORE

Restores files backed up by BACKUP from previous DOS versions (DOS 2.0 through 5.0).

Syntax:

```
RESTORE drive1 target [/S] [/P] [/N]
```

Parameters and Switches:

drive1	Identifies the drive containing the backup files.
target	Identifies the files to be restored, and the drive to which they are to be restored. *target* must include a drive name; it may specify files by including a path and/or filename(s).
/S	Restores files to all subdirectories.
/P	Prompts for permission to restore read-only files, or those changed since the last backup.
/N	Restores only those files that no longer exist on the destination.

Figure 24.7. *RESTORE command summary.*

25

DOS's Antivirus Programs

Introduction

Viruses aren't just exciting stories for the six o'clock news. They are very real problems that have caused many PC users grief.

Why Virus Protection?

Here's an example of how pernicious a virus can be. Some friends had a virus in one of their computers without knowing it, and one unfortunate day, the computer wouldn't boot. When they tried to boot from an emergency floppy boot disk, the virus installed itself on the disk—still without them realizing what was happening. They decided to see whether the boot disk would work on their other machines. Each time they tried to boot another computer, the virus immediately infected the new computer and wiped out its hard disk. In all, four hard disks were erased in just a few minutes.

When they finally realized that something extraordinary was afoot, they called a friendly expert who told them to trash the infected floppy disk, along with all the others they had tried out. Then, they reformatted their hard disks, reinstalled DOS, and—don't miss this point—restored all their files from backups. They were up and running in short order because they had a company policy of regular backups. (P.S. Now they also have a company antivirus policy.)

The virus could have invaded the original system by many routes. Perhaps it was downloaded from an online service or installed with some new software. It might have been built in when the system was new. Viruses can occupy your system for a long time before doing anything except spreading themselves to other systems. Many viruses wait for some kind of triggering event, such as the creator's birthday, before swinging into action.

Microsoft includes several antivirus utilities in DOS 6. If you use them correctly, these utilities will identify a virus almost as soon as it enters your computer, prevent it from doing any harm, and remove it from your system. In this chapter you will learn to:

- Recognize the difference between a virus scanner and a virus monitor
- Decide when to use a virus scanner
- Decide when to use a virus monitor
- Scan your drives for known viruses
- Scan your drives for unknown viruses
- Monitor system activity for virus-like behavior
- Decide what to do if a virus is detected or suspected
- Update your virus software with the newest virus information from Microsoft

Microsoft Antivirus Features

DOS 6's antivirus programs protect your system in two ways. A virus scanner scans memory and your disks for resident viruses, whereas a virus monitor monitors all system activity for virus-like behavior. Both types of programs take up time in your system; you can tailor antivirus options to minimize the time or maximize the protection.

The Virus Scanning Programs

The two virus scanning programs are MSAV (Microsoft Anti-Virus) and MWAV (Microsoft Windows Anti-Virus). You can install either or both programs during Setup. You probably don't need both; install MSAV if you prefer DOS, MWAV if you prefer Windows. Some minor differences exist between the two programs, but both are capable of detecting known and unknown viruses.

Known Viruses

A *known virus* is one that has already been discovered and analyzed by antivirus specialists. They have given it a name, such as Stoned or Michelangelo. They have identified a *signature* for it—a series of bytes contained in the virus program that are used to recognize it. A virus might have several known *strains*—slight variations of the same basic program. More than a thousand viruses have been identified so far. Many of them haven't been seen for a while and are probably extinct, but there's no way of predicting when or where one will crop up again.

Microsoft's antivirus programs scan for known viruses by examining memory and your disks for the thousand or so known virus signatures. This might take several minutes on a large hard drive. You can limit the search to those areas most likely to be infected by a virus: the partition tables of hard drives, the boot records of floppies, and program files. Very few viruses hide themselves in other places.

The scanner can remove many known viruses without damaging the infected files or system areas; this is called *cleaning* a virus. However, some viruses damage files or system areas when they invade them, and of course, the scanner can't undo the damage. Such files need to be deleted; you usually can restore them from a backup or reinstall them from their original program disks.

Unknown Viruses

It's perhaps even more important to scan for unknown viruses than for known ones because the very latest viruses are unknown until they get detected, analyzed, named, and added to the virus scanners.

The scanners detect unknown viruses by looking for changes in program files indicating that they might have been infected by a virus. Most program files don't change after they're installed, so any change at all could indicate a virus infection.

The first time you use a Microsoft antivirus scanner on a drive, it creates a file named CHKLIST.MS in each directory, recording the size, attributes, and date/time stamps for all the program files in that directory. It also records a *checksum*, a unique value calculated from the contents of the file; if the contents change, the checksum changes, and the virus scanner knows that the file has changed even if its size, attributes, and date/time stamp remain unchanged.

Warning: If an unknown virus already exists in your system when the scanner records the CHKLIST.MS data, it will not be identified. Fortunately, Microsoft's virus monitor (VSAFE), which is described next, can block it from doing any damage.

Each subsequent scan compares the recorded data in CHKLIST.MS against the program files. Any difference causes the scanner to report a verify error and lets you decide how to handle it.

Many program changes are legitimate. Some programs write in their own program files when you do such things as change the program options or reconfigure its screens. If you have programs like this, you will soon learn to ignore verify errors for them.

If you update an application to a new version, the next scan produces verify errors for the changed program files. Because you know that you updated the program, you can ask the scanner to update CHKLIST.MS with its new values.

When you get a verify error for a program that you haven't upgraded or reconfigured, you should pay serious attention to it. You may choose to delete the file right away; or, you may choose to stop the scan while you do some additional investigation and decide what action to take.

Monitoring for Viruses

Microsoft's antivirus monitor, called VSAFE, must be loaded as a Terminate-and-Stay resident program. VSAFE runs under DOS, DOS Shell, and Windows. It monitors all system activity looking for viruses. Consequently, it slows your entire system down; you're choosing security over speed when you load VSAFE. You can compromise by monitoring only activities most likely to be undertaken by a virus, such as modifying a hard disk partition table or doing a physical format on a hard disk.

When VSAFE identifies a suspicious behavior, it blocks the activity and displays an alert box asking you whether to continue or stop. If you know that the activity is safe—if you're using FDISK to rework the hard disk partition table, for example—you can tell VSAFE to let the activity continue. If not, stop the activity, reboot to remove the potential virus from memory, and run your virus scanner immediately to locate and remove the virus.

When to Use the Antivirus Programs

If you want maximum protection, you should scan memory and your program files every time you boot. If you're using MSAV, you can add an MSAV command to AUTOEXEC.BAT. For Windows, you can install MWAV in the StartUp group so that it runs every time you start up Windows.

Viruses often travel in the boot sectors of floppy disks. When you insert a disk that comes from another system—whether it's new software or just an old disk borrowed from a friend—you should scan it before booting from it, copying from it, installing a program from it, starting up a program that's on it, or using it in any other way. In other words, scan it as soon as you insert it in the disk drive. (You'll see a little later how to set up VSAFE to do this automatically whenever you insert a floppy into your system.)

Scan new or rented computers as soon as you receive them because a dealer might not scan a computer before delivering it to you. It could have been infected in the shop or, in the case of a rental, by the previous user.

You also should rescan your system when you expose it to the possibility of a virus invasion:

- If you sign on to a bulletin board service (even a nationally known one such as CompuServe or Prodigy), or any type of online service, especially if you download something from it.

- If you link your computer to another one via INTERLNK or similar software.

- If you sign on to a network and copy anything from a network drive to one of your local drives, or run a program located on a network drive.

- If you restore a file from its backup after deleting an infected version of the file. (The backup might also have been infected.)

- If you install or upgrade any software, especially software not sealed in its original package.

Note: Scanning when you install or upgrade software also gives the scanner an opportunity to record CHKLIST.MS data for the new files.

Scanning after each of these events takes a lot of time, and most people don't care to be quite so rigorous. If you choose to scan less often but you expose your system to the outside world on occasion, be sure to install and use VSAFE regularly. You might want to insert a VSAFE command in AUTOEXEC.BAT to start it up every time you boot.

Using MSAV

The MSAV command can be entered directly at the DOS prompt in a batch program such as AUTOEXEC.BAT, or from DOS Shell using the File, Run option. Try starting MSAV now:

1. Exit all programs and get to the DOS command prompt.

2. Enter **MSAV** to start the program.

   The dialog box opens. (See Figure 25.1.)

Figure 25.1.
The Main Menu dialog box.

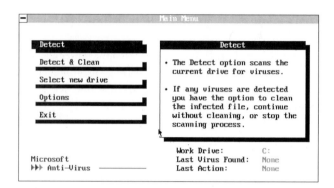

How to Scan Your Hard Drive for Viruses

1. Enter **MSAV** at the DOS command prompt.

   The MSAV dialog box opens.

2. If the Work Drive (in the lower right corner) does not indicate your hard drive, press F2.

   A drive list appears in the upper-left corner.

3. Choose your hard drive from the drive list.

   MSAV reads the selected drive and Work Drive changes to show the new selection.

4. Choose Options to open the Options dialog box.

5. Enable the options that you want to use; disable the options that you don't want to use.

   A check mark appears next to enabled options.

6. Choose OK to close the dialog box.

7. If you have enabled the Prompt while Detect option, choose either Detect or Detect & Clean and start the scan.

   If you have disabled Prompt while Detect, choose Detect to report on viruses but not to remove them, or choose Detect & Clean to report viruses and remove those that can be removed.

8. If you have enabled Prompt while Detect, respond to any virus alerts that are displayed.

9. When the summary report is displayed, choose OK to close the dialog box.

Selecting a Drive

From the Main Menu dialog box, you can scan only one drive at a time. The selected drive is always shown next to the words Work Drive: in the lower-right corner of the dialog box. The drive that was current when you started MSAV is selected by default. You can change the drive by pressing the Select New Drive button.

> **Note:** The functions at the bottom of the MSAV dialog box are activated by pressing the appropriate function key. To get help, press F1; to change drives, press F2; and so on.

Try changing to another drive:

1. Insert a disk in drive A. (The contents of the disk do not matter, but it should be formatted.)

2. Press F2 to choose the Select New Drive function.

   A drive list appears in the upper-left part of the dialog box.

3. Double-click drive A or type the letter **A**.

   MSAV reads the disk. The Work Drive changes to A.

4. Now switch back to drive C.

Selecting Options

MSAV gives you a number of options that allow some flexibility in how the scan is performed. Open the options dialog box on your screen while you read about these options:

1. Click the Options button or type the letter **O**.

   The Options Setting dialog box opens. (See Figure 25.2.)

Figure 25.2.
The MSAV Options Setting dialog box.

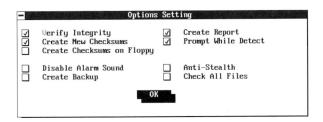

The first group of three options controls scanning for unknown viruses. The group of the two below it represents miscellaneous options. The third group controls whether or not MSAV operates automatically. The final group deals with unusual situations. A check mark indicates that an option is selected.

Verify Integrity

When this option is enabled, MSAV checks for unknown viruses during the scan. Disabling it saves a great deal of scanning time but takes the risk of missing an unknown virus. It is enabled by default, and I recommend that you leave it enabled.

Create New Checksums

When this option is enabled, MSAV creates CHKLIST.MS entries for any new program files it finds during a scan. It is enabled by default. If you disable it before running MSAV for the first time, you disable MSAV's capability to scan for unknown viruses right from the start because it can't create the CHKLIST.MS files. Leaving this option enabled keeps your CHKLIST.MS files up-to-date as you add new software to your system. I recommend that you leave it on.

Create Checksums on Floppy

MSAV ordinarily checks only hard drives for unknown viruses because the CHKLIST.MS system makes sense on a floppy disk only when you use it over and over again. If you have floppies that you use on a regular basis and you want MSAV to scan them for unknown viruses as well as known viruses, select this option so that MSAV will create the necessary CHKLIST.MS files.

Disable Alarm Sound

Ordinarily, MSAV beeps every time it encounters a known virus or a suspected unknown virus. It's an especially annoying beep, something like a Bronx cheer, which is meant to get your attention. If you don't like the beep, enable this option to turn it off.

Create Backup

This option causes MSAV to create a backup of an infected file, using the extension .VIR. You might consider doing this if you have a file infected with an unknown virus, but you can't afford to delete the file. Turning the file into a .VIR file makes it nonexecutable so that the virus can't be loaded into memory. You can then safely keep the infected file, although I would remove it from the hard drive and isolate it on its own floppy. It may be that your unknown virus will become a known virus within a short time, and you will be able to clean it from your file and regain use of your file. You'll see how to add new virus definitions to your system later in this chapter.

Create Report

MSAV normally displays a summary report at the end of a scan. The summary contains details about how many files were scanned, how many were infected with known viruses, how many were cleaned, and so on. The summary doesn't say anything about unknown viruses, and it disappears as soon as you close its dialog box. The Create Report option causes MSAV to generate a more detailed report on disk, containing summary information as well as a list of files suspected of containing unknown viruses. A sample of the disk report is shown in Figure 25.3. It is stored as an ASCII text file named MSAV.RPT in the root directory of the drive that was scanned. You can view it and print it using EDIT.

Figure 25.3.
A sample MSAV.RPT report.

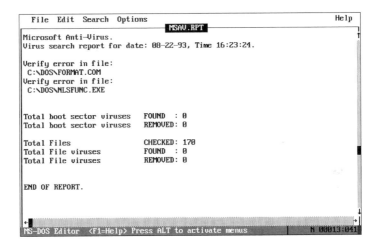

```
 File  Edit  Search  Options                                    Help
                         ┌─────MSAV.RPT─────┐
Microsoft Anti-Virus.
Virus search report for date: 08-22-93, Time 16:23:24.

Verify error in file:
 C:\DOS\FORMAT.COM
Verify error in file:
 C:\DOS\NLSFUNC.EXE


Total boot sector viruses    FOUND  : 0
Total boot sector viruses    REMOVED: 0

Total Files                  CHECKED: 170
Total File viruses           FOUND  : 0
Total File viruses           REMOVED: 0


END OF REPORT.


MS-DOS Editor   <F1=Help>  Press ALT to activate menus          N 00013:041
```

You'll see a little later in this chapter how to scan for viruses without using the dialog box, which you might want to do if you run MSAV from AUTOEXEC.BAT. When you suppress the dialog box, MSAV.RPT becomes your only evidence of any viruses that were found.

Prompt While Detect

Prompt While Detect controls whether MSAV reports viruses to you or handles them automatically. When you enable this option, MSAV displays an alert box each time it encounters a virus. If you leave this option disabled, MSAV's behavior depends on whether you initiated the scan with the Detect or the Detect & Clean button. If you choose Detect, MSAV merely notes viruses in its reports and goes on. If you choose Detect & Clean, it also cleans whatever viruses it can.

Note: If a report shows that viruses were found but not cleaned, you should rerun the scan with this option turned on so that you can deal with the infected files.

Anti-Stealth

A *stealth virus* is a particularly sneaky virus that can infect a file without changing the size, date/time stamp, attributes, or checksum. Scanning for stealth viruses takes only a few seconds more than a regular scan. Those few seconds probably won't make any difference to you, and the extra measure of protection can definitely be worth it. I recommend that you always use this option.

Check All Files

This option causes MSAV to scan data files as well as program files. You can save scanning time by turning this option off because most viruses infect program files. But, if you want that extra measure of protection, leave it on and spend the extra time.

Now that you know a bit about the options, enable the ones that you will use for your practice scan:

1. Enable the following options:

   ```
   Verify Integrity

   Prompt While Detect

   Anti-Stealth
   ```

   A check mark appears next to an option when it is enabled.

2. Disable all other options.

3. Choose OK to close the dialog box.

Running the Scan

Now that you have selected your options, you're ready to start the scan:

1. Choose Detect.

   The Main Menu dialog box acts as a progress screen. The fields in the lower-right corner show the drive being scanned, the last virus that was found, and the action taken on that virus.

   Because you have enabled Prompt While Detect, you may see some alert boxes during the scan. (See Figure 25.4 for a typical example.) If you encounter any kind of virus alert, choose Stop to stop the scan. Read the next section called "How to Handle a Virus." Then, do this exercise again.

Figure 25.4.
A sample virus alert
dialog box.

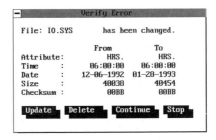

If no viruses are detected, a summary dialog box appears when the scan is completed.

2. Choose OK close the dialog box.

3. Press F3 to exit the scanner.

How to Handle a Virus

Figure 25.4 shows a typical alert box for an unknown virus. Choose Update if you know the file has changed legitimately and you want to update CHKLIST.MS with the new values. Choose Delete to delete the file because you suspect it contains a virus. Choose Continue to ignore the message and continue the scan. Choose Stop to stop the scan so that you can investigate why the file has changed.

If MSAV finds a known virus, the Virus Found dialog box tells you the name of the virus and enables you to choose to Clean the virus (if possible), Continue without handling the virus, Stop the scan, or Delete the file. If you can't clean the virus, you should delete the file and restore it from its backup. Write down the filename before you choose the Delete button, just in case you forget the name of the file by the end of the scan. After restoring the file from its backup, rescan the drive to make sure that the restored file isn't also infected.

Other MSAV Commands

The Delete command deletes all the CHKLIST.MS files from the selected drive. You might want to do this occasionally to eliminate obsolete entries from the files. Create new files by using the Create New Checksums option the next time you scan the drive.

The List command lets you review the list of known viruses that MSAV can detect. This list comes in handy when a virus is going around, and you want to make sure that your scanner is capable of detecting and cleaning it. If the virus in question is not on the list, you can probably upgrade your virus definitions to include it.

Using MSAV in Batch Mode

Figure 25.5 shows the MSAV command summary. It includes several switches that you might find useful.

MSAV

Scans memory and disks for viruses; removes viruses if possible.

Syntax:

MSAV [drive ... ¦ path ¦ /A ¦ /L] [/S ¦ /C] [/R] [/A] [/L] [/N] [/P] [/F]

Parameters and Switches:

none Opens the Microsoft Anti-Virus window so you can select drives and options.

drive Identifies a drive to scan; all program files on the drive are scanned.

path Identifies the top of a branch; all program files in the branch are scanned.

/A Scans all drives except A and B.

/L Scans all drives except A, B, and network drives.

/S Scans without removing viruses. This is the default.

/C Scans and removes any viruses found.

/R Creates a report file (MSAV.RPT) that lists the number of files checked, number of viruses found, number of viruses removed, and names of files suspected of containing unknown viruses.

/N Turns off the information display while scanning.

/P Runs MSAV in nongraphic, command-line mode.

/F Turns off the display of filenames being scanned. Use this switch only with the /N or /P switch.

Note:

The Command Reference at the back of this book describes some additional switches that are rarely used. /VIDEO displays a list of video and mouse options and /videomouse selects a video/mouse option.

Figure 25.5. *MSAV command summary.*

You can bypass the MSAV window and begin the scan immediately by adding either the /N switch or the /P switch. With /P, MSAV displays progress messages on the command prompt screen while it works, as in Scanning memory for viruses... and Scanning files for viruses... The scanning summary report is displayed at the end.

With /N, MSAV displays the text of the /MSAV.TXT file, if it exists; otherwise, it simply displays working... No report is displayed at the end. Instead, exit code 86 is set if any virus was detected. (Exit codes are explained in Chapter 37, "Programming Logic in Batch Programs.") Use /N if you're setting up MSAV in a batch file for an inexperienced user. You can place whatever message you think is pertinent in MSAV.TXT. Store MSAV.TXT in the same directory as MSAV.EXE for a single-user system. For a multiple-user system, if you have set up separate configuration blocks for the users, you can create separate MSAV.TXT files for the different users. In the configuration block, set an environment variable named MSDOSDATA to point to the location of MSAV.TXT. So, for example, Peter's MSAV.TXT could be in PETERDIR and Judi's MSAV.TXT could be in JUDIDIR.

Note: MSDOSDATA also affects MSBACKUP. See Chapter 23, "MSBACKUP and MWBACKUP," for details.

With both the /P and the /N switches, MSAV displays the names of the files being searched unless you add the /F switch.

The MSAV.INI file controls the options that are in effect, although some of the options, such as Prompt While Detect and Disable Audible Alarm, don't pertain to batch mode. You can edit this file with any ASCII editor, or you can set up the options in interactive mode and save them as you exit the MSAV window. The /R switch creates a disk report regardless of the setting of Create Report.

Suppose you want to run MSAV in batch mode suppressing all messages except those in MSAV.TXT, create a disk report, scan all local drives, clean any viruses found, and suppress the filename display. You would use this command:

```
MSAV /N /R /L /C /F
```

Tip: If this command appears in a batch file, the next command could be IF ERRORLEVEL 86 to determine whether any viruses were detected.

Some of the other MSAV parameters cause MSAV to run automatically, although not in batch mode. The MSAV window appears, but the scan starts immediately and you have no chance to select options or press buttons. When the scan is done, MSAV terminates before you can read the on-screen report. The command-line parameters that cause this to happen are /s, /c, *path*, or any parameter that specifies more than one drive to be scanned.

Using MWAV

Figure 25.6 shows the MWAV dialog box, which is quite similar to MSAV's, with the following exceptions: the drive list is always available, and you can select multiple drives for one scan, but you can't generate a disk report. Also, MWAV lets you choose to wipe deleted files. Wiping a file over-writes the file's clusters with zeros to totally obliterate them. That eliminates the virus from the available clusters. MWAV's options are saved in MWAV.INI.

Figure 25.6.
The MWAV dialog box.

Using VSAFE

VSAFE is DOS's virus monitor a TSR that monitors all your system activity, looking for behavior that indicates the presence of a virus. A virus monitor can trap viruses that enter your system after your last scan and set to work immediately. It can also trap viruses that your scanner misses.

But, there's a down side. A virus monitor takes time from your other programs, although with a 486 or better you won't notice any slowdown. A monitor also takes up memory space that you might not be able to spare. Chapter 29, "Managing Memory," and Chapter 30, "Additional Memory Facilities for 386, 486, and Pentium Computers," show you ways that you can free up more memory space for your applications. Using those techniques, you might find plenty of room to load VSAFE along with your other TSRs and applications.

The VSAFE command loads the VSAFE TSR. You can insert the appropriate command in AUTOEXEC.BAT to load VSAFE every time you boot. But, if you don't want to use it all the time, you can load it from the command prompt when you want to monitor system activity for awhile.

Load the VSAFE TSR now:

1. Exit any programs that you are using and get to a primary command prompt.

2. Enter **VSAFE** to load the TSR.

A message confirms that VSAFE was loaded, and tells you how much memory it is using.

If you will be using VSAFE with Windows, you also need to load the MWAVTSR.EXE driver, which enables VSAFE to display alert boxes on the Windows screen. Because MWAVTSR.EXE is a TSR, you should load it as you start up Windows, not later. If you're using Windows 3.1 or later, or Norton Desktop for Windows, you can add a program item for MWAVTSR.EXE to the StartUp group. Or, you can add MWAVTSR.EXE to your WIN.INI file as explained in the following procedure.

How to Load MWAVTSR.EXE from WIN.INI

1. Edit WINDOWS\WIN.INI using an ASCII text editor such as EDIT.

2. Find the [Windows] section.

3. Find the load= line. (If it's not there, insert one.)

4. Add **MWAVTSR.EXE** to the end of the line.

5. Exit the editor and save the file.

6. If Windows is currently running, exit and restart it so that the new driver is loaded.

The VSAFE Options

After you've loaded VSAFE, you can view and select VSAFE's options on the DOS command prompt screen by pressing the Alt+V hotkey. If Windows is running, find the VSAFE Manager window (which should have been opened when you started Windows) and choose the Options button.

Try opening the Options dialog box now:

1. Press Alt+V.

    The Options dialog box opens.

2. Leave the dialog box on your screen while you read about the options.

Figure 25.7 shows the dialog box that appears on the Windows screen. The DOS version is similar. These options control just how much monitoring VSAFE does. The default options are checked in the figure. Any changes you make are remembered for future sessions.

Figure 25.7.
The VSAFE Options dialog box.

HD Low-Level Format

Enabling this option causes VSAFE to warn you of any attempts to perform a low-level (physical) format on a hard drive.

Resident

When this option is enabled, VSAFE warns you when a program attempts to make itself memory-resident. You can try it out right now if you'd like:

1. Press 2 to enable the option. Make sure an X appears next to the option in the dialog box, indicating that the option is enabled.

2. Press Esc to close the dialog box and return to the command prompt.

3. Enter the command **DOSKEY /REINSTALL** to attempt to install a new copy of the DOSKEY TSR.

   You should get a beep (almost like a phone ringing) and a VSAFE Warning Message.

4. Choose Stop to prevent the TSR from loading.

   The command prompt returns.

General Write Protect

This option causes VSAFE to warn you whenever a program attempts to write to a disk. You'll probably find that this is more protection than you want on an everyday basis.

Problem: When I try to start Windows, I get a hard disk error or a message that my hard drive is write protected.

You will encounter this problem if you have VSAFE loaded and the General Write Protect option enabled. Windows needs to create temporary files on your hard disk as it loads, and this VSAFE option prevents it from doing so.

Choose Cancel to close the dialog box. Then, exit Windows. You may have to respond to a series of error messages, as Windows is unable to save its group files during its shut-down procedure.

When you get back to the DOS command prompt, press Alt+V to open the VSAFE options dialog box. Then, press 3 to turn off the General Write Protect option. (Make sure the check mark is off.) You can now start Windows with no problems.

If you get this message when you are not using VSAFE, your hard disk might be defective. Exit Windows and run SCANDISK to find out.

Check Executable Files

This option causes VSAFE to check each executable file that is loaded for known and unknown viruses. (It can check for unknown viruses only if you have scanned for them previously so that the CHKLIST.MS files have been created.)

Boot Sector Viruses

This option causes VSAFE to scan for known viruses in the boot sector of every floppy disk you insert in your system.

Protect HD Boot Sector

This option causes VSAFE to warn you when any program attempts to write to a hard disk boot sector, which includes the partition table.

Protect FD Boot Sector

This option is similar to the preceding one but applies to floppy disk boot sectors.

Protect Executable Files

When you enable this option, VSAFE warns you of any attempt to change an executable file.

What Happens when VSAFE Detects a Suspicious Action?

When VSAFE detects one of the actions for which it is monitoring, it blocks the action and displays an alert box similar to that shown in Figure 25.8. You can choose to stop or continue the action. In this particular case, you also can choose to update the CHKLIST.MS file because VSAFE detected a change in a program file while monitoring for the Check Executable Files option.

Figure 25.8.
The VSAFE alert box.

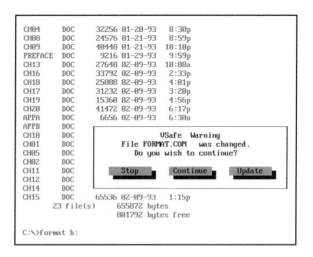

If you choose the Stop button, VSAFE blocks the action. You might then see some kind of error message from the program that was blocked, especially if it's a legitimate program. If you suspect that the action was not legitimate, close your files and programs, reboot to clear memory, and scan for viruses. If you can't find a virus, but VSAFE continues to detect suspicious behavior, contact the Microsoft Product Support Team for assistance.

Unloading VSAFE

There are situations in which you need to disable VSAFE entirely. For example, you must unload VSAFE to install or upgrade DOS or Windows; the SETUP program will fail if VSAFE is present. You use the /U switch on the VSAFE command to unload the TSR, but it must be the last TSR that you loaded.

How to Unload VSAFE

1. Exit Windows or any other shell.

2. Enter the following command:

   VSAFE /U

3. If a message says that VSAFE can't be unloaded because other TSRs were installed after it, and if you don't load VSAFE from AUTOEXEC.BAT, reboot to unload VSAFE.

4. If the /U switch doesn't unload VSAFE, and the VSAFE command is included in AUTOEXEC.BAT, do the following:

   a. Edit AUTOEXEC.BAT.

   b. Insert the word **REM** in front of the VSAFE command.

   c. Exit the editor and save the file.

   d. Reboot.

   e. When you're ready to load VSAFE again, remove REM from the command, save the file, exit the editor, and reboot.

Try unloading VSAFE now:

1. Exit Windows if it's running.

2. Enter the following command:

   VSAFE /U

3. If a message says that VSAFE can't be unloaded because other TSRs were installed after it, and if you don't load VSAFE from AUTOEXEC.BAT, reboot to unload VSAFE.

4. If the /U switch doesn't unload VSAFE, and the VSAFE command is included in AUTOEXEC.BAT, do the following:

   a. Edit AUTOEXEC.BAT.

   b. Insert the word **REM** in front of the VSAFE command.

   c. Exit the editor and save the file.

   d. Reboot.

Note: When you're ready to load VSAFE again, remove REM from the command, save the file, exit the editor, and reboot.

Options for Loading VSAFE

Figure 25.9 shows a command summary for the VSAFE command. The /n+ and /n- switches turn the various VSAFE options on and off. The numbers correspond to the preceding list of monitoring options. That is, /1+ causes VSAFE to monitor for attempts to perform a low-level format, and /3- tells VSAFE not to monitor for disk writes.

VSAFE

Loads (or unloads) the VSAFE TSR, which continuously monitors your computer for virus-like activity.

Syntax:

```
VSAFE [/option+ ¦ -] ... [/U]
```

Parameters and Switches:

/option+ ¦ -	Specifies how VSAFE monitors for viruses; use + or - following an option to turn it on or off.
/U	Removes VSAFE from memory; don't use with any other switches.

Note:

Several minor switches are detailed in the Command Reference at the back of this book. /NE and /NX prevent VSAFE from loading into expanded and extended memory. /Akey and /Ckey specify the VSAFE hotkey. /N enables VSAFE to monitor network drives. /D turns off checksumming.

Figure 25.9. *VSAFE command summary.*

Updating Your Virus List

New viruses become known all the time, and you're much more likely to catch a new one still making the rounds than one that's three years old. It's important for you to keep updating your known virus list. Microsoft maintains a bulletin board from which you can obtain the latest virus signatures. See your *DOS User's Guide* for information on how to contact the bulletin board and download new signatures.

When you add new signatures, your antivirus software can recognize the new viruses, but it can't clean them. You must install an updated version of the antivirus software to be able to clean the new viruses. Your *DOS User's Guide* includes a form that you can use to order updates.

On Your Own

This chapter has shown you how to use MSAV or MWAV and VSAFE to protect your system from viruses. If you would like to practice these techniques on your own, use the following items as a guide:

1. Scan all your hard disks for known and unknown viruses.

2. Scan some of your floppies for known viruses.

3. Load VSAFE and select those options that you might like to work with. Keep VSAFE loaded as you continue to work with your system.

4. If you would like to scan one or more drives each time you start up, edit your AUTOEXEC.BAT file to do the scan. Don't forget to use some of the MSAV switches to automate the scan.

5. If you would like to start up VSAFE every time you boot, edit AUTOEXEC.BAT to insert the VSAFE command. Use the option switches to set the options you want to work with as VSAFE is loaded.

6. If you will be using VSAFE with Windows, edit WIN.INI to load MWAVTSR.EXE.

26 Using UNDELETE

Introduction

It's always best to recover deleted files by restoring them from backups. However, the Delete Sentry program cap-tures file deletions and moves the deleted files to its own hidden SENTRY directory for a few days. From there, they are easily recovered by the UNDELETE program with nearly 100 percent accuracy.

Deleting and Undeleting Files

Does this scene sound familiar? You spend all morning developing spreadsheet data for this afternoon's marketing meeting and, just as you're heading out the door for lunch, you hit the wrong key and delete the entire file. All is not lost. If you have installed UNDELETE, you can recover the file in just a few keystrokes. If you haven't installed UNDELETE, you might still be able to recover the file, although it might take a little more effort.

DOS deletes a file by marking the file's directory entry as reusable. (It changes the first character of the file name to Σ.) DOS also changes the file's FAT entries, marking each of them with zero to indicate an unused cluster. But, it doesn't erase the data in the clusters, nor does it erase the rest of the directory entry.

To undelete a file, DOS must recover the file's clusters while they still contain the original data. If other files are using the clusters, DOS can't retrieve the deleted file. Deletion protection programs try to preserve the original clusters (or at least keep track of where they were).

DOS 6 provides two levels of deletion protection. The higher level, Delete Sentry, interferes with the normal deletion process. It moves the file from its former directory to a special hidden directory, where it is preserved for a while. The lower level, deletion-tracking, saves a list of a deleted file's clusters. The file is retrievable if the clusters haven't been reused, but deletion-tracking doesn't preserve the clusters. If you don't use either protection method, you might be able to undelete a file by using the information in the deleted directory entry (if DOS hasn't reused it for a new file) to try to recover the file's data.

Both protection methods work with DOS, DOS Shell, and Windows. The difference between DOS and Windows is how you undelete the files, not how you protect them.

This chapter shows you how to use Delete Sentry to protect your deleted files for a short while and how to undelete files using the various deletion methods. You will learn how to:

- Install and configure Delete Sentry
- Recover files protected by Delete Sentry
- Recover files catalogued by deletion-tracking
- Recover files from deleted DOS directory entries
- Purge the Delete Sentry directory
- Uninstall Delete Sentry

Peter's Principle: Use it, but don't count on it.

Never rely on deletion protection in lieu of a good system of regular backups. As I've said several times in this book, a good backup system is your best line of defense against data loss. It will protect your files in situations when Delete Sentry won't:

- When files are replaced by a copy or move operation
- When files were deleted a long time ago and the data no longer exists on the disk
- When files are damaged or destroyed by hardware failure, software failure, viruses, or an external disaster such as fire or flood

Use a deletion protection system such as Delete Sentry only to protect those files that you haven't yet had a chance to back up.

Using Delete Sentry

If you want to use Delete Sentry or Deletion-Tracking, you must load the UNDELETE TSR and specify which drives should be protected. Figure 26.1 shows the command summary for loading UNDELETE.

UNDELETE

Enables or disables deletion protection; reports protection status.

Syntax:

`UNDELETE /LOAD ¦ /U ¦ /S[drive] ... ¦ /T[drive[-entries] ... ¦ /STATUS`

Parameters and Switches:

/LOAD	Loads the UNDELETE TSR with the default protection method.
/U	Unloads the UNDELETE TSR.
/S[drive]	Loads the UNDELETE TSR, setting the current and default method of deletion protection to Delete Sentry; adds *drive* to the list of drives protected by Sentry.
/T[drive]	Loads the UNDELETE TSR, setting the current and default method of deletion protection to deletion-tracking; adds *drive* to the list of *drives* protected by tracking.
entries	Specifies the maximum number of entries in the deletion-tracking file for *drive*; may be 1 to 999. The default depends on the drive size.
/STATUS	Displays the drives protected by the current protection method.

Figure 26.1. *UNDELETE command summary (loading the TSR).*

You set up Delete Sentry by loading its TSR with a command using the following syntax:

```
UNDELETE /S[drive]...
```

For example, the following command installs Delete Sentry to protect drive D:

```
UNDELETE /SD
```

Try installing Delete Sentry for your boot drive now:

1. Because Delete Sentry is a TSR, exit all programs and shells before installing it. Make sure you are at a primary command prompt.

2. Enter **UNDELETE** /**SC** (if C is your boot drive).

   You see a response such as the following:

   ```
   UNDELETE loaded.
   Delete Protection Method is Delete Sentry.
   Enabled for drives : C
   ```

Network Note: To use Delete Sentry on a network drive, you must have read, write, create, and delete file access in the drive's root directory.

The UNDELETE program keeps a list of protected drives. The next time you load Delete Sentry, drive C is still protected even if you don't specify it. Suppose that you include drive D the next time you load Delete Sentry:

```
UNDELETE /SD
```

The response indicates that Delete Sentry now protects both C and D:

```
UNDELETE loaded.
Delete Protection Method is Delete Sentry.
Enabled for drives : C D
```

You could have protected C and D in the first command by specifying two /S switches:

```
UNDELETE /SC /SD
```

When you specify /S without a drive name, Delete Sentry adds the current drive to its list of protected drives. If C is the current drive, the following command is equivalent to UNDELETE /SC:

```
UNDELETE /S
```

If you plan to use Delete Sentry, load it once with an /S switch for each drive you want to protect. Then, you can insert the following command in AUTOEXEC.BAT to keep loading Undelete using the same configuration:

```
UNDELETE /LOAD
```

By default, Delete Sentry doesn't protect all deleted files. It protects only files that have a positive archive attribute (that is, they have been modified since the last time they were backed up). In addition, it doesn't protect the files that DOS creates and deletes for its own purposes, such as .TMP files (temporary files).

Checking the Drive List

If you forget which drives Delete Sentry protects, you can use the /STATUS switch to find out. Try it now:

1. Enter **UNDELETE /STATUS**.

   You should see a message something like the following:

   ```
   Delete Protection Method is Delete Sentry.
   Enabled for drives : C
   ```

In the next section, you'll learn how to recover files from Delete Sentry. But, because you have just loaded it, you probably haven't captured any deleted files yet. Before you go on, delete a few files so that you'll have some files to practice recovering in the next section.

1. Create a new directory called PRACTICE as a child of the root directory and copy all the .HLP files from the DOS directory, changing their extensions to .XXX. (Reminder: You can do this in one XCOPY command.)

2. Change to the PRACTICE directory.

3. Delete all the files in PRACTICE, but don't delete the directory itself.

Listing Files Available for Recovery

How to Recover a File Using Delete Sentry

1. List all the files available for recovery by entering a command with the following syntax:

   ```
   UNDELETE [filespec] /LIST
   ```

   If you have been using Delete Sentry, UNDELETE automatically lists only those files that are recoverable from Delete Sentry.

2. Decide which files from the list you want to recover.

3. Re-enter the command without the /LIST switch.

   UNDELETE lists one recoverable file at a time and asks if you want to recover it.

4. For each file that you don't want to recover, enter N.

---

5. For each file that you do want to recover, enter Y.

   If the recovered file duplicates an existing filename in the same directory, UNDELETE asks you to provide a new filename.

6. When you have recovered all the files that you want, press Esc to terminate UNDELETE.

You also use the UNDELETE command to recover files from Delete Sentry. (See Figure 26.2.)

UNDELETE

Recovers deleted files; lists recoverable files; clears a SENTRY directory.

Syntax:

```
UNDELETE [filespec] [/DT ¦ /DS ¦ /DOS ] [/LIST ¦ /ALL]

[/PURGE[drive]]
```

Parameters and Switches:

none	Offers to recover all deleted files in the current directory using the highest available method for that drive.
filespec	Identifies the file(s) that you want to recover; the default is all deleted files in the current directory.
/DT	Recovers only those files listed in the deletion-tracking file (PCTRACKR.DEL), prompting for confirmation on each file.
/DS	Recovers only those files listed in the Delete Sentry directory (SENTRY), prompting for confirmation on each file.
/DOS	Recovers only those files found in the DOS directory, prompting for confirmation on each file.
/LIST	Lists recoverable files, but does not offer to recover them. The files listed depend on *filespec* and the recovery method.
/ALL	Recovers files without prompting. The files recovered depend on filespec and the recovery method.
/PURGE[drive]	Empties the SENTRY directory on *drive*; the default is the current drive.

Figure 26.2. UNDELETE *command summary (Recovering and Purging Files).*

When you use the /LIST switch, _UNDELETE lists all the files available for recovery. Try it:

1. Make sure you are in the PRACTICE directory.

2. Enter the following command:

   UNDELETE /LIST

   The response might look something like the following:

```
Directory: C:\PRACTICE
File Specifications: *.*
Delete Sentry control file contains  5 deleted files.
Deletion-Tracking file not found.
MS-DOS directory contains   6 deleted files.
Of those,   4 files may be recovered.
Using the Delete Sentry method.

DEFRAG    XXX      9,227  5-31-94  6:22a  ...A  Deleted:  2-11-95 11:13a
DOSSHELL  XXX    161,323  5-31-94  6:22a  ...A  Deleted:  2-10-95 10:35a
HELP      XXX    296,844  5-31-94  6:22a  ...A  Deleted:  2-10-95 10:35a
MEMMAKER  XXX     17,237  5-31-94  6:22a  ...A  Deleted:  2-11-95 11:13a
QBASIC    XXX    130,881  5-31-94  6:22a  ...A  Deleted:  2-11-95 11:13a
```

UNDELETE looks for files using every undelete method, then selects the best method—in this case, Delete Sentry—to list the available files. The first part of the report shows the results of all three undelete methods. You can ignore everything but the Delete Sentry information.

Delete Sentry displays not only the file's directory information, but also the date and time it was deleted. This information comes in particularly handy if more than one file of the same name is listed.

Note: The expression ...A indicates that the file is not system, not hidden, and not read-only, but it had a positive archive attribute at the time it was deleted.

Note: UNDELETE /LIST works regardless of whether the Delete Sentry TSR is currently loaded. As long as there is a SENTRY directory on the drive, UNDELETE shows you the files available for recovery.

If you add a filespec to the command, UNDELETE lists only the files that match the filespec. Try listing just the entry for MEMMAKER.XXX:

1. Enter **UNDELETE MEMMAKER.XXX /LIST**.

   UNDELETE reports only on files named MEMMAKER.XXX.

More than one file of the specified name might be listed if you have created and deleted a file with this name several times in the same directory. Their date and time stamps can help you decide which one you want to recover.

You can add a path name to the command, with or without a filespec, to list a different directory.

Undeleting with Delete Sentry

Suppose that you want to undelete one or more of the files listed by UNDELETE. Enter the same command without /LIST. Try undeleting some of the files in your PRACTICE directory:

1. Enter **UNDELETE MEMMAKER.XXX** to recover the specified file.

   This command produces a report with the same beginning as the preceding example, but it doesn't list the files. Instead, it shows one file at a time and asks whether you want to undelete it:

   ```
   MEMMAKER XXX    17,237  5-31-94  6:22a  ...A  Deleted:  2-11-95 11:13a
   This file can be 100% undeleted. Undelete (Y/N)?
   ```

   If you answer N, UNDELETE continues to the next file that matches the filespec, if any.

2. Enter Y.

   You see the following message:

   ```
   File successfully undeleted.
   ```

But, if the directory already contains a file with the name you're trying to recover, you see the following message instead:

```
The filename already exists. Type a different filename.
Press F5 to bypass this file.
```

You can enter a new file name, or decide to forget it and press F5. If you enter the file name MEMMAKER.YYY, you see the following message:

```
MEMMAKER YYY    17,237  5-31-94  6:22a  ...A  Deleted:  2-11-95 11:13a
File successfully undeleted.
```

> **Note:** If several deleted files match the filespec you have entered, UNDELETE lists them one at a time and asks if you want to recover them. You don't have to go through the entire list. Press Esc to terminate UNDELETE when you have recovered all the files you want.

Purging the SENTRY Directory

How to Purge the SENTRY Directory

If you use Windows:

1. Open Undelete in the Microsoft Tools group.

2. Choose the Drive/Dir button.

    The Change Drive and Directory dialog box opens.

3. Select the directory that used to contain the files to be purged.

4. Choose OK.

    All deleted directories and files in the selected directory are displayed in the file list.

5. Choose the files to be purged from SENTRY. (Note: Only files with the Perfect rating are in the SENTRY directory.)

6. Choose File, Purge Delete Sentry File.

If you don't use Windows:

1. Switch to the drive that you want to purge.

2. Enter **UNDELETE /PURGE**.

3. A message asks you to confirm that you want to purge the files.

4. Enter Y to purge the files.

    All the files on the drive are purged. You cannot purge files selectively if you don't use Windows.

One of the main reasons for deleting files is to free up space on your disk. You might think that Delete Sentry clogs up your drive with deleted files, but that's not completely true. Each time you load Delete Sentry, it purges any file that has been in SENTRY for at least seven days. When SEN-TRY takes up more than 20 percent of a drive, Delete Sentry purges the oldest files until it's within that limit. (The oldest files are those with the oldest deletion date/time.) Also, if DOS doesn't have enough space to store new data, Delete Sentry purges the oldest files to make enough free space.

Warning: Automatic purging takes place only if the Delete Sentry TSR is loaded. If you have a SENTRY directory but don't always load Delete Sentry, you may get Disk Full errors when DOS tries to write files. Reload the TSR to make the space available again.

You can purge all the files from SENTRY by using an `UNDELETE /PURGE` command. You see messages such as the following:

```
Delete Sentry control file contains  123 deleted files.

Confirm purging of SENTRY files on drive C (Y/N)?
```

You would answer Y to empty SENTRY, or N if you decide not to empty it. The file count shows all the deleted files preserved on the drive. There's no way to purge individual files or directories with the DOS version of UNDELETE. You can do it in the Windows version, however. Select just the files you want to purge and choose the Purge Delete Sentry File command on the File menu.

What's in SENTRY?

SENTRY is a hidden directory and ordinarily doesn't show up in DOS directory listings. But, there are ways to view the contents of hidden directories under DOS and under some applications. If you happen to view the SENTRY directory, you see strange file names such as the following:

```
#A1B2C3E MS          17 01-13-93      6:42a
#A1B2C3F MS          89 01-13-93      5:18p
#A1B2C3G MS         339 02-09-93      9:37a
#A1B2C3H MS         421 02-09-93      9:40a
```

Even though they have strange names, these are your deleted files. Delete Sentry assigns generic file names to the files it preserves. It maintains a control file that relates the original file name and directory to the generic name in the SENTRY directory.

UNDELETE's Destination Directory

How to Recover a Deleted Directory and Its Files

If you have been using Delete Sentry without Windows:

1. Make a new directory with the same name and path as the deleted directory.

2. Recover the files for the directory as usual.

If you use Windows:

1. Open Undelete in the Microsoft Tools group.

2. Choose the Drive/Dir button.

    The Change Drive and Directory dialog box opens.

---

3. Select the parent of the deleted directory.

4. Choose OK.

   All deleted directories and files in the parent directory are displayed in the file list.

5. Select the directory to be recovered.

6. If the Undelete button is available, choose the button to recover the directory. (If the button is not available, the directory cannot be recovered.)

7. Choose the Drive/Dir button again and select the recovered directory.

   When you close the dialog box, the recovered directory's deleted files appear in the file list.

8. Select the files you want to recover and choose the Undelete button.

Note: If you have not been using Windows or Delete Sentry, you will not be able to recover the directory.

The DOS version of UNDELETE always recovers files to the same directory from which they were deleted. If you have deleted or renamed a directory, you can't recover its files until you create another directory with the same name and path. When you use DELTREE to delete a whole branch, all its files move to SENTRY. You have to remake the directories before you can recover their files.

When UNDELETE Can't Recover a File

You may not be able to undelete a file even though its drive is protected by Delete Sentry. Delete Sentry might have already purged it, especially if your disk is getting so full that DOS often needs to request more space from Delete Sentry. In addition, files with the extensions .TMP, .VM?, .WOA, .SWP, .SPL, .RMG, .IMG, .THM, and .DOV are not protected by Delete Sentry. (Delete Sentry assumes that files with these extensions are temporary.) And, by default, UNDELETE protects only those deleted files with a positive archive attribute; other files can be restored from their backups.

Tip: If you want to delete a group of files, without UNDELETE preserving them and possibly having to purge other files to make room for them in the SENTRY directory, turn off their archive attributes before deleting them.

If Delete Sentry can't find a file you want to recover, you can restore it from its backup, if you have one; or, try to undelete it using the DOS directory method, described later in this chapter.

Using Deletion-Tracking

How to Recover a File Using Deletion-Tracking

1. If you have been using only Deletion-Tracking on the drive, list all the files available for recovery by entering a command with the following syntax:

   UNDELETE [*filespec*] /LIST

   If you have been using Delete Sentry on the drive, add the /DT switch to force UNDELETE to use the deletion-tracking method, as in:

   UNDELETE [*filespec*] /LIST /DT

2. Decide which files from the list you want to recover.

3. Re-enter the command without the /LIST switch.

   UNDELETE lists one recoverable file at a time and asks if you want to recover it. UNDELETE warns you when a file cannot be completely recovered because all of its clusters are no longer available.

4. For each file that you don't want to recover, enter N.

5. For each file that you do want to recover, enter Y.

   If the recovered file duplicates an existing filename in the same directory, UNDELETE asks you to provide a new filename.

6. When you have recovered all the files that you want, press Esc to terminate UNDELETE.

If you are upgrading from DOS 5, you probably will recognize deletion-tracking as the old method of protecting deleted files. A drive protected by deletion-tracking has a system file, PCTRACKR.DEL, in its root directory. PCTRACKR.DEL keeps a list of each deleted file's clusters. Undeleting the file restores any of its clusters that DOS hasn't reused.

There's almost no reason to use deletion-tracking when Delete Sentry is available. Delete Sentry does a much better job of protecting deleted files. If you load it all the time so that it can do automatic purging, you probably will never notice the disk space it uses. But, if you have been using DOS 5's deletion-tracking program and don't want to switch to another method, you can use deletion-tracking with DOS 6. Use /T instead of /S on the UNDELETE command to load deletion-tracking. You can't mix /T and /S switches in a command; you can't load both the Delete Sentry TSR and the deletion-tracking TSR. The following command loads the deletion-tracking TSR and adds drive C to its drive list:

```
UNDELETE /TC
```

Note: The default number of entries in a Deletion-Tracking file depends on the size of the drive. To increase or decrease the number of entries available in the Deletion-Tracking file, add *-entries* to the /T switch. For example, to include 500 entries in the Deletion-Tracking file for drive D, use the switch /TD-500 when you load UNDELETE.

Listing Files Protected by Deletion-Tracking

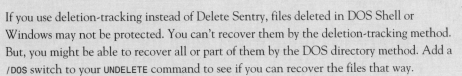

Problem: I deleted some files in DOS Shell, and UNDELETE doesn't list them for recovery. How can I recover these files?

If you use deletion-tracking instead of Delete Sentry, files deleted in DOS Shell or Windows may not be protected. You can't recover them by the deletion-tracking method. But, you might be able to recover all or part of them by the DOS directory method. Add a /DOS switch to your UNDELETE command to see if you can recover the files that way.

If you have been using only deletion-tracking and you need to recover a file that you just erased, you can probably undelete it safely and successfully. But, if you have done some other things on your computer since you erased the file—even if it has been only a few minutes since you erased it—you could end up recovering the wrong data using the deletion-tracking method. (The reasons are explained in the following section.) You would be wise to restore the file from its backup instead. Use the following procedures only if you do not have a valid backup of the file.

When you enter the UNDELETE /LIST command on a system that's using deletion-tracking, the messages look something like the following:

```
Directory: C:\PRACTICE
File Specifications: *.*

Delete Sentry control file not found.
Deletion-tracking file contains    5 deleted files.
Of those,       5 files have all clusters available,
                0 files have some clusters available,
                0 files have no clusters available.
MS-DOS directory contains   6 deleted files.
Of those,   4 files may be recovered.

Using the Deletion-tracking method.
```

```
DEFRAG    XXX      9,227  5-31-94  6:22a  ...A  Deleted:  2-11-95 11:13a
DOSSHELL XXX    161,323  5-31-94  6:22a  ...A  Deleted:  2-10-95 10:35a
HELP      XXX    296,844  5-31-94  6:22a  ...A  Deleted:  2-10-95 10:35a
MEMMAKER XXX     17,237  5-31-94  6:22a  ...A  Deleted:  2-11-95 11:13a
QBASIC    XXX    130,881  5-31-94  6:22a  ...A  Deleted:  2-11-95 11:13a
```

These messages indicate that you have been using deletion-tracking, not Delete Sentry. Five files are available for undeletion by deletion-tracking in the indicated directory. UNDELETE has compared the list of clusters in the deletion-tracking file against the FAT and determined that all the clusters belonging to these files are available. You could go on to undelete some of the files using a command like the following:

```
UNDELETE D*.XXX
```

UNDELETE shows one file at a time and asks whether you want to delete it, like this:

```
DEFRAG    XXX      9,227  5-31-94  6:22a  ...A  Deleted:  2-11-95 11:13a  All of the
clusters of this file are available. UNDELETE (Y/N)?
```

If you answer N, UNDELETE continues to the next file, if any. If you answer Y, you should see the following message:

```
File successfully undeleted.
```

Recovering Partial Files

Sometimes deletion-tracking can recover only part of a file. When you enter the UNDELETE /LIST command, the response might look like the following:

```
Deletion-tracking file contains    3 deleted files.
Of those,        1 files have all clusters available,
                 1 files have some clusters available,
                 1 files have no clusters available.
```

The list of files might show the following:

```
   T4      CAT    17  1-13-93  6:42a  ...A Deleted:  2-12-94  5:45a
* BIGTIME ABC 39,152  3-10-93  3:10a  ...A Deleted:  2-12-94  7:32a
**ZIGZAG  BMP    630  3-10-93  3:10a  ...A Deleted:  2-12-94  7:29a
* indicates some clusters of the file are available.
** indicates no clusters of the file are available.
```

You can't recover ZIGZAG.BMP because none of its clusters are available. Some of BIGTIME.ABC's clusters can't be recovered, but you could recover the rest. You should consider the following points when deciding whether to recover part of a file:

- The part that's available is not necessarily the beginning of the file, nor even a continuous segment. It might just be a cluster here and a cluster there.

- As always, restoring a file from its backup is a much better way to recover it, even if the backup is slightly outdated.

- There's no sense in partially recovering a file that doesn't contain text, as it will be unusable.

Warning: Never recover part of a program file. Attempting to run the program could actually do harm to your system.

- If it's a file from a word processor, desktop publisher, or database manager, it may be missing special header information that such programs build into their documents. In that case, you won't be able to open the file for editing under its original application. However, you can try to edit it as an ASCII text file, clean out any garbage, and recover as much text as possible.

Even when UNDELETE says a file is completely available, it might not recover the correct data. Another file may have overwritten some clusters and then been deleted. Because the clusters appear to be available to UNDELETE, it reports that the entire file can be recovered. However, it recovers the other file's data from the clusters.

Recovering Files Deleted under DOS 5

If you have just upgraded from DOS 5 and were using deletion-tracking, you might still have files in PCTRACKR.DEL that were deleted under DOS 5. But, if you have switched to Delete Sentry with DOS 6, UNDELETE won't offer to recover files by the deletion-tracking method. If you need to recover a file that was deleted before you upgraded and switched to Delete Sentry, add the /DT switch to the UNDELETE command to force UNDELETE to access the PCTRACKR.DEL file. Suppose that you deleted GRFALLS.DRW a few days ago under DOS 5. The following command will recover it if the clusters are still available:

```
UNDELETE GRFALLS.DRW /DT
```

Tip: After about a week of using Delete Sentry, you can delete PCTRACKR.DEL. Its data will be too outdated to be useful anymore. PCTRACKR.DEL is a system file located in the root directory of each drive that it protects. You must turn off the system attribute before you can delete it or use DELTREE PCTRACKR.DEL.

Using the DOS Directory Method

How to Recover a File from the DOS Directory

1. If you have never used Delete Sentry or deletion-tracking on the drive, list all the files available for recovery by entering a command with the following syntax:

   `UNDELETE [filespec] /LIST`

   If you have used Delete Sentry or deletion-tracking on the drive, add the /DOS switch to the command to force UNDELETE to use the DOS directory method, as in:

   `UNDELETE [filespec] /LIST /DOS`

2. Decide which files from the list you want to recover.

3. Re-enter the command without the /LIST switch.

   UNDELETE lists one recoverable file at a time and asks if you want to recover it.

4. For each file that you don't want to recover, enter N.

5. For each file that you do want to recover, enter Y.

   UNDELETE asks you to provide the first character for the filename.

6. Enter a first character for the filename.

   If the first character doesn't cause the filename to duplicate an existing one, UNDELETE recovers the file. Otherwise, UNDELETE asks for another first character.

7. When you have recovered all the files that you want, press Esc to terminate UNDELETE.

The least reliable method of undeleting files is to search a directory for deleted entries. UNDELETE uses this method only if it can't find a SENTRY directory or a PCTRACKR.DEL file. Even if you include a specific file name and that file appears in the DOS directory but not in SENTRY or PCTRACKR.DEL, UNDELETE will not use the directory method if there is a SENTRY directory or a PCTRACKR.DEL file on the drive.

If a file has been purged from SENTRY or PCTRACKR.DEL, its old directory entry may exist, and you can still recover it by the directory method. You can force DOS to use the directory method by including the /DOS switch on the UNDELETE command, as in:

`UNDELETE \TEST1\*.* /DOS /LIST`

The response to your command might look like the following:

```
Directory: C:\

File Specifications: *.*
    Delete Sentry control file not found.
    Deletion-tracking file not found.
MS-DOS directory contains     5 deleted files.
    Of those,    3 files may be recovered.

Using the MS-DOS directory method.

**   ?ONFIG   TMP      778  1-05-93 10:24a  ...A
     ?OC2D31  TMP    7,059 12-05-92  4:27p  ...A
**   ?MF030D  TMP       18 12-05-92  4:27p  ...A
     ?OREAD   TXT   22,016 12-06-92  6:00a  ....
** indicates the first cluster of the file is unavailable and can't be recovered with the
UNDELETE command.
```

The list includes all files in the C:\TEST1 directory whose file names start with Σ. In the list, ? indicates that character. Even though the directory entry is still there, a file can't be undeleted if another file is using its first cluster, as indicated by ** in the list.

The list might include some unexpected file names. Delete Sentry and deletion-tracking suppress temporary files, but the directory method displays them. You might encounter a lot of temporary files made and deleted by DOS, Windows, and your applications; they tend to have generic-looking file names like ~MS396AX.TMP.

Suppose that you want to undelete one or more files. You can use the UNDELETE command without /LIST, as follows:

```
UNDELETE C:\TEST1\*.* /DOS
```

This command produces a display that begins the same way, but it lists one file at a time and asks whether you want to undelete it, as follows:

```
?REP    BAT    63 12-03-92  9:54a  UNDELETE (Y/N)?
```

If you answer N, UNDELETE proceeds to the next file. If you answer Y, it asks you the following:

```
Please type the first character for ?REP    .BAT:
```

After you type a character that creates a unique file name in the directory, you probably will see the following message:

```
File successfully undeleted.
```

Note: UNDELETE lists files that can't be undeleted, but you don't get a chance to undelete them.

Deleted Directories

After you have deleted a directory, the DOS version of UNDELETE can never again recover its files using the directory method. Making a new directory with the same name and path doesn't help because the old deleted directory entries will not be in the new directory. The Windows version of UNDELETE, however, may be able to recover the deleted directory as well as its files.

Problems with the Directory Method

The `File successfully undeleted` message can be deceiving with the directory method. After UNDELETE finds the directory entry and the first cluster, it still has to guess where to find the remaining clusters for the file. The longer you wait and the more work you do with the disk, the more likely it is that UNDELETE won't find the right clusters, especially if the file was fragmented.

You can be reasonably sure of getting your file back correctly with this method only if you recover it immediately after deleting it. If you have done anything else on the system, restore the file from its backup if that's possible.

Warning: Don't run a program recovered by the DOS directory method; if it contains the wrong information, it could damage your system.

Undeleting Files without Prompts

If you include a specific filename in the UNDELETE command, UNDELETE recovers the file without any further prompts. For example, suppose that UNDELETE /LIST reveals that the following files are available for recovery:

```
Directory: C:\PRACTICE
File Specifications: *.*
Delete Sentry control file contains  5 deleted files.
Deletion-Tracking file not found.
MS-DOS directory contains   6 deleted files.
Of those,   4 files may be recovered.
Using the Delete Sentry method.


DEFRAG    XXX      9,227  5-31-94  6:22a  ...A  Deleted:  2-11-95 11:13a
DOSSHELL  XXX    161,323  5-31-94  6:22a  ...A  Deleted:  2-10-95 10:35a
HELP      XXX    296,844  5-31-94  6:22a  ...A  Deleted:  2-10-95 10:35a
MEMMAKER  XXX     17,237  5-31-94  6:22a  ...A  Deleted:  2-11-95 11:13a
QBASIC    XXX    130,881  5-31-94  6:22a  ...A  Deleted:  2-11-95 11:13a
```

To recover DEFRAG.XXX without any further interaction, you could enter UNDELETE DEFRAG.XXX.

To recover all the files without further interaction, enter UNDELETE /ALL. If you're using the DOS directory method only, UNDELETE automatically assigns the first character of each filename, probably using # as the character. You still get the prompt if you use the filename and /DOS.

Undeleting Files from DOS Shell

DOS Shell includes an Undelete program item in the Disk Utilities directory. Selecting this item opens a dialog box in which you can enter the parameters you want to use on the UNDELETE command. The /LIST switch is the only default parameter. If you want to add a filespec, be sure to insert it in front of the /LIST switch, as filespecs must precede any switches in the UNDELETE command. When you press Enter, the DOS command prompt screen appears and the job continues as you have already seen.

Working with Windows Undelete

Figure 26.3 shows the Undelete window, which opens when you open Undelete from the Microsoft Tools group. The file list shows all the files available for undeletion by all methods. When the condition is Perfect, the file is protected by Delete Sentry. Lesser conditions indicate that the file is protected by deletion-tracking. If the first character of the filename is a question mark, the DOS directory method is being used. The listing occasionally shows files from the directory that can't be undeleted. Their entries are dimmed and their condition is Destroyed.

Figure 26.3.
The Windows Undelete window.

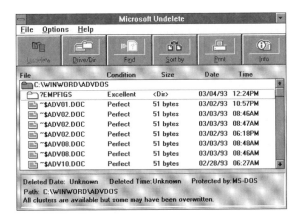

To undelete files, select them in the file list and choose the Undelete button. You can change drives and directories by pressing the Drive/Dir button.

Windows Undelete Features

The Find button opens a dialog box in which you can enter a filespec and/or text to search for. The entire current drive is searched. You also can select a group of files to search for, such as the pbrush (Windows Paintbrush) group, which searches for *.PCX and *.BMP files.

The Sort By button lets you choose sort criteria for the file list. The Print button causes the current file list to be printed on the default printer. The Info button opens a dialog box that provides additional information about the currently selected file, such as its first cluster number.

Figure 26.4 shows the File menu. Most of the commands duplicate the buttons you have already seen, but a few of the commands are unique. The Undelete To command lets you select the directory where you want to place the recovered file. The Purge Delete Sentry File command purges the selected files from Delete Sentry.

Figure 26.4.
The Windows Undelete File menu.

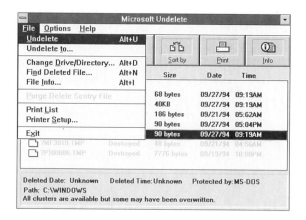

Figure 26.5 shows the Options menu. Choose Select By Name to enter a filespec to select files to be undeleted or purged. Choose Unselect By Name to enter a filespec that deselects files that have already been selected.

The Configure Deletion Protection option opens a dialog box in which you can select Delete Sentry, Delete Tracker, or Standard (which is the DOS directory entry method). If you choose one of the protection methods, an additional dialog box gives you the opportunity to specify which files you want to protect, how many days files should stay in SENTRY, and similar options. Undelete updates the UNDELETE.INI file based on your choices, but you have to reboot to put them into effect.

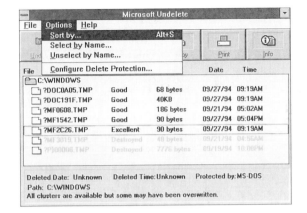

Figure 26.5.
The Windows Undelete
Options menu.

Undeleting Directories

You may be able to recover a deleted subdirectory using Windows Undelete. The entry named ?EMPFIGS in Figure 26.3, shown previously, is a deleted directory, as you can see both by its icon and by the size column. This directory is not being protected by any method, but it can be recovered via the DOS directory method. After it has been recovered, its files can be recovered as well. In fact, they may be protected by Delete Sentry.

Working with UNDELETE.INI

How to Configure Undelete

If you use Windows:

1. Open Undelete in the Microsoft Tools group.

2. Choose Options Configure Delete Protection.

   The Configure Delete Protection dialog box opens.

3. Select Delete Sentry, Delete Tracker, or Standard.

4. Choose the OK button.

   If you chose Delete Sentry or Delete Tracker, a configuration dialog box opens.

5. Use the dialog box to configure UNDELETE.

6. Choose OK to save the new configuration.

   A message advises you to reboot to put the changes into effect.

7. Close all applications, exit Windows, and reboot.

If you don't use Windows:

1. Open C:\DOS\UNDELETE.INI for editing by an ASCII text editor such as EDIT.
2. Change individual lines in the file as appropriate to configure UNDELETE.
3. Save the file and exit the editor.
4. Enter **UNDELETE /U** to unload UNDELETE.
5. Enter **UNDELETE /LOAD** to load UNDELETE with the new configuration.

UNDELETE stores all its configuration information in a file called UNDELETE.INI. You can edit this file using an ASCII text editor such as EDIT to change the configuration. Be very careful not to change the basic structure of the file; all you should do is change the settings for the various items. For example, if Delete Sentry is set up to protect drives C and D, you will find the following section in UNDELETE.INI:

```
[sentry.drives]
C=
D=
```

To remove protection for drive D, delete the line that says D=. But be careful not to delete or change the header [sentry.drives].

To preserve files regardless of their archive attributes, change FALSE to TRUE in the following line:

```
archive=FALSE
```

To change the percentage of space that SENTRY may take up on the drive, change the number in the following line:

```
percentage=20
```

To change the number of days that files are kept in SENTRY, edit the number of days in this line:

```
days=7
```

The following line determines which file types are preserved and which are ignored. The *.* at the beginning of the line tells Delete Sentry to preserve all files. Then each -*filespec* removes a certain file type from protection. In other words, the line tells Delete Sentry to preserve all files *except* .TMP files, .VM files, .WOA files, and so on.

```
sentry.files=*.* -*.TMP -*.VM -*.WOA -*.SWP -*.SPL -*.RMG -*.IMG -*.THM -*.DOV
```

You can add your own exceptions to the line. For example, suppose you don't want to protect *.BAK files. You would add -*.BAK to the end of the line.

On Your Own

This chapter has shown you how to use UNDELETE to protect your files and recover them when necessary. The following items will help you practice these techniques on your own.

1. Load the Delete Sentry TSR to protect your boot drive.

2. Check to see which drives are protected by UNDELETE at this time.

3. Create a practice directory, copy some files to it, and delete those files. Then, recover them.

4. If you have Windows and have installed the Windows version of Undelete, try deleting and recovering files using Windows. Try deleting and recovering a directory using Windows.

5. If you don't want to continue using Delete Sentry, unload the TSR and purge the SENTRY directory. (Don't do this if you use Delete Sentry on a regular basis.)

27

CHKDSK and SCANDISK

Introduction

CHKDSK did two great things for a drive: It fixed problems that could cause data loss, and it reclaimed wasted space. SCANDISK does all that plus more: It rescues data from sectors that have been physically damaged.

What CHKDSK and SCANDISK Do

Both CHKDSK and SCANDISK examine the FAT and directory structure on a drive, looking for errors and inconsistencies that could keep you from accessing files. They can fix most of the problems they find. They also find clusters that haven't been deleted but don't belong to any file (lost clusters); you can convert these clusters into files or delete them. You may be able to reclaim many kilobytes of wasted space on your drive this way.

SCANDISK is much newer than CHKDSK and does a better job at identifying and fixing problems with the FAT and directory structure. It also tests the surface of a disk, identifies damaged clusters, and moves as much data as possible to good clusters, blocking out the bad clusters so that they'll never be used again.

SCANDISK is new with DOS 6.2. If you have upgraded to version 6.2 or later, you won't need CHKDSK for repairing disks, although its reports still come in handy sometimes. If you use an earlier DOS version, you'll need to continue using CHKDSK to diagnose and repair problems.

> **Warning:** You should have a surface scanning facility. If you don't want to upgrade to DOS 6.2, you can find excellent surface scanners included with third-party utility packages, such as Disk Doctor that comes with The Norton Utilities. It is especially important to scan the surface of your disk before installing a data compression program such as DblSpace or DrvSpace.

This chapter shows you how to use both CHKDSK and SCANDISK. You will learn how to:

- Decide when to use a disk checking facility
- Run CHKDSK
- Run SCANDISK
- Deal with common problems reported by either CHKDSK or SCANDISK

When To Use CHKDSK or SCANDISK

You should run CHKDSK or SCANDISK periodically to check for errors and lost clusters. If you use your system full-time, you may want to run CHKDSK or SCANDISK weekly. For less active systems, biweekly or monthly may do. You also should run CHKDSK or SCANDISK if you see any evidence of problems, such as the following:

- Data drops out of a file
- Unexpected data appears in a file
- A program that was working fine starts to malfunction
- A file disappears from a directory
- A directory contains meaningless information
- A directory disappears unexpectedly
- A program crashes, which could strand pieces of temporary files

Checking a Drive for Problems

CHKDSK and SCANDISK can be fooled by open files, so you must terminate all running programs (except TSRs) before starting them. In particular, exit Windows or the DOS Shell and start CHKDSK or SCANDISK from a primary command prompt.

Try using CHKDSK on a floppy disk in drive A:

1. Insert any formatted disk in drive A.
2. Exit any programs or shells and get to a primary command prompt.
3. Enter the following command to start CHKDSK:

   `CHKDSK A:`

   CHKDSK examines the disk and produces a report. It might report some problems with the disk, but it won't fix them. Problems are explained in the next section.

   Whether or not problems are reported, the remainder of the report looks like the following example. The first few lines describe your disk space in terms of bytes:

   ```
   1,457,664 bytes total disk space
     923,648 bytes in 27 user files
     534,016 bytes available on disk
   ```

   The next group of lines show the disk space in terms of allocation units (clusters):

   ```
       512 bytes in each allocation unit
     2,847 total allocation units on disk
     1,043 available allocation units on disk
   ```

   The final two lines tell you about your memory usage, but only the first 640KB bytes:

   ```
   655,360 total bytes memory
   611,248 bytes free
   ```

   Finally, with DOS 6.2 and later, a message suggests that you use SCANDISK instead:

```
Instead of using CHKDSK, try using SCANDISK.  SCANDISK can reliably detect
and fix a much wider range of disk problems.  For more information,
type HELP SCANDISK from the command prompt.
```

> **Note:** The memory report is left over from earlier versions of DOS. You'll see a much better way to find out about available memory in Chapter 29, "Managing Memory."

SCANDISK is newer and better than CHKDSK. However, if it finds third-party compression software such as Stacker present, it won't repair any disks (even uncompressed ones) and it won't do a surface scan. If you use a third-party compression program, skip the following exercise. (SCANDISK is compatible with DOS's disk compression programs, DblSpace and DrvSpace; so, if you're using one of those programs, go ahead and do the following exercise.)

Try running SCANDISK on the same disk if you have DOS 6.2 or later:

1. Exit all programs and shells and get to a primary command prompt.

2. Start SCANDISK with the following command:

   SCANDISK A:

   The SCANDISK window opens and you see each item checked off as SCANDISK completes the test. (See Figure 27.1.)

Figure 27.1.
The SCANDISK window.

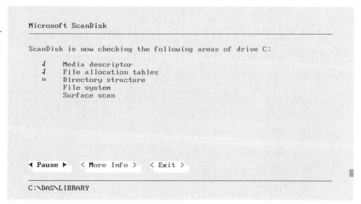

If any error messages appear, choose Stop to terminate the scan and read the next section.

If you don't stop the scan, SCANDISK finishes checking the FAT and directory structure and asks if you want to scan the surface of the disk.

3. A surface scan of a floppy disk may take several minutes. If you want to try a surface scan, choose Yes. Otherwise, choose No.

   If you choose to do a surface scan, a progress screen displays SCANDISK's progress as it works on the drive.

When SCANDISK is done, it displays a summary report. You can choose to examine a more detailed report or to exit.

4. Choose Exit to terminate SCANDISK.

Handling Disk Problems

The most common error reported by CHKDSK and SCANDISK is a *lost allocation unit*. This occurs when a FAT entry indicates that the cluster belongs to some file, but the chain cannot be traced backward to a specific file's directory entry.

Clusters get lost in a number of ways. Any type of mistake in the FAT or directory structure often creates lost clusters. Suppose that a directory entry gets damaged so that it no longer points to the first cluster of the file. That file's clusters are no longer associated with the directory entry, and CHKDSK and SCANDISK will report them as lost allocation units. Suppose that the FAT entry for the second cluster of a file gets damaged so that it no longer points to the third cluster. The third cluster, and all subsequent clusters, are now lost. These types of mistakes happen most often because of malfunctioning hardware, power surges, and improperly parked heads.

You can have lost clusters, however, without having any other mistakes on the drive. Probably the most common way of losing clusters is to interrupt DOS when it's deleting files. If you reboot, eject a disk, or shut off the power before DOS finishes zeroing all the FAT entries belonging to a deleted file, the remaining entries become lost allocation units. Lost clusters also can occur when a program hangs up and you have to reboot without closing files properly.

Lost clusters happen more often than you would expect. After you have used your system for a few months, they could be tying up many kilobytes of disk space. Those clusters are not available for new data; they're just wasted space on your drive. CHKDSK and SCANDISK can free that space.

CHKDSK and SCANDISK offer two ways to recover the space from lost clusters. They will convert them into files or they will delete them. If you're not missing any data, and if CHKDSK or SCANDISK doesn't report any other problems on the drive, you can safely delete the clusters. If you are missing some data or if CHKDSK reports other types of problems, you should recover the lost clusters into files; you may be able to locate and rescue your missing data.

Problem: While recovering files with SCANDISK or CHKDISK, I got the message
`Insufficient room in root directory.`

A root directory has a limited number of entries; the maximum depends on the disk size. SCANDISK or CHKDSK may recapture hundreds of lost chains at the same time if you have allowed them to build up on your disk, or if another error in the FAT or directory structure has caused hundreds of files to be abandoned. All of these files are placed in the root directory.

When you get this message, it's time to examine and deal with all the FILE*nnnn*.CHK files that have been created so far. Delete as many as possible and copy to other directories the ones you want to keep. Then, reenter the SCANDISK or CHKDSK /F command to recover more lost allocation units.

Dealing with Lost Clusters with CHKDSK

CHKDSK reports any problems after the two heading lines. A lost clusters message looks something like the following:

```
Volume MICROMATE   created 10-27-1994 10:30a
Volume Serial Number is 1A4F-4156
Errors found, F parameter not specified
Corrections will not be written to disk

    45 lost allocation units found in 13 chains.
     92160 bytes disk space would be freed

84,768,768 bytes total disk space
    88,064 bytes in 6 hidden files
   126,976 bytes in 41 directories
71,376,896 bytes in 1793 user files
13,084,672 bytes available on disk

     2,048 bytes in each allocation unit
    41,391 total allocation units on disk
     6,389 available allocation units on disk

   655,360 total bytes memory
   627,424 bytes free
```

In this example, CHKDSK found 45 lost clusters in 13 chains. If you decide to zero the clusters, you would gain 92,160 bytes (90KB) of available space. If you decide to convert them into files, CHKDSK would create 13 files, one for each chain.

CHKDSK doesn't recover the lost clusters or fix any other problems in response to the preceding command. You have to rerun it with the /F (fix) switch to fix any problems it finds, as in:

```
CHKDSK /F [drive]
```

When you use the /F switch, you see these messages:

```
Volume MICROMATE   created 10-27-1992 10:30a
Volume Serial Number is 1A4F-4156

    45 lost allocation units found in 13 chains.
Convert lost chains to files (Y/N)?
```

If you type N, CHKDSK deletes the lost clusters so that the space is made available for new data. If you type Y, CHKDSK converts each lost chain into a file in the root directory named FILE*nnnn*.CHK, where *nnnn* is a serial number starting with 0000. You then can examine each file and decide whether to delete or keep it. Examine the files using DOS's EDIT command or your word processor. Nontext files will be unreadable, and even text files might be partially unreadable. You may have to remove some garbage from the text files that you want to keep.

Dealing with Lost Clusters with SCANDISK

When SCANDISK encounters lost clusters, it displays a Problem Found dialog box like the one in Figure 27.2. Choose Save to recover the clusters into files, or Delete to delete the clusters. The results are the same as with CHKDSK. You also can choose Don't Fix It to ignore the problem or More Info to find out more about the lost clusters before deciding.

Figure 27.2.
The Problem Found
dialog box.

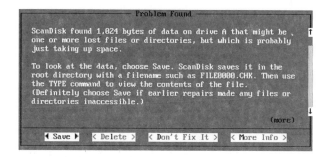

Only part of the message is shown in the dialog box. Scroll down by using the scroll bar or Page Down to read the rest of the message. You also can choose More Info to read a more detailed explanation of the problem.

Whenever SCANDISK corrects a disk, it offers to store undo information so that the corrections can be removed if you don't like them. If you choose Save or Delete in response to the message in Figure 27.2, the dialog box shown in Figure 27.3 opens. Choose Drive A (or Drive B if it's available) to store the undo information or Skip Undo to ignore it. Whatever you choose here controls the rest of this SCANDISK session. If more mistakes are found as the scan continues, you don't get another chance to decide whether or not to store undo information. You also can choose More Info to see more information about the undo feature before you make up your mind.

Figure 27.3.
The Create Undo Disk
dialog box.

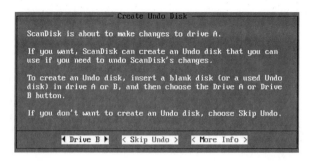

```
┌──────────────────── Create Undo Disk ────────────────────┐
│  ScanDisk is about to make changes to drive A.           │
│                                                          │
│  If you want, ScanDisk can create an Undo disk that you can │
│  use if you need to undo ScanDisk's changes.             │
│                                                          │
│  To create an Undo disk, insert a blank disk (or a used Undo │
│  disk) in drive A or B, and then choose the Drive A or Drive │
│  B button.                                               │
│                                                          │
│  If you don't want to create an Undo disk, choose Skip Undo. │
│                                                          │
│   ◀ Drive B ▶    < Skip Undo >    < More Info >          │
└──────────────────────────────────────────────────────────┘
```

If you choose to store undo information, you must provide a blank, formatted floppy in drive A or B. SCANDISK stores the undo information on the floppy.

You can undo SCANDISK's changes only if you haven't made any changes to the drive since running SCANDISK. If you have added, expanded, shrunk, or deleted even one file, the FAT has changed and the undo information (which includes the old FAT) will be invalid. Keeping that restriction in mind, you can undo SCANDISK's changes by entering the following command:

SCANDISK /UNDO *undo-drive*

The *undo-drive* is the name of the drive containing the undo disk, not the name of the drive to be repaired.

Cross-Linked Files

Perhaps the second most common error—one that CHKDSK cannot fix but SCANDISK can—is cross-linked files, in which two files appear to have some clusters in common. For example, suppose that the FAT shows that FILEA occupies clusters 201, 202, 203, and 204; but FILEB occupies clusters 1096, 1097, 203, and 204. Clusters 203 and 204 cannot belong to both files; one of the chains is incorrect. In all likelihood, FILEB should chain from 1097 to 1098 and beyond.

CHKDSK can't fix cross-linked files because it can't guess which chain is correct and which is not. Your best bet to fix cross-linked files is to delete both files and restore them from their backups. If that's not possible, and if they are not program files, you may be able to recover at least one of them with the following procedure.

SCANDISK does steps 2 and 3 of the procedure for you if you ask it to fix the cross-linked files. You still have to examine and edit the repaired files and handle all the other CHK files.

Looking Ahead: Other types of errors that CHKDSK and SCANDISK can locate and fix are much less common. They are discussed in Chapter 47, "Advanced Rescue Techniques."

How to Recover Cross-Linked Files with CHKDSK (if you don't have SCANDISK)

Warning: Don't use this procedure on a cross-linked program file. Running an incorrectly fixed program could damage your hard disk. Delete the file and restore or reinstall it. (This includes files with extensions .COM, .EXE, .BIN, .DLL, .SYS, and .OVL.)

1. Recover all lost allocation units into files. Then exit CHKDSK. (You'll come back to the recovered files later.)

2. Make a copy of each cross-linked file, giving each copy a new name but the same extension as the original. The new files will not be cross-linked, but each one will contain a copy of the common clusters.

3. Delete the cross-linked files. These deletions clear up the problem in the FAT.

4. Examine each copy using whatever application made the original. You probably will find that one of the files is fine and the other isn't.

5. Edit the damaged file to remove any superfluous data. Use the same application that created the file in the first place.

6. Examine the FILE*nnnn*.CHK files recovered by CHKDSK. If any of them contain data that belongs to the damaged file, use the file's original application to insert the data where it belongs.

7. Handle all other FILE*nnnn*.CHK files as you would normally.

8. Restore the original names of the files that you have recovered.

Archaic CHKDSK Functions

CHKDSK was one of the early DOS utilities, and it includes some functions that were handy at one time but have now been replaced by better utilities. Besides reporting the amount of memory installed, it can perform a couple of obsolete tricks:

- It can report on file fragmentation—but DEFRAG is better.
- It can list all the files on the disk—but DIR and TREE are better.

SCANDISK's Surface Scan

When a disk is first formatted at a low level, the surface is tested and any weak spots, which can't hold data reliably, are identified and marked out in the FAT. But, bad areas can develop after the disk is formatted and in use. You might encounter a `Disk read error` or `Disk write error` message when a new bad spot has developed. You won't be able to access a file stored in that area without using SCANDISK, even though most of the file is fine. SCANDISK can read files sector by sector, rescuing as many sectors as possible. Only the data in sectors that are actually damaged will be lost.

After it finishes checking the FAT and directory structure, SCANDISK offers to scan the surface of the disk. (See Figure 27.4.) If it finds any problems, it moves as much data as it can read accurately away from the damaged clusters. It also marks the damaged clusters in the FAT so they'll never be used again. In many cases, SCANDISK won't be able to rescue an entire file, but it may be able to rescue a large percentage of it. As long as you have backups, you should delete the rescued files and restore them from their backups. Otherwise, you might need to use a rescued text file and retype any data that was lost. As always, do not run a program file that might be incomplete or incorrect; it could damage your hard disk.

Figure 27.4.
*SCANDISK's surface
scan message.*

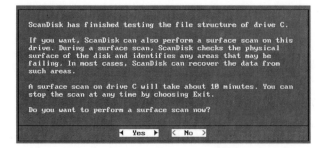

Don't wait until you start getting error messages to scan the surface of your hard drives. Run SCANDISK often to identify and bypass problems before they cause you to lose data. For the average computer, check the surface of your hard drives about once a month.

On Your Own

This chapter has shown you how to use CHKDSK and SCANDISK to test a disk and correct some of the most common errors. The following items can guide you in practicing CHKDSK and SCANDISK on your own:

1. Check your hard drive with CHKDSK. Recover any lost allocation units reported and fix any cross-linked files. Find out the size of your hard disk allocation unit. (If any other errors are reported, read Chapter 47 before trying to fix them.)

2. If you don't use a third-party compression program, scan your hard disk with SCANDISK. Include the surface scan and fix any errors that are reported.

28 Optimizing Your System

Introduction

DOS 6 gives you a number of tools to improve the overall performance of your system.

What Can DOS Do?

One of the advantages of learning to use your operating system, instead of just depending on your applications, is that you can take several steps to make your system faster and more efficient. With DOS 6 utilities, you can make better use of memory so that you have more room to load and run programs. You can squeeze almost twice as much data onto your hard drive. You also can speed up all your disk drives, which improves the speed of your whole system.

This chapter overviews the various DOS tools for optimizing your system. You'll learn how to use each tool in detail in the next few chapters.

Better Memory Management

Memory space in a DOS system is always tight, even if the system has many megabytes of extended or expanded memory. Traditionally, programs must run in *conventional memory*, which is limited to 640KB no matter how much memory is installed on your system. After you have loaded DOS, a handful of device drivers, and perhaps some other TSRs in conventional memory, you may not have enough room left to load and run a large application like a desktop publisher. If you have a 286-based machine, DOS 6 can provide a little relief from the conventional memory crunch. It can make a huge difference on a 386 or higher machine.

The original PCs were limited to 1MB of memory unless you added an expanded memory board. 286s and higher machines, however, can extend memory for several megabytes. For any system with extended memory, DOS 6 includes HIMEM, a driver that gives DOS access to and control of the extended memory area. You can even load DOS into extended memory instead of conventional memory, freeing up 45KB or more of conventional memory for other programs to use. Chapter 29, "Managing Memory," explains the various types of memory—including conventional, extended, and expanded—and shows you how to load and use HIMEM.

If you have a 386 or higher machine, you can do a lot more to free up conventional memory space. The EMM386 driver enables you to load and run programs in *upper memory*, the area that comes in between conventional and extended memory. If you have any programs that need expanded memory, EMM386 also can use extended memory to emulate expanded memory. DOS 6 even includes a program called MEMMAKER that will set up your system to use HIMEM and EMM386 so that you don't have to do it yourself. Chapter 30, "Additional Memory Facilities for 386, 486, and Pentium Computers," shows you how to use EMM386 and MEMMAKER.

Note: If you use Windows, you'll find that the techniques you learn in Chapter 30 improve Windows performance, too.

Caching the Hard Drive

Your hard drive is so slow, compared to memory and the microprocessor, that your system often has to wait for data to be read and written. A *caching* program helps to ease the bottleneck by saving disk data in memory, so that DOS can read from and write to memory instead of the hard disk.

DOS 6 includes a caching program named SmartDrive that creates a cache in extended memory. With SmartDrive, your applications might run so much faster that you actually notice the difference. SmartDrive saves any data you work on in its cache. The next time you want to use the same data, SmartDrive provides the data from the cache instead of reading it from the hard drive. Reading the data from the cache is much faster than reading it from the drive. Chapter 31, "Caching the Drives," explains how to load and use SmartDrive.

> **Note:** If you use Windows, you'll learn some techniques in Chapter 31 to balance SmartDrive with Windows memory needs.

Using a RAM Drive

Another way to cut down on disk accesses is to create a *RAM drive*, which is like a disk drive except that it is located in memory instead of on disk, making it about 100 times faster. You can use a RAM drive just like any other drive, but it loses all its data when you reboot or shut off the power. You have to load it with data after booting and move any important data to a real drive before you reboot or shut down. Because the possibility of a power outage or system hang-up always exists, most people keep only temporary files in a RAM drive; they keep their important data files in a more secure place.

With DOS 6, you can create RAM drives using DOS's RAMDRIVE driver. You can control the size of each RAM drive and whether it is located in conventional, expanded, or extended memory. DOS assigns a drive name to each RAM drive, just like it does to your real drives. Chapter 32, "RAM Drives," shows you how to create and use RAM drives.

Defragmenting

DOS is often forced to fragment files to fit them into the available space on a disk. Fragmentation doesn't hurt a file, but your drive takes longer to read a fragmented file, because it has to move the read-write heads more. If you have a lot of fragmentation on your hard disk, you might notice your programs running slower.

DOS 6 includes a program called DEFRAG that defragments the files on a drive. DEFRAG moves the clusters around to bring file fragments together, adjusting the FAT and directories as necessary. Defragmenting your hard drive once a month or so is one of the steps you should take to keep your system in optimum shape. Chapter 33, "Defragmenter," shows you how to use DEFRAG.

Note: One way to improve Windows performance is to give it a Permanent Swap File. DEFRAG can be an essential tool in creating a Permanent Swap File for Windows, as you'll learn in Chapter 33.

Data Compression

No matter how large your hard drive is, you will soon fill it up. Compressing the drive can free up a lot of space for more files. *Data compression* condenses repetitious data in a file so that it takes up less room. For example, if the word "the" appears several times in a file, all but the first occurrence are replaced by a code that refers back to the first one.

The amount that you can compress a file depends on how much repetitious data it contains. A program file usually contains very little repetition, so program files don't compress very much. A text file contains quite a bit of repeated information. Common strings of characters such as "the", "and", and "are" may appear hundreds of times. Text files often can be compressed to less than half their uncompressed size. Black-and-white bit-mapped graphic files, which consist entirely of black dots and white dots, realize the most compression of all.

DOS 6.0 and early editions of DOS 6.2 provide a disk compression program called DblSpace. DOS 6.22 replaces DblSpace with DrvSpace. You'll learn how to use both DblSpace and DrvSpace in Chapter 34, "DriveSpace and DoubleSpace."

Note: One way to improve Windows performance is to give it a Permanent Swap File. But, a Permanent Swap File cannot be compressed. Chapter 33 shows you how to make room for a Permanent Swap File on a compressed drive.

29

Managing Memory

Introduction

Running out of usable memory in a PC is very easy to do, even if you have 4MB of RAM or more! DOS 6 includes several tools to help you get the most from the memory you have.

DOS's Memory Crunch

How can you run out of memory space when you have 4MB, 8MB, or more? The answer lies in DOS's basic architecture, which uses only the first 640KB of RAM (called *conventional memory*) to load and run your applications, no matter how much RAM you have. If you're also letting your device drivers and TSRs (such as PRINT and DOSKEY) reside in conventional memory, you could very easily get an Out of Memory message when you try to load an up-to-date word processor or spreadsheet.

The goal of good memory management is to move as many things as possible out of conventional memory to maximize the amount of space available to your applications. DOS provides several tools to help you do that. This chapter deals with tools that you can use on any system. Chapter 30, "Additional Memory Facilities for 386, 486, and Pentium Computers," describes additional tools that are available for 386 and higher computers.

In this chapter, you will learn how to:

- Identify the different types of memory
- Display your memory layout with the MEM command
- Load DOS's extended memory manager, HIMEM.SYS
- Move DOS out of conventional memory

You will also learn the following terms:

- conventional memory
- high memory area (HMA)
- expanded memory
- extended memory
- RAM
- ROM
- upper memory

Note: Windows uses memory differently than DOS does. If you get a Windows Out of Memory message with 4MB or more of RAM, it may be that you've run out of stack space. Exiting, rebooting, and restarting Windows usually solves the problem.

What Is Memory?

Memory is the storage device inside your computer in which programs reside while they are being executed. The basic part of memory is a set of chips located on the motherboard close to the microprocessor so that data can travel quickly between the two devices. Memory is completely solid-state; unlike a disk drive, it has no moving parts to slow it down.

You can't run programs from a disk or any other storage device; each program must be loaded into memory for execution. When you enter a command such as WORD (to start Microsoft Word for DOS), DOS loads the Word program into conventional memory. When Word terminates, its memory space is made available for the next program you want to run. When you load a memory-resident program, such as a TSR or a driver, it stays in memory until you specifically remove it or reboot. If you load enough memory-resident programs into conventional memory, you might not be able to load a program such as Word when you want to run it.

Many people confuse memory and disk space. Your disk drives provide long-term storage for your programs and data files. Memory is a short-term storage area where DOS must store a program while executing it. Even though a program must be loaded into memory, the data it processes can be stored on a slower device, such as a disk. If a program also can keep its data in memory, however, it will run much faster because it doesn't have to wait for data to be read from and written to the slower device.

The Types of Memory

In the early days of personal computers, a new computer typically came with 16KB of memory. You could expand it in 16KB increments, up to a maximum of 64KB. Programs were necessarily limited, not only in what tasks they could accomplish, but also in how they interacted with their users. Color monitors, graphic user interfaces, and mice were unheard of. Those early programs also ran very slowly and had to keep most of their data on external storage devices.

In the late 1970s, Intel developed the 8088 microprocessor chip, which could access an incredible 1MB of memory. IBM adopted the 8088 for the first IBM PCs. The PC clones soon followed, all based on the 8088 with its 1MB of memory.

IBM and a new little company called Microsoft developed an operating system called the *Disk Operating System* (*DOS*) for the new machine. Intel, IBM, and Microsoft decided to divide the 1MB memory area into two parts, as shown in Figure 29.1. The first 640KB, called *conventional memory*, is where DOS and its applications run. This area was 10 times as much memory space as previous personal computers had. The remaining 384KB, called *upper memory*, was reserved for DOS's use in accessing hardware devices such as your monitor.

Figure 29.1.
Conventional and upper
memory.

Two basic types of memory devices exist, RAM and ROM. RAM, which stands for *random-access memory*, can be read from and written to. You can write to it again and again; new data replaces older data with no problems. However, RAM is *volatile*; it loses its data when you shut off the power.

ROM, which stands for *read-only memory*, has data stored in it by its manufacturer and can be read from repeatedly, but not written to. A ROM chip usually contains an essential program such as the *basic input-output operating system* (*BIOS*), which provides the elementary instructions to read and write data for your hardware. ROM is not volatile; it retains its memory when the power is off so that its information is available during the early parts of booting, before any programs have been loaded into RAM.

Conventional memory is always made up of RAM because you must be able to repeatedly load programs and data there. Upper memory may contain some RAM and some ROM, depending on what devices your system has. The BIOS chip, which is usually referred to as ROM-BIOS, is located in upper memory. Other devices might be the memory on your video card, your fax/modem, and so on. A lot of upper memory is empty, available for you to install additional devices.

As soon as 640KB of memory became available, people began to think of ways to use it. Programs got bigger, faster, and fancier. Memory-resident programs began to appear—device drivers and TSRs such as ANSI.SYS and PRINT. When you load a memory-resident program, it stays in memory for the rest of the session and any other programs you load have to fit into the remaining space. Within a few years, programs were bumping up against that 640KB ceiling with no way to get around it.

Expanded Memory

An early solution to the memory crunch was called *expanded memory*. (See Figure 29.2.) This memory is an extra set of RAM chips located on a separate board and treated just like any other hardware device. As indicated in the figure, expanded memory is accessed through upper memory. Notice that you can access only a portion of it at a time, but you can switch from portion to portion to take advantage of all the available space. A device driver called an *expanded memory manager* controls access to expanded memory and does the switching. Expanded memory is relatively slow compared to conventional or upper memory, but it is still considerably faster than a disk drive.

Figure 29.2.
Expanded memory.

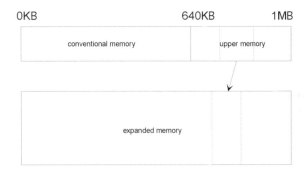

Even if your system has expanded memory, you may not be using it. A program must be specifically designed to take advantage of expanded memory. If you don't have any such programs, your expanded memory is lying fallow.

Because expanded memory is a separate device and can't be accessed directly by DOS, you can't load and run programs there. But, you can keep your data files there. For example, a word processor that takes up 600KB in conventional memory can keep the documents that it is working on in expanded memory.

Extended Memory

Just as expanded memory was gaining a foothold, Intel developed another solution to the 640KB ceiling. The 286 chip, in addition to being a much better and faster processor, could directly access 16MB of memory. Memory above the 1MB mark, which is all RAM, is called *extended memory*. The 386 and 486 have pushed the limit even further, allowing several gigabytes of memory. (A gigabyte is more than a billion bytes.) Theoretically, you could load and run programs throughout this memory space. Sadly, DOS must adhere to its original design and has no way to directly access the extra space. DOS still suffers from the 640KB ceiling, with some interesting exceptions that you'll discover later in this book. This is why you can run out of memory even though you have many megabytes of unused RAM.

Note: Several new operating systems have been designed to take advantage of the full range of extended memory, including OS/2, Windows NT, and Windows 95. There will be more in the near future. Eventually, DOS may be displaced in favor of these more modern systems.

Still, your extended memory doesn't have to go to waste. DOS can treat extended memory as a separate device and access it through upper memory, using an *extended memory manager* to handle the details. As with expanded memory, DOS can't load and run programs in extended memory, with one exception—the high memory area, which is explained in the next section.

386 and higher PCs have a minimum of 1MB of RAM. The first 640KB makes up conventional memory. The next 384KB goes into extended memory. (Upper memory does not use RAM from the PC's memory chips. It accesses memory on your hardware cards.) So, unless you have a 286 or older machine, you have at least 384KB of extended memory, and probably a lot more.

The High Memory Area

Because of a quirk in the way DOS addresses memory, it turns out that it can directly access not just 1MB, but nearly 64KB beyond that. When a PC has extended memory, a small portion (almost 64KB) is directly addressable by DOS, permitting you to run programs there. DOS's extended memory manager, named HIMEM.SYS, turns that part of extended memory into the *high memory area* (HMA), where it can load and run one program at a time. Normally, you load DOS into the HMA, freeing up 45KB or more of conventional memory for other programs.

> **Note:** Extended memory, HIMEM.SYS, and the HMA are available only on 286 and higher PCs. The original PCs and XTs can have expanded memory boards, but not extended memory.

Viewing Your Memory Layout

You can find out how much of each type of memory you have, and how it's being used, with the MEM command. To take a look at your PC's memory layout, enter MEM with no parameters.

You see a message like the following:

```
Memory Type      Total =  Used  +  Free
— — — — — — — —   — — —    — — —    — — —
Conventional      640K     112K     528K
Upper               0K       0K       0K
Reserved          384K     384K       0K
Extended (XMS)  3,072K    3072K       0K
— — — — — — — —   — — —    — — —    — — —
Total memory    4,096K    3568K     528K
Total under 1 MB  640K     112K     528K
```

```
Largest executable program size   527K   (540,096 bytes)
Largest free upper memory block     0K        (0 bytes)
```

The system in the preceding example has 640KB of conventional memory, of which 528KB is currently free. It has 384KB of upper memory, which appears next to Reserved because this system uses upper memory for its original purpose—to access RAM and ROM associated with hardware adapters. Because upper memory is not available to run programs, it is not counted in the Total under 1 MB line. You'll see how to make upper memory available to programs in the next chapter.

The system has 3MB of extended memory, none of which is free. It has no expanded memory. Altogether, this system has 4MB of memory, of which about 528KB is free. The largest executable program size is 527KB because that is the largest fragment of conventional memory available. (It appears that there is a 1KB fragment somewhere.) The final line in the report mentions *upper memory blocks*, which are explained in Chapter 30.

MEM without any switches gives you a general feel for how much memory is available, but you can't see what specific programs are loaded. Adding the /C (classify) switch to the MEM command causes MEM to add details about programs. You can also add the /P switch to break the report into pages if your monitor displays only 24 lines per screen. Try it on your system:

1. Enter **MEM /C /P**.

   MEM displays the first page of a report showing the programs that are currently loaded into memory.

2. If the last line says Press any key to continue, press a key to see the remainder of the report.

The report starts off with a table of the programs that are currently loaded into memory. Yours might be somewhat different from the one in the following example, depending on what drivers, TSRs, and other programs you are currently using.

```
Modules using memory below 1 MB:
    Name         Total    =  Conventional  +  Upper Memory
    ————      ——————      ——————          ——————

    MSDOS      61,037   (60K)     61,037   (60K)       0  (0K)
    SETVER        784    (1K)        784    (1K)       0  (0K)
    ANSI        4,208    (4K)      4,208    (4K)       0  (0K)
    COMMAND     5,760    (6K)      5,760    (6K)       0  (0K)
    MOUSE      13,616   (13K)     13,616   (13K)       0  (0K)
    GRAB       23,760   (23K)     23,760   (23K)       0  (0K)
    GRAPHICS    5,872    (6K)      5,872    (6K)       0  (0K)
    Free      540,208  (528K)    540,208  (528K)       0  (0K)
```

You can see in this table that MSDOS, SETVER, ANSI, and the others are loaded into conventional memory. MSDOS occupies 60KB, SETVER occupies 1KB, and so on. There is 520KB of conventional memory available to run a program.

Note: MEM does not count itself when reporting the programs in memory because it terminates as soon as it finishes displaying the report. By the time you see the report, MEM is already out of memory and its space is available for the next program.

Loading HIMEM

Because DOS can't access extended memory directly, you need a manager to make your extended memory available under DOS. DOS includes an extended memory manager called HIMEM. If your machine has extended memory, you may want to use HIMEM to access and control it.

Note: You may be using a third-party extended memory manager such as QEMM or 386MAX. These products offer more features than HIMEM. If you are already using a third-party manager, you should skip the rest of this chapter. If you're not sure, look in the MEM report that you just displayed for QEMM or 386MAX, or ask the person who set up your system.

HIMEM not only creates and controls the HMA, it also manages the rest of extended memory, so that programs running under DOS can safely store and use data there without conflicting with each other. You load HIMEM from CONFIG.SYS with the following command:

```
DEVICE=C:\DOS\HIMEM.SYS
```

Note: Be sure to include the correct path for your DOS directory. When DOS processes CONFIG.SYS, no search path is available, so you have to tell DOS where to find the desired file.

Most people put the HIMEM.SYS command first in CONFIG.SYS so that HIMEM can seize immediate control and make extended memory available to other programs that are loaded from CONFIG.SYS.

Loading DOS into the HMA

HIMEM enables one program to use the HMA. If you permit a small program—10KB, for example—to load into the HMA, you do not free up much room in conventional memory. One way to guarantee that a sizable program uses the HMA is to load DOS up there, which you can do with the following CONFIG.SYS command:

```
DOS=HIGH
```

Making this the second command in CONFIG.SYS, right after you load HIMEM, guarantees that DOS gets into the HMA before some other program does. How much conventional memory space you save depends on how your DOS is configured. You could save as much as 64KB. A small portion of DOS stays in conventional memory.

If your system has extended memory and uses a third-party manager, is it using HIMEM? Is it loading DOS into the HMA? Look in the report from MEM /C for these indications:

- In the memory summary, look for a line labeled Extended (XMS). If there is no such line, you do not have extended memory, and you can skip the rest of this chapter (as well as Chapter 30).

- In the table of loaded programs, look for HIMEM. If it's not there, you're not using HIMEM. You'll see how to load it in the next exercise.

- Does the last line of the report say MS-DOS is resident in the high memory area? If so, your system loads DOS into the HMA. If not, you'll see how to load it in the next exercise.

If you have extended memory and are not using HIMEM or loading DOS into the HMA, do the following exercise, which walks you through the process of loading them.

> **Warning:** Do not do this exercise if your system uses a third-party extended memory manager such as QEMM or 386MAX.

1. Switch to the root directory of your boot drive.

2. Make an insurance copy of CONFIG.SYS called CONFIG.SAV.

3. Open CONFIG.SYS for editing in an ASCII text editor such as DOS's EDIT.

4. If there is no DEVICE command for HIMEM.SYS, insert the following line as the first line of the file:

```
DEVICE=C:\DOS\HIMEM.SYS
```

5. If DOS is not currently being loaded into the HMA, insert the following command immediately after the `HIMEM` command:

   `DOS=HIGH`

6. Save the file and exit the editor.

7. Reboot to force DOS to execute the new CONFIG.SYS.

   If DOS is unable to boot for some reason, see the Problem Solver that follows.

8. If DOS booted successfully with the revised CONFIG.SYS, enter `MEM /C /P` to see your new memory layout.

   You should see HIMEM loaded into conventional memory. Notice also that you now have more conventional memory free because DOS is loaded into the HMA. You also can see a difference in the use of extended memory. With HIMEM in control, most of extended memory is available. The HMA represents the 64KB in use. The final line of the report shows that DOS is now located in the HMA.

Problem: I added a command to CONFIG.SYS to load HIMEM, and now I can't boot. What's wrong, and how can I boot?

The default settings for HIMEM apparently are not correct for your system. HIMEM includes a number of parameters, described in Appendix A, "Device Drivers," at the back of this book, to tailor HIMEM for particular hardware configurations. Most likely, you need to use the `/MACHINE` parameter. If that doesn't work, try out some of the other parameters. (It doesn't hurt to experiment with these parameters.) If you can't figure out which parameters to use, your hardware dealer or manufacturer, or Microsoft's Product Support Team, may be able to help you.

To boot in the meantime, press Ctrl+Alt+Delete, then press F8 when you see the message `Loading MS-DOS....` Bypass the command that loads HIMEM.SYS, but execute all other commands in CONFIG.SYS and execute all of AUTOEXEC.BAT. You will then be able to edit CONFIG.SYS to try out some of these suggested solutions. Don't forget that each time you change CONFIG.SYS you must reboot to put the changes into effect.

Problem: I tried to run a program and got the message `Packed file corrupt`. What happened to my program?

Your program is fine. When you load DOS into the HMA, you free up the first 64KB of conventional memory for other programs to use. Some programs can't function when loaded that low in memory. To run the program, you need to use the `LOADFIX` command to load the program above the 64KB line. Simply insert the word **LOADFIX** in front of the command that starts up the program, as in the following:

```
LOADFIX AUDIT README.TXT
```

On Your Own

This chapter has introduced you to a variety of terms concerning memory in a PC. Make sure that you understand each of these terms:

- conventional memory
- high memory area (HMA)
- expanded memory
- extended memory
- RAM
- ROM
- upper memory

30 Additional Memory Facilities for 386, 486, and Pentium Computers

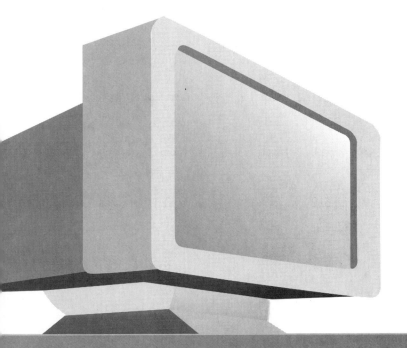

Introduction

If you have a 386 or higher computer, you may be able to move most of your drivers and TSRs out of conventional memory space using the tools included in DOS 6.

DOS and 386, 486, and Pentium Machines

DOS 6 includes several programs to optimize memory in a 386 or higher PC. If you don't have expanded memory but you have a program that requires some, you can use part of extended memory as expanded memory. You also can load and run programs in the unused portions of upper memory, freeing up even more space in conventional memory. DOS even provides a program that will set up your CONFIG.SYS and AUTOEXEC.BAT to make the best possible use of upper memory.

This chapter shows you how to apply these facilities to your best advantage in your PC. You will learn how to:

- Use extended memory to simulate expanded memory
- Load device drivers and TSRs into upper memory instead of conventional memory
- Use MEMMAKER to optimize upper memory, if necessary

Note: If you have a more extensive memory manager, such as QEMM or 386Max, you don't need the features discussed in this chapter. Skip this chapter, but see your memory manager's manual for tips on how to make the best use of your PC's memory.

Providing Expanded Memory

Because almost all new computers have extended memory, and very few have expanded memory, up-to-date applications rarely require expanded memory. But, you might have an older application, such as an early version of Ventura Publisher, that needs some expanded memory. If you can't load a certain application—especially if you used it successfully before upgrading your hardware—check its documentation to see if it requires expanded memory.

DOS 6 includes a driver named EMM386 that can be used to provide expanded memory when you have only extended memory. If you load EMM386 with no parameters or switches, it turns 256KB of extended memory into expanded memory. A program can request and receive more expanded memory space on a temporary basis if enough extended memory is available. When the program is done with expanded memory, all but the basic 256KB reverts back to extended memory.

You load EMM386 with the following command in CONFIG.SYS:

```
DEVICE=C:\DOS\EMM386.EXE
```

EMM386 requires HIMEM, so this command must follow the command that loads HIMEM. If you put the EMM386.EXE command right after the DOS=HIGH command (or right after the HIMEM.SYS command if you're not using DOS=HIGH), EMM386 can take 256KB of extended memory before other programs take it all.

If you would like to try converting some extended memory to expanded, follow these steps:

> **Warning:** Do not try this exercise if your system uses a third-party extended memory manager such as QEMM or 386Max.

1. Switch to the root directory of your boot drive.

2. Make an insurance copy of CONFIG.SYS called CONFIG.SAV.

3. Open CONFIG.SYS for editing in an ASCII text editor such as DOS's EDIT.

4. Insert the following line after the line that loads HIMEM:

   ```
   DEVICE=C:\DOS\EMM386.EXE
   ```

5. Reboot.

   If DOS is unable to boot for some reason, see the Problem Solver in the section titled "Loading DOS into the HMA" in Chapter 29, "Managing Memory."

6. Enter MEM.

   The MEM report should show that you now have 256KB of expanded memory (and 256KB less extended memory). Notice also that EMM386 is using some conventional memory and some reserved memory.

7. To get rid of the expanded memory, replace CONFIG.SYS with CONFIG.SAV and reboot.

Using Upper Memory Blocks

In Chapter 29, you saw that the memory range from 640KB to 1MB, called *upper memory*, was traditionally reserved for DOS's use in accessing hardware devices. Very few systems, however, actually use the entire 384KB. The unused space is valuable because, unlike expanded and extended memory, DOS can run programs there. EMM386 has a second function that enables you to load and run programs in unused upper memory space. Most people manage to load all their device drivers and TSRs into upper memory, leaving more than 600KB of conventional memory for applications.

Figure 30.1 shows an example of how upper memory may be laid out in a system. Device memory and ROM-BIOS don't necessarily occupy consecutive locations; the unused space could be divided into chunks called upper memory blocks (UMBs).

Figure 30.1.
Typical upper memory configuration.

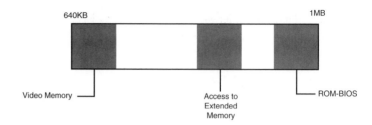

The empty blocks in upper memory have no RAM associated with them; they are just reserved space. EMM386 takes enough RAM from extended memory to supply upper memory for the programs that you want to load. If it can't make a large enough UMB available to load a particular program, because the UMB space doesn't exist or because it can't get enough extended memory, DOS loads the program into conventional memory without warning you. In that case, you don't free up the conventional memory space that would be made available by loading the program in question into upper memory.

If you have a 386 or higher PC, you might already be using upper memory. Your MEM report can tell you:

1. Enter **MEM** **/C** **/P**.

   MEM displays a report of your memory usage. The top part of the report shows which programs are loaded into conventional memory and which are loaded into upper memory:

   Modules using memory below 1MB:

Name	Total		=	Conventional		+	Upper Memory	
MSDOS	17,741	(17K)		17,741	(17K)		0	(0K)
HIMEM	1,168	(1K)		1,168	(1K)		0	(0K)
EMM386	3,120	(3K)		3,120	(3K)		0	(0K)
COMMAND	2,928	(3K)		2,928	(3K)		0	(0K)
SETVER	640	(1K)		0	(0K)		640	(1K)
MTMCDS	10,320	(10K)		0	(0K)		10,320	(10K)
SHARE	17,904	(17K)		0	(0K)		17,904	(17K)
MSCDEX	27,952	(27K)		0	(0K)		27,952	(27K)
SMARTDRV	28,832	(28K)		0	(0K)		28,832	(28K)
Free	630,403	(615K)		630,403	(615K)		0	(0K)

   In this example, SETVER, MTMCDS, SHARE, MSCDEX, and SMARTDRV are occupying upper memory; the other programs are in conventional memory.

Some programs cannot be loaded into upper memory; this includes a small portion of MS-DOS, HIMEM, EMM386, and COMMAND. If your system also loads several other programs into conventional memory, or if it is not using upper memory at all, MEMMAKER can help you take full advantage of upper memory. MEMMAKER is explained in the next section.

> **Note:** Even if your system's memory appears to be very well laid out right now, read the next section anyway (but don't do the exercises). You may need to run MEMMAKER the next time you add a driver or TSR to your system.

Using MEMMAKER

Setting up and using upper memory blocks requires a number of commands in CONFIG.SYS and AUTOEXEC.BAT, and in SYSTEM.INI if you are using Windows. DOS 6 provides a program called MEMMAKER to do the work for you. MEMMAKER analyzes your system, figures out the best way to use the available UMBs, and inserts or adapts the necessary commands in CONFIG.SYS, AUTOEXEC.BAT, and SYSTEM.INI.

MEMMAKER adapts any driver and TSR commands in your startup files to load the referenced programs into upper memory. Before running MEMMAKER, edit CONFIG.SYS and AUTOEXEC.BAT to insert all the commands to load drivers and TSRs that you want MEMMAKER to adapt. (Edit SYSTEM.INI only if you understand how this file works.) However, don't worry about loading every possible driver and TSR at this time. You can rerun MEMMAKER later if you decide to add more drivers and TSRs to your system.

MEMMAKER includes an option to undo its work, so feel free to try it out. If you don't like the results, you can undo them.

1. Exit any programs or shells that you are running and get to a primary command prompt.
2. Enter **MEMMAKER** at the DOS command prompt.
   MEMMAKER displays a Welcome screen.
3. After reading the Welcome screen, press enter to continue.
   MEMMAKER offers you the choice of a custom or express setup.
4. Press Enter to choose Express.

> **Note:** You may be able to squeeze more programs into upper memory with a custom setup, but most people don't need to do this.

MEMMAKER asks if your system needs expanded memory.

5. Press Enter to answer No. (If you're sure that one of your programs needs expanded memory, press the space bar to change No to Yes. Then, press Enter to answer Yes.)

MEMMAKER begins working on your memory layout. It does a fairly good job of keeping you informed of what's happening as it works. It reboots your system several times while experimenting with the best setup, but MEMMAKER always warns you when it's about to reboot.

Problem: My system froze in the middle of running MEMMAKER.

Some systems get stuck when MEMMAKER tries to reboot it—for example, when MEMMAKER tries out a technique that is not right for your system. If you see that your system is stuck, turn the power off and on to force it to restart. MEMMAKER always resumes control when the computer restarts. When MEMMAKER returns, it suggests that you choose the option Try again with conservative settings. You should choose this option unless you want to try the more aggressive settings (and risk freezing up) a second time.

When MEMMAKER is ready for its final reboot using the new settings for your system, it asks you to watch for any error messages during booting.

6. Watch the boot messages carefully. You can press the Pause key during booting to give yourself time to read messages. (Press any other key to resume after a pause.)

After the final reboot, you have the chance to tell MEMMAKER whether it worked.

7. If you answer Yes, MEMMAKER displays a table comparing your old memory use with your new. You see exactly how much conventional memory you're saving with the new settings.

8. Press Enter to accept the new settings and exit MEMMAKER. You also can press Esc at that time to undo MEMMAKER's work and restore your original system.

9. Enter **MEM** /**C** /**P** to see what programs are now loaded into upper memory.

A typical listing looks like this:

```
Modules using memory below 1 MB:
Name      Total         =   Conventional  +  Upper Memory
----      ------            ------           ------
MSDOS     16,621  (16K)     16,621  (16K)       0  (0K)
HIMEM      1,152   (1K)      1,152   (1K)       0  (0K)
EMM386     3,120   (3K)      3,120   (3K)       0  (0K)
COMMAND    3,680   (4K)      3,680   (4K)       0  (0K)
SETVER       816   (1K)          0   (0K)     816  (1K)
ANSI       4,240   (4K)          0   (0K)   4,240  (4K)
MOUSE     13,616  (13K)          0   (0K)  13,616 (13K)
GRAB      23,744  (23K)          0   (0K)  23,744 (23K)
GRAPHICS   5,872   (6K)          0   (0K)   5,872  (6K)
SMARTDRV  27,264  (27K)          0   (0K)  27,264 (27K)
Free     713,952 (697K)    630,656 (616K)  83,296 (81K)
```

```
Memory Summary:

Type of Memory        Total      =      Used      +       Free
_____        _____       _____      _____
Conventional      655,360   (640K)      24,704    (24K)    630,656   (616K)
Upper             158,848   (155K)      75,552    (74K)     83,296    (81K)
Reserved          234,366  (2,29K)     234,368   (229K)          0     (0K)
Extended (XMS)  3,145,728 (3,072K)   1,429,504 (1,396K)  1,716,224 (1,676K)
_____        _____       _____      _____

Total Memory    4,194,304 (4,096K)   1,764,128 (1,723K)  2,430,176 (2,373K)
Total under 1 MB  814,208   (795K)     100,256    (98K)    713,952   (697K)
Largest executable program size                           630,560   (616K)
Largest free upper memory block                            67,952    (66K)
MS-DOS is resident in the high memory area.
```

Compare these figures with those in Chapter 29, which are taken from the same system before running MEMMAKER. The available space in conventional memory has jumped to 616KB. The programs currently in conventional memory—a small portion of DOS, HIMMEM, EMM386, and COMMAND—can't be run from upper memory. All other drivers and TSRs have been loaded in upper memory, and there's still quite a bit of space left up there (81KB).

Looking Ahead: If you need more upper memory space than MEMMAKER creates for you in the express setup, Chapter 44, "Squeezing Even More Out of Memory," explains how to do a custom setup.

MEMMAKER's Changes

A typical CONFIG.SYS after being modified by MEMMAKER looks something like the following:

```
DEVICE=C:\DOS\HIMEM.SYS
DOS=HIGH
DEVICE=C:\DOS\EMM386.EXE   NOEMS
BUFFERS=15,0
FILES=50
DOS=UMB
DEVICEHIGH  /L:1,12048 =C:\DOS\SETVER.EXE
STACKS=9,256
DEVICEHIGH  /L:1,9072 =C:\DOS\ANSI.SYS
SHELL=C:\DOS\COMMAND.COM  C:\DOS\  /E:1024  /P
```

The following sections explain what MEMMAKER did to this file.

Loading HIMEM and EMM386

MEMMAKER inserted commands in CONFIG.SYS to load HIMEM and EMM386. If the HIMEM command already exists in the file, MEMMAKER doesn't change it, although it may move the HIMEM command to a better position. The EMM386 command in this example has a NOEMS ("no expanded memory") switch to request upper memory support without expanded memory support. If you tell MEMMAKER that you need expanded memory, it uses the RAM switch instead of NOEMS to request both types of support.

> **Tip:** If you specify neither RAM nor NOEMS, EMM386 provides expanded memory support, but not upper memory support, as explained in Chapter 29.

> **Looking Ahead:** The EMM386 command includes a number of parameters and switches to control such things as the minimum and maximum amounts of expanded memory. The Command Reference explains these advanced options.

The *DOS* Command

Notice the file contains two DOS commands. The DOS=HIGH command loads DOS into the HMA, as explained in Chapter 29. MEMMAKER deals only with upper memory and does not insert DOS=HIGH in CONFIG.SYS. You must put the command there yourself, before or after running MEMMAKER.

The DOS=UMB command makes the upper memory blocks available to DOS. MEMMAKER inserts this command in CONFIG.SYS for you. You also can use DOS=HIGH,UMB.

The *DEVICEHIGH* Commands

MEMMAKER converts most other DEVICE commands into DEVICEHIGH commands to load device drivers into upper memory blocks. The /L switches tell DOS exactly where to load the program in upper memory to make the best use of the available space.

The AUTOEXEC.BAT File

After you run MEMMAKER, your AUTOEXEC.BAT file will resemble the following, although yours will contain adaptations of the commands that you inserted before running MEMMAKER:

```
PATH C:\DOS;C:\WINWORD;C:\NDW;C:\WINDOWS;C:\HSG
CD MOUSE
LH /L:1,20304 MOUSE BON
CD \HSG
LH /L:1,23744 GRAB
CD \
PROMPT $P$G
SET TEMP=C:\WINDOWS\TEMP
LH /L:1,20560 GRAPHICS
```

MEMMAKER converts almost every command that loads a TSR into an LH (Loadhigh) command, which loads the TSR into upper memory. The /L and /S switches control exactly where the program is loaded.

The LH command isn't limited to AUTOEXEC.BAT. You can use it any time you load a TSR. For example, suppose that you decide to use VSAFE for a while by entering a VSAFE command at the command prompt. Type **LH VSAFE** to load VSAFE into upper memory instead of conventional memory. You can use LH to load DOSKEY, PRINT, and any other TSR into upper memory.

Note: It's possible to get the message Packed File Corrupt after running MEMMAKER. Don't worry, nothing is terribly wrong and the solution is simple. See the Problem Solver in the section titled "Loading DOS into the HMA" in Chapter 29.

Note: The /L switch helps to squeeze programs into tight spaces in upper memory. MEMMAKER may also insert a /S switch with the /L switch. These switches are quite complicated, and you can freeze up your system by using them incorrectly. Fortunately, you don't need them. If the space is available, the LH command will load a program into upper memory just fine without /L and /S. If not, DOS ignores the LH and loads the program into conventional memory.

If you decide to add TSRs to AUTOEXEC.BAT and drivers to CONFIG.SYS, you can insert the LH and DEVICEHIGH commands yourself. If one or more of the new programs don't fit into upper memory and are loaded into conventional memory (which you can tell from MEM /C /P), MEMMAKER may be able to squeeze them in. You can rerun MEMMAKER as many times as necessary, as you continue to change your system's configuration.

Undoing MEMMAKER

If you have programs that no longer work after letting MEMMAKER reconfigure your system, you can return to your former configuration with this command:

```
MEMMAKER /UNDO
```

You still can make use of upper memory by following these steps:

1. Insert commands to load HIMEM and EMM386 in CONFIG.SYS. (Use the NOEMS switch on the EMM386 command if you don't want expanded memory support; otherwise, use the RAM switch.)

2. Insert the DOS=UMB command.

3. Change all other DEVICE commands into DEVICEHIGH commands. (Don't try to use the /L or /S switches.)

4. In AUTOEXEC.BAT, insert LH in front of any command that loads a TSR. (Don't try to use the /L or /S switches.)

If you still have problems with one or more programs, change one DEVICEHIGH or LH command at a time to load that driver or TSR into conventional memory. Reboot after each change and see if that driver or TSR makes a difference. Eventually you should locate the program that is causing the problem. You might want to talk to its manufacturer about getting an updated version that's compatible with upper memory.

On Your Own

If you optimized your PC's memory during this chapter, you don't need to do it again. Just make sure you know how to run MEMMAKER or use the LH and DEVICEHIGH commands, in case you add new drivers and TSRs to your system.

31

Caching the Drives

Introduction

Other than upgrading your hardware, the single best thing you can do to speed up your system is to cache your drives.

About Caching

A *disk cache* (pronounced "cash") is a memory area reserved for holding data that DOS reads from or writes to a disk. The buffers that you learned about in Chapter 21, "Configuring Your System," provide a simple form of caching. SmartDrive, the disk-caching program provided with DOS and Windows, does more sophisticated caching than buffers do.

Note: SmartDrive requires extended memory. You may want to skip to Chapter 32, "RAM Drives," if you don't have extended memory.

Moving data around in memory is much faster than accessing a disk drive. Disk caching may be the best way to improve your system's performance because it dramatically reduces the number of disk accesses.

This chapter shows you how to use SmartDrive. You will learn how to:

- Understand what SmartDrive does
- Install SmartDrive on your computer
- Decide whether you need to use double-buffering with SmartDrive
- Specify which drives should be cached and the level of caching
- Force SmartDrive to write delayed writes
- Interpret SmartDrive's messages

Warning: Do not use SmartDrive if you are already using third-party drive caching software such as NCache. Caching your disk data twice will slow your system down and could lead to data loss. If you have installed third-party software, skip this chapter.

What Does SmartDrive Do?

SmartDrive positions itself between DOS and your disk drives so that it can process read and write requests from DOS. (See Figure 31.1.) When DOS tries to read data from a disk, SmartDrive intervenes. If the desired data is already in the cache, SmartDrive passes the data to DOS from the cache, saving the time it would normally take to read from the disk. If the desired data is not in the cache, DOS goes ahead and gets it from the disk.

Figure 31.1.
SmartDrive, DOS, and
your drives.

SmartDrive copies the data into its cache to make it available for future reads and writes. If the cache is full, the new data replaces some existing data in the cache. One of the things that makes SmartDrive so smart is that it knows how to identify and replace the least used data in its cache.

> **Note:** No data is actually lost by replacing data in the cache. The data still exists on disk and can be reread again, if needed. Replacing cached data simply means that it will take longer to access that data the next time it is requested. That's why SmartDrive replaces the data that is least likely to be needed again.

SmartDrive also can do write caching. When DOS tries to write data to a disk, SmartDrive intervenes and writes it in the cache instead, replacing some existing cache data if necessary. SmartDrive writes the data to the disk from the cache.

SmartDrive does not necessarily pass the written data to the disk immediately. It holds the write cached data until you are not typing, printing, or accessing a disk. During a pause in this kind of activity, SmartDrive writes out cached data, writing the oldest portions first. This *delayed writing* improves system performance by giving priority to reading and processing; writing takes place when the system isn't busy.

SmartDrive writes from the cache to the disk at several other times:

- When data has been delayed for five seconds.
- When SmartDrive needs room in the cache for new data.
- When you press Ctrl+Alt+Del. (SmartDrive immediately writes all delayed data before the system reboots.)
- When you enter the command SMARTDRV /C. (The /C switch forces SmartDrive to write all delayed data.)

DOS 6.2 has added one more write time to this list: whenever the command prompt is displayed. This additional write time guarantees that when a program terminates, its data is written before any other program can be started up. It also decreases the likelihood that you will turn off the computer before delayed writes are written.

What if the system crashes with some delayed writes pending? You lose any data that was in the cache but had not yet been written to the drive. If you're word processing, you might lose part of a document or some changes that you made to a document that was already saved. If you're updating a database or spreadsheet, you might lose some of the updates. You'll have to decide for yourself if the increased speed is worth the risk of data loss in case of a system crash.

A partial data loss can be especially difficult to cope with if you're working on a transaction-based application in which a new transaction updates several types of records. For example, in an accounts receivable system, a new item might be posted to a customer record, an invoice due record, and an accounting record. If the system goes down when only one of those records has been updated, the records are out of synch and can cause problems. For this reason, I recommend that you disable write caching when using a transaction-based application that involves multiple updates.

You also don't want to use delayed write caching with a floppy drive. Losing data by changing the disk before DOS writes the delayed data is easy to do.

Caches and Buffers

Recall that DOS also stores read/write data in its own data buffers. Even with a caching program, DOS needs to keep some information in its buffers. Because DOS looks through all the buffers before going to SmartDrive, you will save time if you drastically reduce the number of buffers in a cached system. If you use SmartDrive, you should change your CONFIG.SYS BUFFERS command to use only 10 to 15 buffers.

Starting SmartDrive

You must load an extended memory manager such as HIMEM.SYS before you start SmartDrive. SmartDrive loads into upper memory if possible. (You don't need to specify LH.) If you load HIMEM from CONFIG.SYS when you boot, you can start up SmartDrive now.

> **Note:** You can't load SmartDrive twice. If it's already loaded on your PC, entering the SMARTDRV command a second time does no harm. It merely displays the startup messages without loading SmartDrive.

1. To start SmartDrive, enter the following command:

    SMARTDRV

    The exact response you get depends on your system configuration. A typical response looks like this:

    ```
    Microsoft SMARTDrive Disk Cache version 5.01
    Copyright 1991,1993 Microsoft Corp.

    Cache size: 1,048,576 bytes
    Cache size while running Windows: 262,144 bytes
    ```

```
           Disk Caching Status
  drive   read cache   write cache   buffering
  ------------------------------------------------


  A:       yes           no            no
  B:       yes           no            no
  C:       yes           yes           no


  Write behind data will be committed before command prompt returns.


  For help, type "Smartdrv /?".
```

The cache sizes are default values that depend on the amount of extended memory in your system. The values shown here are for a system with 1MB to 2MB of extended memory available when SmartDrive is loaded. SmartDrive gives up some extended memory when Windows starts because Windows works best when it has at least 2MB of extended memory available.

Hard drives (including hard drives linked by INTERLNK) are both read cached and write cached by default. Floppy drives are read cached but not write cached by default. CD-ROM drives are read cached with DOS 6.2 and 6.22, but not with earlier versions; they can't be write cached, of course. Other types of drives, such as RAM, network, and compressed drives, cannot be cached.

Note: SmartDrive can cache a CD-ROM drive only if MSCDEX (DOS's CD-ROM driver) is loaded before you load SmartDrive. If you load both SmartDrive and the CD-ROM driver (such as MSCDEX) from AUTOEXEC.BAT, be sure the MSCDEX command comes first.

SmartDrive's Double-Buffering Feature

Some drives do not function well with SMARTDRV's normal setup. For such drives, SMARTDRV needs to use a double-buffering technique that slows it down a bit but protects your system from data loss. Double-buffering creates a small buffer in conventional memory and passes all data through it on its way to the cache; this prevents address mixups that can occur when certain types of drives try to access the cache directly.

Note: Drives with bus-mastering controllers that do not conform to Microsoft's Virtual DMA Services (VDS) standard need double-buffering. This group includes some SCSI drives, some ESDI drives, and a few other types of drives.

Don't install double-buffering automatically; some drives won't function with double-buffering in place. You can use the SMARTDRV disk caching status to see whether your system needs to use double-buffering. If any line in the buffering column says yes, you definitely need double-buffering. If a line says –, SMARTDRV is unable to determine whether you need it, and you should install it for safety's sake. Install it by loading the SMARTDRV.EXE driver from CONFIG.SYS with a command like the following:

```
DEVICEHIGH=C:\DOS\SMARTDRV.SYS DOUBLE_BUFFER
```

You still need the SMARTDRV command to start up SMARTDRV, as explained earlier.

Choosing the Caching for Drives

In the SmartDrive command, you can choose the type of caching for each drive instead of settling for the defaults. Adding a *drive* parameter to the SmartDrive command turns on read caching, but not write caching, for the indicated drive. *Drive+* turns on both read and write caching for that drive. *Drive–* turns off all caching for the drive. You can't turn on write caching without read caching.

Suppose that you have two floppy drives (A and B) and three hard drives (C, D, and E). If you want drives B and C to be read cached only, drives A and E to have read and write caching, and drive D to have no caching, you would use the following command to start SmartDrive:

```
C:\DOS\SMARTDRV A+ B C D- E+
```

You get a response similar to the following:

```
Microsoft SMARTDrive Disk Cache version 5.01
Copyright 1991,1993 Microsoft Corp.

Cache size: 1,048,576 bytes
Cache size while running Windows: 262,144 bytes

             Disk Caching Status
  drive   read cache   write cache   buffering
  ---------------------------------------------

  A:       yes          yes           no
  B:       yes          no            no
  C:       yes          no            no
  D:       no           no            no
  E:       yes          yes           no

Write behind data will be committed before command prompt returns.
For help, type Smartdrv /?.
```

Because you want default caching for drives B and E, you could leave those drive names out and start SmartDrive with the following command:

```
C:\DOS\SMARTDRV A+ C D-
```

Changing Drive Caching after SmartDrive is Installed

After SmartDrive is loaded, you can use the SmartDrive command to change the type of caching for a drive. To turn off all caching for drive A, for example, enter the following:

SMARTDRV A-

This command changes caching for drive A only; other drives are not affected. Try turning off write caching for your boot drive and disabling all caching for drive A:

1. Make a note of your current drive caching status so that you can restore it. (Hint: You could press PrintScreen to print SmartDrive's startup message.)

2. Enter **SMARTDRV A- C**

   In the resulting message, the Disk Caching Status table might look something like this:

   ```
            Disk Caching Status
   drive   read cache   write cache   buffering
   -------------------------------------------

   B:       yes          no            no
   C:       yes          no            no
   ```

3. Enter a SMARTDRV command to restore your former disk caching status.

SmartDrive Results

Use the SmartDrive command with the /s (for status) switch to see the caching status of your drives. The report contains more information than SmartDrive's startup messages. Try it now:

1. Enter **SMARTDRV /S**.

The response may appear as follows:

```
Microsoft SMARTDrive Disk Cache version 5.01
Copyright 1991,1993 Microsoft Corp.

Room for 128 elements of 8,192 bytes each
There have been 5,727 cache hits
        and 3,111 cache misses

Cache size: 1,048,576 bytes
Cache size while running Windows: 262,144 bytes
```

```
           Disk Caching Status
    drive   read cache   write cache   buffering
    ---------------------------------------------

    A:      yes          no            no
    B:      yes          no            no
    C:      yes          yes           no

    For help, type Smartdrv /?.
```

As you see, SmartDrive not only tells you the caching setup, but also the latest caching statistics. A *hit* means that SmartDrive found data in the cache and avoided a disk access; a *miss* is the other way around. A hit ratio of 5,700 to 3,100 is pretty good; SmartDrive has prevented a majority of this system's disk accesses so far. Your hit ratio could reach 9 to 1 or higher, depending on the kind of processing you're doing.

Forcing SmartDrive to Write Cached Data

The /C switch forces SmartDrive to write out any write-cached data. Try it now:

1. Enter **SMARTDRV /C**.

   You might see the hard drive light flash if SmartDrive writes cached data.

If you are write caching and have not upgraded to DOS 6.2, always use this command before you park your heads and turn off your system. If you are write caching a floppy drive, use it before you remove a disk.

Sometimes your system hangs up, and you can't enter the SMARTDRV /C command. If you can reboot with Ctrl+Alt+Del, you have no problem. SmartDrive senses this key combination and writes out all data immediately. If you can't reboot with Ctrl+Alt+Del, you have to use a reset button or turn off the system. When that happens, delayed data is lost.

Windows and SmartDrive

Both DOS and Windows come with a SMARTDRV.EXE file. If you have Windows 3.1 or later, compare the date/time stamp on SMARTDRV.EXE in your Windows directory with that of the same file in your DOS directory. Use the latest version of SmartDrive.

Note: You cannot start SmartDrive when Windows is running. It must be loaded before you start up Windows.

Controlling the Cache Size

The SmartDrive command includes parameters to control the cache size, as you can see in Figure 31.2. You can specify the initial size of the cache and the minimum size when Windows is running. If you run only Windows, give it free reign to manage the cache by specifying a 0 minimum size. However, if you go back and forth between Windows and DOS, save some cache space so that not all of your DOS data will be eliminated when you start up Windows. Table 31.1 shows the default cache sizes.

Table 31.1. Default cache sizes.

Extended Memory	Initial Cache	Smallest Cache (when Windows is running)
Up to 1MB	All extended memory	0 (no cache)
Up to 2MB	1MB	256KB
Up to 4MB	1MB	512KB
Up to 6MB	2MB	1MB
6MB or more	2MB	2MB

The bigger the cache is, the better; so, give it as much space as you can. For example, if you have three megabytes of extended memory that is not used for any other purpose, you could install SmartDrive with the following command:

```
SMARTDRV 3072 512
```

If the specified cache doesn't fit in extended memory, SmartDrive adjusts the cache size to fit the available space.

Tailoring SMARTDRV

The /E, /L, and /B parameters can be used to adjust the balance between SmartDrive efficiency and the amount of memory space it uses. These parameters can be used only on the command that starts up SmartDrive; you can't change these features after SmartDrive is loaded.

If you need SmartDrive to use less conventional memory space, set /E to less than the maximum 8KB. This setting causes SmartDrive to move less data at the same time, hence slowing it down; but, it also uses that much less space in conventional memory. You also can cut down on conventional memory usage by reducing the size of the read-ahead buffer, which is 16KB by default. If you usually access large sequential files that are not fragmented, increasing the size of the read-ahead buffer can increase your hit ratio, if you can afford the space in conventional memory.

SMARTDRV

Starts or configures SmartDrive, which creates a disk cache in extended memory; writes cached data.

Syntax:

SMARTDRV [*drive*[+ | –]...] [/E:*element*] [*InitCache*] [*WinCache*] [/B:*buffer*] [/L]

Parameters and Switches:

none	If SmartDrive is not already loaded, loads the TSR portion of the program with default values. Displays caching status of drives.
drive	Identifies a disk drive for which you want to control caching (do not follow the drive letter with a colon).
+ ¦ –	+ enables both read and write caching for drive; – disables both read and write caching for drive. See Notes for defaults.
/E:*element*	Specifies in bytes the amount of the cache that SmartDrive moves at one time; may be 1024, 2048, 4096, or 8192; the default is 8192. The larger the value, the more conventional memory SmartDrive uses.
InitCache	Specifies in kilobytes the size of the cache when SmartDrive starts and Windows is not running. The default depends on your system's memory.
WinCache	Specifies in kilobytes the smallest size to which SmartDrive reduces the cache when Windows starts. The default depends on your system's memory (see Notes).
/B:*buffer*	Specifies the size of the read-ahead buffer; may be any multiple of element; the default is 16KB.
/L	Prevents SmartDrive from automatically loading into upper memory, even if there are UMBs available.
/S	Displays additional information about the status of SmartDrive.

Figure 31.2. SMARTDRV *command summary.*

Ordinarily, SmartDrive loads itself into upper memory if possible. In some systems, especially when double-buffering is needed, loading SmartDrive in upper memory could actually slow it down. If you're using double-buffering and upper memory blocks, and if you have the room in conventional memory, try the /L switch to see whether it affords even more performance improvement.

> **Note:** The SMARTDRV command includes several additional switches. /R clears the contents of the cache. /Q suppresses messages when SmartDrive loads, whereas /V requests full messages. /S causes additional status information to be displayed.
>
> With DOS 6.2 only, /F writes delayed data each time a command ends and the command prompt returns, whereas /N does not. /F is the default; use the /F switch to restore the default setting after using /N. /U tells SmartDrive not to load the CD-ROM caching module when loading the rest of the program; this saves a little memory space. /X disables all write caching on all drives.
>
> All these switches are explained in detail in the Command Reference.

Measuring SmartDrive's Performance with SMARTMON

DOS 6.2 includes a Windows utility called SMARTMON that displays SmartDrive's performance and lets you adjust your SmartDrive configuration on the fly. Figure 31.3 shows the window that opens when you start up SmartMon. This window by default always stays on top of your other applications so that you can monitor your cache performance as you do other work.

Figure 31.3.
SmartDrive Monitor
window.

The Cache Memory control group shows you the size of the cache, as well as the size that Windows can reduce it to. These numbers can't be changed in the SmartMon window. You must adjust the SMARTDRV command and reboot in order to change the cache size. The Commit button forces SmartDrive to write all delayed data; it is equivalent to the SMARTDRV /C command. The Reset button clears the cache and is equivalent to the SMARTDRV /R command.

The Drive Controls group lets you turn caching on and off for your various drives. The Cache Hit Rate graph samples your cache hit ratio every so often (every 500 msec by default) and displays the result as a bar graph. You can see the graph moving and changing as you perform various activities in Windows.

The status bar shows two messages. On the left, it tells you whether the cache is idle or busy. On the right, it shows the average hit ratio. Both of these messages are adjusted as you continue to work on your applications.

> **Tip:** The SmartMon window might block out important messages from the application you are currently using. You may wonder why your application is just sitting there, when in fact there may be an error message you cannot see. If you don't like SmartMon's window always on top, pull down the control menu and click Always On Top to deselect this feature. Or you can minimize it. The minimized icon continues to show the percentage of cache hits, switching from showing the current percentage (in red on a color monitor) to showing the average (in black).

Logging

You can record a log of cache activity by clicking the Log button. A typical log file looks like this:

ticks,	total,	hits,
71276556,	193252,	145827
71278369,	193276,	145847
71280401,	193291,	145859
71303799,	193795,	146341

The first column shows when the measurement was taken, expressed as the number of clock ticks since you booted, the second shows the total number of disk accesses at that time, and the third shows the number of cache hits at that time.

By default, the log is stored in \DOS\SMARTMON.LOG. If that file already exists, the new logging data is added to the end of the file; if it doesn't exist, SmartMon creates it. Logging continues until you click the Stop Log button or until a time limit is reached. The default time limit is two hours; if you log cache activity for two hours, the log file will be enormous.

SmartMon Options

The Options button opens the dialog box shown in Figure 31.4. The Cache Hit Rate group controls how often SmartMon measures the hit rate and how often it displays the result. The Log File group determines the filespec and the time limit for logging. The Drive Control group determines whether any changes you make in the Drive Controls group are automatically recorded in your SMARTDRV command in AUTOEXEC.BAT. You could also specify another file for them to be saved in.

Figure 31.4.
SmartDrive Monitor
Options dialog box.

Disk Buffers

You can't use SmartDrive without extended memory. But if you don't have extended memory, you can set aside some disk-buffering space in conventional memory to speed up disk access a little. Disk buffers are somewhat like a dumb cache.

DOS always reads from disk into a buffer before transferring the data to the program that requested it. Similarly, DOS always writes data from a program into a buffer before writing it to disk. If only one buffer is allocated, it must be used for all reads and writes, so it's unlikely that the data DOS wants next is already present in the buffer. However, if 30 buffers are allocated, the probability of finding desired data in a buffer goes up dramatically. If 99 buffers are allocated (the maximum), the probability goes up even more, but generally, system performance goes down because DOS spends more time searching the buffers for desired data than it would take to access the disk.

If you also allocate some look-ahead buffers, DOS will read additional sectors when a program requests one. This practice increases the probability of finding the next desired sector in a buffer when unfragmented files are read sequentially.

Figure 31.5 shows the syntax of the BUFFERS command, which belongs in CONFIG.SYS. If you don't specify BUFFERS, DOS allocates a default number of buffers based on your system configuration. It's a sure bet that the default number is not what you want. If you are using a more intelligent caching system, such as SmartDrive, cut the number of buffers back to about 15. If not, use Table 31.2 to determine the number of buffers to allocate. Include some look-ahead buffers if you tend to read unfragmented files in sequential order.

BUFFERS

Specifies the number of disk buffers.

Syntax:

```
BUFFERS=read-write[,look-ahead]
```

Parameters:

  read-write   Specifies the number of read-write buffers. Range is 1 to 99. Default (if the BUFFERS command is omitted) depends on your system configuration.
  look-ahead   Specifies the number of look-ahead buffers. Range is 0 to 8. Default is 0. If either *read-write* or *look-ahead* is outside its range, *look-ahead* defaults to 0.

Figure 31.5. *BUFFERS configuration command summary.*

Table 31.2. Buffer allocation recommendations.

Disk Size	Number of Buffers
< 40MB	20
40MB to 79MB	30
80MB to 119MB	40
<TE>> 119MB	50

Generally, the buffers are located wherever DOS is located. If DOS is loaded into the HMA, the buffers also are created there. However, if the HMA doesn't have enough room for all the buffers you have requested, they are all moved to conventional memory. You can usually fit around 40 buffers along with DOS in the HMA; each buffer is the size of a sector, half a kilobyte. If conventional memory is tight in your system, it pays to experiment with the number of buffers you can get away with in the HMA. Use the MEM /D /P command to determine whether they are in conventional memory. You'll see the line BUFFERS=nn in the report. If the size of that area is only 512 bytes, the buffers are in the HMA.

On Your Own

Use the following items to adapt your system for SmartDrive:

1. If you have decided to use SmartDrive but have not added it to your AUTOEXEC.BAT file, do so now.

2. If AUTOEXEC.BAT already contains a SMARTDRV command, fine-tune the command to control drive caching and cache size.

3. If your system needs double-buffering and your CONFIG.SYS does not load SMARTDRV.EXE, add the necessary command to CONFIG.SYS now.

4. Enter a command to write all delayed data.

5. Display a SmartDrive caching report.

6. If you have Windows, start up SMARTMON and measure the effectiveness of various caching options. (You might have to reboot several times to try out various cache sizes.)

32

RAM Drives

Introduction

If you have some memory to spare, you can speed up your system by creating a RAM drive. However, this chapter explains why you may not want to do that.

About RAM Drives

If you create a RAM drive in memory every time you boot, and copy the programs and files that you use most often into that drive, those programs will run much faster because they aren't slowed down by the drive hardware. However, you also can give yourself some major headaches. First, you must remember to copy any modified data from the RAM drive to a real drive before shutting down. Second, if your system goes down, you lose any modified data that is not saved on a real drive.

Therefore, most people don't keep any important data on a RAM drive. The most common use of a RAM drive is to hold the temporary files created by DOS, DOS Shell, Windows, and applications such as Microsoft Word. Windows writes and deletes numerous temporary files, and letting it use a RAM drive can make a significant difference in system performance.

When you keep your temporary files on a RAM drive, if the system goes down, the temporary files disappear as RAM is cleared. When you keep temporary files on a hard drive, they get abandoned on the drive and you can find them there later. Which way is better? When the system goes down, you stand to lose any work that you have done but not yet saved. If you're working with an application that creates readable temporary files, you might be able to locate the correct temporary file and rescue work from it that might otherwise be lost. But if they're not readable, the temporary files don't do you any good and waste space on your hard drive. You'll have to decide for yourself, from a knowledge of your own applications, whether you want to keep the temp files on your hard disk, where you can rescue data from them, or keep them in a RAM drive, where they will be deleted automatically.

Byte for byte, you get more performance improvement out of a SmartDrive cache than a RAM drive. Don't create a RAM drive in extended memory, unless you have enough room to satisfy all other program needs and to let SmartDrive have a cache of at least 2MB.

This chapter shows you how to create and use a RAM drive. You will learn how to:

- Create a RAM drive during booting
- Instruct DOS and Windows to store their temporary files on the RAM drive

Deciding Where to Place the RAM Drive

In a modern PC with 4MB or more of extended memory, you'll most likely place the RAM drive in extended memory. If you have real expanded memory rather than the simulated type supplied by EMM386, and it isn't being used for any other purpose, it makes a perfect RAM drive. Otherwise, place it in extended memory. Don't let it be put in conventional memory; that space is too valuable.

Setting Up a RAM Drive

You set up a RAM drive by loading the RAMDRIVE.SYS driver from CONFIG.SYS. To use all default settings, you don't have to include any parameters or switches in the command. However, that would create the RAM drive in conventional memory. Use /A to place the RAM drive in expanded memory, or /E to place it in extended memory.

If you have plenty of extended memory (at least 4MB), try creating a RAM drive:

1. Make an insurance copy of CONFIG.SYS as CONFIG.SAV.

2. Open CONFIG.SYS for editing with an ASCII text editor.

3. Insert the following command. (If you load HIMEM from CONFIG.SYS, place this command somewhere after the HIMEM and DOS=HIGH commands.)

   `DEVICEHIGH=C:\DOS\RAMDRIVE.SYS /E`

4. Reboot and watch the messages during booting. (Hint: You can give yourself time to read a message by pressing the Pause key during booting. Press any other key to continue booting.)

   The RAMDRIVE startup message looks something like this:

   ```
   Microsoft RAMDrive version 3.07 virtual disk D:
       Disk size: 64k
       Sector size: 512 bytes
       Allocation unit: 1 sectors
       Directory entries: 64
   ```

   In this example, DOS assigned the drive name D to the RAM drive.

The default RAM drive is 64KB, has 512-byte sectors, and has room for 64 entries in the root directory. A 64KB RAM drive is fine for some applications, such as Microsoft Word for DOS, but it doesn't do you much good with Windows. Windows needs at least 2MB for its temporary files; if 2MB is not available, Windows Print Manager mixes up the data in your print jobs and your printouts will be useless.

You can include a size parameter on the RAMDRIVE.SYS command to control the size of the RAM drive. Specify the amount in kilobytes, from 4KB to 32,767KB (32MB). The following command sets up a 2MB RAM drive in extended memory. It will have 512-byte sectors and 64 entries in the root directory:

`DEVICEHIGH=C:\DOS\RAMDRIVE.SYS 2048 /E`

Even though the RAM drive is created in extended memory, the RAMDRIVE program is loaded into conventional memory, taking up about 5KB. If your system is set up to use UMBs, you can load it into upper memory by using DEVICEHIGH instead of DEVICE.

Note: If RAMDRIVE doesn't fit into upper memory simply by using the DEVICEHIGH command, MEMMAKER might be able to squeeze it in. Add the DEVICE command to CONFIG.SYS, then run MEMMAKER to reconfigure upper memory.

Using the RAM Drive

Ordinarily, you use a RAM drive just like any other drive. A RAM drive shows up in drive lists such as those for DOS Shell, MSAV, and BACKUP. Figure 32.1 shows how the RAM drive looks on the Shell screen. You can assign a volume label to the drive with LABEL, copy or move files to and from the drive, delete files from the drive, and so on. DriveSpace or DoubleSpace will even compress it.

Figure 32.1.
A RAM drive in the Shell.

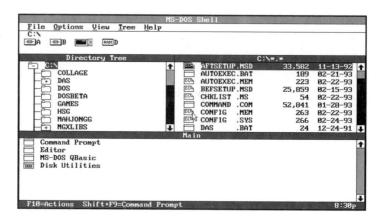

However, you shouldn't do the following to a RAM drive:

• Don't format it; it's ready to go as soon as it's created.

• Don't cache it; because it's in memory, a RAM drive already is running at maximum speed. Caching actually slows it down.

• Don't scan it for viruses; it will be scanned when memory is scanned.

• Don't defragment a RAM drive; fragmentation is not a problem when read-write heads are not involved.

- Don't use DISKCOPY and DISKCOMP with a RAM drive; they pertain to floppy disks only.
- Don't protect it with Delete Sentry or deletion-tracking if you are using it solely for temporary files.

Directing Temporary Files to a RAM Drive

DOS and Windows use a variable named TEMP to tell them where to place their temporary files. You set the TEMP variable with a SET command, as follows:

```
SET TEMP=D:\
```

This command establishes the root directory of drive D as the place to write temporary files. You place this command in AUTOEXEC.BAT to establish the RAM drive as the location for temporary files.

Overriding the Default Parameters

The RAMDRIVE command includes several parameters that let you control the size of the drive, its sector size, the number of directory entries, and so on. (See Figure 32.2.)

RAMDRIVE.SYS

Uses an area of your computer's random-access memory (RAM) to simulate a hard disk drive.

Syntax:

```
DEVICE[HIGH]=[path]RAMDRIVE.SYS [DiskSize [SectorSize [NumEntries]]] [/E ¦ /A]
```

Parameters and Switches:

path	Identifies the location of the RAMDRIVE.SYS file. The default is the root directory of the boot drive.
DiskSize	Specifies, in kilobytes, how much memory to use for the RAM drive. Valid values are 4 to 32767, or available memory, whichever is smaller. The default is 64.

SectorSize	Specifies disk sector size in bytes. May be 128, 256, or 512 (the default). Microsoft recommends that you use 512. If you include *SectorSize*, you must include *DiskSize*.
NumEntries	Specifies the number of files and directories you can create in the root directory of the RAM drive. May be 2 to 1024; the limit you specify is rounded up to the nearest sector size boundary. The default is 64. If you include *NumEntries*, you also must include *SectorSize* and *DiskSize*.
/E	Creates the RAM drive in extended memory. Be sure to use this switch (or /A) to keep the RAM drive out of conventional memory.
/A	Creates the RAM drive in expanded memory.

Figure 32.2.   RAMDRIVE *command summary.*

To create a 3MB RAM drive in extended memory, you would enter the following command:

```
DEVICE=C:\DOS\RAMDRIVE.SYS 3072 /E
```

To allow up to 256 entries in the root directory, you would need to add both the sector size and the number of entries to the command:

```
DEVICE=C:\DOS\RAMDRIVE.SYS 3072 /E 512 256
```

On Your Own

If you have sufficient memory space and would like to try a RAM drive, the following items guide you in setting it up:

1. Insert the command to load RAMDRIVE.SYS in CONFIG.SYS.

2. Reboot and determine what drive letter DOS assigned to the RAM drive.

3. If you want to use your RAM drive for temporary files, insert the necessary SET command in AUTOEXEC.BAT.

4. Reboot to put the SET command into effect.

How Data Compression Works

Data compression schemes take advantage of the fact that most files include a lot of repetition. A data compression program stores a string of bytes only the first time it appears in a file. It replaces other appearances of that string with a code pointing to the first occurrence. The code takes a lot less space than the data it replaces, so the entire file is smaller and there's more room on the drive for other files.

For example, if the first sentence in this section were the first sentence in a file, DriveSpace or DoubleSpace would replace each string marked by brackets below:

```
Data compression schemes [ta]ke advan[ta]ge of t[he] fact [th][at] most fil[es] includ[e]
[a ]lot[ of ]repeti[ti][on].
```

Even from this short example, you can see that as you continue on in a file, more strings and longer strings can be replaced with codes. When DOS needs to read the file, DriveSpace or DoubleSpace decompresses it, replacing each code with the appropriate string of characters. The same data compression scheme is used by DOS 6's backup programs.

DriveSpace or DoubleSpace also eliminates a lot of wasted space by allocating file space in sectors instead of clusters. A small file on a compressed hard disk uses up only 512 bytes instead of 2,048 or more. This savings alone can be 1.5KB for each of the small files on a disk.

The Compressed Drive

When you run DriveSpace or DoubleSpace for the first time, it creates a compressed drive, which looks and behaves like a real drive but is not really a drive. It actually is a file, called a *Compressed Volume File* (CVF), residing on the real drive, known as the *host* drive. The CVF is a system, hidden, and read-only file in the root directory of the host drive.

The CVF and the host drive each have their own drive letters, assigned by DriveSpace or DoubleSpace. Suppose that after you compress drive C, DriveSpace or DoubleSpace assigns the letter C to the CVF and K to the host drive. Any time you write a file to drive C, DriveSpace or DoubleSpace compresses the file and puts it into the CVF. When you read a file from drive C, DriveSpace or DoubleSpace decompresses it for you. You can still read and write uncompressed files to any free space left on drive K, if you wish.

Some files can't be compressed; DriveSpace or DoubleSpace stores them on the host drive. These include the Windows swap file, IO.SYS, MSDOS.SYS, DBLSPACE.BIN, and some DriveSpace/DoubleSpace files. These files usually are system or hidden files, so your host drive looks empty if you list nonsystem and nonhidden files. They are all important files, however; don't delete any of them.

Compressing an Existing Drive

When you compress an existing drive with DriveSpace or DoubleSpace, it creates the CVF on the host, compresses all or most of the files on the drive, and stores them in the CVF. Then, DriveSpace or DoubleSpace assigns the host's original drive letter to the CVF and a new letter to the host. This drive assignment process, called *mounting* the DriveSpace/DoubleSpace drive, makes the data in the CVF available through its original drive letter. Therefore, you don't have to change the batch programs, commands, macros, and path names that you're accustomed to using.

DriveSpace or DoubleSpace must remount the compressed drive(s) every time you boot or reboot. You see messages from DriveSpace or DoubleSpace during the boot process. Sometimes, after you use a DriveSpace/DoubleSpace function like DEFRAGMENT, you see a message saying that DriveSpace or DoubleSpace is remounting the drive.

Setting Up DriveSpace or DoubleSpace

The first time you run DriveSpace or DoubleSpace, it performs the following tasks:

- Sets up the core program, DRVSPACE.BIN or DBLSPACE.BIN, to be loaded every time you boot
- Installs DriveSpace's or DoubleSpace's system files in the root directory of your boot drive (regardless of which drive is being compressed)
- Installs a command in CONFIG.SYS to position the core program properly in memory
- In DOS 6.2 or 6.22, runs SCANDISK on the drive to be compressed

All this takes place automatically the first time you compress a drive on your hard disk. You can't set up DriveSpace or DoubleSpace without compressing at least one hard drive.

> **Warning:** It's very important to scan a drive for problems before compressing it. Otherwise, there's a small chance that you could lose the data on the drive. Be sure to step up to DOS 6.2 or 6.22 before installing one of these data compression utilities. DOS 6.0 does not include SCANDISK and does not check the drive first. If you installed DoubleSpace before stepping up to DOS 6.2 or 6.22, back up all the data on the drive (very important) and run SCANDISK on the drive immediately.

Don't install DriveSpace or DoubleSpace if you're already using some other type of data compression system. You may need to uninstall the other product from your system first if you want to convert to DOS's data compression utility. If you need to convert from another compression product to DriveSpace or DoubleSpace, read section 7 of the README.TXT file included in your DOS directory.

Getting Started

Don't install DoubleSpace or DriveSpace just to see what it's like. The installation process takes a long time, and there's a small chance that the installation could fail and you could have to restore your drive from your backups. And, if you decide not to continue using compression, the process of removing DoubleSpace or DriveSpace can take longer than installing it and can also lead to failure.

You can't compress drives that are too full. DriveSpace and DoubleSpace need a minimum of 1.2MB of free space to compress the boot drive. If you don't have that much space available, move some files to floppy disks to free up the space. After the drive is compressed, there will be room to move them back to the drive.

If you're sure that you want to install data compression, this section guides you through the process. The following procedure shows you how to install DOS 6.22's DriveSpace. If you're installing DoubleSpace from DOS 6.2, the process is nearly identical except that you use the command DBLSPACE instead of DRVSPACE. (Reminder: Don't install DoubleSpace from DOS 6.0.)

How to Compress Your First Hard Drive

1. Back up the drive to be compressed.

2. Exit all programs and get to the primary DOS command prompt.

3. Enter **DRVSPACE**.

   The Welcome screen appears.

4. Choose Continue.

   DriveSpace asks if you want to use Express or Custom Setup.

5. Choose Express Setup.

   DriveSpace gives you one more chance to change your mind.

6. Press C to continue.

   DriveSpace displays a progress screen while it compresses the drive.

If you want to install DriveSpace or DoubleSpace at this time, follow the steps below:

1. Bring your backups up to date. Make sure that you have backup copies of every important file on the drive to be compressed.

2. Exit from Windows or DOS Shell.

3. If you normally use a network, connect to the network and its drives so that DriveSpace knows about any drive letters you usually use.

4. Enter the following command:

   DRVSPACE

   DriveSpace greets you with a Welcome screen and then displays the Setup selection screen. (See Figure 34.1.) Express setup does most of the work for you, automatically compressing drive C.

Figure 34.1.
The Setup selection screen.

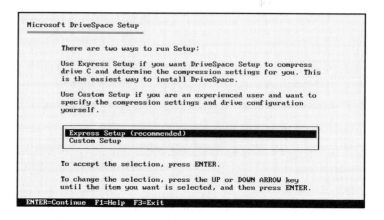

```
Microsoft DriveSpace Setup

          There are two ways to run Setup:

          Use Express Setup if you want DriveSpace Setup to compress
          drive C and determine the compression settings for you. This
          is the easiest way to install DriveSpace.

          Use Custom Setup if you are an experienced user and want to
          specify the compression settings and drive configuration
          yourself.

          ┌────────────────────────────────────────────────┐
          │ Express Setup (recommended)                      │
          │ Custom Setup                                     │
          └────────────────────────────────────────────────┘

          To accept the selection, press ENTER.

          To change the selection, press the UP or DOWN ARROW key
          until the item you want is selected, and then press ENTER.

 ENTER=Continue  F1=Help  F3=Exit
```

Note: If you don't want to compress drive C, you must choose Custom Setup to compress another drive. This exercise uses the Express Setup. If you choose Custom Setup, you must choose a drive to be compressed before going on to step 5.

When you choose Express Setup, a message warns you to back up the drive before continuing. You can choose to exit (so you can back up your drive) or Continue.

5. If you really backed up your files in step 1, choose Continue.

   The next screen gives you a last chance to back out.

6. Press C to continue.

Note: If you have a disk in drive A, DriveSpace asks you to remove it so that DriveSpace can reboot your system as necessary.

During Compression

As DriveSpace compresses your drive, it displays a number of messages and activity screens. All you can do is watch (or go away). Even turning off the power to your computer doesn't cancel the compression process. When you turn the power back on, DoubleSpace picks up where it left off.

First, DriveSpace runs SCANDISK on your drive; be sure to fix any problems it finds. Then, it begins the actual compression. It keeps you informed about the progress of the compression—what file is currently being compressed, the time left and estimated finish time, the percentage of the drive not yet compressed, and so on.

After compression is done, DriveSpace runs its own DEFRAG function on the compressed drive and adjusts the size of the CVF. When finished, DriveSpace displays a final screen that contrasts the original free space on the drive and the new amount; it also shows you the compression ratio and the time that it took to compress the drive. After you have read the screen, press Enter and DriveSpace will reboot your computer again. Setup is now complete, and your new compressed drive is ready to be used.

Note: A 2 to 1 compression ratio means that, for every 2 bytes in the uncompressed file, only 1 byte was needed in the compressed file.

Tip: Run MEMMAKER after installing DriveSpace or DoubleSpace to move the compression software out of conventional memory.

Compressing Additional Drives

How to Compress Additional Drives

1. Back up the drive to be compressed.

2. Exit all programs and get to the DOS primary command prompt.

3. Enter **DRVSPACE**.

   The DriveSpace window opens.

4. Choose Compress Existing Drive.

   DriveSpace displays a list of your uncompressed drives.

5. Select the drive you want to compress and press Enter.

   DriveSpace displays the default compression settings.

6. To accept the settings, press Enter.

   DriveSpace gives you one more chance to change your mind.

7. Press C to continue.

   DriveSpace displays a progress screen while it compresses the drive.

After the first time you run DriveSpace or DoubleSpace and compress a drive, entering the DRVSPACE or DBLSPACE commands brings up a screen like the one in Figure 34.2. This screen lists all the compressed drives on your system and provides you with some pull-down menus for performing various DriveSpace functions. To compress another drive, choose the Compress menu by clicking Compress in the menu bar, or by pressing Alt+C. (See Figure 34.3.) Then, choose the Existing Drive option.

Figure 34.2.
Selecting a compressed drive.

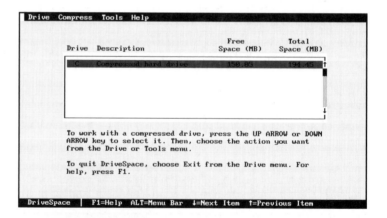

Figure 34.3.
The Compress menu.

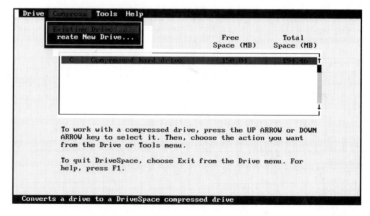

Selecting a Drive

The screen in Figure 34.4 appears after you select Compress Existing Drive. The directions on the screen tell you how to select a drive for compression. The drives listed are the only ones you can compress. You might wonder why your other drives are not on the list. You can't compress network drives or CD-ROM drives. You can't compress drives that are too full. DriveSpace needs a minimum of 1.2MB of free space to compress the boot drive; other drives must have about 665KB or more free.

Figure 34.4.
Selecting a drive
to compress.

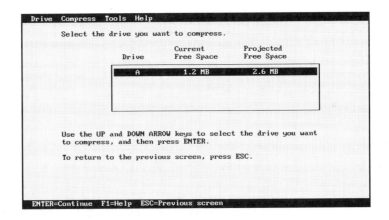

Tip: To compress a drive that doesn't have enough free space, move some of the files to another drive or a floppy disk temporarily. After compression, there should be enough free space on the compressed drive to move them back.

Figure 34.5 shows the screen that appears next. By default, DriveSpace keeps 2MB of uncompressed space on the host drive to hold files that can't be compressed, but you can request a different amount. You also can change the drive letter that DriveSpace assigns to the host drive. However, if you don't have a strong reason to do otherwise, you should accept the settings that DriveSpace suggests for both parameters. Follow the directions on the screen to change or accept the settings shown.

Note: Although this screen mentions a new drive, it really is the original host drive with a new drive letter.

After you agree to the compression settings, DriveSpace warns you to back up your files then gives you one more chance to exit. If you choose to continue, DriveSpace compresses the drive in much the same manner that it compressed your first one.

Figure 34.5.
Compression settings.

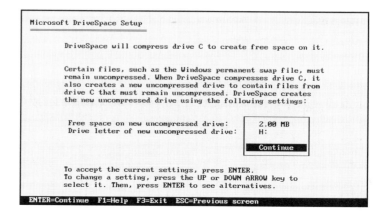

```
 Microsoft DriveSpace Setup
 ─────────────────────────

       DriveSpace will compress drive C to create free space on it.

       Certain files, such as the Windows permanent swap file, must
       remain uncompressed. When DriveSpace compresses drive C, it
       also creates a new uncompressed drive to contain files from
       drive C that must remain uncompressed. DriveSpace creates
       the new uncompressed drive using the following settings:

       Free space on new uncompressed drive:    ┌──────────────┐
       Drive letter of new uncompressed drive:  │  2.00 MB     │
                                                 │  H:          │
                                                 │ ┌──────────┐ │
                                                 │ │ Continue │ │
                                                 │ └──────────┘ │
                                                 └──────────────┘
       To accept the current settings, press ENTER.
       To change a setting, press the UP or DOWN ARROW key to
       select it. Then, press ENTER to see alternatives.

 ENTER=Continue   F1=Help   F3=Exit   ESC=Previous screen
```

Interacting with Other DOS Utilities

DriveSpace and DoubleSpace are designed to interact smoothly with other DOS utilities. You will see your new compressed drive, as well as the host drive, in drive lists such as DOS Shell's, for example. You can create new directories on the compressed drive, move and copy files to and from the drive, delete and undelete files, and so on.

You cannot format a compressed drive with the FORMAT command; you must use DriveSpace's or DoubleSpace's own formatting function (see the Command Reference).

You can, and should, back up your compressed drive on a regular basis, just like any other drive. You can scan and repair a compressed drive with SCANDISK and check it for viruses with the Microsoft Anti-Virus programs. You can cache the host drive with SmartDrive; the compressed drive will be cached too.

Because it's organized differently, fragmentation does not slow down a compressed drive as it does an uncompressed one. A compressed drive does not need to be defragmented on a regular basis. What's more, you can't run DEFRAG on a compressed drive. If you want to defragment a compressed drive, you must use the compression software's own defragmentation function, which is explained in Chapter 33, "Defragmenter."

Converting from DoubleSpace to DriveSpace

As mentioned earlier in this chapter, if you are using DOS 6.0's DoubleSpace, you should upgrade it immediately. If you have upgraded to DOS 6.22, you should convert to DriveSpace. You might or might not have the conversion software in your system, depending on which version of DOS 6.22 you installed. If you don't have the conversion software, you can order it from Microsoft—see your DOS *User's Guide* for instructions.

> **Note:** If the `DRVSPACE` command doesn't start the conversion process, as explained in the following paragraph, you don't have the conversion software.

Once you have the conversion software, enter the `DRVSPACE` command and follow the directions on the screen. DriveSpace converts all the DoubleSpace volumes it can find to its own format. Be sure to back up your files first! The process could tie up your computer for three hours or more. You might want to start it at the end of the work day.

After you make the conversion, you'll find that the DBLSPACE program files still exist on your drive. Don't delete them; DriveSpace needs them for two functions:

- To restore files that were backed up using Backup's compression option while you were using DoubleSpace
- To access files that were compressed by DoubleSpace on removable volumes (such as floppy disks) that were not present in the system when you converted to DriveSpace

SCANDISK also needs the DoubleSpace program files to scan and repair any DoubleSpace volumes that you have not converted to DriveSpace.

Working with Compressed Drives

DriveSpace's menus provide several commands for managing your compressed drives. You can, for example, check the directory and FAT structure and view statistical information about the compressed drive. Choose Drive Info to display information about the drive, such as the amount of free space available on the drive. Most of the information in the display is self-explanatory, but the Space free figure needs some explanation.

When an uncompressed drive has 2MB of free space, there are 2,097,152 unused bytes on the drive, and you can add just that amount of data to it—no more. The situation isn't quite the same for a compressed drive, where DriveSpace or DoubleSpace estimates the amount of uncompressed data that can be added to the drive. If DriveSpace or DoubleSpace reports 20.13MB of free space, for example, it calculates that you can add files that total 20.13MB when uncompressed. This estimate assumes that the new files will compress according to the estimated compression ratio for the drive, which is not always true. You may be able to add only 15MB of program files to the drive, because they usually can't achieve a 1.8 to 1 compression ratio. On the other hand, you probably could add 50MB or more of graphic files to the drive because their compression ratios tend to be greater than 10 to 1.

DIR and Compressed Drives

Other DOS programs coordinate with DriveSpace or DoubleSpace when you use them on compressed drives. For example, if you use DIR on a compressed drive, it reports the estimated amount of space available on the drive, not the actual amount. You can add a /CH switch to the DIR command to display compression ratios for the files. The report looks something like the following:

```
Volume in drive D has no label
Volume Serial Number is 13EF-2218

Directory of D:\FRENCH
.               <DIR>        02-21-94   12:28p
..              <DIR>        02-21-94   12:28p
CHKLIST  MS         54 12-22-94    3:58p   4.0 to 1.0
FLASHCRD BAS     30,896 05-05-94   10:42a   2.3 to 1.0
FLASHCRD EXE     91,084 05-05-94   10:43a   1.3 to 1.0
VOCAB    BAS     31,265 05-05-94   11:42a   2.2 to 1.0
VOCAB    EXE     91,242 05-05-94   11:42a   1.3 to 1.0
WORK     BAS     13,054 05-04-94   11:59a   1.6 to 1.0
                    1.4 to 1.0 average compression ratio
         8 file(s)     257,595 bytes
                    21,102,592 bytes free
```

In this example, CHKLIST.MS has a 4 to 1 compression ratio; whereas the two EXE files have only a 1.3 to 1 compression ratio. The average compression ratio for this listing (not the entire drive) is 1.4 to 1.

> **Note:** DIR /CH also works with drives compressed by third-party programs such as Stacker. DIR's /C switch also displays compression ratios, but don't use it. The /CH switch produces more accurate results.

The file sizes shown in the listing are the uncompressed sizes, so that you can see how much space a file would take if loaded in memory, or moved or copied to an uncompressed drive.

Additional DriveSpace and DoubleSpace Features

This discussion has scratched only the surface of DriveSpace and DoubleSpace, just enough so that you can create and use a compressed volume. When you're ready for more, you may want to learn how to do the following:

- Create and use empty compressed volumes
- Create and use compressed volumes on floppy disks
- Defragment a compressed volume

- Delete a compressed volume
- Reformat a compressed volume
- List information about all your drives, not just the compressed ones
- Change the estimated compression ratio for a compressed drive
- Change the size of a compressed drive
- Uncompress a drive

All of these functions are explained in Chapter 45, "A Second Look at DrvSpace and DblSpace."

On Your Own

If you installed DriveSpace or DoubleSpace during this chapter, make sure that you know how to do the following things:

- Display the reports produced by DriveSpace or DoubleSpace
- Include compression information in your directory listings

35

Putting It All Together before Advancing

Introduction

HIMEM, SmartDrive, VSAFE, UNDELETE, BACKUP... How do you bring the various DOS facilities together into a coordinated system to optimize your work and protect your data?

A Look at CONFIG.SYS and AUTOEXEC.BAT

As you add more and more facilities to your PC, your CONFIG.SYS and AUTOEXEC.BAT can become pretty disorganized. You might be adding commands to them yourself, and your various application installation programs might add more commands without your knowledge. It pays to take a look at CONFIG.SYS and AUTOEXEC.BAT every once in a while to make sure that you understand all the commands that are in there, that they're in a good sequence, and that no out-dated commands are left over from software that you have removed. If you're using upper memory, make sure that as many commands as possible have been adapted for upper memory. If not, rerun MEMMAKER to adapt them.

This chapter looks at two sample systems: a smaller 286-based system that uses extended memory, but not upper memory; and a larger Pentium-based system, complete with CD-ROM drive. Your system might fall somewhere between these two, or it might have even more bells and whistles than our Pentium example, but the examples shown here should help you in analyzing your own startup files.

The questions to ask yourself as you read this chapter are:

- Am I taking full advantage of my PC's memory capacity?
- Do my startup files contain any unnecessary commands?
- Are the commands in the best order?
- Are there any commands that I don't understand?

Setting Up a 286 System

A well-designed CONFIG.SYS for a 286 computer with 2MB of extended memory might look something like the following:

```
DEVICE=C:\DOS\HIMEM.SYS
DOS=HIGH
DEVICE=C:\DOS\SETVER.EXE
DEVICE=C:\DOS\ANSI.SYS
BUFFERS=15
FILES=50
STACKS=9,256
```

The commands used in this example are as follows:

- `DEVICE=C:\DOS\HIMEM.SYS` loads the extended memory driver first, so that it can provide extended memory support to other programs.

- `DOS=HIGH` loads DOS into the HMA before any other program tries to load in that location.

- `DEVICE=C:\DOS\SETVER.EXE` was installed by DOS's SETUP program. You may or may not need SETVER in your system.

- `DEVICE=C:\DOS\ANSI.SYS` loads the ANSI.SYS driver because this system uses at least one program that requires that driver. (Your system might also require it. But, if you haven't used it so far, you probably don't need it.)

- `Buffers=15` requests only 15 buffers because this system uses SmartDrive, which is loaded from AUTOEXEC.BAT as you'll see next.

- `Files=50` requests 50 file handles because this system uses a program that needs them. You may be able to get away with fewer file handles; retain whatever `Files` command is in your current CONFIG.SYS.

- `Stacks=9,256` was installed by some program that needed it and should not be modified or deleted (unless you don't have that program any more).

An AUTOEXEC.BAT file for the same system might contain at least the following commands. (Your AUTOEXEC.BAT file probably contains additional commands to set up TSRs and other features with which you want to work.)

```
@ECHO OFF
PATH C:\DOS;C:\WINDOWS;C:\
DOSKEY
SMARTDRV
UNDELETE /LOAD
VSAFE
MSAV
```

The purpose of each of these commands is as follows:

- `@ECHO OFF` turns off command echoing for the remainder of the commands in the file.

- `PATH` establishes the program search path for this system.

- `DOSKEY` sets up the DOSKEY program to record command history.

- `SMARTDRV` loads the SmartDrive caching system with a 1MB cache (by default) in extended memory and with default caching parameters.

- `UNDELETE /LOAD` loads the Delete Sentry deletion protection system according to its current configuration.

- `VSAFE` loads the VSAFE virus monitor.

- `MSAV` starts up the Microsoft Anti-Virus scanner so that the system is scanned for viruses right away. This command opens the first dialog box only; the user must complete the scan and terminate MSAV.

Setting Up a 386 or Higher System

With a 386, 486, or Pentium-based PC, you can use EMM386 to provide upper memory support and to load drivers and TSRs into UMBs. Running MEMMAKER will set up EMM386 for you. A typical CONFIG.SYS adapted by MEMMAKER might look like the following:

```
DEVICE=C:\DOS\HIMEM.SYS
DEVICE=C:\DOS\EMM386.EXE NOEMS
BUFFERS=15,0
FILES=50
DOS=UMB
LASTDRIVE=E
FCBS=4,0
DOS=HIGH
STACKS=9,256
DEVICEHIGH /L:1,5888 =C:\DOS\RAMDRIVE.SYS 3092 /E
DEVICEHIGH /L:1,12048 =C:\DOS\SETVER.EXE
DEVICEHIGH /L:1,6696 =C:\DEV\MTMCDS.SYS /D:MSCD001 /P:300 /A:0
DEVICEHIGH /L:1,9072 =C:\DOS\ANSI.SYS
DEVICEHIGH=C:\DOS\DRVSPACE.SYS /MOVE
```

These commands accomplish the following tasks:

- `DEVICE=C:\DOS\HIMEM.SYS` loads the extended memory driver before any other program is loaded.

- `DEVICE=C:\DOS\EMM386.EXE` provides upper memory support; the NOEMS switch suppresses this program's expanded memory facility. (Without the switch, EMM386.SYS converts 256KB of extended memory into expanded memory.)

- `Buffers=15` requests only 15 buffers because this system uses SmartDrive, which is loaded from AUTOEXEC.BAT as you'll see next.

- `Files=50` requests 50 file handles because this system uses a program that needs them. You may be able to get away with fewer file handles; retain whatever `Files` command is in your current CONFIG.SYS.

- `DOS=UMB` makes the upper memory blocks available to DOS.

- `LASTDRIVE=E` reserves space for five drive names.

- `FCBS=4,0` reserves space to track four files by the FCB method.

- `DOS=HIGH` loads DOS into the HMA.

- `Stacks=9,256` was installed by some program that needed it and should not be modified or deleted (unless you don't have that program any more).

- `DEVICEHIGH...RAMDRIVE.SYS` creates a 3MB RAM drive in extended memory. This RAM drive is used for DOS and Windows temporary files, as you can determine from the AUTOEXEC.BAT file.

- `DEVICEHIGH...SETVER.EXE` loads the SETVER program into upper memory.

- `DEVICEHIGH...MTMCDS.SYS` loads a device driver for the CD-ROM drive. (This driver came with the CD-ROM drive and is not part of DOS.)
- `DEVICEHIGH...ANSI.SYS` loads ANSI.SYS into upper memory.
- `DEVICEHIGH...DRVSPACE.SYS` was inserted by DriveSpace when it was installed.

The commands that load RAMDRIVE.SYS, SETVER.EXE, MTMCDS.SYS, ANSI.SYS, and DRVSPACE.SYS have been modified by MEMMAKER to load these drivers in specific locations in upper memory.

The AUTOEXEC.BAT file for this system might look like the following:

```
@ECHO OFF
PATH C:\DOS;C:\WINDOWS;C:\

REM Direct temporary files to the RAM drive:
SET TEMP=D:\

SMARTDRV 4096
LH /L:1,53968 UNDELETE /LOAD
LH /L:1,63088 VSAFE
LH /L:1,65288 SHARE
LH /L:1,52700 MSCDEX /D:MSCD001
```

These commands accomplish the following tasks:

- `@ECHO OFF` suppresses command echoing for the rest of the commands in the file.
- `PATH` establishes the program search path.
- `SET`, as the comment indicates, directs the DOS and Windows temporary files to RAM drive D. Because the RAM drive is 3MB, it has plenty of room for the Windows temporary files. In this 16MB system, there also is plenty of extended memory left for a 4MB SmartDrive cache.
- `SMARTDRV` loads the SmartDrive caching system with a 4MB cache in extended memory and with default caching parameters.
- `LH...UNDELETE` loads the UNDELETE TSR in upper memory.
- `LH...VSAFE` loads the antivirus monitor in upper memory.
- `LH...SHARE` loads a program called SHARE, which keeps applications that are running simultaneously in Windows from contending for the same files. SHARE is included in your DOS package and it's a good idea to load it if you run Windows most of the time.
- `LH...MSCDEX` starts up DOS's CD-ROM software.

Two more commands are executed as Windows begins. The Windows StartUp group (not shown here) loads the MWAVTSR.EXE program to support VSAFE and starts up the MWAV virus scanner so that memory and the hard drive are scanned for viruses every time the system is started up.

Daily Shutdown

You need to consider not only your startup routines, but also what you want to do before shutting down. For example, you may want to run a differential or incremental backup. If you are using SmartDrive with delayed writes in DOS 6.0, you probably should force delayed data to be written before shutting off the power. (DOS 6.2 writes all delayed data before displaying the command prompt. So, if you're careful to never shut down except at a command prompt, you don't need to flush delayed writes.)

If you use MSBACKUP, you may want to make a SHUTDOWN.BAT file that runs the backup program for you. You can use DOS Editor to create the file, which can be as simple as the following:

```
MSBACKUP DAILY.SET
```

The MSBACKUP command starts up the program and opens the first dialog box. You still have to complete the backup in the dialog boxes. When the command prompt returns, you can shut down your system.

Weekly Shutdown

Once a week, you may want to run a more extensive shutdown program in which you do a full backup, run SCANDISK, and run DEFRAG. (Be sure to run SCANDISK on all your local hard drives, including compressed drives.) If you use MSBACKUP, the batch file may appear as follows:

```
MSBACKUP DAILY.SET
SCANDISK
DEFRAG /B
```

When the MSBACKUP program opens with the DAILY setup, be sure to reset the backup type to Full to do a full backup. When MSBACKUP asks whether you want to save changes to DAILY.SET, choose No and the normal Differential or Incremental type will be restored.

Introduction to the Advanced Chapters

This chapter completes the basic portion of this book. You have learned all the DOS features you need in order to control your PC, protect its data, and recover from trouble. By now, you can accomplish all of the following tasks:

- Use DOS Shell (if you don't have a more sophisticated shell) to manage disks, directories, files, and programs

- Manage disks, directories, files, and programs at the DOS command prompt
- Protect your files by using facilities such as Delete Sentry, Backup, and Microsoft Anti-Virus
- Make better use of your PC's memory facilities by using such facilities as EMM386 and MEMMAKER
- Make better use of your hard drive by using such facilities as DEFRAG and DriveSpace

The next part of this book takes a more detailed look at many of these same facilities, examining options that can help make your system even more productive. For example, you learn how to compress a floppy drive, more ways to redirect command output, and how to set up CONFIG.SYS and AUTOEXE.BAT for multiple configurations.

You'll also learn several DOS facilities that have not yet been introduced, such as the following:

- Write your own batch programs
- Control the DOS environment
- Connect two computers via INTERLNK
- Set up your PC for international use
- Update your old BASIC programs (if you program in BASIC) to QBASIC
- Partition your hard drive with FDISK

On Your Own

Review your own CONFIG.SYS and AUTOEXEC.BAT files. You should now understand the commands in both files, why they are there, and what they accomplish.

5

Advanced DOS

36 DOS at Your Command

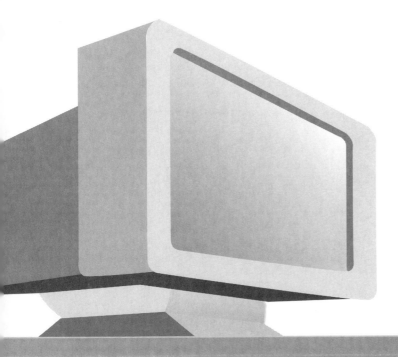

Introduction

The better you understand DOS commands, the more effective your PC work will be, whether you spend most of your time working at the command prompt or in the Shell. Better commands are more powerful commands, which in turn provide more powerful batch programs as well as DOS Shell and Windows program items, putting the full power of DOS at your command.

Getting the Most out of the Command Prompt and DOS Shell

You have learned the basics of working at the command prompt, including all the extra features that DOSKEY provides. But, there's still more that you can do to add extra zing to your commands, both at the command prompt and in DOS Shell program items. In this chapter, you'll learn how to:

- Redirect input, append redirected output to a file, and pipe output to another command
- Page through a displayed file or command output with MORE
- Use FIND to locate and display specified lines from a file or from command messages
- Sort a file with SORT
- Define DOS Shell program items with multiple commands
- Make DOS Shell program items more flexible with replaceable parameters
- Control the amount of memory that is allocated to DOS Shell program items
- Understand the contents of DOSSHELL.INI

Redirecting Input and Output

Suppose you want to print the directory listing for the root directory of your boot drive. You can redirect the output from the DIR command to the PRN device using the > symbol. Try this yourself:

1. Make sure your printer is ready to go.
2. Switch to the root directory of your boot drive.
3. Enter **DIR /A-D > PRN**. (The /A-D switch lists all files, including system and hidden files, but no subdirectories.)

   The directory should print.

> **Note:** Refer back to Table 12.1 in Chapter 12, "Working at the Command Prompt," for a list of DOS's device names.

Now suppose you want to save the directory in a file instead. You can redirect it to a filename:

1. Enter **DIR /A-D > DIRSAVE.TXT**.

   DOS creates the DIRSAVE.TXT file in the current directory. This is a plain-vanilla ASCII file that can be viewed by TYPE, edited by EDIT, printed by PRINT, and so forth.
2. To see the contents of DIRSAVE.TXT, enter **TYPE DIRSAVE.TXT**.

   DOS displays the contents of the file on your monitor.

> **Tip:** Assign the extension .TXT to files that you create by redirection. The .TXT extension is associated with EDIT in DOS Shell and with Notepad in Windows, which makes it easier to view files in those two settings.

Now suppose you want to *add* the listing of the DOS directory to DIRSAVE.TXT. You can't use the > symbol, because that *replaces* an existing file. Table 36.1 shows the complete list of redirection symbols you can use in DOS commands. The >> symbol lets you append something to the end of an existing file. Try it:

1. Enter **DIR /A-D DOS >> DIRSAVE.TXT**. (Reminder: Don't forget that you can recall and edit the former **DIR** command with DOSKEY.)

   DOS adds the new directory to the end of the file.

2. Type **DIRSAVE.TXT** to see the results.

   The file is now too long to fit on your screen, but you should be able to see that the DOS directory has been added to the end of it. You'll see how to break the file into pages in the next section.

Table 36.1. Redirection symbols.

Symbol	Description
< *source*	Redirects input to come from a specified file or device
> *destination*	Redirects output to a specified file or device; an existing file is overwritten
>> *destination*	Redirects output to a specified file or device; an existing file is appended
command1 ¦ *command2*	The output from *command1* becomes the input to command2 (piping)

> **Note:** The symbols shown in Table 36.1 are reserved by DOS and can't be used in any names you create, such as filenames or directory names.

Paging with MORE

If you wanted to examine the DIRSAVE.TXT file in detail, you could open it in EDIT and scroll around in it, making changes if you wish. But, if you just want to scan its contents, it's easier to

TYPE it. You can combine TYPE with DOS's MORE command to break the output into pages.

How to Break Command Output into Pages

1. Enter a command in the following format, where command produces the output that you want to break into pages:

   command ¦ MORE

2. DOS stores the command output in a temporary file (which could take a while if command produces a lot of output), then displays the first page on your monitor, followed by -- MORE --.

3. Each time you want to see the next page, press a key. (Press Ctrl+Break to end the display without viewing the remaining pages.)

MORE has no parameters. By default, it reads a file from the keyboard and displays it on the monitor, one page at a time. There are two ways to redirect MORE's input to a source other than the keyboard. You can redirect a file to MORE using the < input redirection symbol. Or, you can redirect the output of another command to MORE using the ¦ piping symbol. Try each of these methods:

1. Enter the command **MORE < DIRSAVE.TXT**.

   DOS displays the first page of the DIRSAVE.TXT file with the message -- MORE -- at the bottom.

2. Press any key to see the next page.

   DOS displays the second page of DIRSAVE.TXT.

3. Keep pressing a key until you have seen the entire file.

4. Enter the command **TYPE DIRSAVE.TXT ¦ MORE**.

   DOS displays the first page of DIRSAVE.TXT again.

5. Press any key to see the second page.

6. Press Ctrl+Break to kill the display and return to the command prompt.

Piping command output to MORE comes in handy with several DOS commands that don't include /P switches to page the output. Try it with ATTRIB and TREE:

1. Enter **ATTRIB DOS*.* ¦ MORE**.

   DOS lists the attributes of every file in the DOS directory, one page at a time.

2. Enter **TREE \ ¦ MORE**.

   DOS displays the directory tree for your hard drive, one page at a time.

The Temporary Pipe Files

To pipe, DOS must create two temporary files, generating filenames such as ABOABOBH and ABOABOBN. The temporary files are automatically deleted after the command is completed or interrupted with Ctrl+Break; but, if you restart the computer or power it down during the command, the temporary files may be abandoned on your hard drive. You can safely delete them.

DOS writes temporary files in the current directory unless you have specified a standard temporary directory by entering a command like this (probably in AUTOEXEC.BAT):

```
SET TEMP=path
```

If your temporary files are directed to a relatively slow drive, you could experience a long pause when piping a lot of output to another command. The pause occurs while DOS is writing the temporary files on the drive. Chapter 32, "RAM Drives," shows you how to direct temporary files to a RAM drive for speedier processing.

A piping command will fail if DOS can't write its temporary files because the drive is too full or the disk is write protected. (The SET command is explained in Chapter 43, "DOS and the Environment.")

Adding Comments to a Text File

When you're creating a text file via redirection, as with DIRSAVE.TXT, it sometimes helps to insert headings in it. Recall that a command in the form ECHO *text* displays *text* on your monitor. If you redirect ECHO *text*, the *text* is redirected to the file or device. You can use ECHO to place comments in a text file you are building via redirection. The special command ECHO. (the word ECHO terminated by a period with no space in between) displays a blank line. Redirecting ECHO. places a blank line in the file.

Let's create a new DIRSAVE.TXT with comments in it:

1. Enter the command **ECHO Root directory of drive C: > DIRSAVE.TXT**.

   DOS replaces DIRSAVE.TXT with the comment. Notice that you weren't warned when the file was replaced.

> **Warning:** The > redirection symbol will replace an existing file without warning. For safety's sake, use >> unless you're positive that you want an existing file replaced. Chapter 37, "Programming Logic in Batch Programs," shows how to test for the existence of a file and issue commands accordingly.

2. Enter the command **ECHO. >> DIRSAVE.TXT**.

   DOS adds a blank line to the end of the file.

3. Enter the command `DIR /A-D >> DIRSAVE.TXT`.

   DOS adds the directory listing to the end of the file.

4. Enter the command `ECHO. >> DIRSAVE.TXT` twice.

   DOS adds two blank lines to the end of the file.

5. Enter the command `ECHO DOS directory on drive C: >> DIRSAVE.TXT`.

   DOS appends the comment to the file.

6. Enter `ECHO. >> DIRSAVE.TXT`.

   DOS appends a blank line to the file.

7. Enter `DIR /A-D DOS >> DIRSAVE.TXT`.

   DOS appends the directory of DOS to the file.

8. Enter `TYPE DIRSAVE.TXT ¦ MORE` to see the file.

   Notice the headers and blank lines that you have inserted in the file.

What Happens When You Redirect Input and Output?

Not all input and output is affected by the redirection symbols—only input that normally comes from the keyboard, and output that normally goes to the monitor.

To be more precise, many DOS utilities request standard I/O services from DOS. When standard I/O is requested, DOS reads from and writes to a device that it calls CON (for console), which is usually defined as the keyboard and monitor.

Redirection works with any programs that request standard I/O services from DOS, which include many of the DOS utilities and perhaps some of your applications. However, many applications use their own I/O techniques, not DOS's standard ones, when communicating with the keyboard and monitor; they are not affected by redirection.

What's more, not all DOS utility input and output can be redirected. For example, the TYPE and COPY commands don't use standard input; but, because they are designed to read from a file or device, input redirection is not necessary. (TYPE's output can be redirected, though, as you have already seen.) Similarly, the PRINT command's print output can't be redirected to a file, because it does not use the standard I/O device. The only part of PRINT's output that can be redirected is the confirmation message that is normally displayed on the standard output device.

Standard Error Output

If a DOS utility encounters an error situation such as a missing file, it sends the error message not to the standard output device, but to a standard *error* output device, which DOS also displays on CON. Because redirection affects only standard output, not standard error output, error messages are not redirected. You can see the difference for yourself. Try displaying the directory listing for a nonexistent file:

1. Enter the command **DIR XXXX.XXX**.

   The response includes both types of output. The first three lines (the headers) are standard output. The last line is standard error output.

   ```
   Volume in drive C is HARD DRIVE
   Volume Serial Number is 171D-78E4
   Directory of C:\
   File not found
   ```

2. Now try redirecting the command. If you redirect it to the device named NUL, the standard output simply disappears. Enter the command **DIR XXXX.XXX > NUL**.

   All you see on the screen is `File not found`.

You might not always find this feature desirable, but knowing that it exists lets you take occasional advantage of it. For example, you could write a DOSKEY macro to tell you whether or not a file exists:

```
DOSKEY ISFILE=DIR $1 $G NUL
```

This command defines a macro named ISFILE that looks for the filespec requested in replaceable parameter 1, redirecting the standard output to nowhere. (When defining a DOSKEY macro, you must use $G to represent a > symbol.) Only the error message `File not found` will be displayed if the specified file doesn't exist. If it does exist, nothing is displayed.

> **Note:** You can redirect all keyboard input and monitor output, including both standard and error output, by redefining CON using the CTTY command, a technique that's explained in Chapter 48, "Console Control."

Just to keep you on your toes, some programs use standard output to issue error messages (CHKDSK is one), and some programs use standard error output to issue standard messages (MORE is one). These aren't just flaky decisions by the program developers, but are based on whether the messages in question are appropriately redirected when standard output is redirected. For example, if you redirect CHKDSK's output, the assumption is that you want to obtain a hard copy or a file copy for documentation purposes, and that you want error messages included in the documentation.

Redirecting Output to PostScript Printers

PostScript printers require special drivers, and DOS will not be able to print to them in their native modes. But, most of these printers can be set to emulate a standard parallel printer (such as an Epson or IBM printer) that DOS can handle, even if it can't take advantage of the printer's bells and whistles. Check your printer's documentation to find out how to make it emulate a standard parallel printer.

Using ECHO to Automate Commands

If you enter the DATE command without a new date, DATE displays the current system date and asks for a new one. You press Enter to keep the current date, as in the following example:

```
C:\>DATE
Current date is Sat 08-27-1994
Enter new date (mm-dd-yy):
```

When you just want to find out what the system date is, having to press Enter to complete the transaction can be irritating. When executed from a batch program, it can be downright inconvenient. But, you can automate the command by piping a carriage return (also known as a blank line) to it. DOS reads the carriage return from the pipe instead of the keyboard, so it doesn't wait for your response. Try it yourself:

1. Enter the command ECHO. ¦ DATE.

   DOS displays the date and automatically returns to the command prompt.

2. You can do the same thing with the TIME command. Enter ECHO. ¦ TIME.

   DOS displays the time and automatically returns to the command prompt.

This technique can also be used to automate the DEL command for deleting all the files in a directory. When you enter DEL *.*, DOS asks Are you sure (Y/N)?. You must enter a Y to proceed. You can automate the command by piping a Y to it, as in ECHO Y ¦ DEL *.*. DOS reads the Y from the pipe, instead of waiting for keyboard input, and deletes the files immediately. (Caution: don't try this at home until you're ready to delete a complete directory.)

The DOS Filters

DOS designates three of its utilities as filters—programs that read data from the standard input device, manipulate the data in some way, and write it to the standard output device. The three DOS filters are MORE, which breaks standard output into display pages; SORT, which puts lines in order; and FIND, which locates lines containing text strings. You have already learned how to use MORE. SORT and FIND are explained in this section.

What's a Line?

The three filters operate on lines of data, as delimited by carriage returns. In an ASCII file such as a batch file or CONFIG.SYS, the lines are obvious. But, many word processors store a carriage return in a file only when you press the Enter key to end a paragraph. Even though the word processor breaks paragraphs into several lines on the monitor and in print, DOS sees each paragraph as only one line. An exception to this rule is when the word processor saves a file in ASCII format instead of its native format. Then, it might insert carriage returns in each paragraph to turn the displayed line breaks into real ones. So, when applying any of the DOS filters to files created by word processors, the rule of thumb is to be sure you know in what format the file is stored.

Sorting Lines with SORT

SORT's major reason for existence used to be to sort the output of the DIR command. But, DIR's /O parameter now does a much better job of sorting directory information. SORT can still be useful on simple lists, such as an index with only one level of entries; but, for any kind of complex job, you need a more sophisticated sort program.

Figure 36.1 shows the format of the SORT command. If you just enter the word SORT with no parameters or redirection, the utility reads from the standard input device, sorts the lines, and displays them on the standard output device. In case you ever find a need to do this, the sidebar explains how to enter data from the keyboard.

SORT

Sorts ASCII data and displays results.

Format:

```
SORT [/R] [/+n] [< source] [> destination]
```

Parameters and Switches:

source	Identifies a file or device containing data you want to sort; the default is CON, which accepts input from the keyboard until you type Ctrl+Z.
destination	Identifies a file or device to which you want to send sorted data; default is CON, which displays sorted data on the screen.
/R	Reverses the sort order.
/+n	Starts sorting in column *n*; default is column 1.

Figure 36.1. SORT *command summary.*

Entering Files from CON

Most DOS utilities that read input from CON look for an individual key press such as Y or N, or for a single line terminated by the Enter key. But, the three DOS filters actually look for a complete file to be entered from CON if you don't redirect the input to a stored file. In addition, you can use CON as the source for a COPY command, which also requires a file. A file is one or more lines terminated by an end-of-file marker (hex 1A, which is depicted on the screen as ^Z).

Before EDIT, most experienced DOS users knew how to enter a file via CON, as that was a quick-and-dirty way to create a short ASCII file such as a simple batch file. It was also a character-building experience, somewhat akin to boot camp or freshman hazing, because you could work on only one line at a time and could not go back to modify or correct lines that were already entered without restarting the entire file from the top.

Now that EDIT is available, you never have to enter files via CON; but, if you haven't installed EDIT or prefer doing it the hard way, here are the instructions:

1. After you enter the MORE, SORT, FIND, or COPY command, DOS puts the cursor at the beginning of the next line and waits for you to start inputting data.

2. Type each line carefully. Inspect and correct it before pressing Enter. After you press Enter, there's no going back. (MORE and FIND process the line immediately, then wait for the next line. The result is somewhat strange and probably not what you wanted or expected.)

3. When the last line has been entered, press F6 or type Ctrl+Z and press Enter to record the end-of-file mark. (FIND and SORT require the end-of-file mark to appear at the beginning of a new line.) DOS will then process the file.

Redirecting SORT I/O

Most of the time, you redirect SORT input to a file or receive the input from a previous command via piping. Output is frequently redirected to a file or piped to another command. Try sorting the contents of the DIRSAVE.TXT file:

1. Enter **SORT < DIRSAVE.TXT ¦ MORE**.

   DOS sorts the contents of the file in alphabetical order and displays the results on your screen, one line at a time. (The result is useless in this particular case, but it gives you a chance to see what SORT does.)

> **Note:** The DOS HELP documentation indicates that you can specify an input filename without using redirection, but that's not true. You must use the < symbol to read SORT data from an input file.

To save the same output in a file called SORTDIR.TXT instead of displaying it on screen, you could enter the command `SORT < SAVEDIR.TXT > SORTDIR.TXT`.

SORT Collating Sequence

SORT's collating sequence is determined by the current code page. (Code pages are explained in Chapter 49, "Another Country Heard From.") Table 36.2 shows the collating sequence for the keys found on a 101-key keyboard using the English code page (read down the first column, then read down the second column, and so on). SORT ignores the difference between uppercase and lowercase letters.

Table 36.2. SORT collating sequence (standard English keys).

(space)	*	4	>	h	r	\
!	+	5	?	i	s	]
"	,	6	@	j	t	^
#	-	7	a	k	u	_
$	.	8	b	l	v	'
%	/	9	c	m	w	{
&	0	:	d	n	x		
'	1	;	e	o	y	}
(	2	<	f	p	z	~
)	3	=	g	q	[	

SORT Limitations

Unfortunately, SORT is severely limited in function:

- It does alphanumeric sorts only, which produces erroneous results when sorting numeric values.
- It locates the beginning of the data to be sorted strictly by position. It can't identify fields delimited by commas or tabs, the format used by many database and mail-merge files.

- Every line in the file is considered a separate record. There is no way to identify multiline records, such as a name-and-address file might contain.
- It uses all the data from the beginning column through the end of the line as the sort key. You can't limit the length of the sort key, and you can't use primary and secondary sort keys.

Why You Can't Do a Two-Key Sort

This last point bears some extra discussion, because you might think you can accomplish a two-key sort by sorting first by the secondary key and then by the primary key. But, a simple example shows why such a technique would work only by accident. Suppose that you have some name-and-address records that you want to sort by name and, for those records with identical names, by city. A sample set of records might look like this after sorting by city:

JONES	MARY	45 PINE ST	GRAND RAPIDS, MI
ADAMS	PETER	2314 FIR ST	LAS VEGAS, NV
JONES	MARY	316 LOCUST ST	PITTSBURGH, PA
ADAMS	PETER	16 FOREST RD	SILVER SPRING, MD
ADAMS	PETER	5064 ELM ST	TULSA, OK

Now, if you could sort by the name in columns 1 through 20 only, the result would be as desired. Whenever identical names were encountered, the records would retain their city order:

ADAMS	PETER	2314 FIR ST	LAS VEGAS, NV
ADAMS	PETER	16 FOREST RD	SILVER SPRING, MD
ADAMS	PETER	5064 ELM ST	TULSA, OK
JONES	MARY	45 PINE ST	GRAND RAPIDS, MI
JONES	MARY	316 LOCUST ST	PITTSBURGH, PA

But that's not what happens in fact, because SORT won't stop at column 20. It goes right on into column 21, 22, and so on, to resolve identical records. The end result sorts the records by name and, for identical names, by street address, because that's the data that starts in column 21:

ADAMS	PETER	16 FOREST RD	SILVER SPRING, MD
ADAMS	PETER	2314 FIR ST	LAS VEGAS, NV
ADAMS	PETER	5064 ELM ST	TULSA, OK
JONES	MARY	316 LOCUST ST	PITTSBURGH, PA
JONES	MARY	45 PINE ST	GRAND RAPIDS, MI

There is no way to use SORT to order these records by name first and city second.

Using Other Sort Programs

As we said at the outset, SORT will do for small, simple jobs; but, for anything complex, you need another sort program. You might already have a sort utility that will better meet your needs. All the major word processors, database managers, and spreadsheets include sort facilities, with WordPerfect's being especially full of features. Most of these sorters can be used on any file that is in the application's native format or in ASCII format.

Locating Lines with FIND

The remaining DOS filter, FIND is meant to help you locate files by searching for a particular phrase in their contents. (See Figure 36.2.) For example, you could search for files containing the phrase `Norton Utilities`.

FIND

Searches for a specific string of text in a file or files.

Format:

`FIND [/V] [/C] [/N] [/I] "string" [filespec ...]`

Parameters and Switches:

"string"	Specifies the group of characters you want to search for. The quotation marks are required.
filespec	Identifies a file to be searched.
/V	Displays all the lines not containing the specified string.
/C	Displays only a count of all the lines that contain the specified string.
/N	Includes line numbers in the display.
/I	Ignores case.

Notes:

If you omit *filespec*, FIND takes input from the DOS standard input source, usually the keyboard or a pipe.

Figure 36.2.   *FIND command summary.*

You can do a lot more with FIND. By combining its capabilities with other commands via piping, you can select only certain lines from a command's output for display. For example, you can display just the line containing the date from the DATE command, or just the line containing the amount of space left on the drive from the DIR command.

Locating Files by their Contents

Suppose that you can't remember the name of the file containing a letter about a defective compact disc. The current directory has three files that might be right: DISCLET, CDRETURN, and CDCOMP. You could find out which one includes the expression "compact disc," and the context of the expression, with a command like this:

```
C:\>FIND "compact disc" /I DISCLET CDRET CDCOMP
_____ C:\DISCLET
_____ C:\CDRET

I have just received the enclosed compact disc, opened it, and listened to it only once.
Unfortunately, it skips in several places. I am returning it to take advantage of your
"Full Replacement" guarantee. Over the last few years, I have purchased more than 100
compact discs from your service and this is the first problem I have ever encountered.

_____ C:\CDCOMP

It will be some time before I can afford a new CD ROM drive. At the present, I have two
high-density diskette drives (one of each) and a 40MB hard disk. By the time I can afford
a compact disc-style drive, maybe they'll be able to write as well as read. Wouldn't that
be great!
```

Although it looks like FIND displayed lines that don't contain "compact disc," remember that in text documents such as these, each paragraph is one line, so each paragraph that contains "compact disc" is displayed in its entirety. FIND wrapped the long paragraphs into shorter lines on the screen. You can see in this example that DISCLET does not mention "compact disc." The other two files do mention it, and it's clear which one is the desired letter. When doing a search like this, it's a good idea to include the /I switch (ignore case) so that you'll match references to "Compact disc" and "Compact Disc," as well as "compact disc."

In the following exercise, you find some .TXT files that contain the phrase "CD":

1. Switch to the DOS directory.

2. Enter **DIR *.TXT**.

   DOS displays a list of .TXT files in the directory. Use these filenames in the following command.

3. Enter **FIND /I "CD"**, followed by the filenames for the .TXT files in your DOS directory. For example, if your DOS directory contains README.TXT, COUNTRY.TXT, NETWORKS.TXT, and OS2.TXT, you would enter the command **FIND /I "CD" README.TXT COUNTRY.TXT NETWORKS.TXT OS2.TXT**.

   DOS displays any lines from the specified files that contain the phrase "CD." Such a listing could tell you which .TXT files you want to read or print.

Searching All Files for a Text String

Unfortunately, FIND does not let you use a global filespec, so it's difficult to search all the text files in a directory for a particular text string. You must type out each filespec individually, as you did in the preceding exercise, and you can't exceed the 127-character command limit. But, take heart. Chapter 37 shows you how to use a global filespec with FIND by combining it with the FOR command.

Locating Lines in Command Output

You have seen how to use FIND to display certain lines from a file. If you pipe a command's output to FIND, you can specify which lines should be displayed. The rest of the lines simply disappear. For example, suppose that you want to display the current time or date without seeing the rest of the output from an automated TIME or DATE command. You could do it by finding the line containing the word "Current." Try it yourself:

1. Enter the command **ECHO. ¦ TIME ¦ FIND "Current"**.

   DOS displays Current time is *time*. The rest of the normal TIME messages do not appear.

2. Enter **ECHO. ¦ DATE ¦ FIND "Current"**.

   DOS displays Current date is *date*. The rest of the normal DATE messages do not appear.

There are many other applications of this particular technique. Try some of these commands:

1. Enter **DIR ¦ FIND "free"** to see how much space is left on your drive.

2. Enter **CHKDSK ¦ FIND "disk space"** to see your total disk capacity.

3. Enter **MEM ¦ FIND "executable"** to see your current largest executable program size.

4. Enter **SMARTDRV /STATUS ¦ FIND "cache"** to see your current cache hits and misses. (This command causes one other line to be displayed, too. Just ignore the extra line.)

5. Enter **DOSKEY /H ¦ FIND "DIR"** to see only all the commands in your DOSKEY command history that contain the phrase DIR.

Tip: Some of these commands are handy to keep around. Consider making them into DOSKEY macros. For example, you might define a macro named ST (for System Time) this way:

```
DOSKEY ST=ECHO. $B TIME $B FIND "Current"
```

Locating Files in a Directory Listing

The `DIR` command displays files that match a global filename or that have certain attributes. But, how can you find all files created on April 1, or all files containing "RA" anywhere in their names (not just in the first two letters)? Piping DIR output to FIND can help you with these types of tasks. Try listing all files that contain "ME" anywhere in their name:

1. Make sure the DOS directory is current.

2. Enter `DIR ¦ FIND "ME"`.

   You should see entries for such files as HIMEM.SYS, MEM.EXE, MEMMAKER.EXE, and README.TXT.

> **Note:** Because FIND is normally case-sensitive, it's important to use all capitals inside the quotes when searching DIR output, unless you use /L (for lowercase) with DIR or /I (to ignore case) with FIND.

3. Try limiting the output to just .EXE files with this command `DIR *.EXE ¦ FIND "ME"`.

   You should see entries for MEM.EXE and MEMMAKER.EXE.

Expanding this command to cover an entire branch or drive creates problems because of the way that DIR usually lists its output, with the directory name on a separate line from the filename. FIND would list only the file entries and you would have no idea what directories they belong to. But, when /S is used with /B, the complete path is included with each filespec.

Try finding all the files on your hard drive that contain the letters "ME" anywhere in their names. To do this enter the command `DIR \ /S /B ¦ FIND "ME" ¦ MORE`.

   There could be a long pause while DOS creates a temporary piping file containing a listing of all the files on drive C. Then, FIND might display a long list of files. You can't see the size, time, and date information, but at least you can see where to find each file.

Working with DOS Shell

You learned in Part 2 of this book how to run programs from the Shell as well as how to define program items. In this section, you'll learn some advanced techniques for defining program items, and you'll learn how to work with DOS Shell's initialization file, DOSSHELL.INI.

Defining Program Items

Your personalized program list can make a big difference in the effectiveness of the Shell. By adding to it the items you use often, especially those that are candidates for task swapping, you'll create a convenient, flexible, and fast way to start up programs. Program items can be particularly helpful for inexperienced DOS users, as they are one of the easiest ways to start up a program, and you can make them quite flexible.

Figure 36.3 shows the two dialog boxes that you use to define a program item; the second box appears when you press the Advanced button. The Program Title and Commands are required, but everything else is optional.

Figure 36.3.
Defining a program item.

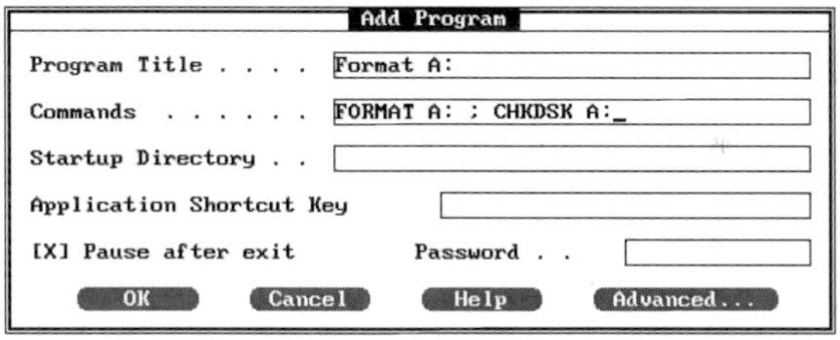

```
┌──────────────────── Add Program ─────────────────────┐
│                                                       │
│  Program Title . . . .  [Format A:                 ]  │
│                                                       │
│  Commands  . . . . . .  [FORMAT A: ; CHKDSK A:_    ]  │
│                                                       │
│  Startup Directory . .  [                          ]  │
│                                                       │
│  Application Shortcut Key  [                       ]  │
│                                                       │
│  [X] Pause after exit        Password . .  [       ]  │
│                                                       │
│    ( OK )    ( Cancel )    ( Help )    ( Advanced... ) │
└───────────────────────────────────────────────────────┘
```

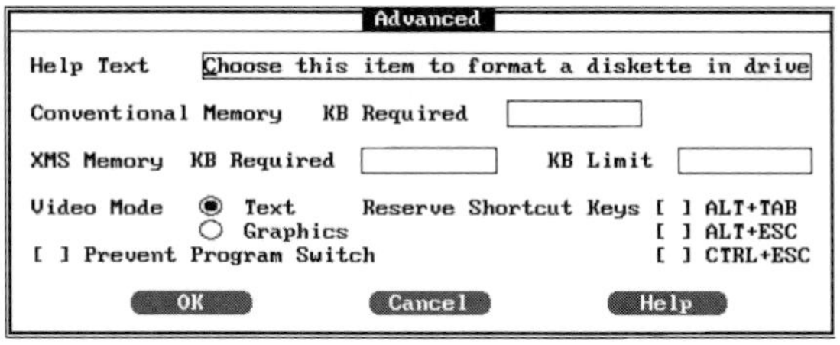

```
┌────────────────────── Advanced ──────────────────────┐
│                                                       │
│  Help Text    [Choose this item to format a diskette in drive]│
│                                                       │
│  Conventional Memory   KB Required  [          ]      │
│                                                       │
│  XMS Memory  KB Required  [       ]    KB Limit [    ] │
│                                                       │
│  Video Mode  ● Text     Reserve Shortcut Keys [ ] ALT+TAB │
│              ○ Graphics                       [ ] ALT+ESC  │
│  [ ] Prevent Program Switch                   [ ] CTRL+ESC │
│           ( OK )         ( Cancel )       ( Help )     │
└───────────────────────────────────────────────────────┘
```

Combining Two or More Commands in the Command Line

The example in the figure shows how you can combine two or more commands in the Commands field. Separate them by semicolons surrounded by spaces. In the example, the program item would execute first the FORMAT command and then the CHKDSK command. Replaceable parameters (%1 through %9) are permitted, along with any other parameters and switches that are appropriate for the command. Each individual command can have up to 127 characters, and the entire Commands field is limited to 255 characters.

If you work with the shell, try out a combined command:

1. Start DOS Shell and activate the program list.
2. Choose File, New to open the New Program Object dialog box.

3. Choose Program Item and choose OK.

   The Add Program dialog box opens.

4. For Program Title enter `Virus Scan Floppy`.

5. For Commands, enter `MSAV A: /C /R ; MORE < A:\MSAV.RPT`.

   This command scans the disk in drive A for viruses, cleans any known viruses it finds (`/C`), and issues a written report (`/R`). Then, it displays that report.

6. Choose OK to close the dialog box.

   The new program item appears in your program list.

7. Place any formatted disk in drive A.

8. Open the Virus Scan Floppy program item.

   DOS scans the floppy and displays the report.

Memory Requirements

The Advanced dialog box includes several items that specify memory requirements for the program item when task swapping is in effect. These items are used only with task swapping.

Conventional Memory KB Required specifies the minimum amount of memory that must be present for the program to be loaded; the default is 128KB. Entering a figure here does not affect how much memory is allocated to the program when it's loaded; DOS always gives it all available memory. But, it does affect how much memory is saved on disk when you switch to another task; that can be a key factor in how many tasks you can start up under the task swapper, as well as the amount of time it takes to swap tasks. If you know that a program requires only 7KB to run, by all means enter a 7 under Conventional Memory KB Required so the task swapper doesn't save the default 128KB for this program.

When you start up DOS Shell, it requests all available extended memory from HIMEM.SYS and does its own management of the extended memory facility. The two extended memory fields, XMS Memory KB Required and XMS Memory KB Limit, identify the minimum and maximum amounts of extended memory that should be allocated to a program during task swapping. The defaults are 0 and 384KB, respectively. When a task is swapped out, its extended memory is held for it (unlike conventional memory, which is swapped out to disk); no other task can access that area of extended memory. So, the amount of extended memory that is set aside for one task influences whether or not another task can be loaded. For this reason, do try to fill in these two XMS fields for all programs that require extended memory, if you can determine what their requirements are.

Video Mode affects how much memory is assigned to the video buffer. It should always be Text (even if the program uses graphics mode), unless you are using a CGA monitor and are having trouble switching to a program. The Graphics setting allocates more memory for the video buffer, which some CGA monitors need in some situations.

Task Switching Limitations

Some programs are not fully compatible with task swapping, and you can establish limitations in the Advanced dialog box. Enable Prevent Program Switch to eliminate task swapping altogether for this program item. After such an item is started, the user must exit it to return to the Shell screen or any other task. If you just need to inhibit one or more task swapping hotkeys because the program uses them for other functions, all you must do is select the pertinent keys under Reserve Shortcut Keys.

Replaceable Parameters

You can use replaceable parameters in a program item definition much as you do in a DOSKEY macro definition. Use the expressions %1 through %9 to indicate replaceable parameters. When it finds a replaceable parameter in the Commands field of the Add Program dialog box, DOS opens the dialog box shown in Figure 36.4. Here you define a dialog box to be displayed whenever the program item is opened, so that the user can enter a value for the replaceable parameter.

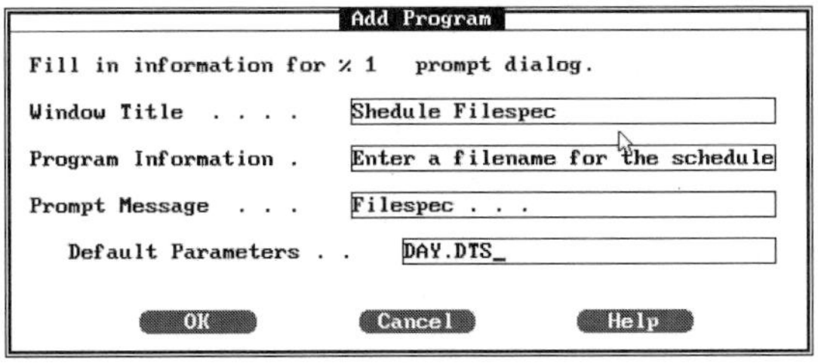

Figure 36.4.
Defining dialog box for
a program item.

```
                        ▌Add Program▐
    Fill in information for %1    prompt dialog.

    Window Title  . . . .    Shedule Filespec
    Program Information .    Enter a filename for the schedule
    Prompt Message  . . .    Filespec . . .
        Default Parameters . .    DAY.DTS_

            ▙  OK  ▟        ▙ Cancel ▟        ▙ Help ▟
```

The first three fields determine the text to be placed in the dialog box. The last field sets a default value for the replaceable parameter. In addition to a fixed default value such as the one shown in the figure, two special parameters are available: %F and %L. %F fills in as a default value the filename that is selected in the file list when the program item is opened. %L fills in the value that was used the last time the item was executed. In any case, the user can overtype the default value when executing the program item.

Try inserting a replaceable parameter in your Virus Scan Floppy program item:

1. Highlight Virus Scan Floppy in the program list.
2. Choose File, Properties.

   The Program Item Properties dialog box opens, showing your definition for Virus Scan Floppy.

3. In the Commands box, replace A: with %1 twice, so that the command reads
   ```
   MSAV %1 /C /R ; MORE < %1\MSAV.RPT.
   ```

4. Choose OK.

The Add Program dialog box changes so that you can define a dialog box for the replace-able parameter.

5. Enter **Virus Scan Floppy** in the Window Title box.

6. Enter **Enter the name of the drive to be scanned** in the Program Information box.

7. Enter **Drive Name . . .** in the Prompt Message box.

8. Enter **A:** in the Default Parameters dialog box.

9. Choose OK.

The dialog box closes and you are back at the Shell screen.

10. Open Virus Scan Floppy.

The Virus Scan Floppy dialog box opens showing **A:** as the default drive name.

11. Choose OK.

The program executes as before.

A Trip Through DOSSHELL.INI

DOSSHELL.INI is the key to the Shell setup. This very important setup file is designed to be edited by an ASCII editor such as DOS's EDIT. Figure 36.5 shows the beginning of the file (EGA/VGA version), which contains a significant warning: Don't let your editor shorten the long lines or the file will no longer be valid. Here are a few more warnings for you:

• Make a backup copy before viewing or modifying the file, just in case the editor damages it.

• If you view or modify it with a word processor, be very careful that it gets saved in ASCII mode and does not get formatted in any way.

• Don't modify any punctuation marks, especially brackets ([ ]) and braces ({ }), unless you know exactly what you're doing. They're crucial to the structure of the file.

Savestate Section

The savestate section shows the status of various Shell parameters. (See Figure 36.6.) You can see the direct relationship between parameters such as screenmode and displayhiddenfiles, and menu-controllable features such as the display mode (Options Display) and the file display options (Display Hidden/System Files).

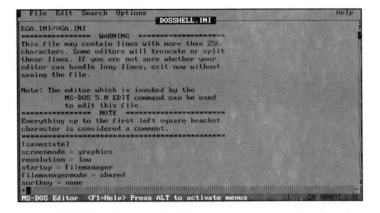

Figure 36.5.
Beginning of
DOSSHELL.INI.

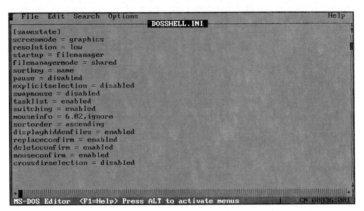

Figure 36.6.
DOS Shell
parameter status.

Programstarter Section Program List Definitions

The programstarter section contains the definitions of the items on the program list. In Figure 36.7, you can see the definition of a program group titled Manage Daily Schedule, which has the Ctrl+D hotkey and executes this command:

```
<MS Last>SCHEDULE %1
```

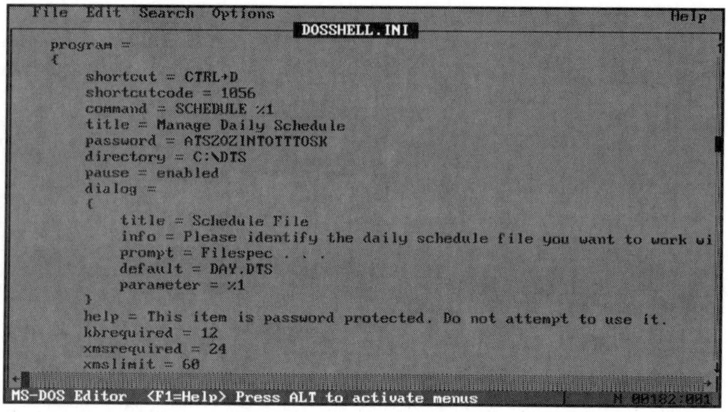

Figure 36.7.
Program group and
item definitions.

```
 File  Edit  Search  Options                                        Help
                            ┌─────────────┐
                            │ DOSSHELL.INI │
     program =
     {
          shortcut = CTRL+D
          shortcutcode = 1856
          command = SCHEDULE %1
          title = Manage Daily Schedule
          password = ATSZOZINTOTTTOSK
          directory = C:\DTS
          pause = enabled
          dialog =
          {
               title = Schedule File
               info = Please identify the daily schedule file you want to work wi
               prompt = Filespec . . .
               default = DAY.DTS
               parameter = %1
          }
          help = This item is password protected. Do not attempt to use it.
          kbrequired = 12
          xmsrequired = 24
          xmslimit = 60
 MS-DOS Editor  <F1=Help> Press ALT to activate menus              N 00182:001
```

Program Passwords in DOSSHELL.INI

This item's password was originally defined as "A Stitch in Time." DOSSHELL.INI has slightly encrypted it by moving all lowercase letters up six letters in the alphabet and converting them to uppercase so that "a" becomes "G." (Uppercase letters are unchanged.) This is not enough encryption to fool anyone who really wants to access the password. Not only that, but the encrypted version will also work as the password to access the program item. You can see why the password protection offered by DOS Shell won't fool too many people.

Color Schemes

At the end of the programstarter section, each of the color schemes is defined. (See Figure 36.8.) You can edit this section to alter the predefined color schemes or add new ones. It doesn't take too much effort to figure out what each field represents on the screen and the correct format to define a new color scheme. It usually takes a bit of trial and error to put together colors that are effective under all circumstances.

The 16 available colors are white, red, brown, green, blue, cyan, magenta, black, and bright versions of each of these (brightwhite, brightred, and so forth). Brightblack appears as gray on most screens, and brightbrown appears as yellow. White is grayish, while brightwhite is white.

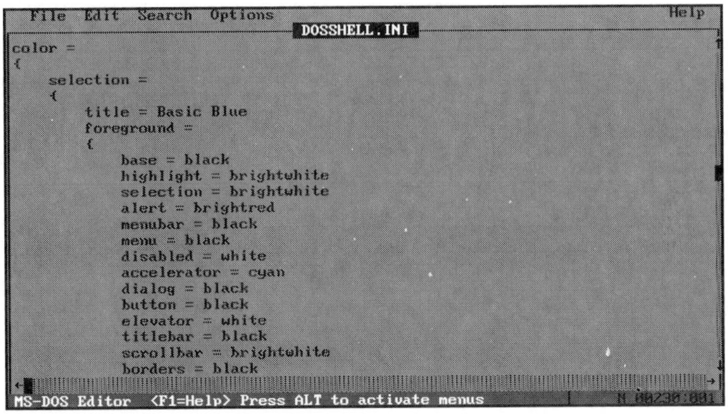

Figure 36.8.
Screen color definitions.

File Associations

The final section of DOSSHELL.INI, which shows the file associations, comes in handy for discovering file associations that you weren't aware of. When you first install DOS, you can see the associations predefined by Microsoft. (See Figure 36.9.) Later on, you might want to review this section to see what associations are currently in effect.

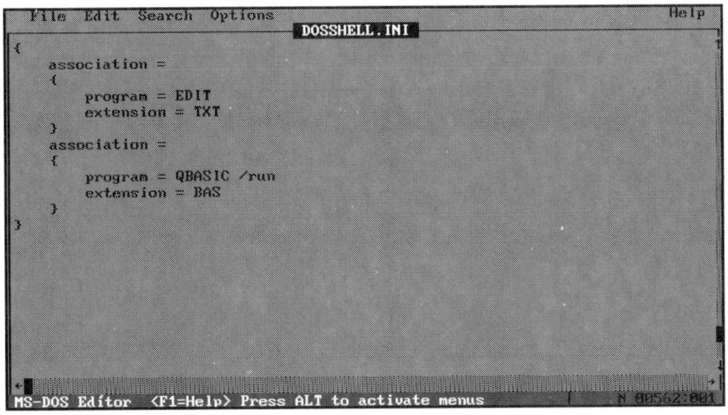

Figure 36.9.
File association definitions.

On Your Own

This chapter has shown you a number of techniques that can be used at the DOS command prompt and in DOS Shell. You can use the following items to practice these techniques on your own.

1. Create a text file containing a list of all the hidden and system files on your hard drive. Include the system date, the system time, and a descriptive comment at the beginning of the file.

2. Create a DOSKEY macro to display how much memory any given program occupies in your system. (Hint: Use FIND in conjunction with MEM /C and a replaceable parameter.)

3. Create a DOSSHELL program item called Vault File to move the currently selected file to the disk in drive A, to add its name to a file called VLIST.TXT in the root directory of your boot drive, and to sort VLIST.TXT.

4. Review your DOSSHELL.INI file. Review your program definitions and file associations.

5. Delete any program items and files that you created in this chapter that you don't want to keep. Program Items: Virus Scan Floppy, Vault File. Files: DIRSAVE.TXT, VLIST.TXT.

37 Programming Logic in Batch Programs

Introduction

You learned some elementary batch programming earlier, but DOS includes several features that give you the power to make logical decisions in your batch programs.

Introduction to Programming Logic

A batch program can include commands to link to other batch programs, read keyboard input, make decisions, and create loops for repetitive processing. For experienced programmers, the commands available in DOS will be familiar, if somewhat awkward when compared to the facilities available in BASIC or C. This chapter introduces a touch of programming logic concepts (just the basics) for readers who have never programmed before. In this chapter, you will learn how to:

- Link to other batch programs
- Test conditions and decide what to do next
- Create loops in batch programs
- Display menus and read input from the keyboard

Linking Batch Files

As batch programs get more complex, it's often convenient for one batch file to link to another. For example, suppose that you have a program named LATT.BAT that displays the attributes of all the files on drive A. Now, you're creating a batch program that overwrites drive A, and you want to list the files and their attributes first. You could copy the lines from LATT.BAT into the new batch file, or you could simply link to LATT.BAT to do the listing.

Linking offers some very real advantages:

- You save disk space by not copying the lines into another file
- If you improve LATT.BAT, the improvements carry through to all programs that link to it

The major disadvantages are that the link itself takes time, which slows down the program making the link; future modifications to LATT.BAT could make it inappropriate to some programs that link to it; and if you move, rename, or delete LATT.BAT, the link will no longer be valid.

You'll use LATT.BAT in the exercises in this section. Take the time now to create this file:

1. Create a new directory called BATCH as a child of the root directory on drive C.
2. Switch to C:\BATCH.
3. Open a new file called LATT.BAT for editing with a text editor such as EDIT.
4. Type and save these lines:

```
@ECHO OFF

ECHO Press any key to see an attribute list of the files on drive A

PAUSE

ATTRIB A:\*.* /S ¦ MORE
```

5. Format a new disk in drive A. (Warning: Don't use a disk containing files that you want to keep.)

6. Use XCOPY to copy all C*.COM from drive C to A. Use the /S switch to copy files from the entire directory tree.

7. Enter **LATT** to try out your new batch program.

   DOS should display the attributes of all the files on the drive. Leave the disk in the drive while you read the next section.

Chaining Versus Calling

You can link to another batch program in two ways, as shown in Figure 37.1. When you *chain* to another program, you transfer completely to that program, causing the first batch program to be terminated. When the chained program ends (without chaining to another program), the batch job terminates, and DOS resumes control. However, when you *call* another batch program, you transfer to it temporarily; when it's finished, you return to the original batch program, picking up with the instruction after the one that did the calling.

Figure 37.1.
Calling and chaining to other batch files.

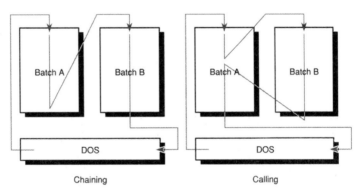

Chaining   Calling

Chaining

Any time you include a command in one batch program that executes another batch program without using any special instructions, a chain takes place and the first batch program is automatically terminated. Try it yourself:

1. Make sure you are in the BATCH directory.

2. Create a new batch file named PR.BAT and type in these lines:

```
@ECHO OFF
ECHO Linking to LATT.BAT
LATT
ECHO Return from the link
```

3. Try out your new program:

You should see these messages:

```
Linking to LATT.BAT

Press any key to see an attribute list of the files on drive A

Press any key to continue . . .

[followed by the attribute list]
```

Notice that you don't see the message Return from the link. That's because you chained to LATT and never returned to PR.BAT.

Note: A batch program executes other types of programs, such as COM and EXE programs, without chaining. In the preceding batch program, ECHO, PAUSE, and ATTRIB cause programs to be executed without chaining. Only links to other batch programs cause chaining to take place.

Calling

To call another batch file, use a command in the following format:

```
CALL batch-command
```

Try calling LATT.BAT instead of chaining to it:

1. In PR.BAT, insert **CALL** in front of the LATT command.

2. Execute PR again.

This time, you should see the final message Return from the link.

Include whatever parameters on the CALL command that you would use when executing the program from the command prompt. For example, if LATT had been written with a replaceable parameter to accept an optional drive name, you could use the following command:

```
CALL LATT A:
```

Note: Redirection is ignored in a CALL command, as it is in any command that executes a batch program.

> **Note:** You might also need to use CALL when defining a program item in DOS Shell. When you reference a batch file without CALL, DOS links to the batch file and never returns to the program item. There's no problem if the batch file is the only command in the Commands field, or if it's the last one. But, if it's not the last one, you need to use CALL so that DOS will return to the list of commands when the batch program terminates.

Passing Replaceable Parameters

You can use replaceable parameters in a linking command; DOS replaces them before executing the link. For example, the following command passes two parameters from the calling program to FMT.BAT:

```
CALL FMT %3 TOTMASTER
```

As usual, the %3 will be replaced by the third parameter from the command line that executed the calling program; if that parameter is A:, the CALL command as executed becomes:

```
CALL FMT.BAT A: TOTMASTER
```

The called batch program, FMT.BAT, treats the A: as %1 and TOTMASTER as %2. It has no awareness that the A: was originally %3 to the calling program.

Replaceable parameters are not automatically passed from the linking program to the linked program. You must include in the linking command any parameters to be passed to the linked program, and they must be in the correct order and format for the linked program, just as if you executed the same program from the command prompt.

Multiple Links

When you link to a second batch program, it may link to another. There is no limit to the number of links you can make in a batch job. Program A may chain to Program B, which calls Program C, which chains to Program D, and so on. Your batch jobs will be easier to manage, revise, and debug if you limit them to a few links, however.

Recursion

A batch file can link to itself, creating a situation called *recursion*. The batch job will repeat endlessly until something interrupts it, such as a condition becoming true or someone pressing Ctrl+Break. You can take advantage of recursion to create a quick-and-dirty screen-saver program for your DOS prompt screen:

> **Note:** A screen-saver protects your monitor by not letting it display the same thing for so long that the display "burns in" on the monitor screen.

1. Create a batch file called SS.BAT and type in the following lines:

   ```
   @ECHO OFF
   ECHO Out to lunch
   ECHO Will be back eventually
   CALL SS
   ```

2. Execute SS.BAT.

   The two messages scroll rapidly on your screen.

3. Press Ctrl+Break to kill the program.

   DOS asks `Terminate batch job (Y/N)?`.

4. Press Y to terminate SS.BAT.

Killing a Batch Job with Links

If you press Ctrl+Break (or Ctrl+C) during a batch job involving links, DOS displays its usual message:

```
Terminate batch job (Y/N)?
```

If you enter Y, the entire batch job (including all linked programs) is killed. If you enter N, only the current command is killed.

Branching

DOS includes some commands that let you decide what to do next in a batch program based on a specific condition. Some typical conditions are as follows:

- Does the C:\AUTOEXEC.BAT file exist?
- Did the preceding command succeed?

- Did the user enter Y or N?
- Does %1 equal /s?

Types of Branches

Branches can range from extremely simple to fairly complex (although not as complex as you can achieve in true programming languages such as BASIC or C).

Bypass Branches

Figure 37.2 illustrates the simplest kind of branch, in which you execute a routine if the condition is true, but bypass it if the condition is false, or vice versa. This branch is called a *bypass branch*, because only one path (the true path or the false one) causes a routine to be executed. The other branch bypasses that and goes on to the next step. Notice that both branches end up at the same place eventually.

Figure 37.2.
Bypass decision logic.

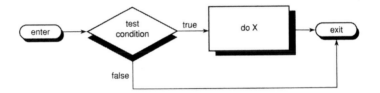

Here are some typical bypass decisions:

- If C:\AUTOEXEC.BAT exists, rename it as C:\AUTOEXEC.OLD.
- If the preceding command failed, issue a warning message.
- If the user entered a Y, format the floppy disk in drive A.
- If %1 equals SORT, sort the source file.

Alternative Branches

Another common type of branch has two paths, as illustrated in Figure 37.3. One routine is executed if the condition is true, and another routine is executed if it's false. Here are some typical alternative branches:

- If C:\AUTOEXEC.BAT exists, copy it to A:; otherwise, create a new A:\AUTOEXEC.BAT
- If the preceding copy command succeeded, delete the source files; otherwise, display an error message and terminate

- If the user entered a 1, display AUTOEXEC.BAT; otherwise, display CONFIG.SYS
- If %3 equals /P, print the target file; otherwise, display it on the monitor

Figure 37.3.
Alternative decision logic.

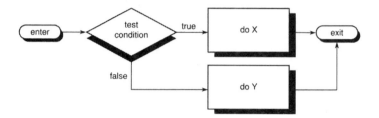

The *IF* Command

Figure 37.4 shows the IF command, which is used for decision-making in batch programs.

IF

Executes a command if (and only if) a condition is true.

Syntax:

```
IF [NOT] condition command
```

Parameters:

condition	The condition to be tested, which must be one of the following:
ERRORLEVEL *n*	The condition is true if the preceding program's exit code equals or exceeds *n*.
EXIST *filespec*	The condition is true if the specified file exists.
string1==string2	The condition is true if the two text strings are equal.
command	The command to be executed if the condition is true.

Note:
NOT negates the result of the condition so that the command is executed if the condition is false.

Figure 37.4. *IF command summary.*

Exit Codes

Many programs set an exit code when they terminate. The exit code is a number between 0 and 255 that indicates whether the program achieved its function or what type of error occurred. No fixed meanings for exit codes exist; each program defines the exit codes it issues, although a 0 generally means that the program was completely successful. The FORMAT program provides a typical example of exit codes:

0	The disk was successfully formatted (no errors)
3	The user interrupted with Ctrl+C or Ctrl+Break
4	Some (unspecified) type of error occurred, and the disk was not successfully formatted
5	A problem was identified and reported to the user, who chose to cancel the format job

Unfortunately, not all of the DOS programs set exit codes, so it's not always possible to test for successful completion of an individual command in a batch file. Appendix B, "Exit Codes," lists the exit codes set by the DOS utilities. If a DOS command isn't in the list, it doesn't set an exit code.

Your application programs and third-party utilities also may set exit codes. Check their documentation to find out.

The ERRORLEVEL Condition

In an IF command, the ERRORLEVEL condition tests the exit code of the preceding program. You specify a number, as in IF ERRORLEVEL 3, and the condition is true if the exit code equals or exceeds that number.

Create a program to format the disk in drive A and, if that fails for any reason, display the message Try again with another floppy.

1. Make sure the floppy in drive A is the one that you have used in previous exercises in this chapter.

2. Create a file named FMT.BAT that contains the following lines:

```
@ECHO OFF
FORMAT A: /Q /U /V:""
IF ERRORLEVEL 1 ECHO Try again with another floppy
```

3. Enter FMT to start FMT.BAT.

4. When FORMAT asks you to press a key to continue, press Ctrl+Break to terminate the program.

You see the message Try again with another floppy.

5. Run FMT again; but, this time, don't interrupt it.

   You don't see the message at the end, because the exit code was 0.

Note: Because FORMAT doesn't use exit codes 1 and 2, you could just as easily write IF ERRORLEVEL 3. But, it's more common to use IF ERRORLEVEL 1 to discriminate between 0 (complete success) and all other exit codes.

You can include NOT in an IF command to negate the result of the condition; that is, the condition is true only if the exit code is less than the specified number. The following routine displays a message only if the format is successful:

```
FORMAT A:
IF NOT ERRORLEVEL 1 ECHO Remove the floppy from drive A:
```

It's easy to get tangled up in IF ERRORLEVEL logic, especially when you reverse it with NOT. A logic chart like the ones in Figure 37.5 can help you analyze a command, determine when it will be true and when false, and decide what's going to happen in each case.

Figure 37.5.
Sample IF logic charts.

condition	IF ERRORLEVEL 3	
exit codes	0, 1, 2	3, 4, ...
result	false	true
action	continue	kill program

condition	IF NOT ERRORLEVEL 2	
exit codes	0, 1	2, 3, ...
result	true	false
action	delete files	display message

The Short Life of the Exit Code

The exit code lasts only until another program changes it. Even if the next program doesn't set specific exit codes, the exit code may be reset to 0. Commands such as CALL and ECHO don't reset the exit code, but other commands may (especially nonbatch commands). Therefore, if you're going to process an exit code, do it immediately.

The IF command does not reset the exit code. You can use several IF commands in a row to process various exit code possibilities after a command such as FORMAT or XCOPY.

IF and Bypass Branches

The IF command is perfectly set up for a simple bypass branch. If the condition is true, it executes a single command and goes on to the next line. If the condition is false, it goes on to the next line. To execute more than one command when the condition is true, which is often the case, you can use CALL to execute another batch program, as in the following:

```
IF ERRORLEVEL 1 CALL BADFORM
```

All the examples you have seen so far are bypass branches. To accomplish alternative branches, you need to use the GOTO command, which is explained next.

Telling DOS Where To Go

Suppose that you're trying to accomplish an alternate decision like this: If the last command was successful, call GOODFORM; otherwise, call BADFORM.

The following program will not work:

```
IF NOT ERRORLEVEL 1 CALL GOODFORM
CALL BADFORM
```

It doesn't work because the CALL BADFORM command is executed in both cases.

The GOTO command is used to branch away from the current sequence of commands to another point in the program. (See Figure 37.6.) To accomplish an alternative branch, you jump to another section of the program for the true path. Only the false path goes on to the next line after the IF statement:

GOTO

When used in a batch program, sends DOS to a line with the specified label.

Syntax:

```
GOTO label
```

Parameter:

label   Identifies the line to go to. It must refer to another line in the same program that starts with :label, as in :ENDING.

Figure 37.6. *GOTO batch command summary.*

```
IF NOT ERRORLEVEL 1 GOTO GOODFORM
REM If DOS reaches the next line, the FORMAT command
failed for some reason.
...
...   (commands to handle FORMAT error)
...
GOTO NEXTSTEP
:GOODFORM
...
...   (commands to handle a successful format)
...
:NEXTSTEP
...
...
...
```

In the preceding routine, if the condition is true, indicating that the exit code is 0, you branch to the GOODFORM label in the same program. Several commands may be in the GOODFORM section. At the end, you fall into NEXTSTEP, which continues the batch processing. If the condition is false, the GOTO command is not executed, and you fall through into the commands that process an exit code greater than 0. At the end of that false branch is an extremely important command: GOTO NEXTSTEP. This command branches around the GOODFORM routine. Without it, you would fall into GOODFORM after the false branch was completed, which is not desired when you're trying to create an alternate branch.

> **Tip:** GOTO must refer to a line starting with a colon and then *label*. DOS ignores all but the first eight characters of any line beginning with a colon, so you can add explanatory comments to label lines to document your program logic. Notice that the labels :PRACTICE1 and :PRACTICE2 would both be read by DOS as :PRACTIC, and both labels would be considered identical. DOS would branch to the first :PRACTIC it encounters.

GOTO is also essential in creating multiple alternatives. For example, the following routine tries to display the exit code resulting from the FORMAT command:

```
FORMAT A:
IF ERRORLEVEL 5 ECHO Exit code is 5
IF ERRORLEVEL 4 ECHO Exit code is 4
IF ERRORLEVEL 3 ECHO Exit code is 3
IF ERRORLEVEL 0 ECHO Exit code is 0
```

However, the following is what the output looks like when the exit code is 4:

```
Exit code is 4
Exit code is 3
Exit code is 0
```

Because these IF commands come one after the other, DOS executes each one in turn, regardless of the outcome of the preceding one. IF ERRORLEVEL 5 is false, so that message is not displayed. IF ERRORLEVEL 4 is true, so its message is displayed. IF ERRORLEVEL 3 and IF ERRORLEVEL 0 also are true, and their messages are displayed as well. The result is not what you wanted.

Modify your FMT.BAT program to completely process the exit codes from the FORMAT command:

1. Revise FMT.BAT so that it contains these lines:

```
@ECHO OFF
FORMAT A: /Q /U /V:""
IF ERRORLEVEL 5 GOTO HANDLE5
IF ERRORLEVEL 4 GOTO HANDLE4
IF ERRORLEVEL 3 GOTO HANDLE3

REM If DOS reaches this line, the exit code must be 0
ECHO Exit code is 0
GOTO NEXTSTEP

:HANDLE3 This routine handles an exit code of 3
ECHO Exit code is 3
GOTO NEXTSTEP
:HANDLE4 This routine handles an exit code of 4
ECHO Exit code is 4
GOTO NEXTSTEP

:HANDLE5 This routine handles an exit code of 5
ECHO Exit code is 5

:NEXTSTEP The program ends here
```

2. Start FMT.BAT.

3. When FORMAT asks you to press any key to continue, press Ctrl+Break to terminate FORMAT.

   You should see the message Exit code is 3.

4. Run FMT.BAT again, but don't interrupt it this time. (Let it format the disk.)

   You should see the message Exit code is 0 at the end.

It's important to test from the highest exit code to the lowest, so that the first true condition encountered is the one that equals the exit code.

Testing for Files

Sometimes it's handy to test for the presence or absence of a file before deciding what to do next. For example, you could test for the existence of AUTOEXEC.BAT:

1. Create a batch file called TEST.BAT that contains these lines:

```
@ECHO OFF
IF EXIST A:\AUTOEXEC.BAT GOTO PRESENT
ECHO There is no AUTOEXEC.BAT file on drive A
GOTO ENDING


:PRESENT
TYPE A:\AUTOEXEC.BAT ¦ MORE


:ENDING
```

2. Run TEST.BAT.

   You should get the message There is no AUTOEXEC.BAT file on drive A.

3. Copy AUTOEXEC.BAT to drive A.

4. Run TEST.BAT again.

   You should see a listing of A:\AUTOEXEC.BAT.

IF [NOT] EXIST also can be used in bypass decisions. The following command copies A:\AUTOEXEC.BAT to C:\ only if it doesn't already exist on C:\:

```
IF NOT EXIST C:\AUTOEXEC.BAT COPY A:\AUTOEXEC.BAT C:\
```

> **Tip:** Suppose that you want to find out whether the current directory has a subdirectory named TEMP. IF EXIST TEMP will not work because EXIST doesn't identify subdirectories. However, the special filename NUL is valid for every existing directory, so use the following command to see whether TEMP exists:
>
> ```
> IF EXIST TEMP\NUL command
> ```

Comparing Text Strings

At first glance, comparing two text strings may seem totally useless: IF APPLES==APPLES is obviously true, and IF APPLES==ORANGES is just as obviously false. However, one or both of those text strings can be a replaceable parameter, giving you the power to check out the parameters entered on the command line.

The following batch program tests to see whether the first parameter is /F; if so, the batch program reformats the disk in drive A before copying files to it. If the first parameter is anything but /F, the disk is not formatted.

```
@ECHO OFF
IF "%1"=="/F" FORMAT A:
COPY C:\MYAPP\*.* A:
```

Testing for Null Values

You don't always have to put quotes around *string1* and *string2*, but it's a good practice. In the preceding example, if quotes were omitted and someone omitted the parameter when running the batch program, the IF command would look like the following:

```
IF ==/F FORMAT A:
```

The condition ==/F is not acceptable and would cause a syntax error that would make the rest of the program fail. Putting quotes around *string1* and *string2* avoids this problem. With quotes, a null parameter yields this command, which is perfectly acceptable:

```
IF ""=="/F" FORMAT A:
```

Because a null does not equal /F, the FORMAT A: command would not be executed.

Note: If you use quotes, both parameters must be quoted.

You also can use quotes to test for a null parameter. To find out whether %3 is null, use a command like the following:

```
IF "%3"=="" GOTO CONTINUE
```

When the user omits the third parameter, DOS interprets the command as follows:

```
IF ""=="" GOTO CONTINUE
```

Because a null does, in fact, equal a null, the GOTO CONTINUE command is executed.

You can create a program that either prints or displays AUTOEXEC.BAT, depending on whether the user enters a P as the first parameter:

1. Create a batch program called PD.BAT that contains these lines:

   ```
   @ECHO OFF
   IF "%1"=="P" GOTO PRINT-IT
   TYPE C:\AUTOEXEC.BAT | MORE
   GOTO ENDING
   ```

```
:PRINT-IT
TYPE C:\AUTOEXEC.BAT > PRN


:ENDING
```

2. Enter **PD** without any parameter.

   PD displays your AUTOEXEC.BAT file.

3. Enter **PD P**.

   PD prints your AUTOEXEC.BAT file.

Nested IFs

You can nest an IF command inside another IF command. The inner IF command is executed when the outer IF command is true. The following GOTO command is executed if the current exit code is equal to or greater than 4, but less than 5; in other words, if it is 4:

```
IF ERRORLEVEL 4 IF NOT ERRORLEVEL 5 GOTO CODE4
```

The IF ERRORLEVEL 5 command is executed only if the IF ERRORLEVEL 4 command is true, and the GOTO command is executed only if both IF commands are true. The following GOTO command is executed if %1 is neither Y nor N:

```
IF NOT "%1"=="Y" IF NOT " %1"=="N" GOTO BADINPUT
```

Case is important in string comparisons. In the preceding command, a lowercase y or n would not be considered the same as Y or N, and the GOTO instruction would be executed. You could adjust the command to permit users to enter either uppercase or lowercase letters as follows:

```
IF NOT "%1"=="Y" IF NOT "%1"=="y" IF NOT "%1"=="N" IF NOT "%1"=="n"
GOTO BADINPUT
```

Loops

A loop is a routine that can be executed more than once. Two types of loops are possible—open and closed. An open loop tests a condition and terminates itself when the condition becomes true. A closed loop repeats continuously with no way out until someone interrupts it from outside, usually by pressing Ctrl+Break or by rebooting. Most closed loops are mistakes, but you may find occasion to use one on purpose.

Figure 37.7 diagrams the logic of an open loop. You perform an action (such as a FORMAT command) and then test a condition (such as whether the exit code is 0). If the condition is false, you repeat the loop. When it's true, you exit the loop and go on with the program. The loop is executed until the condition becomes true. An open loop affects the condition in some way, so that it may be true the next time it's tested.

Figure 37.7.
Loop logic.

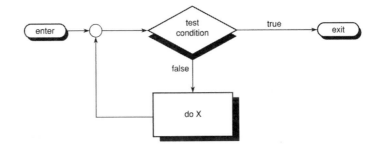

In some routines, it makes more sense to test the condition at the beginning of the loop instead of at the end. This test allows for the possibility that the condition is true from the start, and the routine should never be executed.

Sample Loop

Suppose that you want to execute FORMAT until it is successful. This type of loop is usually completed the first time; but, if the first disk is bad or some other problem occurs, the loop will be repeated:

1. Create a batch file named RF.BAT that contains the following lines:

```
@ECHO OFF
:FORMATLOOP
FORMAT A: /Q /U /V:""
IF NOT ERRORLEVEL 1 GOTO ENDING
REM If DOS reaches this line, FORMAT was not successful
ECHO FORMAT failed for some reason.
ECHO To try again, press any key
ECHO To quit, press Ctrl+Break
PAUSE
GOTO FORMATLOOP
:ENDING
```

2. Start RF.BAT.

3. Press Ctrl+Break when FORMAT asks you to press a key to continue.

   You should see the message:

   ```
   ECHO FORMAT failed for some reason.

   ECHO To try again, press any key

   ECHO To quit, press Ctrl+Break
   ```

4. Press any key to try formatting the disk again.

5. Repeat step 3.

6. Press Ctrl+Break a second time to kill the batch program.

Loops Involving SHIFT

It's often handy to repeat a command several times. For example, it would be handy to be able to delete several unrelated filespecs in one deletion command. The SHIFT command gives you the ability to do that.

SHIFT, which has no parameters of its own, causes all the command-line parameters to be shifted down one position, so that the value that was formerly substituted for %1 is now substituted for %0; the value that was %2 is now %1; and so on. When you include SHIFT in a loop, each loop processes the next parameter on the command line.

Let's create a program to delete any number of filespecs:

1. Create a file called MDEL.BAT that contains the following lines:

   ```
   @ECHO OFF
   :DELLOOP Deletes any number of files
   IF "%1"=="" GOTO ENDING
   DEL %1
   SHIFT
   GOTO DELLOOP
   :ENDING
   ```

   Each loop starts by checking for a null value in the first parameter. If it's null, the program jumps to ENDING and terminates. If it's not null, a DEL command is issued for that parameter. Then all the parameters are shifted down, so the next one becomes %1, and the program returns to the beginning of the loop.

2. Copy the following files to drive A, renaming them as shown:

   ```
   C:\DOS\README.TXT (rename this file as A:\A.XXX)
   C:\DOS\HELP.HLP (rename this file as A:\B.XXX)
   ```

3. Enter the command **MDEL A:\A.XXX A:\B.XXX**.

   DOS deletes the two files.

SHIFT can also be used in a program to process more than nine parameters. Nine replaceable parameters are more than enough for most batch files; but, should you want more than that, the SHIFT command can be used to process an unlimited number of parameters.

Using FOR to Create Loops

Another looping technique uses the FOR command instead of IF. (See Figure 37.8.) When you get used to its ugly-duckling format, you will discover that there is a swan in there somewhere. One big advantage of FOR is that it can be used at the command prompt; it's the only way to create repetitive processing at the command prompt.

FOR

Repeats a command for each item in a set.

Syntax:

```
FOR %x ¦ %%x IN (set) DO command
```

Parameters:

%x ¦ %%x	Identifies a replaceable variable that can be used in *command*; it may be any non-numeric character. Use %x at the command prompt and %%x in a batch program.
(set)	Identifies a set of variables to replace %x or %%x. The parentheses are required.
command	Specifies the command to repeat, including its parameters and switches.

Figure 37.8. *FOR command summary.*

You could, for example, write a command to delete any number of filespecs from the command prompt:

1. Copy the following files to drive A, renaming them as shown:

   ```
   C:\DOS\README.TXT (rename this file as A:\A.XXX)
   C:\DOS\HELP.HLP (rename this file as A:\B.XXX)
   ```

2. Enter **FOR %F IN (A:\A.XXX A:\B.XXX) DO DEL %F**.

   DOS first substitutes A:\A.XXX in DEL %F, creating the command DEL A:\A.XXX. Then, it substitutes A:\B.XXX, creating the command DEL A:\B.XXX.

When FOR is used in a batch program, you must double the percent sign—%%x instead of %x—so that DOS will not delete the % from the command.

602 Part 5 • Advanced DOS

Tip: Because of the way DOS handles the symbol % in a batch file, DOS ends up deleting every single occurrence of this symbol, even if it isn't attached to a digit to represent a replaceable parameter. You occasionally may need to use the % symbol in a batch file without having it deleted. For example, you may need to reference a file named TEN%ERS. Double the % symbol to keep it from being deleted. To print the file named TEN%ERS from within a batch file, use the following command:

```
PRINT TEN%%ERS
```

DOS will replace the %% with % before processing the command.

Global Filespecs in the Item Set

When a global filespec appears in the item set, DOS issues a separate command for each matching filename. If 100 filenames match the global filespec, 100 separate commands are generated. Suppose that you have a batch program called STAMP that changes the time/date stamp of a single file. You could change all the files in the MYDOCS directory with this command:

```
C:\>FOR %X IN (C:\MYDOCS\*.* ) DO CALL STAMP %X
```

You must use CALL in a FOR command (even at the command prompt) to apply a batch program to the item set. In each generated STAMP command, the individual filename is passed as the first parameter. (STAMP should use %1 to access this parameter.)

Note: If you reference a batch file without using CALL, the job will be terminated after the first execution of the batch file, defeating the purpose of the FOR command.

FOR and FIND

Do you find it frustrating that FIND will not accept a global filespec? How can you search all the files in the current directory, or all the .DOC and .TXT files, when you can't use a global filespec in the command? The answer lies in combining FIND with FOR. FOR will turn the global filespecs in the item set into specific filenames and generate a separate FIND command for each one.

Try to find all the .TXT files in your DOS directory that contain the expression "CD". To do this Enter the command **FOR %F IN (C:\DOS*.TXT) DO FIND "CD" /I %F**.

When you issue a command like this, be prepared to press Pause (or Ctrl+S) to page the output. Piping it to MORE doesn't help; piping has no effect with the FOR command.

Tip: FOR provides a simple way to test a variety of different cases with the IF command. The following command jumps to GOODINPUT if %1 is Y, y, N, or n:

```
FOR %%X IN (Y y N n) DO IF "%1"=="%%X" GOTO GOODINPUT
```

The CHOICE Command

Many batch programs need to ask the user a simple Yes-No question or display a menu for the user to choose an item from. The user types a character at the keyboard, and the program branches based on the user's choice. Figure 37.9 shows the format of the CHOICE command, which displays a message and a prompt on the monitor screen, reads a single character from the keyboard, and sets the exit code to indicate what character was entered.

CHOICE

Lets a user choose between options during a batch program.

Syntax:

```
CHOICE [/C:list] [/N] [/S] [/T:char,sec] [text]
```

Parameters and Switches:

/C:list	Defines a *list* of characters that the user can type to select choices. The colon is optional.
/N	Causes CHOICE not to display any prompt.
/S	Causes CHOICE to distinguish between uppercase and lowercase; otherwise case is ignored.
/T:char,sec	Causes CHOICE to pause for *sec* seconds before defaulting to *char*. The colon is optional. *Char* must be a character from *list*. *Sec* must be between 0 and 99. Don't include any spaces in this parameter.
text	Specifies *text* to be displayed before the prompt.

Figure 37.9. *CHOICE command summary.*

For example, suppose that this command appeared in a batch program:

```
CHOICE Do you want to prepare another disk
```

The message on the screen appears as follows:

```
Do you want to prepare another disk [Y,N]?
```

If the user enters Y or y, CHOICE sets the exit code to 1; if N or n, 2. If the user presses Ctrl+Break or Ctrl+C, CHOICE sets the exit code to 0. Any other input causes a beep, and CHOICE keeps waiting for an acceptable response.

Suppose that you're writing a batch program to format a floppy disk and copy some files to it. You can write a program that warns the user if the disk already contains files:

1. Create a batch file named FD.BAT that contains the following commands:

```
@ECHO OFF
IF NOT EXIST A:\*.* GOTO FORMAT
ECHO The disk contains these files:
DIR A:\ /S /B /P
CHOICE Do you want to format the disk?
IF ERRORLEVEL 2 GOTO NEXTDISK
IF ERRORLEVEL 1 GOTO FORMAT


:FORMAT
FORMAT A: /Q /V:""
XCOPY C:\DOS\README.TXT A:
GOTO ENDING


:NEXTDISK
ECHO Try again with another disk


:ENDING
```

2. Make sure the disk in drive A is the one that you have been using throughout this chapter.

3. Run FD.

    FD formats the disk and copies the README.TXT file to it.

4. Run FD again.

    This time, FD warns you that the file contains data and asks if you want to format it.

5. Press N.

    You see the message `Try again with another disk`.

CHOICE Variations

Include the /C:*list* parameter to define a list of choices instead of the default Y and N. For example, if you want the user to enter **A**, **B**, or **C** in response to a menu (displayed by ECHO commands), you would specify /C:ABC. If for some reason you don't want to permit lowercase a, b, and c as acceptable alternatives, include the /S (for "sensitive") switch. CHOICE displays the prompt [A,B,C]?, and sets the exit code to 1 if the user enters an A, 2 for a B, and 3 for a C.

If you leave out the *text* parameter, no message is displayed with the prompt. You may want to do this if you have already used ECHO commands to display a menu. In fact, you can suppress the prompt itself with the /N switch.

Use the /T parameter to set up a default choice to be taken if the user doesn't type anything within a specific time limit. For example, to choose option A after 10 seconds, include /T:A,10 in the CHOICE command.

Using DOSKEY Macros to Override DOS Commands

DOSKEY macros take precedence over any other kind of program, including internal commands and batch programs. You can use this feature to override a DOS program with a DOSKEY macro. For example, suppose that you want the people in your workgroup to always use XCOPY instead of COPY. You can create a COPY macro that intercepts all COPY commands and turns them into XCOPY commands:

```
DOSKEY COPY=XCOPY $*
```

Note: DOSKEY replaces the $* parameter with all the parameters from the invoking command line. So, whatever filespecs and switches were entered with the COPY command are passed on to the XCOPY command.

Sometimes, you just want to disable a command so that inexperienced people can't use it. You could replace it with a message like the following:

```
DOSKEY FDISK=ECHO Please don't use this command; call J. North on extension 457.
```

These macros don't completely disable the commands they supersede. You can still execute COPY and FDISK commands by preceding them with spaces. DOSKEY ignores commands that start with spaces.

> **Tip:** DOSKEY macros are not as flexible as batch files, so you might want to override a command with a batch file instead of a DOSKEY macro. But, how can you do that when batch files have lower priority than internal commands, .COM, and .EXE files? You can use DOSKEY to capture the command and call the batch file. For example, suppose you want to redirect FORMAT commands to a batch file that guides an inexperienced user through the formatting process. The following command creates a DOSKEY macro that will do the trick:
>
> ```
> DOSKEY FORMAT=FORMHELP.BAT
> ```

Floppy Batches

DOS reads and executes one batch command at a time. When execution of one command is finished, DOS returns to the batch file to read the next command. This practice can cause some complications when you are executing a batch program from a floppy disk. If you change disks during the execution of a command, DOS must ask for the disk containing the batch file in order to continue the job. You see the following message:

```
Insert disk with batch file
Press any key to continue . . .
```

This message appears even if no more commands are in the batch file, because DOS doesn't know the batch file is empty until it tries to read a command and discovers the end-of-file mark.

If you remove the floppy disk containing the batch file without inserting another disk, you see the following message, which always appears when DOS tries to read an empty drive:

```
Not ready reading drive A
Abort, Retry, Fail?
```

When this message appears, insert the batch file disk in the drive and press R for Retry.

Clobbering the Batch File

If you know, or even suspect, that a batch program will be executed from a floppy disk, watch out for commands that might process that same disk. Some commands, such as FORMAT is used to branch away from the current sequence of commands to another point in the program. (See Figure 37.6, shown previously.) To accomplish an alternative branch, you jump to another section of the program for the true path. Only the false path goes on to the next line after the IF statement:

```
IF NOT ERRORLEVEL 1 GOTO GOODFORM
REM If DOS reaches the next line, the FORMAT command
failed for some reason.
...
...  (commands to handle FORMAT error)
```

```
...
GOTO NEXTSTEP
<MS Last>:GOODFORM
...
...   (commands to handle a successful format)
...
<MS Last>:NEXTSTEP
...
...
...
```

In the preceding routine, if the condition is true, indicating that the exit code and has the potential for clobbering the batch file, be sure to include a warning message in the program and give the user a chance to change disks or cancel the program.

Looking Ahead: Chapter 43, "DOS and the Environment," shows you how to execute a batch program one line at a time, which can help you pinpoint a command or routine that is not performing as you expected.

On Your Own

Try your hand at writing a couple of programs on your own:

1. Write a program to defragment a floppy disk. Start by displaying the contents of the floppy and making sure the user wants to continue. (Hint: Copy all the files to a temporary directory (don't forget hidden and system files), reformat the floppy, copy all the files back again, and delete the temporary directory.)

2. Write a program to update all the time/date stamps on a floppy to today's date and time. (Hint: Use FOR to apply the COPY command to every file. Don't forget to include the /B switch in the COPY command so that you don't truncate your files. Be sure to test and debug your program on files that don't matter.) When you're sure the program is working and not truncating any files, adapt it to work on any directory, with the pathname of the directory to be entered with the command. Be sure to test it on practice directories only so that you don't change time/date stamps that you might need.

3. Write a program to display the exit code from the preceding program. You should be able to run this program after any other program to find out its exit code, if any.

4. Delete any programs that you wrote in the chapter that you don't want to keep.

38

Starting Up DOS

Introduction

DOS 6 introduced a variety of new features for the startup files—CONFIG.SYS and AUTOEXEC.BAT. You now have a great deal more control over the boot process than before.

Controlling the Booting Process

It used to be that if you changed CONFIG.SYS or AUTOEXEC.BAT and then found that you couldn't boot with the new setup, you had to boot from your emergency boot floppy. But, with DOS 6, you can boot from your hard drive, execute the functional parts of your startup files, and bypass the nonfunctional parts. This makes it a lot easier to fix the problem and get going again.

Also new with DOS 6, you can now set up alternate configurations in CONFIG.SYS so that you can select the configuration that you want to use each time you boot. If you need different configurations for different applications, or if you have several people sharing your computer, each with different needs, it's now much easier to select the configuration that you want to boot.

This chapter shows you how to use DOS 6's startup features. You will learn how to:

- Bypass the startup files entirely when booting
- Set up CONFIG.SYS so that individual commands are offered each time you boot
- Set up CONFIG.SYS so that a user can choose among several configurations on a menu during booting

Bypassing the Startup Files

How to Bypass the Startup Files during Booting

To completely bypass both CONFIG.SYS and AUTOEXEC.BAT:

1. Boot or reboot.

2. When you see the message `Starting MS-DOS...`, press F5.

To completely bypass CONFIG.SYS, AUTOEXEC.BAT, and DRVSPACE.BIN or DBLSPACE.BIN:

1. Boot or reboot.

2. When you see the message `Starting MS-DOS...`, press Ctrl+F5.

    DOS displays these messages:

    `You pressed CTRL+F5 or CTRL+F8 to bypass DRVSPACE.BIN. Therefore, none of your compressed drives are available.`

    `MS-DOS is bypassing your CONFIG.SYS and AUTOEXEC.BAT files.`

    DOS boots without executing the files. You will be able to use DOS internal commands (such as `COPY`), but you will not be able to access any programs on your compressed drive. If your DOS directory is located on your compressed drive, you cannot access DOS utilities such as EDIT. In addition, the drivers and TSRs that you normally load will not be in place.

To execute CONFIG.SYS and AUTOEXEC.BAT one line at a time:

1. Boot or reboot.

2. When you see the message `Starting MS-DOS...`, press F8.

   DOS displays each line of CONFIG.SYS followed by `[Y,N]?`. (If your CONFIG.SYS includes a startup menu, the menu is displayed first.)

3. For each line of CONFIG.SYS, type Y to execute the line or N to bypass it.

   When CONFIG.SYS is completed, DOS asks `Process AUTOEXEC.BAT [Y,N]?`.

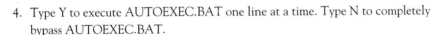

Note: You can press Esc at any time to execute the remainder of the commands in CONFIG.SYS and AUTOEXEC.BAT. Press F5 at any time to bypass the remaining commands in the startup files.

4. Type Y to execute AUTOEXEC.BAT one line at a time. Type N to completely bypass AUTOEXEC.BAT.

   If you type Y, DOS displays each line of AUTOEXEC.BAT followed by `[Y,N]?`.

5. Type Y to execute each line or type N to bypass it.

To bypass DRVSPACE.BIN or DBLSPACE.BIN and execute CONFIG.SYS and AUTOEXEC.BAT one line at a time:

1. Boot or reboot.

2. When you see the message `Starting MS-DOS...`, press Ctrl+F8.

   Because you bypassed DRVSPACE.BIN or DBLSPACE.BIN, your compressed drives are not mounted. If CONFIG.SYS and AUTOEXEC.BAT are on your compressed drive, DOS will not be able to execute them. DOS asks if you want to execute AUTOEXEC.BAT; if you answer Y, the `DATE` and `TIME` commands are executed because there is no AUTOEXEC.BAT file.

   If CONFIG.SYS and AUTOEXEC.BAT are available in the root directory of the unmounted boot drive, they are executed one line at a time as explained in the preceding procedure.

You saw earlier in this book (in Chapter 21, "Configuring Your System") how to press F8 during booting to execute CONFIG.SYS and AUTOEXEC.BAT one line at a time, skipping lines that you think are causing problems. That technique will usually help you isolate the command that needs to be corrected. But, if not, you might need to bypass CONFIG.SYS and AUTOEXEC.BAT entirely, boot your most basic system, restore your old startup files, and then reboot with the system that you used to use.

When you boot DOS 6, the message `Starting MS-DOS...` appears on the screen for a few seconds. To bypass both CONFIG.SYS and AUTOEXEC.BAT, press and release F5 or hold down a Shift key. You see the following message:

`MS-DOS is bypassing your CONFIG.SYS and AUTOEXEC.BAT files.`

When you do this, DOS may not be able to find COMMAND.COM if it's not in the root directory of the boot drive. If DOS can't find COMMAND.COM, it asks you where to find the command processor. Type the full filespec, including the drive name and path, as in `C:\DOS\COMMAND.COM`.

Try bypassing your startup files now:

1. Exit any programs that are running and get to the primary command prompt.

2. Press Ctrl+Alt+Delete to reboot.

3. When you see the message `Starting MS-DOS...`, press F5.

    You see the message `MS-DOS is bypassing your CONFIG.SYS and AUTOEXEC.BAT files.`

4. Reboot again to return to your normal system. (Don't bypass the startup files this time.)

When the system is successfully booted with F5, the only directory in your program search path is C:\DOS (so that you can run DOS utilities such as EDIT to fix your startup files). Devices that need installable device drivers, such as your mouse, will not work. Programs can't use extended or expanded memory because there are no memory managers. Worst of all, if you must load a utility from CONFIG.SYS in order to access your hard drive—a third-party drive manager or a third-party compression program that doesn't load as part of the core system—you won't be able to access your hard drive, not even the DOS directory. But, the COPY command will work, and if you saved your old CONFIG.SYS and AUTOEXEC.BAT before revising them, you should be able to restore them. For example, if you saved them as CONFIG.SAV and AUTOEXEC.SAV, the commands `COPY CONFIG.SAV CONFIG.SYS` and `COPY AUTOEXEC.SAV AUTOEXEC.BAT` restore your former startup files. Then, you can successfully reboot.

If you use DrvSpace or DblSpace, your compression software loads when the core DOS programs load. It is not bypassed by the F5 key, and you will be able to access your compressed drives. However, if you suspect that it's your compression software that is causing the problem, you can bypass it during booting by pressing Ctrl+F5 or Ctrl+F8 when you see the `Starting MS-DOS...` message. Ctrl+F5 bypasses DrvSpace or DblSpace *and* both startup files. Ctrl+F8 bypasses DrvSpace or DblSpace and executes CONFIG.SYS and AUTOEXEC.BAT one line at a time. (As with F8, you can subsequently press Esc to execute the remainder of the startup files without prompting, or press F5 to skip the remainder of the startup files.)

> **Tip:** DOS pauses two seconds while displaying `Starting MS-DOS...` to give you plenty of time to press F5, F8, Ctrl+F5, or Ctrl+F8. If the pause annoys you and you're sure you won't need it, insert a `SWITCHES /F` command in CONFIG.SYS to eliminate it.
>
> If you're responsible for setting up the startup files for other, less experienced users, and you want to prevent them from bypassing the startup files, place `SWITCHES /N` in their CONFIG.SYS files. This doesn't prevent them from using Ctrl+F5 or Ctrl+F8, which bypass DoubleSpace or DriveSpace as well as the startup files. Use the command `DBLSPACE /SWITCHES=N` or `DRVSPACE /SWITCHES=N` to disable Ctrl+F5 and Ctrl+F8.

Prompting for CONFIG.SYS Commands

You can set up individual CONFIG.SYS commands so that DOS will prompt you for confirmation every time you boot. Insert a question mark (?) at the end of the command name to do this. For example, you could set up a RAM drive to be installed only when you say so by inserting the following command in CONFIG.SYS:

```
DEVICE?=C:\DOS\RAMDRIVE.SYS
```

If MEMMAKER has adapted the command with /L and /S switches, the question mark goes right after DEVICEHIGH, as follows:

```
DEVICEHIGH? /L:1,8902 /S =C:\DOS\RAMDRIVE.SYS
```

Using Configuration Blocks

DOS 6 includes a set of new commands for CONFIG.SYS that let you display a menu, input a choice from the keyboard, and execute a block of commands according to which menu item was chosen. In a typical scenario, suppose you have one program that requires expanded memory. You don't want to borrow extended memory every time you boot, only when you plan to work with that one program. You can set up CONFIG.SYS so that, when you boot, you see this screen:

```
MS-DOS 6.22 Startup Menu
========================

    1. Set up expanded memory
    2. Don't set up expanded memory

Enter a choice: 2        Time remaining: 05
```

```
F5=Bypass startup files F8=Confirm each line of CONFIG.SYS and AUTOEXEC.BAT [N]
```

If you choose option 1, CONFIG.SYS borrows some extended memory to create expanded memory. If you choose option 2, no expanded memory is created. If you don't choose either option, perhaps because you walked away from the computer after turning it on, Time Remaining counts down to 0 and option 2 is chosen by default.

Figure 38.1 shows the CONFIG.SYS file that creates the preceding menu. Notice first that it is broken into sections, called *blocks*, headed by names in square brackets, as in [MENU] and [COMMON].

```
[MENU]
MENUITEM=EXPAND, Set up expanded memory
MENUITEM=NORMAL, Don't set up expanded memory
MENUDEFAULT=NORMAL,5


[COMMON]
DEVICE=C:\DOS\HIMEM.SYS
DOS=HIGH
BUFFERS=10,0
FILES=30



LASTDRIVE=E
FCBS=4,0


[EXPAND]
DEVICE=C:\DOS\EMM386.EXE RAM


[NORMAL]
DEVICE=C:\DOS\EMM386.EXE NOEMS


[COMMON]
DOS=UMB
DEVICEHIGH /L:1,12048 =C:\DOS\SETVER.EXE
STACKS=9,256
SHELL=C:\DOS\COMMAND.COM C:\DOS\ /P
DEVICEHIGH=C:\DOS\DRVSPACE.SYS /MOVE
```

Figure 38.1. *Multiple configuration CONFIG.SYS.*

The Configuration Blocks

The [MENU] block contains the commands that create the menu. The [COMMON] blocks contain commands that are executed no matter which menu item is chosen. The [EXPAND] block contains the command that is executed when the first menu item is chosen; the EMM386 command in this block uses the RAM switch to set up both upper memory blocks and expanded memory. The [NORMAL] block contains the command that is executed when the second menu item is chosen; the EMM386 command in this block uses the NOEMS switch to set up upper memory blocks only.

The sequencing of the blocks is important. The first [COMMON] block installs HIMEM.SYS, among other things. This must happen before you can load EMM386 in the [EXPAND] or [NORMAL] block. Then, the second [COMMON] block loads several drivers into upper memory; these commands must be executed after the EMM386 command.

Defining a Menu

To define a menu, you create a block labeled [MENU]. For each item in the menu, insert a command in the following format:

```
MENUITEM=blockname[,menu-text]
```

The blockname identifies the block of commands to be executed if this item is chosen. blockname can be up to 70 characters long and contain any printable characters except the following characters:

```
space , \ / ; = [ ]
```

menu-text identifies the text to be displayed in the menu, and can be up to 70 characters long. If you don't define any menu text, the block name is displayed.

The MENUDEFAULT command established a default if the user doesn't make a choice within so many seconds. The command format is as follows:

```
MENUDEFAULT=blockname[,timeout]
```

blockname identifies the configuration block to be executed by default. timeout establishes the number of seconds to wait before taking the default, from 0 to 90 seconds. If you omit timeout, DOS waits forever. The default is taken when the user presses Enter without typing a menu choice.

If you would like to try creating your own startup menu, follow the steps shown below:

1. Copy your CONFIG.SYS as CONFIG.SAV.
2. Open CONFIG.SYS for editing.

3. Insert the following commands at the beginning:

```
[MENU]
MENUITEM=Peter, Peter (default)
MENUITEM=Judi
MENUITEM=Scott
MENUDEFAULT=Peter, 5


[COMMON]
```

4. Insert the following commands at the end:

```
[PETER]


[JUDI]


[SCOTT]
```

> **Note:** This example displays a menu but doesn't actually do anything different for the three menu choices.

5. Save the file and exit the editor.

6. Exit any programs (such as DOS Shell) and get to the primary command prompt.

7. Reboot.

    DOS displays the menu and pauses.

8. Press 2 to choose Judi.

    DOS finishes booting.

9. Reboot again.

    DOS displays the menu and pauses.

10. Don't make a menu choice. Let it time out.

    After five seconds, DOS chooses the default item and finishes booting.

11. To restore your former CONFIG.SYS, copy CONFIG.SAV as CONFIG.SYS.

Submenus

Let's take a look at another common scenario. Three people share one computer. Peter does a lot of international work and needs to set up the keyboard, monitor, and printer to handle international characters. Scott does mostly multimedia work and needs to load multimedia drivers. Judi sometimes does multimedia work, sometimes works with a database that runs faster with a RAM drive, and sometimes does both.

Rather than display all of Judi's choices on the main menu, you can display a second menu, called a *submenu*, when Judi's configuration is chosen. To define a submenu, insert a command in the main menu in this format:

```
SUBMENU=blockname[,text]
```

The `blockname` should refer to a block that defines menu items for the submenu.

The revised CONFIG.SYS might look something like this:

```
[MENU]
MENUITEM=Peter, Peter (default)
SUBMENU=Judi
MENUITEM=Scott
MENUDEFAULT=Peter, 5

[COMMON]
DEVICE=C:\DOS\HIMEM.SYS
DEVICE=C:\DOS\EMM386.EXE NOEMS
DOS=HIGH
BUFFERS=10,0
FILES=30
LASTDRIVE=E
FCBS=4,0
DOS=UMB
DEVICEHIGH /L:1,12048 =C:\DOS\SETVER.EXE
STACKS=9,256
SHELL=C:\DOS\COMMAND.COM C:\DOS\ /P
DEVICEHIGH=C:\DOS\DRVSPACE.SYS /MOVE

[PETER]
COUNTRY=351,860,C:\DOS\COUNTRY.SYS
DEVICEHIGH=C:\DOS\DISPLAY.SYS CON=(EGA,437)

[JUDI]
MENUITEM=Multimedia
MENUITEM=Database
MENUITEM=Both
MENUDEFAULT=Database,5

[SCOTT]
DEVICEHIGH=C:\DEV\MTMCDS /D:MSCD001 /P:300 /A:0
DEVICEHIGH=C:\DEV\MTMSBS

[MULTIMEDIA]
INCLUDE SCOTT

 [DATABASE]
DEVICEHIGH=C:\DOS\RAMDRIVE.SYS /E

[BOTH]
INCLUDE SCOTT
INCLUDE DATABASE

[COMMON]
```

In the [MENU] block, notice that the second item is a SUBMENU command, not a MENUITEM command. The [PETER] block contains the commands that set up the computer for international characters; these commands are explained in Chapter 49, "Another Country Heard From."

The [SCOTT] block contains the commands that install drivers for the multimedia hardware. These are not DOS commands; they are unique to the hardware that is installed on the PC. The [JUDI] block contains MENUITEM commands that create the submenu. There is an additional block for each submenu item.

The [MULTIMEDIA] block uses a command you haven't seen before, called INCLUDE. INCLUDE blockname causes the contents of the specified block to be executed as part of this block. In this case, the IN-CLUDE command to include all the commands from the BLOCK named [SCOTT]. We could have just copied the actual commands into the block, but this makes it easier to revise them later on. They only have to be changed in one place. The [DATABASE] block executes the command for setting up the RAM drive. And, the [BOTH] block includes the multimedia commands as well as the RAM drive command.

The [COMMON] block at the end is not a mistake. It's a good idea to insert at the end of CONFIG.SYS a [COMMON] block, even if it's empty. This way, when you install new applications that add commands to CONFIG.SYS, the new commands go into a common block instead of your last alternate configuration block.

Adding Color to the Menu

When you define a menu or submenu, you can also define the colors of the text and the background screen. The MENUCOLOR command defines the colors for the menu screen:

```
MENUCOLOR=text[,background]
```

The codes used to define the colors are shown in Table 38.1.

Table 38.1. Color codes.

Code	Color	Code	Color
1	Black	9	Gray
2	Blue	10	Bright blue
3	Green	11	Bright green
4	Cyan	12	Bright cyan
5	Red	13	Bright red
6	Magenta	14	Bright magenta
7	Brown	15	Yellow
8	White	16	Bright white

The default background color is black. To display bright blue text on a white background, you would include this command in the [MENU] or submenu block:

```
MENUCOLOR=10,8
```

Looking Ahead: Chapter 43, "DOS and the Environment," shows you how to deal with alternate configurations in AUTOEXEC.BAT.

On Your Own

This chapter has shown you how to bypass the startup files during booting, as well as how to create multiple configurations in CONFIG.SYS. The following items can help you practice these techniques on your own:

1. Reboot and bypass your startup files.
2. Adapt your CONFIG.SYS to display a menu with white letters on a blue background. The menu should include at least three items. One of the items should lead to a submenu. (Don't actually change your configuration, however.)
3. Restore your former CONFIG.SYS.

39

Directory Management

Introduction

DOS provides several advanced directory techniques that give you even more power over your directory structure.

Advanced Techniques for Managing Directories

You have learned the basics of managing directories, but there are several advanced techniques that can help you get even more out of your directory structure. Some of these techniques are primarily time-savers, such as deleting all the files in a branch without deleting the branch itself. Others solve unusual problems, such as making a directory on your hard drive look like a separate drive to a program that works only with drives. Specifically, in this chapter, you will learn how to:

- Delete files throughout a branch without deleting the branch
- Save and restore the program search path in a batch program
- Substitute drive names for path names, and vice versa
- Find out the real name for a substituted path

Recommendations for Directory Structure

You can do a number of things to optimize your directory structure for ease of use and fast file access.

To keep paths short, avoid creating more than three or four levels of subdirectories. The longer the path, the more chance of making a typing error. Also, DOS commands are limited to 127 characters, and you would run out of command space when trying to copy the following:

```
C:\JNFILES\WP\DOCS\DOSBOOK\FIGURES\FIG3-1.PCX
```

to

```
D:\STORAGE\BACKUPS\JNF\DOCS\DOSBOOK\FIGURES\SAVE3-1.PCX
```

The time to access a file on your hard disk will be shortest if all your directories are located near the beginning of the disk (the ones in the search path being the first ones), with the files you use most often (such as the DOS program files) coming immediately after. This means that the read-write heads don't have to move very far to find a directory and then a desired file. However, it's difficult to arrange your hard disk that way using only DOS commands. If you notice your disk access time slowing down as you add more directories and files to your hard disk, you may consider getting one of the third-party utilities that reorganizes a disk for faster access, such as the Norton Utilities' SpeedDisk.

> **Note:** Another major factor in disk access speed is file fragmentation, which is discussed in Chapter 33, "Defragmenter."

Using DELTREE to Delete Files Instead of Branches

> **Tip:** If you create a temporary directory in a batch program, then delete the directory using DELTREE, be sure to use the /Y switch on the DELTREE command to override the confirmation step. With /Y, DOS doesn't ask users to confirm a DELTREE command for a branch they have never heard of.

You saw earlier (in Chapter 14, "Managing Directories") how to delete an entire branch with DELTREE. But, you can often take advantage of DELTREE's unique features to delete just the files in a branch without deleting the directories themselves.

Emptying a Directory Without Deleting the Directory

How to Empty a Directory Without Deleting the Directory

1. Switch to the directory to be emptied.

2. Enter **DELTREE** /Y *.*.

DOS deletes all the files in the directory, plus all its subdirectories and their files.

DELTREE refuses to delete the current directory, but it will delete all of its files plus all of its descendants. You can take advantage of this fact to empty a directory. Try it for yourself:

1. Create a directory called PRACTICE and copy the \DOS*.TXT files to it.

2. Create a subdirectory of PRACTICE called EXER1 and copy the \DOS\D*.SYS files to it.

3. Create a subdirectory of PRACTICE called EXER2 and copy the \DOS\M*.HLP files to it.

4. You'll need the PRACTICE branch for several of the exercises in this section, so make a copy of the entire branch called \EXERCISE.

5. Switch to \EXERCISE.

6. Enter **DIR** **/S** **/P** to see the contents of the entire branch.

7. Enter **DELTREE** **/Y** ***.*** to empty the entire branch, leaving only the EXERCISE directory.

> **Note:** DELTREE has a slight quirk: you must place the **/Y** before the filespec, instead of after it, or DELTREE ignores it.

8. Enter **DIR** **/S** to see that the branch is empty.

If you empty the branch headed by the root directory, DELTREE clears the entire directory tree of files and subdirectories. Only the root directory remains.

Deleting the Files but Retaining the Directories

Because DELTREE won't delete the current directory, it also won't delete the path leading to the current directory. That is, it won't delete the parent directory, the parent's parent, and so on. You can take advantage of this fact by deleting all the files in a branch without deleting the directories themselves. Just position yourself in the lowest level subdirectory and use DELTREE to delete the branch.

Note that any subdirectories that are not in the current directory's path will be deleted by this action. Take the PRACTICE branch as an example. If you make EXER1 current and delete the PRACTICE branch, PRACTICE and EXER1 will be emptied of files but will not be deleted; however, EXER2 will be deleted because it is not in EXER1's path. Try this for yourself:

1. Copy the \PRACTICE branch as \EXERCISE.

2. Switch to \EXERCISE.

3. Enter **DIR** **/S** **/P** to see the contents of the branch.

4. Switch to EXER1.

5. Enter **DELTREE** **/Y** **..** to empty the branch.

6. Switch to the parent directory.

7. Enter **DIR** **/S** to see that EXERCISE and EXER1 still exist but are empty.

   Notice that EXER2 has been deleted.

Restructuring a Directory Tree

DOS includes some commands that enable you to restructure your directory tree, establishing alternate names for directories or temporarily connecting directories that aren't normally related to each other. Of these commands, only SUBST should be used. The other commands—APPEND, JOIN, and ASSIGN (which has been dropped from DOS 6, but might still appear in your DOS directory)—are never needed. APPEND can in certain situations cause you to lose data. This chapter shows you how to use only SUBST. The rest are listed in the "Command Reference."

Why APPEND Is Dangerous

APPEND looks great on the surface—it makes the files in a specified list of directories available no matter what directory is current. APPEND resembles the PATH command but applies to data files. However, the fly lands in the ointment when you're modifying a file from an appended directory, as illustrated in Figure 39.1.

Figure 39.1.
Directory mix-ups with APPEND.

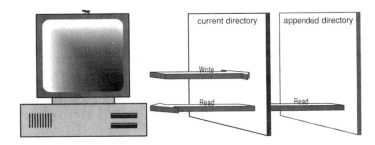

The problem occurs when an application updates a file by saving a new copy instead of rewriting the existing copy. To the application, the file appears to be in the current directory; only DOS knows about the appended directory. Therefore, the application saves the updated version in the current directory, and DOS doesn't reroute it to the appended directory. The overall result is that the new version is in the wrong directory, and the original version, in the right directory, has not been updated. This can happen not only to the data files you work on but also to the support files that are essential to an application's functions (such as DOSSHELL.INI).

In case you think this is a rare problem, you should understand that most applications update files this way—all the major word processors, desktop publishers, graphics developers, text editors, spreadsheet programs, and so on. The most common exceptions are database managers, which tend to update files in place rather than save new copies.

The slight convenience that APPEND offers is not worth the dangers.

Making a Directory Look Like a Drive

Suppose that you're working with an early version of a program that expects its program files to be on drive A and its data files to be on drive B. (This was very common in the early days of PCs, which didn't yet have hard drives.) Your best bet is to upgrade your software, but if you can't, you may be able to work around your existing software. Rather than having to work with exceptionally slow floppy drives, you can fool the program into using directories on your hard drive. The SUBST command can be used to substitute a path name for a drive name. (See Figure 39.2.) For example, the following command substitutes C:\ASHAM for drive A:

```
SUBST A: C:\ASHAM
```

SUBST

Reassigns a drive name to refer to a path.

Syntax:

```
SUBST [drive: path] ¦ [drive: /D]
```

Parameters and Switches:

none	Displays substitutions currently in force.
drive	Identifies drive name to be reassigned.
path	Specifies path to be referred to by *drive*.
/D	Drops the indicated substitution.

Note: The following commands all operate on the underlying structure of a disk and cannot be used on a substituted drive, which is really a directory, not a complete drive: ASSIGN, BACKUP, CHKDSK, FDISK, FORMAT, LABEL, MIRROR, RECOVER, RESTORE, SYS. DISKCOPY and DISKCOMP cannot be used on a substituted drive if the real drive is not removable. DOS displays an error message if you try to use any of these commands inappropriately.

Figure 39.2. *SUBST command summary.*

Try this technique on your PC:

1. Insert any formatted disk in drive A.

2. Enter **DIR A:** to see what's on drive A.

3. Enter **SUBST A: C:\PRACTICE**.

DOS does not confirm the substitution.

4. Enter **DIR A:** again.

You see the contents of C:\PRACTICE, which DOS now thinks is drive A. Notice that you now cannot access the real drive A. Every command that references A accesses C:\PRACTICE instead.

5. Enter SUBST with no parameters to see a list of all your substitutions.

You see the message A: => C:\PRACTICE.

6. Enter **SUBST A: /D** to drop the substitution.

7. Enter **DIR A:** again.

You see the directory of the real drive A.

Note: SUBST cannot refer to the current drive. If you want to substitute a path name for the current drive name, you must switch to another drive first. Similarly, you must switch to another drive before you can drop the substitution for the current drive name.

Creating a Virtual Drive with SUBST

SUBST also solves problems with programs that don't recognize paths. (For example, early versions of WordStar didn't.) You can use SUBST to assign a fake drive name to a directory. For example, to assign the drive name F: to the C:\WIDGETS directory, you would enter SUBST F: C:\WIDGETS. The assigned drive name does not have to be a real drive in your system. If you use a nonexistent drive name, you create a *virtual drive*; that is, it acts just like a separate drive, even though it is really a directory.

Choosing a Drive Name for SUBST

In the previous example, we used a drive name that doesn't exist. We could have used a real drive such as A or B, but that would have made the real drive unavailable as long as the substitution was in effect.

Whatever drive name you choose must be available. Although DOS offers the potential of 26 drive names (A through Z), it doesn't automatically make all of them available. By default, DOS permits either five drive names (A through E) or the number of drive names that you actually have drives for (including RAM drives), whichever is larger. You must use the LASTDRIVE command in CONFIG.SYS to make more drive names available. (See Figure 39.3.)

LASTDRIVE

Specifies the highest drive letter and, therefore, the maximum number of drives that your system can access.

Syntax:

`LASTDRIVE=x`

Parameter:

x   Specifies a drive letter, A through Z. The minimum value is the highest drive letter in use by your system.

Figure 39.3. `LASTDRIVE` *CONFIG.SYS command summary.*

Suppose that you have a common setup—two floppy disk drives (A and B) and one hard drive. The names D and E are available for `SUBST` and `ASSIGN` commands. But, what if you have four hard disk drives (C through F)? By default, no virtual drive names are available for `SUBST` and `ASSIGN` commands. You can make two virtual drive names (G and H) available by inserting the following command in C:\CONFIG.SYS:

`LASTDRIVE=H`

DOS maintains a drive name table in memory, with each entry taking nearly 100 bytes. You can conserve valuable memory space by requesting only as many drive names as you actually need. If you make all possible drive names available by inserting `LASTDRIVE=Z` in CONFIG.SYS, when in fact you need only four drive names, you're wasting a couple of kilobytes of memory space.

Network Note: When your PC belongs to a network, you need the `LASTDRIVE` command to create a large enough drive name table so that you can log on to your network drives. Your network administrator can tell you the appropriate `LASTDRIVE` command.

Switching Disk Drives with SUBST

How to Switch Drives A and B

1. Change to drive C (or any drive that isn't A or B).

2. If you want to be able to access drive B by using the name A, enter **SUBST A: B:**.

Note: As long as the substitution is in effect, you will not be able to access the real drive A.

3. If you want to be able to access drive A by using the name B, enter **SUBST B: A:**.

Note: As long as the substitution is in effect, you will not be able to access the real drive B.

4. To drop the substitution, change to any drive other than the substituted one and enter **SUBST A: /D** or **SUBST B: /D**.

SUBST also can help you solve a problem that crops up occasionally. Suppose that you want to install an application from 3 1/2-inch disks, which fit only in your B drive, but the application must be installed from the A drive. You can make the installation work by substituting B:\ for A: before starting up the installation program:

```
C:\>SUBST A: B:\
C:\>A:
A:\>INSTALL
```

After the installation program is finished, you must switch away from drive A before you can drop the substitution:

```
A:\>C:
C:\>SUBST A: /D
```

Tip: If you need to boot from a disk that fits only in your B drive, more drastic measures are called for. You have to switch the cables inside the box to your A and B drives and, for 286 or higher machines, run the SETUP program to redefine the drives. (See your hardware manual or your dealer for instructions on how to access and use SETUP for your machine.)

TRUENAME

When you have masked the true directory structure with SUBST, you may be confused about what the current directory is, or in what directory a file resides. DOS includes an undocumented command called TRUENAME that shows the true path of a directory or file. (See Figure 39.4.)

TRUENAME

Identifies the true location of a directory or file.

Syntax:

```
TRUENAME [drive ¦ path ¦ filespec]
```

continues

```
Parameters:

none       Displays the true name of the current drive and directory.

drive      Displays the true name of drive.

path       Displays the true name of the indicated directory.

filespec   Displays the true filespec of the indicated file.
```

Figure 39.4. *TRUENAME command summary.*

To find out the true name of the current directory, enter TRUENAME with no parameters. The result appears as follows:

```
A:\>TRUENAME
C:\LOCKOUT\
A:\>
```

To find out the true location of a file, enter the filespec as a parameter:

```
A:\>TRUENAME LOCKOUT.DAT
C:\LOCKOUT\LOCKOUT.DAT
A:\>
```

This message would be displayed even if the current directory does not contain a file named LOCKOUT.DAT. All TRUENAME does is fill in the true path; it doesn't check to see whether the file exists.

On Your Own

This chapter has shown you how to manage your directory structure with commands such as DELTREE and SUBST. If you would like to practice these techniques on your own, you can use the following items as a guide:

- Delete all the files in the \PRACTICE\EXER2 directory.
- Empty the PRACTICE branch.
- Substitute \PRACTICE for drive A.
- Find out the true name of a file on drive A.
- Drop the substitution.
- What is the highest drive name you can access on your PC? Make sure you know how to make more drive names available.

When you have finished practicing, delete the PRACTICE branch before going on to the next chapter.

40 Advanced Copying Techniques

Introduction

DOS's copying commands can be used for plain vanilla copying, but each command also offers unique features that cannot be found elsewhere in DOS or Windows.

Handling Those "Other" Copying Tasks

You learned earlier how to copy files using DOS Shell, the COPY command, the XCOPY command, and even Microsoft's Backup programs. COPY and XCOPY have additional features that enable you to deal with copying tasks that you won't encounter every day. COPY, for example, can be used to concatenate (combine) text files and to change the date/time stamp on a file. XCOPY can select files for copying based on their archive attributes, date stamps, and time stamps.

In addition, the REPLACE command can compare two directories and select files to copy either because they are missing in the destination directory, or because they are present in the destination directory and need to be replaced.

This chapter shows you how to use these advanced features of DOS's copying commands. You will learn how to:

- Use XCOPY in a batch program to copy a set of files to several floppy disks
- Use XCOPY to prune and graft a directory branch
- Use COPY to concatenate files
- Use COPY to change a file's date/time stamp
- Use REPLACE to copy missing files to a directory
- Use REPLACE to update files in a directory

The *XCOPY* Command

Figure 40.1 shows the syntax of the XCOPY command (which some people call "ex-copy;" some call "cross-copy;" and some call "extended copy").

XCOPY

Copies files and subdirectories.

Syntax:

XCOPY *source* [*destination*] [/A ¦ /M] [/D:*date*] [/P] [/W]

Parameters and Switches:

source   Identifies the file(s) you want to copy.

---

destination	Specifies the location where the copy should be written; the default is the current directory.
/A	Copies only source files with positive archive attributes; does not change the archive attributes.
/M	Copies only source files with positive archive attributes; turns off the archive attributes.
/D:*date*	Copies only source files created or modified on or after date.
/P	Prompts you for permission to copy each selected file.
/W	Displays a message and waits for you to press a key before beginning to copy files.

Figure 40.1. *XCOPY command summary.*

XCOPY Versus DISKCOPY

You often may need to copy an entire disk. The DISKCOPY command makes a track-by-track copy of one floppy disk to another disk of exactly the same size. XCOPY also can be used to copy whole diskettes, which it does on a file-by-file basis, with the following advantages:

- You don't need to use the same size source and destination disks. You could copy a 1.2MB disk to a 1.44MB disk, for example.

- XCOPY doesn't copy the source disk's formatting, which may not be accurate for the destination disk. For example, DISKCOPY copies bad sector markings from the source to the destination, blocking out sectors on the destination diskette that aren't really bad.

- DISKCOPY fails if there are bad sectors on the destination disk; XCOPY doesn't.

- DISKCOPY destroys any existing files on the destination disk; XCOPY doesn't.

- With DISKCOPY, if files are fragmented (split into separate parts) on the source, they have the same fragmentation on the destination. XCOPY actually defragments files as it copies them, as long as the destination disk was empty to start with.

Don't use XCOPY to duplicate the installation disks for software, however. It's often important that such duplicates be exact, track-by-track copies of the originals, and you should make such copies by using DISKCOPY.

Avoiding Disk Full Termination

One disadvantage that both COPY and XCOPY share is the irksome habit of terminating themselves when the destination disk is full. Suppose that you have indicated that all *.DOC files should be copied to drive A, and COPY or XCOPY copies about half of them before the disk is full. Then, it quits, returning you to the DOS prompt. Now what do you do? If you insert another disk in the A drive and reenter the same COPY or XCOPY command, the same files will be selected and copied a second time because the program has no way of knowing that some of the files are not wanted. Your only recourse is to figure out which files have not yet been copied and copy them one by one.

You can avoid this problem in several ways. One way is to use DOS Shell, which enables you to continue a copy operation after changing the destination disk. Another solution uses Backup as explained in Chapter 23, "MSBACKUP and MWBACKUP." A third solution uses the archive attributes with XCOPY. The drawback to this solution is that it alters the archive attributes of the source files, which can affect your backup system later on. Nevertheless, it may be the best solution for the problem.

How to Copy a Large Set of Files to Floppy Disks using XCOPY

1. If you normally back up the files to be copied using an incremental or differential backup, do so now, because this procedure will turn off their archive attributes.

2. Enter **ATTRIB** *filespec* **+A** to turn on the archive attributes for all the files in the drive. To copy files throughout a branch, add the /S switch to this command.

3. Enter **XCOPY** *filespec* *d:* /M /W to start copying the files to drive *d*. To copy files throughout a branch, add /S to this command. /M selects files with the attribute, then turns it off after the file is copied.

   XCOPY pauses and displays the message Press any key to begin copying file(s).

4. Insert a blank, formatted disk in the drive and press a key.

   XCOPY begins copying files to the disk. Eventually, you see the message Disk Full and XCOPY terminates.

5. Repeat steps 3 and 4 until all the files have been copied.

To try the procedure, you will copy a large set of files from the DOS directory to floppy disks. You'll need at least two blank, formatted floppy disks for this exercise.

1. If you normally back up the files in your DOS directory using an incremental or differential backup, do so now, because this exercise will turn off their archive attributes.

2. Switch to the DOS directory.

3. Enter **ATTRIB** *.* **+A** to turn on the archive attributes for all the files in the drive.

> **Note:** XCOPY won't copy hidden or system files. To include hidden and system files in the copy, you would have to add -H and -S to this command to turn off those attributes. But first, use ATTRIB *.* > PRN (or a temporary filename) to document the files' attributes. After the copy, use the document to identify which files need to have their hidden or system attributes restored.

4. Enter **XCOPY *.* A: /M /W** to start copying the files to drive A. (Substitute **B:** for **A:** if you want to copy the files to drive B.)

   XCOPY pauses and displays the message Press any key to begin copying file(s) because you used the /W switch.

5. Insert a blank, formatted disk in the drive and press a key.

   XCOPY begins copying files to the disk. Eventually, you see the message Disk Full and XCOPY terminates.

6. Enter **ATTRIB *.*** to see the attributes of all the files in the drive.

   Notice that the archive attribute is off for those files that have been successfully copied (because you used the /M switch) but is on for all the uncopied files.

7. Repeat steps 4 and 5 until all the files have been copied.

A batch file for this procedure may look something like the one that follows. %1 is the filespec of the files to be copied. This procedure includes hidden and system files in the copy and prints out the original attributes of the source files so that they can be restored later, if necessary.

```
@ECHO OFF
REM Record the current attributes in case we want to
REM restore them when the job is done.
ECHO Current attributes for the %1 files: > PRN
ECHO. > PRN
ATTRIB %1 /S > PRN

REM Turn on the archive attributes for all %1 files.
REM Also, turn off their hidden and system attributes.
ATTRIB %1 /S +A -H -S

:COPYLOOP
REM Copy all the %1 files that have positive archive
REM attributes. Turn off attributes as you copy:
ECHO Insert the next target diskette in drive A:
PAUSE
XCOPY %1 A: /S /M

REM Repeat loop if XCOPY terminated unsuccessfully
REM for any reason, such as a disk full error.
IF ERRORLEVEL 1 GOTO COPYLOOP

:ENDING
ECHO ***************************************************
ECHO *                                                 *
```

```
ECHO *   The archive, hidden, and system attributes    *
ECHO *   have been removed from the source files.      *
ECHO *   Check the printout and restore attributes as  *
ECHO *   needed.                                        *
ECHO *                                                  *
ECHO ****************************************************
```

You could make this job more flexible by adding the following features:

- Accept the destination drive name or path as %2.

- Accept Y or N as %3 to indicate whether hidden and system files should be copied, or accept the Y or N from the keyboard with the CHOICE command.

Pruning and Grafting

The tree surgeon's terms, *pruning* and *grafting*, are used in PCs to describe the movement of a directory or branch from one parent to another. If you don't have a third-party utility to prune and graft, you can do it using XCOPY and DELTREE.

How to Prune and Graft a Directory

1. If the source branch includes hidden and system files, enter **ATTRIB** *source-path\directory-name*.* ***/S > PRN*** to document hidden and system attributes so that they can be restored later, if necessary.

2. Enter **ATTRIB** *source-path\directory-name*.* ***/S*** to turn off the hidden and system attributes.

3. Enter **XCOPY** *source-path\directory-name destination-path\directory-name ***/S*** to copy the directory and its files to the new location. Use the same *directory-name* for both the source and the destination, so that the moved branch has the same name that it had before.

4. Enter **DELTREE** *source-path\directory-name* to delete the old directory or branch.

5. Use the printout to restore the hidden and system attributes to the appropriate files in their new location.

In the following exercise, you will create a directory called PRACTICE as a child of the DOS directory, then move it to be a child of the root directory.

1. Create a directory called \DOS\PRACTICE and copy all the \DOS*.TXT files to it.

2. Enter **XCOPY \DOS\PRACTICE*.* \PRACTICE** to copy the directory as a child of the root directory.

> **Note:** It's important to specify the destination directory name in this command. If you specified simply the root directory as the destination, DOS would copy all the files from \DOS\PRACTICE into the root directory; it would not create a new subdirectory.
>
> To move an entire branch instead of just one directory, you would add the /S switch to this command.

3. Enter **DIR \PRACTICE** to see the new directory and its contents.
4. Enter **DELTREE /Y \DOS\PRACTICE** to delete the old directory.

   You have now pruned and grafted the directory.

You'll continue using the \PRACTICE directory in the next section.

Concatenating Files

One of COPY's unique features is its capability to concatenate (combine) files. Figure 40.2 shows the syntax of COPY that you use for this function.

COPY (for concatenation)

Combines two or more files into one.

Syntax:

```
COPY [switches] source [+...] [destination] [switches]
```

Parameters and Switches:

source	Identifies the file(s) to be copied.
destination	Identifies the new file to be created.
/A	Uses ASCII mode for the copy.
/B	Uses binary mode for the copy.

Note:
The /A or /B switch affects the filespec preceding it and all subsequent filespecs until it reaches a filespec that is followed by another /A or /B switch.

Figure 40.2. *COPY command summary (for concatenation).*

Try concatenating some of the .TXT files in the \PRACTICE directory:

1. Switch to the \PRACTICE directory.

2. Enter **COPY README.TXT + WHATSNEW.TXT + NETWORKS.TXT COLLECT.TXT**.

   You see these messages as DOS creates the new file:

   ```
   README.TXT
   WHATSNEW.TXT
   NETWORKS.TXT
           1 File(s) copied
   ```

   The message says 1 `File(s) copied`, because only one file was created (or replaced).

3. Enter **DIR *.TXT** to see the new file as well as the old ones. Notice that COLLECT.TXT's size indicates that it is a sum of README.TXT, WHATSNEW.TXT, and NETWORKS.TXT. Notice also that COLLECT.TXT was created just a few moments ago according to its time and date stamp.

The following command may or may not have the same effect:

```
C:\DOCS>COPY *.TXT COLLECT.TXT
```

Because a global source filespec is used with a single destination filespec, the plus sign is not necessary. COPY will concatenate all matching source files into the one destination file. This match may include more files than you intended. The order of the files will be as they appear in the directory. If NETWORKS.TXT appears first, it will be the first file copied to COLLECT.TXT.

> **Note:** When creating a file, DOS places it in the first available directory entry, which may be the former entry of a deleted file. For this reason, the order of entries in a busy directory seems arbitrary. Even if you write CHAPTER1 first, CHAPTER2 next, and CHAPTER3 last, these three files could appear in any order in the directory.
>
> You can sort directory entries to a limited extent when you optimize the drive using DEFRAG (see Chapter 33, "Defragmenter").

Appending Files

Sometimes, you want to concatenate files by appending them to an existing file. For example, suppose that you want to append WHATSNEW.TXT and NETWORKS.TXT to README.TXT, instead of creating a new file:

1. Make sure you're in the \PRACTICE directory.

2. Enter **COPY README.TXT + WHATSNEW.TXT + NETWORKS.TXT /Y**. (The /Y bypasses COPY's normal overwrite confirmation feature for README.TXT.)

You see these messages:

```
README.TXT
WHATSNEW.TXT
NETWORKS.TXT
        1 File(s) copied
```

3. Enter **DIR *.TXT** to see the effects of the copy command. Notice README.TXT's size, date stamp, and time stamp.

Note: In this case, if COPY can't find README.TXT, it will concatenate NETWORKS.TXT into WHATSNEW.TXT (if WHATSNEW.TXT exists). When a destination file is not specifically identified, COPY uses the first file from the left end of the command that it finds.

The following command is legitimate but may not have the same result because a different set of files may be identified and they may appear in a different order. The destination file will be the first file in the directory that matches the *.TXT filespec:

```
C:\DOCS>COPY *.TXT
```

A variation on this command controls the destination file by specifically identifying it:

```
C:\DOCS>COPY *.TXT README.TXT
```

Problem: I was concatenating files and got the message Content of destination lost before copy. Have I destroyed my file somehow?

When one of the source files is also the destination file, COPY opens it and begins appending each source file to it. After the first file is appended, the destination file is irrevocably changed. If COPY then finds the destination file's entry in the directory and realizes that it matches the filespec for a source file, it also realizes that it can't append the destination file to itself.

This message looks devastating, but in fact it's perfectly normal. It means that, because the destination file has already been changed, it can't be used as a source file. In fact, things are progressing just as they should. You can safely ignore this message.

The Effect of Concatenation on Certain File Types

Because README.TXT, WHATSNEW.TXT, and NETWORKS.TXT are ASCII (unformatted) text files, they concatenate with no problems. Other types of files are not so easy, as you'll see in the following paragraphs.

Data Files

Suppose that PART1.DOC, PART2.DOC, and PART3.DOC were created by a word processor and stored in its native format. They probably have header and trailer information surrounding the text itself. When you concatenate them, all three sets of headers and trailers are included in the file, creating a hybrid that can no longer be processed by the original word processor. The same problem exists with files created by most of today's applications: desktop publishers, spreadsheets, databases, and so on.

To concatenate such files to be usable, don't use COPY; concatenate the files from within the application so that it can create and remove headers and trailers as appropriate.

Binary Files

As with application data files, you do not produce a usable product by concatenating binary files such as executable program modules. Concatenating two program modules will not only produce an invalid program module, it may create a program that could damage your data. Here again, if you want to combine files, use the proper tools. For example, use a linkage editor to combine two executable program modules.

Peter's Principle: Use the original application to concatenate files.

The only files that concatenate logically via COPY are ASCII text files. For all other types of files, you'll achieve better results by using the files' original application to combine them.

Updating Date/Time Stamps

When DOS copies a file, it doesn't update the file's date/time stamp, because the time and date identify the file's version. When you concatenate files, however, the current time and date are assigned to the newly created file because it is a new version.

You can trick DOS into assigning the current time and date to a file by pretending to concatenate it with a command in the following syntax:

```
COPY source-filespec /B +,, [destination]
```

Be sure to use a single source filespec, because a global one would cause a real concatenation to take place. Therefore, if you want to update the date/time stamp on a group of files, do them one at a time; you can use the FOR command to get it all done with one command.

The two commas after the plus force DOS to stop concatenating. If the destination is included, the copy is made and only the destination file receives the new date/time stamp. If there is no destination, the source file receives the new date/time stamp.

Warning: The /B switch is important to prevent DOS from truncating the file, as explained under "The ABCs of /A and /B" later in this chapter. Don't leave it out, or you could lose data.

Note: You can add the /Y switch to this command to overwrite copy protection with DOS 6.2 and 6.22.

Try updating the date/time stamp on NETWORKS.TXT:

1. Enter **DIR NETWORKS.TXT** to see its current date/time stamp.
2. Enter **COPY NETWORKS.TXT /B +,,** to update the date/time stamp to the current system date and time.
3. Enter **DIR NETWORKS.TXT** to see the new date/time stamp.

Tip: The following batch program changes the date/time stamp to any value you want on a group of files, where %1 is the new time; %2 is the new date; and %3 through %9 are optional filespecs, which can be global.

```
@ECHO OFF
TIME %1 > NUL
DATE %2 > NUL
FOR %%F IN (%3 %4 %5 %6 %7 %8 %9) DO COPY /B %%F+,,
ECHO The system time and date have been changed.
ECHO Please reset the correct time:
TIME
ECHO Please reset the correct date:
DATE
```

Matched Concatenations

COPY permits a special technique in which it will concatenate files with matching filenames but different extensions. An example should make this clear:

```
COPY *.TXT + *.ADD *.NEW
```

This command causes COPY to concatenate FORM.TXT with FORM.ADD to create FORM.NEW, TEACH.TXT with TEACH.ADD to create TEACH.NEW, and so on. If the directory contains TEACH.ADD but not TEACH.TXT, or vice versa, an error message is displayed and TEACH.NEW is not created.

The following are some variations on matched concatenations:

- You can specify more than two source files:

```
COPY *.1 + *.2 + *.3 + *.4  *.ALL
```

- You can omit the destination filespec to concatenate into the first filespec:

```
COPY *.TXT + *.ADD
```

The ABCs of /A and /B

The /A and /B switches can be important in copying and concatenating files; in order to use them properly, you have to understand a bit about DOS file storage.

Clusters and Slack

DOS stores files in disk storage blocks called clusters or allocation units. Every disk has a fixed cluster size, which depends on the size of the disk and the program that formatted it. For example, a small-capacity (360KB) floppy disk has 512-byte clusters, but a large-capacity disk such as an 360MB hard disk may have 4096-byte clusters (or larger). The cluster size is set during formatting.

DOS allocates disk space to files in whole clusters. If a file doesn't use a complete cluster, the left-over space at the end of the cluster is called *slack*. On a disk with 2048-byte clusters, a one-byte file will occupy one whole cluster, with 2047 bytes of slack. A 15KB file will occupy eight clusters, with 1KB of slack at the end of the last cluster. Slack space is wasted space; it can't be allocated to any other file. It may contain leftover data from a previous file (or files) that occupied more of the cluster.

Avoiding Slack when Accessing Files

When DOS reads a file for copying, printing, concatenation, or some other operation, it wants to read only the valid file data and ignore the slack. DOS has two methods of identifying the end of legitimate data in a cluster:

- The ASCII method depends on an end-of-file (EOF) mark—which is ^Z or hex 1A—appearing as the last character in the file. When using the ASCII method, DOS scans the data it reads and stops when it encounters hex 1A. (If a file has no EOF mark, DOS uses the file's size to decide when to stop reading.)

- The binary method uses the file's size as recorded in its directory entry. If the directory entry says that the file is 3,267 bytes, DOS will read exactly 3,267 bytes from the disk. Any hex 1A characters in the data are read just like other data.

The problem with the ASCII method is that it works only with files that do not contain inadvertent EOF marks as part of their data, as may happen with binary files, worksheets, graphics files, and other application files. The only files that work reliably with the ASCII method are true ASCII files—files containing only ASCII character data and no formatting information. The binary method, however, always works.

DOS also has ASCII and binary methods of writing files. With the ASCII method, DOS adds the EOF mark to the end of the file. With the binary method, it doesn't.

Some DOS utilities (especially the older and more elementary ones) use the ASCII method, and others use the binary method. Utilities designed to work with ASCII format files, such as TYPE and PRINT, use the ASCII method. Utilities that should work with any type of file, such as XCOPY and MOVE, use the binary method.

COPY Methods

COPY sometimes uses one method and sometimes the other. It uses the binary method for most copy processes. For processes that make sense only with ASCII files, such as concatenation and copying to CON or PRN, it uses the ASCII method. You can force it to use the other method with the /A and /B switches.

You can force COPY to use the ASCII method to read a source file by including the /A switch before or after the source filespec. You can force COPY to use the ASCII method of writing a file, which adds an EOF mark to the end of the copy, by including the /A switch after the destination filespec. The EOF mark is never essential to DOS programs, but you may have some other software that requires it. (Most modern programs don't.)

You can force COPY to use the binary method to read a source file by including the /B switch before or after the source filespec. If you have a reason to concatenate binary files, you have to use the /B switch to force COPY to read the source files in binary mode, because COPY concatenates in ASCII mode by default.

You can force COPY to write a file in binary mode, which omits the EOF mark, by placing a /B after the destination filespec. You need this switch when concatenating binary files if you don't want DOS to add an EOF mark to the end of the new file.

Date Stamping Non-ASCII Files

You need the /B switch when updating the date/time stamp on a non-ASCII file. If you don't use /B, the concatenation process will truncate the file at the first byte containing hex 1A. Without /B, DOS also adds an EOF mark to the end of the file. Specify a /B before the filespec to make sure that the whole file is copied with the new date/time and that no EOF mark is added. The following example updates the date/time stamp on the file named DEFRAG.COM:

```
COPY /B DEFRAG.COM+,,
```

Problem: When I tried to change the time/date stamp on a file, COPY lost part of the file.

You use COPY's concatenation feature to change the time/date stamp on a file, which automatically performs an ASCII concatenation unless you include the /B switch in the command. In an ASCII copy, COPY stops as soon as it recognizes an end-of-file mark. This will most likely truncate any file that contains non-ASCII data.

You can't recover your former file by using DOS utilities now that it has been damaged. You will have to restore it from your most recent backup. If the truncated data is text data, you may be able to rescue some of it using a recovery utility that lets you rescue data from the unused clusters on a disk, such as the Norton Utilities' UnErase.

To avoid this problem in the future, always include /B in the COPY command when updating a file's time/date stamp.

Peter's Principle: Always use the /B switch when updating date/time stamps.

This switch isn't necessary when updating ASCII files, but it's a good habit to get into because it's essential when updating non-ASCII files. You could make a DATESTMP macro to do COPY /B %1+,, and then type DATESTMP DEFRAG.COM.

Copying Files to a Device

Be sure to use /B when copying a non-ASCII file to a device, as COPY by default uses ASCII mode with many devices, and any non-ASCII values in the file may not be handled correctly.

The *REPLACE* Command

REPLACE has two special functions, both based on its capability to select files by comparing the contents of the source and destination directories:

- It will replace files that are present in the source directory but are missing in the destination directory (*replace* is used here in the sense of restoring something that has been lost).
- It will replace files that exist in both the source and destination directories (*replace* here has the sense of substituting one item for another).

Figure 40.3 shows the syntax of the REPLACE command.

REPLACE

Replaces or adds files from one directory to another.

Syntax:

```
REPLACE filespec path [/P] [/R] [/W] [/S] [/U] [/A]
```

Overwrites files in the destination directory with matching files from the source directory or add files that aren't there.

Parameters and Switches:

filespec	Identifies the source file(s).
path	Identifies the destination directory.
/P	Prompts for confirmation before replacing a file.
/R	Replaces files that are read-only in the destination directory as well as nonread-only files.
/W	Waits for you to press a key before beginning to search for source files.
/S	Searches all subdirectories of *path* to find files to be replaced.
/U	Examines the date/time stamps of source and destination files and replaces (updates) files in the destination directory only if they are older than the source files that replace them.
/A	Replaces missing files on the destination directory. Don't use with /R, /S, or /U.

Figure 40.3. *REPLACE command summary.*

Replacing Missing Files

Suppose that you deleted several files from C:\PROPS, and you have changed your mind. Suppose also that it's too late to undelete them, but you have copies on a network drive. (If the copies were made with a backup program, this won't work, but you can restore them.) The REPLACE command may be the easiest way to restore them. The following command will select all *.PLS files that exist on G:\PROPS but do not exist on C:\PROPS:

```
REPLACE G:\PROPS\*.PLS C:\PROPS /A /P
```

Because you used the /P switch, REPLACE will display each filespec and let you decide whether or not to copy it. This helps us avoid unwanted restorations.

Try deleting and replacing some files in the \PRACTICE directory:

1. Delete \PRACTICE\NETWORKS.TXT and WHATSNEW.TXT.

2. Enter **REPLACE \DOS*.TXT \PRACTICE /A /P**.

3. Answer Yes to each confirmation message.

Peter's Principle: Always use the /P switch on the REPLACE command.

The powerful REPLACE command can end up replacing many more files than you intended, perhaps overwriting newer files of the same name. The /P switch gives you the chance to review the name of each file selected for replacement, a sensible precaution when performing this type of operation.

Replacing Existing Files

Suppose that you have installed an application in several places on your hard disk. Now you receive an update. The following command seeks out and replaces all the files on the hard disk that have the same name as the files on the disk in drive A:

```
REPLACE A: C:\ /R /S /P
```

Try replacing the files in your PRACTICE directory with the original ones in the DOS directory:

1. Enter **REPLACE \DOS*.TXT \PRACTICE /P**.

   DOS displays each file name for you to approve before replacing it.

2. Enter **DIR \PRACTICE** to see the effects of the REPLACE command. Notice that README.TXT has been restored to its original size and date/time stamp. Notice also that NETWORKS.TXT has its original date/time stamp.

REPLACE's /U (update) switch causes a file to be replaced only if its date/time stamp indicates that it is an older version than the matching source file.

On Your Own

This chapter has shown you several advanced techniques with the XCOPY, COPY, and REPLACE commands. If you would like to practice these techniques on your own, you can use the following items as a guide:

1. Copy a large group of files to a set of floppy disks.

2. Move the \PRACTICE directory to be a child of the DOS directory.

3. Concatenate all the files in \DOS\PRACTICE into one file called ONMYOWN.TXT.

4. Update the date/time stamp of \DOS\PRACTICE\README.TXT.

5. Write a FOR command to update the date/time stamps of all the files in the \DOS\PRACTICE directory.

6. Delete some of the files in \DOS\PRACTICE, then replace them from the DOS directory.

7. Before ending your work on this chapter, delete the \DOS\PRACTICE directory.

41 INTERLNK

Introduction

DOS 6's new INTERLNK feature lets you hook up two computers and access one from the other. For example, you can copy and move files from one computer to the other, run programs that are installed on only one of them, and use the one computer's printer from the other.

Linking Two Computers via INTERLNK

INTERLNK was designed to let you access a desktop computer from your notebook so that you can transfer and print the files you've developed on the road. But, it comes in handy anytime you have two computers close to each other that aren't networked.

When you connect two computers with INTERLNK, one is the *server* and one is the *client*. (See Figure 41.1.) The server can do nothing on its own while the connection is in force. The only thing you can enter from its keyboard is the command to break the connection. The client does all the work. It can access the server's drives and parallel ports as if they were part of its own configuration. INTERLNK assigns drive names and port names so that it can do this. For example, if the client normally had one hard drive, drive C, INTERLNK would assign the drive name D to the server's drive C. The client can copy files from its hard drive to the server's hard drive by copying them from drive C to drive D.

Figure 41.1.
The client-server connection.

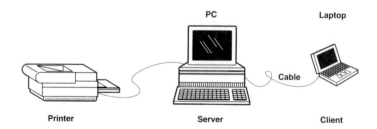

Client drives and ports
A:
B:
C:
D: = Server drive C:
E: = Server drive D:
LPTI: = Server port LPTI

In this chapter you'll learn how to:

- Create the link between two computers
- Access the server computer's drives and ports from the client computer
- Break the link between the two computers

Overview of the INTERLNK Procedure

There are three main steps to establishing a link between two computers:

- First, cable the two computers together.
- Then, run the INTERSRV program on the server. This sets up the computer in server mode.
- Finally, load the INTERLNK.EXE driver on the client via CONFIG.SYS. This completes the connection.

Suppose you have a notebook computer that you frequently connect to your desktop PC to transfer files back and forth. You could set up alternate configurations in your notebook's CONFIG.SYS so that you could boot with or without INTERLNK.EXE. Or, you could include a question mark (?) after the word DEVICE or DEVICEHIGH in the DEVICE command, so that DOS asks if you want to load INTERLNK.EXE each time you boot. (Both of these techniques are explained in Chapter 38, "Starting Up DOS.") Or, if you have upper memory to spare on your notebook, you could just load INTERLNK.EXE every time you boot, whether or not you plan to link to your desktop.

INTERLNK does not try to make a connection when the client is not cabled to another computer or when the other computer is not yet in server mode. In that case, you need to take one more step to complete the connection when you connect the two computers—you enter the INTERLNK command on the client when you're ready to go.

Note: If you link your computers together frequently, you might appreciate the extra features of third-party linking software such as Norton pcANYWHERE. Such software also enables you to control your office computer from your home over the telephone line by using a modem.

Cabling the Two Computers

You can cable the computers together through either their serial ports or their parallel ports. You must use the same type of port on each one, of course, but they don't have to have the same port number. You could, for example, cable LPT1 on the client to LPT3 on the server.

Use one of these types of cable:

- 3-wire serial cable
- 7-wire null-modem cable
- Bidirectional parallel cable

If you would like to try INTERLNK during this chapter, cable them together now:

1. Locate the appropriate cable.
2. Connect the two computers via their serial or parallel ports.

Setting Up the Server

Figure 41.2 shows the INTERSVR command, which you use to place a computer in server mode. If you want to use all the default settings, just enter the word INTERSVR. All the server's drives and ports are made available for redirection when you don't specify otherwise. To redirect just hard drive C, you could use this command:

```
INTERSVR C:
```

Or, you could do it by not redirecting to drives A and B:

```
INTERSVR /X=A /X=B
```

Note: INTERSVR does not redirect network drives, CD-ROM drives, or any other drives that use a redirection interface.

INTERSVR

Loads the INTERLNK server software and redirects drives and printer ports; copies INTERLNK files from one computer to another.

Syntax:

```
INTERSVR [drive ... ] [/X=drive ...]
```

```
[/LPT[n] ¦ /COM[n] ] [BAUD:rate] [/V] [/RCOPY]
```

Parameters and Switches:

none   Loads the server program and displays the server screen.

drive   Identifies server drive(s) to redirect. By default, INTERSVR redirects all the
            server's drives.

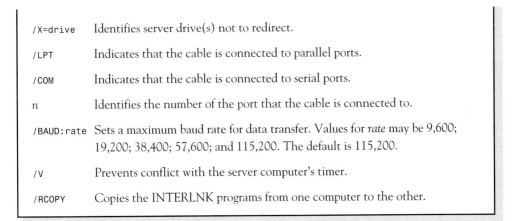

/X=drive	Identifies server drive(s) not to redirect.
/LPT	Indicates that the cable is connected to parallel ports.
/COM	Indicates that the cable is connected to serial ports.
n	Identifies the number of the port that the cable is connected to.
/BAUD:rate	Sets a maximum baud rate for data transfer. Values for *rate* may be 9,600; 19,200; 38,400; 57,600; and 115,200. The default is 115,200.
/V	Prevents conflict with the server computer's timer.
/RCOPY	Copies the INTERLNK programs from one computer to the other.

Figure 41.2. *INTERSVR command summary.*

How to Link Two Computers before Booting the Client Computer

1. Cable the two computers together.

2. Enter the INTERSVR command on the server computer.

   A drive and port table appears on the server computer's screen. However, the new drive and port names are not shown because the connection has not yet been made.

3. If you haven't already done so, edit the client computer's CONFIG.SYS to load INTERLNK.EXE.

4. Reboot the client computer, being sure to load INTERLNK.EXE if it is an option.

   INTERLNK.EXE searches out the cable link and completes the connection, displaying a list of the remapped drives and ports from the server computer. The drive table on the server computer's screen also shows the remapped drive and port list.

5. You can now access the server computer's drives and ports using the names shown on the screen.

6. When you're finished with the connection, press Alt+F4 on the server computer. Then, remove the cable.

7. If you need to clear INTERLNK.EXE from the client computer's memory to make room for other programs, edit CONFIG.SYS if necessary to remove the command, then reboot.

When you don't include a port name on the command, INTERSVR scans all the server's ports looking for the cable. You'll use up more memory space this way because it installs the routines for handling both serial and parallel ports; but, the server's memory space is probably not a problem because it can't do anything else while INTERSVR is running. However, you should avoid scanning the serial ports if a mouse is attached to one of them; INTERSVR can damage the mouse driver in this situation. Suppose you have a serial mouse on COM1 and a cable to your laptop on COM2. You should enter the INTERSVR command this way:

INTERSVR /COM2

Suppose instead you have a serial mouse on COM1 and a cable to your laptop on LPT2. You could use either the /LPT switch to let INTERSVR scan your parallel ports, or specify /LPT2.

With a serial connection, INTERSVR transfers data at 115,200 baud. If that's too fast for your computer, use the /BAUD parameter to set a lower baud rate.

Tip: If one of your computers freezes up during the connection, INTERLNK may be conflicting with your computer's timer. Use the /V switch the next time you try.

If you want to try connecting two computers during this chapter, set up the server computer now:

1. If the cable is connected to COMn, enter **INTERSVR /COM**n.

2. If the cable is connected to LPTn, enter **INTERSVR /LPT** or **INTERSVR /LPT**n, whichever you prefer.

Figure 41.3 shows what the server computer's screen looks like when you first load INTERSVR and no connection has been established. You can see the drives and ports that will be redirected, but they have not received their client names yet. The Client column is filled in when INTERLNK completes the connection. Notice the instruction to press Alt+F4; this is how you break the connection later on.

Figure 41.3.
The INTERSVR screen.

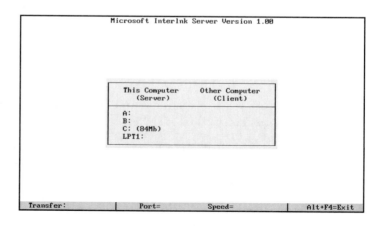

Setting Up the Client

Figure 41.4 shows the command that you insert in CONFIG.SYS to load the INTERLNK.EXE driver. INTERLNK scans for a server computer as soon as it is loaded. If it finds one, it completes the connection and you can begin accessing the server. If not, it merely loads itself and waits. Use the /AUTO switch if you want INTERLNK.EXE to load only if it can find a connection during booting.

INTERLNK.EXE

Completes an INTERLNK connection of client and server computers; redirects server drives.

Syntax:

```
DEVICE[HIGH]=[path]INTERLNK.EXE [/DRIVES:n] [/NOPRINTER]

[/COM[n] ¦ /LPT[n]] [/AUTO] [/NOSCAN]

[/BAUD:rate] [/V]
```

Parameters and Switches:

path	Identifies the location of the INTERLNK.EXE file. The default is the root directory of the boot drive.
/DRIVES:*n*	Specifies the number of server drives to be redirected to the client computer. The default is 3. If $n = 0$, INTERLNK redirects only printers.
/NOPRINTER	Inhibits redirection of printers. By default, INTERLNK redirects all available parallel printer ports.
/COM[*n*]	Specifies the port by which the client computer is cabled to the server computer; if *n* is not specified, INTERLNK scans all serial ports for the connection.
/LPT[*n*]	Specifies the port by which the client computer is cabled to the server computer; if *n* is not specified, INTERLNK scans all parallel ports for the connection.
/AUTO	Installs INTERLNK.EXE in memory only if it can establish an immediate link with the server computer. By default, INTERLNK.EXE is installed even if the connection can't yet be completed.
/NOSCAN	Installs INTERLNK.EXE in memory, but prevents it from establishing a connection. By default, INTERLNK tries to establish a connection with the server as soon as you install it.

/BAUD:*rate*	Sets a maximum baud rate for serial communication. Valid values are 9,600; 19,200; 38,400; 57,600; and 115,200. The default is 115,200.
/V	Prevents conflicts with a computer's timer. Specify this switch if you have a serial connection between computers and one of them stops running when you use INTERLNK to access a drive or printer port.

Figure 41.4.   *INTERLNK.EXE configuration command summary.*

Note: Inserting INTERLNK.EXE in your usual CONFIG.SYS file could change other drive assignments that come later in CONFIG.SYS, for RAMDRIVE.SYS and DRIVER.SYS commands, for example. If you don't insert it in its own configuration block, you might want to put it last in CONFIG.SYS so that the changed drive assignments don't invalidate your current batch programs and DOSKEY macros.

Identifying the Connected Port

As with the server, you should not let INTERLNK.EXE scan the client's serial ports if you have a serial mouse. Specify /LPT to limit the scan to the parallel ports, or specify /COM*n* to identify a specific serial port. These switches also save memory space by loading only the port software that's actually needed. You can save more space with the /NOPRINTER switch if you don't plan to access the server's printers.

If you don't know which port you'll be using, specify /NOSCAN to prevent the scan. This forces you to use the INTERLNK command to complete the connection.

If you are following the exercises in this chapter, load INTERLNK.EXE now:

1. Open \CONFIG.SYS for editing by an ASCII text editor.
2. If the cable is connected to the client's COM*n* port, enter the following command in CONFIG.SYS. Insert this command after the command that loads EMM386.EXE, if there is one:

```
DEVICEHIGH=C:\DOS\INTERLNK.EXE /COMn
```

3. If the cable is connected to the client's LPT*n* port, enter the following command in CONFIG.SYS. Insert this command after the command that loads EMM386.EXE, if there is one:

```
DEVICEHIGH=C:\DOS\INTERLNK.EXE /LPTn
```

4. Save the file, exit the editor, and reboot the client computer.

   When INTERLNK.EXE loads, it locates the cabled port and completes the connection to the server computer. You'll see a report like this on the client's monitor (your drive and port names might be different):

```
Microsoft INTERLNK Version n.nn
Port=LPT1
Drive letters redirected: 3 (D: through F:)
Printer ports redirected: 1 (LPT2:)


This Computer     Other Computer
   (Client)          (Server)


   _____        _____
      D:      equals    A:
      E:      equals    B:
      F:      equals    C: (360Mb MS-DOS 6.22)
   LPT2:      equals  LPT2:
```

   This tells you that the cable is attached to the client's LPT1 port. The client should use drive name D to access the server's drive A, drive name E for the server's drive B, drive name F for the server's drive C, and LPT2 to access the server's LPT2. You can also see that the server's drive C is 360 megabytes and is partitioned by DOS 6.22. An equivalent table appears on the server's video screen, and stays there as long as the link is in force.

Note: Only one computer needs to be running DOS 6. The other must have DOS 3.0 or later. You can copy the necessary INTERLNK program files to a computer that does not have DOS 6. You'll see how under "Copying the INTERLNK Software" later in this chapter.

5. Try out some commands that access the server's hard drive. In the following two commands, *d:* is the name of the server's hard drive as identified in the drive assignment table.

```
DIR d:
TREE d:
```

6. Don't break the connection yet; keep it running while you read the next section.

Redirected Drives

By default, INTERLNK redirects three of the server's drives. Include the /DRIVES parameter to request a different number of drives. INTERLNK redirects server drives starting with A unless the INTERSVR command specified the drives to be redirected. For example, suppose you want to access only drive C on the server. The INTERSVR command should look like this:

```
INTERSVR C:
```

The INTERLNK.EXE command should look like this:

```
DEVICE[HIGH]=C:\DOS\INTERLNK.EXE /DRIVES:1
```

Suppose the server has three hard drives (C, D, and E), and you want to access those drives but not the floppy drives. You don't need to do anything special in the INTERLNK.EXE command, which redirects three drives by default, but you do need to specify the drives to be redirected on the INTERSVR command, like this:

```
INTERSVR C: D: E:
```

> **Tip:** To access only printer ports on the server, include /DRIVES:0 in the INTERLNK.EXE command.

If you need to use the /V switch on the INTERSVR command, include it in the INTERLNK.EXE command too.

Completing the Connection with INTERLNK

If INTERLNK.EXE can't complete the connection when you boot the client computer, you need the INTERLNK command to complete it when the server is set up. (See Figure 41.5.)

INTERLNK

Completes an INTERLNK connection of client and server computers; redirects server drives.

Format:

```
INTERLNK [drive1 = [drive2]]
```

Parameters:

none	Completes the link, if necessary; displays a status report, including the current drive and printer assignments.
drive1	Identifies a client drive name to be assigned to *drive2*.
drive2	Identifies a server drive to be accessed by the name *drive1*.

Figure 41.5.   *INTERLNK command summary.*

How to Link Two Computers after Booting the Client Computer

1. If you haven't already done so, edit the client computer's CONFIG.SYS to load INTERLNK.EXE.

2. Reboot the client computer, being sure to load INTERLNK.EXE if it is an option. During booting, INTERLNK.EXE displays a message that it cannot complete the connection.

3. When you're ready to link the computers, cable them together.

4. Enter the INTERSVR command on the server computer.

   A drive and port table appears on the server computer's screen. However, the new drive and port names are not shown because the connection has not yet been made.

5. Enter the INTERLNK command on the client computer.

   INTERLNK searches out the cable link and completes the connection, displaying a list of the remapped drives and ports from the server computer. The drive table on the server computer's screen also shows the remapped drive and port list.

6. You can now access the server computer's drives and ports using the names shown on the screen.

7. When you're finished with the connection, press Alt+F4 on the server computer. Then, remove the cable.

8. If you need to clear INTERLNK.EXE from the client computer's memory to make room for other programs, edit CONFIG.SYS if necessary to remove the command, then reboot.

When the connection is established, the report shown earlier appears on the client computer. You can enter an INTERLNK command at any time during the link to rework the drive name assignments. For example, suppose you want to refer to the server's drive C as drive D, not F, so that some batch programs work properly. You could enter this command:

```
INTERLNK D:=C:
```

INTERLNK displays a new drive assignment table to confirm the change. You can't use this feature to add new drive names to the list, merely to rework the names that were already reassigned. If you omit the second drive name, as in INTERLNK D:=, the redirection is canceled.

> **Tip:** Enter the INTERLNK command (without parameters) at any time during the link to redisplay the drive name table on the client computer.

If you want to print from Windows on a redirected parallel port, use Windows Control Panel to assign the port to LPT*n*.DOS.

You can't use any programs on the redirected drives that deal with drive architecture and clusters instead of directories and files. For example, you can't run FORMAT, UNFORMAT, CHKDSK, or DEFRAG. Even UNDELETE is forbidden.

Breaking the Link

When you're finished working with the linked computers, press Alt+F4 on the server computer's keyboard to break the link. The server computer returns to its normal mode.

If you have been following the exercises in this chapter, break the connection now by pressing Alt+F4 on the server computer.

Copying the INTERLNK Software

You can copy the INTERLNK software to any computer that's running DOS 3 or later. You can use disks to transfer the files, but you can also do it via the INTERSVR command with the /RCOPY switch. You must use the 7-wire, null-modem cable with this feature. After the two computers are cabled, enter this command on the computer that contains DOS 6:

```
INTERSVR /RCOPY
```

No other parameters can be used with /RCOPY. INTERSVR guides you through the process of setting up the target computer to receive the INTERLNK files. (The MODE command must be available on the target computer.)

On Your Own

This chapter has shown you how to link two computers together via INTERLNK. If you would like to practice the techniques you have learned here, the following items can be used as a guide:

1. Set up your client computer to load INTERLNK.EXE.

2. Set up the server computer before you boot the client, so that the connection is completed during booting.

3. Try it again; but this time set up the server after the connection is completed, so that you must complete the connection using the INTERLNK command.

4. Eliminate INTERLNK.EXE from the client's CONFIG.SYS. Or, if you want to keep it, consider setting it up as an optional command or alternate configuration.

42 Windows on DOS

Introduction

You can run your DOS applications in the Windows multitasking environment to take advantage of the many Windows enhancements.

DOS and Windows Working Hand in Hand

Windows runs on top of DOS, so many of the DOS features that you've learned in this book serve to optimize Windows as well as DOS. The most common example is SmartDrive, DOS's disk caching system, which helps to speed Windows applications too. The first part of this chapter reviews some of the DOS features that can help to make Windows run faster and better.

Many people use both Windows and DOS applications on a regular basis. You can run most of your favorite DOS applications under Windows to give them the extra advantage of the Windows multitasking environment. This means, among other things, that you don't have to exit your currently running Windows applications to run something in DOS. Just start up the DOS application right on your Windows desktop and switch back and forth between it and your other applications. In 386 Enhanced mode, you can even copy data from one to the other. This chapter shows you how to run DOS applications under Windows.

In this chapter, you will learn how to:

- Use DOS facilities to optimize the Windows operating environment
- Run one or more DOS applications under Windows
- Define the operating environment for a DOS application under Windows using the PIF Editor
- Copy and paste text between a DOS application and other applications when Windows is running in 386 Enhanced mode

Optimizing Windows

Like DOS, Windows needs as much memory as it can get. In addition, because it uses your hard drive as virtual memory, it also needs as much disk space as it can get. Anything you can do to free up memory— especially conventional memory—as well as drive space, will improve Windows performance.

Freeing Up Memory

First and foremost, use all the DOS features available to you to get as many programs as possible out of conventional memory. Chapter 29, "Managing Memory," and Chapter 30, "Additional Memory Facilities for 386, 486, and Pentium Computers," describe how you can move DOS into the HMA and most of your device drivers and TSRs into upper memory, making available more than 600KB of conventional memory.

Second, make sure you're not loading any drivers, TSRs, or other programs that you don't really need. Check your CONFIG.SYS and AUTOEXEC.BAT files. If they load software that you no longer use, remove those commands from the files. Also make sure that you're not allocating more files, buffers, and drive names than you need. Chapter 21, "Configuring Your System," explains the contents of CONFIG.SYS.

If you're currently loading a RAM drive, consider whether you want to keep it. A RAM drive smaller than 2MB does not do Windows any good, and in fact, can do some harm if you use Print Manager. Windows can put that space to better uses unless it has memory to spare. I recommend that you don't load a RAM drive unless you have at least 8MB of RAM. With 8MB, you can safely set up a 2MB RAM drive. With 12MB or more, increase the size of the RAM drive to 4MB. Redirect Windows temporary files to the RAM drive with a command such as the following in AUTOEXEC.BAT (where E: is the name of the RAM drive):

```
SET TEMP=E:\
```

Chapter 32, "RAM Drives," explains RAM drives and how to direct TEMP to them.

Freeing Up Disk Space

Windows needs disk space, not only for its swap files, but also for its temporary files. If your hard drive is crammed, it could be slowing Windows down. Examine your directory structure on a regular basis and delete any unnecessary files.

> **Tip:** Before you start Windows, look on your drive for filenames in the form ~*xxxxxx*.TMP and ~WOA*xxxx*.SWP. These are Windows temporary files that get abandoned whenever Windows hangs up and you have to reboot. You can safely delete them, but only when working from the primary command prompt. Important: Never delete a .TMP or .SWP file when Windows is running!

Run SCANDISK (or CHKDSK) every so often and handle lost allocation units. These can tie up many kilobytes of space on your drive. Chapter 27, "CHKDSK and SCANDISK," explains lost allocation units.

Defragment your hard drive with DEFRAG (or a third-party utility) to combine the free space into one location. This lets Windows create and access its temporary and swap files without having to deal with file fragmentation, which slows down access times. Chapter 33, "Defragmenter," explains DEFRAG.

If you haven't already done so, consider compressing the hard drive so that the existing data takes up less room, making more room available to Windows. Chapter 34, "DriveSpace and DoubleSpace," and Chapter 45, "A Second Look at DrvSpace and DblSpace," explain DOS' compression utilities.

Note: You can't compress the Windows swap file, but compression utilities leave room for the swap file on the host if Windows is installed at the time you compressed the drive.

Tip: If the drive containing your Windows program is crowded but another drive offers plenty of room, you can tell Windows to use the other drive for its temporary and swap files. The following command, for example, tells Windows to use D:\TEMP for its temporary files:

```
SET TEMP=D:\TEMP
```

The following entry in the [386Enh] section of SYSTEM.INI tells Windows to place its temporary swap file for 386 Enhanced mode on drive D:

```
PagingDrive=D
```

If you have a permanent swap file, the above entry won't affect it.

In Real and Standard modes, Windows creates swap files for DOS applications. The following entry in the [NonWindowsApp] section of SYSTEM.INI tells Windows to place its DOS swap files in D:\DOSSWAP:

```
Swapdisk=D:\DOSSWAP
```

Another way to free up disk space for swap files is to direct temporary files to a RAM drive, as explained in the previous section.

Using SmartDrive

SmartDrive's disk caching is as important to Windows as it is to DOS. Be sure to load SmartDrive before starting Windows. If you use a third-party disk caching system, make sure it's compatible with your version of Windows; some third-party utilities are not.

Windows needs extended memory even more than it needs drive caching. If it runs short of extended memory, its performance is seriously degraded and you won't be able to load any more applications. In this situation, it borrows as much memory from the SmartDrive cache as it can. When you load SmartDrive, two memory sizes are specified or implied. The first is the size of the cache under DOS. The second is the minimum cache under Windows. The default values, which are based on your memory size, are well thought-out. (See Table 42.1.) There's really no reason for you to override them with your own values.

Table 42.1. SmartDrive cache sizes.

Extended Memory	DOS Cache	Windows Minimum Cache
1MB	All extended memory	None
2MB	1MB	256KB
4MB	1MB	512KB
6MB	2MB	1MB
More than 6MB	2MB	2MB

Running DOS Applications under Windows

If you use both Windows applications and DOS applications, you might be tempted to exit Windows when you want to use a DOS application. But wait—there are some good reasons to start your DOS applications under Windows, especially if you run Windows in 386 Enhanced mode.

In 386 Enhanced mode, you can use many of the Windows features with your DOS application. You can run the application on the full screen, as it appears in DOS; or, in a window that can be sized, moved, minimized, and so on. You can have several DOS applications going at once, and they might be able to continue processing even when you switch away from them. The Windows Clipboard is available to DOS applications so that you can copy data from one to the other, as well as between DOS and Windows applications. And if an application freezes up, you can kill it without having to reboot your computer.

In Real or Standard mode, you can start just one DOS application, which runs on the full screen. Other applications are suspended while the DOS application is on the screen. When you switch away from it to a Windows application, its processing is suspended. The real advantage over DOS is that you don't lose your place in your applications as you switch from one to the other, as you would if you exited Windows to run the DOS application.

Note: Many DOS applications include a feature that lets you execute a DOS command, such as a File, Run command or a Shell to DOS command. Don't use this feature when running the application under Windows because it will impede the performance of the entire application. Instead, switch to another Windows task to run a different DOS command.

Starting a DOS Application

Try opening up DOS's editor under Windows:

1. Start up Windows.

2. In Program Manager, pull down the File menu and choose Run.

   The Run dialog box opens.

3. Type `EDIT \DOS\README.TXT` and press Enter.

   The DOS editor takes over the full screen with DOS's README.TXT file open.

4. Press Alt+Tab to switch back to Program Manager.

   Notice the MS-DOS Editor window minimized at the lower-left corner of your desktop.

5. Press Alt+Tab or double-click the icon to return to the editor.

6. Exit the editor to close the DOS task and return to the desktop.

Warning: Never run from Windows a DOS application or utility such as CHKDSK, SCANDISK, or DEFRAG that reorganizes the drive's directory structure. Also, avoid the DOS utilities that artificially manipulate the directory structure: SUBST, JOIN, APPEND, and ASSIGN. SHARE and FASTOPEN also should never be started from within Windows. Never start a disk caching program from within Windows; your disk caching program should be started up before you start Windows. Do not run undelete or backup programs that aren't designed to run under Windows.

Some memory-resident programs can safely be started up under Windows, but many can't. If you want to run a DOS TSR under Windows, talk to the manufacturer about whether it is compatible, and if so, how to access it under Windows.

Tip: It's easy to forget that you're running Windows when the task is in full-screen mode. You can define the prompt that is displayed in any DOS application running Windows by setting the environment variable named WINPMT before you start Windows, using the same facilities that you use with the `PROMPT` command. For example, the following command creates a DOS application prompt that displays the message `DOS running under Windows...type EXIT to return to the desktop`, followed by the current drive and directory:

```
SET WINPMT DOS running under Windows...type EXIT to return to the desktop $P$G
```

If you load ANSI.SYS, you can use all of its facilities to add color and graphics to the command prompt screen, position the cursor, and so on, as part of the WINPMT definition.

There are several other ways to start up a DOS application under Windows:

- Choose File, Run from File Manager
- Double-click the program name in File Manager
- Drop a data file on the program name in File Manager (for example, drop README.TXT on EDIT.EXE)
- Create a program item for the application and open the program item

Note: There is a program item for MS-DOS Editor in the Applications group.

All of these methods have about the same effect, and they all have a potential problem. So far, you have been opening an application that runs until you intentionally close it. But, as you know, many DOS utilities simply display a message and terminate themselves. Watch what happens when you run such a program using one of the previously mentioned methods:

1. Choose File, Run to open the Run dialog box.
2. Enter **MEM** to display your memory usage.

   If you can read the message before the task terminates and the desktop returns, you're a much faster reader than I am. (Or, your computer is a lot slower.)

Tip: If you have been using the Clipboard and Windows can't load a new application because there is not enough memory, copy one character to the Clipboard to reduce the amount of memory it is using. Sometimes this makes enough difference that you can load the application.

There is a way to run a DOS application that doesn't automatically terminate the task when the program terminates. Opening the MS-DOS Prompt program item (in the Main group) gives you a command prompt screen. You can then run several programs in a row, if you wish. You must enter **EXIT** to close the task. Try running MEM by using the MS-DOS Prompt item:

1. Open the Main group.
2. Open the MS-DOS Prompt program item.

   A command prompt screen appears. Notice the boxed message at the top of the screen (see Figure 42.1 for the 386 Enhanced mode version). Unfortunately, this message scrolls off the screen as you enter commands.

Figure 42.1.
MS-DOS command prompt
screen under Windows (386
Enhanced mode).

Note: In Real or Standard mode, the boxed note does not include the last item because MS-DOS applications must occupy the full screen in Real and Standard mode. Press Alt+Enter to switch to a window.

3. Enter `MEM`.

   This time, you can read the result.

4. Try a few more noninteractive commands such as `VER`, `BREAK`, `PATH`, and `VERIFY`.

5. Enter `EXIT` to close the task and return to the desktop.

Running a DOS Task in a Window

When Windows runs in 386 Enhanced mode, you can display your DOS tasks on the full screen or in a window. Displaying them in a window can be slightly harder to read, but it's often easier to see other running tasks and switch among your tasks. If you use 386 Enhanced mode, try running DOS EDIT in a window:

Note: If you're not sure what mode your Windows program uses, pull down Program Manager's Help menu and choose About Program Manager. The operating mode is displayed near the bottom of the dialog box.

1. Start up DOS EDIT for \DOS\README.TXT.

2. With the editor on your screen, press Alt+Enter.

   The desktop returns with the Editor in a window. (See Figure 42.2.)

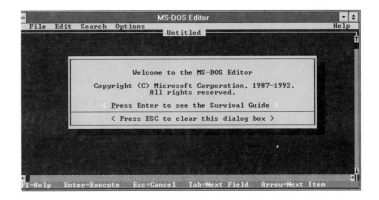

Figure 42.2.
DOS window on the
Windows desktop.

3. Try each of these tasks:

   Move the window

   Make it smaller

   Make it larger

   Minimize it

   Restore it

4. Have you noticed that the window has a maximum size that is not the full size of your screen? That's because it doesn't need the full screen to show the complete command prompt screen. Try maximizing the window.

   The maximized window leaves quite a bit of the desktop showing.

5. Notice how easy it is to change tasks. Click the Program Manager window.

   The Program Manager window becomes the active window.

6. Open a second editor task for a new, untitled file.

   The new editor task takes over the full screen.

7. Press Alt+Enter.

   Now you can see both editor tasks on your desktop.

8. Size the two windows so you can see them both at once. (Hint: You'll have to unmaximize the first one.)

9. Activate the first editor task.

10. Press Alt+Enter to return it to the full screen.

11. Press Alt+Tab to activate the second task.

12. Press Alt+F, X to terminate the task.

13. Activate the remaining editor task and terminate it also.

Note: Displaying a DOS application in a window takes up more system resources (memory and processor time) than running it on the full screen. If you start getting `Out of Memory` messages, return your DOS tasks to full screen status.

Tip: You can control the size of the text displayed in the DOS window, which also determines the maximum size of the window. Press Alt+Spacebar to pull down the window's Control menu. Choose Fonts to open a dialog box in which you can choose from among 10 font sizes, from 4×6 (very small) to 16×12 (very large).

Problem: My mouse won't work with my DOS applications when I run them under Windows.

If an application isn't designed to use a mouse under DOS, it can't use a mouse in DOS under Windows either. You can use your mouse to pull down and select items from the window's Control menu, however. And, when you choose the Control menu's Edit Mark function, you can use the mouse to select text to be copied to the Clipboard.

If a DOS application ordinarily uses a mouse but the mouse doesn't function when you run the application in Windows, you're loading the wrong mouse driver. You may need to install an upgraded mouse driver that will work in the Windows environment.

Program Information Files

Windows knows how to configure a DOS application by checking its Program Information File (PIF). This file contains such information as how much memory the application needs and the text to be displayed in its title bar.

Windows considers a PIF to be an executable program. When you want to run a DOS application, you can execute its PIF or the program itself. You execute a PIF in the same way that you execute any other program; for example, you can double-click it in File Manager, enter its name in a File, Run command, or define a program item that executes it.

When you execute a .COM, .EXE, or .BAT file for a DOS application, Windows checks the current directory and the program search path for a PIF with the same name. If found, it executes the PIF. If not found, it starts up the application using the default PIF, called _DEFAULT.PIF. You'll see _DEFAULT.PIF toward the end of this chapter.

Windows supplies a few PIFs for common DOS applications: EDIT.PIF, DOSPRMPT.PIF (which opens the command prompt task that you used earlier), and QBASIC.PIF, along with _DEFAULT.PIF. Many newer DOS applications include PIFs in their packages; you copy the PIF to your hard disk if you want to be able to run the application under Windows. You can also define your own PIFs and edit the ones that you already have. You use the PIF Editor to create or modify a PIF.

The PIF Editor

Figure 42.3 shows an example of a PIF as displayed in the PIF Editor. In the example, the PIF Editor is in 386 Enhanced mode, and the PIF on display is EDIT.PIF, which configures the MS-DOS Editor. Figure 42.4 shows the Advanced dialog box that opens when you choose the Advanced button.

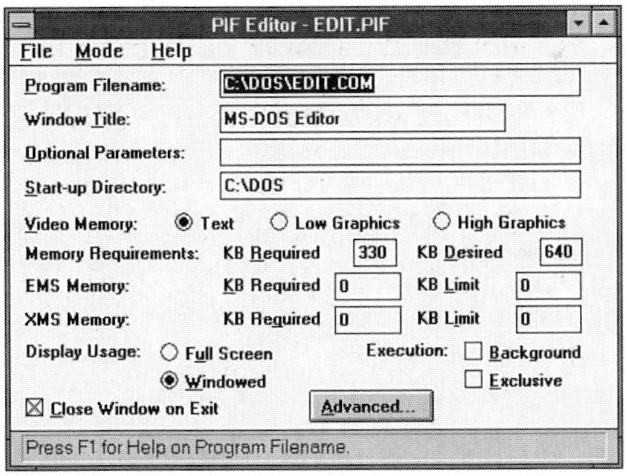

Figure 42.3.
Sample PIF in the PIF Editor (386 Enhanced mode).

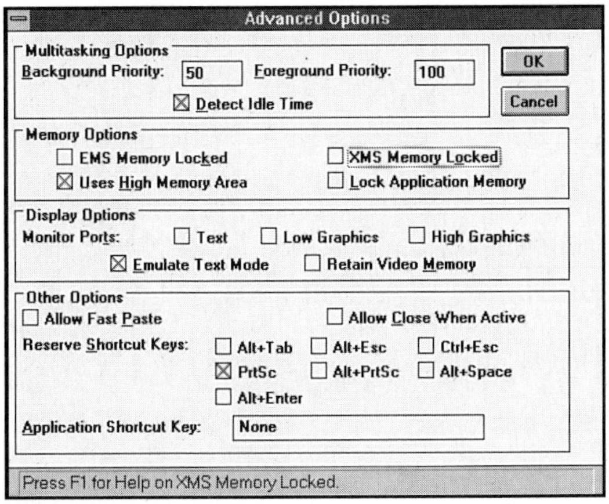

Figure 42.4.
Advanced PIF options in 386 Enhanced mode.

Try opening the PIF Editor yourself:

1. Open Main group and then the PIF Editor.

   The editor window appears, but no PIF file is open.

2. Choose File, Open.

   The Open dialog box lists the PIF files in the default (Windows) directory.

3. Double-click EDIT.PIF.

   The information from EDIT.PIF appears in the PIF Editor window. If you're running Windows in Real or Standard mode, the information displayed is somewhat different from the information shown in Figures 42.3 and 42.4.

Program Filename

The only required field in the PIF is the Program Filename. This field tells Windows what program to run when you execute the PIF. It can reference a batch file (.BAT) or an executable file (.COM or .EXE). It must include the complete program filespec, including path and extension. You can leave out the path if the program is in the Windows directory or a directory on the search path.

If possible, assign the PIF the same filename as the program's filename, as in EDIT.PIF and EDIT.COM. When you start up a DOS application by its program name rather than by a PIF—if you double-click EDIT.COM in the File Manager window, for example—Windows looks for a PIF of the same name. If it doesn't find the PIF, it uses the default PIF (called _DEFAULT.PIF), which might not have the best settings for the application.

Tip: You can specify an environment variable (enclosed in percent signs) in this field instead of a filename. Windows will use the value of the variable as the program filename each time you execute the PIF.

For example, suppose you edit text files with EDLIN.EXE, EDIT.COM, or NED.EXE, depending on which project you're working on. You could place %EDITOR% in the Program Filename field. The following commands in AUTOEXEC.BAT could be used to set the EDITOR environment variable, using EDIT.COM as the default:

```
CLS
ECHO Text editors...
ECHO.
ECHO      A EDIT.COM
ECHO      B EDLIN.EXE
ECHO      C NED.EXE
ECHO.
```

```
CHOICE /C:ABC /T:A,5 Choose an editor
IF ERRORLEVEL 1 IF NOT ERRORLEVEL 2 SET EDITOR=C:\DOS\EDIT.COM
IF ERRORLEVEL 2 IF NOT ERRORLEVEL 3 SET EDITOR=C:\DOS\EDLIN.EXE
IF ERRORLEVEL 3 IF NOT ERRORLEVEL 4 SET EDITOR=C:\DOS\NED.EXE
IF ERRORLEVEL 4 SET EDITOR=C:\DOS\EDIT.COM
```

You can reset EDITOR after AUTOEXEC.BAT finishes, of course, but you must do so before starting Windows. After you have started Windows, you can obtain only a secondary command prompt to enter a SET command, and the variable will be dropped as soon as you exit the secondary command environment. (Chapter 43, "DOS and the Environment," explains secondary command prompts and environment variables.)

Window Title

The Window Title field identifies the text that appears in the window's title bar when this PIF is executed. If you don't provide a title, Windows uses the name of the program (without the extension). If you also include a Description in the properties for a program item that executes this PIF, the Description overrides this field.

Tip: You can specify an environment variable (enclosed in percent signs) in this field instead of a title. Windows will use the value of the variable as the window title each time you execute the PIF.

Optional Parameters

Use the Optional Parameters field to include parameters and switches in the command. To create a PIF to edit \DOS\README.TXT, for example, you would enter **\DOS\README.TXT** in this field.

To display a dialog box for parameters when the PIF is executed, enter a **?** in this field. Optional parameters included in the properties of a program item that executes this PIF override the optional parameters specified here. If you execute the PIF from the File, Run command, any parameters or switches included in the command line override parameters and switches specified here.

Tip: You can specify an environment variable (enclosed in percent signs) in this field instead of parameters and switches. Windows will use the value of the variable as the optional parameters each time you execute the PIF.

Start-up Directory

The Start-up Directory field identifies a directory that Windows should switch to before starting up the program. If a program item that executes the PIF includes a Startup Directory, that directory overrides this one.

> **Tip:** You can specify an environment variable (enclosed in percent signs) in this field instead of a directory path name. Windows will use the value of the variable as the start-up directory each time you execute the PIF.

Video Memory

The Video Memory field determines how much memory is set aside to save the video screen when you switch away from the task, with Text mode requiring the least amount of memory and High Graphics requiring the most. Use the least amount necessary for the application to free up memory for other operations. My recommendation is that you set this field to Text mode unless you know for a fact that it needs a higher mode. If you have trouble changing tasks, if part of your video display disappears, or if you get an Out of Memory message, terminate the application and try a higher mode.

In the 386 Enhanced mode PIF, one of the advanced options is Retain Video Memory. If you enable this option, Windows does not swap the application's video memory out to disk when you switch away from the task and so does not need to swap it back in when you return to the task. This makes it much faster to switch out of and back into the application, but it frees up less memory for other tasks when this task is not active. You'll have to decide whether you have enough extended memory available to take advantage of this option. If you try it and then have difficulty running other tasks under Windows, you should disable this option again.

Memory Specifications

Three sets of fields identify the memory requirements for conventional, expanded (EMS), and extended (XMS) memory. For each type of memory, you can specify the minimum and maximum amounts. Table 42.2 shows the default settings.

Table 42.2. Default memory specifications for Windows PIFs.

Type	KB Required	KB Limit
Conventional	128KB	640KB
Expanded	0KB	1024KB
Extended	0KB	1024KB

Note: In 386 Enhanced mode, Windows automatically converts extended memory into expanded memory when a program requests it. So even if a PC has no built-in expanded memory, a program can obtain as much expanded memory as extended memory permits.

In Real and Standard modes, the PIF does not include settings for EMS (expanded) memory because only one DOS application can be executed at a time and Windows gives it all built-in expanded memory—memory that exists on an expanded memory board and is managed by an expanded memory driver. Windows does not simulate expanded memory in Real and Standard modes (and EMM386.EXE is ignored).

The minimum setting, called KB Required, does not determine how much memory is allocated to the program. Windows always allocates as much conventional, expanded, and conventional memory as the program requests, as long as that much memory is available. But if the requested memory isn't available, Windows allocates what it can, and that's where the minimum setting comes in. Windows won't load a program if the specified minimum amounts of memory aren't available, displaying an insufficient memory message. If the specified minimum is too small, Windows might attempt to load and execute the program and a freeze-up could result.

The maximum setting, called KB Desired or KB Limit, determines the maximum amount of conventional, expanded, or extended memory to allocate to the program. A -1 in this field permits the program to have as much memory as it requests up to the amount currently available. My recommendation is that you enter a **-1** in the KB Desired field to allocate as much conventional memory as the program needs; this can cause Windows to free up some additional conventional memory for the program. Enter **0** for EMS and XMS memory unless you know that they need expanded or extended memory.

Note: Many applications that use extended memory when running under DOS can't use it under Windows because they don't adhere to Windows' standards for accessing extended memory. If you have such an application, you're better off running it under DOS.

In the 386 Enhanced mode Advanced Options, you can prevent Windows from swapping the application's memory out to disk when you switch away from the task. The options are called EMS Memory Locked, XMS Memory Locked, and Lock Application Memory (for conventional memory). Enabling these options speeds task swapping, but robs other tasks of memory, and can slow down all of Windows or prevent another application from loading. In some cases, locking extended memory can harm an application because it needs more XMS memory than is physically available and Windows provides the extra memory by swapping data back and forth between memory and the hard disk.

The Uses High Memory Area option appears in the same section of the Advanced Options dialog box. This option is enabled by default. If an application knows how to use the HMA, if this option is enabled, and if the HMA is not already in use, the application could access another 64KB of memory space. Frankly, those three conditions don't exist very often, but there's no harm in leaving the option enabled.

Display Usage

The Display Usage field determines whether the application starts up on the Full Screen (as you have seen in the exercises) or Windowed. Windowed mode uses more system resources but makes it easier to work with multiple applications. No matter which mode you select here, you can always switch to the other mode by pressing Alt+Enter.

> **Note:** Some applications can run only on the Full Screen (usually because they display a logo or other graphic when starting up). You'll get an error message if you try to switch them to Windowed mode.

Execution and Multitasking Priority

The Execution options determine whether the application continues to execute when another application is active. For example, if the application involves long calculations, sorts, or data transfers, you might want to be able to do other work while the application is completing its task. (Other applications will run more slowly when this application is consuming part of the system's resources, but that can be better than having to sit and wait while the application completes its work.) To allow the application to execute while another application is active, enable the Background option.

To give the application total control when it is active so other applications can't execute in the background, enable the Exclusive option. This option can be crucial for applications that are sensitive to timing, such as games and telecommunications applications, which don't function well when sharing time with other applications. However, in most cases, setting the Foreground Priority to the maximum of 10000 is a better way to give an application as much processing time as it needs. Using the Foreground Priority method lets Windows allot time to other tasks when this task is idle—that is, when it is waiting for you.

In the Advanced Options dialog box, the Background and Foreground Priority options determine how much time Windows allocates to the task in relation to other currently running tasks. The lowest priority is 0 and the highest is 10000. By default, the Background Priority is 50 and the Foreground Priority is 100.

A task's priority number determines its position in the list of tasks, but it does not request a specific percentage of processing time. If task A has a priority of 50 and task B has a priority of 100, and no other tasks are running, task B has the highest priority and would receive no more time if its priority was 10000. When many tasks are running, however, a 10000 priority guarantees a task the highest priority.

The Detect Idle Time option enables Windows to stop giving time to the application if it is not currently doing anything—for example, if it is simply waiting for you to activate it and enter a command. Detect Idle Time makes your other applications run faster but could cause the idle application problems if it needs to update the time regularly, as with a pop-up alarm. Many newer DOS applications are aware of this Windows feature and make themselves look busy to Windows if they need processing time. You should leave this option enabled unless you know that the application doesn't function correctly without it.

Tip: You can change an application's execution settings while the application is running. Pull down the Control menu and choose setting to open the dialog box shown in Figure 42.5, where you can choose Exclusive and/or Background and alter the application's priorities.

Figure 42.5.
Settings dialog box for a
DOS application running
under Windows.

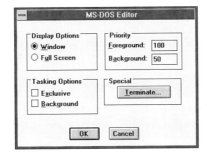

Close Window on Exit

You have already seen the effect of Close Window on Exit. If you're setting up a PIF for an application that displays a final message, disable this option so that the DOS command prompt stays on the screen until you enter the EXIT command.

Tip: If you're having trouble loading a DOS application, disable Close Window on Exit so you can read any messages that the application displays before terminating.

Display Options

In 386 Enhanced mode, the Display Options section of the Advanced Options dialog box contains several options concerning your video monitor. The Retain Video Memory option was already described under Video Memory.

The Monitor Ports options determine whether Windows loads an extra TSR to monitor your video board. Only a very few applications need these options when running on an EGA (not VGA or higher) monitor. Leave these three options disabled unless an application displays nonsense when you return to it after activating another task. In that case, enabling High Graphics for the application should clear up the problem.

> **Note:** Monitoring ports slows Windows noticeably. Avoid this option unless you have no choice.

The Emulate Text Mode option can make your text-mode applications run faster. Leave it enabled unless you have trouble with your video or mouse in a text mode application.

Copying and Pasting

In 386 Enhanced mode, you can copy and paste text among DOS applications and Windows applications using the Windows Clipboard. If you find that you're losing text when you paste into a particular DOS application, disable Allow Fast Paste for that application; otherwise, leave this option enabled for speedier pasting actions.

The following exercise shows you how to copy and paste text in a DOS application running under Windows. If you don't run Windows in 386 Enhanced mode, skip this exercise.

1. Start up two copies of the MS-DOS Editor program item in the Applications group.

2. In one Editor item, open the file named \DOS\README.TXT.

3. Press Alt+Spacebar to pop up the Control menu for the Editor item.

   Even when the item occupies the full screen, it has a Control menu when it runs under Windows. Pressing Alt+Spacebar switches the item into windowed mode and pulls down its Control menu.

4. Choose Edit from the Control menu.

   A submenu appears.

5. Choose Mark from the submenu.

   The title bar changes to say Mark MS-DOS Editor. The word Mark added to the title tells you that you have now overridden the application's functions and are in the midst of a Windows copy function.

6. Drag your mouse over some text to highlight it.

   As soon as you start dragging, the title bar changes to say Select MS-DOS Editor.

7. Press Enter to copy the selected text to the Windows Clipboard.

   The highlight disappears and the title bar returns to normal.

8. Activate the other Editor task.

9. Position the cursor where you would like to paste the text.

10. Click the control menu box or press Alt+Spacebar to pull down the control menu.

11. Choose Edit.

    The Edit submenu appears. Notice that the Paste command is available.

12. Choose Paste.

    Windows pastes the text from the Clipboard into the document at the cursor position.

13. Close both Editor tasks without saving the files.

Note: Unlike Windows applications, you can't scroll the DOS windows while selecting text, so you can copy only one screenful of data at a time.

Allow Close when Active

By default, you can't close a DOS application's window without exiting the application normally. You can't, for example, pop up the window's Control menu and choose Close. Double-clicking the window's Control menu box has no effect. This prevents you from terminating the application before it has a chance to safely close any files it has opened.

However, some applications don't work with files and don't need this type of protection. It's often quicker to terminate the application by closing its window from the outside than to reactivate the application and exit it from within. If you were creating a PIF to run MSD or HELP, for example, you could safely close the window without exiting the application. Enable Allow Close when Active to make it possible to terminate the application by closing its window.

Reserving Shortcut Keys for the Application's Use

Windows assigns its own functions to the keys shown in Table 42.3, overriding any functions that the application may assign to those keys. Windows applications know to avoid those keys, but many DOS applications were not designed with Windows in mind and might use one or more of the shortcut keys for other purposes.

Table 42.3. Windows shortcut keys.

Shortcut	Action
Alt+Enter	Toggles a DOS application between Full Screen and Windowed mode
Alt+Esc	Switches to the next task on the task list
Alt+Tab	Switches to the next task on the task list
Ctrl+Esc	Displays the Task List
Alt+Spacebar	Pops up the window's Control menu
PrintScreen	Copies the screen to the Windows Clipboard
Alt+PrintScreen	Copies the active window to the Windows Clipboard

If an application needs one or more of these keys for its own purposes, you can override the Windows function by enabling the appropriate option under Reserve Shortcut Keys in the PIF window.

Tip: To permit a DOS application to print screens on the printer instead of capturing them to the Windows Clipboard, enable PrtSc under Reserve Shortcut Keys. You can still capture the active window to the Clipboard using Alt+PrintScreen.

Assigning an Application Shortcut Key

You can assign to an application a shortcut key that activates the application when it is running in the background. To assign a shortcut key, click the Application Shortcut Key text box and press the key combination you want to use. You can use almost any combination of Ctrl and/or Alt plus a character or function key, with the Shift key if desired, as in Ctrl+F5, Alt+Shift+;, or Alt+Ctrl+P. If your key combination is invalid, Windows displays a warning message when you try to close the Advanced Options dialog box.

Tip: Once you have defined a shortcut key, you can't delete it by just erasing it from the text box. Place the cursor in the box and press Shift+Backspace. The word None in the text box tells you that the former key has been eliminated.

An application shortcut key can conflict with some application's use of the shortcut keys. Word for Windows, for example, uses Ctrl+I to toggle italics on and off. There are other ways to invoke italics, but Ctrl+I is one of the most convenient. Suppose you start up a DOS application that uses Ctrl+I as its application shortcut key. Now when you're working in Word for Windows, Ctrl+I no longer toggles italics on and off; instead, it switches you to the DOS application. Most people would find that inconvenient.

To avoid these types of conflicts, try to assign application shortcut keys that aren't used in your Windows applications. You're safest with "eccentric" combinations using Ctrl+Alt plus a symbol such as * or [. However, you might find it simpler to switch tasks using some other method.

Real and Standard Mode PIF Options

If your Windows program runs in Real or Standard mode, your PIF window contains somewhat different options, as shown in Figure 42.6. Several options are the same as in 386 Enhanced mode: Program Filename, Window Title, Optional Parameters, Start-up Directory, XMS Memory, and Close Window on Exit. Three fields are similar, but offer fewer options: Video Mode, Memory Requirements, and Reserve Shortcut Keys. Many options, such as Display Usage and Execution, are not available because you can't multitask a DOS application in Real or Standard mode. On the other hand, Real and Standard mode PIFs offer a few options not found on the 386 Enhanced mode PIF; these options are described in the following paragraphs.

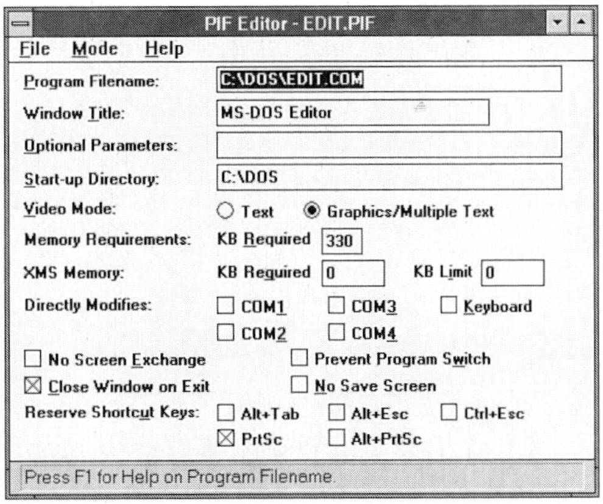

Figure 42.6.
Sample PIF in the PIF Editor (Real and Standard mode).

If your system runs sometimes in Real or Standard mode and sometimes in 386 Enhanced mode, you might want to define PIFs to run in either mode. In the PIF Editor window, use the Mode menu to switch to the other mode; this changes the PIF Editor window only, not the current Windows operating mode. Try switching modes now:

1. Start up the PIF Editor.
2. Pull down the Mode menu.

   The current mode is marked by a check mark. Note that Standard means both Real and Standard mode.

3. Choose the other mode.

A dialog box warns you that the mode will not match the current operating mode.

4. Choose OK.

The window changes to show the PIF format for the selected mode.

When you switch modes, PIF Editor remembers Program Filename, Window Title, Start-up Directory, and Close Window on Exit. Any other common parameters, such as Optional Parameters and XMS Memory, are not carried over from one mode to the other and must be defined in both modes.

Note: When you save the PIF using the File, Save or File, Save As command, you save both modes. If you have edited only one mode, the other mode receives default values.

Saving the Screen Image

In Real and Standard mode, only two video mode options are available: Text and Graphics/Multiple Text. If an application saves several pages of text in video memory, which makes it faster to move about in a document, then you need to select the Graphics/Multiple Text option to set aside enough memory space to hold the multiple pages when you switch away from the application. Notice that there is no option to retain video memory in Real and Standard mode; the application's video memory will be swapped out, so it's important to allocate enough memory to hold it.

If you're defining a PIF for a text-based application and you're not sure if it works with multiple pages, select the Text option first. If you find that the application has trouble switching away and returning—particularly if it loses data when it returns—edit the PIF to select the Graphics/Multiple Text option.

Many newer DOS applications are aware of Windows and don't need to have their screen images saved; they refresh their own screens when they sense that they have been reactivated by Windows. Enable No Save Screen to save both time and memory space by telling Windows not to save or restore the screen image when switching tasks.

Note: If you return to a blank screen in an application, disable the No Save Screen option in the application's PIF.

Working with Applications that Directly Access COM Ports and the Keyboard

Applications that are not aware of Windows may assume that they have free rein of your PC, and access your monitor, keyboard, and ports directly. Windows handles attempts to access the monitor and the parallel ports. But you must warn it if an application will attempt to access a COM port or the keyboard directly. Check the appropriate box(es) in the Directly Modifies section. This warns Windows that there could be a conflict with other programs using the same device.

In the case of the keyboard, any program that directly accesses the keyboard prevents you from using the Windows shortcut keys, whether or not you enable the keyboard option. Enabling the option simply saves a little memory space by letting Windows know that it doesn't have to load the functions that process the shortcut keys.

Printing Screens in Real and Standard Mode

In Real and Standard mode, the PrintScreen key copies the entire screen to the Windows Clipboard, whereas Alt+PrintScreen copies the current window only to the Clipboard. You have already seen how to override these functions and enable DOS's usual PrintScreen functions in the Reserve Shortcut Keys section. Enable No Screen Exchange if you don't need to copy screens to the Clipboard; you save a small amount of memory with this option enabled.

Preventing Program Switching

You can save a little more memory space by enabling Prevent Program Switch. With this option enabled, you must exit the application to return to the desktop and your other applications.

The Default PIF

Windows loads the default PIF when you run a DOS application that doesn't have its own PIF. Figure 42.7 shows the default PIF, which is named _DEFAULT.PIF. The Program Filename, _DEFAULT.BAT, is a dummy name; there is no DEFAULT.BAT. The dummy name is there just to satisfy the requirement that every PIF must have a value in this field. Other than that, the default PIF uses all default values. If you make any changes to this PIF—such as changing the Display Usage to Windowed—you affect all applications that use DEFAULT.PIF because they have no PIF of their own.

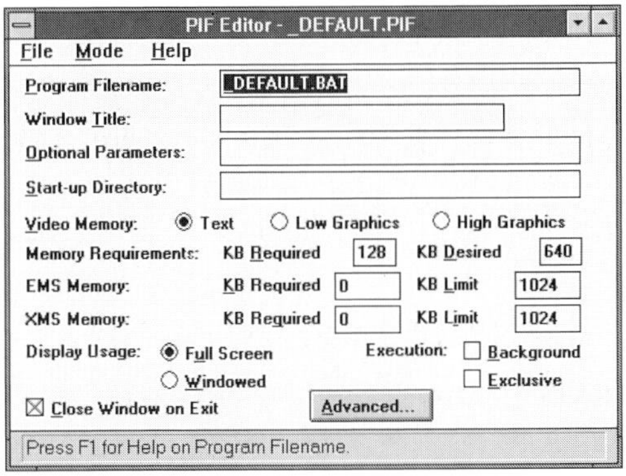

Figure 42.7.
The default PIF.

On Your Own

This chapter has shown you what DOS features can help optimize Windows, as well as how to run DOS applications under Windows. The following items help you apply the information you have learned to your own Windows setup:

1. If you use DOS applications under Windows, check each one to see if it has a PIF. If so, take a look at the PIF and see if there are any options that you want to change. If not, consider defining PIFs for the applications so they don't use the default PIF.

2. Make sure you know how to do the following tasks:

   a. Start a DOS application in Windows.

   b. Switch between full-screen mode and windowed mode.

   c. Copy and paste text between a DOS application and other applications in 386 Enhanced Mode.

3. Design a prompt for your DOS command prompt screen running under Windows, so that you never forget that you're multitasking. Enter a command in AUTOEXEC.BAT to define the command prompt every time you boot.

4. Make sure you know what DOS programs should not be started up under Windows.

43

DOS and the Environment

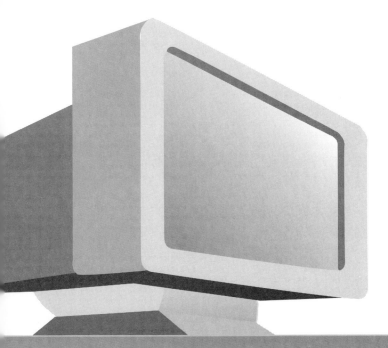

Introduction

DOS's environment gives you the power to set named variables to communicate with many applications and utilities. You can also use them in your own batch programs.

DOS's Environment

DOS sets aside a memory buffer called the *environment* that it uses for storage of crucial variables such as the path and the prompt. Other programs also may store and access variables in the DOS environment. For example, Microsoft Windows uses the TEMP variable to locate its temporary files.

You also can create environment variables and access them in batch programs. In fact, you may find occasion to start up a second command interpreter just to obtain a new environment for a batch program.

This chapter shows you how to control and access the DOS environment. You will learn how to:

* Display all the variables in the environment
* Recognize the environment variables that DOS sets automatically
* Set variables to control DOS utilities such as DIR and XCOPY
* Create and use your own environment variables
* Use the CONFIG variable to establish alternate configurations in AUTOEXEC.BAT
* Control the loading of the primary command interpreter
* Control the size of the environment
* Load a secondary command interpreter
* Redirect the output of a batch program
* Test a batch program by executing it conditionally

Environment Variables

An environment variable has a name and a value. In the following example, TEMP is the variable name, and C:\ DOS is its value:

```
TEMP=C:\DOS
```

The name and value can be any length, as long as they don't exceed the amount of space left in the environment. They can contain any characters, including spaces. DOS always translates and stores the name in uppercase letters, but the value will be stored exactly as entered.

Displaying Environment Variables

Figure 43.1 shows the SET command, which controls environment variables. SET with no parameters displays the current contents of the environment. Take a look at the variables that are currently in your environment. To do this enter SET with no parameters.

DOS displays a complete list of the variables in your environment.

SET

Sets or changes values of environment variables or displays current values.

Syntax:

```
SET [variable=[string]]
```

Parameters:

none	Displays the current values of all environment variables.
variable	Identifies the environment variable to be set.
string	Specifies a new value for an environment variable; if omitted, the current value is cleared.

Figure 43.1. *SET command summary.*

Tip: To see the setting of a particular variable without viewing the entire list, enter `SET ¦ FIND /I "name"`, as in `SET ¦ FIND /I "PROMPT"`.

DOS's Environment Variables

DOS has a number of environment variables that it uses. Some of them are set automatically by DOS, and others are used by DOS if you set them.

PATH

The PATH variable is set when you enter a `PATH` command and contains your current search path. If you don't set a PATH, DOS establishes PATH=C:\DOS by default. DOS accesses this variable whenever it must search for a program file. When no PATH variable is in the environment, there is no search path.

PROMPT

The PROMPT variable is set when you enter a PROMPT command and shows the current format of the command prompt. DOS accesses this variable every time it displays the command prompt. If no PROMPT variable exists, DOS displays the default command prompt, which is just the current drive name (not the current directory) followed by a right angle bracket. The PROMPT command and the meaning of the symbols it uses are discussed in Chapter 12, "Working at the Command Prompt."

TEMP

The TEMP variable, which you must create with a SET command, tells DOS where to store temporary files (such as pipe files). If no TEMP variable is available, DOS stores temporary files in the current directory. Microsoft Windows also uses the TEMP variable to locate its temporary files. Windows needs at least 2MB of available space for its temporary files; if you direct TEMP to a drive that doesn't have enough room, you will have problems with Windows Print Manager.

The DOS programs that use TEMP will run faster if you create a RAM drive of at least 2MB in extended or expanded memory and set TEMP to point to it. That way, DOS can write its temporary files without doing any real disk access. However, SmartDrive gives you better performance improvement than a RAM drive, so don't steal space from SmartDrive to create a RAM drive. If you have expanded memory not needed by any other programs, or if you have more than 4MB of extended memory so that SmartDrive can create a 2MB cache and still have 2MB left over, go ahead and create the RAM drive. If it turns out to be drive E, you would place the following command in AUTOEXEC.BAT:

```
SET TEMP=E:\
```

DIRCMD

The DIRCMD variable, which you must create with a SET command, establishes default parameters for the DIR command. DOS accesses DIRCMD whenever a DIR command is entered. When no DIRCMD variable is available, DOS uses the default DIR parameters and switches.

You can define any combination of DIR's parameters and switches in DIRCMD. Many people set this variable so that DIR sorts directory listings in alphabetical order with all the subdirectories listed first. If you would like to do that, follow these steps:

1. Open \AUTOEXEC.BAT for editing.
2. Enter the following command somewhere in AUTOEXEC.BAT:

   ```
   SET DIRCMD=/O
   ```
3. Save the file and exit the editor.
4. Reboot.
5. Enter DIR to see an example of a sorted listing.

COPYCMD

The COPYCMD variable sets up default parameters for COPY, XCOPY, and MOVE. It is used primarily to bypass DOS's default overwrite protection by setting the /-Y switch. I don't recommend that you do this. You can always include /-Y in commands when you want to temporarily bypass overwrite protection.

MSDOSDATA

You use MSDOSDATA to identify a default directory for Backup's setup and catalog files as well as for Microsoft Anti-Virus's MSAV.TXT file. Chapter 23, "MSBACKUP and MWBACKUP," explains how to use MSDOSDATA for backup and Chapter 25, "DOS's Antivirus Programs," explains its use with Microsoft Anti-Virus.

COMSPEC

The COMSPEC variable is set by DOS to show the location of the command interpreter. DOS accesses this variable whenever it needs to reload the memory-resident portion of the command interpreter after some other program has overwritten it. You see how DOS decides on the value for COMSPEC later in this chapter.

CONFIG

When CONFIG.SYS uses a startup menu and multiple configuration blocks, DOS sets the CONFIG variable to the *blockname* that was selected during booting. You can access this variable in AUTOEXEC.BAT to tailor the remainder of the configuration for the chosen block. You will see some examples of how CONFIG is used in "Using the CONFIG Variable" later in this chapter.

Creating an Environment Variable

The following command creates an environment variable named TEMP and sets its value to C:\DOS:

```
C:\>SET TEMP=C:\DOS
```

Because both the name and the value can have spaces, make sure that there is no space before or after the equal sign unless you want that space included in the name or the value. DOS sees "TEMP" and "TEMP " (with a trailing space) as two different variables. When looking for the place to store its temporary files, it accesses "TEMP" but not "TEMP ".

Try creating an environment variable named MYNAME:

1. Enter **SET MYNAME=name**, where *name* is your name.

2. Enter **SET** to see your new variable.

The SET command receives no confirmation messages unless the environment space is exceeded, in which case the following message is displayed:

```
Out of environment space
```

You'll see how to increase your environment space later in this chapter.

Modifying and Deleting Environment Variables

To change a variable's value, enter a SET command with the same name and the new value. To delete an environment variable, enter a SET command with the same name and nothing after the equal sign, as in the following:

```
SET TEMP=
```

Note: Rebooting deletes all environment variables except the ones DOS sets and those set in AUTOEXEC.BAT.

Accessing Environment Variables

You can access environment variables from batch programs in much the same way as you use replaceable parameters. Use a parameter in the following format:

```
%variable-name%
```

For example, to switch to the directory defined as TEMP from within a batch program, use the following command:

```
CD %TEMP%
```

Note: You can't access environment variables from the command prompt or from DOSKEY macros.

Try writing a short batch program to access MYNAME:

1. Open a new file named HELLO.BAT for editing in a text editor such as EDIT.

2. Enter the following program:

```
@ECHO OFF
ECHO Hello %MYNAME%
```

3. Save the file and exit the editor.

4. Enter **HELLO** to execute the program.

   DOS should display Hello *name*.

Appending a Variable

When a batch program installs a new program or a new function on your system, it may want to add to environment variables such as PATH, PROMPT, or COPYCMD without completely replacing the value that's currently set. You can incorporate the current value into the new value by including the variable reference in the SET command. For example—and this is the most common application of this technique—the following command uses the PATH variable to add the C:\PROGS directory to the end of the current search path:

```
PATH=%PATH%;C:\PROGS
```

The expression %PATH% causes the current value of the PATH variable (the current search path) to be filled into the command. Then, C:\PROGS is appended to it. You could just as easily insert C:PROGS at the front of the search path.

> **Note:** Many application installation programs use this technique to add their application to your program search path. Some applications insert their application at the beginning of your search path rather than at the end. If you don't like your setup, check your PATH command in AUTOEXEC.BAT and adjust it to suit your system needs.

Preserving and Restoring Environment Variables

Sometimes a batch program needs to temporarily change the value of an environment variable. For example, it might need to temporarily change the program search path. A well-behaved program restores the former value of the variable before terminating. You can preserve the current value of the variable at the beginning of the program and restore it at the end. The following example shows how you would preserve and restore COPYCMD:

```
REM Save the current prompt:
SET SAVECOPYCMD=%COPYCMD%
REM Make sure we didn't run out of environment space
IF %SAVECOPYCMD%=%COPYCMD% GOTO CONTINUE
```

```
.
. (commands to deal with inadequate environment space)
.
:CONTINUE
.
. (the remainder of the program)
.
REM Restore the previous prompt:
SET COPYCMD=%SAVECOPYCMD%

REM Remove unneeded variable:
SET SAVECOPYCMD=
```

The same technique can be used to preserve and restore any environment variable.

> **Note:** If the preceding batch program is terminated before the command
> `SET COPYCMD=%SAVECOPYCMD%` is executed—if you press Ctrl+Break for example—the
> COPYCMD variable would not be restored.

Environment Variables versus Replaceable Parameters

Using an environment variable instead of a numeric replaceable parameter, such as %1, has several
advantages:

- You can use as many variables as you want (up to the size limit of the environment).
- An environment variable is more permanent than a replaceable parameter. It outlasts the
  batch job and can be accessed by other batch jobs.

Using the CONFIG Variable

When you set up multiple configuration blocks in CONFIG.SYS, DOS sets the CONFIG environment variable to show which block was selected during booting. You can access that variable from
AUTOEXEC.BAT (or any other batch program) to branch based on which configuration was chosen. For example, if CONFIG.SYS contains three blocks, PETER, JUDI, and SCOTT, you could
branch to different startup routines in AUTOEXEC.BAT in the following way:

```
@ECHO OFF
    commands for all blocks
GOTO %CONFIG%

:PETER
    commands that should be executed for the PETER block
GOTO ENDING

:JUDI
    commands that should be executed for the JUDI block
GOTO ENDING
```

```
:SCOTT
    commands that should be executed for the SCOTT block
:ENDING
```

> **Tip:** If your blocknames are the user's names, you can also use CONFIG to personalize messages to the user. For example, you could display a welcoming message like this:
>
> ```
> ECHO Hello, %CONFIG%...the PC has been set up for your configuration.
> ```
>
> You could tailor the PATH command to include a directory with the user's name:
>
> ```
> PATH=%PATH%;C:\%CONFIG%
> ```
>
> You could even include the user's name in the command prompt:
>
> ```
> PROMPT %CONFIG%'s configuration$_$P$G
> ```

Controlling the Command Interpreter and the Environment

The environment is established when the command interpreter is loaded during booting. By default, DOS's command interpreter, COMMAND.COM, is loaded with 256 bytes in the environment. To control the command interpreter and/or environment size, you must include a SHELL command in CONFIG.SYS. (See Figure 43.2.)

SHELL

Loads a command interpreter.

Syntax:

```
SHELL=filespec [parameters][switches]
```

Parameters and switches depend on which command interpreter is indicated. The following are available for COMMAND.COM:

```
SHELL=[path]COMMAND.COM [path][device][/E:n][/P]
```

Parameters:

filespec   Identifies the command interpreter.

path	Identifies the location of the command interpreter if it's not in the root directory of the boot drive.
device	Identifies a device to be used for standard input and output; default is CON.
/E:*n*	Identifies the size of the environment in bytes, from 160 to 32,768; the default is 256.
/P	Establishes the command interpreter as the primary command interpreter.

Figure 43.2.   *SHELL configuration command summary.*

When no SHELL command appears in CONFIG.SYS, DOS loads COMMAND.COM from the root directory of the boot drive. If it's not there, it looks in the \DOS directory. It sets COMSPEC according to where it found the command interpreter.

Problem: When I try to boot, DOS says Bad or missing command interpreter, Enter correct name of Command Interpreter (such as C:\COMMAND.COM). What's wrong, and how can I finish booting?

DOS can't find COMMAND.COM in the root directory of your boot drive, or in the \DOS directory on that drive, and CONFIG.SYS does not include a SHELL command to tell DOS where to find the command interpreter. It may be that your COMMAND.COM was damaged or deleted, or that your SHELL command was removed from CONFIG.SYS. Or, it could be that your hard drive is damaged in some way so that DOS can't access the DOS directory. You won't be able to finish booting from this disk until you tell DOS where to find the command interpreter.

If you usually use COMMAND.COM from the root directory or the DOS directory, that file must be missing or damaged, or DOS can't access your hard drive. You must boot from an emergency boot floppy that contains the command interpreter, then copy it to the root directory of your boot drive, and reboot.

If you usually use COMMAND.COM from another directory, or if you usually use a third-party command interpreter such as NDOS, enter the full filespec of the command interpreter. If DOS finishes booting, edit CONFIG.SYS to insert (or repair) the appropriate SHELL command, then reboot from the hard disk. (When DOS loads a command interpreter entered in response to this message, it does not execute AUTOEXEC.BAT, so you will have to work with the minimum, default system.) If you enter a filespec and DOS continues to ask for a filespec, you will have to boot from an emergency boot floppy so that you can locate and correct the problem.

Because the default environment size is only 256 bytes, you will quickly run out of environment space if you create and use your own environment variables in addition to those that DOS uses.

Use SHELL in any of the following cases:

- You want to use a command interpreter other than DOS's COMMAND.COM.
- The command interpreter is located neither in the root directory nor in \DOS on the boot drive.
- You want to use a nondefault environment size.

Environment Size

For a larger environment, you must include a SHELL command in CONFIG.SYS with the /E switch included in it. To use the default command interpreter and create a 1KB environment size, use the following command:

```
SHELL=COMMAND.COM /E:1024 /P
```

Warning: The environment is located in conventional memory, which is valuable space, so don't request more environment space than you need.

Warning: If you omit the /P switch and subsequently enter an EXIT command, the system will hang up. If you include /P, EXIT is ignored.

Command Interpreter in Another Location

If the command interpreter is not in the root directory of the boot drive, you must specify its location twice:

- You must include its path with the first parameter (COMMAND.COM) so that DOS knows where to find the command interpreter during booting.
- You must include the path again (without the filespec) as the second parameter, so that DOS knows where to find the command interpreter when it needs to reload the transient part of it. This parameter causes DOS to set the COMSPEC variable in the environment.

To use C:\DOS\COMMAND.COM as the command interpreter with the default environment size, you would put the following command in CONFIG.SYS:

```
SHELL=C:\DOS\COMMAND.COM C:\DOS /P
```

The second parameter causes DOS to create the following environment variable:

```
COMSPEC=C:\DOS\COMMAND.COM
```

Using a Third-Party Command Interpreter

It's possible to use a command interpreter other than COMMAND.COM. For example, the Norton Utilities includes NDOS, with many more features than COMMAND.COM. The SHELL statement is used to establish an alternative command interpreter such as NDOS, in which case COMMAND.COM is not loaded.

Loading a Secondary Command Interpreter

Sometimes, the best way to solve a problem is to start up a secondary command interpreter, even if it's another instance of COMMAND.COM. For example, you might temporarily need additional environment space, you might need to change to a different command interpreter, or you might want to redirect the output of a batch program, all of which can be accomplished by loading a secondary command interpreter, as you'll see in the following paragraphs.

The COMMAND command starts up COMMAND.COM as a secondary command interpreter. (See Figure 43.3.) The following command starts up a secondary COMMAND.COM with a 2KB environment; because no other location is specified, the COMSPEC variable will be inherited from the parent environment.

```
COMMAND /E:2048
```

As long as you don't use the /P switch, the secondary command interpreter is a child of the primary one. The primary command interpreter remains in memory and resumes control when you terminate the secondary one. To terminate the secondary command interpreter and return to the primary one, enter the following one-word command:

```
EXIT
```

COMMAND

Starts a new version of the DOS command processor COMMAND.COM.

Syntax:

```
COMMAND [path] [ctty] [/E:n] [/Y [/C command] ¦ [/K filespec]]
```

Parameters and Switches:

path	Identifies the location of the command processor.
ctty	Identifies the device for command input and output. The default is the current device.
/E:*n*	Specifies the environment size in bytes for the new command processor, from 160 to 32,768.
/Y	Executes the batch program indicated by /C or /K one line at a time, asking if you want to execute each line.
/C *command*	Loads a secondary command processor, performs *command*, and exits the secondary command processor.
/K *filespec*	Runs the specified program before displaying the DOS command prompt.

Figure 43.3. *COMMAND command summary.*

Try loading a secondary command interpreter on your system:

1. Enter **COMMAND** /E:1024 to load the command interpreter with a 1KB environment.

2. Enter **PROMPT $D $T $G** to change the command prompt to show the date and time.

    You see the new command prompt immediately.

3. Enter **SET EXERCISE=Trying out a secondary command interpreter**.

4. Enter **SET** to see your environment variables.

    Notice that all your normal variables are present, but the PROMPT variable reflects your current command prompt. In addition, you should see the EXERCISE variable.

5. Enter **EXIT** to return to the parent command interpreter.

    The command prompt returns to its former setting.

6. Enter **SET** to see your environment variables.

    They should appear as they did before you started the secondary interpreter. In particular, the EXERCISE variable is gone.

Specifying COMSPEC

If you specify a location for COMSPEC when you start a secondary command interpreter, the new environment is empty except for the COMSPEC variable. You will have no PATH, PROMPT, or any other variable that existed in the parent environment. You should notice the difference immediately, because your prompt changes to DOS's default prompt—that is, it shows only the current drive, not the current directory. One quick way to reset your path and prompt is to rerun C:\AUTOEXEC, but that also can load some TSRs for the second time, which may not be desirable.

Try specifying a COMPSPEC when loading a secondary command interpreter:

1. Enter **COMMAND C:**\ to load the secondary command interpreter.

2. Enter **SET** to see your environment variable.

   The only two variables are PATH and COMSPEC, and PATH is empty.

3. Enter **EXIT** to return to your normal environment.

Omitting COMSPEC

If you don't specify a location for COMSPEC, the secondary environment inherits the parent environment's variables. It can modify, add, and delete variables as desired without affecting those in the parent environment. When you return to the parent command interpreter, its environment is in exactly the same condition as when you left it. This is the main reason for starting up a secondary command interpreter. For example, suppose that you must create a batch program that changes the prompt, the search path, and the TEMP directory. You want to restore the original parameters before ending the batch program. The easiest way to do it is as follows:

```
@ECHO OFF
REM Preserve current environment:
COMMAND
 .
 .    (remainder of batch program)
 .
REM Restore original environment:
EXIT
```

Suppose that you are creating a batch program that needs a 2KB environment. Starting a secondary command interpreter not only gives you the extra environment space temporarily, it also eliminates all extra environment variables automatically when you exit back to the parent command interpreter:

```
@ECHO OFF
REM Establish a larger environment:
COMMAND /E:2048
.
.    (remainder of batch program)
.
REM Return to original environment:
EXIT
```

Dynamic Environment Allocation

When COMMAND creates a secondary environment, DOS initially allocates the default or requested amount of environment space. However, if you set variables in excess of that space and the adjacent memory area is available, DOS will dynamically allocate to the environment as many bytes as necessary to create the variables you request. You could set many thousands of bytes of environment variables this way, but keep in mind that you're removing available space from conventional memory, which could prevent programs from being loaded.

> **Note:** If /E is not specified, the default environment size is 256 bytes or the number of bytes necessary to inherit all the parent's variables, whichever is greater.

Starting COMMAND.COM when Another Command Interpreter Is Primary

Suppose that NDOS is loaded as the primary command interpreter and you now need to run a program that requires the presence of COMMAND.COM. To start up COMMAND.COM as a secondary command interpreter, enter the following command:

COMMAND C:\ [switches]

You need to specify the COMSPEC path so that the COMMAND environment doesn't inherit NDOS's COMSPEC variable, which could lead to trouble when DOS attempts to reload the transient portion of COMMAND from the wrong directory. Because the COMSPEC path is specified, no variables are inherited from the parent environment, so you may want to set at least the path and prompt before continuing.

To return to NDOS again, enter the following command:

EXIT

Loading a New Primary Command Interpreter

Suppose that you want to replace the primary command interpreter with COMMAND.COM. You need to include the /P (for primary) switch as follows:

```
COMMAND  C:\ [switches] /P
```

This method has some effects similar to rebooting. AUTOEXEC.BAT is executed from the root directory of the current drive. (If you're not on drive C, you probably don't have an AUTOEXEC.BAT available, and the DATE and TIME commands will be executed instead.) The EXIT command will not terminate this interpreter. Although you can't get back to the previous command interpreter, it continues to take up space in memory, which could cause a shortage of memory space. If memory is tight, it's better to modify the SHELL statement in CONFIG.SYS and reboot to get the command interpreter and environment you want.

Executing a Command with COMMAND.COM

The /C command switch causes COMMAND to start up a secondary command interpreter just long enough to run the indicated command and then exit to the parent command interpreter again. You use this feature primarily to redirect output that can't otherwise be redirected.

Recall that you can't redirect the output of a batch program or pipe the output of a FOR command. However, you can redirect the output of COMMAND. Try it with your HELLO.BAT program:

1. Enter **COMMAND /C HELLO > HELLO.TXT**.

   DOS redirects the output of the HELLO command to the file named HELLO.TXT. As a result, you don't see any messages on your screen. The secondary command processor terminates and the primary command prompt returns.

2. Type **HELLO.TXT** to see the result.

3. Delete HELLO.TXT.

Chapter 7, "Selecting Files in the Shell," showed you how to combine FIND with FOR to search a set of files for a specified phrase. However, you were unable to pipe the output to MORE, because FOR can't be piped. Here again, COMMAND can be used to accomplish the redirection. Try it for yourself:

1. Switch to the DOS directory.

2. Enter `COMMAND /C FOR %F IN (*.TXT) DO FIND /I "network"%F ¦ MORE`.

   Page through the result. (If you get tired of paging through it, press Ctrl+Break to end the display.) Notice that you get enough information here to decide which files to read or print if you want to find out more about networks from the DOS .TXT files.

Unless you have directed TEMP to a RAM drive, this command could result in a long pause while MORE builds a temporary file of the entire output from the FOR command.

> **Note:** If you redirect the COMMAND command without the /C switch, all standard output of the secondary command interpreter is redirected until you exit back to the primary interpreter again. This includes the command prompt, which no longer appears on the monitor, but is recorded in the redirected output. You can still enter commands and data, even though you can't see the command prompt.

Testing a Batch Program with COMMAND.COM

Starting with DOS 6.2, you can test the logic of a batch program by executing it line-by-line, by specifying the /Y switch before the /C or /K parameter. Try this with HELLO.BAT:

1. Enter `COMMAND /Y /C HELLO`.

   DOS starts a secondary command interpreter, then asks if you want to execute HELLO, like this:

   ```
   hello [Y/N]?
   ```

2. Press Y to start executing HELLO.

   DOS asks if you want to execute the first line of HELLO, like this:

   ```
   echo off [Y/N]?
   ```

3. Press Y to execute the ECHO OFF command.

   DOS asks if you want to execute the next line of HELLO:

   ```
   echo Hello, name [Y/N]?
   ```

4. Press N to suppress this command.

   DOS does not execute the ECHO command. As that was the last command in the program, the program terminates, the secondary command interpreter terminates, and you return to the primary command interpreter.

On Your Own

This chapter has shown you how to set and use environment variables, as well as how to control the loading of the command interpreter. If you would like to practice the techniques that you learned in this chapter, you can use the following items as a guide.

1. View your current list of environment variables.

2. Set the ONMYOWN environment variable to the value ITEM2.

3. Write a batch program to display the value of the ONMYOWN variable as part of the command prompt.

4. Set the default switches for the DIR command so that DOS displays files in reverse chronological order and includes hidden and system files in the listing.

5. Set the default switches for the COPY, MOVE, and XCOPY commands to override DOS's normal overwrite protection.

6. Set the default switches for Backup and Anti-Virus to use the C:\ directory instead of their normal directories. Examine the result in Backup.

7. If you have at least 4MB of RAM and are not currently using a RAM drive for temporary files, set up a 512KB RAM drive and direct DOS to use it for temporary files. Try out a command such as DIR C:\ /S /B ¦ FIND "MEM" both before and after setting up the RAM drive; you should notice a significant difference in the amount of time it takes this command to execute.

8. Make sure you know how large your environment space is. If you would like more space, insert (or edit) the appropriate command in CONFIG.SYS.

9. Execute the HELLO program, redirecting the output to your printer.

10. Execute the HELLO program one line at a time.

11. When you're ready to go on, remove the RAMDRIVE command from CONFIG.SYS if you inserted it in step 7. Then, reboot to restore your normal environment. Finally, delete HELLO.BAT and the batch program that you wrote for step 3.

44

Squeezing Even More Out of Memory

Introduction

If you're having trouble taking full advantage of DOS's memory features for the 386 and higher PCs, you may need to use some of the advanced features of HIMEM, EMM386, and MEMMAKER.

Customizing Upper Memory

You learned earlier how to load HIMEM, load DOS into the HMA, and use MEMMAKER to configure your startup files to load EMM386 and fit as many TSRs and drivers as possible into upper memory. But, if HIMEM or EMM386 won't load on your system or if MEMMAKER doesn't get enough of your TSRs and drivers out of conventional memory, there are a variety of things you can do to relieve the situation.

In this chapter, you will learn how to:

- Use switches on the HIMEM command to control how it loads and seizes control of extended memory
- Turn expanded memory on and off after EMM386 is loaded
- Make available areas of upper memory that DOS usually reserves
- Find out how much space a program occupies in memory
- Run MEMMAKER in Custom mode instead of Express mode
- Understand why you sometimes can't unload a TSR without rebooting

Problems in Using HIMEM.SYS

If you find that HIMEM doesn't work for you in its default configuration—for example, if HIMEM.SYS won't load, if your system freezes up when you try to boot after installing HIMEM or if you notice a negative change in system performance—you may need some switches on HIMEM's DEVICE command. Figure 44.1 shows HIMEM's switches.

HIMEM.SYS

Manages extended memory, including the high memory area (HMA).

Syntax:

```
DEVICE=[path]HIMEM.SYS [/A20CONTROL:ON ¦ OFF]

[/CPUCLOCK:ON ¦ OFF] [/EISA] [/HMAMIN=size] [/INT15=x]

[/MACHINE:machine] [/SHADOWRAM:ON ¦ OFF] [/VERBOSE]
```

Parameters and Switches:

path   Identifies the location of the HIMEM.SYS file. The default is
                                  the root directory of your boot drive.

/A20CONTROL:ON ¦ OFF	Specifies whether HIMEM is to take control of the A20 line even if A20 is already on. If you specify /A20CONTROL:OFF, HIMEM takes control of the A20 line only if A20 is not already in use when HIMEM loads. The default setting is /A20CONTROL:ON.
/CPUCLOCK:ON ¦ OFF	Specifies whether HIMEM can affect the clock speed of your computer. If your computer's clock speed changes when you install HIMEM, /CPUCLOCK:ON may correct the problem but slow down HIMEM. The default setting is /CPUCLOCK:OFF.
/EISA	Specifies that HIMEM.SYS should allocate all available extended memory. This switch is necessary only on an EISA (Extended Industry Standard Architecture) computer with more than 16MB of memory; on other computers, HIMEM allocates all available extended memory.
/HMAMIN=size	Specifies (in kilobytes) how large a program must be to use the HMA. Valid values are 0 through 63; the default is 0, which forces HIMEM to give the HMA to the first program that requests it. This switch has no effect when Windows is running in 386 enhanced mode.
/INT15=x	Allocates (in kilobytes) extended memory for the interrupt 15h interface. Valid values are 64 through 65535, but not more than your system's available memory. The default value is 0. If x is less than 64, HIMEM uses 0.
/MACHINE:machine	Specifies which A20 handler to use.
/SHADOWRAM:ON ¦ OFF	Specifies whether to enable shadow RAM. If your computer has less than 2MB of memory, the default is OFF (disabled).
/VERBOSE	Directs HIMEM.SYS to display status and error messages while loading. By default, HIMEM.SYS does not display these messages. You can abbreviate /VERBOSE as /V.

Figure 44.1.   *HIMEM.SYS configuration command summary.*

Loading the Correct Driver for the HMA

If HIMEM won't load at all or your system freezes up when you boot with HIMEM, the most likely problem is the /MACHINE switch. This switch causes HIMEM to load a driver to manage the circuit (or *line*) that addresses the HMA. This connection between the processor and the HMA is called the A20 line. (The ones that connect the processor and conventional and upper memory are numbered A00 through A19.) Because it manages the A20 line, the driver is called the *A20 handler*.

Microsoft includes several A20 handlers in HIMEM.SYS. They are listed under HIMEM.SYS in the Command Reference at the back of this book, and in DOS's online Help library. HIMEM.SYS attempts to load the correct handler for your hardware, but it can't sense the correct handler for some computers. When that happens, you have to use the /MACHINE switch to load the correct handler. If you're not sure which handler to use, it doesn't hurt to experiment. If you can't find it by trial and error, your hardware dealer or Microsoft's Product Support team may be able to help you find the right one.

> **Note:** If you're having trouble loading HIMEM, add the /VERBOSE switch to the DEVICE command so that HIMEM displays status messages as it tries to load. The messages may give you a clue as to what's going wrong and what's going right.

If you're loading the right driver but still can't gain access to the HMA, try using /A20CONTROL:ON. This switch lets HIMEM seize control of the A20 line, even if some other program is already using it.

Controlling the Clock Speed

In some rare cases, HIMEM changes your computer's clock speed, which might affect the performance of other software. If this is a problem in your computer, try the /CPUCLOCK:ON switch, which slows HIMEM down a bit but prevents it from changing your clock speed.

Making Memory beyond 16MB Available in EISA Computers

HIMEM can't access memory beyond the 16MB mark in EISA (Extended Industry Standard Architecture) PCs unless you include the /EISA switch on the HIMEM command.

Controlling Older Programs that Address Extended Memory Directly

When extended memory was first available and no standards had yet been established, some software used a mechanism called INT15h (interrupt 15h) to access extended memory. If you're still using such a program, it may conflict with HIMEM over memory space, and you could end up losing data. The best solution would be to upgrade your software to a newer version that is compatible with HIMEM. But, if that's not possible, you can set aside some extended memory to be accessed by INT15h with the /INT15 parameter. If the program requires 128KB of extended memory, for example, you would include /INT15=128 on your HIMEM command. Extended memory set aside for INT15h is not available to your other software, so don't allocate any more than necessary.

Making Sure that DOS Loads into the HMA

Only one program can load into the HMA at a time. By default, DOS loads high the first program that requests it, no matter how small the program. Because DOS processes the DOS=HIGH command late in CONFIG.SYS, no matter what the command's position in the file, another program could possibly take over the HMA. If it's a sizable program, that's fine. But, if it's less than 43KB, you're better off loading DOS in the HMA. If your system is experiencing this problem, add a parameter to the HIMEM command that says /HMAMIN=40. This prevents any program smaller than 40KB from loading into the HMA.

Shadowing ROM-BIOS

ROM-BIOS is one of the most essential elements in your system and, unfortunately, ROM access is slower than RAM access. Many computers speed up BIOS access by copying it from ROM to RAM and accessing it in RAM. The copy in RAM is called Shadow RAM.

When HIMEM loads, it automatically shuts off Shadow RAM in systems with less than 2MB of RAM, to gain more extended memory for other uses. Shutting off Shadow RAM can significantly slow your entire system. If you don't need the extra memory for other functions, you can prevent HIMEM from disabling Shadow RAM by including /SHADOWRAM:ON on the HIMEM command.

Note: /SHADOWRAM:ON does not create Shadow RAM in systems that don't already have it. It simply prevents HIMEM from disabling an existing Shadow RAM feature.

Note: HIMEM includes several other switches that are rarely needed. They are described in the Command Reference at the back of this book.

Finding Extra Space in Upper Memory

Usually, MEMMAKER can fit all your TSRs and drivers in upper memory with no problem. After using MEMMAKER, a peek at conventional memory with MEM /C should tell you if any programs are loading there that should go into upper memory. If so, there are a few things you could try to make more upper memory space available.

Most of these items are most easily set up by rerunning MEMMAKER and choosing Custom setup instead of Express. Table 44.1 shows the options that MEMMAKER offers when you do a Custom setup. The options that can help you find more space in upper memory are described in the following paragraphs.

Table 44.1. Custom setup options.

Option	Description
Specify drivers and TSRs	Choose this option if you want to exclude some of your drivers and TSRs from being loaded into upper memory.
Aggressive scan	Choose this option if you want MEMMAKER to use the upper memory range from F000-F7FF, which is otherwise excluded. The Express setup will use this memory range; if you have trouble after the Express setup, you could try turning this option off.
Optimize for Windows	Choose this option if you never run DOS-based programs under Windows. If you don't use Windows or if you run DOS-based programs under Windows, turn this option off.
Use monochrome region	Choose this option if you don't have a monochrome or SuperVGA monitor. If you're having trouble after MEMMAKER uses the monochrome region, rerun MEMMAKER and turn this option off again.
Keep current inclusions and exclusions	If your EMM386.SYS driver is currently set up to include or exclude certain areas of upper memory, choose this option

Option	Description
	to retain them. Turning this option off gives MEMMAKER more free rein in upper memory, but it may not work well with your system.
Move extended BIOS data	Choose this option to move the extended area to upper memory BIOS data area to upper memory. If you have problems after MEMMAKER uses this option, rerun MEMMAKER and turn it off.

Aggressive Scan

EMM386 scans upper memory for available space when it loads. Normally, it does not scan the upper memory block starting at F000h, which belongs to ROM-BIOS. Scanning this region can hang up your computer during booting. But, if you need more memory space there may be some in that block that ROM-BIOS is not using. If you choose Aggressive Scan, MEMMAKER adds a /HIGHSCAN switch to the EMM386 command so that EMM386 will scan the F000h block. If your system hangs after you try this, reboot using F8 to bypass the command that loads EMM386, remove the /HIGHSCAN switch from the EMM386 command and try again.

Use Monochrome Region

The upper memory block starting at address B000h is normally used by monochrome video adapters, CGA adapters, and other adapters running in monochrome mode. Some SVGA monitors also use this block in high resolution graphics mode. If you don't have a monochrome or CGA adapter, if you don't use your monitor in monochrome mode, and if you don't have an SVGA monitor, you can safely use this region as a UMB.

If you choose this option and you use Windows, you should insert a command in your SYSTEM.INI file to load a special driver called MONOUMB.386. Insert the following command in the [386Enh] section of SYSTEM.INI:

```
DEVICE=C:\DOS\MONOUMB.386
```

Warning: You can disable your system by using the EMM386.EXE parameters incorrectly. If that happens, you can reboot and use F8 to bypass the EMM386.EXE command in CONFIG.SYS, and then edit the command.

Excluding Upper Memory Regions

Some systems are already using some portions of upper memory for their own purposes and MEMMAKER should not have access to those areas. You can block specific address ranges from MEMMAKER's use by inserting X parameters on the EMM386 DEVICE command (see Figure 44.2) before running MEMMAKER in Custom mode, then enabling the option Keep Current EMM386 Memory Exclusions and Inclusions. For example, if you know that your system uses address range B800 through BB00, but that the rest of the monochrome region is available, you would add this parameter to the DEVICE=EMM386.EXE command:

```
X=B800-BB00
```

EMM386.EXE

Provides access to the upper memory area and uses extended memory to simulate expanded memory.

Syntax:

```
DEVICE=[path]EMM386.EXE [ON ¦ OFF ¦ AUTO] [expanded-memory] [MIN=size] [Mx]

[[X=mmmm1-nnnn1]...] [RAM ¦ NOEMS] [HIGHSCAN] [/VERBOSE]
```

Parameters and Switches:

path	Identifies the location of the EMM386.EXE file. The default is the root directory of the boot drive.
ON ¦ OFF ¦ AUTO	ON loads and activates the EMM386 driver; OFF loads the driver but deactivates it; AUTO places the driver in automatic mode, which enables expanded-memory support and upper memory block support only when a program calls for it. Use the EMM386 command to change this value after the driver has been loaded.
expanded-memory	Specifies (in kilobytes) the maximum amount of extended memory that you want EMM386.EXE to provide as expanded memory. Values are 64 through 32768 (or the amount of free extended memory). The default value is the amount of free extended memory unless you specify NOEMS. EMM386.EXE rounds the value down to the nearest multiple of 16.

MIN=*size*	Specifies (in kilobytes) the minimum amount of expanded memory that EMM386.EXE will provide. Values are 0 through *expanded-memory*. The default value is 256 unless you specify NOEMS.
M*x*	Specifies the base address of the expanded-memory page frame. Valid values are 1 through 14. If your computer has less than 512KB of memory, *x* must be less than 10.
RAM	Requests both expanded memory and UMB support and specifies a range of segment addresses in extended memory to use for UMBs.
NOEMS	Provides UMB support, but not expanded memory support.
HIGHSCAN	Scans the highest region of upper memory area for available memory blocks.
/VERBOSE	Directs EMM386.EXE to display status and error messages while loading. By default, EMM386.EXE does not display only error messages. You can abbreviate /VERBOSE as /V.

Figure 44.2.   *EMM386.EXE configuration command summary.*

Then you would run MEMMAKER, select Custom setup and select Use Monochrome Region and Keep Current EMM386 Memory Exclusions and Inclusions.

Turning Expanded Memory On and Off

After you have installed EMM386 from CONFIG.SYS during booting, you can turn it on and off with the EMM386 command as long as it isn't currently in use. (See Figure 44.3.) You may want to turn it off to make more extended memory available to an application and then turn it on again when you're ready to run an application that needs expanded memory.

Note: Although EMM386.EXE will not work with a 286, you can purchase third-party memory managers that will accomplish the same functions (and more) on a 286. Most third-party memory managers also provide many more features than EMM386.EXE for 386 and more modern systems.

EMM386

Controls expanded memory support.

Syntax:

```
EMM386 [ON ¦ OFF ¦ AUTO] [W=ON ¦ W=OFF]
```

Parameters and Switches:

none	Displays the status of EMM386 support.
ON	Enables the EMM386.EXE driver.
OFF	Disables the EMM386.EXE driver without unloading it.
AUTO	Lets programs control enabling and disabling of EMM386.EXE driver.
W=ON	Enables Weitek coprocessor support.
W=OFF	Disables Weitek coprocessor support. Default is W=OFF.

Note:

You must have a 386 or higher processor and must have installed the EMM386.EXE device driver before you can use this command.

You cannot turn EMM386 off when it is providing UMBs or when any program is currently using expanded memory.

Figure 44.3. *EMM386 command summary.*

You can load EMM386.EXE but turn it off (or place it in AUTO mode) by including the OFF or AUTO parameter in the CONFIG.SYS command that loads it. Then, you can use the EMM386 command to turn it on when it's needed.

> **Note:** Some programs, notably Windows 3.0, have their own emulators and don't work well with EMM386.

If you try to turn EMM386 off when it is providing access to upper memory blocks, or when some program is using its expanded memory, you see the following message:

```
Unable to de-activate EMM386 as UMBs are being provided and/or EMS is being used.
```

Problems with UMBs

Not all programs work well in UMBs. Some try to expand themselves after loading and can't get the space to do so. Some make assumptions about where they are located in memory. If your system locks up during or after booting, bypass the startup files and see whether you can figure out which programs caused the problem.

> **Tip:** All TSRs and device drivers included with DOS 6 run from UMBs with no problems.

You can see how much space a program actually takes up in memory by loading the program in memory (conventional or upper) and using the following command:

```
MEM /MODULE:program-name
```

For example, to find out how much space DOSKEY is using in memory, you could use the following command:

```
MEM /MODULE:DOSKEY
```

The report looks something like the following:

```
DOSKEY is using the following memory:
  Segment  Region      Total      Type
  ------   ------   --------------- --------
   0D5EB     1          4144  (4K)  Program
                    ---------------
  Total Size:         4144  (4K)
```

From this report, you can see that DOSKEY occupies 4,144 bytes. The Region number appears only if the program is in upper memory. Sometimes, you see that a program is occupying two or more locations in memory, perhaps in different regions in upper memory. The Total Size shows how much space the program needs altogether.

If you suspect that a program is not loading correctly and want to exclude it from upper memory, edit the command that loads it to change DEVICEHIGH to DEVICE (in CONFIG.SYS), or remove the LH from in front of it (in AUTOEXEC.BAT). Also delete any /L and /S parameters that MEMMAKER added to it.

Handling TSRs

A TSR (Terminate-and-Stay-Resident) program is a program that stays in memory after it is loaded, whether it is active or not. Many TSRs scan keyboard input for commands or hot keys pertaining to their functions. DOSKEY provides a good example: when you press the up-arrow key at the command prompt, it recalls the preceding command from the command history.

When you press a key with no TSRs installed, DOS sends the keystroke to its own keystroke handler for processing. When you load a TSR that scans keyboard input, the TSR inserts itself in the normal chain of keystroke processing so that it looks at the keystrokes first, processes what it recognizes, and passes unfamiliar ones on to DOS's keystroke handler.

When you load a second TSR that scans keyboard input, it inserts itself in the chain after the first one. The chain gets longer and longer as you load more TSRs:

```
TSR #1 → TSR #2 → TSR #3 → DOS's keystroke handler
```

This chain prevents you from unloading any TSR except the last one loaded. If you were able to unload a TSR in the middle of the chain, the chain would be broken and your keystrokes would never reach DOS's keystroke handler. In fact, the system would probably freeze up.

Not all TSRs behave as they should in the chain, and you may find that your system locks up anyway. Usually this is because two or more TSRs don't get along well together. Perhaps one is stealing the other's keystrokes or is not passing the correct information along. If this starts happening in your system, try installing your TSRs in a different order. If that doesn't work, bypass TSRs one at a time until you find the one that is causing the problem. Talk to its developers about how to load it with your other TSRs; they probably are aware of the problem and have found (or are working on) a solution.

45

A Second Look at DrvSpace and DblSpace

Introduction

Once you have installed DrvSpace or DblSpace, you can compress additional drives (including floppies), maintain your compressed drives, and even uncompress them.

Beyond the Basics with DrvSpace and DblSpace

If you have compressed your only hard drive, you might not ever have to think about DrvSpace or DblSpace again. The compression software loads each time you boot, and mounts the compressed drive so that you can access it; you shouldn't even be aware of its presence, except that you can store a lot more data on your drive.

But DblSpace and DrvSpace have many additional functions. You can, for example, compress additional drives, including floppy drives. You can change the size of your compressed drive, expanding or shrinking it as needed. Or, you could decide that you don't want to compress your drive after all. This chapter shows you how to handle all these functions, and more. You will learn how to:

- Compress an additional hard drive
- Compress a floppy drive
- Create a compressed volume out of the empty space on a drive
- View information about your compressed drives
- Resize a compressed drive
- Defragment a compressed drive
- Change the estimated compression ratio for a compressed drive
- Reduce the amount of memory that DrvSpace or DblSpace uses
- Delete and undelete a compressed drive
- Uncompress a drive

The DriveSpace or DoubleSpace Core Program

When you install DriveSpace or DoubleSpace, the DRVSPACE.BIN or DBLSPACE.BIN program file becomes the third file in DOS's kernel, joining the traditional IO.SYS and MSDOS.SYS. If it is present on the boot drive when you boot, it is loaded along with the other two core files, before CONFIG.SYS is processed. It immediately seizes control of its compressed volumes, so that by the time CONFIG.SYS is processed, the compressed drives are already available. This avoids the boot problems experienced by some older third-party compression software, which must be loaded via CONFIG.SYS.

DOS initially loads DRVSPACE.BIN or DBLSPACE.BIN at the top of conventional memory. A program called DRVSPACE.SYS or DBLSPACE.SYS then moves it to a more appropriate location. If your system is set up to use upper memory blocks and if DRVSPACE.SYS or DBLSPACE.SYS is loaded with a DEVICEHIGH command, DRVSPACE.SYS or DBLSPACE.SYS moves DRVSPACE.BIN or DBLSPACE.BIN into upper memory. (DOS loads it at the top of conventional memory to start with so that it won't leave an unusable gap in conventional memory when it's moved to upper memory.) If DRVSPACE.BIN or DBLSPACE.BIN can't be moved to upper memory, DRVSPACE.SYS or DBLSPACE.SYS moves it lower down in conventional memory. After installing DriveSpace or DoubleSpace, you'll find the following command in CONFIG.SYS; this is the command that loads DRVSPACE.SYS or DBLSPACE.SYS, whose only function is to move DRVSPACE.BIN or DBLSPACE.BIN:

```
DEVICE=C:\DOS\DRVSPACE.SYS /MOVE
```

or

```
DEVICE=C:\DOS\DBLSPACE.SYS /MOVE
```

If your system is set up for upper memory, run MEMMAKER after installing DoubleSpace to convert this command into a DEVICEHIGH command that will load DRVSPACE.BIN or DBLSPACE.BIN into upper memory.

The *DRVSPACE* or *DBLSPACE* Command

When you're working with DrvSpace or DblSpace, you can work from a window with menus and dialog boxes, or you can enter commands to accomplish the same functions at the DOS command prompt. This chapter shows you how to use both methods. These commands have so many options that it is difficult to summarize them in one figure. Instead, I will show you the syntax for each function as we discuss that function. I'll show you DRVSPACE commands; but, if you're using DblSpace, all you have to do is substitute DBLSPACE for DRVSPACE as the command name.

Note: Don't forget that the Command Reference at the back of this book documents the complete DblSpace and DrvSpace commands.

Compressing Additional Hard Drives

After DrvSpace or DblSpace is installed and the first compressed drive is created, the DRVSPACE or DBLSPACE command opens the window shown in Figure 45.1. All your compressed drives are shown in the list. You use this window to perform maintenance on a compressed drive, such as resizing the drive, and to compress more drives.

Figure 45.1.
DriveSpace or DoubleSpace window.

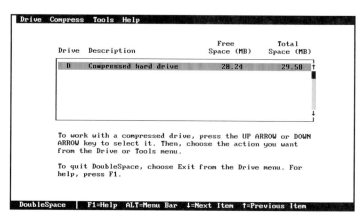

How to Compress an Additional Hard Drive

1. Back up all the important files on the drive to be compressed.

2. Make sure that the drive to be compressed has at least 1.1MB of free space. If not, move some files to floppy or another compressed drive so that you can compress the drive.

3. Enter **DBLSPACE** or **DRVSPACE** to open the DblSpace or DrvSpace window.

4. Choose Compress Existing Drive.

   DblSpace or DrvSpace lists all your drives that are eligible for compression. If none are listed, you have no drives that can be compressed.

5. Select the drive to be compressed. Then, follow the directions on the screen.

   DblSpace or DrvSpace compresses the selected drive.

You can compress additional hard drives by using the commands on the Compress menu: Compress Existing Data or Create New Drive (to compress the free space). DrvSpace or DblSpace asks you to choose the drive to be compressed, then compresses the drive as before. When it's done, you'll see the new compressed drive in the drive list in the main DrvSpace or DblSpace window.

Alternatively, you could enter a command in this format at the DOS command prompt:

```
DRVSPACE /COMPRESS drive1 [/NEWDRIVE=drive2] [/RESERVE=megabytes]
```

This command compresses the existing files on a drive. The *drive1* parameter identifies the host drive; *drive2* identifies the new name for the host drive, if you don't want to use the DrvSpace or DblSpace default. Use the /RESERVE parameter to specify how much uncompressed space to keep on the host drive; if you omit it, DrvSpace or DblSpace leaves only the minimum on the host drive.

> **Note:** The small amount of time that compression and decompression take impedes some time-sensitive applications, such as animators and sound synthesizers. Such applications should not be stored on compressed drives.

To create a compressed drive out of the free space on a drive, enter a command in this format:

```
DRVSPACE /CREATE drive1 [/NEWDRIVE=drive2] [/SIZE=megabytes ¦ /RESERVE=megabytes]
```

For example, to create a compressed drive out of 10MB of free space on drive D, you would enter this command:

```
DRVSPACE /CREATE D /SIZE=10
```

If you would like to compress an additional hard drive, which could take several hours (and could fail, causing you to have to restore the drive's data from its backups), the following exercise guides you through the process:

1. Back up all the important files on the drive to be compressed.

2. Make sure that the drive to be compressed has at least 1.1MB of free space. If not, move some files to floppy so that you can compress the drive.

3. Enter **DBLSPACE** or **DRVSPACE** to open the DblSpace or DrvSpace window.

4. Choose Compress Existing Drive.

   DblSpace or DrvSpace lists all your drives that are eligible for compression. If none are listed, you have no drives that can be compressed.

5. Select the drive to be compressed. Then, follow the directions on the screen.

   DblSpace or DrvSpace compresses the selected drive.

Compressing a Floppy

You can create a compressed drive on a floppy disk. Suppose that you need to ship a large group of files to a client who also has DrvSpace or DblSpace. You'll save a lot of disk space by compressing them. Or, suppose you want to back a finished project off your hard drive, but keep a vault copy on floppy disks for a year or so. You'll need a lot fewer vault disks if you compress them.

You could use Backup for these tasks, but DrvSpace or DblSpace offer some real advantages. With DrvSpace or DblSpace, you simply copy files back and forth; you don't have to deal with backup catalogs when you want to access files on the floppies. Furthermore, you can add, delete, and modify files on the floppies. With Backup, once the backup set is made, it can't be modified. But, there are tradeoffs. DrvSpace or DblSpace doesn't offer many of Backup's bells and whistles, such as error correction code. Furthermore, because DrvSpace or DblSpace automatically decompresses any data that you read from a compressed drive, you can't telecommunicate the data in compressed form. With Backup, you can.

To be compressed, a floppy must be formatted and have at least .65MB of free space. Also, DrvSpace or DblSpace can't compress a 360KB floppy. If a floppy drive doesn't show up in DrvSpace or DblSpace's drive list, the disk that's currently in it doesn't meet these requirements.

To create a compressed drive on a new floppy, insert the disk in the drive and select the Compress Existing Drive command. (You can't use the Compress Create New Drive command on a floppy.) DrvSpace or DblSpace displays a list of drives that are available for compression. (See Figure 45.2.) Select the floppy drive and press Enter. After you confirm the command, DrvSpace or DblSpace converts nearly the entire disk into a compressed drive, mounts the drive, and adds it to the drive list in the DrvSpace or DblSpace window.

Figure 45.2.
Compress Existing Drive
screen.

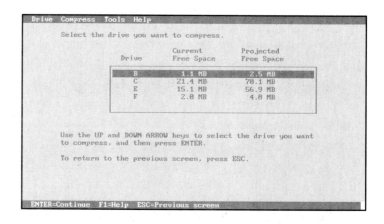

Alternatively, you could enter the DRVSPACE /COMPRESS command shown in the preceding section.

If you have already installed DrvSpace or DblSpace and would like to try compressing a floppy, follow these steps:

1. Find a floppy disk that has at least 1.1MB of free space on it. (A formatted but empty floppy is a good choice.)

2. Insert the floppy in the appropriate drive.

3. Make a backup copy of any important files on the disk.

4. Enter **DBLSPACE** or **DRVSPACE**.

   The DblSpace or DrvSpace window opens.

5. Choose Compress Existing Drive command.

   DblSpace or DrvSpace displays a list of eligible drives, including the floppy. (If the floppy isn't listed, it doesn't have enough free space.)

6. Select the floppy from the list and press Enter.

   DblSpace or DrvSpace suggests that you back up the drive first.

7. Choose Continue.

   DblSpace or DrvSpace displays a time estimate.

8. Press C to continue.

   DblSpace or DrvSpace compresses the drive. When it's done, the new compressed drive appears on your drive list.

As with hard drives, the floppy disk receives a new name for the host drive, and the CVF takes on the old drive name. For a disk in the first floppy disk unit, drive A accesses the compressed volume, whereas the host drive might be called drive L.

The drive is automatically unmounted when you remove the disk from it. If the next disk you insert is not compressed, it receives its normal drive letter. But, when you insert another compressed disk, DrvSpace or DblSpace automatically mounts it.

> **Note:** With DOS 6.0 only, DblSpace does not automatically mount compressed floppies. After inserting the disk in the drive, you must enter the `DBLSPACE /MOUNT d:` command, as in `DBLSPACE /MOUNT A:`.

After a floppy has been compressed, it can be mounted and read by any system that has a compatible version of DrvSpace or DblSpace installed on it. By "installed," I mean that the system must actually have compressed at least one hard drive so that DblSpace or DrvSpace is loaded as part of the core system.

If you compress a floppy with DrvSpace, you can use it on any system that also has DrvSpace installed; but you won't be able to access the compressed data on a system that uses DblSpace, another data compression program, or no compression at all. If you compress a floppy with DblSpace, it can be accessed by any system that has DblSpace installed on it, but not by a system that uses another data compression program or no compression.

A system with DrvSpace installed on it will be able to read a floppy created by DblSpace but not write to it. You must mount the disk manually using the command shown previously. To write to the floppy, you must convert the DblSpace volume to a DrvSpace volume using the following procedure.

How to Convert a DblSpace Floppy to DrvSpace

1. Enter **DRVSPACE /MOUNT A:** to mount the drive. (Substitute **B:** for **A:** if the disk is in drive B.)

2. Enter **DRVSPACE** to open the DrvSpace window.

3. Choose the floppy drive from the drive list.

4. Choose Tools Convert DoubleSpace.

Note: With DOS version 6 only, DblSpace installs in the uncompressed portion of a floppy a READTHIS.TXT file that explains that the disk contains a compressed drive, and how to mount it. If you list the directory of the unmounted disk, you'll see the READTHIS.TXT file.

Tip: The Drive menu contains an Unmount command that you can apply to both hard drives and floppies, but there's very little reason to use it. There's also an /UNMOUNT switch for the DRVSPACE command.

Files on the Host Drive

DrvSpace or DblSpace leaves a certain amount of space on the host drive for storing uncompressed files. By default, it leaves 2MB on your hard drive; but you can specify the amount of space to leave when the compressed drive is first created, and you can resize the compressed drive later on.

Note: Even if the host drive had only 1.2MB of free space when DrvSpace or DblSpace compressed its data, after compression there will be enough space to leave 2MB or more for the host drive.

If the host drive is the boot drive, the DOS core system files will be stored in the uncompressed area along with DRVSPACE.INI or DBLSPACE.INI. All of these files are hidden, but you can see them by including the /A switch with DIR. You'll also see DRVSPACE.nnn or DBLSPACE.nnn, which is the compressed volume file. The nnn is 000 if you compressed the existing data; otherwise, it's a higher number.

Warning: Don't delete, move, or otherwise manipulate the DRVSPACE or DBLSPACE files. You could lose contact with your compressed drive and all its data.

If you compress a drive containing the Windows permanent swap file, DrvSpace or DblSpace places the swap file in the uncompressed space because it won't work if it's compressed. If you have any other files that should not be compressed, you'll have to move them from the compressed drive to the uncompressed drive after DrvSpace or DblSpace finishes. If you discover later that one of your programs doesn't work properly on the compressed drive, you can move it to the host drive, resizing the compressed drive to make more room on the host drive if necessary. You might have to reconfigure or even reinstall the program to reflect the changed drive name.

Problem: After compressing my hard drive, one of my applications issues a copy-protection message and refuses to run.

One way to copy protect a program is to memorize its location when it is installed. Programs protected in this fashion might refuse to run after being compressed, not because they have been compressed, but because they have been moved. You will have to reinstall this application.

Maintaining Compressed Drives and Their Hosts

The Drive menu and the Tools menu contain several options for maintaining compressed drives. These options are also available as switches on the DRVSPACE command.

Caching a Compressed Drive

SMARTDRV will not cache a compressed drive. Instead, it caches the host drive, and that causes any data on the compressed drive to also be cached. When you have a compressed drive, SMARTDRV's status report looks something like this:

```
           Disk Caching Status
drive   read cache   write cache   buffering
─────────────────────────────────────────────
  A:        yes          no           no
  B:        yes          no           no
  C:*       yes          no           no
  H:        yes          no           no

*Compressed drive cached via host drive.
```

In this example, H is the host drive for compressed drive C.

> **Warning:** Do not write-cache compressed drives or their hosts. If the system goes down before DOS has the time to write delayed data to a compressed drive, serious data loss could result.

If you use SMARTDRV and have a compressed drive, you can take a look at your caching status for the drive. To do this, enter **SMARTDRV** to see how your host drive and compressed drive are being cached.

Viewing Compressed Drive Information

Figure 45.3 shows the dialog box that opens when you select a compressed drive and choose the `Drive Info` command.

You can also see this information at the command prompt by entering a command in this format:

Figure 45.3.
Compressed Drive Information dialog box.

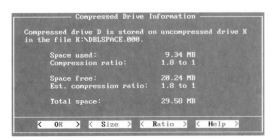

```
DRVSPACE [/INFO] drive
```

The `/INFO` switch is optional because, if you enter a `DRVSPACE` or `DBLSPACE` command with a drive name and no switch to identify the desired function, `/INFO` is the default. (If you also omit the drive name, the DrvSpace or DblSpace window opens.)

Try examining the information for your compressed drives:

1. Enter **DRVSPACE** or **DBLSPACE** to open the compression program's window.

2. Select the drive you want information on.

3. Choose Drive Info.

   DblSpace or DrvSpace displays compression information about the drive.

For information about all your non-network drives, compressed and otherwise, use this command instead:

```
DRVSPACE /LIST
```

The list indicates whether the drives are local hard drives, compressed drives, floppy drives, removable media with no disk inserted, spare drive names that are available for DrvSpace or DblSpace, and so on. (RAM drives are described as local hard drives.) Space used and free space are shown for each drive, if appropriate. For each mounted compressed drive, the report shows the compressed volume name (and its host drive). This function is not available via the DrvSpace or DblSpace window.

Try viewing all the drives on your system:

1. Insert a floppy disk in drive A. (Use a compressed floppy if you have one.)

2. Get to the DOS command prompt.

3. Enter **DRVSPACE** **/LIST** or **DBLSPACE** **/LIST**.

Resizing the Drive

Suppose you want to install a 2MB Windows Permanent Swap File on the host drive, but you have only 1.3MB left on the drive. If there is room available in the compressed drive, you could shrink it to make more room available on the host drive.

On the other hand, suppose you have 5MB available on the host drive and you're running out of space on the compressed drive. You could expand the compressed drive to take up some of the space available on the host drive.

You can press the Size button in the Information dialog box or choose the Drive Change Size command to open a dialog box that lets you change the size of the currently selected drive. (See Figure 45.4.)

Figure 45.4.
Change Size dialog box.

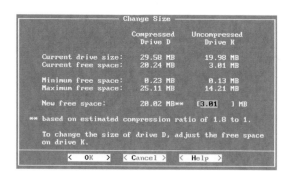

To change the size from the command prompt, enter a command in this format:

DRVSPACE /SIZE=megabytes drive

or

DRVSPACE /SIZE /RESERVE=megabytes drive

For example, to change the size of drive C to 60MB, enter this command:

DRVSPACE /SIZE=60M C:

The specified size refers to the size of the CVF on the host drive, not the estimated capacity. If you don't specify a size, as in DBLSPACE /SIZE C:, DrvSpace or DblSpace makes the drive as small as possible.

To change drive C so that there is 20MB left on the host drive, enter this command:

DRVSPACE /SIZE /RESERVE=20 C:

If you specify /RESERVE=0, DrvSpace or DblSpace makes the compressed drive as large as possible.

If you want to make the drive smaller—and especially if you want to shrink it to its smallest possible size—you should defragment it first, as explained in the next section.

Defragmenting a Compressed Drive

Defragmenting a compressed drive will not improve its access speed as it does with a regular drive. But, defragmenting can help to bring all the empty space together when you want to make the drive smaller. To defragment a compressed drive, choose the Tools Defragment command or enter a command in this format:

DRVSPACE /DEFRAGMENT [drive]

If you omit the drive name, the current drive is defragmented. Add an /F switch to the command to more fully defragment the drive.

> **Note:** Defragmenting a large compressed drive that contains a large amount of data could take several hours.

If you want to make the drive as small as possible, you need to defragment it especially rigorously. Use the procedure shown on this page to do that.

How to Completely Defragment a Compressed Drive

1. Use the DOS DEFRAG command to defragment the host drive.

2. Use the DRVSPACE /DEFRAGMENT command with the /F switch to fully defragment the compressed drive.

3. Use the DRVSPACE /DEFRAGMENT command without the /F switch to fine tune the defragmentation.

Changing the Estimated Compression Ratio

The compression ratio shows how much space was saved by compression. For example, a compression ratio of 2.3:1 means that, for every 2.3KB in the uncompressed file, only 1KB was written in the compressed file. Some types of files compress more than others. A typical word-processing document, for example, achieves a compression ratio around 2:1. A bit-mapped graphic might compress as high as 20:1. Other types of files might compress at only 1.1:1. The overall compression ratio on your compressed drive depends on the mixture of file types you have stored there. It will probably be around 2:1.

When a program such as DIR or CHKDSK reports the available space on a compressed drive, the actual number of bytes would be meaningless. What's more important is how much data you can store on that drive. To compute this, DrvSpace or DblSpace calculates an estimated compression ratio based on the data that's already on the drive, then multiplies that by the number of free bytes on the drive. The result estimates how many bytes of *uncompressed data* you can write to the drive. It may or may not be accurate, depending on the nature of the files that you write to the drive. DIR, CHKDSK, and other programs that report available space use the estimated space figure provided by DrvSpace or DblSpace.

In addition, the DIR command includes a new switch that displays compression ratios on a compressed drive. The /C switch displays compression information based on an 8KB cluster size. If you add an H to it, as in /CH, it displays compression information based on the host drive's cluster size, which is more accurate. A DIR /CH listing looks something like this:

```
Volume in drive D has no label
 Volume Serial Number is 13EF-2218
 Directory of D:\FRENCH

.              <DIR>       02-21-94  12:28p
..             <DIR>       02-21-94  12:28p
CHKLIST  MS         54 12-22-94   3:58p   4.0 to 1.0
FLASHCRD BAS     30896 05-05-94  10:42a   2.3 to 1.0
FLASHCRD EXE     91084 05-05-94  10:43a   1.3 to 1.0
VOCAB    BAS     31265 05-05-94  11:42a   2.2 to 1.0
```

```
VOCAB    EXE    91242 05-05-94  11:42a   1.3 to 1.0
WORK     BAS    13054 05-04-94  11:59a   1.6 to 1.0
                1.4 to 1.0 average compression ratio
         8 file(s)    257595 bytes
                    21102592 bytes free
```

You can see the compression ratio for each file, as well as the average compression ratio for the listed files. The size listed for each file is the uncompressed size; this tells you how much space the file will take up when you read it into memory, or copy or move it to an uncompressed drive. The space estimate on the last line is provided by DrvSpace or DblSpace.

You can also sort the DIR listing by compression ratio. The /OC switch lists files from lowest to highest ratio, and /O-C lists them from highest to lowest.

Note: If you apply the SUBST command to a compressed drive, DrvSpace or DblSpace no longer provides space estimates for the drive, and the actual number of bytes will be shown.

DrvSpace or DblSpace updates the estimated compression ratio to match the actual compression ratio every time it mounts the drive. But, you can change the estimated compression ratio if you think you know something that DrvSpace or DblSpace doesn't. For example, suppose you are trying to install an application that includes 40MB of TIF files and only about 6MB of program and other files. Your compressed drive has a current compression ratio of 2.1:1 and DblSpace or DrvSpace reports that there is 30MB left on the drive. The new application's setup program refuses to install the application because there is not enough space on the drive. Because TIF files compress at about 20:1, you know that there is plenty of room on the drive. You can change the estimated compression ratio to complete the installation task.

To change the estimated ratio, press the Ratio button in the Information dialog box or choose Drive, Option, Change Ratio. (See Figure 45.5.)

Figure 45.5.
Change Compression Ratio
dialog box.

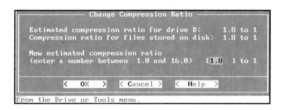

You could also enter this command:

```
DRVSPACE /RATIO[=r.r] [drive ¦ /ALL]
```

The ratio can range from 1.0 to 16.0. If you omit it, DrvSpace or DblSpace adjusts the estimated ratio to the current ratio. /ALL sets the specified compression ratio for all mounted compressed drives. If you don't specify either a drive name or /ALL, DrvSpace or DblSpace sets the ratio for the current drive.

To adjust the estimated ratios for all mounted drives to match their actual ratios, you would enter this command:

DRVSPACE /RATIO /ALL

To finish the installation example described earlier, you would enter **DRVSPACE /RATIO=16.0 C:** so that DblSpace or DrvSpace would report enough room on the drive. After installing the new application, you would enter **DRVSPACE /RATIO C:** to recalculate the actual compression ratio.

Formatting a Compressed Drive

When you first create a compressed drive, it doesn't need to be formatted. But, you can reformat it to delete all its data. You must use DrvSpace or DblSpace's format function, not DOS's FORMAT program.

> **Warning:** You can't unformat a compressed drive.

To format a compressed drive, choose the Drive Format command or enter a command in this format:

DRVSPACE/FORMAT *drive*

Scanning the Drive for Errors

With DOS 6.2, you scan a compressed drive just as you scan an uncompressed one, with SCANDISK as explained in Chapter 27, "CHKDSK and SCANDISK." However, when you try to scan a compressed drive, SCANDISK insists that you scan the host drive first. Choose Yes to scan the host drive and, when that scan is finished, choose Next Drive to scan the compressed drive.

With DOS 6.0, you check the directory structure on a compressed drive by using the Tools Chkdsk command from the DblSpace window, or enter a command in this format:

DBLSPACE /CHKDSK [/F] [*drive*]

Use the /F switch if you want DblSpace to correct any errors it finds.

With DOS 6.2, if you choose the ChkDsk function, a message tells you to run SCANDISK on the drive.

Freeing Up Memory

Two DrvSpace or DblSpace options can help to free up some of the memory space that DrvSpace or DblSpace uses: Last Drive and Removable Media Drives.

DrvSpace or DblSpace automatically reserves a number of drive names on your system so that it can mount drives as necessary, but it usually reserves many more drive names than you need. Because each drive name it reserves takes up 24KB of memory space, it pays to eliminate some of the extra names. Choose the Tools, Options command to see and change the last drive name. For example, suppose you have created only one compressed drive and don't intend to create any more. Furthermore, you're not using any RAM drives or other psuedodrives, so that your highest drive name, not counting the names assigned by DrvSpace or DblSpace, is C. You could safely change the DrvSpace or DblSpace's last drive name to D and save 168KB of memory space.

The Tools, Option command also lets you change the number of removable media drives you have. DrvSpace or DblSpace counts all your floppy drives, removable cartridge drives, and Flash memory card drives and sets aside enough memory space so that you could mount a compressed drive on each one. You can save some memory space by cutting the number back to the number of removable media drives that you actually intend to use compressed drives on. For example, suppose you have two floppy drives and no other removable media drives. If you want to use compressed drives on drive A but not drive B, you could reduce the number of removable media drives to 1. If you plan never to create compressed drives on floppy disks, cut the number to 0.

Deleting a Compressed Drive

If you want to delete a complete compressed drive with all its data from the host drive, choose the Drive Delete command or enter a command in this format:

```
DRVSPACE /DELETE drive
```

Deleting the drive also unmounts it. If it was created by compressing existing data and assigned the host drive's original name, the host drive resumes its original name. If it was created out of free space and assigned a new drive name, that drive name is now available for other uses.

A deleted CVF can be recovered by UNDELETE, just like any other file in DOS. If you recover it, you'll have to mount it to use it again.

Uncompressing a Drive

To uncompress a drive, choose the Tools Uncompress option or enter the command **DRVSPACE /
UNCOMPRESS d:** (but not in DOS 6.0). But first, back up all the important files on the drive. As with
compression, there is some chance of failure during uncompression, and it pays to protect your data.

If DblSpace or DrvSpace determines that the drive does not have enough room to store all the
uncompressed files, it refuses to begin the process. You must remove enough files from the drive to
make sufficient room. You can move them to another drive or delete them.

When you uncompress the last compressed drive on your PC, DrvSpace or DblSpace offers to remove its program from memory. If you answer yes, the compression software will no longer be loaded
when you boot. However, it will still be available in the DOS directory and you can reinstall compression at any time. If you still have compressed floppies, you should not remove the compression
software from memory so that your floppies can still be mounted and accessed.

The uncompress function was new with DOS 6.2. DOS 6.0 does not have a command to uncompress
a drive. The procedure on this page shows you how to uncompress a drive and remove DblSpace
from memory with DOS 6.0.

How to Uncompress a Drive with DOS 6.0

1. Copy any files that you want to keep to another location. (You can use Backup with its
   compression option to do this.)

2. Delete the compressed volume.

   DrvSpace or DblSpace unmounts the volume when it is uncompressed so that the host
   drive assumes its original name.

3. Restore the files to the host drive.

On Your Own

If you have installed DblSpace or DrvSpace, you might want to practice some of the techniques in
this chapter. The items that are bold in the following list could take a long time (perhaps several
hours); you might want to try them only if you really want to compress the drive in question.

1. **Compress an additional hard drive.**
2. Create a new drive by compressing the free space on a drive.

3. Compress a floppy. Then, remove the floppy so that it is unmounted and reinsert it to remount it.

4. View a list of all your drives, compressed or not.

5. Shrink the compressed drive on a floppy down to its minimum size. Then, expand it to its maximum size.

6. **Fully defragment your main compressed drive.**

7. Change the estimated compression ratio for one of your compressed drives to any fictitious number. Then, have DblSpace or DrvSpace calculate the actual compression ratio.

8. Reduce the amount of memory used by DrvSpace or DblSpace, if possible.

9. **Uncompress any of the drives that you compressed in items 1, 2, and 3 that you don't want to keep as compressed drives.**

46

Additional Techniques for Handling Data

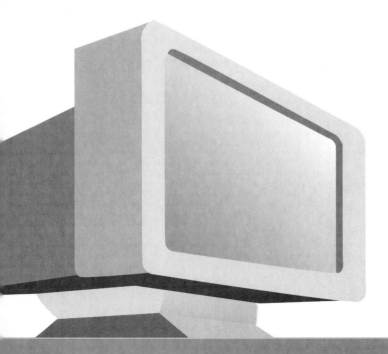

Introduction

You've learned the basics of formatting disks and comparing files, but you may encounter situations where the basics aren't enough, especially when you have to interact with older systems.

Beyond the Basics

The FORMAT command is normally used on disks for your own system. But sometimes you have to prepare a disk to send to a colleague who has a different drive density or an earlier version of DOS. FORMAT includes a number of switches and parameters to assist you in these situations.

FC is an excellent tool for comparing two ASCII files, as you have already learned. Sometimes, however, you want to ignore certain types of differences. For example, you might want to ignore case and spacing differences (that is, uppercase vs. lowercase) when comparing two copies of AUTOEXEC.BAT. If the two files contain the same commands, regardless of case and spacing, they are functionally identical. FC includes switches and parameters to ignore such things as case and spacing. It also gives you some recourse when FC is unable to resynchronize the two files using its default setup.

You may wonder how you can copy a file using DOS's verification feature and still end up with errors in the file. This chapter explains how DOS's verification method works and why it isn't fool-proof.

In this chapter, you will learn how to:

- Format disks for lower density drives
- Format disks for very early versions of DOS
- Ignore case and spacing when comparing two ASCII files
- Extend the resynchronization facility when comparing two ASCII files
- Recognize that DOS's verification feature sometimes misses errors

Formatting at Nondefault Capacities

You have probably used FORMAT many times to prepare disks for your own drives, but what if you want to send a disk to a colleague whose drives are the same size but a different capacity? For example, what if your 3 1/2-inch drive handles 1.44MB disks (high-density), but your colleague's 3 1/2-inch drive handles only 720KB (double-density) disks. If your friend's drives are a higher density than yours, there's no problem. Just format the disk for your drive; your friend's drive will be able to read it. Any 1.44MB 3 1/2-inch drive can read a 720KB disk. And, any 1.2MB 5 1/4-inch drive can read a 360KB disk.

However, the reverse is not true. A double-density drive cannot read a high-density disk. So, if you have a high-density drive and your colleague has a double-density drive, you must take some extra steps to prepare a disk for transmitting to that double-density drive.

Figure 46.1 shows some additional parameters and switches for the FORMAT command. The /F switch is the most popular way to specify a nondefault capacity for a disk. For example, if you want to format a 720KB disk in a 1.44MB drive A, you would specify FORMAT A: /F:720.

FORMAT

Prepares a disk for use or reuse.

Syntax:

```
FORMAT drive [/U] [/V[:label]] [/B] [/F:size]
```

Parameters and Switches:

drive	Identifies the drive to format.
/U	Does an unconditional format.
/V[:*label*]	Specifies the volume label for the formatted disk. Label can be up to 11 characters. If you omit /V or use /V but omit *label*, DOS prompts you for the volume label after formatting is complete. Do not use with /F:160 or /F:320.
/B	Reserves space for system files on a newly formatted disk.
/F:*size*	Overrides the default capacity of the disk. Sizes supported by DOS are:

160KB	5 1/4-inch, single-sided, double-density, 8 sectors per track, 40 tracks
180KB	5 1/4-inch, single-sided, double-density, 9 sectors per track, 40 tracks
320KB	5 1/4-inch, double-sided, double-density, 8 sectors per track, 40 tracks
360KB	5 1/4-inch, double-sided, double-density, 9 sectors per track, 40 tracks
1.2MB	5 1/4-inch, double-sided, high-density, 15 sectors per track, 80 tracks
720KB	3 1/2-inch, double-sided, double-density, 18 sectors per track, 40 tracks
1.44MB	3 1/2-inch, double-sided, high-density, 18 sectors per track, 80 tracks
2.88MB	3 1/2-inch, double-sided, quad-density, 36 sectors per track, 80 tracks

Figure 46.1. FORMAT *command summary.*

Using the nondefault capacity does not always produce accurate results. To increase the probability of success:

- Use a disk that has never been formatted before
- Use a disk that was manufactured for the capacity at which you want to format it; don't format a 1.44MB disk at 720KB, for example

If you enter a size that's not appropriate for the drive (such as /F:1.2 for a 3 1/2-inch drive), you'll see a message such as Parameters not supported on drive or Incompatible parameters. If the disk isn't the right capacity for the format you've selected, FORMAT might try to format the disk (and "discover" a lot of bad sectors), or it might display the message Invalid media or track 0 bad, disk unusable.

> **Tip:** FORMAT's /AUTOTEST switch executes FORMAT with no prompts. But, be careful— you don't get a chance to change the floppy in the drive before it starts to work.

It's unlikely that you have any unformatted double-density disks sitting around if you have high-density drives, so I won't include an exercise here. If you encounter the situation in which you need to do this, your best bet is to buy some new disks (or get your friend to send you some) that are the right capacity.

Formatting for Older Versions of DOS

DOS 1.0 and earlier versions used only 5 1/4-inch disks formatted with only 8 sectors per track and 40 tracks per side. Single-sided disks could hold 160KB and double-sided disks could hold 320KB. Theoretically, you can format a 160KB or 320KB disk by including /F:160 or /F:320 on the FORMAT command. However, be aware that your drive may not be able to accurately prepare the disk. These older disks did not have disk labels, so don't assign the disk a label when you format it.

Ordinarily, you make a disk bootable by including the /S switch on the FORMAT command. But, FORMAT copies the current system to the disk, which is not appropriate if you're preparing a disk for an earlier version of DOS. If the destination computer is using DOS 5.0 or higher, you don't have to do anything special when formatting the disk. The recipients can use the SYS command to install their DOS version on the disk. But, before DOS 5.0, the DOS boot files had to be the first files on the disk; so, if you're preparing a bootable disk for such a system, use the /B switch, which leaves room on the disk for the boot files to be added at a later time by the SYS command.

Expanding FC's Resynchronization Buffer

The FC command includes a number of switches to control how the comparison is made. (See Figure 46.2.) You'll learn how to use these switches in this section.

FC

Compares two files and displays lines or bytes that don't match.

Syntax:

```
FC filespec1 filespec2 [/LBlines] [/resynch] [/C]  [/T] [/W]
```

Parameters and Switches:

filespec1	Identifies the first file to compare.
filespec2	Identifies the second file to compare.
/LB*lines*	Specifies the number of lines in the resynch buffer; the default is 100.
/*resynch*	Specifies the number of lines that must match before files are resynchronized; the default is 2.
/C	Ignores case.
/T	Does not assume tab stops every eight positions and ignores the tab character itself.
/W	Ignores white space.

Figure 46.2. FC *command summary.*

When looking for a matching set of lines after a mismatch, FC uses the contents of the resynch buffer, which holds about 100 lines by default. If no match is found within the buffer, you are notified that the resynchronization failed. You can use /LB*lines* for a larger buffer if necessary; if resynchronization fails, try /LB200 and see whether that works. You probably won't be able to fit a buffer much larger than 200 lines into memory.

Problem: When I tried to use FC, I got the message `FC: Out of memory`.

FC can't find enough memory for its resynch buffer. Try specifying a smaller buffer by using the `/LB` switch.

You can use the *`/resynch`* parameter switch to change the number of lines that must match to resynchronize the file. `/1` sets the number to 1, so only one line must match; `/5` requires five successive matching lines. You may see identical lines identified as mismatches in the output if any number other than 1 is used. If one matching line isn't enough to resynchronize the file, those lines aren't considered a match.

Suppose you compared two files containing the following data:

MEMBERS4

Doherty,Greg,97 Poplar Drive,30038

Fernandez,Davida,95 Poplar Drive,30038

Fernandez,Judi,33 Main Street,30038

Fisher,King,42 Poplar Drive,30038

Gold,Esther,52 Oak Terrace,30033

Gold,Marv,52 Oak Terrace,30033

MacQuown,Dori,41 Spring Drive,30033

MacQuown,Frank,41 Spring Drive,30033

Tabler,Barbara,28 Elm Street,30033

Tabler,George,28 Elm Street,30033

Zoundts,Richard,12 Main Street,30038

MEMBERS6

Doherty,Greg,97 Poplar Drive,30038

Fernandez,Judi,33 Main Street,30038

Gold,Esther,52 Oak Terrace,30033

Gold,Marv,52 Oak Terrace,30033

MacQuown,Dori,41 Spring Drive,30033

MacQuown,Frank,41 Spring Drive,30033

Von Huben,Willie,18 Front Street,30033

Zoundts,Richard,12 Main Street,30038

If you compare these two files using the default resynch parameters, the results look like this:

```
Comparing files MEMBERS4.TXT and MEMBERS6.TXT
***** MEMBERS4.TXT
Doherty,Greg,97 Poplar Drive,30038
Fernandez,Davida,95 Poplar Drive,30038
Fernandez,Judi,33 Main Street,30038
Fisher,King,42 Poplar Drive,30038
Gold,Esther,52 Oak Terrace,30033
***** MEMBERS6.TXT
Doherty,Greg,97 Poplar Drive,30038
Fernandez,Judi,33 Main Street,30038
Gold,Esther,52 Oak Terrace,30033
*****

***** MEMBERS4.TXT
MacQuown,Frank,41 Spring Drive,30033
Tabler,Barbara,28 Elm Street,30033
Tabler,George,28 Elm Street,30033
Zoundts,Richard,12 Main Street,30038
***** MEMBERS6.TXT
MacQuown,Frank,41 Spring Drive,30033
Von Huben,Willie,18 Front Street,30033
Zoundts,Richard,12 Main Street,30038
*****
```

This report tells you that the lines between "Doherty,Greg" and "Gold,Esther" are mismatched. Notice that the line starting with "Fernandez,Judi" is contained in both mismatched sets. It is not used to resynchronize the files because it is not followed by another matching line, and by default, FC looks for two matching lines in a row.

If you compare the same two files using the switch /1, the results are somewhat different:

```
Comparing files MEMBERS4.TXT and MEMBERS6.TXT
***** MEMBERS4.TXT
Doherty,Greg,97 Poplar Drive,30038
Fernandez,Davida,95 Poplar Drive,30038
Fernandez,Judi,33 Main Street,30038
***** MEMBERS6.TXT
Doherty,Greg,97 Poplar Drive,30038
Fernandez,Judi,33 Main Street,30038
*****

***** MEMBERS4.TXT
Fernandez,Judi,33 Main Street,30038
Fisher,King,42 Poplar Drive,30038
Gold,Esther,52 Oak Terrace,30033
***** MEMBERS6.TXT
Fernandez,Judi,33 Main Street,30038
Gold,Esther,52 Oak Terrace,30033
*****
```

```
***** MEMBERS4.TXT
MacQuown,Frank,41 Spring Drive,30033
Tabler,Barbara,28 Elm Street,30033
Tabler,George,28 Elm Street,30033
Zoundts,Richard,12 Main Street,30038
***** MEMBERS6.TXT
MacQuown,Frank,41 Spring Drive,30033
Von Huben,Willie,18 Front Street,30033
Zoundts,Richard,12 Main Street,30038
*****
```

Compare this report with the previous one. Notice that the line beginning "Fernandez,Judi" now is used to resynchronize the files in the first section of the report. Then the next section of the report shows the mismatching lines that come between "Fernandez,Judi" and "Gold,Esther."

Now let's look at what happens if we use /5 instead of /1:

```
Comparing files MEMBERS4.TXT and MEMBERS6.TXT
***** MEMBERS4.TXT
Doherty,Greg,97 Poplar Drive,30038
Fernandez,Davida,95 Poplar Drive,30038
Fernandez,Judi,33 Main Street,30038
Fisher,King,42 Poplar Drive,30038
Gold,Esther,52 Oak Terrace,30033
Gold,Marv,52 Oak Terrace,30033
MacQuown,Dori,41 Spring Drive,30033
MacQuown,Frank,41 Spring Drive,30033
Tabler,Barbara,28 Elm Street,30033
Tabler,George,28 Elm Street,30033
Zoundts,Richard,12 Main Street,30038
***** MEMBERS6.TXT
Doherty,Greg,97 Poplar Drive,30038
Fernandez,Judi,33 Main Street,30038
Gold,Esther,52 Oak Terrace,30033
Gold,Marv,52 Oak Terrace,30033
MacQuown,Dori,41 Spring Drive,30033
MacQuown,Frank,41 Spring Drive,30033
Von Huben,Willie,18 Front Street,30033
Zoundts,Richard,12 Main Street,30038
*****
```

In this last example, FC never manages to resynch the files because it cannot find five matching lines in a row. Therefore, the entire files are considered to be mismatched. This report probably won't do you as much good as one of the earlier examples if you're trying to find out what lines are in one file that aren't in the other. A larger resynch parameter like /5 is more useful to a programmer trying to identify the differences between two program files.

Comparing Two Files for Sense

Sometimes you want to compare two files for sense, rather than a strict character by character comparison. For example, if you compare two name and address files, you really don't care if one file uses uppercase and the other uses lowercase, or if one file indents the lines and the other one doesn't.

You care whether they include the same names and whether any of the addresses are different. Fortunately, FC has switches to ignore such incidentals as case and spacing.

Suppose you want to compare CLIENTS.CRD with MAILING.CRD, ignoring both case and spacing. You would enter FC CLIENTS.CRD MAILING.CRD /W /T /C. The /W switch tells FC to ignore white space—that is, extra spacing between words or between lines. The /T switch tells FC to notice the differences between tab characters and equivalent spaces. And, the /C switch tells FC to ignore case.

If you would like to try ignoring spacing and case, follow the steps below:

1. Switch to C:\.

2. Open AUTOEXEC.BAT for editing.

3. Save the file as AUTOEXEC.TOO.

4. Change the case of any one command. Just change the command name itself from uppercase to lowercase or vice versa.

5. Insert a tab in front of one line, but not the same line where you changed the case.

6. Insert some extra spaces in another line.

7. Insert a blank line between two lines.

8. Save the file and exit the editor.

9. Enter FC AUTOEXEC.BAT AUTOEXEC.TOO ¦ MORE.

   All the lines that you changed should be reported as different.

10. Now enter FC AUTOEXEC.BAT AUTOEXEC.TOO /W /T /C ¦ MORE.

   No differences should be found.

Understanding DOS's Verification

Your system provides several levels of protection to ensure that the data it reads and writes is not corrupted by hardware or media problems.

CRCs

In normal use, a drive controller does a *cyclic redundancy check* (CRC) each time it writes a sector. It performs a calculation on all the bytes in the sector and stores the result in the sector control area immediately preceding the sector. Then, it rereads the sector, recalculates the value, and compares it to the stored value. If they differ, the controller reports a write error to DOS. Later, when the sector is read, the CRC is performed again. If the calculated value doesn't match the stored value, a read error is reported. The CRC will catch all errors that occur after the data is transferred to the disk controller, but you may want to be even more exacting than that.

DOS's Verification

You also can ask DOS to verify each sector it writes. When DOS verifies, it makes sure that each sector is written correctly by comparing it to the data in memory. If verification fails, DOS reports a write error to you.

General Verification

Normally, DOS depends on the hardware's CRC verification and doesn't verify what it writes to disk. You can force it to verify all writes by using VERIFY ON at the command prompt. To find out the current state of verification, enter VERIFY (with no parameters). To turn verification off, enter VERIFY OFF.

Find out if verification is currently on or off in your system:

1. Enter **VERIFY**.

   DOS responds with VERIFY OFF or VERIFY ON.

2. If you would like to change the status of your verification, enter **VERIFY ON** or **VERIFY OFF**.

General verification will slow down your entire system, but not noticeably. However, you may prefer to verify only in specific instances.

Specific Verification

The COPY, XCOPY, and DISKCOPY commands let you use the /V switch to request verification for a single command. This switch works regardless of the setting of VERIFY, but it's redundant when VERIFY is ON. As with VERIFY ON, it takes a bit more time, but the delay may be worth it to you in some cases.

On Your Own

Use the following items as a guide to practicing on your own some of the techniques discussed in this chapter:

1. If you have multiple versions of CONFIG.*xxx* (for example, CONFIG.SYS and CONFIG.SAV), compare them to see if you can figure out the differences. Do the same with multiple versions of AUTOEXEC.*xxx*.

2. Does your system boot with verify on or off? If you would like to change your default verify setting, enter the appropriate command in AUTOEXEC.BAT.

47

Advanced Rescue Techniques

Introduction

No matter how careful you are or how many preventive measures you take, eventually you're going to lose some data. Whether it's from malfunctioning hardware, a virus, or a simple typo in a command, you have to do your best to recover it.

DOS's Recovery Tools

DOS 6 includes a number of diagnostic and recovery tools that can help you deal with errors in the system areas and directory tree, accidentally deleted files, and accidentally reformatted disks. DOS's tools can handle most of your recovery needs. However, you may need to turn to outside solutions in some cases.

You have already learned how to use the most common tools:

- SCANDISK and CHKDSK for recovering lost clusters and cross-linked files
- SCANDISK for rescuing data from damaged sectors
- UNFORMAT for recovering data from a reformatted disk
- UNDELETE for recovering erased files
- Backup for restoring files from their backups

This chapter shows you some features of CHKDSK, SCANDISK, and UNFORMAT that you might need less often. You'll also see how to use MSD to obtain useful diagnostic information about your computer. You will learn how to:

- Handle the following errors when reported by SCANDISK or CHKDSK: Allocation error, Invalid subdirectory entry, and Bad sectors in the FAT
- Unformat a disk when the mirror image file is missing
- Use MSD

Handling Structural Problems with SCANDISK and CHKDSK

By far the most frequent problems reported by SCANDISK and CHKDSK are lost allocation units and cross-linked files. You saw how to handle them in Chapter 27, "CHKDSK and SCANDISK." In this section, you'll learn how to handle some less common problems.

Invalid Allocation Units

A value in a file's FAT chain represents an invalid allocation unit if it is 0, 1, or larger than the number of allocation units on the disk. Although 0s are valid for unused clusters, they should not show up in a file chain.

Figure 47.1 shows a sample FAT with an invalid allocation unit in the file that starts in cluster 46; cluster 49 contains the value 1, which breaks the chain. In this case, SCANDISK or CHKDSK knows the file has more clusters from the size of the directory entry, but it has no way to find the rest of the file's chain. (We can guess by inspecting the FAT that the next cluster should be 50, but SCANDISK and CHKDSK can't make this kind of guess.)

0-7:			3	4	4	<EOF>	<EOF>	<EOF>
8-15:	0	10	11	12	13	14	15	16
16-23:	17	18	19	<EOF>	21	22	23	24
24-31:	25	26	18	28	29	30	31	32
2-39:	33	34	35	36	37	38	39	40
40-47:	<EOF>	0	0	0	0	<EOF>	47	48
48-50:	49	1	51					

Figure 47.1. *Sample FAT data.*

Any other clusters that belonged to the file are orphaned; you may be able to find them among the lost clusters on the disk.

Figure 47.2 shows how SCANDISK reports an invalid allocation unit. It points out that the beginning of the file is all right, but that there is a problem somewhere in the chain.

Figure 47.2.
SCANDISK's report of an invalid allocation unit.

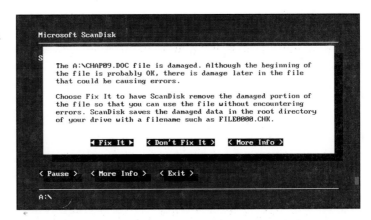

CHKDSK notifies you about invalid allocation units as follows:

```
C:\BOOK1\CHAPTER.CPY
     First allocation unit is invalid, entry truncated

C:\BOOK1\STUDY.STY
    Has invalid allocation unit, file truncated

19 lost allocation units found in 4 chains
     38912 bytes would be freed
```

If the first allocation unit is invalid, no part of the file can be saved directly. At least one chain of lost allocation units probably belongs to this file. The invalid allocation unit in the second example is not the first cluster in the file, so at least part of the file can be found. Unless the invalid entry is at the end of the file, at least one lost chain should have data from this file.

How SCANDISK and CHKDSK Fix Invalid Allocation Units

Your best solution to an invalid allocation unit is to make a note of the filename, finish the scan, then restore the file from its backup. You should let SCANDISK or CHKDSK fix the problem only if you don't have a good backup. Neither SCANDISK nor CHKDSK can do a perfect job of fixing this error.

To let SCANDISK fix the error, choose Fix It in the dialog box. For CHKDSK, rerun CHKDSK with the /F switch. SCANDISK will recover lost allocation units automatically; but, with CHKDSK, be sure to convert all lost allocation units into files. One of the resulting .CHK files might contain the data that has been lost from this file.

When it tries to repair a file that has an invalid allocation unit, SCANDISK or CHKDSK replaces the invalid entry with an end-of-file marker and adjusts the file size in the directory to match the new number of clusters. Now you can access the file (if possible) and find out how much data you have lost; then examine the .CHK files to recover what you can. As always, don't try to run a program file that has been treated this way.

Note: With SCANDISK, an invalid allocation unit also causes an allocation error (discussed next), because the file's size in the directory entry does not match the number of clusters in its chain. If you let SCANDISK fix the invalid allocation unit, also let it fix the allocation error.

You should examine the repaired file by using the application that originally created it. But, many applications store header information at the beginning of the files they create, as well as trailer information at the end. When SCANDISK or CHKDSK fixes the file, it cuts off the trailer information and the application might not be able to open the file. If you encounter this problem, try opening a new file and inserting the damaged file into it. If that also won't work, try opening the file in a text editor such as EDIT, deleting any data that isn't ASCII text, and saving the file as an ASCII text file. You should then be able to insert it into a new file created by the original application. You can also insert the .CHK file into the same document. (You might have to convert it to ASCII text first, too.)

Allocation Errors

SCANDISK or CHKDSK reports an allocation error when it detects that the size recorded for the file in the directory entry doesn't match the number of allocation units assigned to it. CHKDSK displays a message like the following:

```
A:\NEWSTUDY.DOC
    Allocation error, size adjusted
```

If you haven't used /F, the size in the directory entry isn't really adjusted, even though the message says that it is.

Figure 47.3 shows the message that SCANDISK displays when it encounters an allocation error. As you can see, it tells you that the file's size information is incorrect.

Figure 47.3.
SCANDISK's report of an
allocation error.

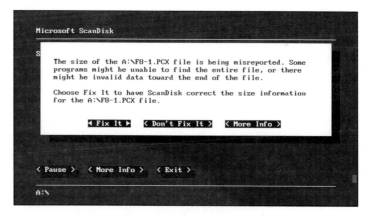

How CHKDSK Fixes an Allocation Error

As always, you should restore the file from its backup rather than trying to fix it. If you don't have a valid backup, choose Fix It from the SCANDISK dialog box or rerun CHKDSK with the /F switch. Save any lost chains as files, because the end of the file might be cut off by the repair.

SCANDISK or CHKDSK fixes an allocation error by adjusting the file's size in the directory entry. The entire last cluster is considered part of the file, because neither SCANDISK nor CHKDSK can tell where the file ends and slack begins.

If the recorded size really was wrong and the number of allocation units in the FAT was correct, CHKDSK's repair may add slack (garbage) to the end of the file. If the recorded size was correct and the FAT included too few or too many allocation units for the file, the resulting file is incorrect; it is either too long or too short. Either the file now contains garbage at the end, or some lost allocation units are on the disk. At any rate, now you can access the file to figure out what to do next.

Dealing with Allocation Errors

After the repair, examine the damaged file under its original application. (You might have to convert it to an ASCII file and insert it into a new document.) You might have to delete unwanted garbage at the end, or locate and insert missing data from the .CHK files created by SCANDISK or CHKDSK.

> **Warning:** If SCANDISK or CHKDSK detects an allocation error on a program file, delete the file and reinstall the program from its original disk. Never try to fix or run a program file that was repaired by CHKDSK or SCANDISK.

Invalid Subdirectory Entry

Subdirectories are stored as files with a special directory attribute. They can be corrupted in many of the same ways that files can. If the .. directory entry shows the wrong cluster number for the parent, for example, DOS can't find the linkage from that subdirectory to its parent. If the parent's link to the child is corrupted, DOS can't locate the subdirectory.

SCANDISK may identify several related problems that crop up from one damaged subdirectory entry. In addition to finding the invalid entry, for example, it may find the orphaned subdirectory itself. Figure 47.4 shows a typical SCANDISK message for an invalid subdirectory entry.

Figure 47.4.
SCANDISK's report of an
invalid subdirectory entry.

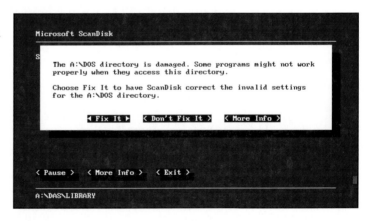

When CHKDSK detects an invalid subdirectory entry, the message depends on the severity of the problem. You might see the following:

```
C:\BOOK1\CHAP03.DOC
    Invalid subdirectory entry
```

In this case, CHKDSK can fix the problem. It may be a corrupted entry for the backlink to the parent directory, for example. CHKDSK can search the tree, find the address of the parent that way, and fix the subdirectory entry. In this case, no files or allocation units are lost.

An invalid subdirectory entry message also may be followed by some lines like the following:

```
324 lost allocation units in 5 chains
   165888 bytes disk space would be freed
 Convert lost directory to file (Y/N)?
```

The final line of this message usually indicates that you can't access anything in the subdirectory, and all of its files appear to be lost chains, as do all of its subdirectories and their files. CHKDSK can't do anything to fix this subdirectory entry.

How SCANDISK and CHKDSK Repair an Invalid Subdirectory Entry

If SCANDISK finds a lost chain on the disk that contains directory entries, it assigns a generic name to the directory (DIR00001 for the first one) and creates an entry for it in the root directory. It repairs invalid subdirectory entries whenever it can and deletes those that it can't repair.

CHKDSK doesn't go quite as far in repairing an invalid directory entry. If it doesn't ask about converting the subdirectory to a file, CHKDSK with the /F switch can find the information it needs. It quietly fixes the problem without losing any data.

However, if CHKDSK asks and you press Y to convert a lost directory to a file, DOS makes the cluster that formerly contained the subdirectory into a file. Because they are no longer linked to the directory structure, allocation units for all files in the branch headed by that subdirectory are lost. You should respond with a Y when CHKDSK asks whether you want to convert them to files.

Dealing with Invalid Subdirectory Entries

Because SCANDISK recovers lost subdirectories as subdirectories, you don't need to remake them or rescue their files, but you do need to correct the subdirectory names.

If CHKDSK offers you the opportunity to convert an invalid subdirectory into a file, you may say yes for safety's sake, although you can do very little with the resulting file. However, it is important to recover lost allocation units into files if you can't restore the branch from backups.

To restore the branch after running CHKDSK, remake all the subdirectories and then examine all the .CHK files and copy them to their former subdirectories with their correct names. As a final step, delete any .CHK files you don't need anymore.

Bad Sectors in the Disk's Administrative Areas

SCANDISK's surface scan may be able to rescue data from bad sectors. However, because a disk's administrative information, such as the FATs and the boot record, must reside in a particular position, SCANDISK can't fix them by moving the data to another spot. Figure 47.5 shows the message that appears when SCANDISK encounters this type of problem. All you can do is select OK, which terminates the scan.

Figure 47.5.
SCANDISK's report of a
bad sector in the root
directory.

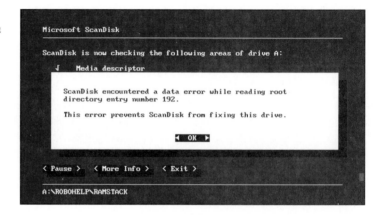

CHKDSK doesn't check for bad sectors or other surface problems on a disk. However, if the disk's administrative area has developed problems, you might see one of the following messages:

```
Bad sector in FAT
```

or

```
Probable nonDOS disk
```

The `Probable nonDOS disk` message may reflect a bad spot in the boot record. Either message indicates a problem too major for CHKDSK to handle.

If the problem is with a floppy disk and you have a valid backup, you probably will just throw away the damaged one. However, if the problem is on a hard disk, you will want to go further to rescue it. A third-party utility such as Norton Disk Doctor might be able to succeed where CHKDSK can't. Even if you can't repair the disk, you may be able to recover the data from it before repairing or replacing it.

Rebuilding Disks without Mirror Image Information

If you have never reformatted a floppy disk in error, you may be unique among your fellow computer users. You learned in Chapter 17, "Formatting and Unformatting Disks," how to use the UNFORMAT program to rescue accidentally reformatted disks. How much of the data on the disk can be recovered depends on several factors:

- Whether the format was unconditional
- Whether the disk contains unformatting information
- Whether any data was added to the disk after formatting
- Whether the disk contained fragmented files if no formatting information was recorded

Unformatting a disk without image information might be necessary in the following situations:

- You reformatted the disk with a third-party format program that did not save image information.
- You used the /U and /Q switches together on the FORMAT command.
- The formatting program was unable to save image information because the disk was too full.
- The image file is corrupted or missing.

Figure 47.6 shows the switches and parameters that can be used on the UNFORMAT command to rebuild a disk from scratch.

UNFORMAT

Restores a disk reformatted by the FORMAT command; undeletes deleted directories; displays partition table.

Syntax:

UNFORMAT *drive* [/L] [/TEST] [/P] [/PARTN] [/J]

Parameters and Switches:

drive	Identifies the drive to be unformatted.
/J	Verifies image file.
/L	Lists every file and subdirectory found by UNFORMAT; without this switch, only fragmented files and directories are listed.
/TEST	Shows how UNFORMAT would re-create the information on the disk, but does not actually unformat the disk.
/P	Sends output messages to LPT1.
/PARTN	When used with /L, displays partition table.

Notes:
When you unformat a hard disk, the sectors must be 512, 1024, or 2048 bytes.
With /L, /TEST, or /P, UNFORMAT bypasses mirror information and searches the clusters (very slowly) for subdirectories.

Figure 47.6.   *UNFORMAT command summary.*

The first thing UNFORMAT does is search the disk for image information. The image file is not a regular file with a directory entry. FORMAT placed it in the last available clusters on the disk. UNFORMAT simply reads the data in the clusters from the end to the beginning, looking for image information. If UNFORMAT can't find image information in its normal location, you see messages such as the following:

```
Unable to find the Mirror control file. If you want to
search for the Mirror image file through the entire
hard drive, press Y, or press N'to cancel the UNFORMAT command.
```

If you would like, the rest of the disk (which is not necessarily the hard drive) will be searched; even on a floppy disk, the search takes a long time. If you think that the mirror image information should be on the disk, press Y to let UNFORMAT continue its search. Otherwise, press N to terminate UNFORMAT. Then, you can restart UNFORMAT with switches that cause it to rebuild the disk.

> **Tip:** When used with /L or /P, UNFORMAT might be able to restore a deleted directory, even if the disk has not been reformatted. This method of re-creating directories, however, is slow and uncertain; sometimes, it creates strange directories, and it truncates fragmented files, even in existing directories.
>
> A better way of recovering the deleted directory is to undelete it. Unfortunately, the DOS version of UNDELETE can't recover deleted directories, but the Windows version may be able to do so. The Norton Utilities' UnErase utility also can recover directories.

How UNFORMAT Rebuilds a Disk

When UNFORMAT doesn't use image information, it searches the disk for subdirectories and uses their backlinks (the .. entries) to locate their parents. By this means, it can rebuild the entire directory tree. When a subdirectory is recovered, its files are also recovered as much as possible. However, UNFORMAT can find only the first fragment of any fragmented files.

When image information is not available, the biggest problem lies with the files in the root directory. They can't be recovered because their directory entries were obliterated when the new root directory was installed. First-level subdirectories will be discovered in the data area, and UNFORMAT knows they belong to the root directory because they backlink to cluster 0; but, there is no way to discover their names. UNDELETE restores them to the root directory using generic names in the form SUBDIR.*n*. You can examine and rename them. You will not be able to recover the files from the root directory, however, unless you use a third-party utility that enables you to examine available clusters and make up files from them.

When it is not using an image file, UNFORMAT lists on-screen the complete path of any subdirectories it finds. It lists fragmented files and asks whether each should be truncated or deleted. (If you include the /L switch, it lists all files, fragmented or otherwise.)

Starting the Rebuilding Process

To rebuild the disk, start by entering **UNFORMAT** *d:* /TEST. The /TEST switch causes UNFORMAT to simulate the rebuilding process. It goes through all the steps and displays all the messages, but it doesn't actually make any changes to the disk. The messages should tell you whether it's worthwhile to try rebuilding the disk for real. If you decide to go ahead with it, enter **UNFORMAT** *d:*. You see the following messages:

```
  CAUTION !!

This attempts to recover all the files lost after a
format, assuming you've not been using the Mirror command.

This method can't guarantee complete recovery of your files.

The search-phase is safe: nothing is altered on the disk.
You will be prompted again before changes are written to the disk.

Using drive A:

Are you sure you want to do this?
If so, press Y; anything else cancels.
?
```

At this point, you can back out and nothing happens. If you enter Y, however, UNFORMAT begins searching the available clusters for subdirectories. The display shows you the percentage of the disk that has been searched and the number of subdirectories that has been found. When the search is finished, you see the number of files and subdirectories found in the root directory. It may find subdirectories that were removed long ago that you don't want; you can remove these later. The messages appear as follows:

```
Searching disk...
n% searched.  n subdirectories found.
Files found in the root: n
Subdirectories found in the root: n
```

Next, UNFORMAT checks the entire directory tree looking for files. Any first-level subdirectories that have been removed will have lost their names. You see the names UNFORMAT creates in the list:

```
Walking the directory tree to locate all files...
Path=A:\
Path=A:\SUBDIR.1\
Path=A:\SUBDIR.1\CHAPS\
Path=A:\SUBDIR.1\
etc.

Files found: n

Warning! The next step writes changes to disk.

Are you sure you want to do this?
If so, press Y; anything else cancels.
?
```

This is your last chance to back out. If you choose to go ahead, UNFORMAT begins recovering subdirectories and files. If only the first fragment of a file is available, you see messages like the following:

```
Checking for file fragmentation...
Path=A:\
Path=A:\SUBDIR.1\
Path=A:\SUBDIR.1\CHAPS\
GETTY2.DOC   2560  9-25-94  11:32am  Only    512 bytes
are recoverable. Truncate or Delete this file?
```

You can decide whether UNFORMAT should save what it can (truncate), or just delete the file.

Using MSD

The MSD (Microsoft Diagnostics) program displays some vital statistics about your system. Figure 47.7 shows the main MSD menu screen, which appears when you enter the MSD command at the DOS command prompt.

Figure 47.7.
MSD's main screen.

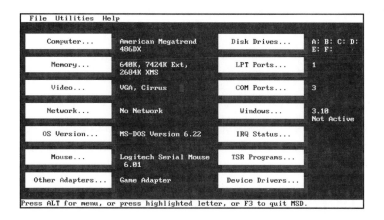

Note: You can start up MSD under Windows, but the information it displays may not be accurate. MSD detects the presence of Windows and warns you when this is the case.

You can choose each button on the screen to see detailed information about that item. For example, Figure 47.8 shows the dialog box that appears if you choose the Video button. As you can see in the figure, the information is quite detailed. Although it's interesting to explore your system with MSD, you usually don't need this level of information. However, if you are experiencing a system-wide problem with DOS or Windows, Microsoft's Technical Support team may ask you for some information provided by MSD.

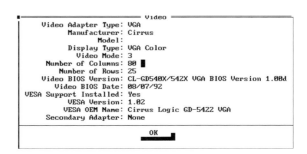

Figure 47.8.
MSD's Video dialog box.

MSD provides especially detailed information on your system's memory usage. Take a look at this information for your system:

1. Exit all programs and get to the primary command prompt.

2. Enter **MSD**.

   The MSD main screen appears.

3. Choose the Memory button.

   MSD displays a map of upper memory. The legend at the top of the display tells you how to interpret the symbols in the map. You can scroll through the map to see all of upper memory.

4. Choose OK to close the memory map.

5. For an even more detailed look at your system's memory, choose Utilities, Memory Block Display.

   In the resulting dialog box, a map of memory is displayed on the right and a list of the currently loaded programs on the left.

6. Move the highlight up and down in the list on the left and watch the effect on the memory map.

   As you move the highlight through the list of programs, the | -- | indicator moves through the map to indicate exact location of the highlighted program. You can scan through all of conventional and upper memory on this map.

7. Choose Close to close the Memory Block Display.

Note: Utilities, Memory Block Display shows what's in RAM. Choose Utilities, Memory Browser for a similar display of ROM.

MSD's File menu lets you view (but not edit) your system startup and .INI files, such as AUTOEXEC.BAT and SYSTEM.INI. (See Figure 47.9.) You can also print a report of any of the MSD displays. Figure 47.10 shows the dialog box that appears when you choose File, Print Report.

All the items marked by X will be included in the report. You can Tab to fields and use the spacebar to select an item to enable or disable. Notice that you can also select the port for the printer or save the report in a file. When you have set up the report the way you want it, choose OK to print it.

Figure 47.9.
MSD's File menu.

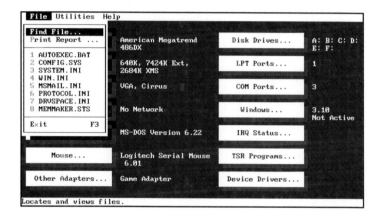

Figure 47.10.
MSD's Print Report dialog box.

On Your Own

The following items will help you practice some of the techniques you have learned in this chapter:

1. Check your hard drives and correct any errors you find.

2. Prepare a practice floppy with several directories and files on it. (Be sure to use practice data only. Don't take the chance of destroying any data that you need.) Format the floppy without saving a mirror file, then rebuild it from scratch.

3. Prepare another practice floppy with several directories and files on it. (Again, be sure to use practice data only.) Delete one of the directories, then try to recover it using UNFORMAT. If you have Windows, also try deleting and recovering a directory with the Windows version of UNDELETE.

4. Explore your system with MSD. Find out, for example, the addresses of your COM ports, how many cylinders your hard drive has, and whether your computer has a DMA controller.

48

Console Control

Introduction

The DOS command-prompt screen, by default, is about as interesting as yesterday's blackboard: plain text on a bland background, 24 lines per screen, and no graphics. The keyboard types the characters shown on the keycaps and very little else. But, you can do a lot to jazz up both the screen and the keyboard.

Dressing Up DOS

Several DOS features give you control over the monitor and the keyboard. You can add color and (somewhat limited) graphics to the screen, flash blinking messages at users, even splash a colorful banner across the top of the screen showing the date, time, and other useful information. You can redefine keys on the keyboard to type international characters such as é, graphics characters such as ☺, even complete macros such as DIR *.* /S /B /P /A /O or CD \NORTH\ALASKA. The techniques in this chapter can make your own work, as well as the batch programs you create for others, more exciting and more effective.

In this chapter, you will learn how to:

- Add color to the command-prompt screen
- Control the position of the cursor on the command-prompt screen
- Display simple graphics (such as boxes) on the command-prompt screen
- Turn character wrapping on and off
- Redefine keys on your keyboard
- Use a different console device
- Use DOS's power-management features to preserve your portable PC's battery
- Adjust the size and position of the characters on your screen
- Adjust the keyboard typematic rate

DOS and Your Video Monitor

DOS supports several types of video: monochrome display adapter (MDA), color graphics adapter (CGA), enhanced graphics adapter (EGA), and the video graphics array (VGA). Other types of video adapters are usually compatible with one or more of these. A video adapter or monitor with more features than these basic types (such as more pixels or a two-page display for desktop publishing) is usually accompanied by software to help you take advantage of its features.

The CON Driver

DOS's command-prompt interface uses the built-in CON device driver to interact with whatever video adapter is installed. CON provides simple text-oriented services so that DOS can write messages to the command-prompt screen. CON uses functions built into the video controller to drive the hardware, which keeps DOS independent of the actual video equipment and lets the operating system function regardless of what display adapter is used. Unfortunately, the result is the dull-as-dishwater monochrome screen that DOS users love to hate.

The Video Buffer

Every video adapter card has a memory area called the video buffer. Whatever will be displayed on the screen must first be stored in the video buffer. The video is said to be memory-mapped because every byte in its buffer corresponds to a specific location on the screen.

In text mode, the video buffer contains two bytes for each screen character position. The first byte contains the ASCII value of the character to be displayed, and the second byte contains its attributes (color, blinking, and so on). Figure 48.1 shows the beginning of a typical buffer. In this case, it contains the message sanity! starting in the first character position on the screen. The first byte shows the ASCII value of the letter S. The next byte shows its attributes; 07 represents DOS's usual white-on-black style. The third byte shows the ASCII code for the letter a; the fourth byte shows its attributes.

s		a		n		i		t		y		!	
83	07	97	07	110	07	105	07	117	07	121	07	33	07

Figure 48.1.   *Video buffer in text mode.*

On color systems, the attribute byte specifies the foreground and background colors, as well as the foreground intensity and blinking/steady status. On monochrome systems, the attribute can be used to specify intensity, underlining, blinking, and normal or reverse video in text mode. Programs that run in graphics mode handle their attributes differently; they work with smaller screen elements than text mode.

What ANSI.SYS Offers

The CON driver can't use color. It just pokes ASCII codes into even-numbered (character) bytes of the video buffer, and doesn't affect any odd-numbered (attribute) bytes, so the current attributes are never changed.

The ANSI.SYS device driver is sort of a super-CON; it gives you many more options to take advantage of your video and keyboard features. ANSI.SYS gives you a way to specify color and the other video attributes. It also lets you control the cursor position and clear the screen. It lets you use 43 or 50 lines (if the monitor can handle that), and 40 columns instead of 80. Additional features enable you to manipulate the meanings of the keyboard keys.

Some programs depend on ANSI.SYS to provide enhanced video and keyboard services. Their documentation advises you that ANSI.SYS must be loaded. Other programs use the PC's video BIOS, which contains even more efficient screen functions. Even a nonprogramming user, however, can use ANSI.SYS to spice up displays, the command prompt, and batch files. The results affect only programs that use the DOS command-prompt screen, such as DIR, MORE, and CHKDSK. It doesn't affect utilities and applications that provide their own screens, such as DOS Shell, EDIT, and SCANDISK.

The ANSI.SYS Device Driver

You load ANSI.SYS from the CONFIG.SYS file with a `DEVICE` or `DEVICEHIGH` command. Figure 48.2 shows the command format. After ANSI.SYS is installed, it scans all standard output looking for its own commands.

ANSI.SYS

Provides functions that control screen colors, cursor position, and key assignments.

Syntax:

```
DEVICE[HIGH]=[path]ANSI.SYS [/X] [/K]
```

Parameters and Switches:

path Identifies the location of the ANSI.SYS file. The default is the root directory of the boot drive.

/X   With a 101-key (extended) keyboard, forces DOS to recognize that the extended (gray) cursor control, deletion, and insert/overlay keys have different scan codes than the numeric keypad keys for the same functions.

/K   Causes ANSI.SYS to treat a 101-key keyboard like an 84-key keyboard.

Figure 48.2. *ANSI.SYS DEVICE command summary.*

You might want to use the /X switch if you assign different characters to keys that have duplicates, such as the up-arrow key, Home, and the + (plus) key. If you don't specify the /X switch, two matching keys are mapped the same; for example both + (plus) keys will have the same effect. If you specify /X, you can assign different functions to each one. Key mapping is covered in detail later in this chapter.

Install ANSI.SYS now, so that you can try out the techniques in this chapter:

1. Edit CONFIG.SYS to include `DEVICEHIGH=C:\DOS\ANSI.SYS /X`.
2. Reboot.

Note: Use /K if you have a program that does not recognize the extended keys on the 101-key keyboard. If you use the /K switch with the SWITCHES command, use /K with ANSI.SYS also.

Sending Commands to ANSI.SYS

When ANSI.SYS is installed, it remains in memory, taking about 4KB. It continuously monitors all standard output, looking for escape sequences, which it recognizes as commands. An escape sequence begins with an Esc character, followed by a left square bracket, and ends with a specific terminator character. In between are the codes that make up the command. The details of specific commands are covered later, but the following is an example that sets a color screen to display cyan letters on a red background:

```
Esc[31;46m
```

The code 31 means a red background, and 46 means a cyan foreground. The terminator character, m, must be used with all escape sequences that control color; it tells ANSI.SYS what function is desired. To set the colors back to the defaults, send Esc[m (without any color specification) to standard output.

Note: The case of terminator characters is significant. Using M instead of m to affect color won't work.

You'll try out this command soon, but first you must learn how to send an escape sequence to standard output.

Typing the Escape Character

You can't just press Esc at the keyboard to start an escape sequence; it cancels the current command and starts another. How you enter Esc depends on how you decide to send the escape sequence to ANSI.SYS. The useful commands that produce standard output are PROMPT, TYPE, and ECHO.

Using PROMPT

In the PROMPT command, you can type normal text as well as special characters that represent untypeable items. Table 48.1 shows the complete set of PROMPT special characters, which can be typed in uppercase or lowercase. The command PROMPT PG establishes the familiar prompt that shows the current drive and path followed by the greater-than symbol.

Table 48.1. PROMPT command special characters.

$B	| (bar or piping sign)
$D	Current date
$E	Escape
$G	> (greater-than sign)
$H	Backspace (to delete character)
$L	< (less-than sign)
$N	Current drive
$P	Current drive and path
$Q	= (equal sign)
$T	Current time
$V	DOS version number
$$	$ (dollar sign)
$_	↵Enter (Enter)

To use PROMPT to send an escape sequence, you use $E to specify the Esc character. If you have a color monitor, try out a few prompt commands on your screen:

1. Enter PROMPT $E[36;41m$P$G.

   The prompt is displayed in cyan text on a red background.

2. Enter CLS.

   This turns the entire screen red and displays the prompt (in cyan) in the upper left corner.

3. Enter PROMPT $E[36;41m$PGE[m. (Reminder: You can recall and edit the previous PROMPT command with DOSKEY.)

   Sets cyan text on a red background, displays the standard prompt, and then turns the color off so that the default colors are restored for all except the prompt itself.

4. Enter CLS to spread the background color to the entire screen.

   Now the prompt is displayed in cyan on red, but the rest of the screen is black.

When you're working hard on a PROMPT command to manipulate colors, it's easy to forget to include PG (or whatever you want to use to define the prompt text). If you forget it, you end up with no prompt text. That's ok, though; you can still enter commands, even if you can't see the command prompt. Try it:

1. Enter PROMPT $E[36;41m.

   Your prompt disappears.

2. Enter CLS to spread the background color to the entire screen.

   The screen turns red, but you still don't have a prompt.

3. Enter PROMPT PG to regain your prompt.

The disadvantage of using PROMPT to send commands to ANSI.SYS is that it eliminates your previous prompt unless you are careful to reset it. However, PROMPT is often the quickest way to try out escape sequences and see the effect right away.

Using a Text File

When you TYPE a file, DOS sends it to standard output. Any escape sequences are diverted by ANSI.SYS. You can create a text file containing one or more escape sequences, and then TYPE it to put them all into effect.

You can use any text editor to create a file containing escape sequences, as long as you know how to enter the Esc character into it. To TYPE correctly, of course, the file must be saved in ASCII form; DOS's EDIT program saves all files in this form. In EDIT, first press Ctrl+P, and then press Esc to type an escape character. You see a left arrow on the screen, but it functions as the Esc character when you TYPE the file.

> **Tip:** Pressing Ctrl+P followed by Esc also works in WordStar. In Microsoft Word for DOS, enter the ASCII code for Esc: Hold down the Alt key, and press 2 and then 7 on the numeric keypad (make sure NumLock is on). When you release the Alt key, a left arrow appears on the screen. In WordPerfect for DOS, press Ctrl+V followed by Esc, which appears on screen as ^[.

The second character in every ANSI.SYS escape sequence must be a left square bracket, [. This is followed by the characters of the command itself, followed by the terminator letter. Try creating a file named COLORTST to set the screen colors:

1. Start up EDIT for a new file named COLORTST.

2. Type the following line into the file, where ← represents the escape character:

   ←[30;46m

3. Save the file and exit the editor.

4. Enter **TYPE COLORTST**.

   The next prompt appears in black text on a cyan background.

5. Enter **CLS** to spread the background color.

   Nice to get rid of that red, isn't it?

Using a Batch File

It's often useful to include ANSI.SYS escape sequences in batch programs. The ECHO command, which sends text to standard output, is more convenient than PROMPT because it doesn't reset the prompt. (Unfortunately, you can't use ECHO outside a batch file, because it offers no method to type an Esc character.)

The following exercise displays the message Sorting Records in cyan on red, and then restores the black on cyan color scheme:

1. Open the editor to create a new file named COLOR.BAT.

2. Enter the following lines into the file:

   ```
   @ECHO OFF
   ECHO ←[36;41mSorting Records←[30;46m
   ```

3. Save the file and exit the editor.

4. Enter **COLOR** to execute the batch program.

   The message appears in cyan on red. Then, the black on cyan color scheme is reset.

The ANSI.SYS Codes for Screen Colors

A number of ANSI escape sequences control various screen features. One set controls the color background and foreground, as well as the text attributes. Another set controls cursor position and clears the screen. Still another set lets you control the graphics mode of your display.

The escape sequences for screen colors require the use of numeric codes. Table 48.2 shows the complete set of attribute and color codes. Each color sequence requires the same terminator character: lowercase m.

Table 48.2. Color display codes.

Attributes:

0	Normal text
1	High-intensity text
2	Low-intensity text
4	Underline on (monochrome only)
5	Blink
7	Inverse
8	Invisible text (foreground displays same color as background)

Color codes:

Color	Foreground	Background
Black	30	40
Red	31	41
Green	32	42
Yellow	33	43
Blue	34	44
Magenta	35	45
Cyan	36	46
White	37	47

Exactly how a color appears depends on the monitor; for example, normal yellow looks brown on many screens. You can include as many codes as you need in each escape sequence; separate them with semicolons.

The attributes apply only to the foreground color on most systems. The high-intensity attribute produces a brighter foreground color, quite different from the normal color; so, 16 foreground colors are available. But, on some systems, attribute 5 causes a high-intensity background rather than a blink.

On some systems, low intensity produces still another color, but it's the same as high intensity on most systems. If you use attribute 8, the foreground color is stored as usual, but foreground material is displayed using the background color.

> **Tip:** If you are preparing a batch file for other users, check out the colors and attributes on their monitors if you can. They might be different from yours.

Suppose that you want to have a blinking foreground of high-intensity yellow on a magenta background. This command, stored in an ASCII file and TYPEd to the screen, produces the following result:

```
←[1;5;33;45m
```

Suppose that a batch file displays the message Sorting Members . . . while it works. You could use the following line in the batch file to make the message more noticeable:

```
ECHO ←[5;33;45mSorting Members . . .[m
```

Screen and Cursor Control

By default, the cursor goes to the beginning of the next line when a command terminates. You can position it somewhere else—perhaps in a message box, at the top of the screen to display the date, or at the bottom to display a copyright notice—through an ANSI command. The escape sequences for cursor position require a variety of special terminator characters, as shown in Table 48.3. You might need to include row and/or column information. As always, the case of the terminator character is critical.

Table 48.3. Screen and cursor control sequences.

s	Save current cursor position
u	Restore saved cursor position
xxA	Cursor up xx rows
xxB	Cursor down xx rows
xxC	Cursor right xx columns
xxD	Cursor left xx columns
H	Cursor to upper left (0,0)
xx;yyH	Cursor to specified position
xx;yyf	Cursor to specified position
2J	Clear screen, cursor to upper left
K	Clear from cursor position to end of line
6n	Display cursor position in form ←[xx;yyR

When controlling the cursor position, be careful not to position it in front of or on top of existing text to avoid confusing users. Careful testing of cursor control changes is recommended.

Creating a Banner

You can use many of the cursor-positioning features in a PROMPT command to create a banner across the top of each screen. Figure 48.3 shows a screen with a sample banner. The command that produces this banner is shown on the screen. The banner is regenerated each time the prompt appears, so the time is kept reasonably up-to-date.

Figure 48.3.
Sample banner screen.

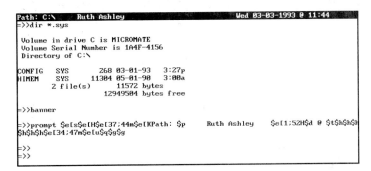

```
Path: C:\    Ruth Ashley                      Wed 03-03-1993 @ 11:44
=>>dir *.sys

  Volume in drive C is MICROMATE
  Volume Serial Number is 1A4F-4156
  Directory of C:\

CONFIG   SYS       268 03-01-93    3:27p
HIMEM    SYS     11304 05-01-90    3:00a
        2 file(s)        11572 bytes
                     12949504 bytes free


=>>banner

=>>prompt $e[s$e[H$e[37;44m$e[KPath: $p       Ruth Ashley      $e[1;52H$d @ $t$h$h$h$h
$h$h$h$e[34;47m$e[u$q$g$g

=>>
=>>
```

This PROMPT command comprises a mixture of ANSI.SYS escape sequences, PROMPT special characters, and straight text. An explanation of each part follows:

$E[s	Saves the current cursor position
$E[H	Moves cursor to upper left corner
$E[37;44m	Sets the banner to white on blue
$E[K	Erases the top line from cursor position
Path:	Displays the indicated text
$P	Inserts the current drive and path here
Ruth Ashley	Displays the indicated text
$E[1;52H	Moves the cursor to row 1 column 52
$D	Displays the current date
@	Displays the indicated text (@)
$T	Displays the current time
HHHHHH	Backspaces six times to remove seconds and hundredths from the time
$E[34;47m	Sets rest of screen to blue on white
$E[u	Restores the saved cursor position
QG$G	Displays the new prompt (=>>)

To try a banner, be sure to load DOSKEY first, if it isn't active; DOSKEY greatly simplifies experimenting with PROMPT commands.

> **Note:** The time displayed in this banner will not stay perfectly current, as it is refreshed only when the command prompt is redisplayed.

If you would like to try your own banner, follow the steps in this exercise:

1. Enter `PROMPT $E[s$E[H$E[37;44m$E[KPath:  $P    your name    $E[1;52H$D @` `$T$H$H$H$H$H$H$E[34;47m$E[u$Q$G$G`.

2. Enter `CLS`.

Displaying a Message Box

You can also use ANSI.SYS to create a colored box containing a message. This makes an interesting, attention-getting display. Figure 48.4 shows a text file containing escape sequences to control the display of a red box with black text. This example uses a separate line for each sequence, but you can combine them if you prefer. You can also modify the commands, changing the position, color, size, and text to fit your needs. Use TYPE *filespec* in a batch file to produce the box. Alternatively, you can put the necessary escape sequences in ECHO commands in the batch file.

Figure 48.4.
Creating a colored
message box.

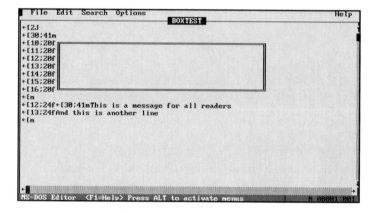

The box itself is drawn using the IBM extended character set (see Appendix B, "Exit Codes"), which bears some explanation. A single byte, representing one text character on a monitor or printer, can hold a value from 0 to 255 (0FFH). The values from 0 through 127 are standardized as ASCII code, representing letters, digits, punctuation marks, and so on. The values from 128 through 255 have not been standardized, and can have different effects with different hardware and software setups. For example, DOS interprets these values according to the IBM extended character set, but Windows doesn't. When displaying a message from a DOS batch program using ECHO commands, you can count on the IBM extended character set to work.

Because a keyboard doesn't have keys for the extended characters, you can type one by holding down the Alt key and typing the byte's value on the numeric keypad. For example, to type the upper left corner of the double-line box, press Alt+201. This method works for any byte value, not just the extended ones.

Explanations of the escape sequences in the file shown in Figure 48.4 follow:

←[2J   Clears the screen with cursor in upper left corner

←[30;41m   Sets the colors to black text on red background

The new colors affect only positions where text or spaces are typed. We limit that to the box itself by positioning the cursor for each line of text. The balance of the screen retains its former colors.

←[10;20f   Positions cursor at row 10 column 20; rest of line draws top of box

←[11;20f   Positions cursor at row 11 column 20; rest of line draws next line of box

The next five commands draw box sides.

←[16;20H   Positions cursor at row 16 column 20; rest of line draws bottom line of box

←[m   Resets default colors

←[12;24f←[30;41m Positions cursor and sets text color; rest of line displays a message in box

←[13;24f   Positions cursor; rest of line displays another message in box

←[m   Resets the colors

The cursor-positioning sequence using the f terminator is exactly the same as with H. If you omit the row and column values, f has no effect, and H defaults to the home (0,0) position.

If you would like to try this display box yourself, follow these steps:

1. Use EDIT to create a new file named BOXTEST.
2. Use Figure 48.4, shown previously, as a guide to type the contents of BOXTEST.
   The codes that you use to create the box are as follows:

Alt+201	Upper left corner
Alt+200	Lower left corner
Alt+187	Upper right corner
Alt+188	Lower right corner
Alt+205	Horizontal line
Alt+186	Vertical line

> **Tip:** You don't have to press Alt+205 repeatedly. Press it once; then, select the character; press Ctrl+Insert to copy it to the clipboard; press right arrow to position the cursor; then, press Shift+Insert as many times as you want to insert the character from the clipboard. You can use a similar technique to type Alt+186 several times.

3. Save the file and exit the editor.

4. Enter **TYPE BOXTEST** to display the box.

Character Wrap

By default, when a command on the screen reaches column 80, characters wrap around to the next line. In earlier versions of DOS, characters were stacked up in column 80, so you could see only the most recently entered character. Turning off character wrap hides characters at the ends of long lines. Use the following commands to enable and disable the character wrap function:

←[=7h   to enable

←[=7l   to disable

Character wrapping affects not only the commands you type, but also the output of commands that display long lines, such as FIND and TYPE.

Screen Mode (Graphics)

Every video adapter and screen has a default mode. If you do any BASIC programming, you know that the screen mode can be changed to achieve different effects. Another set of escape sequences lets you change the screen mode using ANSI commands. The results might vary on different monitors. Table 48.4 lists the values you can use to specify screen modes; use terminator character h, as in

←[=modeh

For example, to use a PROMPT command to change the screen mode to monochrome text with only 40 characters per line, you would enter PROMPT $E[=0h$P$G.

Table 48.4. Screen modes.

Mode	Meaning
0	Monochrome text, 40×25
1	Color text, 40×25
2	Monochrome text, 80×25

Mode	Meaning
3	Color text, 80×25
4	Medium-resolution graphics (4 color), 300×200
5	Same as 4, with color burst disabled
6	High-resolution graphics (2 color), 640×200
13	Color graphics, 320×200
14	Color graphics (16 color), 640×200
15	Monochrome graphics, 640×350
16	Color graphics (16 color), 640×350
17	Color graphics (2 color), 640×480
18	Color graphics (16 color), 640×480
19	Color graphics (256 color), 320×200

If you change the screen mode to one not supported by your system, you might see a strange color pattern, or the system might hang up. You might have to reboot to restore normal operation.

ANSI Keyboard Control

ANSI escape sequences also give you control over your keyboard. You can switch the meanings of any two keys, for example. You can set up a key or key combination (such as Ctrl+D) to type an extended character, or even a string of characters. Table 48.5 shows how to refer to some keys in ANSI.SYS commands. The ones in parentheses are not valid on all keyboards. The complete list is included in the online help for the ANSI.SYS driver.

Table 48.5. Selected key codes.

Key	Normal	⇧Shift	Ctrl	Alt
F1	0;59	0;84	0;94	0;104
F2	0;60	0;85	0;95	0;105
F3	0;61	0;86	0;96	0;106
F4	0;62	0;87	0;97	0;107
Home	0;71	55	0;119	
Up	0;72	56	(0;141)	

continues

Table 48.5. continued

Key	Normal	⇧Shift	Ctrl	Alt
PageUp	0;73	57	0;132	
Left	0;75	52	0;115	
PrtSc			0;114	
Pause/Break				0;0
BkSp	8	8	127	(0)
Enter	13		10	(0;28)
Tab	9	0;15	(0;148)	(0:165)
(Grey keys)				
Home	(224;71)	(224;71)	(224;119)	(224;1051)
Up	(224;72)	(224;72)	(224;141)	(224;152)
PageUp	(224;73	(224;73)	(224;132)	(224;153)
Left	(224;75)	(224;75)	(224;115)	(224;155)
(Keypad Keys)				
Enter	13		10	(0;166)
/	47	47	(0;142)	(0;74)
*	42	(0;144)	(0;78)	
-	45	45	(0;149)	(0;164)
+	43	43	(0;150)	(0;55)
5	(0;76)	53	(0;143)	
(Typeable characters)				
a	97	65	1	0;30
b	98	66	2	0;48
z	122	90	26	0;44
1	49	33		0;120
0	48	41		0;129
-	45	95	31	0;130
=	61	43		0;131

Assigning a value to a particular key *remaps* that key. Assigning a string of text to a key can be used to set up keyboard macros. The remapping affects only the DOS command prompt interface.

Remapping can be done via a PROMPT command, an ECHO command, or in a TYPEd text file, just as with other ANSI.SYS escape sequences.

Remapping Individual Keys

Many key combinations are unassigned. You can remap them to type extended characters. Or, you might want, simply, to relocate a key. You could change a QWERTY keyboard to the more efficient Dvorak layout, for example.

To remap keys, use an ANSI command in this format:

```
Esc[key;new-valuep
```

The *key* parameter identifies the key or key combination to be remapped. You can identify it by the current character it types (if any), placed in quotes, or by its key code (from Table 48.5). The *new-value* parameter identifies the new value for the key, which you can specify as a character in quotes, or as a numeric code from 0 through 255. Appendix B shows the extended characters that result when you use 128 through 255. For example, to set Ctrl+F1 to type the upper left corner of a double-line box, you could use either of the following escape sequences:

```
←[0;94;"╔"p
←[0;94;201p
```

In both commands, 0;94 identifies the Ctrl+F1 key combination. The first command uses quotes surrounding the result of Alt+201, and the second uses the value 201 to specify the desired character.

Suppose you must frequently type the letter Ä (Alt+142). You might want to assign it to Alt+A:

1. Enter **PROMPT $E[0;30;142p$P$G**.
2. Type Alt+A.

    You should see the letter Ä.
3. Press Esc to clear the command line.
4. Switch to the root directory.
5. Enter **COPY AUTOEXEC.BAT HÄGEN.XXX**. (Use Alt+A to type the Ä.)
6. Enter **DIR** to see the new file in your directory.
7. Enter **DEL HÄGEN.XXX** to delete the file.

If you want to drive someone crazy, you could swap their "t" and "h" keys:

```
ECHO ←["t";"h"p
ECHO ←["h";"t"p
```

An enhanced keyboard includes several keys that duplicate other keys. If you want the duplicates treated the same, don't do anything. If you want to give one of the sets a different value, however, use the /X switch in the DEVICE=ANSI.SYS command.

You used the /X switch when you loaded ANSI.SYS earlier in this chapter, so you can now set up your numeric keypad to type international characters:

1. Enter **PROMPT $E[0;71;148p$P$G**.

2. Turn off NumLock and press Home on the numeric keypad.

    You should see ö.

This command works only if ANSI.SYS was loaded with /X. On an enhanced 101-key keyboard, the extra keys—such as gray cursor control keys—are the extended keys. These keys (and a few others) appear in parentheses in the key-code table. If you've disabled them with /K, or if you don't have an enhanced keyboard, then these keys are not available for remapping.

Assigning Strings to Keys

You can assign strings of text to keys. For example, you can assign complete commands, including the Enter key, so that you can run a DOS command with a single key or key combination. You could establish a complete set of function key "macros" to run the commands you need most often. These commands aren't the same as DOSKEY macros—for example, you can't use replaceable parameters in them—but you could set them up to run DOSKEY macros for you.

To assign a simple text string, use a sequence in the following format:

```
Esc[key;"string"p
```

Try assigning your company name to Shift+F1:

1. Enter **PROMPT $E[0;84;"name"p$P$G**, but replace *name* with any name you'd like.

2. Press Shift+F1.

    You should see whatever you entered between the quotation marks in the PROMPT command.

    You can string together quoted values and numeric values, using semicolons to separate them.

3. To cause the CD \ command to be issued when you press F12, enter **PROMPT $E[0;134;"CD \";13p$P$G**.

Note: The value 13 sends the carriage return to enter the CD \ command.

4. Press F12 to switch to the root directory.

5. If you use DOSKEY, you know that pressing F7 lists the stored command history. There is no comparable function key to list DOSKEY macros. You could set up F10 to list them with the command PROMPT $E[0;68;"DOSKEY /M";13p$P$G.

6. Press F10 to list your DOSKEY macros.

We've looked at some of the most useful ANSI.SYS functions in this chapter. You'll discover even more uses for these functions as you continue to apply them.

Controlling the CON (Console) Mode

You can change the number of lines and columns displayed on your monitor with a MODE command; the change affects only those applications that use the command prompt screen. Applications such as EDIT, DOS Shell, and MSBACKUP are not affected. Figure 48.5 shows the MODE format for modifying the console, which includes the screen and the keyboard.

Specifying Lines and Columns

If you want to use more than the default 25 screen lines, you can use the LINES=*n* parameter. ANSI.SYS must be loaded before you change the number of lines. A VGA screen can support 43 or 50 lines, while EGA can handle 43.

You can also set up your screen for 40 or 80 columns. The larger characters (40 columns) can be read from further away, but they can interfere with the layout of formatted output, such as a DIR /W listing.

Try a few of these settings on your screen:

1. Enter **MODE CON COLS=40**.

   Your screen should switch to a large typeface.

2. Enter **MODE CON COLS=80 LINES=43**.

   Your screen should switch back to normal-sized characters, but 43 lines per screen.

3. Enter **DIR** to see the difference in line density.

> **Tip:** To find out which line settings are valid for your screen, start up DOS Shell, choose Options Display, and look at the listing of display modes in text mode.

4. Enter **MODE CON LINES=24**, unless you want to keep the current setting.

Controlling Keyboard Response

PC keyboards have a typematic feature that causes keys to repeat when held down. If you hold any key down for more than half a second, the key starts to repeat at about 20 times per second. Many people take advantage of the typematic feature when moving the cursor with the arrow keys and when backspacing to delete text. But, some people have difficulty controlling the typematic feature because it moves a little too fast for them. They end up erasing too much text or moving the cursor too far.

MODE

Configures system console devices.

Syntax:

```
MODE [display-adapter]

MODE CON[:] [COLS=c] [LINES=n]

MODE CON[:] RATE=r DELAY=d
```

Parameters:

none	Displays status of all devices.
display-adapter	Specifies an adapter mode, which must be one of the following values:
	`40` or `80` Sets number of characters per line.
	`BW40` or `BW80` Selects the color adapter with color disabled, and sets the number of characters per line.
	`CO40` or `CO80` Selects the color adapter with color enabled, and sets the number of characters per line.
	`MONO` Selects a monochrome adapter with 80 characters per line.
`COLS=c`	Specifies the number of characters per line (40 or 80).
`LINES=n`	Specifies the number of lines per screen (24, 43, or 50).
`RATE=r`	Specifies the repeat rate of keyboard characters; range is `1` to `32`, which is approximately 2 to 30 characters per second. Default is `20`.
`DELAY=d`	Specifies the elapsed time in quarters of seconds before keyboard repeat starts; values are `1`, `2`, `3`, and `4`. Default is `2` (for 0.5 second).

Figure 48.5. MODE *command summary (Console functions). Specifying Lines and Columns*

You can set a slower typematic rate; in fact, you can set a faster one, if DOS's normal speed is a little too slow for you. The MODE command lets you modify both the DELAY, which sets the start of the repeat, and the RATE, which controls how fast it repeats.

Try setting the typematic rate for your keyboard:

1. Hold down a character key, and notice how long it takes to start repeating and how quickly it repeats.

2. Enter **MODE CON RATE=2 DELAY=4**.

3. Hold down the key again and notice the difference.

4. Enter **MODE CON RATE=20 DELAY=2** to reset the normal typematic rate, unless you want to work at this slower rate.

Note: If you prefer the slower typematic rate, enter the appropriate MODE command in your AUTOEXEC.BAT file to set the rate you like the most every time you boot.

Switching the Standard Console Devices

The console device is the device in which you type commands and DOS displays standard output and standard error output. Normally, console device is CON, which represents the keyboard and video monitor. But suppose you have a device attached to COM4 that you want to use as CON for a while. You can change to some other device by using the CTTY command, which has the following format:

CTTY *device*

The device can be any standard DOS device name: COM1 through COM4, LPT1 through LPT3, PRN, AUX, PRN, and CON. For example, to control DOS via a remote terminal device connected to COM4, you would enter the following:

CTTY COM4

As soon as you enter this command, you can no longer enter commands at the keyboard. You must enter them through COM4; messages appear not on the video monitor, but on the device attached to COM4. To switch back to the normal console device, enter the following command via the device attached to COM4:

CTTY CON

Note: If you switch console control away from CON and then find that you can't enter commands from the new device, you can still reboot from the keyboard. Rebooting restores CON as the console device.

Preserving Your Laptop Batteries

DOS 6's POWER program can help to save battery power in your laptop or notebook computer by reducing power consumption when you're not actually using it. To use POWER, you must load the POWER.EXE device driver via CONFIG.SYS with a command in this format:

```
DEVICE[HIGH]=C:\DOS\POWER.EXE [ADV[:advtype] ¦ STD ¦ OFF] [/LOW]
```

The *advtype* can be MAX for maximum savings, REG to balance power conservation with application and device performance, and MIN for a little power conservation without interfering with system performance. If you load POWER.EXE with no parameters, or if you use ADV without a value, ADV:REG is assumed.

If your computer supports the Advanced Power Management (APM) specification, you can use STD to specify that the hardware's power-management features should be used. But, STD turns off power management if your system does not support the APM specification. OFF turns off power management in all cases.

Note: Your computer will realize more power savings if it supports the APM specification—about 25 percent, compared to about 5 percent.

Use the /LOW switch to load POWER.EXE into conventional memory, even though upper memory blocks are available.

The *POWER* Command

When you have loaded the POWER.EXE driver, you can use the POWER command to view and change the current POWER setting. When you enter the command without any parameters, POWER displays the current power setting. To change the setting, enter POWER with the ADV parameter, STD, or OFF. For example, if POWER seems to interfere with the application you are currently trying to use, try entering the following:

```
POWER ADV:REG
```

If that doesn't work, try

```
POWER ADV:MIN
```

If that doesn't work, and your laptop supports the APM specification, try

```
POWER STD
```

If it still doesn't work, turn the power management off with the following command:

```
POWER OFF
```

> **Tip:** My notebook has its own power management system that shuts off the screen, even when I'm using the AC adapter instead of batteries. When I plug in the AC adapter, I enter **POWER OFF** to disable the power savings feature, so that my screen doesn't go blank while I'm staring at it wondering what to say next. But, if you try this, be sure to develop the habit of entering **POWER ADV:MAX** when you unplug the AC adapter.

On Your Own

1. Design your own command prompt screen and insert a PROMPT command into AUTOEXEC.BAT, so that it is set up during booting.

2. Create a keyboard macro to enter a MEM /C /P command whenever you press Alt+M.

3. See if you can turn BOXTEST into a batch program. Insert your own message in the box. Try displaying the box in a different color, using a different style of border, and perhaps even using the flashing attribute.

4. Restore your CONFIG.SYS by removing from this chapter any commands that were inserted that you don't want to keep: ANSI.SYS and POWER.EXE.

5. Delete any files that you created in this chapter, but don't want to keep: BOXTEST, BOXTEST.BAT, COLORTST, COLOR.BAT.

49

Another Country Heard From

Introduction

DOS-compatible computers are usually set up for the country in which they are manufactured or purchased. But, you can configure yours for other countries on a temporary or permanent basis.

Communicating in Other Languages

If you bought your system in the United States, your keyboard, monitor, and printer probably handle standard American English characters.

Numeric values, dates, and times most likely appear in the traditional American formats. If you bought your system in some other country, its character set, numeric, date, and time formats probably reflect the standard for that country.

However, you might want to use your computer to prepare, read, or produce text for people from other countries who prefer, for example, to see the time and date in a more familiar form. You might have to prepare correspondence or reports for people in other countries, or use characters common in other languages that don't appear on your keyboard.

This chapter covers various ways you can adapt DOS to deal with the problems of international communication. You will learn how to:

- Use another country's formats for the date, time, numbers, and sorting sequence
- Set up your keyboard to type international characters
- Use another country's keyboard layout
- Use another country's character set (code page)

Overview

DOS provides a gamut of commands that affect the way it deals with internationality. The KEYB command lets you emulate or interpret a country-specific keyboard. The COUNTRY command causes the system to use numeric formats of another country or region.

Your monitor and printer have code pages built into them. A code page is a table that tells the device which character corresponds to each one-byte code (from 0 through 255). With the standard English code page, code 66 is a "B"; code 123 is a "{"; code 156 is a "£"; and code 168 is a "¿". Changing the code page tells DOS to use a different set of characters for the same codes.

DOS provides six software code pages, which can be downloaded to devices to replace the hardware (built-in) code pages. The first 128 values (from 0 to 127) are the same in each because these are the values standardized as ASCII code. The extended characters vary from code page to code page. An appendix in your DOS *User's Guide* shows the contents of each code page.

You might be able to use a different code page without much preparation with the COUNTRY or KEYB command. If you expect to change code pages often, it's best to set up the system so you can switch easily.

International Formats

The date, time, and numeric formats in other countries are frequently different from those in the United States. For example, the year may be first, a different currency symbol may be used, or the use of commas and decimal point characters in numeric values may be reversed. You can tell DOS to use formats specific to another region or country. (These formats affect commands such as DATE, TIME, and DIR, as well as applications like DOS Shell and Backup. They do not affect Windows.)

If a country uses characters such as é and ü, they may be placed differently in the sort sequence than they are in a U.S.-oriented code page. If you use these characters very often, you will want them sorted according to their country's standards. (The sort sequence affects commands like SORT and DIR, and applications that run under DOS, but not Windows or its applications.)

Table 49.1 lists the countries DOS supports, their codes, and the time and date formats they use.

Table 49.1. Countries and formats.

Country	Code	Date	Time
Belgium	032	05/01/1992	17:15:25,00
Brazil	055	05/01/1992	17:15:25,00
Canadian-French	002	1992-01-05	17:15:25,00
Croatia	038	1992-01-05	17:15:25,00
Czech Republic	042	1992-01-05	17:15:25,00
Denmark	045	05-01-1992	17.15.25,00
Finland	358	05.01.1992	17.15.25,00
France	033	05.01.1992	17:15:25,00
Germany	049	05.01.1992	17:15:25,00
Hungary	036	1992-01-05	17:15:25,00
Int'l English	061	05/01/1992	17:15:25.00
Italy	039	05/01/1992	17.15.35,00
Latin America	003	05/01/1992	05:15:25.00p
Netherlands	031	05-01-1992	17:15:25,00
Norway	047	05.01.1992	17:15:25,00
Poland	048	1992-01-05	17:15:25,00
Portugal	351	05-01-1992	17:15:25,00

continues

Table 49.1. continued

Country	Code	Date	Time
Serbia/Yugoslavia	038	1992-01-05	17:15:25,00
Slovakia	042	1992-01-05	17:15:25,00
Slovenia	038	1992-01-05	17:15:25,00
Spain	034	05/01/1992	17:15:25,00
Sweden	046	1992-01-05	17.15.25,00
Switzerland	041	05.01.1992	17,15,25.00
United Kingdom	044	05/01/1992	17:15:25.00
United States	001	01/05/1992	05:15:25.00p

Note: Character sets for Arabic, Israel, Japan, Korea, People's Republic of China, and Taiwan are available with special versions of DOS. Microsoft can tell you how to order special DOS versions.

The COUNTRY configuration command tells DOS to use a particular country's formats. Figure 49.1 shows the syntax of this command, which you include in the CONFIG.SYS file.

COUNTRY

Specifies the country format for date and time displays, currency symbol, sort order, punctuation, and decimal separators.

Syntax:

```
COUNTRY=country[,[page] [,filespec]]
```

Parameters:

country	Specifies the code that identifies the country.
page	Specifies a code page.
filespec	Identifies the file containing country information.

Figure 49.1. *COUNTRY configuration command summary.*

The COUNTRY command must include the country code. (See Table 49.1, shown previously.) The code is often (but not always) the same as the international dialing code for the country. The code page parameter is largely ignored in this command; it's left over from earlier days. Code pages are now controlled by other commands, as you'll see later in this chapter. But, even though you omit the code page, you must include its comma in your commands. For example, to use the Hungarian formats, you would include the following command in CONFIG.SYS. Notice the two commas between COUNTRY=036 and C:\DOS\COUNTRY.SYS.

```
COUNTRY=036,,C:\DOS\COUNTRY.SYS
```

When you load the COUNTRY.SYS driver, DOS must be able to find the COUNTRY.SYS file. If it is stored in the root directory of the boot drive, there is no problem. However, most people store all the DOS files in a \DOS directory, so the command must usually include a complete filespec.

In the following exercise, you set up your computer to use the Latin American formats:

1. Insert the following command in CONFIG.SYS:

   COUNTRY=003,,C:\DOS\COUNTRY.SYS

2. Exit all programs and get to the primary command prompt. Then reboot.

3. Enter **DIR** to see a list of files in the root directory.

   Notice the format of the dates.

4. Start up DOS Shell and notice the dates in the file list.

5. Exit DOS Shell.

6. To set a new date, you must use the Latin American format. Enter **DATE 31/12/95** to set the date to the last day of 1995.

7. Restore today's date.

8. Remove the COUNTRY command from CONFIG.SYS, and reboot to restore your normal configuration.

Typing International Characters

A code page includes 256 characters. Many of these can't be typed directly, however. The default code pages built into your monitor have many characters available that don't correspond to keyboard keys or key combinations. You can type any code by holding down the Alt key, typing the code on the numeric keypad (make sure NumLock is on), and releasing Alt. For example, suppose that the standard English code page (437) is current, and you have to type the character è. Just hold down the Alt key and type **138** on the numeric keypad. When you release Alt, the character appears on the screen. It will even print on a standard printer.

You can use extended characters in commands at the DOS command prompt. You could use the FIND command to search files for "Börg," for example. You could name a directory MAÑANA or a file HÔPITAL. These names show up correctly in DOS Shell's file list, Windows File Manager, file lists displayed by applications, and so on.

Try typing these names yourself:

1. At the DOS command prompt, type **B**, followed by Alt+148 to type the ö, followed by **rg**.

2. Press Esc to clear the command line.

3. Type **MA**, followed by Alt+165 to type Ñ, followed by **ANA**.

4. Press Esc to clear the command line.

With font-oriented software, such as word processors or desktop publishing software, the font controls the character set in documents; characters may be different from the installed code page. In fact, the same code might produce different characters, depending on which font you're using. Also, keep in mind that Windows uses a different character set.

Note: Windows uses the ANSI character set instead of DOS's ASCII character set. The ANSI set does not include the line drawing characters, but instead provides more international characters and symbols. Unfortunately, if you try to open a document that was prepared by a Windows application and contains enhanced characters in a DOS application, such as EDIT, the enhanced characters will be interpreted according to the ASCII character set and will be wrong. Many Windows applications, including Microsoft Word for Windows, permit you to save a file in DOS text format, which adapts the document so that it can be read by a DOS editor such as EDIT. (The document loses formatting such as bold and italics type when saved in DOS text format.)

When you're working at the DOS command prompt, you might want to set up shortcuts for extended characters you must type often, using the ANSI.SYS features. The following command assigns the ä character to Ctrl+A, so that you can type it easily at the DOS prompt:

```
PROMPT $E[1;"ä"p$P$G
```

In creating the command, use Alt+132 to type the ä. Chapter 48, "Console Control," covers the use of ANSI.SYS escape sequences in detail.

Note: Remapped keys are effective only on the DOS command-prompt screen; you can't use them in the Shell or in other software. But, typing Alt+*number* works in many places.

Using International Keyboard Layouts

If you use many non-English characters in your work, you may want to tell DOS you have a keyboard layout that lets you type those characters directly. You may even want to change your keycaps. The KEYB command identifies the keyboard layout you want to use. DOS then assigns different codes to your keypresses, interpreting the characters according to the specified keyboard layout (regardless of what the keycaps say). The keyboard layout affects the DOS command prompt screen and applications that run under DOS, such as DOS Shell and EDIT. It does not affect Windows or Windows applications.

Table 49.2 lists the keyboard layouts available with DOS 6.22, along with the default code page and the alternate code page that can be used with each. (Code pages are explained in the next section.) The ID column shows the ID code for keyboards when the country or region has more than one keyboard layout available. An appendix in your DOS *User's Guide* shows the exact layout of each keyboard.

Table 49.2. Keyboard codes and code pages.

Country/Region	Code	Standard	Alternate	ID
Belgium	BE	850	437	
Brazil	BR	850	437	
Canadian-French	CF	863	850	
Czech	CZ	852	850	
Denmark	DK	850	865	
Finland	SU	850	437	
France	FR	850	437	120,189
Germany	GR	850	437	
Hungary	HU	852	850	
International	+	437	850	
Italy	IT	850	437	141,142
Latin America	LA	850	437	
Netherlands	NL	850	437	
Norway	NO	850	865	
Poland	PL	852	850	

continues

Table 49.2. continued

Country/Region	Code	Standard	Alternate	ID
Portugal	PO	850	860	
Slovak	SL	852	850	
Spain	SP	850	437	
Sweden	SV	850	437	
Switzerland (French)	SF	850	437	
Switzerland (German)	SG	850	437	
United Kingdom	UK	437	850	166,168
United States	US	437	850	
Yugoslavia (Croatia, Slovakia, Slovenia)	YU	852	850	

The *KEYB* Command

Figure 49.2 shows the format of the KEYB command. You can use it at the command prompt or install it from CONFIG.SYS. The keyboard code identifies which keyboard layout to use. If installed through CONFIG.SYS, KEYB must include the complete path if KEYBOARD.SYS is not in the root directory of the boot drive. When used at the command prompt, you can depend on the established path to locate the KEYBOARD.SYS file.

Tip: If your system is set up for it, use LH to load KEYB into a UMB. You can't load KEYB.COM into upper memory from CONFIG.SYS because it is not loaded with a DEVICE command.

Tip: If you always use a nonstandard layout, put the appropriate KEYB command in your CONFIG.SYS or AUTOEXEC.BAT file so that it becomes the default.

Try loading the Latin American keyboard now:

1. Enter **KEYB LA**.

2. Try out these keys on your keyboard:

Press = to type ¿

Press + to type í

Press ; to type ñ

3. To see what keyboard is currently installed, enter **KEYB** with no parameters.

    DOS displays a message like this:

    ```
    Current keyboard code:  LA   code page:  850
    ```

    Because you have not yet loaded a code page, you see the following line as well:

    ```
    Active code page not available from CON device
    ```

KEYB

Loads the KEYB TSR, which lets your keyboard emulate keyboard layouts for other languages.

Syntax:

```
KEYB [code [,[page] [,filespec]]]
```

From CONFIG.SYS:

```
INSTALL=[path]KEYB.COM [code[,[page],[filespec]]]
```

Parameters and Switches:

none	Displays the current keyboard code and code page and the current console code page.
code	Identifies the country whose keyboard you want to use. (See Table 49.2.)
page	Identifies the code page you want to use; the default is the current code page.
filespec	Identifies the location and name of the keyboard definition file; the default is KEYBOARD.SYS in the current directory or on the search path.
path	Specifies the path if not in the root directory.

Figure 49.2. KEYB *command summary.*

After a keyboard layout is installed, you might find it difficult to type your old familiar DOS commands using the nonstandard layout. For example, with the Latin American layout, the / key produces a hyphen (-); you have to press Shift+7 to type a /. At least at first, you might find it easier to switch back to the US layout to type DOS commands, and switch into the other layout when you want to type international text. You can switch between it and the default (U.S.) layout. Ctrl+Alt+F1 activates the built-in keyboard driver, and Ctrl+Alt+F2 goes back to the installed one.

1. Press Ctrl+Alt+F1 to activate your built-in keyboard layout.
2. Try typing =, +, and ;.

   These keys produce the standard characters.

3. Press Ctrl+Alt+F2 to activate the Latin American keyboard.
4. Try typing =, +, and ; again.

   Now these keys produce the Latin American characters.

Note: Why do the Latin American characters appear when DOS clearly said that the 850 code page was not available? Because these characters are also available in the standard 437 code page. There are really only a few characters that are different between the 437 and the 850 code page. The other code pages also have only minor differences.

Note: Some countries have a standard typewriter layout that differs from the keyboard layout; pressing Ctrl+Alt+F7 activates this layout.

Using Code Pages

What is the relationship between the keyboard layout and the code page? The keyboard layout determines the code that is generated by each key; the code page determines what character is displayed on your monitor for each code.

Each keyboard layout is associated with two code pages—a standard and an alternate. (See Table 49.2, shown previously.) These are the code pages capable of displaying the characters generated by the keyboard. For the best results, install the standard code page for the keyboard you want to use. If you want to switch among several keyboard layouts, code page 850 (multilingual code page) may be your best bet; it is the standard or alternate code page for every keyboard layout. You can get away with code page 437 (the English code page) for many layouts; it's probably your built-in code page, so you don't have to do anything to use it.

Any code pages other than your built-in one must be prepared first. If the code page has already been prepared when the KEYB command is entered, KEYB switches to it automatically. For example, suppose that code pages 850 and 852 have been prepared. The following command switches to the

Polish keyboard layout and monitor code page 852, the default for the Polish layout:

```
KEYB PL
```

The following command switches to the Polish layout and monitor code page 850:

```
KEYB PL,850
```

How to Load a Code Page

Several commands must be coordinated in order to use any code pages other than the built-in one. If either KEYB or COUNTRY needs a software code page, the code page must be prepared before it can take effect. The CONFIG.SYS file must install a device driver for the monitor (DISPLAY.SYS) in order to use the code page.

After the environment is established, several commands are needed to handle the code pages. You can put these commands in AUTOEXEC.BAT if you use them every time, or you can enter them individually at the DOS prompt. The NLSFUNC command establishes National Language Support, which makes switching code pages easier. The MODE command installs specific software code pages, preparing them for use by DOS. Additional MODE commands can change code pages or display the current status. The CHCP command uses National Language Support to switch code pages.

Monitor Code Pages

Standard monochrome and CGA monitors cannot use monitor code pages. However, all EGA, VGA, LCD, and more advanced types can. Before you can use software code pages on your monitor, you must load the driver DISPLAY.SYS. (See Figure 49.3.)

As with most device drivers, you can use DEVICEHIGH instead to load the driver into upper memory if your system is set up for it. The following command loads DISPLAY.SYS for an LCD monitor:

```
DEVICE=C:\DOS\DISPLAY.SYS CON=(LCD)
```

The following command loads DISPLAY.SYS and lets DOS determine the monitor type; it specifies the default code page, so that you can switch back to it, and allows for two software code pages:

```
DEVICEHIGH=C:\DOS\DISPLAY.SYS CON=(,437,2)
```

DISPLAY.SYS

Supports code-page switching for your screen and keyboards.

Syntax:

```
DEVICE[HIGH]=[path]DISPLAY.SYS CON=([type][,codepage][,max ])
```

Parameters:

path	Identifies the location of the DISPLAY.SYS file. The default is the root directory of the boot drive.
type	Specifies the display adapter in use. Valid values are EGA and LCD. EGA includes both EGA and VGA adapters. If you don't specify *type*, DISPLAY.SYS checks the hardware to determine the display adapter in use.
codepage	Specifies the code page built into your hardware.
max	Specifies the number of code pages to be loaded, in addition to the one built into the hardware. Valid values are 0 through 6 for EGA, 0 through 1 for LCD.

Figure 49.3.   `DISPLAY.SYS` *DEVICE command.*

If you omit the hardware code page in the command, you cannot switch back to it after loading a different one. This doesn't matter if you expect to install a software code page and use it all the time. The number of code pages determines the amount of memory reserved for switching code pages; it defaults to 1. If you want to switch back and forth between the hardware code page (437) and the multilingual code page (850), you need to store only one software code page. However, if you want to switch back and forth between 850, 852, and 860, you need to store three code pages in memory.

Load DISPLAY.SYS now:

1. Insert the following command in CONFIG.SYS:

   ```
   DEVICEHIGH=C;\DOS\DISPLAY.SYS CON=(,437,1)
   ```

2. Exit all programs and get to the primary command prompt. Then reboot.

Now you will be able to load a software code page in the next section.

Preparing Code Pages

Before any software code page can be used, it must be prepared. This process installs the code page in memory and makes it available to the system, including the COUNTRY and KEYB commands. Figure 49.4 shows how MODE is used to manage code pages.

MODE

Prepares, selects, refreshes, or displays the numbers of the code pages for printers and monitors.

Syntax:

```
MODE CON CP PREP = ((page [...]) filespec)

MODE CON CP SEL = page

MODE CON CP REF

MODE CON CP [/STA]
```

Parameters and Switches:

PREPARE	Prepares *page*(s) for *device*. Abbreviate as PREP.
page	Specifies a code page.
filespec	Identifies the name and location of the code page information (.CPI) file.
SELECT	Loads a code page for use. Abbreviate as SEL.
REFRESH	Reinstates the prepared code pages if they are lost as the result of a hardware or other error. Abbreviate as REF.
/STATUS	Displays the numbers of the current code pages prepared or selected for device. Abbreviate as /STA.

Notes:

Using this format without PREP, SEL, REF, or /STA has the same effect as using /STA.

The code page information files provided by DOS are as follows:

EGA.CPI	For EGA or VGA monitor, or IBM PS/2.
LCD.CPI	For IBM PC Convertible liquid crystal display.

Figure 49.4. *MODE command summary (for code pages).*

Each command specifies one device, followed by the word CODEPAGE, followed by the action to be taken. The PREP command installs the code page. To install the multilingual code page for the console, you would use the following command:

```
MODE CON CODEPAGE PREP=((850) C:\DOS\EGA.CPI)
```

If you specified the hardware code page in the device driver configuration command, you can switch back and forth between it and an installed code page. If you install several code pages in one or more MODE commands, you can switch among them.

Try installing the multilingual code page now:

1. Enter **MODE CON CODEPAGE PREPARE=((850) C:\DOS\EGA.CPI)** if you use an EGA or VGA monitor, or **MODE CON CODEPAGE PREPARE=((850) C:\DOS\LCD.CPI)** for an LCD monitor.

Switching Code Pages

When you switch to a different code page, the monitor uses the new code page table to translate one-byte code values into displayed characters. Some characters already on the screen may switch to the new character set.

If you change to a different code page while a program is running, there may be an internal conflict. To avoid this problem, exit all programs before changing code pages.

Warning: If you are using the task swapper, don't switch code pages while any task is active. It causes more problems than it is worth.

The CODEPAGE SELECT format of the MODE command makes the prepared code page active. The following command makes the multilingual code page active:

```
MODE CON CODEPAGE SEL=850
```

To make the hardware code page active again, use the following command:

```
MODE CON CODEPAGE SEL=437
```

If you didn't specify the hardware code page in the device driver command, you can't return to it after you select a different code page.

Try loading the multilingual code page:

1. Enter **MODE CON CODEPAGE SEL=850**.
2. Now load the Latin American keyboard layout by entering **KEYB LA**.
3. To see which keyboard and code page are loaded, enter **KEYB** with no parameters.

You see these messages:

```
Current keyboard code: LA    code page: 850
Current CON code page: 850
```

4. Now try typing some characters that are unique to the multilingual code page: type Alt+157 to type Ø; type Alt+189 to type ¢; and type Alt+226 to type Ô.

5. Switch back to the hardware code page by entering **MODE CON CODEPAGE SELECT=437**.

6. Try typing Alt+157, Alt+189, and Alt+226 again. You'll get different characters this time.

Complete Code Page Example

Suppose that you need to use the Portuguese keyboard and formatting conventions some of the time, using the alternate Portuguese code page (860). Because you work in English as well and need the built-in code page (437), you want to be able to switch between the two code pages.

You would insert the following commands in your CONFIG.SYS file:

```
COUNTRY=351,860,C:\DOS\COUNTRY.SYS
DEVICEHIGH=C:\DOS\DISPLAY.SYS CON=(,437)
```

The COUNTRY command establishes the numeric and other formats for country 351, which is Portugal. Its alternate code page is specified. The DEVICEHIGH command reserves memory for one software code page. It also defines 437 as the hardware code page, so that you can switch back to it as needed.

Because you aren't sure which keyboard or code page you'll use first, leave those commands for the DOS prompt. The following command goes into AUTOEXEC.BAT:

```
MODE CON CODEPAGE PREPARE=((860) C:\DOS\EGA.CPI)
```

This MODE command installs the software code page for the specified device.

After the AUTOEXEC.BAT file has been executed, you are set up to switch your keyboards and your code pages. You can type the following commands at the DOS prompt to manage the keyboard and monitor code pages:

MODE CON CODEPAGE SELECT=860	Switches console to code page 860
MODE CON CODEPAGE SELECT=437	Switches console to code page 437
[LH] KEYB PO	Switches to Portuguese layout
KEYB US	Switches to U.S. English layout

If you use these commands or similar ones at the keyboard, you might want to set up DOSKEY macros to make them easier to use. The following batch file contains two DOSKEY macro definitions:

```
DOSKEY C8=MODE CON CODEPAGE SELECT=860
DOSKEY C4=MODE CON CODEPAGE SELECT=437
```

You could map the commands to key combinations, if you prefer. For example, this command sets up Shift+F1 to switch to monitor code page 860 and restores the usual prompt:

```
PROMPT $E[0;84;"MODE CON CODEPAGE SELECT=860"p$P$G
```

You can switch between keyboards using Ctrl+Alt+F2 to access the memory-resident one (Portugal), and Ctrl+Alt+F1 to return to the built-in one.

National Language Support

DOS's National Language Support feature makes code-page switching easier, both internally and externally. Although you still use MODE to install the code pages, you don't have to use MODE to change code pages. To use National Language Support, you must load NLSFUNC as a TSR. Figure 49.5 shows the command syntax. You don't have to specify the filespec if it's already included in the COUNTRY command in your CONFIG.SYS file; otherwise, it defaults to COUNTRY.SYS in the root directory of the boot drive.

NLSFUNC

Starts the program that loads country-specific information for national language support (NLS).

Syntax:

```
NLSFUNC [filespec]
```

Parameters and Switches:

none   Uses the default file for country-specific information.

filespec   Identifies the file containing country-specific information.

Figure 49.5. *NLSFUNC command summary.*

The NLSFUNC program can be loaded at the DOS prompt or through the CONFIG.SYS INSTALL command. Using INSTALL lets you make sure that the TSR is loaded before COMMAND.COM. This can help if the language support functions don't seem to work. If you use the INSTALL method, it must follow the DEVICE command that loads DISPLAY.SYS. (When you use INSTALL, you can't load the TSR into upper memory blocks.)

After National Language Support is installed, you can use the CHCP command to change code pages. (See Figure 49.6.) CHCP, without a parameter, displays the number of the active code page, even if NLSFUNC hasn't been loaded.

CHCP

Changes the code page for all devices or displays the number of the current code page.

Syntax:

```
CHCP [page]
```

Parameters:

none   Displays the number of the current code page.

page   Changes to the specified code page.

Figure 49.6. *CHCP command summary.*

Another Complete Code Page Example Using NLSFUNC and CHCP

Suppose that you want to use National Language Support to work with the multilingual code page and the Latin American keyboard layout. The same commands are needed in your CONFIG.SYS file:

```
COUNTRY=003,,C:\DOS\COUNTRY.SYS
DEVICEHIGH=C:\DOS\DISPLAY.SYS CON=(,437,1)
```

And, you still need to prepare the code page with this command:

```
MODE CON CODEPAGE PREPARE=((850) C:\DOS\EGA.CPI)
```

Now try loading NLSFUNC and switching code pages:

1. Enter **LH NLSFUNC** to load the language support.
2. Enter **CHCP 850** to select the multilingual code page.
3. Enter **KEYB LA** to load the Latin American keyboard.
4. Enter **KEYB** to see which keyboard and code page are loaded.

Manipulating Code Pages

Occasionally, DOS may lose track of a code page. In that case, use the MODE command to refresh the code page. The following command reinstates the last active code page for the printer:

```
MODE CON CP REF
```

If the monitor has locked up, you probably will have to reboot to free it. In that case, the commands in your CONFIG.SYS and AUTOEXEC.BAT files are processed again. Then, you can switch code pages at the keyboard with a MODE command, or with CHCP (if NLSFUNC was loaded).

Displaying Code Page Information

Several commands give you information on the status of your system; you can use any of these at the DOS prompt or through the Shell as needed.

The KEYB command, with no options, displays the current keyboard information in this format:

```
Current keyboard code: BE   code page: 850
Current CON code page: 850
```

The messages give you both the keyboard layout and the code page in effect. If KEYB has not been used, you see a message like the following instead:

```
KEYB has not been installed
Active code page not available from CON device
```

The CHCP command, with no options, displays just the current code page in the following format:

```
Active code page: 850
```

The report is produced even if NLSFUNC isn't in memory.

The MODE command with no parameters displays information on all the attached devices and any current code pages. It provides lots of information. Therefore, use MODE ¦ MORE, or redirect the output so that you can see it all.

The /STATUS switch of the MODE command gives you information on a specific device. For example, the command MODE CON CODEPAGE /STATUS gives the following output:

```
Active code page for device CON is 850
Hardware code pages:
  code page 437
Prepared code pages:
  code page 850

MODE status code page function completed
```

In most cases, the /STATUS switch is optional; you get exactly the same information whether or not you use it.

On Your Own

This chapter has shown you how to set up your system for international use. If you would like to practice on your own, try setting up your PC for French Canadian formats and keyboard layout, using the appropriate code page.

When you're finished practicing, restore your system to its normal setup (unless you want to continue using an international setup).

50

Printing Through DOS

Introduction

You'll do most of your printing via your applications, but when you redirect a directory listing to the printer, when you press PrintScreen to capture a CHKDSK message, and when you print a DOS help topic, you're using DOS's print facility.

DOS's Very Basic Printing Services

When you print a file from an application such as a word processing document or a worksheet, the application probably provides its own printer driver. The developers of print-oriented applications put a lot of effort into their printer drivers to make the best use of the popular printer models.

DOS is hardly print-oriented, but it provides some primitive printing services so that you can capture screen prints with the PrintScreen key, print ASCII text files (such as README files), redirect standard output to the printer, and echo the monitor in print. Although DOS assumes that you have a basic printer attached to LPT1, you can get it to use other types of printers, including a laser printer attached to a serial port.

This chapter discusses various techniques for printing under DOS. You will learn how to:

- Echo on the printer everything that appears on the screen
- Print a copy of the current screen, in text or in graphics mode
- Configure the columns and lines per inch on your printer when printing from DOS
- Configure PRINT and manage its print queue

Printer Types

DOS uses only the most basic printer capabilities. For this reason, it can print on almost any PC-compatible printer. Most modern printers can emulate a basic printer of some type. If DOS doesn't seem to communicate with your printer, check its documentation and find out how to emulate an IBM, Hewlett-Packard, Epson, or Diablo printer; DOS handles these types very well.

DOS can't communicate directly with PostScript printers, but most PostScript printers will emulate one of these printers. You might have to set a switch on the printer itself to make it emulate an Epson (or whatever). Don't forget to return the printer to its normal setting when using it with software that has a PostScript driver.

DOS expects a parallel printer and uses LPT1 as the default printer port; device PRN refers to the same port. When you use echo printing or screen printing, the output is sent to PRN. You can redirect a parallel port to a serial port using a MODE command, as explained later in this chapter.

Echo Printing

You learned earlier how to redirect a command's output to your printer for documentation purposes, but sometimes you want to document an entire series of commands and their output. You might want to print a series of directory lists or diagnostic reports, for example, or to document a work session.

Echo printing copies to the default printer everything that crosses the screen: prompts, commands, error messages, and command output. It affects only commands and messages that cross the command-prompt screen. If you start up some other program while echo printing is in effect, echo printing resumes when that program terminates. Ctrl+PrintScreen toggles echo printing on and off. Try it on your PC:

1. Make sure your printer is ready to print.

2. Press Ctrl+PrintScreen.

3. Enter **DIR**.

    DOS echoes the `DIR` command, its output, and the next command prompt on the printer.

4. Enter **DIR \DOS**.

    DOS continues echoing everything on the printer.

5. To eject the last page, type **Ctrl+L** and press enter.

    You'll get an error message, but you'll also get your last page.

6. Press Ctrl+PrintScreen again to turn off echo printing.

If no printer is attached or redirected to LPT1, the system hangs up; make the printer available or reboot to continue. After echo printing is in effect, press Ctrl+PrintScreen or Ctrl+P to cancel it.

Note: You can't turn echo printing on or off from within a batch program or DOSKEY macro. Ctrl+P or Ctrl+PrintScreen must be pressed at the command prompt.

Text Screen Printing

Echo printing must be turned on before the text you want to capture crosses the screen. If the text is already displayed, you can capture it with a screen print. Just press the PrintScreen key (Shift+PrintScreen on some keyboards) and all the text on the screen is printed on the default printer. Printing graphics screens, such as DOS Shell's default screen, requires the `GRAPHICS` command, which is explained later in this chapter.

Try printing your screen now:

1. Press PrintScreen or Shift+PrintScreen.

    You should get a printout of your current screen.

2. Enter **ECHO ^L > PRN** (where ^L indicates that you pressed Ctrl+L) to eject the page.

Problem: My system froze up when I pressed PrintScreen.

If you press PrintScreen with no printer available on LPT1, your system may just beep or it may hang up waiting for a printer. If it hangs up, either make the printer available or reboot.

Configuring a Printer

Every printer has a standard vertical spacing measured in lines per inch (lpi), and horizontal spacing measured in characters per line. Most printers use 6 lpi and 80 characters per line by default. You can modify the spacing for many printers with a MODE command. (See Figure 50.1.) For parallel printers, you can set the vertical spacing at 6 or 8 lpi and the horizontal spacing at 80 or 132 characters per line. (This command doesn't work on serial printers and many laser and inkjet printers.)

MODE

Configures a parallel printer to use specific vertical and horizontal spacing and retry action.

Syntax:

```
MODE LPTn [COLS=c] [LINES=l] [RETRY=r]
```

Parameters:

LPT*n*   Identifies the parallel port: LPT1 to LPT3. You can use PRN instead of LPT1.

c   Specifies the number of columns per line: 80 or 132.

l   Specifies the number of lines per inch: 6 or 8.

r   Specifies the retry action if a time-out error occurs. Valid values are as follows:

E   Returns an error

B   Returns "busy"

P   Continue retrying until printer accepts output

R   Returns "ready"

N   No retry value (default)

Figure 50.1. MODE command summary (parallel printer configuration).

Try setting your printer to maximum print density:

1. Enter **MODE LPT1 COLS=132 LINES=8**.

   MODE acknowledges the command.

2. Enter **DIR > PRN** to see if the MODE command worked on your printer.

The RETRY parameter tells DOS how to react if DOS senses the printer, but the printer isn't ready to receive signals. By default, it simply gives up. The P parameter tells it to continue trying until the printer becomes available. This can cause your system to hang up when you try to print something and the printer is turned off, out of paper, off-line, or some other problem exists. To break out of the loop, make the printer available or press Ctrl+C.

After you configure the printer with MODE, it applies to all uses of that printer, including all applications that use DOS's printing services. Many applications use their own printer drivers, but the current print mode is restored when an application terminates.

Using Serial Printers

To use a serial printer for printing directly under DOS, you must first tell DOS the communications characteristics of the device. If the serial printer is your only printer or you want to use it as DOS's default device, you also must redirect LPT1 to it.

Configuring the Serial Port

A serial port—also known as a communications port—may be attached to a printer, a mouse, a modem, or some other device. To use a serial port with DOS, you must define its communications characteristics with a MODE command. (See Figure 50.2.) This section shows how to use MODE to set up a serial port for a printer. The same parameters are used to set it up for any serial device.

You can't guess at communications characteristics. You must use the correct values for the attached device. In most cases, the device's documentation tells you exactly how to write the MODE command. The following example configures a printer at 9,600 baud with no parity, 8 data bits, 1 stop bit, and continuous retry:

```
MODE COM1 BAUD=96 PARITY=N DATA=8 STOP=1 RETRY=P
```

The configuration affects all uses of the COM port until another MODE command changes it.

MODE

Configures a serial (COM) port for use by a device such as a serial printer.

Syntax:

```
MODE COMn BAUD = baud [PARITY = parity] [DATA = data]

[STOP = stop] [RETRY = retry]
```

Parameters:

COMn
: Identifies the serial port; *n* may be 1 to 4.

baud
: Specifies the transmission rate in bits per second (baud rate). (See Notes for values.)

parity
: Specifies how the system uses the parity bit to check for transmission errors. (See Notes for values.)

data
: Specifies the number of data bits per character. Values may be 5 through 8; the default value is 7.

stop
: Specifies the number of stop bits that identify the end of a character. Values may be 1, 1.5, or 2. If the baud rate is 100, the default is 2; otherwise, the default is 1.

retry
: Specifies the action to take if a time-out occurs when Mode attempts to send output to the port. (See Notes.)

Notes:

Values for baud rate are as follows:

11 or 110	110 baud
15 or 150	150 baud
30 or 300	300 baud
60 or 600	600 baud
12 or 1,200	1,200 baud
24 or 2,400	2,400 baud
48 or 4,800	4,800 baud
96 or 9,600	9,600 baud
19 or 19,200	19,200 baud

Values for *parity* may be N for no parity, E for even parity, O for odd parity, M for mark, or S for space. E is the default.

Values for *retry* are as follows:

E   Returns an error if the port is busy.

B   Returns busy if the port is busy.

P   Continues retrying until the port accepts output.

R   Returns ready if the port is busy.

N   Takes no retry action (default value).

Do not use any value for *retry* if you use MODE over a network.

Some values that are valid for MODE are not supported by all computers. These include: BAUD = 19; PARITY = S; PARITY = M; DATA = 5; DATA = 6; and STOP = 1.5.

If you omit any parameter except *baud*, MODE defaults to the most recent value for this port. If no previous MODE command has specified a value, MODE uses the default values. There is no default value for *baud*; you must specify this parameter.

Figure 50.2. *MODE command summary (configuring serial ports).*

You can't guess at communications characteristics. You must use the correct values for the attached device. In most cases, the device's documentation tells you exactly how to write the MODE command. The following example configures a printer at 9,600 baud with no parity, 8 data bits, 1 stop bit, and continuous retry:

```
MODE COM1 BAUD=96 PARITY=N DATA=88  STOP=1 RETRY=P
```

The configuration affects all uses of the COM port until another MODE command changes it.

Note: Some of MODE's functions require a small (0.5KB) TSR to be installed. Configuring a serial port is one of these memory-resident functions. Whichever MODE command installs the TSR results in the following message:

```
Resident portion of MODE loaded
```

The TSR needs to be loaded only once, then all of MODE's memory-resident functions can use it. This TSR can't be loaded in upper memory blocks. DOS ignores LOADHIGH when applied to a MODE command.

Redirecting a Serial Printer

If you want DOS to use a serial printer as PRN (for screen prints, echo printing, and so on), you must redirect LPT1 to it, using a command like the following:

```
MODE LPTn=COMn
```

For example, MODE LPT1=COM1 tells DOS that any data directed to LPT1 should be sent to COM1 instead. Of course, you can specify any valid serial (COM) and parallel (LPT) ports in the command. But, to use the serial printer as the default printer, you must redirect LPT1.

> **Note:** This MODE command format redirects parallel ports to serial ports only. It can't be used to redirect a serial port, nor can it redirect a parallel port to any other type of port.

Many applications depend on DOS's printing services, so you may need to redirect LPT1 even if you don't plan on screen prints or echo printing. The MODE command that sets the COM port's characteristics must precede the redirection command or DOS can't use the port.

To undo a redirection, enter **MODE LPT***n* (without the =COM*n*). You see a message like the following:

```
LPT1: not rerouted.
```

In summary, if your primary or only printer is a serial printer connected to COM2, you would insert the following commands in AUTOEXEC.BAT so that you use DOS's printing services:

```
MODE COM2 BAUD=96 PARITY=N DATA=8 STOP=1 RETRY=P
MODE LPT1=COM2
```

Viewing Redirection Status

The MODE command with no parameters displays status information for all the devices it controls. In addition, MODE generally displays status information for a device when you enter **MODE** followed by the device name and no other parameters. The following are some examples:

MODE CON	Displays status information about the console
MODE COM1	Displays status information about the first serial port

However, the following command will not display status information about the indicated parallel printer. Instead, it will undo any redirection applied to the printer:

```
MODE LPT1
```

To see status information for parallel printers, you must include the /STATUS switch (which can be abbreviated /STA), as in the following:

```
C:\>MODE LPT1 /STA
Status for device LPT1:
- - - - -
LPT1: rerouted to COM1:
Retry=NONE
Code page operation not supported on this device
```

The /STATUS switch may be used with the other device names, but it is not necessary.

The *PRINT* Command

You have seen how to use PRINT to print ASCII text files. Recall that the first PRINT command after booting loads the PRINT TSR, establishes the print queue, and identifies the printing device.

Configuring PRINT

If you do a lot of printing via the PRINT command, you might want to configure other PRINT features in the initializing command. (See Figure 50.3.) You can control such features as print-buffer size, print-queue size, and the balance between PRINT's processing (in the background) and any other work you are doing (in the foreground).

> **Note:** PRINT can be configured only by its initializing command. It can't be reconfigured without rebooting.

The /B switch sets the size of the print buffer; a larger buffer speeds up printing, but decreases the amount of available memory. Don't forget that you can use LH to load PRINT, its buffer, and its print queue into upper memory.

> **Tip:** If space is tight in upper memory, insert the PRINT command—including the desired buffer size and print queue size parameters—in AUTOEXEC.BAT, and run MEMMAKER to find the optimal location for it. If MEMMAKER can't squeeze it in upper memory, set smaller buffer and queue sizes and try again.

The rest of the configuration switches control how DOS does time-slicing when PRINT runs in the background. A clock tick is about 1/18 of a second. Normally, DOS will abort the PRINT command if the printer isn't available within one clock tick; if you want more time, increase it with the /U parameter. The /M parameter specifies how many clock ticks are allowed for printing one character. If you have an extremely slow printer and PRINT often aborts with an error message, you might want to specify a higher value here. The /S switch specifies how much background printing is done before DOS checks for a foreground action. If you increase this value from the default 8, print speed is increased but your foreground work may be impeded.

PRINT

Manages background printing.

Syntax:

```
PRINT [/D:device] [/B:buffer] [/U:ticks1] [/M:ticks2]

[/S:ticks3] [/Q:qsize] [/T] [filespec ...] [/C] [/P]
```

Parameters and Switches:

none	Displays the contents of the print queue or loads the TSR.
/D:*device*	Identifies the printer port on which to print. Valid values are LPT1, LPT2, LPT3, COM1, COM2, COM3, and COM4. LPT1 is identical to PRN. If used, /D must precede *filespec* on the command line.
/B:*buffer*	Sets the size, in bytes, of the buffer used to store data before printing; may be 512 to 16,384; 512 is the default.
/U:*ticks1*	Specifies the maximum number of clock ticks to wait for a printer to be available; may be 1 to 255; the default is 1. If the printer is not available in *ticks1* clock ticks, the job is not printed. (There are about 18 clock ticks per second.)
/M:*ticks2*	Specifies the maximum number of clock ticks to print a character on the printer; may be 1 to 55; the default value is 2. If a character takes longer than *ticks2* clock ticks to print, DOS displays an error message.
/S:*ticks3*	Specifies the number of clock ticks the DOS scheduler allocates for background printing before returning to foreground work; maybe 1 to 255; the default value is 8.
/Q:*qsize*	Specifies the maximum number of files in the print queue; may be 4 through 32. The default value is 10.
/T	Removes all files from the print queue.
filespec	Identifies a text file to place in the print queue; may be up to 64 characters.
/C	Removes file(s) from the print queue.
/P	Adds file(s) to the print queue.

> Notes:
>
> /T empties the queue. If any filespecs precede /T, they are removed from the queue. If any follow /T, they are added or canceled depending on whether /P or /C applies to them.

Figure 50.3. *PRINT command summary*

Controlling the Print Queue

Normally, the print queue holds up to 10 files. Each new file is placed at the end of the queue; if the queue is empty, the file is printed immediately. You can include several filespecs separated by spaces, or even a global filespec to queue several files at the same time. A message warns you when the queue is full.

The /Q switch, which belongs on the initializing command, sets the size of the print queue; if you often need to queue up more than 10 files, you may want to specify a larger number. On the other hand, if you need to save every possible byte of conventional memory, each entry in the print queue requires 64 bytes. You can save 384 bytes by reducing the print queue to its minimum size of four entries.

You can see the current queue by entering **PRINT** with no parameters. The /T switch, with no filenames, terminates the queue immediately, right in the middle of the current file.

Try using a minimum print queue (if you load PRINT from your AUTOEXEC.BAT file, skip this exercise):

1. If you have already loaded print, exit all programs and reboot to clear PRINT from memory.

2. Enter **LH PRINT /Q:4** to load PRINT with a four-file print queue.

   PRINT asks for the name of the print device.

3. Enter the name of your print device (just press Enter to accept PRN as the device).

4. Switch to the DOS directory.

5. Enter **PRINT *.TXT**.

   The first four *.TXT files are loaded into the print queue. You also see the message PRINT queue is full.

6. Enter **PRINT** to see the status of the PRINT queue.

7. Enter **PRINT /T** to empty the print queue.

Problem: I entered a PRINT command and nothing printed.

Try entering **PRINT** with no parameters to see the status of the print queue. PRINT will include any error messages in the status report.

Note: When /T is entered, PRINT stops shipping data to the printer, but the printer keeps printing until its own buffer is empty. A printer with a large buffer might print several pages before stopping. You can stop the printer and empty its buffer immediately by turning it off.

You can cancel files from the queue by issuing another PRINT command with the /C switch before or just after the filename to be removed. All filenames following /C are removed from the queue; if a filename precedes it, that one is removed as well. To add files to the queue in the same command, use /P. Just like /C, it applies to all filenames following it and the one immediately before it. Files named in a PRINT command without either /P or /C are added to the queue.

You can't directly change the order of files in the print queue. To force a later file to be printed quickly, you would have to cancel any files preceding it in the queue and then add them to the queue again following that file.

Try moving a file up in the queue:

1. Enter **PRINT *.TXT** to place four files in the queue.
2. Enter **PRINT** to see the order of the files in the queue.

    Notice that README.TXT is not at the beginning of the queue.

3. Enter **PRINT /T README.TXT *.TXT** to move README.TXT to the front of the print queue. (This command empties the queue with /T, adds README.TXT to the queue, then adds other .TXT files to the queue.)

4. Enter **PRINT** to see the current status of the print queue.

    You should see that README.TXT is now being printed.

5. Enter **PRINT /T** to empty the queue.

Printing GRAPHICS Screens

DOS normally can't print graphics screens that can be displayed by CGA, EGA, and VGA monitors; it may try to convert them to text characters. You can use several third-party software programs to capture, print, and even modify graphics screens. On occasion, however, you may want to print a graphics screen from a CGA, EGA, or VGA monitor using PrintScreen. The GRAPHICS command might make this possible. DOS can't handle video modes that aren't supported by the BIOS; many SuperVGA graphics can't be handled, for example. Some applications reprogram the VGA display to a different mode; these displays can't be printed under DOS. Windows screens also cannot be printed via DOS.

> **Note:** In Windows, the PrintScreen key stores a copy of the current screen on the Windows Clipboard, from which you can paste it into any application that is compatible with the Clipboard and graphics images.

How GRAPHICS Works

The GRAPHICS command loads a TSR that lets DOS print supported graphic screens on several types of printers. After GRAPHICS is loaded, the signal generated by the PrintScreen key is intercepted. If the screen is in text mode, the request is passed back to the BIOS for standard text-screen printing. If the screen is in graphics mode, however, GRAPHICS takes over. It scans each pixel on the screen, translates it for the printer, and prints it. Both the number of pixels (screen resolution) and the number of dots per inch (printer resolution) affect the result. Some graphic displays are printed sideways for best effect.

Your DOS directory includes a file called GRAPHICS.PRO that includes printer profiles for the printer types DOS supports, including details on translating different video formats for printing. This is an ASCII file; you can examine it with EDIT or print it with PRINT.

The GRAPHICS Command

Figure 50.4 shows the format of the GRAPHICS command. GRAPHICS with no parameters is equivalent to GRAPHICS HPDEFAULT; DOS prepares to print graphics screens on a printer that recognizes the PCL (page control language) commands used by most Hewlett-Packard printers. Table 50.1 shows a complete list of the available printer-type parameters.

Table 50.1. GRAPHICS printer types.

Type	Printers Included
COLOR1	IBM PC Color Printer with black ribbon
COLOR4	IBM PC Color Printer with RGB ribbon
COLOR8	IBM PC Color Printer with CMY ribbon (cyan, magenta, yellow)

continues

Table 50.1. continued

Type	Printers Included
DESKJET	Hewlett-Packard DeskJet
HPDEFAULT	Any Hewlett-Packard PCL printer (the default)
GRAPHICS	IBM Personal Graphics Printer, Proprinter, or Quietwriter; also most Epson dot-matrix printers
GRAPHICSWIDE	Any GRAPHICS printer with a wide carriage
LASERJET	Hewlett-Packard LaserJet printer
LASERJETII	Hewlett-Packard LaserJet II printer
PAINTJET	Hewlett-Packard PaintJet printer
QUIETJET	Hewlett-Packard QuietJet printer
QUIETJETPLUS	Hewlett-Packard QuietJet Plus printer
RUGGEDWRITER	Hewlett-Packard RuggedWriter printer
RUGGEDWRITERWIDE	Hewlett-Packard RuggedWriter Wide printer
THERMAL	IBM PC-convertible Thermal printer
THINKJET	Hewlett-Packard ThinkJet printer

If GRAPHICS.PRO isn't in the same directory as GRAPHICS.COM or the current directory, you have to tell DOS where it is by using the `filespec` parameter.

Try printing a graphics screen from DOS Shell on your printer. (If your monitor can't display the Shell screen in graphics mode, skip this exercise.)

1. Decide which printer type from Table 50.1 most closely resembles your printer.
2. Enter **GRAPHICS** *type* **/R**.
3. Start DOS Shell.
4. Press PrintScreen or Shift+PrintScreen.

   DOS should start printing a copy of the DOS Shell screen. If not, or if it doesn't complete the job, the graphics *type* might not be compatible with your printer.

GRAPHICS Switches

Normally, screens are printed with a white background; this is easy on a printer because the background is simply ignored. The typical DOS screen, however, is displayed on the monitor with a dark background. If you want the screen print prepared with a dark background, use the /R switch; the result will more closely match the displayed screen. (Many printers don't do a very good job on solid black areas, however.)

GRAPHICS

Loads the Graphics TSR to enable DOS to print graphics screens.

Syntax:

```
GRAPHICS [type] [filespec] [/R] [/B] [LCD] [/PRINTBOX:size]
```

Parameters and Switches:

none	Loads the Graphics TSR with default values.
type	Identifies the printer type. See notes for possible values. The default is HPDEFAULT.
filespec	Identifies the printer profile file; default is GRAPHICS.PRO.
/R	Specifies that images should be printed as they appear on-screen (a positive image). Default is to print a reverse (or negative) screen image, which sometimes looks better in print.
/B	Prints background in color for printers COLOR4 and COLOR8.
/LCD	Prints image using LCD aspect ratio instead of CGA aspect ratio. The effect of this switch is the same as /PRINTBOX:LCD.
/PRINTBOX:size	Specifies the size of the printbox. You can abbreviate /PRINTBOX as /PB. size may be STD or LCD. This must match the first operand of the PRINTBOX statement in your printer profile.

Notes:

You can't print a graphics screen to a PostScript printer via DOS.

After GRAPHICS is loaded, press Shift+PrintScreen or PrintScreen (depending on the keyboard) to print the screen. The number of shades of gray depends on both monitor and printer. If the monitor is 640×200 or better, the screen will be printed sideways.

Figure 50.4. *GRAPHICS command summary.*

Note: Some applications, such as DOS Shell, are displayed as black (or color) on white, but print the reverse. You have to use the /R switch to "unreverse" them.

When you print to a color printer, GRAPHICS also uses white for the background by default. The /B switch tells it to use a color; this is valid only for COLOR4 and COLOR8 printers. If you examine the GRAPHICS.PRO file, you see listings of how each displayed color is printed.

Aspect Ratio

The aspect ratio is the ratio of the vertical and horizontal dimensions. An LCD monitor has a different aspect ratio than a VGA or other type of monitor. If you print screens using the wrong aspect ratio, graphics appear distorted. For example, circles appear as ellipses.

Normally, you can trust GRAPHICS to choose the correct aspect, as they are specified in GRAPHICS.PRO for each printer as the PRINTBOX value. If you find that the ratio is not for your printer, check GRAPHICS.PRO to see whether your system can handle both LCD and STD; the values follow the word PRINTBOX for each screen resolution. Either /LCD or /PB:LCD specifies the LCD aspect ratio. Use /PB:STD to specify a standard one.

You may have to reboot to replace the GRAPHICS profile. If the new profile takes less space in memory, it can be loaded over the existing one. If not, you see an error message, and you have to reboot and start over.

Tip: After you decide on the correct GRAPHICS command for your system, load it through AUTOEXEC.BAT so it is always available. If you can't load it in upper memory and can't afford the conventional memory space on a regular basis, make a batch program or DOSKEY macro to load GRAPHICS as you need it.

On Your Own

This chapter has shown you how to print through DOS. The following items help you practice these printing techniques:

1. Turn on echo printing and enter several DOS commands. Turn off echo printing again.

2. Print the DOS command prompt screen.

3. Print the DOS Shell screen (or another GUI screen) if your printer is compatible with the GRAPHICS command.

4. Set your screen to its maximum number of lines per screen.

5. Set your screen to 40 characters per line.

6. Load PRINT with a larger buffer and a 20-file print queue. Start printing several text files, then empty the print queue.

51 Configuring Disks and Networks

Introduction

Working together with CMOS and ROM-BIOS, DOS usually handles your disk drives perfectly. But, when it doesn't, you have to give it some extra help. The DRIVPARM command and the DRIVER.SYS device driver let you redefine your disk drives. Running DOS on a network also requires special considerations.

Defining Drives for DOS

Your PC's CMOS chip maintains the physical descriptions of your drives that are essential to accessing them during system startup. Your ROM-BIOS then provides the low-level software that actually reads and writes data on the drives (as well as your other devices). When DOS boots, it is able to access your drives because of the facilities provided by CMOS and ROM-BIOS.

In rare cases, a PC might have a drive that cannot be defined correctly in CMOS, or that is not supported by ROM-BIOS. Then, you must use the DRIVPARM or DRIVER.SYS driver to define the drive for DOS. You can also use DRIVER.SYS to set up extra logical drive names for floppy disk drives to make file moves and copies more convenient. You learn when and how to use these configuration commands in this chapter.

Attaching a PC to a network requires both hardware and software adaptations. The network operating system handles most of the software needs, but you have to consider a few DOS features when running DOS under a network. These features are covered in this chapter.

In this chapter, you will learn how to:

- Define a block device such as a disk drive or tape drive with DRIVPARM
- Configure a logical floppy disk drive with DRIVER.SYS
- Assign an extra drive name to a floppy drive
- Recognize when you need extra information in order to install DOS 6.22 with a networked system
- Identify DOS commands that should not be used on a network
- Load SHARE to protect files in a network

Configuring Physical Disks

The DRIVPARM command, which goes in CONFIG.SYS, is used to define a block device when DOS is not capable of accessing it correctly without extra help. (See Figure 51.1.) A *block device* is a device that reads and writes more than one character at a time, such as a floppy disk drive, a hard disk drive, or a tape drive.

DRIVPARM

Specifies new parameters for an existing physical drive.

Syntax:

```
DRIVPARM /D:drive [switches]
```

Switches:

/D:*drive* Specifies the physical drive number: 0=A; 1=B; 2=C, etc. This switch is required.

/F:*type* Identifies the type of drive. Valid values are as follows:

  0 360KB or less

  1 1.2MB

  2 720KB (default)

  5 Hard disk

  6 Tape

  7 1.44MB

  8 Read/write optical disk

  9 2.88MB

/H:*heads* Specifies the number of heads (or sides).

/S:*sectors* Specifies the number of sectors per track.

/T:*tracks* Specifies the number of tracks.

/C Indicates that the drive has change-line support.

/N Indicates a nonremovable drive.

/I Indicates an electronically compatible 3 1/2-inch drive.

Figure 51.1. DRIVPARM *configuration command summary.*

Usually, if a block device needs to be defined by DRIVPARM, the manufacturer provides the exact information. All you have to do is add it to your CONFIG.SYS file.

One reason you might have to redefine a device is because it does not use the default number of heads, sectors, and tracks. Table 51.1 shows the defaults for the disk types that DOS supports. If the device you are installing doesn't use the default values, specify the correct values from the device documentation. If you specify wrong or inconsistent values, DOS might be able to read from the drive, but it will do erratic or bad formatting on the drive.

Table 51.1. Standard floppy disk parameters.

Capacity	Heads	Sectors	Tracks
160KB	1	8	40
180KB	1	9	40
320KB	2	8	40
360KB	2	9	40
720KB	2	9	80
1.2MB	2	15	80
1.44MB	2	18	80
2.88MB	2	36	80

Warning: If you specify your boot drive in the DRIVPARM command and give it the wrong parameters, you may not be able to start up your system, or it may start up as usual and then destroy the root directory when it writes to the disk. Be sure that you have a valid backup and a recovery disk handy before redefining the boot drive. You'll be able to start up using F8 to bypass DRIVPARM, but if the root directory has been destroyed, you'll need the backup and the recovery disk to continue.

Suppose you install as drive A a 1.44MB drive that has 2 heads, 20 sectors per track, 72 tracks, and change-line support. You would insert the following command in CONFIG.SYS:

```
DRIVPARM /D:0 /F:7 /C /S:20 /T:72
```

Suppose that you install a 2.88MB drive as drive B and DOS has difficulty recognizing the new drive. You would include the following command in CONFIG.SYS:

```
DRIVPARM /D:1 /F:9 /C
```

This command sets the parameters for drive 1 (the B drive) to use the default values for drive type 9 (2.88MB), and says that the drive has change-line support, which is explained in the next section.

Change-Line Support

A *change line* is a mechanism that lets DOS know that a drive door has been opened, signaling that a disk may have been changed. Most 360KB and below disk drives do not have this feature.

If DOS thinks that a drive has change-line support, it saves time by referring to a cache of the directory instead of rereading the disk when it needs to access a drive that has not been opened since the directory was cached. If the drive has been opened, DOS rereads (and caches) the drive's directory structure.

A malfunctioning change-line mechanism could threaten the integrity of data on your floppy disk. If DOS accesses one floppy disk using another floppy disk's directory, data could be read from or written to the wrong clusters. If you suspect this is happening, repair or replace the drive, or use DRIVPARM to tell DOS that the drive does not have change-line support.

Configuring Logical Floppy Disks

The DRIVER.SYS device driver creates a logical floppy disk drive based on a physical one. It assigns a new drive letter, the next one in sequence. Two major uses of DRIVER.SYS are as follows:

- To force DOS to recognize and assign a logical drive name to an external disk drive
- To assign an alternate logical drive name to a disk drive

> **Note:** To create a logical drive name for a hard disk, use the SUBST command, which is explained in Chapter 39, "Directory Management."

Figure 51.2 shows the switches you can use with the DRIVER.SYS device driver. Notice that you can use DEVICE or DEVICEHIGH to load the driver. You can use more than one DRIVER.SYS command to define multiple logical drives. Each loaded driver takes about 240 bytes in memory. The primary use of this command is to assign alternate names to drives, as explained in the next section.

DRIVER.SYS

Creates a new logical drive corresponding to a physical disk drive.

Syntax:

```
DEVICE[HIGH]=[path]DRIVER.SYS /D:drive [switches]
```

Parameters and Switches:

path   Identifies the location of DRIVER.SYS if it is not in the root directory of the
              boot drive.

/D:drive   Specifies the number of the physical floppy disk drive: 0 = first; 1 = second;
              up to 127.

/F:type   Identifies the type of drive.

   0 360KB or less

   1 1.2MB

   2 720KB (default)

   7 1.44MB

   9 2.88MB

/H:heads   Specifies the number of heads (or sides).

/S:sectors   Specifies the number of sectors per track.

/T:tracks   Specifies the number of tracks.

/C   Indicates that the drive has change-line support.

Figure 51.2. *DRIVER.SYS DEVICE command summary.*

Creating an Alternate Drive Name

Many computers these days have floppy drives of two different types, such as 1.2MB and 1.44MB.
You can't directly move or copy files from one disk to another of the same type, because DOS rejects
a command such as the following:

```
XCOPY B:\*.* B:
```

You can use DRIVER.SYS to assign a second logical drive name to a physical drive, so that you can move and copy files from one disk to another in that drive using MOVE, COPY, and XCOPY commands. This command sets up a second drive letter for the second disk drive (drive B) with a 1.44MB capacity:

```
DEVICE=C:\DOS\DRIVER.SYS /D:1 /F:7
```

Be sure to notice which drive letter DOS assigns to the drive during booting. A message like the following appears when the driver is loaded:

```
Loaded External Driver for Drive E
```

This message tells you that the alternate name for the drive is E. With the logical drive created in this example, you could use the following command to copy files:

```
XCOPY B:\*.* E:
```

You are prompted to insert one disk at a time (starting with the target disk so that DOS can check it out). The messages look something like the following:

```
C:\>XCOPY B:*.* D:
Insert diskette for drive D: and press any key when ready
Insert diskette for drive B: and press any key when ready
Reading source file(s)...
Insert disk for drive D: and press any key when ready
B:CHAP02.CHP
 ...
B:APPP.CHP

Insert diskette for drive B: and press any key when ready
        7 File(s) copied

Insert disk for drive D: and press any key when ready
```

> **Tip:** When you are copying more than one file, use XCOPY rather than COPY. You have to do a lot less disk swapping, because XCOPY fills memory with files before writing any; COPY handles each file separately.

Setting Up Two Alternate Drive Names

Suppose that your computer has two floppy disk drives, 1.2MB and 1.44MB, and two hard drives. You can include the following commands in your CONFIG.SYS file:

```
DEVICE=C:\DOS\DRIVER.SYS /D:0 /F:1
DEVICE=C:\DOS\DRIVER.SYS /D:1 /F:7
```

When the system boots, you see the following messages on the screen:

```
Loaded External Disk Driver for Drive E

Loaded External Disk Driver for Drive F
```

You can refer to drives E and F as needed during your DOS work; they have exactly the same characteristics as drives A and B. Most importantly, you can copy files from drive A to drive E (which is the same physical drive), and from drive B to drive F.

> **Note:** DOS keeps track of which logical drive name was used last. If drive E is in effect and you enter DIR A:, you see the following message:
>
> ```
> Insert diskette for drive A: and press any key when ready
> ```

You can switch from one drive name to another just as you switch drives anywhere in DOS. For example, if drive E is currently in effect, you can switch to drive A by entering A:.

Adding an External Floppy Disk Drive

If you install a drive that DOS doesn't recognize automatically, either DRIVPARM or DRIVER.SYS can be used to tell DOS that you have added the drive to your PC. For example, the following command specifies a 1.2MB external drive as the third disk drive:

```
DEVICE=C:\DOS\DRIVER.SYS /D:2 /F:1 /C
```

If you want to be able to copy files in that drive, you need a second, identical DEVICE command to set up a second logical drive.

Choosing between DRIVER.SYS and DRIVPARM

If you use DRIVER.SYS to change the parameters of a physical drive, a new logical drive name is assigned to the drive. It is better to redefine drive characteristics with DRIVPARM, which lets you continue to use the drive's original name. DRIVPARM also takes up less space in conventional memory.

Problem: I installed a new (or used) floppy drive and DOS doesn't recognize it.

If you add a floppy disk drive not supported by the BIOS, a driver supplied with it may not work. For example, suppose that you get a 2.88MB drive at a swap meet for your drive A and your BIOS doesn't support it (most older ones don't). As a first step, add the following DRIVPARM command to CONFIG.SYS:

```
DRIVPARM /D:0 /F:9 /C
```

If you still have access problems, try using DRIVER.SYS to define it; then two logical drive names will refer to the same floppy disk drive. Use a configuration command like the following:

```
DEVICE=C:\DOS\DRIVER.SYS /D:0 /F:9 /C
```

It's possible that you may need both commands.

Running DOS on a Network

A network is a collection of two or more computers linked to each other via hardware and software; the way in which they are connected varies radically from network to network. But, the hardware always includes network adapter cards in each computer, and cables to connect them. The software includes the network operating system and a file server, which manages file access. It may also include other servers to handle printers and communications.

Each computer in a network is called a *workstation* or *node*. The workstations can range from a simple keyboard and monitor with no local resources (such as disks or printers), to a full-fledged PC with extensive local facilities in addition to its network connection. Some PC networks can handle Macintosh computers as well. A workstation typically can transfer messages and files to other workstations, access files on network drives (such as a departmental database), and access at least one shared printer.

An individual user is assigned access rights to the shared resources on the network. Kevin might be allowed to read a network drive but not update it, for example, whereas Donna can both read and update the drive but not reformat it.

Many workstations can also operate independently of the network, using most DOS commands on the their local drives. (This is not true of diskless workstations, which have access only to network drives.) Neither the processing nor the commands differ from everyday DOS when the programs and data are contained locally. However, time does become a factor when transferring data across connections, particularly if several users are doing it at the same time.

Special network commands set up the system when it is turned on. The network operating system often has its own startup file, much like AUTOEXEC.BAT, which is executed automatically when you start up the network. Some DOS commands, such as JOIN and SUBST, may be used to set up the required access paths for the network. Although these commands are valid, they should not be used on a network for any purpose other than what is required to establish the network, as they can cause trouble within DOS.

Upgrading a Networked System to DOS 6.22

If you're upgrading from DOS 5.0 or later, and your network works with your current version of DOS, upgrading to DOS 6.22 will not affect your network. If you're upgrading from an earlier version of DOS, you might experience trouble, depending on how old your network software is.

Your DOS 6.22 upgrade package includes a file called NETWORKS.TXT that specifies details for many network systems. If your system is networked, you should check this file *before* trying to upgrade to DOS 6.22. For many systems, it contains instructions on what to do before installing your new version of DOS. You can display and read or print NETWORKS.TXT from the floppy disks. You don't have to install DOS 6.22 to be able to access the file.

DOS Command Limitations

Most DOS commands work the same under a network as on an independent computer. However, some DOS commands can't be used over a network connection. Other commands can't be used to refer to network drives. Table 51.2 lists these commands.

Table 51.2. DOS command network restrictions.

Do not use the following on network drives:
CHKDSK
DEFRAG
DISKCOMP
FDISK
RECOVER (from earlier DOS versions)
SYS

Do not use the following across network connections:

FASTOPEN

FORMAT

LABEL

UNFORMAT

A command that can't be used on a network drive can be used to refer to local drives on a networked computer. Any DOS command that can't be used across network connections can be used to refer only to local drives.

If your system includes a token-ring network, and if you are having trouble running MEMMAKER, add the /T switch to the MEMMAKER command to disable detection of the token-ring network.

Sharing and Locking Files

When working on a network, it is possible that two people might try to access the same file at the same time. They might even try to make simultaneous changes to the file. For example, several people might try to update a departmental database simultaneously. It's up to the network software to prevent any conflicts that might occur in this situation. Some network operating systems depend on DOS's SHARE command to resolve such conflicts. Figure 51.3 shows the command format for SHARE.

SHARE might also be required by a Windows OLE 2.0 application, such as Word for Windows 6.0, where more than one application might try to access the same file for update via OLE 2.0. Some Windows applications also require SHARE in order to open multiple instances of the application. For example, you can open Word for Windows in more than one window only if you have loaded SHARE.

The SHARE command specifies the amount of space reserved for storing file specifications and a maximum number of files that can be locked at a time. If your network requires SHARE, it was probably placed in your AUTOEXEC.BAT file when the network was installed.

Note: Windows for Workgroups had SHARE built into it, so you don't need to load it.

SHARE

Installs file locking and sharing functions on a hard disk, usually used in a network or multitasking environment. After SHARE is installed, it validates all read-and-write requests.

Syntax:

From the command prompt:

`SHARE [switches]`

From CONFIG.SYS:

`INSTALL=[path]SHARE.EXE[switches]`

Parameters and Switches:

path	Identifies the location of the SHARE.EXE file if it is not in the root directory of the boot drive.
/F:space	Specifies the space (in bytes) for recording file sharing information; default is 2,048.
/L:locks	Specifies the number of files that can be locked at the same time; default is 20.

Figure 51.3. SHARE *command summary.*

On Your Own

You won't need to practice most of the techniques in this chapter. If you need to redefine a drive, for example, you need to insert the command in your startup file only once. However, if you have only one 3 1/2-inch or 5 1/4-inch floppy drive, practice assigning to it a second drive name and copying and moving files between disks in that drive.

52

The Multimedia PC

Introduction

It's all the rage—the adult toy...er...tool of the 1990s. But exactly what is a multimedia PC and how can you take advantage of the burgeoning wealth of CD software taking over your dealer's shelves?

New Concepts in Multimedia

Back in the early 1970s (prehistoric times by PC standards), I worked with some multimedia programmer training courses. Each course started with a printed introduction, then a 10-minute video overviewing the topic, followed by a series of printed lessons. Some of the courses also included a 10-minute audio that you listened to during one of the lessons. That was the state-of-the-art in multimedia. And it truly was *multi*media, consisting of at least two, and sometimes three, methods of communication.

By contrast, today's multimedia as realized on the personal computer offers the viewer a totally interactive experience, with text, sound, graphics, photos, videos, and animation all used to educate, inform, persuade, or entertain (sometimes all at once). The viewer often has complete control over the order of presentation. Microsoft's Cinemania, for example, documents thousands of movies and the people who make them. You could start by looking up Tootsie, check out a couple of reviews, view the complete credits, take a look at what Academy Awards it received, view a film clip from the movie (with sound), click Dustin Hoffman's name to jump to his biography, click a term such as black comedy to read about it in detail, switch to Hoffman's filmography, click a title to jump to that film, and so on. (Some people extend the "and so on" for hours at a time, following Byzantine trails from performer to movie to director to another movie to another performer...and so on.)

This chapter introduces you to the multimedia PC and the DOS commands that you need in order to interact with your multimedia hardware and software. There aren't very many of them; most multimedia programs are run from Windows rather than DOS. In this chapter, you will learn:

- What hardware is commonly used with the multimedia PC
- What software you'll need for your multimedia PC
- How to load DOS's MSCDEX CD-ROM driver
- How to use DOS's MSD (Microsoft Diagnostics) program to locate interrupts (IRQ) for your multimedia hardware

Multimedia Hardware

You can limp along with a 386SX and a cheap (single-speed) CD-ROM drive. You don't even need a sound board; you can download a free program called SPEAK.EXE from most major online services that lets you play sound clips on your built-in PC speaker. But, the effect is much like watching one of the first films—which were nicknamed *flickers* for good reason—accompanied by a recording made by Edison himself.

The Multimedia PC Marketing Council, Inc. has defined the industry standard for an MPC (multi-media PC). The upgraded standard, called MPC2, includes:

- A 486SX 25MHz processor
- 160MB hard disk
- 4MB RAM
- Double-speed CD-ROM drive
- SuperVGA 640×480 video with 64KB colors
- 1.44MB floppy disk
- Joystick
- 16-bit sound board with 8-note synthesizer and MIDI playback (you'll need speakers too)

Any software bearing the MPC2 logo can assume that your PC has these devices. But the truth is, even that's not enough. To get the most from the video components of your MPC software, you need the fastest processor you can afford (at least a 486DX), a triple-speed CD-ROM drive, and a high-speed, high-resolution monitor. To get the most from the audio components, you probably need much better speakers than the ones that came with your sound board.

If you get into creating your own multimedia-ware, you'll find you need even more hardware. Your sound board lets you record your own sounds, but you'll need a microphone and lots (pronounced "humongous amounts") of room on your hard drive. An average 10 second sound bite takes 880KB to store on disk.

To record video clips from your camcorder or VCR, you need a video capture card. Video eats up even more drive space. A 10-second video, compressed, needs 5.5MB of drive space. And, to play it back properly, the drive must be very fast, which means that it probably can't be compressed. Compression utilities such as DriveSpace must decompress a file each time you access it. When you're working with a document in your word processor, you won't notice the slight increase in access time, but when you're playing back a video, you will. You'll also want a fast hard drive if you're going to create your own animation. (A high-quality, color scanner and a pressure-sensitive digitizer pad also come in handy when you're creating your own animation; it's difficult to draw smooth curves with a mouse.)

Note: Defragment your hard drive regularly to make sure it's running at its fastest possible speed. See Chapter 33, "Defragmenter," for a description of DOS's DEFRAG program.

The Software

At the very least, you need drivers to manage your CD-ROM drive, sound board, and other MPC hardware. Each item should come with its own driver and an installation program, on disk, that installs the driver in your CONFIG.SYS file. If the manufacturer doesn't provide an installation program, follow the steps in the procedure on this page to install the driver yourself.

How to Install a New Device Driver

1. Read the hardware documentation. The driver will almost certainly require parameters and switches on the `DEVICEHIGH` command. Decide what parameters and switches are needed for your PC. (If the documentation is not clear, you might need to call the manufacturer or experiment to find the proper settings.)

2. Open CONFIG.SYS for editing in an ASCII text editor such as EDIT.

3. Insert a `DEVICEHIGH` command for the driver somewhere *after* the `EMM386.EXE` and `DOS=UMB` commands. The command should take this form:

   `DEVICEHIGH=`*path\filespec parameters and switches*

4. Repeat step 3 for each device driver that you are installing at this time.

5. Save the file and exit the editor.

6. Reboot to execute your revised CONFIG.SYS.

7. If DOS is unable to complete the boot process (always a possibility when you install a new device driver), reboot and press F8 to execute CONFIG.SYS one line at a time. Bypass your new `DEVICEHIGH` command(s) so that you can complete the boot process. Then, go back to step 1 and try again.

8. When DOS successfully reboots, try out your new devices. If they don't work, go back to step 1 and try again.

9. When the new devices work, you might want to run MEMMAKER to optimize upper memory. (If `MEM /C` shows that the device drivers are successfully loading into upper memory, you don't need to run MEMMAKER.)

You'll need a lot more software, usually called *authoring software*, if you want to record your own sound and video files; create animation; develop sophisticated graphics; view, manipulate, and manage photographs; and bring it all together into a game, educational package, or marketing presentation. DOS does not include any software to create or play back multimedia CDs. Windows 3.1 includes some basic facilities:

- Media Player to play audio CDs
- Sound Recorder to record and play sound waves (these are .WAV files)

It also includes several utilities to manage MPC facilities, such as Drivers to load hardware drivers and Sounds to relate sound wave files to events that occur while you work in Windows and its applications. You're probably used to the default sound waves, such as "ta-da" when you start Windows and a chime when you exit it. But, you can change these sounds to any sound waves on your system (and you can download a plethora of sound waves from BBSs and online services).

Multimedia programs, such as Microsoft Cinemania or Compton's Multimedia Encyclopedia, include their own playback software. All you need to do is load the CD in your CD-ROM drive and enter the correct command to install it and/or start it up.

The MSCDEX Program

DOS does include one important multimedia utility, called MSCDEX, that enables it to access and manage a CD-ROM drive. (See Figure 52.1.) You must load MSCDEX from the command prompt or AUTOEXEC.BAT. Most likely, the program that installed your CD-ROM driver in CONFIG.SYS also installed the correct MSCDEX command in AUTOEXEC.BAT. If not, you should insert it yourself, but you have to take a look at the /D switch for the device driver in CONFIG.SYS. You use the same /D switch in the MSCDEX command, so that DOS knows for which drive to load MSCDEX. (If you have more than one CD-ROM drive, include an MSCDEX command for each one.) Suppose that the device driver is loaded with this command:

```
DEVICEHIGH=\DEV\MTMCDS.SYS /D:MSCD001 /P:300 /A:0
```

The MSCDEX command would look like this:

```
LH C:\DOS\MSCDEX /D:MSCD001
```

MSCDEX

Makes CD ROM drives available to DOS.

Syntax

MSCDEX /D:*signature* [...] [/E] [/K] [/S] [/V] [/L:*drivename*] [/M:*buffers*]

Parameters and Switches

/D:*signature*	Identifies the signature of the CD-ROM device driver.
/E	Lets the device driver use expanded memory.
/K	Recognizes CD-ROM disks encoded in Kanji.
/S	Permits MS-NET and Windows for Workgroups servers to share CD-ROM drives.
/V	Displays a memory report when MSCDEX starts up.
/L:*drivename*	Specifies the drivename to assign to the CD-ROM drive; if more than one drive are included in the command, specifies the name of the first one, and the other drives receive successive names.
/M:*buffers*	Specifies the number of buffers to allocate to the drive.

Figure 52.1. MSCDEX *command summary.*

DOS assigns a drive name to the CD-ROM drive when it loads the device driver; watch the boot messages to see the drive name. If you miss it, you can start up DOS Shell to see the drive list; CD-ROM drives have their own icons in the drive list, so it's easy to figure out which is your CD-ROM drive.

Choosing an IRQ

DOS interacts with your PC's devices via *interrupts*. An interrupt is pretty much like a phone call from the device to DOS. When a device wants attention—when you press a key on your keyboard, for example—it sends a signal on its interrupt line. DOS answers the signal and handles the interruption.

Your PC has 16 hardware interrupt lines, called IRQ0 through IRQ15. Essentially, this means that DOS can handle up to 16 hardware devices at a time. (There are exceptions; some devices can share an interrupt line without conflicting with each other.) When you install a new device driver, it might seek out an unused interrupt line (if you're lucky), or you might have to tell it what line to use (if you're not so lucky). You can use DOS's MSD (Microsoft Diagnostics) program to locate unused IRQs.

Start the program by entering **MSD** with no parameters. Figure 52.2 shows the initial MSD screen, which acts as a main menu for MSD. Choose IRQ Status to see the screen shown in Figure 52.3, which displays the status of all 16 IRQs.

Figure 52.2.
MSD main screen.

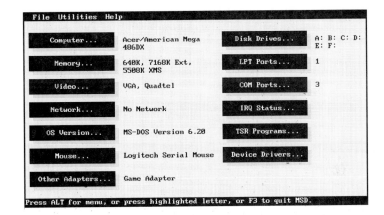

Figure 52.3.
IRQ status window.

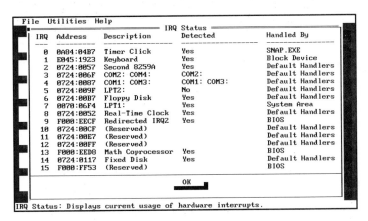

In the example, the Timer is using IRQ0, the keyboard communicates with DOS via IRQ1, and so on.

Notice that IRQ5 is set aside for LPT2, but this system has no device on LPT2. You may be able to borrow this IRQ for one of your multimedia devices. But, if you do, you won't be able to attach a device to LPT2 that operates at the same time as the multimedia device. Suppose, for example, that you assign your CD-ROM device to IRQ5. The device driver seizes IRQ5 when it boots. You could not then use LPT2 to connect this computer to another computer via INTERLNK, unless you reboot and bypass the CD-ROM device driver until you complete the INTERLNK task. But, in this particular system, there may be no reason to usurp IRQ5. IRQ10 through 12 are available, as is IRQ15.

How do you tell the device which IRQ to use? Check the documentation. The installation program might ask you for an IRQ during the setup process. Or, you have to set a jumper or dip switch according to the manufacturer's directions.

Optimizing CONFIG.SYS and AUTOEXEC.BAT

If you install a device using an installation program provided by the manufacturer, take a look at your CONFIG.SYS and AUTOEXEC.BAT files after completing the installation. Make sure that:

- The device driver is being loaded into high memory. If not, adapt the DEVICE command yourself or run MEMMAKER to optimize it.
- Any obsoleted device drivers have been removed.
- If you use multiple configurations, the device driver is loaded in all the appropriate configuration blocks.
- The PATH command reflects the best search order for your system. (Some setup programs insert their own directory at the beginning of the search path, quite rudely in my opinion.)
- Any obsoleted directories have been removed from the search path.

53

Upgrading to QBASIC

Introduction

If you program your PC in BASIC, DOS 5 introduced a new language environment called QBASIC with many more facilities than the earlier BASICA or GW-BASIC.

QBASIC Features and Facilities

For people who write applications, BASIC and the PC have always gone hand-in-hand. QBASIC is a more advanced language than many earlier forms of BASIC, including GW-BASIC and BASICA, which were supplied with earlier versions of DOS. With QBASIC, you can create structured programs that not only execute more efficiently but also are easier to code and debug.

QBASIC is an interpretive version of Microsoft QuickBASIC; unlike the full QuickBASIC, it has no compiler. But, any programs you create under QBASIC can be compiled under QuickBASIC. Also, QuickBASIC source code will run under QBASIC.

Many differences exist between the earlier supplied forms of BASIC and QBASIC. The major differences concern the user interface, data types, line numbers, and new statements that enable you to create control structures. This chapter is not designed to teach QBASIC programming. Instead, it is intended for BASIC programmers and discusses only the major differences between QBASIC also unstructured versions of BASIC. You will learn how to:

- Use the QBASIC editor
- Convert your old BASIC programs to QBASIC's storage format
- Use the following QBASIC features:

    Subscript ranges

    RECORD data type

    Block IF

    CASE structures

    DO loops

    Named constants

    Long integers

    Fixed-length string variables

    New string functions: UCASE$, LCASE$, LTRIM$, RTRIM$
- Create subprograms and functions by using the QBASIC editor
- Use global and local variables in subprograms and functions
- Test and debug a QBASIC program by using the QBASIC editor

This chapter does not teach BASIC programming. If you're not already a BASIC programmer, you should skip to the next chapter.

QBASIC's Interface

The QBASIC programming environment is provided by the same full-screen ASCII text editor accessed by DOS's EDIT command. But, EDIT starts up the editor in its document mode; whereas QBASIC normally opens the editor in its programming mode (see Figure 53.1), which is quite a bit different. You can start up QBASIC in document mode by adding the /EDITOR switch to the QBASIC command.

Figure 53.1.
QBASIC Editor screen.

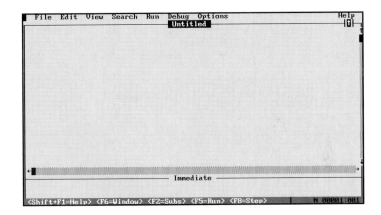

Start up the editor on your PC:

1. At the DOS command prompt, enter **QBASIC**.

   The editor starts up with the Welcome dialog box. Notice that it looks similar to, but not the same as, EDIT's opening window.

2. Press Esc to clear the Welcome dialog box.

The QBASIC Editor

The QBASIC menus assist you in creating, testing, and debugging QBASIC programs. The File menu lets you open and save files, as well as exit QBASIC. The Edit menu includes commands to cut and copy text, and create subprograms and functions. The View menu lets you view and edit any procedure of the current program, split the screen so you can see two parts of the same program, and switch immediately to the output screen. The Search menu commands will find and replace text strings. Run menu commands execute all or part of a program. The Debug menu offers several tools, such as tracing and stepping through a program. The Options menu includes commands to modify the display and set the status of Syntax Checking.

The screen includes two windows. The larger window is the standard program-editing area. Its title bar shows Untitled unless the currently loaded program has a name. The smaller window, called the Immediate window, holds one line at a time, which is executed as soon as you press Enter. You can use the Immediate window to test parts of your program as you work.

Try entering some BASIC statements in the Immediate window:

1. Click the Immediate window or press F6 to activate it.

    The cursor appears in the Immediate window.

> **Note:** Notice the reminder `<F6=Window>` on the status bar to remind you that pressing F6 switches windows.

2. Enter `C=5*25`.

    QBASIC calculates C, but you can't see the result yet.

3. Enter `PRINT C`.

    QBASIC switches to the output screen, which is the DOS command prompt screen, and displays 125. A note at the bottom says to press any key to continue.

4. Press a key to return to the QBASIC window.

    The two statements you entered still appear in the Immediate window; but, so far, there are no statements in the program, which is displayed in the Untitled window.

The status line shows the position of the cursor as well as some of the function keys that you can use. Once the window contains statements, pressing F1 gets context-sensitive help on the QBASIC word containing the cursor. Table 53.1 includes a complete list of the hotkeys available when the editor window is active. Different hotkeys are available when you aren't in edit mode.

Try getting help for the `PRINT` command:

1. In the Immediate window, position the cursor on the word `PRINT`.

2. Press F1.

    A Help window opens and displays the PRINT, LPRINT Statements topic. There are now three windows open on your screen.

3. Press F6 several times and watch the cursor move among the three windows.

4. Press Esc to close the Help window.

Table 53.1. Hotkeys in QBASIC Editor.

Key	Unshifted Key	Shift+Key	Ctrl+Key
F1	Help	Using Help	
F2	View SUBs	Next Procedure	Previous Procedure
F3	Repeat Find		
F4	Output Screen		
F5	Continue	Run Start	
F6	Next Window	Previous Window	
F7	Execute to cursor		
F8	Step		
F9	Breakpoint		
F10	Procedure Step		Zoom
Del	Clear	Cut	
Ins	Overtype/Insert	Paste	Copy

Smart Editor Effects

The editor begins to work on your program lines as soon as you type them. When you press Enter or move the cursor to another line, any QBASIC words are converted to uppercase and spaces are inserted around equal signs and operators. If Options Syntax Checking is turned on, you are informed immediately of any syntax errors. You can press F1 to view the correct format of the current statement. The editor automatically keeps the capitalization pattern of names consistent by converting all to the layout of the latest typed one. If a reference is made to a different procedure, the editor inserts the required DE-CLARE statement at the beginning of the program. If the main program includes a DEFtype statement, the editor includes it automatically at the beginning of other procedures.

Try entering a short program using the editor:

1. Switch to the Untitled window.

2. Using only lowercase letters, enter **input "enter the first multiplier> ", a**.

   As soon as you press Enter, QBASIC converts the word input to uppercase.

3. Using only lowercase letters, enter **input "enter the second multiplier> ", b**.

QBASIC converts the word input to uppercase.

4. In all capital letters, type C=A*B.

When you press Enter, QBASIC inserts spaces in the statement and changes the a and b in the first two statements to uppercase to match the third statement.

5. Type PRINT C.

You can copy or cut lines by selecting them and using the Edit menu or the hotkeys. Copied or cut lines are stored in the clipboard until another copy or cut replaces them; you can paste the clipboard contents as often as you need. You can even copy or move lines to another program or procedure, because the clipboard is unaffected by anything except another cut or copy, or exiting QBASIC.

Try copying lines in the program you are developing:

1. Select all four lines.

2. Choose Edit, Copy.

3. Position the cursor on the first blank line.

4. Choose Edit, Paste.

5. Edit the new lines to read as follows:

```
INPUT "Enter the third multiplier> ", D
INPUT "Enter the fourth multiplier> ", E
F = D * E
PRINT F
```

6. Press F5.

The output screen appears with the message Enter the first multiplier>.

7. Enter any number.

The message Enter the second multiplier> appears.

8. Enter any number.

QBASIC displays the product of the two numbers and displays the message Enter the third multiplier>.

9. Repeat steps 2 and 3 for the third and fourth multiplier.

After displaying the second product, QBASIC displays the message Press any key to continue.

10. Press any key to return to the QBASIC window.

Converting a GW-BASIC or BASICA Program

QBASIC stores programs in ASCII format; so, if your existing programs are stored in GW-BASIC's or BASICA's default binary format, you'll have to convert them. Start up the other BASIC editor, call up the program, and save it in ASCII format with the BAS extension. To save a GW-BASIC file as OLDPAY.BAS in ASCII form, for example, you would complete the following steps:

- Start up GW-BASIC.
- Load the file.
- Enter **SAVE "OLDPAY.BAS",A**.
- Type **SYSTEM** to exit GW-BASIC.

Now you can start up QBASIC, use the File, Open command to open the program, and run it from within the QBASIC editor.

Running Programs

The easiest way to run a loaded program under QBASIC is to press F5. Alternatively, you can choose Run Start. A program converted from a different form of BASIC should run with no problems unless it uses any of the few features not supported by QBASIC. (See Table 53.2.) If your program uses any of these features, you have to modify it to run under QBASIC. A message prompts you to press F1 for help if a syntax error occurs.

Table 53.2. QBASIC incompatibilities.

Statements not supported:
DEF USR
EXTERR(n)
LIST
LLIST
MERGE
MOTOR
USR

continues

Table 53.2. continued

Major features not supported:

```
CALL (offvar,var1...)
CHAIN (ALL, MERGE, DELETE, linenumber)
CLEAR (,n)
DRAW (var=;)
PLAY (var=;)
VARPTR (#filename)
```

Other possible problems:

QBASIC has additional reserved words

PEEK and POKE in Data Segment may have different effects

Line Numbers

In QBASIC, line numbers are not required, but they are permitted. If you use GOTO to transfer control, you can reference a line number if you like; just number the target line as in other BASICs. If you prefer, you can use a label, which is a QBASIC word followed by a colon. For example, the statement GOTO ERRORLINE transfers control to a line beginning with ERRORLINE: and continues from there. Any string of up to 40 letters and digits that is not a QBASIC reserved word, and is not used for another purpose in the program, can be used as a label. The trailing colon tells QBASIC that the string is a label.

New Constant and Variable Types

You have more choices for constants and variables in QBASIC than in GW-BASIC or BASICA. The names can have up to 40 characters, in any combination of uppercase and lowercase letters, digits, and the period. If the same string of characters is used, however, QBASIC assumes it is the same name even if the capitalization is different. The editor helps you be consistent by converting all strings of the same characters to the same capitalization format. If you use FIRSTNAME$, then later type Firstname$, all other occurrences of FIRSTNAME$ are converted to Firstname$.

As in the earlier forms of BASIC, you can use the DEFtype statement to specify names as string (DEFSTR), integer (DEFINT), single-precision (DEFSNG), or double-precision (DEFDBL) numbers. Any DEFtype statements you use in the main program are automatically copied to any procedures you create later. If you add a DEFtype statement to the main program after creating procedures, the procedures aren't updated, however. Data type suffixes on names override the DEFtype statements.

Constants

You can create named constants with a CONST statement, which looks much like an assignment statement:

```
CONST ConstantName=value
```

The `ConstantName` and the `value` must be of the same type. You can use CONST Logo$ = "IBM" or CONST TotalLines% = 400, for example. The value can't include a variable name or function, but it can include expressions and other constant names if necessary.

QBASIC won't let you change the value assigned to a constant. If you define CONST Rate=.0935, you cannot specify Rate=Rate+.01 later in the program. Of course, you can use literal constants of any type, just as in other forms of the BASIC language.

Numeric Variables

In addition to the standard numeric variable types, QBASIC provides the long integer, which can handle values between –2,147,483,648 and 2,147,483,647. (Standard integers must be between 32,768 and 32,767.) The long integer is stored in four bytes of memory, while the standard integer takes only two bytes. Even though the long integer takes as much space as a single-precision value, it is stored in two's complement form and allows for more efficient execution of the program.

You can use the DEFLNG statement to reserve initial letters for a long integer or use the type character & at the end of the name. Once declared by its appearance in a statement, a long integer is used just like other integers.

String Variables

String variables can be declared and used much as in earlier forms of BASIC. In QBASIC, you also can define fixed-length string variables using a form of the DIM statement:

```
*DIM StringName AS STRING * n
```

The following statement defines a 30-character variable named Fullname:

```
DIM Fullname AS STRING * 30
```

It overrides any DEFSTR statement; in addition, you cannot use the $ type character on the name. Fixed-length strings are useful in many file and database applications. If you want an array of fixed-length strings, include the array dimension following the StringName. The following statement defines an array of 50 string variables, each 30 characters long:

```
DIM Fullname(50) AS STRING * 30
```

When data is placed in a fixed-length string variable, it is left-justified and padded with blanks on the right. If a value is too long for the variable, it is truncated on the right with no warning.

Additional String Functions

QBASIC supports the standard string functions, as well as several new ones. The UCASE$ and LCASE$ functions change the string's letters to all uppercase or all lowercase. The following statement converts the value in Fullname (a string variable) to all uppercase and assigns it to the variable Fixname$ (a variable-length string):

```
Fixname$=UCASE$(Fullname)
```

In this case, the resulting value in Fixname$ is as long as the fixed-length string variable.

The LTRIM$ and RTRIM$ functions let you remove leading or trailing spaces and/or tabs from a string. The following statement removes any number of trailing spaces from the string Fullname and assigns the result to Fixname$:

```
Fixname$=RTRIM$(Fullname)
```

The resulting value in Fixname$ has no trailing spaces, so it may be shorter than the fixed-length string that provided the value.

Array Variables

Arrays can be defined and used just as they are in unstructured BASICs. Alternatively, you can specify the subscript range in a TO clause. The following statement sets up a 12-element array with the specified subscripts:

```
DIM MONTH(1 TO 12)
```

The following statement sets up a 61-element array with subscripts ranging from 1940 to 2000:

```
DIM YEAR(1940 TO 2000)
```

You can define arrays that contain several different data types in one element by using the user-defined or record data type, described in the following sections.

Record Data Type

QBASIC supports a user-defined data type called a record data type, which is defined with the TYPE block and creates a record. It can contain any combination of existing data types, so that the result can contain several values. The record data type is especially useful in defining an array that contains several data types in each element or in defining a record of mixed data for use in files:

```
TYPE usertype
    element1 AS typename1
    element2 AS typename2
    ...<CE>END TYPE
```

The usertype is a standard QBASIC name that is not used for any other purpose in the procedure. Each element is a data item within the record; each can be accessed individually by the program. The typename specifies the type (and hence the length) of the individual element; it can be INTEGER, LONG, SINGLE, DOUBLE, STRING * n, or another already defined usertype. For example, the following block defines user data type GPA to contain three different elements:

```
TYPE GPA
    StudentNumber AS STRING * 6
    StudentHours AS INTEGER
    StudentPoints AS SINGLE
END TYPE
```

The usertype defines a data type, not a variable name, so it can't be used directly in statements. It can be used only as a typename in its own definition, or as an element in another TYPE block. To use data in the defined format, declare a variable as that data type. For example, after defining the data type above, you could use the following statement to define Student as a 12-byte variable; six bytes for the string, two bytes for the integer, and four bytes for the single-precision value:

```
DIM Student AS GPA
```

To reference a part of the record, join the variable name with the element name, connecting them with a period as in the following example:

```
Student.StudentHours = Student.StudentHours + NewHours
```

Records in Arrays

A variable of a user-defined data type can be used in an array. The following statement sets up an array of 180 elements, each 12 bytes long:

```
DIM Student (180) AS GPA
```

Student(25).StudentNumber refers to the six-character string in the twenty-fifth occurrence of the array.

The following example defines data type Employee and uses it for the array variable Worker:

```
TYPE Employee
    EmpNumber AS STRING * 9
    EmpSalary AS SINGLE
    EmpDependents AS INTEGER
END TYPE
DIM Worker(240) AS Employee
```

The program refers to elements of the record by connecting them to the variable name with a period. For example, Worker(Next%).EmpSalary refers to the EmpSalary element of the array component indicated by the value of Next%.

Records in Files

Record data types can be used instead of FIELD variables in QBASIC programs, which lets you create and modify file data much more easily, without all the restrictions on FIELD variables. For compatibility, QBASIC supports the FIELD statement, of course.

New Flow of Control Facilities

In earlier forms of BASIC, a program had an essentially linear form with branching. The single-line IF statement handled decision making, and GOTO statements and line numbers let you create a morass of decision-based loops. The WHILE...WEND statement allowed some looping control. QBASIC provides more techniques and statements to handle flow of control in your program in a structured, efficient manner.

Expanded *IF* Statement

QBASIC can handle all the earlier formats of IF, including the one-line IF...THEN and IF...THEN...ELSE statements. It's often hard to read these IF statements, much less debug them. So QBASIC includes an expanded, multiline IF block that conforms to structured programming principles. Here's the format:

```
IF condition THEN
    statements to be executed if condition is true
[ELSE
    statements to be executed if condition is false]
END IF
```

The line beginning with IF starts the block; it must include the conditional expression and the word THEN. When the condition is true, statements on all lines down to ELSE are executed; if there is no ELSE statement, statements on all lines down to END IF are executed. When the conditional expression is false, statements on all lines between ELSE and END IF are executed; if there is no ELSE statement, control passes to the statement following END IF. The following example executes several commands if the condition is true:

```
IF TotalBill! >= CreditLimit! THEN
    PRINT OverLimitMessage$
    OverFlag$ = "Y"
    CALL warningflash
END IF
```

The following example executes only one set of statements, depending on the condition's value:

```
IF ApplicantAge% < 21 THEN
    PRINT MinorMessage$
    AgeProblem$ = "Y"
ELSE
    PRINT NoProblemMessage$
```

```
        AgeProblem$ = "N"
END IF
```

Another QBASIC option makes it easier to code complex nested IFs. You can include the ELSEIF element, which is evaluated only if the preceding IF statement is false, as follows:

```
IF condition THEN
     statements to be executed if condition is true
[ELSEIF condition-n THEN
     statements to be executed if condition-n is true]...
[ELSE
     statements to be executed if all conditions are false]
END IF
```

The following example uses ELSEIF to include a second condition and allow execution of one of three possible sets of statements:

```
IF ApplicantAge! < 21 THEN
     PRINT MinorMessage$
     AgeProblem$ = "Y"
ELSEIF ApplicantAge% > 65
     PRINT SeniorMessage$
     AgeProblem$ = "Y"
ELSE
     PRINT NoProblemMessage$
     AgeProblem$ = "N"
END IF
```

You can use as many ELSEIF elements as needed to fully create the desired branches.

Tip: You can optimize processing time by arranging the IF and ELSE conditions from the most likely to the least likely to occur.

Using a Case Structure

You may be familiar with using ON...GOTO or ON...GOSUB to handle multiple branching situations. While such situations can often be handled with a nested IF or ELSEIF, QBASIC provides a special statement block that is designed for just such situations. The SELECT CASE statement lets you name a variable, then execute specific blocks of statements based on its value; the entire block sets up a case structure. The simplest format is as follows:

```
SELECT CASE variable
     [CASE valuelist
          statements to execute if variable = any value in valuelist]...
     CASE ELSE
          statements to execute if variable <> any value in valuelist
END SELECT
```

When the SELECT CASE block is executed, the CASE variable has a single value. One CASE block or CASE ELSE block is processed, then control jumps to the END SELECT statement and continues from there. You can include as many values as you like (separated by commas) in each *valuelist*, and as many CASE blocks as you need. The CASE ELSE block specifies statements to be executed if the value of the CASE variable is not equal to any of the specified values in any of the CASE statements.

For example, suppose that you have a menu or multiple-choice question to display. The input value is a single character, supposed to be A through D. A different subprogram is executed for each situation. You could handle it in a CASE block as follows:

```
SELECT CASE MenuChoice$
    CASE "A", "a"
        CALL DoSubA
    CASE "B", "b"
        CALL DoSubB
    CASE "C", "c"
        CALL DoSubC
    CASE "D", "d"
        CALL DoSubD
    CASE ELSE
        CALL DoBadChoice
END SELECT
```

This example lets you enter uppercase or lowercase letters. If a character that is not in the desired range is typed, subprogram DoBadChoice asks you to try again. If you prefer, you can include a set of statements, as many as needed, following each CASE statement.

Actually, SELECT CASE doesn't limit you to a single variable and valuelist for each case. The complete format follows:

```
SELECT CASE variable
    [CASE expressionlist
      statements to execute if any expression is true]...
    CASE ELSE
      statements to execute if no expressions are true
END SELECT
```

The *expressionlist* lets you use more than a single value or list of values to determine which block is executed. To include a condition, assume the variable name and type the word **IS** followed by the rest of the relational operation. You might use CASE IS > 65 or CASE IS <= 20, for example. To specify a range, use the TO keyword, as in CASE 1 TO 5 or CASE "X" TO "Z". You can even combine expressions, as in CASE 0, 18 TO 20, IS > 65. Just make sure each individual value or expression is valid, and separate them with commas.

Loop Structures

In earlier forms of BASIC, loops are created with FOR...NEXT, with GOTO statements, and with WHILE...WEND statements. While these forms are still available for consistency, QBASIC's DO blocks allow easier structuring and clearer code than WHILE...WEND. A DO block begins with a DO statement and ends with a LOOP statement. All statements in between are executed during the loop. The block includes either a WHILE or an UNTIL element, added to either the DO or the LOOP statement. A DO

WHILE...LOOP block is equivalent to a WHILE...WEND block.

The WHILE or UNTIL element includes a conditional expression. The expression is tested at the beginning of the loop if it is included on the DO statement, and at the end if it is included on the LOOP statement. The loop is executed repeatedly as long as the condition is true when WHILE is used, or until the condition becomes true when UNTIL is used. Use the following DO format if you want the condition to be tested before the block is executed the first time:

```
DO [WHILE¦UNTIL] condition
    statements to be executed
LOOP
```

Use the following format if you want the block to be executed at least once, regardless of the truth of the condition:

```
DO
    statements to be executed
LOOP [WHILE¦UNTIL] condition
```

Contents of Loop

Any statements can be used within a DO...LOOP block. You can use IFs, FOR...NEXT, WHILE...WEND, nested DOs, even subprogram references. Nested DO loops can be of any type; inner loops don't have to match the outer loop's structure. The only rule is that an inner loop of any kind (even FOR...NEXT) must end before its outer loop does.

If you must terminate a loop before the condition causes it to end, use an EXIT DO statement. When EXIT DO is executed, control passes immediately to the statement following the LOOP statement that marks the end of the current DO block.

Modular Programming

Earlier versions of BASIC are essentially linear; statements are executed in sequence unless a branch directs execution to another location in the program.

QBASIC enables you to work with modules. Execution of a program always starts and ends in the main module. The program can include as many procedure modules as you need, either subprograms or functions. Each procedure is a separate, named entity called by the main module.

When a subprogram is created, you give it a name. Using that name as a statement, or including it in a CALL statement, starts its execution. After the statements in the subprogram are executed, control returns to the statement following the one that called it, much like a GOSUB procedure.

A user-defined function is also given a name. You then use it just like you use the built-in functions. Defining a QBASIC function has much the same effect as the DEF FN statement, but it allows more than one program line.

Note: For compatibility with other versions, GOSUB and DEF FN both work in QBASIC. You can reference a label in a GOSUB statement instead of a line number.

A subprogram or function is a separate procedure, so variables in the main module (or any other procedure) have no effect in other procedures unless you make them global (COMMON SHARED). You can pass specific values to either a subprogram or a function in an argument list. (Global variables and passing values are covered later in this chapter.)

Examining a Modular Program

A modular program has a main module, along with several functions and subprograms. When you open the program file, you can examine the main module in the editing window. If you press F2 or choose View SUBs, you can select another procedure to view and edit in the window. You can use Shift+F2 to see the next procedure directly, or Ctrl+F2 to see the previous one without going through the SUBs dialog box again.

Creating a Procedure

To create a subprogram or function, choose Edit New SUB or Edit New Function. If the cursor rests on text, you'll see the current word in the dialog box like the one in Figure 53.2. You can accept that as the procedure name or type in a name and choose OK. The resulting window is an editing window for the procedure. QBASIC puts in the first line (SUB or FUNCTION) with the name you provided, followed by an empty set of parentheses and the last line (END SUB or END FUNCTION). You can add whatever you need between these two lines. If you used any DEFtype statements in the main program, they are copied to the beginning of each procedure when you start creating it.

Figure 53.2.
New Procedure Specification dialog box.

Tip: Type SUB *ProcedureName* in a program and press Enter. You'll get to the editing window for the new procedure immediately.

After a procedure has a name and has been saved, you can view or edit it by choosing View SUBs or by pressing F2. The resulting dialog box, like the one shown in Figure 53.3, lets you choose from all the procedures for the current program. You can even delete them if necessary. When the program is saved, a DECLARE statement for each new procedure is generated and added to the beginning of the main module.

Figure 53.3.
View SUBs dialog box.

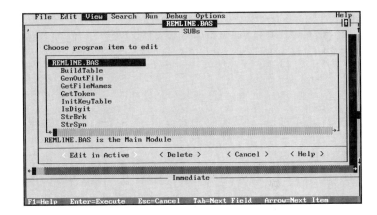

Global Variables

By default, all variables used in a procedure are local variables; they apply only to the procedure in which they appear. A variable named TaxRate in the main program has no effect on a variable named TaxRate in a subprogram or function unless you make special arrangements. You can tell QBASIC up front to make certain variables available to all procedures; these are called global variables.

Global variables must be declared in the main program in a COMMON SHARED statement, with the following format:

```
COMMON SHARED VariableList
```

You can include as many variables as needed, separating them with commas. Multiple COMMON SHARED statements may be used.

> **Tip:** Use one COMMON SHARED statement for all variables used together for easier program maintenance.

Suppose that your main program includes the following statement:

```
COMMON SHARED PrimeRate!, CreditLimit!
```

If the value of PrimeRate! is set in one procedure, it is the same in every procedure used by the program. If the variable were local, the value would apply only in the procedure in which it was set.

Subprograms

A subprogram is a block of code between SUB and END SUB statements. When you choose Edit, New SUB, these lines are included automatically. If you type a SUB statement as part of the main module, the smart editor assumes you want to create a new subprogram and puts you in a new editor window to create it; the effect is the same as choosing Edit, New SUB. Once defined, subprograms can be called by the main module or by other subprograms. When execution reaches the END SUB statement, it returns to the statement following the one that started the subprogram.

The general format for a subprogram is as follows:

```
SUB subprogramname [(parameters)]
    [local variable or constant declarations]
    statements to be executed
END SUB
```

Subprograms can be used to handle many complex operations. You might use a subprogram to print headers on each page of a printed report. Another subprogram might print footers.

The following is an example of a subprogram that plays "Happy Birthday":

```
SUB birthday
' Play a tune
PLAY "L4 C8C8DCFE2 C8C8DCGF2"
PLAY "C8C8>C<AFED2 B-8B-8AFGF2"
END SUB
```

A subprogram is invoked by naming it in a CALL statement or by using its name as a statement in the main program or another procedure. If the subprogram has no parameters, you can use CALL or omit it. The preceding subprogram could be run by either of the following statements:

```
CALL birthday
birthday
```

Each time a subprogram is invoked, any local variables in it are reset to their default values. Any global variables maintain their current values. If you want the subprogram to hold its local values between executions, add the word STATIC to the first line. The following statement causes local variables in taxwithholding to keep their values when the subprogram ends, and use them again the next time it is executed:

```
SUB taxwithholding STATIC
```

A subroutine should use static variables when it accumulates a value as the program progresses. For example, you might use a static subroutine to print the footer and page number at the bottom of each page of a report. Each time the routine is executed, the page number is increased by 1.

The main program finds out about subprograms through DECLARE statements, which must precede any executable statements in the program. When you create a subprogram, QBASIC generates an initial DECLARE statement for the program using information currently available in the SUB statement:

```
DECLARE SUB subprogramname (parameters)
```

If there are no parameters, an empty set of parentheses is used. If you change the content of the parameter list later, be sure to change it in the DECLARE statement as well.

Passing Values

Sometimes, a subprogram has to use specific values passed from the calling program. If you use the CALL statement, the values to be passed must be enclosed in a single set of parentheses. If you omit the word CALL, you also omit the parentheses around the value list.

You can pass constants in the form of named constants, quoted strings, numeric values, or expressions. You can also pass local variables or expressions by including them as arguments. Every passed local variable can be changed in the subprogram, and the changed value will be available back in the calling procedure. If you want to prevent a passed variable from being changed, create an expression by enclosing it in an individual set of parentheses in the calling statement.

In the following example, changes to Taxrate do not affect the calling program when control returns:

```
CALL taxwithholding (Gross, Dependents, (Taxrate))
```

Any changes to variables used only in passed expressions are not carried back to the calling procedure.

The arguments are received by the subprogram into a parameter list; every parameter is represented by a variable name. Arguments are passed to parameters by position, not by name. That is, the first argument is passed to the first parameter, the second argument to the second parameter, and so on. Because of the positional relationship, any that are skipped must be represented by a comma. The matched items must be of the same data type. That is, a string argument must be paired with a string parameter, an integer argument must be paired with an integer parameter, and so forth. The following are some examples of valid sets.

Calling statement:

```
MakeMailingLabel Name$, Address1$, City$, State$, Zip$
```

Subprogram:

```
SUB MakeMailingLabel (Line1$, Line2$, City$, State$, Zip$)
```

Calling statement:

```
CALL FigureTax (Total#, TaxRate!, TypeTax$)
```

Subprogram:

```
SUB FigureTax (BaseAmount#, CurrentRate!, TaxType$)
```

FigureTax can refer to `BaseAmount#`, `CurrentRate!`, and `TaxType$`; but not to `Total#`, `TaxRate!`, or `TypeTax$`. However, when control returns to the main module, `Total#`, `TaxRate!`, and `TypeTax$` contain the values the corresponding variables held when control exits the FigureTax subprogram.

Try creating a subprogram named DOUBLER:

1. On the next blank line in your program, enter the statement **SUB DOUBLER**.

   As soon as you press Enter, QBASIC opens a window for the subprogram. The first and last lines are filled in for you.

2. Edit the subprogram to read as follows:

```
SUB DOUBLER (INVAR, OUTVAR)
OUTVAR = INVAR *2
END SUB
```

3. Press F2.

   QBASIC displays a list of the main program (which is still called Untitled) and all the subprograms.

4. Choose Untitled.

   The main program returns.

5. Enter the following two lines at the end of the main program:

```
CALL DOUBLER (F,G)
PRINT G
```

6. Press F5 to test your program. Enter variables as requested.

   After QBASIC displays the second product, it doubles that product and displays the result.

7. Press a key to return to the QBASIC editor.

Functions

Functions calculate and return a single value, much like the DEF FN statement of GW-BASIC and BASICA. The difference is that a function name need not begin with FN and the FUNCTION procedure can use as many statements as it needs.

Like the subprogram, each function must be defined by a DECLARE statement. When you begin a new function through QBASIC, the appropriate DECLARE statement is generated and positioned in the main program automatically. You have to keep the parameter list up-to-date yourself if you change it later.

Creating a Function

To create a function, choose Edit, New FUNCTION or type a FUNCTION statement and press Enter. After QBASIC has a name for the function, you are placed in an editor window for defining the function.

The format of a function is as follows:

```
FUNCTION functionname [(parameters)]
    [local variable or constant declarations]
    statements to be executed
    functionname = expression
END FUNCTION
```

The following is an example of a function that calculates a random integer between 1 and the value of the integer argument:

```
FUNCTION RANDINT%(N%)
    RANDOMIZE TIMER
    RANDINT% = INT(RND*N%)+1
END FUNCTION
```

This function could be invoked by a statement such as the following:

```
CurrentValue = RANDINT%(GUESS%)
```

Debugging Innovations

QBASIC offers several features that help in debugging files. When a program terminates with an error, you see the critical program line highlighted in the editor document window. You can see the line in context; it may even give you information you need to fix the problem. More likely, you will have to do more in the way of debugging.

The Immediate Window

The Immediate editor window not only lets you check statements during program entry, it also permits variable checking when a program ends with an error. You can enter PRINT statements in the Immediate window to find the current values of crucial variables.

Tracing a Program

The Debug menu includes three commands that control tracing. Trace On is a toggle that turns it on or off; a dot next to the command indicates trace is on. When tracing is in effect, the program runs in slow motion; the statement being executed is highlighted. By watching the screen, you can see if the statements are processed in the order you expect. You can use Ctrl+Break to interrupt the trace and pause the program. The Immediate window is available to check values, and you can press F4 to see any screen output. Pressing F5 resumes the trace.

Debug, Step sets up a process whereby execution pauses after each statement is executed. Choosing Debug, Step or pressing F8 executes the next statement. If the statement produces screen output, you can press F4 to see the result on the output screen; any key returns you to the program window. At any time, you can use Run, Start to start over.

Try stepping through the program you have written:

1. Choose Debug, Step.

   QBASIC highlights the first statement in the program.

2. Press F8 to execute the statement.

   QBASIC displays the message `Enter the first multiplier>`.

3. Enter a number.

   QBASIC highlights the second statement.

4. Continue pressing F8 and entering multipliers until the program is completed.

5. Press a key to return to the editor.

The Debug Procedure Step command (F10) is similar, but it executes each function or subprogram as a single instruction. This will speed the stepping process when all your functions and subprograms have already been debugged.

Breakpoints

A breakpoint is a spot where you want execution to pause. You can insert breakpoints in a program at points where you want to check the program's progress. For example, you might insert a special PRINT command, then flag it as a breakpoint. When you run the program, the output will be generated and the program will pause.

To set a breakpoint, position the cursor in the line, then press F9 or choose Debug Toggle Breakpoint. The line will appear in red or inverse video, depending on your monitor. You can set as many breakpoints as you wish. To remove a breakpoint, place the cursor on the line again, and press F9 or choose Debug Toggle Breakpoint. To clear all breakpoints when debugging is complete, choose Debug Clear All Breakpoints.

Running QBASIC Programs Directly from the DOS Prompt

You can run a QBASIC program directly from the DOS Prompt without opening the editor by including /RUN *filename* in the QBASIC command. Try running the program you created in this chapter from the command prompt:

1. Choose File, Save to save the program. Name it PRACTICE.BAS.

2. Exit QBASIC.

3. At the DOS command prompt, enter **QBASIC /RUN PRACTICE.BAS**.

   The program should run.

> **Tip:** You can redirect the output of the QBASIC /RUN *filename* command, as in QBASIC /RUN
> PRACTICE.BAS > PRN.

Including such a command in a batch program executes the QBASIC program from within the batch program; you return to the batch program when the QBASIC program ends. You could chain a series of QBASIC programs by referencing them from a batch program. Use the DOS environment to pass variables between the batch program and the QBASIC program and between the chained QBASIC programs. The ENVIRON function sets an environment variable, as in ENVIRON ALTDIR$=C:\ALTERED$. The ENVIRON$ function returns an environment variable, as in OPEN ENVIRON$(ALTDIR$)\NAMELIST.TXT$ AS 1.

On Your Own

This chapter has shown you how QBASIC differs from earlier forms of BASIC that were included in the DOS package. If you would like to try out some of these new QBASIC features on your own, use the following items as a guide:

1. Modify the program you wrote in this chapter to accept numbers between 2 and 30 only.

2. Modify the program to create a subprogram that keeps a running total of the values of the doubled products (as produced by the DOUBLER subprogram). Display the running total after displaying the doubled product.

3. Convert some of your old BASIC programs to QBASIC's storage format.

54

FDISK

Introduction

Every hard disk must be partitioned after physical formatting and before logical formatting. It must be partitioned even if it will have only one partition. FDISK is DOS's partitioning program.

Partitioning Your Hard Drive with FDISK

Before DOS 4, hard disk drives were limited to 32MB, so it was common to partition a large hard disk into several logical drives. Nowadays, most DOS users don't bother. Nevertheless, FDISK still has the facility to create multiple partitions and multiple logical drives per partition. FDISK also lets you view partition information for your hard drives.

FDISK can be used to set up a non-DOS partition. For example, suppose you want to be able to use UNIX as well as DOS. After physically formatting the hard disk, you can use FDISK to create a DOS partition and a non-DOS partition; then you install UNIX in the non-DOS partition. When you boot from the DOS partition, DOS is installed. When you boot from the UNIX partition, UNIX is installed.

This chapter shows you how to use FDISK. You will learn how to:

- Create a primary DOS partition
- Create a secondary DOS partition
- Establish logical drives on partitions
- Identify the active (boot) partition
- Delete a partition
- View partition information

Warning: Do not attempt to change your hard disk's partition structure if the disk contains data. You could lose the ability to access your data. After you have formatted and started using your disk, use FDISK only to view partition information. If you really must repartition your hard drive, back up all the data, repartition it, and then restore.

Starting FDISK

To start FDISK, enter the command FDISK with no parameters. If your only hard disk has not yet been partitioned, you must do this from a floppy disk that contains the FDISK.EXE program. Figure 54.1 shows the first FDISK screen that appears, which acts as a main menu for the four FDISK functions.

Figure 54.1.
FDISK Options screen.

```
                        MS-DOS Version 6
                     Fixed Disk Setup Program
                (C)Copyright Microsoft Corp. 1983 - 1993

                          FDISK Options

    Current fixed disk drive: 1

    Choose one of the following:

    1. Create DOS partition or Logical DOS Drive
    2. Set active partition
    3. Delete partition or Logical DOS Drive
    4. Display partition information


    Enter choice: [1]




    Press Esc to exit FDISK
```

Note: If your system has two or more hard disks, a fifth option lets you select the disk you want to work with.

Creating a DOS Partition

Choose option 1 to create a partition on the hard disk. The next screen lets you choose to create a *primary* DOS partition or an *extended* partition. (See Figure 54.2.) There can only be one of each per hard disk. The primary DOS partition can contain only one logical drive, which will be your drive C. The extended partition can have multiple logical drives. You must create the primary DOS partition before you create an extended one. And, you must create the extended partition before you can create logical drives on it.

Figure 54.2.
Create DOS Partition or Logical DOS Drive screen.

```
              Create DOS Partition or Logical DOS Drive
    Current fixed disk drive: 1

    Choose one of the following:

    1. Create Primary DOS Partition
    2. Create Extended DOS Partition
    3. Create Logical DOS Drive(s) in the Extended DOS Partition


    Enter choice: [1]



    Press Esc to return to FDISK Options
```

Creating the Primary Partition

When you choose to create the primary DOS partition, FDISK asks if you want to include the entire hard disk in the partition and make it the boot drive. If you enter Yes, you're done partitioning the hard disk. Drive C is established and you can exit FDISK and format it.

Tip: If you use a tape backup system, your life will be easier if you limit the size of your partitions to the maximum size of a backup tape. For example, if your maximum tape size is 250MB, make your partitions 250MB also. If you plan to compress the drive or compress the backup data on the tape, you should adjust the sizes accordingly. For example, if you plan to compress the backup data but not the hard drive, and you think the data will achieve a 2 to 1 compression ratio, then you could make the partition 500MB.

Note: You can create a primary partition only if the hard drive does not already have one.

If you want to set up more than one logical drive on your hard disk, or if you want to set aside some space for a non-DOS partition, you must enter No to the quick-and-easy setup. Then, FDISK lets you specify how much space you want to include in the primary partition. Because this partition can have only one logical drive, FDISK creates the drive automatically when you create the partition.

Note: If you reserved space on the hard disk for another operating system such as UNIX, you must now set up that partition using the other operating system.

When you're done with FDISK, you have to format the primary partition using FORMAT (or a third-party alternative such as the Norton Utilities' Safe Format) with the /s switch so that you'll be able to boot from this partition.

Creating the Extended Partition

If you reserved space for an extended partition, choose option 1 on the main menu again. This time, choose to create the extended partition. Again, FDISK will offer to use the rest of the space for the extended partition. You can have only one extended partition, so enter Yes unless you want to re-serve space for a non-DOS operating system.

After creating the extended partition, you establish one or more logical drives on it. You must designate how much space to allot to each logical drive. Each logical drive receives a drive name (D, E, and so on). When you're done with FDISK, you must format each logical drive separately with the FORMAT command (or a third-party alternative). There's no need to use the /S switch when formatting logical drives in the extended partition.

Setting the Active Partition

If you created a non-DOS partition for an alternative operating system, you need to designate which partition to boot from. On FDISK's main menu, choose the second option, Set Active Partition. FDISK displays the partitions that are eligible as boot drives and lets you choose the one you want to boot from.

Suppose you set up the DOS partition as the active partition. How can you access the operating system in the other partition? As far as DOS is concerned, that partition doesn't exist. It cannot access any part of it. When you want to boot the other operating system, start FDISK, choose Set Active Partition, and select the non-DOS partition. When you reboot, the other operating system takes over and your DOS partition will be inaccessible.

To return to DOS, you must use the other operating system's partitioning program to set the active partition back to the DOS partition.

Deleting a Partition

If you want to rework the partitioning of your hard disk, you must delete the current partitions to make room for new ones. Deleting a partition does not delete the data in it; FDISK simply deletes the entry from the partition table. If you create exactly the same partition again, you'll be able to access the old data (as long as you don't format the restored partition).

However, if you create a new partition that uses some or all of the old partition's space but doesn't exactly coincide with the old partition, you'll lose access to the old partition's data when you format the new partition. Data stored in the new partition will wipe out the old partition's data in the tracks.

On FDISK's main menu, choose the third option, Delete Partition or Logical Disk Drive, to delete a partition. (See Figure 54.3.) You must delete all the logical drives on the extended partition before you can delete the partition itself. If you delete the primary partition, you also delete the DOS boot drive, and you won't be able to boot DOS from the hard disk anymore. You could still boot from the non-DOS partition if it is set up as the active partition.

Figure 54.3.
*Delete DOS Partition or
Logical DOS Drive screen.*

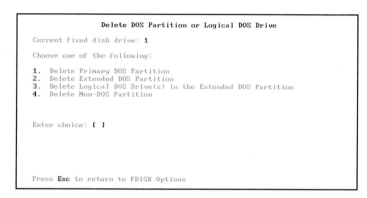

Notice that you can delete a non-DOS partition from this menu. If you want to eliminate a partition belonging to another operating system, you can do it with FDISK. You can add that space to one of your DOS partitions, but you'll have to delete the partition and create a new, larger one, which will make you lose contact with all the data currently in that partition.

Viewing Partition Information

To see how your partitions are laid out, choose the fourth option on FDISK's main menu, Display Partition Information. In the example in Figure 54.4, the hard disk contains a primary partition and an extended partition. The primary partition is drive C. The drives on the extended partition aren't shown on this screen.

Figure 54.4.
*Display Partition
Information screen.*

```
                    Display Partition Information

      Current fixed disk drive: 1

      Partition  Status   Type    Volume Label  Mbytes   System   Usage
      C: 1         A     PRI DOS                   50     FAT16     45%
         2               EXT DOS                   62               55%


      Total disk space is   112 Mbytes (1 Mbyte = 1048576 bytes)

      The Extended DOS Partition contains Logical DOS Drives.
      Do you want to display the logical drive information (Y/N)......?[Y]



      Press Esc to return to FDISK Options
```

The status column shows which partition is active. In this case, drive C is the boot drive. The Usage column shows the percentage of the drive that contains data. The System column shows how the drive is formatted. FAT16 means that the drive was formatted by DOS and its FAT entries are 16 bits long. Smaller drives formatted by DOS show up as FAT12 because they have smaller FAT entries; because they have fewer clusters, the maximum value in a FAT entry fits in 12 bits. Drives larger than 32MB and drives partitioned and/or formatted by third-party systems might show other values in the System column.

If the disk has an extended partition, FDISK asks if you want to see its logical drive information. If you answer Y, a screen similar to Figure 54.5 appears. You can see the size, system, and usage information for each logical drive in the extended partition.

Figure 54.5.
Display Logical DOS Drive Information screen.

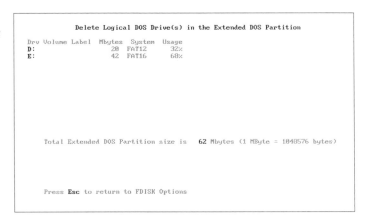

Try viewing the partition information for your hard disk:

1. Enter **FDISK** to start FDISK.

   The FDISK Options menu appears

2. Choose 4, Display partition information.

   Your partition information is displayed. You should be able to tell how many partitions you have, and which one is active.

3. Press Esc to return to the Options menu.

4. Press Esc again to exit FDISK.

Exiting FDISK

Whenever you change the partition table, you need to reboot when you exit FDISK so that the new partition table takes effect. After rebooting, you have to format any new drives.

On Your Own

This chapter has shown you how to use FDISK to view and manage the partitions on your hard disks. I wouldn't suggest practicing these techniques until your hard disk actually needs partitioning.

55

Riding the Internet with DOS

Introduction

People all over the world are talking to each other and sharing information via their PCs, not through a unified online service, but through an unplanned (and often disorganized) linkage of computers known as Internet.

What Is Internet?

It's almost easier to describe what it isn't than what it is: it isn't a planned service, organized and supervised by an administering group. No one created Internet, it just happened. And nobody runs it except its users. It started from two major sources: universities and government agencies, both of which have enormous needs to share information. With the advent of modems and telecommunications, college professors, students, and government employees began dialing in to each others' large computers, uploading and downloading data. Then the people doing the calling began sending messages to each other—and Internet was born.

Nowadays, Internet provides a worldwide network of computers of all shapes and sizes that anyone can access. It's not just university and government computers now; you'll find news services, *bulletin board systems* (BBSs) from all over the world, shopping services, companies, libraries, and more. The latest estimates are that more than 3 million computers are accessible via Internet. When you sign on to the *Net* (also known as *Cyberspace*) from your den, within the time an hour or so (presuming you know how to travel around the network smoothly) you can:

- Download a report on genetic engineering from a university in Glasgow
- Read the front page of the *New York Times*
- Read and answer letters from friends all over the world
- Wish your cousin in Hanover a happy birthday
- Check the latest stock market quotes
- Make travel reservations
- Buy a new printer
- Download the latest shareware personal information manager
- Participate in a live conference on Little League management
- Upload a completed report to your client 3,000 miles away
- Upload a letter to the President with copies to your senators and representative

And—as they say—much, much more!

Internet Resources

Because Internet grows and changes daily, there's no way to catalog a complete list of resources. We can, however, describe five major types of features: databases, newsgroups, e-mail, chatting, and other services.

Note: There are several guides to Internet resources available, both online and in your bookstore or library.

Databases

Do you need to see a copy of the Constitution at 3 a.m., or find out what government grants are available for inventing a better mousetrap? Perhaps you'd like to know who won the World Series in 1927, or how to treat chicken pox. All that information is available in Internet databases.

No one knows how many databases are available on the Internet, but they number in the thousands. To help people locate the information they seek in some kind of reasonable fashion, several database search facilities are available: Gopher, WAIS, and Archie are the most widely available. Some search facilities, such as Gopher, give you access to databases via a series of menus and submenus. Others, such as WAIS (wide area information server, pronounced "ways"), let you do a keyword search. For example, you might search for "chicken pox" or "mousetrap." Some facilities, such as Archie, let you search without waiting online for the results, which are returned to you via e-mail.

Newsgroups

For many users, newsgroups are what Internet is about. A newsgroup is a group of people who want to share information on a particular topic such as needlework, their favorite hockey team, organic gardening, poetry, using Lotus 1-2-3, or genealogy. Newsgroup members post messages on a bulletin board that all other group members can read and answer. When you sign on to Internet, you usually check your newsgroups to see if any new messages have been posted.

Some newsgroups are moderated; the moderator screens messages for appropriateness to the group's stated subject, as well as for unacceptable language. Many newsgroups are not moderated and, as they say, anything goes. But, inappropriate behavior in an unmoderated group often results in the perpetrator getting "flamed" (told off, and usually in no uncertain terms) by other members of the group.

E-mail

It's almost ironic—people whose mothers begged them in vain to write to Aunt Dorothy now write dozens of letters a week to friends, coworkers, family, and often perfect strangers. E-mail (electronic mail) letters travel through Internet so fast that correspondents can often exchange two or three messages a day, if they wish. The old-fashioned kind of mail, delivered by the post office, has become known as "snail mail" by contrast.

When people send you e-mail, a mail server somewhere stores the mail until you sign on. As part of your welcome messages, you receive a notice that you have e-mail waiting. You can download the e-mail or read it online, depending on how much time you're willing to spend online. After you have downloaded or read your mail, you can delete it from the server. To send your own e-mail, you can compose it offline and sign on to send it, or you can compose it online and send each letter as you finish it.

Mailing Lists

A mailing list is something like a newsgroup, except that the members communicate by e-mail instead of posting messages on a bulletin board. Mailing lists generally concentrate on a specified topic such as railroad travel, much as newsgroups do. Rather than addressing all the members of the group individually, you send your mail to the group address and the server distributes it to all the members of the group.

Belonging to a mailing list can generate more e-mail than you ever wanted to receive. Each time you sign on, you might find dozens of letters waiting for you. Unlike personal e-mail, of course, there's no need to answer every letter, but even reading them can be a chore.

Chatting

Chatting represents the most immediate form of Internet contact in which two or more people who are simultaneously online hold a live, and often lively, discussion by typing messages back and forth on their keyboards. At any time of the day or night, you can find people all over the world to chat with. Internet offers a number of commands to find out who is online right now, to find out if a specific person is online, and to set up a two-person chat or a conference among a group of people, which can be open to the public or private. But, most people access chat areas through their online service, as explained shortly.

One popular type of chat conference is a game room, in which participants play trivia, Dungeons and Dragons, or some other online game. Fantasy chat conferences, in which participants travel back to Merry Olde England or forward to the Starship Enterprise, are also popular. Some chat groups meet on a regular basis, much as a club or professional society does.

Chatting can be fascinating; some people get addicted to it. More than one devoted Internet user has gone broke, quite literally, by spending several hours a day online with new friends around the world, while the phone bill and online service bill grow to astronomical proportions.

Other Services

Newsgroups, e-mail, chatting, mailing lists, and databases only begin to describe the resources available to you on Internet. Many companies and agencies provide a wide variety of specialized services, from travel reservations to stock market quotes, from shopping services to product technical support, from the Commerce Business Daily (the U.S. Government's daily listing of requests for proposals from contractors) to United Press International. You can access many of your favorite magazines online; check your credit rating; download an amazing variety of photos, sound clips, video clips, and software; check the latest movie reviews; and even earn your college degree. There is almost no limit to the kinds of services you can find on Internet right now, and there will be even more tomorrow.

Accessing Internet

Internet is available to anyone who has access to a computer and a modem. But you also need telecommunications software to run the modem, and you need some kind of gateway into Internet. For home users, the gateway often takes the form of a BBS or some other kind of online service; but, if you have access to your company's or university's computer, you probably don't need an outside service.

A Word about Modems

Any modem will do; but the faster, the better. Data transfer rates are measured in *bauds*, with a baud representing approximately one bit per second. Five years ago, modems typically operated in the range of 300 to 1,200 baud, and that was too slow to make Internet feasible to most home users. Today, speeds from 2,400 to 9,600 baud are common. Modems in the stores right now are usually capable of 14,400 baud, with 28,800-baud modems just beginning to make their appearance.

Whenever you connect with another modem, the baud rate that you use depends on the top speed of both modems. If your modem is capable of 14,400 baud, but the other modem's top speed is only 9,600 baud, then your modem must operate at 9,600 baud also. (All modems can operate at slower speeds than their maximum.) Many online services have not yet upgraded their modems to the highest speeds available today; in fact, you might find yourself limited to 2,400 baud by your service.

Does the baud rate make that much difference? Yes, it does. A file that takes only five minutes to download at 9,600 baud takes 20 minutes at 2,400 baud. When you're paying an hourly rate for your online service, plus telephone charges that could include toll rates, that extra time can really add up to a lot of money.

If you're paying for your own Internet access, I recommend buying the fastest modem you can afford. You might not be able to use its top speed with your service right now, but your modem is going to last you several years and your service will probably continue to upgrade its facilities during that time.

Telecommunications Software

Your telecommunications software controls your modem and provides the interface you need to dial phone numbers and communicate with another computer. If you're accessing Internet through your work or school, you don't have to worry about the telecommunications package; you'll use whatever is installed on the system you're using. But, if you're working at home, or even if you're dialing into the computer at work or at school, you need a telecommunications program on your home computer.

A communications program probably came with your modem, but it might not be the right choice for accessing Internet. Many of the programs that are supplied with fax/modems are more oriented toward faxing than online communications, and many are "lite" packages—they have a reduced feature set.

> **Note:** Some of the national online services, such as America Online and CompuServe, provide their own telecommunications software to subscribers. Their programs are especially well designed to aid nontechnical users in easy access to their services.

When looking for the right communications package, consider these points:

- Does it run under DOS or Windows? (And which do you prefer? Many of the DOS interfaces are not mouse-enabled and you must use commands to get your work done.)

- How easy is it to install and set up for your modem? Telecommunications software can be terribly difficult to set up. I have known programs that would take a telecommunications specialist several hours to install. Other programs do all the work for you, seeking your modem and sensing its characteristics automatically; a complete amateur can install them in just a few minutes. If you're smart, you'll talk to your friends about their software before choosing a program for yourself.

- What protocols does it support? A protocol determines how two computers upload and download files. Common protocols are Kermit, XModem, YModem, and ZModem. The fastest of these is ZModem, and you'll want to use it if it's available.

- If you'll be chatting on Internet, does it include chat features such as a split screen and backwards scrolling? Split screen lets you type your next message on one part of the screen while messages from others are scrolling onto another part. Without a split screen, your typing intermingles with the arriving messages and can be nearly impossible to read. Backwards scrolling lets you reread earlier messages (including your own).

- Does it let you compose e-mail offline? Composing e-mail online can run your bill up very quickly.

Other features that can come in handy include:

- A personal address book so that you can select addresses for your e-mail instead of typing them out. Internet addresses are notoriously unfriendly—some examples are coralcee@lamar.colo.edu and 30900512.3899210@dca.com—and an address book can save you both time and errors.

- A script or macro feature, which memorizes keystrokes that you repeat often (such as your sign-on routine) so that you don't have to type them every time.

- An automated e-mail handling routine that signs on to Internet, uploads any e-mail that you have written, downloads any e-mail that is waiting for you, and signs off again as quickly as possible.

- Will it sign off automatically after completing an upload or download? Because uploads and downloads can take many boring minutes, if you can set up your software to sign off automatically at the end of a file transfer, you can wander away from the computer and do something else while it's working.

The Gateway to Internet

Your telecommunications software gives you the ability to dial in to a telephone number, but the software at the other end of the line must provide the gateway to Internet. It is that software that determines what Internet resources are available to you.

Some gateways provide full Internet access; you can reach any Internet resource that you know how to find. Others provide limited access. They might offer a limited set of newsgroups, a limited set of mailing lists, Gopher and WAIS database searches but not Archie, local chatting (with other users of the same gateway) but not IRC (Internet chatting), and limited access to other services. For many people, the restricted access provides more than enough features, and it is often much easier to use.

If you're accessing Internet through a computer at school or work, the gateway is already in place and you don't have to worry about it. You might find that you need to learn some UNIX commands, though, as many such gateways are based on UNIX, not DOS.

If you're accessing Internet on your own, you must subscribe to a BBS or online service that gives you Internet access. You should be able to find many local BBSs that provide at least some Internet access. In addition, national online services such as CompuServe, America Online, and Delphi offer partial or full Internet access.

> **Note:** Many BBSs provide resources much like Internet's without actually accessing Internet itself. Most provide e-mail and newsgroups, many provide mailing lists, and some provide chat facilities and other services. In some cases, they are linked into a network of other BBSs, perhaps even a worldwide network, so that you can reach hundreds of thousands of people without entering Internet. You may find that a local BBS provides all the resources you need. However, only Internet provides services on the massive scale described in this chapter.

In selecting a gateway, consider these factors:

- Does it have a local phone number? You don't want to have to pay long-distance rates for your online time, especially if you plan to chat.

- What does it cost? Theoretically, Internet is free. But, you have to pay for the online service. In most cases, you pay a monthly rate that gives you a set number of online hours, such as $10 per month for 10 hours, and you pay an hourly rate for any hours over the monthly minimum.

- Are there any surcharges? Some online services charge extra for prime-time (daytime) access and certain services.

- Do you have to dial into a telephone network such as Sprint or Tymnet, and is there a separate charge for that service. In many areas, the answer to both of these questions is yes, although there is usually no charge for network access outside of prime time.

- Does it offer the Internet resources that you want?

- If it includes chatting, does it provide access to Internet chatting or local chatting only? You might prefer to chat only with the people who belong to your own local bulletin board. Or, you might be happiest with a service such as America Online, which does not provide access to Internet chatting yet (although it is planned), but which has more than a million subscribers and thousands of people chatting online at almost any hour of the day or night. Or, you might want full access to international chatting so you can talk to friends and family around the world.

Some Internet Warnings

Internet can be fun, educational, rewarding, and profitable. But, it can also be irritating or downright dangerous. Here are some potential problem areas that require some intelligent caution:

- Viruses can and have happened on Internet; if you download anything—especially software—check your system for viruses often.

- Never give your password to anyone! If you receive an e-mail or other type of message from someone asking for your password for verification purposes, DO NOT provide your password. Save the message and notify your online service immediately. If you do give someone your password, they could run up thousands of dollars on your account before you become aware of it.

- For the same reason, be sure to create an obscure password. Don't use your spouse's name, your dog's name, your birthday or social security number, or anything else that someone else could figure out just by talking to you for a few minutes.

- Some people travel in disguise on the Net—men masquerade as women, teenagers as adults, nonentities as celebrities, clerks as millionaires, and in all cases, vice versa. You would be wise to exercise some caution in talking to strangers until you feel confident that they are who they say they are.

- Internet is traveled by people of many different outlooks and emotional makeups. You'll most likely receive messages and e-mail that you consider offensive, no matter how open-minded you are. If it's any comfort to you, so does everyone else. The best response is no response at all. Or, if you find something especially disturbing, report it to your online service.

How Do I Access Internet through DOS?

There are no DOS commands to access Internet directly. You use DOS (or Windows) to start your telecommunications program. The telecommunications program, in turn, accesses the gateway to Internet.

6

Command
Reference

Command
Reference

Conventions

The following typographical conventions are used in this command reference:

ALL CAPS	Text that must be typed as shown, although it can be in uppercase or lowercase.
italics	Text that must be replaced by the indicated value when you type the command; that is, *filespec* must be replaced by a filespec.
[square brackets]	Optional material; everything that is not enclosed in square brackets is required.
...	An ellipsis (...) indicates that the preceding parameter can be repeated as many times as desired; that is, *filespec*... indicates that you can enter one or more filespecs.
¦	A vertical bar indicates a mutually exclusive choice between two items; that is, /B ¦ /C indicates that you can enter /B or /C, but not both.

Throughout this reference, icons appear next to the command names. These icons represent the type of command:

(I)   Internal command (contained in COMMAND.COM)

(E)   External command (has its own program file(s))

(B)   Batch program command (makes sense only when used in a batch program)

(C)   CONFIG.SYS command (can be used only in CONFIG.SYS)

APPEND

Enables programs to access files in specified directories as though those files were in the current directory.

Syntax 1

```
APPEND [path[;path...]] [/X[:ON ¦ :OFF]] [/PATH:ON ¦ :OFF]
```

Appends *path* to the current directory.

Parameters and Switches

none	Displays list of appended directories.
path	Identifies the directory to append.
/X	Specifies whether DOS is to search appended directories for program files. The default setting is OFF. /X has the same effect as /X:ON.
/PATH	Specifies whether DOS is to search appended directories for a data file when the data filespec includes a path. The default setting is ON.

Notes

If *path* does not include a drive name, DOS assumes that the directory is on the drive that is current when it executes APPEND.

When /X is ON, DOS searches for programs first in the current directory, then in any appended directories, and finally in the search path.

If you are going to use /X:ON at any time during a session, you must use /X:ON the first time you use this Syntax. After that, you can use /X:OFF and /X:ON anytime.

Each new APPEND command in this Syntax cancels all previous APPEND commands. If you want to append more than one directory to the current directory, do them all in one APPEND command. If you want to change the setting of the /X or /PATH switch, be sure to include in the command any path that should still be appended.

If you are going to use APPEND and ASSIGN in the same session, you must use APPEND first even if none of the same drives are involved.

Using DIR for the current directory does not list appended directories.

> **Warning:** Many application programs, when called on to save an updated file, actually create a new file rather than writing over the old one. Even if the original file was in an appended directory, the updated version is stored in the current directory—thus not replacing the earlier version. For this reason alone, APPEND can be a dangerous command. Many experts advise against using APPEND. Anything you want to do with APPEND you can do by judicious use of path names and the PATH command.

Do not use APPEND with when you are running Windows or Windows SETUP.

Examples

```
APPEND D:\MYDIR\TOKEN
```

Appends the specified directory.

```
APPEND \NEWDIR /X
```

Appends directory NEWDIR (on the current drive) and turns on /X so that DOS looks for program files in NEWDIR if they aren't in the current directory.

```
APPEND \NEWDIR;A:\BDIR /X:OFF /PATH:OFF
```

Appends directory NEWDIR on the current drive and directory BDIR on drive A to the current directory. Turns off /X so that DOS searches for program files first in the current directory and then in the search path. Turns off /PATH so that when a data filespec includes a path, DOS searches for the file in the specified directory only.

Syntax 2

```
APPEND /E
```

Assigns the list of appended directories to an environment variable named APPEND.

Notes

If used, this command must be the first APPEND command after starting your system. Notice that you can't use a *path* with this Syntax.

Syntax 3

```
APPEND ;
```

Cancels the existing list of appended directories.

ATTRIB

Chapter 16

Displays or changes file and directory attributes or removes all attributes.

Syntax 1

Displays or changes file and directory attributes.

```
ATTRIB [+R ¦ -R] [+A ¦ -A] [+H ¦ -H] [+S ¦ -S] [filespec] [/S]
```

Parameters and Switches

none	Shows the attributes of all files in the current directory.
+R	Turns on the read-only attribute.
-R	Turns off the read-only attribute.
+A	Turns on the archive attribute.

-A	Turns off the archive attribute.
+H	Turns on the hidden attribute.
-H	Turns off the hidden attribute.
+S	Turns on the system attribute.
-S	Turns off the system attribute.
filespec	Identifies file(s) or a directory to process. You can use wild cards to identify files but not directories. When *filespec* appears with no attribute switches, ATTRIB displays the current attributes of the file(s) or directory.
/S	Processes all files in the branch headed by the current directory.

Notes

The read-only attribute prevents a file from being overwritten or deleted. The hidden attribute prevents a file from being accessed by many commands. The system attribute combines hidden and read-only characteristics. The archive attribute indicates that a file has not been backed up.

If a file has the hidden or system attribute, you can't change any of its other attributes unless you turn off or confirm the hidden or system attribute, either in a preceding command or in the same command in which you change the other attributes.

DOS automatically sets the archive attribute when it creates or modifies a file. Many backup programs can select files for processing based on their archive attributes and turn off the attribute after backing up a file.

If you use /S with filespec, ATTRIB ignores /S and processes the specified file(s) or directory only.

Examples

```
ATTRIB +H \D1
```

Turns on the hidden attribute for directory D1 (unless D1 is a system directory).

```
ATTRIB -H -S -R TESTFILE.*
```

Turns off the hidden, system, and read-only attributes for all files in the current directory that match the filespec.

```
ATTRIB +A /S
```

Turns on the archive attribute for all files in the current directory and its subdirectories (except system and hidden files).

```
ATTRIB *.EXE
```

Displays the attributes of all files that match the filespec in the current directory.

Syntax 2

Removes all attributes from files.

```
ATTRIB , [filespec] [/S]
```

Parameters and Switches

none	Removes all attributes of all files in the current directory.
filespec	Identifies file(s) to process. You can use wild cards to identify files.
/S	Processes all files in the branch headed by the current directory.

Examples

```
ATTRIB ,
```

Turns off attributes for all files in the current directory.

```
ATTRIB , /S
```

Turns off all attributes for all files in the current directory and its subdirectories.

```
ATTRIB , MYSYS.EXE
```

Turns off all attributes for file MYSYS.EXE in the current directory.

BREAK

Chapter 21

Controls extended break checking.

Syntax

```
BREAK[=][ON ¦ OFF]
```

Parameters

none	Displays the current status of extended break checking.
ON	Turns on extended break checking.
OFF	Turns off extended break checking.

Notes

When BREAK is off, DOS checks for the use of a Break key (Ctrl+Break or Ctrl+C) only while reading from the keyboard, writing to the screen, or writing to the printer. When BREAK is on, DOS also checks for the Break key during other operations, such as reading from or writing to disks. This additional checking, however, may slow down such operations.

BREAK is off by default.

You can use BREAK with one of its parameters either at the command prompt or in CONFIG.SYS.

Examples

`BREAK ON`

Turns on extended break checking.

`BREAK=OFF`

Turns off extended break checking.

`BREAK`

Displays current status of break checking. Don't use this form in CONFIG.SYS.

BUFFERS

Chapter 21

Specifies the number of disk buffers.

Syntax

`BUFFERS=read-write[,look-ahead]`

Parameters

read-write	Specifies the number of read-write buffers. The range is from 1 to 99. The default (if the BUFFERS command is omitted) depends on your system configuration.
look-ahead	Specifies the number of look-ahead buffers. The range is from 0 to 8. The default is 0. If either *read-write* or *look-ahead* is outside its range, *look-ahead* defaults to 0.

Notes

DOS uses read-write buffers to hold data while reading and writing from a disk. Before actually reading or writing on the disk, DOS looks to see whether the desired data already is in a buffer; the more buffers there are, the more likely it is that DOS can reduce the number of disk accesses.

If you also allocate some look-ahead buffers, DOS will read additional sectors whenever it reads from a disk. This increases the likelihood that the next data to be read can be found in a buffer.

The optimum number of buffers depends on your system configuration. A reasonable number improves performance. Using too many not only takes up too much memory but actually slows down reading and writing because searching all the buffers may take longer than accessing the disk.

If you also use SmartDrive, allocate about 15 read-write buffers and no look-ahead buffers.

Each buffer uses about 500 bytes of memory. If DOS is loaded in the HMA (see the DOS command), the read-write buffers are loaded with DOS in the HMA if there is enough room for all of them. Otherwise, they appear in conventional memory. BUFFERS=10 leaves enough room in the HMA for DOS, DoubleSpace, and the buffers. Note that some application installation programs increase your BUFFERS setting to a number that is beneficial for their applications.

Examples

BUFFERS 30, 5

Allocates 30 read-write buffers and 5 look-ahead buffers.

BUFFERS 15

Allocates 15 read-write buffers and no look-ahead buffers.

CALL

Chapter 37

Calls a second batch program without ending the first one.

Syntax

CALL *batch-command*

Parameter

batch-command   The command needed to start the called batch program.

Notes

The *batch-command* should be exactly the same as the command that starts the batch program from the command prompt, including any desired parameters.

After the called program ends, DOS returns to the command following CALL in the original program.

To start one batch program from another without returning to the original batch program when the second program ends, simply include *batch-command* in the original program without CALL, just as you would enter *batch-command* at the DOS prompt.

A batch program can call itself.

Examples

`CALL NEWDAY`

Starts a batch program called NEWDAY.BAT. When NEWDAY finishes, DOS returns to the original program on the line following this CALL command.

`CALL NEWDAY JAN 1999 2`

Starts a batch program called NEWDAY.BAT and passes command line parameters to it to replace %1 (JAN), %2 (1999), and %3 (2). When NEWDAY ends, DOS continues executing the original program on the line following this CALL command.

`NEWDAY`

Starts a batch program called NEWDAY.BAT. Because CALL has not been used, DOS does not return to the original program when NEWDAY ends.

CD

Chapter 14

Changes the default directory or displays the name of the default directory. CHDIR is an alternate form of this command.

Syntax

`CD [drive:] [path]`

Parameters

none	Displays the name of default directory on the current drive (the current directory).
drive	Displays the name of the default directory on the specified drive. *Drive* must end with a colon.
path	Specifies the name of the new default directory. *Path* must represent an existing directory.

Notes

DOS establishes a default directory for each drive in the system. To change the default directory for a drive that is not the current drive, include the drive name in *path*.

A double dot (..) in *path* specifies the next higher level of the directory tree. For example, .. represents the parent of the current directory; ..\.. represents the grandparent of the current directory.

Examples

```
CHDIR
```

Displays the name of the current directory.

```
CD E:
```

Displays the name of the default directory on drive E.

```
CD \
```

Changes the current directory to the root directory of the current drive.

The following examples assume that the current drive is C: and that the current directory is \OFFICE\MYDIR. (The examples are independent of each other and are not meant to be read in sequence.)

```
CD NEWDIR
```

Changes the current directory to C:\OFFICE\MYDIR\NEWDIR.

```
CD ..
```

Changes the current directory to C:\OFFICE.

```
CD ..\YOURDIR
```

Changes the current directory to C:\OFFICE\YOURDIR.

```
CD \NEWDIR
```

Changes the current directory to C:\NEWDIR.

```
CD E:\XDIR
```

Changes the default directory on drive E to XDIR. The current drive and directory are unchanged.

CHCP

Chapter 49

Changes the code page for all devices or displays the number of the current code page.

Syntax

```
CHCP [page]
```

Parameters

none	Displays the number of the current code page.
page	Changes to the specified code page.

Notes

A code page is a character set for a keyboard or monitor. DOS provides six different software code pages so that you can type and display characters for languages other than U.S. English.

The default code page for the United States is page 437. This is also the built-in code page for most hardware sold in the U.S. The alternate code page for the U.S. is 850, which contains more international characters.

If you use the COUNTRY command in the CONFIG.SYS file, DOS establishes default and alternate code pages appropriate for the country specified.

Before you can use CHCP to change a code page, you must take these steps:

- In CONFIG.SYS, load the proper driver so that your monitor can use software code pages.
- Load NLSFUNC to allow changing code pages with CHCP.
- Use MODE to load monitor code pages.

CHCP changes code pages for all applicable devices at once and can choose between the two pages available for the current country only no matter how many code pages have been loaded. Use MODE to change to other code pages or to change the code page for one device at a time.

Examples

```
CHCP
```

Displays the number of the current code page.

```
CHCP 850
```

Changes the current code page to page 850.

CHDIR

See CD.

CHKDSK

Chapters 27 and 47

Reports disk status, reports and fixes problems in the FAT and directory structure, and reports file fragmentation. If you have DOS 6.2 or above, use the more versatile SCANDISK instead.

Syntax 1

```
CHKDSK [drive] [/F] [/V]
```

Reports disk status and reports and fixes disk structure problems.

Parameters and Switches

none	Checks the current drive.
drive	Checks the specified drive.
/F	Fixes errors in the drive's FAT and directory structure, if possible.
/V	Lists each file while checking the drive.

Notes

This syntax of CHKDSK automatically analyzes and reports on a drive's space usage and any errors in the FAT and directory structure. If no errors are found, the report summarizes space usage only.

CHKDSK finds logical errors in the FAT and directory structure, such as lost allocation units or cross-linked files; it does not find physical errors, such as bad sectors. (See SCANDISK.)

If CHKDSK /F finds lost allocation units (clusters that are marked as containing data but do not belong to any file), it asks whether you want to convert them to files. If you press Y (or Enter), CHKDSK converts each chain to a file named FILE*nnnn*.CHK. If you press N, CHKDSK immediately makes the clusters available for future use.

Never run CHKDSK on drives on which you have used ASSIGN or SUBST or on network drives.

Do not use CHKDSK /F when files may be open. You must not start CHKDSK /F from another program (such as a word processor) or when Microsoft Windows or DOS Shell is running. You may need to reboot to eliminate TSRs before using CHKDSK /F.

With DOS 6.2 and up, the SCANDISK program is preferable to CHKDSK because it can identify and fix more errors.

Examples

CHKDSK

Checks the current drive and reports FAT and directory structure errors and space usage.

CHKDSK E: /F

Checks drive E, reports space usage and FAT and directory structure errors, and attempts to fix errors.

CHKDSK /V

Checks the current drive and reports FAT and directory structure errors, reports space usage, and lists every file on the drive.

Syntax 2

CHKDSK *filespec*

Reports on file fragmentation in the current directory only.

Parameter

filespec   Checks specified file(s) for fragmentation.

Notes

A fragmented file resides in several different areas on the disk. Excessive file fragmentation can slow down performance. You can use DEFRAG to clean up file fragmentation.

Example

`CHKDSK *.*`

Lists any fragmented files in the current directory.

CHOICE

Chapter 37

Enables user to choose options during a batch program.

Syntax

`CHOICE [/C:list] [/N] [/S] [/T:char,sec] [text]`

Parameters and Switches

/C:*list*	Defines a list of characters that the user can type to select choices. The colon is optional.
/N	Causes CHOICE not to display any prompt.
/S	Causes CHOICE to distinguish between uppercase and lowercase; otherwise case is ignored.
/T:*char,sec*	Causes CHOICE to pause for *sec* seconds before defaulting to *char*. The colon is optional. *Char* must be a character from *list*. *Sec* must be between 0 and 99. Don't include any spaces in this parameter.
text	Specifies text to be displayed before the prompt.

Notes

CHOICE prompts for input by displaying *list* enclosed in brackets with the characters separated by commas and followed by a question mark, as in [A,B]?. Without /S, the list appears in uppercase.

If you omit /C, CHOICE uses Y/N as a default list.

If you use /N, CHOICE displays *text* with no prompt.

You must enclose *text* in quotation marks if it includes a slash (/).

With /T, CHOICE defaults to *char* after *sec* seconds. Otherwise, it waits forever for the user to type a character from *list* (or press Ctrl+C or Ctrl+Break). If the user enters any other response, CHOICE beeps and continues to wait.

CHOICE sets the ERRORLEVEL parameter according to the user's response: 1 for the first character in *list*, 2 for the second character, and so on. If the user presses Ctrl+C or Ctrl+Break, CHOICE sets ERRORLEVEL to 0. If an error occurs, such as a bad parameter in /T, CHOICE sets ERRORLEVEL to 255.

You can use the IF command to test the value of ERRORLEVEL and decide what to do next.

Examples

```
CHOICE /C:ABC /S Which do you want?
```

Displays Which do you want [A,B,C]? and waits for a response. Acceptable responses are A, B, C, Ctrl+C, and Ctrl+Break.

```
CHOICE /C:ABC Which do you want?
```

Displays Which do you want[A,B,C]? and waits for a response. Acceptable responses are A, B, C, a, b, c, Ctrl+C, and Ctrl+Break.

```
CHOICE /T:y,3 Are you done
```

Displays Are you done[Y,N]? and waits for a response. Acceptable responses are Y, y, N, n, Ctrl+C, and Ctrl+Break. If user doesn't respond within three seconds, CHOICE defaults to y and continues.

CLS

Chapter 20

Clears the screen.

Syntax

CLS

Notes

CLS sets the entire screen to the current background color, with the command prompt and cursor at the top left.

COMMAND

Chapter 43

Starts a new version of the DOS command processor COMMAND.COM.

Syntax

`COMMAND [path] [ctty] [/E:n] [[/Y] /C command ¦/K command]`

Parameters and Switches

path	Identifies the location of the command processor.
ctty	Identifies the device for command input and output. The default is the current device.
/E:*n*	Specifies the environment size in bytes for the new command processor, from 160 to 32,768.
/Y	Conditionally executes the program identified by /C *command* or /K *command*.
/C *command*	Loads a secondary command processor, performs *command*, and exits the secondary command processor.
/K *command*	Loads a secondary command processor and performs *command* before displaying the command prompt.

Notes

DOS's default command processor, loaded when the system starts, is COMMAND.COM, located in the root directory of the boot drive. See the SHELL command for details about booting with other options, such as a different location or a different command processor.

COMMAND loads a new version of COMMAND.COM as a child of the current processor. This is called a secondary command processor. When you are through using the secondary processor, the EXIT command closes it and returns you to the parent processor.

See the CTTY command for information about changing console devices.

When you specify /C *command*, DOS loads the secondary command processor, performs the specified command, and then exits to the parent command processor. When you specify /K *command*, DOS loads the secondary processor, performs the specified command, and prompts for more commands. It does not exit from the secondary command processor until you enter an EXIT command. Both /C and /K can run batch programs, internal commands, and external programs.

If you precede /C or /K with /Y, DOS displays the program name or DOS command followed by [Y,N]? Type Y to execute the program/command or N to bypass it. If it's a batch program, DOS displays a similar prompt for each line in the file, letting you choose whether or not to execute that command. You can use this facility to debug a batch program, testing the commands one at a time until you find the one that's not working properly.

Each instance of the command processor has its own set of environment variables. When DOS loads a secondary processor, it copies the parent's environment, but you can change the child environment without affecting the parent.

If you don't use /E, DOS allocates 256 bytes for the environment. If the environment size requested (by /E or by default) is too small to contain all of the parent environment variables, DOS increases the environment to the size needed to contain all of them.

Path is used to set the COMSPEC environment variable, which determines where DOS looks when it needs to reload the transient part of COMMAND.COM. When you omit *path*, DOS uses the parent environment's COMSPEC. If *path* is invalid or points to a directory that does not contain COMMAND.COM, DOS displays an error message and sets COMSPEC to \COMMAND.COM.

When you use *path* to set the COMSPEC environment variable, the secondary environment does not inherit the parent's environment variables.

Path sets COMSPEC for reloading the transient portion of COMMAND.COM only. It does not tell DOS where to find COMMAND.COM to execute COMMAND. If COMMAND.COM is not in the current directory or search path, you need to specify a path with the command name, as in D:\OLDDOS\COMMAND.

The COMMAND command is often used in conjunction with the SHELL command, which you can look up here.

Examples

```
COMMAND C:\DOS /E:1024
```

Loads a secondary copy of COMMAND.COM from the current directory (or from the program search path), sets COMSPEC to C:\DOS\COMMAND.COM, and requests 1,024 bytes for its environment. The parent's environment variables are not inherited.

```
COMMAND /C FOR %X IN (C:\ D:\) DO DIR %X*.BAT > PRN
```

Redirects the output of a FOR command to the printer. Note that the text from FOR through BAT is the command associated with /C.

```
C:\NEWDOS\COMMAND C:\NEWDOS COM1 /K C:\STARTUP.COM
```

Loads C:\NEWDOS\COMMAND.COM, sets COMSPEC to C:\NEWDOS, changes the input/output device to COM1, runs STARTUP.COM, and then waits for new commands from COM1. The secondary command processor does not inherit the parent's environment variables.

```
COMMAND /Y /C C:\BATCHES\FILESAVE.BAT
```

Loads a secondary copy of COMMAND.COM, executes C:\BATCHES\FILESAVE.BAT, prompting you for permission to execute each line, then terminates the secondary command processor.

COMP

Compares two files or two sets of files.

> **Note:** This command is not provided with DOS 6. See FC for a better file comparison facility.

Syntax

```
COMP [filespec1] [filespec2] [/D ¦ /A] [/L] [/N=n] [/C]
```

Parameters and Switches

none	Prompts for filespecs and switches.
filespec1	Identifies the first file(s) to be compared.
filespec2	Identifies the second file(s) to be compared.
/D	Reports differences in decimal format.
/A	Reports differences is ASCII (character) format.
/L	Reports line numbers instead of offsets.
/N=*n*	Compares only the first *n* lines.
/C	Ignores case differences.

Notes

COMP compares files byte by byte. When two files are identical, COMP reports that the files compare OK.

When you compare multiple files by using wild cards, COMP compares each *filespec1* to a *filespec2* with the same wild card characters; that is, COMP A*.* B*.* compares AFILE.DAT with BFILE.DAT, ATYPE.TXT with BTYPE.TXT, and so on.

COMP won't compare files with different file sizes unless you specify /N.

COMP stops comparing two files after finding 10 mismatches.

COMP reports each mismatched byte. By default, the report shows, in hexadecimal, the offset of the byte and the value of that byte in each file.

If you use /L or /N, COMP reports errors by line number instead of offset. This is useful in text files in which each text line ends in a carriage return. It isn't very helpful with binary files, such as graphics or executable program files, in which lines are not marked.

Use /D to force COMP to report byte values in decimal instead of hex. Use /A to force COMP to report byte values as ASCII characters (non-printable characters show up as spaces).

Microsoft is phasing out COMP in favor of the FC command, which is newer and more flexible. But COMP is still useful for a quick check to see whether files are identical.

Examples

```
COMP AFILE.BAT BFILE.BAT
```

Compares AFILE.BAT and BFILE.BAT (provided that the files are the same size) and reports up to 10 differences by showing offset and mismatched values in hexadecimal.

```
COMP AFILE.BAT BFILE.BAT /D
```

Compares AFILE.BAT and BFILE.BAT as in the previous example but reports mismatched bytes in decimal format.

```
COMP AFILE.BAT BFILE.BAT /A /N=19
```

Compares AFILE.BAT and BFILE.BAT, reporting mismatched bytes in ASCII format; compares up to 19 lines even if the files are different sizes. If one (or both) of the files is less than 19 lines, the comparison ends when COMP reaches the end of the shorter file.

```
COMP AFILE.* BFILE.*
```

Compares each file named AFILE with a file named BFILE with the same extension. COMP compares AFILE.BAT, for example, to BFILE.BAT (if it exists), and compares AFILE.D1 to BFILE.D1 (if it exists).

COPY

Chapters 15 and 40

Copies one or more files; concatenates files.

Syntax 1

```
COPY source [/A] [/B] [destination] [/A] [/B] [/V] [/Y ¦ /-Y]
```

Copies file(s).

Parameters and Switches

source	Identifies file(s) to copy.
destination	Identifies location and name of copies.
/A	Treats files as ASCII text files, whose sizes are determined by end-of-file markers.
/B	Treats files as binary files, whose sizes are determined by the directory entries.
/V	Verifies files after copying.
/Y	Overwrites destination files without warning.
/-Y	Requests permission to overwrite destination files.

Notes

This Syntax of COPY creates destination files with the same date/time stamp as their sources, but it sets the archive attribute for each destination file. See Syntax 2 to see how to assign the current date and time to the new copy.

Destination may include a path and a new file name. If *destination* does not include a path, COPY uses the current directory. If *destination* does not include a file name, COPY uses the original file name for the copy. If you omit *destination* altogether, COPY puts the new file in the current directory using the same file name as the source file.

If the destination directory is the same as the source directory, *destination* must assign a new name to the copy. (A file can't be copied to itself.)

In versions of DOS before 6.2, if the file identified by *destination* already exists, COPY overwrites it. In effect, this means it deletes *destination* and creates a new file with the specified name. (You may be able to use a third-party undelete utility to recover the data from the newly deleted file.)

In DOS 6.2 and up, if the file identified by *destination* already exists, COPY's action depends on several factors. By default, if the command was entered from the command prompt, COPY asks if you want to overwrite the destination file, but if the command was entered from a batch program, COPY overwrites the destination file without warning. However, if the COPYCMD environment variable is set to /Y, COPY overwrites files without asking. If the COPYCMD environment variable is set to /-Y, COPY asks you before overwriting files. You can override the default action or the COPYCMD environment variable for a specific command by including /Y or /-Y in the command.

The /Y and /-Y switches are not available before DOS 6.2.

When DOS asks if you want to overwrite an existing destination file, you can enter Y to overwrite the file, N to preserve the file (the copy is not made), or A to overwrite this file and all subsequent files affected by the current COPY command. In other words, A terminates file protection for the remainder of this COPY command.

If *source* identifies multiple files (by using wild cards) but *destination* provides only one file name, DOS concatenates (combines) the *source* files in *destination*. See Syntax 2 for more information about concatenating.

To copy multiple files from source to separate files with new names, you must use wild-cards in *destination* also. If *source* is *.BAT, for example, *destination* might be *.OLD.

Source and *destination* may be device names. When *source* is CON, COPY accepts input from the keyboard until you enter an end-of-file character. (You enter this character by pressing Ctrl+Z or F6.) When *destination* is a printer port, such as LPT1, to which a printer is attached, DOS prints the source files.

In this syntax, when /A or /B follows *source*, it also applies to *destination* unless another switch follows *destination*.

COPY reads the file size in the directory entry to determine how many bytes are in the file. When /A applies to *source*, COPY stops copying if it finds an end-of-file marker before reaching the file size. It does not copy the marker. If /B applies to *source*, COPY continues copying until it reaches the file size. /B is the default when copying files; /A is the default when concatenating or when source is CON.

Binary files, such as EXE or COM files, may inadvertently contain end-of-file markers as data. It is important to copy them as binary files to avoid truncating them.

When /A applies to *destination*, COPY adds an end-of-file marker to the file; with /B, COPY does not add the end-of-file marker.

Examples

```
COPY MYFILE.DAT YOURFILE.DAT
```

Copies MYFILE.DAT to create (or overwrite) YOURFILE.DAT. Both files are in the current directory. The file size of MYFILE.DAT in its directory entry determines how many bytes DOS copies. YOURFILE.DAT does not end with an end-of-file marker unless MYFILE.DAT does.

```
COPY MYFILE.* YOURFILE.*
```

Copies each file matching the source filespec into a file named YOURFILE with the same extension as the source file. MYFILE.A1, for example, is copied to YOURFILE.A1.

```
SET COPYCMD=/Y
COPY /-Y MYFILE.* YOURFILE.*
```

The first command sets COPYCMD to /Y, which turns off file protection for all subsequent COPY, XCOPY, and MOVE commands. These commands will now overwrite files without warning. The second command copies all files that match MYFILE.* in the current directory, naming the copies YOURFILE.* in the same directory. It overrides the COPYCMD setting, requesting file protection for any existing YOURFILE.* files, so that COPY asks you before overwriting any files.

Syntax 2

```
COPY source1 + [source2] [+...] [/A] [/B] [destination] [/A] [/B] [/V] [/Y ¦ /-Y]
```

Concatenates files.

Parameters and Switches

source1	Identifies the first file(s) to be concatenated.
source2	Identifies additional file(s) to be concatenated.
destination	Identifies the file(s) to hold the concatenated data.
/A	Treats files as ASCII text files.
/B	Treats files as binary files.
/V	Verifies files after concatenation.
/Y	Overwrites destination files without warning.
/-Y	Requests permission to overwrite destination files.

Notes

You can repeat + *source2* as needed. Source filespecs can include wild cards.

Because the destination file is a new creation, COPY assigns the current date and time to it. You can fake a concatenation to assign the current date and time to a file (see the examples).

If you omit *destination*, COPY concatenates all source files into the first source file that actually exists. If *source1* does not exist, for example, but *source2* does, COPY puts the concatenated data in *source2*; if neither *source1* nor *source2* exists, but there is an existing *source3*, *source3* receives the data.

In this syntax, when you use wildcards in two or more source file names, COPY concatenates files with matching wildcard characters. COPY AFILE.* + BFILE.* CFILE.*, for example, concatenates AFILE.DAT with BFILE.DAT to create or replace CFILE.DAT and concatenates AFILE.NEW with BFILE.NEW to create or replace CFILE.NEW. COPY AFILE.* + BFILE.* concatenates AFILE.BAT and BFILE.BAT into AFILE.BAT (if it exists).

/A is the default for this syntax. An /A or /B switch applies to the preceding file name and all succeeding file names until COPY reaches a file name followed by another /A or /B switch.

As in Syntax 1, when /A applies to a source file, COPY stops copying if it finds an end-of-file marker, without copying the marker. If there is no marker, or if /B applies, COPY determines the source file size from the directory entry. When /A applies to a destination file, COPY inserts an end-of-file marker at the end of the file; with /B, no marker is inserted unless one is copied from the source file.

When you concatenate data into one of the source files, you may receive the message Content of destination lost before copy. This is a normal message. It does not necessarily mean that you have lost data. It indicates that COPY has discovered that the destination file also qualifies as a source file but can't be used as a source because it is being used as the destination.

Examples

```
COPY C:\DS1\MYFILE.* NEWFILE.CAT
```

Concatenates all specified files to create (or overwrite) NEWFILE.CAT in the current directory. For each source file, COPY ends the copy if it finds an end-of-file marker. COPY also writes an end-of-file marker at the end of NEWFILE.CAT.

```
COPY MYFILE.DAT + YOURFILE.DAT OURFILE.DAT /V /-Y
```

Concatenates MYFILE.DAT and YOURFILE.DAT to overwrite OURFILE.DAT and verifies the result. COPY treats these files as ASCII text files and adds an end-of-file marker to the new file. If OURFILE.DAT already exists, COPY asks if you want to overwrite it.

```
COPY MYFILE.DAT +YOURFILE.DAT +OURFILE.DAT
```

Concatenates MYFILE.DAT, YOURFILE.DAT, and OURFILE.DAT into MYFILE.DAT if it exists. If MYFILE.DAT does not exist, concatenates YOURFILE.DAT and OURFILE.DAT into YOURFILE.DAT. If neither MYFILE.DAT nor YOURFILE.DAT exists, copies OURFILE.DAT to itself as though concatenating. COPY treats these files as ASCII text files and adds an end-of-file marker to the concatenated data.

```
COPY MYFILE.DAT/B+YOURFILE.DAT OURFILE.DAT
```

Concatenates MYFILE.DAT and YOURFILE.DAT to create (or overwrite) OURFILE.DAT. COPY treats these files as binary files, copying all characters from the source files, and does not append an end-of-file marker.

```
COPY MYFILE.DAT+YOURFILE.DAT /B OURFILE.DAT
```

Concatenates MYFILE.DAT and YOURFILE.DAT to create (or overwrite) OURFILE.DAT. COPY treats MYFILE.DAT as an ASCII text file but YOURFILE.DAT and OURFILE.DAT as binary files.

```
COPY MYFILE.DAT+,, /B NEWFILE.DAT
```

Concatenates MYFILE.DAT with nothing (signified by the double commas) to create or overwrite NEWFILE.DAT. The effect is to copy MYFILE.DAT as NEWFILE.DAT and to assign the current date and time to NEWFILE.DAT. Both files are treated as binary files. The commas mark the end of the source list; without them, COPY would consider NEWFILE.DAT a source file.

```
COPY MYFILE.DAT +,, /B
```

Concatenates MYFILE.DAT with nothing to overwrite MYFILE.DAT. The effect is to update the date/time stamp for MYFILE.DAT. /B ensures that COPY copies the entire file, including end-of-file markers, but does not add a new end-of-file marker. The +,, is necessary to indicate that this is a concatenation, not a copy.

COUNTRY

Chapter 49

Specifies the country format for date and time displays, currency symbol, sort order, punctuation, decimal separators, and code pages.

Syntax

COUNTRY=*country*[,[*page*] [,*filespec*]]

Parameters

country	Specifies the code number that identifies the country.
page	Identifies a code page (character set).
filespec	Identifies the file containing country information.

Notes

The default country (if COUNTRY is not included in CONFIG.SYS) is the United States.

Country codes, date and time formats, and appropriate code pages are documented in the on-screen help for COUNTRY.

Each country has two possible code pages associated with it. One of them is the default code page, the other is the alternate. If you omit *page*, DOS uses the default code page.

Changes such as date and time formats take effect as soon as COUNTRY is executed in the CONFIG.SYS file, but no software code page can be used until you have followed all the steps outlined in the CHCP command. Until you load the drivers and prepare and install the code pages, DOS continues to use the default hardware page.

If you omit *filespec*, DOS looks for country information in COUNTRY.SYS in the root directory of your startup drive.

Examples

COUNTRY=039

Changes the country to Italy; uses default code page 850 (once all the necessary steps are taken); looks for country information in \COUNTRY.SYS on the boot drive.

COUNTRY=351,860,C:\DOS\COUNTRY.SYS

Changes the country to Portugal; uses alternate code page 860 (once all the necessary steps are taken); looks for country information in C:\DOS\COUNTRY.SYS.

COUNTRY=047,C:\OLD\SPECIAL.SYS

Changes the country to Norway; uses default code page for Norway (850) (once all the necessary steps are taken); looks for country information in C:\OLD\SPECIAL.SYS.

CTTY

Chapter 48

Changes the console device.

Syntax

CTTY *device*

Parameter

device   Specifies the new console device.

Notes

The console device receives command input and displays command output. Normally, this device is CON, which represents your keyboard and monitor.

Device can be PRN, LPT1, LPT2, LPT3, CON, AUX, COM1, COM2, COM3, or COM4. LPT1 through LPT3 refer to the parallel printer ports. PRN is the same as LPT1. COM1 through COM4 refer to serial ports. AUX refers to the auxiliary port.

If you specify a COM port, you must establish the communications parameters of the port with the MODE command before issuing the CTTY command.

If the console device is not CON, DOS can't respond to command input from your keyboard. You may need to reboot to return control to your keyboard and monitor.

See COMMAND for another way to change your console device.

Not all input and output is transferred by this command, just standard DOS command input and output. You can, for example, reboot from the keyboard.

Examples

CTTY AUX

Uses a remote terminal connected to the auxiliary port for command input and output.

CTTY CON

Transfers input and output functions back to your keyboard and monitor (when entered from the current console device).

DATE

Chapter 12

Displays the system date and lets you change it.

Syntax

DATE [date]

Parameters

none	Displays date in standard format and asks for a new date.
date	Changes to date.

Notes

The system date affects directory entries and is used by MSBACKUP, XCOPY, and many other applications.

When DOS asks for a new date, press Enter to retain the current date.

The COUNTRY command determines the date format. By default, the allowable formats for entering the date are the U.S. standards: mm/dd/yy, mm-dd-yy, and mm.dd.yy. In each of these, yy can be a two-digit year from 80 to 99 (interpreted as 1980 through 1999) or a four-digit year between 1980 and 2099.

DOS always computes the weekday (such as Sun or Mon) from the system date; don't try to enter the weekday.

Examples

DATE

Displays the system date and asks you to enter a new date.

DATE 12-15-97

Changes the system date to December 15, 1997.

DATE 12/15/2003

Changes the system date to December 15, 2003.

DBLSPACE

Chapters 34 and 45

Compresses hard disk drives and floppy disks; manages compressed drives.

Syntax 1

`DBLSPACE`

Starts the DoubleSpace setup program, which installs DoubleSpace and compresses and mounts a drive.

> **Warning:** As of DOS 6.22, DriveSpace has replaced DoubleSpace. If you already use DoubleSpace to handle compressed files, you can continue to do so using the `DBLSPACE` commands or you can convert to DriveSpace. If you want to begin using compressed files, use DriveSpace instead of DoubleSpace. (See the command `DRVSPACE`.)

Notes

The first time you use DBLSPACE, you must use this syntax. DBLSPACE sets up your system for file compression, placing the DBLSPACE core program (DBLSPACE.BIN) and other files in the root directory of your boot drive. It also places a `DEVICEHIGH=DBLSPACE.SYS` command into your CONFIG.SYS file so that DBLSPACE.BIN moves to upper memory, if possible; otherwise, it moves to the bottom of conventional memory. DBLSPACE also compresses at least one hard disk drive. You can't install DoubleSpace without compressing at least one hard disk drive.

When you use Syntax 1 again, it loads the DoubleSpace program and displays a dialog box with pull-down menus, from which you can compress other drives or manage compressed drives.

After installation, you can accomplish DoubleSpace functions without opening the dialog box by using other `DBLSPACE` command syntaxes.

When DoubleSpace compresses existing data, it creates a large file named DBLSPACE.000 that holds the compressed data. (This is a system, hidden, and read-only file.) The original drive now contains the DBLSPACE.000 file, other files that are not appropriate for compression (such as a Windows swap file), and some free space. The compressed data file is called a *compressed volume file* (CVF) and is accessed and referred to by the original drive letter. The original drive, called the *host drive*, is accessed by a new letter assigned by DoubleSpace. (If you're not sure what letter DoubleSpace assigned to a host drive, use DBLSPACE /INFO or /LIST syntaxes 9 and 10.)

Assigning drive letters to the compressed and host drives and establishing access is called *mounting* the compressed drive. DoubleSpace automatically mounts all compressed hard disk drives when you boot your system. With DOS 6.2, it also mounts floppy disk drives automatically. With DOS 6.0, you must mount a compressed floppy disk every time you insert it. (See Syntax 11.) When a compressed drive is not mounted, you can't access it because no drive letter is assigned to it.

DoubleSpace can't compress a drive that's completely full. Your boot drive must have at least 1.2MB of free space; other drives, including floppies, must have at least 1.1MB.

If your drive had a SENTRY directory, there is a SENTRY directory on both the compressed and host drive after compression. Files deleted before compression cannot be recovered, however. Files deleted after compression can be undeleted as usual by Delete Sentry. (You need to add the new drive letter as a drive protected by Delete Sentry, however, if you want to protect the uncompressed host drive.)

If your drive had a PCTRACKR.DEL file, it is left on the host drive, but any files deleted before compression are probably unrecoverable because their clusters have been reused by the CVF. Files deleted after compression can be undeleted as usual by deletion-tracking. (You need to add the new drive letter as a drive protected by deletion-tracking, however, if you want to protect the uncompressed host drive.)

If you use a SMARTDRV command naming a compressed drive, you will see a message telling you that you must cache the host drive. You don't need to change the command; DoubleSpace and SmartDrive work together to cache the compressed drive through the host drive.

Warning: Avoid write caching a compressed drive; delayed writes could result in data loss on the compressed drive if your system goes down before the writes can be completed. If you installed SmartDrive before upgrading to DOS 6.2 and up, you might be write caching your compressed drive. Change your SmartDrive configuration so that the compressed drive is not write cached.

The following command formats manage DoubleSpace drives from the command prompt. All these functions also can be accomplished from the DoubleSpace dialog box, which opens when you enter the DBLSPACE command with no parameters (Syntax 1).

Syntax 2

```
DBLSPACE /CHKDSK [/F] [drive]
```

Checks the directory structure of a compressed drive (DOS 6.0 only).

Parameters and Switches

/CHKDSK	Requests the CHKDSK function; abbreviate as /CHK.
/F	Fixes errors found on the compressed drive.
drive	Identifies the compressed drive to be checked; the default is the current drive.

Notes

DoubleSpace's /CHKDSK function has been replaced by the SCANDISK program in DOS 6.2 and up.

In DOS 6.0, this command checks the internal structure of the compressed volume file. Use DOS's CHKDSK command to check the compressed drive's file allocation tables.

Examples

```
DBLSPACE /CHK
```

Checks the internal structure of the current drive, if it's a compressed drive. Reports errors but doesn't fix them.

```
DBLSPACE /CHK /F D
```

Checks the internal structure of compressed drive D, correcting errors if possible.

Syntax 3

```
DBLSPACE /COMPRESS drive1 [/NEWDRIVE=drive2] [/RESERVE=size] [/F]
```

Compresses the files on an existing hard disk drive, floppy drive, or other removable media, and mounts the drive.

Parameters and Switches

/COMPRESS	Requests the COMPRESS function; abbreviate as /COM.
drive1	Identifies the existing drive you want to compress.
/NEWDRIVE=*drive2*	Specifies the drive letter you want to use for the host drive; abbreviate as /NEW. (Use Syntax 10 to find out what drive letters are available). Without /NEW, DoubleSpace selects a drive letter for the new drive.
/RESERVE=*size*	Specifies, in megabytes, how much space to leave uncompressed on the host drive; abbreviate as /RES. Without /RES, DoubleSpace leaves 2MB on a hard disk drive if possible.
/F	Suppresses the final report so that you return to the command prompt automatically.

Notes

When DoubleSpace compresses a floppy disk, it adds a file called READTHIS.TXT to the host drive. This file explains to the recipient that the disk contains compressed data and how to access the data. (READTHIS.TXT doesn't show up in a DOS 6.2 or later system with DoubleSpace installed because the compressed drive on the floppy is mounted automatically. It shows up on systems using DOS 6.0 or earlier, and on systems where DoubleSpace is not installed.)

Whether you specify /RES at this point, you can increase or decrease the amount of uncompressed space later. (See Syntax 14.)

Refer to Syntax 1 for more information about what happens when you compress a disk.

Examples

```
DBLSPACE /COM A
```

Compresses the floppy disk in drive A; after compression, assigns the host drive an available drive letter.

```
DBLSPACE /COM D /RES=2.5 /NEW=L
```

Compresses drive D, leaving 2.5MB of free space (if possible); assigns the host drive the letter L.

Syntax 4

```
DBLSPACE /UNCOMPRESS drive
```

Uncompresses a drive.

Parameters and switches

/UNCOMPRESS	Requests the UNCOMPRESS function.
drive	Identifies the compressed drive to be uncompressed.

Notes

The UNCOMPRESS function uncompresses the data in the CVF, storing it on the host drive. If there's not enough room on the host drive to hold all the uncompressed data, you might need to delete some of the compressed files or move them to other drives first. After uncompressing, the compressed drive is unmounted and deleted. The host drive's original name is restored.

When the last compressed drive is uncompressed, DBLSPACE.BIN is removed from memory. But it is not deleted from the boot directory.

Syntax 5

```
DBLSPACE /CREATE drive1 [/NEWDRIVE=drive2] [/SIZE=size1 ¦ /RESERVE=size2]
```

Creates a new, empty, compressed drive out of free space on an uncompressed drive.

Parameters and Switches

/CREATE	Requests the CREATE function; abbreviate as /CR.
drive1	Identifies the host drive.
/NEWDRIVE=drive2	Specifies the drive letter for the new CVF; abbreviate as /NEW. Without /NEW, DoubleSpace selects a drive letter for the new CVF.
/SIZE=size1	Specifies the number of megabytes to be allocated to the compressed volume file (before compression); abbreviate as /SI.
/RESERVE=size2	Specifies how many megabytes of free space to leave on the uncompressed drive; abbreviate as /RES.

Notes

You can't use /CREATE on a floppy disk.

When you create a CVF out of free space instead of existing data, DoubleSpace assigns the new drive letter to the new volume instead of the host drive (which retains its existing drive letter).

You can create a new, empty volume on a drive that already contains a compressed volume file. The original CVF is named DBLSPACE.000 and has the original drive letter. The new CVF is DBLSPACE.001 (assuming this is the second CVF on the drive) and receives a new drive letter. The remaining uncompressed space is on the host drive, which keeps the drive letter assigned to it when DBLSPACE.000 was created.

If you don't specify /SIZE or /RES, DoubleSpace uses all but 1MB of free space.

Examples

```
DBLSPACE /CR E
```

Creates a new, empty compressed volume file on host drive E, leaving 1MB of free space; assigns an available drive letter to the new compressed volume file.

```
DBLSPACE /CR E /NEW=L /RES=1.5
```

Creates a new, empty, CVF on host drive E, leaving 1.5MB of free space on E (if possible) and assigning the drive letter L to the new CVF.

Syntax 6

```
DBLSPACE /DEFRAGMENT [drive] [/F]
```

Defragments the compressed drive.

Parameters and Switches

/DEFRAGMENT	Requests the DEFRAGMENT function; abbreviate as /DEF.
drive	Specifies the compressed drive to defragment; the default is the current drive.
/F	Defragments more fully (available in DOS 6.2 and up only).

Notes

Defragmenting is not necessary to improve performance on a compressed drive. It does, however, consolidate the drive's free space. If you want to reduce the drive's size (see Syntax 14), you should use DBLSPACE /DEF first.

If you run DOS's DEFRAG on a DoubleSpace drive, DOS automatically runs the DBLSPACE /DEF command as soon as DEFRAG is finished.

Example

```
DBLSPACE /DEF /F
```

Defragments the current (compressed) drive.

Syntax 7

```
DBLSPACE /DELETE drive
```

Deletes a compressed drive, erasing all its files.

Parameters and Switches

/DELETE	Requests the DELETE function; abbreviate as /DEL.
drive	Specifies the compressed drive to delete.

Notes

Deleting a DoubleSpace drive also unmounts it. If you delete DBLSPACE.000, the original drive letter is restored to the host drive. If you delete any other CVF, the drive letter from the deleted volume becomes available for other uses.

If you change your mind after deleting a DoubleSpace drive, you may be able to recover it using DOS's UNDELETE command. Look for a deleted file named DBLSPACE.nnn on the host drive.

If you are able to restore the file with UNDELETE, you still can't access its data until you mount it. See Syntax 11.

Example

```
DBLSPACE /DEL F
```

Deletes the compressed drive referred to as drive F.

Syntax 8

```
DBLESPACE /FORMAT drive
```

Formats a compressed drive.

Parameters and Switches

/FORMAT	Requests the FORMAT function; abbreviate as /FOR.
drive	Specifies the compressed drive to format.

Notes

Formatting a compressed drive deletes all the files it contains. You can't unformat a compressed drive if you change your mind.

Example

```
DBLSPACE /FOR G
```

Formats compressed drive G, erasing all its data.

Syntax 9

```
DBLSPACE [/INFO] drive
```

Displays information about a compressed drive.

Parameters and Switches

/INFO	Requests the INFO function; this is the default when no other DBLSPACE function is specified.
drive	Identifies the drive about which you want information.

Notes

The information displayed includes the host drive, the CVF's file name, the total space, used space, and free space on both the CVF and the host drive, the actual average compression ratio, and the estimated compression ratio. Free space on the CVF is an estimate of uncompressed bytes that could be compressed into the remaining space in the CVF, based on the estimated compression ratio.

Example

`DBLSPACE D`

Displays information about compressed drive D.

`DBLSPACE /INFO`

Displays information about the current drive.

Syntax 10

`DBLSPACE /LIST`

Lists and describes all your computer's non-network drives, including DoubleSpace volumes.

Parameters and Switches

`/LIST`	Requests the `LIST` function; abbreviate as `/L`.

Notes

This syntax lists each available drive letter and describes its status in terms such as `Local hard drive`, `Compressed hard drive`, `Floppy drive`, `Removable-media with No disk in drive`, `Available for DoubleSpace`, and so on. (RAM drives are described as local hard drives.) Space used and free space are shown for each drive if appropriate. For each mounted compressed drive, the report shows the compressed volume name and its host drive.

Syntax 11

`DBLSPACE /MOUNT[=nnn] drive1 [/NEWDRIVE=drive2]`

Mounts a compressed volume.

Parameters and Switches

`/MOUNT`	Requests the `MOUNT` function; abbreviate as `/MO`.
nnn	Identifies the extension of the volume to be mounted; default is 000.
drive	Specifies the drive that contains the compressed file you want to mount.
`/NEWDRIVE=drive2`	Specifies the drive letter to be assigned; abbreviate as `/NEW`. Without `/NEW`, DoubleSpace assigns an available drive letter.

Notes

When you mount a DBLSPACE.000 file, the host's drive letter is assigned to the compressed drive, and a new letter is assigned to the host drive. When you mount any other DBLSPACE.*nnn* file, the new letter is assigned to the compressed drive.

DBLSPACE automatically mounts drives when it compresses or creates them. It may unmount and mount a drive when it is performing certain functions on that drive. It automatically mounts compressed hard drives when the system boots. The only time you need to mount a hard drive is if you have unmounted it or deleted and recovered it. (See Syntax 14 and Syntax 7.)

DOS 6.2 (and up) automatically mounts floppy drives also. But with DOS 6.0, you need to mount a floppy disk each time you insert it into the drive.

Examples

```
DBLSPACE /MO A
```

Mounts a disk in drive A, assigning drive letter A to DBLSPACE.000 and an available drive letter to the uncompressed portion of the disk.

```
DBLSPACE /MO=001 E /NEW=L
```

Mounts a compressed drive, assigning drive letter L to E:\DBLSPACE.001 and retaining E as the drive letter of the host drive.

Syntax 12

```
DBLSPACE /RATIO[=r.r] [drive ¦ /ALL]
```

Changes the estimated compression ratio of one or all compressed drives.

Parameters and Switches

/RATIO=*r.r*	Specifies the new ratio; from 1.0 to 16.0; the default is the current overall compression ratio for the drive; abbreviate as /RA.
drive	Identifies the drive.
/ALL	Specifies that you want to change the ratio for all currently mounted compressed drives.

Notes

DoubleSpace uses the estimated compression ratio to estimate how many bytes of uncompressed data would, when compressed, fit into the CVF. This affects reports from functions such as DIR and DOS Shell.

If you don't specify drive or /ALL, DoubleSpace changes the ratio of the current drive.

Use Syntax 9 (/INFO) to find the estimated and actual compression ratio of a drive.

Examples

```
DBLSPACE /RA /ALL
```

Changes the estimated compression ratio of all currently mounted compressed drives to match each one's average compression ratio.

```
DBLSPACE /RA=3 D
```

Changes the estimated compression ratio of compressed drive D to 3.0 to 1.

Syntax 13

```
DBLSPACE /SIZE[=size1 ¦ /RESERVE=size2] drive
```

Resizes the compressed volume file.

Parameters and Switches

/SIZE	Requests the SIZE function; abbreviate as /SI.
size1	Specifies the new size of the CVF in megabytes (before compression). Do not use with /RESERVE.
/RESERVE=size2	Specifies in megabytes the amount of free space you want DoubleSpace to leave on the host drive; abbreviate as /RES; do not use if you specify size1. If size2 is 0, the compressed drive is increased to its maximum possible size.
drive	Identifies the compressed drive to resize.

Notes

If you specify neither size1 nor /RES, DoubleSpace makes the compressed drive as small as possible.

Examples

```
DBLSPACE /SI=30 D
```

Changes the size of compressed drive D to 30MB (if possible) before compression.

```
DBLSPACE /SI /RES=10 D
```

Changes the size of compressed drive D to leave 10MB of free space on its host drive (if possible). You should defragment the compressed drive before doing this.

```
DBLSPACE /SI /RES=0 D
```

Makes compressed drive D as large as possible.

```
DBLSPACE /SI D
```

Makes compressed drive D as small as possible. You should defragment the compressed drive before doing this.

Syntax 14

`DBLSPACE /UNMOUNT [drive]`

Unmounts a drive.

Parameters and Switches

/UNMOUNT	Requests the UNMOUNT function; abbreviate as /U.
drive	Specifies the drive to be unmounted; the default is the current drive.

Notes

The unmounted drive becomes unavailable until mounted again. If the host drive letter was swapped to the CVF, the original drive letter now reverts to the host drive, and the host's letter becomes available for other uses. If the letters were not swapped, the CVF's letter becomes available for other uses.

You don't need to unmount a floppy drive before removing it from the disk drive.

Example

`DBLSPACE /U D`

Unmounts compressed drive D. If D was assigned to DBLSPACE.000, it now refers to the host drive. Otherwise, the host drive letter remains unchanged and D becomes an available drive letter.

Syntax 15

`DBLSPACE [/AUTOMOUNT=0 ¦ 1 ¦ x] [/DOUBLEGUARD=0 ¦ 1] [drive1 /HOST=drive2] [/LASTDRIVE=x]`
`[/MAXFILEFRAGMENTS=n] [/MAXREMOVABLEDRIVES=n] [/ROMSERVER=0 ¦ 1] [/SWITCHES=F ¦ N]`

Sets default settings in DBLSPACE.INI.

Parameters and Switches

/AUTOMOUNT	Indicates whether or not DoubleSpace should mount floppies automatically.
/DOUBLEGUARD	Enables or disables the DoubleGuard feature, which constantly checks for damage to DoubleSpace's memory buffers.
/HOST	Specifies the drive name (*drive2*) for the host of a compressed drive (*drive1*).

/LASTDRIVE	Specifies the highest drive name that DoubleSpace can use when mounting drives.
/MAXFILEFRAGMENTS	Specifies the maximum number of fragments that a CVF can be split into on the host drive.
/MAXREMOVABLEDRIVES	Specifies the number of additional compressed drives DoubleSpace should reserve space for during booting.
/ROMSERVER	Enables or disables the check for a ROM BIOS Microsoft Real-Time Compression Interface (MRCI) server.
/SWITCHES	Controls whether or not a user can bypass DoubleSpace during booting.

Notes

DBLSPACE.INI contains default settings for DoubleSpace. Because it's a hidden, system, an read-only file, you can't edit it directly. (It would be dangerous to remove the hidden, system, and read-only attributes.) Use these commands to change the settings in DBLSPACE.INI.

You can view DBLSPACE.INI using DOS's EDIT, even though you can't edit it. By viewing it, you can find out what your current settings are for these parameters.

With DOS 6.2 and up, DoubleSpace by default mounts removable drives (such as floppy drives) automatically. DoubleSpace must set aside memory space for each drive that might be automounted. The command DBLSPACE /AUTOMOUNT=0 sets DBLSPACE.INI so that removable drives are not mounted automatically, saving memory space. DBLSPACE /AUTOMOUNT=1 restores the default setting. You can also identify specific removable drives to be automounted with DBLSPACE /AUTOMOUNT=A, DBLSPACE /AUTOMOUNT=B, and so on. (See Syntax 11 for a command that mounts a compressed drive that hasn't been mounted automatically.)

With DOS 6.2 (or later) DoubleGuard constantly checks DoubleSpace's memory buffers for corruption and, if detected, halts your computer to prevent damage to your compressed drive. DoubleGuard slows down your system somewhat. You can disable DoubleGuard with the command DBLSPACE /DOUBLEGUARD=0. You can enable it again with DBLSPACE /DOUBLEGUARD=1.

Warning: Disabling DoubleGuard could result in damage to your compressed data.

If you receive the message Compressed drive x is currently too fragmented to mount, the CVF known as drive x has been split into more fragments than specified in the MAXFRAGMENTS setting in DBLSPACE.INI. It can't be mounted or used until you resolve the problem. You can increase the number of allowed fragments by entering the command DBLSPACE /MAXFRAGMENTS=n, where n is the new number of fragments. Or you can remove the CVF's attributes, defragment the host drive, and restore the CVF's attributes again (very important).

The MAXREMOVABLEDRIVES parameter determines the maximum number of additional compressed drives that DoubleSpace can handle (whether they are removable or not) after booting. This controls not only how many compressed volumes you can mount from removable drives, but also how many new compressed volumes you can create without rebooting. The default maximum is 2. Lowering it saves memory space but impacts your ability to create new compressed drives.

The MRCI check looks for a ROM BIOS Microsoft Realtime Compression Interface server. Some systems use MRCI as an interface to DoubleSpace's compression services. If your system includes an MRCI ROM BIOS, you need to set this switch to 1. However, this check can impede a ROM BIOS that doesn't use MRCI, so don't enable MRCI checking unless you're sure that your system needs it. Enable MRCI checking with the command DBLSPACE /ROMSERVER=1. Disable it again with DBLSPACE /ROMSERVER=0.

By default, when a user presses Ctrl+F5 during booting, DOS displays each line in CONFIG.SYS and AUTOEXEC.BAT and asks if it should be executed. It also asks if DoubleSpace should be loaded. When a user presses Ctrl+F8 during booting, DOS bypasses CONFIG.SYS, AUTOEXEC.BAT, and DBLSPACE.BIN without asking. You can disable the DoubleSpace portion of these bypasses by entering the command DBLSPACE /SWITCHES=N. When bypassing is disabled, Ctrl+F5 still conditionally executes CONFIG.SYS and AUTOEXEC.BAT, and Ctrl+F8 still bypasses CONFIG.SYS and AUTOEXEC.BAT.

The command DBLSPACE /SWITCHES=F shortens the time that DOS waits for the user to press a bypass key, which speeds up booting slightly.

Once you have entered /SWITCHES=N and/or /SWITCHES=F, there is no command to remove them from DBLSPACE.INI. You must edit the file and remove the SWITCHES parameter to return to the default settings.

See SWITCHES for a command that disables your ability to bypass AUTOEXEC.BAT and CONFIG.SYS.

DEBUG

Starts a program that lets you test and debug an executable program file.

Syntax

```
DEBUG [filespec [parameters]]
```

Parameters

none	Starts DEBUG without loading a program.
filespec	Loads a program for debugging. The *filespec* may include a path; it must include the extension (usually .EXE or .COM).

parameters	Provides any parameters for the program to be loaded.

Notes

When DEBUG starts, it displays its own command prompt, a hyphen (–). You enter DEBUG commands at the hyphen. You can exit DEBUG with the command Q (for quit).

See DEBUG on-screen help for other DEBUG commands.

Examples

DEBUG

Starts DEBUG without loading a program.

DEBUG MYCAL.COM JAN

Starts DEBUG; loads a program called MYCAL.COM found in the current directory; passes the parameter value JAN to MYCAL.COM.

DEFRAG

Chapter 33

Reorganizes files on a drive to optimize file performance; sorts directory entries.

Syntax

DEFRAG [*drive*] [/F ¦ /Q¦ /U] [/S*order*] [/B] [/H] [/SKIPHIGH] [/LCD ¦ /BW ¦ /G0]

Parameters and Switches

none	Opens the DEFRAG dialog box so you can select the drive and options.
drive	Identifies the drive to optimize.
/F	Defragments files and free space.
/Q	Optimizes free space only.
/U	Defragments files only.
/S*order*	Sorts directory entries; *order* specifies the sort field (see Notes).
/B	Reboots when DEFRAG ends.
/H	Permits DEFRAG to move hidden files.
/SKIPHIGH	Loads the DEFRAG program in conventional memory.
/LCD	Displays dialog boxes in LCD color scheme.
/BW	Displays dialog boxes in black-and-white color scheme.
/G0	Suppresses graphics characters in dialog boxes.

Notes

Excessive file fragmentation can slow down system performance. DEFRAG brings all fragmented files' clusters together (if space permits).

/F also moves all empty space to the end of the drive, decreasing the likelihood of future fragmentation.

/Q moves all empty space to the end of the drive but does not defragment files. It is the quickest to optimize free space. This is an undocumented switch and may not be present in all versions. You can't use /F, /U, or /S with /Q.

DEFRAG doesn't move system files because these files must often stay where they are. If you don't use the /H switch, it also doesn't move hidden files. Unmovable files can cause other files to be fragmented, especially if you have used the /F switch.

Before starting DEFRAG, do the following:

- Delete all unnecessary files from the drive.
- Delete any delete-tracking files, such as PCTRACKR.DEL. (They would not be valid after DEFRAG.)
- Purge all unneeded files from SENTRY (or other deletion protection facilities).
- Quit all programs, including Microsoft Windows. (Do not run DEFRAG from a secondary DOS prompt provided by another program.)
- Run CHKDSK /F (DOS 6.0) or SCANDISK (DOS 6.2 and up) to clean up lost allocation units.
- Disable any program that might write to the disk while DEFRAG is running, such as a program scheduled to update a file automatically.
- Remove system attributes from files that should be defragmented and moved. Do the same for hidden files if you are not using the /H switch. (But keep in mind that many system and hidden files should not be moved.)

If you specify both *drive* and /F, /Q, or /U in the command line, DEFRAG immediately begins defragmenting. Otherwise, the DEFRAG dialog box opens. In the dialog box, you can choose drive, defragmentation type, and sort order. You can specify other functions, such as /H, /B, or /SKIPHIGH, only on the command line; there is no opportunity to choose them in the dialog box.

/S sorts the directory entries for each directory on the drive; but it doesn't move the files themselves around. The values for *order* are as follows:

N	By name (alphanumeric order)
N-	By name (reverse alphanumeric order)
E	By extension (alphanumeric order)
E-	By extension (reverse alphanumeric order)
D	By date and time, earliest first

D-	By date and time, latest first
S	By size, smallest first
S-	By size, largest first

DEFRAG loads into upper memory, if possible, unless you specify /SKIPHIGH.

You should always reboot after DEFRAG to clear caches and buffers of old directory information. You must reboot if you're using FASTOPEN.

You can't use DEFRAG to optimize network drives or drives created with INTERLNK.

DEFRAG is intercepted by your compression software if the specified drive is compressed. The compression program's defragmenting function is executed in its place.

DEFRAG sets an exit code as follows:

0	DEFRAG was successful.
1	An internal error occurred.
2	There was not enough free space on the disk. DEFRAG needs at least one free cluster.
3	The user pressed Ctrl+C or Ctrl+Break to stop DEFRAG.
4	A general error occurred.
5	A read error occurred.
6	A write error occurred.
7	An allocation error occurred. (Run CHKDSK /F (DOS 6.0) or SCANDISK (DOS 6.2 and up) to correct this error.)

Examples

`DEFRAG`

Opens the DEFRAG dialog box.

`DEFRAG /B`

Opens the DEFRAG dialog box; reboots when DEFRAG ends.

`DEFRAG D:`

Opens the DEFRAG dialog box so you can choose defragmentation type.

`DEFRAG C: /F /B`

Defragments files on drive C and eliminates free space between files; reboots when DEFRAG ends.

`DEFRAG C: /U /SD-`

Defragments files on drive C but does not eliminate free space between files. Sorts directory entries by date and time, with the latest first.

DEL

Chapter 16

Deletes a file or a set of files. ERASE is interchangeable with DEL.

Syntax

```
DEL filespec [/P]
```

Parameters and Switches

filespec	Identifies file(s) to delete.
/P	Prompts for confirmation before each deletion.

Notes

DEL can't delete files with the system, hidden, or read-only attribute.

You can delete all the files in one directory (except system, hidden, and read-only files) by using *.* as *filespec* or by using a path without a file name. Without /P, DEL asks whether you really want to erase all the files.

See UNDELETE for information about possibly restoring a deleted file.

Examples

```
DEL OLDFILE.EXE
```

Deletes OLDFILE.EXE from the current directory (unless OLDFILE.EXE is a system, hidden, or read-only file).

```
DEL C:\OFFICE\OLDFILE.* /P
```

Deletes all files named OLDFILE with any extension from directory C:\OFFICE except those with system, hidden, or read-only attributes. DEL displays each file name and asks whether you want to delete it.

```
DEL *.*
```

Asks whether you really want to delete all files in the directory. If you answer Y, DEL deletes all files in the current directory except system, hidden, and read-only files.

```
DEL C:\OFFICE
```

Asks whether you really want to delete all files in the directory. If you answer Y, DEL deletes all files in C:\OFFICE except system, hidden, and read-only files.

```
DEL C:\OFFICE\*.* /P
```

Displays each file name in C:\OFFICE (except system and hidden files) and asks you if you want to delete it. If you answer Y for a read-only file, DEL tells you `Access denied`.

DELOLDOS

Chapter 4

Removes old version(s) of DOS from the drive.

Syntax

`DELOLDOS [/B]`

Parameters and Switches

none	Presents warning message in color.
/B	Presents warning message in black and white.

Notes

When you install DOS 6, SETUP saves any previous DOS version it finds on the boot drive in a directory called OLD_DOS.*n*. If you install DOS several times for some reason, you may have several such directories, with *n*=1 for the first, 2 for the second, and so on.

When you are sure that you can live with DOS 6, you can remove all these OLD_DOS.n directories at once by running DELOLDOS.

When you start DELOLDOS, a warning screen appears. If you do not want to continue, press any key except Y.

> **Warning:** If you have backups from earlier versions of DOS, be sure you have saved the old versions of RESTORE or MSBACKUP before you use DELOLDOS. See Chapter 24, "Restore and Compare," for details on how to save and use these older versions.

DELTREE

Chapter 14

Deletes a directory and all its files and subdirectories; deletes files in a directory.

Syntax

`DELTREE [/Y] path ¦ filespec [...]`

Parameters and Switches

/Y	Carries out DELTREE without first prompting you for confirmation.
path	Specifies the directory at the top of the branch that you want to delete.
filespec	Specifies file(s) and directories that you want to delete.

Notes

You can't use DELTREE to delete the current directory. You can, however, delete the files in the current directory and all its children.

DELTREE deletes files and subdirectories regardless of their attributes. When DELTREE deletes a directory, it deletes the entire branch headed by the directory with no regard to filenames or attributes within that branch.

You can use wildcards. DELTREE deletes every file and subdirectory (with all its contents and children) whose name matches the global name.

DELTREE always prompts you for confirmation before deleting a file or a branch. (In the prompt, it calls a file a subdirectory.)

When DELTREE is successful, it returns an exit code of 0.

Examples

```
DELTREE C:\TEST1
```

Deletes the TEST1 directory on drive C, including all its files and subdirectories and their files. Prompts before deleting the branch. (If TEST1 is a file, deletes the file.)

```
DELTREE C:\HOLD\*.1
```

If C:\HOLD contains any files with names matching the filespec, deletes them, prompting before each one. If C:\HOLD has any child subdirectories with names matching the filespec, deletes them along with all their files and subdirectories; prompts before deleting each branch.

```
DELTREE /Y D:\TEST D:\TEMP D:\PRACTICE
```

If D:\TEST, D:\TEMP, and D:\PRACTICE are subdirectory names, deletes the three branches headed by these subdirectories. If the three names are filenames, deletes the three files.

DEVICE

Chapter 21

Loads a device driver into conventional memory.

Syntax

```
DEVICE=filespec [parameters]
```

Parameters

filespec	Identifies the device driver to load.
parameters	Specifies any command line parameters required by the device driver.

Notes

You must not load COUNTRY.SYS and KEYBOARD.SYS with the DEVICE command. Use the COUNTRY command to load COUNTRY.SYS and the KEYB command to load KEYBOARD.SYS. If you try to load either of them with DEVICE, your system halts and you must bypass these commands in CONFIG.SYS to re-start it.

See Appendix A, "Device Drivers," for directions on loading the device drivers included in DOS. For third-party device drivers, see the manufacturer's instructions.

See DEVICEHIGH to load device drivers into upper memory instead of conventional memory.

Examples

```
DEVICE=C:\DOS\ANSI.SYS
```

Loads the device driver ANSI.SYS into conventional memory.

```
DEVICE=C:\DOS\DISPLAY.SYS CON=(EGA,437,3)
```

Loads the device driver DISPLAY.SYS into conventional memory. Note that CON=(EGA,437,3) represents parameters that DISPLAY.SYS requires for its operation.

DEVICEHIGH

Chapter 30

Loads a device driver into upper memory, if possible.

Syntax

```
DEVICEHIGH [[/L:region[,min][;region[,min]...]] [/S]] filespec [parameters]
```

Parameters and Switches

filespec	Identifies the device driver.
/L	Loads the device driver into specific region(s) of upper memory.

region	Identifies a region in upper memory.
min	Specifies the minimum size required in a region when the device driver is running.
/S	Shrinks the UMB to its minimum size while the driver is loading.
parameters	Specifies any command line parameters required by the device driver.

Notes

See DEVICE for information and warnings about loading device drivers.

If you have an 80386 or later processor, have loaded EMM386.EXE, and requested UMB support, you may have upper memory blocks (UMBs) available. DEVICEHIGH loads a device driver into available UMBs. If not, DEVICEHIGH loads the driver into conventional memory, if possible.

Since this command will be executed before any PATH command, always include an absolute path with *filespec* unless the driver is located in the root directory of the boot drive.

See MEMMAKER for a command that converts DEVICE commands to DEVICEHIGH. The /L and /S switches are used by MEMMAKER; avoid trying to use them unless you understand what they do.

DOS 5's DEVICEHIGH command, which has a different syntax, still works with DOS 6.

Examples

```
DEVICEHIGH=C:\DOS\ANSI.SYS
```

Loads the ANSI.SYS driver into upper memory if available.

DIR

Chapter 14

Displays a list of a directory's files and subdirectories.

Syntax

```
DIR [filespec] [/P] [/W] [/A[attrib]] [/O[order]] [/S] [/B] [/L] [/C[H]]
```

Parameters and Switches

none	Lists the complete directory of the current drive in the default format.
filespec	Specifies the directory and file(s) to list.
/P	Displays one page at a time.

/W	Displays the listing of names only in wide format, with as many as five names per line.
/A[attrib]	Displays entries that meet the criteria in *attrib*.
/O[order]	Displays entries in the order specified by order.
/S	Lists contents of subdirectories too.
/B	Suppresses heading and summary information and lists filespecs only.
/L	Displays directory listing in lowercase.
/C	Displays the compression ratio of files stored on compressed volumes.
/CH	Displays a more accurate compression ratio of files stored on DBLSPACE or DRVSPACE volumes.

Notes

The DIRCMD environment variable establishes default switches for the DIR command (see SET). These notes describe DOS's defaults when you don't set DIRCMD.

When you use /W, the listing does not show size, date, or time. In this format, DIR encloses subdirectory names in brackets, as in [DOS].

DIR does not list system or hidden files or subdirectories unless /A requests them.

When you include the /A switch, DIR lists only those files and subdirectories that have the specified attribute(s). /A without *attrib* requests all files regardless of their attributes. Permissible values for *attrib* are as follows:

H	Lists hidden files or subdirectories
-H	Lists nonhidden files or subdirectories
S	Lists system files or subdirectories
-S	Lists nonsystem files or subdirectories
D	Lists subdirectories (no files)
-D	Lists files (no subdirectories)
A	Lists files and subdirectories with the archive attribute
-A	Lists files or subdirectories without the archive attribute
R	Lists read-only files or subdirectories
-R	Lists nonread-only files or subdirectories

You can use multiple attributes. Don't put spaces between multiple values in *attrib*; /AHS-R lists files and subdirectories that are both hidden and system but not read-only.

By default, DIR lists entries in the order that they appear in the directory. /O without *order* displays directories first, sorted by name and extension, then files sorted by name and extension. Values for *order* are as follows:

A	Lists entries in alphanumeric order by name
-A	Lists entries in reverse alphanumeric order by name
E	Lists entries in alphanumeric order by extension
-E	Lists entries in reverse alphanumeric order by extension
D	Lists entries by date and time, earliest first
-D	Lists entries by date and time, latest first
S	Lists entries by file size, smallest first
-S	Lists entries by file size, largest first
G	Lists all subdirectories before all files
-G	Lists all files before all subdirectories
C	Lists entries by compression ratio, lowest first
-C	Lists entries by compression ratio, highest first

You can specify more than one sort order. Don't put spaces between multiple *order* codes. DIR sorts by the first value first; within that, by the second value, and so on. For example, if you use /OES, DIR sorts entries by extension, then by size (smallest first) within each extension.

/S produces a listing for each subdirectory in the branch (except hidden and system subdirectories). You can get a more compact listing by combining /S with /B.

/S combined with /A includes an entry for a hidden or system subdirectory in the parent directory's listing but does not list the subdirectory's contents. The only way to list the contents of a hidden or system subdirectory is to specify the subdirectory's name in *filespec*.

You can override DIRCMD settings for a single command by putting a minus sign in front of the switch letter. If DIRCMD requests /W as the default, for example, you can turn off the /W switch for a single DIR command, by using /-W in the command line.

Examples

These examples assume that you have not set DIRCMD.

```
DIR /P
```

Lists the current directory (except system or hidden files and subdirectories), pausing after each full screen until you press any key.

```
DIR E:\WIN\*.BAT /S
```

Lists all files and subdirectories with extension BAT in E:\WIN and its subdirectories (except hidden and system files and subdirectories).

```
DIR MYFILE.* /OE /B > PRN
```

Prints a listing (with no heading and no summary) of all files and subdirectories named MYFILE with any extension in the current directory (except system and hidden ones). DIR sorts the listing alphanumerically by extension.

```
DIR /A
```

Lists all subdirectories and files in the current directory, including system and hidden ones.

```
DIR /A-RA /W
```

Lists, in wide format, all subdirectories and files in the current directory, including system and hidden ones, that have the archive but not the read-only attributes.

```
DIR /O-GND
```

Lists all subdirectories and files in the current directory except hidden and system ones. DIR displays the files first, then subdirectories. Within each of these groups, DIR sorts alphanumerically by name and within name by date and time.

```
DIR MYFILE.BAT /B /S
```

Lists all files in the current branch that have the name MYFILE.BAT except system or hidden files, or those in system or hidden sub-directories. The listing does not include headings or summaries for the directory or for any subdirectory listed, but displays the full path for each file and subdirectory. This is a good way to find a missing file on a drive.

DISKCOMP

Chapter 18

Compares two floppy disks.

Syntax

```
DISKCOMP [drive1] [drive2] [/1] [/8]
```

Parameters and Switches

drive1	Identifies one drive that holds a disk for comparison.
drive2	Identifies a second drive that holds a disk for comparison.
/1	Compares only the first side of the disks, even if they are double-sided.
/8	Compares only the first 8 sectors per track, even if the disks contain more sectors per track.

Notes

DISKCOMP works with floppy disks only.

If you omit *drive2*, DISKCOMP uses the current drive as *drive2*. If you omit *drive1* and *drive2*, DISKCOMP uses the current drive as both *drive1* and *drive2*. When *drive1* and *drive2* are the same drive, DISKCOMP prompts you to change disks as necessary.

The disks must have the same format. However, the /1 and /8 switches can make certain types of disks appear to have the same format by ignoring either the second side or additional sectors per track.

DISKCOMP compares disks track by track, not file by file. When you use COPY or XCOPY to copy all files from one disk to another, the data probably does not reside in the same locations on both disks, so DISKCOMP does not recognize the disks as identical.

DISKCOMP ignores differences in volume serial numbers.

If you have just copied a disk with DISKCOPY and DISKCOMP finds the copy not identical to the original, the problem may be due to bad sectors or a failing drive or memory chip.

DISKCOMP sets an exit code as follows:

0	The disks are the same.
1	DISKCOMP found differences.
2	The user pressed Ctrl+C or Ctrl+Break to stop DISKCOMP.
3	A critical error occurred.
4	An initialization error occurred.

In a batch program you can follow DISKCOMP with an IF command to test ERRORLEVEL and decide what to do next.

Examples

```
DISKCOMP A: B:
```

Compares the disk in drive A to the disk in drive B.

```
DISKCOMP A: A:
```

Compares the disk in drive A to a second disk that you will swap into drive A. (DISKCOMP tells you when to swap disks.)

```
DISKCOMP
```

Compares the disk in the current drive to a second disk that you will swap into the same drive.

DISKCOPY

Chapter 18

Copies one floppy disk to another.

Syntax

```
DISKCOPY [drive1] [drive2] [/1] [/M] [/V]
```

Parameters and Switches

drive1	Identifies the drive holding the source disk.
drive2	Identifies the drive holding the destination disk.
/1	Copies the first side only of the source disk.
/M	Uses only conventional memory to make the copy.
/V	Verifies that copied data is correct.

Notes

DISKCOPY works with floppy disks only. If the destination disk is unformatted, DISKCOPY formats it to match the source disk.

If you omit *drive2*, DISKCOPY uses the current drive as *drive2*. If you omit *drive1* and *drive2*, DISKCOPY uses the current drive as both *drive1* and *drive2*. When *drive1* and *drive2* are the same drive, DISKCOPY prompts you to change disks as necessary.

DISKCOPY creates a new serial number for the destination disk and displays the number when the copy is complete.

DISKCOPY copies the original disk exactly. Any fragmented files on the source disk are fragmented on the destination disk. After DISKCOPY, the destination disks FAT is identical to the sources FAT. Any bad sector markings on the source are duplicated on the destination (little harm done); but the destination's original bad sector markings, if any, are overwritten (usually causing DISKCOPY to fail).

When you make a single-drive copy under DOS 6.2 (or later) without /M, DISKCOPY copies the entire source disk to a temporary file, if there's room on the drive identified in the TEMP environment variable. It then asks you to swap disks and creates the destination disk from the temp file. It offers you the option of making more destination disks from the same data before deleting the temporary file. This process is much faster than earlier versions of DISKCOPY.

DISKCOPY sets an exit code as follows:

0	The copy was successful.
1	A non-fatal read/write error occurred.

2	The user pressed Ctrl+C or Ctrl+Break to stop DISKCOPY.
3	A critical error occurred.
4	An initialization error occurred.

In a batch program, you can follow DISKCOPY with an IF command to test ERRORLEVEL and decide what to do next.

Examples

```
DISKCOPY A: B:
```

Copies the disk in drive A to the disk in drive B.

```
DISKCOPY A: A:
```

Copies the disk in drive A to a second disk that you will swap into drive A.

```
DISKCOPY /V
```

Copies the disk in the current drive to a second disk that you will swap into the drive. Verifies that copied data is correct.

DOS

Chapter 21

Loads DOS into the High Memory Area (HMA) and specifies that DOS manages upper memory blocks (UMBs).

Syntax

```
DOS=[HIGH ¦ LOW] [,] [UMB ¦ NOUMB]
```

Parameters

| HIGH ¦ LOW | Specifies whether DOS should load itself into the HMA; the default is LOW. |
| UMB ¦ NOUMB | Specifies whether DOS should manage upper memory blocks (UMBs); the default is NOUMB. |

Notes

You can use one or both parameters. When you use both, either can come first, but you must separate them by a comma.

You must install an extended memory manager such as HIMEM.SYS before you can use either HIGH or UMB. You must install an upper-memory-block provider before you can use UMB. If you have an 80386 or higher processor, you can use EMM386.EXE to provide access to upper memory blocks.

When you use HIGH, DOS attempts to load part of itself into the HMA, freeing conventional space. If DOS is unable to use the HMA, it defaults to LOW.

When you load DOS in the HMA, some programs may have trouble loading in conventional memory. See LOADFIX for details.

Examples

DOS=HIGH

DOS loads itself into the HMA.

DOS=UMB

DOS can access upper memory blocks when loading programs and device drivers.

DOS=HIGH,UMB

DOS loads itself into the HMA and can load programs and device drivers into UMBs.

DOSKEY

Chapter 13

Saves and provides access to commands and macros entered at the DOS command prompt.

Syntax

```
DOSKEY [/BUFSIZE=size] [/INSERT ¦ /OVERSTRIKE] [/HISTORY] [/MACROS] [mname=text]
[/REINSTALL]
```

Parameters and Switches

none	Loads the DOSKEY TSR with default values for BUFSIZE and /INSERT ¦ /OVERSTRIKE; immediately begins recording commands in the DOSKEY buffer.
/BUFSIZE=size	Specifies the size of the DOSKEY buffer. This parameter is effective only when loading or reinstalling the DOSKEY TSR.
/INSERT	Sets default typing mode to insert.
/OVERSTRIKE	Sets default typing mode to overstrike. (This is the default if you don't specify /INSERT or /OVERSTRIKE.)
/HISTORY	Lists all commands in the DOSKEY buffer; abbreviate as /H.
/MACROS	Lists all current macros; abbreviate as /M.
mname=text	Defines a macro named mname. Text defines command(s) to execute when you run mname.
/REINSTALL	Installs a new copy of DOSKEY.

Notes

DOSKEY is a TSR that saves each command subsequently typed at the DOS prompt. When the buffer is full, each new command overlays the oldest command in the buffer. The minimum *size* for the DOSKEY buffer is 256 bytes; the default is 512 bytes.

DOSKEY lets you edit commands at the prompt using the following editing keys:

Left arrow	Moves the cursor left one character.
Right arrow	Moves the cursor right one character.
Ctrl+Left arrow	Moves the cursor left one word.
Ctrl+Right arrow	Moves the cursor right one word.
Home	Moves the cursor to the beginning of the command line.
End	Moves the cursor to the end of the command line.
Esc	Clears the command line.
Insert	Toggles insert mode on and off.
Backspace	Deletes the character to the left of the cursor.
Delete	Deletes the character at the cursor.
Ctrl+Home	Deletes from the cursor to the beginning of the command line.
Ctrl+End	Deletes from the cursor to the end of the command line.

When insert mode is on, typing inserts text at the cursor. When overstrike mode is on, typing replaces the text at the cursor. The insert key toggles between the two typing modes, but each time you press Enter, it returns to the default.

If you don't specify the typing mode when installing or reinstalling DOSKEY, /OVERSTRIKE is the default. You can change the default (without reinstalling DOSKEY) by entering a DOSKEY command with the /INSERT or /OVERSTRIKE switch.

DOSKEY lets you recall commands from the buffer. Use these keys to recall a command:

Up arrow	Recalls the previous command in the buffer.
Down arrow	Recalls the next command in the buffer.
Page Up	Recalls the oldest command in the buffer.
Page Down	Recalls the newest command in the buffer.
F7	Displays a numbered list of all saved commands.
Alt+F7	Deletes all the commands in the buffer.
F8	Recalls the next command in the buffer that starts with the letters on the command line.
F9	Prompts for a command number, then recalls that command.

DOSKEY displays a recalled command at the DOS prompt. You can edit and enter the command as though you had just typed it.

To recall a command without scanning the entire list, type the first few letters and press F8. Keep pressing F8 until DOSKEY recalls the desired command.

To recall a command by number, press F7 to scan the numbered list, find the command you want, then press F9 so you can enter its number.

DOSKEY lets you include two or more commands on a command line. Separate commands by pressing Ctrl+T, which displays as ¶. Use this feature to create more effective entries in your command history. The command DIR A: ¶ DIR B: [PP] DIR C:, for example, which displays directories for the default directories on drives A, B, and C, can be recalled and entered as a single command.

A macro consists of one or more commands that you can execute by entering the macro name. Macro definitions can contain these special characters:

$G	Redirects output; equivalent to the redirection symbol for output (>). (If you use the redirection symbol itself, it redirects the output of the DOSKEY command instead of being stored as part of the macro.)
GG	Appends output to the end of a file; equivalent to the append redirection symbol for output (>>).
$L	Redirects input; equivalent to the redirection symbol for input (<).
$B	Sends output to the next command; equivalent to the pipe symbol (¦).
$T	Separates commands; equivalent to the DOSKEY command separator (Ctrl+T).
$$	Specifies the dollar-sign character.
$n	Represents a parameter to be specified when the macro is run; n may be 1 through 9. These are similar to the batch parameters %1 through %9.
$*	Represents all parameters. $* is replaced by everything on a command line following a macro name.

A macro may have the same name as a DOS command. To run the macro, type its name at the DOS prompt. To use the DOS command instead, insert one or more spaces between the prompt and the command. Use this feature to override DOS commands that you want to adapt for some reason.

DOSKEY macros and the command history share the same buffer. Newly defined macros may overlay commands in the buffer, but neither commands nor new macros ever overlay existing macros. DOSKEY limits the number of macros you can create to save about half of the buffer for the command history.

A batch program cannot execute a macro (although it can include a DOSKEY command to create one).

A macro cannot be more than 120 characters long.

/REINSTALL installs a new copy of DOSKEY with an empty DOSKEY buffer. The previous copy of DOSKEY remains in memory, although inaccessible, wasting memory space.

Examples

```
DOSKEY
```

If this is the first DOSKEY command after booting, it installs the DOSKEY TSR with a 512-byte buffer and overstrike as the default typing mode. Otherwise this command has no effect.

```
DOSKEY /BUFSIZE=1024 /INSERT
```

If this is the first DOSKEY command after booting, it installs the DOSKEY TSR with a buffer size of 1024 bytes and a default typing mode of insert. Otherwise the command only changes the default typing mode to insert (and /BUFSIZE has no effect).

```
DOSKEY /H /M
```

Displays the command history and lists all current macro definitions.

```
DOSKEY /H > TEMP.BAT
```

Copies the command history to TEMP.BAT.

```
DOSKEY ACOPY=COPY $1 $2 $T DIR $2 $G PRN
```

Defines a macro ACOPY that copies a file then prints a directory listing for the new file name.

```
ACOPY JUNEDAT.NEW JUNEDAT.OLD
```

Executes the ACOPY macro, copying JUNEDAT.NEW to JUNEDAT.OLD and printing a directory listing for JUNEDAT.OLD.

DOSSHELL

Chapter 5

Starts DOS Shell, a graphical user interface to DOS.

Syntax

```
DOSSHELL [/T[:resolution[n]] ¦ /G[:resolution[n]]] [/B]
```

Parameters and Switches

/T	Starts DOS Shell in text mode.
/G	Starts DOS Shell in graphics mode.

/B	Starts DOS Shell in black and white.
resolution	Specifies the screen-resolution category.
n	Specifies screen resolution when there is more than one choice within a category.

Notes

DOS Shell is not included in DOS 6.2 and later, but if you don't have a copy from an earlier version of DOS, you can request it from Microsoft (see the *User's Guide* for details).

DOS Shell requires at least 384KB of conventional memory.

If you want to run both DOS Shell and Microsoft Windows, start the Shell from within Windows, not vice versa.

If the file DOSSHELL.INI is not in the same directory as DOSSHELL.EXE, set the environment variable DOS Shell to show the path for DOSSHELL.INI before you start up DOS Shell. (See the SET command.)

Resolution can be L, M, or H for low, medium, or high resolution, respectively. The default value depends on your hardware. Possible values for *n*, as well as the default value, depend on your hardware.

If you start DOS Shell without /T or /G and cannot read the screen, press F3 to get back to the command prompt and try using /T for text mode. Once DOS Shell is running, you can adjust the display mode (T or G) and screen resolution by using the Options, Display command. When you set values using Options, Display, DOS Shell them in DOSSHELL.INI and they become the default settings. (Command line switches and parameters override the default settings but do not set new defaults.)

Examples

```
DOSSHELL /T:L
```

Starts DOS Shell in text mode with low resolution (25 lines per screen).

```
DOSSHELL /G /B
```

Starts DOS Shell in black-and-white graphics mode with default resolution.

```
DOSSHELL
```

Starts DOS Shell with default settings from DOSSHELL.INI.

DRIVPARM

Chapter 51

Redefines parameters for an existing physical drive.

Syntax

`DRIVPARM=/D:n [/C] [/F:type] [/H:heads] [/I] [/N] [/S:sectors] [/T:tracks]`

Parameters and Switches

`/D:n`	Identifies the drive to be redefined.
`/C`	Indicates that the drive has change line support; valid for removable drives only.
`/F:type`	Specifies the drive type.
`/H:heads`	Specifies the number of heads.
`/I`	Indicates an electronically compatible 3 1/2-inch drive.
`/N`	Indicates a non-removable drive.
`/S:sectors`	Specifies number of sectors per track.
`/T:tracks`	Specifies number of tracks.

Notes

Normally DOS senses block devices such as floppy disks, hard disks, and tape drives while booting, but occasionally DOS is wrong. If DOS has trouble accessing one of your block devices, especially in formatting it, include the DRIVPARM command in CONFIG.SYS so that DOS always accesses the drive correctly.

In /D, n should be 0 for drive A, 1 for drive B, 2 for drive C, and so on.

Change-line support, indicated by /C, means that a disk drive can detect when its door is open. If you omit /C, DOS treats the drive as if it has no change-line support and checks the disk serial number every time it accesses the drive.

Warning: Never specify that a disk drive has change-line support when it doesn't. Doing so could cause DOS to overwrite valuable data because it doesn't know you changed disks.

In /F, *type* can have one of these values:

0	360KB or less
1	1.2MB
2	720KB
3	8-inch single density
4	8-inch double density
5	Hard disk
6	Tape drive

7	1.44MB
8	Read/write optical disk
9	2.88MB

If you don't use /F, disk type defaults to 2 (720KB).

The following table shows the defaults for *heads*, *sectors*, and *tracks* when /F indicates a floppy disk (types 0, 1, 2, 7, or 9). To specify other values, use the /H, /S, and/or /T switches as necessary.

Type	Capacity	Heads	Sectors	Tracks
0	160KB	1	8	40
0	180KB	1	9	40
0	320KB	2	8	40
0	360KB	2	9	40
2	720KB	2	9	80
1	1.2MB	2	15	80
7	1.44MB	2	18	80
9	2.88MB	2	36	80

Use /I if the drive is a 3 1/2-inch floppy disk drive using your existing drive controller, but your ROM BIOS does not support 3 1/2-inch floppy disks.

Wrong or inconsistent values can result in erratic or bad formatting on the drive. If you must redefine a drive, get the right values from your drive's documentation or manufacturer.

If you redefine your boot drive incorrectly, your system may not boot or it may boot and destroy the root directory. Be sure to have valid backups before redefining the boot drive.

Examples

```
DRIVPARM /D:1 /C
```

Defines drive B as a 720KB drive (by default) with change-line support.

```
DRIVPARM /D:4 /F:6 /H:1 /S:40 /T:28
```

Defines the fifth drive as a tape drive with one head that writes 28 tracks of 40 sectors per track.

DRVSPACE

Chapters 34 and 45

Compresses hard disk drives and floppy disks; manages compressed drives.

Note: DRVSPACE is available with DOS 6.22 only. See DBLSPACE for DOS 6.0's compression program. The DRVSPACE and DBLSPACE commands are identical except for the /CHKDSK function, which DRVSPACE does not offer.

Syntax 1

DRVSPACE

Starts the DRVSPACE setup program, which installs DriveSpace and compresses and mounts a drive. If DriveSpace is already installed, opens the DriveSpace window.

Notes

The first time you use DRVSPACE, you must use this syntax. DRVSPACE sets up your system for file compression, placing the DRVSPACE core program (DRVSPACE.BIN) and other files in the root directory of your boot drive. It also places a DEVICEHIGH=DRVSPACE.SYS command into your CONFIG.SYS file so that DRVSPACE.BIN moves to upper memory, if possible; otherwise, it moves to the bottom of conventional memory. DRVSPACE also compresses at least one hard disk drive. You can't install DriveSpace without compressing at least one hard disk drive.

When you use Syntax 1 again, it loads the DriveSpace program and displays a dialog box with pull-down menus, from which you can compress other drives or manage compressed drives.

After installation, you can accomplish DriveSpace functions without opening the dialog box by using other DRVSPACE command formats.

When DriveSpace compresses existing data, it creates a large file named DRVSPACE.000 that holds the compressed data. (This is a system, hidden, and read-only file.) The original drive now contains the DRVSPACE.000 file, other files that are not appropriate for compression (such as a Windows swap file), and some free space. The compressed data file is called a *compressed volume file* (CVF) and is accessed and referred to by the original drive letter. The original drive, called the *host drive*, is accessed by a new letter assigned by DriveSpace. (If you're not sure what letter DriveSpace assigned to a host drive, use DRVSPACE /INFO or /LIST, syntaxes 8 and 9.)

Assigning drive letters to the compressed and host drives is called *mounting* the compressed drive. DriveSpace automatically mounts all compressed hard disk drives when you boot your system. It also mounts floppy disk drives automatically unless you turn off the Automount parameter. (See Syntax 14.)

DriveSpace can't compress a drive that's completely full. Your boot drive must have at least 1.2MB of free space; other drives, including floppies, must have at least 1.1MB.

If your drive had a SENTRY directory, there is a SENTRY directory on both the compressed and host drive after compression. Files deleted before compression cannot be recovered, however. Files deleted after compression can be undeleted as usual by Delete Sentry. (You need to add the new drive letter as a drive protected by Delete Sentry, however, if you want to protect the uncompressed host drive.)

If your drive had a PCTRACKR.DEL file, it is left on the host drive, but any files deleted before compression are probably unrecoverable because their clusters have been reused by the CVF. Files deleted after compression can be undeleted as usual by deletion-tracking. (You need to add the new drive letter as a drive protected by deletion-tracking, however, if you want to protect the uncompressed host drive.)

If you use a SMARTDRV command naming a compressed drive, you will see a message telling you that you must cache the host drive. You don't need to change the command; DriveSpace and SmartDrive work together to cache the compressed drive through the host drive.

> **Warning:** Avoid write-caching a compressed drive; delayed writes could result in data loss on the compressed drive if your system goes down before the writes can be completed. If you installed SmartDrive before upgrading to DOS 6.22, you might be write-caching your compressed drive. Change your SmartDrive configuration so that the compressed drive is not write-cached.

The following command syntaxes manage DriveSpace drives from the command prompt. All these functions also can be accomplished from the DriveSpace dialog box, which opens when you enter the DRVSPACE command with no parameters (this Syntax).

Syntax 2

```
DRVSPACE /COMPRESS drive1 [/NEWDRIVE=drive2] [/RESERVE=size] [/F]
```

Compresses the files on an existing hard disk drive, floppy drive, or other removable medium, and mounts the drive.

Parameters and Switches

/COMPRESS	Requests the COMPRESS function; abbreviate as /COM.
drive1	Identifies the existing drive you want to compress.
/NEWDRIVE=*drive2*	Specifies the drive letter you want to use for the host drive; abbreviate as /NEW. (Use Syntax 10 to find out what drive letters are available.) Without /NEW, DriveSpace selects a drive letter for the new drive.
/RESERVE=*size*	Specifies, in megabytes, how much space to leave uncompressed on the host drive; abbreviate as /RES. Without /RES, DriveSpace leaves 2MB on a hard disk drive, if possible.

/ F   Suppresses the final report so that you return to the
                            command prompt automatically.

Notes

When DriveSpace compresses a floppy disk, it adds a file called READTHIS.TXT to the host drive. This file explains to the recipient that the disk contains compressed data and how to mount the disk and access the data. (READTHIS.TXT doesn't show up when the recipient has a DOS 6.22 system with DriveSpace installed because the compressed drive on the floppy is mounted automatically. It shows up on systems where DriveSpace is not installed.)

Whether or not you specify /RES at this point, you can increase or decrease the amount of uncompressed space later. (See Syntax 13.)

Refer to Syntax 1 for more information about what happens when you compress a disk.

Examples

```
DRVSPACE /COM A
```

Compresses the floppy disk in drive A; after compression, assigns the host drive an available drive letter.

```
DRVSPACE /COM D /RES=2.5 /NEW=L
```

Compresses drive D, leaving 2.5MB of free space (if possible); assigns the host drive the letter L.

Syntax 3

```
DRVSPACE /UNCOMPRESS drive
```

Uncompresses a drive.

Parameters and switches

/ UNCOMPRESS   Requests the UNCOMPRESS function.

drive   Identifies the compressed drive to be uncompressed.

Notes

The UNCOMPRESS function uncompresses the data in the CVF, storing it on the host drive. If there's not enough room on the host drive to hold all the uncompressed data, you might need to delete some of the compressed files or move them to other drives first. After uncompressing, the compressed drive is unmounted and deleted. The host drive's original name is restored.

When the last compressed drive is uncompressed, DRVSPACE.BIN is removed from memory but it is not deleted from the boot directory. You will be able to run DRVSPACE to compress drives later.

Syntax 4

```
DRVSPACE /CREATE drive1 [/NEWDRIVE=drive2] [/SIZE=size1 ¦ /RESERVE=size2]
```

Creates a new, empty, compressed drive out of free space on an uncompressed drive.

Parameters and Switches

/CREATE	Requests the CREATE function; abbreviate as /CR.
drive1	Identifies the host drive.
/NEWDRIVE=drive2	Specifies the drive letter for the new CVF; abbreviate as /NEW. Without /NEW, DriveSpace selects a drive letter for the new CVF.
/SIZE=size1	Specifies the total size, in megabytes, of the compressed volume file; abbreviate as /SI.
/RESERVE=size2	Specifies how many megabytes of free space to leave on the uncompressed drive; abbreviate as /RES.

Notes

You can't use /CREATE on a floppy disk.

When you create a CVF out of free space instead of existing data, DriveSpace assigns the new drive letter to the new volume instead of the host drive (which retains its existing drive letter).

You can create a new, empty volume on a drive that already contains a compressed volume file. The original CVF is named DRVSPACE.000 and has the original drive letter. The new CVF is DRVSPACE.001 (assuming this is the second CVF on the drive) and receives a new drive letter. The remaining uncompressed space is on the host drive, which keeps the drive letter assigned to it when DRVSPACE.000 was created.

If you don't specify /SIZE or /RES, DriveSpace uses all but 1MB of free space.

Examples

```
DRVSPACE /CR E
```

Creates a new, empty compressed volume file on host drive E, leaving 1MB of free space; assigns an available drive letter to the new compressed volume file.

```
DRVSPACE /CR E /NEW=L /RES=1.5
```

Creates a new, empty, CVF on host drive E, leaving 1.5MB of free space on E (if possible) and assigning the drive letter L to the new CVF.

Syntax 5

```
DRVSPACE /DEFRAGMENT [drive] [/F]
```

Defragments the compressed drive.

Parameters and Switches

/DEFRAGMENT	Requests the DEFRAGMENT function; abbreviate as /DEF.
drive	Specifies the compressed drive to defragment; the default is the current drive.
/F	Defragments more fully.

Notes

Defragmenting is not necessary to improve performance on a compressed drive. It does, however, consolidate the drive's free space. If you want to reduce the drive's size (see Syntax 14), you should use DRVSPACE /DEF first.

If you run DOS's DEFRAG on a DriveSpace drive, DOS automatically runs the DRVSPACE /DEF command as soon as DEFRAG is finished.

Example

```
DRVSPACE /DEF /F
```

Defragments the current (compressed) drive.

Syntax 6

```
DRVSPACE /DELETE drive
```

Deletes a compressed drive, erasing all its files.

Parameters and Switches

/DELETE	Requests the DELETE function; abbreviate as /DEL.
drive	Specifies the compressed drive to delete.

Notes

Deleting a DriveSpace drive also unmounts it. If you delete DRVSPACE.000, the original drive letter is restored to the host drive. If you delete any other CVF, the drive letter from the deleted volume becomes available for other uses.

If you change your mind after deleting a DriveSpace drive, you may be able to recover it using DOS's UNDELETE command. Look for a deleted file named DRVSPACE.nnn on the host drive.

If you are able to restore the file with UNDELETE, you still can't access its data until you mount it. (See Syntax 11.)

Example

```
DRVSPACE /DEL F
```

Deletes the compressed drive referred to as drive F.

Syntax 7

```
DRVSPACE /FORMAT drive
```

Formats a compressed drive.

Parameters and Switches

/FORMAT	Requests the FORMAT function; abbreviate as /FOR.
drive	Specifies the compressed drive to format.

Notes

Formatting a compressed drive deletes all the files it contains. You can't unformat a compressed drive if you change your mind.

Example

```
DRVSPACE /FOR G
```

Formats compressed drive G, erasing all its data.

Syntax 8

```
DRVSPACE [/INFO] drive
```

Displays information about a compressed drive.

Parameters and Switches

/INFO	Requests the INFO function; this is the default when no other DRVSPACE function is specified.
drive	Identifies the drive about which you want information.

Notes

The information displayed includes the host drive, the CVF's file name, the total space, used space, and free space on both the CVF and the host drive, the actual average compression ratio, and the estimated compression ratio. Free space on the CVF is an estimate of uncompressed bytes that could be compressed into the remaining space in the CVF, based on the estimated compression ratio.

Example

```
DRVSPACE D
```

Displays information about compressed drive D.

```
DRVSPACE /INFO
```

Displays information about the current drive.

Syntax 9

```
DRVSPACE /LIST
```

Lists and describes all your computer's non-network drives, including DriveSpace volumes.

Parameters and Switches

/LIST	Requests the LIST function; abbreviate as /L.

Notes

This syntax lists each available drive letter and describes its status in terms such as Local hard drive, Compressed hard drive, Floppy drive, Removable-media with No disk in drive, Available for DriveSpace, and so on. (RAM drives are described as local hard drives.) Space used and free space are shown for each drive if appropriate. For each mounted compressed drive, the report shows the compressed volume name and its host drive.

Syntax 10

```
DRVSPACE /MOUNT[=nnn] drive1 [/NEWDRIVE=drive2]
```

Mounts a compressed volume.

Parameters and Switches

/MOUNT	Requests the MOUNT function; abbreviate as /MO.
nnn	Identifies the extension of the volume to be mounted; default is 000.
drive	Specifies the drive that contains the compressed file you want to mount.
/NEWDRIVE=drive2	Specifies the drive letter to be assigned; abbreviate as /NEW. Without /NEW, DriveSpace assigns an available drive letter.

Notes

When you mount a DRVSPACE.000 file, the host's drive letter is assigned to the compressed drive, and a new letter is assigned to the host drive. When you mount any other DRVSPACE.nnn file, the new letter is assigned to the compressed drive.

DRVSPACE automatically mounts drives when it compresses or creates them. It may unmount and mount a drive when it is performing certain functions on that drive. It automatically mounts compressed hard drives when the system boots. The only time you need to mount a hard drive is if you have unmounted it. (See Syntax 13.) DriveSpace automatically mounts floppy drives also unless you have changed the AutoMount parameter in DRVSPACE.INI. (See Syntax 14.) If AutoMount = 0, you need to mount a floppy every time you insert a compressed disk in the floppy drive.

Examples

```
DRVSPACE /MO A
```

Mounts a disk in drive A, assigning drive letter A to DRVSPACE.000 and an available drive letter to the uncompressed portion of the disk.

```
DRVSPACE /MO=001 E /NEW=L
```

Mounts a compressed drive, assigning drive letter L to E:\DRVSPACE.001 and retaining E as the drive letter of the host drive.

Syntax 11

```
DRVSPACE /RATIO[=r.r] [drive ¦ /ALL]
```

Changes the estimated compression ratio of one or all compressed drives.

Parameters and Switches

/RATIO=r.r	Specifies the new ratio; from 1.0 to 16.0; the default is the current overall compression ratio for the drive; abbreviate as /RA.
drive	Identifies the drive.
/ALL	Specifies that you want to change the ratio for all currently mounted compressed drives.

Notes

DriveSpace uses the estimated compression ratio to estimate how many bytes of uncompressed data would, when compressed, fit into the CVF. This affects reports from functions such as DIR and DOS Shell.

If you don't specify drive or /ALL, DriveSpace changes the ratio of the current drive.

Use Syntax 8 to find the estimated and actual compression ratio of a drive.

Examples

```
DRVSPACE /RA /ALL
```

Changes the estimated compression ratio of all currently mounted compressed drives to match each one's average compression ratio.

```
DRVSPACE /RA=3 D
```

Changes the estimated compression ratio of compressed drive D to 3.0 to 1.

Syntax 12

```
DRVSPACE /SIZE[=size1 ¦ /RESERVE=size2] drive
```

Changes the size of a compressed drive.

Parameters and Switches

/SIZE	Requests the SIZE function; abbreviate as /SI.
size1	Specifies the new size of the CVF in megabytes. Do not use with /RESERVE.
/RESERVE=size2	Specifies in megabytes the amount of free space you want DriveSpace to leave on the host drive; abbreviate as /RES; do not use if you specify size1. If size2 is 0, the compressed drive is increased to its maximum possible size.
drive	Identifies the compressed drive to resize.

Notes

If you specify neither size1 nor /RES, DriveSpace makes the compressed drive as small as possible.

Examples

```
DRVSPACE /SI=30 D
```

Changes the size of compressed drive D to 30MB (if possible).

```
DRVSPACE /SI /RES=10 D
```

Changes the size of compressed drive D to leave 10MB of free space on its host drive (if possible). You should defragment the compressed drive before doing this.

```
DRVSPACE /SI /RES=0 D
```

Makes compressed drive D as large as possible.

```
DRVSPACE /SI D
```

Makes compressed drive D as small as possible. You should defragment the compressed drive before doing this.

Syntax 13

```
DRVSPACE /UNMOUNT [drive]
```

Unmounts a drive.

Parameters and Switches

/UNMOUNT	Requests the UNMOUNT function; abbreviate as /U.
drive	Specifies the drive to be unmounted; the default is the current drive.

Notes

The unmounted drive becomes unavailable until mounted again. If the host drive letter was swapped to the CVF, the original drive letter now reverts to the host drive, and the host's letter becomes available for other uses. If the letters were not swapped, the CVF's letter becomes available for other uses.

You don't need to unmount a floppy drive before removing it from the disk drive.

Example

```
DRVSPACE /U D
```

Unmounts compressed drive D. If D was assigned to DRVSPACE.000, it now refers to the host drive. Otherwise, the host drive letter remains unchanged and D becomes an available drive letter.

Syntax 14

```
DRVSPACE [/AUTOMOUNT=0 ¦ 1 ¦ x] [/DOUBLEGUARD=0 ¦ 1] [drive1 /HOST=drive2] [/LASTDRIVE=x]
[/MAXFILEFRAGMENTS=n] [/MAXREMOVABLEDRIVES=n] [/ROMSERVER=0 ¦ 1] [/SWITCHES=F ¦ N]
```

Sets default settings in DRVSPACE.INI.

Parameters and Switches

/AUTOMOUNT	Indicates whether or not DriveSpace should mount floppies automatically.
/DOUBLEGUARD	Enables or disables the DoubleGuard feature, which constantly checks for damage to DriveSpace's memory buffers.
/HOST	Specifies the drive name (*drive2*) for the host of a compressed drive (*drive1*).
/LASTDRIVE	Specifies the highest drive name that DriveSpace can use when mounting drives.

/MAXFILEFRAGMENTS	Specifies the maximum number of fragments that a CVF can be split into on the host drive.
/MAXREMOVABLEDRIVES	Specifies the number of additional compressed drives DriveSpace should reserve space for during booting.
/ROMSERVER	Enables or disables the check for a ROM BIOS Microsoft Real-Time Compression Interface (MRCI) server.
/SWITCHES	Controls whether or not a user can bypass DriveSpace during booting.

Notes

DRVSPACE.INI contains default settings for DriveSpace. Because it's a hidden, system, and read-only file, you can't edit it directly. (It would be dangerous to remove the hidden, system, and read-only attributes.) Use these commands to change the settings in DRVSPACE.INI.

You can view DRVSPACE.INI using DOS's EDIT, even though you can't edit it. By viewing it, you can find out what your current settings are for these parameters.

DriveSpace by default mounts removable drives (such as floppy drives) automatically. DriveSpace must set aside memory space for each drive that might be automounted. The command DRVSPACE /AUTOMOUNT=0 sets DRVSPACE.INI so that removable drives are not mounted automatically, saving memory space. DRVSPACE /AUTOMOUNT=1 restores the default setting. You can also identify specific removable drives to be automounted with DRVSPACE /AUTOMOUNT=A, DRVSPACE /AUTOMOUNT=B, and so on. (See Syntax 10 for a command that mounts a compressed drive that hasn't been mounted automatically.)

DoubleGuard constantly checks DriveSpace's memory buffers for corruption and, if detected, halts your computer to prevent damage to your compressed drive. DoubleGuard slows down your system somewhat. You can disable DoubleGuard with the command DRVSPACE /DOUBLEGUARD=0. You can enable it again with DRVSPACE /DOUBLEGUARD=1.

Warning: Disabling DoubleGuard could result in damage to your compressed data.

If you receive the message Compressed drive x is currently too fragmented to mount, the CVF known as drive x has been split into more fragments than specified in the MAXFRAGMENTS setting in DRVSPACE.INI. It can't be mounted or used until you resolve the problem. You can increase the number of allowed fragments by entering the command DRVSPACE /MAXFRAGMENTS=n, where n is the new number of fragments. Or you can remove the CVF's attributes, defragment the host drive, and restore the CVF's attributes again (very important).

The MAXREMOVABLEDRIVES parameter determines the maximum number of additional compressed drives that DriveSpace can handle (whether they are removable or not) after booting. This controls not only how many compressed volumes you can mount from removable drives, but also how many new compressed volumes you can create without rebooting. The default maximum is 2. Lowering it saves memory space but impacts your ability to create new compressed drives.

The MRCI check can impede a ROM BIOS that doesn't use MCRI, so don't enable MRCI checking unless you're sure that your system needs it. Enable MRCI checking with the command DRVSPACE /ROMSERVER=1. Disable it again with DRVSPACE /ROMSERVER=0.

By default, when a user presses Ctrl+F5 during booting, DOS displays each line in CONFIG.SYS and AUTOEXEC.BAT and asks if it should be executed. It also asks if DriveSpace should be loaded. When a user presses Ctrl+F8 during booting, DOS bypasses CONFIG.SYS, AUTOEXEC.BAT, and DRVSPACE.BIN without asking. You can disable the DriveSpace portion of these bypasses by entering the command DRVSPACE /SWITCHES=N. When bypassing is disabled, Ctrl+F5 still conditionally executes CONFIG.SYS and AUTOEXEC.BAT, and Ctrl+F8 still bypasses CONFIG.SYS and AUTOEXEC.BAT.

The command DRVSPACE /SWITCHES=F shortens the time that DOS waits for the user to press a bypass key, which speeds up booting slightly.

Once you have entered /SWITCHES=N and/or /SWITCHES=F, there is no command to remove them from DRVSPACE.INI. You must edit the file and remove the SWITCHES parameter to return to the default settings.

See SWITCHES for a command that disables your ability to bypass AUTOEXEC.BAT and CONFIG.SYS.

ECHO

Chapter 20

Turns command echoing features on or off or displays a message.

Syntax

ECHO [message ¦ ON ¦ OFF]

Parameters and Switches

none	Displays the current setting of ECHO.
ON ¦ OFF	Turns command echoing on or off.
message	Displays message on the screen.
ECHO.	This special ECHO command displays a carriage return (a blank line). Be sure there is no space between ECHO and the period.

Notes

When command echoing is on, DOS displays the command prompt when it is ready to receive and process a command. When processing a batch program, DOS displays a command prompt line (the prompt and the command) followed by a blank line for each command in the program. Command echoing is on by default. Use `ECHO ON` to turn it on when it is off.

Turning off command echoing suppresses the command prompt, but you can still type and enter commands. When executing a batch program, it suppresses the command line and the blank line that normally follows it. Only command output is displayed. Use `ECHO OFF` to turn it off.

ECHO with *message* displays *message* as ECHO's command output, so *message* displays even when command echoing is off.

A batch program can change command echoing only for the duration of the program. If command echoing is on when a batch program starts, it is automatically turned on when the program ends; if it's off when the program starts, its turned off when the program ends.

`ECHO OFF` doesn't take effect until DOS processes the next line. To suppress echoing `ECHO OFF`, or any other single line in a batch program, put @ in front of the line.

Examples

```
@ECHO OFF
ECHO.
ECHO This batch program formats disks in drive A.
ECHO You will need new 5.25 inch disks.
ECHO.
ECHO ON
```

This sequence of commands in a batch program turns ECHO off (without displaying the `ECHO` command), then displays a blank line, a two-line message, and another blank line. Then it turns ECHO on again.

```
ECHO. > PRN
ECHO Beginning of Weekly Report > PRN
ECHO. > PRN
```

Prints a blank line, then the message, then another blank line.

EDIT

Chapter 19

Starts the DOS Editor, which creates and changes ASCII text files.

Syntax

```
EDIT [filespec] [/B] [/G] [/H] [/NOHI]
```

Parameters and Switches

none	Starts the Editor with default screen characteristics and no startup file.
filespec	Opens an ASCII text file. If the file does not exist, creates it; if it does exist, displays its contents.
/B	Uses black-and-white screen mode.
/G	Uses fast-screen updating for a CGA monitor.
/H	Displays the maximum number of lines for your monitor.
/NOHI	Enables the use of an eight-color monitor.

Notes

EDIT does not work if QBASIC.EXE is not in the current directory, in the search path, or in the same directory as EDIT.COM. If you delete QBASIC.EXE to save space, you cannot use the DOS Editor.

If the DOS Editor does not display properly on your monitor, or does not display shortcut keys on the bottom line, try using /B or /NOHI (or both).

Examples

```
EDIT ANYFILE.BAT /B
```

Creates or loads ANYFILE.BAT; displays black-and-white mode.

```
EDIT
```

Starts the Editor in default mode without a startup file.

EMM386

Chapters 30 and 44

Controls expanded memory support.

Syntax

```
EMM386 [ON ¦ OFF ¦ AUTO] [W=ON ¦ W=OFF]
```

Parameters and Switches

none	Displays the status of EMM386 support.
ON	Enables the EMM386.EXE driver.
OFF	Disables the EMM386.EXE driver without unloading it.

AUTO	Lets programs control enabling and disabling of EMM386.EXE driver.
W=ON	Enables Weitek coprocessor support.
W=OFF	Disables Weitek coprocessor support. Default is W=OFF.

Notes

You must have a 386 or higher processor and must have installed the EMM386.EXE device driver before you can use this command. See EMM386.3XE in Appendix A for an explanation of the driver.

You can't turn EMM386 off when it is providing UMBs or when any program is currently using expanded memory.

Some programs, including Microsoft's Windows 3.0 in Standard mode, require that EMM386 be off.

You can't use OFF and W=ON in the same EMM386 command.

The Weitek coprocessor support requires the HMA. If you have used DOS=HIGH, you may not be able to enable Weitek coprocessor support. (See the DOS command.)

Examples

EMM386 OFF

Disables expanded memory support without unloading the EMM386 driver.

EMM386 AUTO

Lets programs enable or disable expanded memory support as needed.

ERASE

See DEL.

EXIT

Chapter 43

Quits a secondary command processor.

Syntax

EXIT

Notes

In a secondary command processor started by COMMAND without /P, EXIT closes the secondary version and returns to the parent. In a secondary command processor started by another program, such as Microsoft Windows or DOS Shell, EXIT closes the secondary command processor and returns to the starting program. In other circumstances, EXIT has no effect.

See the COMMAND command for more information about parent and child command processors.

EXPAND

Chapter 4

Expands files from the DOS installation disks.

Syntax

```
EXPAND [filespec ... [destination]]
```

Parameters

none	Prompts for *filespec* and *destination*.
filespec	Identifies a compressed file that you want to expand on the DOS setup disks.
destination	Specifies the location and/or name of the expanded file(s).

Notes

Most of the files on the installation disks provided with DOS 6.22 are compressed. You can recognize a compressed file on these disks because the last character of the name is an underscore (_). DOS 6.22's SETUP program expands these files. If you need to get a fresh copy of one of them, look at PACKING.LST on Disk 1 to find out which disk the file is on, what its compressed file name is, and what its expanded file name should be. Then put the correct disk in a drive and use EXPAND to copy the file to the DOS directory.

EXPAND does not decompress files compressed by other disk-compression programs, such as DoubleSpace, DriveSpace, or PKZIP.

You can list more than one *filespec*, but you cannot use wild cards. When the command line contains more than one *filespec*, EXPAND assumes the last one is *destination*. When expanding more than one file, *destination* must be a directory, not a file name.

For a single *filespec*, *destination* can be a directory or a file name. EXPAND prompts for *destination* if you omit it.

If *destination* is a directory, the expanded file's name is the same as the compressed file's name. If the name ends in an underscore, you must change it to the proper name before using it as a DOS 6 file.

Examples

```
EXPAND A:\SORT.EX_ C:\DOS\SORT.EXE
```

Expands SORT.EX_ from the disk in drive A; puts the expanded file in C:\DOS with the name SORT.EXE.

```
EXPAND A:\SORT.EX_
```

Expands SORT.EX_ from the disk in drive A; prompts you for the destination.

```
EXPAND CGA.IN_ CGA.VI_ C:\DOS
```

Expands the files CGA.IN_ and CGA.VI_ found in the current directory and puts the expanded files into C:\DOS. The expanded files have the same names as the originals because the destination is a directory; before you can use them, you need to rename them as CGA.INI and CGA.VID, respectively.

FASTHELP

Chapter 12

Provides on-screen information about DOS commands or lists all commands.

Syntax

```
FASTHELP [command]
```

Parameters

none	Lists all available commands with a short description of each.
command	Displays a syntax summary for command.

Notes

FASTHELP *command* produces a short report showing the purpose and the syntax of *command*, along with a description of its parameters and switches. *Command* /? produces the same report as FASTHELP command.

FASTHELP does not provide as much information, notes, or examples as HELP does.

You can edit the FASTHELP.HLP file using any ASCII text editor to customize it for your installation by adding information about DOS commands or including non-DOS commands so that this information is also available through FASTHELP. The added information affects only the listing produced by FASTHELP without a specific command name.

Examples

```
FASTHELP
```

Provides a paged list of commands and a short description of each.

```
FASTHELP COPY > PRN
```

Prints a short description of COPY and its parameters and switches. You can get the same description by entering COPY /? > PRN.

FASTOPEN

Starts FASTOPEN, which makes it faster to open frequently accessed files.

Syntax

```
FASTOPEN drive[=n] [...] [/X]
```

Parameters and Switches

drive	Identifies drive(s) to be tracked by FASTOPEN.
n	Number of files to track for the drive, from 10 to 999; the default is 48.
/X	Stores drive information in expanded memory instead of conventional memory.

Notes

Every time you open a file, FASTOPEN records its name and location. If you reopen the file, FASTOPEN saves time by retrieving its location from the buffer instead of the disk's directory structure.

FASTOPEN works on hard disks only and does not work on network drives.

The total number of files being tracked for all drives must not exceed 999. FASTOPEN requires approximately 48 bytes per file.

You must restart DOS to change the FASTOPEN parameters; you cannot run FASTOPEN twice in one session.

You can install FASTOPEN from the command prompt or from CONFIG.SYS (see INSTALL).

If you use DEFRAG while FASTOPEN is running, you must reboot after DEFRAG so that FASTOPEN doesn't try to use the original locations for relocated files.

Warning: Some experts consider FASTOPEN unreliable, and some software refuses to operate with FASTOPEN present. Using the FASTOPEN command from DOS Shell can lock up your system.

Examples

```
FASTOPEN C:=100
```

Loads FASTOPEN, tracking 100 files on drive C.

```
FASTOPEN C:=100 D: E:=300 /X
```

Loads FASTOPEN, tracking 100 files on drive C, 48 (by default) on drive D, and 300 on drive E. Keeps FASTOPEN records in expanded memory.

FC

Chapter 16

Compares two files and displays lines or bytes that don't match.

Syntax

```
FC [/B] [/L] [/A] [/C] [/LBlines] [/N] [/T] [/W] [/resynch] filespec1 filespec2
```

Parameters and Switches

filespec1	Identifies first file to compare.
filespec2	Identifies second file to compare.
/B	Compares files in binary mode, byte by byte, without attempting to resynchronize after a mismatch. This is the default mode with files having the extensions .EXE, .COM, .SYS, .OBJ, .LIB, or .BIN. Don't use any other switches in binary mode (all other switches pertain to ASCII mode).
/L	Compares files in ASCII mode, comparing line by line and attempting to resynchronize after finding a mismatch. This is the default mode for files that do not have the extensions .EXE, .COM, .SYS, .OBJ, .LIB, or .BIN.
/A	Abbreviates output by showing only the first and last line for a series of mismatched lines; the default shows all mismatched lines.
/C	Ignores case.

/N	Displays line numbers when showing mismatched lines during an ASCII comparison.
/LB*lines*	Specifies the number of lines in the resynch buffer; the default is 100.
/T	Does not expand tabs to spaces. The default is to expand tabs with stops at each eighth character position.
/W	Ignores white space (see notes).
/*resynch*	Specifies the number of lines that must match before files are resynchronized; the default is 2.

Notes

You can use wildcards in either filespec. If you use a wildcard in *filespec1* only, FC compares all the specified files to the file named by *filespec2*. If you use wildcards in both filespecs, FC compares files that have the same wildcard characters in their names. (See the examples.)

In ASCII mode, FC tries to find a place to continue the comparison after a mismatch. It fills its resynch buffer with lines from each file, then searches the first file and the buffer for matching lines. If it finds a match, the files are said to be resynchronized and the comparison continues from that point; otherwise, FC gives up. (Notice that it might not search the rest of the files.) The /*resynch* parameter determines how many lines in a row must match for resynchronization. The /LB parameter determines the size of the resynch buffer. Increasing *lines* or decreasing *resynch* can improve your chances of resynchronizing.

Because of resynchronization, extra lines in one file don't cause FC to treat all subsequent lines as mismatches.

For an ASCII comparison, FC reports differences by displaying the name of the first file, the last line that matches in both files, the mismatched lines in the first file, then the first line to match in both files; then it lists the same information for the second file.

If *resynch* is greater than 1, some matching lines may count as mismatched and show up in the listing of mismatched lines. The files are not resynchronized until the specified number of consecutive lines match.

If you use /W, FC ignores tabs and spaces at the beginning of a line. Also, consecutive tabs or spaces (white space) anywhere count as one space. In other words, some extra spaces or tabs in a line will not cause a mismatch.

In binary mode, FC reports differences by showing, in hexadecimal, the address relative to the beginning of the file and the mismatched bytes, first from *filespec1*, then *filespec2*.

If the two filespecs default to different comparison modes and you haven't specified /B or /L, FC uses the default comparison mode for *filespec1*. When you use wildcards for *filespec1*'s extension, FC defaults to ASCII comparisons.

Examples

```
FC /LB200 /W JANUARY.DOC NEWYEAR.DOC
```

Makes an ASCII comparison of JANUARY.DOC and NEWYEAR.DOC; stops if more than 200 consecutive lines don't match; ignores white space. Two lines are required for re-synchronization.

```
FC /B *.OLD EXTRA.SAV
```

Makes binary comparisons of each file with extension OLD in the current directory to the file EXTRA.SAV.

```
FC OLD.EXE E:\*.*
```

Makes a binary comparison of OLD.EXE in the current directory to OLD.EXE in E:\.

```
FC /C /1 *.OLD *.SAV
```

Makes ASCII comparisons, ignoring case, of each file in the current directory with extension .OLD to the file with the same name but extension .SAV. Only one line is required for synchronization.

FCBS

Chapter 21

Allocates file control blocks.

Syntax

```
FCBS=n
```

Parameter

n	Specifies number of FCBs to allocate; can be 1 through 255; default is 4.

Notes

Early DOS versions used file control blocks (FCBs) for file handling. Some older programs still control files this way; such programs may require you to use the FCBS command in CONFIG.SYS.

See the FILES command for the newer file handling method.

Example

```
FCBS=8
```

Specifies that DOS can have up to eight file control blocks open at the same time.

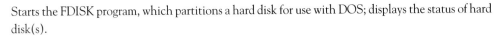

FDISK

Chapter 54

Starts the FDISK program, which partitions a hard disk for use with DOS; displays the status of hard disk(s).

Syntax

FDISK [/STATUS] [/MBR]

Parameters and Switches

none	Starts the FDISK program.
/STATUS	Displays an overview of the partition information of your hard disk(s). Does not start FDISK.
/MBR	Rebuilds the Master Boot Record. Does not start FDISK.

Notes

Do not experiment with partitioning. If you accidentally delete or change a drive or partition, you could lose the data from it.

Once you start it, the FDISK program prompts you for information about the tasks you want to accomplish.

FDISK does not work on a drive formed by using ASSIGN, JOIN, or SUBST, on a network drive, or on an INTERLNK drive.

Use FDISK /MBR if you suspect that the Master Boot Record has a virus attached to it and you can't find another way to remove it. /MBR removes the virus; it does not repair any damage already done to the Master Boot Record. Reboot immediately after using FDISK /MBR.

Examples

FDISK /STATUS

Displays the status of partitions on your hard drive(s).

FDISK /MBR

Rebuilds the Master Boot Record on your hard drive.

FDISK

Starts the FDISK program.

FILES

Chapter 21

Sets the number of files that DOS can access at one time using file handles.

Syntax

`FILES=n`

Parameter

n   Specifies the number of file handles; can be 8 through 255; default is 8.

Notes

DOS uses file handles to keep track of open files. Many programs need more than eight file handles and require you to specify `FILES` in CONFIG.SYS.

Each allocated file handle after the original 8 increases the size of DOS by 39 bytes.

Example

`FILES=20`

Allows DOS to have up to 20 files open at once.

FIND

Chapter 36

Searches for a specific string of text in a file or files, and displays lines containing the string.

Syntax

`FIND [/V] [/C] [/N] [/I] "string" [filespec ...]`

Parameters and Switches

"string"	Specifies the group of characters you want to search for. The quotation marks are required.
filespec	Identifies a file to be searched.
/V	Displays all the lines not containing the specified string.
/C	Displays only a count of all the lines that contain the specified string.

/N	Includes line numbers in the display.
/I	Ignores case.

Notes

If you omit *filespec*, FIND takes input from the DOS standard input source, usually the keyboard or a pipe.

You can't use wildcards in *filespec*. You can, however, list more than one *filespec*, separating them by spaces. You also can use FIND in a FOR command to search multiple files. (See FOR.)

If the search string contains quotation marks, use two quotation marks to search for one. That is, "David ""Daffy"" Jones" searches for David "Daffy" Jones.

/C and /V together display a count of the lines that do not contain the specified string. If you use /C and /N together, FIND ignores /N.

FIND matches strings based solely on the values of the bytes they contain. It does not make allowances for tabs, carriage returns, hyphenation, and other features often inserted by word processors and other applications. Try to search for a string that cannot be broken at the end of a line or otherwise formatted by the application that created the file.

Examples

```
FIND /I /N "TENTH" TEST1.BAT TEST2.BAT
```

Displays every line containing the word "tenth" in files TEST1.BAT and TEST2.BAT. The search ignores case, so it will find "TENTH," "tenth," or "Tenth." The line number displays with each line.

```
DIR *.* ¦ FIND /V -93
```

Displays every line from the directory listing that does not contain –93. This could produce a list of all files in the current directory not created or modified during 1993.

```
FOR %F IN (*.BAT) DO FIND /I "FORMAT" %F
```

Searches all .BAT files in the current directory and lists all lines that contain the word "format," ignoring case.

FOR

Chapter 37

Repeats a command for each item in a set.

Syntax

```
FOR %x ¦ %%x IN (set) DO command
```

Parameters and Switches

x	Identifies a replaceable variable which can be used in *command*. May be any non-numeric character. Use %x at the command prompt and %%x in a batch program.
(set)	Identifies a set of variables to replace *x*. The parentheses are required.
command	Specifies the command to repeat, including its parameters and switches.

Notes

FOR repeats *command* for each item in *set*. Use the replaceable variable (%x or %%x) in *command* to indicate where to substitute items from *set*.

Separate items in *set* by spaces.

When *set* contains a filespec with wildcards, FOR repeats *command* for each file that matches the filespec.

Command cannot be another FOR command.

You can redirect *command*s output using > or >>, but you cannot use | to pipe its output.

Examples

```
FOR %R IN (A B C D) DO DIR %R:\ >PRN
```

Prints directory listings for the root directories of drives A, B, C, and D when used at the command prompt.

```
FOR %%R IN (A B C D) DO DIR %%R:\ >PRN
```

Prints directory listings for the root directories of drives A, B, C, and D when used in a batch program.

```
FOR %F IN (*.SAV *.OLD) DO FIND ECHO %F
```

For each file with extension .SAV or .OLD in the current directory, displays the lines in which ECHO occurs; used at the command prompt.

```
FOR %%F IN (*.SAV *.OLD) DO FIND ECHO %%F
```

For each file with extension .SAV or .OLD in the current directory, displays the lines in which ECHO occurs; used in a batch program.

FORMAT

Chapter 17

Prepares a disk for use or reuse.

Syntax

FORMAT *drive* [/Q] [/U] [V[:*label*]] [/S ¦ /B] [/F:*size*] [/T:*tracks* /N:*sectors*] [/1] [/4]
[/8] [/C] [/AUTOTEST] [/BACKUP]

Parameters and Switches

drive	Identifies the drive to format.
/Q	Does a quick format.
/U	Does an unconditional format.
/V[:*label*]	Specifies the volume label for the formatted disk. *Label* can be up to 11 characters. If you omit /V, or use /V but omit *label*, DOS prompts you for the volume label after formatting is complete. Do not use with /8.
/S	Makes the disk bootable.
/B	Reserves space for system files on a newly formatted disk.
/F:*size*	Overrides the default capacity of the drive. Specify *size* in bytes, as 360KB or 1.2MB. Don't use this switch with /T, /N, /1, /4, or /8.
/T:*tracks*	Specifies the number of tracks on the disk; must be used with /N. Don't use with /F.
/N:*sectors*	Specifies the number of sectors per track; must be used with /T. Don't use with /F.
/1	Formats a single-sided disk. Don't use with /F.
/4	Formats a 360KB disk in a 1.2MB drive. If used with /1, formats 180KB disk in a 1.2MB drive. Don't use with /F.
/8	Formats a 5 1/4-inch disk with 8 sectors per track (for DOS 2.0 or earlier). Don't use with /F or /V.
/C	Retests bad clusters when formatting.
/AUTOTEST	Performs format without any prompts and does not produce a disk space report.
/BACKUP	Performs format without any prompts except the volume label prompt; does produce disk space report.

Notes

If you specify /U (but not /Q), or if the disk capacity is being changed, or if the disk is unformatted, DOS performs an unconditional format. It lays out new sectors, tests the surface for bad spots, installs a boot sector, and creates the root directory and FATs. Any data already on the disk is lost. (For an unformatted disk, it's faster to specify /U than to let DOS discover that the disk is unformatted.)

If you don't specify /U or /Q for an already formatted disk, and the disk capacity is not being changed, DOS performs a safe format. It zeros the FAT, clears the root directory, checks for bad clusters, and saves information for UNFORMAT. Existing data is not destroyed. This is faster than an unconditional format, and UNFORMAT may be able to recover existing data if necessary.

When checking for bad clusters, FORMAT assumes that clusters already marked bad are still bad; it doesn't retest them unless you specify /C. A disk written by DISKCOPY may have bad cluster markings copied from the original disk. Using /C when formating can correct mismarkings but it may slow down formatting, especially if a lot of clusters are marked bad. Prior to DOS 6.2, FORMAT always rechecked bad clusters.

If you specify /Q for an already formatted disk and the disk capacity is not being changed, DOS performs a quick format. This is the same as a safe format except that it doesn't check for bad clusters. This is even faster than a safe format, and UNFORMAT may be able to recover existing data if necessary.

For the fastest format, use both /Q and /U. DOS does a quick format, if possible, but doesn't save UNFORMAT information. UNFORMAT may not be able to recover the existing data from the disk.

If a used disk has been producing sector not found errors or read/write errors, format it with /U to renew the sectors. Note that all previous data will be destroyed permanently.

Don't format a disk at a capacity higher than it's manufactured for. Do not, for example, format a 360KB floppy disk as 1.2MB. (It's permissible to format a 1.2MB disk as 360KB, however.) Some 360KB drives have trouble reading a disk formatted as 360KB in a 1.2MB drive.

When you don't use any capacity switches (/F, /T, /N, /1/, /4, or /8), an unconditional format uses the drive's capacity; a safe or quick format uses the disk's current capacity.

Permissible values for *size* and their meanings are as follows:

160 or 160K or 160KB	160KB, single-sided, double-density, 5 1/4-inch disk
180 or 180K or 180KB	180KB, single-sided, double-density, 5 1/4-inch disk
320 or 320K or 320KB	320KB, double-sided, double-density, 5 1/4-inch disk
360 or 360K or 360KB	360KB, double-sided, double-density, 5 1/4-inch disk
720 or 720K or 720KB	720KB, double-sided, double-density, 3 1/2-inch disk
1200 or 1200K or 1200KB or 1.2 or 1.2M or 1.2MB	1.2MB, double-sided, high-density, 5 1/4-inch disk

| 1440 or 1400K or 1400KB or 1.4 or 1.4M or 1.4MB | 1.44MB, double-sided, high-density, 3 1/2-inch disk |
| 2880 or 2880K or 2880KB or 2.8 or 2.8M or 2.8MB | 2.88MB, double-sided, extra-high-density, 3 1/2-inch disk |

DOS versions before 5.0 required that the two DOS system files on a system disk be contiguous. If you format a disk to which you might later copy system files for a version of DOS earlier than 5.0, you need to use /B to reserve a block of space large enough for both files. (See the SYS command.) You don't need /B if you use /S or if this disk is never going to be used to hold system files for a version of DOS earlier than 5.0.

After FORMAT finishes formatting a disk, it asks you if you want to format another one. If you answer yes, DOS formats the next disk using the current options; you don't have a chance to change options.

If you use /AUTOTEST or /BACKUP, FORMAT does not prompt you to insert a disk and does not ask if you want to format another. /AUTOTEST also does not prompt for a volume label nor produce a disk space listing. Either of these switches make FORMAT more usuable in a batch program and faster to use at the DOS prompt; but they can be hazardous if you don't have the correct disk already inserted in the correct drive.

When *drive* refers to a hard disk drive, FORMAT warns you that all data will be lost and gives you a chance to stop.

You can't use FORMAT on a drive prepared by SUBST. You cannot use FORMAT remotely on a network drive or on an INTERLNK drive.

If the volume label includes spaces, enclose it in quotes, as in /V:"Don's Disk". You can also suppress the label by including a null value in quotes, as in /V:""; this prevents FORMAT from asking for a label during the formatting process.

FORMAT sets an exit code as follows:

0	The format was successful.
3	The user pressed Ctrl+C or Ctrl+Break to stop the process.
4	A fatal error occurred (any error other than 0, 3, or 5).
5	The user chose not to continue after a warning message.

Examples

```
FORMAT A:
```

Formats the disk in drive A, using the default capacity. Uses safe format if disk already is formatted (you may be able to unformat the disk); otherwise, uses unconditional format.

```
FORMAT B: /F:360K /S /V:DATA1993 /U
```

Formats the disk in drive B as a 360KB bootable disk, using unconditional format (you cannot unformat the disk). Assigns a volume label of DATA1993.

GOTO

Chapter 37

When used in a batch program, sends DOS to a line with the specified label.

Syntax

```
GOTO label
```

Parameter

label   Identifies the line to which the batch program should jump.

Notes

Normally DOS processes a batch program line-by-line. GOTO changes the order of processing by directing DOS to a line that consists of a colon followed by *label*. DOS goes on to execute commands beginning on the next line after that.

Label can include spaces but not other separators, such as semicolons or equal signs. GOTO looks at the first eight characters of *label* only, so :NEXTCOMMAND and :NEXTCOMMANDS are both equivalent to :NEXTCOMM.

Examples

```
GOTO :ENDPROG
```

Directs DOS to go to a line consisting of :ENDPROG and continue processing from that point.

```
GOTO %CONFIG%
```

Directs DOS to go to a line containing a label that matches the CONFIG environment variable.

GRAPHICS

Chapter 50

Loads the GRAPHICS TSR to enable DOS to print graphics screens.

Syntax

```
GRAPHICS [type] [filespec] [/R] [/B] [LCD] [/PRINTBOX:size]
```

Parameters and Switches

none	Loads the GRAPHICS TSR with default values.
type	Identifies the printer type. See notes for possible values. The default is HPDEFAULT.
filespec	Identifies the printer profile file; default is GRAPHICS.PRO.
/R	Specifies that images should be printed as they appear on the screen (a positive image). Default is to print a reverse, or negative, screen image, which sometimes looks better in print (see Notes).
/B	Prints background in color for printers COLOR4 and COLOR8.
/LCD	Prints image using LCD aspect ratio instead of CGA aspect ratio. The effect of this switch is the same as /PRINTBOX:LCD.
/PRINTBOX:*size*	Specifies size of printbox. You can abbreviate /PRINTBOX as /PB. *Size* may be STD or LCD. This must match the first operand of the PRINTBOX statement in your printer profile.

Notes

Valid printer types include the following:

COLOR1	IBM PC Color Printer with black ribbon
COLOR4	IBM PC Color Printer with RGB ribbon
COLOR8	IBM PC Color Printer with CMY ribbon
DESKJET	Hewlett-Packard DeskJet printer
HPDEFAULT	Any Hewlett-Packard PCL printer
GRAPHICS	IBM Personal Graphics Printer Proprinter or Quietwriter; also most Epson dot-matrix printers
GRAPHICSWIDE	Any GRAPHICS printer with a wide carriage
LASERJET	Hewlett-Packard LaserJet printer
LASERJETII	Hewlett-Packard LaserJet II printer
PAINTJET	Hewlett-Packard PaintJet printer
QUIETJET	Hewlett-Packard QuietJet printer
QUIETJETPLUS	Hewlett-Packard QuietJet Plus printer
RUGGEDWRITER	Hewlett-Packard RuggedWriter printer
RUGGEDWRITERWIDE	Hewlett-Packard RuggedWriter Wide printer
THERMAL	IBM PC-convertible Thermal printer
THINKJET	Hewlett-Packard ThinkJet printer

Choose the printer type that seems closest to your printer. GRAPHICS doesn't work with a PostScript printer, however, unless it can emulate one of the listed printers.

If you omit *filespec*, GRAPHICS looks for GRAPHICS.PRO in the same directory as GRAPHICS.COM or in the current directory.

Once GRAPHICS is loaded, you can print a graphics screen by pressing PrintScreen.

Normally a black-and-white graphics print looks best and prints fastest with black letters on a white background. With some graphics programs, such as DOS Shell, you need to use /R to get this effect.

Normally you can trust GRAPHICS to specify the right aspect ratio for your printer (LCD or STD). If you find that the ratio is not quite right (if circles come out as ovals, for example), check the printer profile to see if your monitor can handle both LCD and STD. You can use either /LCD or /PB:LCD to specify the LCD aspect ratio. Use /PB:STD to specify a standard one.

You may need to reboot to change printer profiles if the new profile is larger than the original one.

Examples

`GRAPHICS`

Loads the GRAPHICS TSR with default values: printer type HPDEFAULT, profile GRAPHICS.PRO, using negative screen image, and PB size determined by GRAPHICS.PRO.

`GRAPHICS GRAPHICS`

If the GRAPHICS TSR is not already loaded, loads it for GRAPHICS type printer, with default values for printer profile, negative screen image, and PB size. If the TSR already is loaded, switches to the GRAPHICS printer type.

`GRAPHICS /R`

If the GRAPHICS TSR is not already loaded, loads it with default values for printer type, printer profile, and PB size, but using a positive screen image. If the GRAPHICS TSR already is loaded, switches to a positive screen image.

HELP

Chapter 12

Starts DOS's command help program.

Syntax

`HELP [topic] [/B] [/G] [/H] [/NOHI]`

Parameters

none	Displays a table of contents showing subjects for which help is available.
topic	Displays the article describing syntax of topic. Topic can be any subject from the HELP table of contents, including all DOS commands.
/B	Specifies a black-and-white (monochrome) display.
/G	Updates a CGA screen faster (but may cause snow).
/H	Displays as many lines as possible on your video screen.
/NOHI	Specifies that your monitor does not support high intensity.

Notes

HELP provides much more information than FASTHELP, but you may want to use FASTHELP for quick, compact information about command syntax.

You can go directly to the Notes or Examples for a command by specifying HELP command--NOTES or HELP command--EXAMPLES, as in HELP PATH--NOTES or HELP PATH--EXAMPLES.

Examples

HELP

Loads HELP and displays the table of contents.

HELP COPY

Loads HELP and displays the first article (syntax) for the COPY command.

IF

Chapter 37

Performs conditional processing in batch programs.

Syntax

IF [NOT] expression command

Parameters and Switches

NOT	Performs command only if expression is false. Otherwise DOS performs command only if expression is true.

expression	Identifies an ERRORLEVEL, EXIST, or equality condition that IF can evaluate as true or false. The three forms of expression are:

ERRORLEVEL *n*

string1==string2

EXIST *filename*

command	Identifies a command for DOS to perform.

Notes

The expression ERRORLEVEL *n* is true if the previous program returned an exit code equal to or greater than *n*. Otherwise the expression is false. For example, ERRORLEVEL 1 is false if the exit code is 0 but true for exit codes of 1 or higher.

The expression EXIST *filespec* is true if *filespec* identifies an existing file; otherwise it's false.

The expression *string1==string2* is true if *string1* is identical to *string2*. The test is case-sensitive; for example, the statement x==X is false.

One or both strings can be replaceable parameters, as in %1==Y or %FACTOR%==X. Put quotation marks around both *string1* and *string2* if either represents a replaceable parameter that might be null, as in "%1"="Y". A null string would cause a syntax error in the IF command.

Examples

```
FORMAT A:
IF ERRORLEVEL 6 GOTO UNKNOWN
IF ERRORLEVEL 5 GOTO UENDED
IF ERRORLEVEL 4 GOTO FATAL
IF ERRORLEVEL 3 GOTO INTERRUPT
IF ERRORLEVEL 1 GOTO UNKNOWN
ECHO ****FORMAT SUCCESSFUL
GOTO ENDING
:UNKNOWN
ECHO ****FORMAT ENDED WITH UNKNOWN ERROR CODE
GOTO ENDING
:UENDED
ECHO ****USER DECIDED NOT TO PROCEED WITH FORMAT
GOTO ENDING
:FATAL
ECHO ****FATAL ERROR WHILE FORMATTING
GOTO ENDING
:INTERRUPT
ECHO ****USER INTERRUPTED FORMAT
:ENDING
```

This batch program uses several IF commands to display different messages depending on which exit code FORMAT provides.

```
IF NOT EXIST MAKEBAT.DAT NEWPROG.BAT
ECHO FILE ALREADY EXISTS: NEWPROG CAN'T RUN
```

If the file named MAKEBAT.DAT does not exist, the batch program named NEWPROG runs and DOS never returns to perform the next line of the batch program. If the file does exist, NEWPROG does not execute; DOS displays the message on the next line.

```
IF %1==T TYPE %2
IF %1==P PRINT %2
```

This program either types or prints a user-specified file. The action taken depends on the value passed by the user in %1. Notice that nothing happens if the user enters an incorrect parameter, such as t, p, X, or no parameter.

INCLUDE

Chapter 38

Includes the contents of a configuration block at this point in CONFIG.SYS.

Syntax

```
INCLUDE=blockname
```

Parameter

blockname   Identifies the configuration block.

Notes

The INCLUDE command is used only when CONFIG.SYS contains multiple configurations. See the MENUITEM, MENUDEFAULT, MENUCOLOR, and SUBMENU commands for information about setting up and using menus for multiple configurations in CONFIG.SYS.

A configuration block contains a set of CONFIG.SYS commands. A blockname enclosed in square brackets identifies the start of a configuration block. The block ends at the next [blockname] (or the end of the file).

DOS may need to perform the same commands for several of your configurations. Define these commands in a separate block and use INCLUDE=blockname to perform them within another configuration block.

Example

```
INCLUDE=BASIC
```

Processes the commands from the [BASIC] block, then continues with the rest of the current configuration block.

INSTALL

Chapter 49

Loads a TSR from CONFIG.SYS.

Syntax

```
INSTALL=filespec [parameters]
```

Parameters

filespec	Identifies the memory-resident program that you want to install.
parameters	Specifies any parameters and switches needed by the program.

Notes

A program loaded with INSTALL takes slightly less memory than the same program loaded from a batch program or from the command prompt because it does not receive its own environment area in memory.

> **Warning:** Some programs may not run correctly when loaded with INSTALL. Don't install programs that use environment variables or shortcut keys or that require COMMAND.COM to be present to handle critical errors.

The DOS TSRs that can safely be loaded with INSTALL are: FASTOPEN.EXE, KEYB.COM, NLSFUNC.EXE, and SHARE.EXE.

DOS processes all INSTALL commands after processing any DEVICE commands and before loading the command processor, regardless of the order of the commands in CONFIG.SYS.

Example

```
INSTALL=C:\DOS\SHARE.EXE /L=25
```

Loads the Share TSR and passes it the /L=25 parameter.

INTERLNK

Chapter 41

Completes an INTERLNK connection of client and server computers; redirects server drives.

> **Note:** See INTERLNK.EXE in Appendix A for an explanation of the INTERLNK device driver.

Syntax

```
INTERLNK [drive1 = [drive2]] [...]
```

Parameters

none	Completes the link, if necessary; displays a status report, including the current drive and printer assignments.
drive1	Identifies a client drive name to be assigned to *drive2*.
drive2	Identifies a server drive to be accessed by the name *drive1*.

Notes

You must load the INTERLNK.EXE device driver from CONFIG.SYS on the client computer, start INTERSVR on the server computer, and cable the two computers before you can use this command. See INTERSVR for more information about linking two computers.

Use this command to complete the link between the two computers, to display the status of the link, and/or to reassign a client drive name.

The INTERLNK command can reassign drive names originally assigned when the INTERLNK device driver was loaded. Both drives must be in the list of those connected by the INTERLNK device driver. If the server has drives A, B, and C assigned to the client's drive letters D, E, and F, respectively, INTERLNK can rearrange these assignments, but it cannot assign a server drive D, even if it exists, to a client drive letter.

If you omit *drive2*, the client's drive assignment is canceled.

Drive name colons are optional.

Examples

```
INTERLNK
```

Completes the connection between a server and client computer.

```
INTERLNK F:=D:
```

Reassigns the client's drive name F to server's drive D, provided that these are both drives that were reassigned when INTERLNK.EXE was loaded.

```
INTERLNK F=
```

Cancels the assignment of the client's drive name F.

INTERSVR

Chapter 41

Loads the INTERLNK server software and redirects drives and printer ports; copies INTERLNK files from one computer to another.

Syntax 1

INTERSVR [*drive ...*] [/X=*drive ...*] [/LPT[*n*] ¦ /LPT:[*address*] ¦ /COM[*n*] ¦ /COM:[*address*]] [BAUD:*rate*] [/B] [/V]

Loads the INTERLNK server software, redirecting drives and printer ports.

Parameters and Switches

none	Loads the server program and displays the server screen.
drive	Identifies server drive(s) to redirect. By default, INTERSVR redirects all the server's drives.
/X=*drive*	Identifies server drive(s) not to redirect.
/LPT	Indicates that the cable is connected to a parallel port.
/COM	Indicates that the cable is connected to a serial port.
n	Identifies the number of the port that the cable is connected to.
address	Identifies the address of the port that the cable is connected to.
/BAUD:*rate*	Sets a maximum baud rate for data transfer. Values for *rate* can be 9,600, 19,200, 38,400, 57,600, and 115,200. The default is 115,200.
/B	Displays the INTERLNK server screen in black and white.
/V	Prevents conflict with the server computer's timer.

Notes

To connect two computers so they can share drives and printer ports, cable either two serial ports or two parallel ports together. Then start up INTERSVR on one computer (called the *server* computer) and load the INTERLNK device driver from CONFIG.SYS on the other computer (called the *client* computer). If you load the device driver on the client computer before starting up INTERSVR, you will need to use the INTERLNK command to complete the connection. (See INTERLNK.)

When the INTERLNK device driver is installed, it assigns unused client computer drive letters to the server's drives. For example, if the client computer already has drives A, B, and C, and the server computer also has three drives, the client computer would use the letters D, E, and F to access the server computers drives. Similarly, the client's unused parallel port names (such as LPT2) are assigned to the server's parallel ports.

The INTERSVR command can change the order of the drive assignments and/or exclude some drives from being accessed by the client computer. For example, INTERSVR C: B: A: causes INTERLNK to assign drive letter D to the server's drive C, E to server drive B, and F to server drive A. INTERSVR /X=A: /X=B: prevents INTERLNK from assigning drive letters to the server's floppy drives.

INTERLNK does not redirect network drives, CD-ROM drives, or any other drives that use a redirection interface. These drives cannot be accessed directly by the client.

The /LPT or /COM switch tells INTERSVR which server port is connected to the client computer. (INTERLNK has a similar switch to identify the client port.)

If you specify neither /LPT nor /COM, INTERSVR scans all parallel and serial ports for a connection with the client.

If you use /LPT without *n* or *address*, the INTERLNK server uses the first parallel port that it finds connected to a client.

If you use /COM without *n* or *address*, the INTERLNK server uses the first serial port that it finds connected to the client.

If you start INTERSVR from Windows and are using a serial mouse, include either /LPT or a /COM switch that designates the specific port connected to the client to avoid letting INTERSVR scan the port the mouse is attached to, which can disable the mouse driver.

Use /V if you have a serial connection between two computers and one of them stops running when you use INTERLNK to access a drive or printer port.

These commands do not work on drives connected through INTERSVR: CHKDSK, DEFRAG, DISKCOMP, DISKCOPY, FDISK, FORMAT, MIRROR, SYS, UNDELETE, and UNFORMAT.

INTERSVR assumes control of the server computer and does not permit any other program to run on that computer. (Multitasking and task-switching are disabled.) You press Alt+F4 on the server to break the link.

Drive name colons are optional.

Examples

INTERSVR /X=A: /COM2

Starts INTERSVR for the computer cabled to COM2; lets the client access all drives except A.

INTERSVR C D /LPT

Starts INTERSVR for the computer cabled to one of the parallel ports; lets the client access the server's drives C and D only.

Syntax 2

```
INTERSVR /RCOPY
```

Copies the INTERLNK program files from one computer to another.

Notes

This command installs INTERLNK on a computer that doesn't already have it. The two computers must be connected through serial ports by a seven-wire null-modem cable. You can use INTERLNK with earlier versions of DOS, but the target computer's DOS must include the MODE command.

If you are using a port other than COM1 on the target computer, make sure that you're not running the SHARE program on that computer. If you are, reboot without SHARE.

The INTERLNK files are copied to the current directory on the target computer.

Enter the `INTERSVR /RCOPY` command at the source computer's command prompt. INTERSVR displays detailed instructions telling you what to do next.

KEYB

Chapter 49

Loads the KEYB TSR, which enables you to use a nonstandard keyboard layout.

Syntax

```
KEYB [code [,[page] [,filespec]]] [/E] [/ID:id]
```

Parameters and Switches

none	Displays the current keyboard code and code page, and the current console code page.
code	Identifies the country whose keyboard you want to use.
page	Identifies the code page (character set) you want to use; the default is the current code page.
filespec	Identifies the location and name of the keyboard definition file; the default is KEYBOARD.SYS in the current directory or on the search path.
/E	Indicates that you have installed an enhanced keyboard on an 8086 computer.
/ID:*id*	For countries with more than one keyboard layout, specifies which layout is in use.

Notes

KEYB identifies the layout of the keyboard, whether or not you have actually installed that keyboard. If you have a standard US keyboard, for example, and you use KEYB to emulate a Latin American keyboard, the key marked with a semicolon produces ñ.

You can use KEYB to change the keyboard without using COUNTRY. Use COUNTRY if you want to change other country-related information as well.

If you don't specify *page*, the default page for the country is used. Whether or not you specify *page*, however, the characters displayed for ASCII values above 127 are those from the current console code page. (See CHCP and MODE for more information about changing code pages for console and printer.)

If you are changing both the keyboard layout and the code page, you must prepare the code page before changing the keyboard layout (see the `MODE CP PREP` command).

You don't need *filespec* if your keyboard file is KEYBOARD.SYS and it's in a directory in the search path.

You can switch from the current KEYB configuration to the default keyboard configuration (US for most keyboards sold in the United States) by pressing Ctrl+Alt+F1. You can change back to the KEYB configuration by pressing Ctrl+Alt+F2. You can switch to typewriter mode by pressing Ctrl+Alt+F7.

Appropriate values for *code*, *page*, and *id* are as follows:

Country	Code	Page	Id
Belgium	BE	850	437
Brazil	BR	850	437
French-Canada	CF	850	863
Czechoslovakia (Czech)	CZ	852	850
Czechoslovakia (Slovak)	SL	852	850
Denmark	DK	850	865
Finland	SU	850	865
France	FR	850	437
		120	189
Germany	GR	850	437
Hungary	HU	852	850
Italy	IT	850	437
		141	142
Latin America	LA	850	437
Netherlands	NL	850	437

Norway	NO	850	865
Poland	PL	852	850
Portugal	PO	850	860
Spain	SP	850	437
Sweden	SV	850	437
Switzerland (French)	SF	850	437
Switzerland (German)	SG	850	437
United Kingdom	UK	850	437
		166	168
United States	US	850	437
Yugoslavia	YU	852	850

KEYB sets an exit code as follows:

0	Keyboard definition file was loaded successfully.
1	Invalid keyboard code, code page, or syntax was used.
2	Keyboard definition file is bad or missing.
4	An error occurred while communicating with the CON device.
5	The requested code page has not been prepared.

You can install KEYB.COM from CONFIG.SYS instead of using the KEYB command at the command prompt. (See INSTALL.)

Examples

```
KEYB
```

Displays current keyboard country and code page and the current CON code page.

```
KEYB PO, 850
```

Starts KEYB, emulating the keyboard for Portugal and using code page 850.

```
KEYB FR,,C:\COUNTRY\KEYBOARD.SYS /ID:189
```

Starts KEYB, emulating the French keyboard with ID 189 and using the current code page; uses the keyboard definition file found in C:\COUNTRY.

LABEL

Chapter 18

Displays and changes the volume label of a disk.

Syntax

`LABEL [drive] [label]`

Parameters

none	Displays the volume label of the current drive and lets you change or delete it.
drive	Identifies the location of the disk whose label you want to display and/or change; the default is the current drive.
label	Specifies a new volume label for the disk; the *label* can contain up to 11 characters (see Notes for restrictions).

Notes

If you don't specify *label*, DOS displays the disk's current label and serial number, if any, and prompts for a new label. If you press Enter, the current label is deleted.

A volume label can include spaces, but not tabs. Consecutive spaces become one space. Don't use these characters in a label:

* ? / \ | . , ; : + = [ ] ( ) & ^ < > "

LABEL doesn't work on drives created with ASSIGN, JOIN, or SUBST.

Examples

`LABEL`

Displays the volume label (and serial number, if any) of the disk in the current drive and prompts for a new label.

`LABEL B:TAX 1993`

Changes the label on the disk in drive B to TAX 1993.

LASTDRIVE

Chapter 39

Specifies the highest drive letter, and therefore the maximum number of drives, that your system can access.

Syntax

`LASTDRIVE=x`

Parameter

x   Specifies a drive letter, A through Z. The minimum value is the highest drive letter in use by your system.

Notes

The default number of drives is five (A through E) or the number you actually have, whichever is greater.

Compressed drives, RAM drives, network drives, and other types of extra drives in your system (such as secondary drive names created by DRIVER.SYS) all need drive letters. You may need to use LASTDRIVE to make more drive letters available in your system.

To allocate more drives, you can use LASTDRIVE in CONFIG.SYS with the highest drive letter that you need. DOS allocates about 100 bytes of memory per drive, so don't waste memory by making LASTDRIVE any higher than it needs to be.

Example

```
LASTDRIVE = K
```

Enables your computer to access up to 11 logical drives.

LH

Chapter 30

Loads a program into upper memory; LOADHIGH is interchangeable with LH.

Syntax

```
LH [[/L:region[,min][;region[,min]]...] [/S]] filespec [parameters]
```

Parameters and Switches

filespec	Identifies the program to load.
/L:region	Loads the program into specific region(s) of upper memory.
min	Specifies the minimum size required in a region when the program is running.
/S	Shrinks the UMB to its minimum size while the program is loading. This switch is normally used only by MEMMAKER.
parameters	Specifies any command line parameters required by the program.

Notes

If you have an 80386 or later processor, have loaded EMM386.EXE, and have requested UMB support (see the DOS command), you may have upper memory blocks (UMBs) available. LH loads a program into upper memory if available. If not, LH loads the program into conventional memory, if possible.

By default, LH loads a program into the largest free UMB and makes all other UMBs available for the program's use. The /L and /S switches can be used to override this default action, but probably should be used only by MEMMAKER.

See MEMMAKER for a command that automatically converts appropriate commands in AUTOEXEC.BAT to LH, generating /L and /S as needed for optimal memory configuration.

Examples

```
LH C:\TEST1\NEWDATA
```

Loads the NEWDATA program into upper memory if available. Otherwise, loads it into conventional memory if possible.

LOADFIX

Chapter 29

Loads and runs a program above the first 64KB of memory.

Syntax

```
LOADFIX command
```

Parameter

command	Specifies a command that starts a program, including any desired parameters and switches.

Notes

If you load DOS or device drivers into the HMA, other programs might be loaded into the low parts of conventional memory where DOS and device drivers normally reside. A few programs don't work well when loaded in the first 64KB of memory. If you receive the message Packed file corrupt when starting a program, try forcing it to load above the 64KB mark by using LOADFIX.

Example

```
LOADFIX DREPORT JAN /C
```

Loads a program named DREPORT above the 64KB mark. JAN /C represent information passed to the DREPORT program from the command line.

LOADHIGH

See LH.

MD

Chapter 14

Creates a new directory. Can be used interchangeably with MKDIR.

Syntax

MD [*path*]*dirname*

Parameters

path	Identifies the parent of the new directory.
dirname	Identifies the name of the new directory.

Notes

path can include a drive name. If not, DOS creates *dirname* on the current drive.

Without *path*, DOS creates *dirname* as a subdirectory of the current directory.

dirname's full path, from the root directory up to and including *dirname*, including backslashes, can't be more than 63 characters.

dirname must be unique within the parent. You can't duplicate a directory or file name belonging to the parent.

Examples

MD NEWSTUFF

Creates directory NEWSTUFF as a subdirectory of the current directory.

MD E:\NEWSTUFF

Creates directory NEWSTUFF as a subdirectory of the root directory on drive E.

MD \NEWSTUFF

Creates directory NEWSTUFF as a subdirectory of the root directory on the current drive.

```
MD ..\NEWSTUFF
```

Creates directory NEWSTUFF as a subdirectory of the parent of the current directory.

MEM

Chapter 29

Displays current memory use.

Syntax

```
MEM [/CLASSIFY ¦ /DEBUG ¦ /FREE ¦ /MODULE program] [/PAGE]
```

Switches

none	Displays summary information about your system's used and free memory.
/CLASSIFY	Lists currently loaded programs and their memory usage along with summary information. Abbreviate as /C.
/DEBUG	Lists programs and drivers currently loaded into memory. For each module, shows size, segment address, and module type. Displays summary information also. Abbreviate as /D.
/FREE	Lists the free areas of memory; shows the segment address and size of each free area of conventional memory and the largest free UMB in each region of upper memory. Displays summary information also. Abbreviate as /F.
/MODULE	Shows how a program is currently using memory. Lists the memory areas the program occupies and shows the address and size of each. Abbreviate as /M.
program	Identifies a program currently loaded in memory.
/PAGE	Pauses after each screen. Abbreviate as /P.

Notes

MEM displays the status of extended memory if installed.

MEM displays the status of expanded memory only if your system has expanded memory that conforms to LIMS 4.0 EMS standards.

MEM displays the status of upper memory only if a UMB provider, such as EMM386 is installed and DOS=UMB is included in CONFIG.SYS. MEM does not display the status of upper memory if you run MEM under Windows 3.0.

Examples

```
MEM /C /P
```

Lists programs currently loaded and shows memory usage of each; pauses after each screen.

```
MEM /M DOSKEY
```

Shows the segment address, size, and module type of each area of memory being used by DOSKEY. If any portion of DOSKEY is in upper memory, shows the region of each UMB being used by DOSKEY.

MEMMAKER

Chapter 30

Optimizes memory by moving device drivers and TSRs to upper memory.

Syntax

```
MEMMAKER [/B] [/BATCH] [/SWAP:drive] [/T] [/UNDO]
[/W:size1, size2] [/SESSION]
```

Parameters and Switches

none	Starts MEMMAKER.
/B	Runs MEMMAKER in black-and-white mode.
/BATCH	Runs MEMMAKER in batch mode, using default values at all prompts. If an error occurs, MEMMAKER restores your CONFIG.SYS, AUTOEXEC.BAT, and if necessary Windows SYSTEM.INI files. Puts all status messages into MEMMAKER.STS file.
/SWAP:drive	Identifies your startup drive; see Notes.
/T	Disables the detection of IBM Token-Ring networks. Use this switch if your computer has such a network and you have problems running MEMMAKER.
/UNDO	Undoes MEMMAKER's most recent changes, restoring your previous CONFIG.SYS, AUTOEXEC.BAT, and if necessary, Windows SYSTEM.INI files.
/W:size1, size2	Specifies, in kilobytes, how much upper memory to reserve for Microsoft Windows' translation buffers. (Windows needs two areas of memory for translation buffers.) The default value is 12, 12.
/SESSION	The SESSION switch is added to the MEMMAKER command by MEMMAKER. Don't use it yourself.

Notes

You must have a 386 (or higher) processor to run MEMMAKER.

Don't use MEMMAKER if you use Windows applications only.

You can't run MEMMAKER from another program, such as Microsoft Windows or DOS Shell. Before you start MEMMAKER, exit from any other program you may be running. Also, be sure that your CONFIG.SYS and AUTOEXEC.BAT files do not start any unnecessary programs but that they do load any hardware devices or TSRs that you normally use.

Unless you use /BATCH, MEMMAKER's dialog boxes prompt you for options, such as whether to use express or custom optimization. Custom optimization requires many choices from the user.

If you use a disk-compression program, the drive letter of your startup disk may change after your computer starts. You must then use /SWAP to let MEMMAKER know where to find your CONFIG.SYS and AUTOEXEC.BAT files (and, if necessary, Windows' SYSTEM.INI). You don't need this switch with DoubleSpace, DriveSpace, or Stacker 2.0 or higher.

If you do not use Windows, you can save upper memory space by specifying /W:0,0.

If your system doesn't work properly after MEMMAKER runs, or if you don't like the new memory configuration, you can return to your previous configuration by starting MEMMAKER with the /UNDO switch.

When you use /UNDO, MEMMAKER restores CONFIG.SYS, AUTOEXEC.BAT, and SYSTEM.INI from its backup versions of these files. If you have made any changes to these files since running MEMMAKER, your changes are lost.

Examples

MEMMAKER

Starts MEMMAKER, displays the Welcome screen, and begins prompting for options.

MEMMAKER /SWAP:D

Starts MEMMAKER and specifies that the current drive D was the original boot drive.

MENUCOLOR

Chapter 38

Sets the colors for a startup menu.

Syntax

MENUCOLOR text[,background]

Parameters

text   Specifies the text color.

background   Specifies the background color; default is 0 (black).

Notes

You can use MENUCOLOR in a main menu block or a submenu block of a multiple configuration CONFIG.SYS file only.

If you leave a space after the comma, MENUCOLOR ignores background.

Values for *text* and *background* are as follows:

0	Black
1	Blue
2	Green
3	Cyan
4	Red
5	Magenta
6	Brown
7	White
8	Gray
9	Bright blue
10	Bright green
11	Bright cyan
12	Bright red
13	Bright magenta
14	Yellow
15	Bright white

The effect of using a value higher than 7 for *background* can vary with different monitors or display cards. When *background* = 12, for example, you may get a blinking red background instead of a bright red background.

Example

MENUCOLOR 9

Produces a menu with bright blue text on a black background.

MENUCOLOR 10,7

Produces a menu with bright green text on a white background.

MENUDEFAULT

Chapter 38

Specifies the default menu item on a CONFIG.SYS startup menu and sets a time-out value.

Syntax

```
MENUDEFAULT=blockname[,time]
```

Parameters

blockname	Identifies the default menu item.
time	Specifies the number of seconds DOS waits for a user to choose a menu item; can be 0 to 90.

Notes

You can use MENUDEFAULT only in a main menu block or a submenu block of a multiple configuration CONFIG.SYS.

When you use MENUDEFAULT, DOS displays the menu with the default item highlighted and the number corresponding to *blockname* already inserted at the prompt.

When you use time in a main menu block, DOS also displays a countdown from time to 0. When the countdown reaches 0, DOS proceeds to *blockname*. In a submenu block, DOS currently ignores time.

When you don't use MENUDEFAULT, the menu screen is displayed with the first item highlighted and 1 already inserted at the choice prompt, there is no countdown, and DOS waits until the user presses Enter before proceeding.

Setting time to 0 effectively cancels the user's ability to choose; the startup menu goes directly to *blockname* whenever the system boots.

Examples

```
MENUDEFAULT WINDOWS,10
```

Goes to configuration block [WINDOWS] if the user doesn't make a choice within 10 seconds.

MENUITEM

Chapter 38

Defines an item on a CONFIG.SYS startup menu.

Syntax

```
MENUITEM blockname[,text]
```

Parameters

blockname   Specifies the name of the configuration block associated with this item.

text   Specifies the text to be displayed for this menu item; default is blockname.

Notes

You can use MENUITEM only in a main menu block or submenu block of a multiple configuration CONFIG.SYS.

A menu block can contain up to nine items. DOS numbers the items in the order of their appearance in the menu block. You can replace MENUITEM by SUBMENU (see the SUBMENU command) for one or more items if you want more, or more detailed, choices.

There must be a block named blockname defined elsewhere in CONFIG.SYS. If DOS can't find blockname, the item is not included in the menu.

Blockname can be up to 70 characters long and can include any printable characters except spaces, backslashes (\ ), slashes (/), commas (,), semicolons (;), equal signs (=), and square brackets ([]).

Text can be up to 70 characters long and can contain any printable characters.

Examples

```
[MENU]
MENUITEM BASIC, BASIC STARTUP
MENUITEM WINDOWS, GO DIRECTLY TO WINDOWS
MENUITEM NETWORK
```

This menu block produces this startup menu:

```
1.  BASIC STARTUP
2.  GO DIRECTLY TO WINDOWS
3.  NETWORK
```

MKDIR

See MD.

MODE

Chapters 48, 49, and 50

Configures system devices.

Syntax 1

```
MODE LPTn [COLS = cols] [LINES = lines] [RETRY = retry]
```

```
MODE LPTn [cols],[lines],[retry]
```

Configures a printer attached to a parallel printer port.

Parameters

LPTn	Identifies the parallel port; *n* can be 1 to 3.
cols	Specifies the number of characters (or columns) per line; can be 80 or 132; the default is 80.
lines	Specifies the number of lines per inch; can be 6 or 8; the default is 6.
retry	Specifies the action to take if a time-out occurs when DOS attempts to send output to a parallel printer. See Notes.

Notes

See Syntax 6 for MODE LPTn without any other parameters.

You can use PRN interchangeably with LPT1.

If you use the first, fuller version of this syntax, the parameters can be in any order.

If you use the second, abbreviated, version of this syntax, you must use the parameters in the order shown, with the accompanying commas. If you leave out a parameter, be sure to indicate its place by the appropriate commas (trailing commas can be omitted).

Values for *retry* are as follows:

E	Returns an error if the port is busy.
P	Continues retrying until the printer accepts output.
R	Returns ready if the port is busy.
N	Takes no retry action.

Do not use any value for *retry* if you use MODE over a network.

If you omit a parameter, MODE uses the most recent value as the default. If no previous MODE command has specified a value, MODE uses 80 for *cols*, 6 for *lines*, and N for *retry*.

Examples

```
MODE LPT1 132, 8, P
```

Configures LPT1 with 132 columns and 8 lines per inch; tells MODE to continue to retry if the port is busy when trying to access the printer.

```
MODE PRN ,,E
```

Configures LPT1 with default column and line values; returns an error if the port is busy when trying to access the printer.

Syntax 2

```
MODE COMn BAUD = baud [PARITY = parity] [DATA = data]
[STOP = stop] [RETRY = retry]

MODE COMn baud,[parity],[data],[stop],[retry]
```

Configures a serial port.

Parameters

COMn	Identifies the serial port; n can be 1 to 4.
baud	Specifies the transmission rate (baud rate). (See Notes for values.)
parity	Specifies how the system uses the parity bit to check for transmission errors. (See Notes for values.)
data	Specifies the number of data bits per character. Values can be 5 through 8; the default value is 7.
stop	Specifies the number of stop bits that identify the end of a character. Values can be 1, 1.5, or 2. If the baud rate is 100, the default is 2; otherwise, the default is 1.
retry	Specifies the action to take if a time-out occurs when DOS attempts to send output to the port. (See Notes.)

Notes

If you use the first, fuller version of this syntax the parameters can be in any order.

If you use the second, abbreviated, version of this syntax, you must use the parameters in the order shown, with the accompanying commas. If you leave out a parameter, be sure to indicate its place by the appropriate comma (trailing commas can be omitted). (See Examples.)

Values for *baud* are as follows:

11 or 110	110 baud
15 or 150	150 baud
30 or 300	300 baud
60 or 600	600 baud
12 or 1,200	1,200 baud
24 or 2,400	2,400 baud
48 or 4,800	4,800 baud
96 or 9,600	9,600 baud
19 or 1,920	19,200 baud

Values for *parity* can be N for no parity, E for even parity, O for odd parity, M for mark, or S for space. E is the default.

Values for *retry* are as follows:

E	Returns an error if the port is busy
B	Returns "busy" if the port is busy
P	Continues retrying until the port accepts output
R	Returns "ready" if the port is busy
N	Takes no retry action (default value)

Do not use any value for *retry* if you use MODE over a network.

Some values that are valid for MODE are not supported by all computers. These include: BAUD = 19; PARITY = S; PARITY = M; DATA = 5; DATA = 6; and STOP = 1.5.

If you omit any parameter except *baud*, MODE defaults to the most recent value for this port. If no previous MODE command has specified a value, MODE uses the default values shown above. There is no default value for *baud*; you must specify this parameter.

Examples

```
MODE COM1 24, O, 8, 2, P
```

Configures COM1 as 2,400 baud, odd parity, 8 data bits per character, and 2 stop bits; continues trying to access the port if it is busy.

```
MODE COM2 96,,,,E
```

Configures COM2 with 9,600 baud, using default values for parity, data bits, and stop bits; returns an error if port is busy.

Syntax 3

```
MODE [display][,shift [,T]]
MODE [display][,lines]
MODE CON [COLS = cols] [LINES = lines]
```

Selects and configures the active display adapter.

Parameters

none	See Syntax 6.
display	Specifies a display category, including color characteristics and characters per line. (See Notes.)
shift	Shifts screen to left or right; valid values are L and R.
T	Provides a test pattern to be used in aligning screen correctly.

<table>
<tr><td>lines</td><td>Specifies the number of lines per screen; can be 25, 43, or 50. Not all monitors support 50. The ANSI.SYS device driver must be installed before you can set the number of lines.</td></tr>
<tr><td>cols</td><td>Specifies the number of columns per screen (characters per line); can be 40 or 80.</td></tr>
</table>

Notes

Not all monitors permit shifting and/or test patterns.

Valid values for *display* are as follows:

`40` or `80`	Characters per line
`BW40` or `BW80`	CGA adapter with color disabled, 40 or 80 characters per line
`CO40` or `CO80`	Color monitor with color enabled, 40 or 80 characters per line
`MONO`	Monochrome adapter with 80 characters per line

This syntax of the `MODE` command controls the display for the DOS command prompt screen and some others; but many applications such as DOS Shell override them with their own settings.

Examples

`MODE 40, 43`

Sets monitor to 40 characters per line, 43 lines per screen.

`MODE BW80, 25`

Sets monitor to black-and-white with 80 characters per line, 25 lines per screen.

`MODE ,43`

Leave color and characters per line unchanged; sets monitor to 43 lines per screen.

Syntax 4

`MODE CON RATE=rate DELAY=delay`

Sets the keyboard typematic rate.

Parameters

rate   Specifies the rate at which a character repeats when you
                         hold down a key; can be 1 to 32. These correspond to about
                         2 to 30 characters per second respectively. For IBM AT-
                         compatible keyboards, the default value is 20. For IBM
                         PS/2-compatible keyboards, the default value is 21.

delay   Specifies how long you press a key before repeat begins.
                         Values are 1, 2, 3, and 4, representing 0.25, 0.50, 0.75, and 1
                         second respectively; default is 2.

Notes

If you use this syntax, you must specify both rate and delay.

Example

```
MODE CON RATE = 32 DELAY = 3
```

Specifies that, when you hold down a key for 0.75 seconds, the character begins repeating at approximately 30 times per seconds, until you release the key.

Syntax 5

```
MODE LPTn[= COMm]
```

Redirects output from a parallel port to a serial port.

Parameters

LPT*n*   Identifies the parallel port; *n* can be 1 to 3.

COM*m*   Identifies the serial port; *m* can be 1 to 4.

Notes

When LPT*n* has been redirected, any output sent to LPT*n* goes instead to COM*m*; presumably a serial printer is connected to COM*m*.

To end redirection, use MODE LPT*n* without =COM*m*.

If *n* = 1, the COM port becomes the system's default printer port, PRN.

Be sure to configure COM*m*, using Syntax 2, before issuing this command.

Examples

```
MODE COM1 96,N,8,1
MODE LPT1=COM1
```

The first command establishes communications parameters for COM1. The second command then redirects all output from LPT1 to COM1.

```
MODE LPT1
```

Undoes any redirection applied to LPT1. From now on, all output directed to LPT1 will actually go to LPT1.

Syntax 6

```
MODE [device] [/STATUS]
```

Displays the status of one or all of the devices installed on your system or ends redirection.

Parameters and Switches

none	Displays the status of all devices installed on your system.
device	Identifies a device whose status you want to display. Device can be CON, LPTn, or COMm.
/STATUS	Requests the status of a device; abbreviate as /STA.

Notes

Without /STA, if device is a parallel printer that has been redirected (see Syntax 5), the redirection is canceled. With /STA, the status of the redirected printer is shown and it remains redirected.

If device is not a redirected parallel printer, the status of the device is displayed with or without /STA.

Without device, the status of all devices is shown and any redirection is not affected.

Examples

```
MODE CON
```

Displays the status of the console device.

```
MODE LPT1
```

If LPT1 has been redirected to a serial port, ends the redirection.

```
MODE LPT1 /STA
```

Displays the status of LPT1 without undoing any redirection applied to it.

Syntax 7

```
MODE device CODEPAGE PREPARE = ((page [...]) filespec)
MODE device CODEPAGE SELECT = page
```

```
MODE device CODEPAGE REFRESH
MODE device CODEPAGE [/STATUS]
```

Manages code pages.

Parameters and Switches

device	Identifies the device to which the command applies.
CODEPAGE	Identifies this as a code page command; abbreviate as CP.
PREPARE *page*	Prepares page(s) for device; abbreviate as PREP. Specifies a code page; can be 437 (American), 850 (Multilingual or Latin I), 852 (Slavic or Latin II), 860 (Portuguese), 863 (French-Canadian) or 865 (Nordic).
filespec	Identifies the name and location of the code page information file for *device*. (See Notes.)
SELECT	Loads a code page for use; page must already be prepared with a MODE CP PREP command; abbreviate as SEL.
REFRESH	Reinstates the prepared code pages if they are lost as the result of a hardware or other error; abbreviate as REF.
/STATUS	Displays the numbers of the current code pages prepared or selected for device; abbreviate as /STA.

Notes

Using this syntax without PREPARE, SELECT, REFRESH, or /STATUS has the same effect as using /STATUS.

You must load the device driver(s) DISPLAY.SYS (for the console) and/or PRINTER.SYS (for printers) to reserve buffer space before MODE can prepare or select code pages. You can't prepare more pages for device than you specified when loading the device driver.

You can use a combination of COUNTRY, NLSFUNC, and CHCP to select a code page for both console and printer(s) at once.

Examples

```
MODE CON PREP = ((850 437) C:\DOS\EGA.CPI)
```

Prepares code pages 850 and 437 for the console, using information found in C:\DOS\EGA.CPI.

```
MODE CP
```

Displays current code page status.

MORE

Chapter 36

Displays a file or output from a program pausing after each screen.

Syntax

```
MORE < filespec
command ¦ MORE
```

Parameters

filespec	Identifies an ASCII text file whose contents you want to display one screen at a time.
command	Specifies a command (including any necessary switches and parameters) whose output you want to display one screen at a time.

Notes

Before using a pipe (¦), you should set the TEMP environment variable. (See SET.)

You can pipe output to MORE from commands such as SORT and TYPE or with other programs that produce ASCII text as standard output, but not from a command that invokes a batch program.

Examples

```
MORE < TESTA.BAT
```

Displays the contents of TESTA.BAT, pausing after each screen.

```
TREE ¦ MORE
```

Displays the directory structure of the current drive, pausing after each screen.

```
TYPE TESTA.BAT ¦ SORT ¦ MORE
```

Sorts the contents of TESTA.BAT and displays them, pausing after each screen.

MOVE

Chapter 15

Moves one or more files to another location; renames a file or directory.

Syntax 1

```
MOVE [/Y ¦ /-Y] filespec [...] destination
```

Moves and renames files.

Parameters

filespec	Identifies the file(s) you want to move or rename.
destination	Identifies the file or directory to which you want to move file(s) or the new name for the file.
/Y	Overwrites destination files without warning.
/-Y	Requests permission to overwrite destination files.

Notes

MOVE assumes that the last entry on the command line is *destination*. Any other entries on the line are filespecs. *Filespec* can include wildcards.

If you move more than one file, *destination* must be a directory, not a file name. *Destination* can't include wildcards.

If you move only one file, *destination* can be (or include) a new file name; in that case, the file is moved and/or renamed. In DOS 6.0, if the file identified by *destination* already exists, MOVE overwrites it without warning.

In DOS 6.2 and up, if the file identified by *destination* already exists, MOVE's action depends on several factors. By default, if the command was entered from the command prompt, MOVE asks if you want to overwrite the destination file, but if the command was entered from a batch program, MOVE overwrites the destination file without warning. However, if the COPYCMD environment variable is set to /Y, MOVE overwrites files without asking. If the COPYCMD environment variable is set to /-Y, MOVE asks you before overwriting files. You can override the default action or the COPYCMD environment variable for a specific command by including /Y or /-Y in the command.

The /Y and /-Y switches are not available before DOS 6.2.

When DOS asks if you want to overwrite an existing destination file, you can enter Y to overwrite the file, N to preserve the file (the move is not made), or A to overwrite this file and all subsequent files affected by the current MOVE command. In other words, A terminates file protection for the remainder of this MOVE command.

MOVE will not process system or hidden files. It does move read-only files, but it will not overwrite one in *destination*. The read-only and archive attributes of the source files are copied to the destination files.

When moving a file to the same drive, MOVE moves only the directory entry; this is much faster than copying and deleting the file. When moving to a different drive, of course, MOVE must copy the file and delete the original.

If the move is unsuccessful because the *destination* is a read-only file or the destination drive is full, MOVE doesn't delete the original file. MOVE tells you when a move is unsuccessful.

Example

```
MOVE AFILE.* *.BAT C:\ACCOUNT
```

From the current directory, moves all files named AFILE with any extension and all files with extension .BAT to directory ACCOUNT on drive C. No system or hidden files are moved.

```
MOVE AFILE.NEW AFILE.OLD
```

In the current directory, changes the name of AFILE.NEW to AFILE.OLD.

Syntax 2

```
MOVE directory newname
```

Renames a directory.

Parameters

directory	Identifies the directory you want to rename.
newname	Specifies the new name.

Notes

You can't rename the current directory.

Newname must produce a unique name for the new directory. You can't duplicate the name of a file or subdirectory of the parent.

Newname must not specify a different path for the directory.

Examples

```
MOVE C:\T1 C:\ACCOUNT
```

If T1 is a directory name, renames directory T1 on drive C; the new name is ACCOUNT. (If T1 is a file name, see Syntax 1.)

```
MOVE T1 TESTING
```

If T1 is a child of the current directory, renames it as TESTING. (If T1 is a file name, see Syntax 1.)

MSAV

Chapter 25

Scans memory and disks for viruses; removes viruses when found.

Syntax

```
MSAV [drive ... ¦ path ¦ /A ¦ /L] [/S ¦ /C] [/R] [/N] [/P] [/F] [/VIDEO]
[/videomouse ...]
```

Parameters and Switches

none	Opens the MSAV dialog box so that you can select drives and options.
drive	Identifies a drive to scan.
path	Identifies the top of a branch.
/A	Scans all drives except A and B.
/L	Scans all drives except A, B, and network drives.
/S	Scans without cleaning viruses.
/C	Scans and cleans any viruses found.
/R	Creates a report file (MSAV.RPT) that lists the number of files checked, number of viruses found, number of viruses cleaned, and names of files suspected of containing unknown viruses.
/N	Turns off the information display while scanning.
/P	Runs MSAV in non-graphic, command-line mode.
/F	Turns off the display of file names being scanned. Use this switch only with the /N or /P switch.
/VIDEO	Displays a list of video and mouse options. This option does not perform any virus scan or load the dialog box; to scan for viruses you must enter MSAV again after you see the list.
/videomouse	Uses *videomouse* option (see Notes for values).

Notes

MSAV identifies more than 1,000 known viruses and also can detect unknown viruses. It maintains a CHKLIST.MS file in each scanned directory to help it identify unknown viruses by changes in the directory's files. It can't clean unknown viruses; some known viruses also can't be cleaned.

The first scan you run after starting up MSAV also scans memory for viruses.

From the MSAV dialog box, you can choose options that are not on the command line, such as scanning for stealth viruses or turning off the warning beep. Also, from the dialog box you can see a list of known viruses and read about particular ones.

If you specify drive without /N or /P, the dialog box appears and you can, if you want, select options and even choose to scan a different drive. After a drive is scanned, you have another opportunity to choose options and drives for another scan.

If you use *path* without /N or /P, the dialog box appears but the scan begins immediately. When it ends, the dialog box closes. You don't have a chance to choose other options or to continue to scan another path or drive.

Values for *videomouse* are as follows:

25	Sets screen to 25 lines; this is the default value.
28	Sets screen to 28 lines. Use this switch with VGA display adapters only.
43	Sets screen to 43 lines. Use this switch with either EGA or VGA display adapters.
50	Sets screen to 50 lines. Use this switch with VGA display adapters only.
60	Sets screen to 60 lines. Use this switch with Video 7 display adapters only.
IN	Uses a color scheme even if a color display adapter is not detected.
BW	Uses a black-and-white color scheme.
MONO	Uses a monochrome color scheme.
LCD	Uses an LCD color scheme.
FF	Uses the fastest screen updating with CGA display adapters; can cause snow.
BF	Uses the computer's BIOS to display video; try this switch if the quality of the display is poor.
NF	Disables the use of alternate fonts.
BT	Allows use of a graphics mouse in Windows.
NGM	Uses default mouse character instead of graphics character. Try this if snow appears on-screen.
LE	Exchanges left and right mouse buttons.
IM	Disables the mouse.
PS2	Resets the mouse if the mouse cursor disappears or locks up.

/VIDEO overrides any other parameters or switches and displays only the video/mouse option list.

A summary report is displayed every time you use MSAV, whether or not you use /R to generate MSAV.RPT. MSAV.RPT is more detailed because it contains the names of files suspected of containing unknown viruses; the summary report does not include this information. Sometimes the summary report flashes on the screen too rapidly to be read; if you have a problem with this, be sure to use /R to get a readable report.

MSAV.RPT is saved in the root directory of the scanned drive. If you name more than one drive to be scanned, an MSAV.RPT is generated for each drive.

See your DOS *User's Guide* for instructions on keeping your Anti-Virus software current.

When run with the /N switch, MSAV sets exit code 86 if any viruses were detected; otherwise, it sets exit code 0.

Examples

MSAV /A

Starts MSAV, scanning memory and all drives except A and B.

MSAV C: D: /BW /43

Starts MSAV in black-and-white mode with 43 lines per screen, scanning memory and drives C and D.

MSAV C:\DOS /C /R

Scans memory and the files in the branch headed by C:\DOS, removing any viruses found; stores a report in C:\MSAV.RPT.

MSBACKUP

Chapters 23 and 24

Backs up and restores data on your computer.

Syntax

MSBACKUP [*setup*] [/BW ¦ /LCD ¦ /MDA]

Parameters and Switches

none	Opens the main MSBACKUP dialog box and loads DEFAULT.SET.
setup	Specifies a setup file to load when opening the MSBACKUP dialog box; the file's extension must be .SET; the default is DEFAULT.SET.

/BW	Uses a black-and-white color scheme for the MSBACKUP dialog boxes.
/LCD	Uses a video mode compatible with laptop displays.
/MDA	Uses a monochrome display adapter.

Notes

You create a setup file using the MSBACKUP dialog boxes.

Even though you specify setup, you have a chance to modify settings and file selections in the MSBACKUP dialog box before starting the backup. Opening the dialog box also gives you access to configuration, compare, and restore functions.

MSBACKUP can't restore files backed up by versions of DOS before 6.0. (See RESTORE.)

In DOS 6.22 and up, MSBACKUP uses a different method of file compression than DOS 6.0 and 6.2 did. Therefore, DOS 6.22 and up cannot restore files backed up by DOS 6.0 or 6.2 with compression. (Equally, files backed up with compression from DOS 6.22 can't be read by MSBACKUP from DOS 6.0 or 6.2.) See Chapter 24 for techniques to recover files from earlier versions of DOS.

Examples

```
MSBACKUP
```

Opens the MSBACKUP dialog box and loads DEFAULT.SET.

```
MSBACKUP DAILY
```

Opens the MSBACKUP dialog box and loads DAILY.SET.

MSCDEX

Makes CD-ROM drives available to DOS.

Syntax

```
MSCDEX /D:signature [...] [/E] [/K] [/S] [/V] [/L:drivename] [/M:buffers]
```

Parameters and Switches

/D:signature	Identifies the signature of the CD-ROM device driver.
/E	Lets the device driver use expanded memory.
/K	Recognizes CD-ROM disks encoded in Kanji.
/S	Permits MS-NET and Windows for Workgroups servers to share CD-ROM drives.
/V	Displays a memory report when MSCDEX starts up.

/L:*drivename*	Specifies the drivename to assign to the CD-ROM drive; if more than one drive are included in the command, specifies the name of the first one, and the other drives receive successive names.
/M:*buffers*	Specifies the number of buffers to allocate to the drive.

Notes

You must load a device driver for each CD-ROM drive from CONFIG.SYS before enabling the drive(s) with the MSCDEX command.

The command that loads your CD-ROM device driver from CONFIG.SYS should include a /D:*signature* parameter that identifies the CD-ROM device. Use the same /D parameter in this command to relate the MSCDEX command to the device driver.

If you have more than one CD-ROM device, each must have a unique signature.

If you use Windows, enter the MSCDEX command before starting Windows. Most people include the MSCDEX command in AUTOEXEC.BAT.

If you don't specify a drive name, MSCDEX assigns the next available drive name to the CD-ROM drive. You might need to use LASTDRIVE to increase the number of available drive names. (See LASTDRIVE.)

SmartDrive for DOS 6.2 and later can cache your CD-ROM drives and significantly improve their speed. If you have DOS 6.2 or later and use SmartDrive, be sure to place the MSCDEX command(s) before the SMARTDRV command in your AUTOEXEC.BAT file so that SmartDrive identifies the CD-ROM drives and sets up caching for them. (See SMARTDRV.)

Examples

```
DEVICEHIGH=C:\CDROM\MTMCDS.SYS /D:MSCD0000 (in CONFIG.SYS)
MSCDEX /D:MSCD0000 (in AUTOEXEC.BAT)
```

The first command loads the MTMCDS.SYS device driver and assigns the CD-ROM drive the signature MSCD0000. (This command is unique to the device driver that came with the CD-ROM drive; yours might be quite different.) The second command loads MSCDEX for the MSCD0000 device.

```
DEVICEHIGH=C:\CDROM\MTMCDS.SYS /D:MSCD0000 (in CONFIG.SYS)
DEVICEHIGH=C:\CDROM\MTMCDS.SYS /D:MSCD0001 (in CONFIG.SYS)
MSCDEX /D:MSCD0000 /D:MSCD0001 /V /K (in AUTOEXEC.BAT)
```

The first two commands load device drivers for two CD-ROM drives, identified as MSCD0000 and MSCD0001. The third command loads MSCDEX for both devices, displays a memory report, and specifies that CD-ROM volumes encoded in Kanji should be recognized.

MSD

Displays or reports technical information about your computer.

Syntax

MSD [/F *filespec* ¦ /P *filespec* ¦ /S [*filespec*] ¦ [/I] [/B]]

Parameters and Switches

filespec	Specifies a file to hold the MSD report.
/F	Prompts for identification information, then writes a complete MSD report to *filespec*; do not use with any other switch.
/P	Writes a complete MSD report to *filespec* without any prompting; do not use with any other switch.
/S	Writes a summary MSD report. If *filespec* is present, writes report to *filespec*. If *filespec* is absent, writes report to the monitor. Do not use with any other switch.
/I	Specifies that MSD should not initially detect hardware; use this switch if you have problems starting MSD or MSD does not run properly; do not use with any other switch except /B.
/B	Runs MSD in black and white instead of color; do not use with any other switch except /I.

Notes

MSD provides information about your computer's model and processor, memory, video type, DOS version, mouse, other adapters, disk drives, LPT ports, COM ports, IRQ status, TSRs, and device drivers.

If /F, /P, and /S are all omitted, MSD opens a dialog box where you can select the information you want to view.

Examples

MSD

Opens MSD's dialog box that lets you access data about your computer.

MSD /F MYSYSTEM.TXT

Prompts you for name, company, address, and other identification information. Creates a report in MYSYSTEM.TXT that includes the identification data and the technical information about your computer.

NLSFUNC

Chapter 49

Starts the program that loads country-specific information for national language support (NLS).

Syntax

```
NLSFUNC [filespec]
```

Parameters

none	Uses the default file for country-specific information. (See Notes.)
filespec	Identifies the file containing country-specific information.

Notes

If CONFIG.SYS contains a COUNTRY command, it defines the default file; otherwise, the default file is COUNTRY.SYS in the root directory of your startup drive.

There is no error message if the country-specific information file is missing, because NLSFUNC doesn't actually access the file. The error message shows up later, when CHCP tries to use information from the file.

You also can load NLSFUNC by installing NLSFUNC.EXE in CONFIG.SYS. (See INSTALL.)

Examples

```
NLSFUNC
```

Starts the national language support TSR using the default file for country-specific information.

```
NLSFUNC C:\OLDDOS\COUNTRY.SYS
```

Starts the national language support TSR using the COUNTRY.SYS file from C:\OLDDOS for country-specific information.

NUMLOCK

Specifies whether the NumLock setting of the numeric keyboard is initially on or off.

Syntax

```
NUMLOCK=ON | OFF
```

Parameters

ON	Turns on the NumLock setting.
OFF	Turns off the NumLock setting.

Notes

You can use NUMLOCK only in a menu block of CONFIG.SYS.

When the NumLock setting is on, the numeric keypad produces numbers. (This can also affect the duplicate keys on an enhanced keyboard. If you have this problem, try loading ANSI.SYS with /X in CONFIG.SYS.) When the NumLock setting is off, the numeric keypad produces alternate functions (cursor movement, insert, and delete).

Without the NUMLOCK command, most computers start up with the NumLock setting off. In any case, pressing the NumLock key toggles the NumLock setting on and off.

Example

NUMLOCK=ON

Turns NumLock on during booting, so that typing on the numeric keypad produces numbers.

PATH

Chapter 12

Defines a search path for external executable files (including batch files).

Syntax

```
PATH [path [;path]...]
PATH ;
```

Parameters

none	Displays the current search path.
path	Identifies a directory to search for program files.
;	When used as the only parameter, clears the search path.

Notes

When a command name includes a path, as in C:\DOS\FORMAT A:, DOS ignores the search path and looks for the program only in the specified directory.

When a command name does not include a path, DOS looks for the program first in the current directory, then in the directories on the search path, if any. It searches the directories in the order shown on the search path. DOS stops searching when a specified program is found even though another program with that name may exist in another directory on the search path.

If it can't find the program in the current directory or any directory on the search path, DOS displays a `Bad command or file name` error message.

DOS doesn't search for internal programs, which are part of COMMAND.COM, or for DOSKEY macros, which are stored in memory.

Be sure that each *path* specifies a complete, absolute path name, including the drive name.

PATH doesn't produce an error message if *path* isn't valid. DOS displays an `Invalid directory` error message when it encounters an invalid path name while searching.

The search path created by PATH is assigned to an environment variable named `PATH`.

Each time the `PATH` command defines a search path, it completely replaces the former search path. If you want to add another directory to the current search path, be sure to include the complete current search path in the command.

The `PATH` command can't be more than 127 characters long, which limits the search path itself to 122 characters.

Examples

`PATH C:\;C:\DOS;D:\BOOK\APPS`

Sets a search path so that DOS looks for programs first in the current directory, next in the root directory on drive C, then in C:\DOS and finally in D:\BOOK\APPS.

`PATH ;`

Clears the search path. After this, DOS looks for programs in the current directory only.

`PATH %PATH%;C:\WORKOUT`

Adds the directory named C:\WORKOUT to the end of the current search path. Note that this command uses the `PATH` environment variable and therefore works only in a batch program.

PAUSE

Chapter 20

Temporarily suspends processing of a batch program and prompts the user to press any key to continue.

Syntax

`PAUSE`

Notes

The key pressed by the user in response to PAUSE serves only to continue the program unless it is one of the break keys (Ctrl+C or Ctrl+Break). See CHOICE for a command that lets users enter a meaningful response.

Example

```
ECHO Load Form 301/B in the printer
PAUSE
```

After displaying the message from ECHO, the program pauses until the user presses a key, giving the user as much time as necessary to load the forms.

POWER

Chapter 48

Reduces power consumption in laptops when applications and devices are idle.

Syntax

```
POWER [ADV:option ¦ STD ¦ OFF]
```

Parameters and Switches

none	Displays the current power setting.
ADV:option	Conserves power when applications and hardware drivers are idle; option can be MAX, REG, or MIN (see Notes).
STD	Uses only the power-management features, if any, of your computer's hardware.
OFF	Turns off power management.

Notes

You must install POWER.EXE as a device driver from CONFIG.SYS before you can use the POWER command.

The power manager conforms to the Advanced Power Management (APM) specification.

If your computer does not support the APM specification, STD turns off power management.

Use ADV:MAX for maximum power conservation. Use ADV:REG to balance power conservation with application and device performance. If performance is not satisfactory with MAX or REG, try ADV:MIN.

Examples

```
POWER ADV:MIN
```

Sets power conservation to a minimum to improve application performance.

```
POWER OFF
```

Turns off power conservation.

PRINT

Chapter 16

Manages background printing.

Syntax

```
PRINT [/D:device] [/B:buffer] [/U:ticks1] [/M:ticks2] [/S:ticks3] [/Q:qsize] [/T]
[filespec ...] [/C] [/P]
```

Parameters and Switches

none	Displays the contents of the print queue or loads the TSR.
/D:device	Identifies the printer port on which to print. Valid values are LPT1, LPT2, LPT3, COM1, COM2, COM3, and COM4. LPT1 is identical to PRN. If both /D and *filespec* are used, /D must precede *filespec*.
/B:buffer	Sets the size, in bytes, of the buffer used to store data before printing; can be 512 to 16384; 512 is the default.
/U:ticks1	Specifies the maximum number of clock ticks to wait for a printer to be available; can be 1 to 255; the default is 1. If the printer is not available in *ticks1* clock ticks, the job is not printed. (There are about 18 clock ticks per second.)
/M:ticks2	Specifies the maximum number of clock ticks to print a character on the printer; can be 1 to 55; the default value is 2. If a character takes longer than *ticks2* clock ticks to print, DOS displays an error message.
/S:ticks3	Specifies the number of clock ticks the DOS scheduler allocates for background printing before returning to foreground work; maybe 1 to 255; the default value is 8.
/Q:qsize	Specifies the maximum number of files in the print queue; can be 4 through 32; the default value is 10.
/T	Removes all files from the print queue.
filespec	Identifies a text file to place in the print queue; can be up to 64 characters.
/C	Removes specified file(s) from the print queue.
/P	Adds specified file(s) to the print queue.

Notes

The first time you use the PRINT command after booting, DOS loads a memory-resident portion of the PRINT program to retain the print parameters. You can use the /D, /B, /U, /M, /S, and /Q switches only the first time you use the PRINT command. To change values for any of these switches, you have to reboot and issue a new PRINT command.

If you don't specify /D when loading the memory-resident program, PRINT prompts you for the name of the printer port.

The actual printing occurs in the background—that is, DOS continues processing other applications while taking small blocks of time (defined by /S) to print the contents of the queue.

Increasing buffer decreases the amount of memory available for other purposes but speeds up printing. Increasing any of the ticks values speeds up printing but may slow down other work.

/P applies to the *filespec* preceding it, if any, and all following *filespecs* until it reaches a *filespec* controlled by /C, if any. /C applies to the *filespec* preceding it, if any, and all following filespecs until it reaches a *filespec* controlled by /P, if any.

When neither /C nor /P applies to a *filespec*, /P is assumed.

/T empties the queue. If any *filespecs* precede /T, they are added to the queue, then removed from the queue when /T is processed. If any follow /T, they are added to the queue.

Examples

`PRINT /D:LPT2 /B:2048`

If this is the first PRINT command, loads the PRINT TSR with a buffer of 2048 bytes. All subsequent PRINT commands will send files to the LPT2 queue.

`PRINT LETTER1.TXT`

Adds LETTER1.TXT to the print queue; if the PRINT TSR is not yet loaded, loads PRINT with the default values but prompts for printer name.

`PRINT /C LETTER1.TXT LETTER2.TXT LETTER3.TXT /P`

Removes LETTER1.TXT and LETTER2.TXT from the print queue and adds LETTER3.TXT to the queue.

`PRINT /T`

Removes all files from the print queue.

`PRINT /T REP1.TXT REP2.TXT`

Removes all files from the print queue. Then places REP1.TXT and REP2.TXT in the queue.

PROMPT

Chapter 12

Changes the command prompt.

Syntax

PROMPT [*text*]

Parameters

none	Resets the prompt to the current drive letter followed by >.
text	Specifies text and information to be shown as the prompt.

Notes

Special codes you can use in the prompt are as follows:

$Q	= (equal sign)
$$	$ (dollar sign)
$T	Current time
$D	Current date
$P	Current drive and path
$V	DOS version number
$N	Current drive
$G	> (greater-than sign)
$L	< (less-than sign)
$B	¦ (pipe)
$_	Enter (line feed)
$E	ASCII escape code (code 27)
$H	Backspace (deletes a character already written in the prompt)

The default prompt is equivalent to PG.

$_ lets you define a multiple-line prompt. T_PG, for example, displays the current time on one line, then goes to the beginning of the next line to display the current drive and path followed by >.

$E, the ASCII escape code, lets you code ANSI.SYS escape sequences as part of your prompt. $E[2J, for example, clears the screen and places the cursor in the upper left corner (with no prompt text). You must load the ANSI.SYS driver in CONFIG.SYS to process ANSI.SYS escape sequences in a prompt; otherwise, the escape sequences are treated just like any other text. There are hundreds of ANSI.SYS escape sequences to control such things as the colors of the screen's background and text, what happens when you press Ctrl+Shift+X, and so on. They are documented in DOS 6's on-screen HELP system; look up the ANSI.SYS topic.

You could use $H, the backspace character, to erase unwanted characters from $D or $T. THHH, for example, displays the time as *hh:mm:ss* instead of the usual *hh:mm:ss.nn*.

Examples

```
PROMPT USING $V$G
```

Defines a prompt that says USING followed by the DOS version number and >.

```
PROMPT $T$_TIME$Q$$
```

Defines a two-line prompt. The first line shows the time; the second line says TIME=$. (The cursor follows $.)

```
PROMPT
```

Sets the prompt to the stripped down value: the current drive (only) followed by >.

```
PROMPT $P$G
```

Sets the prompt to the default value, the current drive and directory followed by >.

QBASIC

Chapter 53

Starts the QBASIC programming environment, which allows the writing, testing, and running of QBASIC programs.

Syntax

```
QBASIC [/B] [/EDITOR] [/G] [/H] [/MBF] [/NOHI] [[/RUN] filespec]
```

Parameters and Switches

none	Loads the QBASIC environment.
/B	Displays QBASIC in black and white.
/EDITOR	Invokes the DOS text editor instead of the QBASIC program editor.
/G	Provides the fastest update of a CGA monitor.
/H	Displays the maximum number of display lines possible on your screen.

/MBF	Converts the built-in functions MKS$, MKD$, CVS, and CVD to MKSMBF$, MKDMBF$, CVSMBF, and CVDMBF, respectively. This provides compatibility with data files written in some earlier versions of BASIC.
/NOHI	Allows the use of a monitor that doesn't support high-intensity video. Do not use this switch with Compaq laptop computers.
/RUN	Runs *filespec* before displaying the file. Don't use this switch without *filespec*.
filespec	Specifies a QBASIC program to load; without /RUN, displays the program; with /RUN, runs the program before displaying it.

Notes

/EDITOR has the same effect as starting the DOS text editor with the EDIT command.

If your monitor does not display shortcut keys on the bottom line when you run QBASIC, use /B (for CGA monitors) and/or /NOHI (for systems that do not support bold or high-intensity characters).

Examples

QBASIC TESTPROG

Starts the QBASIC environment, loading and displaying the file TESTPROG.BAS.

QBASIC /B

Starts the QBASIC environment with a black-and-white color scheme. No file is loaded.

QBASIC /RUN TESTPROG

Starts the QBASIC environment, loading and running TESTPROG.BAS. When the program ends, it is displayed in the QBASIC editor.

RD

Chapter 14

Deletes a directory. You can use RMDIR interchangeably with RD.

Syntax

RD *path*

Parameter

path   Identifies the directory you want to delete.

Notes

Before you can delete a directory using RD, you must delete all its files and subdirectories. The directory must be empty except for the . and .. entries.

If a DIR command shows that the directory is empty but you still can't delete it, use DIR /A (or DOS Shell) to see whether there are hidden or system files or subdirectories.

RD will not delete the current directory; make some other directory current before entering the RD command.

You cannot delete the root directory.

To delete a directory along with all its files, its subdirectories, and their files and subdirectories in one command, see DELTREE.

Examples

RD \DDIR

Deletes directory DDIR, a subdirectory of the root directory on the current drive.

RD DDIR

Deletes directory DDIR, a subdirectory of the current directory.

REM

Chapter 20

Identifies a comment, or remark, in a batch file or CONFIG.SYS.

Syntax

REM [*comment*]

Parameter

comment   Specifies text you want to include in the batch file or in CONFIG.SYS without affecting operations.

Notes

You can use REM commands to provide documentation or notes in a batch file or in CONFIG.SYS. Sometimes it is convenient to put REM in front of a command that you want to disable temporarily. You then can easily restore the command by removing REM from the line.

Examples

```
REM Next run the daily backup.
```

A note to remind yourself (and others) of the purpose of the next several commands.

```
REM DEL TEMP.*
```

This DEL command has no effect; no TEMP files are erased by this command when the batch program runs.

REN

Chapter 16

Changes the name of a file or files. You can use RENAME interchangeably with REN.

Syntax

```
REN filespec newname
```

Parameters

filespec	Identifies the file(s) to be renamed.
newname	Specifies the new name(s) for the file(s).

Notes

Filespec can include a drive and/or path name, but *newname* can't.

REN doesn't work if *newname* already exists (as a file or subdirectory) in the same directory as the file being renamed. (For a command that replaces an existing *newname*, see MOVE).

If you use wildcards in both names, the wildcard characters from the original name replace the wildcards in *newname*. In REN A*.* B*.*, for example, AFILE.DAT becomes BFILE.DAT, ACCOUNT.EXE becomes BCCOUNT.EXE, and so on.

Filespec can't identify a directory; for a command that renames directories, see MOVE.

Examples

```
REN JET.NEW JET.SAV
```

Changes the name of JET.NEW (in the current directory) to JET.SAV.

```
REN D:\YEARDATA\NEWDATA.* OLDDATA.*
```

For each file in D:\YEARDATA that has the name NEWDATA (with any extension), changes the name to OLDDATA (with the same extension as before).

RENAME

See REN.

REPLACE

Chapter 40

Replaces or adds files from one directory to another.

Syntax 1

```
REPLACE filespec path [/P] [/R] [/W] [/S] [/U]
```

Overwrites files in the destination directory with matching files from the source directory.

Parameters and Switches

filespec	Identifies the source file(s).
path	Identifies the destination directory.
/P	Prompts for confirmation before replacing a file.
/R	Replaces files that are read-only in the destination directory as well as nonread-only files.
/W	Waits for you to press a key before beginning to search for source files.
/S	Searches the entire branch headed by *path* to find files to be replaced.
/U	Examines the date/time stamps of source and destination files and replaces (updates) files in the destination directory only if they are older than the source files that replace them.

Notes

REPLACE ignores system and/or hidden files in both the source and destination directory.

Without /R, an attempt to replace a read-only destination file produces an error message and terminates REPLACE.

If you use wildcards in *filespec*, each file matching the specification replaces file(s) with the same name in the destination directory or branch.

With /U, you can be sure that you will not overwrite a more recent version. If you want to be sure that both JOHN and MARY have the latest version of TILE.DAT, for example, use REPLACE JOHN\TILE.DAT MARY /U followed by REPLACE MARY\TILE.DAT JOHN /U.

REPLACE sets an exit code as follows:

0	Successful completion
1	DOS version not compatible with REPLACE
2	Source files not found
3	Source or Destination path not found
5	Destination file(s) not accessible (read-only)
8	Insufficient memory
11	Incorrect syntax on command line

Examples

In these examples, assume that neither the source files nor the destination files are system or hidden files.

```
REPLACE NEWDATA.921 \DIR92
```

If \DIR92\NEWDATA.921 exists and is not read-only, replaces it with NEWDATA.921 from the current directory.

```
REPLACE DONNA\NEWDATA.* JUDI /R
```

Copies NEWDATA.BAT from DONNA to JUDI if NEWDATA.BAT exists in both directories; copies NEWDATA.COM from DONNA to JUDI if NEWDATA.COM exists in both directories; copies NEWDATA.EXE from DONNA to JUDI if NEWDATA.EXE exists in both directories; and so on. Makes the replacement even when a JUDI file is read-only.

```
REPLACE A:\BUDGET.LST C:\ /S /R /W
```

Waits for you to press a key before beginning and then looks in every directory in the branch headed by C:\ for a file named BUDGET.LST; each occurrence of this file (even if it's read-only) is replaced by BUDGET.LST from the root directory of drive A.

Syntax 2

```
REPLACE filespec path /A [/P] [/W]
```

Replaces files missing from the destination with files from the source directory.

Parameters and Switches

filespec	Identifies the source file(s).
path	Identifies the destination directory.
/A	Specifies that you want to add missing files to the destination directory instead of overwriting existing files.
/P	Prompts for confirmation before replacing a file.

/W	Waits for you to press a key before beginning to search for source files.

Notes

With /A, REPLACE adds each source file matching the specification to the destination directory unless there's already a file with that name in that directory.

You can specify only one destination directory; the /S switch (to process an entire branch) is not available.

Example

```
REPLACE \DONNA\NEWDATA.* \JUDI /A /P
```

For each NEWDATA file (with any extension) in DONNA, if a file with the same name does not exist in JUDI, copies the file to JUDI, prompting for confirmation before adding each file.

RESTORE

Chapter 24

Restores files backed up by BACKUP from previous DOS versions (DOS 2.0 through 5.0).

Syntax

```
RESTORE drive1 destination [/S] [/P] [/B:date] [/A:date] [/E:time] [/L:time] [/M]
[/N] [/D]
```

Parameters and Switches

drive1	Identifies the drive containing the backup files.
destination	Identifies the files to be restored, and the drive to which they are to be restored. *Destination* must include a drive name; it may specify files by including a path and/or file name(s).
/S	Restores files to all subdirectories.
/P	Prompts for permission to restore read-only files or those changed since the last backup.
/B:*date*	Restores only those files last modified on or before *date*.
/A:*date*	Restores only those files last modified on or after *date*.
/E:*time*	Restores only those files last modified at or earlier than *time*.
/L:*time*	Restores only those files last modified at or later than *time*.
/M	Restores only those files modified since the last backup.

/N	Restores only those files that no longer exist on the destination.
/D	Displays a list of files that would be restored but does not restore any. Even though no files are restored, you must specify *destination* when you use /D.

Notes

RESTORE cannot restore the system files IO.SYS and MSDOS.SYS. RESTORE does not work with drives that have been redirected with ASSIGN or JOIN.

RESTORE prompts you to insert disks from a backup set in the order in which they were created. It searches each disk for files that match the specifications.

If you know which disks contain the files you want, you can skip disks by confirming when RESTORE asks if it is OK.

You can cancel the RESTORE operation before it reads all the disks by pressing Ctrl+C.

A file can be spanned across two (or even more) disks. If you cancel RESTORE, be sure you don't do so when it has restored only part of a spanned file.

Files are restored to the directory with the same path that they were backed up from, but it doesn't have to be on the same drive. For example, if you backed up files from drive D, you can use RE-STORE to put them on drive E. RESTORE will create any directories needed on the destination drive in order to restore the files to the same path they came from.

When you specify a date or time switch, RESTORE looks at the date/time stamp on the destination file, not the source file. Suppose you want to restore any BANDLIST.* file that you modified after 4/15/93. Use RESTORE A: C:\BANDLIST.* /A:4/16/93.

> **Warning:** Use time switches carefully. The times apply to every day, not just the day specified in a date switch. /A:4/16/93 /L:3:00P restores destination files modified on 4/16/93 after 3:00 p.m., on 4/17/93 after 3:00 p.m., on 4/18/93 after 3:00 p.m., and so on.

/M restores files modified since the last backup, according to the archive attributes on the destination drive. Files deleted since the last backup are not re-created. Files unchanged since the last backup are not restored. This could shorten restore time by not bothering to restore unmodified files.

RESTORE sets an exit code, as follows:

0	Successful completion
1	RESTORE could not find files to restore
3	User stopped the operation by pressing Ctrl+C or Ctrl+Break
4	RESTORE stopped because of an error (such as disk full)

Examples

```
RESTORE A: C:\*.BAT
```

Restores all files with extension .BAT that were originally in the root directory of the backed up drive to the root directory on C.

```
RESTORE A: C:\*.BAT /S
```

Restores all files with extension .BAT to drive C, including those backed up from subdirectories; each file is restored to a directory with the same path name as the one from which it was backed up, creating directories as need to reproduce the correct path names.

```
RESTORE A: C:\PROWORD\*.DOC /M
```

Looks for any file with the extension .DOC backed up from directory \PROWORD. When RE-STORE finds such a file both in the backup set and in C:\PROWORD, and the destination file has been modified since backup, the modified version is replaced by the backup version. (Note that files created or deleted since the backup are not affected.)

RMDIR

See RD.

SCANDISK

Chapter 27

Detects and repairs problems on a drive.

Syntax 1

```
SCANDISK [drive ... ¦ /ALL] [/CHECKONLY ¦ /CUSTOM ¦ /AUTOFIX [/NOSAVE]] [/SURFACE]
[/MONO] [/NOSUMMARY]
```

Checks and fixes one or more drives.

Parameters and Switches

none	Opens the SCANDISK dialog box; checks the current drive; displays messages about any errors it finds so that you can decide how to handle them; also asks if you want to perform a surface test.
drive	Indicates a drive to be checked.
/ALL	Processes all local drives.
/CHECKONLY	Checks the indicated drives and reports on errors but does not attempt to repair them.

/CUSTOM	Uses the settings in the [Custom] section of SCANDISK.INI to configure the scan.
/AUTOFIX	Repairs any errors it finds without asking you; lost clusters are saved unless you specify /NOSAVE.
/NOSAVE	Specifies that lost clusters should be deleted when /AUTOFIX is used.
/SURFACE	Performs the surface scan without prompting.
/MONO	Displays the SCANDISK dialog box in black and white.
/NOSUMMARY	Suppresses the summary report at the end of the scan; also suppresses the prompt for an Undo disk if SCANDISK fixes a drive problem. (Fixes can't be undone.)

Notes

SCANDISK can check the logical structure of a drive as well as test its surface. The logic test looks for errors and logical anomalies in the drive's FAT and directory structure, much as CHKDSK does (but it does a better job than CHKDSK). The surface test tests each sector for physical flaws. If physical errors are found, SCANDISK can fix the problem by moving as much data as possible to a safer location on the disk and marking the damaged sectors as unusable. (Some data may already be damaged and cannot be rescued.)

SCANDISK can check hard drives, RAM drives, floppy drives, memory cards, and DriveSpace or DoubleSpace compressed drives. It can't check CD-ROM drives, network drives, or drives created by INTERLNK, ASSIGN, SUBST, or JOIN.

If SCANDISK finds lost clusters (clusters that are marked as containing data but do not belong to any file), it asks whether you want to save them or delete them. If you choose to save them, SCANDISK converts each chain of lost clusters to a file named FILE*nnnn*.CHK. If you choose to delete them, SCANDISK immediately makes the clusters available for future use.

If you specify /AUTOFIX, SCANDISK automatically saves lost clusters unless you also specify /NOSAVE.

When SCANDISK repairs cross-linked files (two or more files sharing the same clusters), it makes a new copy of each file, giving separate copies of the shared clusters to each file. It then deletes the cross-linked files. One of the new files may be correct, but the others will contain at least some invalid data and may be missing some data. If the damaged file contains text data, be sure to save any lost clusters that are also detected; you may be able to recover the missing data there.

Don't run SCANDISK under Windows (or any other program). Open files could mislead SCANDISK, and fixing a spurious error could result in severe data loss. If SCANDISK detects that you are attempting to run it under another program, it refuses to run without the /CHECKONLY switch. (Even /CHECKONLY could result in incorrect reports.)

SCANDISK opens a dialog box to keep you informed of progress and to report results. Use /MONO to display the dialog box in black and white.

If you don't specify /SURFACE, SCANDISK prompts you before performing a surface test.

If an error is found and you haven't specified /AUTOFIX, SCANDISK asks if you want to fix the problem or ignore it.

If you choose to fix an error, SCANDISK prompts you to save information so the repair can be undone if necessary. If you want to save undo information, you must provide a floppy disk (but not in the drive being scanned). See Syntax 3 for the command that uses the undo information to reverse the fixes. (The undo information includes the damaged FAT and directory structure.)

SCANDISK prompts for an Undo disk with the first repair only. After one repair has been made, the FAT and directory structure have been changed, and the changed versions would not help to restore the disk to its original, unrepaired state.

You can scan a mounted DriveSpace or DoubleSpace compressed drive just like any other type of hard drive. But you can perform additional tests by scanning the unmounted DriveSpace or DoubleSpace compressed volume file (CVF). When scanning an unmounted CVF, SCANDISK checks the volume header, the file structure, the compression structure, and the volume signatures. Unmount the volume and specify the volume name, as in DRVSPACE.000 or DBLSPACE.000, instead of its mounted drive name. Do not use the /ALL or /SURFACE switches.

SCANDISK.INI contains configuration information for SCANDISK. You can edit this file using an ASCII text editor such as EDIT. The file contains its own documentation on the meaning of its variables and how to change them.

SCANDISK sets an exit code:

0	No problems were detected.
1	There was a syntax error in the SCANDISK command.
2	SCANDISK encountered an out-of-memory error or some kind of internal error.
3	The user canceled SCANDISK (but not during a surface scan).
4	The user chose to do a surface scan but canceled it after it started.
254	Problems were detected and corrected.
255	Not all problems were corrected.

Examples

All the examples assume that the commands are entered from a primary command prompt.

```
SCANDISK A:
```

Performs a logic scan on the disk in drive A; if any errors are detected, prompts you before correcting them; if any corrections are made, prompts you for an Undo disk. After the logic scan is complete, prompts you for a surface scan. Displays a summary report at the end.

```
SCANDISK /CHECKONLY /SURFACE
```

Scans the current drive for errors but does not offer to correct them. Performs the surface test without asking. Displays a summary report at the end.

```
SCANDISK /ALL AUTOFIX /NOSAVE /NOSUMMARY
```

Performs a fully automated logic scan on the current drive, fixing errors automatically; lost clusters are deleted; does not prompt for an Undo disk; does not prompt for a surface scan; does not display a summary report.

```
DRVSPACE D: /UNMOUNT
SCANDISK D:\DRVSPACE.OOO /CUSTOM
DRVSPACE D: /MOUNT
```

The first command unmounts the DriveSpace volume known as drive D. The second command scans that volume using the default parameters and switches contained in SCANDISK.INI. (The drive name D now refers to the host drive.) The third command mounts the volume again.

Syntax 2

```
SCANDISK filespec /FRAGMENT
```

Reports on file fragmentation.

Parameters and Switches

filespec	Identifies file(s) to be examined.
/FRAGMENT	Indicates that you want a fragmentation report instead of the normal disk scan.

Notes

A fragmented file resides in several different areas on the disk. Excessive file fragmentation can slow down performance. You can use DEFRAG to clean up file fragmentation.

When you use the /FRAGMENT switch, the SCANDISK dialog box does not appear and no logic or surface scan is done.

Filespec can contain wild-card characters.

SCANDISK /FRAGMENT examines only one directory per command.

Examples

```
SCANDISK D:\*.*
```

Displays a fragmentation report for all the files in the root directory of drive D.

Syntax 3

```
SCANDISK /UNDO [undo-drive] [/MONO]
```

Restores a drive to its condition before being fixed.

Parameters and Switches

/UNDO	Indicates that SCANDISK's UNDO function is desired.
undo-drive	Identifies where the floppy disk containing the undo information is located.
/MONO	Displays the SCANDISK dialog box in black and white.

Notes

The UNDO function restores a drive to its unrepaired condition by restoring the drive's former FAT and directory structure that was saved on the Undo disk.

> **Warning:** Do not undo SCANDISK repairs if you have changed the drive in any way since the repairs were made; if you have added, modified, or deleted files since you ran SCANDISK, restoring the former FAT and directory structure could cause data loss.

Do not try to identify the name of the drive to be repaired; the Undo disk contains that information. Just identify the location of the Undo disk.

Examples

```
SCANDISK /UNDO A:
```

Uses the Undo disk in drive A to undo repairs to a drive.

SET

Chapter 43

Sets or changes values of environment variables or displays current values.

Syntax

```
SET [variable=[string]]
```

Parameters and Switches

none	Displays the current values of all environment variables.
variable	Identifies the environment variable to be set.
string	Specifies a new value for an environment variable; if omitted, the current value is cleared.

Notes

When you use SET, you may get an error message saying that you are out of environment space. See SHELL and COMMAND for commands that can increase your environment space.

DOS sets some environment variables without the SET command. For example, it sets CONFIG, which keeps track of which option was chosen in a multiple configuration file, when you make that choice; it initializes PATH to C:\DOS; it sets PROMPT to PG; and it sets COMSPEC to C:\ or C:\DOS, depending on where it finds COMMAND.COM . Except for CONFIG, you can override these default values using the PATH, PROMPT, and SHELL commands, respectively.

DOS also uses some environment variables that you create with SET. These include TEMP, which specifies a directory in which temporary files are kept; DIRCMD, which provides a set of default options for the DIR command; COPYCMD, which provides default options for MOVE, COPY, and XCOPY; and MSDOSDATA, which identifies the default directory for MSBACKUP and MSAV.

You can use environment variables in batch programs but not in DOSKEY macros. Surround the variable name by percent signs. %CONFIG%, for example, refers to the current value of CONFIG, which DOS sets when you boot with a multiconfiguration CONFIG.SYS. A command such as GOTO %CONFIG% in a batch program branches to a label that matches the current value of CONFIG. This enables you to customize AUTOEXEC.BAT (and other batch files) to perform different actions depending on which configuration you chose when starting DOS.

When you use an environment variable in an IF equality condition, you usually need to surround the entire variable, including the percent signs, with quotation marks to account for a null value, as in IF "%CONFIG%"=="SHORT". (Don't put quotation marks around environment variables in other settings, however.)

You can use the existing value of an environment variable in a SET command. The command SET PATH=%PATH%;C:\PROGS, for example, adds the directory C:\PROGS to the end of the current search path.

Examples

SET

Displays the current values of all environment variables.

SET TEMP=F:\TEMP

Sets the value of TEMP to F:\TEMP. DOS commands, Windows, and some application programs use the directory specified by TEMP for storing temporary files.

```
SET DNT=C:\OLD_DOS
```

Creates (if it doesn't already exist) an environment variable named DNT and gives it the value C:\OLD_DOS. After this command, any time %DNT% is encountered in a batch file, it is replaced by C:\OLD_DOS.

```
SET TEMP=
```

Clears the environment variable TEMP. (When TEMP is cleared, DOS stores temporary files in the root directory of the current drive.)

SETUP

Chapter 4

Installs DOS from floppy disks.

Syntax

```
SETUP [/B] [/E] [F] [/G] [/H] [/I] [/M] [/Q] [/U]]
```

Parameters and Switches

none	Installs full DOS system on a hard drive, allowing you to select optional programs.
/B	Displays Setup screens in monochrome instead of color.
/E	Allows you to install Windows and DOS optional programs only.
/F	Installs DOS on a floppy disk (a minimal system is installed.
/G	Specifies that Setup should not create an Uninstall disk and does not prompt you to update your Network.
/H	Uses default SETUP options.
/I	Turns off video hardware detection.
/M	Installs a minimal DOS system.
/Q	Copies DOS files to a hard disk.
/U	Installs DOS even if SETUP detects disk partitions that are incompatible with DOS.

Notes

Setup is found on the Setup disks that come with DOS; it is not put on the hard drive when DOS is installed.

Chapter 4 describes in detail how Setup normally runs. The parameters and switches shown here are rarely necessary, except the /E switch.

When you run Setup with /E, it skips directly to the screen that allows you to select the DOS and/or WINDOWS versions of MSBACKUP, UNDELETE, and the Anti-Virus program. If, for example, you originally installed the DOS verion of MSBACKUP, you can add the WINDOWS version. Just put Disk 1 of the SETUP disks in your floppy drive, run SETUP /E from the floppy, and choose the WINDOWS version. Note that the DOS version won't be removed.

Examples

SETUP

Installs DOS on your hard drive. Enables you to choose between DOS and WINDOWS versions of the back up, undelete, and Anti-Virus programs.

SETUP /E

Enables you to choose and install backup, undelete, and Anti-Virus versions without reinstalling all of DOS.

SETVER

Chapter 21

Sets the version number DOS reports to a program or device driver; displays the version table.

Syntax

SETVER [path] [filename.ext version [/DELETE [/QUIET]]

Parameters and Switches

none	Displays the version table from SETVER.EXE in the current directory or search path.
path	Identifies the location of SETVER.EXE.
filename.ext	Identifies a program file.
version	Specifies a DOS version number to be reported to the specified program.
/DELETE	Deletes filename.ext from the version table; abbreviate as /D.
/QUIET	Omits the standard warning message when deleting a program from the version table.

Notes

Some programs check the DOS version number when they start up. They may be programmed to run with a specific version number, such as 5.0. When you run them with DOS 6.0 or later, you get a message saying you are using an incorrect version of DOS. Some of these programs run correctly with DOS 6; you just need to report a different version number to them. Others might not run correctly with DOS 6; fooling them through SETVER may lead to errors or data loss. When you add a program to SETVER, be sure you back up your hard disk before you run the program for the first time.

A version table, consisting of a list of programs and DOS version numbers, is maintained in SETVER.EXE. When you invoke a program listed in the table and the SETVER version table has been loaded, SETVER tells the program that it is running under the DOS version specified in its table entry.

See SETVER.EXE in Appendix A for the CONFIG.SYS command that loads the version table. If you don't load the version table, you can use this SETVER command to view and update the version table, but SETVER will not report version numbers to programs.

The SETUP program for DOS 6 usually inserts a command in CONFIG.SYS to load a version table provided by Microsoft. If you want to delete this command from CONFIG.SYS, first use SETVER (with no parameters) to see if any of the programs in the table are ones that you use or that support ones you use. If you're not sure, don't delete the command that loads SETVER's version table.

Some programs that were part of earlier DOS versions but are not in DOS 6 (such as ASSIGN, EDLIN, and JOIN) are in the version table provided by Microsoft so that you won't get an error message if you try to use them.

If you add the DOS 6 command interpreter (COMMAND.COM) to your version table, you may not be able to boot your system.

When you use SETVER to add to or delete from your current version table, the change does not take effect until you reboot, which loads the revised table into memory when it loads SETVER from CONFIG.SYS. (If CONFIG.SYS does not include a command to load SETVER, the table is not loaded.)

Path does not affect the location of the SETVER program that is loaded to process this command, which is located via DOS's usual program search procedures, but it does affect the location of the SETVER.EXE version table that is displayed and updated. Usually you don't need *path* because you want to update the only copy of SETVER you have. But if you are maintaining two version tables, one in C:\DOS and one in C:\ALTDOS, for example, you might need *path* to view and update the table in C:\ALTDOS.

SETVER sets an exit code, as follows:

0	Successful completion
1	Invalid command switch
2	Invalid file name
3	Insufficient memory
4	Invalid version number format

5	File name not in version table
6	SETVER.EXE file not found
7	Invalid drive (for *path*)
8	Too many command-line parameters
9	Missing command-line parameter(s)
10	Error reading SETVER.EXE file
11	SETVER.EXE file corrupt
12	Specified SETVER.EXE file does not support a version table
13	Version table full
14	Error writing to SETVER.EXE file

Examples

`SETVER MYPROG.EXE 5.0`

Adds an entry to the current version table so that MYPROG.EXE can be told that you are running DOS 5.0.

`SETVER MYPROG.EXE /DELETE`

Removes MYPROG.EXE from the version table.

`SETVER E:\ ¦ SORT ¦ MORE`

Displays the version table from the SETVER.EXE file found in the root directory of E; sorts the entries and pauses after each page.

SHARE

Chapter 51

Loads the SHARE TSR, which installs file-sharing and locking capabilities on your disks and network drives.

Syntax

`SHARE [/F:space] [/L:locks]`

Parameters and Switches

none	Loads SHARE with the default values.
/F:space	Allocates space (in bytes) to record file-sharing information; default value is 2048.
/L:locks	Sets the number of files that can be locked at one time; default is 20.

Notes

SHARE supports file-sharing and locking in network or multi-tasking environments in which programs share files. SHARE validates all read and write requests from programs so that, for example, two programs can't both write to the same file at the same time.

Each open file requires enough space for the length of the absolute path name and file name. The average length of a path name and file name is 20 characters.

You can load SHARE.EXE using INSTALL in CONFIG.SYS instead of this command, if you prefer. This makes SHARE available early in this booting process for systems that encounter sharing problems during booting.

Examples

```
SHARE
```

Loads SHARE with default values.

```
SHARE /F:4096 /L:300
```

Loads share with space for 4096 bytes of file information and allowing up to 300 locked files.

SHELL

Chapter 43

Identifies the command interpreter you want DOS to use.

Syntax

```
SHELL=filespec [parameters]
```

Parameters

filespec	Identifies the command interpreter.
parameters	Specifies command-line parameters or switches for the requested command interpreter.

Notes

Without SHELL, the default command interpreter is COMMAND.COM; DOS looks for it first in the root directory of the startup drive, then in \DOS. You must use SHELL in your CONFIG.SYS file if you want to use another command interpreter or another directory.

See COMMAND for parameters and switches that can be used with COMMAND.COM. If you use some other command interpreter, see its documentation for appropriate parameters and switches.

Two additional switches that can be used with COMMAND.COM in the SHELL command but not when you use COMMAND at the command prompt are:

/P	Makes the new copy of COMMAND.COM the permanent command interpreter. (The EXIT command does not remove it.) When you specify /P, AUTOEXEC.BAT is executed when the command interpreter is loaded; if there is no AUTOEXEC.BAT, the DATE and TIME commands are executed.
/MSG	Loads the COMMAND.COM messages into memory; use this switch when you're loading COMMAND.COM from a floppy and you don't want to read the floppy every time DOS needs to display a message. You can use /MSG only with /P.

Examples

```
SHELL=C:\SYS\COMMAND.COM C:\SYS /E:2048 /P
```

Installs COMMAND.COM from C:\SYS as the primary command processor and specifies an environment size of 2048 bytes.

SHIFT

Chapter 37

Shifts to the left the command-line parameters passed to a batch file.

Syntax

```
SHIFT
```

Notes

The SHIFT command shifts command-line parameters %0 through %9 so that the parameter that was %1 becomes %0, the parameter that was %2 becomes %1, and so on.

Examples

```
:LOOPER
IF "%1" == "" GOTO ENDING
DEL %1
SHIFT
GOTO LOOPER
:ENDING
```

This routine deletes an unknown number of files; you supply the file names on the command line that invokes this batch program. Each time SHIFT executes, a new name from the command line replaces %1. When there are no names left on the command line, %1 becomes a null value, and the IF command sends the program to :ENDING.

```
:COMPARE
IF "%2"=="" GOTO ENDING
FC %1 %2
SHIFT
SHIFT
GOTO COMPARE
:ENDING
```

This program compares an unknown number of file pairs, the names to be supplied from the command line. Two SHIFTs are needed so that both %1 and %2 are replaced by new values each time the loop is executed.

SMARTDRV

Chapter 31

Starts or configures SmartDrive, which creates a disk cache in extended memory; writes cached data.

Syntax 1

```
SMARTDRV [drive[+¦-]...] [/E:element] [InitCache [WinCache]] [/B:buffer] [/R]
[/L] [/Q ¦ /V ¦ /S] [/X] [/U] [/F ¦ /N]
```

Starts or configures SmartDrive.

Parameters and Switches

none	If SmartDrive is not already loaded, loads the TSR portion of the program with default values. Displays caching status of drives.
drive	Identifies a disk drive for which you want to control caching (do not follow the drive letter with a colon).
+ ¦ −	+ enables both read and write caching for *drive*; − disables both read and write caching for *drive*. See Notes for defaults.
/E:*element*	Specifies the number of bytes that SmartDrive reads or writes at one time; may be 1024, 2048, 4096, or 8192; the default is 8192.
InitCache	Specifies in kilobytes the size of the cache when SmartDrive starts and Windows is not running. The default depends on your system's memory (see Notes).
WinCache	Specifies in kilobytes the smallest size to which SmartDrive reduces the cache when Windows starts. The default depends on your system's memory. (See Notes.)

/B:*buffer*	Specifies the size of the read-ahead buffer; may be any multiple of *element*; the default is 16KB.
/R	Clears the contents of the cache.
/L	Prevents SmartDrive from automatically loading into upper memory, even if there are UMBs available.
/Q	Prevents SmartDrive from displaying status messages when it starts up.
/V	Displays status messages when SmartDrive starts.
/S	Displays additional information about the status of SmartDrive.

The following switches are available with DOS 6.2 and up only:

/F	Writes cached data after each command completes. (This is the default with DOS 6.2.)
/N	Does not write cached data when each command completes.
/U	Does not load the CD-ROM caching module.
/X	Disables write-caching for all drives.

Notes

SmartDrive keeps its cache in extended memory. Before using a SMARTDRV command, you must install an extended memory manager such as HIMEM.SYS.

Do not use the SMARTDRV command after Windows has started; Windows does its own cache management.

SmartDrive by default caches drives as follows:

Floppy drives	Read-cached but not write-cached
INTERLNK drives	Read-cached but not write-cached
CD-ROM drives	Read-cached but not write-cached
Hard drives	Both read-cached and write-cached

Other types of drives (RAM, network, memory card) cannot be cached. Compressed drives are not cached per se, but any caching of the host drive also caches the compressed drive.

With DOS 6.0, CD-ROM drives cannot be cached. With DOS 6.2 and up, CD-ROM drives are cached by default only if you load MSCDEX before you load SmartDrive.

You can override default caching with the *drive*[+ ¦ -] switch, either at the time that SmartDrive is loaded or any time after that.

/E, /B, /L, *InitCache*, and *WinCache* can be used only with the command that installs SmartDrive. Using /C or /S with an initial command prevents SmartDrive from loading and may produce a "help" message. (The /C switch is shown in Syntax 2.)

If you use /E, also specify *InitCache* and be sure to put /E before *InitCache* on the command line. Otherwise, the size of your cache may be reduced.

The larger the cache size and the element size, the fewer disk accesses and the more efficient your system.

 When SmartDrive loads, the size of the cache is *InitCache*. When Windows starts, it reduces the cache size to *WinCache* to allow more room for Windows operations. When Windows ends, the cache size returns to *InitCache*.

If you include only one cache size on the SMARTDRV command line, it is used for both *InitCache* and *WinCache*. That is, Windows can't reduce the cache size.

If you don't specify any cache size, SMARTDRV uses the default values shown in the following table:

Extended Memory	InitCache	WinCache
Up to 1MB	All extended memory	0
Up to 2MB	1MB	256KB
Up to 4MB	1MB	512KB
Up to 6MB	2MB	1MB
6MB or more	2MB	2MB

The SmartDrive TSR automatically loads into upper memory if any is available (unless you use /L). You don't need to use LH with SMARTDRV.

Some systems need to load a double-buffering version of SmartDrive. See SMARTDRV.EXE in Appendix A for information on when double-buffering is needed and how to load it.

Examples

SMARTDRV

If SmartDrive is not yet loaded, loads it with default values for cache, element, and buffer sizes, and default caching status for all drives. If SmartDrive is already loaded, displays the status report.

SMARTDRV A- B- C 2048 512 /E:2048

If SmartDrive is not yet loaded, loads it with a cache size of 2048K; allows the cache to be reduced to 512KB when Windows is running; uses the default value (16KB) for *buffer*; specifies that SmartDrive should access data in blocks of 2048 bytes; turns off caching for drives A and B; enables read-caching only for drive C. (Other drives are cached according to the default settings.)

If SmartDrive is already loaded, ignores *InitCache*, *WinCache*, and *element*; changes the caching status for drives A, B, and C; caching status for other drives is unchanged.

```
SMARTDRV /S
```

If SmartDrive is already loaded, displays an extended status report.

Syntax 2

```
SMARTDRV /C
```

Writes all write-cached information from memory to the disk.

Notes

If you're using write caching on any of your drives under DOS 6.0, it's a good idea to write out any write-cached data before turning off the system or pressing a reset button. It's not necessary to do this before pressing Ctrl+Alt+Del; SmartDrive automatically writes cached data when it detects this sequence.

If you are using DriveSpace or DoubleSpace with DOS 6.0, it's especially important to use SMARTDRV /C before shutting down or resetting; you could suffer severe data loss on a compressed drive otherwise.

By default, DOS 6.2's SmartDrive (and later versions) writes cached data whenever it returns to the command prompt, so you don't need to use SMARTDRV /C. However, if you loaded SmartDrive with the /N switch, you do need to use SMARTDRV /C to flush caches as described previously.

SORT

Chapter 36

Sorts ASCII data and displays results.

Syntax

```
SORT [/R] [/+n]
```

Parameters and Switches

/R	Reverses the sort order.
/+*n*	Starts sorting in column *n*; default is column 1.

Notes

SORT does not distinguish between uppercase and lowercase letters in the data to be sorted.

SORT can handle files as large as 64KB.

Normally, characters are sorted according to the ASCII code sequence; numeric digits 0–9 sort before letters A–Z. The placement of special or nonprinting characters depends on their ASCII codes.

If there is a COUNTRY command in CONFIG.SYS, SORT uses the collating-sequence table corresponding to the country code and code-page settings.

By default, SORT accepts data from the standard input device and writes it to the standard output device. You can redirect the input to come from a file or pipe it from a preceding command, and you can redirect the output to a file or a device or pipe it to another command.

Examples

```
SORT
```

Accepts input from the keyboard until you press Ctrl+Z (or its equivalent, F6); sorts the input; then displays the sorted data on the screen. (Notice that the sorted data is not stored in a file; as soon as it is displayed, it is lost.)

```
SORT /+2 < ADDRESS.LST > LPT1
```

Sorts the data in ADDRESS.LST, starting with characters in column 2 of each line, and sends the output to the printer. (Notice that the sorted data is not stored in a file.)

```
TYPE ADDRESS.LST ¦ SORT /+2 > LPT1
```

Has the same effect as the previous example.

```
SETVER ¦ SORT ¦ MORE
```

Lists the contents of SETVER's version table in alphanumeric order, one page at a time.

STACKS

Chapter 21

Supports the use of data stacks to handle hardware interrupts.

Syntax

```
STACKS=number,size
```

Parameters

number

Specifies the number of stacks; valid values are 0 or 8 through 64. For an IBM PC, IBM PC/XT, and IBM PC-Portable, the default value is 0; for all other computers, the default is 9.

size	Specifies the size (in bytes) of each stack. Valid values are 0 or 32 through 512. For an IBM PC, IBM PC/XT, and IBM PC-Portable, the default value is 0; for all other computers, the default is 128.

Notes

You can use the STACKS command in CONFIG.SYS only.

DOS allocates one stack when it receives a hardware interrupt. But if you specify 0 for both number and size, DOS allocates no stacks and each program must have its own stack space to accommodate the computer's hardware interrupt drivers. Many programs operate correctly with number and size set to 0.

If your computer operation becomes unstable when you set *number* and *size* to 0, return to the default values.

If *number* and *size* are not set to 0, and you get a Stack Overflow or Exception error 12 message, increase *number* or *size*.

Example

STACKS=12, 512

Allocates 12 stacks of 512 bytes each for hardware interrupt handling.

SUBMENU

Chapter 38

Defines an item on a startup menu that, when selected, displays another set of choices.

Syntax

SUBMENU=*blockname*[, *text*]

Parameters

blockname	Identifies the name of the configuration block where the submenu is defined.
text	Specifies the text to be displayed for this menu item; default is *blockname*.

Notes

You can use SUBMENU only in a main menu block or submenu block of a multiple configuration CONFIG.SYS. See MENUITEM for a description of a menu block.

There must be a block named [*blockname*] defined elsewhere in CONFIG.SYS. If DOS can't find [*blockname*], this item is not included in the menu.

Blockname may be up to 70 characters long and can include any printable characters except spaces, backslashes, slashes, commas, semicolons, equal signs, and square brackets.

Text may be up to 70 characters long and can contain any printable characters.

Examples

```
[MENU]
SUBMENU BASIC, BASIC STARTUP
MENUITEM WINDOWS
[BASIC]
MENUITEM JOE
MENUITEM MARY
...
```

This startup menu block produces this startup menu:

```
1.  BASIC STARTUP
2.  WINDOWS
```

When a user chooses 1, another menu is produced:

```
1.  JOE
2.  MARY
```

SUBST

Chapter 39

Reassigns a drive name to refer to a path.

Syntax 1

SUBST [*drive: path*]

Causes future references to *drive* to access *path* instead; displays current substitutions.

Parameters

none	Displays substitutions currently in force.
drive	Identifies drive name to be reassigned.
path	Specifies path to be referred to by *drive*.

Notes

Drive does not need to be an existing drive, but it must be within the range of possible drive names for the system (see LASTDRIVE). *Drive* can't be the current drive.

Path must refer to an existing directory on an existing drive. *Path* may include a drive name; if it does not, DOS assumes that *path* is on the drive current at the time SUBST is executed.

Once a substitution is made, any reference to *drive* is redirected to *path*. If *drive* actually exists, you will not be able to access it until you cancel the substitution. (If *drive* contains your DOS directory, you will not be able to use any external DOS commands, including SUBST, and you'll have to reboot to clear the substitution.)

Do not use the following commands on a substituted drive name: ASSIGN, MSBACKUP, CHKDSK, DEFRAG, DISKCOMP, DISKCOPY, FDISK, FORMAT, LABEL, MIRROR, RECOVER, RESTORE, SYS, and UNDELETE /S.

Examples

```
SUBST F: C:\DATADIR
```

Causes any future reference to drive F to access the DATADIR directory on drive C.

```
SUBST A: MYDIR\D1
```

Causes any future reference to drive A to access subdirectory D1 of directory MYDIR on the current drive.

```
SUBST A: B:\
```

Causes any future reference to drive A to access the root directory of the disk in drive B.

```
SUBST
```

Lists all current substitutions.

Syntax 2

```
SUBST drive: /D
```

Cancels the current substitution for *drive*.

Example

```
SUBST A: /D
```

Cancels any substitution for drive A. Future references to drive A will access drive A.

SWITCHES

Chapter 38

Provides special options for various DOS features.

Syntax

```
SWITCHES=[/W] [/K] [/N] [/F]
```

Switches

/W	Specifies that WINA20.386 is in a directory other than the root directory of the boot drive.
/K	Forces an enhanced keyboard (101-key) to behave like a conventional keyboard (84-key).
/N	Prevents a user from using F5 or F8 to bypass or condition-ally execute CONFIG.SYS and AUTOEXEC.BAT.
/F	Skips the two-second delay after displaying the Starting MS-DOS... message during startup.

Notes

Use SWITCHES in CONFIG.SYS only.

Use /W if you are using Windows 3.0 in enhanced mode and have moved the WINA20.386 from the root directory of the boot drive to another directory. You must also add a Device command under the [386Enh] heading in your SYSTEM.INI file, specifying the new location of WINA20.386. If you do not use Microsoft Windows 3.0, do not use the /W switch.

Use /K if you have a program that does not correctly interpret input from an enhanced keyboard. If you install the ANSI.SYS device driver, use the /K switch on the DEVICE command that loads ANSI.SYS also.

The /N switch does not prevent a user from pressing Ctrl+F5 or Ctrl+F8 to bypass DriveSpace or DoubleSpace during startup. You can disable this feature by entering a DRVSPACE /SWITCHES or DBLSPACE /SWITCHES command, which adds a SWITCHES /N command to DRVSPACE.INI or DBLSPACE.INI.

Example

```
SWITCHES=/F /N
```

Forces DOS to skip the two-second delay after the Starting MS-DOS... message and prevents users from bypassing startup commands.

SYS

Copies DOS system files and command interpreter to a formatted disk, making it a bootable disk.

Syntax

```
SYS [path] drive
```

Parameters

path	Identifies the location of the system files; the default is the root directory of the current drive.
drive	Specifies the drive to which you want to copy the system files.

Notes

SYS copies IO.SYS and MSDOS.SYS from the specified directory (or the default directory) and marks them as hidden, system, and read-only files. If SYS finds COMMAND.COM in *path* (or the default directory), it copies the file; otherwise, it displays a message saying that COMMAND.COM could not be copied. If SYS finds DRVSPACE.BIN or DBLSPACE.BIN along the search path, it copies this file also and marks it as system, hidden, and read-only. If SYS doesn't find DRVSPACE.BIN or DBLSPACE.BIN, there is no warning message.

All four files occupy about 193K.

SYS always copies these system files to the root directory of *drive*.

You do not need to reformat the target disk to make room for the system files. SYS moves files around as needed to place the two SYS files at the beginning of the disk where they belong.

SYS does not work on drives that have been redirected by ASSIGN, JOIN, or SUBST. It also does not work on network drives or drives redirected by INTERLNK.

Example

```
SYS A:
```

Copies the system files and command interpreter from the current drive's root directory to the root directory of the disk in drive A.

TIME

Chapter 12

Displays the system time and lets you change it.

Syntax

```
TIME [time]
```

Parameters

none	Displays the system time in standard format and asks for new time.
time	Changes the system time to *time*.

Notes

The system time affects directory entries, MSBACKUP, RESTORE, and many applications.

When you display the time, DOS asks for a new time. To retain the current time, press Enter. To change the time, type the new time and press Enter. You can also change the time in one step by entering the new time as *time*.

By default, the standard display format is the US standard, *hh:mm:ss.nnx* where:

- *hh* represents hours in 2-hour format
- *mm* represents minutes
- *ss* represents seconds
- *nn* represents hundredths of a second
- *x* is A (for a.m.) or P (for p.m.)

When entering a time, you may omit the A or P designation and use the 24-hour format, where hours are 0 (midnight) through 23 (11 PM); or you may use A or P with the 12-hour format. Case is ignored in the A or P designation. Do not enter hundredths of seconds.

When setting time to an exact hour, you can omit the zeros for minutes and seconds. Similarly, when setting time to an exact hour and minute, you do not need to enter seconds.

To change to other time formats, such as *hh.mm.ss.nn*, use the COUNTRY command in your CONFIG.SYS file to specify the country whose date and time formats are to be used as standards.

Examples

`TIME`

Displays the system time and asks you to enter a new time.

`TIME 3:15P`

Changes the system time to 3:15:00.00P.

`TIME 15:15:30`

Changes the system time to 3:15:30.00P.

`TIME 2:12`

Changes the system time to 2:12:00.00A.

`TIME 0`

Changes the system time to 12:00:00.00A (midnight).

`TIME 12`

Changes the system time to 12:00:00.00P (noon).

TREE

Chapter 14

Graphically displays a directory structure.

Syntax

```
TREE [drive ¦ path] [/F] [/A]
```

Parameters and Switches

none	Displays the directory structure starting with the current directory.
drive	Identifies the drive for which you want to display the directory structure.
path	Identifies a branch for which you want to display the directory structure.
/F	Includes in the display the names of the files in each directory.
/A	Specifies that TREE is to use text characters instead of graphics characters to show the lines linking subdirectories. Use this switch with code pages that do not support graphics characters and to send output to printers that don't properly interpret the graphics characters.

Examples

```
TREE
```

Displays the directory structure beginning with the current drive; does not list file names; uses graphics characters for lines connecting directories.

```
TREE A: /F ¦ MORE
```

Displays the directory structure of the disk in drive A, listing all files in all directories and pausing after each page.

```
TREE C:\BOOK /A >LPT1
```

Prints a directory structure of C:\BOOK and its subdirectories, using ASCII text characters instead of graphics characters for lines.

TRUENAME

Chapter 39

Identifies the true location of a directory or file.

Syntax

`TRUENAME [drive ¦ path ¦ filespec]`

Parameters

none	Displays the true name of the current drive and directory.
drive	Displays the true name of *drive*.
path	Displays the true name of the indicated directory.
filespec	Displays the true filespec of the indicated file.

Notes

Use TRUENAME when a directory structure has been masked by ASSIGN or SUBST.

TRUENAME doesn't check to make sure a file exists. It merely inserts the correct path name for the redirected one.

TYPE

Chapter 16

Displays the contents of a file.

Syntax

`TYPE filespec`

Parameter

filespec	Identifies the file that you want to view.

Notes

If *filespec* is not an ASCII text file, the display will probably not be readable; it might beep several times or stop before displaying the entire file.

Examples

`TYPE REPORT.TXT`

Displays the contents of REPORT.TXT on the screen.

```
TYPE AFILE.BAT ¦ SORT >LPT1
```

Prints the sorted contents of AFILE.BAT.

```
TYPE MYLIST ¦ MORE
```

Displays the contents of MYLIST, pausing after each page.

UNDELETE

Chapter 26

Enables deletion protection or restores files previously deleted.

Syntax 1

```
UNDELETE /LOAD ¦ /UNLOAD ¦ /S[drive] ... ¦ /T[drive[-entries] ... ¦ /STATUS
```

Enables or disables deletion protection; reports protection status.

Parameters and Switches

/LOAD	Loads the UNDELETE TSR with the default protection method.
/UNLOAD	Unloads the UNDELETE TSR. May be abbreviated to /U.
/S[drive]	Loads the UNDELETE TSR, setting the current and default method of deletion protection to Delete Sentry; adds drive to the list of drives protected by Sentry.
/T[drive]	Loads the UNDELETE TSR, setting the current and default method of deletion protection to deletion-tracking; adds drive to the list of drives protected by tracking.
entries	Specifies the maximum number of entries in the deletion-tracking file for drive; may be 1 to 999. The default depends on the drive size.
/STATUS	Displays the drives protected by the current protection method.

Notes

UNDELETE offers two levels of deletion protection. The higher level, Delete Sentry, and the lower, deletion-tracking, operate only if the UNDELETE TSR is loaded at the time you delete a file. If you don't use either method, you may still be able to recover a file using information in the DOS directory. (See Syntax 2.)

The UNDELETE.INI file (usually in the same directory as UNDELETE.EXE) contains default values for such things as how long a file should remain available (usually seven days); which files are protected (often *.TMP, *.VM?, and other files are left unprotected); which drives are protected by which method; and which is the default method of protection. You can view and modify UNDELETE.INI using a text editor such as EDIT.

When you use the Delete Sentry method and delete a file, UNDELETE moves the file to a special hidden directory (SENTRY). UNDELETE can easily and accurately restore the file later because its clusters are intact. Each drive protected by Delete Sentry has its own SENTRY directory.

Delete Sentry removes (purges) files from the SENTRY directory after a length of time specified in UNDELETE.INI, or when the directory takes up more than about 20 percent of the drive, or if necessary to make room for new data on the drive. The oldest files are removed first. If Delete Sentry is not loaded, files can't be purged from the SENTRY directory unless you use /PURGE. (See Syntax 2.) If your SENTRY directory is fairly large, you may easily get a `Disk full` message when you disable Delete Sentry.

When you use the deletion-tracking method and delete a file, UNDELETE stores the file's directory entry and FAT chain in a hidden file called PCTRACKR.DEL. UNDELETE can use the information to restore the file if its clusters have not been reused. Each drive protected by the deletion-tracking method has its own PCTRACKR.DEL file in its root directory.

PCTRACKR.DEL's size is fixed, as determined by the number of entries you request it to hold. When it is full, entries for new deletions replace the oldest entries in the file.

For deletion-tracking, the default value for *entries* depends on the disk size, as shown in the following table.

Drive	Entries
360KB	25
720KB	50
1.2MB	75
1.44MB	75
20MB	101
32MB	202
More than 32MB	303

Do not use the deletion-tracking method on a drive redirected by JOIN or SUBST. If you intend to use ASSIGN, you must do so before installing deletion-tracking.

Examples

```
UNDELETE /SC /SD
```

Loads the UNDELETE TSR using the Delete Sentry method; adds C and D to the list of drives protected by this method. (Any drives previously protected by this method remain protected).

```
UNDELETE /U
```

Unloads the UNDELETE TSR.

Syntax 2

```
UNDELETE [filespec] [/DT ¦ /DS ¦ /DOS ] [/LIST ¦ /ALL]
[/PURGE[drive]]
```

Recovers deleted files; lists recoverable files; clears a SENTRY directory.

Parameters and Switches

none	Offers to recover all deleted files in the current directory using the highest available method for that drive.
filespec	Identifies the file(s) that you want to recover; the default is all deleted files in the current directory.
/DT	Recovers only those files listed in the deletion-tracking file (PCTRACKR.DEL), prompting for confirmation on each file.
/DS	Recovers only those files listed in the Delete Sentry directory (SENTRY), prompting for confirmation on each file.
/DOS	Recovers only those files found in the DOS directory, prompting for confirmation on each file.
/LIST	Lists recoverable files, but does not offer to recover them. The files listed depend on *filespec* and the recovery method.
/ALL	Recovers files without prompting. The files recovered depend on filespec and the recovery method.
/PURGE[*drive*]	Empties the SENTRY directory on *drive*; the default is the current drive.

Notes

You don't need to load the UNDELETE TSR to use these recovery functions.

When you don't specify a recovery method, UNDELETE uses the highest available method for the drive. For example, if the drive has a SENTRY directory, UNDELETE uses the Delete Sentry method and ignores any PCTRACKR.DEL or DOS directory information.

No matter which recovery method is selected, UNDELETE displays the number of files that can be recovered by each method, including the DOS directory method, but it will recover only those that are available via the selected method.

When DOS deletes a file, it overwrites the first character of the file name. When you recover a deleted file by the DOS directory method, UNDELETE prompts you for a first character for the file name. But /ALL dispenses with prompting, so UNDELETE provides a first character (#). If the first attempt at providing an initial letter creates a nonunique name, UNDELETE substitutes another character (%), and so on. Characters are substituted in this order:

#%&0123456789ABCDEFGHIJKLMNOPQRSTUVWXYZ

Examples

```
UNDELETE C:\ /DT
```

Undeletes files deleted from the root directory on the C drive and protected by the deletion-tracking method; prompts before each file.

```
UNDELETE C:\WORDS\*.TXT /DS /ALL
```

Undeletes .TXT files deleted from directory C:\WORDS and protected by the Delete Sentry method; undeletes without prompting.

```
UNDELETE D:\ACCOUNT /LIST
```

If drive D is protected by the Delete Sentry method, lists files deleted from D:\ACCOUNT that are recoverable by Delete Sentry; otherwise, if drive D is protected by Delete Tracking, lists files deleted from D:\ACCOUNT that are recoverable by Delete Tracking. If D is not protected by Delete Sentry or Delete Tracking, lists files marked as deleted in the D:\ACCOUNT directory.

UNFORMAT

Chapter 17

Restores a disk reformatted by the FORMAT command.

Syntax

```
UNFORMAT drive [/L] [/TEST] [/P]
```

Parameters and Switches

drive	Identifies the drive to be unformatted.
/L	Bypasses the mirror file and lists every file and subdirectory found by UNFORMAT.

| /TEST | Bypasses the mirror file and shows how UNFORMAT would rebuild the disk, but does not actually rebuild the disk. |
| /P | Bypasses the mirror file and sends output messages to LPT1. |

Notes

If an unconditional format was done, UNFORMAT can't restore the disk.

If you have added data to a disk since it was reformatted, you can unformat it but some of the old files will have been damaged by the new data.

When you unformat a hard disk, the sectors must be 512, 1024, or 2048 bytes.

A safe or quick format stores a copy of the old root directory and FAT in a mirror file, located on the disk where UNFORMAT can find it even after the disk has been reformatted. When used with no switches, UNFORMAT uses information from this file to re-establish the former FAT and root directory, thus reconnecting with the undamaged data in the clusters.

If UNFORMAT can't find a mirror file on the disk, or if you use the /L, /TEST, or /P switches, UNFORMAT rebuilds the disk's directory structure (very slowly) by searching the clusters for subdirectories. It can't figure out the original names of the first level of subdirectories (the root directory's children), so it assigns generic names to them—SUBDIR.1, SUBDIR.2, and so on. Then it tries to undelete the files belonging to each subdirectory, but it can recover only the first fragment of files that were fragmented. It can't recover the files that were in the root directory.

Before DOS 6.0, UNFORMAT included three other switches: /U, /J, and /PARTN. These switches are still valid; you can see them in the fasthelp entry for UNFORMAT, but not in the help file entry. They serve no real purpose in DOS 6.0 and up since they depend on mirror and partition table files saved by the MIRROR program which no longer exists.

Examples

UNFORMAT A:

Unformats the disk in drive A using unformat information created by FORMAT, if found. If no mirror file is found, rebuilds the disk.

UNFORMAT B: /TEST

Simulates rebuilding the disk in drive B, searching for subdirectories and files.

VER

Chapter 12

Displays the DOS version number.

Syntax

VER

VERIFY

Turns write verification on or off.

Syntax

VERIFY [ON ¦ OFF]

Parameters

none	Displays the status of write verification.
ON	Turns write verification on, so that DOS verifies that files are written correctly to a disk.
OFF	Turns write verification off.

Notes

You can use VERIFY either in CONFIG.SYS or at the command prompt.

When verification is on, DOS verifies that any data written to a disk matches the copy of the data in memory. This can reassure you that no errors have been introduced during writing, but it doesn't verify that the data was correct in memory; it also slows down all disk writing slightly.

Examples

VERIFY

Displays the status of the verify switch.

VERIFY ON

Turns on write verification for all future commands.

VOL

Chapter 18

Displays the disk volume label and serial number, if they exist.

Syntax

VOL [drive]

Parameter

none	Displays the volume label and serial number, if any, of the disk in the current drive.
drive	Specifies a drive whose volume label and serial number you want to see.

Example

VOL A:

Displays the volume label and serial number of the disk in drive A.

VSAFE

Chapter 25

Loads (or unloads) the VSAFE TSR, which continuously monitors your computer for virus-like activity.

Syntax

VSAFE [*/option+* ¦ */option-*] [...] [/NE] [/NX] [/*Akey* ¦ /*Ckey*] [/N] [/D] [/U]

Parameters and Switches

/option+ ¦ –	Specifies how VSAFE monitors for viruses; use + or – following an option to turn it on or off. See Notes for the options.
/NE	Prevents VSAFE from loading into expanded memory.
/NX	Prevents VSAFE from loading into extended memory.
/*Akey*	Sets the hotkey that displays the VSAFE options dialog box as Alt+*key*; the default is Alt+V.
/*Ckey*	Sets the hotkey that displays the VSAFE options dialog box as Ctrl+*key*.
/N	Allows VSAFE to monitor network drives.
/D	Turns off checksumming.
/U	Removes VSAFE from memory; don't use with any other switches.

Notes

To use VSAFE with Windows, add the command C:\DOS\MWAVTSR.EXE to the line in your WIN.INI file that starts with LOAD=; this enables VSAFE to pop up virus alerts in Windows.

Don't install DOS, DriveSpace or DoubleSpace, or Windows when VSAFE is running. Disable VSAFE while you run the installation program, then enable VSAFE again.

You can use LH to load VSAFE in high memory.

Valid options are as follows:

1	Warns of low-level formatting that could completely erase the hard disk; default is ON.
2	Warns of an attempt by a program to establish memory residence; default is OFF.
3	Prevents programs from writing to disk; default is OFF.
4	Scans executable files for viruses as DOS loads them; default is ON.
5	Checks all disks for boot sector viruses; default is ON.
6	Warns of attempts to write to the boot sector or partition table of the hard disk; default is ON.
7	Warns of attempts to write to the boot sector of a floppy disk; default is OFF.
8	Warns of attempts to modify executable files; default is ON.

The VSAFE options list, accessed by the hotkey, shows you the status of each option, lets you change options, and lets you unload VSAFE.

Example

VSAFE /7+ /4- /AX

Loads VSAFE, turning on the option to warn of attempts to write to the boot sector of a floppy disk and turning off the option to scan executable files; all other options receive their default status; sets the hotkey to Alt+X.

XCOPY

Chapters 15 and 40

Copies files and subdirectories.

Syntax

XCOPY source [destination] [/A ¦ /M] [/D:date] [/P] [/S [/E]] [/V] [/W]
[/Y ¦ /-Y]

Parameters and Switches

source	Identifies the file(s) you want to copy.
destination	Specifies the location where the copy should be written; the default is the current directory.
/A	Copies only source files with positive archive attributes; does not change the archive attributes.
/M	Copies only source files with positive archive attributes; turns off the archive attributes.
/D:*date*	Copies only source files created or modified on or after *date*.
/P	Prompts you for permission to copy each selected file.
/S	Extends copying to the entire branch headed by the source directory (see Notes).
/E	Copies empty subdirectories when copying to the entire branch (see Notes). Before DOS 6.2, you must use /S if you use /E. With DOS 6.2 and higher, /E can be used without /S.
/V	Verifies each copy.
/W	Displays a message and waits for you to press a key before beginning to copy files.
/Y	Overwrites destination files without warning.
/-Y	Requests permission to overwrite destination files.

Notes

When copying multiple files, XCOPY is considerably faster than COPY.

XCOPY copies empty files (unlike COPY) but not system or hidden files.

XCOPY turns on the archive attribute of each copy but copies the source files' date/time stamps.

When *source* includes a file name, *destination* can include a file name, and the two files can be in the same directory. When the *source* filespec includes wildcards and *destination* is a directory, XCOPY makes a copy of each file matching the filespec. For example, in XCOPY CHAP*.DOC A:, XCOPY copies CHAP1.DOC to A:CHAP1.DOC.

If both *source* and *destination* include global filespecs, XCOPY creates or replaces destination files with the same wildcard characters in their file names. For example, in XCOPY CHAP*.DOC A:CHAP*.BAK, XCOPY copies CHAP1.DOC as A:CHAP1.BAK.

If *source* is global and *destination* is a single file, XCOPY copies each file in turn to the same *destination* file; *destination* ends up as the last *source* file copied.

If *destination* does not identify an existing directory and does not end with \, XCOPY asks you whether *destination* is a directory or a file. (If it ends with \, XCOPY knows that the *destination* is a directory.) If you enter D for directory, XCOPY creates the directory and copies the file(s) to it.

With /S, XCOPY selects source files from the entire branch headed by the source directory, and copies them to comparably named subdirectories in the branch headed by the destination directory, creating destination subdirectories as needed.

With /S but without /E, XCOPY creates a destination subdirectory only if it's needed to hold a copied file. With /E, XCOPY duplicates all of the source branch's subdirectories in the target branch, even if no files are copied to some of the new subdirectories.

With DOS 6.0 (and earlier versions), you can't use /E without using /S. With DOS 6.2 and later, use /E alone.

If you use XCOPY in a batch file or DOSKEY macro to copy files to or from a floppy disk, you can use /W to provide time for someone to insert a disk in the drive before XCOPY starts processing files.

In versions of DOS before 6.2, if the file identified by *destination* already exists, XCOPY overwrites it without warning. In effect, this means it deletes *destination* and creates a new file with the specified name. (You may be able to use a third-party undelete utility to recover the data from the newly deleted file.)

In DOS 6.2 and up, if the file identified by *destination* already exists, XCOPY's action depends on several factors. By default, if the command was entered from the command prompt, XCOPY asks if you want to overwrite the destination file, but if the command was entered from a batch program, XCOPY overwrites the destination file without warning. However, if the COPYCMD environment variable is set to /Y, XCOPY overwrites files without asking. If the COPYCMD environment variable is set to /-Y, XCOPY asks you before overwriting files. You can override the default action or the COPYCMD environment variable for a specific command by including /Y or /-Y in the command.

When XCOPY asks if you want to overwrite an existing destination file, you can enter Y to overwrite the file, N to preserve the file (the copy is not made), or A to overwrite this file and all subsequent files affected by the current XCOPY command. In other words, A terminates file protection for the remainder of this XCOPY command.

The /Y and /-Y switches are not available before DOS 6.2.

XCOPY sets an exit code as follows:

0	Successful completion.
1	No source files were found.
2	The user pressed Ctrl+C to terminate XCOPY.

4	Initialization error. There is not enough memory or disk space, or you entered an invalid drive name or invalid syntax on the command line.
5	Disk write error occurred.

Examples

```
XCOPY J*.* A:\NEWDIR\K*.*
```

Copies all files (except hidden and system ones) whose names start with J from the current directory to A:\NEWDIR; each destination file has the same name as the source file except that the first letter is replaced by K. If NEWDIR does not exist on drive A, XCOPY creates it.

```
XCOPY D:\ACCOUNT E:\ /S
```

If D:\ACCOUNT is a subdirectory, the branch headed by D:\ACCOUNT is copied to a branch headed by the root directory of drive E, with new subdirectories created under E:\ as needed. All files (except system or hidden ones) are copied. No empty subdirectories are created in the new branch.

If D:\ACCOUNT is a file, every file named ACCOUNT on drive D (except hidden and system ones) is copied to a comparably named directory on drive E, with new subdirectories created as needed to hold the new files.

```
XCOPY *.COM A:\ /E /W /Y
```

Waits for you to press a key (giving you time to insert a disk in A). After the keypress, each COM file (except system or hidden ones) from the branch headed by the current directory is copied to a comparably named directory on drive A, with new subdirectories created on A as needed. Source directories that don't contain a .COM file are also created on drive A if they don't already exist there. Comparably named files in A:\ are replaced without warning. (Note that versions of DOS before 6.2 would require the /S switch with the /E switch and could not use the /Y switch.)

```
XCOPY *.DAT \SAVE /A /S
```

Each .DAT file with a positive archive attribute from the branch headed by the current directory (except hidden or system ones) is copied (with its original name) to a comparably named subdirectory in the branch headed by \SAVE. New subdirectories are created as needed to hold the copied files. The archive attributes of the source files are unchanged.

A

Device Drivers

ANSI.SYS

Chapter 48, "Console Control"

Provides functions that control screen colors, cursor position, and key assignments.

Syntax

DEVICE[HIGH]=[*path*]ANSI.SYS [/X ¦ /K] [/R]

Parameters and Switches

path   Identifies the location of the ANSI.SYS file. The default is the root directory of the boot drive.

/X   With a 101-key (extended) keyboard, forces DOS to recognize that the extended (gray) cursor control, deletion, and insert/overlay keys have different scan codes than the numeric keypad keys for the same functions.

/K   Causes ANSI.SYS to treat a 101-key keyboard like an 84-key keyboard. Use this if you have a program that does not recognize the extended keys on the 101-key keyboard. If you use the /K switch with the SWITCHES command, use /K with ANSI.SYS also.

/R   Slows the line scrolling rate slightly for easier reading. The effect is almost unnoticeable.

Notes

After ANSI.SYS has been loaded, any program can use its features by issuing escape sequences that act as commands to ANSI.SYS. (A program's documentation should tell you if it requires ANSI.SYS to be loaded.)

You also can enter an ANSI.SYS escape sequence by including it in a PROMPT command, by putting it in an ASCII text file and displaying the file with TYPE, or by inserting it in an ECHO command in a batch file and running the batch program.

All ANSI.SYS escape sequences begin with the Escape character. The Esc key types the escape character; but, because that key normally acts to terminate a command or program, you can't type it directly at the command prompt or in a file. You can, however, generate an escape character in a PROMPT command by typing $E. In DOS's EDIT and WordStar, you can type an Escape character by pressing Ctrl+P followed by the Esc key; it shows up on the screen as a left arrow. In Microsoft Word, you can type an escape character by holding the Alt key while typing 27 on the numeric keypad. Other editors and word processors may use other techniques; some are not able to do it.

There are hundreds of ANSI.SYS escape sequences to control such things as the colors of the screen's background and text, what happens when you press Ctrl+Shift+X, and so on. They are documented in DOS 6's on-screen HELP system; look up the ANSI.SYS topic.

Example

```
DEVICEHIGH=C:\DOS\ANSI.SYS
```

Loads the ANSI.SYS device driver found in C:\DOS into upper memory, if available; otherwise, loads it into conventional memory, if possible.

```
PROMPT $E[34;57m$P$G
```

Sets up the command prompt screen with blue characters on a white background, and displays the normal command prompt. The escape sequence `$E[34;57m` defines the screen colors.

CHKSTATE.SYS

Used by MEMMAKER to control the optimization process.

Notes

MEMMAKER temporarily adds the CHKSTATE.SYS command to your CONFIG.SYS file. When optimization is complete, MEMMAKER deletes it again.

DBLSPACE.SYS

Chapter 34, "DriveSpace and DoubleSpace," and Chapter 45, "A Second Look at DrvSpace and DblSpace"

Moves DBLSPACE.BIN to an appropriate memory location.

Syntax

```
DEVICE[HIGH]=[path]DBLSPACE.SYS /MOVE [NOHMA]
```

Parameters and Switches

path   Identifies the location of the DBLSPACE.SYS file. The default is the root directory of the boot drive.

NOHMA   Prevents DBLSPACE from sharing HMA with DOS.

Notes

DoubleSpace adds this command to CONFIG.SYS. If your system is set up to access UMBs, you may replace DEVICE with DEVICEHIGH to load this driver into upper memory.

DBLSPACE.BIN manages compressed drives. DOS loads DBLSPACE.BIN into the top of conventional memory at boot time before carrying out any commands in CONFIG.SYS. This may cause conflict with other programs that require the use of this area. The DBLSPACE.SYS driver moves DBLSPACE.BIN to another location in memory to avoid any conflict.

In DOS 6.2 and up, part of DBLSPACE is normally loaded into HMA, reducing the amount of upper or lower memory it requires. This leaves room for only 10 buffers in HMA; if you use more than 10 buffers, they will all be loaded in conventional memory. If you are using a disk cache such as SmartDrive, reduce buffers to 10. Otherwise, use /NOHMA to prevent DBLSPACE from sharing HMA with DOS.

Example

```
DEVICE=C:\DOS\DBLSPACE.SYS /MOVE
```

Moves DBLSPACE.BIN.

DISPLAY.SYS

Chapter 49, "Another Country Heard From"

Supports code-page switching for your screen and keyboards.

Syntax

```
DEVICE[HIGH]=[path]DISPLAY.SYS CON=([type][,codepage][,max¦ ,(max, sub)])
```

Parameters

path	Identifies the location of the DISPLAY.SYS file. The default is the root directory of the boot drive.
type	Specifies the display adapter in use. Valid values are EGA and LCD. EGA includes both EGA and VGA adapters. If you don't specify *type*, DISPLAY.SYS checks the hardware to determine the display adapter in use.
code page	Specifies the code page built into your hardware.

max	Specifies the number of code pages the hardware can support besides the one built into the hardware. Valid values are 0 through 6 for EGA, 0 through 1 for LCD.
sub	Specifies the number of subfonts the hardware supports for each code page.

Notes

See the CHCP and MODE commands for more information about code pages.

Although TYPE accepts the values CGA and MONO, DISPLAY.SYS has no effect with these values, because CGA and MONO adapters don't support multiple character sets.

Code page values supported by DOS are as follows:

437	United States
850	Multilingual (Latin I)
852	Slavic (Latin II)
860	Portuguese
863	Canadian-French
865	Nordic

Most hardware sold in the U.S. uses code page 437.

If you install both DISPLAY.SYS and a third-party console driver in CONFIG.SYS, install the third-party console driver first. Otherwise, the third-party console driver may disable DISPLAY.SYS.

Example

```
DEVICE=C:\DOS\DISPLAY.SYS CON=(EGA,437,(2,1))
```

Loads DISPLAY.SYS for an EGA (or VGA) console with hardware code page 437, permitting two additional code pages, each with 1 subfont. Loads DISPLAY.SYS into conventional memory.

```
DEVICEHIGH=C:\DOS\DISPLAY.SYS CON=(LCD, 437, 1)
```

Loads DISPLAY.SYS for an LCD console with hardware code page 437, permitting one additional code page. Loads DISPLAY.SYS into upper memory, if available; otherwise, into conventional memory.

DRIVER.SYS

Chapter 51, "Configuring Disks and Networks"

Creates a logical drive assigned to a physical floppy drive.

Syntax

```
DEVICE[HIGH]=[path]DRIVER.SYS /D:physical [/C] [/F:type] [/H:heads] [/S:sectors]
[T:tracks]
```

Parameters and Switches

path	Identifies the location of the DRIVER.SYS file. The default is the root directory of the boot drive.
/D:*physical*	Specifies the number of the physical floppy drive. Valid values are 0 through 127.
/C	States that the drive has change-line support. (See the DRIVEPARM command for information about change-line support.)
/F:*type*	Identifies the type of drive. (See Notes for values.)
/H:*heads*	Specifies the number of heads for the disk drive. Valid values are 1 through 99. The default is 2.
/S:*sectors*	Specifies the number of sectors per track. Valid values are 1 through 99. (See Notes for default values.)
/T:*tracks*	Specifies the number of tracks per side. Valid values are 1 through 999. (See Notes for default values.)

Notes

Drive name A is always assigned to physical drive 0. If the system has a second drive, it is physical drive 1, and is assigned the drive name B; otherwise, drive name B also is assigned to physical drive 0.

If you put a new floppy drive on your system and can't get DOS to recognize it, use DRIVER.SYS to assign a drive letter to it. If this is the third floppy drive for your system, its number is 2; if it's the fourth, its number is 3; and so on.

If you want to assign two drive names to the same drive, use DRIVER.SYS to assign the second drive name. One reason for doing this is to make it possible to use COPY or XCOPY to copy files from one disk to another in the same drive.

DOS assigns the next available drive name to a drive defined by DRIVER.SYS. If you add a DEVICE=DRIVER.SYS command to a CONFIG.SYS that also defines a RAM drive, DOS may assign a different letter to your RAM drive than it did previously. It's possible that drive names assigned by DoubleSpace also may change if you add DRIVER.SYS to your CONFIG.SYS file.

Default values for sectors and tracks depend on type. Valid values for type and the defaults associated with each type are as follows:

Type	Drive	Sectors	Tracks
0	160KB/180KB or 320KB/360KB	9	40
1	1.2MB	15	80
2	720KB or other (Default)	9	80
7	1.44MB	18	80
9	2.88MB	36	80

If you specify /H, /S, and / T, you can omit the / F switch. Usually, if you specify / F, you can omit /H, /S, and / T; but, check the disk-drive's documentation to be sure the default values for these switches are correct for your drive.

If you create two logical drives for the same physical drive, be sure that they have the same parameters and switches.

Examples

```
DEVICEHIGH=C:\DOS\DRIVER.SYS /D:1 /C
```

Loads DRIVER.SYS into upper memory, if possible; otherwise, into conventional memory. Assigns the next available drive name to the second floppy drive, using values appropriate for a 720KB 3 1/2-inch floppy disk drive (by default), and specifying that the drive has change-line support. If DOS has already assigned a name to the second floppy drive during booting, this assigns an additional name to the drive:

```
DEVICE=C:\DOS\DRIVER.SYS /D:2 /F:7
DEVICE=C:\DOS\DRIVER.SYS /D:2 /F:7
```

Each of these commands loads the DRIVER.SYS file and assigns the next available drive name to the third floppy drive, using values appropriate to a 1.44MB 3 1/2-inch floppy drive (by default). The effect is to assign two drive names to the drive.

DRVSPACE.SYS

Chapters 34 and 45

Moves DRVSPACE.BIN to an appropriate memory location.

Syntax

```
DEVICE[HIGH]=[path]DRVSPACE.SYS /MOVE [NOHMA]
```

Parameters and Switches

path	Identifies the location of the DRVSPACE.SYS file. The default is the root directory of the boot drive.
NOHMA	Prevents DRVSPACE from sharing HMA with DOS.

Notes

DriveSpace adds this command to CONFIG.SYS when you install DriveSpace. If your system is set up to access UMBs, you may replace DEVICE with DEVICEHIGH to load this driver into upper memory.

DRVSPACE.BIN manages compressed drives. DOS loads DRVSPACE.BIN into the top of conventional memory at boot time, before carrying out any commands in CONFIG.SYS. This may cause conflict with other programs that require the use of this area. The DRVSPACE.SYS driver moves DRVSPACE.BIN to another location in memory to avoid any conflict.

Part of DRVSPACE is normally loaded into HMA, reducing the amount of upper or lower memory it requires. This leaves room for only 10 buffers in HMA; if you use more than 10 buffers, they will all be loaded in conventional memory. If you are using a disk cache such as SmartDrive, reduce buffers to 10. Otherwise, use /NOHMA to prevent DRVSPACE from sharing HMA with DOS.

Example

```
DEVICE=C:\DOS\DRVSPACE.SYS /MOVE
```

Moves DRVSPACE.BIN.

EGA.SYS

Chapter 21, "Configuring Your System"

Saves and restores the display when DOS Shell's task swapper is used with EGA monitors.

Syntax

```
DEVICE[HIGH]=[path]EGA.SYS
```

Parameter

path	Identifies the location of the EGA.SYS file. The default is the root directory of the boot drive.

Notes

If you have an EGA monitor, you must install EGA.SYS before using DOS Shell's task swapper. EGA.SYS may also be required by Microsoft Windows or other task switching software.

If you are using a mouse on a system that has an EGA monitor, you can save memory by installing EGA.SYS before you install your mouse driver.

EMM386.EXE

Chapter 30, "Additional Memory Facilities for 386, 486, and Pentium Computers," and Chapter 44, "Squeezing Even More Out of Memory"

Provides access to the upper memory area, and uses extended memory to simulate expanded memory.

Syntax

```
DEVICE=[path]EMM386.EXE [ON ¦ OFF ¦ AUTO] [expanded-memory] [MIN=size] [W=ON ¦ W=OFF] [Mx
¦ FRAME=address1 ¦ /Paddress1] [Pn=address2] [[X=mmmm1-nnnn1]...] [[I=mmmm2-nnnn2]...]
[B=address3] [L=minXMS] [A=altregs] [H=handles] [D=nnn] [RAM[=mmmm3-nnnn3]] [NOEMS]
[NOVCPI] [HIGHSCAN] [VERBOSE] [[WIN=mmmm4-nnnn4]...] [NOHI] [ROM=mmmm5-nnnn5]
[NOMOVEXBDAT] [ALTBOOT]
```

Parameters and Switches

path	Identifies the location of the EMM386.EXE file. The default is the root directory of the boot drive.
ON¦OFF¦AUTO	ON loads and activates the EMM386 driver; OFF loads the driver, but deactivates it; AUTO places the driver in automatic mode, which enables expanded-memory support and upper memory block support only when a program calls for it. Use the EMM386 command to change this value after the driver has been loaded.
expanded-memory	Specifies (in kilobytes) the maximum amount of extended memory that you want EMM386.EXE to provide as expanded/Virtual Control Program Interface (EMS/VCPII) memory. Values are 64 through 32768 (or the amount of free extended memory). The default value is the amount of free extended memory, unless you specify NOEMS. EMM386.EXE rounds the value down to the nearest multiple of 16.

MIN=*size*	Specifies (in kilobytes) the minimum amount of EMS/VCPI memory that EMM386.EXE will provide. Values are 0 through *expanded-memory*. The default value is 256, unless you specify NOEMS.
W=ON ¦ W=OFF	Enables or disables support for the Weitek coprocessor. The default is W=OFF.
M*x*	Specifies the base address of the expanded-memory page frame. Valid values are 1 through 14. If your computer has less than 512KB of memory, *x* must be less than 10. See Notes for the address associated with each value of *x*.
FRAME=*address1*	Specifies the page-frame base address directly. Valid values are 8000H through 9000H, and C000H through E000H, in increments of 400H. You may specify FRAME=NONE, but this could cause some programs to malfunction.
/P*address1*	Specifies the page-frame base address directly. Valid values are 8000H through 9000H, and C000H through E000H, in increments of 400H.
P*n*=*address2*	Specifies the base address of page *n*. Valid values for *n* are 0 through 255. Valid values for address are 8000H through 9C00H, and C000H through EC00H, in increments of 400H. The addresses for pages 0 through 3 must be contiguous to maintain compatibility with Version 3.2 of LIM EMS. If you use M*x*, FRAME, or /P*address1*, you can't specify addresses for pages 0 through 3 with the /P*n* switch.
X=*mmmm1*-*nnnn1*	Prevents EMM386.EXE from using a particular range of segment addresses for an EMS page or for UMBs. Valid values for *mmmm1* and *nnnn1* are in the range A000H through FFFFH, and are rounded down to the nearest 4KB boundary. This parameter takes precedence over the I parameter if two ranges overlap.
I=*mmmm2*-*nnnn2*	Specifies a range of segment addresses to use for an EMS page or for UMBs. Valid values for *mmmm2* and *nnnn2* are in the range A000H through FFFFH, and are rounded down to the nearest 4KB boundary. The X parameter takes precedence over the I parameter if two ranges overlap.
B=*address3*	Specifies the lowest segment address available for EMS bank-switching. Valid values are in the range 1000H through 4000H. The default value is 4000H.
L=*min*XMS	Ensures that *min* kilobytes of extended memory will still be available after you load EMM386.EXE. The default value is 0.

A=*altregs*	Specifies how many fast alternate register sets (used for multitasking) you want to allocate to EMM386.EXE. Valid values are in the range 0 through 254. The default value is 7. Every alternate register set adds about 200 bytes to the size of EMM386.EXE in memory.
H=*handles*	Specifies how many handles EMM386.EXE can use. Valid values are in the range 2 through 255. The default is 64.
D=*nnn*	Specifies how many kilobytes of memory to reserve for buffered direct memory access (DMA). Discounting floppy-disk DMA, this value should reflect the largest DMA transfer that will occur while EMM386.EXE is active. Valid values for *nnn* are in the range 16 through 256. The default value is 16.
RAM[=*mmmm3-nnnn3*]	Requests both expanded memory and UMB support, and specifies a range of segment addresses in extended memory to use for UMBs. If you do not specify a range, EMM386.EXE selects the addresses.
NOEMS	Provides UMB support, but not expanded memory support.
NOVCPI	Disables support for VCPI (Virtual Control Program Interface) applications. This switch may be used only with the NOEMS switch. When you specify both switches, EMM386.EXE disregards the *expanded-memory* and MIN parameters.
HIGHSCAN	Specifies additional scanning of the upper memory area for available memory. On some computers, this switch may have no effect, or even cause the computer to freeze.
VERBOSE	Directs EMM386.EXE to display status and error messages while loading. By default, EMM386.EXE does not display these messages. You can abbreviate /VERBOSE as /V.
WIN=*mmmm4-nnnn4*	Reserves a range of segment addresses for Windows instead of for EMM386.EXE. Valid values for *mmmm4* and *nnnn4* are in the range A000H through FFFFH, and are rounded down to the nearest 4 KB. The X parameter takes precedence over the WIN parameter if two ranges overlap. The WIN parameter takes precedence over the RAM, ROM, and I parameters if their ranges overlap.
NOHI	Prevents EMM386.EXE from loading into the upper memory area. Normally, a portion of EMM386.EXE is loaded into upper memory. Specifying this switch decreases available conventional memory and increases the upper memory area available for UMBs.

ROM=*mmmm5*-*nnnn5*	Specifies a range of segment addresses that EMM386.EXE uses for shadow RAM. Valid values for *mmmm5* and *nnnn5* are in the range A000H through FFFFH, and are rounded down to the nearest 4KB. Specifying this switch may speed up your system, if it does not already have shadow RAM. (See HIMEM.SYS for an explanation of shadow RAM.)
NOMOVEXBDAT	Prevents EMM386.EXE from moving the extended BIOS data from conventional to upper memory.
ALTBOOT	Tells EMM386.EXE to use a different method of restarting your computer when you press CTRL+ALT+DEL. If you have problems rebooting when EMM386.EXE is loaded, use this switch.

Notes

You must load this device driver with a DEVICE (not DEVICEHIGH) command in CONFIG.SYS. You can use this driver only on computers with a 386 or higher processor.

You must install HIMEM.SYS before loading EMM386.SYS. The DEVICE command that loads EMM386 must come before any DEVICEHIGH commands in CONFIG.SYS.

EMM386 can provide expanded memory to programs by using extended memory to simulate expanded memory. To use EMM386 for this purpose, you don't usually need to specify any of the memory parameters; EMM386 normally runs properly with the default parameters. Extended memory reserved for this purpose (by the MIN parameter or its default) is no longer available for use as extended memory. If EMM386 uses additional extended memory, up to the *expanded-memory* maximum, the additional memory returns to extended memory use when it is no longer needed as expanded memory.

To provide access to upper memory, you must use either the RAM or NOEMS switch. (You also must include DOS=UMB in CONFIG.SYS.) NOEMS gives access to upper memory, while suppressing expanded memory support. RAM provides both upper memory and expanded memory support.

When EMM386.EXE is used with Windows 3.1, the I; X; NOEMS; M*x*; P*address1*; and FRAME parameters have precedence over the EMMINCLUDE, EMMEXCLUDE, and EMMPAGEFRAME settings in the Windows SYSTEM.INI file.

If you have a small computer system interface (SCSI) or enhanced system device interface (ESDI) hard disk or other device, you may have to use SmartDrive double buffering (see SMARTDRV.EXE) with EMM386.

Values for M*x*, and the base addresses associated with them, are as follows:

x	*Base Address*
1	C000H
2	C400H

x	Base Address
3	C800H
4	CC00H
5	D000H
6	D400H
7	D800H
8	DC00H
9	E000H
10	8000H
11	8400H
12	8800H
13	8C00H
14	9000H

Examples

```
DEVICE=C:\DOS\HIMEM.SYS
DEVICE=C:\DOS\EMM386.EXE OFF
```

The first command loads the HIMEM.SYS extended memory manager using all default values; this is a prerequisite to the second command. The second command loads the EMM386.EXE device driver to provide a minimum of 256KB of expanded memory, which is borrowed from extended memory. Additional expanded memory support can be allocated to a program upon request, up to the amount of available extended memory. All other parameters such as page frame addresses, alternate registers, and handles, use their default values. The driver is disabled after loading, so no expanded memory is provided until an EMM386 command enables it or places it in automatic mode.

```
DEVICE=C:\DOS\HIMEM.SYS
DEVICE=C:\DOS\EMM386.EXE NOEMS
DOS=UMB
```

The first command loads the HIMEM.SYS extended memory manager using all default values; this is a prerequisite to the second command. The second command loads the EMM386.EXE device driver to provide upper memory blocks only. (Memory for the UMBs is borrowed from extended memory.) The third command is required to make the UMBs available to DOS:

```
DEVICE=C:\DOS\HIMEM.SYS
DEVICE=C:\DOS\EMM386.EXE MIN=1024 2048 RAM
DOS=UMB
```

The first command loads the HIMEM.SYS extended memory manager using all default values; this is a prerequisite to the second command. The second command loads the EMM386.EXE device driver to provide both expanded memory and upper memory support. A minimum of 1MB of expanded memory is borrowed from extended memory; this can be expanded up to 2MB on individual program request. All other expanded memory parameters use their default values. The third command makes the UMBs available to DOS.

HIMEM.SYS

Chapter 29 "Managing Memory," and Chapter 44

Manages extended memory, including the high memory area (HMA).

Syntax

```
DEVICE=[path]HIMEM.SYS [/A20CONTROL:ON ¦ OFF][/CPUCLOCK:ON ¦ OFF] [/EISA] [/HMAMIN=size]
[/INT15=x] [/NUMHANDLES=n] [/MACHINE:machine] [/SHADOWRAM:ON ¦ OFF] [/TESTMEM:[ON ¦ OFF]
[/VERBOSE]
```

Parameters and Switches

path	Identifies the location of the HIMEM.SYS file. The default is the root directory of your boot drive.
/A20CONTROL:ON ¦ OFF	Specifies whether HIMEM is to take control of the A20 line, even if A20 is already on. If you specify /A20CONTROL:OFF, HIMEM takes control of the A20 line only if A20 is not already in use when HIMEM loads. The default setting is /A20CONTROL:ON.
/CPUCLOCK:ON ¦ OFF	Specifies whether HIMEM can affect the clock speed of your computer. If your computer's clock speed changes when you install HIMEM, /CPUCLOCK:ON may correct the problem but slow down HIMEM. The default setting is /CPUCLOCK:OFF.
/EISA	Specifies that HIMEM.SYS should allocate all available extended memory. This switch is necessary only on an EISA (Extended Industry Standard Architecture) computer with more than 16MB of memory; on other computers, HIMEM automatically allocates all available extended memory.
/HMAMIN=size	Specifies (in kilobytes) how large a program must be to use the HMA. Valid values are 0 through 63; the default is 0, which forces HIMEM to give the HMA to the first program that requests it. This switch has no effect when Windows is running in 386 enhanced mode.

/INT15=*x*	Allocates (in kilobytes) extended memory for the interrupt 15h interface. Valid values are 64 through 65535, but not more than your systems available memory. The default value is 0. If *x* is less than 64, HIMEM uses 0.
/NUMHANDLES=*n*	Specifies the maximum number of extended memory block handles that can be used simultaneously. Valid values are 1 through 128; the default value is 32. Each handle requires an additional 6 bytes of memory. This switch has no effect when Windows is running in 386 enhanced mode.
/MACHINE:*machine*	Specifies which A20 handler to use. (See Notes for valid values.)
/SHADOWRAM:ON ¦ OFF	Specifies whether or not to enable shadow RAM. If your computer has less than 2MB of memory, the default is OFF (disabled).
/TESTMEM:ON ¦ OFF	Specifies whether to test high memory when booting. The default is ON.
/VERBOSE	Directs HIMEM.SYS to display status and error messages while loading. By default, HIMEM.SYS does not display these messages. You can abbreviate /VERBOSE as /V.

Notes

You must load this device driver with a DEVICE (not DEVICEHIGH) command in CONFIG.SYS. The DEVICE command must come before any commands that start applications, or device drivers that use extended memory; for example, you must load HIMEM.SYS before EMM386.

In most cases, you will not need to specify command-line options. The default values for HIMEM.SYS work with most hardware.

In a 286 or newer machine, the twenty-first address line (named A20) gives DOS access to the high memory area (HMA), which is the first 64KB (almost) of extended memory. The HMA can be used to execute programs just like conventional memory, but you must load special software to manage the A20 line.

Usually, HIMEM detects the computer type successfully and loads the correct A20 handler, but there are a few computers that HIMEM can't detect. On such systems, HIMEM uses the default A20 handler (#1, for the IBM AT or compatible). If HIMEM does not work properly on your system, you may need to use /MACHINE to specify the A20 handler. Systems that may require this option include Acer 1100, Wyse, and IBM 7552.

With /MACHINE, you can specify either the machine code, as in /MACHINE=WYSE, or the number of the A20 handler, as in /MACHINE=8.

Machine can be any of these codes, or their equivalent A20 handler numbers, as follows:

Machine Code	A20 Handler	Computer Type
AT	1	IBM AT or 100% compatible
PS2	2	IBM PS/2
PTLCASCADE	3	Phoenix Cascade BIOS
HPVECTRA	4	HP Vectra (A & A+)
ATT6300PLUS	5	AT&T 6300 Plus
ACER1100	6	Acer 1100
TOSHIBA	7	Toshiba 1600 & 1200XE
WYSE	8	Wyse 12.5 MHz 286
TULIP	9	Tulip SX
ZENITH	10	Zenith ZBIOS
AT1	11	IBM PC/AT (alternative delay)
AT2	12	IBM PC/AT (alternative delay)
CSS	12	CSS Labs
AT3	13	IBM PC/AT (alternative delay)
PHILIPS	13	Philips
FASTHP	14	HP Vectra
IBM7552	15	IBM 7552 Industrial Computer
BULLMICRAL	16	Bull Micral 60
DELL	17	Dell XBIOS

Some computer's shadow ROM by copying its information into RAM at startup. This can make ROM code run faster, but it uses some extended memory. If a computer has less than 2MB of RAM, HIMEM usually attempts to disable shadow RAM to recover additional extended memory for other uses. (HIMEM can disable shadow RAM only on certain types of systems.) When HIMEM disables shadow RAM, your computer may run slightly slower than it did before. (See EMM386.EXE for a means of providing shadow RAM, if your computer does not have it built-in.)

Some older applications use the interrupt 15H interface to allocate extended memory, rather than using the XMS (eXtended-Memory Specification) method provided by HIMEM. If you use such an application, you can make sure that enough memory is available to it by making *x* 64KB larger than the amount the application requires.

Normally HIMEM tests expanded memory when CONFIG.SYS runs. To save time, you can use /TESTMEM: OFF to prevent this check. If memory checking is turned off when HIMEM loads, you can still do a memory check by holding down ALT while CONFIG.SYS runs.

Examples

```
DEVICE=C:\DOS\HIMEM.SYS
```

Loads the HIMEM.SYS driver using all default values.

```
DEVICE=C:\DOS\HIMEM.SYS /MACHINE=6 /INT15=64
```

Loads the HIMEM.SYS driver with the Acer 1100 A20 handler, and reserves 64K of memory for processing old-style extended memory requests.

INTERLNK.EXE

Chapter 41, "INTERLNK"

Links a client computer to a server computer and redirects drive and printer port names.

Syntax

```
DEVICE[HIGH]=[path]INTERLNK.EXE [/DRIVES:n] [/NOPRINTER] [/COM[n ¦ address]]
[/LPT[n ¦ address]] [/AUTO] [/NOSCAN] [/LOW] [/BAUD:rate] [/V]
```

Parameters and Switches

path	Identifies the location of the INTERLNK.EXE file. The default is the root directory of the boot drive.
/DRIVES:*n*	Specifies the number of server drives to be redirected to the client computer. The default is 3. If *n* = 0, INTERLNK redirects only printers.
/NOPRINTER	Inhibits redirection of printers. By default, INTERLNK redirects all available parallel printer ports.
/COM[*n* ¦ *address*]	Specifies the port by which the client computer is cabled to the server computer; if neither *n* nor *address* is specified, INTERLNK scans all serial ports for the connection.
/LPT[*n* ¦ *address*]	Specifies the port by which the client computer is cabled to the server computer; if neither *n* nor *address* is specified, INTERLNK scans all parallel ports for the connection.
/AUTO	Installs INTERLNK.EXE in memory only if it can establish an immediate link with the server computer. By default, INTERLNK.EXE is installed even if the connection can't yet be completed.

/NOSCAN	Installs INTERLNK.EXE in memory, but prevents it from establishing a connection. By default, INTERLNK tries to establish a connection with the server as soon as you install it.
/LOW	Loads the INTERLNK.EXE driver into conventional memory, even if upper memory is available. By default, INTERLNK.EXE loads into upper memory, if available.
/BAUD:*rate*	Sets a maximum baud rate for serial communication. Valid values are 9,600; 19,200; 38,400; 57,600; and 115,200. The default is 115,200.
/V	Prevents conflicts with a computer's timer. Specify this switch if you have a serial connection between computers, and one of them stops running when you use INTERLNK to access a drive or printer port.

Notes

The INTERLNK driver can establish a link and redirect a server's drives and printer ports, if the two computers are cabled and the INTERSVR program has already been loaded on the server computer. Otherwise, you'll need the INTERLNK command to complete the connection after these conditions have been met.

If you don't specify /LPT or /COM, the client scans all serial and parallel ports.

> **Warning:** Scanning a serial port that is attached to a mouse can disable the mouse driver. If you are using a serial mouse, either specify / LPT (and not /COM), or specify /COMn, where COMn is not the port the mouse is using.

The position of the DEVICE command that loads INTERLNK.EXE can affect future drive assignments. To make sure that all drives have the same letter assignments that they had before putting this DEVICE command in CONFIG.SYS, be sure that it is the last one in CONFIG.SYS.

You can save memory space by using switches to load only the portions of INTERLNK.EXE that you need. If you specify /NOPRINTER, INTERLNK.EXE doesn't load the code that handles printers. If you specify /LPT, the program does not load the code that supports serial ports. If you specify /COM, the program doesn't load the code that supports parallel ports.

If you redirect LPT1 or LPT2 and print from Microsoft Windows, use Control Panel to assign the printer to either LPT1.DOS or LPT2.DOS.

Some features of DOS may not be available to the client computer, if you are running different DOS versions on the server and client. For example, if you have large partitions on your server computer and are running DOS 3.0 on your client, the partitions will not be available to the client, because DOS 3.0 doesn't support them.

If you use INTERLNK to run an application located on the server computer, be sure the application is configured for the client computer.

These commands do not work with the INTERLNK.EXE device driver: CHKDSK, DEFRAG, DISKCOMP, DISKCOPY, FDISK, FORMAT, SYS, UNDELETE, and UNFORMAT (as well as any other programs that bypass DOS's normal file-handling routines, and deal directly with the system areas, tracks, or sectors).

Examples

```
DEVICE=C:\DOS\INTERLNK.EXE /COM2
```

Loads the INTERLNK.EXE device driver for the client computers COM2 port. If a connection can be established, redirects all of the server's parallel printers and three drives.

```
DEVICE=C:\DOS\INTERLNK.EXE /DRIVES:5 /NOPRINTER
```

Loads the INTERLNK.EXE device driver, and scans all the client computer's serial and parallel ports for a connection. If a connection can be established, redirects five drives and no printers.

POWER.EXE

Chapter 48

Reduces power consumption in a laptop computer when applications and devices are idle.

Syntax

```
DEVICE[HIGH]=[path]POWER.EXE [ADV[:advtype] ¦ STD ¦ OFF] [/LOW]
```

Parameters and Switches

path Identifies the location of POWER.EXE; the default is the root directory of the boot drive.

ADV[:*advtype*] Conserves power when applications and hardware devices are idle. *Advtype* may be MAX, for maximum power conservation, REG to balance application and device performance with power conservation, or MIN to minimize power conservation if performance is unsatisfactory when using REG or MAX. ADV:REG is the default setting.

STD   If your computer supports the Advance Power Management (APM) specification, STD conserves power by using only your computer's power-management features. If your computer does not support the APM specification, STD turns off power management.

OFF   Turns off power management.

Notes

POWER.EXE loads into upper memory, if available; otherwise, it loads into conventional memory.

The power manager conforms to the APM specification.

See the POWER command for more information about power management.

Example

```
DEVICE=C:\DOS\POWER.EXE
```

Loads the POWER.EXE file found in C:\DOS into upper memory, if available, otherwise into conventional memory. Uses the default setting ADV:REG.

RAMDRIVE.SYS

Chapter 32, "RAM Drives"

Uses an area of your computer's random-access memory (RAM) to simulate a hard disk drive.

Syntax

```
DEVICE[HIGH]=[path]RAMDRIVE.SYS [DiskSize [SectorSize [NumEntries]]] [/E ¦ /A]
```

Parameters and Switches

path   Identifies the location of the RAMDRIVE.SYS file. The default is the root directory of the boot drive.

DiskSize   Specifies, in kilobytes, how much memory to use for the RAM drive. Valid values are 4 to 32767, or available memory, whichever is smaller. The default is 64.

SectorSize   Specifies disk sector size in bytes. May be 128, 256, or 512 (the default). Microsoft recommends that you use 512. If you include *SectorSize*, you must include *DiskSize*.

NumEntries	Specifies the number of files and directories you can create in the root directory of the RAM drive. May be 2 to 1024; the limit you specify is rounded up to the nearest sector size boundary. The default is 64. If you include *NumEntries*, you also must include *SectorSize* and *DiskSize*.
/E	Creates the RAM drive in extended memory.
/A	Creates the RAM drive in expanded memory.

Notes

DOS allocates the next available drive letter to the RAM drive.

RAM drives are much faster than hard disk drives, and blindingly fast compared to floppy drives, because your computer can access memory faster than it can a disk. But, you lose all the data in a RAM drive when you turn off or restart your computer. RAM drives are especially suitable to use for temporary files; many people set the TEMP environment variable to a directory on a RAM drive, both for speed and to avoid possibly filling up a hard drive with temporary data.

It's best to create a RAM drive in extended memory, if possible.

To use /A, your system must have expanded memory, and you must load an expanded memory manager such as EMM386 before creating the RAM drive.

If you omit /E and /A, the RAM drive uses conventional memory. This is recommended only on a system with no extended memory, no expanded memory, and no hard disk.

If you use Windows and set TEMP to a directory on a RAM drive, be sure that *DiskSize* is at least 2048KB (2MB) to allow enough space for Windows temporary print files.

If there is not enough room to create the RAM drive as specified, RAMDRIVE.SYS tries to create a drive with a limit of 16 entries in the root directory.

Watch your boot messages for the names of the new RAM drives.

Examples

```
DEVICEHIGH=C:\DOS\RAMDRIVE.SYS 2048 /E
```

Loads the RAMDRIVE.SYS file into upper memory, if available; otherwise, loads it into conventional memory. Creates in extended memory a 2048KB (2MB) RAM drive with 512-byte sectors, and a maximum of 64 entries in the root directory.

```
DEVICE=C:\DOS\RAMDRIVE.SYS 2048 512 128 /A
```

Loads the RAMDRIVE.SYS file and creates in expanded memory a 2048KB (2MB) RAM drive with 512-byte sectors, and a maximum of 128 entries in the root directory.

SETVER.EXE

Chapter 21

Loads the DOS version table into memory.

Syntax

```
DEVICE[HIGH]=[path]SETVER.EXE
```

Parameter

path   Identifies the location of the SETVER.EXE file.

The default is the root directory of the boot drive.

Notes

The SETVER.EXE device driver uses the version table to report appropriate DOS version numbers to programs that require this information. The SETVER command enables you to display and edit the version table. See the SETVER command for more details about the version table.

If you are using SETVER to report a different DOS version to a device driver, the DEVICE (or DEVICEHIGH) command loading SETVER.EXE must appear in CONFIG.SYS before the DEVICE (or DEVICEHIGH) command loading the other device driver.

Examples

```
DEVICEHIGH=C:\DOS\SETVER.EXE
```

Loads the SETVER.EXE file found in C:\DOS into upper memory, if available, rather than conventional memory.

SIZER.SYS

Used by MEMMAKER to determine the size in memory of device drivers and TSRs.

Notes

MEMMAKER temporarily adds SIZER.SYS to your CONFIG.SYS and AUTOEXEC.BAT files. When optimization is complete, MEMMAKER deletes the SIZER.SYS commands again.

SMARTDRV.EXE

Chapter 31, "Caching the Drives"

Provides compatibility for hard-disk controllers that can't work with memory provided by EMM386.EXE or Windows running in 386 enhanced mode.

Syntax

```
DEVICE=[path]SMARTDRV.EXE /DOUBLE_BUFFER
```

Parameter

path   Identifies the location of the SMARTDRV.EXE file; the default is the root directory of the boot drive.

Notes

If you don't use EMM386.EXE, and don't run Windows in 386 enhanced mode, you don't need double-buffering.

If you do use EMM386.EXE, or run Windows in 386 enhanced mode, you probably need double-buffering if you have an SCSI (small computer system interface) device; and, you may need it if you have an ESDI (enhanced system device interface) or MCA (microchannel architecture) device.

When the device driver is loaded for double-buffering, it requires about 2KB of conventional memory.

The SMARDTRV.EXE driver does not provide disk caching. You must use the SMARTDRV command to do that.

Follow these steps to determine whether your system requires double-buffering (your system must be set up to use upper memory blocks):

1. Load the SMARTDRV.EXE device driver for double-buffering.

2. Insert a SMARTDRV command in AUTOEXEC.BAT (unless it already contains one). If your system seems to be running slowly after you start using SMARTDRV, add the /L switch to this SMARTDRV command.

3. Run MEMMAKER.

4. At the command prompt, enter SMARTDRV to display information about your system.

5. Look at the column labeled Buffering. If any line in this column reads yes, you need double-buffering.

6. If every line in the Buffering column says no, you don't need double-buffering, and you can remove the command from CONFIG.SYS.

7. If any line in the Buffering column says –, SmartDrive can't detect whether double-buffering is needed.

B

Exit Codes

Introduction

Many DOS commands set an exit code when they terminate. You can access these codes only if the command was run as part of a batch program. In most cases, an exit code of 0 means that the command functioned correctly, and that the operation was successfully completed. Any other exit code means the operation was not completed correctly.

The IF ERRORLEVEL command enables you to test the code and take action depending on what it is. Chapter 37, "Programming Logic in Batch Programs," explains how to use exit codes in your batch programs.

Command	Exit Code	Meaning
DEFRAG	0	The defragmentation was successful.
	1	Internal error.
	2	No free clusters (DEFRAG requires one free cluster).
	3	User pressed Ctrl+C to stop.
	4	General Error.
	5	Error-reading cluster.
	6	Error-writing cluster.
	7	Allocation error (use CHKDSK /F).
	8	Memory error.
	9	Insufficient memory.
DISKCOMP	0	Disks are the same; normal exit.
	1	Disks are not the same.
	2	User pressed Ctrl+C to stop command.
	3	Critical error.
	4	Initialization error.
DISKCOPY	0	Disk copied successfully; normal exit.
	1	Not a success; nonfatal read/write error during copy.
	2	User pressed Ctrl+C to stop command.
	3	Fatal hardware error.
	4	Initialization error.
FIND	0	Successful search; at least one match found.
	1	Successful completion, but no match found.
	2	Not completed successfully; FIND cannot report whether matches were found.
FORMAT	0	Disk formatted successfully; normal exit.
	3	User pressed Ctrl+C to stop command.
	4	Error; program stopped.
	5	User pressed N in response to Proceed with Format (Y/N).

Command	Exit Code	Meaning
KEYB	0	Keyboard file loaded; normal exit.
	1	Bad keyboard code, code page value, or syntax.
	2	Bad or missing keyboard definition file.
	4	CON device error.
	5	Requested code page not prepared.
MSAV	86	Virus detected when not using the graphical interface.
REPLACE	0	Specified files replaced or added; normal exit.
	1	DOS version incompatible with REPLACE.
	2	No files affected; source files not found.
	3	No files affected; source or target path not found.
	5	Read/write access denied; at least one file not replaced. Use ATTRIB to change access.
	8	Not done; not enough memory to run command.
	11	Not done; bad parameter or invalid format.
RESTORE	0	Files restored; normal exit.
	1	No files found to restore.
	3	User pressed Ctrl+C to stop the command.
	4	Error occurred; command interrupted.
SETVER	0	Mission accomplished; normal exit.
	1	Not done; invalid switch.
	2	Not done; invalid filename.
	3	Not done; not enough memory.
	4	Not done; wrong version-number format.
	5	Not done; entry not found in version table.
	6	Not done; SETVER.EXE not found.
	7	Not done; invalid drive.
	8	Not done; too many parameters.
	9	Not done; missing parameter.
	10	Not done; error reading SETVER.EXE file.
	11	Not done; version table in SETVER.EXE is corrupted.
	12	Not done; SETVER.EXE doesn't support version tables.

continues

Command	Exit Code	Meaning
	13	Not done; no space left in version table.
	14	Not done; error writing to version table.
XCOPY	0	Specified files copied; normal exit.
	1	No file found to copy.
	2	User pressed Ctrl+C to stop command.
	4	Not enough memory or disk space, syntax error, or initialization error.
	5	Write-protected disk or other write error.

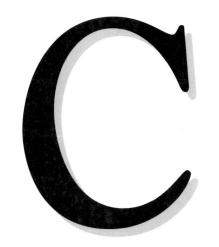

IBM
Extended
Character
Set

Extended Character Set

128	Ç	150	û	172	¼
129	ü	151	ù	173	¡
130	é	152	ÿ	174	«
131	â	153	Ö	175	»
132	ä	154	Ü	176	▓
133	à	155	¢	177	▓
134	å	156	£	178	█
135	ç	157	¥	179	│
136	ê	158	₨	180	┤
137	ë	159	ƒ	181	╡
138	è	160	á	182	╢
139	ï	161	í	183	╖
140	î	162	ó	184	╕
141	ì	163	ú	185	╣
142	Ä	164	ñ	186	║
143	Å	165	Ñ	187	╗
144	É	166	ª	188	╝
145	æ	167	º	189	╜
146	Æ	168	¿	190	╛
147	ô	169	⌐	191	┐
148	ö	170	¬	192	└
149	ò	171	½	193	┴

Extended Character Set

194 ┬	217 ┘	240 ≡
195 ├	218 ┌	241 ±
196 –	219 ■	242 ≥
197 ┼	220 ▄	243 ≤
198 ╞	221 ▌	244 ⌠
199 ╟	222 ▐	245 ⌡
200 ╚	223 ▀	246 ÷
201 ╔	224 α	247 ≈
202 ╩	225 β	248 °
203 ╦	226 Γ	249 ·
204 ╠	227 π	250 ·
205 =	228 Σ	251 √
206 ╬	229 σ	252 η
207 ╧	230 μ	253 ²
208 ╨	231 Υ	254 ■
209 ╤	232 Φ	255
210 ╥	233 Θ	
211 ╙	234 Ω	
212 ╘	235 δ	
213 ╒	236 ω	
214 ╓	237 φ	
215 ╫	238 ∈	
216 ╪	239 ∩	

Glossary

.	A code that represents the current directory.
..	A code that represents the parent of the current directory.
Absolute path	A path that starts from the root directory.
Address	A number that identifies a location in memory or on a disk.
Allocation unit	The smallest unit in which DOS stores a file or part of a file. Also referred to as a *cluster*.
Alphanumeric data	Data made up of letters, digits, and printable special characters.
ANSI	American National Standards Institute, which has established standards for data storage and communication. The standard 256-character ANSI code includes ASCII characters and others.
Anti-virus	A program designed to detect the presence of a virus in a system, prevent the virus from functioning, and remove it if possible. See *virus*.
Archie	An Internet resource for locating information in the worldwide web of databases.
Archive	To make a copy of a file for safekeeping in a different location, usually on removable media. Same as *back up*.
Archive attribute	An attribute indicating whether a file has changed since it was last backed up. The archive attribute is turned on when a file is created and when it is modified.
ASCII	American Standard Code for Information Interchange. A standard 128-character code that represents letters, digits, printable special characters, and some control codes.

Attribute	One of four characteristics that can be assigned to a file or directory and recorded in its directory entry. They include the archive, hidden, read-only, and system attributes.
AUTOEXEC.BAT	A batch file that is executed when the system boots, immediately after CONFIG.SYS is processed.
Back up	To copy a file for safekeeping to another location, often on removable media. The copy also is called a *backup*.
.BAT	An extension that indicates a batch file.
Batch file	A file that contains a series of commands to be executed like a program.
Baud rate	An indication of the speed at which data can be communicated between a computer and other equipment. Also referred to as *bits per second* or *BPS*.
BBS	See *bulletin board system*.
Binary	A numbering system that uses only two digits: 0 and 1. All data in a computer or on a disk is handled and stored in binary.
BIOS	Basic Input Output System. See *ROM-BIOS*.
Bit	The smallest unit of information handled by a computer. A bit can have one or two values, usually represented by 0 and 1. Bit stands for Binary digIT.
Boot	To start up a computer system.
Boot record	A program found in the boot sector. The boot record on the boot drive loads the operating system when you start up the computer or reboot.

Boot sector	The first sector of a disk.
Branch	A directory and all its descendants. See *child directory*.
Buffer	A memory area that holds data temporarily.
Bulletin board	A computer system running software that allows system access to many people at one time through their modems. Such systems typically enable you to carry on a "conversation" by reading and posting messages and to send and receive files. Abbreviated as BBS.
Byte	A series of eight bits, which can form 256 unique combinations. The term *byte* often is used as the equivalent to one character.
Cache	A memory location used to store data for rapid access. A disk cache holds data read from or written to a disk. It is similar to, but more intelligent and efficient than, a read-writer buffer.
CD-ROM	A drive that holds read-only data on a medium similar to that of an audio CD.
Chat	Talking to people who are online on a bulletin board, a network, Internet, or a similar service, at the same time as you are; chatting is done via typed messages that all the people involved in the conversation can read and answer.
Check box	A dialog box option marked by a small box. When the option is turned on, the box contains a checkmark or an X. When the option is off, the box is empty.
Checksum	A number obtained by performing a calculation on the contents of a sector or a file. Checksum usually is used to validate the data.

Child directory	A subdirectory subordinate to another directory, called the parent (see *parent directory*). DOS looks in the parent directory to find the location of the child directory.
Client	A computer that uses another computer's resources (such as its printers and hard drives) via a network or direct connection.
Click	To press and release a mouse button without moving the mouse.
Cluster	See *allocation unit*.
CMOS	Complementary Metal-Oxide Semiconductor. In 286 and higher machines, a battery-powered module that retains information about the computer's hardware for booting purposes.
.COM	An extension used to identify a file as an executable program file. See also .EXE and .BAT.
Command	An instruction processed by DOS's command interpreter (or perhaps an alternative command interpreter).
Command button	A dialog box item that initiates an immediate action when you press it. For example, an OK button to proceed with a program or a Cancel button to cancel the dialog box.
Command processor	A program that can interpret commands entered from a command prompt or a batch file. The command processor carries out internal commands and passes external commands to the proper program.
COMMAND.COM	The command processor included in DOS.
Compressed drive	See *compressed volume file*.

Compressed volume file	CVF or compressed drive. A file that acts like a volume file drive. The CVF is created and managed by a disk-compression program such as DriveSpace or DoubleSpace to contain compressed files.
Compression	Reducing the size of a file or files by eliminating repetition and/or waste space.
CONFIG.SYS	A file that contains commands necessary to configure the system and load device drivers. CONFIG.SYS is executed immediately after the operating system files are loaded during booting.
Console	The standard input/output device; usually a keyboard and monitor combination.
Conventional memory	RAM in the range of 0KB to 640KB. In versions of DOS before DOS 5, programs had to be loaded into conventional memory for execution.
Cross-linked	An allocation unit, or cluster, that appears to belong to two files in the FAT.
CVF	See *compressed volume file*.
DBLSPACE.BIN	One of DOS's core program files. DBLSPACE.BIN manages DoubleSpace CVFs. Introduced in DOS 6.0, it has been replaced by DRVSPACE.BIN in DOS 6.22.
Default	An item, option, or value used if you don't specify otherwise.
Deletion protection	A program that tracks deleted files to assist in undeleting them.

Device driver	A file that contains information used to control hardware devices such as memory, a monitor, a keyboard, a printer, and so on. Some device drivers create and control logical devices such as RAM drives.
Dialog box	A box displayed by a graphical program that enables you to select options and provide information needed by the program.
Directory	A data structure that contains information about the location, sizes, attributes, and so on of files and other directories. Any directory that is not a root directory is a subdirectory.
Directory tree	The entire set of directories on a drive, from the root directory down through its children and their children to the lowest level on the drive.
Disk	See *floppy disk* and *hard disk*.
DOS	The Disk Operating System. An operating system designed for the IBM line of personal computers and their compatibles.
Double-click	To press a mouse button twice in rapid succession without moving the mouse.
Drag	To hold down a mouse button while moving the mouse.
Drive name	A letter assigned to a physical or logical drive.
DRVSPACE.BIN	One of DOS's core program files. DRVSPACE.BIN manages DriveSpace CVFs. It has replaced DBLSPACE.BIN in DOS 6.22.
E-mail	Letters and notes sent electronically via a network, bulletin board, online service, or other connection.

.EXE	An extension used to identify a file as an executable program file. See also .COM and .BAT.
Executable file	A file containing instructions that control the computer. Also known as a *program file*. Executable files usually have the extension .EXE or .COM.
Expanded memory	Also called EMS. An external memory device managed by an expanded memory manager in accordance with Lotus-Intel Microsoft Expanded Memory Standard (LIM EMS).
Extension	A suffix for a file name. An extension can contain from one to three characters. Extensions are connected to the file name by a period.
FAT	See *file allocation table*.
Field	A data item in a dialog box or database record; for example, a ZIP code or a name.
File	A collection of related data stored and handled as a single entity by DOS.
File allocation table	A table maintained by DOS on every floppy disk or table hard drive, used to track the location of files and empty space.
File handle	A memory area that contains the information DOS needs to access an open file.
Filespec	An expression that identifies a file or files. A filespec may include a drive name, path, file name, and extension. The file name and extension may include wild cards.
Floppy disk	A small removable magnetic disk. The most common are 3 1/2-inch hard-body disks and 5 1/4-inch flexible disks.

Floppy drive	A drive that uses floppy disks.
Fragmentation	Storing a file in nonadjacent clusters.
Global filespec	A filespec containing wild-card characters in the file name and/or extension.
Gopher	An Internet resource for locating information in the worldwide system of databases.
Hard disk	A nonremovable storage medium.
Hard drive	A logical drive on a hard disk.
Hardware	The physical equipment that makes up a computer system, including boards, monitor, keyboard, disk drives, printer, modem, mouse, and other possible items.
Hexadecimal	HEX. A number system based on the number 16; hexadecimal numbers have 16 digits, from 0 through F. Computers often turn the binary numbers used internally into relatively more readable hexadecimal numbers for display purposes.
Hidden attribute	An attribute that, when turned on, indicates that a file or directory should not be casually accessible by DIR or other commands.
Hidden file	A file with the hidden attribute turned on.
High memory area	HMA. The first 65,520 bytes of extended memory.
Host drive	The drive on which a compressed volume file resides.
Hot key	A key or key combination that activates a TSR or command.

I/O	See *input/output*.
Icon	A small drawing used instead of words by a graphical program to label an item's type or to represent a command or function that can be invoked by clicking the icon.
Input	Information entered into a computer by a keyboard, mouse, or other input device.
Input/Output	Often abbreviated I/O. Input and output operations or devices.
Interface	A connection between any two parts of a system— for example, between a computer user and a program.
Internet	A worldwide connection of computer networks used to collect, organize, and share information on almost any subject.
Interrupt	A signal sent to a computer to interrupt its current activity and request immediate processing. An *external interrupt* is from the outside world, such as a disk drive. An *internal interrupt* reports that an unusual situation has arisen—usually an error condition. A *software interrupt* is a request from a program for a service.
IO.SYS	One of DOS's system files that contains the core of the DOS program.
IRQ	An external interrupt. See *interrupt*.
Kilobyte	1,024 bytes. Abbreviated as K or KB.
Logical drive	An area of a disk or of memory treated as a separate drive although it has no separate physical existence.
Lost allocation	An allocation unit that is marked in the FAT as unit used but does not seem to belong to a file.

Mailing list	On Internet, a group of people who broadcast e-mail to each other on a particular topic.
Megabyte	A kilobyte squared (1,048,576 bytes). Abbreviated as M or MB.
Memory	An internal storage device used to store the programs being executed, as well as their data.
Memory-resident	Also called TSR. A program that remains loaded in memory until the end of the session (or until you specifically unload it). It usually monitors input and/or processing, looking for specific events that it is designed to handle.
Menu	A list of commands for you to choose from. Menus usually appear in graphical programs, which enable you to choose items by using the mouse or the keyboard.
Modem	A hardware device that enables communication between two computers over a telephone line.
MPC	Multimedia PC. A computer equipped with devices such as CD ROM drive, sound board, and joystick to play multimedia software. See also *multimedia*.
MSDOS.SYS	One of DOS's systems files that contains the core of the DOS program.
Multimedia	Software involving multiple elements such as sound, video, graphics, and photos. See also *MPC*.
Newsgroup	An Internet bulletin board where members can read and store messages on a particular topic.
Node	A single computer in a network.

Numeric keypad	A set of keys arranged like those on a 10-key adder and used to enter numeric data. The numeric keypad often shares the same functions as the cursor-movement keys, with the Shift and NumLock keys used to select between the two functions.
Operating system	A program that manages all of a computer's operations, controlling other programs' access to the computer's basis resources such as memory and the disk drives. The operating system also provides the user interface.
Option button	A list of items in which one, and only one, item is always selected. Option buttons usually appear in dialog boxes.
Output	Data sent from a program to a storage or output device, such as a printer, a monitor, a disk, and so on.
Parallel port	A port through which data passes eight bits (one byte) at a time. Frequently used to communicate with printers.
Parameter	A variable data item entered as a part of a command. The parameter provides information to a program, such as a filespec that tells a copy command what files to copy.
Parent directory	A directory that contains an entry for a subordinate directory. See *child directory*.
Partition	A division of a hard disk.
Partition table	A table stored at the beginning of a hard disk that identifies the partitions on the disk.
Path	A list of directories that DOS must go through to find a directory or file.
PIF	Program Information File; a file that defines the parameters for running a DOS application under Windows.

Pipe	Directing the output from one program as input to another.
Port	An address used to communicate with another device such as a printer, modem, or mouse.
Processor	The hardware device that carries out program instructions.
Program	See *executable file*.
Program group	A list of programs that can be opened from the DOS Shell screen.
Program search path	See *search path*.
Prompt	A message from a program requesting input from a user.
Protocol	A set of rules to govern how two computers transfer data with each other; there are several standard protocols, such as XMODEM, YMODEM, ZMODEM, and Kermit.
Queue	A list of items for attention; particularly, a list of files waiting to be printed by the Print command.
Radio button	See Option button.
RAM	Random-access memory. Memory that can be written to and read from. Data stored in RAM is not permanent; it disappears when the system is turned off or rebooted.
RAM disk	A logical drive created in RAM to provide rapid access to data that would otherwise require disk access. Data in a RAM drive disappears when the system is turned off or rebooted.

Read-only attribute	A read-attribute that indicates whether a file or directory can be written to. When the read-only attribute is turned on, programs are not supposed to modify or delete the file.
Read-write head	The physical device that reads and writes data on a disk or tape drive.
Reboot	To reload the operating system; in DOS, you normally reboot by pressing Ctrl+Alt+Del.
Relative path	A path that starts from a drive's current directory.
ROM	Read-only memory. A type of memory in which data is stored permanently; the data cannot be erased or replaced. ROM retains its data even when the power goes out.
ROM-BIOS	A collection of programs stored in ROM that DOS uses to perform the basic input and output operations of the computer.
Root directory	The primary directory on a disk; the top level of the directory tree.
Scroll	To move data on-screen or within a box or window.
Scroll bar	A bar at the right side or bottom of a screen, box, or window that enables you to use a mouse to move data up or down or from side to side.
Scroll box	A box in the scroll bar that indicates the position of the displayed data relative to the entire file or list; you usually can move the data by dragging the scroll box.
Search path	A list of directories that DOS should scan when looking for a program file that is not in the current directory. Some newer DOS programs also use the search path to look for data files.

Sector	A portion of a track on a disk, usually 512 bytes. A sector is the smallest amount that can be read or written at one time.
Serial port	A port through which data passes one bit at a time. Usually used to connect with a modem, a mouse, or some special type of printer.
Server	A computer whose resources (such as its printers and hard drives) are made available to other computers via a network or direct connection.
Shell	A program that replaces DOS's basic command prompt and command processor. DOS's Shell program provides a graphical interface from which you can perform many DOS functions.
Software	Computer programs.
Stack	A memory area used to store temporary information. Stacks often hold information needed to return to a program after an interrupt.
Subdirectory	Any directory on a disk except the root directory.
Switch	A parameter included in a command to turn a program feature on or off. Most switches begin with a slash (/).
SYS	An extension often used for device drivers and other programs loaded in CONFIG.SYS.
System attribute	An attribute that tells DOS whether a file or directory should be both hidden and read-only.
System file	A file with the system attributes turned on; one of the files that contains DOS's core program—IO.SYS, MSDOS.SYS, and DRVSPACE.BIN.

Task swapping	Switching between two or more programs without losing your place in any of the programs.
Telecommunications	Communication between two computers over a phone line.
Track	On a disk, one of the set of concentric circles on which the drive writes data.
Tree	See *directory tree*.
TSR	See *memory-resident*.
Undelete	To recover data that has been deleted.
Unformat	To restore data removed from a disk by the FORMAT command.
Upper memory	The area of memory from 640KB to 1024KB (1MB). In earlier versions of DOS, upper memory was reserved for DOS's system use, but it now can be used to load and execute programs in 386 and higher machines.
User interface	The way in which a user and a program communicate with each other. DOS provides two interfaces: the command prompt and the graphical DOS Shell.
Utility program	A program that helps to manage the computer and its data. Anti-Virus, UNDELETE, and BACKUP are examples of utility programs provided with DOS 6.
Virtual disk	See *RAM disk*.
Virus	A computer program that can duplicate and spread itself from computer to computer, usually without a user's knowledge. Viruses often hide in a system area or program file; they may do harm to a system and its data, intentionally or unintentionally.

WAIS   (Wide Area Information Server) An Internet resource for
                        locating information in the worldwide web of databases.

Wild-card character   A nonspecific character in a filespec. The question mark (?) is
                        matched by any single character. The asterisk(*) is matched by
                        any number of characters or even no characters.

Window   A rectangle area on-screen that displays program output
                        independent of that displayed in other areas of the screen.

WORM   Write Once, Read Many. Similar to a CD-ROM except that
                        the user may write the original data on the disk. Once written,
                        it cannot be overwritten, only read.

Write protection   A physical mechanism that prevents a disk from being
                        modified. On a 5 1/4-inch disk, activating this protection
                        usually involves placing a tab over a notch. On a 3 1/2-inch
                        disk, it usually involves sliding a tab to unblock a cutout on the
                        disk.

Write-delayed cache   A caching system that delays writing data to a disk until system
                        resources are not otherwise occupied, so that reading and other
                        processing has priority.

Index

SYMBOLS

$$ (dollar sign), PROMPT command, 196

$* (macro parameters), 205

$D (current date), PROMPT command, 196

$G (greater-than), PROMPT command, 196

$n (macro parameters), 205

$P (current drive and directory), PROMPT command, 196

$T (current time), PROMPT command, 196

* (asterisk) wildcard, 35

+ (plus signs), directories, 66

- (minus sign), directories, 86

... (ellipsis), commands, 82, 184

< source redirection symbols, 561

> (greater-than symbol), redirecting command output, 180

> destination redirection symbol, 561

>> destination redirection symbol, 561

? (question mark) wildcard, 34-35

[(left square bracket), ANSI.SYS escape sequences, 767

[ ] (brackets)
    DOS commands, 176
    nested, 184

\ (backslash), 238

^ (caret), help text, 155

^Z (end-of-file mark), 643

| (vertical bar), DOS commands, 184

 (DOSKEY history), 200

Ø (DOSKEY history), 200

286 microprocessors, 5
    AUTOEXEC.BAT files, 551
    CONFIG.SYS files, 550-551

386 Enhanced Mode,
667-685
386 microprocessors, 5,
552-553
486 microprocessors, 5,
552-553

A

A switch, 218-219, 248
About Help command (Help
menu), 75-76, 191
absolute paths, 1098
Access Denied error message,
84, 89, 109, 126, 234
access rights, 831
accessing
batch command informa-
tion, 186
command prompt, 172-176
commands, 198
DOS environment
variables, 692-695
EDIT Help, 313
extended memory, 484
external command
information, 186
internal command
information, 186
Internet, 879-882
macros, 198
upper memory, 708
activating
character wrapping, 774
EMM386.EXE com-
mand, 713
expanded memory, 713-716
active partition, 871
Add Group dialog box, 155
Add mode (file selection), 98
adding
attribute codes to A
switches, 219
colors to menus, 618-619
commands to
AUTOEXEC.BAT
files, 331

dates to commands, 184
files to print queues, 130
parameters to paths, 184
program items (DOS
Shell), 157
programs to SETVER
device driver, 339
time to commands, 184
W switches to com-
mands, 178
address books (telecommunications software), 881
addresses, 1098
adjacent files, 95
Advanced dialog box, 575
Advanced Options dialog box,
678, 680
aggressive scanning, 711
All Files command (View
menu), 100
allocating
buffers to disks, 511
extended memory, 709
memory
in PIFs, 676-678
to COMMAND.COM
command inter-
preter, 701
to DOSKEY buffer, 208
to file handles, 342
to stacks, 342-343
to video screens, 676
allocation units (byte sectors),
41-42, 746-748, 1098
Allow Close when Active
option (DOS applica-
tions), 681
alphanumeric data, 1098
Alt key, 10-11
Alt+F7 shortcut key
(DOSKEY history), 200
alternate drive names,
828-829
alternative branches (batch
files), 589-590
Always Format Diskettes
(Backup option), 378
America Online, 880

American Standard Code for
Information Interchange,
see ASCII
annotating
batch files, 322-323
text files, 563-564
ANSI (American National
Standards Institute), 1098
ANSI.SYS device driver, 340,
763-765, 1066-1067
color display codes, 768-770
escape sequences, 768-770
keyboard control, 775-779
sending commands to,
765-768
Anti-Stealth (MSAV option),
424
Anti-Virus (DOS 6
utility), 29
antivirus monitors, 418-420
antivirus programs, 47-48,
418-419, 1098
APPEND command, 625
appended directories, 625
appending
DOS environment
variables, 693
files, 561, 638-639
applications, 14
Archie, 877, 1098
archive attributes, 36,
634, 1098
archives, 1098
array variables, 852
arrays, 853
text messages
redirecting, 182
ASCII (American Standard
Code for Information
Interchange), 16, 1098
ASCII command (Display
menu), 127
ASCII comparisons (files),
260-262
ASCII text files, 130
aspect ratios (printers), 820

assigning
  key commands to interna-
    tional characters, 790
  shortcut keys
    to DOS applications,
      681-683
    to program items (DOS
      Shell), 158
  text strings to keys, 778-779
Associate command (File
  menu), 140
Associate File dialog box, 140
associated files
  opening, 140-141
  starting programs, 137
associating
  blank file extensions with
    programs, 141
  files, 140
  programs with file exten-
    sions, 141
associations (files), 581
asterisk (*) wildcard, 35
attaching paths
  to command names, 179
  to filespecs, 179
ATTRIB command, 248-252
ATTRIB filespec com-
  mand, 248
attribute codes, 219
attributes (files), 35-37, 1099
  changing, 122-123
  viewing, 121-122
Audible Prompts
  Backup option, 378
  Compare option, 411
  Restore option, 402
AUTOEXEC.BAT files,
  331-332, 496-498,
  842, 1099
  286 microprocessors, 551
  386 microprocessors,
    552-553
  486 microprocessors,
    552-553
  backing up, 335
  bypassing, 612
  loading DOSKEY into,
    208-209

Pentium microprocessors,
  552-553
  see also startup files
automating
  commands, 566
  DOS Shell at system
    startup, 332
  DOS Shell startup, 65
  PRINT initialization during
    system startup, 129
  Windows at startup, 332

B

B switch, 222, 644
back ups, 1099
Background option
  (PIFs), 678
backing up
  files, 46
  hard drives, 46
  infected files, 422
  older version files, 400
  startup files, 335
backslash (\), 238
Backtab, 67
Backup
  catalogs, 382-383
    deleting, 388-389
    opening, 394-395
    storing, 386
  configurations, 357-364
  data compression, 377
  default directories, 691
  differential backups, 374
  disk maintenance, 384-385
  drives, 368, 375
  files
    organizing, 385-386
    restoring, 392-411
  freeze troubleshooting, 382
  full backups, 373-375
  incremental backups, 374
  old backup file restoration,
    406-407 412-413
  optimizing loading, 380
  options, 376-379
  password protection, 377

progress screen, 381
  quitting, 379
  recording catalogs, 378
  running, 380-382
  setup files, 365-380
  starting, 356-357
  types, 373-375
BACKUP (DOS 6
  utility), 29
Backup Devices dialog
  box, 359
Backup dialog box, 364
Backup function, 364
backup programs, 48-49
Backup Set Catalog dialog
  box, 394
Bad command or file name
  error message, 178-179
Bad or missing command
  interpreter...error message, 696
banners (screens), 771
BASIC, 844
BASICA (QBASIC conver-
  sion), 849-850
batch files, 1099
  accessing DOS environ-
    ment variables, 692
  alternative branches,
    589-590
  annotating, 322-323
  branches, 589-590
  bypass branches, 589, 593
  calling, 327-329, 586-587
  cancelling, 321
  chaining, 585-586
  clobbering, 606-607
  commands, 186, 321-329
    branching, 593-595
    repeating, 600-601
  conditional command lines,
    590-598
  creating, 318-319
  deleting links, 588-589
  ERRORLEVEL condition,
    591-592
  executing from disks, 606
  exit codes, 591, 594
  finding, 320

formatting, 590-598
global filespecs, 602
GOTO command, 593-595
IF command, 590-598
in ANSI.SYS device dri-
    ver, 768
in DOS Shell, 332
linking, 584-588
loops, 598-603
MSAV command, 426-428
multiple links, 587
naming, 320
pausing, 325-327
recursion, 588
referencing, 602
replaceable parameters,
    329-330, 587
routine bypassing, 589
running, 319
testing
    for existence, 596
    for null values, 597-598
testing logic, 703
text string comparison,
    596-597
batch programs, 25
baud rates, 810, 879, 1099
BBSs (bulletin board
    systems), 881-882
BIN files, 326
binary, 1099
binary files
    comparing, 259-260
    concatenation, 640
BIOS (basic input-output
    operating system),
    480, 1099
bits, 15, 1099
blank file extensions, 141
block devices, 824
boot records, 1099
Boot Sector Viruses (VSAFE
    option), 431
booting, 1099
brackets ([ ])
    DOS commands, 176
    nested, 184

branches
    batch files, 589-590
    directories, 38, 1100
        grafting, 637
        pruning, 637
    directory tree, 221-222
branching batch file com-
    mands, 593-595
Break key, 12
breaking computer links, 660
breakpoints (QBASIC
    debugging), 864
buffers, 341, 502, 1100
    disks, 511-512
    DOSKEY buffer, 199
    resynchronization buffer
        (FC command), 739-744
    SmartDrive program,
        503-504
    video buffer, 763
BUFFERS command, 341,
    511-512
bulletin board systems, 1099
bulletin boards, 1100
buses (circuits), 6
bypass branches (batch files),
    589, 593
bypassing
    batch file routines, 589
    compression software, 612
    EMM386.EXE com-
        mand, 711
    files from recovery, 444
    MSAV window, 427
    startup file items, 382
    startup files, 336-337,
        610-613
    VSAFE actions, 432
byte sectors, 1111
    disks, 14
    drives, 41-42
    partition table, 268
    validity checks, 270
    see also sectors
bytes, 15, 1100

C

C switch (DIR com-
    mand), 729
C:\ command prompt, 173
C:\> command prompt,
    62, 173
cabling computers, 651-652
caches, 1100
caching
    compressed drives, 725-726
    hard drives, 475
    host drives, 726
CALL command, 328,
    586-587
CALL statements, 860-862
calling batch files, 327-329,
    586-587
Cancel button (DOS Shell
    dialog box), 84
cancelling
    batch files, 321
    commands, 253
    disk rebuilding, 756
    drive changes, 81
CapsLock key, 10
caret (^), help text, 155
carriage returns, 567
CASE ELSE block
    (QBASIC), 855
case structures (QBASIC),
    855-856
catalogs
    Backup, 382-383
    deleting, 388-389
    master catalogs, 383
    opening, 394-395
    recording, 378
    restoring, 410-411
    retrieving, 406
    storing, 386
CD command, 213
CD DOS command, 177
CD-ROM drives, 1100
chaining batch files, 585-586
Change Attributes command
    (File menu), 122
Change Attributes dialog box,
    122-123

Change command (Search menu), 306
Change dialog box, 306
Change Size command (Drive menu), 727
Change Size dialog box, 727
change-line support (drives), 827
change-line test (drives), 359
changing
    default directories, 213-214
    disk labels, 274, 294
    DOS environment variables, 692
    drives, 309, 421
        compression ratios, 729-731
        default directories, 214-218
        defaults, 213
        disk caches, 505
    filenames, 233
    files
        attributes, 122-123, 249-250
        multiple attributes, 123-124
    group properties, 154
    hidden file attributes, 250-251
    keyboard response, 779-781
    mouse clicking speeds, 358
    program item properties (DOS Shell), 157
    screen column defaults, 779
    screen line defaults, 779
    screen modes, 774
    system file attributes, 250-251
    text, 306-307
    typematic rates (keyboard), 781
characters
    DOS commands, 176
    filespecs, 33
    international characters, 789-790
    lowercase, 10
    repeating, 12
    uppercase, 10
    wildcards, 34
    wrapping, 774
chat, 1100
chatting (Internet), 878
    Internet gateways, 882
    telecommunications software, 880
CHCP command, 801, 802
Check All Files (MSAV option), 424
check boxes, 1100
Check Executable Files (VSAFE option), 431
checking drives for glitches, 463-465
checksums, 1100
child directories, 38, 1101
CHKDSK | FIND command, 573
CHKDSK program, 26, 351, 746-752
    functions, 469
    locating lost file clusters, 466-467
    recovering cross-linked files, 469
    running, 463
CHKSTATE.SYS, 1067
CHOICE command, 603-605
Choose Drives for Delete Sentry dialog box, 55
chording (mouse), 372
Cinemania, 836, 839
circuits (buses), 6
Clear All Breakpoints command (Debug menu), 864
clearing
    printer memory, 258
    screens, 322
clicking (mouse), 13, 1101
    changing speed, 358
client model, 1101
clients (INTERLNK), 650, 655-658
Clipboard editing keys, 304
clobbering
    batch files, 606-607
    files, 104
clock speed, 708
Close Window on Exit option (PIFs), 679
closed loops (batch files), 598
closing
    EDIT Help, 313
    Help dialog box, 75
    Help window, 192
    Memory Block Display, 758
    menus, 73
    tasks, 148-149
CLS command, 322
clusters (file byte sectors), 41-42, 522-523
    finding, 466-468
    recovering, 465-467
    slack, 642-643
    storing, 642
CMOS (complementary metal-oxide semiconductor module), 6-7, 1101
CMOS chip, 824
code pages (keyboard), 794-802
collapsing directory trees, 86-88
collating sequence (keyboard), 569
color scanners, 837
Color Scheme dialog box, 163
colors
    adding to menus, 618-619
    ANSI.SYS display codes, 768-770
    DOSSHELL.INI file, 580
    GRAPHICS command (color printers), 820
    screens, 162-163, 765-770
.COM files, 1101
combining
    commands, 203-204, 575-576
    files, 637-644
command buttons, 68-69, 1101

command processors,
  342, 1101
command prompts, 20-24
  accessing, 172-176
  C:\ command prompt, 173
  C:\> command
    prompt, 173
  creating, 195-196
  primary command prompt,
    173, 175-176
  restoring, 196
  secondary command
    prompt, 174-176
Command Reference,
  183-184
command-names
  paths, 179
  programs, 177
COMMAND.COM command
  interpreter, 1101
  controlling, 695-698
  loading, 702
  location specification,
    697-698
  memory allocation, 701
  starting, 701
commands, 1101
  ... (ellipsis), 82
  accessing, 198
  adding to
    AUTOEXEC.BAT
    files, 331
  APPEND, 625
  ATTRIB, 248-252
  ATTRIB filespec, 248
  automating, 566
  batch files, 321-329
  BUFFERS, 341, 511
  CALL, 328, 586-587
  cancelling, 253
  CD, 213
  CD DOS, 177
  CHCP, 801-802
  CHKDSK | FIND, 573
  CHOICE, 603-605
  CLS, 322
  combining, 203-204,
    575-576

Compress Existing
  Drive, 722
Compress menu, 720
CONFIG.SYS files, 338
converting to macros, 206
COPY, 230-236,
  637-644, 829
COUNTRY, 786-788
dates, 184
DblSpace, 719
Debug menu, 863-864
DEFRAG, 475,
  533-534, 1090
DEL, 252-255
Delete, 425
DELTREE, 90, 226-228,
  623-624
DEVICE, 339-340, 842
DEVICEHIGH, 496, 518,
  838-839
dimmed commands, 73, 83,
  99, 107
DIR, 216, 807
DIR | FIND, 573
DISKCOMP,
  291-293, 1090
DISKCOPY, 284-291, 1090
Display menu, 127
DISPLAY.SYS DE-
  VICE, 796
DOS command syntax,
  176-180
DOS DEFRAG, 729
DOS=HIGH, 496
DOS=UMB, 496
DOSKEY, 199, 205
DOSKEY /H | FIND
  "DIR", 573
DOSKEY /INSERT, 202
DOSKEY /OVER-
  TYPE, 202
DOSKEY history, 200-201
DOSSHELL, 63-64
Drive Info, 726
Drive menu
  Change Size, 727
  Delete, 732
  Format, 731

Options / Change
  Ratio, 730
  Unmount, 724
DRIVPARM, 824-827
DRVSPACE, 545, 719
DRVSPACE /LIST, 727
DRVSPACE /
  UNCOMPRESS, 733
ECHO, 323-325, 563, 566
EDIT, 299, 845
Edit menu
  Copy, 848
  New FUNCTION, 863
  New Function, 858
  New SUB, 858-860
  Paste, 848
editing, 201-203
EMM386.EXE, 711-712
executing with
  COMMANDCOM,
  702-703
exit codes, 1089-1092
FC, 258-263, 739-744
FCBS, 342
FDISK, 868
File menu
  Associate, 140
  Change Attributes, 122
  Copy, 106
  Create Directory, 82
  Delete Setup, 388
  Deselect All, 99
  Exit, 76, 190
  Move, 106
  New, 311
  Open, 311, 849
  Open Setup, 379
  Print, 190, 311-312
  Print Setup, 387
  Properties, 154
  Purge Delete Sentry
    File, 445
  Rename, 88, 125-126
  Run, 174-175
  Save As, 309
  Save Setup, 379
  Select All, 99
  View File Contents, 126

FILES, 342
FIND, 571-574, 602-603, 1090
Find menu, 191
FOR, 601-603, 641
FORMAT, 271-279, 595, 871
exit code, 1090
nondefault capacities, 736-744
GOTO, 593-595
GRAPHICS, 807, 816-820
Help menu, 75-76, 191
IF, 590-598
INCLUDE, 618
insert editing mode, 202
INTERLNK, 651, 658-660
INTERLNK.EXE, 655-656
internal commands, 177, 320
INTERSVR, 652-654
entering, 654
KEYB, 786, 791-794, 802, 1091
LABEL, 274, 294-296
LASTDRIVE, 628
LH, 497
List, 425
MD, 223
MEM, 482-487
MEM | FIND, 573
MEMMAKER, 493-495
MENUDEFAULT, 615
MIRROR, 281
MODE, 797-813
MORE, 561-562
MOVE, 224
MSAV, 418-428, 1091
MSCDEX, 839-840
MSD, 757
NLSFUNC, 800
Optimize menu, 532
Options menu
Configure Delete Protection, 54
Confirmation, 132
Display, 162, 314
Enable Task Swapper, 144

File Display Options, 163
Help Path, 312
Show Information, 121
output
finding lines, 573
page breaks, 561-562
redirecting, 180-183
suppressing, 182
overtype editing mode, 202
PATH, 185, 194, 842
paths, 178-180
PAUSE, 325-327
POWER, 782
PREP, 798
PRINT, 256-258, 813-816
PROMPT, 195-196, 766-767, 771
Quick Format, 279
RD, 225
recall commands (DOSKEY history), 200-201, 204
RECOVER, 281
REM, 322-323
REN, 247-248
repeating, 600-601
REPLACE, 644-646, 1091
RESTORE, 412-413, 1091
running from secondary command prompt, 175
Search menu
Change, 306
Find, 308-309
Repeat Last Find, 191
sending to ANSI.SYS device driver, 765-768
SET, 688-689
SETVER, 1091
SHARE, 833-834
SHELL, 695
SHIFT, 600-601
SMARTDRV, 502
SMARTDRV /STATUS | FIND, 573
SORT, 567-571
STACKS, 342-343
SUBST, 626-628
time, 184

Tools menu
Defragment, 728
Options, 732
Uncompress, 733
TREE, 214
Tree menu, 87
TRUENAME, 629-630
TYPE, 255-256
UNDELETE, 439, 453
configurations, 457-458
recovering deleted files, 442
UNDELETE /PURGE, 446
UNFORMAT, 280-282, 753-757
Utilities menu, 758
VER, 177
View menu
All Files, 100
Dual File Lists, 116
Program/File Lists, 101
Repaint Screen, 128
Restore View, 128
VOL, 274, 293-296
VSAFE, 428-434
W switch, 178
XCOPY, 236-241, 632-637, 829, 1092
see also DOS commands
see also key commands
Commands command (Help menu), 75
COMMON SHARED statements, 859
COMn (serial ports), 129
Compare dialog box, 411
Compare function, 364, 411-412
comparing
disks, 291-293
drives, 395-397
files, 258-263, 411-412, 739-744
text strings in batch files, 596-597
compatibility tests (disks), 359-362
Compress Backup Data (Backup option), 377

Compress Existing Drive
  command, 722
Compress menu, 542
Compress menu com-
  mands, 720
compressed backup programs
  restoration, 49
compressed drives, 545, 1102
  caching, 725-726
  creating, 721-725
  defragmenting, 728-729
  deleting, 732
  DIR command, 546
  formatting, 731
  information, 726-727
  scanning for errors, 731
compressed files, 57-58
Compressed Volume File, see
  CVF
compressing
  data, 476
  disks, 722-725
  drives, 538, 541-542
  hard drives, 27, 539,
    719-721
compression ratios
  drives, 729-731
  files, 546
compression software, 612
CompuServe, 880
computers
  cabling, 651-652
  clock speed, 708
  laptop battery power,
    782-783
  linking, 651-660
COMSPEC variable, 691,
  700-701
CON device driver, 762
CON mode (screens), 779
concatenation
  binary files, 640
  data files, 640
  files, 637-644
  matched concatena-
    tion, 642
conditional command lines
  (batch files), 590-598

CONFIG variable, 691,
  694-695
CONFIG.SYS, 842, 1102
CONFIG.SYS files, 338
  286 microprocessors,
    550-551
  386 microprocessors,
    552-553
  486 microprocessors,
    552-553
  backing up, 335
  bypassing, 612
  command blocks, 613-619
  command prompts, 613
  commands, 338
  Pentium microprocessors,
    552-553
  see also startup files
configurations
  Backup, 357-364
  blocks, 615
  BUFFERS command, 512
  DOS applications, 672-673
  HIMEM.SYS files, 706-707
  international communica-
    tion, 785-803
  logical floppy disks, 827-831
  menus, 615-616
  mouse, 358-359
  physical disks, 824-827
  PRINT, 813-815
  printers, 808-809
  serial ports, 809-811
  submenus, 616-618
  tests, 362-363
  UNDELETE command,
    457-458
  upper memory blocks, 492
  video, 358-359
Configure Delete Protection
  command (Options
  menu), 54
Configure Delete Protection
  dialog box, 54
Configure Delete Sentry
  dialog box, 55
Confirm Mouse Operation
  dialog box, 138

Confirm on Delete dialog box,
  131-133
Confirmation command
  (Options menu), 132
Confirmation dialog box, 105
console devices, 781-782
consoles, 1102
CONST statement, 851
constants
  passing (modular program-
    ming), 861
  QBASIC, 851
Content of destination lost
  before copy error mes-
  sage, 639
control facilities (QBASIC),
  854-857
controlling
  COMMAND.COM
    command interpreter,
    695-698
  DOS environment, 695-698
conventional memory, 27,
  474, 480, 1102
  loading RAMDRIVE, 518
  PIFs, 676-678
converting
  commands into macros, 206
  DblSpace disks to DrvSpace
    disks, 724
  DoubleSpace to DriveSpace
    (compression program),
    544-545
  extended memory to
    expanded memory,
    490-493
coprocessors, 6
COPY command, 230-236,
  829
  ASCII method (file-
    writing), 643
  B switch, 644
  binary method (file-reading/
    writing), 643
  parameters, 691
Copy command
  Edit menu, 848
  File menu, 106

Copy File dialog box, 107, 111
COPYCMD variable, 691
copying
    backup programs, 49
    different density disks, 291
    directory files, 232
    disks, 284-291
    files, 106-109, 113,
        between drives, 117-118
        to devices, 643-644
        to disks, 634-636
        with COPY command, 230-236
        with XCOPY command, 236-241
    hidden files, 635
    INTERLNK software, 661
    large files, 389-390
    lines in QBASIC Editor, 848
    multiple files, 110-112, 232-233, 239
    program items (DOS Shell), 157-161
    subdirectories, 236
    system files, 635
    text, 304-309, 680-681
correcting disks, 467-468
cost (Internet gateways), 882
COUNTRY command, 786-788
CRC (cyclic redundancy check), 15, 743
Create Backup (MSAV option), 422
Create Checksums on Floppy (MSAV option), 422
Create Directory command (File menu), 82
Create New Checksums (MSAV option), 422
Create Report (MSAV option), 422-423
Create Undo Disk dialog box, 468

creating
    batch files, 318-319
    command prompts, 195-196
    compressed drives, 721-725
    directories, 25, 82-85, 223-224, 237
    directory trees in DOS Shell, 84
    documents, 311
    DOS environment variables, 691-692
    DOS Shell groups, 153
    DOSKEY editing mode defaults, 203
    ECHO messages, 324-325
    emergency startup disks, 46, 56, 274-275
    files with XCOPY command, 237
    functions (modular programming), 863
    groups, 154
    loops (batch files), 601
    macros, 204-209
    parameters for macros, 207
    partitions, 869-871
    passwords for groups, 155
    procedures (modular programming), 858-859
    program items (DOS Shell), 156
    RAM drives, 517
    screen banners, 771
    screen-savers, 588
    setup files, 365-380
    SmartDrive
        performance evaluations, 509-511
        reports, 505-506
    startup menus, 615-616
    virtual drives, 627
cross-linked files, 468-469
Ctrl key, 10-11
current directories, 39
current drives, 39
cursor-movement keys, 9, 12, 301-302

cursors
    control sequences, 770-775
    editing with, 108
    moving
        in Help window, 187
        with keypads, 9
    navigating, 108
Custom setup options (MEMMAKER), 710-711
customizing
    EDIT screen, 314
    file lists, 163-167
    screen colors, 162-163
cutting lines in QBASIC Editor, 848
cutting-and-pasting text, 304-309
CVF (Compressed Volume File), 537, 1102
Cyberspace, 876
cyclic redundancy check, see CRC
cycling
    Help topic screens, 190
    through task lists, 147

D

damaged disk troubleshooting, 351
data compression, 476, 537
Data compression (DOS 6 utility), 28
data files
    concatenation, 640
    drag-and-dropping on program files, 138-140
    scanning for viruses, 424
data management, 25
data protection, 25-26
data recovery, 25-26
data storage, 15-16
data transfers, 6
databases (Internet), 877
date formats (international settings), 787-789

date/time stamps
    commands, 184
    non-ASCII files, 644
    updating, 640-641
DblSpace (compression
    program), 476, 717-734
DblSpace command, 719
DblSpace disks, 724
DBLSPACE.BIN, 1102
DBLSPACE.SYS, 1067-1068
deactivating
    character wrapping, 774
    EMM386.EXE com-
        mand, 713
    expanded memory, 713-716
    file archive attributes, 634
Debug menu (QBASIC
    Editor), 845
Debug menu commands,
    863-864
debugging QBASIC, 863-864
DECLARE statements
    functions, 862
    subprograms, 860
decompressing compressed
    files, 57-58
DEF FN (QBASIC), 858
default parameter overriding,
    519-520
default settings, 1102
defaults
    Backup directories, 691
    directories, 39, 213-214
    directory tree, 66
    DOSKEY editing
        modes, 203
    drives, 213
    menu colors, 619
    PIFs, 676, 685
defining
    drives, 824
    program items, 575-578
DEFLNG statement
    (QBASIC), 851
DEFRAG (DOS 6 utility), 29
DEFRAG (DOS 6.2
    utility), 30
DEFRAG command, 475,
    533-534, 1090

DEFRAG utility, 523-526
    running in batch mode, 534
    sorting directory entries,
        531-532
    starting, 527-529
Defragment command (Tools
    menu), 728
defragmentation (optimiza-
    tion), 475-476
defragmenting
    compressed drives, 728-729
    drives, 523-529
DEFtype statement
    (QBASIC), 850
DEL command, 252-255
Delete command, 425, 732
Delete Directory Confirma-
    tion dialog box, 90
Delete key, 90
Delete Sentry program,
    439-441
    starting, 53-56
    undeleting files, 444
Delete Setup command (File
    menu), 388
deleted files
    protecting, 53-56
    recovering, 254
deleting
    batch file links, 588-589
    catalogs, 388-389
    compressed drives, 732
    directories, 90-91, 225-226
    directory tree branches,
        226-228
    disk labels, 295
    DOS directories, 454
    DOS environment
        variables, 692
    expanded memory, 491
    files, 42-43, 98, 131-132,
        252-255, 624
        for hard drive optimiza-
            tion, 525-527
        from printer queues, 258
    filespecs, 600-601
    groups, 154
    macros, 210

multiple files, 132-134,
    253-254
partitions, 871-872
program items (DOS
    Shell), 160
protected files, 254
setup files, 388
text, 303-304
viruses, 348
deletion keys, 304
deletion protection, 1102
deletion protection programs,
    47-48
Deletion-Tracking program,
    448-451
DELOLDOS program, 57
DELTREE command, 90,
    226-228, 623-624
Deselect All command (File
    menu), 99
deselecting
    files, 94-99
    text, 303
Detect Idle Time option
    (PIFs), 679
DEVICE command,
    339-340, 842
device drivers, 28, 340, 1103
    ANSI.SYS, 340, 763-765,
        1066-1067
    CHKSTATE.SYS, 1067
    CON, 762
    DBLSPACE.SYS,
        1067-1068
    DISPLAY.SYS, 795,
        1068-1069
    DRIVER.SYS, 1069-1071
    DRVSPACE.SYS,
        1071-1072
    EGA.SYS, 1072-1073
    EMM386, 490, 714,
        1073-1078
    HIMEM.SYS, 340,
        1078-1081
    HMA, 708
    installation (multimedia),
        838-839
    INTERLNK.EXE , 338-339,
        655-658, 1081-1083

mouse driver, 13
multimedia, 838-839
MWAVTSR.EXE , 429
POWER.EXE, 1083-1084
RAMDRIVE.SYS,
    1084-1085
SETVER, 339, 1086
SIZER.SYS, 1086
SMARTDRV.EXE,
    1087-1088
device-accessing DOS
    applications, 684
DEVICEHIGH (DOS 6
    utility), 29
DEVICEHIGH commands,
    496, 518, 838-839
devices
    consoles, 781-782
    copying files to, 644
    redirecting command
        output to, 182
dialog boxes, 1103
    Add Group, 155
    Advanced, 575
    Advanced Options,
        678, 680
    Associate File, 140
    Backup, 364
    Backup Devices, 359
    Backup Set Catalog, 394
    Change, 306
    Change Attributes, 122-123
    Change Size, 727
    Choose Drives for Delete
        Sentry, 55
    Color Scheme, 163
    command buttons, 1101
    Compare, 411
    Configure Delete Protec-
        tion, 54
    Configure Delete Sentry, 55
    Confirm Mouse Opera-
        tion, 138
    Confirm on Delete,
        131-133
    Confirmation, 105
    Copy File, 107, 111
    Create Undo Disk, 468

defining program items, 575
Delete Directory Confirma-
    tion, 90
Disk Backup Options, 376
Disk Restore Options, 401
DOS Shell, 68
Drive Info, 726
Drive Selection, 528
Exclude, 369
File Display Options, 163
File to Edit, 142
Find, 191, 308
Help, 69
Include, 369
Information, 730
Move File, 110
MSAV, 419
MWAV, 428
New Procedure Specifica-
    tion, 858
New Program Object, 154
Optimization Com-
    plete, 530
Options (SMARTMON
    utility), 510-511
Password, 155
Print, 192
Print File, 130
Problem Found, 467
Program Group Pro-
    perties, 154
Quick Format, 279
Recommendation, 529
Replace File Confirma-
    tion, 108
Restore, 394
Run, 174
Save As, 309
Screen Display Mode, 162
scrolling, 69-72
Select Backup Files, 369
Select Optimization
    Method, 531
Select Restore Files, 398
Special Inclusions, 367
Special Selections, 372
Video and Mouse Configu-
    ration, 358-359

View SUBs, 859
Virus Found, 425
VSAFE Options, 429
differential backups, 374
digitizer pads (multimedia
    hardware), 837
DIM statement (QBASIC),
    851-852
dimmed commands, 73, 83,
    99, 107
dip switches, 7-8
DIR | FIND command, 573
DIR command, 216,
    248, 807
    C switch, 729
    compressed drives, 546
    order codes, 220
    parameters, 690
DIRCMD variable, 690
directories, 1103
    + (plus sign), 66
    - (minus sign), 86
    appended directories, 625
    attributes, 251-252
    branches, 38, 637, 1100
    children, 38
    contents, 37, 216-222
    copying files between,
        233-235
    creating, 25, 82-85,
        223-224, 237
    current directory, 39
    default directories, 39,
        213-214
    deleting, 90-91, 225-226
    directory tree, 37-39, 66,
        1103, 1112
        collapsing, 86-88
        deleting branches,
            226-228
        displaying, 214-216
        displaying branches, 91
        expanding, 86-88
        listing branches,
            221-222
        reading, 216
        restructuring, 625-630
    displaying, 25

DOS directories, 452-454
    printing, 181
    switching to, 180
drive simulation, 626-627
empty directories, 402
emptying, 623-624
files
    copying, 232
    deleting, 254-255, 624
    listing, 248
    recovering, 446-447
    restoring, 402
    viewing, 66
grafting, 636-637
hiding, 251-252
listing, 38, 223
listings
    finding files in, 574
    sorting, 220
    sorting by compression
        ratios, 730
long directories, 218
parent directories, 38, 1108
path names, 40
paths, 629-630
pruning, 636-637
recovering, 446-447
redirecting, 560-566
removing, 25
renaming, 88-89, 224-225
restoring, 402
root directories, 37, 1110
saving in files, 560
selecting, 85-86
SENTRY directory, 458
    contents, 446
    purging, 445-446
structure optimization,
    622-623
subdirectories, 37-39,
    248, 1111
switching, 40, 179
viewing, 116
Windows directories, 457
**Disable Alarm Sound (MSAV
    option), 422**
**disabling Windows startup
    applications, 363**

**Disk Backup Options dialog
    box, 376**
disk caches, 500
    changing in drives, 505
    logging activity, 510
    programs, 47-48
    selecting for drives, 504-506
    sizing, 507-509
    Windows, 666-667
    writing, 501, 506
disk drives, *see* drives
Disk full error message, 233
**Disk Operating System,
    see DOS**
**Disk Restore Options dialog
    box, 401**
Disk Utilities group, 153
Disk Utilities icon, 153
**DISKCOMP command,
    291-293, 1090**
**DISKCOPY (DOS 6.2
    utility), 29**
**DISKCOPY command,
    284-291**
    exit code, 1090
    vs. XCOPY command, 633
disks, 14-15
    Backup disk maintenance,
        384-385
    bad sectors, 752
    buffers, 511-512
    byte sectors, 14
    changes, 174
    comparing, 291-293
    compatibility tests, 359-362
    compressing, 722-725
    copying, 284-291
    copying files to, 634-636
    correcting, 467-468
    damaged disk troubleshoot-
        ing, 351
    data recovery, 267-268
    DblSpace disks, 724
    different density disks,
        copying, 291
    directory structure, 38
    emergency startup disks,
        46, 56

entry sorting, 531-532
executing batch files
    from, 606
files
    finding, 166
    protecting from
        overwriting, 604
formatting, 266-268,
    271-275, 378
    for lower-density drives,
        736-744
    for older DOS versions,
        738-744
high-level formatting, 266
labels
    changing, 294
    internal labels, 267,
        293-296
    viewing, 293
lost allocation units,
    465-466
low-level formatting, 266
management, 25
memory capacity, 16
optimization methods,
    530-531
physical configurations,
    824-827
protecting
    from corruption, 15
    from overwriting,
        430-431
quick reformats, 270, 277
RAM disks, 1109
rebuilding without mirror
    image files, 753-757
reformatted disk restora-
    tion, 280-282
reformatting, 269-271,
    275-279, 351
safe format, 270
single drive copying,
    287-289
surface scanning, 470
system disks
    formatting, 274-275
    virus scanning, 431
tracks, 1112

unconditional format, 270
undo information storage, 467
Uninstall disks, 48
verifying copies, 290-291
volume labels, 273-274
Windows space optimization, 665-667
write-delayed caches, 1113
write-protected disks, 1113
Display command (Options menu), 162, 314
Display menu commands, 127
display options (monitors), 162
Display Options (PIFs), 680
Display Usage field (PIFs), 678
DISPLAY.SYS DEVICE command, 796
DISPLAY.SYS device driver, 795, 1068-1069
displaying
current directories, 39
current drive, 39
default directories, 213
directories, 25
paths, 629-630
trees, 91, 214-216
DOS environment variables, 688-689
DOS Shell screen, 64
drives
default directories, 214
files, 164
memory status, 218
files, 255-256
associations, 581
attributes, 248-249
by attributes, 218-219
compression ratios, 546
names, 178
paths, 629-630
hidden files, 165-166, 218
keyboard code page information, 802
long directories, 218
memory layout, 482-487

message boxes, 772-774
ROM status, 758
setup files, 371
system
files, 165-166, 218
statistics, 757-759
DO WHILE...LOOP block (QBASIC), 856
DO...LOOP block (QBASIC), 857
documents, 311
DOS, 20, 28, 1103
applications
Allow Close when Active option, 681
assigning shortcut keys, 681-683
configurations, 672-673
copying and pasting text, 680-681
device accessing, 684
Full Screen mode, 678
mouse interaction, 672
printing screens, 685
running in Windows, 667-685
saving screen images, 684
Windowed mode, 678
batch file execution, 321
booting, 334
command limitations for networks, 832-833
command overriding, 605-606
command prompt, 20-21, 24
CRC (cyclic redundancy check), 743
drives, defining, 824
early version removal, 57
environment, 695-698
environment variables
accessing, 692-695
appending, 693
changing, 692
creating, 691-692
deleting, 692

displaying, 688-689
preserving, 693-694
restoring, 693-694
versus replaceable parameters, 694
files
extensions, 33
general verification, 744
specific verification, 744
filters, 566-574
floppy disk parameters, 826
Internet, 875-883
loading
into extended memory, 340-341
into high memory area, 485-487
into HMA, 709
optimization, 473-476
partitions, 869-871
printing, 805-821
running on networks, 831-834
tasks, 670-672
upgrading to QBASIC, 843-865
windows, 671-672
DOS 5 files, 451
DOS 6
single drive copying, 287-288
uncompressing drives, 733
uninstalling, 56
utilities, 28-30
DOS 6.2
single drive copying, 288-289
utilities, 29
DOS 6.22
installation, 46-48
networked system upgrades, 832
utilities, 29
DOS command prompt, 143
DOS commands
| (vertical bar), 184
bracketed statements, 183
ellipsis (...), 184

Help, 185
lowercase italic state-
    ments, 183
nested brackets ([ ]), 184
replaceable items, 185
searching, 191-192
syntax, 176-180
see also commands
DOS core
program files, 267
system files, 724
**DOS DEFRAG com-
mand, 729**
DOS directories
deleting, 454
file recovery, 452-454
printing, 181
searching, 194
switching to, 180
DOS Editor, *see* **EDIT**
**DOS Shell, 22-24, 574-581,
1111**
associated files, 137
automating at system
    startup, 332
automating startup, 65
batch files, 332
command buttons, 68-69
dialog boxes, 68
directories
    creating, 83
    deleting, 90-91
    renaming, 88
    viewing, 116
directory trees, 84
disk copying, 291
drives, 78-82
exiting, 64, 76
File List, 137-138
file recovery, 455
files
    changing attributes,
        122-123
    changing multiple
        attributes, 123-124
    copying, 106-109, 113,
        116-117
    drag-and-drop, 112-116

moving, 106, 110
printing, 128-131
renaming, 125-126
replacement confirma-
    tion, 104-105
selecting, 94-95
viewing, 126-128
viewing attributes,
    121-122
Format command, 279
groups, 153
Help, 68-76
lists, 66
menu bar, 65
MSAV command, 419
multiple files
    copying, 110-112
    moving, 110-112
    selecting, 95-99
parameters, 578
program files, 63
program items
    adding, 157
    assigning shortcut
        keys, 158
    changing properties, 157
    copying, 157, 159-161
    creating, 156
    deleting, 160
    naming, 157
    password protection, 159
    viewing, 579
Quick Format com-
    mand, 279
Run dialog box, 174
screen, 63, 65-68, 144
    displaying, 64
    repainting, 82
    returning to, 137, 145
    views, 115-116
starting, 62-65
status bar, 65
title bar, 65
DOS=HIGH command, 496
DOS=UMB command, 496
DOSKEY, 198
batch files, 319
commands, 200-204
editing modes, 203

history list, 210
loading, 198-200, 208-209
macros
    creating, 204-209
    deleting, 210
    editing, 210
    listing, 210
    overriding DOS
        commands, 605-606
memory allocation, 715
memory requirements, 200
**DOSKEY /H | FIND "DIR"
command, 573**
**DOSKEY /INSERT com-
mand, 202**
**DOSKEY /OVERTYPE
command, 202**
DOSKEY buffer, 199, 208
**DOSKEY command,
199, 205**
**DOSSHELL /B /T com-
mand, 64**
DOSSHELL /B command, 64
DOSSHELL /T command, 64
DOSSHELL command, 63
**DOSSHELL.INI file,
160-161, 578-582**
**double-buffers (SmartDrive),
503-504**
**double-clicking (mouse),
13, 1103**
**double-density installation
disks, 49**
**DOUBLER program (passing
values), 862**
**DoubleSpace (compression
program), 27, 538, 546-547**
converting to DriveSpace,
    544-545
installation, 539-543
running, 541-543
setup, 538-539
utility interaction, 544
drag-and-drop (mouse), 13
data files, 138-140
files, 112-116
dragging (mouse), 1103
Drive Info command, 726
Drive Info dialog box, 726

drive lists, 66, 78
Drive menu commands
    Change Size, 727
    Delete, 732
    Format, 731
    Options / Change
        Ratio, 730
    Unmount, 724
Drive Selection dialog
    box, 528
DRIVER.SYS device driver,
    1069-1071
    alternate drive names,
        828-829
    comparing DRIVPARM,
        830-831
    drives, defining, 824
    external floppy disk
        drives, 830
    logical floppy disk configu-
        rations, 827-831
    two alternate drive names,
        829-830
drives, 14
    alternate drive names,
        828-829
    Backup drives, 375
    cancelling changes, 81
    change line test, 359
    changing, 309, 421
    change-line support, 827
    checking for glitches,
        463-465
    comparing, 395-397
    compressed drives, 545
        caching, 725-726
        creating, 721
        creating on disks,
            721-725
        defragmenting, 728-729
        deleting, 732
        formatting, 731
        scanning for errors, 731
        viewing information,
            726-727
    compressing, 538, 541-542
    compression ratios, 729-731

copying disks from different
    capacities, 291
copying files between, 113,
    117-118
current drives, 39
default directories, 214-218
default drives, 213
defining, 824
defragmenting, 523-529
disk caches, 504-506
double-buffering, 503-504
empty drives, 80-81
external floppy disk
    drives, 830
files
    displaying, 164
    listing, 179
    moving between, 112,
        117-118
hard drives
    compressing, 539
    restoring, 407-409
    virus scanning, 420
host drives, 537, 726
logical drives, 1106
mapping, 529
memory
    optimizing, 732
    status, 218
mounting, 538
moving files between, 112,
    117-118
optimizing, 529-530
phantom drives, 79, 117
protected drives, 440-441
RAM drives, 27, 515-520
reconfiguring, 363
refreshing, 79, 81-82
resizing, 727-728
restoring, 395-397
selecting, 78-82, 421
    for Backup, 368
    for compression, 543
    for defragmentation, 528
switching, 628-629
two alternate drive names,
    829-830
uncompressing, 733

undo-drive, 468
viewing, 727
virtual drives, 627-629
DriveSpace (compression
    program), 546-547
    installation, 539-543
    running, 541-543
    setup, 538-539
    utility interaction, 544
DRIVPARM
    comparing DRIVER.SYS,
        830-831
    drives, defining, 824
DRIVPARM command,
    824-827
DrvSpace, 717-734
DRVSPACE /LIST com-
    mand, 727
DRVSPACE /
    UNCOMPRESS com-
    mand, 733
DRVSPACE command,
    545, 719
DRVSPACE.BIN, 1103
DRVSPACE.SYS,
    1071-1072
Dual File Lists command
    (View menu), 116
Duplicate file name or file not
    found error message, 247

E

E switch, 236
e-mail, 1103
    Internet, 877-878
    telecommunications
        software, 881
ECHO command, 323-325,
    563, 566
ECHO messages, 324-325
echo printing, 806-807
echoing commands, 321,
    323-325
EDIT
    exiting, 178
    finding-and-replacing text,
        306-307

Get Started Help, 312
Help, 312-313
Keyboard Help, 312
lines versus paragraphs,
    300-301
screen customizing, 314
screens, 300
starting, 177, 299-300
Survival Guide Help, 313
EDIT command, 299
    QBASIC interface, 845
    switches, 314
Edit menu (QBASIC
    Editor), 845
Edit menu commands
    Copy, 848
    New FUNCTION, 863
    New Function, 858
    New SUB, 858, 860
    Paste, 848
editing
    commands, 201-203
    macros, 210
    procedures, 858
    setup files, 387
    text, 301-306
    with cursors, 108
EGA.SYS, 1072-1073
EISA (Extended Industry
    Standard Architecture), 708
ellipsis (...), 82, 184
ELSE statements
    (QBASIC), 854
ELSEIF element
    (QBASIC), 855
emergency startup disks, 46,
    56, 274-275
EMM386 device driver, 490,
    496, 714
EMM386.EXE command,
    711-713
EMM386.SYS, 1073-1078
empty directories
    deleting, 90
    excluding from restora-
        tion, 402
empty drives, 80-81
emptying directories, 623-624

EMS Memory Locked (386
    Enhanced Mode
    option), 677
Emulate Text Mode option
    (PIFs), 680
Enable Task Swapper
    command (Options
    menu), 144
END IF statements
    (QBASIC), 854
END SUB statements,
    860-861
end-of-file marks, 643
enhanced keyboard, 9
Enhanced Readability (DOS
    6.2 utility), 30
entering
    files from CON, 568
    INTERSVR command, 654
EOF (end-of-file) marks, 643
Error creating image file error
    message, 288
error messages
    Access Denied, 84, 89,
        109, 126
    Access denied, 234
    Bad command or file name,
        178-179
    Bad or missing command
        interpreter, 696
    Content of destination lost
        before copy, 639
    Disk full, 233
    Duplicate file name or file
        not found, 247
    Error creating image
        file, 288
    FC: Out of memory, 740
    File cannot be copied onto
        itself, 109, 232
    File not found, 231, 254
    Insert DOS disk in
        drive..., 275
    Insufficient room in root
        directory, 465
    Invalid drive specifica-
        tion, 292

Invalid media, 273
Packed file corrupt, 487
permission denied, 225
Read, 268
Sector not found, 267
TARGET diskette bad or
    incompatible, 290
Unable to create direc-
    tory, 239
Unrecoverable read..., 285
Unrecoverable write..., 286
Write, 268
Write-protect error writing
    drive A, Abort, Retry,
    Fail?, 251
You have more than one
    file selected, 111
ERRORLEVEL condition
    (batch files), 591-592
Esc key, 11-12, 147
ESC key command, 765
escape sequences
    ANSI.SYS device driver,
        768-770
    batch files, 768
    sending, 766
    text files, 767-768, 773
Examples (Help topic
    screen), 189
Exclude dialog box, 369
excluding
    COMSPEC from secondary
        command interpreters,
        700-701
    empty directories from
        restoration, 402
    files from restoration,
        396-397
    setup files, 368, 372-373
    spacing and case in file
        comparisons, 743
    upper memory, 712-713
Exclusive option (PIFs), 678
executable files, 1104
    protecting from overwrit-
        ing, 431
    virus scanning, 431

executing
batch files from disks, 606
commands with
COMMANDCOM,
702-703
PIFs, 674-683
startup files line-by-
line, 337
Execution options (PIFs),
678-679
existing file replacement, 646
exit codes, 591, 594,
1089-1092
Exit command (File menu),
76, 190
exiting
DOS Shell, 64, 76
EDIT, 178
FDISK, 873
programs, 172
virus scanner, 424
Expand All command (Tree
menu), 87
EXPAND program, 57, 405
expanded memory, 480-481,
1104
activating, 713-716
converting extended
memory to, 490-493
deactivating, 713-716
deleting, 491
PIFs, 676-678
simulating with extended
memory, 712
expanding
compressed files, 57-58
directory trees, 86-88
resynchronization buffer
(FC command), 739-744
extended character set (IBM),
1094-1095
Extended Industry Standard
Architecture, see EISA
extended memory, 474,
481-482
accessing, 484
allocation, 709
converting to expanded
memory, 490-493

expanded memory simula-
tion, 712
loading DOS, 340-341
PIFs, 676-678
RAM drives, 516-517
extended partition, 870-871
extensions
files, 1104
filespecs, 33-34
external commands, 186
external files, 193
external floppy disk
drives, 830
external programs, 177

F

F1 shortcut key, 358
F3 shortcut key, 192
F5 shortcut key, 174, 337
F7 shortcut key, 200
F8 shortcut key, 107,
200, 336
F9 shortcut key, 126, 200
FASTHELP, 185-192
FAT (file allocation table)
files, 41, 174
FC command, 258-263,
739-744
FC: Out of memory error
message, 740
FCBS command, 342
FDISK (partitioning pro-
gram), 867-874
FDISK command, 868
fields, 1104
file allocation, 1104
File cannot be copied onto
itself error message, 109,
232
File Control Blocks, see
FCBS command
File Display Options com-
mand (Options menu), 163
File Display Options dialog
box, 163
file extensions, program
associations, 141

file handles, 1104
file lists, 66
customizing, 163-167
filtering, 164
sorting, 166-167
starting programs, 137-138
File menu (QBASIC
Editor), 845
File menu commands
Associate, 140
Change Attributes, 122
Copy, 106
Create Directory, 82
Delete Setup, 388
Deselect All, 99
Exit, 76, 190
Move, 106
New, 311
Open, 311, 849
Open Setup, 379
Print, 190, 311-312
Print Setup, 387
Properties, 154
Purge Delete Sentry
File, 445
Rename, 88, 125-126
Run, 174-175
Save As, 309
Save Setup, 379
Select All, 99
View File Contents, 126
File not found error message,
231, 254
File Sort command (Optimize
menu), 532
File to Edit dialog box, 142
filenames
changing, 233
displaying, 178
files, 33, 1104
Add mode, 98
adding to print queue, 130
adjacent files, 95
appending, 561, 638-639
archive attributes, 36, 634
ASCII comparisons,
260-262
ASCII text files, 130

associated files
  opening, 140-141
  starting programs, 137
associating, 140
associations, 581
attributes, 35-37
  changing, 122-123,
    249-250
  displaying, 248-249
  listing, 184
  viewing, 121-122
AUTOEXEC.BAT files,
  331-332, 496-498, 550
backing up, 46, 373-375
Backup files, 385-386
batch files
  accessing DOS environ-
    ment variables, 692
  alternative branches,
    589-590
  annotating, 322-323
  branches, 589-590
  bypass branches,
    589, 593
  calling, 327-329,
    586-587
  cancelling, 321
  chaining, 585-586
  clobbering, 606-607
  commands, 321-329
  creating, 318-319
  deleting links, 588-589
  ERRORLEVEL
    condition, 591-592
  exit codes, 591
  extensions, 1099
  finding, 320
  formatting, 590-598
  GOTO command,
    593-595
  in ANSI.SYS device
    driver, 768
  linking, 584-588
  linking to them-
    selves, 588
  loops, 598-603
  MSAV command,
    426-428

multiple links, 587
naming, 320
passing replaceable
  parameters in, 587
pausing, 325-327
recursion, 588
referencing, 602
replaceable parameters,
  329-330
running, 319
testing for existence, 596
testing for null values,
  597-598
testing logic, 703
binary comparisons,
  259-260
binary files, 326, 640
carriage returns, 567
clobbering, 104
clusters, 522-523
  recovering, 465-467
  slack, 642-643
  storing, 642
.COM format, 1101
combining, 637-644
comparing, 258-263,
  411-412, 739-744
compressed files, 57-58
compression ratios
  displaying, 546
  viewing, 730
concatenation, 637-644
CONFIG.SYS files,
  338, 550
  command blocks,
    613-619
  command prompts, 613
copying, 106-109, 113, 643
  between drives, 117-118
  to devices, 644
  to disks with XCOPY
    command, 634-636
  with COPY command,
    230-236
  with XCOPY command,
    236-241
creating with XCOPY
  command, 237

cross-linked files, 468-469
data files
  concatenation, 640
  drag-and-dropping on
    program files, 138-140
  scanning for viruses, 424
date/time stamps, 640-641
DBLSPACE.BIN, 1102
deleted files
  protecting, 53-56
  recovering, 254
deleting, 42-43, 98,
  131-132, 252-255
  for hard drive optimiza-
    tion, 525-527
  from directories, 624
  from printer queues, 258
deletion protection, 350
Deletion-Tracking files,
  449-450
deselecting, 94-99
disks
  finding, 166
  protecting from
    overwriting, 604
displaying, 255-256
DOS 5 files recovery, 451
DOS core
  program files, 267
  system files, 724
DOSSHELL.INI file,
  160-161, 578-582
drag-and-drop, 112-116
drive displays, 164
entering from CON, 568
excluding from restoration,
  396-397
executable files, 431
existing file replace-
  ment, 646
file chains, 42
filtering, 221
finding, 165, 222
  by context, 572
  in directory listings, 574
fragmented, 42, 1105
global filespecs, 34-35
grabber files, 147

handles, 342
hidden attributes, 36
hidden files
    changing attributes,
        250-251
    copying with XCOPY
        command, 635
    displaying, 165-166
HIMEM.SYS files, 706-710
HLP files, 247
host drive files, 724-725
identifying cluster ends,
    642-643
infected files, 422
installation, 147
invalid allocation units,
    746-748
large files, 389-390
lines, 571-574
listing by attributes,
    218-219
locking (networks),
    833-834
memory allocation, 42
memory allocation errors,
    749-750
mirror image files, 270, 754
missing files replacement,
    645-646
moving, 106, 110, 112,
    117-118
MSAV.INI file, 427
multiple attributes, 123-124
multiple files
    copying, 232-233, 239
    deleting, 132-134,
        253-254
    selecting, 95-99
naming, 33-34, 83
navigating, 301-302
non-ASCII files, 644
nonadjacent files, 95
old versions, 399-400
opening, 311
overwriting, 402
partial file recovery,
    450-451
paths, 629-630

PIFs, 672-673
pipe files, 563
printing, 98, 128-131, 235,
    256-258, 311-312
programs, 180
protected files
    deleting, 254
    listing, 441-444
protecting
    during file replace-
        ment, 646
    from deletion, 438-446
    from overwriting, 234
read-only files, 36, 1110
record data types, 854
recovering, 234, 441-444,
    448-451
    from DOS Shell, 455
    from Windows, 455-457
    without prompts,
        454-456
recovery files, 443
renaming, 125-126, 231,
    238, 247-248
repairing, 748
replacement confirmation,
    104-105
replacing, 104-105, 233-235
restoring, 392-413
resynchronizing, 262-263
saving, 309-310
selecting, 94-95, 100-101
setup files
    creating, 365-380
    deleting, 388
    displaying, 371
    editing, 387
    excluding, 368, 372-373
    finding, 386
    including, 368
    opening, 379
    opening from Restore
        dialog box, 401
    printing, 387
    selecting, 366-373
    storing, 386
    undoing selections, 372
sharing (networks),
    833-834

startup files
    backing up, 335
    bypassing, 336-337
    bypassing during
        booting, 610-613
    bypassing items, 382
    executing line-by-
        line, 337
    protecting, 334-336
    restoring, 336
swap files (Windows), 666
system attribute, 36
system files, 1111
    changing attributes,
        250-251
    copying with XCOPY
        command, 635
    displaying, 165-166
system initialization
    files, 758
system startup files, 758
temporary files, 519, 690
text, 305
text files
    annotating, 563-564
    escape sequences, 773
    in ANSI.SYS device
        driver, 767
    viewing, 52
text strings, 573
undeleting, 444
viewing, 126-128
VIR file, 422
Windows files, 456-457
FILES command, 342
filespecs, 33-34, 1104
    deleting, 600-601
    filtering files by, 221
    listing files by, 443
    path names, 41
    paths, 179
filtering
    file lists, 164
    files by filespecs, 221
filters, 566-574
**FIND command, 571-574,
    602-603, 1090**
**Find command (Search
    menu), 308-309**

Find dialog box, 191, 308
Find menu commands, 191
finding
    batch files, 320
    clusters (files), 466-468
    command output lines, 573
    files, 165, 222
        by context, 572
        disk files, 166
        in directory listings, 574
        lines (files), 571-574
        setup files, 386
        temporary files, 690
    text, 307-309
finding-and-replacing text,
    306-307
flaming, 877
floppy disk drives
    (external), 830
floppy disks, 1104
    logical floppy disks,
        configuring, 827-831
    standard parameters, 826
    see also disks
floppy drives, 1105
focuses (lists), 67-68
fonts (DOS windows), 672
FOR command, 601-603, 641
FOR...NEXT statements
    (QBASIC), 856
Foreground Priority option
    (PIFs), 678
FORMAT command,
    271-279, 595
    exit code, 1090
    nondefault capacities,
        736-744
    partitioning, 871
Format command (Drive
    menu), 279, 731
formats
    international formats,
        787-789
    quick format, 270
    safe format, 270
    unconditional format, 270
formatting
    batch files, 590-598
    compressed drives, 731

disks, 378
    for lower-density drives,
        736-744
    for older DOS versions,
        738-744
    hard disks, 268-269
    system disks, 274-275
fragmented files, 42, 1105
full backups, 373-375
Full Screen mode (DOS
    applications), 678
function keys, 8
functions
    Backup function, 364
    CHKDSK program, 469
    Compare function, 364,
        411-412
    DECLARE statements, 862
    executing with key-
        board, 301
    modular programming,
        862-863
    Restore function, 364,
        392-393

G

gateways, 881-882
general verification (DOS
    files), 744
General Write Protect
    (VSAFE option), 430-431
Getting Started Help
    (EDIT), 313
gigabytes, 16
global filespecs, 34-35, 1105
    batch files, 602
    changing/displaying file
        attributes, 251
    copying files, 232
    filtering files by, 221
global variables, 859
Gopher, 877, 1105
GOSUB (QBASIC), 858
GOTO command, 593-595
government agencies as
    Internet sources, 876
grabber files, 147

grafting directories, 636-637
graphical user interfaces,
    see GUIs
GRAPHICS command, 807,
    816-820
GRAPHICS screens,
    printing, 816-820
GRAPHICS.PRO, 817
greater-than symbol (>),
    redirecting command
    output, 180
groups, 153-163
GUIs (graphical user
    interfaces), 22-24
GW-BASIC (QBASIC
    conversion), 849-850

H

hard disks, 14, 1105
    compressing, 27
    formatting, 268-269
    partitioning, 268
    partitioning with FDISK,
        867-874
    partitions, 1108
hard drives, 14, 1105
    backing up, 46
    caching, 475
    compressing, 539, 719-721
    deleting files, 525-527
    optimizing, 523
    redirecting, 652
    reformatting, 50
    restoring, 407-409
    virus scanning, 420
hardware, 4-13, 1105
    interacting with, 28
    multimedia, 836-838
    troubleshooting, 350
HD Low-Level Format
    (VSAFE option), 430
Help
    contents, 187
    DOS commands, 185
    DOS Shell, 68-76
    EDIT, 312-313

jumps, 187, 190
menus, 190-191
topic screens, 189-190
topics
  printing, 192
  selecting, 74
windows
  closing, 192
  navigating, 187-188
  scrolling, 188-189
Help button (DOS Shell dialog box), 84
Help dialog box, 69
Help index, 74-75
Help menu, 72-76
Help menu commands, 75-76, 191
Help Path command (Options menu), 312
help topic groups, 155
hex 1A (end-of-file mark), 643
Hex command (Display menu), 127
hexadecimal, 1105
hidden attributes (files), 36, 1105
hidden files, 1105
  attributes, 250-251
  copying, 635
  displaying, 165-166, 218
hiding directories, 251-252
high memory area, 482, 1105
high-level formatting (disks), 266
HIMEM command, 496
HIMEM extended memory manager, 474, 484
HIMEM.SYS device driver, 340, 1078-1081
HIMEM.SYS files, 706-710
history list (DOSKEY), 210
HLP files
  listing, 222
  renaming, 247
HMA (High Memory Area), 708-709

host drives, 537, 1105
  caching, 726
  defragmenting, 729
  files, 724-725
hotkeys, 847, 1105
How to Use MS-DOS Help command (Help menu), 191

IBM extended character set, 1094, 1095
icons, 22, 153, 1106
identifying
  file cluster ends, 642-643
  ports for computer linking, 656-657
IF command, 590-598
IF statements (QBASIC), 854-855
Immediate window
  QBASIC debugging, 863
  QBASIC Editor, 846
INCLUDE command, 618
Include dialog box, 369
Include/Exclude list, 371-372
including setup files, 368
incremental backups, 374
infected files (backups), 422
Information dialog box, 730
initializing PRINT program, 128
input, 1106
  redirecting, 560-566
  SORT command, 568-569
Insert DOS disk in drive... error message, 275
insert editing mode commands, 202
inserting
  page breaks into memory reports, 483
  replaceable parameters in program items, 577-578
  text, 302-303
installation
  ANSI.SYS device driver, 764

Delete Sentry program, 440
device drivers (multimedia), 838-839
DOS 6.22, 46-48
DOS core program files, 267
DoubleSpace (compression program), 539-543
DriveSpace (compression program), 539-543
files, 147
keyboard code pages, 797-798
Insufficient room in root directory error message, 465
INT15h, troubleshooting, 709
interacting with hardware, 28
Interactive Batch Programs (DOS 6.2 utility), 29
Interactive Startup (DOS 6.2 utility), 29
interfaces, 1106
  QBASIC, 845-848
  user interface, 1112
INTERLINK.EXE, 1081-1083
INTERLNK, 650, 651
  client setup, 655-658
  server setup, 652-654
  software, 661
INTERLNK (DOS 6 utility), 28
INTERLNK command, 651-660
INTERLNK.EXE driver, 655-658
internal commands, 177, 186, 320
internal labels (disks), 267, 293-296
internal programs, 177
international characters, 789-790
international formats, 787-789
international keyboard layouts, 791-794

Internet, 1106
  access through DOS, 883
  accessing, 879
  chatting, 878, 882
  cost, 882
  databases, 877
  e-mail, 877-878
  gateways, 881-882
  mailing lists, 878
  modems, 879-880
  newsgroups, 877
  passwords, 883
  resources, 876-879
  telecommunications
    software, 880-881
  viruses, 882
**interrupt requests (IRQs),
  841-842**
interrupting
  batch files, 321
  TSR loading, 430
interrupts, 1106
**INTERSVR command,
  652-654**
**Invalid drive specification
  error message, 292**
**Invalid media error mes-
  sage, 273**
IO.SYS file, 1106
**IRQs (interrupt requests),
  841-842, 1106**

J–K

jumpers, 7-8
jumps (Help), 187, 190

**KB Desired memory setting
  (PIFs), 677**
**KB Limit memory setting
  (PIFs), 677**
**KB Required memory setting
  (PIFs), 677**
key commands
  assigning to international
    characters, 790
  ESC, 765
  F1, 358

F3, 192
F5, 174, 337
F7, 106
F8, 107, 336
F9, 126
PrintScreen, 685
task switching keys, 145
**KEYB command, 786,
  791-794, 802, 1091**
keyboard, 8-12
  assigning text strings to
    keys, 778-779
  changing response, 779-781
  Clipboard keys, 304
  code pages, 794-802
  controlling with ANSI.SYS
    device driver, 775-779
  cursor-movement keys,
    301-302
  Delete key, 90
  deletion keys, 304
  function execution, 301
  international layouts,
    791-794
  layouts, 794
  numeric keypad, 1108
  remapping keys, 777-778
  scrolling keys, 69
  selecting
    directories, 85
    drives, 79
    files, 94-95
    multiple files, 98
  SORT collating se-
    quence, 569
**Keyboard command (Help
  menu), 75**
Keyboard Help (EDIT), 312
keypad, 9
kilobytes, 16, 1106
known viruses, 417

L

**LABEL command, 274,
  294-296, 518**
**labeling disks electron-
  ically, 273**

labels (disks), 293-296
**laptop computers, battery
  power preservation,
  782-783**
LASTDRIVE command, 628
**LCASE$ function
  (QBASIC), 852**
**left square bracket ([),
  ANSI.SYS escape se-
  quences, 767**
LH command, 497
line numbers (QBASIC), 850
lines (files)
  copying or cutting
    (QBASIC Editor), 848
  finding, 571-574
  sorting, 567-571
linking
  batch files, 584-588
  computers, 651, 653-654,
    659-660
List command, 425
listing
  BIN files, 326
  Deletion-Tracking files,
    449-450
  directories, 38, 223
    contents, 216-222
    files, 248
    subdirectories, 248
    tree branches, 221-222
  drives
    disk caches, 505-506
    files, 179
  file attributes, 184, 218-219
  Help contents, 187
  hidden files, 218
  HLP files, 222
  protected drives, 441
  protected files, 441-444
  recovery files, 443
  system files, 218
  upper memory pro-
    grams, 494
listings, 574
lists
  DOS Shell, 66
  drive lists, 66, 78

file lists, 66
customizing, 163-167
filtering, 164
sorting, 166-167
focuses, 67-68
program lists, 67
task list, 147
View All Files list, 100
lithium batteries replacement, 7
LOADHIGH (DOS 6 utility), 29
loading
command processors, 342
COMMAND.COM command interpreter, 702
device drivers, 338-339
DISPLAY.SYS device driver, 795
DOS
into extended memory, 340-341
into high memory area, 485-487
into HMA, 709
DOSKEY, 198-200, 208-209
EMM386 device driver, 490, 496
FAT files, 174
HIMEM command, 496
HIMEM extended memory manager, 484
HMA drivers, 708
INTERLNK.EXE driver, 655-658
international keyboard layouts, 792
keyboard code pages, 795
mouse drivers, 13
MWAVTSR.EXE driver, 429
programs into upper memory, 493-495
secondary command interpreters, 698-701
TSRs, 128, 174, 497, 716

UNDELETE TSRs, 439-441
VSAFE virus monitor, 434-435
local variables (modular programming), 861
Lock Application Memory (386 Enhanced Mode option), 677
locking files (networks), 833-834
locking keys, 10
logging disk cache activity, 510
logical drives, 1106
logical floppy disk configurations, 827-831
long directories, 218
long integers (QBASIC), 851
loop structures (QBASIC), 856-857
loops
batch files, 598-603
contents of, 857
lost allocation units (files), 1106
see also clusters
low-level formatting (disks), 266
lowercase characters, 10
LPT1 as default printer port, 806
LPTn (parallel ports), 129
LTRIM$ function (QBASIC), 852

M

macro list (DOSKEY), 210
macros
accessing, 198
command conversion, 206
creating, 204-209
deleting, 210
editing, 210
overriding DOS commands, 605-606

parameters, 207
quitting, 207
replacing, 210
telecommunications software, 881
mailing lists, 878, 1107
Main group program list, 152
main module (modular programs), 858
managing disks, 25
mapping drives, 529
master catalogs, 383
MASV command, 1091
matched concatenations, 642
maximizing
DOS environment, 697
upper memory space, 710-714
MB (megabytes), 16, 1107
MD command, 223
Media Player, 839
MEM | FIND command, 573
MEM command, 482-487
MEMMAKER (DOS 6 utility), 29, 474, 710-711
MEMMAKER command, 493-498
memory, 479, 1107
allocating, 41-42
in PIFs, 676-678
to COMMAND.COM command interpreter, 701
to DOSKEY buffer, 208
to file handles, 342
to stacks, 342-343
to video screens, 676
buffers, 341
caches, 1100
components, 6
conventional memory, 27, 474, 480, 676-678, 1102
dip switches, 7-8
disk caches, 500
disk capacity, 16
DOSKEY requirements, 200
drive status displays, 218

drive optimization, 732
expanded memory, 480-481
  activating, 713-716
  deactivating, 713-716
  deleting, 491
  PIFs, 676-678
extended memory, 474,
  481-482
  accessing, 484
  allocation, 709
  converting to expanded
    memory, 490-493
  expanded memory
    simulation, 712
  PIFs, 676-678
file allocation errors,
  749-750
gigabytes, 16
hard drive caching, 475
high memory area, 482
invalid allocation units,
  746-748
jumpers, 7-8
kilobytes, 16
layout displays, 482-487
megabytes, 16
mirror image file requirements, 278
optimizing, 27, 474-475
printers, 258
RAM drives, 475
reports, 483, 492
slack space, 41
system memory, 758
task swapping require-
  ments, 576
upper memory, 474,
  480, 1112
  accessing, 708
  aggressive scanning, 711
  excluding, 712-713
  maximizing space,
    710-714
upper memory blocks,
  491-493
Windows, 664-665
Memory Block Display
  command (Utilities
  menu), 758

Memory Browser command
  (Utilities menu), 758
menu bar (DOS Shell), 65
MENUDEFAULT com-
  mand, 615
menus, 1107
  closing, 73
  colors, 618-619
  Compress menu, 542
  configurations, 615-616
  Help menu, 72-76, 190-191
  navigating, 72
  Optimize, 531
  startup menus, 615-616
  submenu configurations,
    616-618
  Tree menu, 86
  Windows Undelete
    File menu, 456
    Options menu, 457
message boxes, 772-774
microprocessors, 5
Microsoft Anti-Virus
  program, 26, 52-53
  see also MSAV
Microsoft Diagnostics (MSD),
  841-842
  see also MSD
Microsoft Windows Anti-
  Virus, 53
minus sign (-), directories, 86
MIRROR command, 281
mirror image files
  memory requirements, 278
  searching, 754
  storing, 270
misplaced files, 165
missing file replacement,
  645-646
MODE command, 797, 799,
  802, 806
  printer configuration,
    808-809
  redirection status, 812-813
  serial port configuration,
    809-811
  serial printer redirec-
    tion, 812

modems, 1107
  Internet, 879-880
  telecommunications
    software, 880
modular programming
  functions, 862
  functions, creating, 863
  global variables, 859
  passing values, 861-862
  procedures, creating,
    858-859
  QBASIC, 857-863
  subprograms, 860-861
modular programs, 858
Monitor Ports options
  (PIFs), 680
monitoring keyboard code
  pages, 795-796
monitors, 162, 762-764
monochrome regions
  (UMBs), 711
MORE command, 561-562
mother board, 5
mounting CVFs, 538
mouse, 12-13
  chording, 372
  clicking, 358, 1101
  configurations, 358-359
  double-clicking, 1103
  dragging, 1103
  expanding/collapsing
    directory trees, 88
  interaction with DOS
    applications, 672
  refreshing drives, 82
  scrolling
    dialog boxes, 70
    Help window, 188
  selecting
    directories, 85
    drives, 80
    files, 95
    multiple files, 96-97
mouse drivers, 13
mouse pointer, 12, 114
MOVE command, 224, 691
Move command (File
  menu), 106

Move File dialog box, 110
moving
  cursors, 301-302
    in Help window, 187
    with keypads, 9
  files, 106, 117-118
  list focuses, 67-68
  multiple files, 110-112
  text, 305
MPC (Multimedia PC), 1107
MPC2 standard (Multimedia PCs), 837
MSAV (Microsoft Anti-Virus) program, 348-349, 417
MSAV command, 418-428
MSAV dialog box, 419
MSAV.INI file, 427
MSBACKUP program, see Backup
MSCDEX command (multimedia), 839-840
MSD (Microsoft Diagnostics) program, 757-759, 841-842
MSDOS.SYS files, 1107
MSDOSDATA variable, 691
Multimedia, 1107
  hardware, 836-838
  IRQs (interrupt requests), 841-842
  MSCDEX command, 839-840
  PCs, 835-842
  software, 838-842
Multimedia Encylopedia, 839
multiple attributes (files), 123-124
multiple files
  copying, 110-112, 232-233, 239
  deleting, 132-134, 253-254
  moving, 110-112
  selecting, 95-99
multiple links (batch files), 587
MWAV (Microsoft Windows Anti-Virus) program, 417
MWAV dialog box, 428

MWAVTSR.EXE driver, 429
MWBACKUP program, see Backup

N

N switch, 263
naming
  batch files, 320
  files, 33-34, 83
  groups, 155
  program items (DOS Shell), 157
  virtual drives, 627-629
National Language Support, 800-801
navigating
  cursors, 108
  files, 301-302
  Help window, 187-188
  menus, 72
  scroll bars, 70-72
nested brackets ([ ]), 184
nesting IF command, 598
NETWORKS.TXT (system upgrades), 832
New command (File menu), 311
New Function command (Edit menu), 858, 863
New Procedure Specification dialog box, 858
New Program Object dialog box, 154
New SUB command (Edit menu), 858, 860
newsgroups, 877, 1107
NLSFUNC command, 800
No symbol (mouse pointer), 114
nodes, 1107
  see also workstations
non-ASCII files, 644
non-DOS partitions, 868
nonadjacent files, 95
Notes (Help topic screen), 189

numeric formats (international settings), 787-789
numeric keypad, 1108
numeric variables (QBASIC), 851
NumLock key, 9, 10

O

O switch, 220
objects, 136
OK button (DOS Shell dialog box), 84
On-screen command help (DOS 6 utility), 29
online services, 881
Open command (File menu), 311, 849
open loops (batch files), 598
Open Setup command (File menu), 379
opening
  associated files, 140-141
  catalogs, 394-395
  Disk Utilities group, 153
  files, 311
  Help Index, 74
  objects, 136
  PIF Editor, 674-683
  setup files, 379, 401
operating system, 1108
optimization
  compressing data, 476
  defragmentation, 475-476
  memory management, 474-475
Optimization Complete dialog box, 530
optimization methods (disks), 530-531
Optimization progress screen, 530
Optimize menu, 531
Optimize menu commands, 532
optimizing
  AUTOEXEC.BAT, 842
  Backup loading, 380

CONFIG.SYS, 842
directory structures, 622-623
disk space in Windows, 665-667
drives, 529-530, 732
file printing, 235
hard drives, 523
system memory, 27
task swapping, 677
Windows, 664-667
option buttons, 154, 1108
Optional Parameters field (PIFs), 675
Options / Change Ratio command (Drive menu), 730-734
Options command (Tools menu), 732
Options dialog box (SMARTMON utility), 510-511
Options menu commands
Configure Delete Protection, 54
Confirmation, 132
Display, 162, 314
Enable Task Swapper, 144
File Display Options, 163
Help Path, 312
Show Information, 121
order codes (DIR command), 220
ordering
DOS Shell program, 22
DOS Shell program files, 63
double-density installation disks, 49
organizing Backup files, 385-386
output, 1108
commands, 573
redirecting, 560-566
SORT command, 568-569
standard error output, 565
overriding
default parameters (RAM drives), 519-520

DOS commands, 605-606
Include/Exclude list, 371-372
overtype editing mode (commands), 202
Overwrite Protection (DOS 6.2 utility), 29
overwriting files, 402

P

P switch, 222, 252, 646
Packed file corrupt error message, 487
page breaks
command output, 561-562
inserting into memory reports, 483
parallel ports (printers), 129, 1108
parameters, 1108
ANSI.SYS device driver, 764
ATTRIB command, 249
BUFFERS command, 512
CHCP command, 801
CHOICE command, 603
COMMAND command, 699
COPY command, 637, 691
COUNTRY command, 788
DEFRAG command, 533
DEL command, 252
DIR command, 690
DISKCOMP command, 292
DISKCOPY command, 285
DOS Shell, 578
EDIT command, 299
EMM386.EXE command, 712, 714
FC command, 259, 261, 739
FIND command, 571
FOR command, 601
FORMAT command, 271, 276, 737-744

GOTO command, 593
HIMEM.SYS files, 706-707
IF command, 590
INTERLNK command, 659
INTERLNK.EXE command, 655-656
INTERSVR command, 652
KEYB command, 793
LABEL command, 295
macros, 207
MODE command, 797
MOVE command, 691
MSAV command, 426
NLSFUNC command, 800
null parameters, 597
paths, 184
PIFs, 675
PRINT command, 257
programs, 177-178
REPLACE command, 645
replaceable parameters, 329-330
inserting in program items, 577-578
versus DOS environment variables, 694
RESTORE command, 413
searching, 186
SET command, 689
SHELL command, 695
SMARTDRV command, 508
SORT command, 567
SUBST command, 626
TREE command, 216
TRUENAME command, 630
UNDELETE command, 442
UNDELETE TSRs, 439
UNFORMAT command, 280, 754
VOL command, 294
VSAFE command, 434
XCOPY command, 632, 691
parent directories, 38, 1108
parity values (serial port configuration), 811

partial file recovery, 450-451
partition table (byte sectors), 268
partitioning hard disks, 268, 867-874
partitions, 869-873
partitions (hard disks), 1108
passing
    constants (modular programming), 861
    local variables (modular programming), 861
    values (modular programming), 861-862
Password dialog box, 155
passwords
    Backup files, 377
    DOSSHELL.INI file, 580
    forgotten password recovery, 155
    groups, 155
    Internet, 883
    program items (DOS Shell), 159
Paste command (Edit menu), 848
pasting text in DOS applications, 680-681
PATH command, 185, 189, 194, 842
path names, 40-41
PATH program, 193-195
PATH variable, 689
paths, 1108
    attaching
        to command-names, 179
        to filespecs, 179
    commands, 178-180
    directories, 629-630
    files, 629-630
    parameters, 184
    relative paths, 1110
    replacing, 194
    search paths, 1110
    viewing, 194
PAUSE command, 325-327
Pause key, 11-12

pausing
    batch files, 325-327
    screen contents, 12
PCs (Multimedia PCs), 835-842
Pentium microprocessors, 5
    AUTOEXEC.BAT files, 552-553
    CONFIG.SYS files, 552-553
permission denied error message, 225
PgDn (DOSKEY history), 200
PgUp (DOSKEY history), 200
phantom drives, 79, 117
physical disk configurations, 824-827
PIF Editor, 673-683
PIFs (Program Information Files), 672-673, 1108
    defaults, 685
    executing, 674-683
    Real Mode options, 683-686
    Standard Mode options, 683-686
    switching modes, 683
pipe files, 563, 1109
placing RAM drives, 516
plus signs (+), directories, 66
ports, 1109
    identifying for computer linking, 656-657
    parallel ports, 1108
    printers, 129
    serial ports, 1111
PostScript
    GRAPHICS command, 819
    printers, 566, 806
POWER (DOS 6 utility), 29
POWER command, 782
POWER.EXE, 1083-1084
PREP command, 798
preparing keyboard code pages, 797-798

preserving
    DOS environment variables, 693-694
    laptop computer battery power, 782-783
Prevent Program Switch option (PIFs), 685
primary command prompt, 173, 175-176
primary partition, 870
PRINT command, 256-258, 813-816
Print command (File menu), 190, 311-312
Print dialog box, 192
Print File dialog box, 130
PRINT program, 128, 131
Print Setup command (File menu), 387
printer drivers, 806
printer queues, 130, 258
printers
    aspect ratio, 820
    cleating memory, 258
    configuring, 808-809
    GRAPHICS printer types, 817-818
    ports, 129
    PostScript printers, 806
    redirecting commands to, 181
    redirection status, viewing, 812-813
    serial printers, 809-813
    types, 806-808
printing, 805-821
    ASCII text files, 130
    DOS application screens, 685
    DOS directory, 181
    DOSKEY lists, 210
    echo printing, 806-807
    files, 98, 128-131, 235, 256-258, 311-312
    GRAPHICS screens, 816-820
    Help topics, 192

queues
  controlling, 815-816
  files, cancelling or
    adding, 816
screen contents, 11
setup files, 387
text screen printing,
  807-808
**PrintScreen (GRAPHICS
screens), 817-820**
**PrintScreen key, 11-12,
685, 807**
PRN, 806, 812
**Problem Found dialog
box, 467**
**Procedure Step command
(Debug menu), 864**
procedures, 858-859
**Procedures command (Help
menu), 75**
processors, 1101, 1109
**Program Filename field (PIF
Editor), 674-675**
**Program Group Properties
dialog box, 154**
program groups, *see* groups
**Program Information Files,
see PIFs**
program items (DOS Shell)
  adding, 157
  copying, 157, 159-161
  creating, 156
  deleting, 160
  naming, 157
  password protection, 159
  properties, 157
  shortcut keys, 158
program list
  Disk Utilities group, 153
  Main group, 152
  starting programs, 142-143
program lists, 67, 161
program search path, 178
**Program/File Lists command
(View menu), 101**
programs
  adding to SETVER device
    driver, 339
  antivirus programs, 418-419
    reloading, 48
    unloading, 47-48
  associating with file
    extensions, 141

backup programs, 48-49
batch programs, 25
CHKDSK, 26, 351, 462-463
command-names, 177
DEFRAG, 27
Delete Sentry, 439-441
deletion protection
  programs, 47-48
Deletion-Tracking, 448-451
DELOLDOS, 57
disk caching programs,
  47-48
DoubleSpace, 27
exiting, 172
EXPAND, 57, 405
external programs, 177
file searching, 180
groups, 1109
internal programs, 177
items, 575-578
loading into upper memory,
  493-495
memory allocation, 715
Microsoft Anti-Virus
  program, 26
MSAV (Microsoft Anti-
  Virus), 348-349
MSBACKUP, 355-356
MSD (Microsoft Diagnos-
  tics), 757-759
MWBACKUP, 355
parameters, 177-178
PATH program, 193-195
PRINT, 128, 131
quitting during task
  swapping, 148
reconfiguring, 497-498
running (QBASIC),
  849-850
SCANDISK, 26, 351,
  462-463
searching, 178, 193-195
SETUP, 51
SmartDrive, 27, 500-502
starting
  form DOS command
    prompt, 143
  from associated files, 137
  from data files, 138-141
  from file lists, 137-138
  from program list,
    142-143
switches, 177-178

task swapping, 143
tracing (QBASIC debug-
  ging), 863-864
TSRs, 128, 715-716
upper memory pro-
  grams, 494
virus scanning programs,
  417-418
VSAFE virus monitor,
  428-434
**program starter section
(DOSSHELL.INI file), 579**
**Prompt before Creating
Directories (Restore
option), 402**
**Prompt before Creating Files
(Restore option), 402**
**Prompt Before Overwriting
(Backup option), 377**
**Prompt before Overwriting
Existing Files (Restore
option), 402**
**PROMPT command,
195-196, 766-767, 771**
PROMPT variable, 690
**Prompt While Detect (MSAV
option), 423**
prompts, 1109
  CONFIG.SYS file com-
    mands, 613
  DOS applications in
    Windows, 668
properties
  DOS Shell program
    items, 157
  groups, 154
**Properties command (File
menu), 154**
**Protect Executable Files
(VSAFE option), 431**
**Protect FD Boot Sector
(VSAFE option), 431**
**Protect HD Boot Sector
(VSAFE option), 431**
protected files, 254
protecting
  data, 25-26
  deleted files, 53-56
  disks
    files from over-
      writing, 604
    from corruption, 15

from overwriting,
430-431
drives from deletion, 440
executable files from
overwriting, 431
files
during file replace-
ment, 646
from deletion, 438-446
from overwriting, 234
startup files, 334-336
protocols, 880, 1109
pruning directories, 636-637
**Purge Delete Sentry File
command (File menu), 445**
**purging SENTRY directory,
445-446**

Q

QBASIC
array variables, 852
BASICA, converting,
849-850
CALL statements, 860, 861
CASE ELSE block, 855
COMMON SHARED
statements (global
variables), 859
compared to Quick-
BASIC, 844
constants, 851
control facilities, 854-857
debugging, 863-864
DECLARE statements, 860
DEF FN, 858
DEFLNG statement, 851
DEFtype statement, 850
DIM statement, 851-852
DO WHILE...LOOP
block, 856
DO...LOOP block, 857
ELSE statements, 854
ELSEIF element, 855
END IF statements, 854
FOR...NEXT state-
ments, 856
GOSUB, 858
GW-BASIC, converting,
849-850
IF statements, 854-855
incompatibilities, 849-850

interface, 845-848
LCASE$ function, 852
line numbers, 850
long integers, 851
loop structures, 856-857
LTRIM$ function, 852
modular programming,
857-863
numeric variables, 851
programs, running, 849-850
record data type, 852-854
RTRIM$ function, 852
running programs from the
DOS prompt, 865
SELECT CASE statement,
855-856
string variables, 851-852
UCASE$ function, 852
usertype (record data
type), 853
WHILE...WEND state-
ments, 856
QBASIC Editor, 845-848
**question mark (?) wildcard,
34-35**
**queues (printing),
815-816, 1109**
quick format (disks), 270
Quick Format command, 279
Quick Format dialog box, 279
quick reformats (disks), 277
**QuickBASIC compared to
QBASIC, 844**
**Quit After Backup (Backup
option), 379**
**Quit After Compare (Com-
pare option), 411**
**Quit After Restore (Restore
option), 403**
quitting
Backup, 379
DOS Shell, 76
EDIT, 178
macros, 207
programs, 148, 172
task swapping, 149
virus scanner, 424

R

**RAM (random-access
memory), 480, 1109**

RAM disks, 1109
**RAM drives, 27, 475,
515-520**
64KB default, 517
compared to Smart-
Drive, 516
creating, 517
default parameters,
overriding, 519-520
LABEL command, 518
placing, 516
setup, 517-518
size parameters, 517
temporary files,
directing, 519
**RAMDRIVE.SYS,
1084-1085**
**RAMDRIVE.SYS driver,
475, 517-518**
RD command, 225
Read error message, 268
read-only files, 36, 1110
read-only memory, *see* ROM
read-write head, 1110
reading directory trees, 216
**Real Mode options (PIFs),
683-686**
rebooting, 175, 1110
rebuilding
catalogs, 410-411
disks without mirror image
files, 753-757
**recall commands (DOSKEY
history), 200**
recalling
commands from DOSKEY
history, 200-201
previous commands, 204
**Recommendation dialog
box, 529**
reconfiguring
drives, 363
programs, 497-498
**record data type (QBASIC),
852-854**
record data types, 853-854
record sorting, 570
RECOVER command, 281
recovering
catalogs, 406
cross-linked files, 469
customized program
lists, 161

data, 25-26, 267-268
deleted files, 254
directories, 446-447
DOS 5 files, 451
DOS directory files,
  452-454
files, 234, 441-444
  clusters, 465-467
  from DOS Shell, 455
  from Windows, 455-457
  without prompts,
    454-456
forgotten passwords, 155
partial files, 450-451
Windows directories, 457
recovery tools, 746
recursion (batch files), 588
redirecting
  ASCII text messages, 182
  command output, 180-183
  hard drives, 652
  input, 560-566
  output, 560-566
  serial printers, 812
  server drives during
    computer linking, 658
  SORT command input/
    output, 568-569
redirection status (printers),
  812-813
referencing batch files, 602
reformatted disk restoration,
  280-282
reformatting
  disks, 269-271,
    275-279, 351
  hard drives, 50
refreshing
  drives, 79, 81-82
  keyboard code pages, 802
relative paths, 1110
reloading
  antivirus programs, 48
  deletion protection
    programs, 48
  disk caching programs, 48
REM command, 322-323
remapping keyboard keys,
  777-778
removing
  directories, 25
  disk labels, 295
  early versions of DOS from

hard drive, 57
  expanded memory, 491
  screen snow, 358
  viruses, 348
REN command, 247-248
Rename command (File
  menu), 88, 125-126
renaming
  directories, 88-89, 224-225
  files, 125-126, 231, 238,
    247-248
  HLP files, 247
Repaint Screen command
  (View menu), 128
repainting
  DOS Shell screen, 82
  screens, 79
repairing files, 748
repartitioning hard disks, 269
Repeat Last Find command
  (Search menu), 191
repeating
  batch file commands,
    600-601
  characters, 12
  cursor-movement keys, 12
REPLACE command, 644-
  646, 1091
Replace File Confirmation
  dialog box, 108
replaceable parameters
  batch files, 329-330, 587
  inserting in program items,
    577-578
  versus DOS environment
    variables, 694
replacement confirmation
  (DOS Shell files), 104-105
replacing
  existing files, 646
  files, 104-105, 233-235
  lithium batteries, 7
  macros, 210
  missing files, 645-646
  paths, 194
Resident (VSAFE
  option), 430
resizing drives, 727-728
resources (Internet), 876-879
RESTORE command,
  405-413
  exit code, 1091
  options, 400-403

running, 403-405
Restore dialog box, 394
Restore Empty Directories
  (Restore option), 402
Restore function, 364
Restore progress box, 404
Restore View command
  (View menu), 128
restoring
  catalogs, 410-411
  command prompt
    default, 196
  compressed backup
    programs, 49
  directories, 402
  DOS environment
    variables, 693-694
  drives, 395-397
  files, 392-413
  hard drives, 407-409
  old versions of files,
    399-400
  reformatted disks, 280-282
  startup files, 336
restructuring directory trees,
  625-630
resynchronization buffer (FC
  command), 739-744
resynchronizing
  file comparisons, 740-744
  files, 262-263
retrieving catalogs, 406
retry values (serial port
  configurations), 811
returning
  to DOS Shell screen,
    137, 145
  to Help Index, 74
ROM (read-only memory),
  480, 758, 1110
ROM-BIOS, 1110
  drives, defining, 824
  shadowing, 709-710
root directories, 37, 1110
RTRIM$ function
  (QBASIC), 852
Run command (File menu),
  174-175
Run dialog box, 174
Run menu (QBASIC
  Editor), 845
running
  Backup, 380-382
  batch files, 319

CHKDSK program, 463
commands from secondary
command prompt, 175
DEFRAG utility in batch
mode, 534
DOS applications in
Windows, 667-685
DOS on networks, 831-834
DOS tasks in windows,
670-672
DoubleSpace (compression
program), 541-543
DriveSpace (compression
program), 541-543
Microsoft Anti-Virus, 52-53
Microsoft Windows Anti-
Virus, 53
programs (QBASIC),
849-850
Restore, 403-405
SCANDISK program, 464
SETUP, 49-50
virus scans, 424

S

S switch, 222, 236
safe format (disks), 270
Save As command (File
menu), 309
Save As dialog box, 309
Save Setup command (File
menu), 379
savestate section
(DOSSHELL.INI file), 578
saving
directories in files, 560
files, 309-310
Restore options, 403
screen images (DOS
applications), 684
SCANDISK (DOS 6.2
utilities), 29-30
SCANDISK program, 26,
351, 462-463, 746-752
disk surface-scanning, 470
locating lost file clusters,
467-468
running, 464
troubleshooting cross-
linked files, 468-469

scanners (multimedia
hardware), 837
scanning
compressed drives for
errors, 731
data files for viruses, 424
disk surfaces, 470
executable files for
viruses, 431
hard drives for viruses, 420
system disks for viruses, 431
upper memory, 711
viruses, 52
Screen Display Mode dialog
box, 162
screen images (DOS applications), 684
screen-savers, 588
screens
Backup progress screen, 381
banners, 771
clearing, 322
colors, 162-163, 765,
767-770
columns, 779
CON mode, 779
contents
pausing, 12
printing, 11
control sequences, 770-775
DOS applications, 685
DOS Editor screen, 300
DOS Shell, 63
DOS Shell screen, 22,
65-68, 144
repainting, 82
returning to, 137
views, 115-116
EDIT, 314
Help topic screens, 189-190
line defaults, 779
modes, 774-775
MSD menu screen, 757
Optimization progress
screen, 530
repainting, 79
Setup selection screen
(compression pro-
grams), 540
snow, 358
script (telecommunications
software), 881

scroll bars, 70-72, 1110
scroll boxes, 1110
scrolling
dialog boxes, 69-72
Help window, 188-189
scrolling keys, 69
ScrollLock key, 10
Search command (Find
menu), 191
Search menu (QBASIC
Editor), 845
Search menu commands
Change, 306
Find, 308-309
Repeat Last Find, 191
search paths, 1110
searching
DOS commands, 191-192
DOS directories, 194
external files, 193
file text strings, 573
mirror image files, 754
parameters, 186
program files, 180
programs, 178, 193-195
switches, 186
text, 307-309
Windows files, 456-457
secondary command interpreters, 698-701
secondary command prompt,
174-176
Sector not found error
message, 267
sectors
bad disk sectors, 752
CRCs
see also byte sectors
Select All command (File
menu), 99
Select Backup Files dialog
box, 369
SELECT CASE statement
(QBASIC), 855-856
Select Optimization Method
dialog box, 531
Select Restore Files dialog
box, 398
selecting
adjacent files, 95
Backup
options, 376-379
types, 373-375

directories, 85-86
drives, 78-82, 421
  disk caches, 504
  for Backup, 368
  for compression, 543
  for defragmentation, 528
  to be restored, 395-397
EDIT Help topics, 313
empty drives, 80-81
files, 94-95
  from multiple directo-
    ries, 100-101
  to restore, 395-400
group items, 154
Help topics, 74
multiple files, 95-99
nonadjacent files, 95
Restore options, 403
setup files, 366-373
text, 303
Windows file protection
  methods, 456
sending
  commands to ANSI.SYS
    device driver, 765-768
  escape sequences, 766
SENTRY directory, 458
  contents, 446
  purging, 445-446
serial ports, 1111
  configurations, 809-811
  printers, 129
serial printers, 809-813
servers, 1111
  drives, 658
  INTERLNK, 650, 652-654
SET command, 688-689
SETUP, 51
  running, 49-50
  troubleshooting, 50
setup
  286 microprocessors,
    550-551
  386 microprocessors,
    552-553
  486 microprocessors,
    552-553
  DoubleSpace (compression
    program), 538-539
  DriveSpace (compression
    program), 538-539
  INTERLNK
    clients, 655-658

server, 652-654
international formats, 789
Pentium microprocessors,
  552-553
RAM drives, 517-518
setup files
  creating, 365-380
  deleting, 388
  displaying, 371
  editing, 387
  excluding, 368, 372-373
  finding, 386
  including, 368
  opening, 379, 401
  printing, 387
  selecting, 366-373
  storing, 386
  undoing selections, 372
Setup selection screen
  (compression pro-
  grams), 540
SETVER command, 1091
SETVER device driver,
  339, 1086
Shadow RAM, 709-711
shadowing ROM-BIOS,
  709-710
SHARE command, 833-834
sharing files (networks),
  833-834
Shell Basics command (Help
  menu), 75
SHELL command, 695
SHIFT command, 600-601
Shift key, 10-11
shifting keys, 10-11
shortcut keys, 158, 681-683
Show Information command
  (Options menu), 121
shutdown, 554
simulating
  drives with directories,
    626-627
  expanded memory with
    extended memory, 712
single drive copying, 287-289
size parameters (RAM
  drives), 517
SIZER.SYS, 1086
sizing
  disk caches, 507-509, 667
  drives, 727-728

slack space (memory), 41,
  642-643
SmartDrive, 666-667
  compared to RAM
    drives, 516
  reports, 505-506
SmartDrive (caching pro-
  gram), 27, 29, 475,
  500-502
  performance evaluations,
    509-511
  starting, 502-506
  Windows, 506
SMARTDRV /STATUS |
  FIND command, 573
SMARTDRV command, 508
SMARTDRV.EXE,
  1087-1088
SMARTMON utility,
  509-511
software, 13-14, 1111
  compression software, 612
  INTERLNK software, 661
  Multimedia, 838-842
  troubleshooting, 349-350
SORT command, 567-571
sorting
  directory listings, 220, 730
  disk entries, 531-532
  files
    lines, 567-571
    lists, 166-167
  records, 570
Sound Recorder, 839
Special Inclusions dialog
  box, 367
special purpose keys, 11-12
Special Selections dialog
  box, 372
specific verification (DOS
  files), 744
stacks, 342-343, 1111
STACKS command, 342-343
standard error output, 565
Standard Mode options
  (PIFs), 683-686
Start-up Directory field
  (PIFs), 676
starting
  Backup, 356-357
  COMMAND.COM
    command interpreter, 701
  DEFRAG utility, 527-529

Delete Sentry, 53-56
DOS applications in
  Windows, 668-670
DOS Shell, 62-65
EDIT, 177, 299-300
FDISK, 868-869
programs
  from associated files, 137
  from data files, 140-141
  from DOS command
    prompt, 143
  from file lists, 137-138
  from program list,
    142-143
Restore, 406
SmartDrive program,
  502-506
task swapping, 144-145
startup files
  backing up, 335
  booting without, 337
  bypassing, 336-337,
    610-613
  executing line-by-line, 337
  item bypassing, 382
  protecting, 334-336
  restoring, 336
startup menus, 615-616
static variables (subpro-
  grams), 860
status bar (DOS Shell), 65
STATUS switch (MODE
  command), 802
stealth virus, 424
Step command (Debug
  menu), 864
storing
  catalogs, 386
  clusters (files), 642
  mirror image files, 270
  setup files, 386
  temporary files, 690
  undo information
    (disks), 467
string variables (QBASIC),
  851-852
SUB statements (subpro-
  grams), 860-861
subdirectories, 37-39, 1111
  copying, 236
  invalid entries, 750-751
  path names, 40

submenu configurations,
  616-618
subprograms (modular
  programming), 860-861
SUBST command,
  626-627, 628
suppressing command
  output, 182
surge protectors, 350
Survival Guide Help
  (EDIT), 313
swap files (Windows), 666
switches, 1111
  A switch, 218-219, 248
  activating/deactivating file
    attributes, 249
  ANSI.SYS device
    driver, 764
  ATTRIB command, 249
  B switch, 222, 644
  C switch (DIR com-
    mand), 729
  CHCP command, 801
  CHOICE command, 603
  COMMAND com-
    mand, 699
  COPY command, 637
  DEFRAG command, 533
  DEL command, 252
  DISKCOMP com-
    mand, 292
  DISKCOPY command, 285
  E switch, 236
  EDIT command, 299, 314
  EMM386.EXE command,
    712, 714
  FC command, 259,
    261, 739
  FIND command, 571
  FORMAT command, 271,
    276, 737-744
  GRAPHICS command,
    818-820
  HIMEM.SYS files, 706-707
  INTERLNK.EXE com-
    mand, 655-656
  INTERSVR command, 652
  KEYB command, 793
  MEMMAKER com-
    mand, 497
  MODE command, 797
  MSAV command, 426
  N switch, 263

NLSFUNC command, 800
O switch, 220
P switch, 222, 252, 646
PRINT command, 257
programs, 177-178
REPLACE command, 645
RESTORE command, 413
S switch, 222, 236
searching, 186
SHELL command, 695
SMARTDRV com-
  mand, 508
SORT command, 567
STATUS switch (MODE
  command), 802
SUBST command, 626
TEST switch
  (UNFORMAT com-
  mand), 755
U switch (REPLACE
  command), 646
UNDELETE command, 442
UNDELETE TSRs, 439
UNFORMAT com-
  mand, 754
V switch, 290
VSAFE command, 434
XCOPY command, 632
Y switch, 233, 236
switching
  between directories, 213
  between drives, 213
  between keyboard code
    pages, 798-799
  between keyboard lay-
    outs, 794
  between tasks, 145-147
  console devices, 781-782
  directories, 40, 179
  drives, 628-629
  PIF Editor modes, 683
  to DOS directory, 180
Syntax (Help topic
  screen), 189
syntax checking (QBASIC
  Editor), 847
system statistics, 757-759
system attributes (files),
  36, 1111
system board, 5
system booting, 610
  DOS, 334
  without startup files, 337

system configurations, 363-364
system disks
  formatting, 274-275
  virus scanning, 431
system files, 1111
  attributes, 250-251
  copying, 635
  displaying, 165-166, 218
system initialization files, 758
system rebooting, 175
system shutdown, 554
system software, 13
system startup files, 758
system unit, 4-8

T

TARGET diskette bad or incompatible error message, 290
task list, 147
task swapper versus Windows multitasking, 143
task swapping, 23-24, 62, 1112
  limitations in DOS Shell, 577
  memory requirements for program items, 576
  optimizing in Windows, 677
  programs, 143
  quitting, 149
  starting, 144
task switching keys, 145
tasks
  closing, 148-149
  starting, 144-145
  switching between, 145-147
telecommunications, 1112
telecommunications software (Internet), 880-881
TEMP variable, 519, 690
temporary exits (DOS Shell), 76
temporary files
  directing to RAM drives, 519
  finding, 690
  storing, 690
temporary pipe files, 563

terminate-and-stay-resident, see TSRs
TEST switch (UNFORMAT command), 755
testing
  Backup configurations, 357
  batch files
    for existence, 596
    for null values, 597-598
    logic, 703
  system configurations, 363-364
text
  changing, 306-307
  copying, 304-309
  cutting-and-pasting, 304-309
  deleting, 303-304
  deselecting, 303
  DOS applications, copying and pasting, 680-681
  editing, 301-306
  finding, 307-309
  finding-and-replacing, 306-307
  inserting, 302-303
  moving, 305
  selecting, 303
  strings
    assigning to keys, 778-779
    comparing, 596-597
text boxes, 83
text editor, see EDIT
text files
  annotating, 563-564
  escape sequences, 773
  in ANSI.SYS device driver, 767
text screen printing, 807-808
third party command interpreters, 698-699
time (commands), 184
time formats (international settings), 787-789
time-slicing (PRINT command), 813
title bar (DOS Shell), 65
Toggle Breakpoint command (Debug menu), 864
toggle keys, 10
toggle switches
  Add mode spacebar, 98

Display menu commands, 127
file attributes, 122
tools (recovery tools), 746
Tools menu commands
  Defragment, 728
  Options, 732
  Uncompress, 733
Trace On command (Debug menu), 863
tracing programs (QBASIC debugging), 863-864
tracks (disks), 1112
TREE command, 214, 216
Tree menu, 86
Tree menu commands, 87
troubleshooting
  Backup freezes, 382
  bad disk sectors, 752
  configuration tests, 362-363
  cross-linked files, 468-469
  damaged disks, 351
  disk changes, 174
  FC command, 260
  file copying/moving problems, 118
  file memory allocation errors, 749-750
  file restoration, 404-405
  full disks, 233
  hangups during task swapping, 147
  hardware failure, 350
  HIMEM.SYS files, 706-710
  INT15h, 709
  invalid allocation units, 748
  invalid subdirectory entries, 750-751
  lost allocation units (disks), 465-466
  MEMMAKER command, 494
  SETUP, 50
  software problems, 349-350
  TYPE command, 256
  UMBs (upper memory blocks), 715
TRUENAME command, 629-630
TSRs (terminate-and-stay-resident) programs, 128, 715-716, 1107
  DOSKEY, 198

interrupting loading, 430
loading into upper
  memory, 497
loading restrictions, 174
TXT files, 52
TYPE command, 255-256
typematic rates (keyboard),
  12, 781
typing international characters, 789-790

U

U switch (REPLACE
  command), 646
UCASE$ function
  (QBASIC), 852
UMBs (upper memory
  blocks), 491
  monochrome regions, 711
  troubleshooting, 715
Unable to create directory
  error message, 239
Uncompress command (Tools
  menu), 733
uncompressing drives, 733
unconditional format
  (disks), 270
UNDELETE (DOS 6
  utility), 29
UNDELETE /PURGE
  command, 446
UNDELETE command,
  439, 453
  configurations, 457-458
  recovering deleted files, 442
UNDELETE TSRs
  Deletion-Tracking, 448
  loading, 439-441
undeleting, 1112
  DOS directory files,
    452-454
  files, 444, 449-450
    from DOS Shell, 455
    from Windows, 455-457
    without prompts,
      454-456
  Windows directories, 457
undo-drive, 468
undoing
  MEMMAKER command,

497-498
  setup file selections, 372
Unerase utility, 234
UNFORMAT command,
  280-282, 753-757
unformatting, 1112
Uninstall disks, 48
uninstalling DOS 6, 56
universities as Internet
  sources, 876
unknown viruses, 417-418
unloading
  antivirus programs, 47-48
  deletion protection
    programs, 47-48
  disk caching programs,
    47-48
  VSAFE virus monitor,
    432-433
Unmount command (Drive
  menu), 724
Unrecoverable read...error
  message, 285
Unrecoverable write...error
  message, 286
updating
  date/time stamps
    files, 640-641
    non-ASCII files, 644
  virus lists, 434-435
upgrading
  networked systems to DOS
    6.22, 832
  to DOS 6.22, 46-48
  to QBASIC, 843-865
upper memory, 474,
  480, 1112
  accessing, 708
  aggressive scanning, 711
  excluding, 712-713
  loading RAMDRIVE, 518
  maximizing space, 710-714
upper memory blocks,
  491-493
uppercase characters, 10
Use Error Correction
  (Backup option), 378
user interface, 1112
users, 16
usertype (QBASIC record
  data type), 853
Using Help command (Help
  menu), 75

utilities, 1112
  DEFRAG, 523-527
    sorting directory entries,
      531-532
    starting, 527-529
  DOS 6, 28-30
  DOS 6.2, 29
  DOS 6.22, 29
  DoubleSpace (compression
    program) interaction, 544
  DriveSpace (compression
    program) interaction, 544
  SMARTMON, 509-511
  Unerase, 234
Utilities menu com-
  mands, 758

V

V switch, 290
validity checks (byte
  sectors), 270
values (modular program-
  ming), 861-862
variables
  COMSPEC variable, 691
  CONFIG variable, 691,
    694-695
  COPYCMD variable, 691
  DIRCMD variable, 690
  MSDOSDATA
    variable, 691
  PATH variable, 689
  PROMPT variable, 690
  TEMP variable, 690
VER command, 177
Verify Backup Data (Backup
  option), 376
Verify Integrity (MSAV
  option), 422
Verify Restore Data (Restore
  option), 401-402
verifying disk copies, 290-291
vertical bar (|), DOS
  commands, 184
video configurations, 358-359
Video and Mouse Configura-
  tion dialog box, 358-359
video buffers, 763
video capture card (Multime-
  dia hardware), 837

Video Memory field
(PIFs), 676
video screen (memory
allocation), 676
View All Files list, 100
View File Contents command
(File menu), 126
View menu (QBASIC
Editor), 845
View menu commands
All Files, 100
Dual File Lists, 116
Program/File Lists, 101
Repaint Screen, 128
Restore View, 128
View SUBs dialog box, 859
viewing
compressed drive informa-
tion, 726-727
directories, 66, 116
disk labels, 274, 293
DOS core system files, 724
DOS Shell parameters, 578
DOSKEY memory alloca-
tion status, 715
drive contents, 727
files, 126-128
attributes, 121-122
compression ratios, 730
partition information,
872-873
paths, 194
procedures, 858
program item definitions in
DOS Shell, 579
program memory allocation
status, 715
redirection status (printers),
812-813
system initialization
files, 758
system startup files, 758
TXT files, 52
VSAFE options, 429
views (DOS Shell screen),
115-116
VIR file, 422
virtual drives, 627-629
Virus Found dialog box, 425
virus protection, 348-349
virus scanning programs,
417-418
viruses, 1112

antivirus monitors, 418-420
Internet, 882
known viruses, 417
monitors, 428-434
scanning, 52, 424
stealth virus, 424
unknown viruses, 417-418
updating lists, 434-435
VOL command, 274,
293-296
volume labels (disks),
273-274
VSAFE antivirus monitors,
418-420
VSAFE command, 428-434
VSAFE Options dialog
box, 429
VSAFE virus monitor,
428-435

W

W switch, 178
WAIS (Wide Area Informa-
tion Server), 877, 1113
WHILE...WEND statements
(QBASIC), 856
wildcards, 34, 1113
asterisk (*), 35
in XCOPY command, 239
question mark (?), 34-35
Window Title field
(PIFs), 675
Windowed mode (DOS
applications), 678
Windows
386 Enhanced mode,
667-685
automating at system
startup, 332
Delete Sentry, 54
directory recoveries, 457
disks
caches, 666-667
optimizing space,
665-667
files, 456-457
optimizing, 664-667
running DOS applications
in, 667-685
SmartDrive program, 506
startup applications, 363

swap files, 666
task swapping, 677
Undelete command,
455-457
Undelete File menu, 456
Undelete Options
menu, 457
windows, 1113
DOS windows in Windows,
671-672
Help window, 187-189
Help window (EDIT),
312-313
SCANDISK window, 464
Undelete window, 455-457
Windows multitasking versus
task swapper, 143
workstations, 831
see also nodes
WORM (Write Once, Read
Many), 1113
wrapping characters, 774
Write error message, 268
write-delayed caches
(disks), 1113
Write-protect error writing
drive A, Abort, Retry, Fail?
error message, 251
write-protected disks, 1113
writing disk caches, 501, 506

X–Y–Z

XCOPY command, 236-241,
632-637, 829
exit code, 1092
parameters, 691
XMS Memory Locked (386
Enhanced Mode
option), 677

Y switch, 233, 236
You have more than one file
selected error message, 111

Add to Your Sams Library Today with the Best Books for Programming, Operating Systems, and New Technologies

The easiest way to order is to pick up the phone and call

1-800-428-5331

between 9:00 a.m. and 5:00 p.m. EST.
For faster service please have your credit card available.

ISBN	Quantity	Description of Item	Unit Cost	Total Cost
1-56686-097-0		Peter Norton's Inside the PC, 5th Edition	$24.95	
1-56686-127-6		The Winn L. Rosch Hardware Bible, 3rd Edition	$35.00	
1-56686-265-5		Power User's Pocket Guide to DOS 6.2	$16.00	
1-56686-094-6		Peter Norton's PC Problem Solver, Special Edition	$29.95	
0-672-30291-8		DOS 6 Developer's Guide	$39.95	
1-56686-080-6		The Data Recovery Bible (Book/Disk)	$49.95	
0-672-30524-0		Absolute Beginner's Guide to Multimedia (Book/CD)	$29.99	
0-672-30413-9		Multimedia Madness!, Deluxe Edition	$55.00	
0-672-30269-1		Absolute Beginner's Guide to Programming	$19.95	
0-672-30342-6		Absolute Beginner's Guide to QBASIC	$16.95	
0-672-30324-8		Teach Yourself QBASIC in 21 Days	$24.95	
0-672-30250-0		Moving from QBASIC to C	$24.95	
0-672-30445-7		OS/2 2.11 Unleashed, 2nd Edition	$39.95	
0-672-30464-3		Teach Yourself UNIX in a Week	$28.00	
0-672-30519-4		Teach Yourself the Internet	$25.00	
0-672-30382-5		Understanding Local Area Networks, 4th Edition	$26.95	
0-672-30501-1		Understanding Data Communications, 4th Edition	$29.99	
❏ 3 ½" Disk		Shipping and Handling: See information below.		
❏ 5 ¼" Disk		TOTAL		

Shipping and Handling: $4.00 for the first book, and $1.75 for each additional book. Floppy disk: add $1.75 for shipping and handling. If you need to have it NOW, we can ship product to you in 24 hours for an additional charge of approximately $18.00, and you will receive your item overnight or in two days. Overseas shipping and handling adds $2.00 per book and $8.00 for up to three disks. Prices subject to change. Call for availability and pricing information on latest editions.

201 W. 103rd Street, Indianapolis, Indiana 46290

1-800-428-5331 — Orders   1-800-835-3202 — FAX   1-800-858-7674 — Customer Service